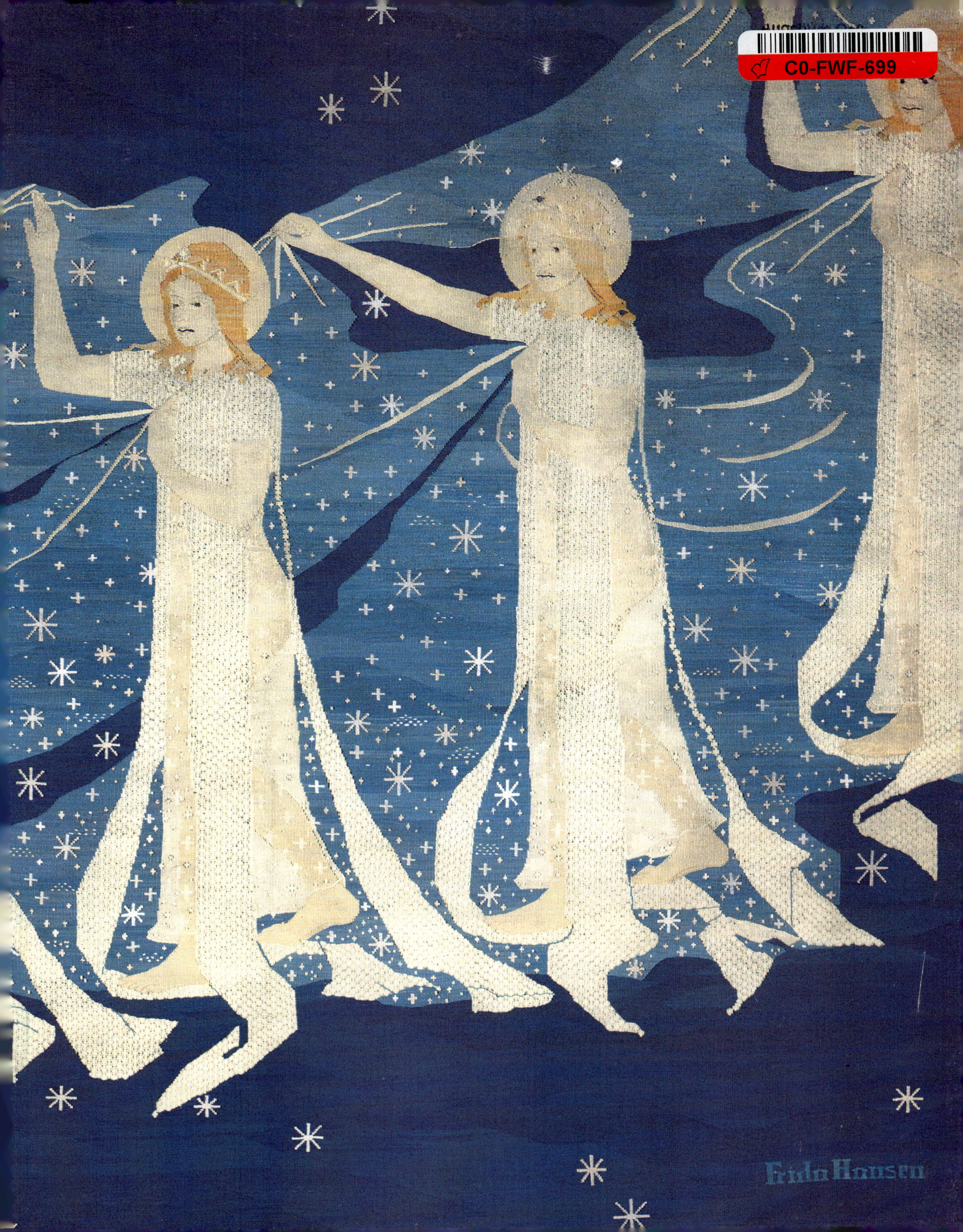
Frida Hansen

Arts of the

19TH CENTURY

1850 to 1905

Arts of the
19TH
CEN

Volume Two
1850 to 1905

TURY

Edited by Françoise Cachin

Geneviève Lacambre
Rodolphe Rapetti
Antoinette Le Normand-Romain
Anne Pingeot
Philippe Néagu
Françoise Heilbrun
Marc Bascou
Philippe Thiébaut
Caroline Mathieu
Georges Vigne

Harry N. Abrams, Inc., Publishers

THE COLOR PHOTOGRAPHS WERE TAKEN BY:
Kiemer & Kiemer: 1; Cuchi White: 2, 273, 278; Dominique Genet: 3, 7, 9, 13, 21–22, 24, 27–29, 34, 78–80, 85, 113–25, 127, 129–37, 144–53, 199, 224–26, 229, 231, 236–37, 239, 241, 248–49, 251, 253–54, 260–62, 268–69; Metropolitan Museum of Art, New York: 4, 23, 39, 51, 69, 83, 201, 214, 234; Musée d'Orsay, Paris: 5, 156, 159–60, 162–63, 170, 174, 178, 189, 193, 196–97, 201, 205, 209, 217–19, 221; Réunion des Musées Nationaux, Paris: 6, 15, 20, 36, 42, 44, 47–48, 55, 57, 64–65, 73, 75–76, 84, 86, 88, 92, 94, 96, 100, 103, 107, 112, 157, 161, 164–66, 168, 172–73, 175, 190, 200, 202, 204, 210, 212, 215, 230, 232–33, 235, 255–56, 258–59, 267; Scala: 8, 31–32, 35, 50, 105; Reinaldo Viegas: 10, 246; J. Évrard/Ch. Bastin: 11, 274–75; Jacques Lathion: 12, 66, 98–99, 102; National Gallery, London: 15; Hugo Maertens: 16; Tate Gallery, London: 17, 30; National Museums and Galleries on Merseyside, Liverpool: 18, 25; City Art Gallery, Manchester: 19; Arxiu Mas: 26; Giraudon: 33, 37, 72; National Museum, Stockholm: 38, 97; Rheinisches Bildarchiv, Cologne: 40; Museum of Art, Providence: 41; Freer Gallery of Art, Washington, D.C.: 43; Art Institute, Chicago: 45, 61, 208; Kunsthalle, Hamburg: 46; Artothek: 49, 67, 104; Phillips Collection, Washington, D.C.: 52, 63; Philadelphia Museum of Art, Philadelphia: 53; Institute of Art, Detroit: 54; André Berthelemy/Studio Jean Cousin: 56; Hinz: 58; National Gallery of Art, Washington, D.C.: 59, 126; Bridgemann Art Gallery: 60; Tretyakov Gallery, Moscow: 62; Bulloz: 68, 91, 93; Národní Gallery, Prague: 70; W. Dräyer: 71, 154; Yale University Art Gallery, New Haven: 74; National Gallery of Scotland, Edinburgh: 77; Rijksmuseum Kröller-Müller, Otterlo: 81; Malcolm Varon: 82; Collection of Mr. and Mrs. Arthur G. Altschul: 87; Kunsthaus, Zürich: 89; Musée Toulouse-Lautrec, Albi: 90; Kunsthistorisches Museum, Vienna: 95; Collection of the Jorma Gallén-Kallela family, Lugano: 102; Bridgestone Museum, Tokyo: 106; Giuseppe Schiavinotto: 108; Koninklijk Museum voor Schone Kunsten, Antwerp: 109; Phototheque des Musées de la Ville de Paris: 111, 182; Museum of Fine Arts, Boston: 128; Bayle: 138; Benoit Roland: 139; Angelo Hornak: 140, 272, 277; Ny Carlsberg Glyptotek, Copenhagen: 141; Ferrante Ferranti: 142, 265–66, 270, 276, 279; Studio Image, Nancy: 143, 238, 240, 244–45, 252; American Antiquarian Society, Worcester: 155; Bibliotheque Nationale, Paris: 158, 169, 171, 183, 192; Private collections: 160, 162–63, 179, 205, 221; Bibliothèque des Arts Décoratifs, Paris: 167, 181; International Museum of Photography at George Eastman House, Rochester: 176, 211, 216; Royal Photographic Society, Bath: 177, 180, 184–85; Victoria & Albert Museum, London: 186; J. Paul Getty Museum, Malibu: 187–88, 195; New York Public Library: 191; Humanity Research Center, Austin: 194; Collège de France, Paris: 198; Museum of Modern Art, New York: 203, 207; Berlinische Galerie, Berlin: 206, 222–23; Musée Carnavalet, Paris: 213; Folkwang Museum, Essen: 220; Christie's New York: 228; Österreichisches museum für Angewandte Kunst, Vienna: 242, 247; Württembergisches Landesmuseum, Stuttgart: 243; Glasgow University: 250; Centre de Recherches des Monuments Historiques, Paris: 257; Deutsches Architekturmuseum, Frankfurt: 263; Sotheby's London: 264; A. F. Kersting: 271.

Project Coordinator, English-language edition: Ellen Nidy
Editor, English-language edition: Bernard Wooding
Design Coordinator, English-language edition: Robert McKee

Library of Congress has cataloged Volume One as follows:

Vaughan, William, 1943-
Arts of the nineteenth century / by William Vaughan ;
introduction, captions, and biographical notes were translated from the French by James Underwood.
p. cm.
First published in French translation under title: L'art du XIXe siècle 1780-1850.
Contents: v. 1. 1780-1850
Includes bibilographical references and index.
ISBN 0-8109-1982-6 (clothbound)
1. Art, European. 2. Art, Modern—19th century—Europe. 3. Art, American. 4. Art, Modern—19th century—United States. I. Title.
N6757.V38 1998
709' .034—dc21 98-3693

Published in 1999 by Harry N. Abrams, Incorporated, New York

Printed and bound in France

Harry N. Abrams, Inc.
100 Fifth Avenue
New York, N.Y. 10011
www.abramsbooks.com

ACKNOWLEDGMENTS

We should like to thank all those who have been kind enough to help us in the production of this book: Arthur G. Altschul, Brigitte Bambusch, Joanna Banham, Georgia B. Barnhill, Patrick Baptiste, Pierre Baudson, Begonia, Caroline Benzaria, Michel Berranger, Daniel Bertin, Béatrice de Boisseson, Joëlle Bossu, Philippe Bouilloud, Michel Bourdon, Joël Boutet, Alexis Brandt, Anne-Marie de Brem, Marie-Hélène Calvignac, Dorine Cardyn, Paige Carter, Philippe Chabert, Pierre Chanel, duc de Chevreuse, Deborah A. Charlton, Béatrice Coti, Simon Cottle, Marie-Laure Crosnier-Lecomte, Deanna Cross, Alain Daguerre de Hureaux, Christian Daguier, Michel Dauvergne, Gérard Delecambre, Claire Denis, Danielle Derrey, Jacqueline Dieuzaide, M. F. Du Bellay, Lorah Dulisse, Bruno Dury, Jacques Evrard, Dennis Farr, Ferrante Ferranti, Radjevi Filatriau, Bruno Foucart, Janos Frecot, Matthias Frehner, Françoise Fur, Aivi Gallén-Kallela, Albert Gallichon, Philippe Garner, Dominique Genet, Oscar Ghez, Maria Teresa Gomes Ferreira, Patrick Guitton, Ingebjørg Gunnarson, Colette Hervin, Nakata Hiroko, Angelo Hornak, Debbie Ireland, André Jammes, Samuel Josefowitz, Martine Kahane, Frédérique Kartouby, J. M. Kearns, Michel Laugel, René Le Bihan, Françoise Leboulenger, Bénédicte Ledru, Olivier Lefuel, André Lejeune, Patricia Lhote, Annie Lotte, Henri Loyrette, Karen Merete Lundsgaard-Leth, duc de Luynes, Ronald Maddox, Dominique Magdelaine, Anne de Margerie, Laure de Margerie, Hugh F. McKean, Odilla Marini, Alain Melchior, Paul Mellon, Nathalie Mengelle, Melissa M. Moore, Dominique Morel, Nelido Negri, Andrew Norris, Eddie Norton, Patricia Oranin, Karen L. Otis, Cécile and Dominique Paillarse, Paula Pergament, Márta Péter, V. Petiouchenko, Alain Pezel, Jean-Claude Pinon, Jean-Dominique Rey, Pamela Robertson, Benoît Roland, Alain de Roquemaurel, P. D. Rose, Daniel Sallet, Jean-Jacques Sauciat, Ofir Scheps, Patrice Schmidt, Hanna-Leena Sihvonen, Cécile Simon, Dusan Spicka, Albert Steen, Ivar Strangar, Matthieu Sturtevant, Christina Thon, G. Tisserand, Michail Y. Treister, Peter Trowles, Jesus Velasco, Vera Vokácova, Christiane van Wersch-Cot, Clive Wainright, Cuchi White, and all the many anonymous collectors and museum curators.

INTRODUCTION

What could be more unjust than the title of the notorious pamphlet by Léon Daudet, "Le Stupide XIXe Siècle" (The silly nineteenth century). This becomes daily more apparent. Today, the period between 1848 and 1914 (an era when Paris played the central role) seems more like a modern equivalent of the Florentine Quattrocento in terms of the number of geniuses, major talents, and innovations that emerged and the profusion of apparently contradictory currents and personalities. In every field—painting, sculpture, architecture, photography, and the decorative arts—this age of industrial dynamism and scientific invention, with its new techniques of mechanical reproduction, its series and multiples, was also one of artistic individualism in which ever greater importance was attached to feelings and impressions. In short, this was the age of the "ego." The sculpture editions of Ferdinand Barbedienne and the creations of Auguste Rodin existed side by side, as did "chromos" and Claude Monet, Henri II sideboards and the furniture crafted by Josef Hoffmann. What other century was so introspective, historicist, and given to recapitulation, yet also so realist and innovative? What era was more eclectic, absorbing so many styles from the past or from remote, even primitive cultures, often in "collage" form (Greco-Japanese objects, classical-neo-Gothic architecture, and primitivist-Symbolist painting), while remaining so well defined? While being radically new, the most avant-garde artists always invoked the great arts of the past as well. Today, we are more aware of the continuity, which in no way detracts from the originality of what was happening (on the contrary). The architect of the first skyscrapers, Louis Sullivan, was a descendant of Viollet-le-Duc; Édouard Manet sought to be the Velázquez of his day and Rodin the Michelangelo of the modern soul; Paul Cézanne wished to "paint Poussin from nature," while William Morris wanted to reinvest industrial publishing with the flavor of medieval craftsmanship.

Perhaps now is the right moment to survey this prodigious period. For a long time there were two viewpoints: that of the traditionalists, for whom modernity tolled the death knell of art, and the one that prevailed from the 1920s to the 1960s, according to which the only kind of history was that of innovations and breakthroughs, a series of forward leaps punctuated by successive "isms." The two viewpoints were mutually exclusive, each being still too caught up in the conflicts of preceding generations. That is no longer the case: from the vantage point of another *fin de siècle*, we are able to take a more dispassionate line. The period we are looking at is far enough away to be the subject of history yet close enough to be still colored with memories, emotions, and even nostalgia for a world that World War I swept away.

These reasons may explain the popularity of the Musée d'Orsay in Paris, which covers precisely the period under discussion here; certainly, they fully justify the choice of authors, all of whom worked for eight years on setting the museum up and were subsequently its curators. As historians of the various arts of the second half of the nineteenth century, sometimes specializing in a particular slice of that period, they are both researchers and connoisseurs, hands-on experts with experience of the actual works. For them, the eye and the mind are in constant communication. The diversity of approach, variety of tone and temperament, and combination of spicy enthusiasm and knowledge that characterize the pages you are about to read say a great deal about the sheer breadth of the period under review. Yet the reader will be struck, nevertheless, by a certain unity of sensibility. This book is no ordinary collection of texts by experts; it is the product of a team of people who have worked together. Representatives of a new generation of art historians, the authors all have certain qualities in common: a breadth of vision, a genuinely international approach, and a desire to set each artist in his or her historical and social context, by discussing the parts played by salons, commissions, dealers, collectors, journals, and critics.

In the various chapters, which examine the different artistic disciplines, the reader will discover some of the things that distinguished this extraordinary half-century: the new importance of prestigious international exhibitions, the powerful role (both positive and negative) of the Académie des Beaux-Arts in France, the influence of a confident, prosperous bourgeoisie, the development of such new arts as iron architecture and photography. Everyone, even the French poets of the 1890s who called themselves *maudits* (the accursed ones), proclaimed a belief in progress, in the union of the beautiful and the useful, and in the democratization and future of art. In short, there was enormous optimism. And it is as if the creators of that supremely fertile half-century had bequeathed something of their vitality, their enthusiasm, and their conviction to the authors who tell you their story in these pages.

FRANCOISE CACHIN

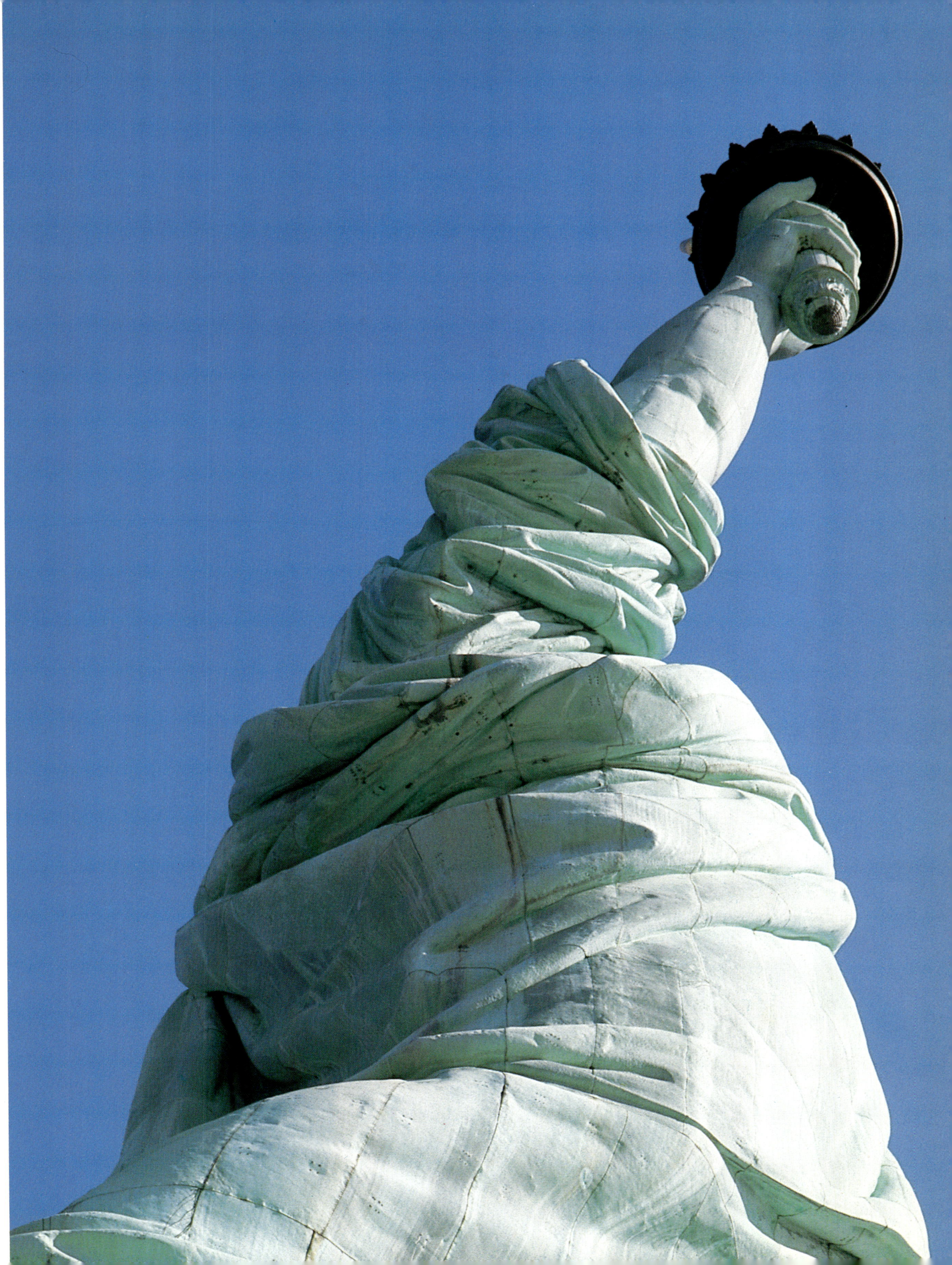

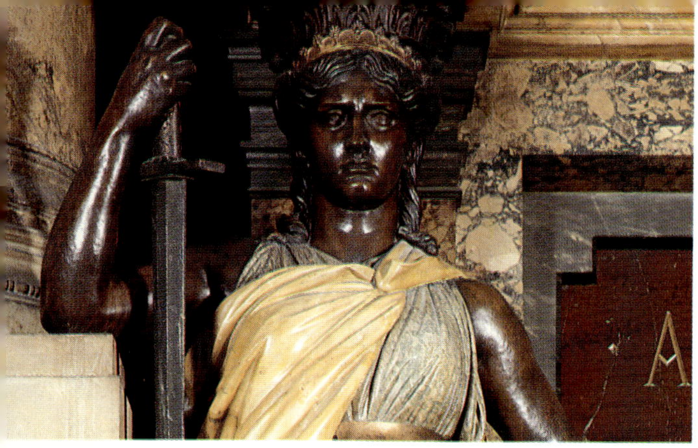

3

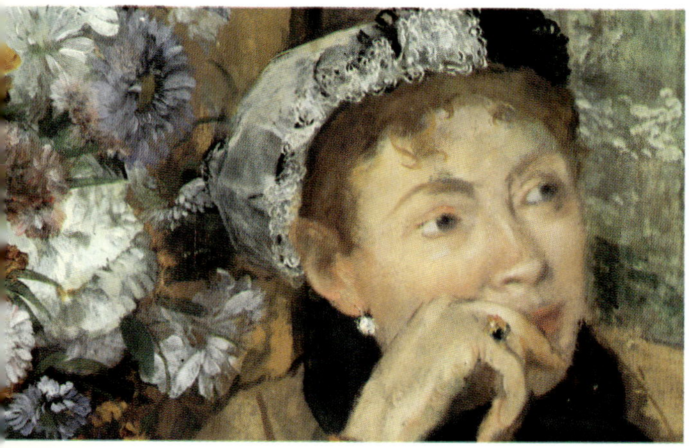

4

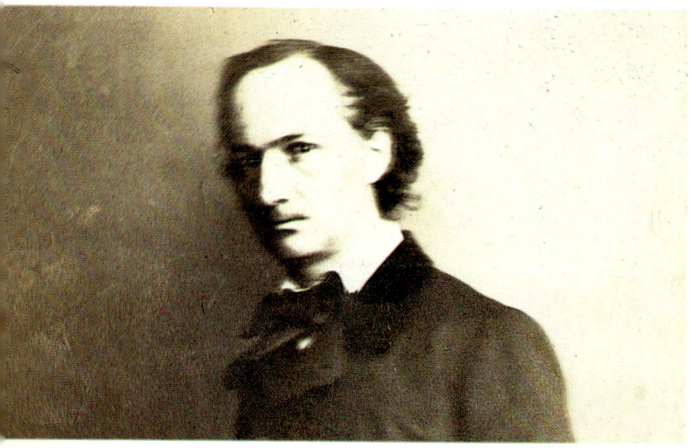

5

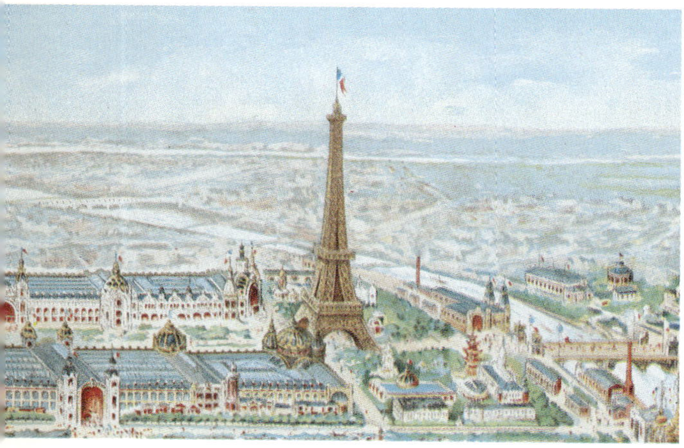

6

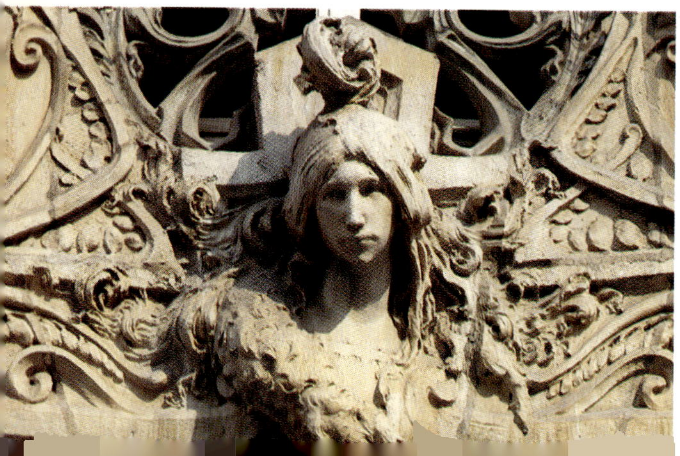

7

TABLE OF CONTENTS

1 (endpaper) Frida Hansen. *The Milky Way.* 1900 Exposition Universelle. Wool and silk tapestry made on a high-warp loom. Museum für Kunst und Gewerbe, Hamburg

2 Frédéric-Auguste Bartholdi. *Liberty Enlightening the World* (detail). 1871–86. Hammered copper, overall height 46 m. New York Harbor

3 Gabriel-Jules Thomas. *Drama* (detail). Polychrome marble and bronze. Opéra, Paris

4 Edgar Degas. *Woman Leaning on Her Elbow Beside a Vase of Flowers* (detail). 1865. Oil on canvas. Metropolitan Museum of Art, New York

5 Nadar (real name, Félix Tournachon). *Portrait of Charles Baudelaire* (detail). c. 1855. Print on salt paper from a glass collodion negative. Musée d'Orsay, Paris

6 Paris, general view of the 1900 Exposition Universelle (detail). Engraving by G. Grivell. Musée d'Orsay, Paris

7 Jules Lavirotte. Entrance of 29 Avenue Rapp, Paris (detail). 1900–1

8 Claude Monet. *The Picnic* (detail). 1865. Oil on canvas. Pushkin Museum, Moscow

9 Alexandre Charpentier. *Bakers* (detail). 1897. Glazed earthenware. Square Scipion, Paris

10 René Lalique. Bodice front (detail). c. 1898–1900. Gold, enamel, opals, and diamonds. Fundação Calouste Gulbenkian, Lisbon

11 Victor Horta. Interior of Hôtel Tassel, Brussels (detail). 1893

12 Edvard Munch. *The Dance of Life* (detail). 1893. Oil on canvas. Nasjonalgalleriet, Oslo

13 Paul Signac. Study for *In the Days of Harmony (Poppies)* (detail). 1895 (?). Oil on wood, overall dimensions 15 x 24 cm. Private collection

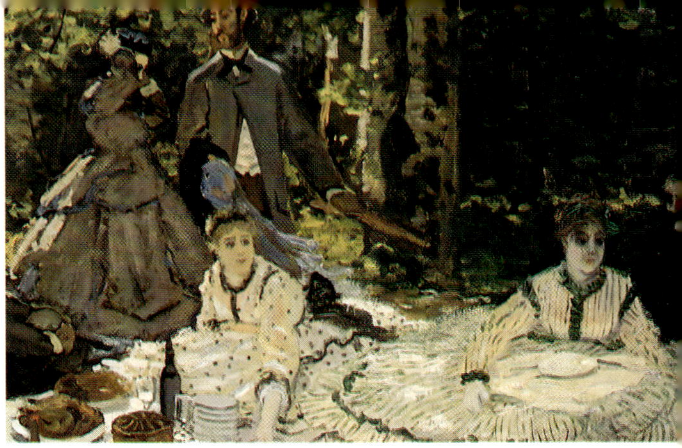

8

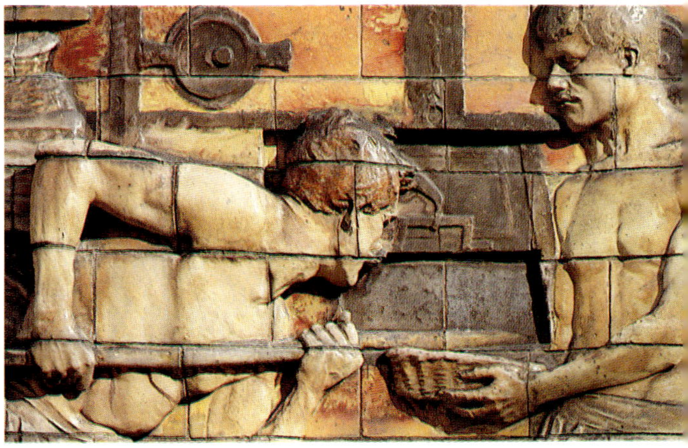

9

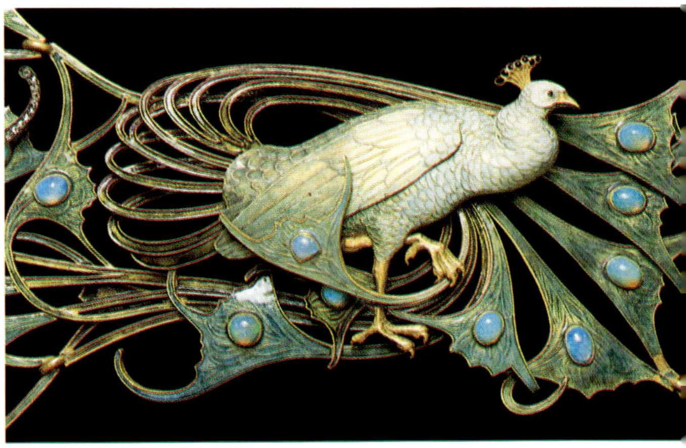

10

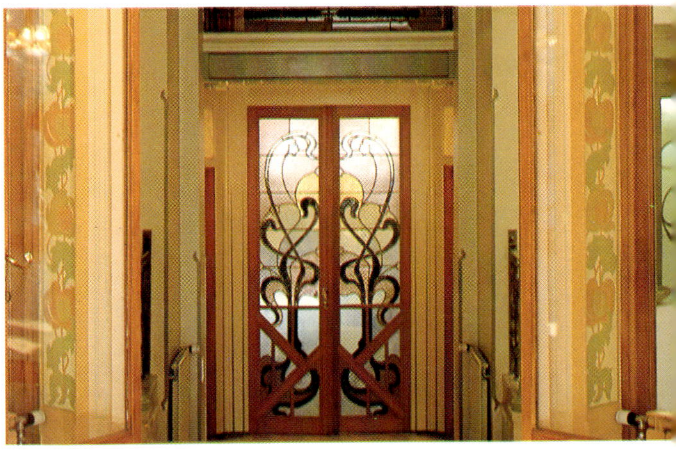

11

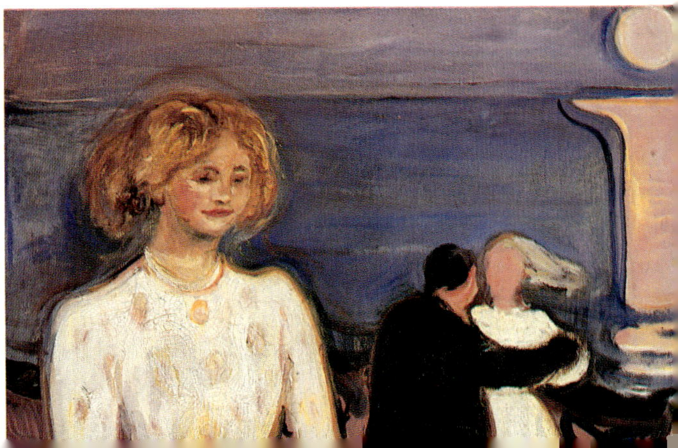

12

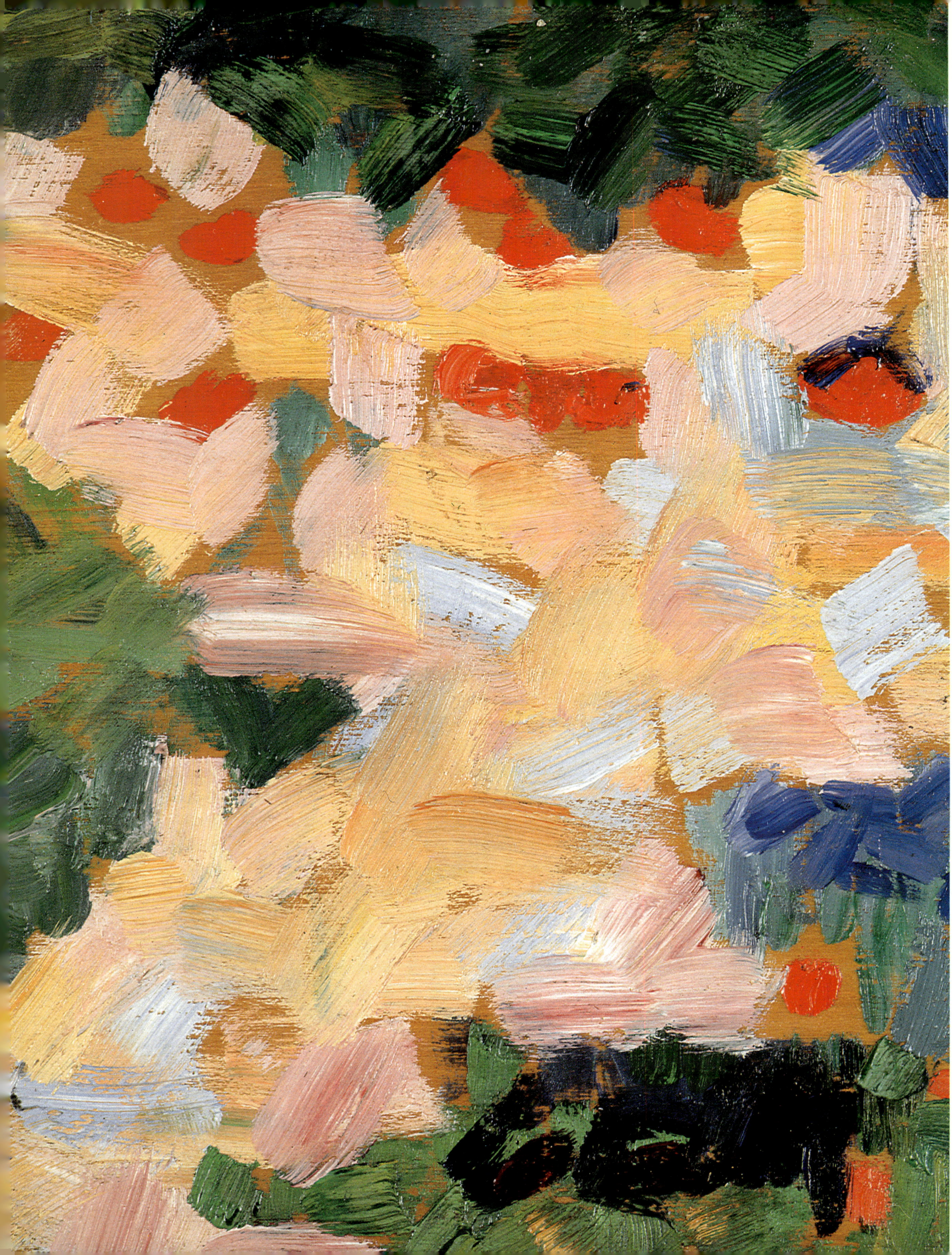

Arts of the
19TH CENTURY
1850 to 1905

PAINTING

THE SALON YEARS

Never had there been more painters than there were during the second half of the nineteenth century. In 1844, the French critic Théophile Thoré wondered whether art was going to be reduced to an industry. The talk was all of "decadence" and "decline." It is true that the growth of museums facilitated constant comparisons with the masterpieces of the past and that the presence in Paris, since 1818, of a museum devoted to living artists (the Musée du Luxembourg) simply added another layer to what was already a ubiquitous hierarchical structure. There was a hierarchy of artists (according to whether or not they were admitted to this "anteroom of the Louvre"), a hierarchy of subjects, inherited from the Académie (with history painting at the top), and a hierarchy of styles of painting (with polish and illusionism prized the most).

Writing in 1880, summing up the 1878 Exposition Universelle in Paris, Ernest Chesneau admitted to considerable pessimism: "Let us have the courage to see and tell things the way they are. The arts throughout Europe are in decline" (Chesneau 1880, 7). With a few exceptions, he blamed this state on inadequate "education of the artist." The debate about the role of institutions (academies, art schools, and exhibitions) had been in full swing since 1848. It was particularly heated in France, where the crisis appears to have been more acute and reactions to it more radical. Charles Baudelaire, concluding his famous essay on the *Salon de 1846*, had suggested the study of modern heroes as a remedy for the decline of painting (Baudelaire 1976, 2:493). Meanwhile the infant Second Republic, in the aftermath of the heady revolutionary days of February 1848, proposed a competition, open to all artists, for a figure to symbolize the Republic. Large numbers of painters set to work. The exhibition at the École des Beaux-Arts from April 27 to May 2, 1848 included a total of 450 painted sketches. Most of the artists involved were bogged down in outdated allegories and disguised studio models. The *National* newspaper of May 1 saw only "grotesque turpitudes." However, Jules Champfleury (the future defender of Realism) did notice, "lost amid a mass of mediocre works, one simple, serious, modest painting" (Champfleury 1894, 98). It was by Honoré Daumier (1808–1879), the well-known satirical lithographer of the July Monarchy (fig. 559).

For his first public appearance as a painter, Daumier chose to illustrate the slogan "La république nourrit ses enfants et les instruit" (The republic feeds its children and teaches them). He adopted a triangular composition giving an impression of stability. It is a portrayal of both the figure of Charity and of the "mother" of journeymen who, at the end of the day, offers bed and board to apprentices and protects them. Note that the sign chosen by Daumier (this was one of the rules of the competition) is that of a stonecutter (bottom right), combined with the three points inscribed by every journeyman after his signature (Chaudonneret 1987, 62). Timeless in character, this splendid composition utilizes only a minimum of accessories: no Phrygian cap or lion, simply the green touch of a laurel wreath, symbol of peace and immortality, and the French flag (the *tricolore*) held unpretentiously in one hand. In this picture, Daumier the painter already shows complete mastery of his technique, characterized by a vigorous play of highlights on fabric and flesh accentuating the muscle structure in an almost sculptural way. Far-removed though it was from the academic model, this sketch was nevertheless chosen by the jury as one of the twenty to be presented in a larger format, but Daumier never completed the large version.

Most of the other prizewinners were of the Ingres allegiance. These included his pupil Hippolyte Flandrin (1809–1864), who came first, and the young Jean-Léon Gérôme (1824–1924), who had attracted attention at the 1847 Salon with his *Young Greeks Engaged in Cockfighting* (*Jeune Grecs faisant battre des coqs*, Musée d'Orsay, Paris) and was the leader of what Champfleury mischievously dubbed the "tracing paper school." One of the other decisions of Ledru-Rollin's provisional government had been to approve (without a competition) the grandiose project proposed by Paul Chenavard (1807–1895) from Lyon, a "painter of the soul" and friend of Charles Blanc, then in charge of the fine arts department of the Ministry of the Interior, for a cycle of grisaille paintings for the Panthéon.

The intention was to portray the broad lines of world history, *The Procession of Mankind Down the Ages,* dominated by a *Social Palingenesis* (this one to be in color; fig. 647)—using a term invented by the philosopher Pierre-Simon Ballanche, also from Lyon, to denote a syncretic vision of all the faiths of the West. The dream of a "museum of the human race" foundered in the conservative reaction that followed the events of June 1848, and the project never got beyond the cartoon stage; these were shown at the 1855 Exposition Universelle, on the walls of the Salle de Sculpture Française in the Avenue Montaigne.

It was in making fundamental changes to the rules of admission to the annual Salon that the Second Republic (1848–52) took decisions of momentous consequence for the future. The questions raised at the time about the right of artists to present their work to the public and the practical means of achieving this (to which was soon added the duty, on the part of the public, of eliminating the poorest works from the show) led to innumerable rule changes and ultimately, in 1881, to the abandonment of the Salon. Set up under Louis XIV, the institution had been thrown into upheaval by the French Revolution, when a demand for wider access redounded to the benefit of artists' societies. This proved to be the beginning of a multiplication of Salons, heralding the gradual loss of importance of such institutions, which exist to this day. The advent of the Second Empire in 1852 brought more and more alternative solutions, together with a growth in art dealing and increasing numbers of individual and group exhibitions outside the official framework.

The Académie jury, so traditional under the reign of Louis-Philippe that Théodore Rousseau had refused to submit work to the Salon, was replaced under the Second Republic by a jury elected by the artists themselves. In 1848 the jury was required only to grade entries and admission was open to all. Though hardly convincing, this exhibition (the last to be held in the Louvre's Salon Carré and adjacent galleries) did enable perpetual "rejectees" such as Gustave Courbet (1819–1877) to show their work. The following year (1849), the elected jury was involved at the admission stage but allowed in large numbers of naturalistic and Realist works. It awarded prizes to the newcomers, which meant that they did not have to submit their works to the jury at future Salons. The Minister for the Interior, the man with overall responsibility for the fine arts department, fell into line to the extent of buying *An After-dinner at Ornans* (*Une après-dinée à Ornans*) by Courbet, which he allocated to the Musée des Beaux-Arts, Lille. Every ambition was allowed, and the same artist's *Burial at Ornans* (*L'Enterrement à Ornans,* Musée d'Orsay) presents a scene from everyday life in the format of a history painting. Interestingly, it was not the only example: this key problem of format and subject matter was posed with renewed intensity under the Second Republic.

Reflecting his awareness of the poverty of the rural population streaming into the cities on the eve of the 1848 revolution, Alexandre Antigna (1817–1878) showed *Lightning* (*L'Éclair*) at the 1848 Salon, a life-sized portrayal of a family under a lean-to, frightened by a storm. The work was purchased for the Musée d'Avignon and is now in the Musée d'Orsay. The same monumental approach and pyramidal composition was used in the artist's *Fire* (*L'Incendie,* fig. 560) in the 1850–51 Salon (which was awarded the supreme honor of being purchased for the Musée du Luxembourg in Paris) and by Jules Breton (1827–1906) in the two large paintings (now destroyed) with which he made his debut, namely *Destitution and Despair* (*Misère et Désespoir*) at the 1849 Salon and *Hunger* (*La Faim*) at that of 1850–51. Breton later abandoned such urban subjects to depict the rustic life of his native Artois village of Courrières, as Courbet devoted himself to Ornans, the small town in the province of Franche-Comté in eastern France in which he had been born and which he was to make famous.

Similarly, Ernest Hébert (1817–1908), while remaining loyal to Italy, where he had spent a long time after winning the Prix de Rome in 1839, nevertheless tackled in his *Malaria* (*Mal'aria,* fig. 561) a particularly poignant subject from rural life (the fever that used to strike the inhabitants of the unhealthy Pontins marshes) with great realism. The expressions (notably on the face of the sufferer on the left), the atmosphere of gloom, heightened by the greenish tones, and the details of the provisions placed in the boat all recall the picturesque scenes cultivated by the previous generation in the wake of Léopold Robert. When it was exhibited at the 1850–51 Salon, Hébert's *Malaria* won him a first-class medal and immediate entry into the Musée du Luxembourg.

But of course not everything had changed, and eclecticism continued to dominate. Isidore Pils (1823–1875), for example, a Prix de Rome laureate in 1838 and one of the winners of the Concours de la République, tried his hand at various subjects, showing a predilection for dramatic moments in religion and history. At the 1849 Salon, slightly behind events (the euphoria of spring 1848 was already a distant memory), he exhibited a small painting illustrating an episode from the Revolution taken from Alphonse de Lamartine's *L'Histoire des Girondins.* It was entitled *Rouget de Lisle Singing the "Marseillaise" for the First Time at the House of Dietrick, Mayor of Strasbourg* (*Rouget de Lisle chantant pour la première fois la Marseillaise chez Dietrick,* fig. 558). Showing a concern for realistic reconstruction reminiscent of the contemporary interiors of Louis-Léopold Boilly, Pils here created a highly effective composition. The picture, known to every French person, evidently passed unnoticed at the time, perhaps because of its small format, though the government did take the precaution of purchasing it. Initially, however, it was hung where few people saw it—in a room in the Ministry of the Interior, from which it emerged after the painter's death—to enjoy a brilliant career as a "Republican icon" under the title *The Marseillaise* from 1880. This was a history painting using the genre-painting format, in keeping with a trend that became more and more pronounced under the Second Empire (1852–70).

Antique subjects also became mere fantasies, and this was a vein in which Gérôme enjoyed great success with collectors. His *Greek Interior* (*Intérieur grec*, fig. 572) at the 1850–51 Salon (now known only through a tiny study with delightfully fresh coloring) is a long way from the heroic compositions of Jacques-Louis David. This is simply an antique gynaeceum offering an excuse for a collection of nude or clothed women in various languid poses and in a setting whose archaeological accuracy is reminiscent of the records or reconstructions of Greek or Roman buildings made by architectural students at the École des Beaux-Arts. Gérôme's "porcelain" manner earned him a commission for the decoration of a Sèvres vase made for Queen Victoria (Musée d'Orsay). *The Four Quarters of the World Offering their Productions at the First International Exhibition in London in 1851* (*Les Quatre Parties du monde présentant leurs productions à la Première Exposition Internationale de Londres en 1851*) is very much a successor (if on a smaller scale) to the decorative scheme devised by Paul Delaroche for the semicircular auditorium of the École des Beaux-Arts or the *Apotheosis of Homer* (*L'Apothéose d'Homère*) by Jean-Auguste-Dominique Ingres. In fact, Gérôme tried to rival Ingres with the less successful composition entitled *Century of Augustus* (*Siècle d'Auguste*, Musée d'Orsay), probably one of the largest new paintings (6 by 10 meters) shown at the 1855 Exposition Universelle in Paris. At the same exhibition the organizers had had no hesitation in reexhibiting Horace Vernet's gigantic *Capture of the Smala of Abd-el-Kader* (*Prise de la Smala d'Abd-el-Kadar,* Château de Versailles), a painting measuring 20 meters in width that Baudelaire, in his *Salon de 1845*, had described as "daubed at a gallop."

In 1855, however, no expense was spared for the special show (the first of its kind devoted to living artists) that was to accompany the Exposition Universelle of that year. The decision had been taken during the early months of the Second Empire, and the intention was to impose the new regime on the European stage and in particular to compete with France's neighbor across the English Channel. With the exception of industrial sculpture, the fine arts had been absent from the 1851 Great Exhibition in the Crystal Palace in London, but in Paris they were the focus of particular attention, with the erection of a special temporary building on the Avenue Montaigne. The Palais de l'Industrie, located in the Champs-Élysées, was to remain in position until the end of the century, housing the Salon.

In 1855, an impressive 12,500 square meters of wall area in the Palais des Beaux-Arts were covered with paintings. The interior, half of which was devoted to France, was designed by Hector Lefuel, the Louvre architect, and consisted of galleries with top-lighting and two enormous halls reminiscent of the Louvre's Salon Carré. One of these was reserved for Prussia, with the cartoons that Peter von Cornelius had designed for the royal cemetery in Berlin, and the other for France.

That year, the Salon was deliberately incorporated into the exhibition, with new works alongside older works, which it was now possible to submit. Thus, Ingres, Delacroix, Decamps, and Horace Vernet in particular were given what amounted to retrospectives.

Europe's favorite court painter, Franz Xaver Winterhalter (1805–1873), had placed himself at the service of Napoleon III, having previously served Louis-Philippe and his family. He presented recent commissions, official portraits of the emperor and empress destined to be copied and dispatched to various public buildings as well as to the French Salon. The centerpiece was the sumptuous group portrait, completed in 1854, of *Empress Eugénie Surrounded by her Ladies-in-Waiting* (*L'Impératrice Eugénie entourée de ses dames d'honneur*, fig. 557). The figures were depicted life-sized, and their multi-colored crinolines were rendered with such brilliance as to send little girls into ecstasies. The critics attacked the artist either in veiled terms, for fear of the censor, or (like Gustave Planche, for example) quite openly. Planche wrote in the *Revue des Deux Mondes* that all one saw here was an over-sized "parody of Watteau." He went on: "The dresses so coquettishly displayed contain absolutely nothing" (1855, 403–4). In other words, Winterhalter was incapable of giving his models the presence, life, and psychological verisimilitude that one expects of the portraitist. Probably what he was aiming at here was more a spectacular imaginative composition recreating his *Florinda* (Royal Collection, Her Majesty Queen Elizabeth II), a medieval-Spanish fantasy completed in 1852 to a commission from Queen Victoria, in which a cloud of female figures in various stages of undress disport themselves in a glade.

None of this bore comparison, of course, with the fascinating portrait work of Jean-Auguste-Dominique Ingres (1780–1867) so well represented in an adjacent gallery. On two walls, arranged symmetrically around *The Apotheosis of Homer* (*L'Apothéose d'Homère*), which had been taken down from the ceiling of the Musée Charles X in the Louvre especially and replaced by a copy, and the new ceiling of the Hôtel de Ville, *The Apotheosis of Napoleon I* (*L'Apothéose de Napoléon Ier*), the Ingres exhibition showed a broad spectrum of the artist's work since the beginning of the century. The public was able to examine at leisure the way in which his works related to one another. The *Virgin of the Host* (*Vierge à l'hostie*), for example (commissioned by the state in 1841, repainted from 1851, and only recently completed), recalled the artist's long-standing passion for Raphael. Here Ingres was thinking particularly of Raphael's *Virgin of the Candelabra*, of which he owned a copy, as well as certain gestures he had used before in *The Vow of Louis XIII* (*Vœu de Louis XIII*) shown at the 1824 Salon and now in the cathedral of Montauban. The painting is moreover a triumph of line, with a subtle play of perfect circles (the shape of the picture itself, the Virgin's face, the host) and a symmetry that is virtually total. Such a work, with that almost pathological preoccupation with style that Baudelaire criticized in Ingres, would not be out of place in the religious gift shops around Saint-Sulpice Church in

Paris, alongside the pious models supplied by the Düsseldorf School. Its strangeness, however (which our eyes find fascinating), meant that it spent more than thirty years locked away in a government reserve.

The altogether official fame of Ingres (he was a pillar of the Institut de France) guaranteed him the highest rewards, notably a *grande médaille d'honneur* at the 1855 Exposition Universelle, yet this did not prevent criticism. Among the most celebrated instances of repudiation was that of his pupil Théodore Chassériau (1819–1856), who had entered Ingres's studio at the age of fourteen and who had been criticizing his master for not being open to new ideas since 1840. Chassériau's own new manner, which drew particularly on a trip to Algeria in 1846, brought him closer to the colorism of Delacroix. In *"Tepidarium," the Room to Which the Women of Pompeii Withdrew to Rest and Dry Themselves After Bathing* (*"Tepidarium," salle où les femmes de Pompéi venaient se reposer et se sécher en sortant du bain*, fig. 15), which found a place in the Musée du Luxembourg after the 1853 Salon and was reexhibited in 1855, observers noted how the artist had managed to give life (which was the major criterion of the day) to an antique location, skillfully combining archaeological precision with warm coloring and an almost orientalizing sensuality reminiscent of a Delacroix harem. The painting recognizably reproduces a bathroom belonging to Venus Genitrix at Pompeii, excavated at the Porta di Stabia in 1826 and immediately published in the third volume of Paul Mazois's *Ruines de Pompéi*, a work the artist was familiar with.

In contrast to Chassériau, who had learned from Delacroix a new way of handling color, the Antwerp painter Hendrik Leys (1815–1869), who had frequented Delacroix's studio in 1835, had preferred a smoother, more detailed manner for his Romantic and often dramatic scenes in the style of Delaroche. Leys had been confirmed in this approach during a trip to Holland and Germany in 1852, where he had been able to study the masters of the Nordic Renaissance (notably Dürer, whose manner he adopted). A precise, almost metallic style of painting characterized his submissions to the 1855 Exposition Universelle, which accorded so well with the wishes of the jury that Leys was one of three foreigners to receive a *grande médaille d'honneur* (the others being the Prussian Cornelius and the Briton Edwin Landseer, a well-known animal painter). He illustrated Goethe's *Faust* (his influence was later to be felt by the French painter James Tissot), and he depicted an obscure episode from Belgian history, *The Months of Berthal de Haze* (*Les Trentaines de Berthal de Haze*, Musées Royaux des Beaux-Arts, Brussels), which necessitated a lengthy explanation in the catalog: "The tinsmith Berthal de Haze, leader of the brotherhood of former arbalesters, who died in 1512, bequeathed his fighting gear to the Church of Our Lady, to wit: his best corslet, his morion, his gorgerin, his crossbow, his quiver, complete with arrows, and his curved dagger, all to be hung up there in the Chapel of the Oath at the end of the month." The artist chose to portray the gear still at the foot of the altar, during the month of prayer, using a strictly narrative frieze composition showing the congregation and the nave of the church viewed from the side as if in section and stressing the reconstituted realism of the costumes.

The same smooth manner, this time associated with strident coloring, characterized the most striking works in the British section. These were by a group of young artists who, weary of the conventions of history painting and genre imagery, had come together in 1848 to form the Pre-Raphaelite Brotherhood. The situation in London with regard to institutions was less rigid and monopolistic than in France, and the Pre-Raphaelites were able to continue as normal exhibiting their works at the Royal Academy of Arts, the most prestigious though not the only society of artists in the country.

For example, one of the three important painters of the group, Dante Gabriel Rossetti (1828–1882), chose in 1850 to offer his painting (scarcely dry and destined to be modified subsequently) representing an *Annunciation* or *Ecce Ancilla Domini!* to the National Institution (which, unlike the Royal Academy, did not have a jury). This was one of the Pre-Raphaelites' boldest attempts to revolutionize iconography by means of an unusual setting (the Virgin is on a bed rather than at her prie-dieu) and above all by means of a symbolic treatment of color, with a predominance of white as the sign of virginity and a small number of notes of primary colors (blue, associated with the Virgin, the red of Christ's blood, and a faintly coppery yellow-gold in the Virgin's auburn hair). The work was unfavorably received, with the critics complaining that it was too full of ideas and in fact constituted more a symbol of virginity and femininity than a religious representation. In Paris in 1855, the intentions of the Pre-Raphaelites largely passed unnoticed; all people saw was the surprising effectiveness of certain effects of light and realistic details. For example, admiration was expressed for the sunset depicted in a small painting by William Holman Hunt (1827–1910), which in Paris bore the title *Lost Sheep* but which had been shown at the Royal Academy in 1853 as *Our English Coasts, 1852* (fig. 567)—a clear allusion to the defenseless state of England's coastline at a time when people feared an invasion by the new regime of Napoleon III. The artist had admittedly made studies from the life in the Hastings area for his cliffs, vegetation, and sheep, just as his friend John Everett Millais (1829–1896) had painted the landscape for his *Ophelia* beside a stream while staying with Hunt on a farm in Surrey in the summer and fall of 1851. The time Millais took over this painting from the life enabled him to represent the flowers he required (some of which were cited by Shakespeare in *Hamlet* and some of which were included for their symbolic value), even if they did not all bloom at the same time! Following a method much used by the Pre-Raphaelites, Millais painted the figure in his London studio during the following winter. There he observed the effect of drowning, again from the life, by having Elizabeth Siddal (the group's favorite model and Rossetti's future wife) pose in a heated bathtub, wearing an old-fashioned dress. More famous among the end-of-the-century Symbolists than in

1855, Millais's *Ophelia* nevertheless inspired Théophile Gautier to enthuse: "What damp freshness, what watery murky greens. What a beautiful black of deep water beneath overhanging trees" (Gautier 1855, 32).

Though similar in certain respects (the studies from nature, the sincerity, the rejection of convention), Courbet's approach was actually very different and his art more radically innovative. We know that when the jury of the 1855 Exposition Universelle rejected some of his large paintings, his response was a vigorous one. With the aid of Alfred Bruyas, a wealthy Montpellier collector who had begun purchasing his works in 1853, Courbet constructed his own Pavillon du Réalisme near the Pont de l'Alma to show "forty paintings from among his works." The Exposition Universelle nevertheless retained eleven works, including several portraits and landscapes together with *The Stone Breakers* (*Les Casseurs de pierres*) from the Salon of 1850–51 (now destroyed), *The Young Ladies of the Village* (*Les Demoiselles de village*), acquired by the duke of Morny before the 1852 Salon (Metropolitan Museum of Art, New York), and two major new works: *The Meeting* (*La Rencontre*, fig. 20) and *The Winnowers* (*Les Cribleuses de blé*, fig. 568). *The Meeting*, which was instantly dubbed *Bonjour Monsieur Courbet* (the artist was already famous, following several scandals at previous Salons), was commissioned by Bruyas and is associated with Courbet's stay at Montpellier during the summer of 1854. The composition is simultaneously narrative and symbolic. It echoes the popular image (well known to Courbet and his friend Champfleury) showing "the burghers of the town speaking to the wandering Jew," and it is capable of a thoroughly Fourierist reading as the meeting of money and genius, one of the "solutions" dear to Bruyas's heart. The location is precisely identified as being near a friend's house on the outskirts of Montpellier, and we see Courbet arriving on foot (leaving for others the coach visible in the background), a free artist returning from the sea, his painting gear on his back.

Courbet possessed a powerful artistic temperament (as Champfleury recognized, even if he was exasperated by his friend's pretensions), and was at his most inspired shortly before the Exposition Universelle. At Ornans he embarked on a "painting of country ways," *The Winnowers*, for which he had people he knew well pose, notably his sister Zoé. In search of collectors, Courbet followed the usual contemporary practice of sending the painting to numerous exhibitions: it went to Brussels, London, Besançon, and finally (in 1861) Nantes, where it was acquired for the local museum. The same did not happen to *The Painter's Studio: A Real Allegory Determining a Seven-Year Phase of my Artistic Life* (*L'Atelier du peintre; allégorie réelle determinant une phase de sept ans de ma vie artistique*, fig. 562) an impractically large canvas (it is over 6 meters long) that was rejected at the Exposition Universelle and formed the centerpiece of Courbet's private exhibition. Delacroix, who appreciated the craftsmanship behind the work, noted in his *Journal* on August 3, 1855: "What they've rejected there is one of the most outstanding works of the age." The painting is in fact one of the last manifestations of history painting, a kind of monumental charade that people are still trying to decode. Courbet gave his friend Champfleury a lengthy description of the work: "I am in the center, painting. On the right is the active contingent, i.e., friends, workers, those who love the world of art. On the left is the other world of commonplace existence, the populace, destitution, poverty, wealth, the exploited, the exploiters, those who live off death." While the figures on the right are easily recognizable as Courbet's friends (Baudelaire, Champfleury, Proudhon), those on the left are variously disguised. The poacher in the foreground can only be Napoleon III, for example, and the whole composition is a kind of lesson in political reconciliation around the artist in touch with nature. The work was very little seen during Courbet's lifetime (unlike *Burial at Ornans*, he did not reexhibit it at the 1867 Exposition Universelle), and it eventually entered the Louvre in 1920. Certainly the format was that of a museum piece.

In the years following the 1855 Exposition Universelle, even if Courbet's exemplary initiative had no real public success, the taste for reality spread through the various painting genres. Even history painting now became anxious to reconstitute the events of the past so faithfully as to invest them with the same presence as if they were happening on the stage. For instance, the Munich painter Karl von Piloty (1826–1886), working in the tradition of Paul Delaroche, depicted an episode from the Thirty Years' War, namely the assassination of the imperial army's General Wallenstein in February 1634. Amid a jumble of silky hangings painted with great brio, this vast composition shows us *Seni Before the Body of Wallenstein* (*Seni devant le cadavre de Wallenstein*), the celestial sphere on the table reminding us that Wallenstein's astrologer, Seni, had read the hero's tragic fate in the stars.

Gérôme, a pupil of Delaroche and subsequently of Charles Gleyre, was after the same effect of viewer participation when in *Ave Caesar, Morituri Te Salutant* or *The Gladiators* (*Les Gladiateurs*, fig. 587) he located his viewpoint on the sand of the arena, almost within reach of the body of one of the victims of the last contest. This painting, which shows a group of gladiators shouting up at the box of Emperor Vitellius in A.D. 69 the famous words "Hail Caesar, those about to die salute thee," was one of the instant successes of the 1859 Salon. The figures are not lifesized, but the concern for archaeological accuracy is pushed to the limit. The artist himself admitted that he drew both on literary texts and antique objects (a small bronze in the Cabinet des Médailles in the Bibliothèque Nationale gave him the gladiators' costumes), and it is said that he even asked an architect to help him with the reconstruction of the Colosseum.

At the same Salon, however, Eugène Delacroix (1798–1863) treated another antique subject quite differently. For the aging Romantic painter, now chiefly occupied in executing the major decorative schemes he had been commissioned to produce (the Chapelle des Saints-Anges in the Saint-Sulpice Church in Paris was to be completed in 1861), the primary quality was still imagination, glorified by a mastery of the means of expression, notably color. In *Ovid in Exile Among the Scythians* (*Ovide en exil chez les Scythes*, fig. 589), in which Delacroix worked out one of the subjects for his decorative scheme for the Palais Bourbon library, the artist makes us empathize with the melancholy nostalgia of the poet banished from Rome by the government. He could not help being sensitive to such ingratitude on the part of the political authorities toward genius, having himself had to wait until 1857 for admission to the Académie des Beaux-Arts. In his enthusiastic description of the work, Baudelaire noted: "The mind sinks into it with slow, avid, sensual delight" (Baudelaire 1976, 636). He also expressed the hope that it would delight young artists such as Eugène Fromentin.

It is yet another type of reference to antiquity that we find in the *Portrait of Madame Moitessier* painted by Ingres (fig. 14). The gesture of the index finger pressed to the temple is that of a female figure in an antique painting from Herculaneum now in the Museo e Gallerie Nazionali di Capodimonte, *Hercules and Telephus*, that was much imitated by artists and of which Ingres possessed a copy (Musée Ingres, Montauban). The composition, whose strict architecture makes the *Portrait of Madame Moitessier* more than just a portrait (indeed, she is the very type of the leisured middle class of the Second Empire), was nevertheless worked out with immense care. Begun about 1845, the portrait was later abandoned; it was taken up again in June 1852 and completed only in 1862, with the choice of the dress decorated with flowers against a white background. Like the jewelry and the setting, this is painted with astounding realism, or rather, as Champfleury (an admirer of Delacroix and critic of Ingres) put it, rendered "with incredible care and indulgence" (Champfleury 1990, 135). Using a mirror, Ingres also shows us the model's profile, which certainly corresponds to the Greek ideal that contemporaries insisted on seeing in this picture.

A couple of years later, about 1861–62, the official portrait of Napoleon III by Ingres's pupil Hippolyte Flandrin evinced the same concern to be faithful to a reality organized in such a way as to become discreetly meaningful. We know that, in addition to sittings at the Tuileries Gardens, the artist used photographs of the location as well as of the imperial costume, which he himself donned for a photograph. Anxious to obtain an ideal perfection, Flandrin selected the elements of the decor, including a bust of Napoleon I in profile and an Empire chair, and repeated the course adopted by David for his 1812 painting of *Napoleon I Standing in his Office* (*Napoléon Ier debout dans son cabinet de travail*, National Gallery of Art, Washington, D.C.). In London in 1862 and in Paris at the 1863 Salon, popular success was important and this was the first "true" portrait of the emperor, an intimate psychological study. It failed to please such Realists as Manet's friend Zacharie Astruc.

In Great Britain, the Pre-Raphaelites and their friends were pushing to the extreme their search for a symbolic, edifying meaning in details, using juxtapositions of meticulously rendered real elements. References to the art of the past were not lacking, even for modern subjects. The blue-green background in the little portrait that Rossetti made of his friend, the poet Robert Browning, in October 1855 echoed their joint interest in fourteenth- and fifteenth-century Italian art and in such Renaissance portraitists as Agnolo Bronzino or François Clouet, whose drawing skills Rossetti echoed, right down to the precise, vivid rendition of the beard and hair. Despite numerous attacks, and at the very time the group was starting to break up, the Pre-Raphaelites attracted many followers. One of these, Henry Wallis (1830–1916), was above all the author of a single masterpiece, *Chatterton*, shown at the Royal Academy in 1856 and in the following year in Manchester (where it had to be guarded by two policemen). The painting shows the dead poet (1752–1770), poisoned by his own hand, lying supine in his London garret. The dramatic effect of the death of this young prodigy at the age of just eighteen is enhanced by the technical perfection of the work as well as by the choice of details (the elegant clothes, the candle that has just gone out) and has been subject to two interpretations: as an apologia for suicide or, as the artist himself wished, as representing the unhappy fate of an unrecognized genius.

Psychological intensity could also be applied to contemporary subjects, as in the works of Ford Madox Brown (1821–1893). Although never a member of the Pre-Raphaelite Brotherhood, Brown was first the master and subsequently the friend of Rossetti, and the two painters influenced each other in a great many ways. He had trained in Belgium with Baron Gustaf Wappers, been influenced by Delaroche and Delacroix in Paris, and subsequently come into contact, in Rome, with the Nazarenes Cornelius and Friedrich Overbeck. He soon freed himself from this eclectic culture by working outdoors, but he never abandoned the polished manner that characterized them all (with the exception of Delacroix). He had no hesitation in using unexpected combinations of colors, as in the famous and fascinating oval composition, *The Last of England* (fig. 566). The picture was inspired by the departure to Australia in 1852 (for the gold rush) of the Pre-Raphaelite sculptor Thomas Woolner. He himself, together with his wife, posed for the emigrating couple, out in the open in cold weather. Even the cabbages hanging from the ship's rail as provisions on the voyage were purchased especially, while the lifeboat on the deck behind bears the name *Eldorado*—in sharp contrast to the sorrowful expressions on the faces of the travelers thus obliged to leave their homeland. Subsequently, the artist was to confirm his intention of going beyond mere anecdote, however poignant, to create history painting, using an approach not unlike that of Courbet. Like Courbet's *Studio* (fig. 562), the ambitious composition *Work* (fig. 19), which Brown began in 1852, continued and altered at the client's request in 1856, and completed only in 1863, can be described as a "real allegory." In 1865 it formed the centerpiece (with an explanation by the artist in the catalog) of a private exhibition that Brown organized in London at 1911 Piccadilly. To paint his chosen location (in the north London suburb of Hampstead), he had carried his huge canvas and set it up in situ throughout the summer of 1852. Hence the sunlight that illuminates some of the protagonists (the "navvies," the orphans with their big sister, and, in the distance on the right, the people carrying election posters), while in the shade of the trees the artist portrays a wealthy couple on horseback and, on the other side of the railings, a family of Irish tramps. On the far right, observing this spectacle of the entire social spectrum, we recognize Thomas Carlyle and Frederick Denison Maurice, whose ideas are illustrated here.

A painting treated with an extreme minuteness of detail, *The Stonebreaker* (fig. 569), with which John Brett (1830–1902) triumphed at the Royal Academy in 1858, was to delight John Ruskin, the theorist of the group. However, the work is not without a certain picturesque quality, which is a long way from the stern grandeur of a painter such as Courbet, who had tackled the same subject at the 1850–51 Salon.

Hunt and Millais aimed higher in the subjects from modern life that they painted about this time. With his *Awakening Conscience*, which is dated 1853 but was retouched several times (notably in 1856, because the collector found the young woman's face too sorrowful), Hunt set out to moralize. This was a topical subject, relating to the growth of urban prostitution, and in his concern for accuracy Hunt even hired a room in a brothel for his work. Ruskin was pleased with the way in which the most unassuming details added to the overall comprehension of the piece. There is no ring on the ruined girl's finger, for instance, the score on the piano includes the word "tears" in its title, and there are numerous indications, apart from the young woman's movement and expression, that some hope of redemption is possible (the ray of sunlight falling in the foreground, the bird escaping the claws of the cat). The significance of what can be seen in the mirror appears to have escaped contemporaries (possibly the composition is somewhat overloaded); clearly, this scene of sunlit nature represents the innocence on which the young woman has temporarily turned her back. The chemise, underskirt, and cashmere shawl in which she is clad constitute a state of dishabille very like that of one of Courbet's *Young Women on the Banks of the Seine* (*Demoiselles des bords de la Seine*, fig. 578) The reason why this latter painting caused such a stir at the 1857 Salon (horrifying Proudhon, for example) was that it commented ironically on the morals of girls of easy virtue as they wait in a state of sensual nonchalance for a client (for surely there is a man visible in the rowboat in the background?). Again, the subject was corruption in the urban society of the day.

Millais for his part intended his contemporary *Blind Girl* (fig. 565) as a response to Hunt. What he was describing was the poverty of country life, rendered even more pathetic by his subject's disability. The verdant landscape and double rainbow are forever alien to her and she has her back to them, but the other senses are alert. She is touching a blade of grass as she listens to birdsong, and has a small musical instrument in her lap; her companion is smelling a flower. The subtle symbolism of what might at first glance appear to be a simple genre scene recurs with even greater clarity in *The Valley of Eternal Rest* (fig. 564), in which Millais combines a sunset landscape actually observed, a view of a cemetery painted elsewhere, and two nuns digging a grave and meditating on death. Even if each of these elements was painted from the life, including the models dressed up as nuns, the composition as a whole was worked out in advance for its content.

This concern for direct observation led Hunt to leave for Palestine in 1854 in search of biblical locations. It was to the south of the Dead Sea, at Kharbet Esdun (then identified as the site of Sodom), that he painted the desolate landscape of his *Scapegoat* (fig. 18). Hunt depicts the animal as an exile living in this uninhabited place, bearing the sins of the Jewish people (according to the Old Testament another goat was sacrificed, and it is this one, drowned in the sea, whose horns can be seen on the left). The white goat, symbol of purity, a trickle of blood on its horns, prefigures the Messiah wearing the crown of thorns who, through his Passion, was to redeem the sins of the world. This personal interpretation of the Holy Scriptures surprised people when the work was submitted to the Royal Academy in 1856, but the image nevertheless has a haunting quality about it. This is one of the great inventions of the period.

The passion for truth that Ruskin advocated found a distinctive echo in America with the landscape artist Frederick Edwin Church (1826–1900), a pupil of Thomas Cole who devoted himself to portraying the great natural sights of North America and the Andes. For his *Niagara Falls* (fig. 582), for example, of which he made a careful study from the life in 1856, he shrewdly chose an elongated composition devoted mainly to water and sky, creating a powerful effect and suggesting a flood as the symbolic origin of the New World, which offered humanity a second beginning. America was a new Jerusalem, the Hudson Valley, where Church settled, was a new Eden, and his house, Olana, named after a location near Mount Ararat, was the new center of the world. This breadth of vision (by which Church established the legitimacy of American landscape) earned the artist enormous success when he exhibited *Niagara Falls* in a private gallery in New York and subsequently in London in 1857; ten years later (in 1867) the painting won him a medal at the Exposition Universelle in Paris.

In France this search for national identity, this concern to put down roots in one's own territory, had been in evidence since the 1830s among such artists as Théodore Rousseau (1812–1867) and his successors, prompted by the English example of John Constable and Richard Parkes Bonington or that of the seventeenth-century Dutch masters. In the process, they deliberately rejected any reference to the Italian landscape, the very basis of historical landscape, which had been an academic genre since 1818 and was to be swept away as obsolete in the 1863 reform of the École des Beaux-Arts. They likewise detached themselves from the picturesque quality associated with Romantic trips to the French provinces in order to concentrate on essentials, namely the representation of nature. Charles Le Roux (1814–1895), Jules Dupré (1811–1889), and Narcisse-Virgile Diaz de la Peña (1807–1876) encountered Théodore Rousseau before 1840. Charles Le Roux, who often painted the huge skies of his native region around the Loire estuary, also succeeded in capturing the trembling of light in the branches in *The Edge of the Wood, Cherry Trees in Autumn* (*Lisière des bois, cerisiers en automne*, shown at the 1855 Exposition Universelle, fig. 584). The effects obtained by Dupré and Diaz by means of impasto combined with color contrasts were even more spectacular. This is seen to best effect in Dupré's *Sluice Gate* (*La Vanne*, exhibited at the 1867 Exposition Universelle) and Diaz's *Jean de Paris Heights, Forest of Fontainebleau* (*Les Hauteurs du Jean de Paris; forêt de Fontainebleau*, 1867, fig. 581), one of the greatest masterpieces of the Barbizon School.

The so-called Barbizon School was dominated by the restless and highly poetic personality of Théodore Rousseau, who finally settled in the little town on the edge of the forest of Fontainebleau in 1848. Rousseau often reworked his paintings, which were begun in situ and continued in the studio. An example was his *Village of Becquigny* (*Le Village de Becquigny*, fig. 571), which he started in 1862, then altered in 1863 after having discovered Japanese prints. According to his friend and biographer Alfred Sensier, that discovery prompted the artist to "change the whole harmony of his village: from being gentle and northern as it was, he dreamed of a blue sky like the colored sapphires of the East . . . He redid his sky, repainting its reflections and highlights and leaving only the silhouettes of his former village. Everything except the fixed shapes of his parent configurations became Japanese in terms of coloring" (Sensier 1872, 272). However, it is difficult to assess this experiment, because Rousseau reworked the painting yet again after the 1864 Salon, where his bold ideas had met with incomprehension.

The Dutch tradition of landscape filled with domestic animals had found many disciples in France. Here too the transfer from a picturesque art with "porcelain" animals of a painter like Jacques-Raymond Brascassat to a more naturalistic art was effected by such personalities as Rosa Bonheur (1822–1899) or above all Constant Troyon (1810–1865), who also cast a knowledgeable eye on the rustic life of the outskirts of Paris in his *Grape Harvest Beside the Seine at Suresnes* (*Les Vendanges sur les bords de la Seine, à Suresnes*, fig. 593) painted in 1862.

As for Jules Breton, following the large *misérabiliste* canvases (showing scenes from the lives of poor people) he had painted under the Second Republic, he devoted himself to chronicling the rural life of Courrières, his native village in the Artois region of northern France. In *The Burning Rick* (*La Meule en feu*, 1852–56, fig. 570), there is still some sentimentality in the heroic scene of solidarity as the people struggle to save the precious harvest.

A similar search for emotion and narrative effect characterized *The Shipwreck Victim* (fig. 586) by Dutchman Jozef Israëls (1824–1911). This picture was hailed as a masterpiece at the 1861 Salon in Paris and above all at the International Exhibition in London in 1862. As with *The Burning Rick*, which denounced the lack of means to combat fires, *The Shipwreck Victim* contains an implicit social message: the need to have more lifeboats stationed along the coast. Van Gogh recalled this sad procession over the dunes, led by the widow and orphans, during his time in the Borinage district of Belgium, where he himself witnessed mining accidents.

Even if Israëls sometimes came very close to the French painter Jean-François Millet (1814–1875) in his intimist scenes of rural life, he never achieved the same grandeur. Millet had been overwhelmed by the 1848 revolution and, having taken up residence in Barbizon as early as the end of 1849, he had sent a monumental *Sower* (*Semeur*, Kofu Museum, Japan) to the 1850–51 Salon. As a consequence, he was associated with Courbet in the minds of the conservative critics who prevailed under the Second Empire. They saw his Salon works as a dangerous apologia for the poor.

Certainly, Millet gave a new monumentality to the representation of the men and women of the countryside in their traditional activities, insisting on the moral dignity of his models. He abandoned the spirit of the pastoral scenes painted in the style of François Boucher or Jean-Honoré Fragonard that had tempted him in the 1840s, and he deliberately moved away from the picturesque quality of Romantic painting. Without using large formats, he elevated the modern peasant to the status of a subject of history painting. The government may not have considered him a worthy candidate for the Musée du Luxembourg, but he did not lack private admirers, and particularly after 1864 dealers also began to take an interest in his work. His *Angelus* (fig. 580) is a case in point. If the "Monsieur américain" who had asked him to complete the picture in 1857 never showed up to take delivery of his order, the work nevertheless found a buyer in 1859 and subsequently passed between collectors and dealers at a rapid rate. Francis Petit had it in 1864, Paul Durand-Ruel in 1869, Georges Petit in the 1880s, and it was finally sold by Sedelmeyer on July 1, 1889, together with the Secrétan Collection, for a record price. The sale caused an international stir at a time when naturalism had itself achieved official status.

This painting, one of the best-known works of the nineteenth century, perhaps contains an element of nostalgia. Indeed, Millet wrote to a friend of his in 1865: "*The Angelus* is a painting I did while thinking how, when working in the fields in the old days, my grandmother would without fail, as soon as she heard the bell toll, make us stop what we were doing in order to say the Angelus for those poor dead people, reverently holding our hats in our hands." However, the very organization of the scene, beneath its apparent simplicity, soon made the work a "lesson in social and political morality," as Léon Gambetta called it in 1873: the position of the woman on the same side as the church where the bells are tolling and the light that bathes her serve to show that she is more directly affected by religion than the man, who waits respectfully but indifferently. The division of labor between the sexes is also documented: digging for the man, gathering for the woman. At the 1857 Salon, with *Gleaners* (*Des glaneuses*, Musée d'Orsay), and to an even greater extent in 1863, with the impressive *Man with a Hoe* (*Homme à la houe*, The J. Paul Getty Museum, Malibu), Millet's art, with its way of evoking the darkest depths of poverty, divided the critics. While the conservative press poked fun at the cretinous faces of his countryfolk, Jules Castagnary, the theorist of naturalism, defended his qualities of sincerity and truth and came down on the side of *Gleaners*, finding it to be a "very beautiful, very simple work of art, free of all bombast" (Castagnary 1892, 1:24).

It is an illuminating exercise to compare these two works with *Hunger, Madness, Crime* (*Faim, Folie, Crime*), painted in 1854 by the Belgian Antoine Wiertz (1806–1865), an anguished and somewhat pretentious artist who cultivated a visionary Romanticism. In 1850 Wiertz had managed to persuade the Belgian government to provide him with a large studio, which after his death became a curious museum of his work. Alongside colossal historical compositions, in which the artist sought to outdo his hero Peter Paul Rubens, we find genre scenes that occasionally look forward to Symbolism and often resemble the illustrations of Victor Hugo (indeed Wiertz depicted Esméralda and Quasimodo, characters from Hugo's novel *Notre-Dame de Paris*). These scenes tend to be macabre in the extreme. *Hunger, Madness, Crime* shows a hallucinating mother cutting up her child prior to cooking its limbs.

If the very rules of the Paris Salon (which under the Second Empire quickly reverted to the system of having submissions judged by an academic jury) encouraged artists to work within recognized genres, paintings of a more personal nature sometimes reflected a sincere realism, notably in the field of portraiture. While pursuing somewhat laborious studies in Paris under Martin Drolling and subsequently under François-Édouard Picot (he eventually won the Prix de Rome in 1858, just before the top age limit of thirty), the Alsace-born painter Jean-Jacques Henner (1829–1905) earned his living practicing the art of the provincial portrait. He also experimented with a number of tightly composed realistic scenes painted at Bernwiller, using relations as models. At the opposite end of the spectrum from Courbet's "manifesto" paintings, these are almost naive portrayals of family life, intended for personal use. In the impressive little painting representing *The Artist's Mother Praying Beside the Body of her Daughter Madeleine* (*La Mère de l'artiste priant devant le corps de sa fille Madeleine*, fig. 575), which dates from 1852, the dead girl under her shroud occupies the whole width of the composition, her head dominated only by the crucifix on the right, and the artist's restraint in depicting his mother from behind and against the light is expressed symbolically in the winter landscape seen on the left through the misted windowpanes.

It was prior to his arrival in Paris in January 1854 and his entry into the studio of Léon Cogniet on a scholarship from the city of Bayonne that the young Léon Bonnat (1833–1922) painted a number of remarkable portraits that he never exhibited but kept in his studio until his death. In *Family Portrait* (*Portrait de famille*, 1853) he grouped together his brother, his mother, his sister, and a servant standing in the background. The chief protagonists are shown variously occupied in the silence of a provincial afternoon (one is reading, while the others sew, all with lowered gaze, indifferent to one another's presence) in a composition that makes no concessions to the viewer and contains none of those picturesque, narrative ingredients that mark the genre painting. One thinks of Degas and his *Bellelli Family* (*Famille Bellelli*, fig. 610), begun five years later, though not completed until 1867.

Following his course at the École des Beaux-Arts, Bonnat won only a second prize in the Prix de Rome but was nevertheless able, thanks to fresh financial support from friends and from the city of Bayonne, to stay in Italy from 1858 to 1860. His memories of Spanish art (Bayonne is close to the border with Spain) were complemented by his study of the Renaissance painters and, above all, by his discussions on art with the artists who frequented the Villa Medici: Henner, Jules Lefebvre, Jules-Élie Delaunay, the sculptor Henri Chapu, Edgar Degas, and Gustave Moreau. The latter, an older man, brilliant and cultivated, played the role of mentor for these young artists, in particular for Degas, who, before featuring as an independent artist at the heart of the Impressionist group, sought to make his mark as a history painter.

Edgar Degas (1834–1917) had come to Italy, where part of his family lived, in 1856. In Florence in 1858, he painted his portrait of the *Bellelli Family*, which represented his first brush with tradition. Degas worked on the picture for almost ten years before showing it under the title *Family Portraits* at the 1867 Salon in Paris, where it passed unnoticed. However, as Degas himself stressed on several occasions, his aim was to produce a painting worthy of being shown at the Salon rather than a private portrait. He did numerous detail studies (faces, hands) and packed the composition with deliberate meaning. The picture portrays the domestic drama of a family exiled from Naples to Florence, much to the despair of Laura (his seriously depressive cousin) and her irascible husband Gennarro, who had no proper job and whom we see turning almost reluctantly to face his wife and daughters. The youngest, Giulia, sitting on a stool with one leg tucked under her, appears impatient, lending animation to the whole, while in the great tradition of group effigies from the classical era Degas includes a portrait of his grandfather Hilaire Degas, on the wall behind his daughter Laura. Hilaire had just died in Naples (in 1858), hence the dark mourning dress, alleviated only by the girls' white pinafores.

Shortly after his return to Paris, he became interested in genuinely historical subjects. For his *Spartan Girls Provoking Boys* (*Petites Filles spartiates provoquant des garçons*, fig. 590), Degas was probably influenced by Gustave Moreau, who began painting *Tyrtaeus* (*Tyrtée*), a subject drawn from the history of Sparta (about 1860). Degas drew on Plutarch and the book *Voyage du jeune Anacharsis en Grèce* (1787) by the Abbé Barthélemy. Later on, Degas considered exhibiting his picture at the fifth Impressionist exhibition in 1880, though he eventually decided against it. Nevertheless, the catalog lists the title with the date 1860 beside it.

We know from the unfinished version in the Art Institute of Chicago that Degas decided to remove an antique building from the background and some plane trees to the right. At the time, people would have been able to detect a similarity in the approach of Degas in this picture and that of Puvis de Chavannes (1824–1898), whose cartoon for *Ludus Pro Patria* (Musées Royaux d'Art et d'Histoire, Brussels) for the staircase of the Musée de Picardie, Amiens, was presented at the 1880 Salon. In rejecting archaeological or exotic details (Sparta on the horizon is shown as a simple village), Degas was looking for a fresh approach to history painting. This was the man who, according to his niece Jeanne Fèvre, had "a very vivid, very keen, very intelligent sense of ancient Greece" (Fèvre 1949, 51).

While Degas was experimenting with history paintings that never left his studio, such as *Semiramis Building Babylon* (*Sémaris construisant Babylone*, 1860–62, Musée d'Orsay), which may have been an allusion to the radical redesign of Paris being undertaken by Baron Haussmann, Léon Belly (1827–1877) scored a huge success at the 1861 Salon with a modern Orientalist subject that had pretensions in the direction of history painting. Belly's *Pilgrims Traveling to Mecca* (*Pèlerins allant à la Mecque*, fig. 603) should be read as illustrating the universality of religion, despite the division of faiths, for on the left of the caravan, halfway back, we see a reminder of the flight into Egypt, with Joseph on foot beside a donkey bearing the Virgin and Child. Belly had been a regular visitor to Barbizon since 1849 and had made several trips to the Middle East. However, despite a favorable reception at Paris exhibitions from 1855 onward, his naturalistic landscapes of France and Egypt were not deemed worthy of purchase by the government. It took this vast and ambitious canvas, with its striking back-light, to move the state to buy one of his works. Following a brief spell in the apartments of the Minister of State, *Pilgrims* entered the Musée du Luxembourg in 1863. Some years later Belly took a further step by producing a real history painting, which the government bought at the 1867 Salon and allocated to his native city. In the enormous *Sirens* (*Les Sirènes*, 3.63 by 3 meters, Musée de Saint-Omer), a group of buxom Rubenesque nymphs (he had studied the Louvre's Galerie de Medicis in 1865) leave an unconscious Ulysses firmly tied to the mast of his ship. The critics were hardly favorable; Belly's true vocation was landscape and the kind of outdoor painting practiced by his friends (and elders) Troyon, Corot, and Théodore Rousseau. His example clearly illustrates how the gulf between artists and institutions was growing.

Those who followed the example of Courbet found their work rejected, as did Manet, Henri Fantin-Latour, and James McNeill Whistler in 1859, or ignored, which is what happened to Alphonse Legros (1837–1911), to the point where in 1863 he went into voluntary exile in England. Legros was even accused, with *The Shrine* (*Ex-voto*) at the 1861 Salon, of reviving the scandal of *Burial at Ornans*. The memory of Courbet's *Wounded Man* (*L'Homme blessé*, Musée d'Orsay) was clearly evoked by the young Carolus-Duran (1837–1917), both in *Man Asleep* (*L'Homme endormi*, Musée des Beaux-Arts, Lille) at the 1861 Salon and in *The Convalescent* or *The Casualty* (*Le Convalescent* or *Le Blessé*, fig. 27), a fragment of the large composition that had won Carolus-Duran the Prix Wicar in Lille in 1860, leading to a four-year stay in Italy. For the Salon, he settled for a waistcoat open to reveal a white shirt, whereas before he had boldly dressed his subject in a bright-red jacket.

Thanks to the art critic Zacharie Astruc, whom he had got to know in Lille, Carolus-Duran became acquainted with Courbet and subsequently with Manet, and he became part of the group of painters and critics that used to meet at the Brasserie des Martyrs. They were enthusiastic about Manet's submission to the 1861 Salon—not the austere portrait of his parents (Musée d'Orsay) but *Spaniard Playing the Guitar* (*L'Espagnol jouant de la guitare*, Metropolitan Museum of Art, New York). Manet had chosen the subject for its fashionable exoticism (although it was painted from a model posing in the studio) and had treated it with the Spanish masters and Frans Hals in mind. Fernand Desnoyers, the spokesman of the group, was later to write of the time when Legros, Fantin-Latour, Carolus-Duran, and others visited Manet, whom they did not yet know: "The Spanish musician was painted in a certain way, a strange, new way of which the astonished young painters believed that they alone held the secret, a kind of painting midway between that called Realist and that called Romantic" (Desnoyers 1863, 40–41). Although Manet maintained his independence, he was flattered by such recognition and was looked upon as the leader of the school, soon becoming familiar with the writers of the group, Champfleury and Baudelaire. Nowhere is the novelty of Manet's technique more apparent than in *Baudelaire's Mistress Reclining* (*La Maîtresse de Baudelaire couchée*, fig. 599), his strange portrait of the Creole woman, Jeanne Duval, the writer's "aging Infanta," painted in 1862 when she was sick and half-paralyzed. Her hard, swarthy face, ugly enough for Courbet, contrasts with her immense striped crinoline, which is treated broadly, almost sketchily, and the delicate embroidery on the curtain hung over the windows of the Rue Guyot studio that Manet occupied at the time.

To understand just how surprising such a style was at the time, even coming from a pupil of Thomas Couture (Manet had spent six years in his studio), who sought to make his teaching distinct from academism, it should be compared with that of an artist of the same generation, the Swiss Albert Anker (1831–1910). Anker had trained in

Paris from 1854 in the studio of his compatriot Gleyre (where Pierre-Auguste Renoir, Frédéric Bazille, and Claude Monet were to follow him some years later). He quickly found his own direction, which was a long way from the history painting he attempted in the early years of his career, and embraced scenes from the village life of his native Bern canton, showing girls and old men going about their daily occupations. Anker often returned to Paris during the winter, but he kept faith with the Germanic tradition of genre scenes, which (it is worth remembering) had been so successful at the 1855 Exposition Universelle. A typical example of his narrative style (which changed little for the remainder of the century) is *The Test* (*L'Examen*, 1862, fig. 592). In his very pure sense of values and in the serenity that his pictures exude (particularly his portraits of children), he is sometimes reminiscent of Camille Corot as a figure painter. Anker's work heralds the official naturalism of the 1880s through his constant attention to authentic detail and the bright, diffuse light that surrounds his figures.

The year 1863 was marked in Paris by an event of legendary importance: the Salon des Refusés ("Salon of the Refused"), which is often seen as marking the birth of modern art. From the start of the Second Empire, thanks to Count de Nieuwerkerke, the superintendent of fine arts, the Salon had been held on a regular basis (every two years), and the jury had become increasingly strict. Artists became afraid of falling into disrepute with potential clients if their works were rejected. On January 29, 1862, Troyon wrote to Eugène Boudin, who had returned to Le Havre: "The situation is a difficult one, with artists in general rather unsatisfied . . . The poor youngsters have good reason to complain" (Jean-Aubry 1922, 53). While it is commonly thought that only Realists and naturalists suffered from the hostile judgments of the jury, it is worth remembering that the jury's role was in fact to eliminate amateurs, painters with truly poor technique. One of these, Théodore Véron (1820–1898), a self-styled history painter, poet, and critic, aware of the progressive discredit into which this noble art was falling among collectors, relied on the government to give him a chance. Rejected in 1861, he addressed a proposal (which remained without effect) to the authorities that they should accept all submissions and ask the jury to suggest a system of grading from masterpieces to more mediocre works, leaving the public to judge. Véron was soon aiming even higher, addressing Napoleon III directly. On April 11, 1861 he submitted a petition on behalf of rejected artists, in which the emperor underlined the following sentence in red: "To see our works placed in a room reserved for the purpose in the Palais de l'Exposition" (the Palais de l'Industrie never being more than half-filled by the Salon).

That was precisely what the emperor decided after visiting the Palais de l'Industrie on April 22, 1863, a week before the opening of the Salon. On April 24, 1863 the newspaper *Le Moniteur universel* published an article that generated great excitement among artists: "Numerous complaints have reached the emperor on the subject of the works of art rejected by the exhibition jury. Anxious to allow the public to judge the legitimacy of such complaints, His Majesty has decided that the works of art that have been rejected would be exhibited in another part of the Palais de l'Industrie. That exhibition shall be optional." This last provision inevitably provoked endless discussion (would people say the jury had been right, thus further increasing its power?). Many artists withdrew their works, but others, such as Manet and Whistler, did not hesitate. Nor did Johan Barthold Jongkind, Antoine Chintreuil, Fantin-Latour, Legros, and even Jean-Paul Laurens (1838–1921) who, like the two previous artists, had also had a work accepted for the Salon. Opening on May 15, the Salon des Refusés was a huge success—even if in some cases it was as a source of amusement, as with the submissions of Manet and Whistler (1834–1903). The latter, an American artist who divided his time between London and Paris, submitted his *Dame blanche* (later entitled *Symphony in White No. 1: The White Girl*, National Gallery of Art, Washington, D.C.), which had already been turned down by the Royal Academy in London the year before. Excluded from the Salon in 1859, Whistler had in fact taken part in a private exhibition of rejected artists at the house of the Realist painter François Bonvin (1817–1887) at 189 Rue Saint Jacques, along with Fantin-Latour, Legros, and Théodule Ribot—all fervent admirers of Courbet, as well as being regulars at the Brasserie Andler.

In 1863, however, Whistler's reception went beyond the circle of his friends when his *Dame blanche*, which had been well hung, attracted a certain amount of attention. The same fate befell Manet's three paintings, notably *Le Bain*, which has since been known as *Le Déjeuner sur l'herbe* (fig. 597). The outcry provoked by this painting was greater than anything previously provoked by Courbet, who was absent from both 1863 Salons, his *Return from the Meeting* (*Retour de la conférence*), which featured drunken priests in a country lane, having been banned for immorality. Manet for his part was surely echoing Courbet's *Young Women on the Banks of the Seine* in presenting his prostitute with two dandies—an episode which even Baudelaire's friend Thoré described as being "in very daring taste." The rowboat in the background and the fine still life of discarded garments and picnic things both refer to Courbet's painting. Moreover, the artist wanted to offer the jury a nude. But we know that, again, Manet was careful to pay tribute to the art of the past: the idea of combining nude and dressed figures he borrowed from Titian's *Pastoral Concert* (then attributed to Giorgione) in the Louvre, and the poses are in part taken from an engraving by Marcantonio Raimondi based on *The Judgment of Paris* by Raphael. He had friends sit for him in modern dress, and the seated nude is Victorine Meurent, a favorite model of his for the past year. Everyone saw her as a model in repose (who would afterward get dressed again) rather than some ideal figure from antiquity as painted by Alexandre Cabanel, Paul Baudry, or Amaury-Duval, for example, whose three *Venus* pictures delighted visitors to the official Salon that year. *The Birth of Venus* (*La Naissance de Vénus*, fig. 22) by Alexandre Cabanel (1823–1889), which was acquired by the civil list of Napoleon III (and allocated to the national museums in 1879 by judicial decision), illustrates the kind of technique that was popular at the time: polished, smooth, and meticulous—quite unlike the vigorous work of Manet, who was accused of painting mere sketches. There was also the importance attached to drawing, of which the otherwise severe Jules Castagnary recognized the correctness, concluding nevertheless: "M. Alexandre Cabanel is no painter" (Castagnary 1892, 1:114). And yet it was precisely Cabanel who, in 1863, reaped every honor, including election to the Institut de France and appointment to a professorship at the École des Beaux-Arts (reformed at the end of that year), along with Pils and Gérôme. Cabanel's very training (he had studied under the old Neoclassicist Picot and won the Prix de Rome in 1845) made him the distant heir of the technique of David, though in his work David's heroic substance was ditched in favor of a voluptuous imagination that is not without reference to Boucher and other eighteenth-century artists.

The experiment of the Salon des Refusés seems to have been somewhat inconclusive. Certain paintings might also well have been acceptable to the official Salon, such as the *Ruins of Rosemont Castle* (*Ruines du château de Rosemont*, fig. 594) by Johan Barthold Jongkind (1819–1891). A Dutch painter who had come to France to study under Eugène-Gabriel Isabey and even, for a while, under Picot, Jongkind had had a healthy clientele for ten years, like his friend Troyon. Granted, he belonged to the circle of Théodore Rousseau and Boudin and lived a rather bohemian existence. In later years, his honest approach to nature was to have a genuine influence on Monet, for example. Castagnary, who liked his work, wrote in 1863 "For me, he is an artist to his fingertips," though he did add a word of warning: "In him, everything lies in the impression" (Castagnary 1892, 1:170).

One painting accepted by the official Salon in 1863 was *The Morning Wash* (*La Toilette du matin*, fig. 591) by Théodule Ribot (1823–1891), an artist who had exhibited for the first time in 1861 with kitchen scenes, after having been rejected in 1859 (when he had exhibited with Courbet's friends at the house of Bonvin). The painting depicts a *salle d'asile*, a place where young children were looked after. It is a good example of the vigorous, Spanish-influenced style of an artist who had none of the rose-tinted affectations of someone like Cabanel.

This incoherent selection in 1863 (many people pointed out that there was little difference between the two Salons, apart from the provocative works of artists like Manet and Whistler) probably explains why the experiment did not last long. In a clear gesture to liberalism, the government, wishing to limit the power of the Institut, reinstated the annual Salon and partly altered the composition of the jury. The 1864 Salon des Refusés (or more precisely the exhibition of works "not accepted for the award competition") was made up of artists whose names have been entirely forgotten. Despite repeated pleas on the part of rejected artists (notably Paul Cézanne and Frédéric Bazille), the Second Empire never again organized what had turned out to be a flop.

The presence on the jury of artists such as Charles Daubigny (1817–1878) did enable certain new admirers of Manet to be admitted from time to time. Daubigny was one of the few landscape artists to obtain a semi-official position under the Second Empire. This did not prevent him from experimenting with a new way of studying nature by combing the rivers of the Paris region (the Marne, the Oise, and the Seine) on his studio-boat, the *Botin*. He was one of the first to settle at Auvers-sur-Oise, where he received visits from both Daumier and Corot.

Camille Corot (1796–1875), "le bonhomme Corot" as he was affectionately known, who seems the very incarnation of the joy of painting, had begun his career under those adherents of historical landscape, Achille-Etna Michallon and Jean-Victor Bertin. However, on his very first trip to Italy in 1825 he had met the cosmopolitan group of landscapists then assembled in Rome who already wished to break with academic painting and were not interested in the masters of the past. If Corot had peopled the pictures he sent to the Salon with mythological figures, it was to satisfy the constraints of an institution that regarded landscapes without subjects as mere sketches. Even so, he was rejected several times in the last years of Louis-Philippe's reign.

After 1850 Corot's style changed, becoming more lyrical. His misty evocations of locations once visited won him many admirers and not a few imitators, but it is worth remembering that one of his masterpieces, *Souvenir of Mortefontaine* (*Souvenir de Mortefontaine*), which was bought by the civil list of Napoleon III at the 1864 Salon, for a long time served no other purpose than to decorate the Château de Fontainebleau (where the court occasionally resided) before it entered the Louvre in 1889.

Like many artists looking for customers, Corot often sent paintings to exhibitions organized by associations active in provincial cities. His great work *The Evening Star* (*L'Étoile du berger*) was bought by the city of Toulouse at the local exhibition of the Union Artistique. It includes Corot's favorite subjects (trees and ponds), while the flock on the right is more bucolic than realist.

Compared with the very reasonable, not to say modest prices obtained by Corot (given his talent and his age), the record sums of 50,000 francs fetched by the paintings submitted to the 1864 Salon by Ernest Meissonier (1815–1891) are indicative of the prevailing taste. Meissonier had made his name with war scenes in the Dutch style, incorporating figures in eighteenth-century dress painted with meticulous precision and a clear concern for reconstruction and exemplary documentation. At ease only in small formats, he was capable of representing in the style of a portrait gallery both *Napoleon III at Solferino* (*Napoléon III à Solférino*, Château de Compiègne) and *The Retreat from Moscow* (*La Campagne de France*, 1814, fig. 601). The former was commissioned by the state and

Meissonier went to Italy to study the location for it. The latter shows one of five episodes from the wars of Napoleon I that the artist intended to paint. These two works, shown at the 1864 Salon, formed a contrast with more topical paintings of battles and reviews, some of which attained almost panoramic dimensions.

One of the surprises of the 1864 Salon was the sensational debut of Gustave Moreau (1826–1898), who leapt to immediate fame and from then on attracted many loyal admirers. *Oedipus and the Sphinx* (*Œdipe et le Sphinx*) was bought by Prince Napoleon, a noted collector and an admirer of Ingres (one of whose subjects Moreau here revisited) and first purchaser in 1859 of Ingres's *Turkish Bath* (*Bain turc*, fig. 21). Gustave Moreau, a pupil of Picot, was strongly influenced by his friend Chassériau's decorative scheme for the staircase of the Cour des Comptes (now in the Louvre), as well as by the Romanticism of Delacroix. He had admittedly taken part in several Salons in the early years of the Second Empire, from 1852 to 1855. But he had then gone to Italy to complete his training (where he met Degas), before developing at length a number of ideal compositions painted in a more academic manner, such as *Oedipus and the Sphinx* in 1864, *The Young Man and Death* (*Le Jeune Homme et la Mort*, Fogg Art Museum, Cambridge, Mass.), painted in memory of Chassériau, *Jason* in 1865, and finally *Orpheus* (*Orphée*, Musée d'Orsay) in 1866, which was acquired by the Musée du Luxembourg.

Also at the 1864 Salon, Fantin-Latour (1836–1904) presented his *Homage to Delacroix* (*Hommage à Delacroix*, Musée d'Orsay). In front of a portrait of the late master, we see the writers Baudelaire, Champfleury, and Edmond Duranty, and a whole clutch of painters, including Legros, Fantin-Latour himself, Whistler, Manet, and Félix Bracquemond. They were all members of the "young school," which a hostile press still associated with Realism, finding that, more than a homage to Delacroix, this was a declaration in support of the artistic movement treated so badly by the Salon jury. We know that Whistler would have liked Dante Gabriel Rossetti to pose too, but Rossetti did not visit Paris in early 1864. That would have made it harder to interpret the painting as a new Realist manifesto, because around that time Rossetti's painting developed a sumptuously decorative quality that would be difficult to reconcile with such a definition. Like Whistler, Bracquemond, and their friends, Rossetti was one of those artists both in London and in Paris who at a very early stage fell under the spell of the Far Eastern, and particularly Japanese, art revealed at the 1862 International Exhibition in London and who became customers of the Japanese curio shop owned by M. and Mme. Desoye under the Rue de Rivoli arcade in Paris.

As with Whistler, Rossetti was particularly interested in color harmonies, such as the blues and greens in *The Blue Bower* (1865, Barber Institute of Fine Arts, Birmingham), in which his model plays a Japanese instrument against a background of Far Eastern blue-and-white ceramics, or the golds, blonds, and Venetian yellows tempered with red and green of *Monna Vanna*, which Rossetti painted the following year (fig. 30). A sumptuous echo of Raphael's *Portrait of Joan of Aragon* in the Louvre, *Monna Vanna* is built up of many circles, emphasizing its fullness—in the dress, the hair, the fan, the jewelry, the necklace, and even the pot of roses in the background.

On a more modest scale, intended to convince visitors to the 1864 Salon of the skills of an artist looking for portrait customers, was the remarkable *Portrait of Miss L.L.* or *Girl in a Red Jacket* (fig. 28) by James Tissot (1836–1902). The picture marked Tissot's abandonment of historical subjects in the style of the Belgian Leys in favor of the honest realism that was to bring him success. A friend of Degas, who painted a fine portrait of him in 1868 (Metropolitan Museum of Art, New York), Tissot was also a dandy with a solid position in smart society. In 1868 he was commissioned to paint a portrait of *The Rue Royale Group*, in which his models appear frozen as if posing for a photographer. Compromised during the Paris Commune, Tissot continued for ten years or so to make a brilliant career as a society painter in London.

Degas himself also abandoned historical subjects in favor of close observation of modern life. In *Woman Leaning on an Elbow Beside a Vase of Flowers* (*Femme accoudée près d'un vase de fleurs*, fig. 23) he introduces us into a typical middle-class home in the country, possibly that of his friends the Valpinçons in southern Normandy. His model is relaxing informally after gathering this large bouquet in her garden, the gloves that protected her hands from scratches now carelessly laid on the table beside the water jug. The off-center composition here is probably not influenced by Japanese prints. Nor can we be certain that Degas was bowing in the direction of Courbet's *Trellis* (*Le Treillis*, Toledo Museum of Art, Toledo), of which it seems likely he was unaware—Courbet had painted *The Trellis* in Saintonge at the house of Étienne Baudry, a young writer he had met through Castagnary, and the picture had only been exhibited at Saintes, in 1863, under the title *Woman with Flowers* (*Femme aux fleurs*).

The new painting was not at all averse to flowers, and Courbet, Fantin-Latour (who had a ready British clientele for his still lifes), and Manet all painted many pictures with flowers in them. Among the best-known bunches (this time wrapped in florist's paper, like those that Degas later placed in the hands of his dancers as they took their bow) is the one being presented by a black servant to *Olympia* (fig. 34) in the most vociferously decried painting of the 1865 Salon. Manet had painted it in 1863, in fact, but had apparently not dared submit it in 1864. Exhibited at the same time as *Christ Insulted by the Soldiers* (*Jésu insulté par les soldats*, Art Institute of Chicago), with which it contrasted in the most scandalous way, *Olympia* is nevertheless another painting packed with allusions to past masterpieces, notably Titian's *Venus of Urbino* and Goya's *Naked Maja* (*La maja desnuda*). This whole tradition, from the odalisque to the black slave, continues (particularly with Ingres) throughout the nineteenth century, but what was surprising here was the absence of any exoticism, of either period or location, and the portrayal of a modern prostitute. A poem by Zacharie Astruc accompanied the title of the painting in the Salon catalog, but the work is also a perfect illustration of the poems of Baudelaire. The style of the painting shocked people as much as the subject, the absence of the traditional model, and Manet's self-confessedly almost naive respect for what he saw.

The same reproach of clumsy, even amateurish technique was leveled against Courbet. Wishing to pay tribute to his friend and defender, the philosopher Proudhon, who had died in January 1865, Courbet had hastily assembled a few documents and shown Proudhon in a family setting just after his release from prison in 1853. His *Portrait of P. J. Proudhon in 1853* was treated sarcastically by the press, and the artist subsequently reworked the painting, adding some greenery in the background and replacing the figure of Proudhon's wife with a work basket.

The critics of course preferred the academic style of William Bouguereau (1825–1905), who succumbed to the temptation of *misérabiliste* subjects with his *Poor Family* (*Famille indigente*) at the 1865 Salon. Here were recognizably studio models (albeit more chubby than poverty-stricken), and the artist's skill at painting hands and feet was greeted with rapturous enthusiasm.

This contrast between widely different techniques was noted in other countries too, with Italy offering an equally significant example. In 1859 the elderly painter Francesco Hayez (1791–1882), who had long been president of the Brera academy in Milan, exhibited one of his best-known compositions, *The Kiss* (*Il bàcio*). The painting instantly satisfied the desires of a public sensitive to a sentimentality that was still Romantic. A late example of a Troubadour style in the Ingres manner, *The Kiss* demonstrated an extraordinary degree of skill in the treatment of fabrics—very different from the dabbing technique being experimented with about the same time by a group of young artists who gathered to talk painting at the Michelangiolo Café in Florence's Via Cavour (Degas frequented the same establishment during his stay in the city). A few members of the group traveled extensively, and thanks to them these young people were aware of artistic developments in London and Paris, receiving news, for example, of the Exposition Universelle in Paris in 1855 and of the disputes surrounding Realism. They also had a number of examples to hand, thanks to the Demidov Collection in the nearby Villa San Donato, which they were able to visit. Consequently, they were familiar with the art of Corot and the Barbizon School, and they liked the violent contrasts of light and shade in the paintings of Decamps. Their technique was profoundly influenced by these artists.

In a society marked by extreme patriotic fervor (this was the time of the final upheavals preceding Italian unification), their ideal was a contemporary art that would give expression to the society from which it sprang. This resulted in a new simplicity of subject matter and a taste for freshness and honesty in what were often very small-format works. Odoardo Borrani (1833–1905), like Telemaco Signorini and Diego Martelli, the future theoretician of the group and chronicler of the French Impressionists (and whose portrait was painted by Degas and Federico Zandomeneghi), signed up in the Tuscan artillery in 1859. Borrani was interested in local landscape and in the intimist portrayal of how political events impinged on everyday life. One of his masterpieces was *The Red Shirt Makers*, a back-lit composition of four young society ladies working for the brave soldiers of Garibaldi. A certain kinship with the work of Degas and Tissot, as well as the Pre-Raphaelites, marks the delicate realism of Silvestro Lega (1826–1895), who dropped the Ingres-like manner of his early years to make a series of outdoor studies and intimist scenes, the most famous of which are *The Visit* (fig. 32) and *The Pergola* (Pinacoteca di Brera, Milan). Both painted in 1868, these works were highly appreciated at exhibitions in Turin, Florence, and Parma for their remarkable evocation of local life. But the man whose work best typifies the technique of these artists (as a group they were known as the Macchiaioli, from the verb *macchiare*, "to blot or speckle") was Giovanni Fattori (1825–1908). Fattori's small paintings passed unnoticed at the time and were "discovered" by twentieth-century critics. In *The Palmieri Rotunda* (fig. 31), painted in 1866, the smart ladies looking out to sea at Livorno, sheltered from the sun by the rotunda of a well-known thermal establishment, are mere patches of flat color—rigorously solid and at the same time supremely elegant. As a portraitist and a painter of military as well as rural subjects, Fattori was among those who persisted in this original technique, while others, such as Telemaco Signorini (1835–1901), turned more deliberately in the direction of *verismo*, the Italian version of naturalism. Despite painting *The Asylum* in 1865, which was not exhibited until 1870 at the Turin "Promotrice," he pioneered a type of subject matter in the spirit of Émile Zola. At the time, the painting left critics bewildered, though it was admired by Degas in 1865 and toward the end of the century helped to establish its author's reputation.

The particular technique of the Macchiaioli, with its pure contrasting colors, was nevertheless related to that of Claude Monet (1840–1926) when he painted his *Picnic* (*Déjeuner sur l'herbe*, fig. 35) in 1865–66 (a much larger picture, of course) or that of his friend Frédéric Bazille (1841–1870), whose *Family Gathering* (*Réunion de famille*, fig. 611) pictured in the shade on the terrace at Méric, near Montpellier in the south of France, was even accepted by the 1868 Salon. The two painters, like Pierre-Auguste Renoir (1841–1919) and Alfred Sisley (1839–1899), had met in the studio of Gleyre, where with varying degrees of dissatisfaction they remained until it closed at the beginning of 1864. Subsequently, they had completed their training as independent painters in regular visits to Chailly and the forest of Fontainebleau and in lengthy discussions at the Brasserie des Martyrs in Paris, where they met Courbet and Camille Pissarro.

The impact of Courbet on Monet has sometimes been overshadowed by his relations with Manet or his older relationship with Jongkind and Boudin on the Normandy coast, yet Monet's admiration for the champion of Realism is clearly visible in the huge *Picnic* (4.60 by 6 meters), which was unfinished and later rolled up and then cut up. In one of the two large fragments preserved in the Musée d'Orsay it is possible to recognize, seated among the guests in a clearing in the forest of Fontainebleau, the figure of Courbet himself. The overall composition (as preserved in the smaller version in Moscow) did not yet include the master of Ornans, and we know that Bazille posed for four male figures. Monet's painting no longer makes any of the overt references to past painters that gave the daring innovations of Manet, for example, their scandalous and ironical quality. The format alone shows that what Monet sought to achieve was a history painting of the society of his day, in other words of contemporary life.

Courbet himself, at that time, while continuing his provocations (or his dreams of large-scale museum painting), had found a wealthy clientele for his portraits (notably in Trouville on the Normandy coast in the summer of 1865), as well as for his landscapes. One version of his *Wooded Stream* (*Ruisseau couvert*, Musée d'Orsay) showing a tree-lined creek in the Doubs *département*, a work which sparkles with freshness, is a sober picture, perfectly acceptable for drawing room decoration, and was acquired on the civil list of Napoleon III by Count de Nieuwerkerke. But his seascapes, in their restraint and luminosity, represent a quite new boldness of approach. Here there is no subject any more, no distinctive or picturesque location, simply pure exploration of chromatic variations, laid down with a firm brush, for beach, sea, and sky. As in *Low Tide at Trouville* (*Marée basse à Trouville*, fig. 25), the latter takes up most of the canvas, which is painted exclusively in pale colors.

Courbet was undoubtedly influenced by others, notably the discreet Boudin (the "king of skies," as Courbet dubbed him) and the English landscapists, but he added a new vigor. This vigor distinguished him from the works of another artist whom Monet met in Trouville in that summer of 1865: Whistler. Whistler's Trouville landscapes, painted in 1865, show the same interest in the coloring of sky and sea (gray-blue or bold pink) but treated with broad brushstrokes in a sketchy, wholly suggestive manner. More than any other artist, Whistler regarded painting as simply an exercise in color variations—to the point where he gave his compositions titles that evoke only the dominant color notes. Whistler originally dated *The Balcony* 1865, before replacing the traditional signature with a rectangular cartouche featuring a butterfly (a kind of naturalistic stylization of his own initials), the cartouche idea being very obviously borrowed from those used by the Japanese ukiyo-e printmakers. Whistler was in fact one of the earliest enthusiasts of Japanese art, which had recently been discovered in London and Paris as a result of the resumption of trade, interrupted since the middle of the seventeenth century. In *The Balcony, Variations in Flesh-color and Green*, Whistler turned the view from his balcony overlooking the River Thames into a sort of Japanese fairy tale by placing several young women dressed in Japanese costume in poses directly inspired by those found in the prints of Utagawa Kunisada and Katsushika Hokusai, almost contemporary Japanese artists whose works, readily available in the bookshops of Edo (renamed Tokyo in 1868), were the first to reach the West. In the foreground he placed a branch in blossom without showing the vase or pot in which it stood. This was an allusive method that the Japanese loved and that Fantin-Latour was to use some years later in his still life, *Corner of the Table*, shown at the 1873 Salon (fig. 45).

Experiments with atmosphere and luminosity were not the monopoly of artists who were treated badly on a more or less regular basis by the juries of Paris Salons. We also find them in Orientalists, who had now got rid of the Romantic chiaroscuro effects cultivated by Decamps in favor of a more Realist view of North Africa and the Middle East (although of course the exoticism of such works lends them a peculiar charm). In their novel *Manette Salomon*, written in 1865 and published in book form in 1867, the Goncourt brothers created, in addition to their hero Coriolis, who loves Japanese albums, an Orientialist painter based recognizably on Charles de Tournemine (1812–1872). Tournemine specialized in Turkey, the intense luminosity of which he managed to render in his work. The same was true of the painter and writer Eugène Fromentin (1820–1876), whose paintings of that era were based on memories of his three trips to Algeria between 1846 and 1853. Hugely successful in the Salons of the Second Empire, Fromentin became almost the official painter of Eastern subjects. He was to be invited to Egypt in 1869 for the inauguration of the Suez Canal, where he was able to renew his inspiration. His Sahara often appears in festive colors, as in *Arabs Hunting with Falcons* (*Arabes chassant au faucon*, fig. 604), presented to the 1857 Salon, a painting bathed in a luminous atmosphere that won Fromentin the approval of Realist critics.

With a rather sharper feeling for the everyday reality of southern Algeria, a country that fascinated him, Gustave Guillaumet (1840–1887) was capable of being soberly dramatic in, for example, *The Desert* (*Le Désert*, fig. 602), which features a skeleton in the foreground of a totally flat, empty landscape where the only sign of life is a tiny caravan visible on the horizon, a kind of mirage trembling in the heat. In his close observation of the people of the oases of southern Algeria, he invited comparison with Millet. Adopting an atavistic approach, he stripped Oriental subjects of the picturesque quality given them by illustrations of travel writing.

An artist of a quite different generation (he was born sixty years before Guillaumet), old Ingres continued to dominate the artistic life of Paris with his enormous authority until his death in 1867. It was about this time that he completed his *Turkish Bath* (*Bain turc*, fig. 21), the supreme masterpiece of imaginative Orientalism. This was the apogee of a whole series of compositions, from the *Valpinçon Bather* (Louvre), painted in Rome in 1808, by way of various odalisques and harem interiors, that had haunted Ingres all his life (though he never once visited the Islamic world himself, except through picture books and engravings). In December 1859, he had sold an initial, rectangular version of the subject to Prince Napoleon, who had soon returned it to the artist, his wife Princess Clotilde finding the subject unsuitable. Ingres had then transformed the painting, giving it the circular form of a Renaissance-style tondo, before reexhibiting it in his studio in 1864. In the following year, the work passed into the collection of a rich and important Turkish diplomat, the liberal Khalil Bey, who had recently moved into luxurious accommodation in the Rue Taitbout in Paris. Khalil Bey was then putting together a collection of masterpieces, which included works by Delacroix, Chassériau, and Gérôme. Thanks partly to his mistress Jeanne de Tourbey, whose portrait was painted by Ingres's pupil Amaury-Duval (*Madame de Loynes*, 1863), and partly to writer Sainte-Beuve and Prince Napoleon himself, he gained entry to republican literary and artistic circles.

After Sainte-Beuve had given him an enthusiastic account of *Venus Pursuing Psyche in her Jealousy* (*Vénus poursuivant Psyché de sa jalousie*, destroyed in Berlin), a painting rejected by the 1864 Salon as being immoral, Khalil Bey paid a visit to Courbet in his studio and asked the artist for a copy. Courbet apparently suggested at the time that he should paint "something different" or "afterward." The commission led to *Sleep* or *The Lovers* of 1866 (*Le Sommeil* or *Les Amies*, fig. 598). The painting's overtly lesbian implications could not help pleasing a connoisseur who enjoyed good living and who also, like his wealthy fellow countrymen, owned a villa on the island of Lesbos, the actual home of the poet Sappho. This celebrated work did not, like *The Turkish Bath*, go into the sale of Khalil Bey's collection in January 1868, when the diplomat was temporarily declared bankrupt, but was later left to the singer Jean-Baptiste Faure, one of the great Manet collectors. It can be seen, surely, as a sort of modern answer to *The Turkish Bath*, right down to the presence of a precious little still life in the foreground.

On the subject of the large nude, the obligatory "purple passage" of any history painter in the middle years of the century, Courbet sent *The Woman with a Parrot* (*La Femme au Perroquet*, Metropolitan Museum of Art, New York) to the 1866 Salon, thinking (mistakenly) that it would meet the requirements of the superintendent of fine arts, Count de Nieuwerkerke.

However, it would be wrong to reduce Khalil Bey's whole collection to a mere stockpile of prurient subjects. It was in fact a godsend for artists who had exceeded the bounds of acceptability, for it also included *The Assassination of the Bishop of Liège* (Louvre) by Delacroix and another Courbet work from 1867, *The Poachers, Ornans*, in which two huntsmen and their dogs stand out against a subtle background of luminous whites, with the sky and the snow-covered landscape punctuated by colored shadows painted in fresh hues.

It was this visible touch, large or small, laid on with a knife in squares or dots, this refusal to blend everything into an academic finish, that characterized the technique of a whole series of artists of the final years of the Second Empire. Adolphe Monticelli (1824–1886) found his style (derived from Diaz de la Peña, whom he had met in 1856) late in his career. He had been a somewhat reluctant pupil of Delaroche and an assiduous visitor of museums, notably the Louvre, where (like Gustave Ricard, who influenced him for a while) he appreciated Paolo Veronese, Watteau, and Rembrandt. Monticelli worked apart from the official Salon, treating Romantic subjects in a style that was already modern, manipulating his paint in an erratic manner, superimposing thick touches. He turned out large numbers of fantasy compositions to satisfy a clientele of English and American collectors, many of whom were captivated by his enchanted world, in which imaginary characters people gardens of the mind. *Don Quixote and Sancho Panza* (fig. 595) dates from his time in Paris, where he lived until 1870 before finally returning to his native city of Marseille. The portraits and bunches of flowers of Monticelli's mature period were admired by Vincent van Gogh in the early years of his career. As for Jean-Baptiste Carpeaux (1827–1875), the imperial court's favorite sculptor, he was also an enthusiastic painter possessed by a visionary ardor, using spurts of rapidly applied paint to represent crowds, whether at a Tuileries ball or attending a dramatic incident such as *Berezovski's Attempt to Assassinate Czar Alexander II, June 6, 1867* (*L'Attentat de Berezowski contre le tsar Alexandre II, le 6 juin 1867*, fig. 618) or *Monseigneur Darboy* in prison in 1871 (Musée d'Orsay), shortly before the archbishop of Paris was shot by the Commune on May 28 of that year.

Carpeaux admired the art of Delacroix, who died in 1863 and was celebrated the following year at Martinet's in the Boulevard des Italiens (Paris) by the short-lived Société Nationale des Beaux-Arts, which consisted of two hundred painters and sculptors, including himself, Manet, Corot, Pierre Puvis de Chavannes, and Bonvin, and which for a while sought to rival the Salon by offering direct to the public paintings and sculptures in small formats that could easily be accommodated in private drawing rooms.

This experiment, though of short duration, illustrates how the hesitations of the administration were pushing artists in the direction of organizing themselves. After the scandal of *Olympia* (fig. 34) at the 1865 Salon, the following year Manet had his *Fifer* rejected. He showed it to the public in 1867 in the private exhibition that he organized near the Pont de l'Alma alongside the Exposition Universelle (Courbet, repeating his 1855 experiment, also had an exhibition nearby). *The Fifer* was dismissed as naive and derisively compared to a playing-card by people who failed to appreciate the references to Velázquez, whose work Manet had recently been admiring in the Museu del Prado in Madrid. Only the young journalist Émile Zola defended the painting, which he had seen in the artist's studio, thanks to a mutual friend, the painter Guillemet. In an article in *L'Évènement* (May 7, 1866), Zola praised the solidity and strength of Manet's painting and his ability to visualize in "simple, vigorous patches and fragments." Eight months later, in a resonant article in *La Revue du XIXe siècle* (January 1, 1867) under the title "A New Painting Style: Manet," he advised his readers to "compare this simplified painting with the Japanese prints that resemble it in their elegance and in their splendid areas of color" (Zola 1867, 52).

To thank him, Manet suggested that he paint a portrait of Zola, which was hung in the 1868 Salon. The model is set off in a traditional way by a decorative scheme that sums up many of the two men's tastes and common interests. On the left is a Japanese screen; on the right, in a frame, are three symbolically chosen pictures: *Olympia*, an engraving taken from *Los Borrachos* by Velázquez, both in black and white, and beside them a Japanese wrestler by a contemporary ukiyo-e artist, Utagawa Kuniaki II (1835–1888), a print of the kind that had recently become available in the Parisian shops selling Far Eastern curios. The latter is the only one treated in color: the blue-gray of the background and the black of the wrestler's coat, combined with some brief touches of red, themselves become colors, highlighting the fact that one of the principal revelations of Japanese prints was precisely the boldness of such flat areas of color. By contrast, the book that Zola is absentmindedly holding open (and that forms a brilliant patch of white at the center of the portrait) is a volume of Charles Blanc's *Histoire des peintres de toutes les écoles*, from which Manet had taken the subjects of many of his earlier paintings. Finally, in the dazzling still life on the desk to the right, behind the writer's goose quill we see a brochure with a blue cover bearing the name "MANET," which doubles as the signature of the work; this is a copy of Dentu's reprint of the article in which Zola had praised the artist so highly.

In his critique of the 1868 Salon, *Mon Salon*, Zola not only hailed this new work by Manet, whom he had seen wrestling "toe to toe with nature" during sittings (Zola 1974, 104), he also wrote at length about another naturalistic artist who was sometimes accepted and sometimes rejected by the Salon. This was the landscapist Camille Pissarro (1830–1903), who in 1868 exhibited his *Hillside at Jallais (Pontoise)* (*La Côte du Jallais (Pontoise)*, fig. 614). Born in the Danish West Indies, Pissarro had already visited Paris once before settling permanently in France in 1855, arriving in time for the Exposition Universelle. He made his debut at the 1859 Salon, met Monet in that year at the Académie Suisse, a free studio in Paris that he frequented, and two years later met Cézanne and Armand Guillaumin (1841–1927) at the same place. He also knew Corot, briefly presenting himself as Corot's pupil at the 1865 Salon. Various locations in the Paris suburbs where he lived furnished the subjects of Pissarro's paintings, which at this time often still used the dark greens reminiscent of Courbet's undergrowth.

Pissarro's encouragement of the young Paul Cézanne (1839–1906), Zola's faithful friend since their boyhood in Aix-en-Provence, anticipated the role he was to play as patriarch of the group of "independent artists" in 1874.

From 1864 onward, Cézanne was rejected every time he tried to exhibit at the Salon. In 1867, one of his works even had to be withdrawn from an exhibition in Marseille when crowds attempted to slash it. The deliberately provocative subjects of this artist's early work, coupled with his style (very heavy impasto, often applied with a palette knife), certainly were surprising. He later evolved in the direction of calmer subjects and a more rhythmic style, though his brushwork was still unusually vigorous, as in *The Negro Scipio* (*Le Nègre Scipion*, fig. 33), a large study painted from a well-known Académie Suisse model who must have posed in Cézanne's studio about 1867. In this work, which has no true subject and is striking in its sobriety, Monet (who hung it on his bedroom wall) rightly recognized a work of the very first rank.

Despite the success of his large portrait of *Camille* in a green dress (Kunsthalle, Bremen) at the 1866 Salon, Monet himself was having a difficult time. However, his landscape experiments did result in some particularly striking works, such as *The Terrace at Sainte-Adresse* (*La Terrasse à Sainte-Adresse*, fig. 37), which he painted in 1867 near Le Havre. In this work he abandoned the contrasts and somber tones of his early years in favor of a juxtaposition of bright, fresh colors (greens, reds, blues) in a tiered composition with an unusually high horizon such as he might have found in the prints of Hiroshige and his followers. Renoir, who was close to Monet at this time, was to speak of this painting in 1869 as "a bit of Japan with little flags."

Is it possible to see in Monet's *Mapgie* (*La Pie*, fig. 607) an echo of those prints devoted to the seasons, including the snows of winter, or of the rapid drawings found in little Japanese books? This work, one of Monet's masterpieces, was painted in Normandy in the open air (and the cold), probably in the winter of 1868–69. The main reference is of course to Courbet's winter landscapes, but we find here a quite new mastery in Monet's observation of a brief sunny spell following a recent snowfall and the way in which it illuminates the fields on the horizon and casts the bluish shadows of the hedge in the foreground. The barely red chimneys of the house, like the black of the magpie, give striking relief to this "snapshot." On a lesser scale, the same skill at seizing the ephemeral and noting essentials characterized the views of Trouville painted by Eugène Boudin, Monet's discreet mentor. A backlit effect is the principal characteristic of Boudin's *Bathers on Trouville Beach* (*Baigneurs sur la plage de Trouville*, Trouville was a fashionable resort under the Second Empire); the inevitable long dresses are briefly indicated by small patches of color that help to give the painting its liveliness and sense of capturing a moment of life (fig. 36).

Pierre-Auguste Renoir, a friend of Bazille, Monet, and Alfred Sisley (all fellow disciples in the Gleyre studio), had attended the École des Beaux-Arts, and his early works, such as his paintings of Diana the Huntress executed in the spirit of Courbet's *Bathers*, were marked by a desire to try out Salon-worthy subjects. Like his friends, he also experimented with large portraits such as *Lise with Sunshade* (*Lise à l'ombrelle*, Folkwang Museum, Essen), a misty symphony in white that was hung in the 1868 Salon. He sought to attract customers with subjects closer to the successful genre scene, in the manner of *The Letter Breaking It Off* (*Lettre de rupture*) by Alfred Stevens (1823–1906), a Belgian painter living in Paris and a friend of Manet. For instance, Renoir sent the dealer Carpentier a smallish painting, with figures half life-sized, known as *The Sisleys* or *The Engaged Couple* (*Mènage Sisley* or *Les Fiancés*, fig. 40). The painter Sisley is indeed recognizable, but the lively young lady on his arm is not in fact Sisley's companion but Renoir's favorite model at this period, Lise Tréhot. This is an outdoor scene in a town garden, which is suggested in a rather vague way, not unlike a photographer's backdrop. Renoir was not interested in the figures, which he treats in the firm style that he so admired in Manet (and that Bazille also used).

The year 1869 brought a clear turning point, with Renoir and Monet producing a whole series of scenes of modern life painted outdoors. Their subject was La Grenouillère (literally "frogpond"), a sort of "Trouville-on-the-Seine." Situated on the banks of the Île de Croissy on the Seine near Paris (opposite Bougival), La Grenouillère was an elegant establishment built on a barge and combining bathing cabins and a restaurant. It was reached by footbridges and a small island with a tree, from which one watched the bathers. The island forms the centerpiece of a pair of twin compositions by the two artists. Monet's is the more structured, while Renoir's is livelier, more tightly framed, and more picturesque. Both paintings devote much attention to the reflections of trees, people, and sky in the rippling water, and if the figures are still treated in a style that is quite close to Manet's in his 1862 *Concert in the Tuileries Gardens* (*La Musique aux Tuileries*, National Gallery, London), the novelty lies in the application of paint in patches of color, so suggestive of the reflective surface of water.

A work of firm relief and shimmering color, *Negress With Poppies* (*La Négresse aux pivoines*, 1870, Musée Fabre, Montpellier) is one of Bazille's masterpieces. In this painting, Bazille may have been thinking of the servant in *Olympia* (fig. 34) or of Manet's flower still lifes with their predilection for poppies. Alternatively, the picture may have been an act of homage to Courbet, or it may simply have been prompted by the artist's desire to re-pose the black model he had just used for *Woman Washing Herself* (*"La Toilette"*) (Musée Fabre, Montpellier), a work on the traditional theme of the odalisque submitted to the 1870 Salon (and rejected). The large spherical vase containing the flower arrangement invites comparison with the one of similar shape and decoration that Fantin-Latour used in *Studio in the Batignolles Quarter* (*Un atelier aux Batignolles*, fig. 623), a large painting that was exhibited in the 1870 Salon. We know from him that it was made by Laurent Bouvier (1840–1901), one of the earliest Japanese-influenced potters in Paris and a Café Guerbois regular. Fantin-Latour included it in his painting as a symbol of the interest that the most modern artists were now taking in Japanese art, alongside a statue of the Greek goddess Minerva, standing for reason and truth. These were the qualities he recognized in the artists and writers grouped around Manet, leader of what in 1869 Duranty called the "Batignolles school," among whom Fantin-Latour already counted Otto Scholderer (1834–1902; the figure on the left, standing behind Manet). Scholderer lived in Frankfurt, so was the only one in the picture who did not frequent the Café Guerbois. The figure apparently sitting for his portrait is Zacharie Astruc, while the five men behind him are recognizable as (from the left) Renoir, Zola, Edmond Maître, Bazille, and Monet. Composed very much in the style of the visits to the studio that Romantic artists loved to paint, this large work was equally well received at the Salon, where it won Bazille a third-class medal. This time, the portrait gallery did not offend anyone.

Bazille adopted a radically different approach to represent more or less the same people in *Studio in the Rue de la Condamine* (*Atelier de la rue de la Condamine*, fig. 622). Here the artist set out to paint the room in which he had been working since January 1, 1868. Certain details are shown very precisely: the black curtains that he had installed on his return from a vacation in 1869 and that enabled him to work without interruption in a steady light, and the paintings stacked against or hung on the walls (some of which are his own and others are by his friends Monet and Renoir, who were sharing his studio at the time). Prominent among the paintings is a large composition in the style of Courbet, high on the wall above the sofa, a landscape with two figures, one nude and the other clothed. This may be the Renoir that was rejected by the 1866 Salon and of which only the clothed fragment has survived. The tall figure of Bazille himself, leaning on the easel that bears his *View of the Village* (*Vue du village*, Musée Fabre, Montpellier), was apparently painted by Manet (the brushwork is more incisive than in the rest of the painting). Manet is the one wearing a hat, shown giving his young friend some advice. Of the four other young men represented, only Edmond Maître, art-lover and musician (he is shown playing the piano), can be identified with any certainty. Bazille was killed in action at Beaune-la-Rolande on September 28, 1870, during the Franco-Prussian war. His works, which all stayed in the family, remained unknown until the end of the century. After the Bazille retrospective at the 1910 Salon d'Automne, this painting reappeared. At the time, the elderly Monet gave two conflicting accounts of it. Is that Monet himself or Astruc standing behind Manet, and does the group on the left portray Renoir and Zola or Monet and Sisley? Missing from these two paintings of the Batignolles group—Bazille's "intimist" treatment and Fantin-Latour's more official version—are Pissarro, then working in the Paris region, Cézanne, and Degas. The solitary, strange, tormented Cézanne painted works that provoked scorn and incomprehension even among his friends. About 1869–70, however, he was in the neighborhood, having begun the large (and ultimately unfinished) double portrait of *Paul Alexis Reading to Émile Zola* (*Paul Alexis lisant à Émile Zola*, fig. 619) in the latter's garden in this same Rue de la Condamine (Paul Alexis was Zola's new secretary).

It was Zola's clock that Cézanne portrayed in the severe still life *The Black Clock* (*La Pendule noire*, fig. 624), which was probably painted before August 1870, when the two friends left Paris. This is a very rugged example of the concern for spatial organization and geometrization that characterized Cézanne's approach (the folds of the tablecloth are rock-solid), only slightly tempered by the sensuous depiction of the red interior of the shell.

As for Degas, he was very close to Manet at this time, as he was to the Morisot family, one of whose daughters, Berthe, had taken up painting and often posed for Manet—in *The Balcony* (*Le Balcon*), hung at the 1870 Salon, and, in the early summer of 1870, in *Resting* (*Le Repos*, fig. 41). Events dictated that the latter painting was presented only to the 1873 Salon, at which Manet finally received positive recognition with *Le Bon Bock* (Philadelphia Museum of Art). Degas was continuing his experiments in the field of portraiture, using family and friends as models. One of the most successful of these portraits (and one of his best-known works since its entry into the Louvre in 1935) is *Orchestra of the Paris Opera* (*L'Orchestre de l'Opéra*, fig. 42), composed around the figure of bassoonist Désiré Dihau, who was its first owner. The work had been painted before the Franco-Prussian war of 1870, and the artist's family were delighted to see a finished painting at last. Degas had met Dihau in a restaurant near the old Opéra in Rue Le Peletier (Garnier's new building was then under construction). He wanted to set the portrait of his new friend in a wholly naturalistic way in the middle of Dihau's professional world, hence the emphasis on the (largely invisible) orchestra pit. Each of the faces of the musicians is a portrait, sometimes of one the artist's friends who did not work in the orchestra, and the requirements of his subject forced Degas to take liberties with the position of the musicians (the bassoonist does not normally sit in the front row). Nevertheless, the painting conveys an intense feeling of life, with all the players closely observed in their movements, complete with swollen cheeks and tensed hands. As Degas wrote in one of his notebooks, they are alert only to the conductor, who is out of the picture, and indifferent to the shimmering spectacle being played out on stage, where we can just make out feet and heads of ballerinas. The auditorium is suggested only by a stage-side box in which the figure of Emmanuel Chabrier is recognizable, the bright red of the edge of the box balancing the geometry of the double-bass player's chair in the right foreground.

A very different approach had been adopted by Daumier in *At The Theater* (*Le Drame*, fig. 596), an incisive work with the emphasis on the lighting. Daumier used the same subject in an 1864 lithograph, with the bright rectangle of the stage as seen from the balcony by attentive viewers, engrossed in what is taking place below.

It was only in the twentieth century that the merit of these works, which had passed unnoticed in their day, was recognized. Daumier was not discovered as a painter until after his death, and for many years Degas's *Orchestra of the Paris Opera*, which may have been exhibited in Lille during the Franco-Prussian war of 1870 and again at Durand-Ruel's gallery in 1871, graced the home of its chief model. The true glories of the Salons of the last years of the Second Empire were elsewhere. The dream was still of "great art" and, in the case of the finest examples of history painting, it became tinged with idealism.

The prestige of Italy continued, both as the source of antique subjects and as the cradle of Christianity. At the 1869 Salon, *The Plague in Rome* (*La Peste à Rome*, fig. 588) by Jules-Élie Delaunay (1828–1891) occasioned much comment and was purchased for the Musée du Luxembourg. Although the traditionalist Edmond About, writing in *La Revue des Deux Mondes*, felt that this was merely a sketch for a major composition to come, it was in fact a finished painting, using the medium-sized format that seemed reasonable at the time for works not intended for public buildings. It was the mature result of experiments the artist had been carrying out since the beginning of his stay at the Villa Medici in 1857, following the late award of a Prix de Rome in 1856. From the very first overall sketches (such as that of 1861, presented with the submissions from Rome to the École des Beaux-Arts), the composition features a void in the middle, emphasizing the horror of God's vengeance in this episode from the life of St. Sebastian, as told in the *Golden Legend* by Jacobus de Voragine. The architecture is changed, too, to give it greater balance, probably under the influence of friendly discussions with Gustave Moreau.

A painter with a far more academic technique was Jules Lefebvre (1836–1911), who was awarded his Prix de Rome in 1861 and lost no time in climbing the ladder of an official career. Lefebvre also had a solid private clientele and was able to behave in a haughty, not to say scornful manner toward the state authorities, who had to pay a large sum of money at the 1870 Salon for his *Truth* (*Vérité*, fig. 628), which was actually no more than a version of *The Spring* (*La Source*, Musée d'Orsay) by Ingres. Beneath his genuinely assured craftsmanship, Lefebvre's overscrupulous fidelity to realistic portrayal of his studio model (notably her face) led to a sort of vulgarity that was in fact very typical. This kind of art had gradually lost its substance since the heroic days of Davidian Neoclassicism.

Antoine Vollon (1833–1900) had had a difficult start on his arrival in Paris in 1859, when he became friends with Ribot and Bonvin (he was among the artists rejected in 1863). He soon found success, however, with his kitchen interiors and still lifes, thanks to an ability to render shiny materials with a skill and solidity thoroughly typical of the Lyon school in which he had served his apprenticeship. His *Sea Fish* (*Poissons de mer*, fig. 625) at the 1870 Salon, purchased for the Musée du Luxembourg, was acclaimed for a degree of realism bordering almost on trompe l'oeil. Surprisingly, perhaps, Castagnary, the champion of naturalism, criticized them for being "painted from memory" (Castagnary 1892, 1:414). He preferred a truly original work of great power and emotion: *The Condemned Man's Last Day* (*Le Dernier jour d'un condamné à mort*, fig. 617) by newcomer Mihály Munkácsy (1844–1900).

The picture shows the condemned man receiving visits on the eve of his execution, as was the custom in Hungary. Encouraged by his success, in 1872 Munkácsy settled in Paris, where he pursued a brilliant career in the (occasionally tyrannical) orbit of the dealers Goupil and Sedelmeyer. His training had been cosmopolitan, taking in Budapest, Munich, and Düsseldorf, and from a visit to Paris in 1867 he had learned the Realist social lessons of Courbet, here evident in the choice of a subject from his native land. Munkácsy's brown painting, violently lit and punctuated with red, was on the somber side, but it was effective, and it accorded well with the tastes of the newly rich urban middle class (soon to be described by Guy de Maupassant in his novel *Bel-Ami*). Paris was a veritable magnet for artists of all nationalities. Even those intending to pursue their studies in Italy were keen to try their luck in the French capital.

A typical example was the Spaniard Mariano Fortuny (1838–1874). In Rome on a scholarship, Fortuny fell under the spell of the art of Velázquez. Subsequently, on a Spanish military expedition to Morocco in 1860, he discovered the light of the south. He then moved to Paris, where he made the acquaintance of Meissonier. Like Meissonier, he treated genre scenes such as *The Print Collector* (*Collectionneur d'estampes*, fig. 26) painted in 1866. His execution was freer, however, using shimmering colors with extraordinary skill. Launched by Goupil in 1871, he quickly achieved huge international success, particularly in the United States, a success that also benefited his two stepbrothers Raimondo and Ricardo de Madrazo, who survived him by many years.

Another eclectic artist, Anselm Feuerbach (1829–1880) studied in Düsseldorf, Munich, and Antwerp before coming under the influence of Couture (more than that of Courbet) during a stay in Paris from 1851 to 1854. He then moved to Italy, where he lived until 1873, absorbing the art of the Renaissance. Feuerbach wanted to restore history painting, which in his day had rather lost its originality, to fresh greatness. He several times illustrated the theme of renunciation and self-denial, and it was from this angle that he approached the story of *Medea* in 1870 (fig. 626). Medea (her noble face seen in profile, as was customary for Feuerbach) is deliberating whether to leave her children to her faithless partner Jason or kill them herself. This classical group contrasts with the sailors pushing out the boat on the right, who are treated in a much more naturalistic way.

The American Thomas Eakins (1844–1916), a younger artist, stayed in Paris fifteen years later (1866–70), and studied under Gérôme (who was highly esteemed by transatlantic collectors) and Bonnat. After his return to Philadelphia, he purposely moved away from traditional subjects in order to portray modern American life. In this he used sporting subjects, notably rowing, which was very popular at the time and which he practiced with his childhood friend Max Schmitt. These scenes echo the works being painted in France showing people enjoying the pleasures of boating on the Seine, at La Grenouillère or Argenteuil.

The first work that Eakins exhibited in Philadelphia in April 1871 (to initial incomprehension) was *Max Schmitt in a Single Scull* (fig. 51). It shows Schmitt in the foreground, prosaically dressed in a singlet, in an informal pose expressive of exhaustion, with Eakins himself in the background in another boat (on which the artist has written his signature and the date). The river itself (the Schuylkill) is shown without nostalgia, metal bridges and all, and the light effects serve to set off the principal figure in the immensity of American nature. In 1875, with the idea of celebrating modern science, he painted *The Gross Clinic* (Jefferson Medical College, Philadelphia), a solidly naturalistic work that was rejected by Philadelphia's Centennial Exposition in 1876.

The fact was, the weight of convention was less oppressive in Philadelphia or New York than in Paris or Brussels. Another American artist of the period (totally forgotten until he was rediscovered in 1945) was Martin Johnson Heade (1818–1904). Heade, who had traveled in Europe from 1838, succeeded in 1868 in representing the disturbing calm preceding a *Storm Over Narragansett Bay* (fig. 585). The product of ten years of study, this is a work of astonishing restraint. A small number of white sails contrast with a dark sea and sky; the former might almost be a pool of oil, the sails being reflected in it without a ripple. Yet it was not appreciated at the forty-third annual exhibition of New York's National Academy of Design, prompting the discouraged artist to choose less ambitious subjects in future (still lifes and views of swamps).

In France, the events of 1870–71—the war with Prussia, military defeats, the abdication of Napoleon III on September 4, 1870, the siege of Paris, followed in the spring of 1871 by the Commune—wrought havoc on the lives of artists, but had less impact on their style.

Some of those who had enlisted were killed on the battlefield. Following the death of Bazille in the fighting at Beaune-la-Rolande on the Loire, that of Henri Regnault (1843–1871) at Buzenval near Paris was felt as a national disaster, and Meissonier portrayed Regnault among the victims in his allegorical composition, *The Siege of Paris, 1870* (*Le Siège de Paris, 1870*, Musée d'Orsay). An early developer and a skilled draftsman, Regnault won a Prix de Rome in 1866 and divided his scholarship time between Rome and Spain, discovering in the process the shimmering technique of Fortuny, who was to influence him. He was already famous for certain pictures he had sent to the Salon and at the 1870 Salon his *Salome* (Metropolitan Museum of Art, New York) caused a sensation. His third-year submission from Rome, painted in Tangier in 1870, was *Summary Execution under the Moorish Kings of Granada* (*L'Execution sans jugement sous les rois maures de Grenade*, fig. 44). Much admired in London during the 1871 International Exhibition, the painting was later acquired for the Musée du Luxembourg. It reflects the artist's fascination with Granada's Alhambra Palace, as well as his morbid predilection (here, using a historical pretext, taken to an extreme) for severed heads, anticipating certain Symbolist and Parnassian compositions of the final years of the century. The crimson blood splashed on the steps, the decapitated body, and the severed head itself instantly impressed an enthusiastic Théophile Gautier with their realism, which he imagined to have been studied at first hand in Morocco.

Other artists left Paris. Some, like Bonvin, Daubigny, Pissarro, and Monet, met up again in London. Thanks to Daubigny, Monet and Pissarro made the acquaintance of a Parisian dealer there, Durand-Ruel, who had hitherto specialized in the Barbizon School but who now started buying some of their works (which were of course still quite difficult to sell). This transformed their lives but, moreover, it marked the beginning of an exemplary venture, because on his return to Paris Durand-Ruel began to take an interest in the other artists of the Batignolles group: Manet, Sisley, Renoir, Degas, and the rest.

In the English museums that they visited, Pissarro and Monet were able to study at their leisure (though they subsequently denied any influence) the works of Turner and Constable, and at least compare those artists' luminous landscapes with their current preoccupations.

Courbet stayed on in Paris, serving as president of the new Fédération des Artistes. Implicated in the sack of the Colonne Vendôme, he was convicted and sentenced to six months in prison. He was imprisoned in the notorious Sainte-Pélagie prison, but fell seriously ill. Back in Ornans in 1873, before leaving for his Swiss exile, he painted *The Trout* (*La Truite*). The hooked fish was meant as a reminder of his incarceration, but it was also to be a harrowing symbol of his death.

Others who remained in Paris enlisted in the National Guard, notably Manet, Degas, Puvis de Chavannes, Meissonier, and Gustave Doré. Events inspired them to produce works as varied as their temperaments. Pierre Puvis de Chavannes, who for over ten years had been consolidating his status as a great decorator and worthy successor of Chassériau, notably with his large compositions for the Musée d'Amiens, was not always understood in his quest for an ideal, timeless art. However, his two symbolic images of the siege of Paris, *The Balloon* (*Le Ballon*, 1870, fig. 629) and *The Pigeon* (*Le Pigeon*, early 1871, fig. 627), propagated through the medium of engravings, were a huge success because they went right to the heart of the Parisian predicament, cut off as the city was from the rest of the world through the long months of that dramatic winter. The only means of communication with the outside were indeed passenger balloons, couriers, and pigeons, which brought the mail. However, Puvis does not portray them as mere elements in a picturesque scene; he has an austere figure representing the city of Paris in mourning, holding an arm skyward. In one picture she is standing armed on the ramparts, while in the other she dominates the Île de la Cité in the snow, holding against her heart the pigeon that has managed to escape from the falcon (silhouetted at the top of the picture like a Hiroshige eagle), the Prussian army's latest auxiliary. The sketches for these two pendants are in color, but for the finished works the artist chose a severe brown monochrome perfectly adapted to the somber situation. He put the two paintings in black-and-gold frames bearing the symbolic inscriptions "The besieged City of Paris entrusts its appeal to France to the air" and "After escaping the talons of the enemy, the longed-for message fires the heart of the proud city."

Much the same spirit moved Meissonier (who was inspired by the dramatic events of 1871, just as he had been in 1848) to paint a view of *The Tuileries in Ruins* (*Tuileries en ruines*, fig. 615). A fallen stone in the foreground bears an inscription and the date 1871, while through an aperture in the ruined building, beyond an impressive pile of rubble, we see the tiny silhouette of the statue on top of the triumphal arch in the Place du Carrousel, symbolizing past glories.

The inspiration of the great illustrator Gustave Doré (1832–1882) was of a quite different kind. He made some astonishing drawings in Paris during the siege, including *Rounding up the Animals in the Bois de Boulogne* (*Le Rassemblement des troupeaux dans le bois de Boulogne*, Cabinet des Dessins, Musée du Louvre) and *Moving House During the Bombardment* (*Déménagement pendant le bombardement*), recorded in highly realistic detail. For the latter, he focused on the group of a Sister of Charity carrying a child and made a poignant composition by placing her alone against a wall in a snow-covered street, lit by the harsh glare of an invisible street lamp, while the flames of the bombardment are visible on the horizon (fig. 574). At the time of the Commune, Doré was in Versailles, where he soon conceived the idea of representing events allegorically in three paintings. These appeared in his posthumous sale under the collective title *Memories of 1870* (*Souvenirs de 1870*). They were *The Enigma*, with a sphinx (*L'Énigme*, Musée d'Orsay), *The Defense of Paris*, with the angel of the motherland driven back against the gates of the city (*La Défense de Paris*, Vassar College Art Museum, Poughkeepsie), and lastly *The Black Eagle* (*L'Aigle noir*, lost), in which Doré was faithful to the enemy's heraldic bird, where Puvis had chosen a very real falcon.

None of these works linked to the painful events of 1870–71 was of course purchased by the government of the nascent Third Republic, which attempted to make a fresh start—though without responding to Zola's dream (as described in a letter to Cézanne): "This is our reign just beginning." At the 1872 Salon the government bought (for the Musée du Luxembourg) a small nocturnal scene painted with neo-Greek precision by a pupil of Gérôme, Lecomte de Nouy (1842–1923). Entitled *Bearers of Bad News* (*Les Porteurs de mauvaises nouvelles*), the painting illustrated a passage from Théophile Gautier's *Roman de la momie*, which was set in the age of the pharaohs.

THE IMPRESSIONIST PERIOD

Life soon resumed its course, though for some there were real ruptures. Tissot, for instance, remained in London. Manet's friend Théodore Duret, together with Enrico Cernuschi, embarked on a world tour that not only kept the two artists away from Paris, where they were temporarily compromised, but actually took them to Japan, enabling them to bring back illustrated books, ceramics, and bronzes. Monet returned to Paris at the end of 1871, traveling via the Netherlands, where he painted the red-sailed windmills of Zaandam. The writers slipped back into their old habits as soon as things settled down in August 1871, and some of the more loyal patrons of the Vilains Bonhommes restaurant soon made the acquaintance, through Paul Verlaine, of a brilliant youngster named Arthur Rimbaud, who arrived in Paris in September 1871. It was they, together with various poets and journalists linked to the Parnassian movement, that Fantin-Latour portrayed in his new group portrait, *A Corner of the Table* (*Coin de table*, fig. 621) shown at the 1872 Salon. As with Courbet's *Portrait of P. J. Proudhon in 1853* (*Portrait de Proudhon*), which was originally painted in 1865 but was altered prior to its presentation in 1867, Fantin-Latour changed his picture when one of the group, Albert Mérat, withdrew following a quarrel. He was replaced in the picture by a bunch of flowers.

These young people had just founded a new magazine, *La Renaissance littéraire et artistique*, the first issue of which came out in April 1872. Several months later, Armand Silvestre, in his last article on "L'École de peinture contemporaine" (The contemporary school of painting, published on September 28, 1872), devoted considerable attention to the landscapes of Monet, Pissarro, and Sisley, which Durand-Ruel was then publicizing. Silvestre stressed the "immediate caress that the eye receives from them" and the "uncommonly cheerful range of colors" used in them. He acknowledged their debt to Japanese "images," and he went on to remark that "the painting of these three landscapists bears no resemblance to that of any of the masters who have occupied us hitherto; its only apparent forebear, distant in likeness if not in time, and very indirect, is M. Manet."

At the time, Manet was still seen as an artist who worked in the studio and referred continually to paintings he had seen in museums. Not until rather later (under the influence of Monet, in fact) did he too become interested in the way water ripples in sunlight. However, some of the experiments of artists such as Jongkind (in both paintings and etchings), Daubigny, and Daubigny's friend Auguste Ravier, had laid the groundwork for these dazzling innovations. Auguste Ravier (1814–1895) had remained in the Lyon area, near Optevoz, where he entertained Corot, Courbet, and Daubigny; he later moved to nearby Morestel to explore the effects of the setting sun on stretches of water. His many studies (which are difficult to date) reveal experiments with color applied in broad strokes, with picturesque elements, such as tree trunks, gradually disappearing.

Another artist to have captured the interest of Durand-Ruel was Millet. Millet was now increasingly devoting himself to landscapes in which the human figure played a limited role or was absent altogether, notably in his views of Normandy after 1870. He treated space in a quite new way, using a very high horizon in, for example, *Grazing in the Mountains: Auvergne* (*Pâturage sur la montagne. Auvergne*, fig. 606), painted during one of his trips to the Vichy region before war broke out in 1870. The goatherd spinning in the fields (an activity that was new to him), the animals outlined against the horizon, and the clump of chestnut trees are all placed near the top of the composition, beneath a luminous sky, while a few touches indicate the vegetation in the foreground and give a new depth to the landscape.

Millet used the same approach, with open flowers in the foreground, in his *Spring* (*Printemps*, fig. 29), one of the four seasons that Frédéric Hartmann commissioned him to paint in 1863 and that he completed in 1873. Although complex, the composition of this picture is more classical in some ways, with the path running up the center. There is a tiny human presence under a tree in the distance, which is deliberately set among cultivated fields, not far from a grafted tree—another sign of man's labor. But it is very much the role of nature in the seasonal renewal of life that the artist evokes here, with the double rainbow, the stormy sky, and the bright light washing the trees on the horizon in delicate pale greens.

Millet's last work, painted in 1874, presents a more unusual effect of light, treated with rapid, startling, hook-shaped brushstrokes. *Hunting Birds at Night* (*Chasse aux oiseaux la nuit*, fig. 53) represents a pastime of his youth in Normandy, the memory of which haunted him toward the end of his life. He told a young American painter, Will Low, how, using a torch of burning straw, people would dazzle the wild pigeons roosting in flocks in the trees, club them to death, and then gather them up. In their violent movements, the figures are treated with a wholly classical solidity that avoids any suggestion of the picturesque and helps to make this work an apocalyptic vision of the end of the world, death, and hell.

As for the official scene, the Salon had resumed its annual rhythm in 1872, with no relaxation of its conservative attitude toward new trends. In fact, so many works were rejected that the following year saw a repetition of the experiments of 1863 and 1864, with an exhibition of rejected works, which included Jongkind's pictures and Renoir's submissions, which attracted favorable comment.

At the Salon itself, Manet finally scored a positive success with *Le Bon Bock* (Museum of Art, Philadelphia), while *Repose (Berthe Morisot)* (*Le Repos. Portrait de Berthe Morisot*, fig. 41), which he had painted in 1870, drew the by now traditional reproaches to the effect that it was "unfinished." Manet placed his model beneath a triptych print, probably by the Japanese artist Utagawa Kuniyoshi, representing a tortured subject that corresponded to Berthe's state of mind—at the time she had not made a firm commitment to the Impressionist camp (she did so in 1876). Once again, Manet's refined coloring of the white of her dress gave it a rare quality of modernity—a quality that Théodore de Banville was almost alone in appreciating. There was equally little understanding, at the same Salon, for the vigorous contrast of black and white and the thick paint used in Charles Daubigny's impressive winter landscape *Snow* (*La Neige*, fig. 612), with its bare trees and flight of crows against a reddening sky. Daubigny's technique, of course, was developing through contact with the young artists whom he mixed with and encouraged, notably Monet and Pissarro and their friends.

Another exercise in discreet virtuosity against a white ground was Fantin-Latour's large still life *A Corner of the Table* (*Coin de table*, fig. 45), which he submitted to the 1873 Salon. The painting was initially rejected, then eventually accepted, which the artist saw as failure. In fact the work was misunderstood and the artist criticized for its apparent disorder (although it was actually arranged with great care to give an impression of naturalness) and the way in which the various elements represented are cut off (the picture frame to the left, the tablecloth and the rhododendron plant below) in the style of the Japanese prints then so widely admired among artists. Was it to guarantee a good reception by jury and critics that in the following year Fantin submitted a still life of *Flowers and Various Objects* (*Fleurs et Objets divers*, Konstmuseum, Göteborg), in which the untidiness of life (flowers, a fan, a Japanese print) was counterbalanced by a plaster cast of a Hellenistic Aphrodite?

It seems still to have been difficult to gain acceptance with works that were not carefully modulated, like Fantin-Latour's, but that deliberately left broad brushstrokes visible, like those of the landscapists painting their subjects from the life in Paris and its environs: Alfred Sisley, for example, with *View of the Canal Saint-Martin, Paris* (*La Vue du canal Saint-Martin*, 1870, fig. 608) or *Garden at Louveciennes, Snow Effect* (*Le Jardin sous la neige à Louveciennes*, 1874, fig. 52), or Pissarro with *Entrance to the Village of Voisins* (*L'Entrée du village de Voisins*, fig. 630). Durand-Ruel, who had begun to take an interest in such artists, was unable to sell his stock and even had to cease buying in 1873.

A significant work in this new, broad style, which showed a true convergence of views among all the artists involved on the eve of their first independent exhibition, was Pissarro's *Self-Portrait* (*Autoportrait*, fig. 48), which dates from 1873. In this painting, the touch is left visible, not just in the background with its small landscapes hung on the wall (mere juxtapositions of green, blue, and pink rectangles) but also in the luminous beard of the man who succeeded, by virtue of his benevolent authority, in uniting the members of the group (including the rebel Cézanne, with whom he was working in Pontoise at the time) in a common undertaking.

Applied to a vast panorama, this allusive technique accounted for all the spontaneity of *Paris Seen from the Trocadéro* (*Vue de Paris des hauteurs du Trocadéro*, fig. 635) by Berthe Morisot (1841–1895), which is in fact closer to Manet and Degas. Figures and carriages down on the roads beside the Seine are indicated by a few almost calligraphic dabs of paint, while the broad spaces of the Champ-de-Mars, the quays, the paths and lawns, and the bridge (the Pont d'Iéna) are painted with long horizontal brushstrokes.

Despite Manet's strong hostility to such events, Berthe Morisot was one of the most loyal participants in the so-called "Impressionist exhibitions" (she missed only that of 1879, when her daughter Julie was born; Pissarro was represented at all eight). At the instigation of Monet (taking up an old project he had formed with Bazille in 1867), a number of painters, sculptors, and etchers, including Renoir, Sisley, Pissarro, Degas, and Berthe Morisot, came together in 1874 to form a limited cooperative company, the Société anonyme des artistes peintres, sculpteurs, graveurs, etc. They decided to abandon any obligation to the Salon and to organize their own independent exhibitions.

They were not in fact alone in Europe. It should not be forgotten that artists in Russia, rebelling against the oppressive rules imposed by the St. Petersburg Academy, had formed a new organization. The "Revolt of the Fourteen" had ended in repression and the withholding of a diploma. Then, following a short-lived attempt to form a cooperative, in 1870 the Itinerant Art Exhibitions Company had been formed. The so-called Wanderers (in Russian: Peredvizhniki) staged their first exhibition in St. Petersburg in 1871, following it with a second in Moscow in 1872; in subsequent years exhibitions took place in the principal cities of the vast Russian empire. Despite certain bans by the authorities, the artists concerned were able to rely on a good reception from the general public, and with their naturalistic, social, and national subjects they succeeded in gaining acceptance for a series of works that soon became embedded in the popular imagination.

In France, on the contrary, public and critics both had a great deal of fun at the expense of the independent exhibitions organized in Paris. It was a journalist, Alfred Leroy, who in fact coined the nickname "Impressionist," having used the word in his famous satirical article in *Charivari* on April 25, 1874. The trigger had been a work that Monet had painted in Le Havre two years earlier and that was listed in the catalog as *Impression, Sunrise* (*Impression, soleil levant*, fig. 50). As early as 1877, the (initially pejorative) term was adopted by the artists themselves and used as a rallying cry.

The catalog of the first independent exhibition, held in premises loaned by the photographer Nadar in the Boulevard des Capucines, on the corner of Rue Daunou, included thirty names and a total of 165 works. One name, Alfred Meyer, who showed enamels on historical subjects from the time of Étienne Marcel and Charles V, hardly fitted into the naturalistic programme. Meyer never exhibited again with the group and nor did fourteen other artists, including Boudin, Georges Latouche, Lépine, and Giuseppe de Nittis (1846–1884), the Italian painter and admirer of Japanese art who was so adept at depicting the streets of Paris and racecourses from unusual viewpoints. Altogether, fifty-five artists took part in these exhibitions on a more or less regular basis, and some 1,750 works were shown—fewer than the number included in a single annual Salon. Three new names that appeared at the second exhibition in 1876 were Marcellin Desboutin (one of the models for Degas's *Absinthe*), Legros, and above all Gustave Caillebotte (1848–1894), a painter and patron whose financial assistance was to be of considerable importance in organizing future exhibitions. The fourth exhibition in 1879 (there was none in 1878, the year of the Exposition Universelle) again saw some new names: Albert Lebourg (1849–1928), Jean-Louis Forain (1852–1931), Henri Somm, and Federico Zandomeneghi (1841–1917), an Italian artist associated with the Macchiaioli group who, in addition to some views of Venice, entered his *Portrait of Diego Martelli* (fig. 667). This Florentine writer, of whom Degas also painted a portrait in 1879 (National Gallery of Scotland, Edinburgh), showed an unusual understanding of what in 1876 Edmond Duranty called the "new painting" when he gave a remarkable lecture (subsequently published) on the Impressionists in 1880 at the Circolo Filologico in Livorno. Also at the fourth exhibition, Gauguin, who had been recruited by Pissarro, made his first appearance with a sculpture (he arrived too late to be listed in the catalog). The fifth and sixth exhibitions were notable for the participation of Jean-François Raffaëlli. Finally, in 1886 the newcomers were Georges Seurat, Paul Signac, Odilon Redon, and Émile Schuffenecker (1851–1934). While the latter was close to Gauguin (still involved), the other three, each in his own style, opened up fresh avenues of exploration that were very far from the original experiments of the Impressionists.

This twelve-year adventure, which was not without its clashes and debates (Cézanne, for example, took part only in 1874 and 1877) left a large number of masterpieces that, while very different from one another, are now among the most famous works of Western painting. In 1874 Cézanne showed three pieces. One of them, a "sketch" entitled *A Modern Olympia*, loaned for the occasion by the amateur painter, friend of artists, and collector Dr. Paul Gachet, was a provocative and ironic reply to Manet's great painting of ten years earlier. By including a rear view of the prostitute's client in the foreground, Cézanne avoided the scandal experienced by visitors to the 1865 Salon, who had found themselves in this somewhat ignominious role. The other two were landscapes, both painted in Auvers northwest of Paris (where Dr. Gachet lived) in 1873. *La Maison du pendu* (Musée d'Orsay) is Impressionist in spirit and shows the influence of Cézanne's friend Pissarro, while *Study, Auvers Landscape* (*Étude, paysage à Auvers*, fig. 632), which depicts the Four district of the town, is already typical of Cézanne's experiments in giving solidity to the representation of volumes. A very different technique was employed by Pissarro in *White Frost* (*Gelée blanche*), in which, through the subtle use of irregular touches that are virtually illegible close-up, the artist concentrates on the effects of light on ploughed fields. This rural landscape of the Île-de-France region, in which a lone figure labors under a heavy burden, wholly eschews the picturesque. Unlike Courbet or Millet, Pissarro was not seeking to illustrate a social drama; he was only interested in light.

If the *Charivari* critic saw the work as mere "palette scrapings," he laughed a good deal louder at the black "scraps" that were the strollers in Monet's *Boulevard des Capucines* (it is not known whether it was the Moscow version or the Kansas City version that was hung in the first Impressionist exhibition; fig. 634). The picture was painted from Nadar's photographic studio and is itself a snapshot full of life, with some of the passers-by and trees blurred in precisely the way that contemporary photographers of urban landscapes were unable to avoid, given the lengths of their exposure times. His *Impression, Sunrise*, a view of the port of Le Havre one morning (or evening, it has been suggested), with its red sun suspended in the mist, is even more allusive in its approach (1872, fig. 50). Clearly, in hanging so "unpolished" a work in an exhibition that, because it represented a challenge to the official Salon, was bound to attract attention (at least from professionals—there were only 3,500 paying visitors), Monet's intention was to be provocative. The rules governing the new exhibition, in the context of the general reform of institutions, looked attractive, and in a sense anticipated the creation of the Société des Artistes Français in 1880, after the state had abandoned its three-hundred-year monopoly over the national art scene.

One painting that attracted no hostile criticism at the first Impressionist exhibition was *The Theater Box* by Renoir (*La Loge*, fig. 660). This was the first time that Renoir had tackled the theater theme (he also showed a *Dancer*, now in the National Gallery of Art, Washington, D.C.), a highly typical subject of modern life that Daumier and Degas had already illustrated in other ways and that was to tempt so many artists (the attractiveness of the subject undoubtedly had a lot to do with this). Here the artist had had his brother pose with a model and had portrayed them in close-up in one of those compositions that were, in the artist's words, "full to bursting" and for which he had a real predilection.

Despite the insistence of Degas, Manet refused to take part in the first Impressionist exhibition, preferring to exhibit at the Salon. Nevertheless, he took a great interest in what his painter friends were doing, particularly

Monet. The latter, following on from the experiments of the Realist painter Daubigny ten years earlier, studied the play of light and reflections on water. He used to paint from his studio-boat on the Seine at Argenteuil (near Paris). Manet spent the summer of 1874 at Gennevilliers, on the other side of the Seine from Argenteuil. Another artist who joined them was Caillebotte, who lived nearby at Petit-Gennevilliers, and Renoir also joined the group of friends. It was Manet's first experience painting on a plein-air theme, executed at least in part outdoors.

Manet submitted to the 1875 Salon a summer scene that is the most truly Impressionist of his works (fig. 658). Its title—*Argenteuil*—suggests it was an act of homage to Monet. For it, his brother-in-law posed with a model in the role of one of those idle occasional companions that boatmen picked up (hence her rather absent, not to say indifferent air). The landscape, as intensely luminous as the figures and treated in the same tones, is rigorously constructed and given rhythm by the horizontals and verticals of the landing stage and the masts of the boats, shown close up as in certain views of Edo (Tokyo) by Hiroshige, whom Manet no doubt had in mind when he painted the water of the river in so startling a blue as to incur the critics' sarcasm.

This over-cheerful palette and this kind of touch were still not the norm. Even without seeking to compare Manet with Cabanel (whose biblical *Tamar* was nonetheless savaged by the critics), it has to be admitted that artists tending toward Realism, such as Bonvin or Bonnat, presented works that were more reassuring in terms of chiaroscuro technique and polish. Castagnary was aware of the perfection of Bonvin's little painting *The Carcass, Pork-Butcher's Yard,* (*Le Cochon, cour de charcutier,* fig. 640), where the setting matches perfectly the main subject, the flayed animal—a tour de force for those familiar with Rembrandt's masterpiece (which Bonvin had studied back in 1858 from a copy in the Louvre). As for Bonnat, who was sufficiently close to Bonvin to have received as a gift the watercolor study for *The Carcass* (*Le Cochon,* Musée Bonnat, Bayonne), he too was hostile to Italianizing academicism and a skilled exponent of chiaroscuro as practiced by Rembrandt and Spanish artists. These were the foundations on which he had built his teaching since 1865, placing the emphasis on observation and meticulous rendition. Bonnat's cleverly lighted portraits against a neutral ground earned him the title of "king of the likeness" and made him the semi-official portraitist of the Third Republic. His portraits of Adolphe Thiers, Victor Hugo, and Jules Grévy are engraved in the memory of every French person. He delighted the 1875 Salon with his large portrait of *Madame Pasca, Dramatic Actress* (*Madame Pasca, artiste dramatique*), in which the actress is forcefully depicted in all her majesty, just as people knew her from her habitual roles of *grande dame* and noble matron.

It is interesting to note that Bonnat was among the few to champion Manet's submissions (though in vain) to the 1876 Salon. The only other artist to vote with him was Jean-Jacques Henner, whose painting opened up an original approach to the portrayal of idyllic nudes in landscapes of forests or peaceful lakes and anticipated certain aspects of late-nineteenth-century Symbolism, such as that of Émile-René Ménard (1862–1930), who was one of his pupils. No doubt they preferred *The Artist: Portrait of Marcellin Desboutin* (*L'Artiste. Portrait de Marcellin Desboutin,* Museu de Arte, São Paulo) in brown and blond monochrome, while *Le Linge* (The Barnes Foundation Museum of Art, Merion, Pa.) was a further attempt at painting outdoors, in a Paris garden. This was the painting that Symbolist poet Stéphane Mallarmé liked so much. The charming, familiar, everyday subject (a child watching its mother wring out the laundry before hanging it up) was not the same as Monet's laundresses, although it was closely related. Degas painted the same subject—washing being hung out to dry—in the Munich version of *The Laundress* (*La Blanchisseuse*). His model for this work was a girl called Emma Dobigny, whom Corot and Puvis de Chavannes also painted. The artist had probably started tackling this subject before 1870, and on February 13, 1874 Edmond de Goncourt recorded in his *Journal* a visit to Degas, an "odd" painter who showed him a number of laundresses "in their poses and their short skirts . . . talking their language and explaining to us about *firm* ironing, *circular* ironing, and so on" (fig. 639). This highly naturalistic subject from the world of labor Goncourt subsequently attempted to link to his 1867 novel *Manette Salomon,* though in fact it looked forward to Zola's *L'Assommoir* of ten years later. One *Laundress* had already been presented in 1874; at the second Impressionist exhibition in 1876, there were five. The twenty-four works submitted by Degas also included a number of dancers, as well as a large painting executed during his visit to Louisiana in 1872–73, *Portraits in an Office—Cotton Exchange in New Orleans* (*Portraits dans un bureau (Nouvelle Orléans),* fig. 638). This depicts his maternal uncle Michel Musson (foreground), together with various close relatives, in the setting of the office of a cotton trader. The high-angle viewpoint enabled the artist to show each of his protagonists about his individual business. Degas had hoped to find a buyer for this vision of a wealthy America in the person of a Liverpool textile magnate. The plan failed, but when the picture was shown at a provincial exhibition in 1878, it was purchased for the Musée des Beaux-Arts, Pau—the first sign of public recognition of Degas's work.

In the center of one wall of the *salon d'honneur* of Durand-Ruel's gallery, which showed the Impressionists in 1876, spun the flamboyant figure of Camille in a theatrical kimono, surrounded by multicolored fans, in a painting Monet called simply *Japonnerie* (Museum of Fine Arts, Boston). The possibly ironic title concealed a fashionable subject, and the artist hoped to make a lot of money with the picture. Indeed, when it was sold on April 4, 1876 it was the only work to reach a high price. It may have been for similarly commercial reasons that Degas produced (under the modest title *Panneau décoratif*) another large composition, a *Luncheon* (*Déjeuner*) in his Argenteuil garden in 1873. The meal is over, the artist's son Jean is lingering to one side, looking for amusement, a young woman is seen going back into the house, and the silhouette of the sideboard in the foreground, like the high-angle viewpoint, gives the viewer the impression of having himself just got up from the table. This is a moment of life, a truly everyday subject, but one that is somehow reluctant to admit as much, possibly because of the format.

It was Gustave Caillebotte who eventually bought the painting in 1878. Caillebotte, who came from a wealthy family, joined the group in 1876 when he exhibited the powerfully realistic *Floor Planers* (*Raboteurs de parquet*, Musée d'Orsay) and other interior scenes with bold compositions, such as his back-lit man standing in front of an open window. We know that he was generous to his friends, putting together a collection that he bequeathed to France's national museums.

Monet also exhibited landscapes, particularly of the banks of the Seine and bridges at Argenteuil (fig. 631). Alfred Sisley used a very similar technique, as in *The Flood at Port-Marly* (*L'Inondation à Port-Marly*, fig. 633), but coupled it with a discretion that earned him compliments.

In his 1876 brochure entitled *La Nouvelle peinture*, Duranty justified his friends' subjects and technique, briskly rejecting the conventions of the École des Beaux-Arts. Was he thinking of Gustave Moreau when he wrote: "You are clutching at the knees of Prometheus, the wings of the Sphinx"? Moreau had indeed made a name for himself under the Second Empire with compositions on such antique subjects but had not been seen again at the Salon until that very year, 1876, where his Salome pictures struck some as sick and others as so fascinating that they subsequently inspired poets and novelists, notably Joris-Karl Huysmans in the description of the collection belonging to his decadent hero, Des Esseintes.

Moreau had always seen himself as a history painter, yet he declined to take part in the decoration of the Panthéon in Paris, for which he had been approached in 1874 by Philippe de Chennevières, preferring to devote himself to the many Symbolist ideal art projects that he was developing on his own.

Alongside various decorative programs for buildings that had been rebuilt or converted after the fires of the Commune, the Panthéon (empty since the abandonment of the Chenavard project) offered a great deal of wall space that could be used to glorify the nation's history—always a useful thing for a new political regime to do. The choice of artists is indicative of the state of the arts in France at that time. While Paul Baudry (1828–1886), who was tied up with the vast Opéra project, and Gérôme declined, as had Moreau, other artists such as Pierre-Victor Galand, Bonnat, Cabanel, Delaunay, Puvis de Chavannes, and Joseph Blanc set to work. They were soon joined by Humbert, Jean-Paul Laurens, Henry Lévy, Maillard, Hébert, and Jules Lenepveu (1819–1898), who also played a successful part in the decoration of the new Opéra with his auditorium ceiling on an allegorical theme, *The Muses and the Hours of the Day and Night* (*Les Muses et les Heures du jour et de la nuit*; now covered by Chagall's ceiling). Also considered were Henri Lehmann (1814–1882), who was ill, Chenavard, and Millet, who was to die in 1875, but neither they nor Meissonier actually started work. Meissonier, who specialized in miniature epics, was a surprising choice, and despite numerous fresh attempts died in 1891 without completing his commission. He was then replaced by Puvis de Chavannes for a second cycle of the life of St. Geneviève.

After Neoclassical beginnings, Puvis gradually perfected a style that suited mural painting and that he also used in easel paintings with a decorative intention, such as *Girls at the Seaside* (*Jeunes Filles au bord de la mer*, 1879, Musée d'Orsay) and *The Poor Fisherman* (*Le Pauvre Pêcheur*, 1881, Musée d'Orsay). The style was characterized by an absence of perspective and chiaroscuro, and the use of areas of light color. He achieved grandeur and depth of emotion through the austere simplification of figures that are somehow outside time and place.

Puvis remained an isolated figure in France (though he had an enormous influence on the artists of the Symbolist generation, with Gauguin foremost among them), but we find a similar sense of harmony and primitive simplicity in the work of the German painter, Hans von Marées (1837–1887), who sought to portray a new Arcadia. Marées had traveled widely in Europe, not only in Italy but also in France, when he was commissioned to paint the frescoes in the great hall of the Zoological Institute in Naples. The commission came from the institute's founder, a German professor by the name of Anton Dohrn, whom Marées depicted, together with his colleagues and the artist himself, in *The Pergola*. Marées also showed, in other parts of the decorative scheme such as *Orange Picking*, that he was capable of combining nudes with figures in modern dress, indicating that he had learned the lesson (though here it is the men who are nude) of Courbet and Manet.

Courbet had long been a familiar presence in the German-speaking countries, both through his travels and the paintings he sent to exhibitions. Couture had also been influential there, through the pupils who passed through his studio. And the 1869 international exhibition in Munich had seen considerable French participation, including Chenavard, Courbet, and even Manet. Moreover, until 1870 it was common for German artists to visit France, sometimes on the way to Italy (as in the case of Marées) or Spain.

The acute tensions between officialdom and innovative artists that, in France, simply pushed the latter's radical experiments further did not exist in the same way in the German-speaking world. Adolf von Menzel (1815–1905), for example, though he had treated subjects from the life of Frederick the Great with something of the luminous touch of a Meissonier, was at the height of his fame and in possession of all the honors of the Berlin Academy when in 1875 he caused a sensation with his most important work, *The Rolling Mill*. He had always been attracted by the idea of depicting the contemporary world and the busy life of big cities such as Paris (which he had visited in 1855 and again in 1867 and 1868) and Berlin. Men at work were in fact a subject he returned to repeatedly, and for *The Rolling Mill* he did many studies from the life, starting in 1872; he even braved the danger of working in the vicinity of white-hot metal in a factory in Königshütte in Silesia. His vibrant touch lends an almost mythical quality to this representation of the machines and men of emergent industrial civilization—to the point where the picture has even been entitled *Modern Cyclopes*. Menzel's 1872 painting of *The Studio Wall* (fig. 46), with its burden of plaster casts of animals, antiques, and masks of writers and artists (including his own, in the middle of the top row), was an opportunity for him to demonstrate a striking realism, using a novel artificial-light effect, and to restate his aesthetic principles, notably his rejection of academicism.

It was shortly after his return from Paris, where he had been introduced to Courbet by Otto Scholderer (whom Fantin-Latour depicted in 1870 in *A Studio in Les Batignolles*, fig. 623), that Hans Thoma (1839–1924) painted *Evening* or *The Artist's Mother and Sister in the Garden* (1868), with its rural landscape setting. In it he used the Parisian master's dull coloring, placing his figures and the whole of the foreground in the shade, as he was so often to do, and distancing himself from what is otherwise a traditional genre scene by eliminating any kind of narrative element in favor of an almost Symbolist representation of life in his own locality, to which he remained faithful from then on. This tendency was reinforced in 1875 when he painted his *Self-Portrait* (Staatliche Kunsthalle, Karlsruhe), a veritable vanitas, between a skeleton wearing a laurel wreath and a fluttering cupid, while a butterfly, that symbol of the soul, stands out against a verdant background above his head.

In 1875, the very year that saw the death of Millet, who had treated *Spring* (fig. 29) in a similar manner (a tiny human presence in a landscape after a storm), Hans Thoma painted *The Plain of the Main* (fig. 49), which combines monumental simplicity with enormous expressive power. The eye commands a broad sweep (a loop of the river and water meadows) sparkling in the rays of sunlight that penetrate the clouds after rain. The palette-knife treatment of the lumpy paintwork, using a technique inspired by Courbet, gives a primitive solidity to the location, while on the left we glimpse the silhouettes of people ploughing a field, dwarfed by the mass of blossom that is the blackthorn in the foreground. This is Thoma's way of marking man's place in nature, the source of regeneration and life.

Another artist who had known Courbet ten years earlier but had found his own style in recent years was the American, Whistler. In 1875 he painted a firework display in London's Cremorne Gardens in the form of a harmony of color, as the very title indicates: *Nocturne in Black and Gold: The Falling Rocket* (fig. 54). His approach was very different, though poetic and Impressionist in its way, prompting Huysmans to remark, when the painting was exhibited in Paris a few years later, that this was a "dream landscape" and that Whistler was a "supremely lucid artist bringing out the supra-perceptible from the real" (Huysman 1976, 32). Shown at London's Grosvenor Gallery in 1875 with the explanatory words "The Falling Rocket" and then again in 1877 without that tag, the painting was to incur the criticism of Ruskin, the champion of the Pre-Raphaelites, who pronounced the artist to be "a joker who is asking two hundred guineas for hurling a pot of paint in the face of the public." During the trial of the action that Whistler brought against John Ruskin in 1878, the artist pointed out that, although the manual work involved had been swift (only two days), he did not start painting until he had conceived the picture in his mind, and he finished only thanks to the skill he had acquired throughout his life. This was indeed a finished painting and not a sketch.

In 1877, when the third Impressionist exhibition was held, the accusation of slovenliness and ignorance was again launched by the more reactionary journalists against Pissarro, Cézanne, and Monet (Renoir and Caillebotte, among others, escaped this reproach). This time the exhibition attracted more than eight thousand visitors and was adjudged a success. It was held in enormous premises on the first floor of 6 Rue Le Peletier, opposite Durand-Ruel's galleries (not far from the Opéra), and Caillebotte had played a large part in its organization. He himself submitted some large paintings of his own on the subject of modern Paris, including *Paris, A Rainy Day* (*Rue de Paris; temps de pluie*, Art Institute of Chicago), with its life-sized figures under umbrellas, and *The Pont de l'Europe* (fig. 637). In this very large painting, despite the boldness of the perspective effect (which may have been inspired, as regards the great diagonal, by some prints of Yokohama that Caillebotte had pinned up on the wall of his studio), it looks correct, and the smooth painting style appears "normal" (as one critic remarked), and reassuring, with shadows that are clearly drawn. The plume of smoke rising from the Gare Saint-Lazare below is treated simply as a white cloud, obscuring some of the windows of a building in the distance. Critics were more interested in pointing out the recognizable figure of Caillebotte himself, wearing a top hat: here was the millionaire who painted for a hobby.

Beside Caillebotte's highly distinctive paintings, the seven views of the Gare Saint-Lazare submitted by Monet formed a strange contrast, both in their use of impasto and in the way shapes dissolve in light (fig. 636). The views were painted at different times of the day and employ different palettes. The Musée d'Orsay version shows the sun at its zenith, casting the shadow of the great glass roof over the platforms in yellows and grays. The version in the Fogg Art Museum (Cambridge, Mass.) is blue with spots of red, and this time the rails are very clear, back-lit by a reddening sun. This was Monet's first attempt at a series, of which he painted so many from this time on, notably haystacks, poplar trees, and later water lilies.

Also in 1877, blue was the dominant color in Renoir's outdoor views, *The Swing* (*La Balançoire*, Musée d'Orsay) and *Dancing at the Moulin de la Galette* (*Le Bal du moulin de la Galette*). For the latter work, he carried his canvas every day to the garden of this Montmartre establishment where there was outdoor dancing. Young friends (painters, for the most part) and regulars who went dancing there on Sundays served as his models, but what really interested Renoir at that time was studying the way shafts of sunlight filtered through the branches, illuminating the ground and the figures and making forms dissolve.

In the following years, Renoir decided to take his chances at the Salon. He took part in only one of the group's subsequent exhibitions, in 1882, when he showed *The Luncheon of the Boating Party* (*Le Déjeuner des canotiers*). Here the figures are far more individualized and the composition clearer, but this is very much yet another homage to the merry festivities held in and around Paris, this time at the Fournaise restaurant on an island in the Seine at Chatou. If the Impressionists, like Manet, chose modern subjects that lent themselves well to a naturalistic approach while experimenting with new ways of painting (to which the critics, more than the public and collectors, were not yet accustomed), naturalism as such was now practiced more and more widely—to the point of becoming almost the official art, having by about 1880 largely replaced history painting.

In Holland, a school of landscapists and painters of everyday life emerged in the wake of Israëls, with their own exhibition facilities in the form of well-established societies of artists, such as the Pulchri Studio in The Hague, founded in 1847. They profited from their interest in the Barbizon School while looking again at local sources such as Dutch landscape painting of the seventeenth century. One of the most engaging painters of this Hague School was Anton Mauve (1838–1888), to whom a cousin by the name of Vincent van Gogh was to come for advice in 1881. Mauve painted animal subjects and fishing scenes, using a broad technique and applying his paint very quickly. Occasionally, he was outstandingly successful, as in the very fine *Riding on the Beach at Scheveningen* (fig. 665), in which a party of aristocratic-looking horsemen is pictured from behind, descending a dune toward the sea. Mauve has been compared to Manet, but his work is more reminiscent of Jean-Charles Cazin, de Nittis, or Jules Bastien-Lepage; in fact, he is a typical representative of international naturalism. As for Jacob Maris (1837–1899), who had passed through Paris and the Loing valley near Fontainebleau to the south during the Second Empire, after his return to The Hague in 1871 he concentrated on (sometimes imaginary) townscapes with canals, bridges, and windmills. His *Dutch Riverside Town* (fig. 678), for example, painted in 1883, alludes to Vermeer's famous *View of Delft*.

In France, the example of Courbet and Jules Breton, who had given pride of place to the representation of their hometowns (Ornans and Courrières respectively), was followed by the brilliant young painter Jules Bastien-Lepage (1848–1884). He soon dropped conventional subjects (he had entered Cabanel's studio in 1868) in favor of rural scenes of his native village of Damvillers in the Lorraine. When Bastien-Lepage showed *The Haymakers* (*Les Foins*, fig. 651) at the 1878 Salon, he was accused of having stolen the Impressionists' light palette. The artist did not become successful until about 1882, and it was not until the posthumous exhibition of 1885 that the state purchased *The Haymakers* for the Musée du Luxembourg. His portraits, noted for their great psychological insight, enjoyed a swifter success. They stemmed, in fact, from a tradition that was also celebrated at the 1878 Salon by Élie Delaunay's portrait of *Madame Georges Bizet* (fig. 666). Painted a few months after the death of the composer (an old friend of Delaunay's), the portrait depicts his wife in deep mourning, wearing a look of such intensity as to make this almost an allegory of the tragedy she has just experienced. Yet we also get a sense of the elegance and spontaneity of the woman who, following her remarriage to the attorney Émile Straus, was to become the queen of a fashionable salon and a model for heroines in the work of Maupassant and Marcel Proust.

The bright palette so dear to the Impressionists was used with powerful realism and a very bold touch by a former pupil of Cabanel and Fromentin, Henri Gervex (1852–1929), in *Rolla* (fig. 650), which the 1878 Salon rejected for impropriety. It had been on the advice of Degas that the artist had introduced certain details pointing to a night of debauchery (a starched petticoat and pink silk garter flung down beside the bed), and the scandal arose from this modernization of the painting's Romantic subject, a famous poem by Alfred de Musset in which Rolla, having bankrupted himself for the beautiful Marion, eventually commits suicide. Seen as a simple bedroom subject taken from bourgeois life, *Rolla* was clearly unacceptable at the Salon. Was it perhaps the air of sensual abandon surrounding the little girl depicted by Mary Cassatt (1844–1926) in *The Blue Room* (*Le Salon bleu*, fig. 59) that accounted for its rejection by the Exposition Universelle of the same year, or was it the total absence of subject, the bold framing, the high-angle view, or the aggressive colors? Degas, who had made the acquaintance of this American artist then living in Paris, was to persuade her to exhibit with the Impressionists from 1879 onward. Mary Cassatt is known to have played a considerable role in the success that the Impressionists were later to enjoy among her wealthier American friends.

There is a far greater degree of sensual ambiguity in the vast canvas by the Austrian Hans Makart (1840–1884), *Charles V Entering Antwerp* (fig. 677), which was one of the star attractions of the 1878 Exposition Universelle in Paris. Makart, a former pupil of Piloty who lived in Vienna, wanted to revive history painting by making it more appealing. He contrived to conceal the sensuality of this painting beneath a historical disguise, as if in homage to the painters of the past from whom he had drawn his inspiration: Dürer, on the one hand, who had shown the emperor surrounded by beautiful semi-naked girls amid the jubilation of his entry into the conquered city, and on the other hand Rubens, whom Makart had been able to study on a visit to Antwerp in 1877 and whom he sought to equal. An exhibition in the artist's Vienna studio in March 1878 had attracted 34,000 visitors, who had fun spotting, in the procession of lovelies, the local celebrities whom Makart had used as models. Subsequently, from March 1879 to January 1881, the painting was shown in a traveling exhibition that crisscrossed Europe (Berlin, Munich, Dresden, London, and Hanover) before it was eventually acquired by Hamburg's Kunsthalle in 1882.

In Paris in 1879, when it was decided, under the legal settlement of the succession of Napoleon III, to let the nation's museums have certain landscapes by Courbet and Daubigny as well as several paintings by Cabanel, including his famous *Birth of Venus* (*Naissance de Vénus*) from the 1863 Salon, the government kept faith with the aesthetics of academicism by acquiring Bouguereau's *Birth of Venus* (*Naissance de Vénus*), shown at that year's Salon, for the Musée du Luxembourg. Hardly surprisingly, Huysmans savaged the painting right at the beginning of his review, accusing Bouguereau of having "invented gas-filled painting, the blow-up subject" and comparing the figure of Venus to a "poorly inflated toy balloon" (Huysmans 1976, 37). The banality of the work and the atrocious color and drawing were disturbing on the part of someone with teaching responsibilities. Huysmans, of course, preferred the few artists who had "long since abandoned the old routines" (Huysmans 1976, 75), such as a former independent who had now returned to the Salon, Renoir. Renoir's portrait of the actress *Jeanne Samary* (Hermitage Museum, St. Petersburg) was hung too high to be seen, but the *Portrait of Madame Charpentier and her Children* (*Portrait de Madame Charpentier et de ses enfants*, fig. 674) was well positioned, possibly because the model and her husband (who published Gustave Flaubert, Zola, and the Goncourt brothers) were prominent people. The artist, whom the critics all agreed was a superb colorist, had managed to preserve the naturalness of a family scene in a middle class drawing room with its decor of Japanese silks and its bamboo furniture, despite a composition that is more studied than it appears and an obvious desire to produce great art.

At a time when naturalism was triumphant throughout Europe, notably in far-off Russia, where the landscapist Arkhip Ivanovich Kuindzhi (1842–1910) presented a startling effect of light, *After the Storm* (fig. 62), to the seventh Wanderers' exhibition in 1879, the most talented French naturalistic painters were seeking to reintroduce an ideal element into their works. At the last of the official Salons in 1880, prior to the transfer of powers to the new Société des Artistes Français, Bastien-Lepage showed an astonishing *Joan of Arc* (*Jeanne d'Arc*, Metropolitan Museum of Art, New York) while Jean-Charles Cazin (1841–1901), a former pupil of Horace Lecoq de Boisbaudran (as Fantin-Latour, Legros, and Auguste Rodin had been), won a first-class medal with *Ishmael* (*Ismaël*, Musée des Beaux-Arts, Tours) and *Tobias and the Angel* (*Tobie et l'Ange*, fig. 645). Cazin took the bold step of placing his figures in the dunes of the Pas-de-Calais coast, lending a fresh topicality to biblical themes.

The precursory signs of Symbolism were already beginning to emerge in isolated pockets: in France with Puvis de Chavannes and Gustave Moreau, in Great Britain with Edward Burne-Jones, and in Florence, where he had eventually settled in 1874, with the Swiss artist Arnold Böcklin (1827–1901). In fact it was in 1880 that, at the request of Maria Berna of Frankfurt, he painted a "dream picture" that subsequently became known as *The Island of the Dead* (*Die Toteninsel*, fig. 58). Böcklin painted five versions of this subject, of which the Basel one is the earliest. Despite a number of variations (the distance of the island, the narrowness of the entrance), they all exude the same atmosphere of mystery, the same suffocating silence. This made them enormously popular in German-speaking countries, and they also exerted great fascination on artists, from Max Klinger to the Surrealists, notably Giorgio de Chirico and Salvador Dalí.

The British painter Edward Burne-Jones (1833–1898) was at that time slowly developing his great cycles drawn from mythology or literature, in which he placed his figures outside time in order to suggest the permanence of the ideas they conveyed. He had begun his career in the group centered around William Morris and Rossetti. He made many visits to Italy, which helped to mold his style, with its echoes of Andrea Mantegna, Sandro Botticelli, and Michelangelo. In 1875 the British politician Arthur Balfour had asked him to paint a *Perseus* cycle for the music room of his London home. The cycle was never installed, but in 1883 Balfour purchased *The Wheel of Fortune* (fig. 55), which Burne-Jones had begun in 1875 and completed for his exhibition at the Grosvenor Gallery in London in 1883, developing one of the motifs of the predella of a polyptych depicting *The Story of Troy* (City Museum and Art Gallery, Birmingham), much of which was only roughed out. A number of his works had been seen in Paris on the occasion of the 1878 Exposition Universelle, but it was chiefly after 1890 that he became famous in France, thanks to the intervention of Puvis de Chavannes.

Meanwhile the naturalistic vein persisted and evolved in the direction of fresh formal experiments, producing its final masterpieces The list of participants in the Impressionist exhibitions widened to include several newcomers. One, introduced by Degas in 1880 and 1881, was Jean-François Raffaëlli (1850–1924), a painter of suburban scenes that were sometimes *misérabiliste* and sometimes rather tender, such as *The Guests Waiting for the Wedding* (*Les Invités attendant la noce*, fig. 652) which he showed at a private exhibition in 1884. Another, encouraged by Pissarro, was Paul Gauguin (1848–1903), a stockbroker and spare-time artist who made his mark as a sculptor as early as 1879, and was invited to contribute to the fifth Impressionist exhibition the following year as a painter. At the seventh Impressionist exhibition in 1882, to which Gauguin sent thirteen works, the painting that he exhibited under the title *Flowers, Still-life* (*Fleurs, nature morte*) is in fact *The Painter's Home, Rue Carcel* (*L'Intérieur du peintre, rue Carcel*). The whole thing is a little dark, despite the large bunch of zinnias in the foreground, but the organization of the interior is complex, with the artist standing behind a screen, listening to someone playing the piano (probably his wife). It suggests a certain familiarity with the interiors painted by Caillebotte, but also with the compositions of Degas, notably the café scenes he painted which are punctuated with verticals. In 1883, when the Paris stock exchange crashed, he lost his job. He decided to devote himself wholly to painting, with all the material and marital difficulties that the decision was to involve for him.

Renoir's submission to the same exhibition was varied and extensive. In addition to the ambitious *Luncheon of the Boating Party* (fig. 63), exhibited under the title *Lunch at Bougival* (*Un Déjeuner à Bougival*), there were two landscapes that he had brought back from a trip to Algiers in the spring of 1881, including *Banana Plantation near Algiers* (*Champ de bananiers près d'Alger*) with its profuse, almost abstract presentation and two views of Venice testifying to a stay in Italy toward the end of that year. The latter works are rich in reflections on classical art and prelude a change of direction in Renoir's art. He had in fact painted a *Bather* in Capri (Clark Institute, Williamstown) that already heralds the *Large Bathers* (*Les Grandes Baigneuses*) shown at Georges Petit's gallery in 1887, the incisive drawing of which marks Renoir's abandonment of the Impressionist technique. Finally, Manet had just been rewarded a modest second-class medal at the 1881 Salon, the first to be organized by the new Société des Artistes Français, the jury of which thus made amends for a regrettable injustice. He showed his continuing loyalty to the institution by sending two works to the 1882 Salon, one of which was his last masterpiece, *Bar at the Folies-Bergère* (*Un bar aux Folies-Bergère*, fig. 60). We know the conditions under which this was painted in the studio. Manet had a barmaid from this fashionable establishment pose for him; on a marble-topped table he had set out the bottles and glassware that form the dazzling still life in the foreground. All the rest is a reflection in a huge mirror—the room with its chandeliers, the spectators, and the show itself, with an acrobat in green slippers in the top left-hand corner. We also see (at an angle) the barmaid's back and a customer in conversation with her who is actually in the place of the viewer of the painting. The customer, incidentally, is the painter Gaston La Touche (1854–1913), who apparently posed for the figure. The singular power of this cleverly composed picture, painted with the bright, allusive technique of the Impressionists, particularly evident in the reflection of the crowd, stems from the way the fresh-faced young barmaid is isolated in her evident glum indifference.

Some months later, the ailing Manet died at the age of fifty-one. In January 1884 a posthumous exhibition opened at the École des Beaux-Arts. It was an occasion for young artists of all nationalities (who the year before had been able to see a Courbet retrospective) to discover the work of this exceptional artist. We can get an idea of the cosmopolitan liveliness of Paris at this time from Edmond de Goncourt's diary entry for June 17, 1882: "Went to the Salon. A particular painting draws my eye for its craftsmanship, say, for a new effect, or for something or other that is original, and when I go close to read the signature I find it is by a foreigner, an Austrian, a Scandinavian, a Russian, a Spaniard."

Manet's friend Giuseppe de Nittis, an Italian living in Paris, painted an astonishing triptych entitled *Racing at the Bois de Boulogne* (*Courses aux bois de Boulogne*, figs. 662–64) in 1881. Many artists came to France, attracted by the prestige of his school. They attended classes at the Académie Julian and gathered in Brittany (Pont-Aven was already an artists' colony), and at Marlotte and Grez-sur-Loing. On returning to their homeland, the Scandinavians founded their own artists' colonies, such as the one at Skagen on the northernmost tip of Denmark. The Norwegian painter Christian Krohg (1852–1925), who lived for a while in Paris, visited Skagen in 1872 and again in the summers of 1882 to 1884. In Paris, he had been able to absorb the art of Manet, Caillebotte, and Bastien-Lepage and he even presented a work at the 1882 Salon. *The Sick Girl*, whom he painted in 1880–81, with her flushed face bearing the clinical marks of tuberculosis, injects new life into a familiar genre scene with its bold frontality; the red stripes on the blanket echo the color of the girl's lips and eyelids as well as of the rose in her lap, its petals already (symbolically) falling (fig. 644). The Dane Peder Severin Krøyer (1851–1909), one of the Skagen faithful, had during his European tour frequented the studio of Bonnat, with whom he visited the museums of Spain in 1878. Back in Skagen in 1879, Krøyer painted a sardine cannery with a realism rather less conventional than the French were using at the time—more like that of the Dutchman Israëls or the German Max Liebermann (1847–1935). A flowing style, bright colors, and a keen sense of the natural characterize his *Artists' Luncheon*, painted at Skagen in 1883 in tribute to the community of painters that had grouped around Michael Anker. The painting formed the decorative centerpiece of the room in the Brøndum Hotel where they used to meet—a practice established by the Barbizon artists and, later, those of Le Pouldu in Brittany.

It was also in 1882–82 that the British painter George Clausen (1852–1944) visited Brittany and Paris, and there is an echo of Bastien-Lepage's *Poor Fauvette* (*Pauvre Fauvette*, Art Gallery and Museum, Glasgow) in the technique of Clausen's *Women Gathering Stones* of 1887, though they are more touching in their poverty. The expatriate American painter John Singer Sargent (1856–1925) had a similarly cosmopolitan career as a portraitist, spending some time in Paris in the studio of Carolus-Duran. Sargent too had a broad, flowing manner inspired by his admiration for Velázquez, Franz Hals, and Anthony van Dyck (painters who had also inspired Manet in his early years). Sargent exhibited at the Paris Salon until 1884, when his portrait of Madame Gautreau (*Madame X*, Metropolitan Museum of Art, New York) caused a scandal with its revealing décolleté. He demonstrated a remarkable facility in the natural framing of his *Portrait of the Daughters of Edward D. Boit* (fig. 675), one of the American customers who were responsible for his later success.

The American Childe Hassam (1859–1935) made a long trip to Europe in 1883, during which he spent part of the time studying at the Académie Julian. Hassam liked to paint street scenes and was influenced by the naturalism of de Nittis and Jean Béraud (1848–1935) more than by that of Caillebotte. His first major painting, *Rainy Day in Boston*, exhibited at the Society of American Artists in New York in 1886, featured the broad avenues of a modern city, large wet paving stones, regular houses, and even the streetcar serving Columbus Avenue. While they were not necessarily the most inventive, some of those who took part in the Impressionist exhibitions were foreign painters: the Italian Zandomeneghi, for example, or the American Mary Cassatt, whose *At the Opera* (1882, fig. 661) is a particularly well-captured scene from modern life.

There was to be no shortage of innovations at the last Impressionist exhibition in 1886.

1885–1905: A FRESH CONTEXT

Artists and the Public

Toward the mid-1880s certain profound changes became apparent on the art scene. Up until then, public exposure to art had largely been the monopoly of official institutions that generally remained closed to new tendencies and guaranteed not only a certain level of technical mastery in the works exhibited but also a respect for the essential stylistic and iconographic criteria governing traditional taste. The Salon, in France, was *the* artistic event of the year, sufficient in itself to marginalize any independent exhibition ventures, which did not carry the same guarantees and in any case never had the breadth of a complete panorama of the nation's contemporary art.

This situation was transformed in less than a decade, thanks to the development of the art trade. If, in France, the taste of most collectors was still dominated by the Barbizon School, Meissonier, and French Romantics such as Delacroix, Decamps, and Isabey (then known as the "1830 School"), a dealer such as Durand-Ruel was able to set out to promote (with difficulty, it has to be said) Impressionism, the very existence of which was denied in official quarters. About the middle of the 1880s, with the Impressionist group ceasing to exist as an organized movement, there was an attempt to widen the fairly narrow circle of collectors who had constituted the faithful clientele of Impressionism from the outset. With the backing of Mary Cassatt, from 1886 Durand-Ruel held exhibitions in New York of works by Manet, Degas, Renoir, Monet, Sisley, Pissarro, Morisot, Guillaumin, Caillebotte, Seurat, and Signac—alongside the painters of the Barbizon School and the academic artists who accounted for most of his business. Also in that year, Monet and Renoir took part in the fifth Exposition Internationale organized by Georges Petit in his gallery in the Rue de Sèze in Paris. A competitor of Durand-Ruel, Petit had started these exhibitions in 1882 in collaboration with Giuseppe de Nittis, with the idea of presenting innovative trends in European painting. Whistler had a substantial entry in 1887, for example, and between 1882 and 1896 the Petit catalog included such names as Émile Claus (1849–1924), Max Liebermann, Jean-Charles Cazin, Charles Cottet (1863–1925), Fritz Thaulow, Anders Zorn (1860–1920), Jacques-Émile Blanche (1861–1942), and Giovanni Boldini.

Georges Petit's annexation of Impressionism marked the reversal of a trend. From this point on, the art trade helped remove the obstacles blocking the Impressionists' path to recognition by putting them in touch with a clientele of wealthy art-lovers. Another important aspect was the spread of private exhibitions, which had previously been very rare. Monet, for example, had a series of exhibitions with Durand-Ruel and Petit that, from 1891, were wholly or partly devoted to specific themes (haystacks, poplars, cathedrals, water lilies). The private exhibition implied an accolade that tended to take the place of the medal awarded by the jury of the Salon. So it was that the art market absorbed the new trends with increasing rapidity, echoed by abundant press and critical attention. In 1891 the Nabis, a group of young artists who had come out of the Académie Julian, together with a group of

Impressionist and Symbolist painters that included Henri de Toulouse-Lautrec, Henri Rousseau, Gauguin, and van Gogh, were exhibited by Le Barc de Boutteville, a dealer with very varied and forward-looking tastes.

Nevertheless, the key role in this shifting of relations between art and the public fell to the new groups of artists that now began to emerge. To get round the obstacle of official art, two solutions were possible: the creation of an annual Salon with no jury (and consequently open to anyone who wished to take part), or on the other hand the "secessionist" solution of forming a society of artists outside the academic channels usually employed (and open to new tendencies as a matter of principle). The first solution produced only one example of any importance, namely the Société des Artistes Indépendants, founded in Paris in 1884. In terms of scope and frequency, the exhibitions of the Indépendants were comparable to the old Salon, except that all one had to do to be accepted was to pay a small annual subscription to the society. A glance at the art criticism of the period leaves no doubt as to the mediocrity of a large proportion of the artists exhibiting. However, from Neo-Impressionism to Fauvism, the Salon des Indépendants was the theater of every innovation. In 1886 Henri Rousseau (1844–1910) enthusiastically joined the Société des Artistes Indépendants, "the finest society as well as the most legal, because everyone in it has the same rights." Ten years later, Edvard Munch exhibited with them for the first time in Paris. The retrospectives devoted to Albert Dubois-Pillet (1846–1890) in 1891 and Seurat in the following year were responsible for the spread of Neo-Impressionism, then still a very marginal movement.

The year 1844 also saw the creation, in Brussels, of Les XX, a group combining artists of various allegiances. The list of members in fact constitutes a striking résumé of the two tendencies (realist and idealist) then competing for dominance in Belgian painting. Again, the purpose of Les XX was to break out of the straitjacket of a three-yearly cycle of official exhibitions in Brussels, Ghent, and Antwerp and to open up national art as much as possible to outside influences. The sole watchword of the group (which at that time had no equal in any other country) was innovation. "What I find extraordinarily pleasing about Les XX," wrote Félicien Rops, "is their lack of program." Inspired by a very remarkable personality, the attorney Octave Maus, the group played its assigned role of forum for exchange very effectively. Van Gogh exhibited six paintings with them in 1890. Seurat and Pissarro took part in exhibitions of Les XX as early as 1887 and Signac from 1888, thus initiating a Belgian and Dutch development that gave Neo-Impressionism several of its major artists, notably Théo van Rysselberghe, Jan Toorop, Henry van de Velde, and Georges Lemmen.

The formation of fresh associations was a constant feature of the art scene in the last twenty years of the nineteenth century. One that was created in Paris in 1891, at the instigation of Meissonier, Eugène Carrière, and Puvis de Chavannes, was the Société Nationale des Beaux-Arts, which was open to foreign artists; its annual Salon gradually eclipsed the more traditional Salon des Artistes Français. The Munich Sezession of 1892 (followed by those of Vienna and Berlin in 1897 and 1898 respectively) adopted the same principles: a liberal hanging committee that was open to innovative tendencies, and very large exhibitions. But alongside these "new Salons," the object of which was to bait the established order, large numbers of societies grew up that organized their own exhibitions. Examples in Paris were the Société des Peintres-Graveurs, formed in 1891, or the short-lived Salon des Cent, which held ten exhibitions in 1894–95 and came under the auspices of the magazine *La Plume* (The Pen). Clearly, this was bound to lead to a liberalization of artistic life and an acceleration of the process whereby different currents influenced one another. Various publications (some of which emanated directly from artists' groups, such as the Viennese magazine *Ver Sacrum*, the organ of the Sezession) played an active part in this development, while reproductions of works of art (initially through engraving but subsequently through photography) became increasingly widespread.

Once it was possible for new tendencies, championed by powerful personalities, to appear easily, every innovative work of art became tantamount to a stance adopted by its author vis-à-vis the public, the critics, and even society itself, seen as being traditionally hostile to change in the field of art. A series of very violent struggles served as backcloth to the history of painting up until the beginning of the twentieth century. The public, bewildered by this unprecedented proliferation of new aesthetic theories, was largely cut off from the art of its day. The gap between the artist and the rest of society (which in earlier periods had been more often the result of a way of life than of artistic production itself) was here "given" from the outset, as a result of the incongruity of these works compared with what people were use to.

At the same time, the search for style took on a hitherto unknown intensity. The very talented young artist Émile Bernard (1868–1941) exemplified this stylistic versatility and illustrates the rapidity with which innovative currents appeared. Having adopted a technique inspired by Neo-Impressionism, Bernard then laid the foundations of Cloisonnism, a principle to which in the space of a few months he went on to give very varied versions, ranging from a geometrical simplification that anticipated Art Nouveau to a kind of medievalism with mystic overtones.

Although the new exhibitions facilitated the personal encounters that lay at the origin of a more rapid development of forms, it is important not to overlook other factors that played a vital role in the appearance of this phenomenon. The teaching of art was itself becoming more liberal. In Paris, the organization of the École des Beaux-Arts did not change significantly, but a fresh aspect of the last two decades of the century was the importance assumed by the free academies which provided training for artists who did not wish to take the traditional course. What usually happened was that professors who taught at the École des Beaux-Arts, men like Bonnat or Eugène Cormon (1845–1924), also had studios where they gave lessons privately. The Académie Julian, founded in 1868 by the painter Rodolphe Julian, was in fact organized along the lines of the École des Beaux-Arts but with the crucial difference that students were not required to pass a competitive entrance examination before they could attend. In addition to Julian himself, other official celebrities such as Bouguereau, Tony Robert-Fleury, and Jean-Paul Laurens taught there alternately. Over the last twenty years of the nineteenth century, this free academy went from strength to strength. The official channel was structured in such a way that the painter who wished to receive a complete education in his chosen profession found himself obliged to spend several years at the École des Beaux-Arts, devoting himself first to drawing and only subsequently to painting. The examinations and competitions punctuating the progress of every student constituted as many occasions not only to monitor his technical skills but also to influence him in the direction of officially recognized taste. The emergence of a less interventionist approach to art training rendered the old confrontations with official art somewhat obsolete and left the field clear for fresh aesthetic experimentation. It did not, of course, wholly account for the emergence of the latter.

Problems of Style

The search for style, which reached its height about 1890, had about it something of the individualism and thirst for experience of the late nineteenth century. As Impressionism, the new trend that had dominated the previous decade, became commonplace (by the end of the century, innumerable painters were exploiting the vein), its historical protagonists, such as Cézanne, Degas, Monet, Pissarro, and Renoir, all felt the need, about 1886, to develop in the direction of a new manner. The bitter period of struggles and lack of success lay behind them. From now on, the public had other targets at which to direct its wrath. The aesthetic gap between avant-garde and tradition had grown even wider. Significantly, the presence of Seurat and Signac at the eighth Impressionist exhibition (Pissarro had gone to a lot of trouble to recruit them) provoked the withdrawal of Monet, Renoir, and Sisley. The profusion of new tendencies, their coexistence and sometimes even amalgamation with contradictory aesthetic systems explain why this period (unless all we are interested in is the part of it that spawned the art of the twentieth century) was characterized by a deep-seated ambiguity and a lack of unity that refused to fit into the molds of modern ideology. More than the abstract concept of a struggle between avant-garde and tradition, which matches only part of the historical reality, it was defined by the idea of a proliferation of forms unprecedented in its diversity. How, without falling back on some such notion, are we to characterize the hybrid styles that kept appearing around that time and formed the background against which the most brilliant innovations emerged? It was the coexistence of Cézanne and Jean-Paul Laurens that gave the years from 1880 to 1900 their true color. The paradox of the eclecticism of the final years of the century is that, by drawing together fragments of tradition, by attempting to fuse old and new, it ended up challenging the whole notion of historical continuity. In an artist like Léon Frédéric (1856–1940), the blend of stylistic references to Flemish artists and the Pre-Raphaelites was ultimately concealed by an effect of precision that belongs very much to the end of the nineteenth century. There is a mysterious coherence about this questioning of sources, and considerations whereby the innovators were those who were held to have resumed the ties with tradition (Cézanne, for example, was seen by some as a latter-day offshoot of French Classicism) count for little in comparison with this "something new" that informed the most contradictory aesthetic manifestations.

This art that so often seemed cut off from its roots showed a surprising ability to assimilate earlier periods. Already present in the eclecticism of the middle of the century, that ability here assumed mammoth proportions. This drawing on a history of art that was constantly refining itself, using examples from antiquity, the Middle Ages, the Far East, was part of the same desire for renewal. But here too the last years of the century saw an abrupt bringing together of references, often within a single work, to the point where the concept of "revival" was rendered obsolete. Thus the duality of this period, split as it was between the intransigence of ruptures and an eclecticism that sought to draw together the scattered elements of a pictorial tradition, was only on the surface, since in both cases what turned out to be essential was the thirst for experiment. Not only was painting able, as it were by turning back on itself, to absorb whole tracts of its history; its relentless forward rush led it to annex optics (Neo-Impressionism), to draw inspiration from photography (from Degas to the origins of Italian Futurism), to break with the historical inheritance of pictorial techniques, and to explore mythology. Whereas the dominant theme of the previous decade had been truth, that of the final fifteen years of the century was myth. Yet in 1884 Zola wrote: "Little by little, we saw the Salons lighten up. The mahogany Romans and Greeks and the china Nymphs disappeared year by year, while the tide of modern scenes, painted from everyday life, flooded over the walls, bathing them in the sunshine of its bright colors." It is true that the naturalism that dominated literature and the arts up until the dawn of the twentieth century completed the task of sweeping away allegory and mythology as iconographic conventions. But at the same time myths were beginning to be read in different ways, which suddenly went beyond their moral or narrative content alone, as if a mysterious unity with the contemporary era awaited discovery beneath the surface of the fable. Gustave Moreau exploring the obscurities of Greek myth in his lonely final years or Gauguin anthologizing in his *Ancien Culte mahorie* (Ancient Maori religion) beliefs that he said were destined soon to die out both betray that fascination with the stuff of legend that was to disappear with the century. As James George Frazer asserted in *The Golden Bough*, the first edition of which dates from 1890, myth could no longer be seen as the remote image of lost civilizations, even less a pretext for idyllic visions; it was an outcrop of the deep stratum of savagery that lies beneath the surface of society or, conversely, when painting presents a different myth (that of modern man), a profound faith in the progress of civilization. What might be called a "mythic structure" linked these two opposing conceptions. A denial of the objective world—such is the definition that encompasses all the painting of the last twenty years of a century that the inroads of science had thrown into doubt. To keep its head above water, as it were, art, which rested on a representation of external reality, now pursued an anxious search for style, while the continuation of traditional Western illusionism found its redemption in the world of make-believe.

The opening up of exhibition structures, coupled with a greater degree of movement among artists and their works, initially found expression in a widening of French influence. The 1889 Exposition Universelle, which drew several million visitors from all countries to Paris, included in its fine arts coverage a retrospective section that traced the development of French art since 1789. Moreover, French painting was propagated abroad through a number of important exhibitions (Antwerp in 1885, Copenhagen in 1887) in which Bonnat and Carolus-Duran were represented, as well as Raffaëlli, for example, and Monet. France held a dual attraction for foreign artists, particularly for those young painters who wanted to acquire the kind of schooling that was sometimes only precariously available in their country of origin. On the one hand, it was possible to receive high-quality training there, with very simple conditions of entry. A large number of Scandinavian artists, such as Edvard Munch (1863–1944) and Prince Eugene of Sweden (1865–1947), attended the classes that Bonnat gave in his private studio. This kind of liberal training, which each painter could adapt to his own requirements, attracted many artists to Paris who, for a variety of reasons, would not have been able to attend the city's École des Beaux-Arts. On the other hand, the reputation of Paris as a breeding ground for new trends was solidly established—so much so that France was an obligatory way station for anyone wishing to learn about the evolution of contemporary art or to make a name for himself outside his country of origin. France was not the only country that attracted artists for its art training. Germany also exerted a strong pull, particularly on artists from Scandinavia, Russia, and America. The highest reputation was enjoyed by the Düsseldorf School of Fine Arts, though in the 1880s Munich came to acquire the same importance as a result of the exhibitions of its Society of Arts. Perhaps oversimplifying slightly, then, we can say that France enjoyed overall hegemony during this period, barely counterbalanced by the special relations existing between Germany and northern Europe. The aftermath of Pre-Raphaelitism sealed Britain into an isolation that tended to increase with time. Similarly, Spain and Italy seemed to have withdrawn into their respective national cultures. Currently, for example, we know of only one tenuous link between Italian Divisionism and French Neo-Impressionism in the person of Vittore Grubicy de Dragon (1851–1920), an art critic turned painter who traveled extensively in Europe, accompanied by his brother Alberto, pursuing contacts with a number of galleries.

However, the notion of the spread of French art needs to be qualified by taking into consideration the slowness with which the latest artistic trends achieved recognition. Many foreign artists going to live in Paris rarely moved outside a group consisting of their fellow countrymen, and it was often through this cultural "filter" that they encountered modern art. For instance Fritz Thaulow (1847–1906), a Norwegian painter living in Paris, was for many Scandinavians a virtually unavoidable intermediary on the way to any understanding of Parisian intellectual circles. Finally, any intensification of French influence often took place through the image of French art that was then most widespread abroad, the image never evolving as rapidly as the actual situation in painting. The painter Willem Mesdag, who was based in The Hague from 1869 onward, put together a collection there that was later to become a museum representing the principal contemporary trends. Like other wealthy collections built up toward the end of the century, such as those of Alfred Chauchard in Paris, William Walters in Baltimore, or the British railroad magnate James Stuart Forbes, the acquisitions of Mesdag remained confined to Impressionism (from which his own artistic production was not in fact too distant). Max Liebermann, soon to be recognized as the chief protagonist of what came to be known as "German Impressionism," devoted most of his attention to the Barbizon School on his first trip to Paris.

So when we speak of French influence on foreign painting, it should be made clear that such influence was not always exerted through the medium of the latest that France had to offer. This resulted in certain stylistic pairings that are difficult to fit into the linear continuity of a history of painting that takes account only of innovations. During his stay in Paris between 1889 and 1891, Munch experimented with a Divisionist technique that was vaguely inspired by Seurat in paintings whose coloring and composition were closer to Monet or Caillebotte. Moreover, such combinations were not the prerogative of foreign painters. In the work of the Symbolist painter Alphonse Osbert (1857–1939), for example, we find the Neo-Impressionist touch being hijacked for largely decorative purposes, with no true division of color.

But at the same time as France was enjoying this expansionist phase, most other countries saw artists emerge who turned out to be deeply original. The careers of some of these artists became international in scope, even impinging on the Parisian scene. This was no new phenomenon; the newness lay rather in the frequency with which it occurred and in France's receptivity (more, it has to be said, on the part of art critics and collectors than on that of painters themselves) to a certain stylistic foreignness. One thinks in this connection of the Italian Giovanni Boldini (1842–1931) and an artist from Finland, Albert Edelfelt (1854–1905), both of whom were among the top portraitists in Paris at the turn of the century. The Musée du Luxembourg, which housed the national collections of contemporary art, and its curator Léonce Bénédite (1859–1927) had something to do with this. When Bénédite took up his job in 1889, he set about enlarging the collections of foreign painting, which at that time comprised only a few dozen works. Painters admitted to the Luxembourg in the last decade of the century included Homer, Liebermann, Sargent, Thaulow, Fritz von Uhde (1848–1911), George Frederic Watts (1817–1904), Whistler, and Zorn. At the same time, however, Impressionism was still encountering a great deal of resistance from French museums. Whereas in Germany Hugo von Tschudi (1851–1911) had no sooner become head of Berlin's Nationalgalerie (he was appointed in 1896) than he acquired a number of French Impressionist paintings, in France the Caillebotte affair sparked a debate on a national scale. Of the body of paintings by his Impressionist friends that Gustave Caillebotte had bequeathed to the state for the Musée du Luxembourg, twenty-seven works by Monet, Sisley, Pissarro, Cézanne, Renoir, and Manet were turned down. This incomplete acceptance of the Caillebotte donation, coupled with the exhibition of the rejected works in an annex to the Luxembourg from 1897, was to provoke impassioned controversy, proving that Impressionism, the principles of which had been common currency for a decade, nevertheless retained a subversive connotation when it was a matter of its founders receiving official recognition.

The Obsolescence of Categories and the Persistence of the Subject

Division into distinct genres (history painting, religious painting, portraiture, the genre scene, landscape, still life), each of which carried its own demands and usually implied a degree of specialization, had given painting in the nineteenth century a strong framework, both as regarded the organization of the art world proper and in terms of the constraints it imposed on creative artists. The boundaries guaranteeing the persistence of pictorial categories finally collapsed in the 1880s. The fact was, the primacy of history painting hardly seemed appropriate to the tastes of a society dominated by the commercial middle class. On the other hand, the slow decline of the Salon, which found itself progressively supplanted in its role as *the* annual event in the artistic calendar, was eventually to deprive that now obsolete distinction of the only outward sign that might have lent it some justification. As a consequence of this change, there was a fundamental shift in the artistic career. The previously accepted superiority of the history painter (together with its social rewards—honors, the top teaching posts, commissions) no longer obtained, and if the official commission continued to be something special, the criteria governing it became more complex. The progression from the obligatory Prix de Rome stage to Salon distinctions and jobs decorating civic and religious buildings was no longer the dominant career path.

However, the fact that history painting had lost its position as the preeminent, standard genre did not mean that it simply disappeared. For economic reasons, initially, it survived in countries where the current political climate was able to justify some glorification of history. When Jan Matejko (1830–1893) retraced the history of Poland in epic terms, his great history painting was justified by the wave of patriotism currently sweeping the nation. It was a similar story when the Norwegian Gerhard Munthe (1849–1929) drew inspiration from the *Heimskringla* (Sagas of the kings), written by Snorri Sturluson in the thirteenth century (except that here the style owed everything to Norwegian folk art and the "history" was confined to legend). In some countries, on the other hand, the by now widespread practice of outdoor painting and a renewal of interest in national color were to breathe new life into the old tradition. This was particularly the case with the Wanderers in Russia, whose major works fall into the category of history painting.

In France about the same time, the genre went into even more rapid decline. The true "success" artists of the Third Republic were people like Albert Besnard (1849–1934), Alfred Roll, Henri Gervex, and Eugène Carrière (1849–1906), who were able to define an iconography that was particularly theirs or who resolutely adopted modern subjects. Tragedy or the example of virtue appear only rarely in their works. Jean-Paul Laurens, poignant in his isolation, was the true upholder of the great tradition, even deciding deliberately not to neglect mural painting. As with Augustin Thierry, whose *Récits des temps mérovingiens* (Accounts of the Merovingian age) he illustrated, historical or archaeological accuracy was not allowed to clip the wings of poetic inspiration, and the epic atmosphere that breathes through these compositions may blind us to the fact that they are somewhat laboriously detailed. It is in this sense that the historicism of Jean-Paul Laurens looks like a desperate attempt to graft the kind of precision that was a nineteenth-century discovery onto a genre whose end he could feel approaching. A remarkable painter whose sketches and landscapes reveal a confident and inspired mastery, Laurens represents the most solid contribution to the renewal of academic art. Some of the most important and powerful murals in the the Salle des Illustres in the Capitole in Toulouse (fig. 720) and the the Panthéon in Paris (*The Death of St. Geneviève*) were painted by Laurens. As recent studies have shown, this type of official commission was not always as profitable for the artist as one might think. That is probably why, in the most opulent periods of their respective careers, artists as feted as Gérôme and Bouguereau devoted themselves exclusively to easel painting.

The few really good painters who adhered to the tradition of history painting not only assumed its outer shell but in fact attempted to breathe new life into what constituted its underlying essence. Investing the genre with fresh dramatic and expressive tension seemed, at the time, to be the *sine qua non* of its survival. It was what Gérôme had tried to do in 1867 with *The Death of the Duke of Enghien* (*Mort du duc d'Enghien*, City Art Gallery, Sheffield), in which the choice of the climactic instant of the drama marks the artist out as a successor to David and Géricault. Jean-Paul Laurens remembered the lesson. His *St. John Chrysostom* (*Saint Jean Chrysostome*, fig. 56) at the 1893 Salon may be seen as the last significant milestone in nineteenth-century history painting. The traditional accessories of historicism are here abandoned in favor of a new kind of dramatic intensity. A face that is invisible but can be imagined gives voice to the saint's mystical pain; an arm, powerfully outstretched, gestures with clenched fist. Together, they re-create with uncommon force the poetic truth of the history of Christianity's early years in a composition dominated by a feeling of emptiness that enhances the crucial confrontation between the protagonists. The reception accorded to such paintings, which coupled traditional techniques with an injection of theatricality, was not as favorable as one might have expected. Conservative critics were far from being won over by such experiments. *The Holy Women at the Tomb* (Koninklijk Museum voor Schone Kunsten, Antwerp), in which Bouguereau used a violent lighting effect in line with this trend toward bold theatrical effects, was panned by Armand Sylvestre when hung in the 1890 Salon. The evolution of history painting and religious painting was soon stifled between the indifference of the younger generation, which was more interested in formal innovation, and the disapproval of critics who were either too conservative or saved their indulgence for the dominant current of naturalism.

But the disfavor into which history painting had fallen as a category did not mean that it was dead in spirit. By limiting its iconography to visually observable phenomena, Impressionism had shown that it was possible to found (in line with the century's positivism) a pictorial style whose visual coherence was so strong that it could confine itself to the reproduction of simple subjects drawn from everyday life—landscapes or figures in landscapes, indoor scenes, portraits, still lifes. But it would be wrong to pretend that, in dispensing with pictorial narration, Impressionism had broken the thread running through painting up until the dawn of the twentieth century. On the contrary, the persistence of the subject is one of the key characteristics of the art of the last two decades of the nineteenth century, in so far as the ousting of history painting led inevitably to the appearance of forms in which the artist was able to include a philosophical, literary, or narrative element. The fact that literature preceded and permeated the art of its day had much to do with it. The close symbiosis that became established between painting and literature makes it possible, by using the many links, to put certain works back into context, works that, without their intellectual substratum, lose all meaning. These "crossovers" make it possible to draw up a network of correspondences that reveals the full depth of the nineteenth century. We are not talking about painting illustrating literary subjects but of what it tells us about contemporary thought. For example, if the prehistoric men painted by Cormon bring to mind the archaeologist Joseph Déchelette, the *Primitive Man* (*L'Homme primitif*, fig. 748) that Albert Besnard painted for the École de Pharmacie is racked by a painful yearning for the infinite, a solitary anguish that very much belongs to the age.

What might be termed the "narrative viewpoint" was then the rule. The reading that Gustave Kahn gave to Seurat's painting *Le Chahut* (fig. 694), a work that the twentieth century has overlaid with comments of a strictly formal nature, relies heavily on anecdote: "The male dancer is ugly, ordinary, he is the trite exaggeration of the female physiognomy beside him . . . and look at that marvelously hideous spectator, the archetypal fat reveler, sitting just below the dancer, as close as possible, coarsely enjoying the moment of pleasure provided for him . . . if you insist on looking for a symbol you will find one in the contrast between the beauty of the female dancer and her admirer's ugliness; you will find another in the hieratic treatment of this canvas and its subject, a contemporary disgrace." Kahn's interpretation perfectly illustrates the significance that the tiniest detail might acquire in the eye of the contemporary observer. Clearly, the importance of the subject is central to Symbolism. As for the naturalism that invested modern subjects with feeling (a "theme" art if ever there was one), this was a kind of painting that, beneath the outward appearance of creatures and objects, sought to represent their social fate. *Manda Lamétrie, Farmer's Wife* (*Manda Lamétrie, fermière*, fig. 686) by Alfred Roll (1846–1919) has the kind of documentary precision that Zola so much admired: straight frontal view of the model, total absence of picturesque qualities, accurate observation of physical type, and vigorous rendition. We are a long way from the eclogues of

Millet or the melancholy of Bastien-Lepage. This painting is meant to be seen as one of the elements of a social portrait of contemporary France.

Possibly the biggest sign of this renewed interest in the subject lay in the changes that affected religious iconography. About 1890, religious painting underwent all kinds of attempts at restoration. An elimination of the sacred (resulting from historicism) characterized the work of James Tissot, who in 1886–87 underwent a sudden crisis of mysticism and went off to Palestine in order to be able to represent scenes from the life of Christ with the most scrupulous exactitude by depicting them in the locations in which they had originally occurred. But it was the interpenetration of sacred and social that best expressed this determination by artists to find new subjects. The German Fritz von Uhde initiated a wave of scenes from the life of Christ in contemporary urban and rural settings. His painting *Come, Lord Jesus, Be Our Host* (1885) was exhibited along with two other works by him, *Suffer the Little Children to Come unto Me* (1883–84, Museum der Bildenden Künste, Leipzig) and *The Last Supper* (1886, Staatsgalerie, Stuttgart) on the occasion of the Berlin Jubilee in 1886. A work that appeared in 1892, for example, was *The Host* (*L'Hôte*, Musée des Beaux-Arts, Rouen) by Jacques-Émile Blanche (1861–1942), in which the figure of Christ seen blessing the bread in a bourgeois apartment with a vaguely Japanese-influenced decor is said to resemble Louis Anquetin (1861–1932). Another is the *Crucifixion* that Jean Béraud set on the heights of Montmartre; near the cross, a workman dressed in black raises an avenging fist toward Paris. Béraud had in fact launched the genre in France with *Mary Magdalene at the House of the Pharisee* (*La Madeleine chez le pharisien*, fig. 680), shown at the Société Nationale des Beaux-Arts in 1891. In this painting, the diatribe against contemporary wickedness through allusion to the Gospels achieves the acidity of the pamphlet as, in an after-dinner atmosphere, Christ (a portrait of the socialist poet Albert Duc-Quercy) urges clemency toward Mary Magdalene, the modern prostitute, here represented with the features of Liane de Pougy. Among the men grouped around the table we recognize Ernest Renan (whose *Vie de Jésus*, 1863, had provoked disapproval in Catholic circles), Alexandre Dumas *fils*, and the scientist Eugène Chevreul, whose studies of color phenomena formed the basis for Neo-Impressionism. As a denunciation of everything in contemporary thought purporting to deny the existence of the sacred, this polemical "showdown" between religion and the bourgeois life of the day caused an enormous stir. Béraud's updating of the story of Christ would not have the same importance if we did not have evidence of the same phenomenon in other forms—less striking, perhaps, but nevertheless bearing witness to the durability of religious iconography coupled with a need to rediscover, beyond the universally accepted formula of naturalism, a web of meaning having the profundity of the sacred. These closing years of the nineteenth century produced countless scenes in which a dramatization of everyday life rests on some allusion to a plastic theme drawn from religious iconography. The whole of Charles Cottet's work, for example, might be seen in terms of this primitive religious feeling, which the Romantic painters had already sought among the people of Brittany. *Grief Beside the Sea* (*Douleur au pays de la mer*, 1908–9, Museum of Western Art, Tokyo) is a variation on the theme of the lamentation over Christ's body, dramatized in the extreme by a background composed like a stage set and the archaism of a perspective borrowed from the Quattrocento. The work of the Belgian painter Léon Frédéric, in which social parables alternate with fantasies of the sacred, contains innumerable references to plastic configurations derived from religious art. *The People Shall One Day See the Sunrise* (*Le peuple un jour verra le lever du soleil*, 1891), a triptych inspired by the painter's anarchist beliefs, uses in its middle section the subject of the *Crossing of the Red Sea* (*Passage de la mer Rouge*, fig. 676) to illustrate the redemptive suffering of the oppressed.

THE IMPRESSIONISTS AFTER 1886

When the eighth (and last) Impressionist exhibition opened at the gallery of Durand-Ruel in May 1886, the movement had already ceased to exist as a group aiming to promote a particular pictorial style. In that same year, Monet and Renoir were represented at the fifth Exposition Internationale put on by Georges Petit, as well as with Les XX in Brussels. Moreover, the reception accorded to the eighth Impressionist exhibition by both public and critics showed that tastes had moved on. It was the Divisionist technique of Pissarro, Seurat, and Signac that aroused the greatest curiosity. Impressionism had now lost its innovative role; it had been supplanted. This was in fact more a symbol than the actual cause of an evolution on the part of the principal protagonists of Impressionism, who began to move in new directions from the mid-1880s onward. Cézanne, who had withdrawn to Aix-en-Provence, remained a "loner" whose works (apart from a single canvas hung at the 1882 Salon) could be seen only at the shop run by *père* Tanguy, a small-time Parisian art materials supplier. For Monet and Renoir, however, the 1880s marked the beginning of a degree of personal success. Increasingly, critics tended to analyze the works of the Impressionists for their intrinsic qualities, seeking to discern as it were the personal stamp of each of the protagonists of the group. The somewhat generalized attention of the early years gave way to a more discriminating approach, which corresponded to a development on the part of the artists concerned toward more personal styles. The retrospective exhibition that Durand-Ruel devoted to Monet in 1883 encouraged people to view the artist's output as an individual progression leading up to his most recent works. In 1889, Georges Petit (who organized one-man shows for Sisley and Renoir) placed Monet's work alongside the sculptures of Rodin.

For these painters, however, the 1880s were also years of stylistic exploration. Renoir told Ambroise Vollard later about a certain feeling of unease: "I had taken Impressionism to the limit and I had reached the conclusion that I could neither paint nor draw." For its chief protagonists, therefore, the historical end of Impressionism was a period of experimentation that tended to show that the original aesthetic was now exhausted. With the exception of Sisley, who cultivated the surface elements of the Impressionist style right up until the end, simply using brighter and brighter colors and an ever-broader touch, all the former Impressionists had only one thing in common in the years from 1885 to 1890: their striving (sometimes their straining) to go where none had gone before. This new situation is as much in evidence in the changes of direction made by Renoir and Pissarro as it is in the developments followed by Monet, for instance, or Cézanne. This questioning of the very foundations of Impressionism took various forms. With Degas, who admittedly was only ever marginally involved in Impressionism, it found expression in an exploration of fresh techniques, notably on two fronts. The first of these was sculpture, which he practiced more and more assiduously until, at the end of his life, it was his sole means of expression. The second was an exceptional concentration on graphic processes, exploiting their possibilities to the full in a subjective interpretation of reality. He began to work in pastel, notably in his series of forty-five women at their toilet (1880–85; fig. 65) and his allusive landscapes (1878–93).

The approach adopted by Camille Pissarro, who from 1886 to 1890 belonged to the emergent Neo-Impressionist tendency, revealed a more acute concern for what was happening at the time, allied to a greater openness to outside influences. It was Lucien Pissarro who introduced his father to the technique of dividing tones into primary colors, which Seurat had begun to develop in 1884. We know that Pissarro was immediately won over by the new technique, which he saw as radicalizing Impressionism, and that it was he who arranged for Seurat's manifesto piece, *Sunday Afternoon on the Island of La Grande Jatte* (*Un dimanche après-midi à l'île de la Grande Jatte*), to be shown at the eighth Impressionist exhibition. Pissarro's conversion to the new style was almost a warranty, given that at the time he was over fifty years old (to Seurat's twenty-six). What Pissarro saw in the art of Seurat was not only a recognition of Impressionism but also the means of giving an artistic current that was grounded in subjectivity the kind of theoretical basis it had always lacked. The scientific laws of color happened, in fact, to chime admirably with Pissarro's enthusiasm for the modern myth of progress. But more than that, the works that Pissarro painted between 1885 and 1892 show us the artist's concern that Impressionism should welcome and absorb something that might give it the permanence of a style. *Apple Pickers* (*La Cueillette des pommes*, fig. 68) can be seen not simply as a further reflection by the artist on a subject he had painted several times over the course of his career but also as an experimental synthesis of the different "manners" then characterizing all that was most modern in art. The painting further reveals (more clearly than in Seurat's work) decorative rhythms suggestive of the Classicism of Puvis de Chavannes, while Japanese influence dictated a design using simple volumes, the square format (most unusual at the time), and the diagonals structuring the composition in an ornamental fashion.

But this investigation of modern styles was peculiar to Pissarro. Renoir's change of direction between 1884 and 1887, though almost equally abrupt, was nevertheless dictated by a more individual approach. It was Renoir's desire to be a "painter of figures" that persuaded him to give primacy to drawing over color. The spontaneity of

Impressionism, as well as its traditional fondness for landscape, gave way to a gradual elaboration of composition that enabled Renoir to reexamine the problem of the nude in a landscape. For his *Large Bathers* (*Grandes Baigneuses*, fig. 757), painted in 1887, Renoir did a number of preliminary designs. Having been a Delacroix admirer in his early years, Renoir here seems to turn toward Ingres, and the way he neatly outlines his shapes places him in the context of that modern redefinition of the nude that in the 1890s was to preoccupy such artists as Félix Vallotton (1865–1925) and Charles Maurin (1856–1914).

However, Renoir's Ingresque phase was only an interlude. Similarly, Pissarro was unable to adhere to the kind of aestheticism championed by Seurat: "Having experimented with the theory for four years," he wrote to Henry van de Velde in 1896, "and having abandoned it not without difficulty and strenuous effort in order to recover what I had lost without losing what I had been able to learn . . . I cannot . . . join the ranks of the Neo-Impressionists who turn their backs on life in favor of an aesthetic that is diametrically opposed to it and that, while it might suit a person with the right temperament, is not for someone like me, who is keen to avoid any narrow, self-styled scientific theory . . ." On the other hand, the problem which Renoir's new way of painting confronted him with was the disparity it introduced between his figures, which he now treated in a linear fashion, and his still Impressionist treatment of the landscape against which they floated. It is significant that in 1901 he painted a second version of the *Large Bathers* (Musée des Beaux-Arts Jules Chéret, Nice), in which he reverted to the fluidity of Impressionism, still using the subject of the nude, which from now on never ceased to preoccupy him.

The work produced by Monet and Cézanne was the most logical extension of Impressionism, even though Cézanne's primary allegiance was to a wholly personal aesthetic that defied classification. From 1883 Monet, thanks to his recent successes, was able to travel extensively. In 1883–84 he visited the south of France and Italy with Renoir, and in 1886 he went to Holland. Gradually, Monet's life came to assume a balance between his periodic need to discover fresh landscapes (Norway, 1885; London, 1898–1901; Venice, 1908–9) and withdrawal to a place of private inspiration, namely his Giverny estate, to which he dedicated himself from 1883. The Giverny period, which extended to the end of his life, corresponded to a concentration on the problems posed by continuing and going beyond the Impressionist adventure. In 1887 Monet, like Renoir, became preoccupied with the problem of how to tackle the figure, and he produced his two *Plein-Air Figure Studies* (*Essais de figures en plein air*, Musée d'Orsay, Paris), treated "as landscapes," as he explained in a letter to Théodore Duret, written on August 13, 1887. Monet's "journey" here was precisely the opposite of Renoir's, since what he was interested in was finding an equivalent of the fleeting technique of Impressionism with which to tackle the human figure. It is true that, while there may be precedents for the composition in the art of portraiture, the perfunctory treatment of head and hands was without equivalent at the time. But the experiment was taken no further, and it was through landscape that Monet found his way beyond the Impressionist scheme of things. In 1890, using the motif of haystacks in a field, he produced a series of paintings in which he set out to transcribe the variations of light visible at different times of day. Monet's Haystacks, which were exhibited with great success at Durand-Ruel's in 1891, were the first example of the serial method by which Monet went beyond the instantaneous nature of Impressionism to reconstitute the permanence of the motif in a series of successive visions that had validity not merely as autonomous works but also by virtue of their visual interdependence. In this sense, each series should be seen not only as a collection of separate works dealing with the same subject but as a body of elements intended as a whole to present a particular intellectual coherence. Furthermore, the different exhibitions of his series—Haystacks and Poplars (1891–92; fig. 83), Cathedrals (1895), Water Lilies (from 1900), the London series (1904), the Venice series (1912)—gave Monet the opportunity to harmonize these sets that, in themselves, are among the greatest artistic innovations of the turn-of-the-century period. The Water Lilies (fig. 110), with their decorative culmination, represent an extreme development. From 1899 to 1926 Monet worked on this theme with unremitting determination, using different formats and viewpoints, adopting an increasingly flexible treatment, and culminating in a fusion with the motif that seeks to encompass the entirety of the artist's vision. The Rouen Cathedral series of 1893–94 had already seen the canvas filled to overflowing by the model, giving free rein to a subjective treatment of color, the texture of which (almost like absorbent cotton) declares a new awareness of the phenomena of the picture surface.

This kind of solitary pursuit of an artistic ideal is something Monet and Cézanne had in common. If we compare statements they made toward the end of their lives, we find both men talking about their art mainly in terms of the difficulties they had encountered in seeking to express what they really wanted. Cézanne's withdrawal to Aix-en-Provence (which was in fact punctuated by several stays in Paris) was perhaps not so much the result of a choice as the reaction to a deep-seated sense of failure. Every year up until 1888 Cézanne tried to have his works accepted by the Salon jury, yet he succeeded only once (in 1882). The year 1886 marked a turning point in the artist's life, when his father's death placed him at the head of a fortune large enough to allow him to pursue his work without material worries. But that was also the year that saw the publication of *L'Œuvre*, the novel by his friend Zola in which it was possible for Cézanne to recognize himself in the person of Zola's central character, the painter Claude Lantier, a "failed genius." There is no doubt that Zola's judgment on his career contributed to the fact that, in the last twenty years of his life, Cézanne's behavior was marked on the one hand by introspection and on the other by a search for a pictorial solution that would demonstrate in a resounding fashion the viability of his ideas. Cézanne's style had no real connection with Impressionism except between 1872 and 1876, when he was under the influence of Pissarro. Nevertheless, his method continued to owe a great deal not only to outdoor painting but also to a certain spontaneity of execution that was typically Impressionist. This is borne out by his predilection for watercolor (a medium that requires confidence and speed) as well as by his late paintings. In the different versions of *Vallier the Gardener* (*Jardinier Vallier*, fig. 758), a group of works dating from about 1905–6, toward the very end of Cézanne's life, the picture surface looks as if it has been physically assaulted: lumpy layers of overpainting betray both an urgency of execution and numerous revisions. Moreover, some of these paintings have a strip of canvas added to the bottom, which enabled the artist to introduce the red diagonal of the chair. Just as there were no preliminary studies, strictly speaking, for the monumental *Large Bathers* (*Grandes Baigneuses*), here Cézanne strove to reconcile the requirements of construction and composition with an execution that by its immediacy conveys the reaction of the artist before his motif. Cézanne was unable to abandon the direct visual contact with reality that was so much part of the Impressionist credo. The exception of *Large Bathers* (fig. 761), in which both nudes and landscape quite obviously develop outside the context of any observation of nature, may have been an accident. We know that the artist dreamed of elaborating these works by having models pose outdoors, though it was a dream he was never able to realize. Another similarity with Monet is the fact that the last twenty years of Cézanne's productive life were marked by groups of treatments of a single motif: The Card Players (about 1890–94), Montagne Sainte-Victoire (fig. 106), Large Bathers (1899–1906). In Cézanne's case, however, the phenomenon was less wide-ranging. Also, it was not so much a question of painting variations on a theme as of finding out how to achieve the full extent of what he wished to say pictorially. Furthermore, the questions touched on by Cézanne in the course of this development had to do with color only in so far as it affected form and volume—hence the somewhat limited palette and the vibrant touch used to construct both the space and the surface of the work. From the effects of transparency in *Woman with a Coffee Pot* (*La Femme à la cafetière*, fig. 96), which evoke the lightness of watercolor, to the darker tonalities of *Vallier the Gardener*, color is used to suggest structure. If this tendency explains Cézanne's interest in the figure, in his landscapes too he seems equally preoccupied by the three-dimensional requirements of form. The advice he gave in a letter of April 15, 1904 to Émile Bernard illustrates clearly, in its implied discrepancy between a theoretical basis for naturalism and its visual result, both Cézanne's rootedness in Impressionism and the ambiguity that this entailed: "Treat nature in terms of the cylinder, the sphere, and the cone, all set in perspective so that each side of an object or plane is directed at a central point. Lines parallel to the horizon provide breadth . . . Lines at right-angles to that horizon provide depth. The fact is, nature for us humans is more in depth than on the surface, whence the need to put into our vibrations of light, represented by reds and yellows, a sufficient quantity of blue tints to give the feeling of air."

In other words, Impressionism, for Cézanne, was to inject new life into tradition by abolishing the treatment of contour by means of chiaroscuro and replacing it with the treatment of volume by means of color. That is what emerges from his adherence to the classical notion of composition in the three versions of *Large Bathers,* the key work of Cézanne's final period, in which, as he had done previously in the five versions of *Card Players* (*Joueurs de cartes*), the artist explores different possibilities of organizing figures until eventually, in the Philadelphia version (which is probably the last), he arranges his nudes in two pyramid-shaped groups, echoed in the upper part of the composition by the pointed arch formed by the trunks of the trees. The landscape, which is no more than a backdrop, serves to set off this violent geometrization of the figures. The experiment was interrupted by the artist's death, but it was one that the twentieth century was to draw on freely.

NATIONAL SCHOOLS AND NATURALISM

In France, the opening up of painting to outdoor practice may seem to have been an outdated problem ten years after the irruption of Impressionism onto the art scene. As far as most other countries were concerned, however, things were rather different. Outside France, landscape painting was treated eclectically in a variety of ways, blending the new contributions of naturalism, Impressionism, and Neo-Impressionism. The Polish artist Wojcek Weiss (1875–1950), for example, recalling the changes that had occurred in the syllabus of the Warsaw School of Fine Arts after 1893, wrote in his diary: "After Matejko's death we started to turn away from history painting. From the West we were receiving an art that was bright and friendly, the art of an ordinary middle class. We began to become interested in color . . . We went outdoors. We tried to reconstitute our experiences of the moment as faithfully as possible . . . Painting a historical subject was reactionary—indicated a lack of talent. We liked the present moment."

It may be of some use, then, to examine the consequences of this rapid switch from national traditions to a more modern form of art. The dominant feature of landscape painting at the time was the way in which it had been swamped by Impressionism, though this did not apply with regard to the more innovative movements. One consequence of this widespread acceptance of the aesthetic criteria of Impressionism was that it was now admissible to produce paintings in the "sketch style" using the large formats once reserved for the Salon. What this plein-air approach took from Impressionism was its freedom of technique rather than its (intuitive yet thorough) analysis of color. It is possible, for example, to contrast the Norwegian Eilif Peterssen (1852–1928), for example, who trained in Munich, with the Swede Anders Zorn or the Dane Peter Severin Krøyer, both of whom passed through Paris. Zorn and Krøyer favored a blending touch that expressed great manual skill, while for Peterssen it was drawing that underpinned the whole composition. However, the use of light in the work of all three artists remained biased toward a chiaroscuro effect, enabling us to place their works in the naturalist camp. Moreover, the method of observation of nature introduced by Impressionism, which sought to transcribe the tiniest changes of atmosphere, was not present in naturalism, in which landscape usually played only a secondary role. The Impressionist concept, which was extended and powerfully renewed in the work of an artist like Monet, was also to be that of van Gogh. Van Gogh's approach, though it has little in common aesthetically with Impressionism, was nevertheless based on an immediate response to a vision received from the outside world. For all the force of his subjectivity, it is inseparable from the practice of outdoor painting.

The same is true of quite a number of artists who came from naturalism and who generally drew on other sources than those of French Impressionism. It is what, for want of a better term, we might call "atmospheric landscape," a constant of the final years of the century to which it is possible to link not only various Nordic painters such as Erik Werenskiold (1855–1938) or Eilif Peterssen but also the colony of artists working in the little German village of Worpswede. Worpswede offered that rare phenomenon: a profoundly naturalistic aesthetic that turned eventually in the direction of a pantheistic conception. Perhaps it is their echoes of Böcklin that give the landscapes of Fritz Overbeck (1869–1909) and Otto Modersohn (1865–1943) their distinctive character. The feeling of space conveyed by those shrill-colored skies, in which unusual atmospheric effects are observed with scrupulous precision, is truly cosmic. In Belgium, slightly later, the first Laethem-Saint-Martin group pursued the same ambition of forging a style based on nature, though referring on the way to a glorious pictorial past. It is surprising to note that Valérius de Saedeleer (1867–1941), whose intimism is reminiscent of Pieter Bruegel, followed the example of Monet in working in a mobile outdoor studio. In an unexpected reversal, plein air here saw itself as a form of primordial emotion in the face of nature that must result in the simplicity of the old masters. We have reached the exact opposite of what Impressionism sought to do. The importance of outdoor painting, in other words, was purely secondary in the new aesthetic systems of Neo-Impressionism, Synthetism, and Symbolism.

It was probably in the United States that Impressionism met with its greatest response. An agreement between Paul Durand-Ruel and Mary Cassatt on the one hand and the American Art Association on the other led to the great exhibition of April 1886, which introduced the New York public to the works of the French Impressionists. The training of American painters included a tour of Europe that often took them via Germany (William Merritt Chase [1849–1916] studied in Munich in 1872), but even more often via Paris. Childe Hassam, who had settled in Paris in 1886, won a medal at the 1889 Exposition Universelle in that city. Back in New York from 1890, he moved closer and closer to the palette of Renoir. *The Flower-Room* (1894, Arthur G. Altschul Collection, New York), with its broad brushstrokes using very vivid colors that result in an overall chromatic unity, relates to questions preoccupying Monet around the same time. It was to his meeting with Monet on the occasion of the second Impressionist exhibition that John Singer Sargent, a cosmopolitan man of the world whose portraits interpreted Whistler and Velázquez, owed the practice of outdoor landscape painting. This was one of the key elements in the artistic "baggage" that enabled American painters to break away from provincial realism. The work of Winslow Homer

(1836–1910) embodies the specificity of the New World even in its symbolism. When Homer retired to Prout's Neck on the Maine coast in 1883, he adopted a conception of landscape in which attention to atmospheric phenomena occupies a preeminent place. Above all, though, Homer was a recluse, like Albert Pinkham Ryder (1847–1917) and Thomas Eakins. In the 1890s, it was the introspective anguish of the artist that informed his landscapes, with their strongly contrasting colors and graphic clarity of touch.

If the enthronement of naturalism took place in the 1870s, the high point of its development occurred during the last two decades of the century. Furthermore, it was during this period that it spread outward from France to most other countries. The enormous influence of Bastien-Lepage, for example, dates from this period (on the basis of a few works frequently exhibited abroad, he virtually founded international naturalism). At this time, with naturalism well on the way to becoming the dominant style of all major international exhibitions, the idea that most people outside France had of Impressionism was very much vaguer than the stylistic and historical notion we have of it today. Impressionism was seen simply as a type of naturalistic outdoor painting dealing with modern life, and as such it usually encompassed Bastien-Lepage as much as Monet. International naturalism was often seen by its protagonists as a response to French Impressionism. Christian Krohg, for instance, who was seen in his lifetime as the founder of the modern Norwegian school and who was also a journalist, associated the term "Impressionism" with the idea of a free treatment of color coupled with a moral commitment on the part of the artist to a type of painting that was stamped with the mentality of the day.

The success of such conceptions may be explained by the fact that they constituted the happy medium for these end-of-the-century years, satisfying both the positive tendencies of the period and its moral and sentimental inclinations with an art in which technique usually served a narrative purpose. Quite often, for example, we see national myth or religious history transposed into the simple language of naturalism. Before giving expression to the legends of the *Kalevala*, as in his *Lemminkäinen's Mother* (*Lemminkäisen äiti*, 1897, fig. 714) in a Cloisonnist style, the Finnish painter Akseli Gallén-Kallela found in *The Mäntykoski Rapids* (*Mäntykoski*, 1891–94, fig. 101) a curious solution to the encounter between naturalism and legend. Gallén-Kallela's intention in this work was to celebrate the beautiful landscape, symbol of a Finnish identity that Russia was currently seeking to suppress. Blended into this illustration of nationalist feeling was the artist's ambition to re-create, through the mystique of nature, the impression of power conveyed by the location. Initially, he thought of enshrining this idea in the form of an allegory: a nymph playing a harp would have represented the "spirit of the rapids." Of this figure, the artist eventually retained only the four golden strings running from top to bottom of the composition, a decorative symbol applied to the surface of the work like the geometrical border suggesting a tapestry. The two registers (naturalistic and symbolic) are superimposed without mixing, enabling the artist to reconcile his metaphysical requirements with a modern form of representation. International naturalism often served to give expression to a national cultural peculiarity. The fact is, works in which today we can see only the stylistic common denominator were capable of being perceived by contemporary viewers in terms of their specific subject matter. As a style that was accessible to all, naturalism lent itself to articulating the political problems of emergent nationalism or other problems of a social nature. As the middle years of the century had seen art dominated by a certain pantheism, its final decades were marked by a climate of social contention. That probably explains why it was possible for the Bastien-Lepage formula to be echoed almost literally by so very many artists: his peasants were imbued with the same proletarian suffering as were Constantin Meunier's miners at a later date. Even when it did not carry any subversive charge, naturalism was still a profoundly social art. It was the specific study of a milieu (that of decadent sophistication) that interested the young Jacques-Émile Blanche in his *Portrait of Marcel Proust* (fig. 738). If not a clinical examination, the work at least constitutes a veritable chronicle of social mores. In other words, naturalism was more than simply a matter of outdoor painting banishing the old dark colors and the inherited tradition of museum art from drawing room walls. It was the style best suited to the nineteenth century's penchant for social inquiry.

However, each country had its artists who were rooted in local traditions and local tastes. Indeed, outside France there were as many schools claiming to be unique as there were major cities. Before the emergence of Divisionism (and even to a large extent afterward), Italy was a mosaic of distinct schools, each with a life of its own. In Venice, Ettore Tito (1859–1941), like Giacomo Favretto (1849–1887) before him, concentrated on the popular picturesque. Naples was to be marked for many years by the influence of Mariano Fortuny (1838–1874). A similarly complex provincial artistic life characterized Germany, though with an art that was more open to outside influences. The principal centers were Berlin with Walter Leistikow (1865–1908), Dresden with the enduring influence of Gotthard Kuehl (1850–1915), Karlsruhe with Hans Thoma (1839–1924) and Wilhelm Trübner (1851–1917), Leipzig with Max Klinger and Fritz von Uhde, and Munich with Franz von Stück.

Apart from a few major figures such as Joachin Sorolla y Bastida (1862–1923), Isidro Nonell (1873–1911), Joaquin Mir (1873–1940), Santiago Rusiñol (1861–1931), and Ignacio Zuloaga (1870–1945), Spanish painting in the late nineteenth century was peopled by artists who pursued Fortuny's interest in the social picturesque. Efforts to escape the alternatives of history painting and the Rococo inheritance of Fortuny took the form of fairly isolated experiments. Spain had no unifying national movement comparable to Italian Divisionism (one of the most durable aesthetic innovations of the late nineteenth century). Such provincialism gave a particular cast to the art market. Museums bought little, and it was essentially the private collector whom artists had to address. This partly explains the slowness with which taste evolved in countries where international art exhibitions were still a rarity. In 1895, the first Venice Biennale gave Italy (rather belatedly) a degree of exposure to the art of other countries. But exhibitions on a national scale remained few and far between until the creation of the Triennale di Brera in Milan, the first of which (in 1891) saw the appearance of the beginnings of Divisionism in the work of Angelo Morbelli (1853–1919), Gaetano Previati (1852–1920), and Giovanni Segantini (1858–1899). Besides, countries like Spain and Italy, where cultural awareness was still primarily local, showed little concern for social questions, which were the principal vehicle of naturalism. It is no accident that the appearance of Italian Divisionism coincided with a late adoption, in the work of Morbelli, Giuseppe Pellizza da Volpedo, and Emilio Longoni, of an anti-establishment stance. This was a key factor, further reinforced by the fact that the training of Italian and Spanish artists had far less recourse to foreign sources than that of Germans or Scandinavians. It is significant that Sorolla y Bastida, who can be classified under the heading of international naturalism, and Zuloaga, who on the contrary wanted to institute a specifically Spanish art, both studied under Bonnat in Paris. Zuloaga perfectly illustrates how, through naturalism, it was possible for reference to the former glories of national art to manifest itself. Drawing on El Greco and Velázquez in order to break with the omnipresent Fortuny, he gave his painting a kind of Art Nouveau stylization taken from French poster art. Although less eclectic, Rusiñol, who went to live in Paris in 1887, adopted certain subjects derived from Impressionism, treating them with a palette not unlike Whistler's.

In other countries, the problem of overhauling a recent tradition did not arise as acutely. In England, for instance, painting continued to be dominated by the neo-Greek Classicism of Frederic Leighton (1830–1896) and Lawrence Alma-Tadema (1836–1912) and by Pre-Raphaelitism until the end of the century. But in Scotland the "Glasgow Boys," a group that formed about 1880 around William York Macgregor (1855–1923) and James Guthrie (1859–1930), drew their inspiration from Whistler in an attempt to challenge the authority of the Edinburgh Royal Academy and the official taste of Victorian England. In his landscapes with their hazy skies painted with the softness of absorbent cotton, Robert Macaulay Stevenson (1860–1952) came close to Symbolism. In Russia, apart from the Symbolism practiced by Mikhail Vrubel (1856–1910), for example, the Wanderers continued to dominate. Ilya Repin (1844–1930), the leading artist of the school, drew on the contemporary reality of his country for his violently dramatic history painting. His work, thanks to his sense of precise observation, provides an epic vision of the Russian soul. This stability, which looked as if it was destined to confirm the recent conquests of naturalism, nevertheless saw a gradual shift in Russian painting toward a broader construction, as witness the development of Repin himself. His last major work, a monumental canvas representing *The Solemn Meeting of the Council of State on May 7, 1901* (Russian Museum, St. Petersburg), painted twelve years after the *Zaporozhye Cossacks* (fig. 67), shows how Repin abandoned his former precision in favor of a new feeling for color applied in broad flat areas. The same development can be seen in the work of Nicolas Gay (1831–1894), another artist from the Wanderers group, who devoted the last ten years of his life to a curious cycle of paintings inspired by the passion of Christ and generically entitled *Golgotha*. In tackling this theme, Gay developed a technique that was jerky in the extreme, seeking to exploit its plastic potential. His savage treatment of picture layer and color contrasts bears witness to a special concern for expressiveness, the source of which can be traced to the painfully human image of Christ in the contemporary writings of Tolstoy.

Germany, Holland, and Belgium were all countries where a vigorous national tradition went hand in hand with a thorough knowledge of artistic production beyond their borders—particularly in France. Neo-Impressionism and Symbolism were to see the establishment of very direct links between France and Belgium. In addition, the existence of ongoing political and commercial relations, coupled with geographical proximity, had created a network of more complex influences in which local traditions were blended with borrowings from the modern art of the last three decades. The example of the Hague School, for instance, was of particularly importance with regard to German painting of the 1880s. Max Liebermann, Gotthard Kuehl, Fritz von Uhde, and many other German artists of the time made numerous trips to Holland, from which they retained not so much the luminous treatment of the atmosphere as a taste for the intimism of rustic interiors. Superimposing on the requirements of the national school such knowledge as one might have of modern French art was in itself an advance on what was often an ossified tradition. Thus, the fact that many German artists were initially interested in religious painting corresponded to a founding mentality quite as strong as the one that in the first half of the century had given rise to the Nazarenes. *Jesus in the Temple* (Kunsthalle, Hamburg), which Max Liebermann exhibited in 1879, caused a scandal that marked the beginning of that artist's success. The approach adopted by Fritz von Uhde in setting scenes from the life of Christ among the Dutch countryfolk of his day reflected a similar ambition. His works, which set out to bring the social message of the Scriptures up to date, tended in fact to be quite poorly received both by a Christian public accustomed to the Nazarene aesthetic and by Social Democrat critics, who would have liked the artist to propose a religious solution to the poverty of the common people.

In this process of renewal, knowledge of modern artistic trends played a crucial role, since it largely conditioned the stylistic conjunctions that were to occur. The Munich international exhibition of 1879 sealed Germany's exposure to French art. But at the time it was only really Millet, Manet, and Bastien-Lepage who entered the vocabulary of German painting—hence the complexity of the path taken by someone like Max Liebermann. In Paris in 1873, Munkácsy steered him in the direction of a somber palette, but he was attracted by the Barbizon School. During numerous stays in Paris between 1873 and 1878, Liebermann appears to have taken no interest in Impressionism but turned instead toward what corresponded to a German view of French art, notably Courbet and Manet. After 1881, thanks to his contacts with Holland, where he met Jozef Israëls, he inclined toward a more atmospheric type of painting characterized by lighter tones and a sensitivity to outdoor effects. Two traditions seem then to have met in his painting: that of Wilhelm Leibl (1844–1900), based around a meticulous representation of the life of the people, and the more outdoor tradition of Adolf von Menzel. Liebermann thus took the opposite line from Thoma or Böcklin, for example, with their fondness for historical landscape. In the 1890s, however, he adopted a different approach to color, as the silvery delicacy of the previous decade gave way to a search for more violent harmonies. While this time Liebermann's interest in the phenomena of light appeared to stem directly from Impressionism, the molded touch was reminiscent of Courbet and the deliberately monumental treatment of the human figure evoked Manet. His conception of color, however, was still typically Germanic. In his landscapes of the 1890s and the first years of the twentieth century (*The Parrot Man*, fig. 759), Liebermann multiplied contrasts of light and shade. The patches of sunlight on the ground are rendered with broad, luminous impasto dominated by the expressive qualities of color and touch, as in the work of Max Slevogt (1868–1932). This need to dramatize the act of painting came out even more emphatically in the work of Lovis Corinth (1858–1925), whose *Self-Portrait with Skeleton* (fig. 735), a naturalistic paraphrase of Böcklin, is evidence of German painting's ongoing preoccupation with the symbolic through different aesthetic approaches.

The Hague School, through which many German painters discovered the principles of a luminism unknown in their own country, enjoyed enormous prestige. Taking the ideas of the Barbizon School further in its meticulous attention to conveying atmospheric phenomena, it retained Barbizon's nature mysticism (which continued to ensure the success of Millet and Rousseau, for example). Rebellion by the younger generation against official art was unknown in Holland, where the principal founders of the Hague School, Johannes Bosboom (1817–1891), Israëls, and the three Maris brothers (Jacob [1837–1899], Matthias [1839–1917], and Willem [1844–1910]) were venerated as masters by the young artists of the 1890s, and the emergence of what was then known as Dutch Impressionism took place smoothly and seamlessly. The powerful influence of that intimist landscape painting meant that the ties that a man like Matthias Maris formed with England remained peripheral. Similarly, the time that George Hendrik Breitner (1857–1923) spent in Paris in 1889 (when he met Bernard, Toulouse-Lautrec, and Anquetin at Cormon's studio) was of secondary importance compared to the training he received from Willem Maris or Mesdag. Actually, it was Courbet, Manet, and Millet who attracted Breitner on his visit to Paris. He followed up a Japanese-influenced Interiors series with a number of landscapes in which he adopted a geometric treatment of forms that heralded Piet Mondrian. He pursued this vision in urban landscapes in which he broke with his origins by taking his inspiration from photography and adopting a more agitated technique, which Isaäc Israëls (1865–1934) also took up. In the many views of Amsterdam construction sites that Breitner painted between 1895 and 1900, he was not in any way motivated by the idea of social art but instead used the city, its gabled houses, the muscled horses straining with effort, and the workmen in their jackets as so many motifs whose poetry he transcribed in a somber, rugged style that by now had little in common with the transparent style of Mesdag.

SYMBOLISM

In September 1886, Jean Moréas published in the newspaper *Le Figaro* his "Manifesto of Symbolism," which marked the official emergence of what had hitherto been latent tendencies in literature and art. The difficulty of defining Symbolism led to numerous contradictory views as to its precise nature. It was usually characterized by its absolute novelty and its contradictory force with regard to the various artistic currents that had preceded it in the nineteenth century. Today it is perhaps even more difficult to circumscribe that many-sided way of thinking, the ramifications of which extended far beyond the nineteenth century and that, so far as both literature and the plastic arts are concerned, itself constituted a veritable culture. Theorizing about it was the job of writers much more than of painters, whose output reflected an often confused reaction to the new sensibility. The "definition of pictorial Symbolism" given by Gabriel-Albert Aurier in 1891 was more an analysis of the art of Gauguin than something that could be applied universally. Nevertheless, it remains quite unique in its attempt to define the visual characteristics of the pictorial equivalent of literary Symbolism. According to Aurier, the work of art must be: "1) ideaist since its sole ideal will be to give expression to the Idea; 2) symbolist since it will give expression to that idea in forms; 3) synthetic since it will inscribe those forms, those signs, in accordance with a general method of comprehension; 4) subjective since in it the object will never be considered as such but as signifying an idea perceived by the subject; 5) (in consequence) decorative because decorative painting properly so-called, as conceived by the Egyptians very probably, by the Greeks, and by the Primitives, is nothing else but a manifestation of art that is at once subjective, synthetic, symbolist, and ideaist."

"Synthetic" stylization, inspired by the Cloisonnism of Émile Bernard and Gauguin, was determined by a desire to express the idea not in a discursive manner as in allegory but in a kind of art that, through the senses, gave access to knowledge of a higher order. "The symbol is a soul made visible," Rémy de Gourmont was to write. In Symbolist art, whatever its style, the meaning of the work lies beyond the reality represented. The intellectual intentions of Symbolist art mean that it is difficult to consider it outside the symbiosis that it effected with the literature and ideas of the time. The idea of creating a style was not important and was actually quite foreign to the preoccupations of the Symbolists. Rather, the movement should be seen as wishing to reach beyond artistic categories in order to construct a unity of thought that revived the intellectual coherence of its founding years. The desire to give expression to the whole human being was what characterized Symbolism, together with the Wagnerian ambition to constitute an art that would burst out of its own technical limitations to reach many aspects of perception and attain the universality of myth. In the numerous *a contrario* definitions that Symbolism was to give of itself, naturalism and Impressionism were consequently rejected wholesale as being too closely associated with the materialism of modern society. The ideas of the philosopher Hippolyte Taine underpinned this appreciation of the social character of art, which is what determined what could be called the Symbolist reaction. The first man to give a modern cast to a strategy of imagery was Joséphin Péladan. He organized the Rosicrucian salons, which had a great impact on the public and rapidly propagated the idealist and occultist tendencies he championed in his writings. However, the works that attacked head on contemporary society (despised for its bourgeois materialism) were few and far between, the most significant examples being those produced by James Ensor (1860–1949). It was in the field of painting that the reaction was to occur. The iconography of Symbolism largely chimed with a return to the literary or mythological subjects that naturalism might have seemed to have eliminated forever. However, Symbolism breathed new life into them by deliberately using them to mediate a thoroughly modern awareness.

In his *Règle du salon annuel de la Rose-Croix*, published in 1893, Péladan first drew up a list of "subjects held in contempt." These ran from "prosaic, textbook-illustration history painting" to "any representation of contemporary life, whether private or public." He went on to state: "The Order will favor mainly the Catholic ideal and mysticity. Below them, Legend, Myth, Allegory, Dream, the Paraphrasing of great poets, and finally any kind of Lyricism, preferring (as being superior in essence) work of a mural nature." But the key is not so much in this series of iconographical prohibitions as in the higher power attributed to the artist in the "Exhortation" that introduced the 1886 Rosicrucian Salon: "Artist, thou art a priest . . . Artist, thou art a king . . . Artist, thou art a magus." In other words, naturalism, which held up a mirror to the modern world, was to be demolished by an individualistic art in which imagination took pride of place. Many thinking people found the idea of progress disturbing; they were troubled by the irreversible march of science. The scientific optimism of the end of the century bred a new kind of skepticism or, conversely, a fear that the future would see the sacred disappear from the intellectual horizon. Hence Symbolism's propensity for religion, its fascination with memory as captured in myth, and its elitism, which saw itself as a reaction to the intellectual leveling of middle-class society. Without it being entirely clear whether they evoked nostalgia for a world gone for ever or the hope of a new order, the themes of Symbolism sought to bring man back to the deepest part of his nature. Reflecting a continuity in the world perceived in its mysterious unity, myth wove links with the substance that had originally inspired it: life and death, day following night, the vital instinct, existential angst. Odile Redon (1840–1916) tackled mythology only as an illustrator. *The Chariot of Apollo* (*Le Char d'Apollon*), a subject he treated toward the end of his life, producing many versions, is a triumphant vision of the artist as Apollo and of the serene, imperious joy of the creative act. An admirer of Delacroix, Redon wrote of his *Apollo Conquering the Serpent Python* (*Apollon vainqueur du serpent Python*): "This is the triumph of light over darkness. It is the joy of day as opposed to the sorrows of night and shadows, and like the joy of feeling better after distress . . . The attribute defining every god becomes superfluous, so fully does color take upon itself to say all and say it well."

Restoring general value to subjects that were no longer anything but plastic themes emptied of meaning meant giving them back something of their religious force. This search for a new kind of evocative power led to a transposition of Christian iconography. Ensor, painting *Christ's Entry into Brussels in 1889* (fig. 707), gave his own features to the figure of Jesus who, in a carnival atmosphere both joyful and threatening, is seen triumphantly entering the modern Jerusalem that will crucify him. The posters being waved by masked bystanders are packed with allusions to the Belgium of Léopold II. Inspired by Lautréamont and the French Symbolists, the Belgian Henri de Groux (1866–1930), who shared the anarchist opinions of William Degouve de Nuncques (1867–1935), used the latter as his model for *Christ Suffering Abuse* (fig. 706), an image of the independent artist being howled down by society. In both cases, an aggressive metaphor is sustained by a coarse technique in a deliberate insult directed at academicism. This desire to convey a meaning was to lead some artists toward an essentially allegorical Symbolism requiring fresh associations of ideas. Max Klinger (1857–1920) etched several cycles (including *A Glove*, 1881; *A Love*, 1887; *Of Death I* and *II*, 1889–1909) in which he defined a modern vocabulary of allegory. In the series *The Adventures of a Glove*, an amorous adventure serves as point of departure for various fetishist presentations of the object, each associated with one of the fantasies it inspires in the artist (*Desires, Rescue, Triumph, Homage, Fears, Tranquility, Abduction, Amor*). This allegorical presence is in fact typical of Germanic Symbolism, and we find numerous examples in Böcklin, as well as in Franz von Stück (1863–1928). The latter did several paintings on the subject of sin in which Eve and the serpent form a single composite being. But it also informs the hermetism of the Dutch artist Jan Toorop (1858–1928). Once the first markers of this repertoire of images were in place, the symbols could be used for a wide variety of pictorial ambitions. The figure of death, in the form of a skull or skeleton (a figure which features in the work of Félicien Rops [1833–1898], a precursor of Symbolism), is the instrument of a psychological introspection in which the artist pours out his angst. It symbolizes the futility of existence and the derisory reward for creative activity, as when Ensor paints himself as a skeleton in a studio lined with his works (fig. 109). It also symbolizes the oppressive disproportion between man and the mystery of life, which in Munch finds resolution only in a *Scream* of despair, with the screamer having the empty face of death (*Skrik*, fig. 99).

The multiplicity of symbols was matched by an immense variety of stylistic approaches. In fact the sole unifying stylistic feature among the forms that Symbolism assumed as it infiltrated different traditions and sensibilities was an absence of naturalistic preoccupations. An image was treated realistically only if it carried within itself an element of unreality that immediately identified it as something seen in dream. This was the case on one of the most interesting fringes of Symbolism, where a certain precision of style appeared to assert the truth of myth in the face of a modern world that seemed well on the way toward destroying it. The Pole Jacek Malczewski (1854–1929), who depicted the national legend of Elloe, and the Italian Giulio-Aristide Sartorio (1860–1932), with his *Gorgon and the Heroes* (1897), both went in for this kind of fantastic realism (figs. 104, 105). But even here the subjectivity of the period claimed its due, with Malczewski cultivating a certain stridency of color and using dynamic lines, while Sartorio, in his search for monumentality, employed a background of broad bands of somber tones to offset his heroic nudes. The only stylistic lesson of Symbolism was in terms of an individual interpretation of the objective world, which, faithfully expressing the artist's state of mind, could be far from reality. It was this concentration on the mysterious that enabled the isolated approach of a self-taught painter like William Degouve de Nuncques, in whom Edmond Picard found "deep sincerity and a kind of elective primitivism," to gain acceptance.

In the wake of Baudelaire, the Symbolists saw color in the abstract, as it were, in terms of its inherent harmonic force and power of suggestion. While the latest aesthetic innovations tended to banish it, shadow came back into art in the graphic work of Redon and the monochromes of Carrière. Black was not in this instance a dim echo of the bitumens of the Romantic palette but conveyed the secret fascination of darkness. Line, too, aimed at a suggestive quality and laid claim to total freedom, initially in the Cloisonnism of Bernard and Gauguin and subsequently in the linear variations that relate Symbolism to Art Nouveau, as in the work of Aubrey Beardsley (1872–1898) or Toorop. When he used the word "caricature" in connection with *Madeleine in the Forest of Love* (fig. 657), Émile Bernard emphasized the expressiveness that lay behind both Syncretism and the aesthetics of Seurat. Command of this vocabulary was believed to give access to the viewer's unconscious, but the converse approach also existed and in certain instances painters were able to harness the power of the unconscious mind. The late works of Gustave Moreau, even when they were preceded by several small-format studies, were an attempt to find form through color, the contrasts and occasionally even the accidents of which may generate the composition. It is only after this initial phase that the drawing is overlaid like a grid on the color harmony from which the figuration has sprung. Eventually, the insistence on the need for symbols in art led artists in the direction of stylistic conceptions known at the time as "decorative" (in contrast to naturalism), whether these were close to the linear tendencies of Art Nouveau or on the contrary proceeded from a reformulation of the styles of the past. The many historicist aspects of Symbolism (for example, the references to Italian pre-Renaissance art found in the Pre-Raphaelites) were in fact so many invocations of a golden age of the human mind. In the eclogues of Émile-René Ménard, the poetic translation of pagan antiquity is coupled with a pictorial reference to the landscape with figures of French Classicism, the rhythms of which lend a monumental grandeur to the poet's nostalgic visions.

Precursors since 1890

Although Moréas's manifesto may be taken as its birth certificate, the emergence of pictorial Symbolism cannot be linked to any specific event. The Symbolist wave that broke over Europe about 1890 was the work of artists born for the most part between 1860 and 1870, and it came at a time when the initiators of the movement were already at the height of their fame. Puvis de Chavannes, Gustave Moreau, Burne-Jones, and Böcklin enjoyed the privilege of being officially recognized artists while remaining "beacons" for the younger generation up until the threshold of the twentieth century.

In Tuscany, where from 1893 until his death he lived in seclusion in the village of San Domenico di Fiesole, the Swiss painter Böcklin played the role, among local artists, of a grand old man of Symbolism. The young Giorgio de Chirico (1888–1978) took as his starting point this Böcklin tradition as enshrined in the master's final works, in which the precision of pre-Renaissance Italian art and the fervor of his large wooden panels are at variance with the parodical verve and brusque naturalism with which he tackled religious or mythological themes (fig. 722). His *St. Anthony*, for example, a work inspired by a poem from *Des Knaben Wunderhorn* (The boy's magic horn), the collection of German folk tales made by Achim von Arnim and Clemens Brentano, combines a luminous panel in which the humorous cataloging of fishes is reminiscent of Frans Snyders, with a grim predella presenting a disillusioned image of everlasting cruelty.

In France, Odilon Redon, whose etchings had been exciting comment from Huysmans for some time, took up painting only in 1890, while remaining faithful to the same visionary approach. His brilliant color, applied in large flat areas without regard to the model, links him to the Nabis. A small number of private commissions, such as the one from Fontfroide Abbey in 1910–11, gave him the opportunity to stress the decorative nature of an art that found a new kind of serenity in color. Puvis de Chavannes, thanks to his monumental commissions, came to be universally acknowledged as the man who restored the tradition of mural decoration. The image of a nineteenth-century Domenico Ghirlandaio, often invoked to emphasize the Quattrocento aspect of Puvis's work, spread from that time on, while his style evolved smoothly in the direction of linear simplification and an approach to color that went even further toward integrating painting with the flat surface of the wall as support. The extension of the same principles to easel painting in fact did much to propagate the flat, decorative approach, to which the eye had become accustomed through monumental art. The major commissions of his final years—notably for the Boston Public Library (1895–96) and the final phase of the Panthéon in Paris, which was still unfinished at his death (1893–98)—show Puvis looking for modern echoes in history painting, as in *St. Geneviève Watching over the Sleeping Paris* (*Sainte Geneviève veillant sur Paris endormi*, fig. 723), or allegory, as in *Physics* (*La Physique*, fig. 721), which critic Gustave Geffroy called "a magnificent, absolute image of the *scientific* poetry of our time." Compared with Puvis de Chavannes, who enjoyed universal fame, Gustave Moreau, who stopped exhibiting at the Salon in 1880, was something of an isolated figure. Moreau's art, rediscovered in the early 1880s by idealist writers such as Huysmans and Jean Lorrain, nevertheless demonstrates the same ability to go beyond reality while simultaneously revealing the kind of solitary intellectual activity that rather appealed to the individualistic elitism of the period. But in addition to paying homage to pre-Renaissance Italian art, Moreau put into his work his admiration for Indian art and his fascination for a barbaric antiquity. This Hellenism, which in Moreau's work was like an echo of the violence of Romanticism, gave rise to an extra decorative dimension. Mosaics, precious stones, enamels, concretions—the entire arsenal of the Decadent vocabulary was mobilized by the Symbolists to convey their desire for a kind of painting that, without regard to visual homogeneity, alternated between the minute detail of illumination and gestural vigor in an overarching syncretism. Moreau continued this search for pictorial freedom in his teaching at the École des Beaux-Arts, where he taught from 1892 until his death. He was greatly admired by his students. Matisse and the Fauves testified to his lack of aesthetic interventionism, which undoubtedly contributed to the emergence of a treatment of color free from any reference to objective reality.

Burne-Jones and Watts were to Victorian England what Puvis de Chavannes and Moreau were to the France of the Third Republic. As a result of its prestige, Pre-Raphaelitism, which was quickly recognized as a national movement, continued to exert a strong influence on artists of the younger generation, such as George Byam Shaw (1872–1919) and John William Waterhouse (1848–1917). Waterhouse's *Lady of Shalott* (1894, City Art Gallery, Leeds) is in fact a reworking of a theme treated in 1886–87 by William Holman Hunt in a still celebrated painting. Burne-Jones was the prestige of late Pre-Raphaelitism incarnate, leading the German critic Richard Muther to record that at London's Grosvenor Gallery he was the object of a cult as fervent as that of Richard Wagner in Bayreuth. Like Watts, toward the end of his life Burne-Jones conceived large-scale works organized in cycles. His *Perseus Cycle*, begun about 1875, was never completed. The *Troy Triptych* (1870, City Museum and Art Gallery, Birmingham), a huge columned reredos, never got beyond the design stage, and Burne-Jones reused parts of it much later to make separate paintings, such as *The Wheel of Fortune* (fig. 55). Actually it was in the fields of stained glass and mosaic (San Paolo, Rome, from 1881) that the artist was able to satisfy his desire for monumentality. At the same time his aestheticism pushed him in the direction of a drier style and a mannerism that clearly drew on the Italian art of the Quattrocento and Cinquecento, as in *The Garden of Pan* (1886–87, National Gallery of Victoria, Melbourne), a modern transcription of Piero di Cosimo. While Burne-Jones evokes Sandro Botticelli, Watts borrowed his palette from the Venetians of the Renaissance as well as from Joseph Mallord William Turner. A highly independent artist, Watts differed from Burne-Jones in his more modern approach to color. His late paintings, many of which he reworked ten or more years later, occasionally give the impression of a colored magma from which the composition emerges.

The Symbolist Generation

It may seem illusory to attempt any kind of historical synthesis concerning the appearance and development of Symbolism, given that it permeated the art of its day in so diffuse a manner. The creation of the group Les XX in Brussels in 1884, whose founder members included Ensor and Fernand Khnopff (1858–1921), can be seen as a milestone. But the substantial Symbolist presence in Les XX was merely a result of the group's principle of being open to all new artistic tendencies. The same was to apply to the Libre Esthétique group (also led by Octave Maus) that succeeded Les XX after their dissolution in 1893. The Sezession organizations that emerged in Munich, Berlin, and Vienna were not exclusively oriented toward Symbolism, even if their prime movers can today be classified under that heading. The first manifestation of this kind was the Rosicrucian Salon, founded in Paris in 1892 by the self-styled Sâr Péladan. This event invoked a deliberately Symbolist aesthetic and had very precise selection criteria. Péladan, assisted by the painter Antoine de Rochefoucauld (1862–?), himself selected the artists and the works represented. The resounding success of the first Rosicrucian Salon, which was held at Durand-Ruel's, alerted both public and critics, who were bowled over by these new images, to the existence of a powerful current of idealism in contemporary art. Bernard, Ferdinand Hodler, Khnopff, Previati, Toorop, and Vallotton were among those exhibiting.

But while the initiators of Symbolism received recognition, the second generation of artists saw the gap separating them from the public widen. In 1894 the German writer Max Nordau saw Symbolism as the ultimate expression of degeneracy. According to him, two key traits made it possible to state that the tendency revealed abnormal mental states: on the one hand a mysticism that flew in the face of contemporary scientific progress, and on the other the structure of the works themselves, which depended on the association of ideas and gave no indication of having been thought through along the lines of reason. Critics applied themselves to refuting such assertions, coming up with many different theoretical justifications for the new tendencies. Never before had there been so urgent a need for the written word. Add to that the fact that Symbolism grew in the compost of a constant interaction between painting and literature, and you can see why literary and artistic magazines assumed such importance at the time. Consequently, the major dates of any chronology of Symbolism are also those of the reviews of the period, when they were founded and when they carried the most striking texts. In Paris alone more than a hundred literary magazines, all opening their columns to art criticism, saw the light of day between 1880 and 1900. *La Revue indépendante*, started by Félix Fénéon, *La Plume*, *Mercure de France* with contributions by Gabriel-Albert Aurier and Camille Mauclair, and *La Revue blanche*, together with innumerable often short-lived publications, made it their business to reflect this creative disorder. The larger ones also covered foreign literature and art. Belgium, too, experienced the same intellectual ferment in the 1880s, with Albert Mockel's *La Wallonie*, Octave Maus's *L'Art moderne*, and such Flemish-language Symbolist reviews as *Van Nu en Straks*. In Germany, the poet Stefan George published Baudelaire translations in his *Blätter für die Kunst*. Another German publication, *Pan*, founded by Julius Meier-Graefe in 1895, also appeared in French. *The Yellow Book*, which was published in London between 1894 and 1897, made the drawings of Aubrey Beardsley widely known. And there were also many publications in Russia (notably Diaghilev's *Mir Iskusstva* from 1898) and central Europe that, mostly after 1900, propagated the Symbolist aesthetic.

This burgeoning of ideas accurately reflected the young Symbolist generation and its many different aesthetic combinations. The typical cursive stylization of Art Nouveau, for instance, which reached its greatest degree of abstraction in Jan Toorop, assumed a mannerist flavor in the work of the Belgian Émile Fabry (1865–1966). In the work of the Czech Jan Preisler (1872–1918) and the Hungarian Jószef Rippl-Rónai (1861–1927) it was overlaid on flat areas of color reminiscent of Gauguin and the Nabis. After 1890, the Symbolists broadened the expressive scope of painting. Fernand Khnopff, for example, having originally subscribed to an intimist naturalism and been an admirer of Gustave Moreau, found an original way of portraying his private world and his memories, making an emblematic use of objects and illustrating his own secret obsessions. Work after work featured the same views of a deserted Bruges and the head of Hermes conjuring up the world of dream, intertwined with portraits of the artist's sister, all painted with a Pre-Raphaelite delicacy. For all the coarse caricature of Ensor's work and the crude language of his color, he shared Khnopff's fascination for interiors, a recurring theme in Belgian Symbolism from Xavier Mellery (1845–1921) to Léon Spilliaert (1881–1946). Such painting generally dispenses with the texts once thought necessary. *I Lock my Door upon Myself* (fig. 716) is a poetic image of the artist's microcosm and of his deliberate reclusion in memory. Khnopff is undoubtedly the painter who best embodies international Symbolism, not only through his themes but also by virtue of a style in which Belgian, British, and French elements meet and intersect. His prestigious career did much to propagate Symbolism throughout Europe, particularly in Austria. Only Eugène Carrière, toward the end of the century, enjoyed comparable influence. Perhaps it is the way Carrière brought together an allusive style (in which Jean Dolent saw "realities having the magic of dream") with the development of Art Nouveau that accounts for the almost universal enthusiasm with which his work was received. Carrière translated into the intimist language of his day his admiration for the work of Rembrandt and Turner. Though an influential figure in the art world, Carrière did not actually have any followers in the strict sense—unlike Puvis de Chavannes, for example, whose work served as a model for Alexandre Séon (1855–1917), Alphonse Osbert, Émile-René Ménard, and Ary Renan (1858–1900). The latter was a strange artist who took the composition of the typical Puvis landscape and introduced into it a frenzied quality typical of the century's final years. In the work of Maurice Denis (1870–1943) and Paul Sérusier, who were part of the same circle as Gauguin and Redon, the Cloisonnist aesthetic was blended with a fervent Catholicism or, in the case of Paul Ranson (1861–1909), with an esoteric syncretism not unlike that of Édouard Schuré. Félix Vallotton, Aristide Maillol (1861–1944), and the Dane Jens Ferdinand Willumsen (1863–1958; the man who introduced Art Nouveau to Denmark) can be linked to the same group, but it is impossible to categorize the Symbolist generation of 1890 as a whole. It is above all a juxtaposition of individual personalities, a compilation of influences. Péladan's Rosicrucian group was typical of this stylistic diversity. In his *Portrait of Séverine* (*Portrait de Séverine*, fig. 100) Louis-Welden Hawkins (1849–1910), who exhibited with the Rosicrucians in 1894 and 1895, gave a provocative image of the celebrated journalist and apostle of social solidarity, a blend of Pre-Raphaelitism and Ingres-like sophistication with odd hints of naturalism. Jean Lorrain was alive to the eclectism of this work: "The mop of rust-colored hair lends a very Parisian halo to the ecstatic martyr's face: Hawkins stressed its mystical nature by placing the woman against a gold background like some Byzantine Virgin and turning his Madame Séverine into a sort of blessed one—as one might say, a Sainte Gavroche [the *gamin* in Hugo's novel *Les Misérables*]."

In Germany, the work of Franz von Stück, for example, shows the same kind of cross-pollination, blending a deeply Germanic stamp inherited from Böcklin and Hans von Marées with allusions to Khnopff. Similarly, Ludwig von Hoffmann (1861–1945) created a monumental art combining the balance of Puvis de Chavannes with the sensuality of Albert Besnard. In fact it was Austria that produced, late on, the Germanic world's most original contribution to Art Nouveau in the person of Gustav Klimt (1862–1918), the central figure of the Viennese Sezession. Around the turn of the century Klimt, whose early work had been influenced by Makart, evolved a style of his own that juxtaposed a treatment of the human body clearly derived from Khnopff with purely decorative passages that tended toward geometric abstraction. Primarily a decorator (Beethoven frieze for the Sezession building, 1902; decorative scheme for the Vienna University, 1903–7), Klimt effected a literal transposition of decoration to painting that imitated successively fabric, mosaic, and the sparkling of precious stones. The concept of *Malmosaïk* (painting in mosaic form), in which the surface of the painting was divided up into large areas treated alternately in an ornamental or illusionist manner, illustrated Symbolism's slow development in the direction of a problematics of form. It has not been sufficiently stressed the extent to which Symbolism lay behind the stylistic upheavals of the turn of the century. In the work of Frantisek Kupka (1871–1957), for example, who after training in Prague left for Vienna in 1891, the liberation of color and geometrization of form that eventually led to abstraction are inseparable from an originally Symbolist purpose.

The way in which the stylistic components of Art Nouveau led to new plastic solutions is in fact the key contribution of twentieth-century Symbolism. The landscapes of Munch and Hodler produced about 1900 bear witness to this attempt to drop the specific iconography of Symbolism while retaining the structural unity and pursuit of expression that stemmed from it. The break that Ferdinand Hodler (1853–1918) made with the naturalistic realism of his early works coincided with his meeting with the Symbolist poet Louis Duchosal, leading light of the *Revue de Genève*, which championed Wagner and Verlaine. In contrast to the medievalism of his compatriots Cuno

Amiet (1868–1961) and Albert Welti (1862–1912), Hodler adopted a monumental art reminiscent of Puvis de Chavannes. The pantheistic subject matter had already existed in embryo in his early works, but from now on the artist tackled it with a rhythmic order that he dubbed "parallelism." In *The Night* (*Die Nacht*, fig. 712), which Hodler saw as a "great symbol of death," the pyramidal composition is dominated by the enigmatic, black-draped figure seen harrying the prey it has caught sleeping. Edvard Munch adopted a similar horizontal format when he painted *The Dance of Life* (fig. 98), in which under a very high horizon he creates the feeling of an unreal space in which groups of figures are juxtaposed symmetrically. The arrangement of the figures as well as the symbolic way it is used are similar. In *The Frieze of Life*, the vast pictorial cycle in which, from 1893, Munch included his successive works, *The Dance of Life* occupies a key place. It represents a kind of monumental pause, summing up the themes that the artist had set out up until then. In his need for meaningful forms, the Munch of *The Dance of Life* declared his kinship with Synthetism, which he had discovered in Paris back in 1889. A broad band outlines his figures, which stand out against a background of uniform green. As he left naturalism behind him, Munch experimented with the latest tendencies in French art (both Impressionism and Neo-Impressionism). He then spent some time in Berlin (1892–93). Using subject matter that sprang from Germanic Symbolism, he developed a style inspired by Gauguin and Art Nouveau. All Munch's borrowings, however, were given a personal slant by the expressive urgency that filled everything he did. Like Ensor and Khnopff, he sought universal terms in which to convey his individual experience and the privacy of his own psychology. *The Scream* is the outcome of a moment of inexplicable emotional fusion with nature. One of the artist's notebooks explains: "I was walking along the road with two friends—the sun was setting—I experienced a kind of gust of melancholy. The sky suddenly went blood-red. I stopped, leaned on the fence, dead-tired—I saw the clouds blazing like blood and a sword—the sea and the town blue-black—My friends walked on. I stood there, shivering with fear—and I felt as it were one vast, endless scream shooting through nature." Using his initial drawing illustrating the vision in the margin of the text, Munch produced four versions of *The Scream*, one left unfinished, in which he combined pastel, pencil, and tempera. Each of them features the same sinuous figure in the foreground, echoing the tortured symbol of the landscape. This attitude distinguishes Munch from the majority of Scandinavian artists, such as Harald Sohlberg (1869–1935) and Gallén-Kallela, for whom the myth of the homeland always held pride of place. Similarly, in Poland, with its older pictorial tradition, it is possible to contrast Malczewski, who largely assumed the mantle of nationalist Romanticism, with Jozef Pankiewicz (1866–1940), for example, who was influenced by Carrière and Impressionism.

In Italy, the Symbolist current arrived late and became a paradoxical blend of decadent pessimism and the forces seeking to abolish it. The barbarian mythology of Giulio-Aristide Sartorio proclaimed the need for a return to order, glimpsed also in the exasperated Latinity of the writer Gabriele d'Annunzio. The same reaction manifested itself between 1908 and 1910 in Previati's work. The Divisionism of Giuseppe Pellizza da Volpedo (1868–1907), Segantini, Previati, Vittore Grubicy de Dragon, and Plinio Nomellini (1866–1943), which was Symbolism's most original formulation in Italy, involved adherence to a resolutely modern pictorial technique (the division of tone into primary colors) that the French Neo-Impressionists had practiced before them. Here, though, such use of color was applied to a rustic Christianity reminiscent of Millet, to the poem-landscapes painted by Grubicy, and to texts that retained a residue of pagan feeling. Segantini's *Unnatural Mothers* (*Le Cattive Madri*, fig. 95) was inspired by the Indian poem "Pangiavahli," made famous by Arthur Schopenhauer. Division of color was used for decorative ends. Morbelli's fabric, more woven than painted, Segantini's golden fibrillae, and the meandering trails of Previati put color contrasts to emotional use, in contrast to the airy clarity of Seurat. Note, moreover, that the equivalent attitudes found in other countries all fell within the orbit of Symbolism, as with the Czech Viteslaw Karel Masek (1865–1927), for example. Of the new technique, the Italian Divisionists retained only its power to embrace all the different kinds of visual phenomena, without abdicating their subjectivity as painters. Futurism, a late offshoot of this tradition and one of the most important movements of the early twentieth century, was to take over its inordinate desire to achieve a pictorial transcription of time.

NEW AESTHETICS

The search for style that was apparent throughout the period undoubtedly had an effect on technique. Never before had the emergence of a new organization of the picture surface involved such a pushing back of the frontiers of technique, such a desire to present the viewer with an object that was new even down to its actual physical consistency. The period delighted in visual equivalents. Puvis de Chavannes, who in his lifetime was hailed for having revived the art of mural painting, painted canvases to look like frescoes, which were afterward remounted. The chalky, matte quality of fresco painting itself became a stylistic feature linking painting to a mythical tradition, that of monumental decoration, for which the favorite reference at the time was the Italian Quattrocento. It even spread to easel painting, in the work of the many artists who took their aesthetic cue from Puvis, notably Gauguin. This new interest in the phenomena of the picture surface, however, rapidly took the form of a diversification that contributed to a redefinition of the classic techniques of painting and drawing, the boundaries of which were done away with. The result was an endless succession of different media, including charcoal on prepared or unprepared canvas, spirit-based paint on card (Toulouse-Lautrec), tempera on velvet (Pierre Bonnard), and oil paint with traces of pastel. Among certain pupils of Gustave Moreau, such as Georges Rouault (1871–1958) and above all Georges Desvallières (1861–1950), the traditional techniques of drawing (pencil, charcoal, pastel, gouache, watercolor) were occasionally used in works whose monumental dimensions had formerly been the province of oils. Of course, this was a way of practicing a kind of painting that was "different"; technical ideas are not in themselves capable of defining style. Up until the beginning of the twentieth century, fresco had offered a focal point: the swiftness of decision that it demanded seemed likely to generate a style that would be the most spontaneous expression of the artistic gift, while calling for simplification in a way that matched the synthetic tendencies of the period. Furthermore, given the exhaustion of stylistic combinations, studies of fresco painting presented themselves as a return to an original state of painting, which it then seemed reasonable to bring back to what was regarded as its dual initial function: decorative and monumental. The experiments of René Piot (1866–1934), which were an extension of those of Victor Mottez (1809–1897), were equally without sequel, except for a few finished works such as his *Burial Chamber* (*Chambre funéraire*) of 1908 or the decoration of André Gide's villa in 1910.

The art of printing, particularly wood engraving (previously used mainly as a means of reproduction), enjoyed a real revival from 1885. Numerous small magazines published plates by artists such as Auguste Lepère (1849–1918), Georges d'Espagnat (1870–1950), and Vallotton. In 1894, Rémy de Gourmont and Alfred Jarry founded *L'Ymagier*, which set out to renew the visual repertoire and which published not only works by Gourmont, Jarry, and Émile Bernard but also wood engravings from the Renaissance and *images d'Épinal* (an early form of strip cartoon). In the German-speaking world, *Pan* and *Ver Sacrum* (the mouthpiece of the Viennese Sezession) promoted wood engraving in a similar fashion. Woodcut (exploiting the texture of wood sawn with the grain), which went hand in hand with a certain aesthetic ruggedness, produced works (notably by Gauguin) that immediately opened up new perspectives. In the crudeness of their style and execution, the plates that Gauguin cut in 1893–94 to illustrate *Noa Noa* took the possibilities offered by this technique to an extreme. Only Munch, who invented a technique in which pieces of wood were cut out like a puzzle, with as many pieces as there were colors, showed comparable originality.

Neo-Impressionism

In a famous letter of August 28, 1890, written at the request of Maurice Beaubourg, Georges Seurat (1859–1891) summarized his artistic principles in the following terms:

> AESTHETICS:
>
> Art is harmony.
> Harmony is the analogy of opposites, the analogy of similars, of *tone*, of *hue*, of *line*, considered by the dominant and under the influence of light in combinations that are gay, calm, or sad.
> The opposites are:
>
> For tone, one that is { more luminous { lighter { for one that is darker.

For hue, the complementaries, i.e. a certain red contrasted with its complementary, etc.

Red — Green
Orange — Blue
Yellow — Purple

For line, those running at right-angles.

Gaiety of tone is the luminous dominant; of *hue*, the warm dominant; of *line*, lines above the horizontal.

Calmness of tone is equality of dark and light; of hue, warm and cold, and the horizontal for line.

Sadness of tone is the dark dominant; of hue, the cold dominant, and of line downward directions.

TECHNIQUE:

Accepting the phenomena of the length of the impression of light on the retina.

Synthesis is essential as the outcome. The means of expression is the optical Mixture of tones, hues (localities and illuminating color: sun, kerosene lamp, gas lamp, etc.), i.e. of lights and their reactions (shadows), obeying the laws of *contrast*, of shading-off, of irradiation. The context is in the opposite harmony to that of the tones, hues, and lines in the picture.

This classical statement of belief constituted the most apposite response there could be to an Impressionism that was running out of steam. Seurat preached a return to construction, to a slow and careful development of the work of art on the basis of abstract aesthetic rules. From Impressionism he retained only the general principle of attention to the phenomena of light. This was not simply a matter of restoring to painting a structure that the nineteenth century had gradually eroded but of establishing a new order that would harmonize closely with modern times. As Seurat said in a letter to Signac on August 26, 1888: "The only reason for my painting in this way was to find something new, a painting of my own." Seurat's personality and the fact that he deliberately set out to found a school were quite unique in nineteenth-century art. Only Cézanne, with his desire to use purely pictorial means to go beyond the experience of the art of his day, is comparable. But Seurat was a leader surrounded by ardent disciples. Paul Signac (1863–1935), Camille Pissarro and his son Lucien (1863–1944), Maximilien Luce (1858–1941), Henri-Edmond Cross (1856–1910), Albert Dubois-Pillet, and Charles Angrand (1854–1926) all adopted the Neo-Impressionist aesthetic launched by Seurat. His *Sunday Afternoon on the Island of La Grande Jatte*, shown at the last Impressionist exhibition in 1886, served as the manifesto of the new school. Seurat adopted certain elements of the Impressionist tradition (he made outdoor color studies and he retained the light tonality of the Impressionist palette), but his training took place well away from the protagonists of modern art, following a highly personal course from the outset. He studied first under Henri Lehmann, who taught him the Ingresque discipline of line, and up until 1883 he practiced drawing almost exclusively. His conté crayon sheets from 1882–83 are subtle studies of values revealing quite exceptional maturity. Around the same time, Seurat took up color by reading scientific books on optical phenomena. His starting point was Charles Blanc's *Grammaire des arts du dessin*, which echoed the findings of *La Loi du contraste simultané des couleurs* by the physicist Eugène Chevreul, published in 1829. As early as 1867 Blanc, in a body of writing mainly devoted to painting, formulated a number of principles that subsequently formed the theoretical bases of Neo-Impressionism: the distinction between hue and tone (or color and value), the idea of the "optical mixing" effected by the retina, and the colored "vibrations" obtained by juxtaposing different tones of the same hue. Seurat's approach coincided with a renewal of interest in color theories, which had undergone some development in the early part of the nineteenth century. Seurat was thus able to draw on a number of recent works looking at physiological optics, including an article on "The Phenomena of Vision" by David Sutter, which appeared in the magazine *L'Art* in 1880, and N. O. Rood's book *Modern Chromatics*, a French edition of which appeared in 1881. These publications, plus the teachings of the mathematician Charles Henry (1859–1926), formed the "Bible" of the Neo-Impressionists. *Une baignade, Asnières* (fig. 692), hung at the Salon des Indépendants in 1884, was Seurat's first major attempt to apply the principles of Chevreul, which he had first studied in 1878. This was still a work painted "in broad, flat strokes brushed one on top of the other and proceeding from a palette that, like Delacroix's, was made up of pure colors and muddy colors." The words were written by Signac, who so admired the work that he sought the acquaintance of its author. These two men formed the core of a group of artists: they were joined by Camille Pissarro in the following year and subsequently by the *Revue Indépendante* circle round Félix Fénéon and Gustave Kahn. In 1885–86, these artists adopted—a little hesitantly, sometimes—the technique of breaking down tones into primary colors. When the eighth Impressionist exhibition and the Salon des Indépendants in 1886 presented a group of works by Seurat, Signac, and Pissarro in which color separation was applied, the new movement found both detractors and champions among the critics. From that point on, Gustave Kahn, Émile Verhaeren, Paul Adam, and Félix Fénéon poured out an endless stream of articles developing the aesthetic conceptions implicit in these paintings, which were made up of tiny dots of pure colors. Fénéon, who left the most complete body of writing on the subject, immediately placed Neo-Impressionism in a historical perspective as being the most significant successor of Impressionism, because it was rooted in scientific determinism. His analysis dissected Neo-Impressionist technique with extreme subtlety, bringing out the abstract modernity of the new style.

Indeed, in Neo-Impressionism the conflict between representation and abstraction was glaring. Already present in the Puvis-like quality of *Une baignade, Asnières*, the tendency to treat figures as colored silhouettes reached its height in *Sunday Afternoon on the Island of La Grande Jatte* (fig. 61), in which, as Paul Adam put it, "the stiffness of the characters and the incisive shapes help to generate the sound of modernity." The *Posers* (fig. 64) of 1887 are in fact evidence of a wish to demonstrate how well Neo-Impressionist technique could tackle contours, using a reference to the *Three Graces*. However, in *The Circus Parade* (*La Parade de cirque*, 1887–88, Metropolitan Museum of Art, New York) and *Le Chahut* (1889–90, fig. 694), with its play of directional lines against a decorative background, Seurat's art returned to its characteristic fundamental abstraction. Signac, in his *Portrait of Félix Fénéon* (*Portrait de Félix Fénéon*, fig. 82), achieved with extraordinary lucidity a reconciliation between the requirements of representation and the Neo-Impressionist tendency to make of color arranged in geometric rhythms an end in itself. This is what he wrote about it to Fénéon in 1890: "It would be no ordinary portrait but a highly composed picture, very much arranged in lines and hues. An angular, rhythmical pose. A decorative Félix entering hat or flower in hand . . . on a tall, very narrow canvas. A deliberate background of two complementary hues, and a coat in harmony." This working out of the painting according to a preordained plan, in which external reality figures only as a pretext, implies that the traditional antagonism between scientific inquiry and artistic spontaneity had been overcome. This kind of detachment with regard to physical execution, this mechanical "fabrication" that eliminated manual accidents, were to be exalted for their implacable logic.

All this brought painting back to the purity of ideas, rejecting the facile attractions of Impressionist touch, which saw itself as bearing direct witness to the spectacle of nature. Neo-Impressionism, by contrast, wrecked the transitory in order to achieve timelessness. The landscapes of Cross are abstract constructions (*The Îles d'Or*, fig. 84) or visions of Eden (*Nocturne*, fig. 696). The truthfulness of the moment mattered less than an intellectual construction resulting in a consciously sought balance: "To make a sketch from the life first of all is to behave quite illogically and start at the end," Cross wrote in one of his sketchbooks (Louvre-R.F. 36586). Paul Adam, Gustave Kahn, and many other critics regarded Neo-Impressionism as a modernist version of Symbolism, and in 1897 Signac noted in his diary: "Division [of tone] is more a philosophy than a system." The Neo-Impressionists saw scientific theories of color not as a way of getting closer to a more truthful rendition of reality but as a tool enabling them to dominate the totality of visual phenomena. In seeking to penetrate beyond appearances, scientific theory found itself in conflict with the imperfectly codified practice hallowed by custom and prompted a return to the original state of painting: the white ground of a prepared canvas, with paints arrayed on the palette in prismatic order. As early as 1886, Paul Adam saw in this "pure" vision (that is to say one that was in conformity with the conclusions of science) an approach that paralleled the latest developments in the world of ideas: "It is a school of abstraction. It flees the error imposed on our thinking by the education of twenty centuries of dualism, which have created a wholly imaginary objective world existing outside our senses. Modern philosophy is coming round to a single substance: the ideal phenomenon. The Impressionists endeavor to convey its most typical manifestations. To render the primary aspect of a visual sensation, without allowing the understanding to lead the manly science of the eye astray, complicating it with hypothetical features . . . to preserve and fix a vision: that is the goal of these analytical painters."

Cloisonnism and Synthetism

Beyond its orthodox connotation, Neo-Impressionism, considered in its most superficial aspects, was capable of becoming an aesthetic formula. The climate of experimentation that characterized the mid-1880s led Émile Bernard and Vincent van Gogh (1853–1890), for example, to produce, under the influence of Seurat, a number of works using a conception of color division. This revealed two things: the way young artists were keen to follow a modern tradition, and a degree of confusion regarding the respective aims of Impressionism and Neo-Impressionism. The term "Impressionist" was one that critics of the day applied as much to Seurat as to Monet. Before Cloisonnism was properly constituted in 1888, a certain number of works were produced in which the Neo-Impressionist method, by virtue of the alterations it underwent, was interpreted as a style.

Midway between a freedom of execution derived from Impressionism and a wish not to take account of the most modern trends, van Gogh's Parisian works of 1887 were an attempt to exorcise his dark Nuenen period.

Influenced by Signac, whom he met around that time, he devoted the whole year to a series of experimental variations on the dot or dash brushstroke, the aim of which was not so much "optical blending" as the structuring of space. The paintings of late 1887, such as *Portrait of Père Tanguy* (*Portrait du père Tanguy*, fig. 700), in which a newly acquired maturity begins to assert itself, retain traces of this experimental Neo-Impressionist practice in the stark contrast between the network of touches of pure color and the backgrounds against which they are applied. Impressionism itself bore within it certain novel elements that the younger generation of artists took up for themselves, elevating them to the status of stylistic systems. The Japanese influence, already present in Whistler and Manet and drawn upon by Monet in the 1880s for its compositional boldness, was absorbed in a blatant fashion by van Gogh and Gauguin. Examples are the wall covered in ukiyo-e prints against which van Gogh posed *père* Tanguy and the circular shape that Gauguin introduced into *La Belle Angèle* (fig. 75), which can be found in the work of Hokusai and Hiroshige. The interest that Western artists took in Japanese art reached unprecedented proportions, notably with Gauguin and the Nabis. Knowledge of Japanese art had expanded considerably since the pioneering efforts of Philippe Burty and Champfleury, while publications and exhibitions (including the one organized in Paris in 1890 by the École des Beaux-Arts) ensured that examples were widely available. Each issue of the magazine *Le Japon artistique*, published in Paris by Siegfried Bing from 1888 to 1891, carried an essay written by an expert as well as a large number of illustrations. Besides having Japanese objects and prints permanently on display in his gallery, Bing twice organized a Salon des Peintres Japonais in the Palais de l'Industrie in Paris (in 1883 and 1884) and several exhibitions abroad. Van Gogh himself organized an exhibition of Japanese prints in a Paris café and painted several free copies of works by ukiyo-e artists. The fascination for Japan was felt equally strongly by art-lovers and collectors, as can be seen in the work of the Goncourt brothers and the novels of Pierre Loti. The Japanese-influenced style of the late 1880s was characterized by the radical way in which it brought out the formal nature of its sources. Van Gogh, for instance, produced a small number of strictly two-dimensional works, such as *Branch of an Almond Tree in Blossom* (fig. 691), and we also find examples of compositions derived from Japanese prints that had previously been used only in drawing or magazine illustration being transferred wholesale to painting. Thus, having set out from an Impressionist tradition, certain aspects of which they developed, both van Gogh and Gauguin formulated an approach that denied the very principles of Impressionism by asserting the flatness of the painted surface and seeking arbitrary effects of color and stylization.

The continuity of these currents with Impressionism was enshrined in the person of Gauguin. Associated with Pissarro as early as 1874, Gauguin actually took part in the exhibitions of the Impressionist group from 1880. At that time his works either reflected the influence of Cézanne's landscapes or, in his interiors (*Interior, Rue Carcel*, 1881, Nasjonalgalleriet, Oslo), that of Monet. Gauguin moved further and further away from the Impressionist method. It may be that his collaboration with the ceramicist Ernest Chaplet in 1886 led him in the direction of a new approach to drawing and a bolder stylization of shapes, both of which are apparent in the works of his first Pont-Aven period, although his technique remained strictly Impressionist. The artist started writing his *Notes synthétiques*, in which he advocated as creative process the accumulation of documents of various origins (sketches, copies, studies) which the finished work would then "synthesize." This text may be seen as the starting point of Synthetism, the most important aspect of which was the stress it laid on the painter's imaginative interpretation of his or her sources. It was in Pont-Aven in 1888 that Gauguin, in association with Émile Bernard, was to come up with a true embodiment of his theories. For the past year, Bernard and Louis Anquetin had been working on a new way of structuring the picture space. They called it Cloisonnism, and it consisted in treating the surface of the picture in large areas of color separated by strong darker outlines, rather in the manner of a stained-glass window. According to Bernard, whose principles turned out to be related to Symbolism, this kind of linear distortion carried its own expressive charge, determining the character of the work. He eventually arrived at an extremely modern geometrization of forms, as in *Harvest by the Sea* (*Moisson au bord de la mer*, 1891, Musée d'Orsay, Paris). In March 1888, much struck by Bernard's *Breton Women in a Meadow* (*Bretonnes dans la prairie*, fig. 72), Gauguin produced a paraphrase of the work in which Cloisonnism was imbued with religious fervor: this was *The Vision After the Sermon* or *Jacob Wrestling with the Angel*. (*La Vision du sermon* or *La Lutte de Jacob avec l'ange*, fig. 77). As Bernard was later to write: "Gauguin had simply put into practice not the color theory I had been telling him about but the essential style of my *Breton Women in a Meadow*, having first laid down an all-red ground in place of my yellow-green one." Beyond formal borrowings, however, Gauguin here made the Symbolist statement which was the logical conclusion to the stylistic exercises of Cloisonnism. He combined an imagined scene and real figures in a single plane, separating them by the Japanese-influenced diagonal of the trunk of an apple tree. This desire to achieve "great rustic and superstitious simplicity" completed the artist's break with the Impressionist ethic. In 1891, at a time when Gauguin was looked upon as a leader in Symbolist circles, Octave Mirbeau (1848–1917) saw in him "a rich and at the same time disturbing blend of barbaric splendor, Catholic liturgy, Hindu reverie, Gothic imagery, and obscure and subtle symbolism." By associating with Mallarmé, Redon, Carrière, and Charles Morice, Gauguin became familiar with the esoteric tendencies widespread at the time. Idealist literature found an echo in his work, and up until his final paintings Gauguin was marked by the same creative approach based on a system of symbols. The artist's identification with the figure of Christ in several self-portraits, together with his use of Asian art not only as a repertory of forms but also in terms of the sacred concepts those forms represent, put one in mind of the religious Syncretism of Édouard Schuré, for example. In his writings Gauguin claimed repeatedly that his painting possessed a symbolic quality, and a penchant for metaphysical problems was a constant feature of his thinking. In this respect, Gauguin's spells in the South Sea Islands (1891–92 and 1895–1901 in Tahiti, 1901–3 in the Marquesas Islands) corresponded to a search for a mythical Eden, in which he endeavored to recover a sense of the holy that had been destroyed by the Western world, a primitive naivety dominated by the antitheses of life and death. For example, his use of the same figure in several successive works (a frequent feature after the Tahiti period) implied a conception of form as a symbolic entity. The old woman in *Where Do We Come From? What Are We? Where Are We Going?* (*D'où venons-nous? Que sommes-nous? Où allons-nous?*, fig. 734) is depicted in a pose found in several other paintings—*Life and Death* (*La Vie et la mort*, 1889, Mahmoud Khalil Museum, Cairo) and *Arii Matamoe* (1892, private collection)—where it is always associated with the idea of death. The source is a Peruvian mummy that Gauguin saw in the Musée de l'Homme in Paris some time before 1888. In introducing into *Where Do We Come From?* several figures or groups of figures taken from earlier works, Gauguin gave this vast canvas the value of a pictorial summary in which he meant to encapsulate his religious symbolism. Completed rather hurriedly in many sections, the work is painted in the smooth, low-contrast manner that the artist was using at the time, even in smaller paintings such as *Nevermore* (1897; figs. 730, 731). As in several earlier paintings dating from Gauguin's first stay in Tahiti (*Vahine no te vi*, 1892), the visual coherence rests on the juxtaposition of large masses of color that are linked together and create volume without the use of contour.

The distance between this refinement of forms (which, color apart, is reminiscent of Cézanne) and the stylistic evolution that van Gogh went through in the last three years of his life illustrates the variations that could affect Cloisonnism. Even before van Gogh left for Arles in February 1888, assimilation of this new vocabulary had enabled him to break away from Impressionism. In the first landscapes he painted in Arles, the picture surface is divided up into large areas, each of which is treated in a distinct manner, even down to the brushstrokes. His foregrounds sometimes took on a cursive, graphic quality (*View of Arles with Irises in the Foreground*, May 1888, Rijksmuseum Vincent van Gogh, Amsterdam), in which color was heightened with black outlines. Later, under Gauguin's influence, he extended this process to the whole painting, but here van Gogh employed it for certain parts, as in *The Night Café* (*Le Café de nuit*, fig. 74), a composition structured by the use of complementary colors. Gauguin's arrival in Arles and the close collaboration between the two in October-December 1888 gave rise to many new formulations of Synthetism. Common elements emerged, such as the composition viewed from above, which Gauguin had used in *The Vision After the Sermon* (fig. 77), and adopted again in his *Portrait of Van Gogh* (fig. 671). During those few months van Gogh strove to use drawing to give his pictures a decorative framework, though some works still retained the impasto treatment he had inherited from Monticelli. Consequently, his method, largely the product of direct execution in front of the subject, remained close to Impressionism. Soon after Gauguin's departure, however, he started painting small series of pictures in which a single subject gives rise to various stylistic speculations. The five versions of *Portrait of Madame Roulin (the Lullaby)* (*La Berceuse: Madame Augustine Rollin*) include sometimes tiny variations in color or in the arrangement of the background. Van Gogh got into the habit of doing one or more repetitions based on an initial picture painted from the life. The works of the Saint-Rémy period and those painted at Auvers-sur-Oise in the months preceding his suicide in July 1890 continue this quest for style, but in them the teachings of Bernard and Gauguin about the symbolic value of form are subjected to an interpretation that reveals the artist's admiration for Millet. Van Gogh was beginning to achieve recognition through the exhibitions of the Indépendants and Les XX, which showed works by him in 1889 and 1890. In January of that year, Aurier devoted an enthusiastic article to him in the prestigious *Mercure de France*. In Auvers, where the artist produced some twenty-four paintings in just over two months, his suppleness of line reached heights of lyrical effusion, except that in certain canvases, such as *Cornfield with Crows* (*Le Champ de blé aux corbeaux*, fig. 684), it seems suddenly to tighten and acquire a hard angularity. This treatment of form went hand in hand with an increasingly imaginative use of color, which was a resource that van Gogh used quite ascetically. In many paintings, the chromatic scale is restricted in order to set up a certain tension between two extremes, as in the *Portrait of Dr. Paul Gachet* (*Portrait du docteur Gachet*, fig. 76) for example, where the flat area of red offsets nuances ranging from blue to purplish. The panoramic breadth of the landscapes of fields under stormy skies that closed the artist's career then appear as a kind of formal leitmotiv developed with supreme freedom.

Toward the end of 1888, Paul Sérusier showed his friends at the Académie Julian—Maurice Denis, Henri-Gabriel Ibels (1867–1936), Paul Ranson, Pierre Bonnard (1867–1947)—a panel painted in Pont-Aven "at Gauguin's dictation." Denis called it "a shapeless landscape, as a result of having been formulated synthetically in purple, vermilion, Veronese green, and other colors as they came out of the tube, with virtually no white mixed in them." This relic was to become *The Talisman* (*Le Talisman*, fig. 73) around which was soon to form the group known as the Nabis (from a Hebrew word meaning "prophet"). The small Académie Julian group was joined by René Piot, Ker-Xavier Roussel (1867–1944), and Édouard Vuillard (1868–1940), who were then students at the École des Beaux-Arts, and subsequently by Georges Lacombe (1868–1916) and Aristide Maillol (1861–1944) as well as by Mögens

Ballin (1871–1914), Jan Verkade (1868–1946), Jószef Rippl-Rónai, and Félix Vallotton. Sérusier, the senior member of the group, was also the closest to Gauguin, having worked with him in Brittany in 1889–90. On the other hand, the "Exposition des peintres impressionistes et synthétistes" held at the Café Volpini on the fringe of the 1889 Exposition Universelle, in which Gauguin brought together, in addition to twenty of his own paintings, works by such artists as Bernard and Anquetin, introduced the young painters to various aspects of Cloisonnism. Denis was to write: "We found in those unusual works the influence of the Japanese print, the *images d'Épinal,* sign-painting, Romanesque stylization." The fact that Gauguin's lead made any kind of sense to artists of such different mentalities highlights the universal nature of the anti-naturalistic tendency shared by so many artists born after 1860.

Right from 1890, the first works of the Nabis consisted of broad areas of plain color, thicker and fruitier in texture than Gauguin's. Moreover, Redon, van Gogh, and Cézanne provided examples which enabled them to modify in a subtle way the lessons learned in Pont-Aven. Their admiration for Puvis de Chavannes led them to rediscover the darker tonalities—the deep greens, grays, and beiges used by Bonnard in *The Croquet Game* (*La Partie de croquet,* fig. 751), for example—that quickly ousted the pure purple of *The Talisman.* The originality of the Nabis lay less in the novelty of their stylistic theories than in the way in which they used them to arrive quite quickly at a style that was distinct from its sources. Starting from a common base, each one developed according to his particular inclination: Bonnard and Vuillard toward intimism; Roussel toward the eclogue; Sérusier, Denis, and Ranson in the more Symbolist directions of theosophy and Catholic mysticism. Nevertheless, over the last ten years of the lifetime of the group, there did emerge a concerted desire to reach an artistic ideal. The Nabis met regularly, exhibited together, and often used in their letters to one another certain codified expressions meaningless to anyone else.

The doctrine of the Nabis was derived from John Ruskin's idea that art should reach beyond the narrow bounds imposed by convention and affect the whole of society in its everyday life, and the group showed a marked interest in the decorative arts. Bonnard, Vuillard, and Sérusier all painted screens, Denis designed wallpapers, and Ranson produced hangings. In stage set design, the Nabis were part of a vast reform movement that appeared toward the end of the century and was accompanied by the discovery of the new, Symbolist repertoire of Oscar Wilde, Maurice Maeterlinck, and the Scandinavians Bjørnsterne Bjørnson, Henrik Ibsen, and August Strindberg. At André Antoine's Théâtre Libre from 1890, and subsequently at Paul Fort's Théâtre d'Art as well as for Lugné-Poë (a fellow student at the Académie Julian), the Nabis produced many sets in which the illusionist tradition was eclipsed by their experiments in simplification. Maeterlinck's *Pelléas et Mélisande,* first performed at the Théâtre de l'Œuvre in 1893 with sets by Vuillard, and Alfred Jarry's *Ubu Roi,* which brought together Bonnard, Ranson, Sérusier, and Vuillard, are both landmarks in the history of set design. Bonnard, together with Jules Chéret (1836–1932) and Toulouse-Lautrec, created the modern poster. But it was in mural painting that the Nabis achieved their most striking successes, notably with Vuillard and later with Denis and Roussel. From decorations for Paul Desmarais (1892) to the foyer of the Comédie des Champs-Élysées (1913), Vuillard completed several decorative schemes that in their sumptuous coloring and in the perfect match between their style and their modern inspiration represented an intimist response to the monumentality of Puvis.

The writings that Maurice Denis published from 1890 onward constituted a veritable aesthetic treatise. In them he emphasized the decorative aspect of the work of art, as in his celebrated dictum: "Remember that, before being a war-horse, a nude woman, or an anecdote of some kind, a painting is essentially a flat surface covered with colors arranged in a certain order." On the other hand (and this was what brought the Nabis close to Symbolism), line and color must constitute the "plastic equivalent" of the artist's thought. However, with the Nabis this concept of decorative art ultimately led them to question the very act of depiction and the historical heritage that manifested itself in the material structure of the painting. As Verkade was to write in his *Souvenirs*: "A battle cry rang out from studio to studio: No more easel paintings! Down with useless furniture! Painting must not usurp a freedom that cuts it off from the other arts. The painter's work begins where the architect regards his as complete. Walls, walls to decorate! Down with perspective! The wall should remain a surface, it ought not to be troubled by representation of endless horizons. There are no paintings, only decorations." This brought into the province of painting formal characteristics more usually associated with related domains: the matte surface of fresco painting, the cut-out shapes of poster design, the elongated formats associated with interior decoration. Inspired by Japanese prints, the works of Bonnard and Vuillard evoked the two-dimensional look of hangings. Backgrounds and foregrounds were flat and uniform, or treated with an accumulation of decorative motifs from which Vuillard, for example, drew amazing vibrations. For the first time (and in this the Nabis can be seen as a radical extension of Synthetism) the construction of space was achieved through masses of color alone. The illusionistic use of values leading to the shading off of a particular tint as a function of volume or depth, still a feature of Neo-Impressionist theory, was now declared obsolete. Pictorial technique branched out in all directions. It might adopt the asceticism of tempera, leaving the support visible—canvas, paper, velvet, or fabric, as in *The Dressing Gown* (*Le Peignoir,* fig. 92) by Bonnard. It might, by contrast, saturate the surface of the canvas with rich impasto, wholly concealing the grain. This kind of painting, more than any other, asserts the constituents of the work. It maintains a discourse on its materiality, which it both glorifies as a whole and treats harshly if the eye picks out a detail. Never had the beauty of a color so obviously depended on the color next to it.

Around the same time, Henri de Toulouse-Lautrec (1864–1901) began to go beyond his admiration for Degas, producing paintings in which he incorporated elements of poster design, such as the exaggerated line of the rough sketch or flat areas of color. In 1893, Gustave Geffroy wrote: "We shall certainly learn something about his skill at conveying 'people landscapes' and putting colors together if we bear in mind that he has designed and executed several high-quality posters: Bruant, La Goulue, and more recently Le Divan japonais have taken over our streets with compelling authority." *In the Salon of the Rue des Moulins* (*Au Salon de la rue des Moulins*, fig. 90) followed a pastel of the same size using an identical composition, the hatching and velvety texture of which the artist reproduced in the painted version. Lautrec had in common with the Nabis a liking for interiors and artificial light. The urban spectacle, which in his work became a chronicle of manners, was something intimate in their eyes, though we should not forget the caustic caricatures produced by Bonnard, for example. If Lautrec's linear stylization was always more vigorous, closer to a traditional anatomical treatment, the way he arranged his pictures was not fundamentally different. In *Women Dancing at the Moulin-Rouge* (*Femmes dansant au Moulin-Rouge*, 1892, Národní Gallery, Prague), the two dancers form a single patch of blue, run through with vertical brushstrokes, while the figures in the background, despite the diagonal suggesting depth, are treated as flat areas of color and decorative streaking. Similarly, for a long time Bonnard saw his landscapes as a backcloth in front of which he placed his figures; the tendency can still be seen in a work like *The Bourgeois Afternoon* (*L'Après-midi bourgeoise*, fig. 753), painted in 1900. Color, which Denis and Vuillard initially preferred bright, applied in uniform areas inscribed with curvilinear motifs—as in Denis's *Procession Beneath the Trees* (*Procession sous les arbres*, fig. 87)—gradually moved toward less strident harmonies and became iridescent with little flecks while still powerfully asserting the presence of the picture surface. Maillol, whose touch retained something of the gentleness of Impressionism, made his figures stand out clearly against a background designed as successive flat planes in the manner of a stage set, as in his *Two Nudes in a Landscape* (*Deux nus dans un paysage*, fig. 762).

In the early years of the twentieth century, when the modernity of these solutions became outmoded, the approach adopted by Bonnard and Vuillard consisted in working out a system of spatial construction that integrated depth by using successive planes or diagonal lines. This was not unlike the path taken by Monet. Having succeeded, in the Japanese Bridge series, in filling in the pictorial field almost completely, from 1900 Monet began to find his way back to three-dimensionality with his paintings of water lilies (fig. 110). About 1905, Bonnard in fact rediscovered Impressionism and lightened his palette, following a brief period during which he produced a number of works that used darker coloring, as in *Indolence* (*L'Indolente*, 1899, Musée d'Orsay, Paris), which marked a break with the Nabi style. The disappearance in 1903 of *La Revue blanche*, with which the Nabis had been closely associated, enhanced the independence of the former members of the group. While staying well away from the new currents, Bonnard nevertheless, thanks to the coherent development of his art, proved to be one of the key pivots between the nineteenth and twentieth centuries. It is usual to explain his increasingly ardent coloring in terms of a kind of return to Impressionism. However, it was more a matter of a subjective chromaticism in which the painter manifested a desire to break free from "snapshot" notation and from any kind of narrow dependence with regard to external reality, of which he nevertheless idealized the light. Although Bonnard's approach was less directly influential in his day than that of Munch, for example (who was particularly important with regard to Fauvism and Expressionism), it formed one of the most significant links between the end of the nineteenth century and the major movements of the early twentieth century. In many respects the "ruptures" of the period before World War I (Fauvism, Cubism, Expressionism) can be seen as manifestations of a continuity, bringing fresh solutions to a problem which had remained unchanged since the mid-1880s. Technique itself occasionally bore witness to this line of descent, as was the case for the Italian Futurists with regard to Divisionism, or for the Fauves, whose early works were an exaggerated version of the Neo-Impressionist landscape. But this linkage obeyed the same logic without always showing evidence of stylistic borrowing: before discovering Cézanne in 1911, Mondrian admired van Gogh for the freedom of his color, while his conception of the purpose of the work of art was profoundly Symbolist. What twentieth-century artists would try to do was to unite the tendencies that had led to a renewal of the whole vocabulary of the plastic arts. After 1900, the younger generation of artists discovered what was to become the "modern tradition." Between 1900 and 1906 Gauguin, van Gogh, Cézanne, and Seurat all had retrospectives at the Salon des Indépendants, at the newly established Salon d'Automne, and at Ambroise Vollard's gallery. Pondered over by the future Fauves and by the Germans of the Die Brücke group, their principles were to undergo fresh developments. Cézanne's way of constructing space, in conjunction with purity of color seen as an expressive language and the linear stylization inherited from Gauguin and van Gogh, would be the focus of the series of radical changes that gave early-twentieth-century art its underlying structure.

14 Jean-Auguste-Dominique Ingres
Portrait of Madame Moitessier
1844–56
Oil on canvas, 120 x 92 cm
National Gallery, London

15 Théodore Chassériau
"Tepidarium," the Room to Which the Women of Pompeii Withdrew to Rest and Dry Themselves After Bathing (detail)
1853 Salon
Oil on canvas, 171 x 258 cm
Musée d'Orsay, Paris

16 Henri Leys
Study for the Months of Berthal de Haze (detail)
1855
Oil on canvas, overall dimensions 25 x 67 cm
Stedelijke Musea, Bruges

17 John Everett Millais
Ophelia
1851–52
Oil on canvas, 76 x 112 cm
Tate Gallery, London

18 William Holman Hunt
The Scapegoat
1854
Oil on canvas, 86 x 136 cm
Lady Lever Art Gallery, Port Sunlight, Merseyside

19 Ford Madox Brown
Work
1852–63
Oil on canvas, 137 x 197.3 cm
City Art Gallery, Manchester

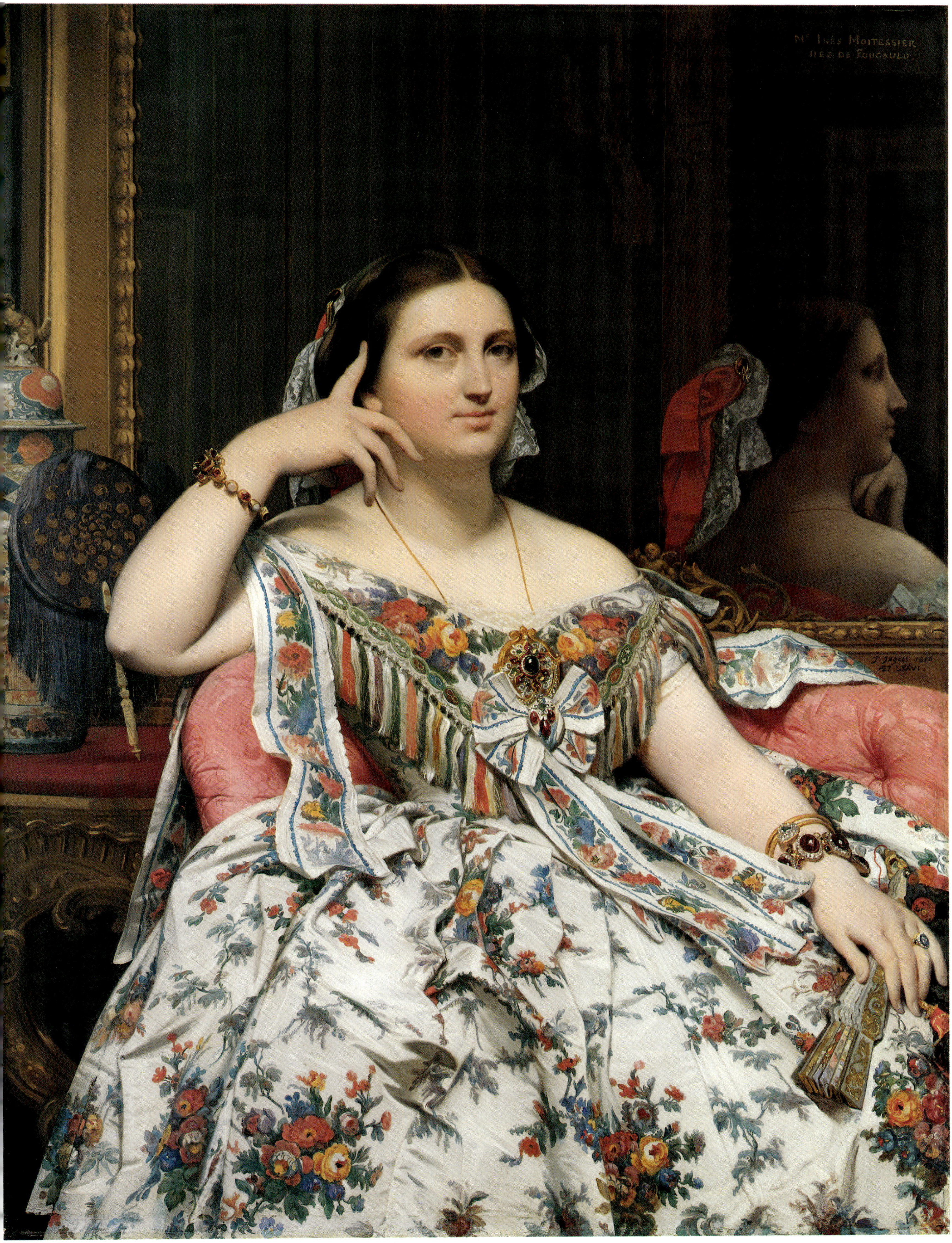

14

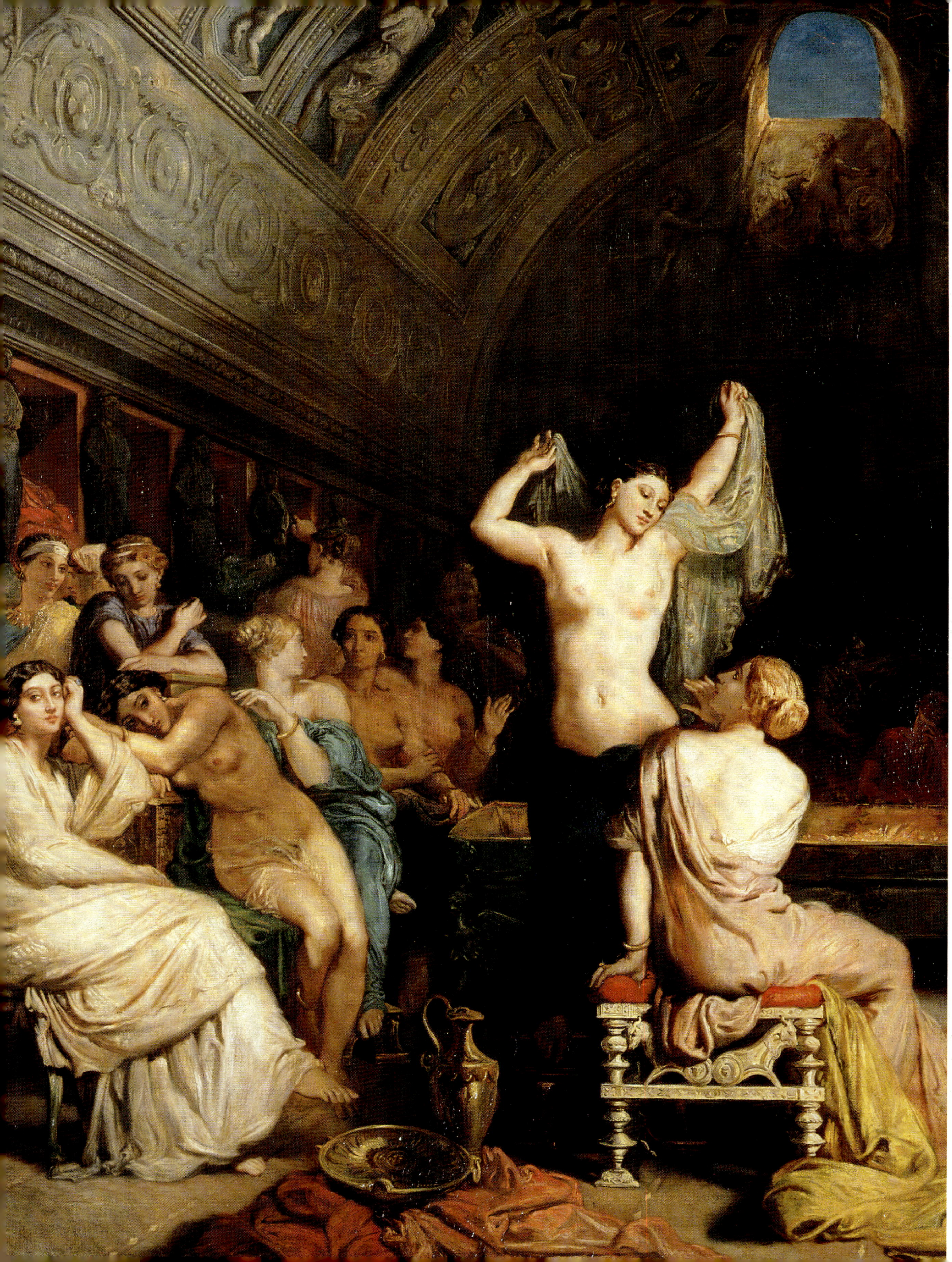

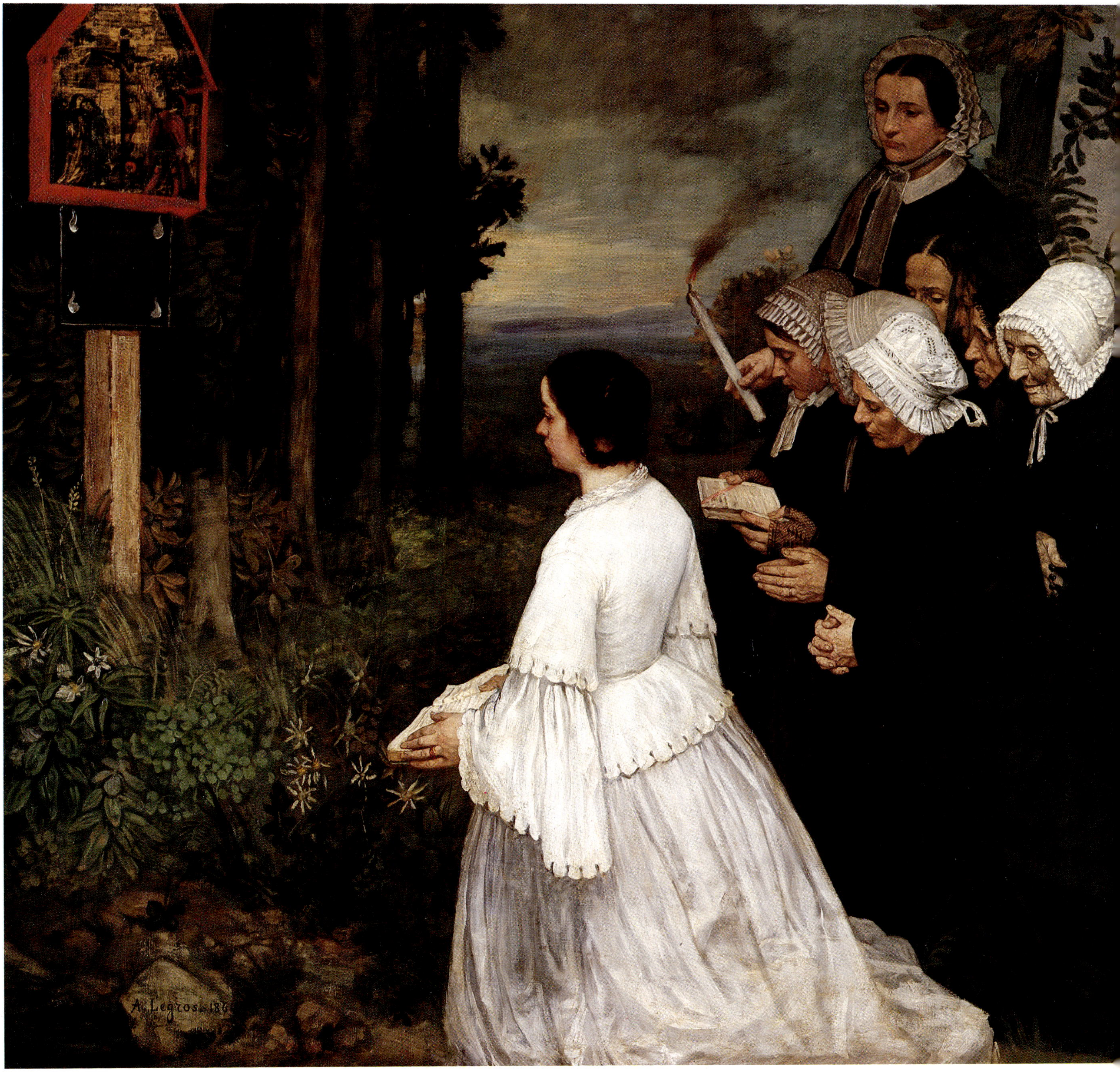

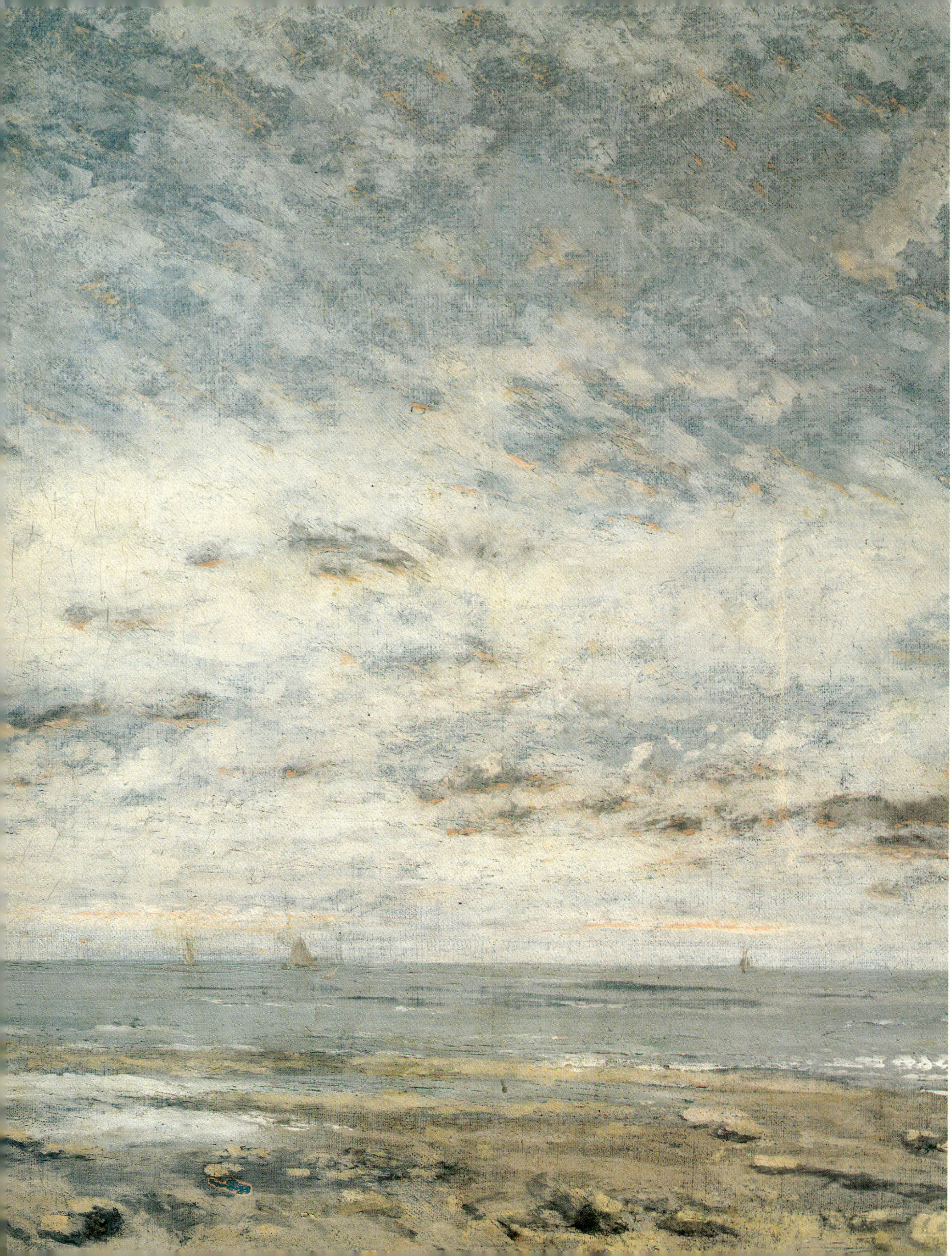

20 Gustave Courbet
The Meeting or *Bonjour Monsieur Courbet*
1854
Oil on canvas, 129 x 149 cm
Musée Fabre, Montpellier

21 Jean-Auguste-Dominique Ingres
The Turkish Bath
1864
Oil on canvas glued onto wood, diameter 110 cm
Louvre, Paris

22 Alexandre Cabanel
The Birth of Venus (detail)
1863 Salon
Oil on canvas, overall dimensions 130 x 225 cm
Musée d'Orsay, Paris

23 Edgar Degas
Woman Leaning on an Elbow Beside a Vase of Flowers,
incorrectly referred to as *Woman with Chrysanthemums*
1865
Oil on canvas, 73.7 x 92.7 cm
Metropolitan Museum of Art (H. O. Havemeyer Collection), New York

24 Alphonse Legros
The Shrine
1860
Oil on canvas, 174 x 197 cm
Musée des Beaux-Arts, Dijon

25 Gustave Courbet
Low Tide at Trouville (detail)
1865
Oil on canvas, overall dimensions 59.5 x 72.5 cm
Walker Art Gallery, Liverpool

26 Mariano Fortuny
The Print Collector (detail)
1866
Oil on canvas, overall dimensions 66.5 x 92 cm
Museu Nacional d'Art Modern de Catalunya, Barcelona

27 Carolus-Duran
The Convalescent or *The Casualty*
1860
Oil on canvas, 99 x 125 cm
Musée d'Orsay, Paris

28 James Tissot
Portrait of Miss L.L. or *Girl in a Red Jacket*
1864 Salon
Oil on canvas, 124 x 99.5 cm
Musée d'Orsay, Paris

29 Jean-François Millet
Spring
1868–73
Oil on canvas, 86 x 111 cm
Musée d'Orsay, Paris

30 Dante Gabriel Rossetti
Monna Vanna
1866
Oil on canvas, 88.9 x 86.4 cm
Tate Gallery, London

31 Giovanni Fattori
The Palmieri Rotunda (detail)
1866
Oil on canvas, overall dimensions 12 x 35 cm
Galleria Nazionale d'Arte Moderna, Florence

32 Silvestro Lega
The Visit (detail)
1868
Oil on canvas, overall dimensions 31 x 60 cm
Galleria Nazionale d'Arte Moderna, Rome

33 Paul Cézanne
The Negro Scipio
c. 1867
Oil on canvas, 107 x 83 cm
Museu de Arte, São Paulo

34 Édouard Manet
Olympia
1863 (1865 Salon)
Oil on canvas, 130.5 x 190 cm
Musée d'Orsay, Paris

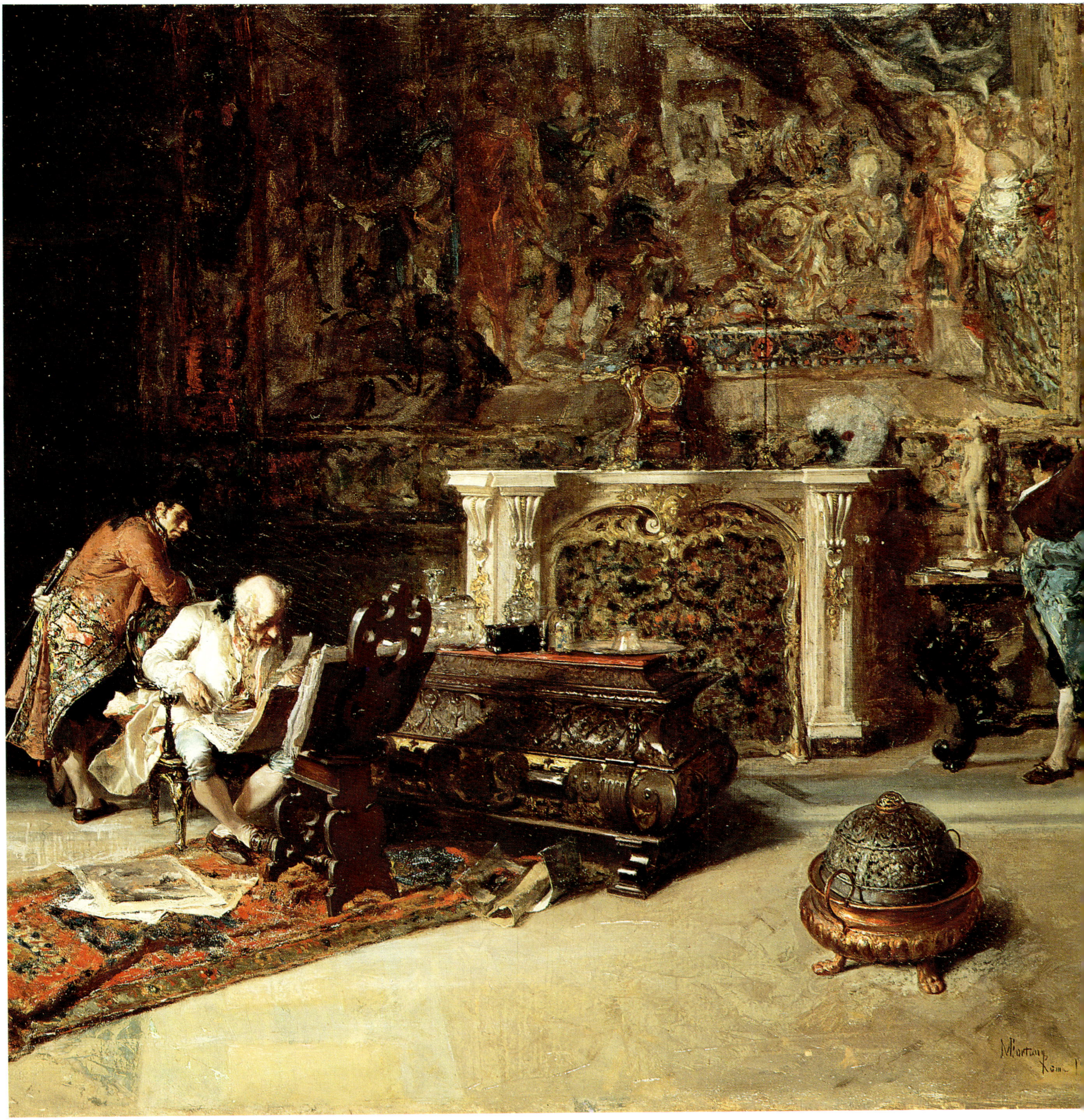

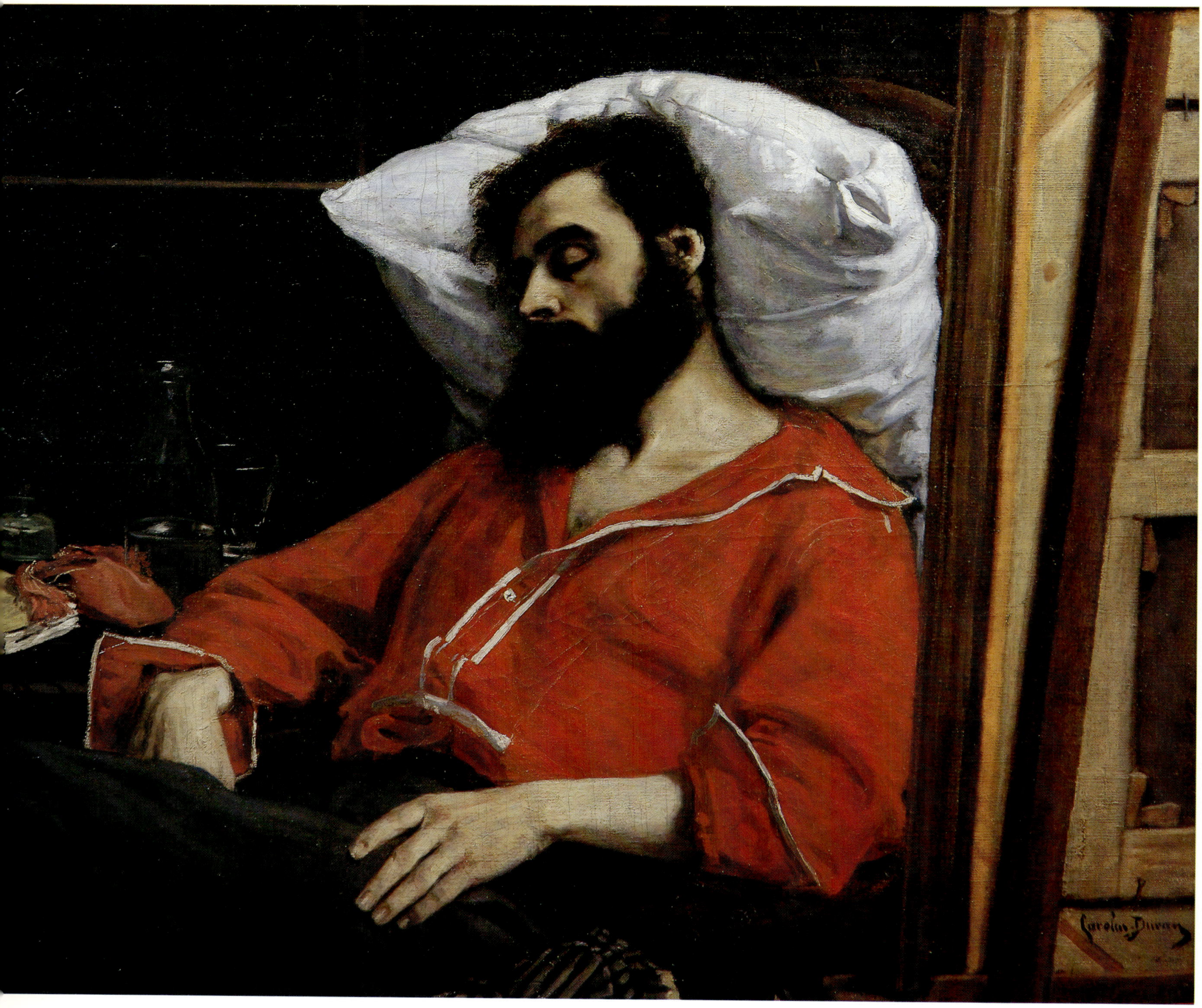

27

→
28

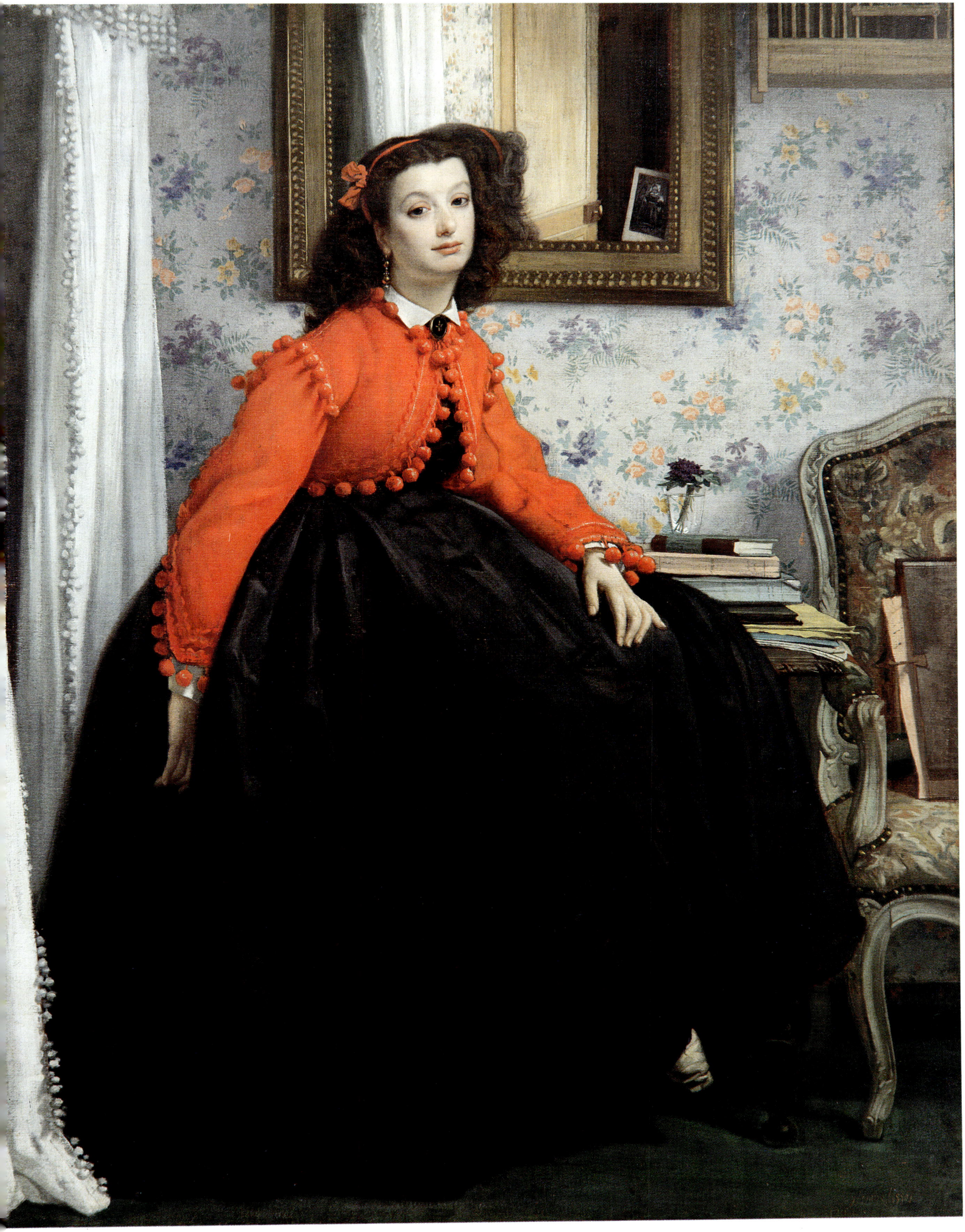

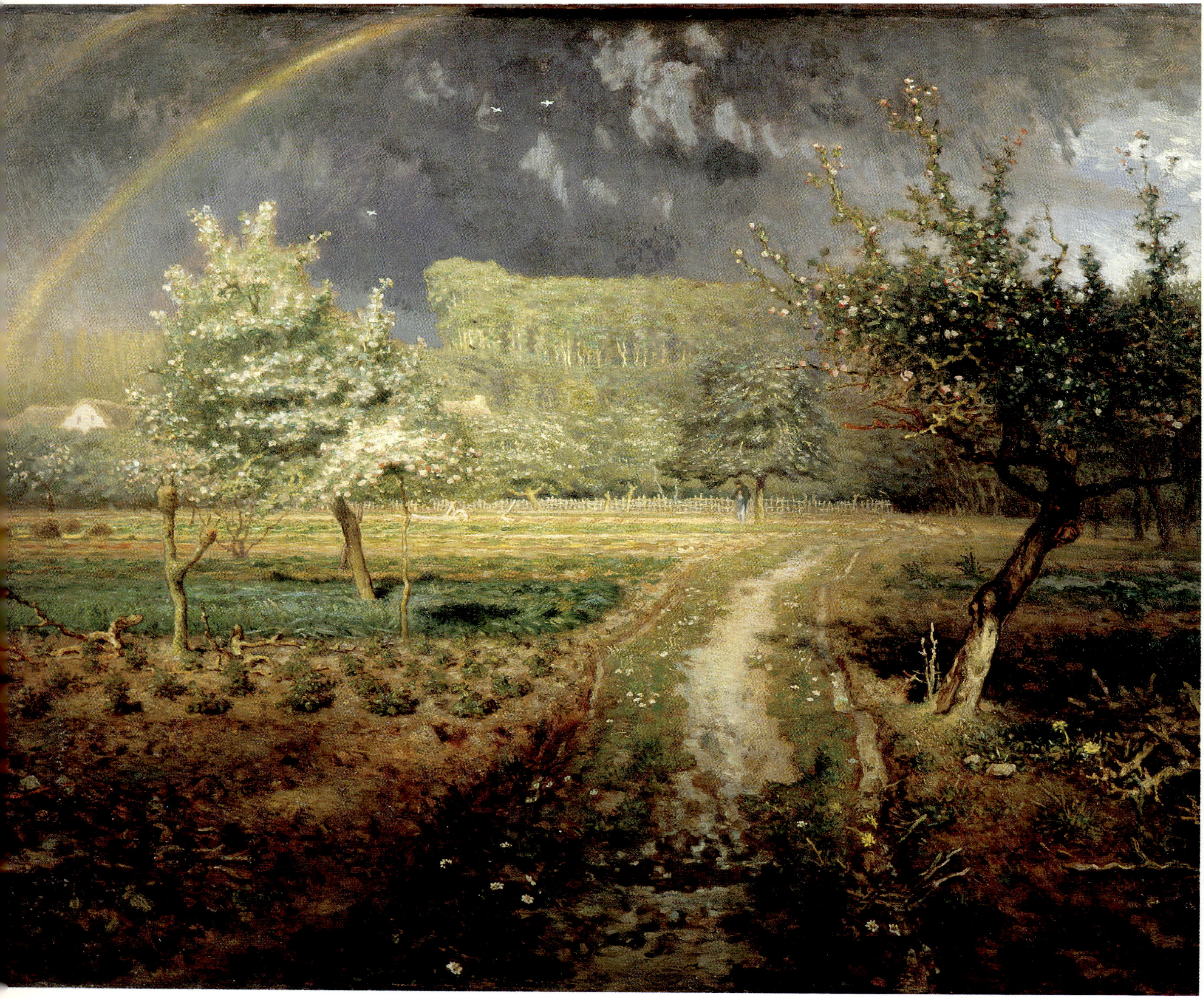

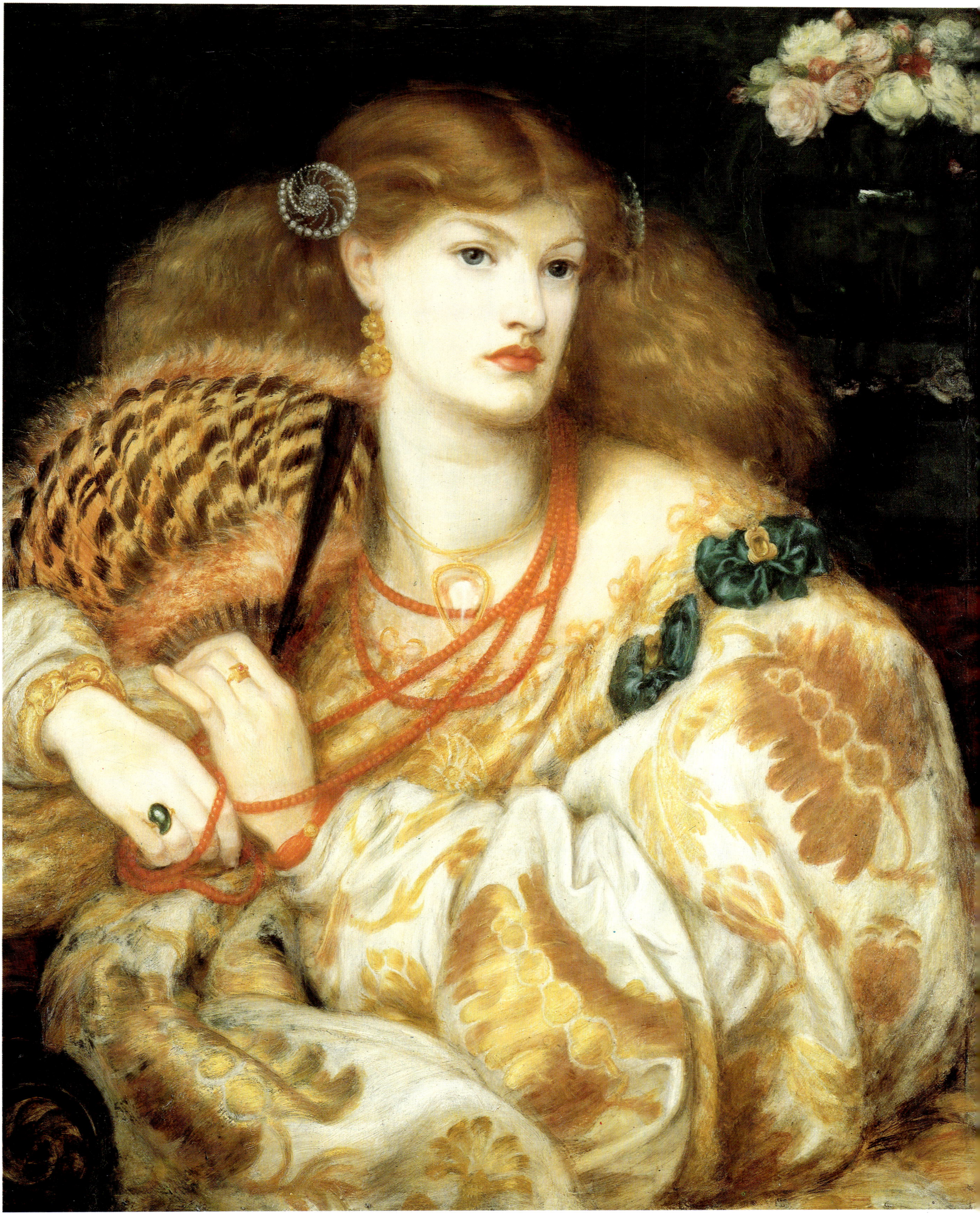

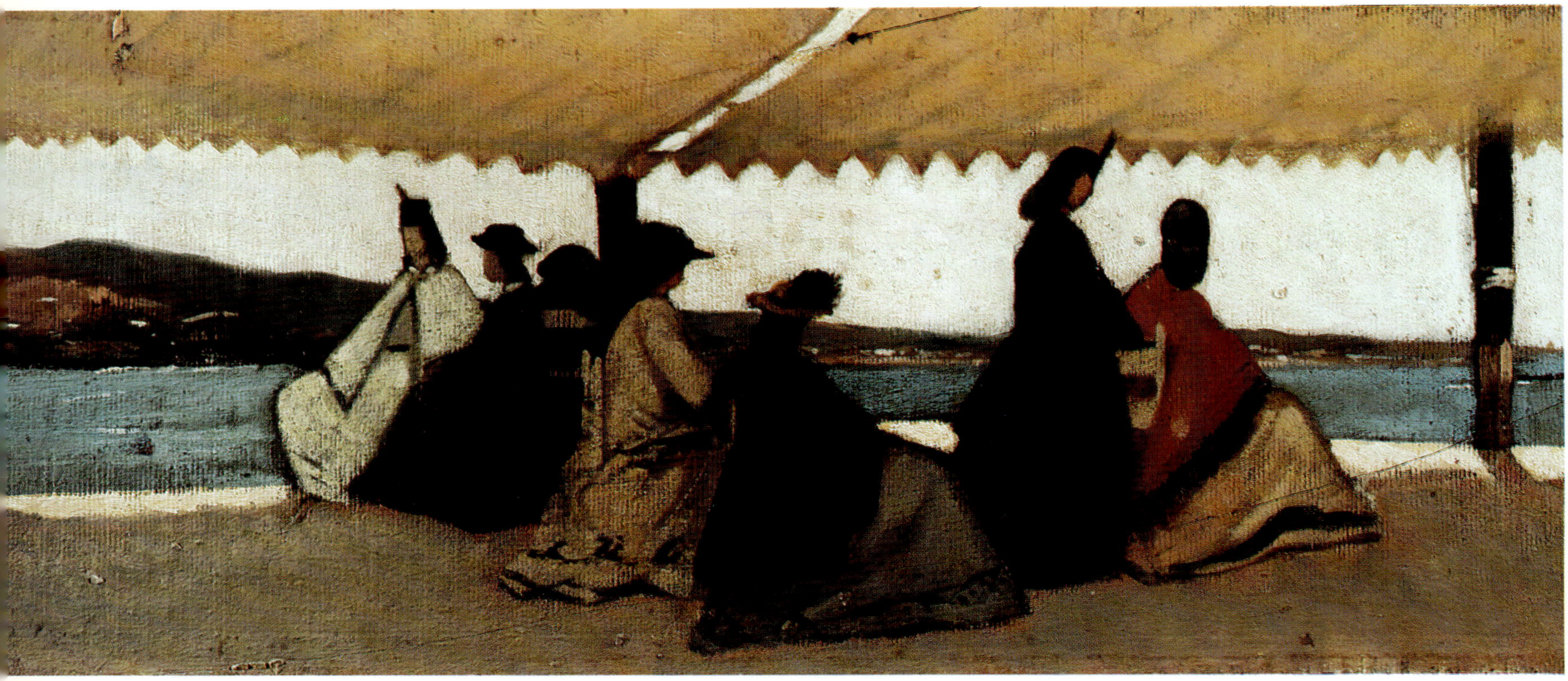

31

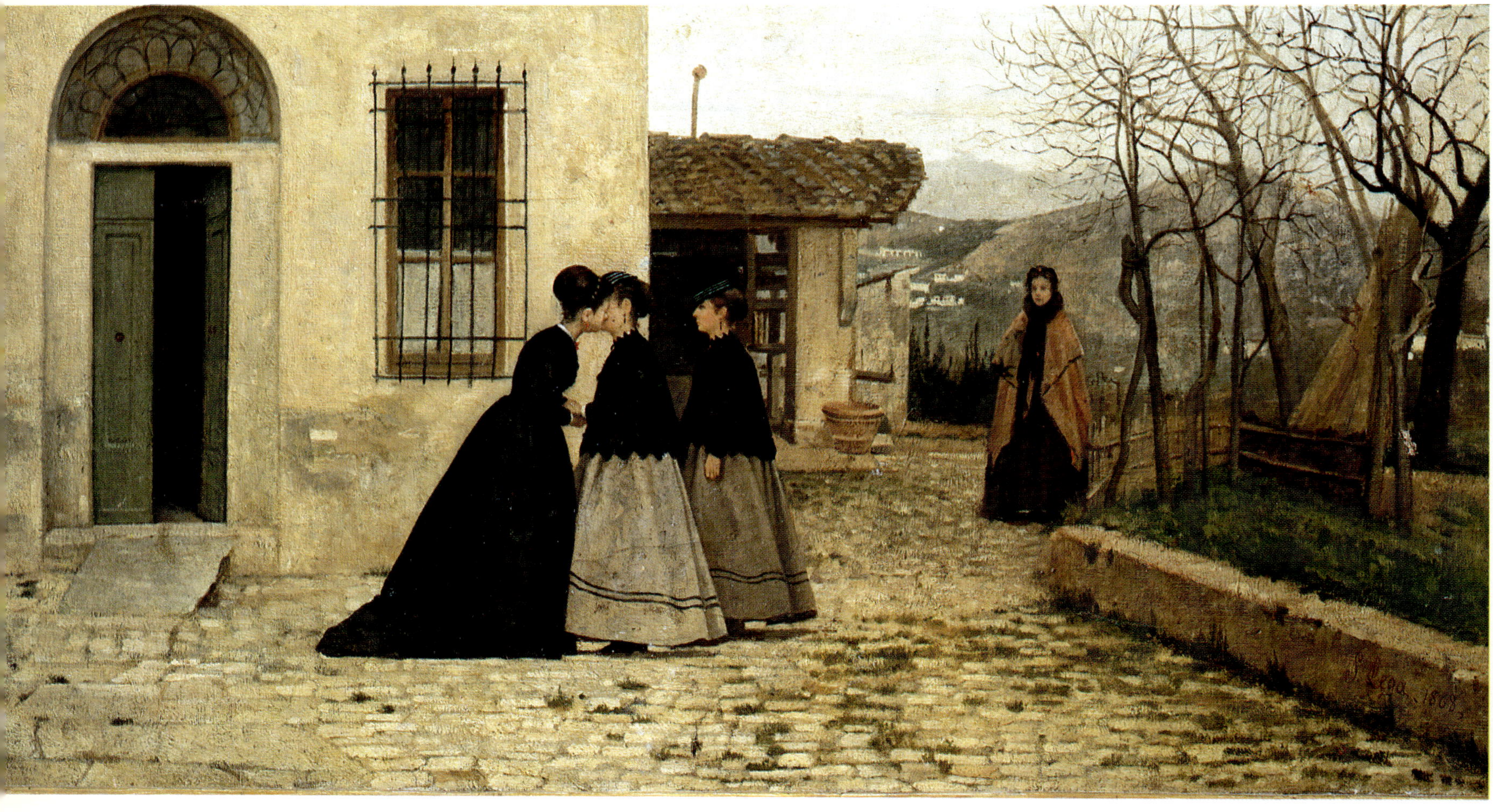

32

→
33

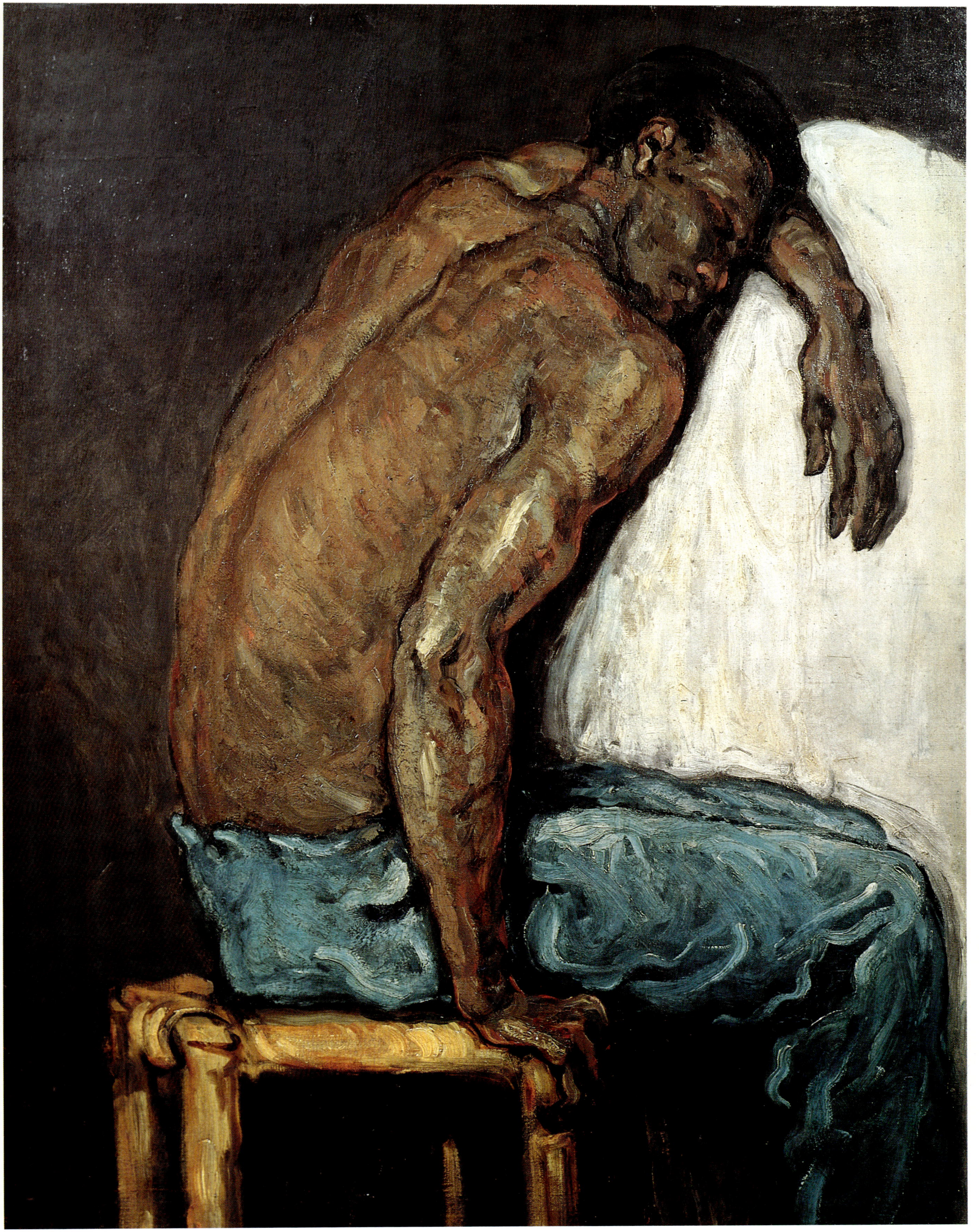

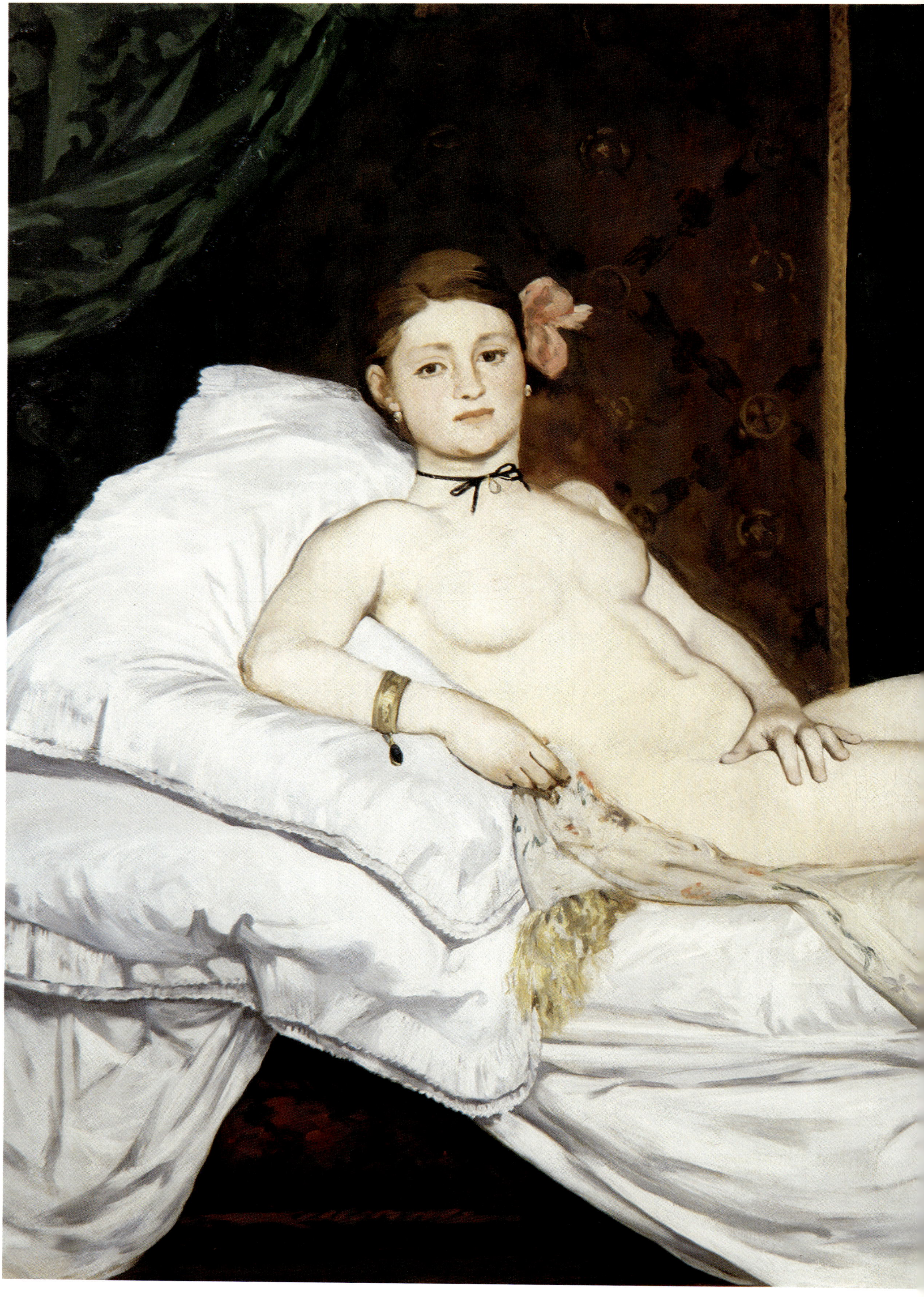

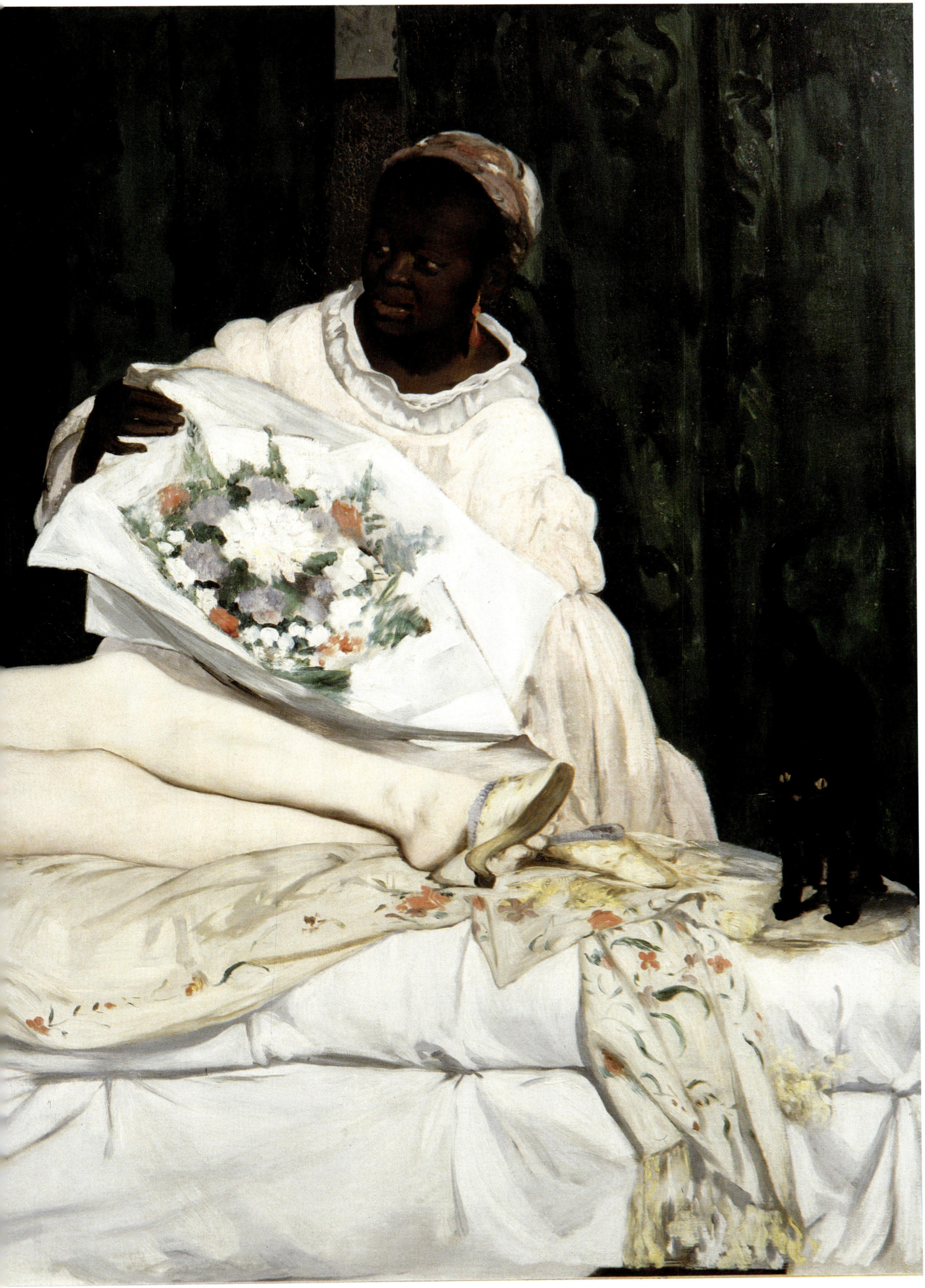

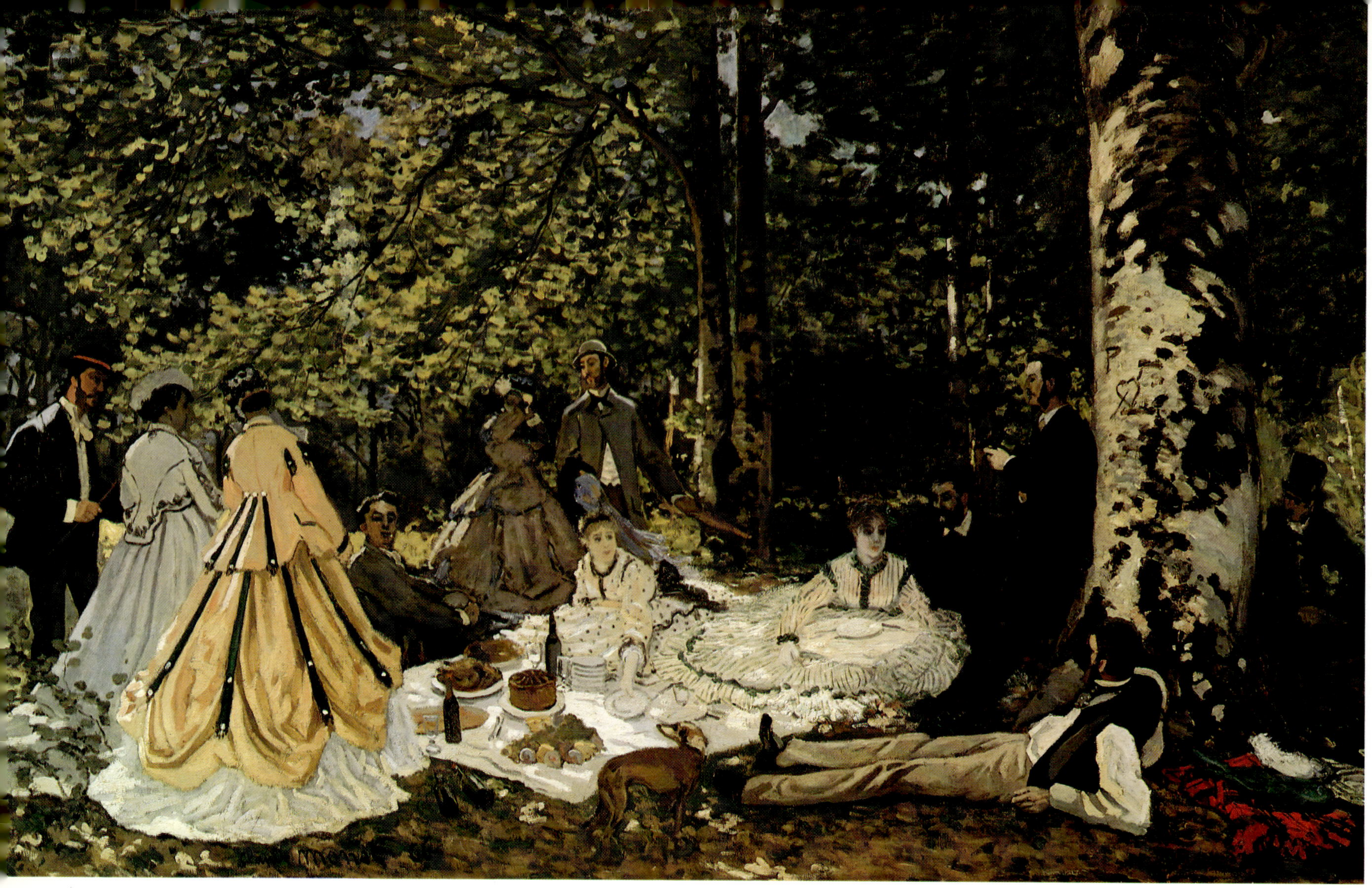

35

36

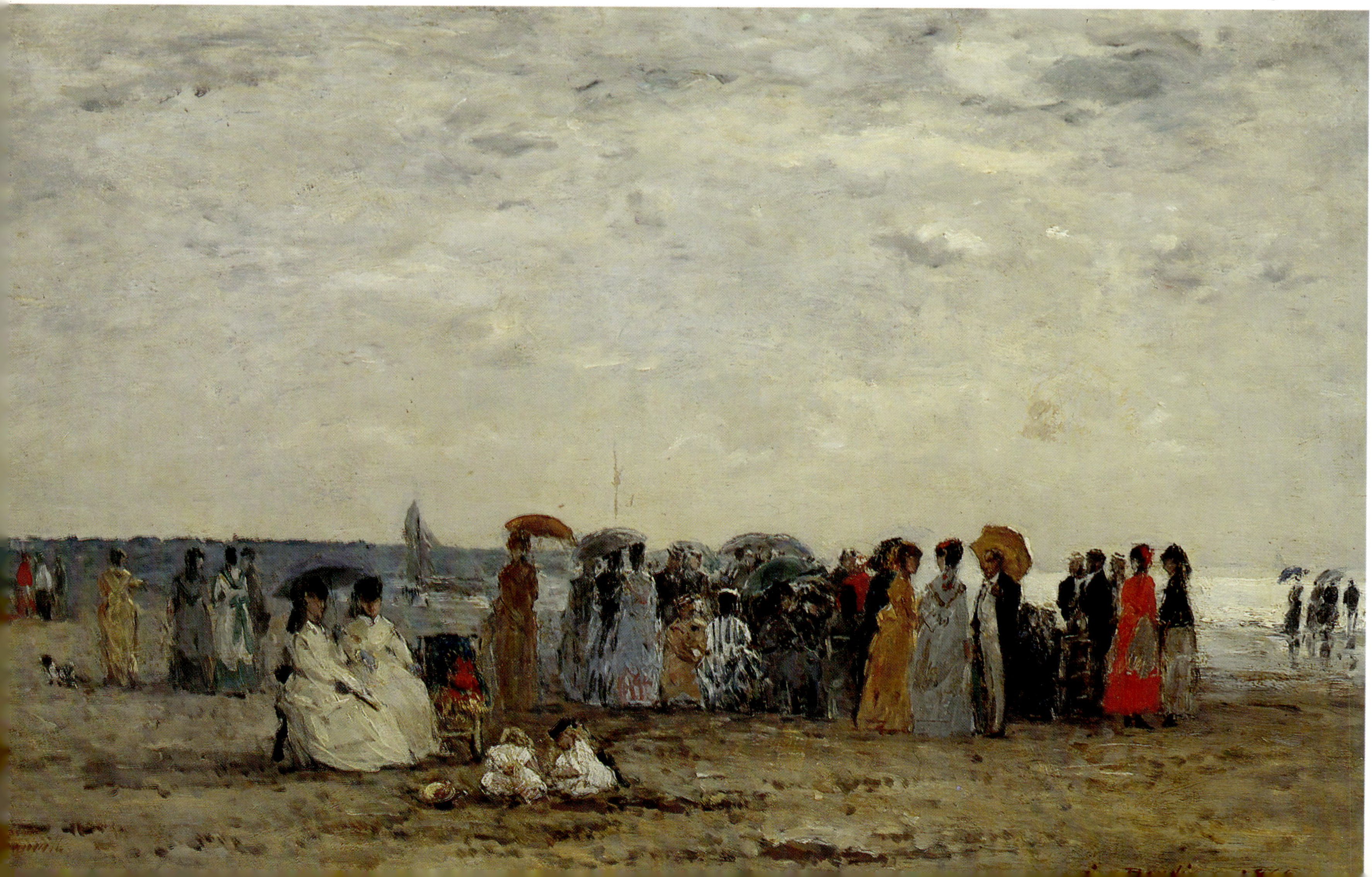

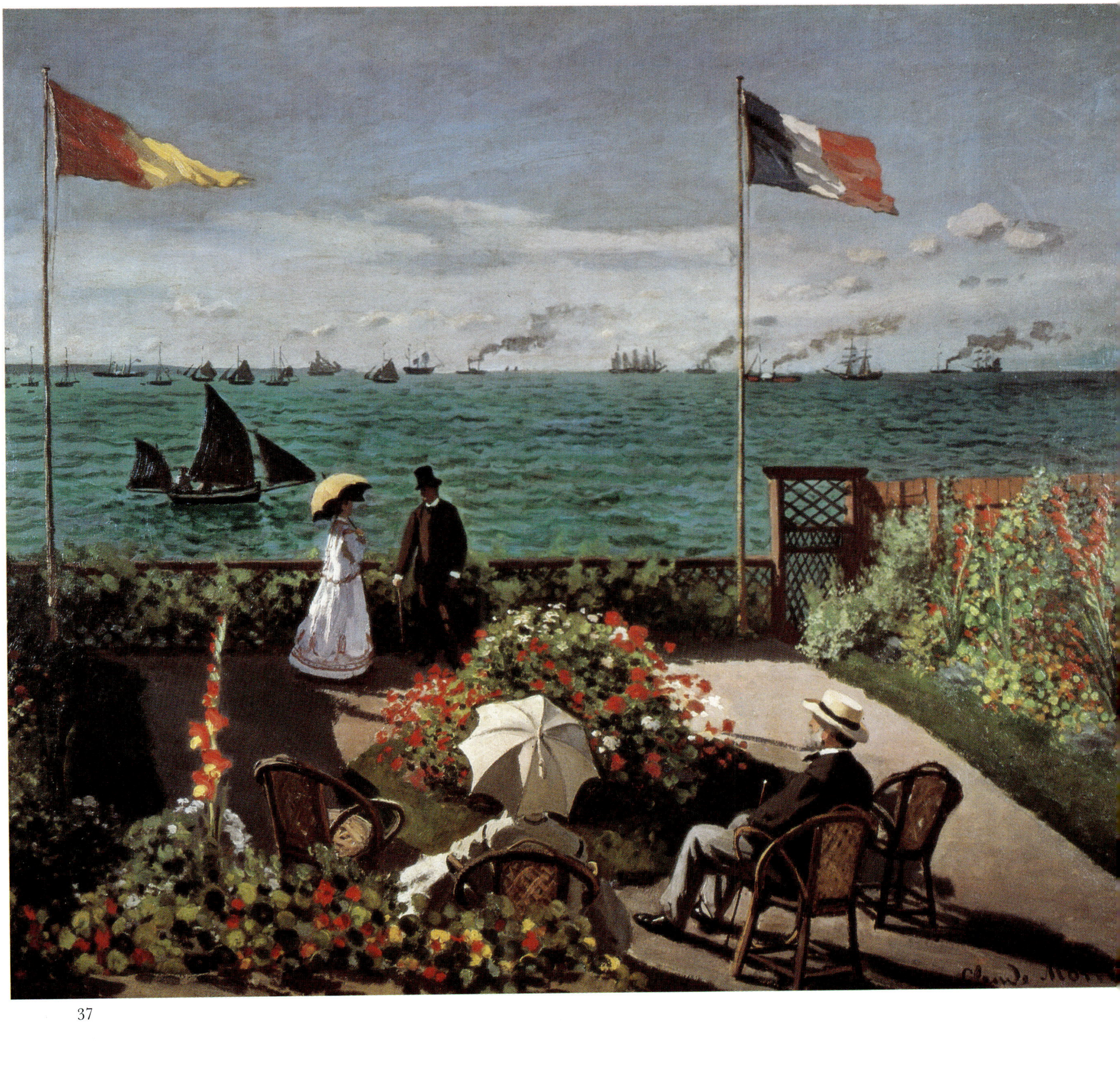

37

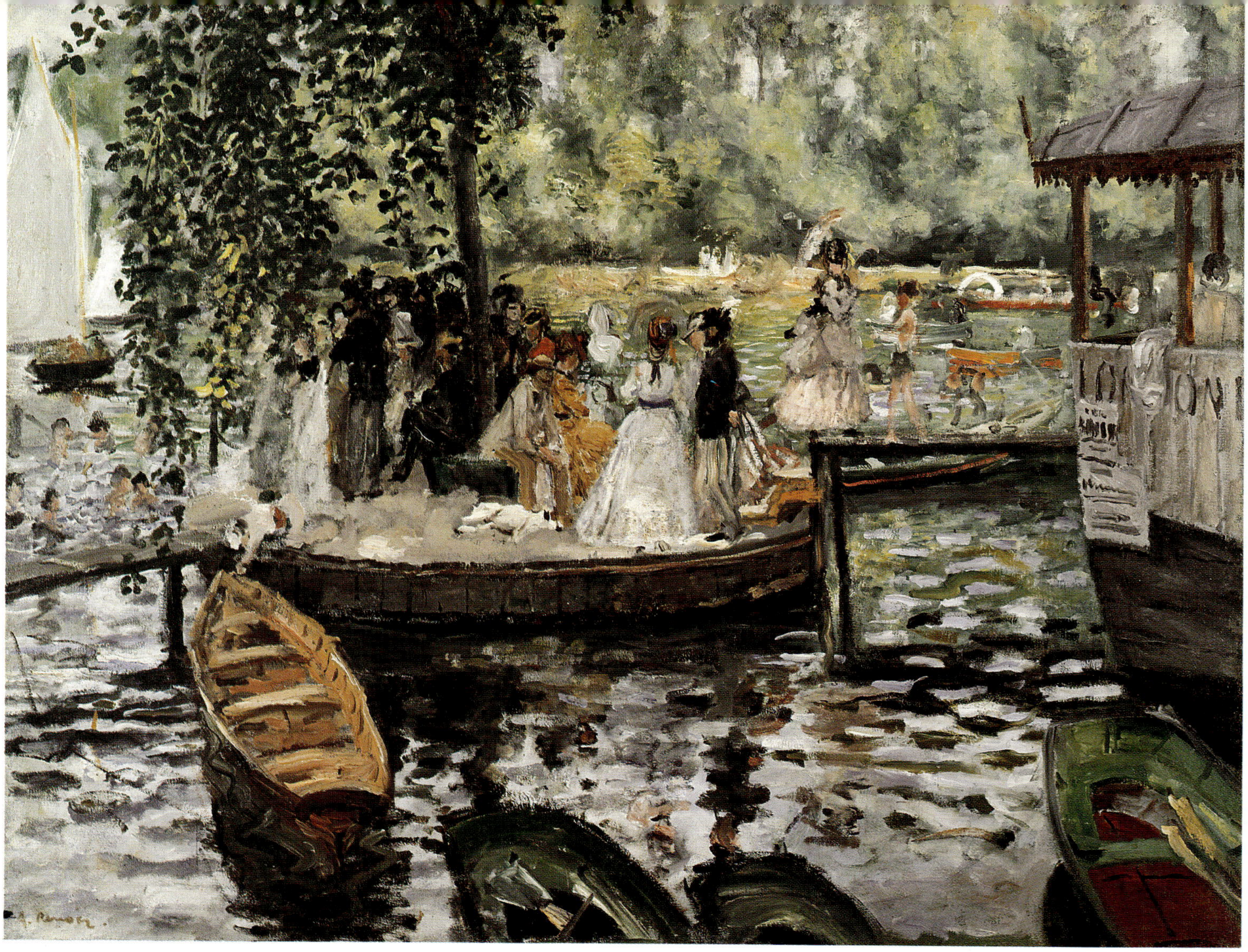

38

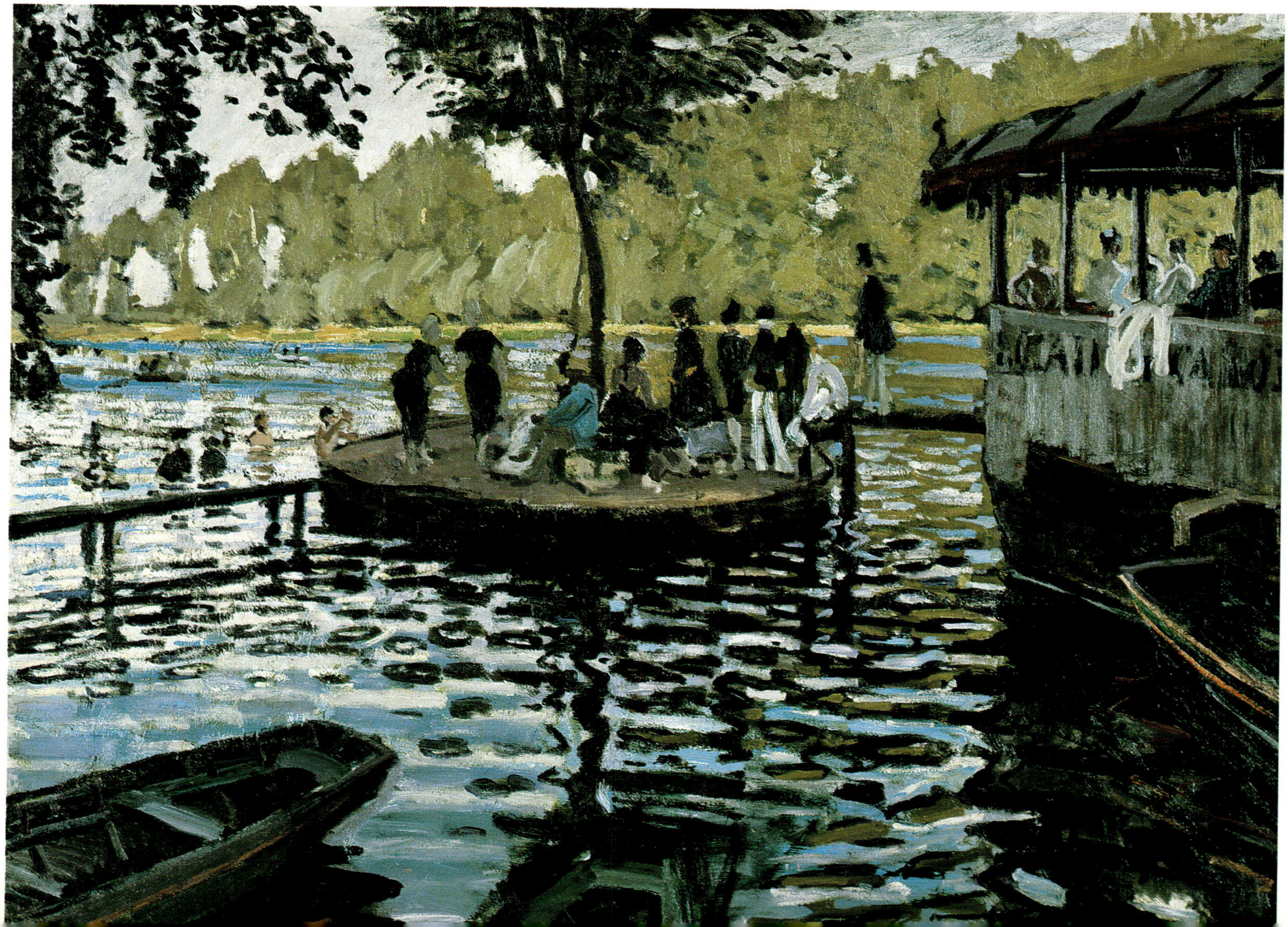

39

→ 40

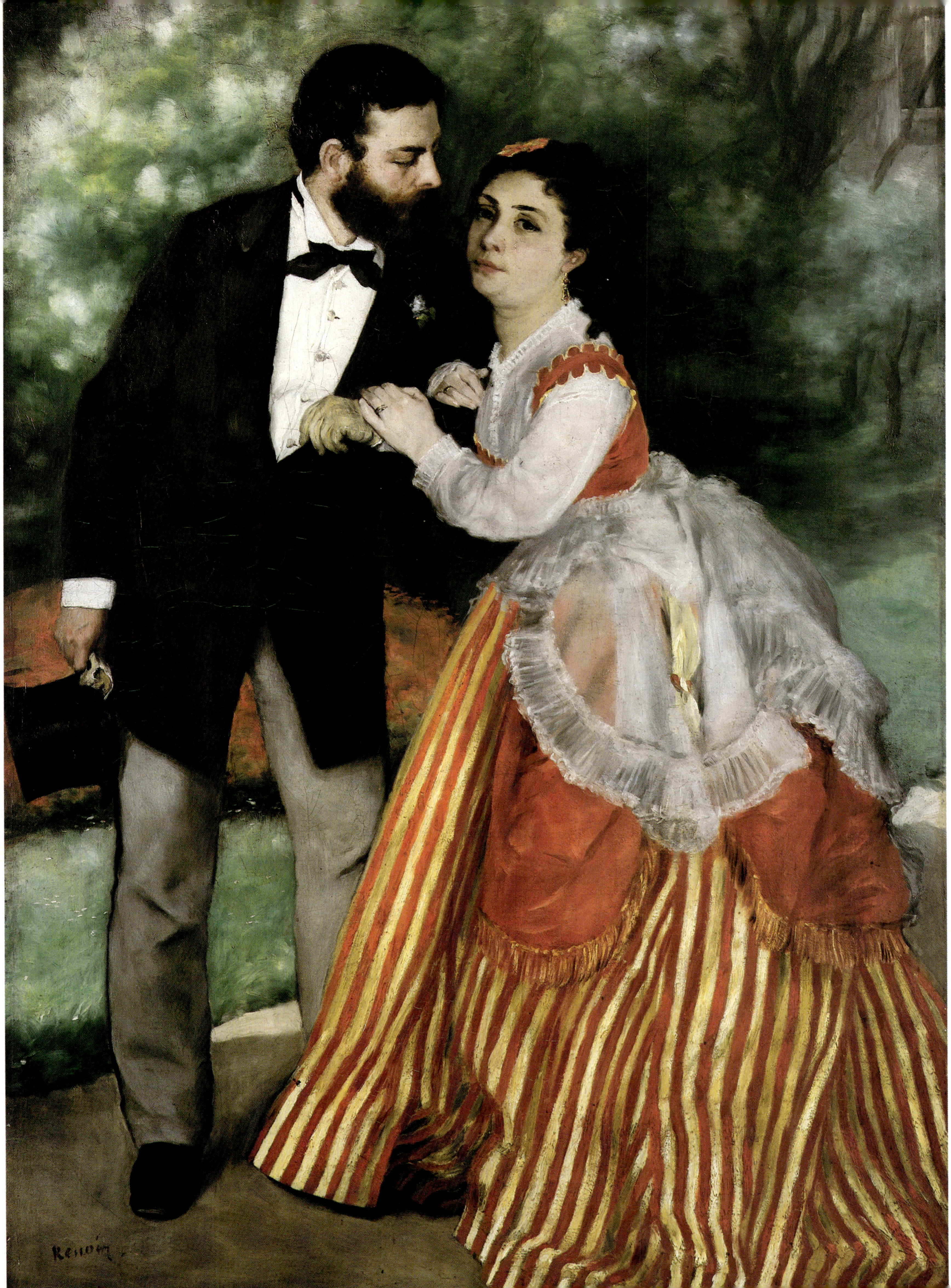
Renoir

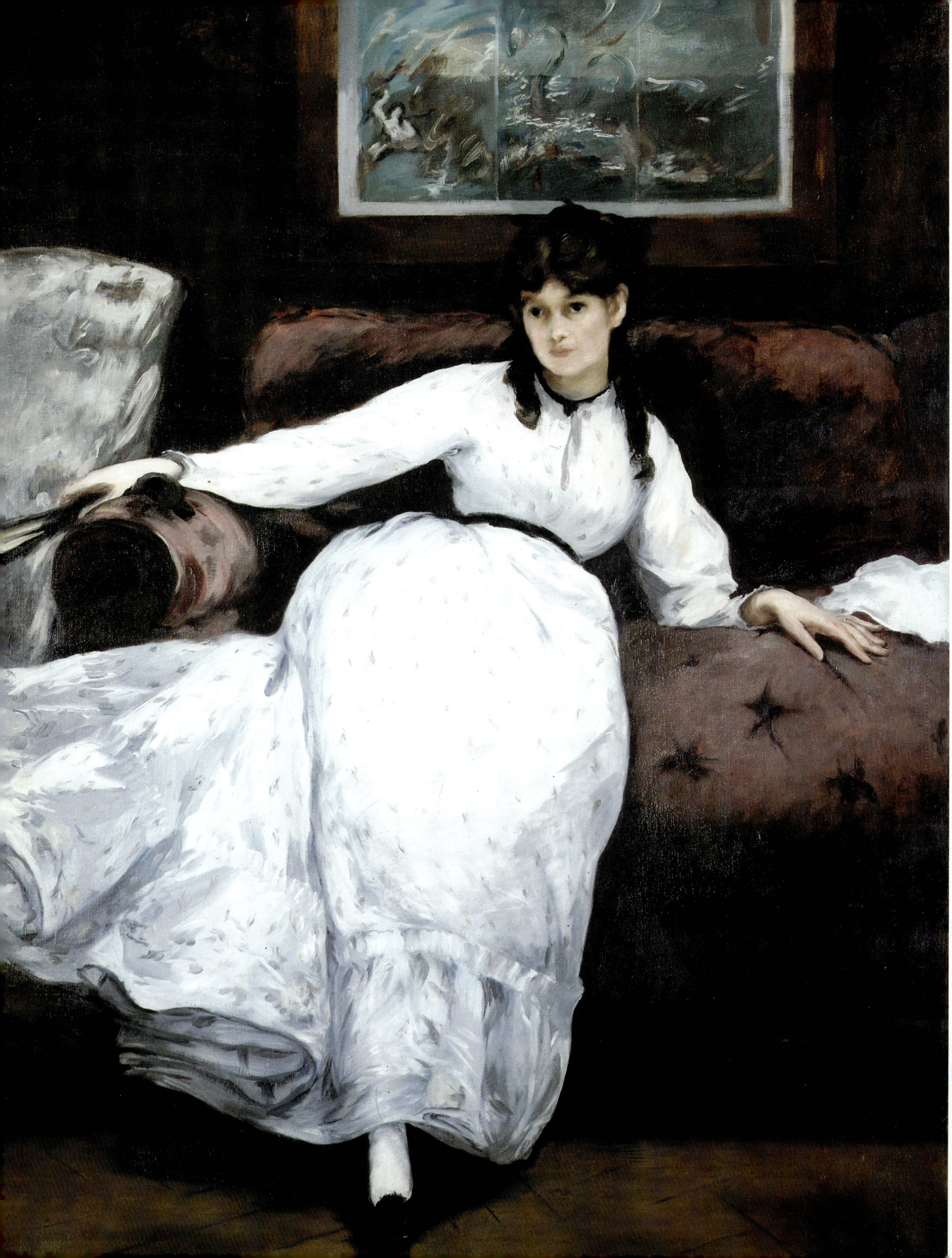

41

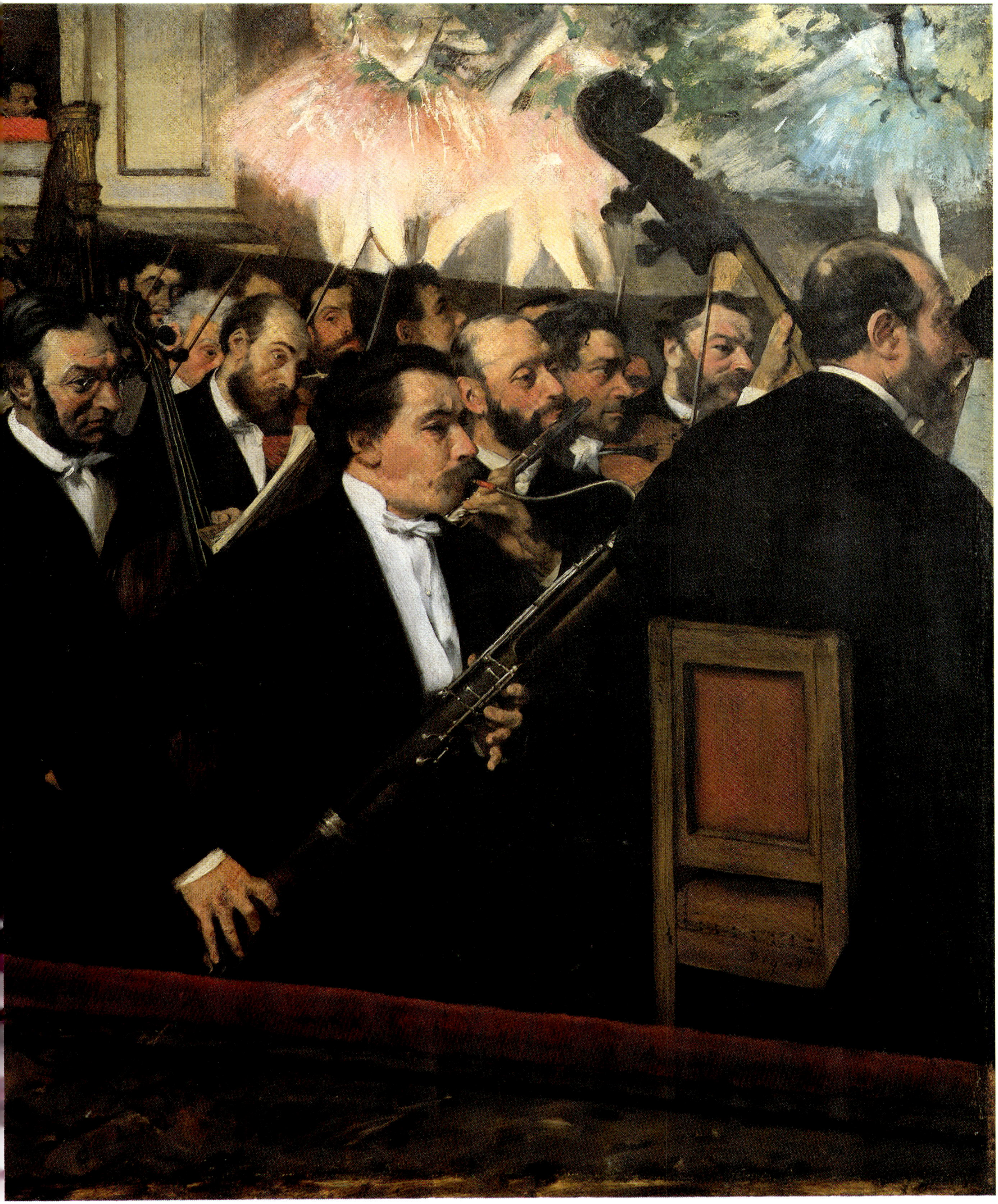

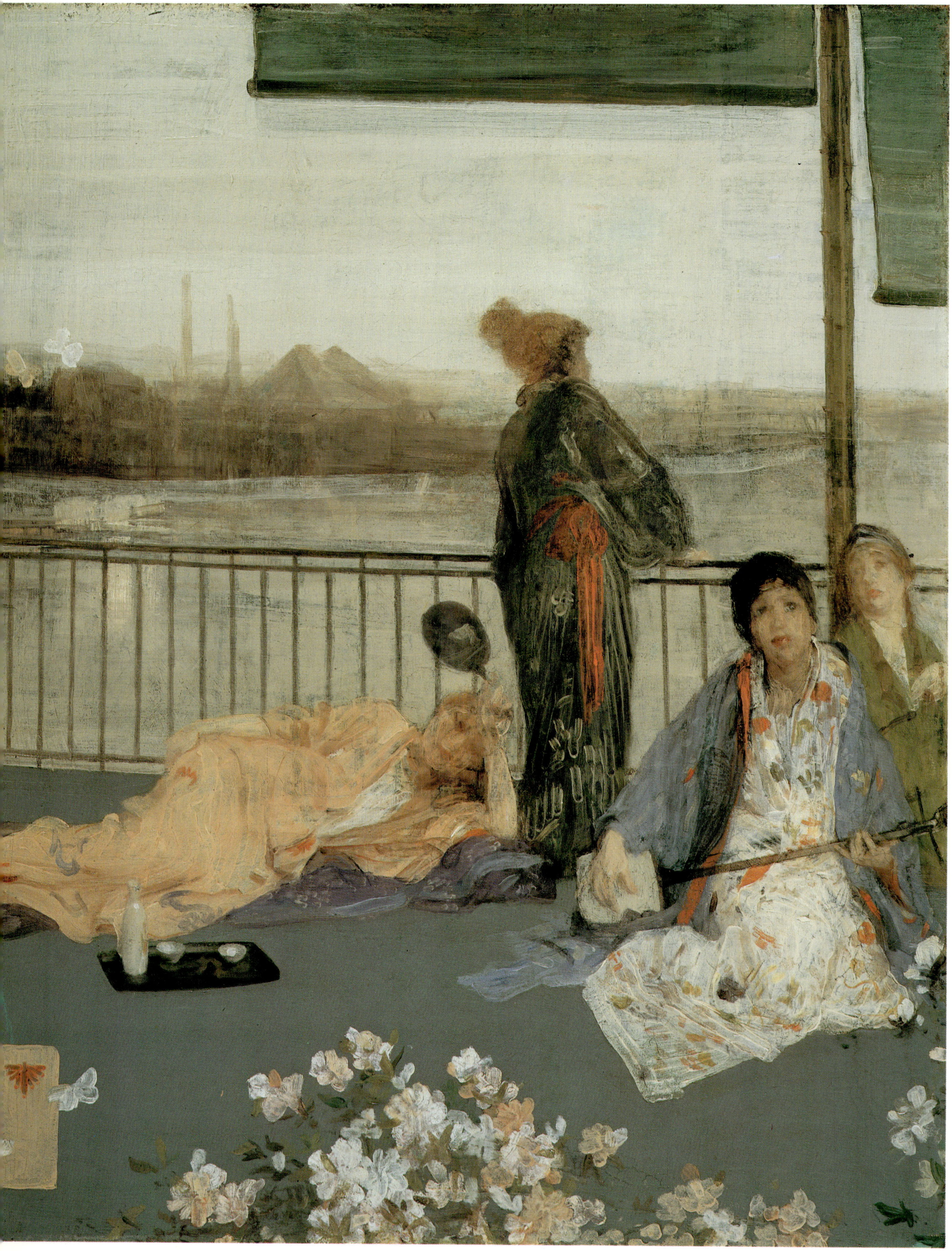

35 Claude Monet
The Picnic
1865
Oil on canvas, 130 x 181 cm
Pushkin Museum, Moscow

36 Eugène Boudin
Bathers on Trouville Beach
1869
Oil on canvas, 31 x 48 cm
Musée d'Orsay, Paris

37 Claude Monet
The Terrace at Saint-Adresse
1867
Oil on canvas, 98 x 130 cm
Metropolitan Museum of Art, New York

38 Pierre-Auguste Renoir
La Grenouillère
1869
Oil on canvas, 66 x 86 cm
Nationalmuseum, Stockholm

39 Claude Monet
La Grenouillère
1869
Oil on canvas, 74.6 x 99.7 cm
Metropolitan Museum of Art (H. O. Havemeyer Collection), New York

40 Auguste Renoir
The Engaged Couple (wrongly titled *Mr. and Mrs. Sisley*)
c. 1868
Oil on canvas, 106 x 74 cm
Wallraf-Richartz Museum, Cologne

41 Édouard Manet
Resting—Portrait of Berthe Morisot
1870
Oil on canvas, 148 x 113 cm
Museum of Art, Rhode Island School of Design, Providence

42 Edgar Degas
Orchestra of the Paris Opera
c. 1870
Oil on canvas, 56.5 x 46.2 cm
Musée d'Orsay, Paris

43 James McNeill Whistler
The Balcony, Variations in Flesh Color and Green
1865
Oil on canvas, 61.4 x 48.8 cm
Freer Gallery of Art, Washington, D.C.

44 Henri Regnault
Summary Execution under the Moorish Kings of Granada
1870
Oil on canvas, 302 x 146 cm
Musée d'Orsay, Paris

45 Henri Fantin-Latour
Corner of the Table
1873
Oil on canvas, 97.2 x 125 cm
Art Institute of Chicago, Chicago

46 Adolf von Menzel
The Studio Wall
1872
Oil on canvas, 111 x 79.3 cm
Kunsthalle, Hamburg

47 Camille Corot
The Woman in Blue
1874
Oil on canvas, 80 x 50 cm
Louvre, Paris

48 Camille Pissarro
Self-Portrait
1873
Oil on canvas, 56 x 46.7 cm
Musée d'Orsay, Paris

49 Hans Thoma
The Plain of the Main (detail)
1875
Oil on canvas, 85.5 x 124 cm
Neue Pinakothek, Munich

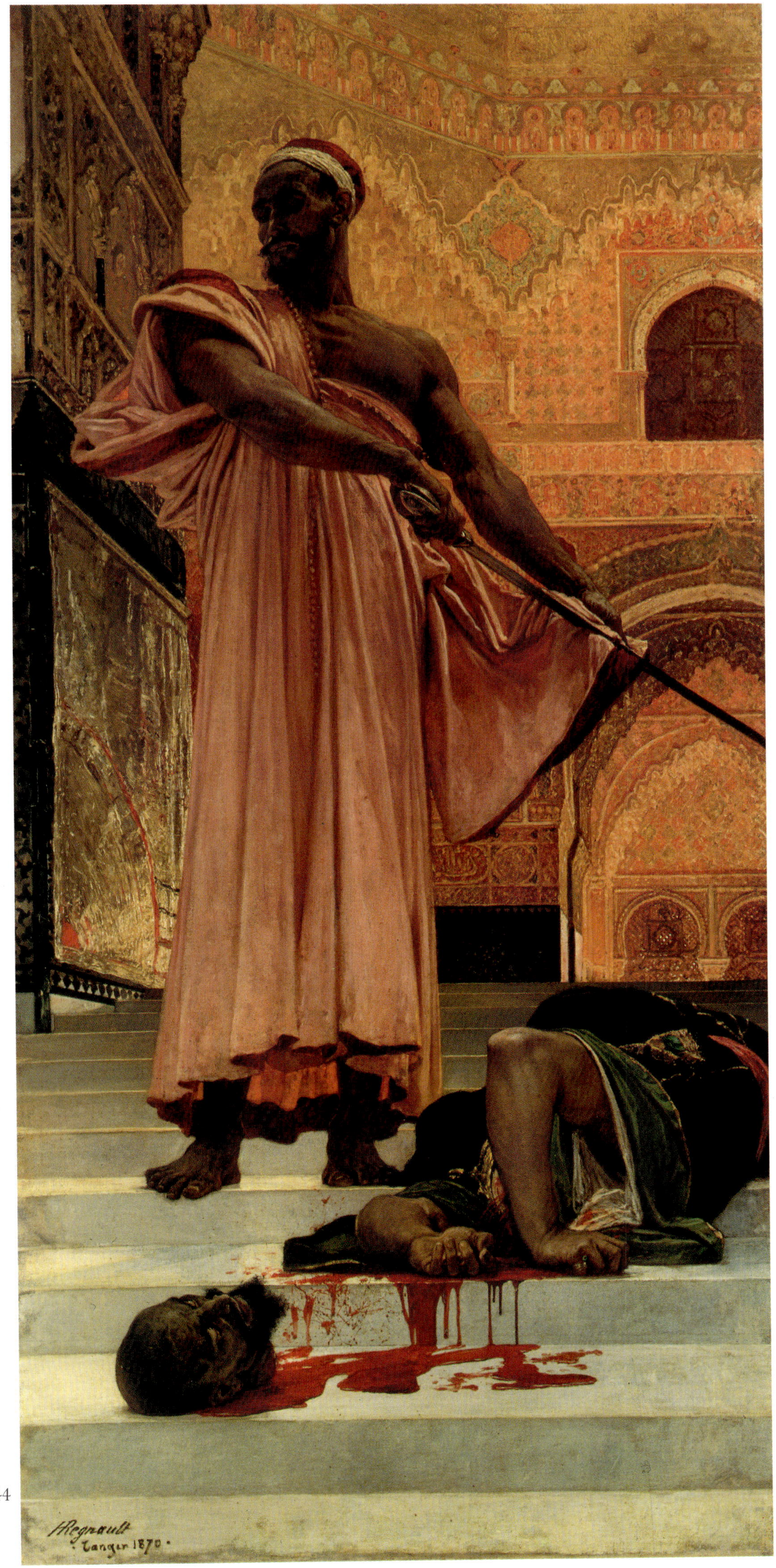
HRegnault
Tanger 1870

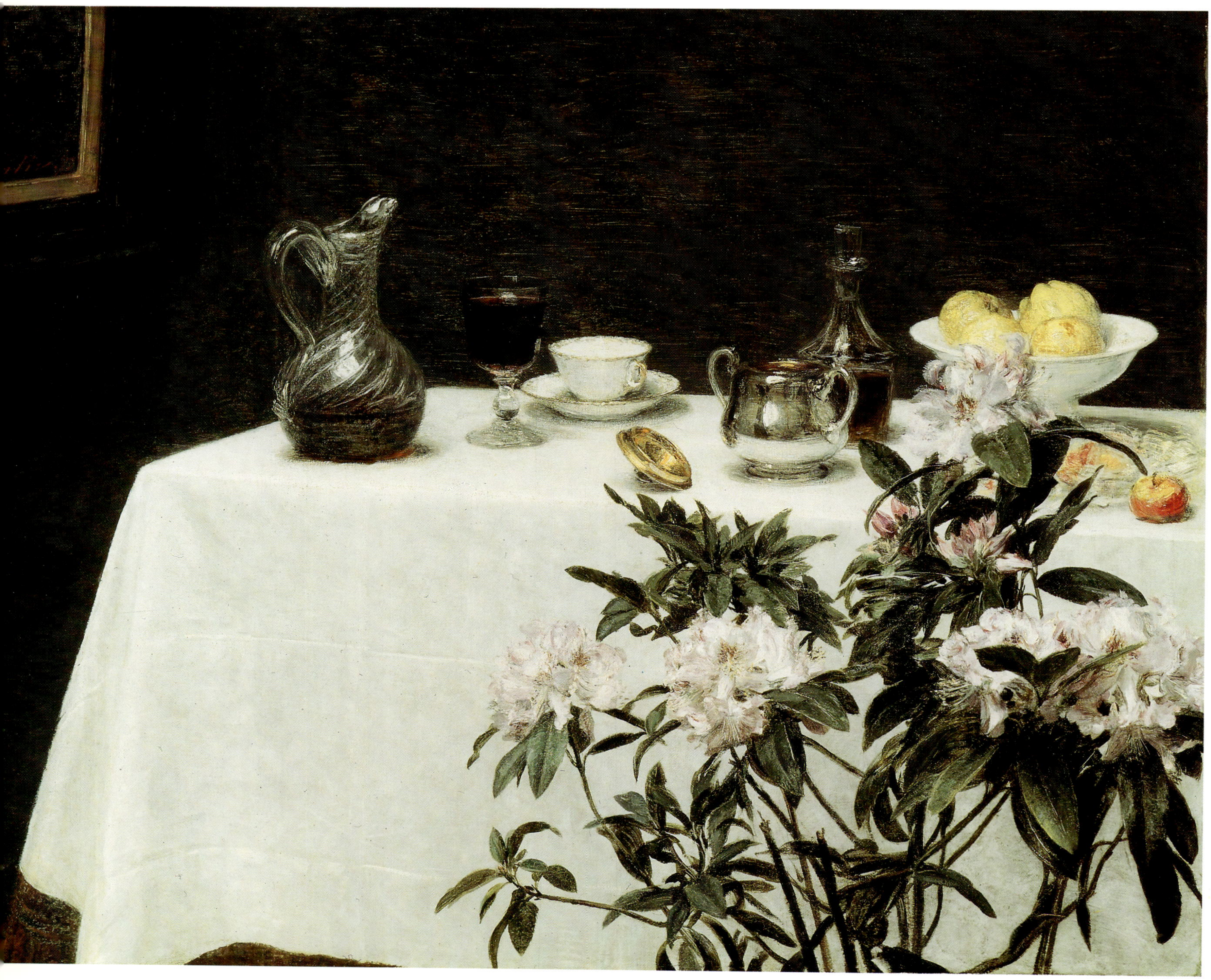

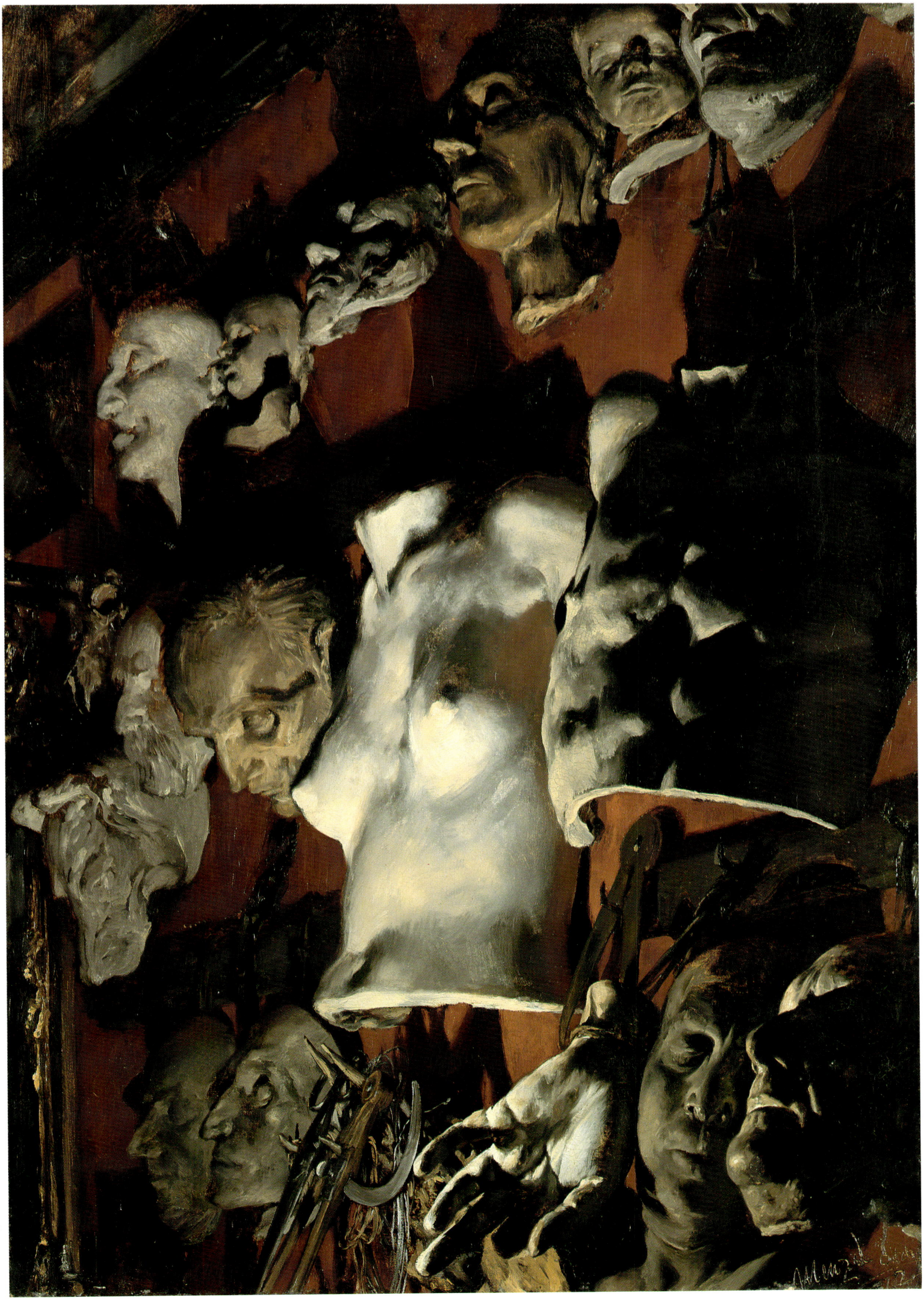

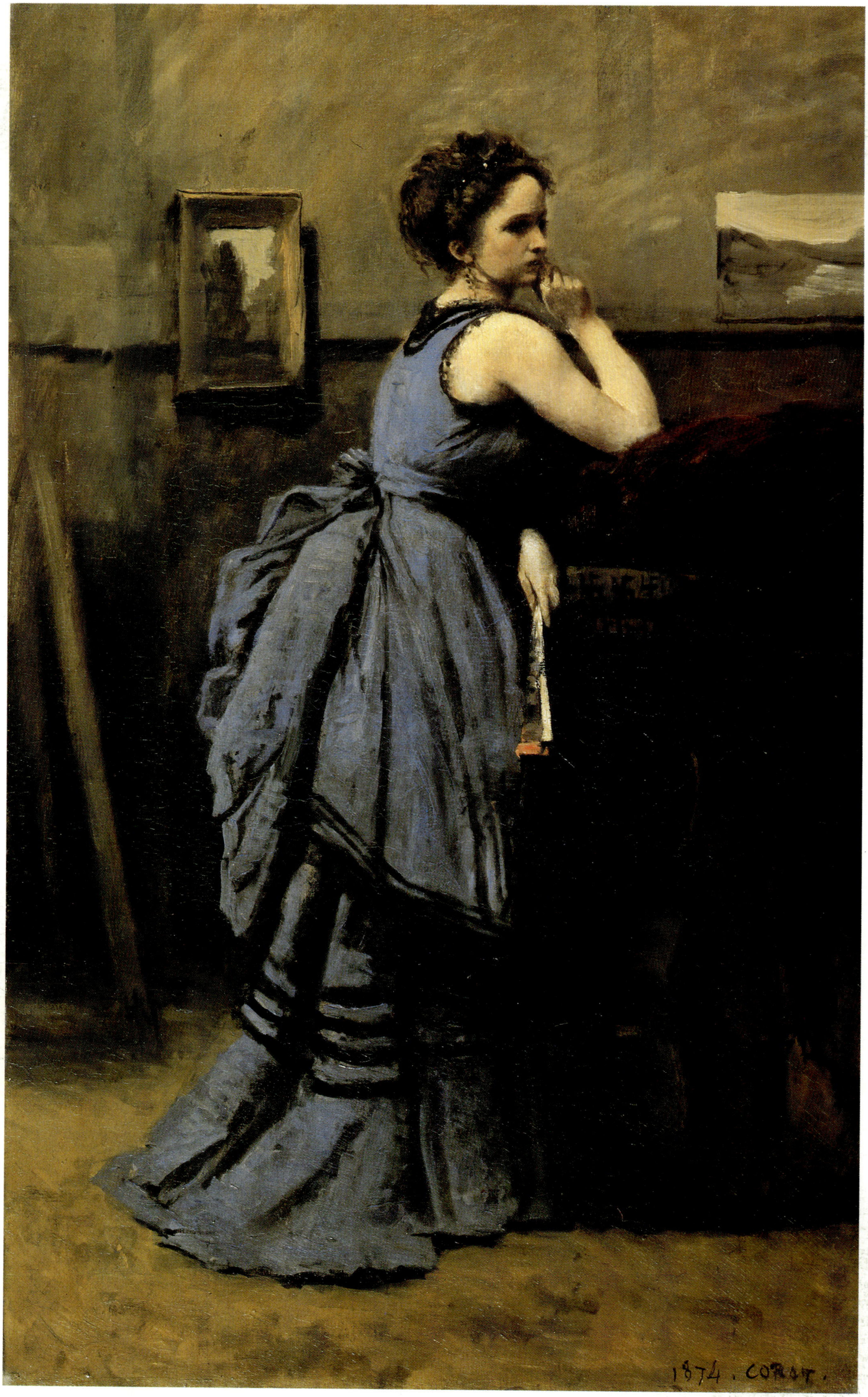

47

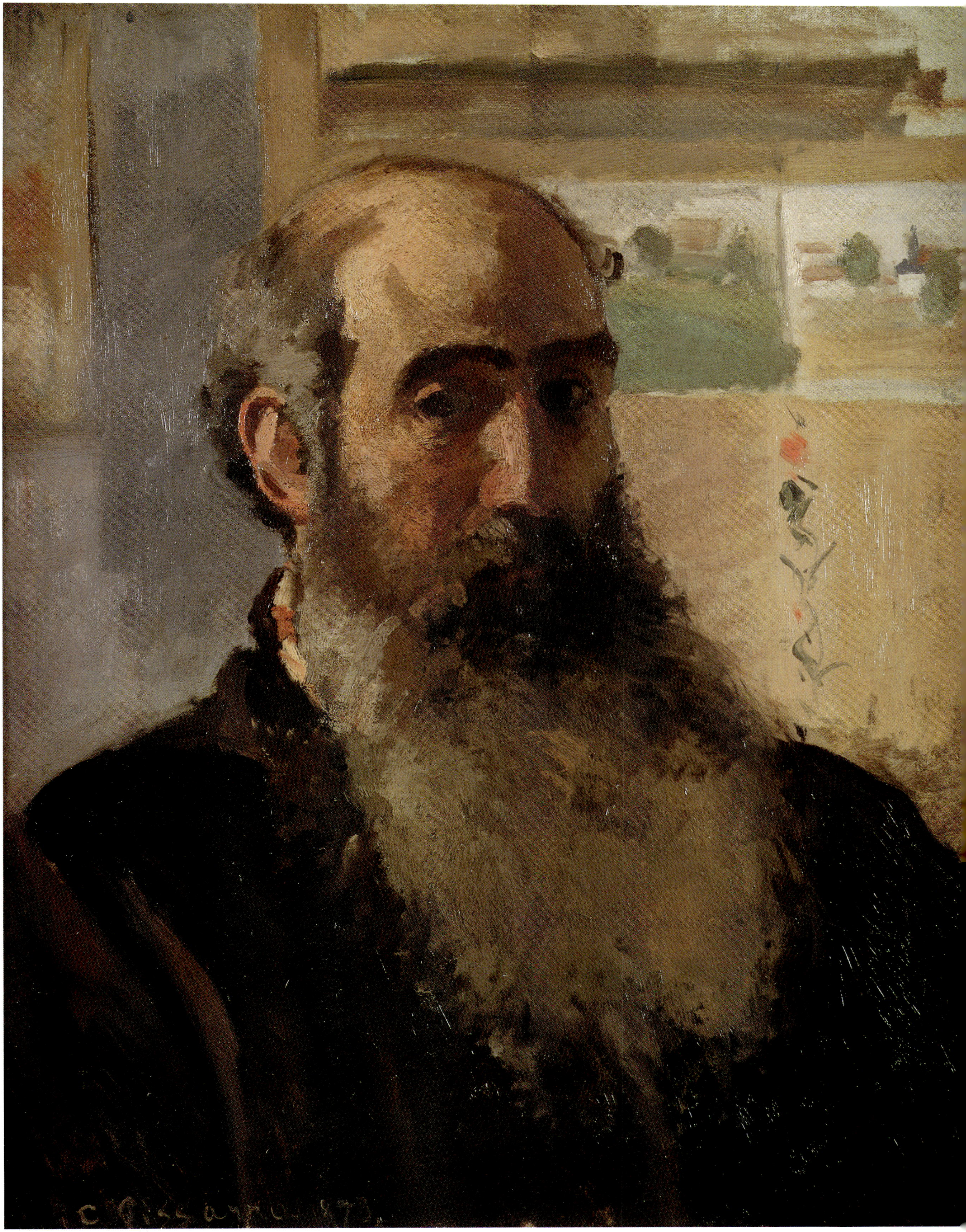
C. Pissarro. 1873.

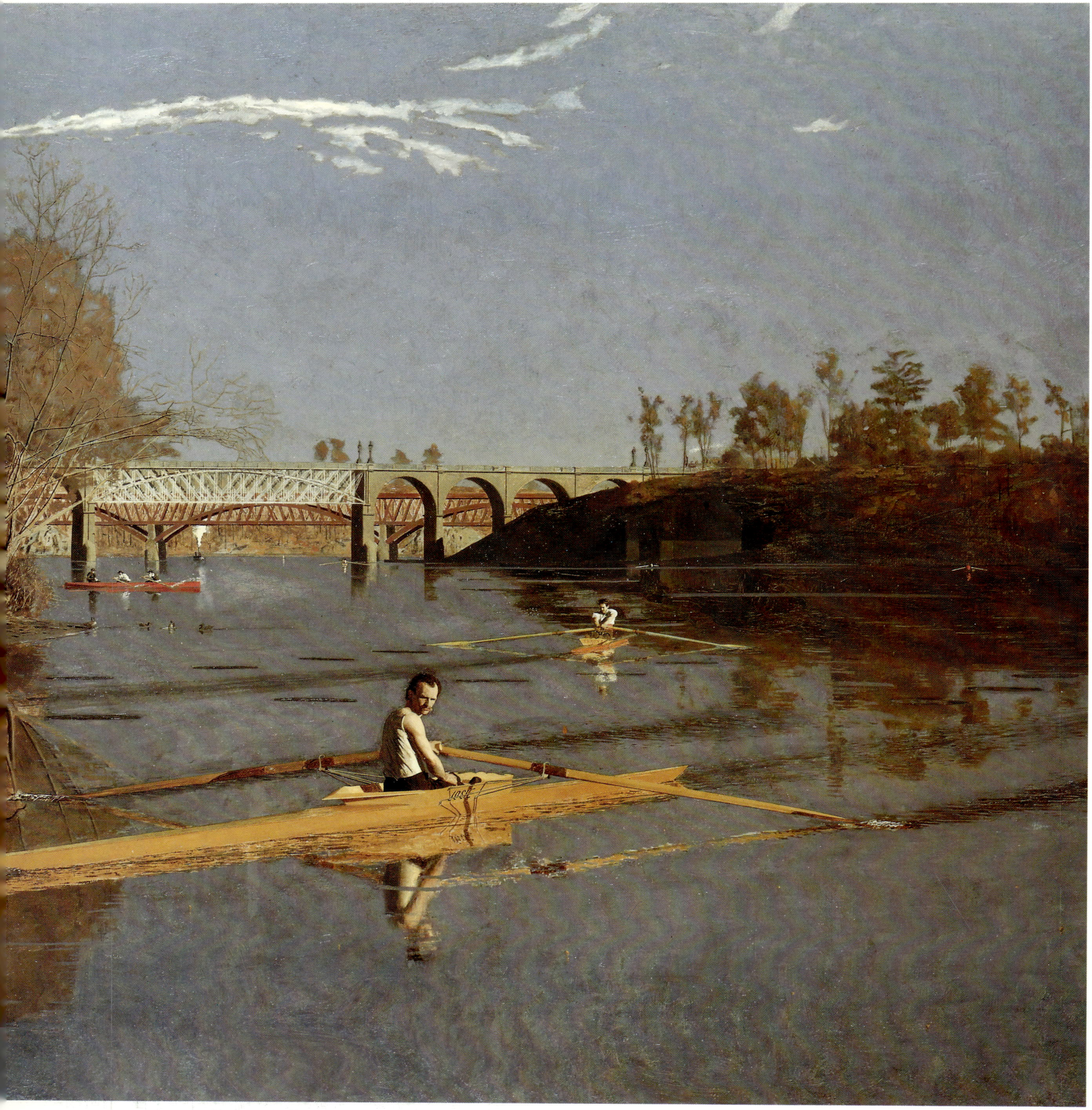

→ 52

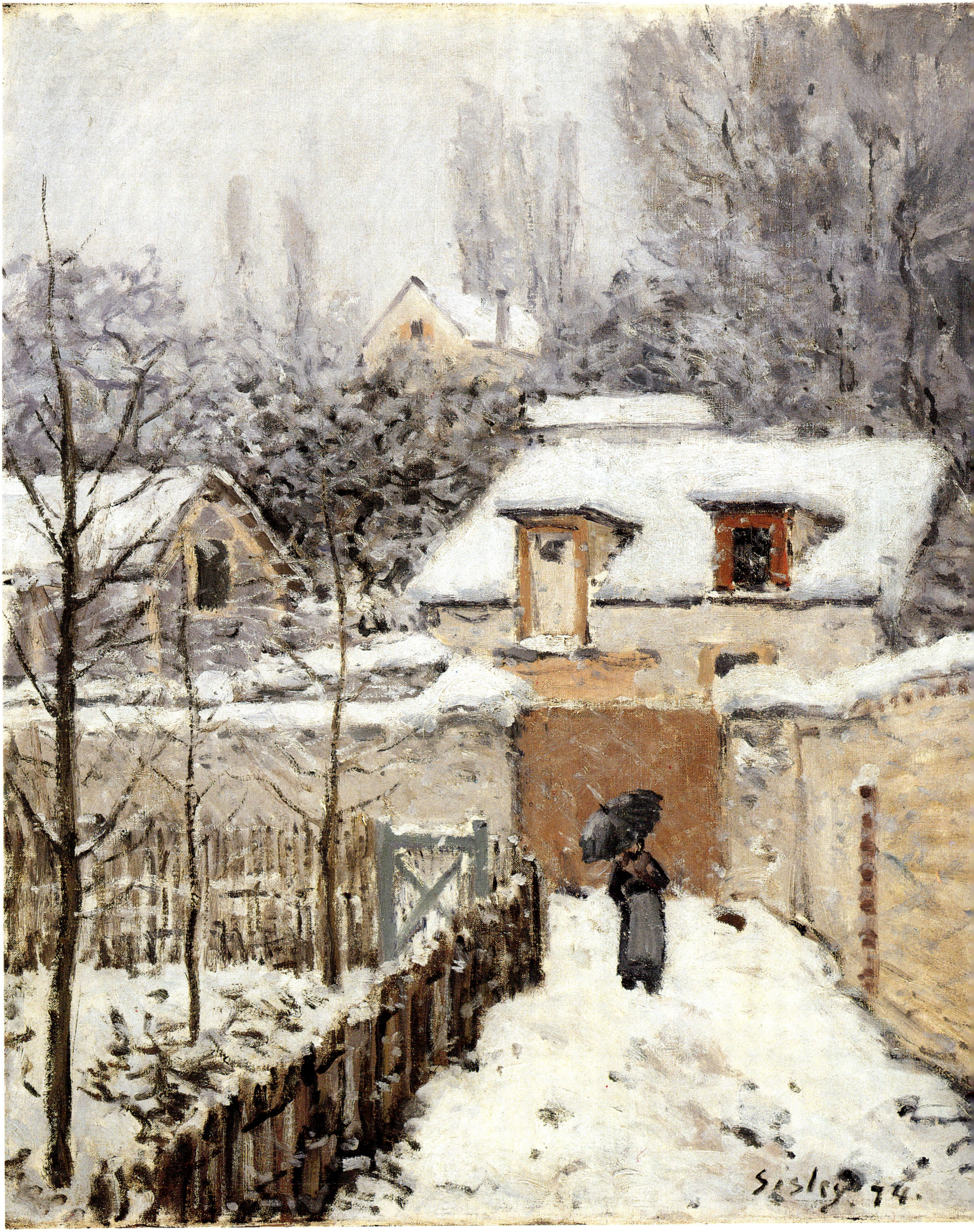
Sisley. 74.

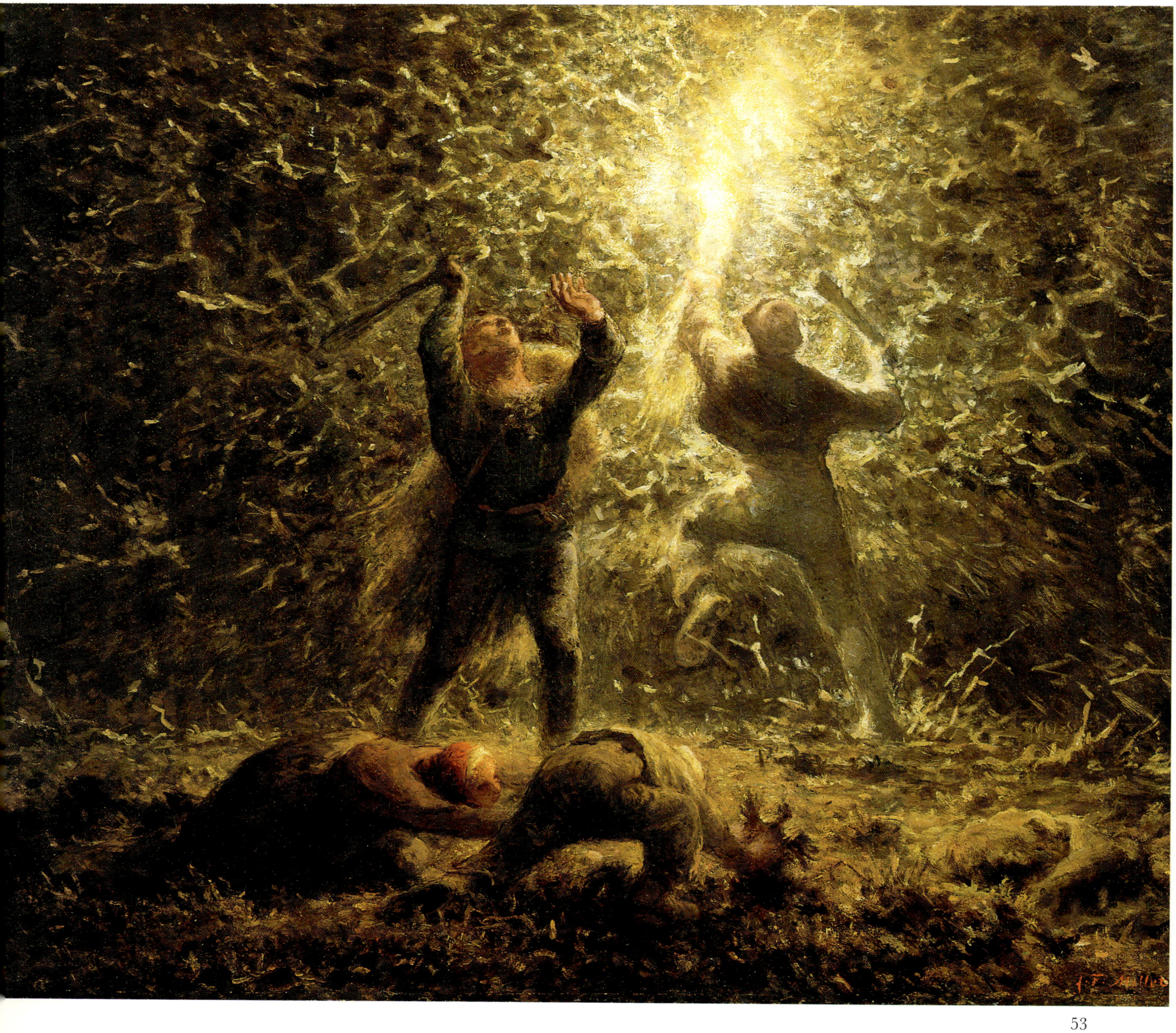

53

→ 54

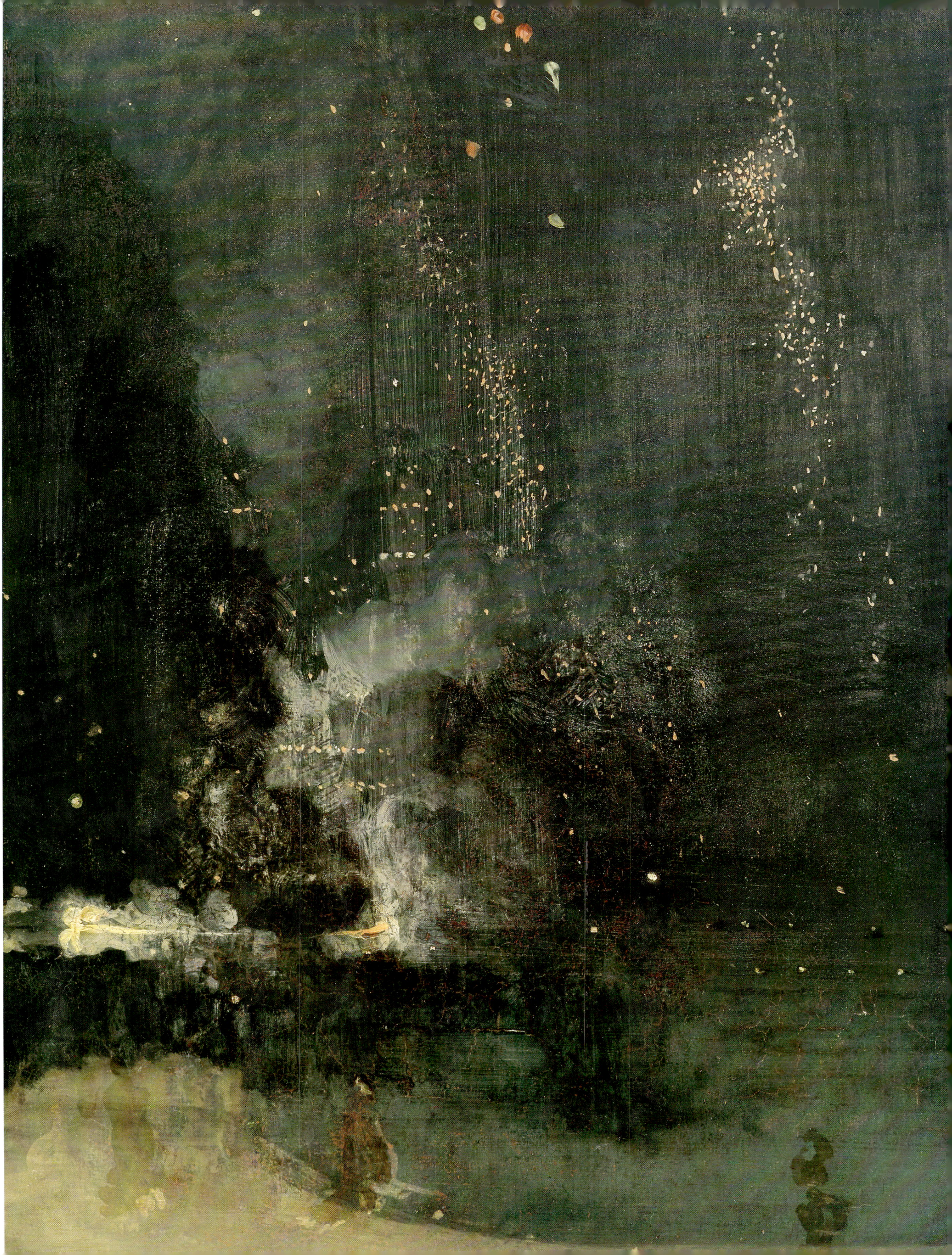

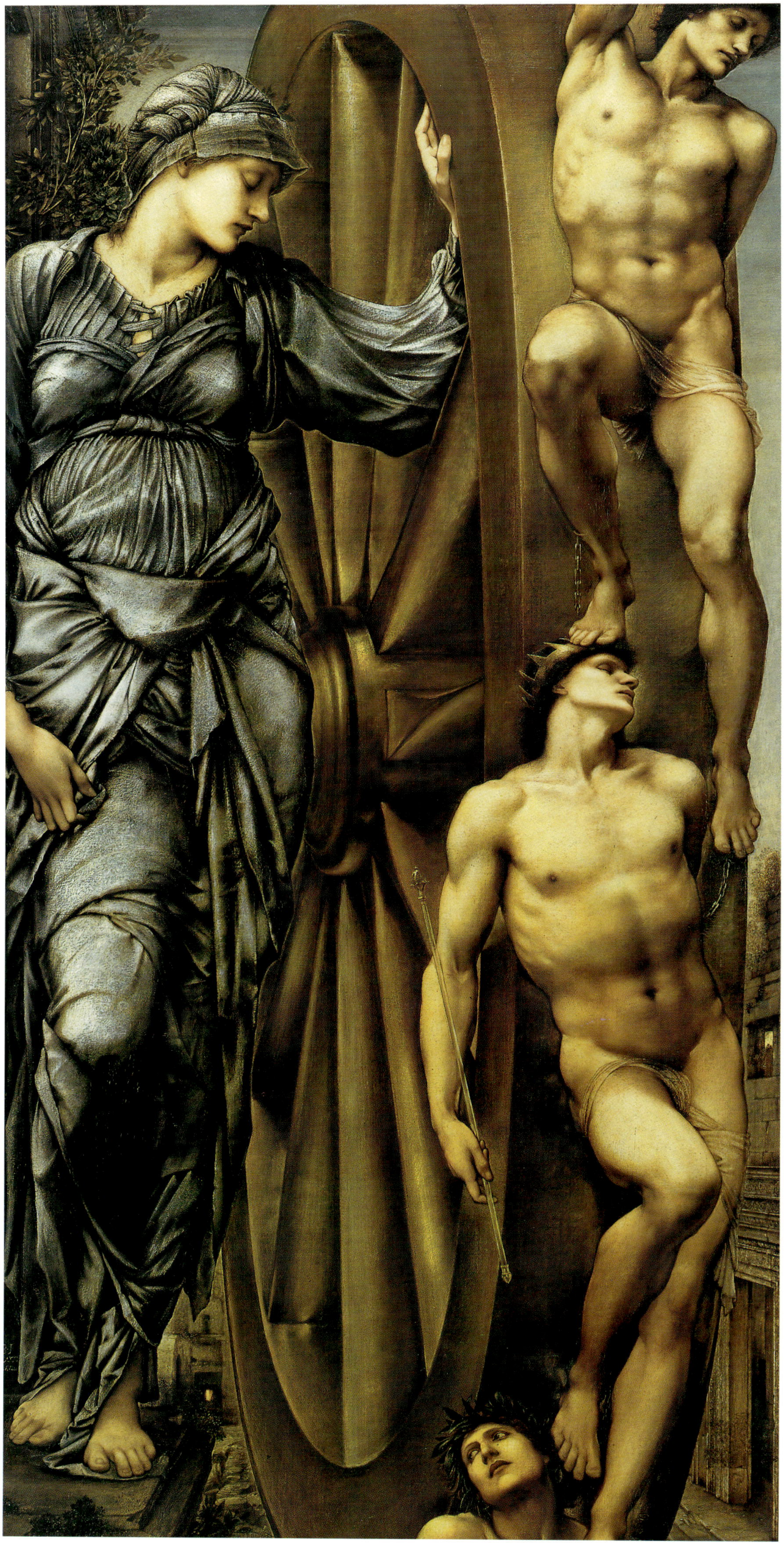

55

50 Claude Monet
Impression, Sunrise
1872
Oil on canvas, 48 x 63 cm
Musée Marmottan, Paris

51 Thomas Eakins
Max Schmitt in a Single Scull (detail)
1871
Oil on canvas, overall dimensions 81.9 x 117.5 cm
Metropolitan Museum of Art, New York

52 Alfred Sisley
Garden at Louveciennes, Snow Effect
1874
Oil on canvas, 65 x 46 cm
Phillips Collection, Washington, D.C.

53 Jean-François Millet
Hunting Birds at Night
1874
Oil on canvas, 73.5 x 92.5 cm
Philadelphia Museum (William L. Elkins Collection), Philadelphia

54 James McNeill Whistler
Nocturne in Black and Gold: The Falling Rocket
1875
Oil on canvas, 60.3 x 46.6 cm
Institute of Arts (Dexter M. Ferry Jr. Collection), Detroit

55 Edward Burne-Jones
The Wheel of Fortune
1875–83
Oil on canvas, 200 x 100 cm
Musée d'Orsay, Paris

56 Jean-Paul Laurens
St. John Chrysostom (detail)
1893 Salon
Oil on canvas, 127 x 160 cm
Musée des Augustins, Toulouse

57 Gustave Moreau
Salome Dancing
c. 1886
Watercolor on black lead with gouache and gold highlights, 33.6 x 21.3 cm
Louvre/Orsay (Graphic Arts Department), Paris

58 Arnold Böcklin
The Island of the Dead
1880
Oil on canvas, 111 x 155 cm
Kunstmuseum (Gottfried Keller Stiftung), Basel

59 Mary Cassatt
The Blue Room
1878
Oil on canvas, 89.5 x 129 cm
National Gallery of Art (Mr. and Mrs. Paul Mellon Collection), Washington, D.C.

60 Édouard Manet
Bar at the Folies-Bergère (detail)
1881–82
Oil on canvas, overall dimensions 96 x 130 cm
Courtauld Institute, London

61 Georges Seurat
Sunday Afternoon on the Island of La Grande Jatte
1884–86
Oil on canvas, 207 x 308 cm
Art Institute of Chicago (Helen Birch Bartlett Memorial Collection), Chicago

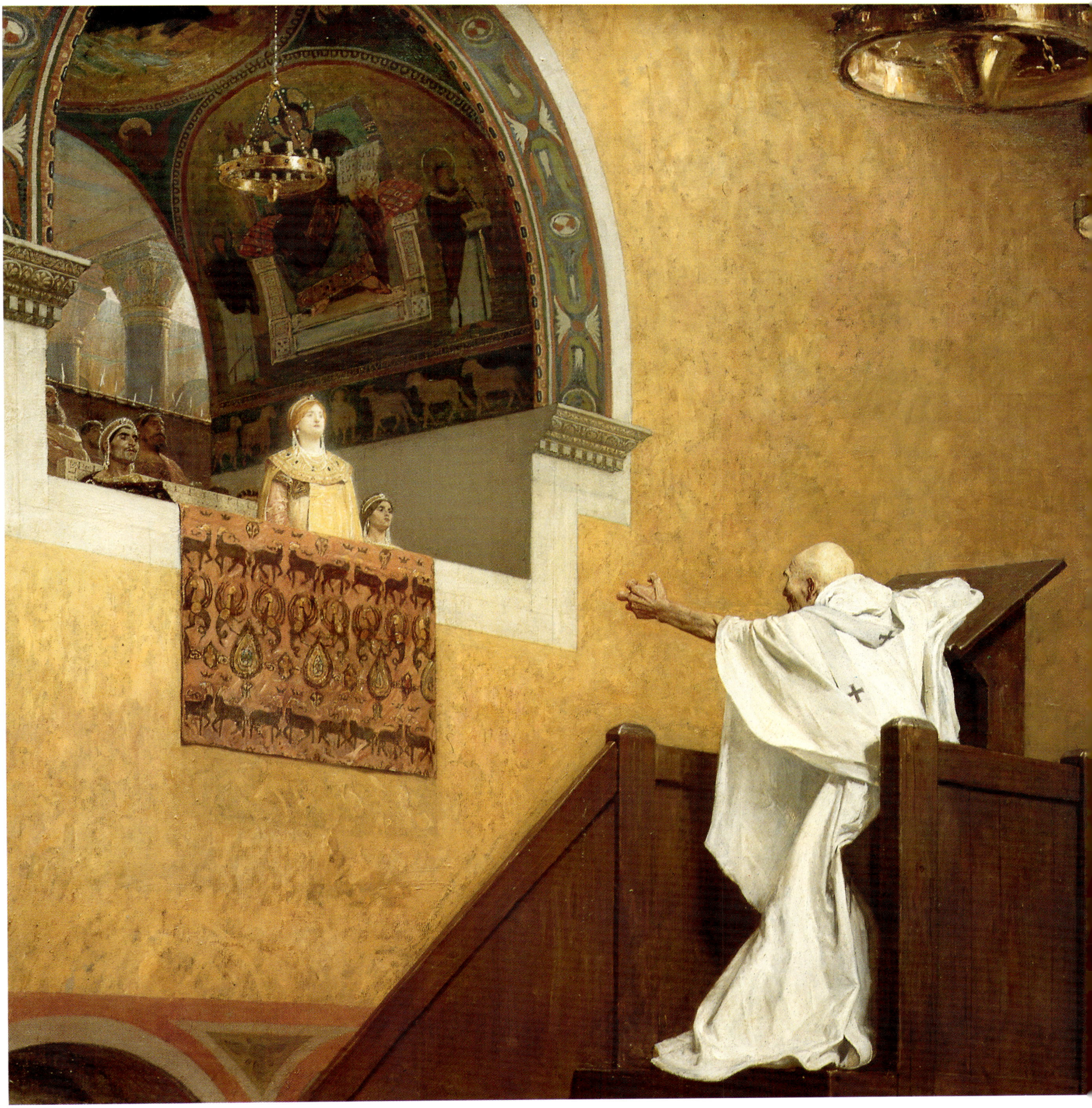

57

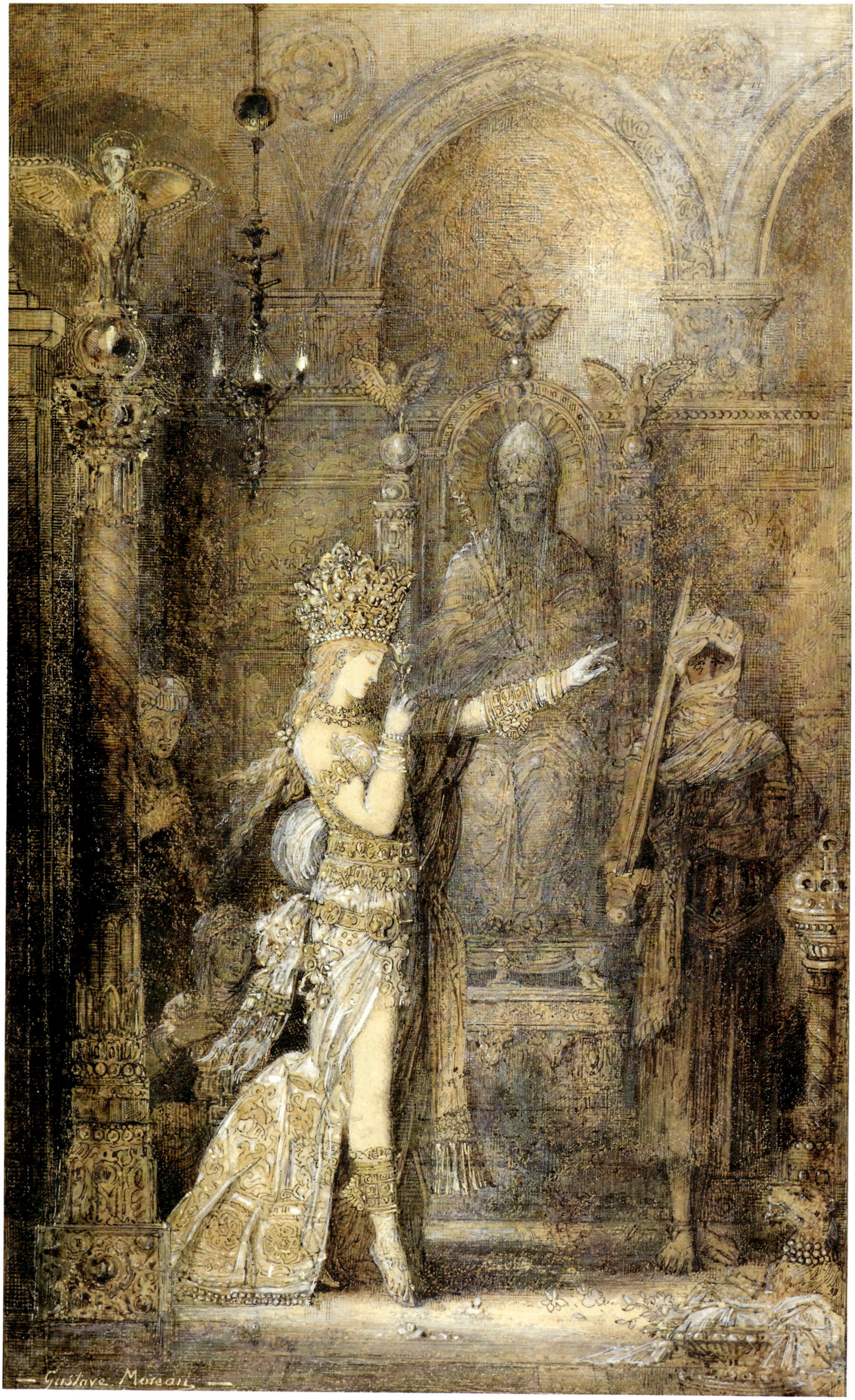

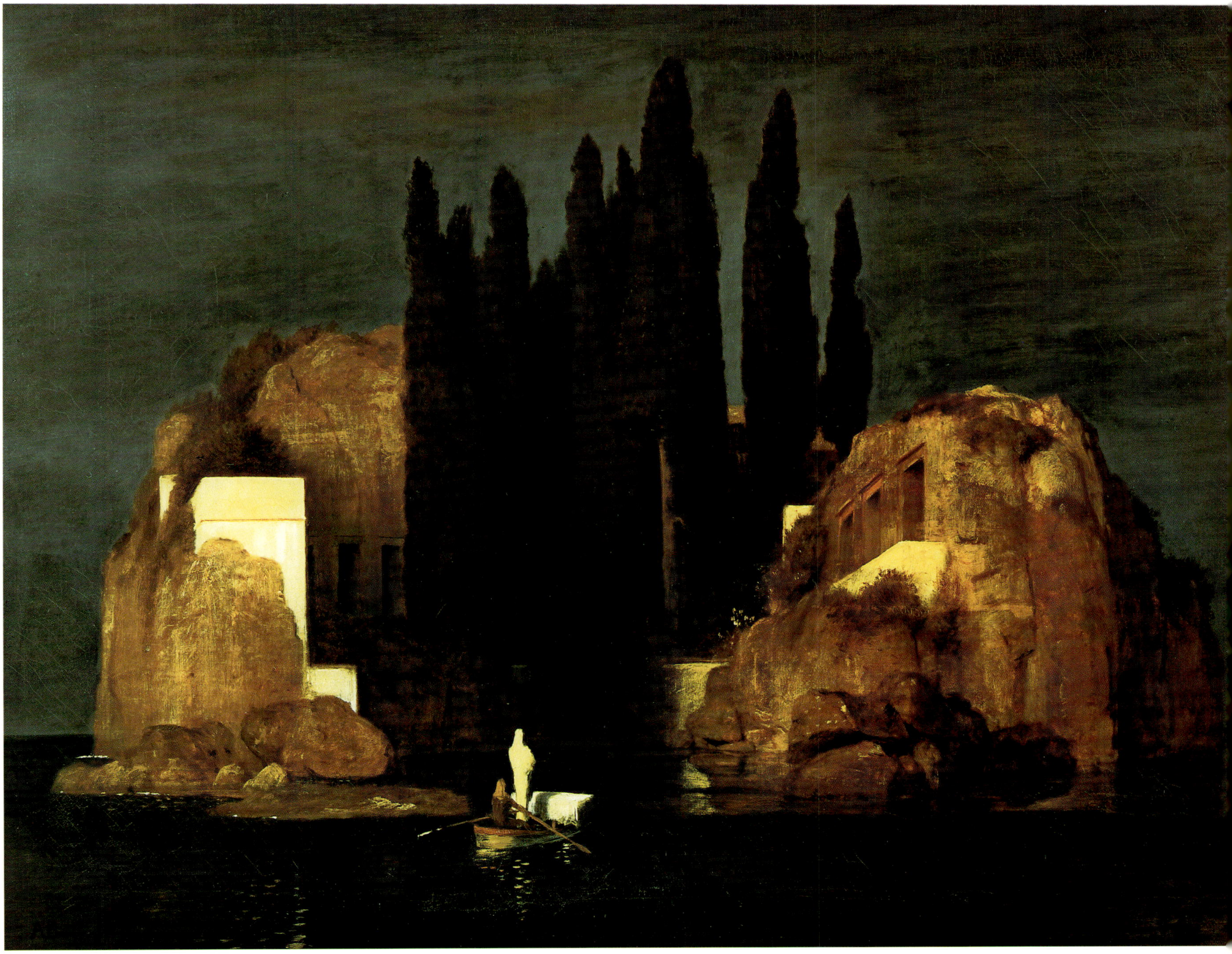

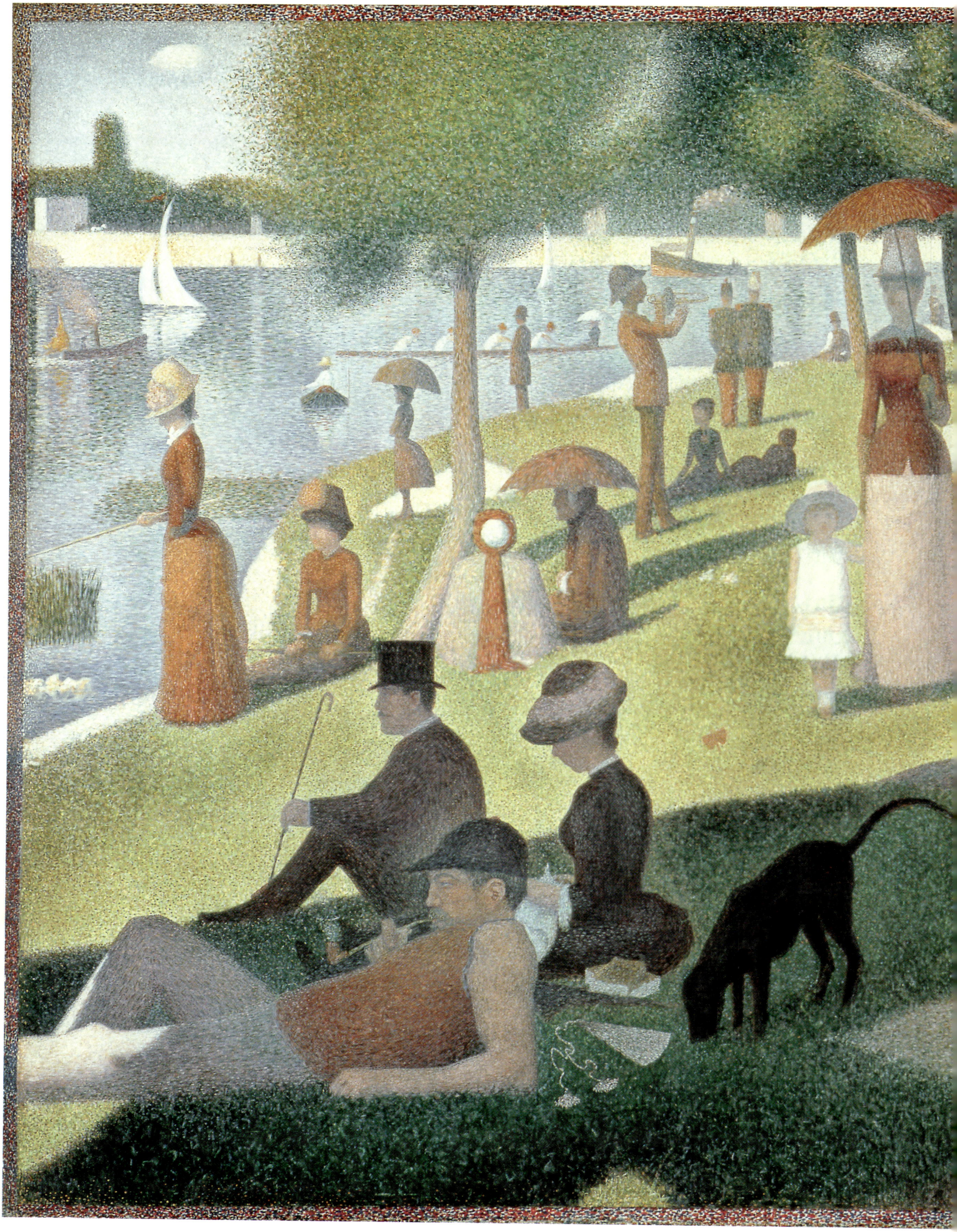

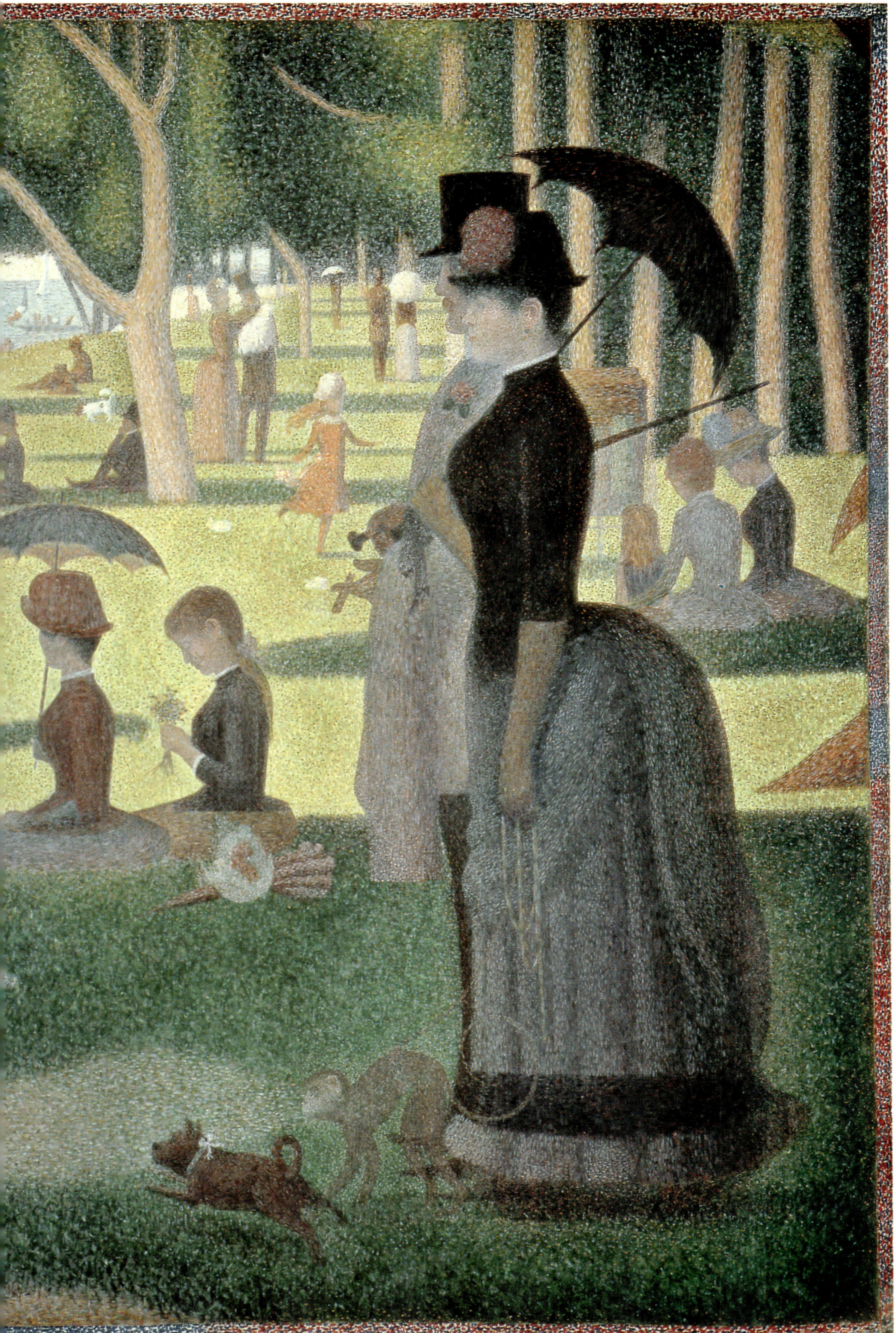

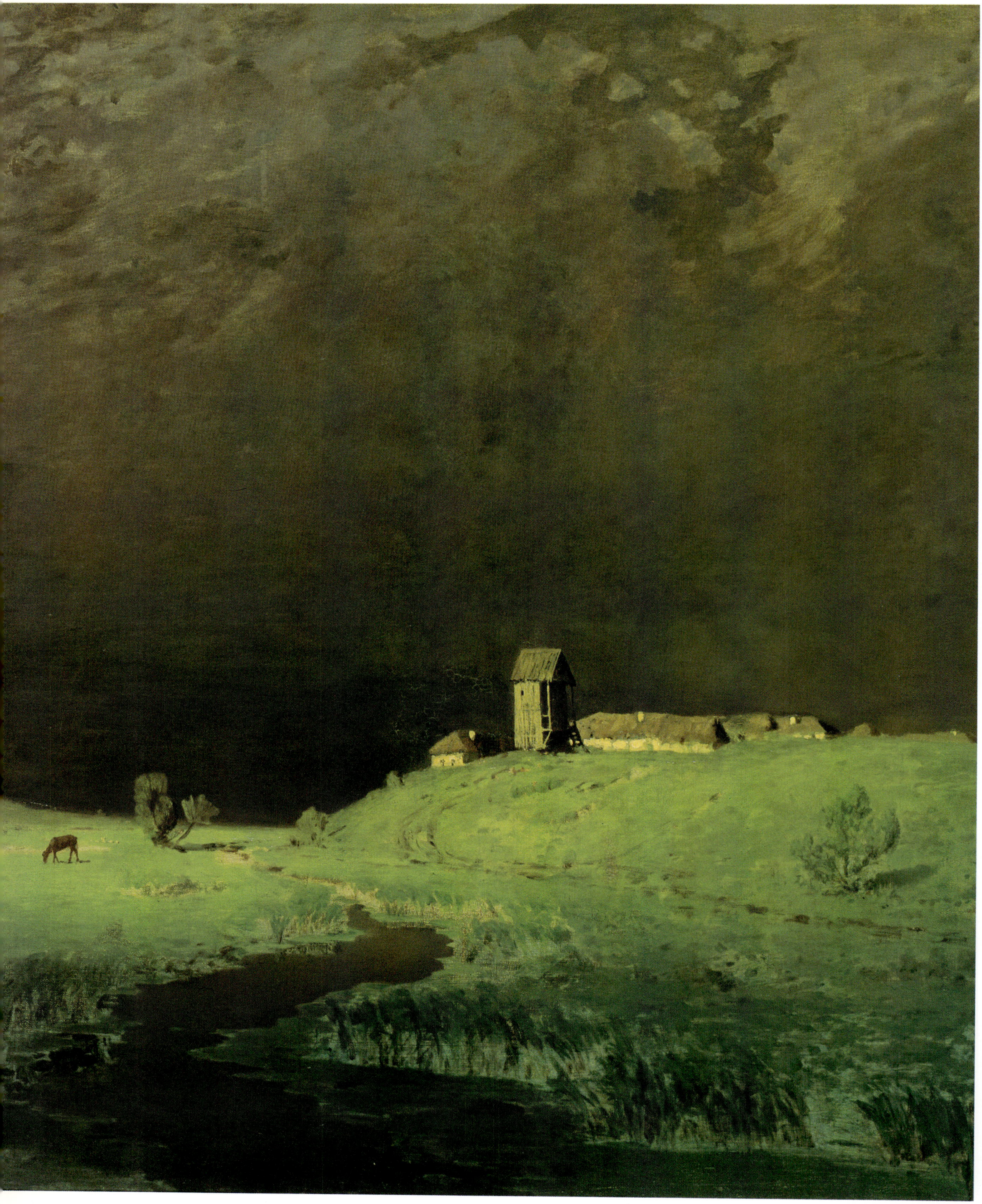

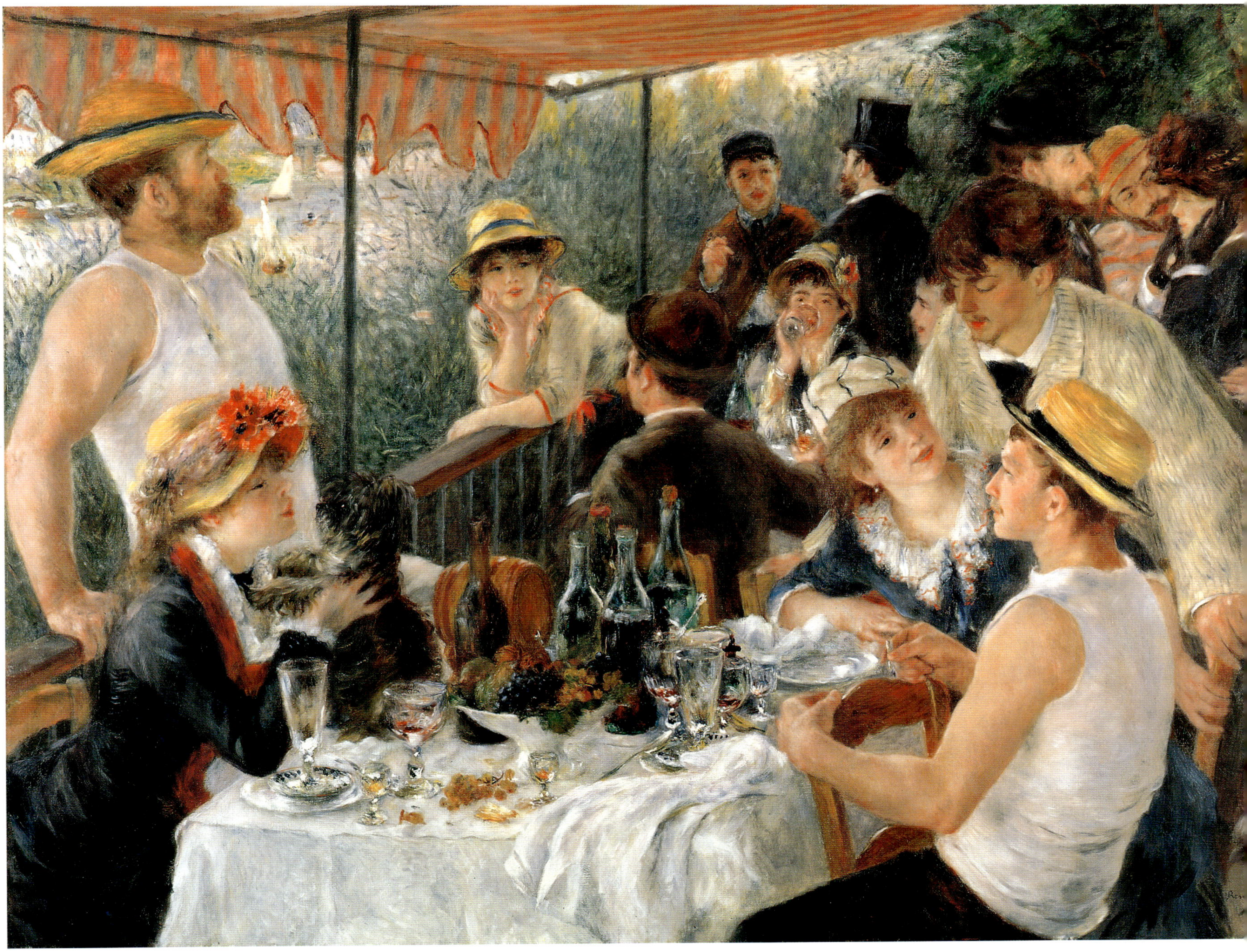

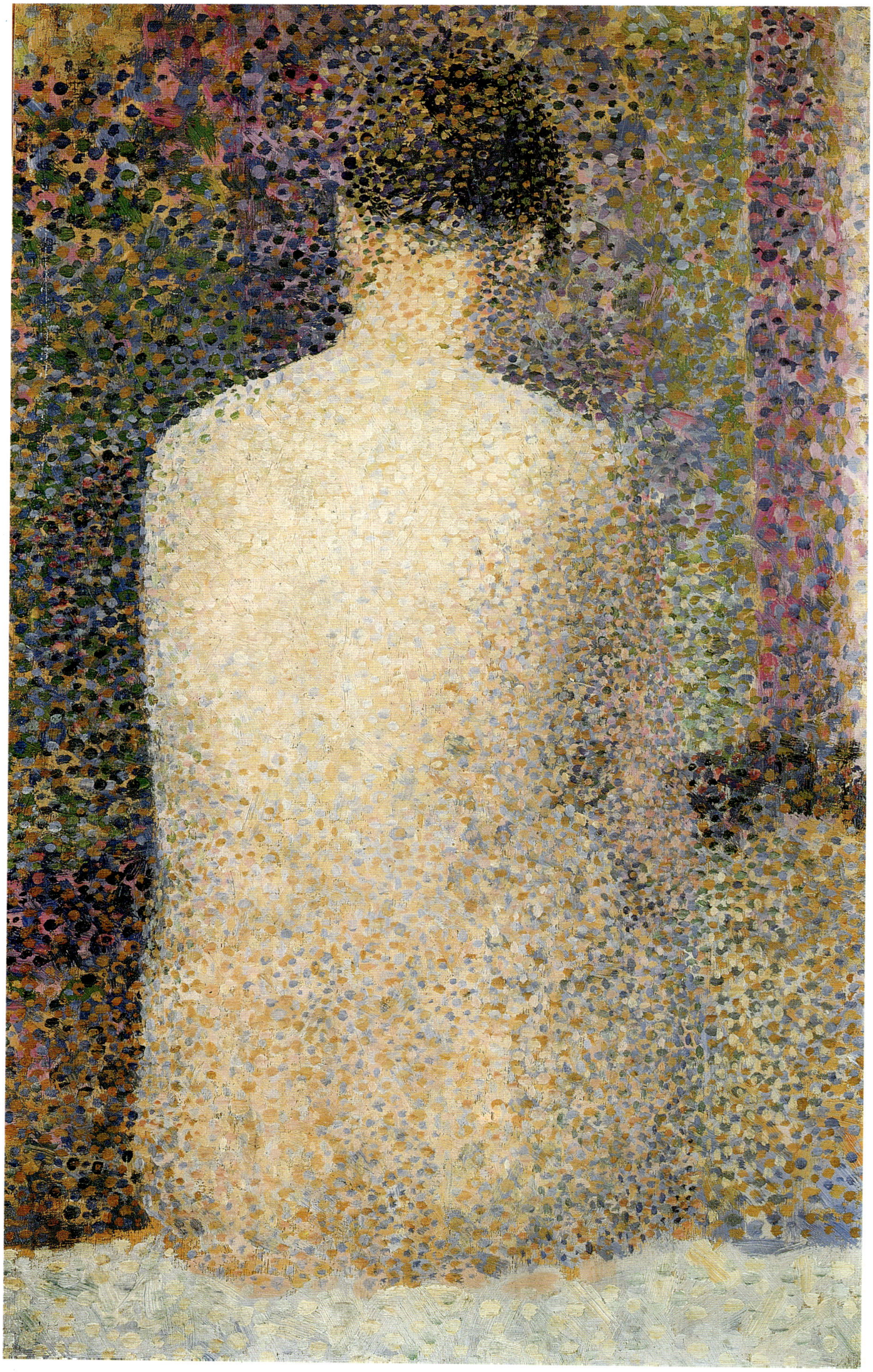

64

→ 65

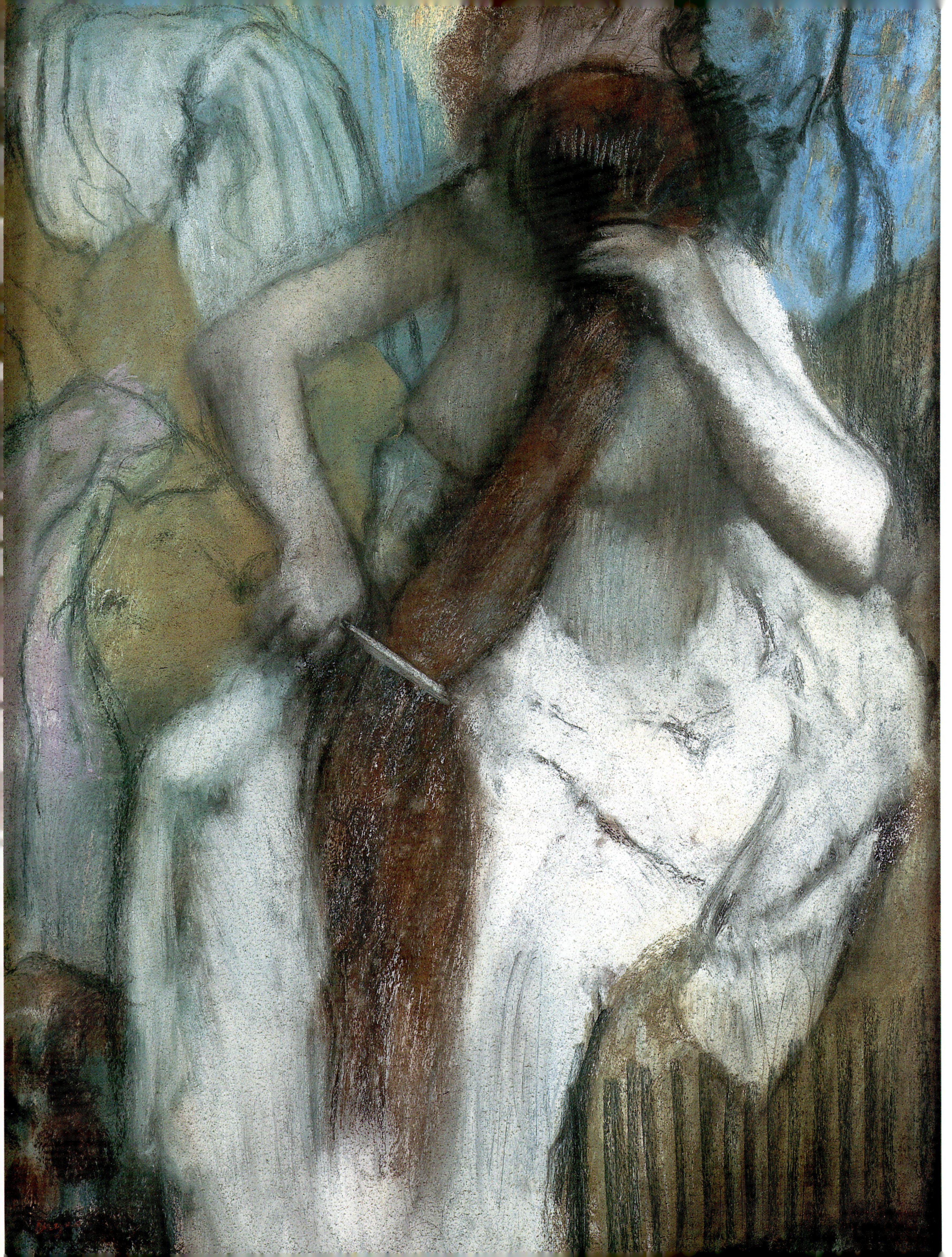

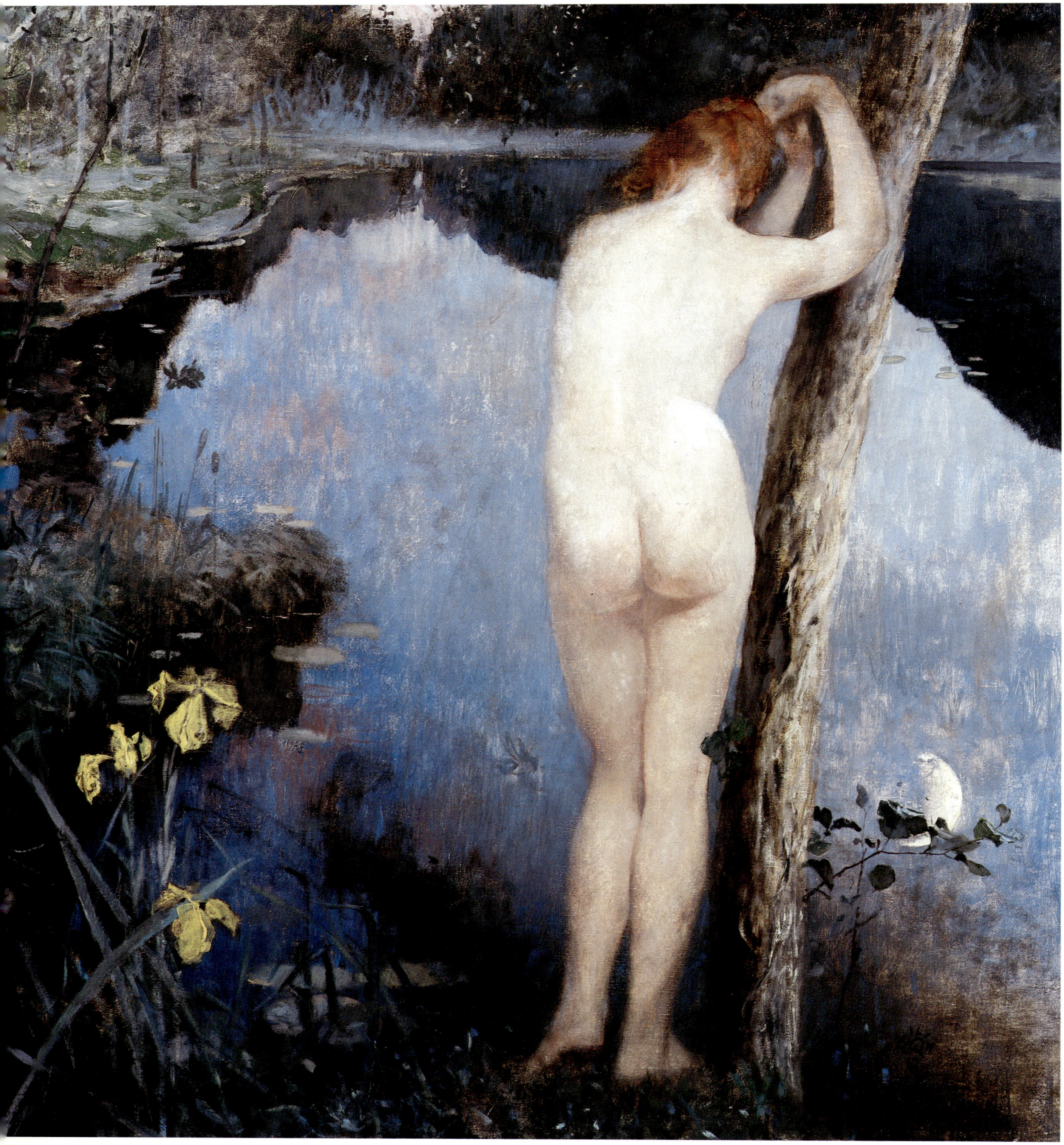

62 Arkhip Ivanovich Kuindzhi
After the Storm (detail)
1879
Oil on canvas, 102 x 159 cm
Tretyakov Gallery, Moscow

63 Pierre-Auguste Renoir
Luncheon of the Boating Party
1881
Oil on canvas, 130 x 173 cm
Phillips Collection, Washington, D.C.

64 Georges Seurat
Poser from Behind
1887
Oil on canvas, 24.5 x 15.5 cm
Musée d'Orsay, Paris

65 Edgar Degas
Woman Combing her Hair
c. 1887–90
Pastel, 82 x 57 cm
Musée d'Orsay, Paris

66 Eilif Peterssen
Nocturne
1887
Oil on canvas, 81.5 x 81.5 cm
Nasjonalgalleriet, Oslo

67 Ilya Repin
Zaporozhye Cossacks (detail)
1880–91
Oil on canvas, overall dimensions 203 x 358 cm
Russian Museum, St. Petersburg

68 Camille Pissarro
Apple Pickers
1886
Oil on canvas, 128 x 128 cm
Ohara Museum of Art, Kurashiki

69 Pierre Puvis de Chavannes
The Shepherd's Song
1891
Oil on canvas, 105 x 110 cm
Metropolitan Museum of Modern Art
(Rogers Fund), New York

70 Henri Rousseau
Myself: Portrait-Landscape
1890
Oil on canvas, 143 x 110 cm
Národní Gallery, Prague

71 Paul Cézanne
Self-Portrait with Palette
1885–87
Oil on canvas, 92.5 x 73 cm
Bührle Foundation, Zurich

72 Émile Bernard
Breton Women in a Meadow
1888
Oil on canvas, 74 x 92 cm
Private collection

73 Paul Sérusier
The Talisman
1888
Oil on canvas, 27 x 21.5 cm
Musée d'Orsay, Paris

74 Vincent van Gogh
The Night Café
1888
Oil on canvas, 70 x 89 cm
Yale University Art Gallery, New Haven

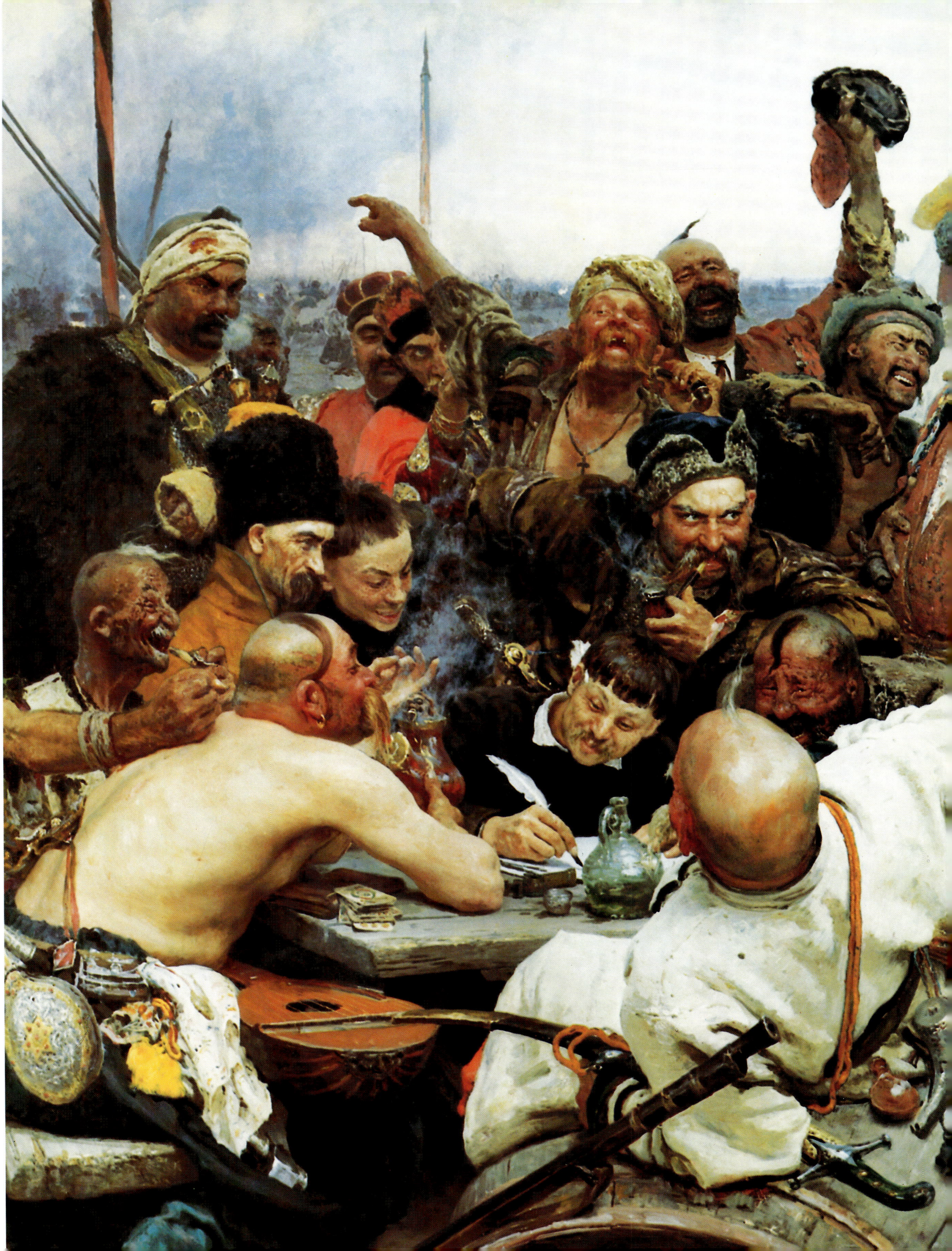

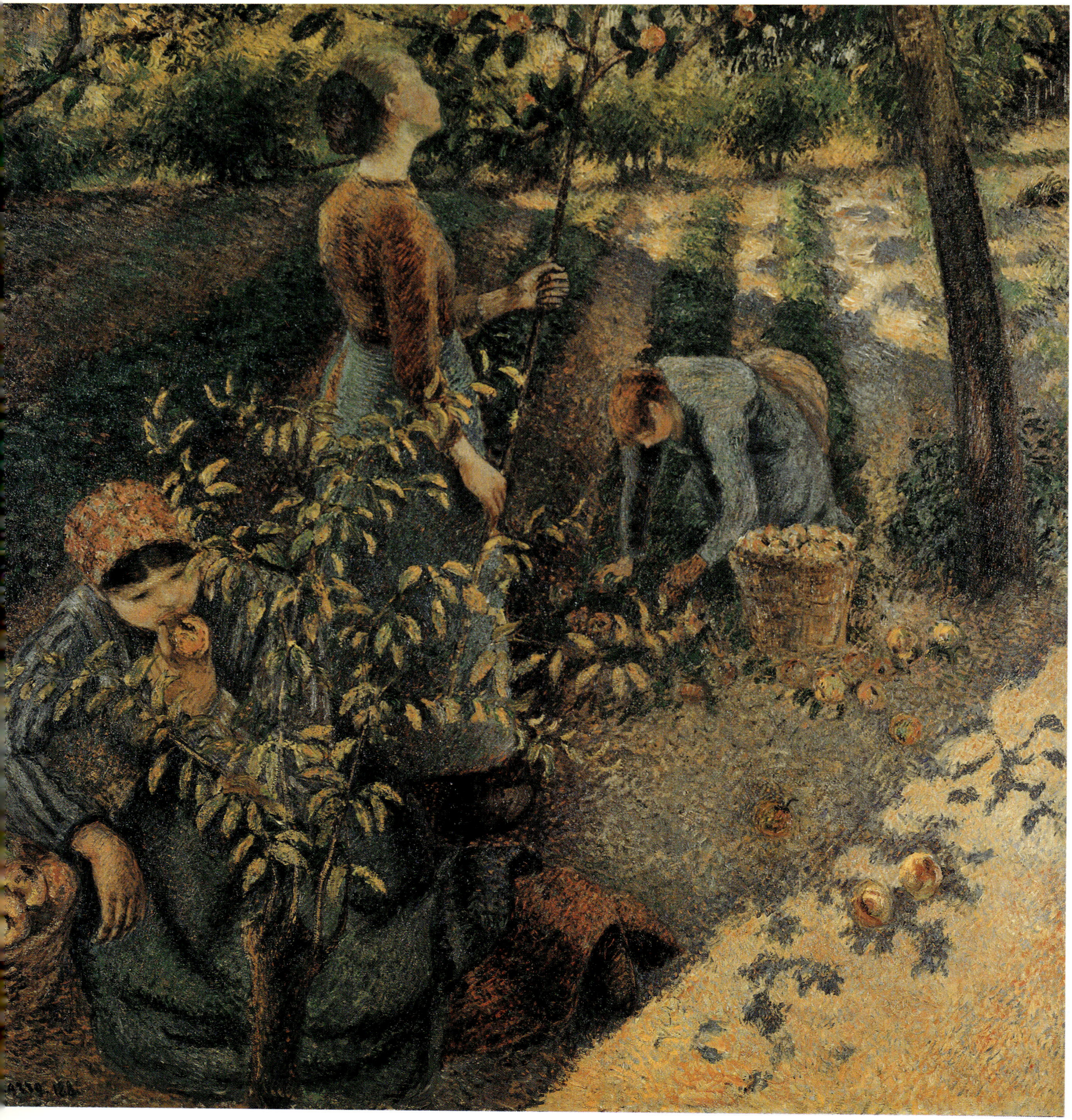

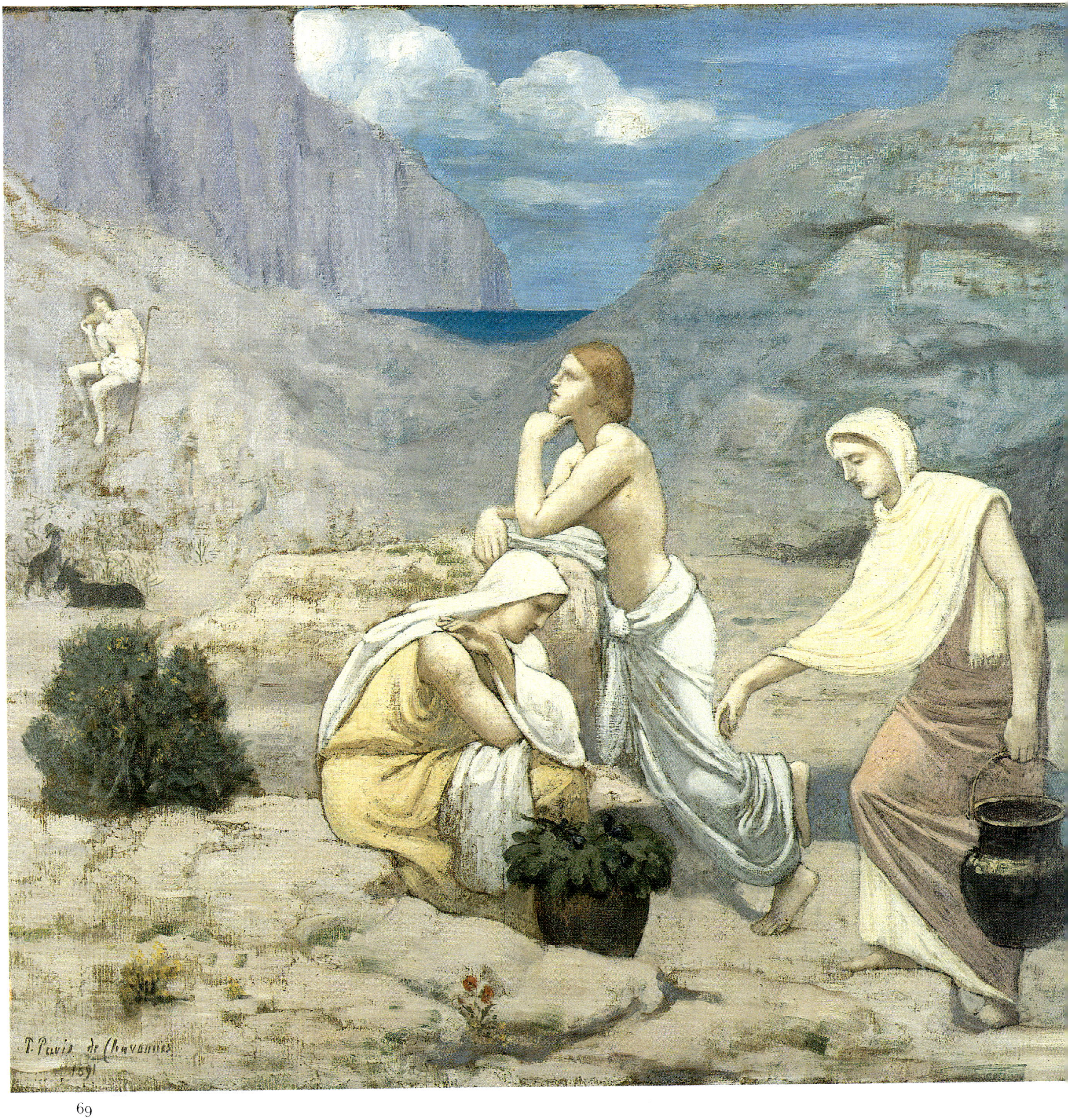
P. Puvis de Chavannes
1891

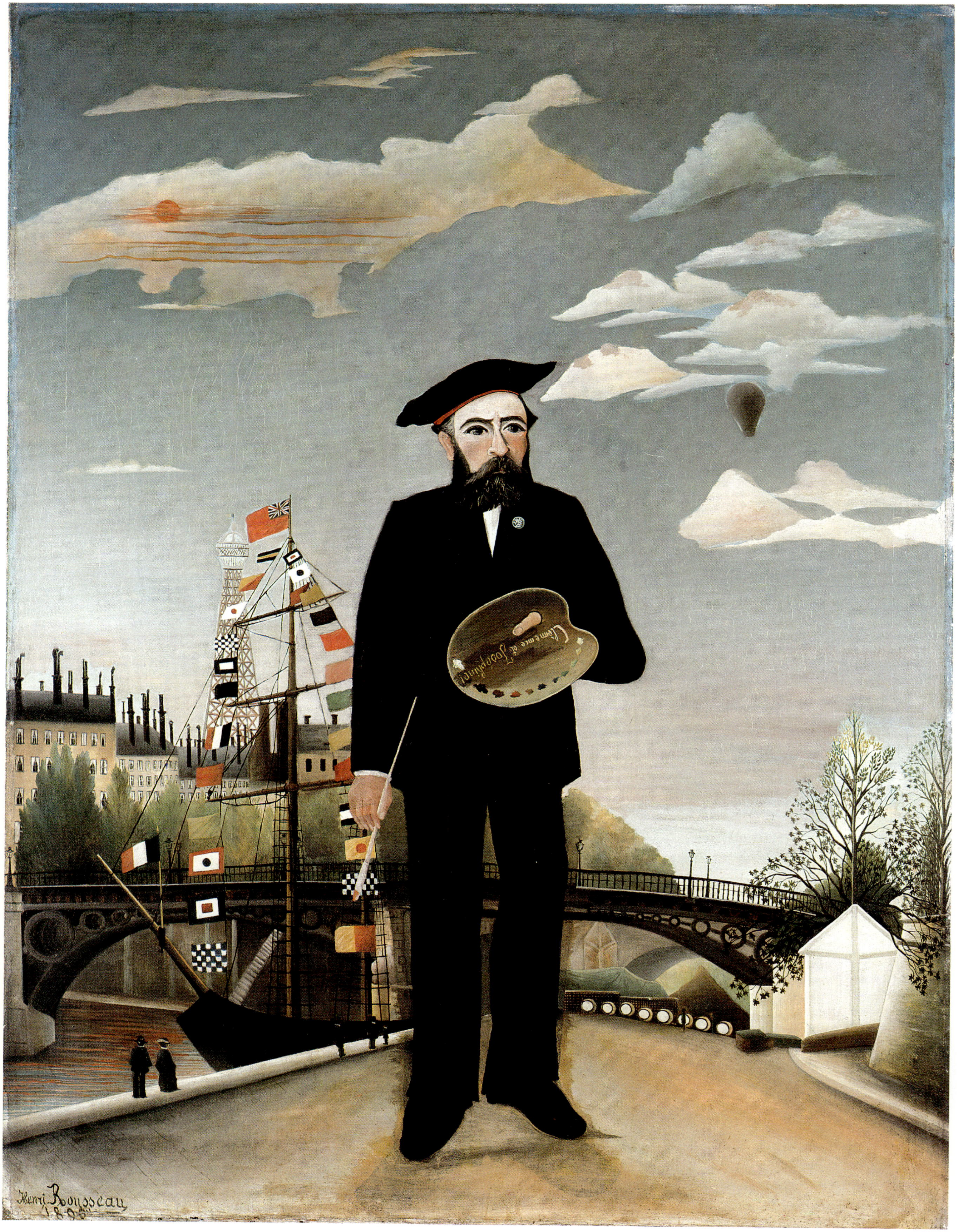
Henri Rousseau

71

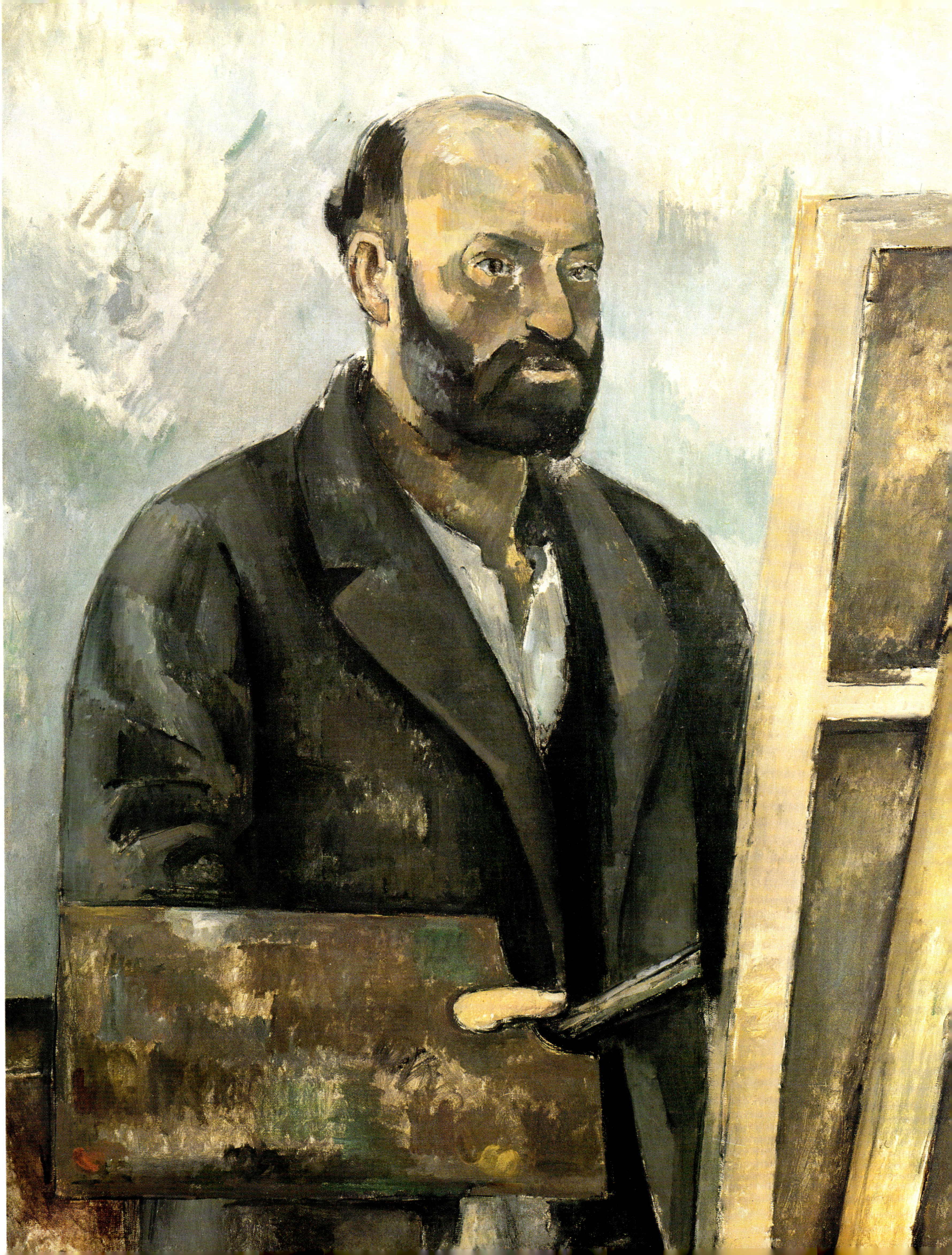

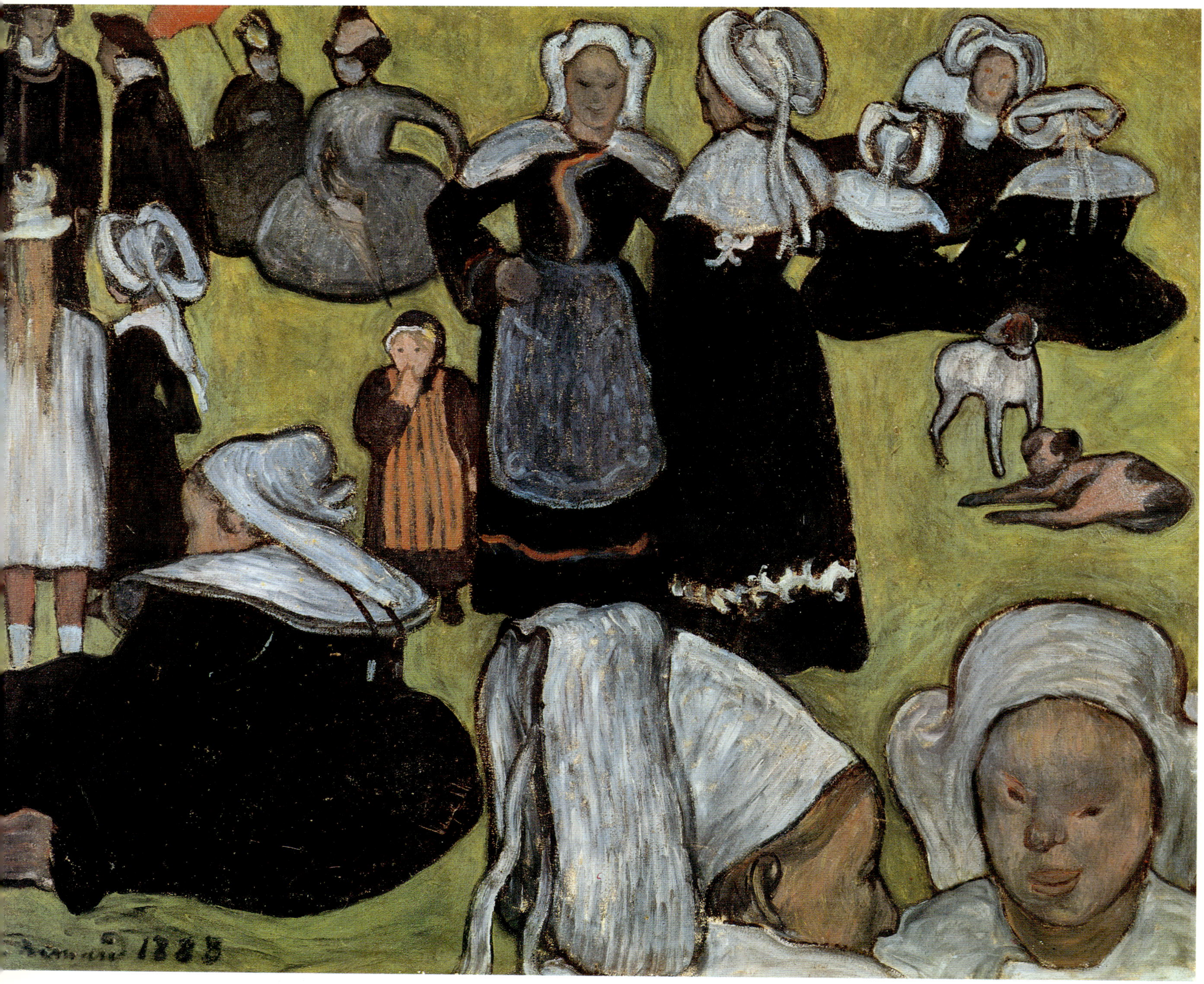
Bernard 1888

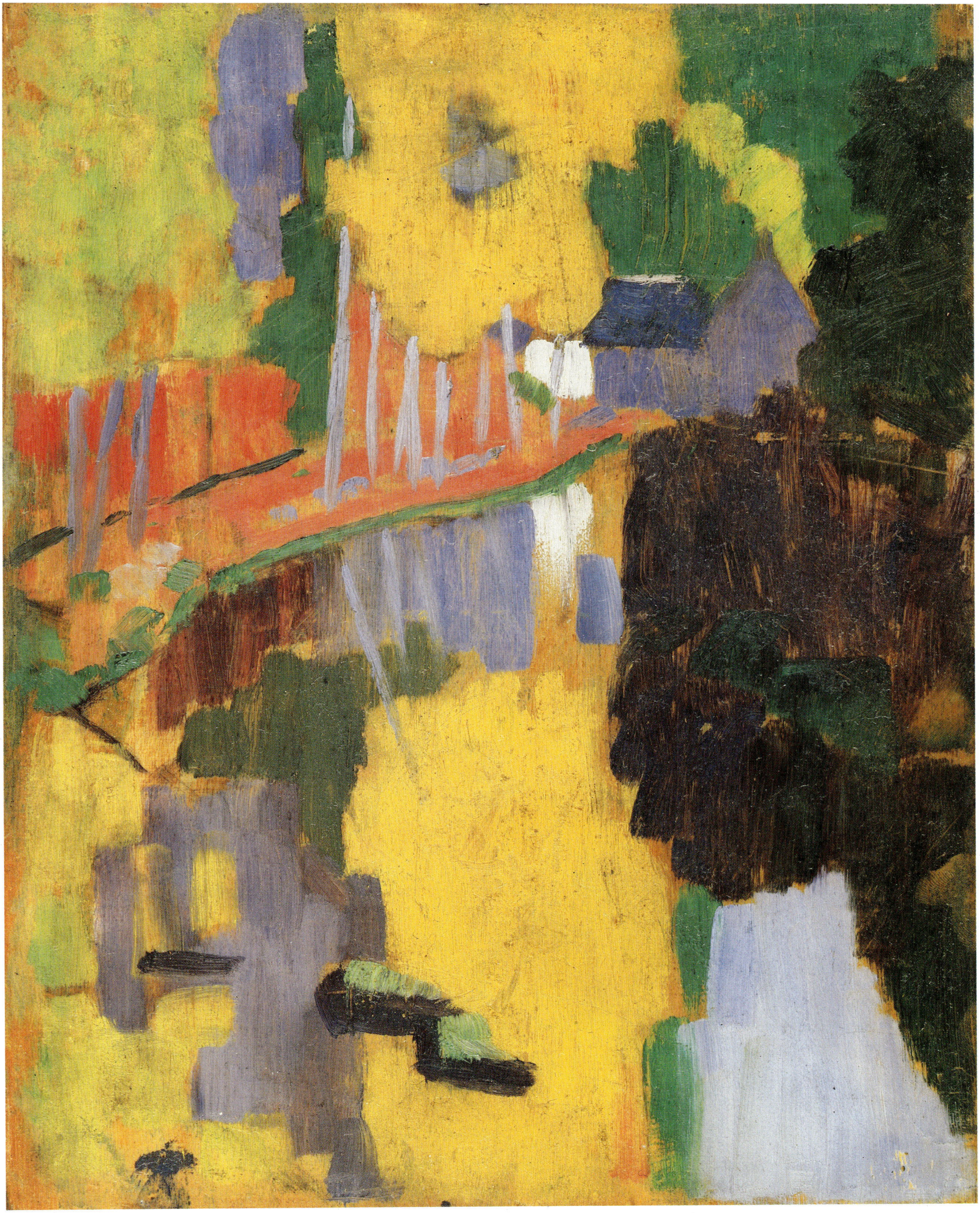

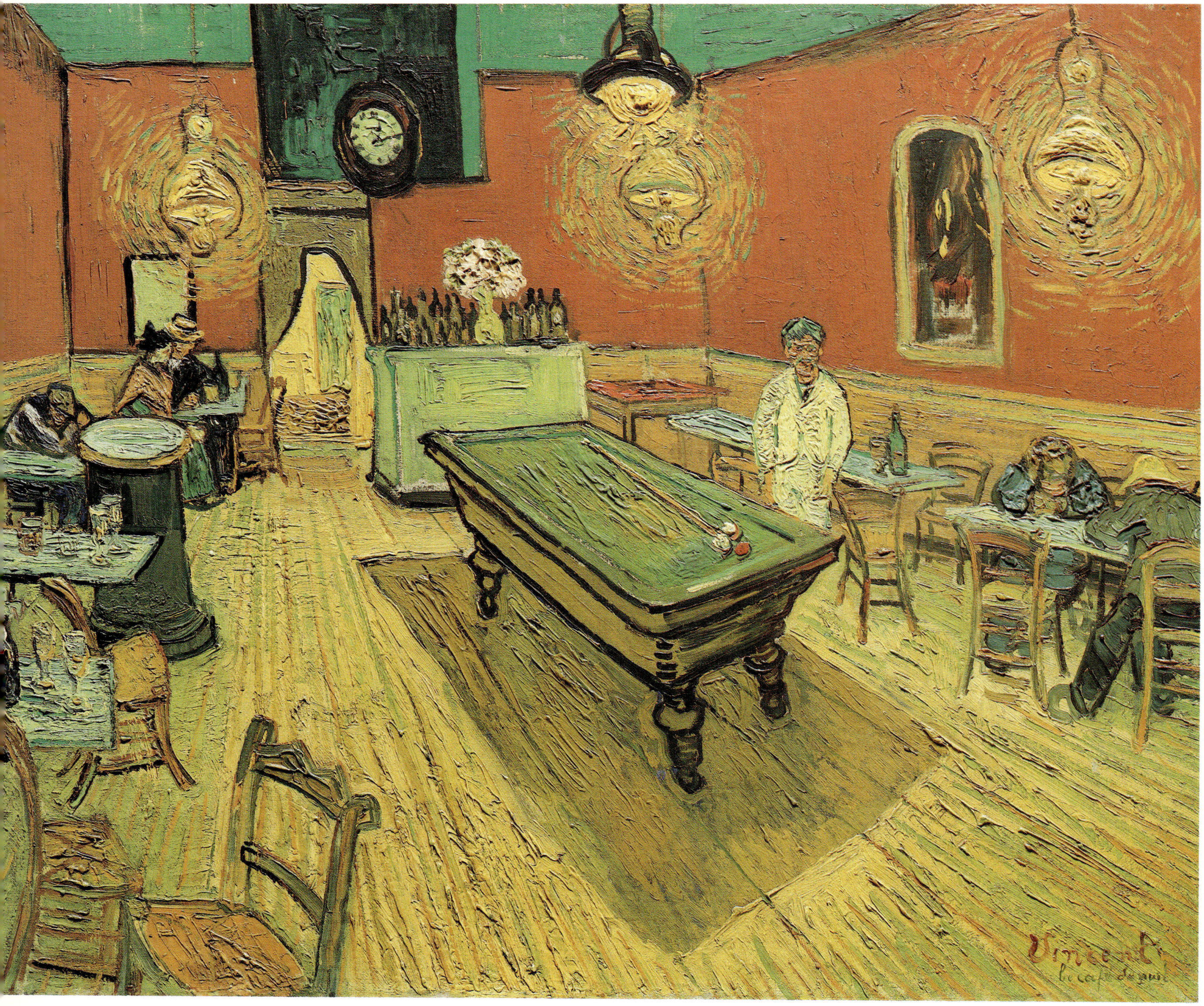

74

→
75

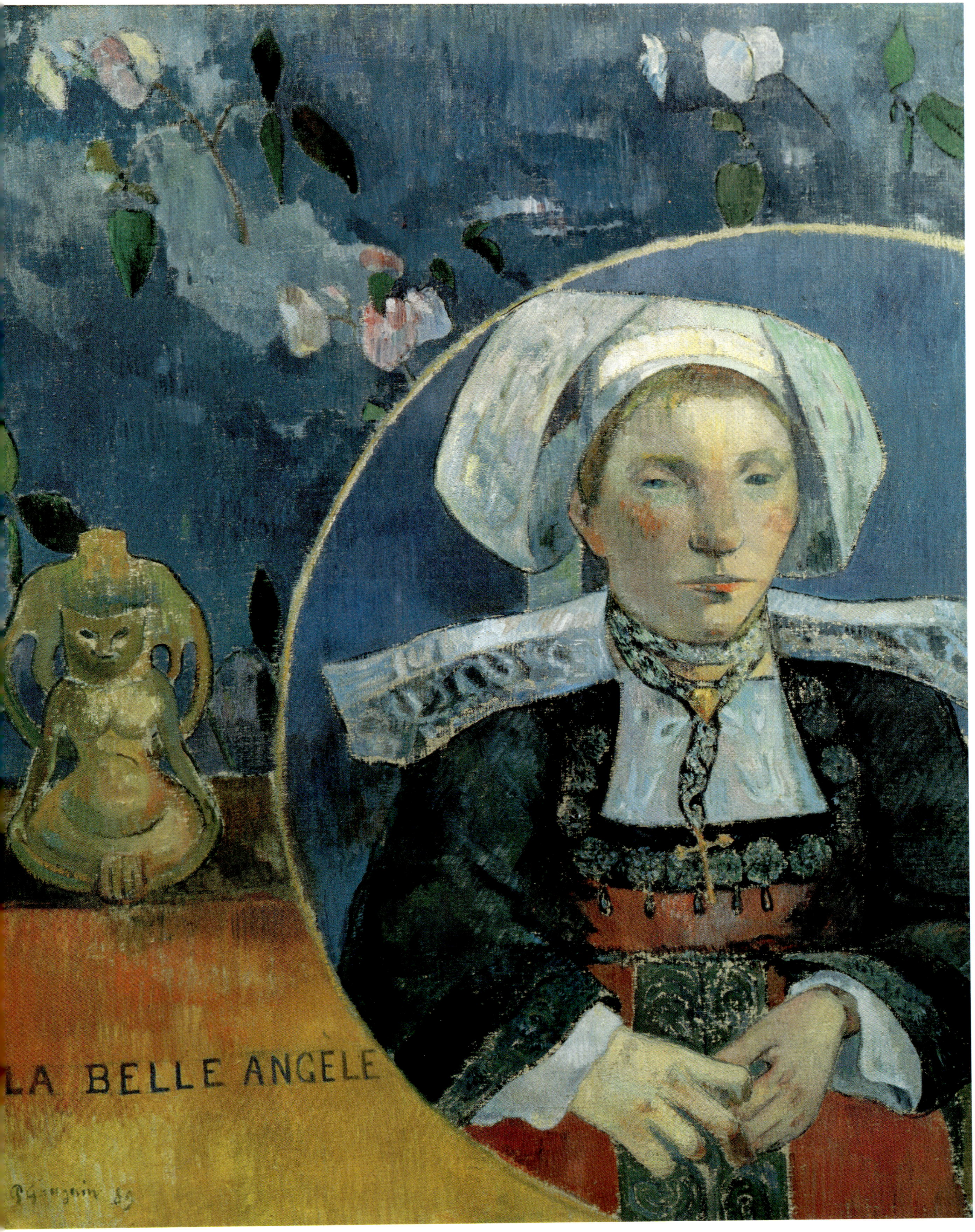
LA BELLE ANGELE
P Gauguin 89

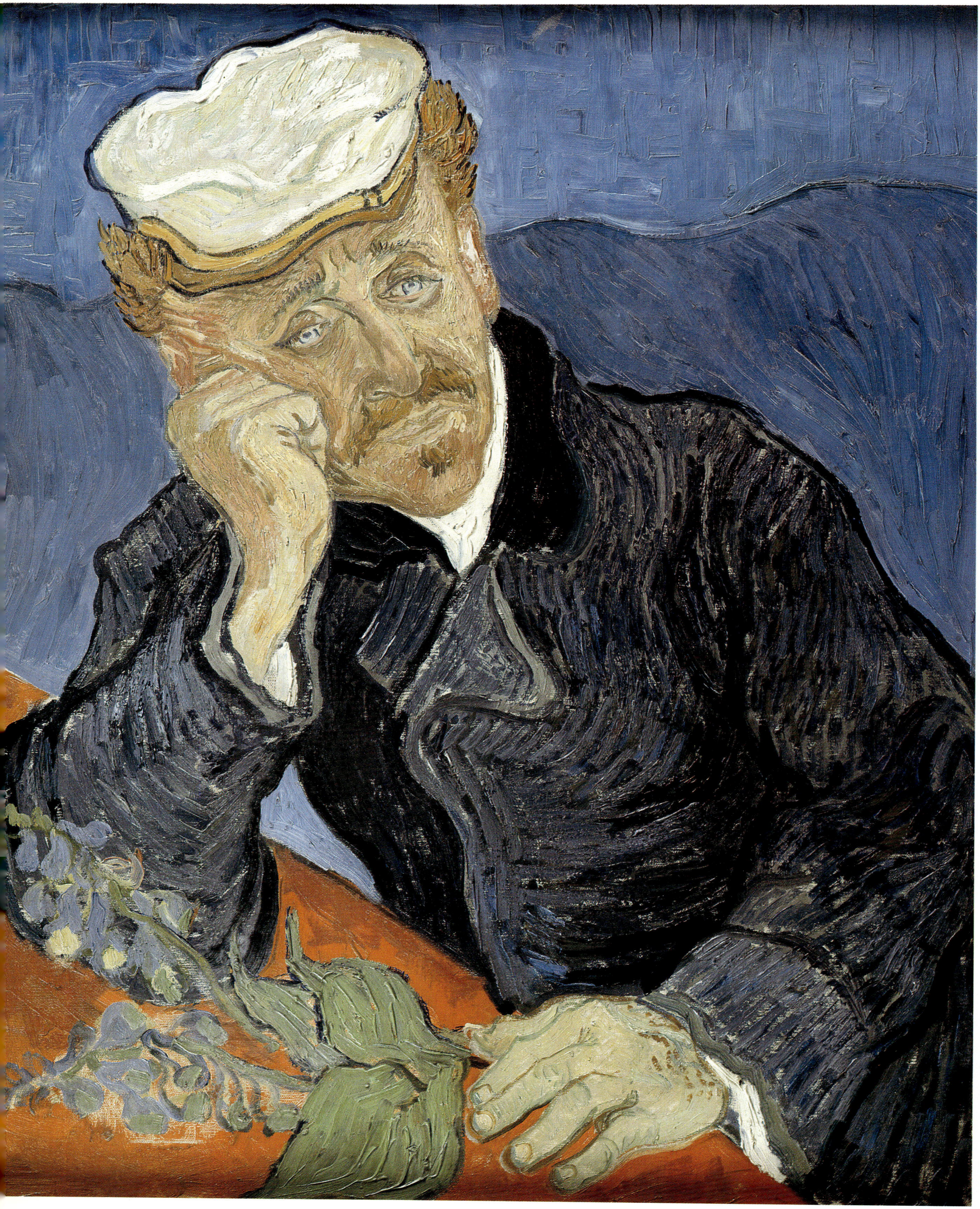

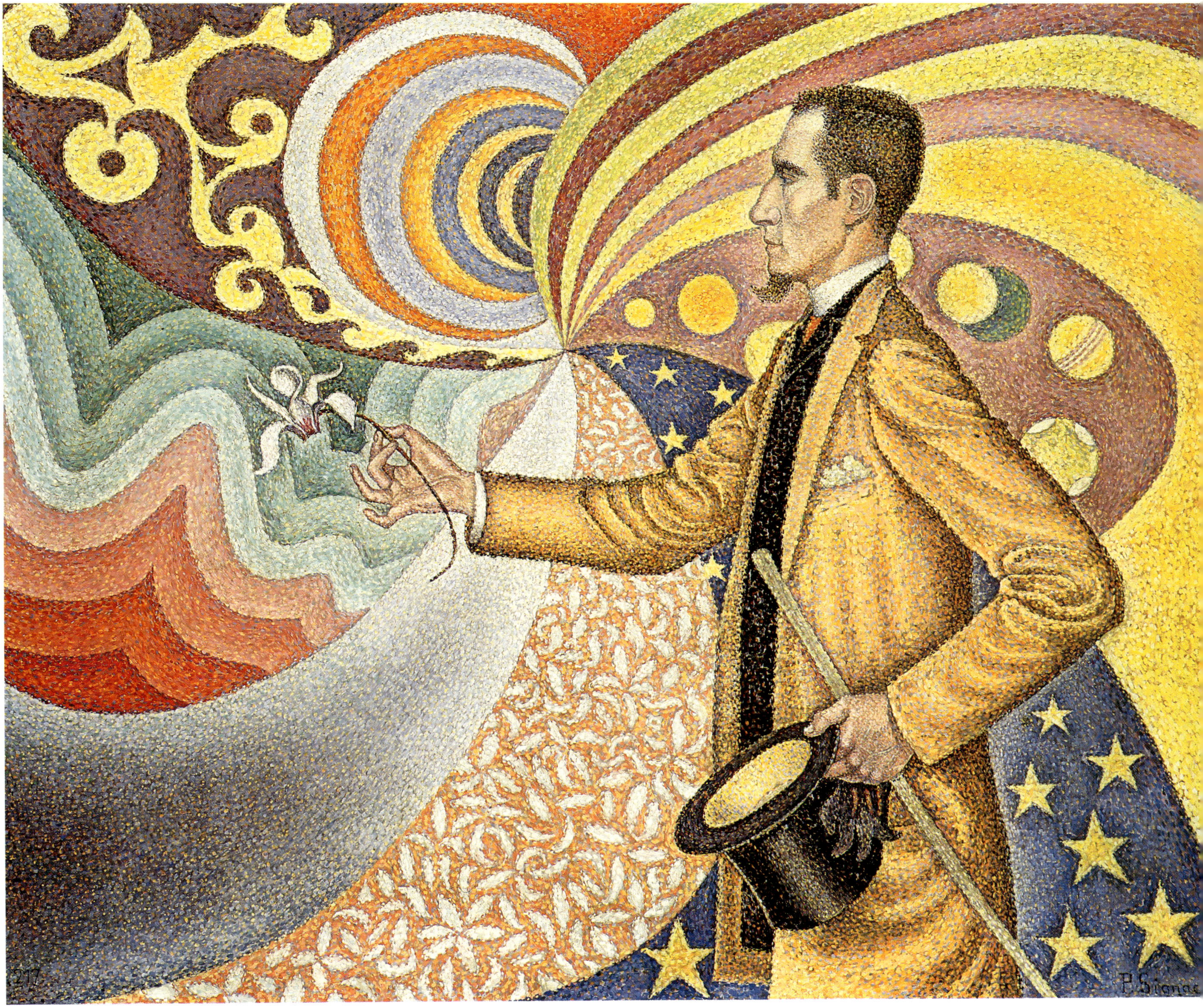

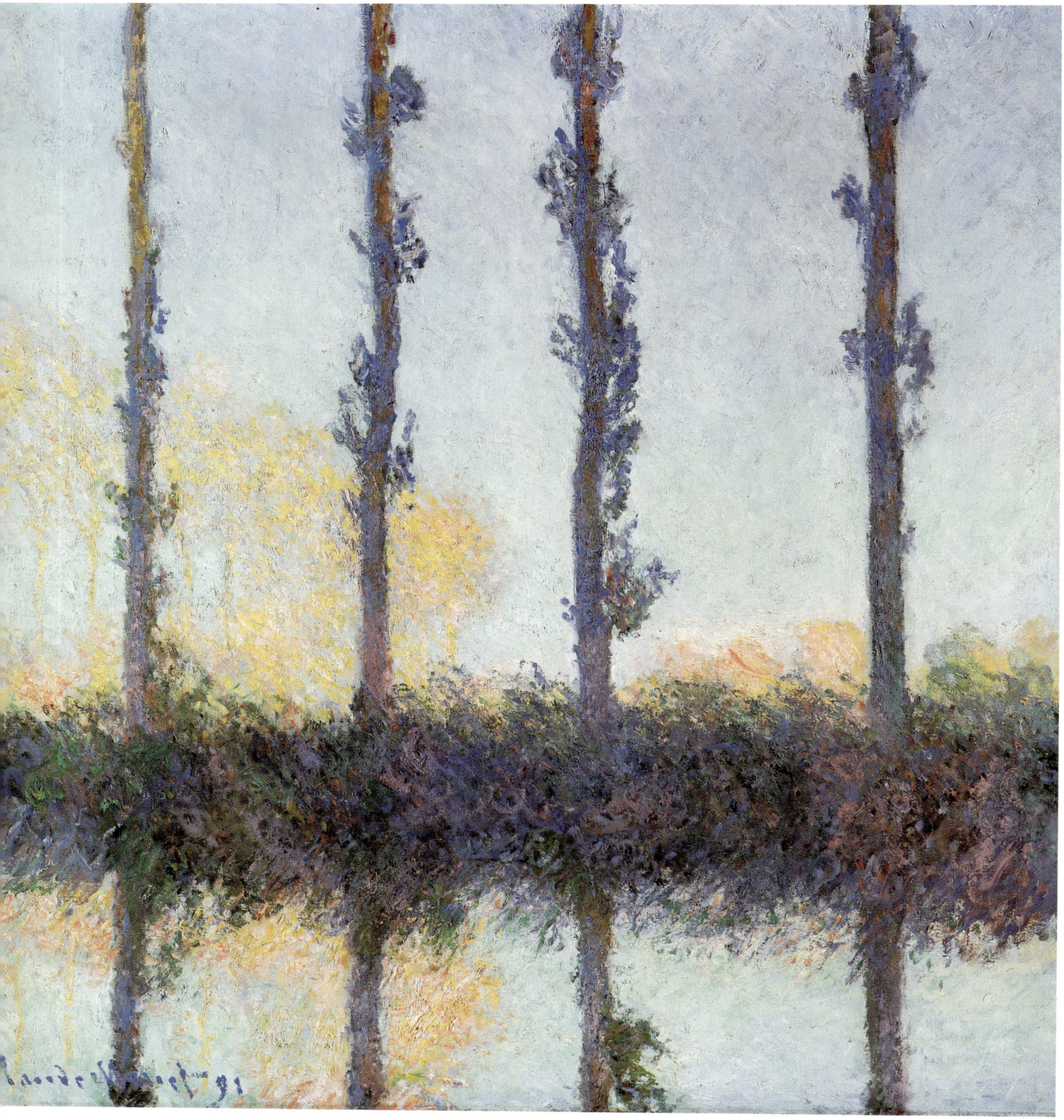

75 Paul Gauguin
La Belle Angèle
1889
Oil on canvas, 92 x 73 cm
Musée d'Orsay, Paris

76 Vincent van Gogh
Portrait of Dr. Paul Gachet
1890
Oil on canvas, 68 x 57 cm
Musée d'Orsay, Paris

77 Paul Gauguin
The Vision After the Sermon
1888
Oil on canvas, 73 x 92 cm
National Gallery of Scotland, Edinburgh

78 George Hendrik Breitner
Moonlight
c. 1887–89
Oil on canvas, 70 x 101 cm
Musée d'Orsay, Paris

79 Robert Macaulay Stevenson
Lambing
Oil on canvas, 54.5 x 65.7 cm
Musée des Beaux-Arts, Brest

80 Émile-René Ménard
The Wanderers
1902
Pastel, 61.5 x 90.5 cm
Musée des Beaux-Arts, Brest

81 William Degouve de Nuncques
The Blind House or *The Pink House*
1892
Oil on canvas, 63 x 43 cm
Rijksmuseum Kröller-Müller, Otterlo

82 Paul Signac
Portrait of Félix Fénéon
1890
Oil on canvas, 74 x 95 cm
Private collection

83 Claude Monet
The Four Trees
1891
Oil on canvas, 82 x 81.5 cm
Metropolitan Museum of Art
(H. O. Havemeyer
Collection), New York

84 Henri-Edmond Cross
The Îles d'Or (detail)
1891–92
Oil on canvas, 59 x 54 cm
Musée d'Orsay, Paris

85 Winslow Homer
Summer Night
1890
Oil on canvas, 61 x 73 cm
Musée d'Orsay, Paris

86 Aristide Maillol
Woman with Parasol
1895
Oil on canvas, 190 x 149 cm
Musée d'Orsay, Paris

87 Maurice Denis
Procession Beneath the Trees
1892
Oil on canvas, 55.9 x 81 cm
Collection of Mr. and Mrs. Arthur G. Altschul

88 Viteslaw Karel Masek
The Prophetess Libuse (detail)
Oil on canvas, 193 x 193 cm
Musée d'Orsay, Paris

89 Félix Vallotton
The Bathing-Pool on a Summer Evening
1892–93
Oil on canvas, 97 x 131 cm
Kunsthaus, Zürich

90 Henri de Toulouse-Lautrec
In the Salon of the Rue des Moulins
1894
Paint on canvas, 111 x 132 cm
Musée Toulouse-Lautrec, Albi

91 Gustav Klimt
The Goldfish
1901–2
Oil on canvas, 181 x 66.5 cm
Musée des Beaux-Arts, Soleure

92 Pierre Bonnard
The Dressing Gown
1892
Paint on fabric, 150 x 50 cm
Musée d'Orsay, Paris

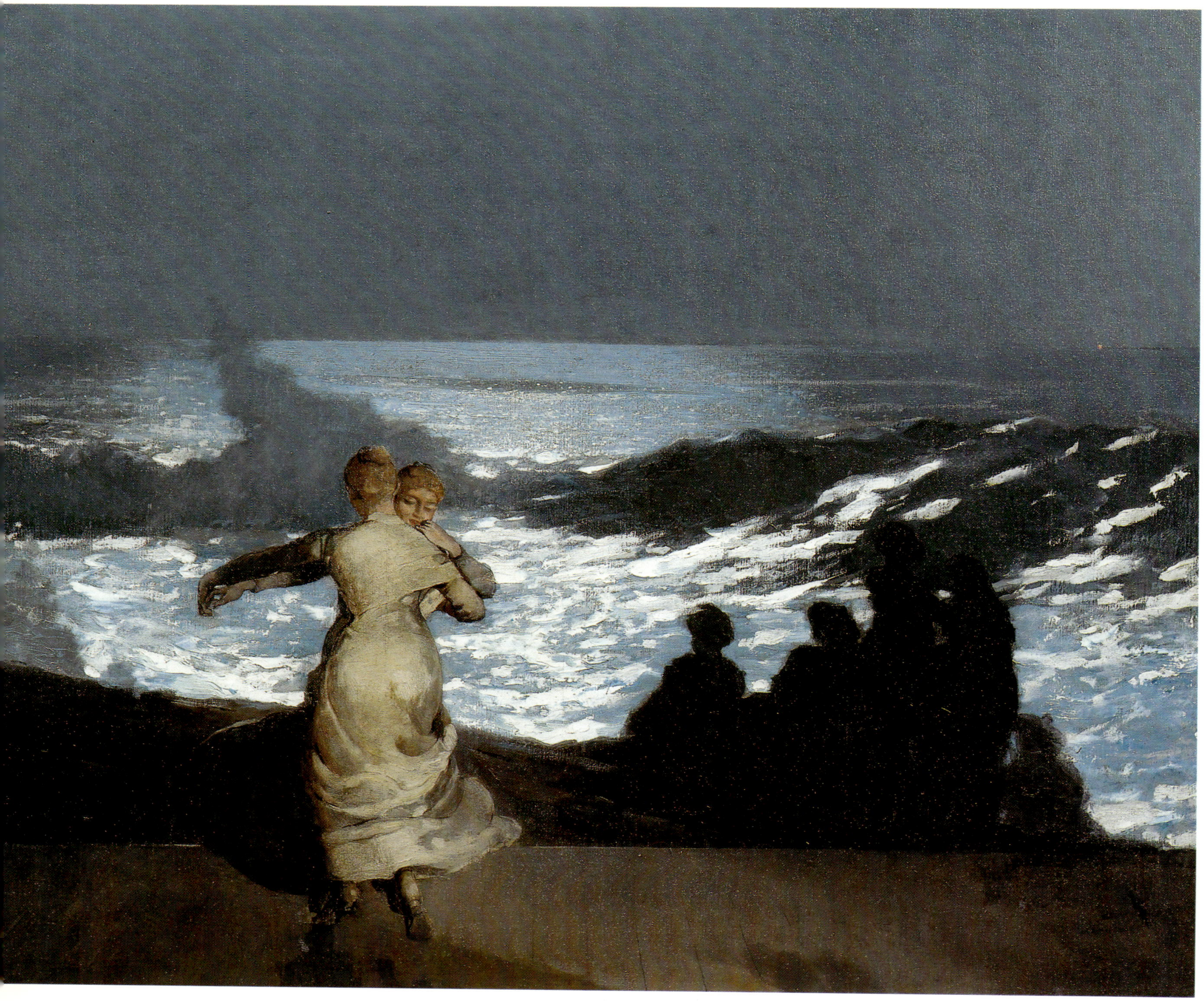

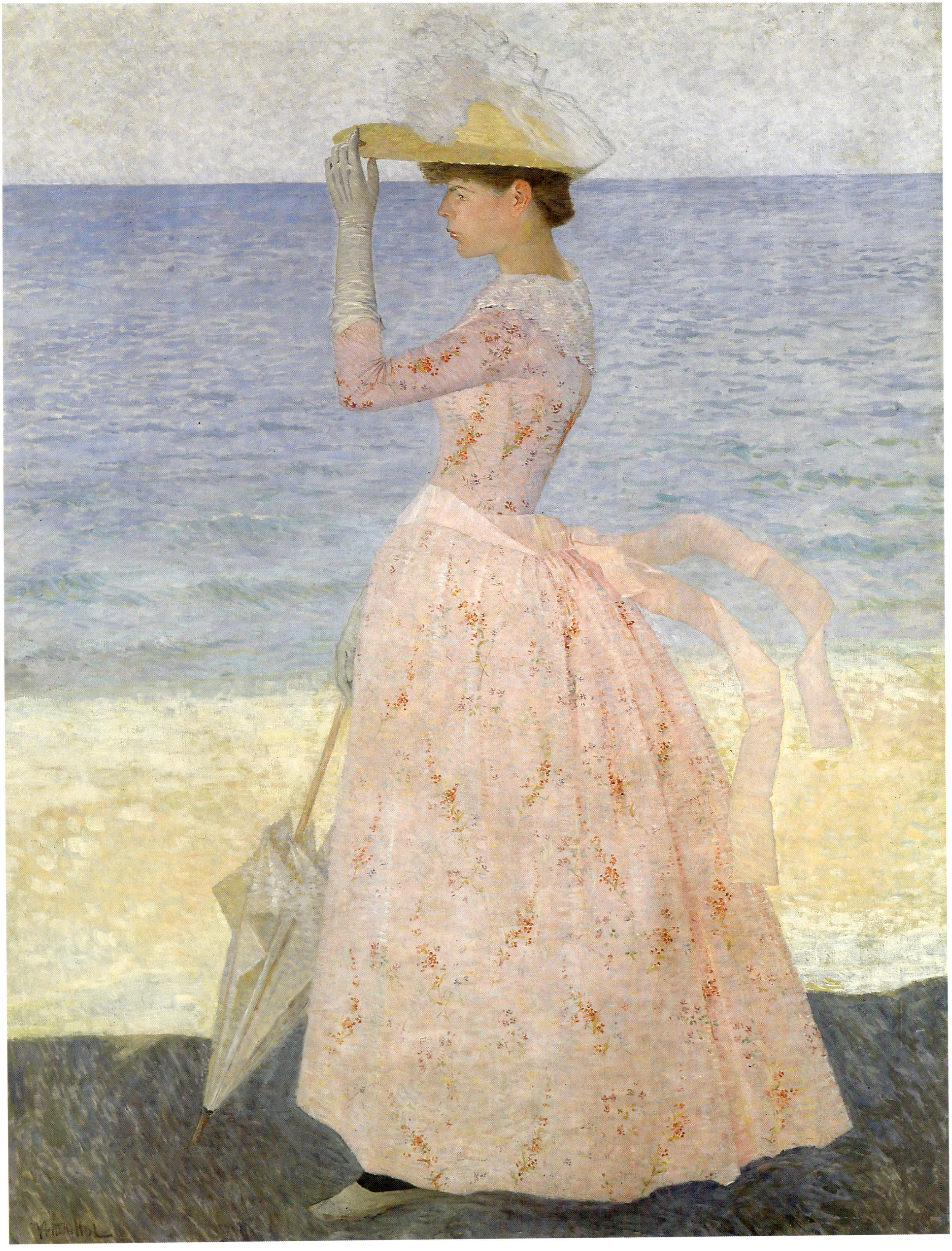

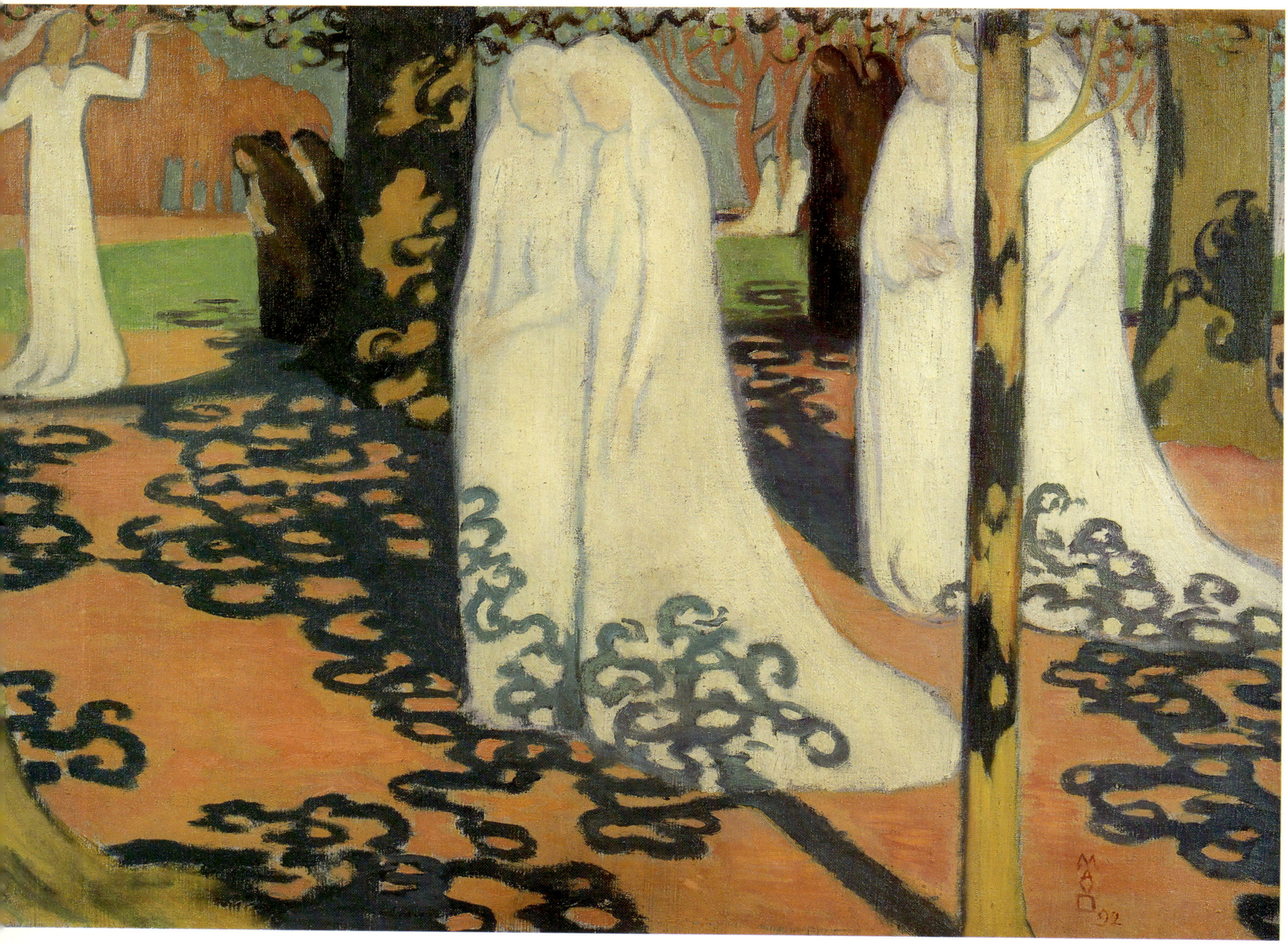
MAVD 92

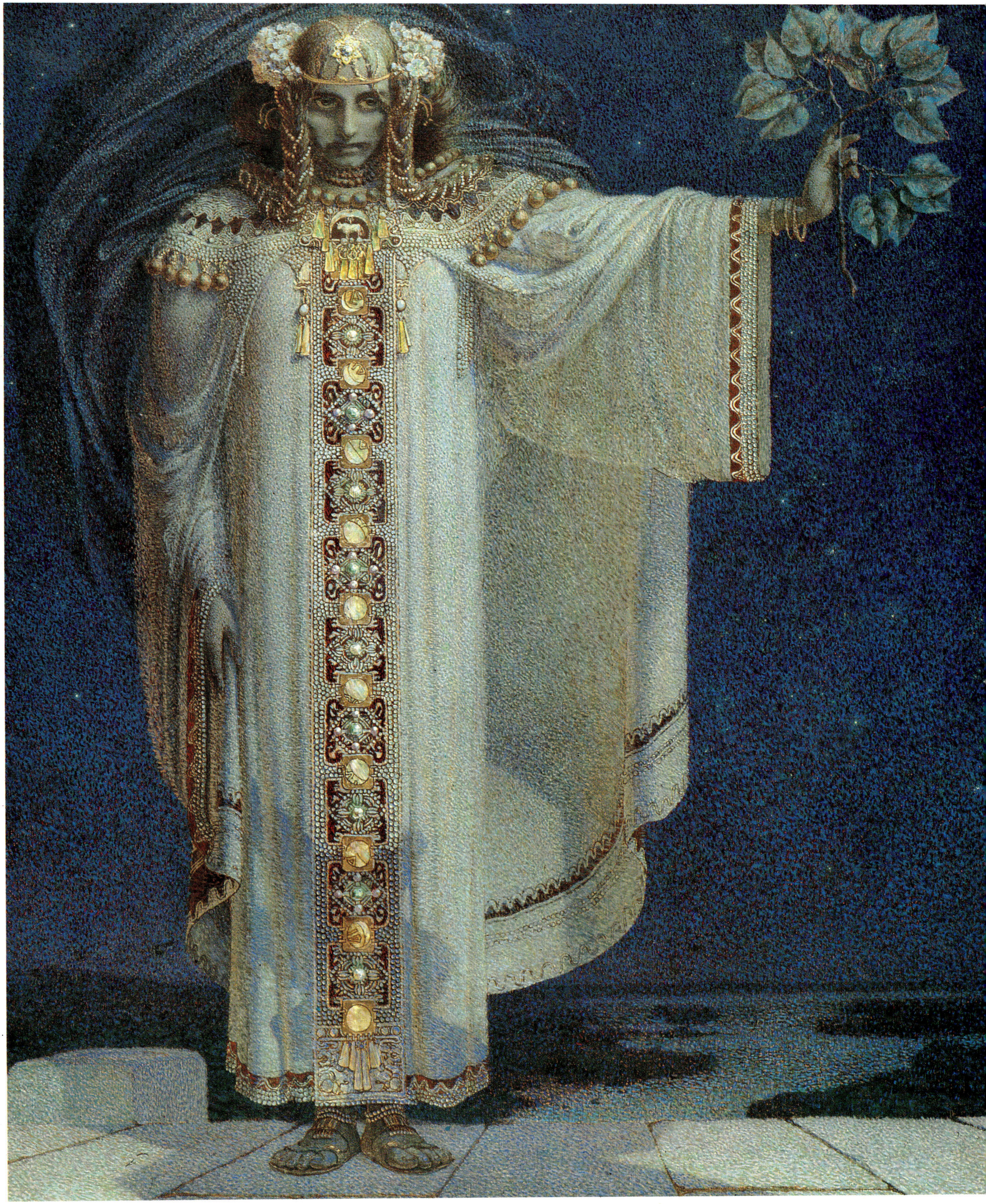

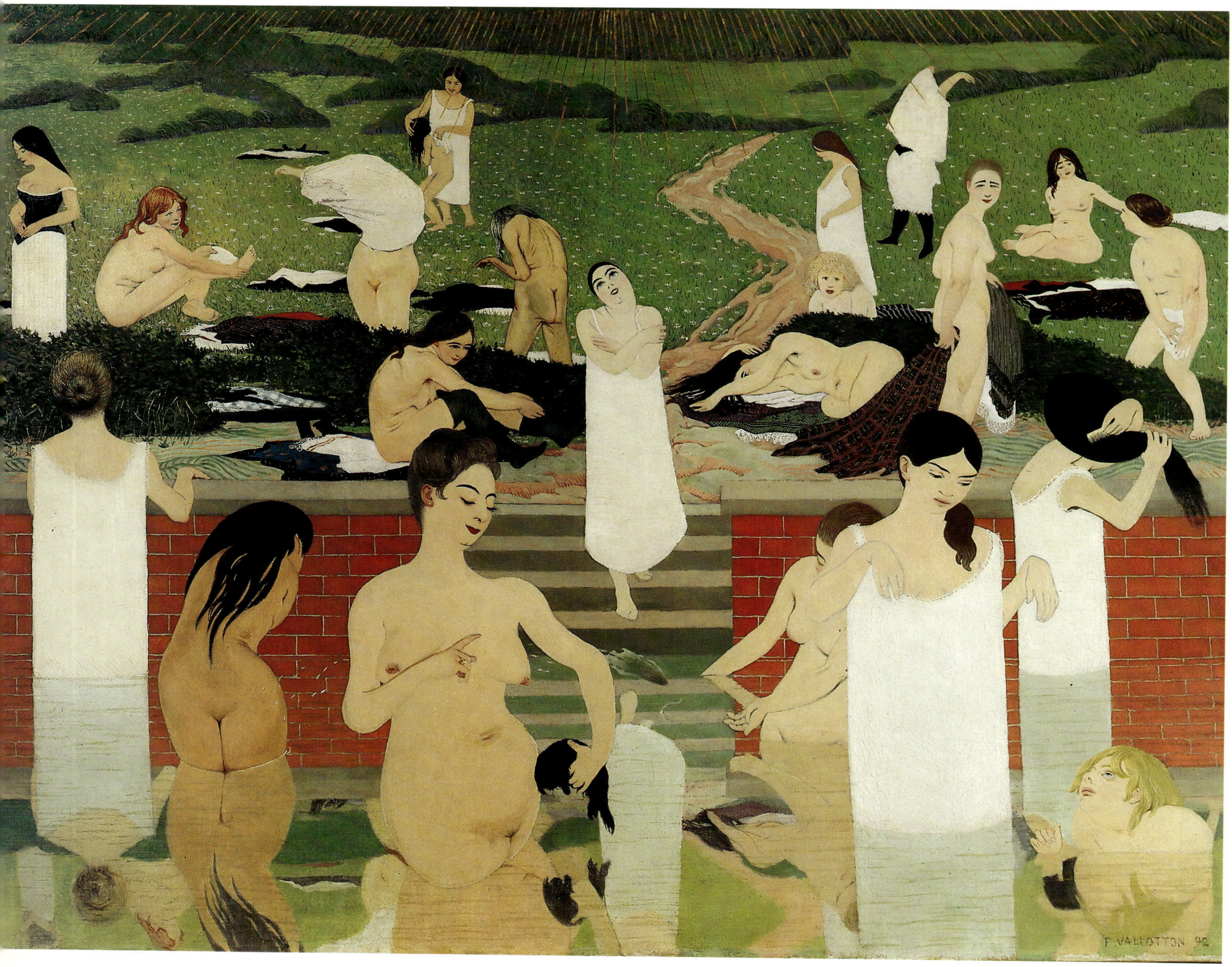
F. VALLOTTON 92

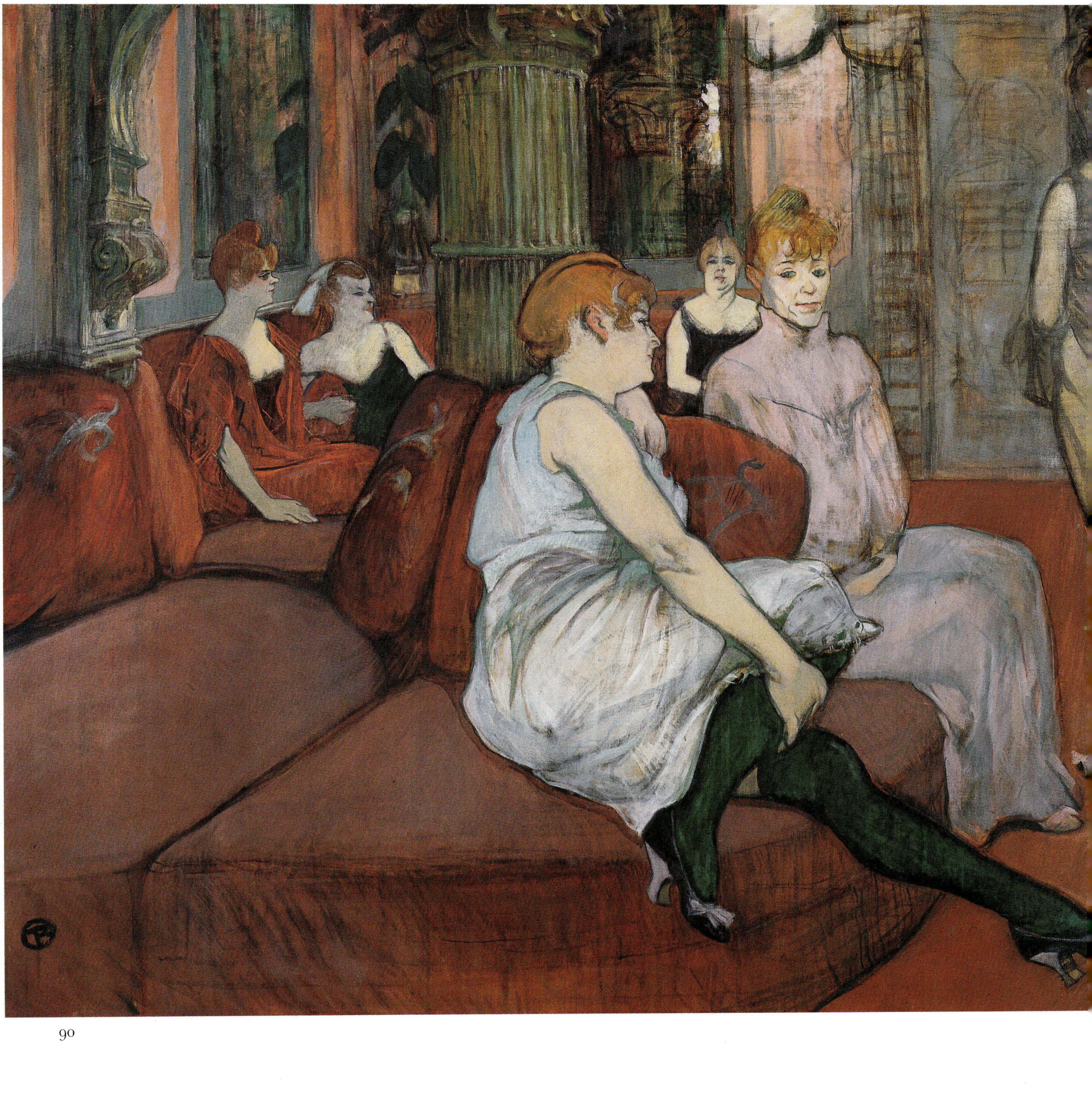

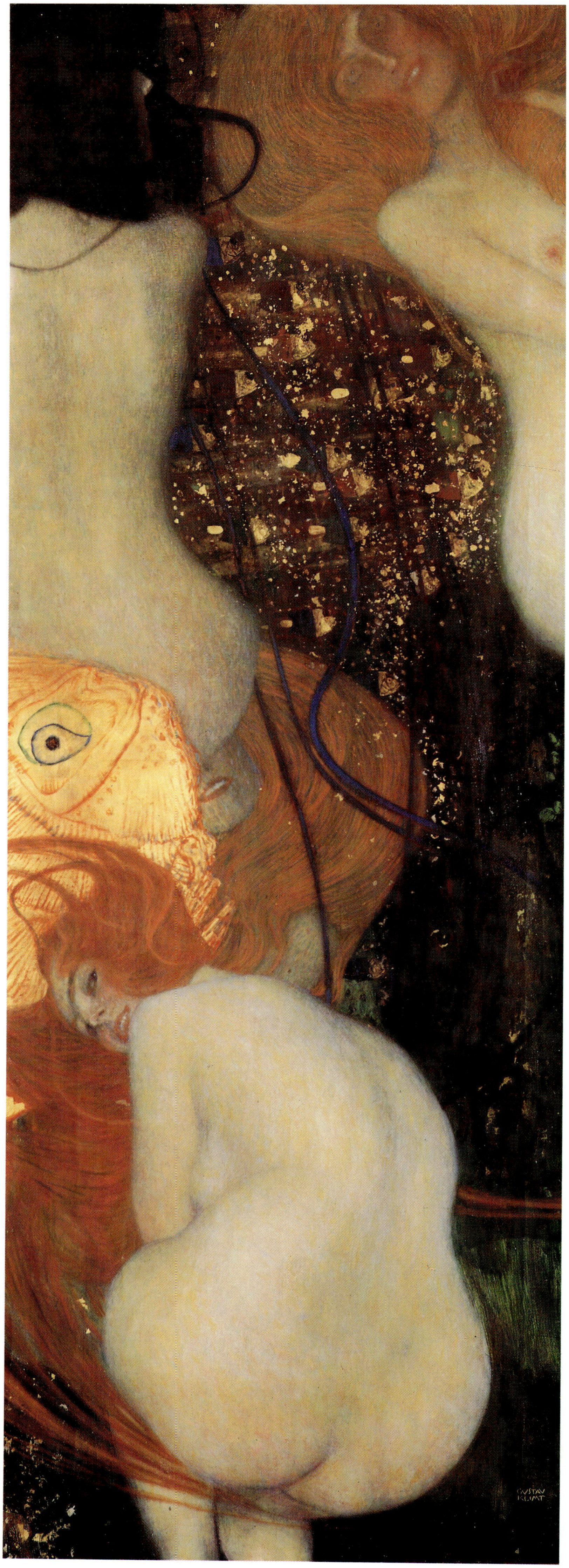

91

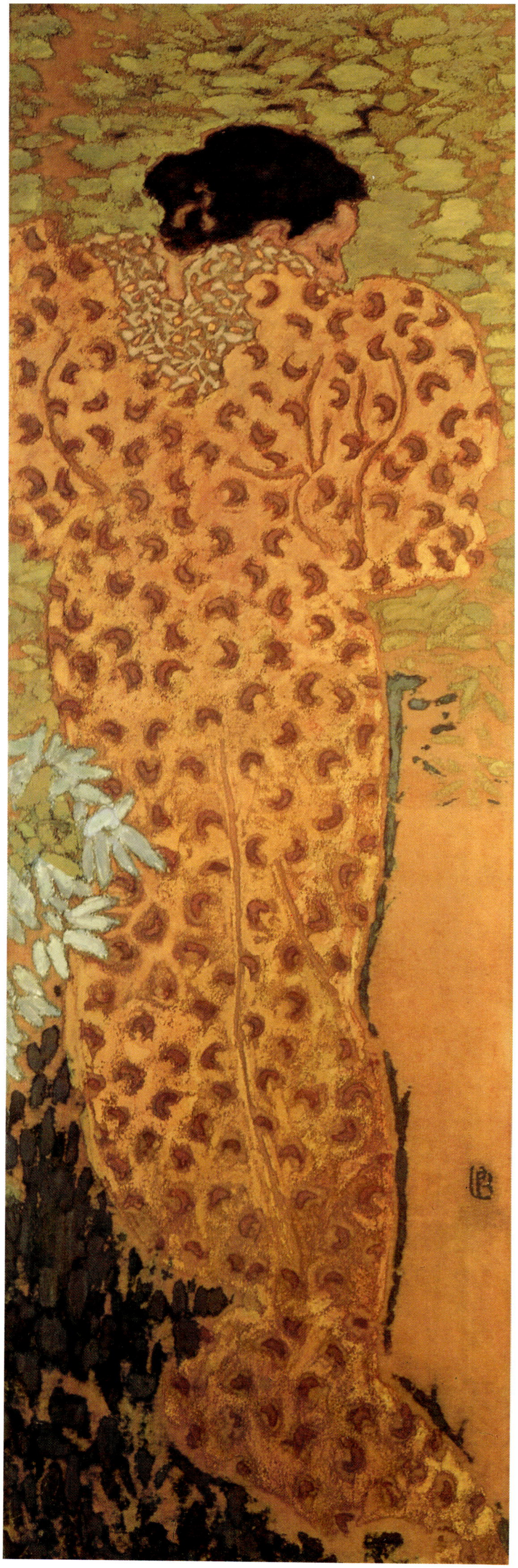

92

→
93

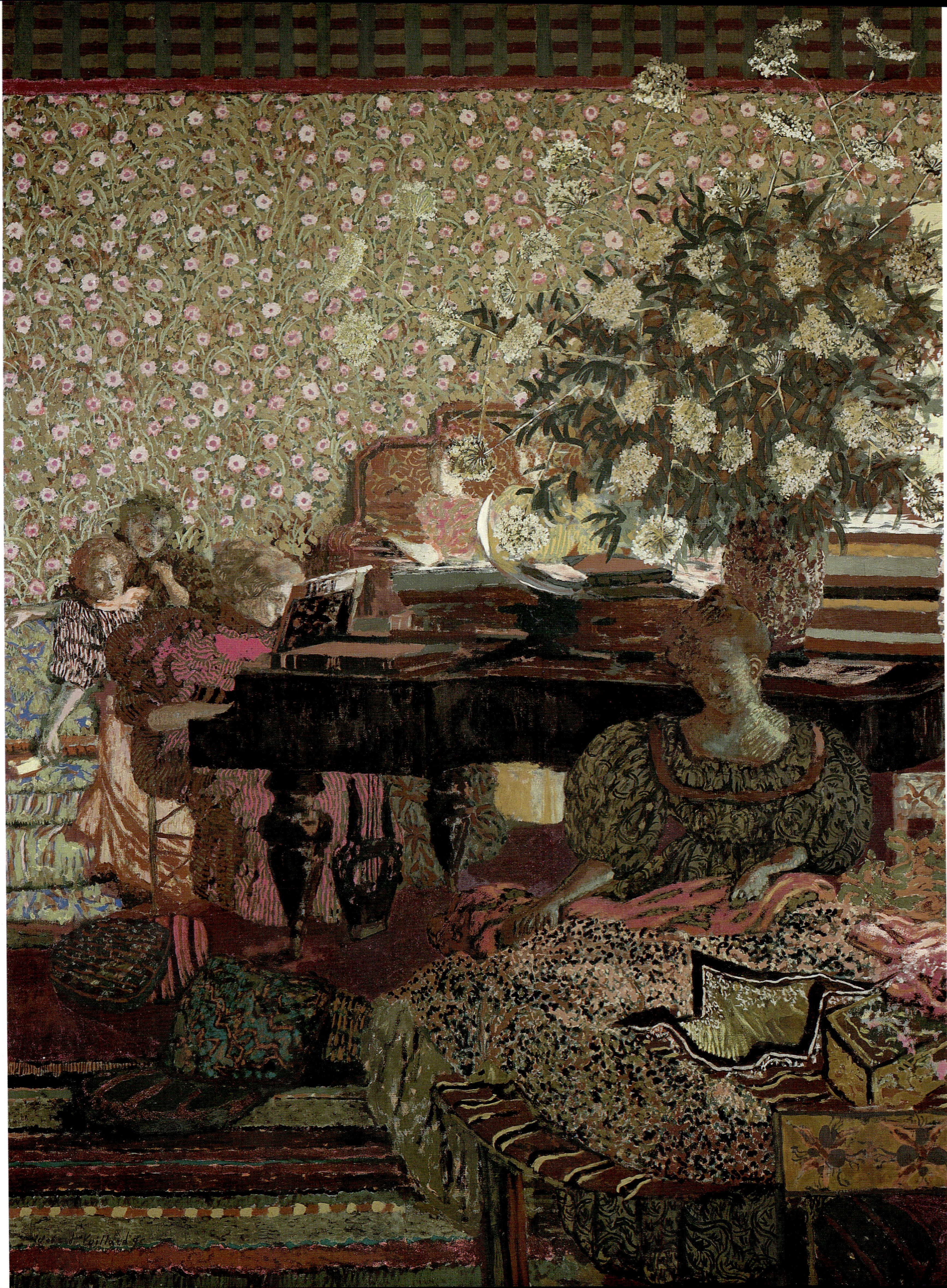

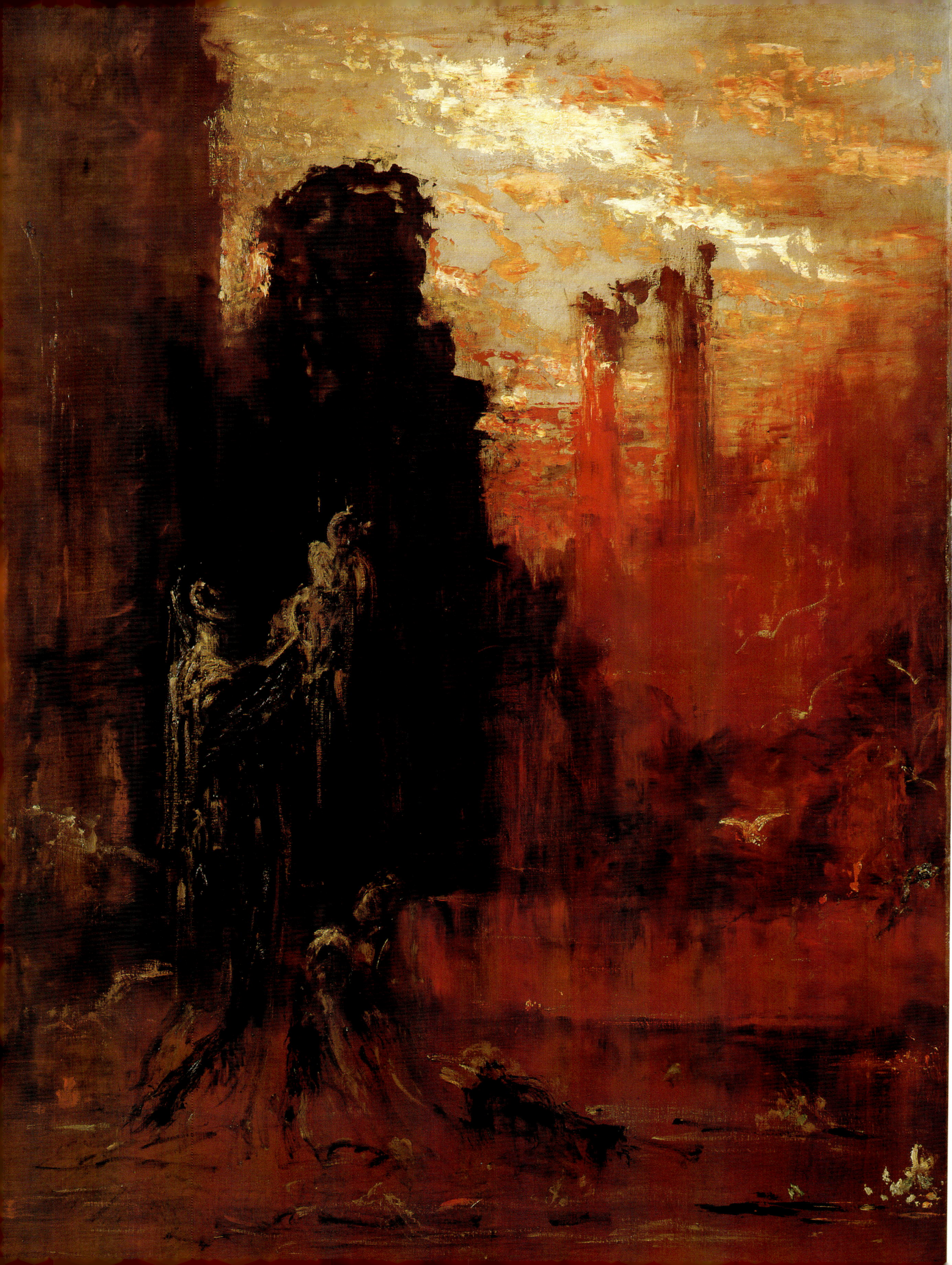

94

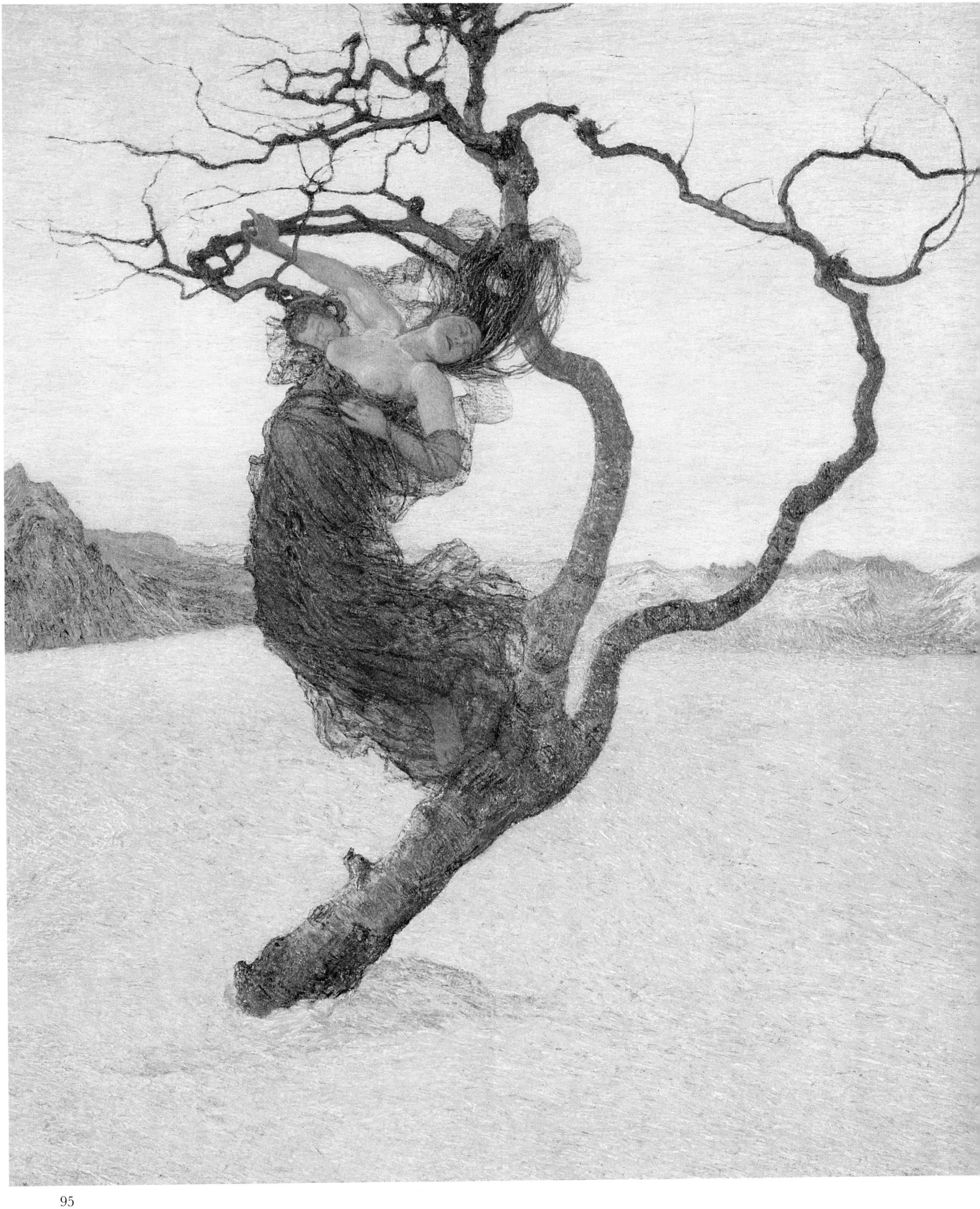

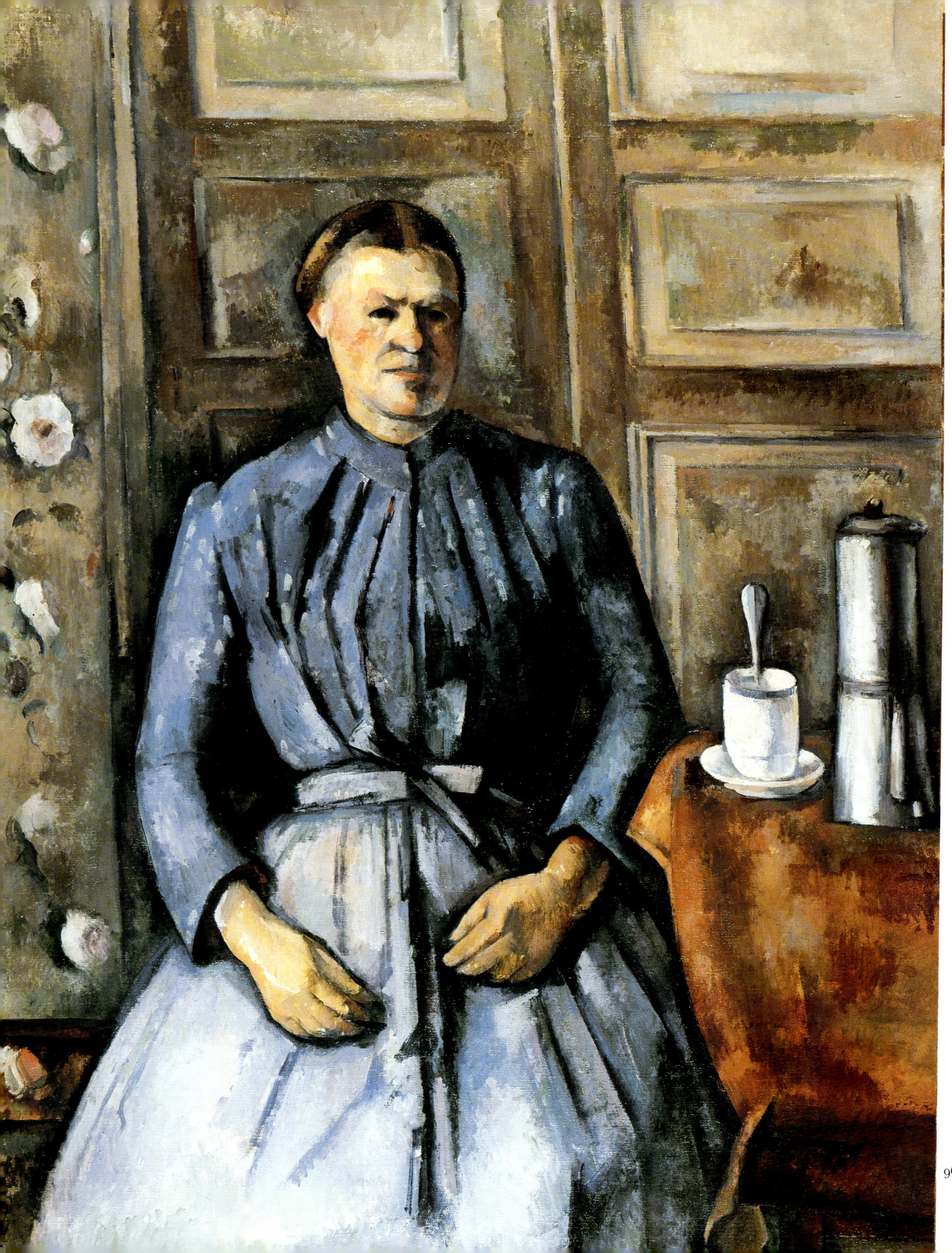

96

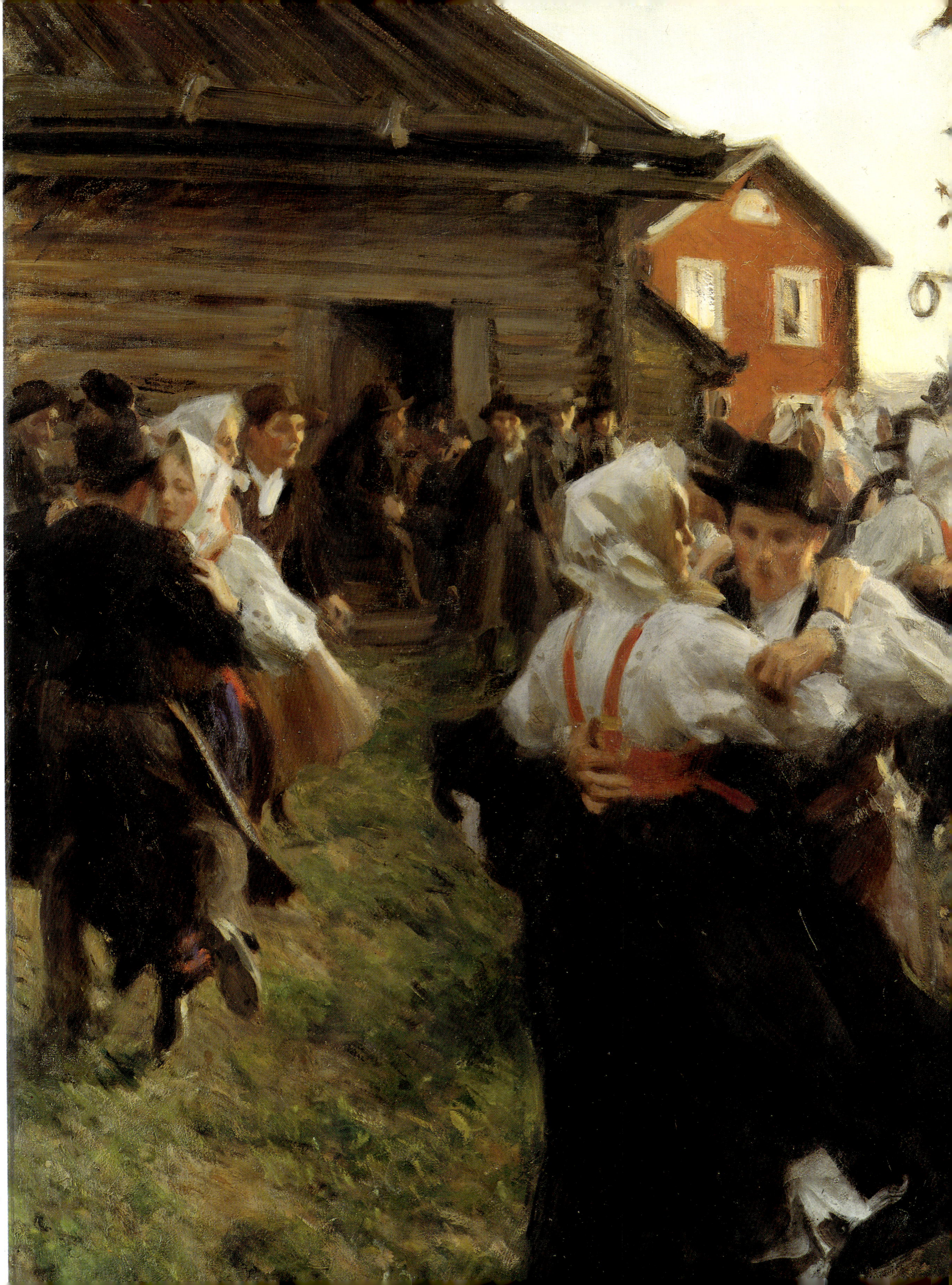

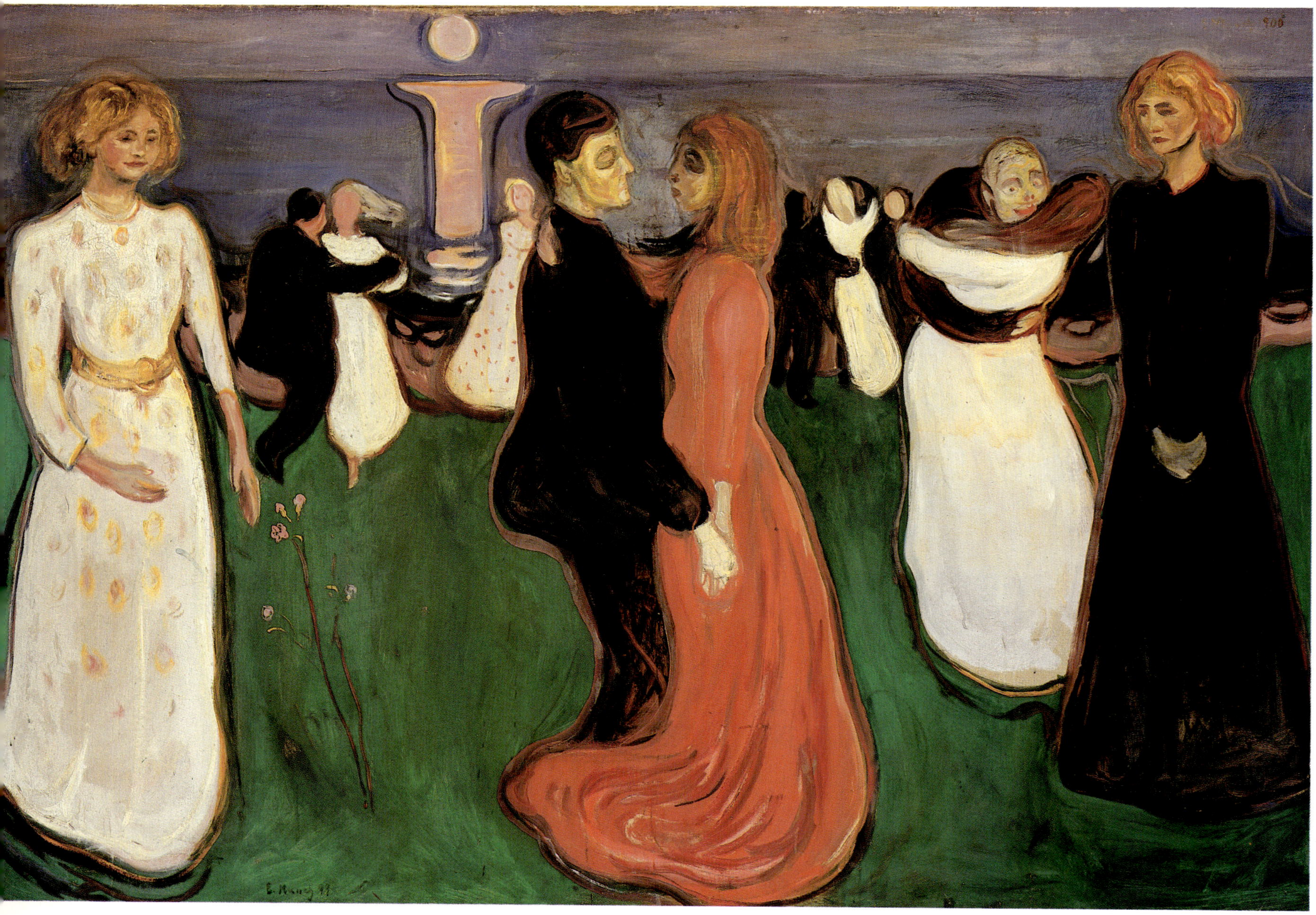

98

→ 99

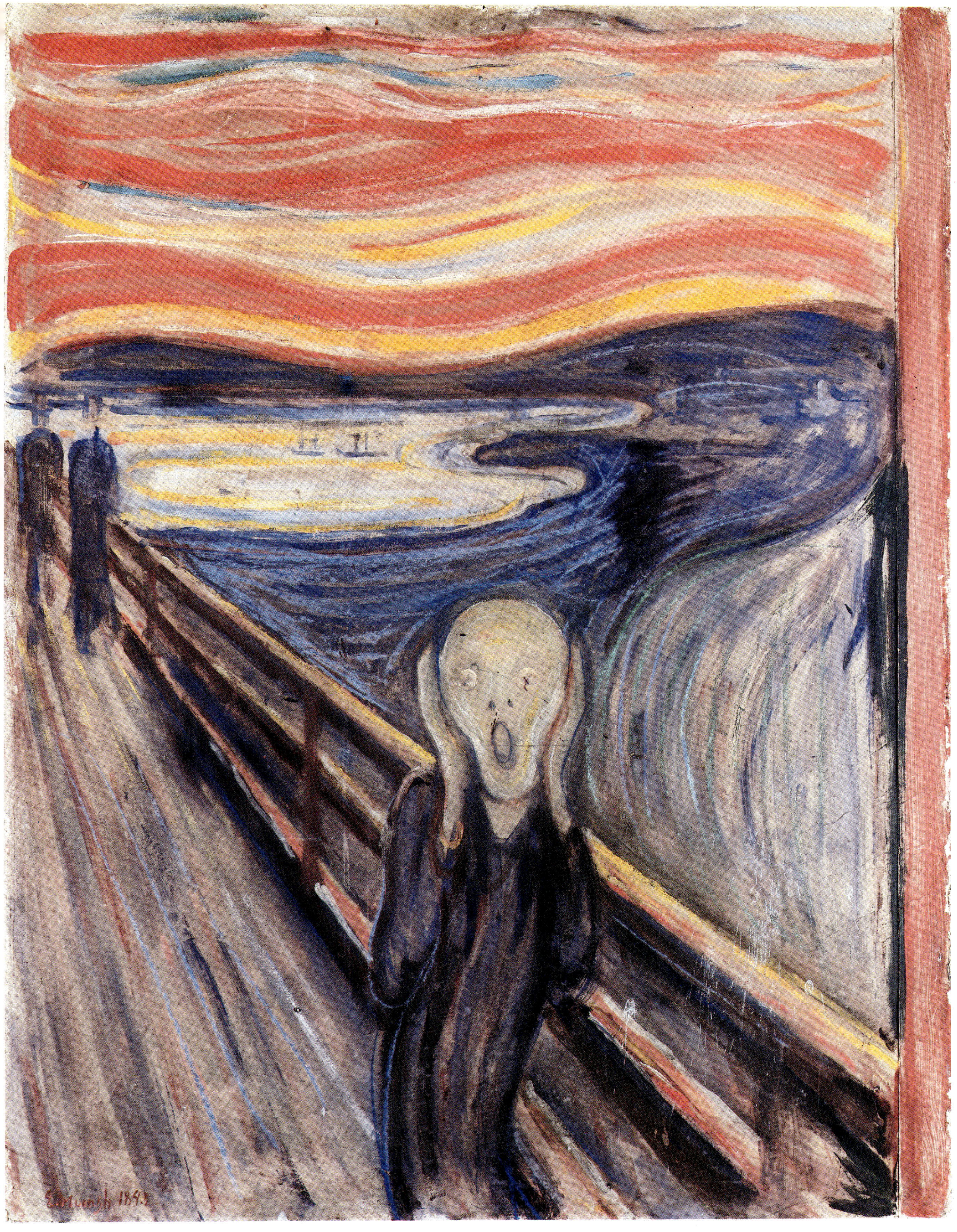

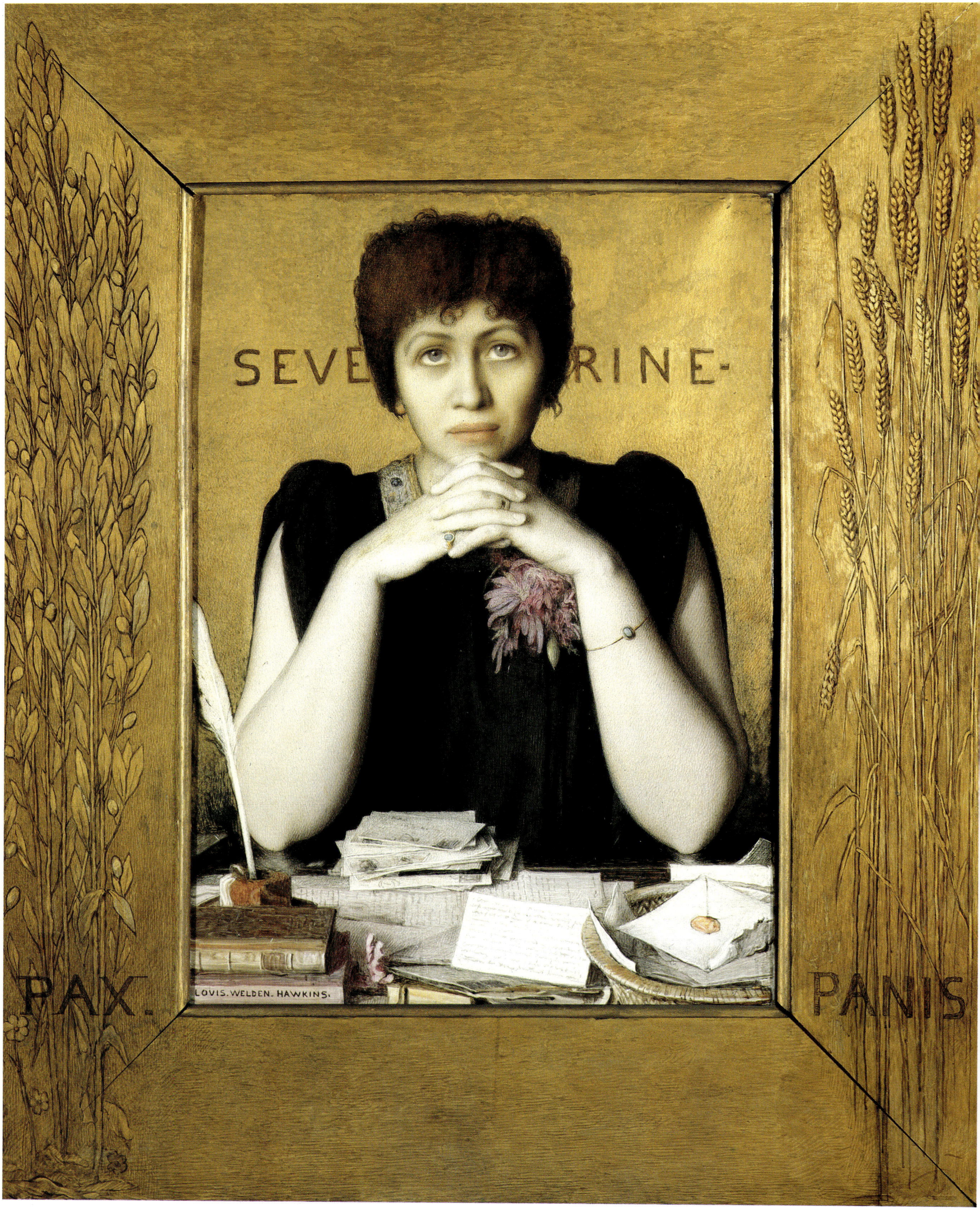
SEVE RINE-
PAX.
PANIS
LOVIS. WELDEN. HAWKINS.

93 Édouard Vuillard
The Piano (decoration in the library of Dr. Vaquez)
1896
Glue-based paint on canvas, 213 x 154 cm
Petit Palais, Paris

94 Gustave Moreau
Moses
c. 1893
Oil on canvas, 173 x 128 cm
Musée Gustave Moreau, Paris

95 Giovanni Segantini
The Unnatural Mothers (detail)
1894
Oil on canvas, overall dimensions 120 x 225 cm
Kunsthistorisches Museum, Vienna

96 Paul Cézanne
Woman with a Coffee Pot
c. 1890–95
Oil on canvas, 130 x 96.5 cm
Musée d'Orsay, Paris

97 Anders Zorn
Midsummer's Day Dance
1897
Oil on canvas, 98 x 140 cm
Nationalmuseum, Stockholm

98 Edvard Munch
The Dance of Life
1899
Oil on canvas, 125 x 190 cm
Nasjonalgalleriet, Oslo

99 Edvard Munch
The Scream
1893
Tempera and pastel on card, 91 x 74 cm
Nasjonalgalleriet, Oslo

100 Louis-Welden Hawkins
Portrait of Séverine
1893
Oil on canvas, 77 x 55 cm
Musée d'Orsay, Paris

101 Akseli Gallén-Kallela
The Mäntykoski Rapids
1891–94
Oil on canvas, 270 x 156 cm
Collection of the Jorma Gallén-Kallela family, Lugano

102 Harald Sohlberg
Summer Night
1899
Oil on canvas, 114 x 136 cm
Nasjonalgalleriet, Oslo

103 Georges Lemmen
Beach at Heist
1891
Oil on canvas, 37.5 x 46 cm
Musée d'Orsay, Paris

104 Jacek Malczewski
Elloe and Ellenai
1908–9
Oil on paper, 218 x 129 cm
Muzeum Narodowe, Poznan

105 Giulio-Aristide Sartorio
Gorgon and the Heroes
1897
Oil on canvas, 305 x 421 cm
Galleria Nazionale d'Arte Moderna, Rome

106 Paul Cézanne
Montagne Sainte-Victoire and Château Noir
1904–6
Oil on canvas, 65.5 x 81 cm
Bridgestone Museum, Tokyo

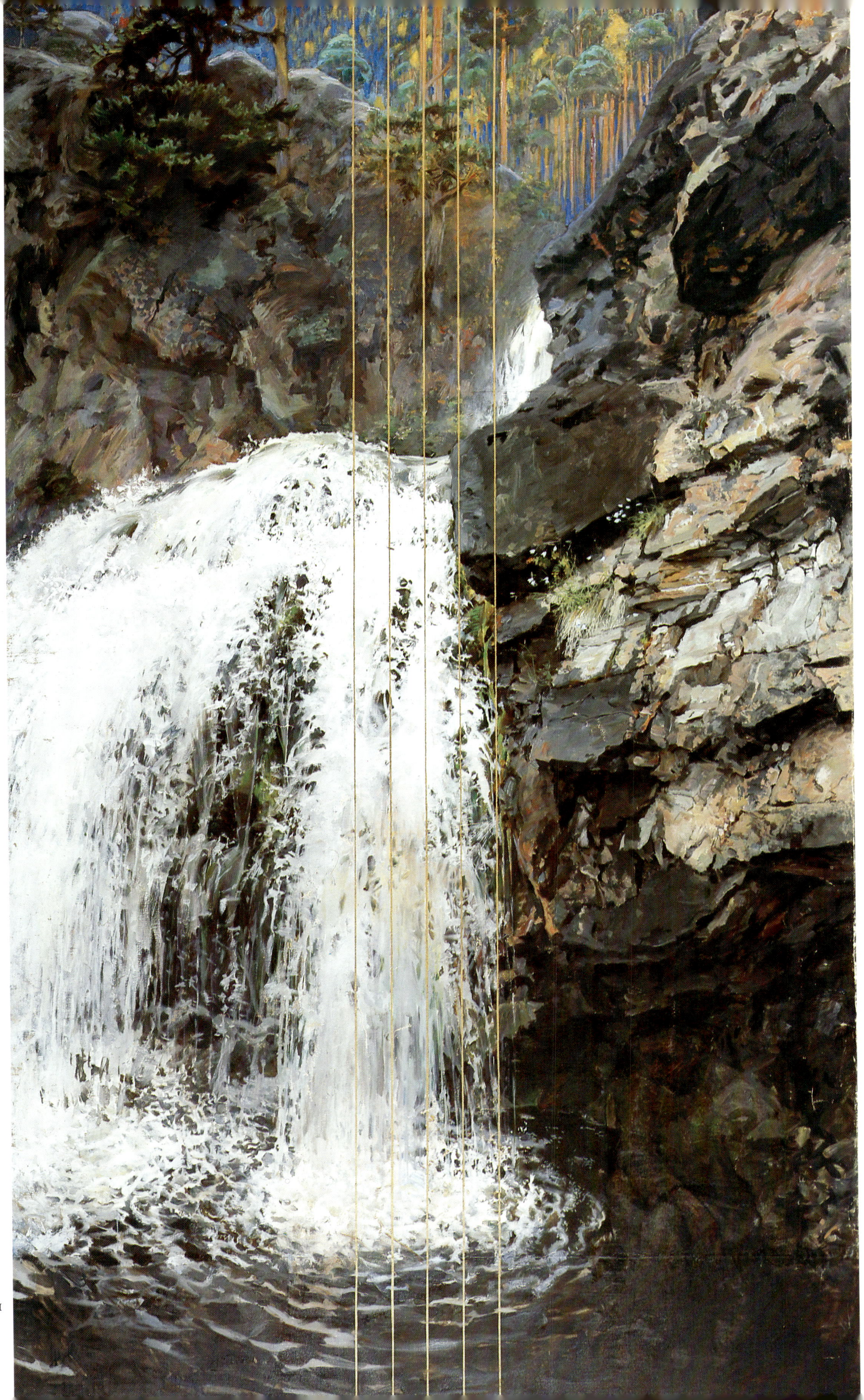

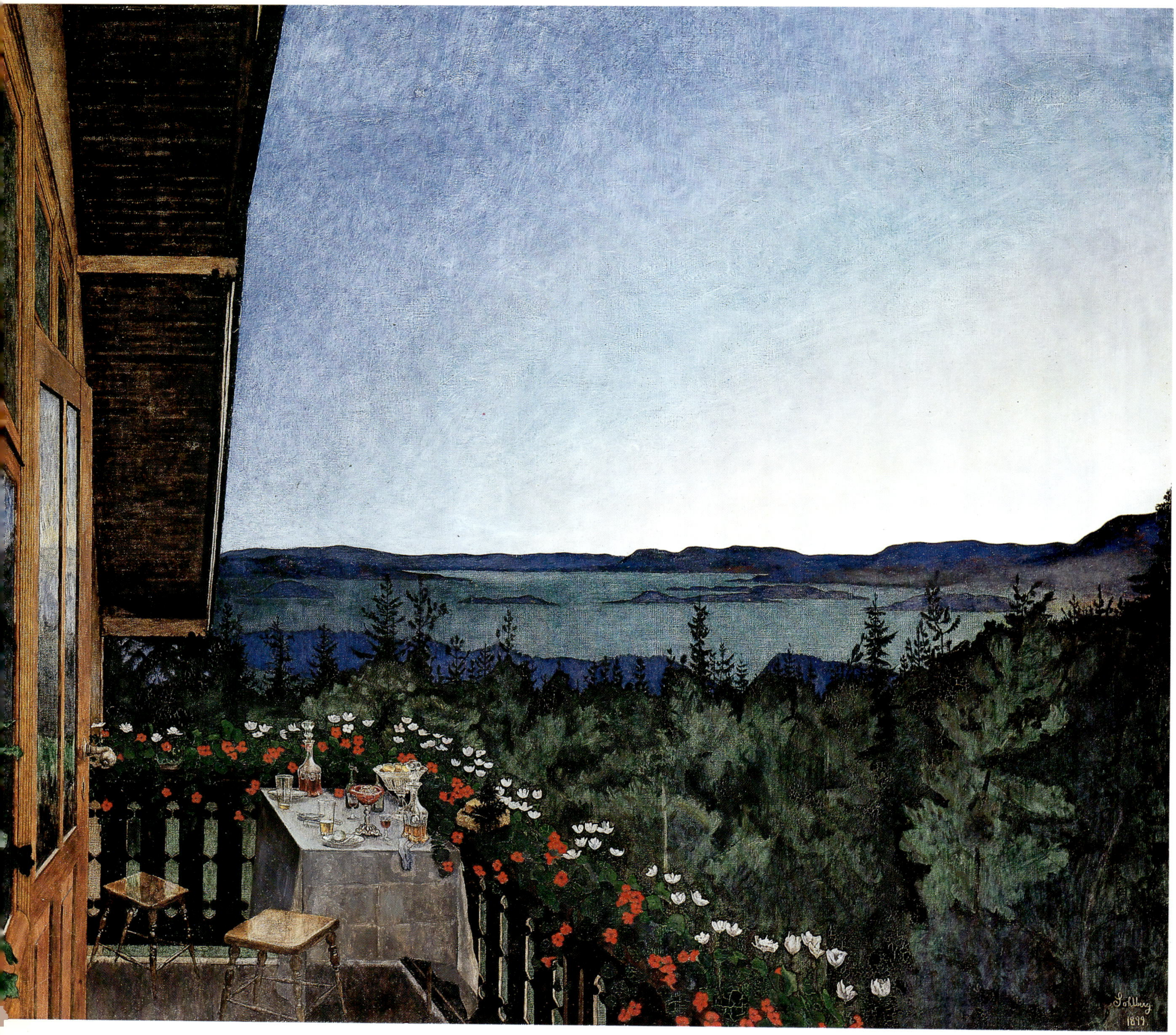

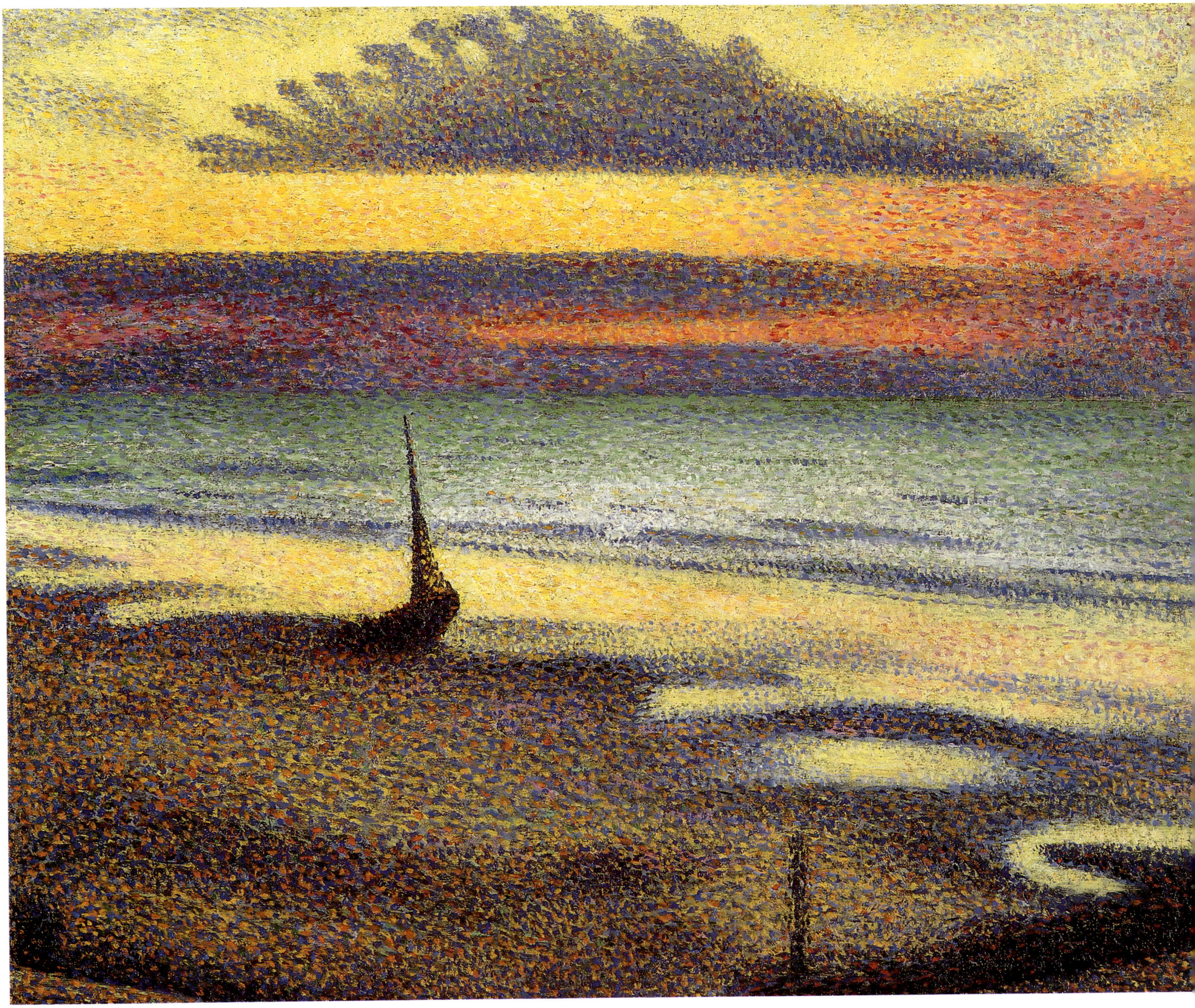

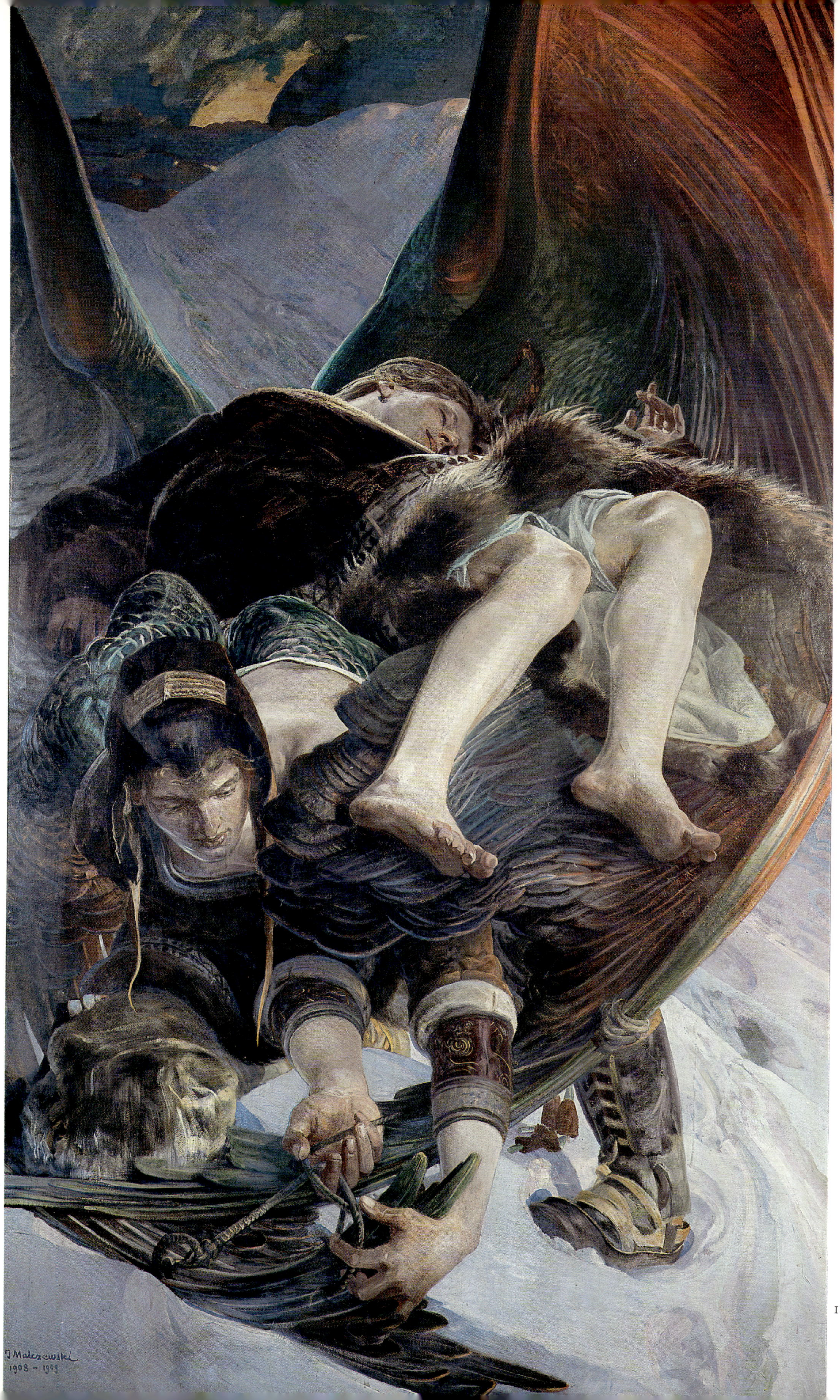
J. Malczewski
1908 – 1909

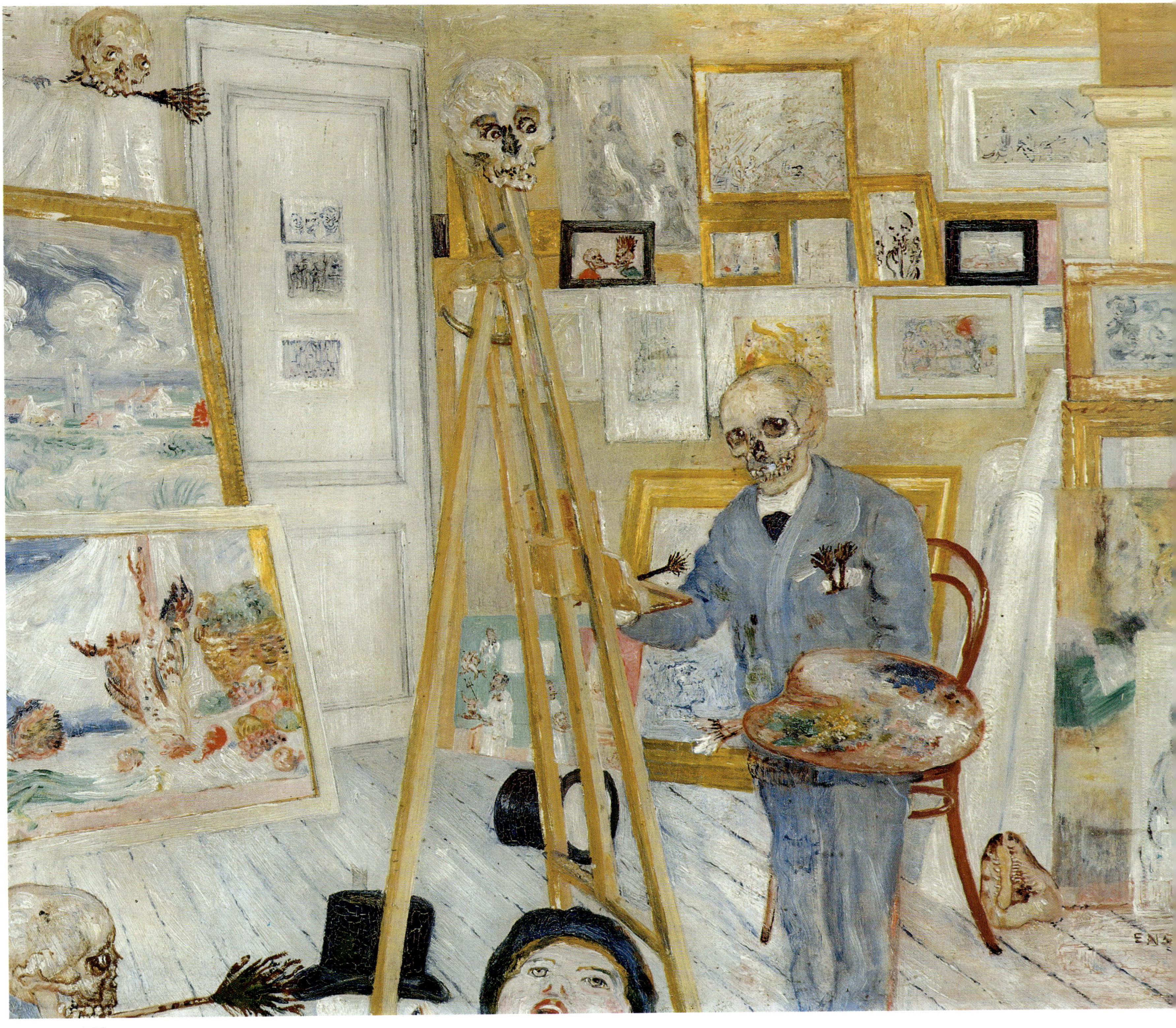
ENS

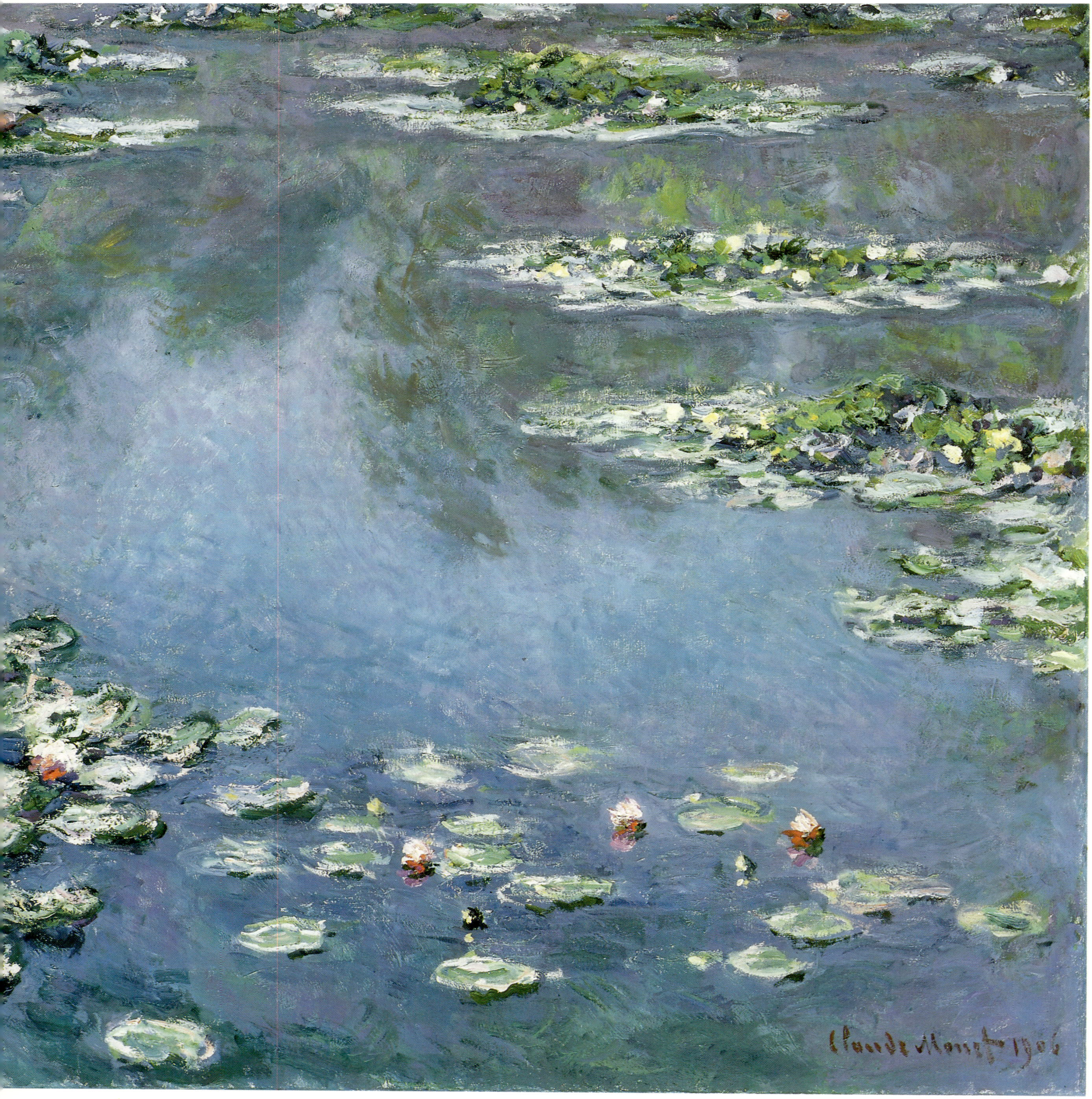
Claude Monet 1906

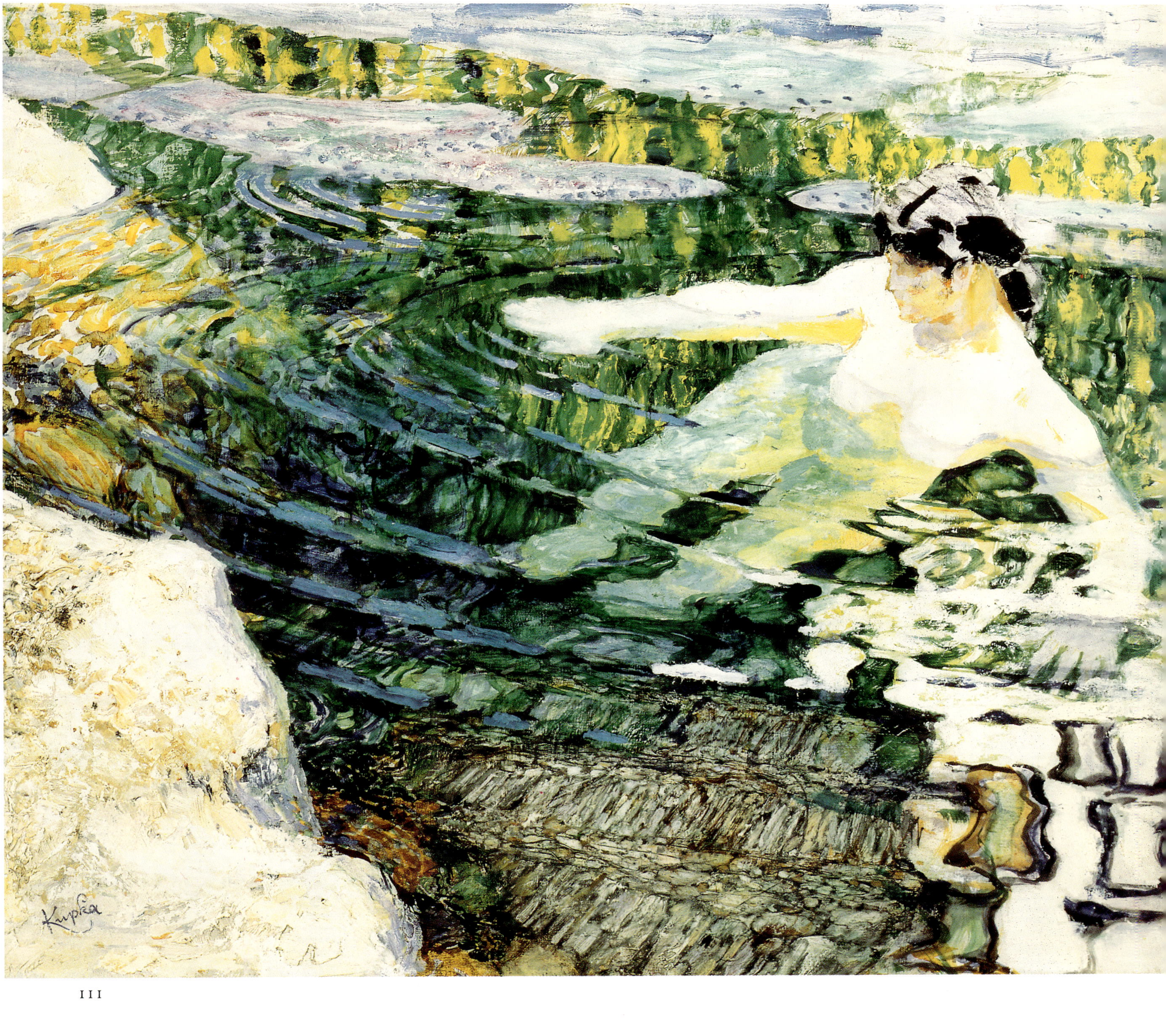

III

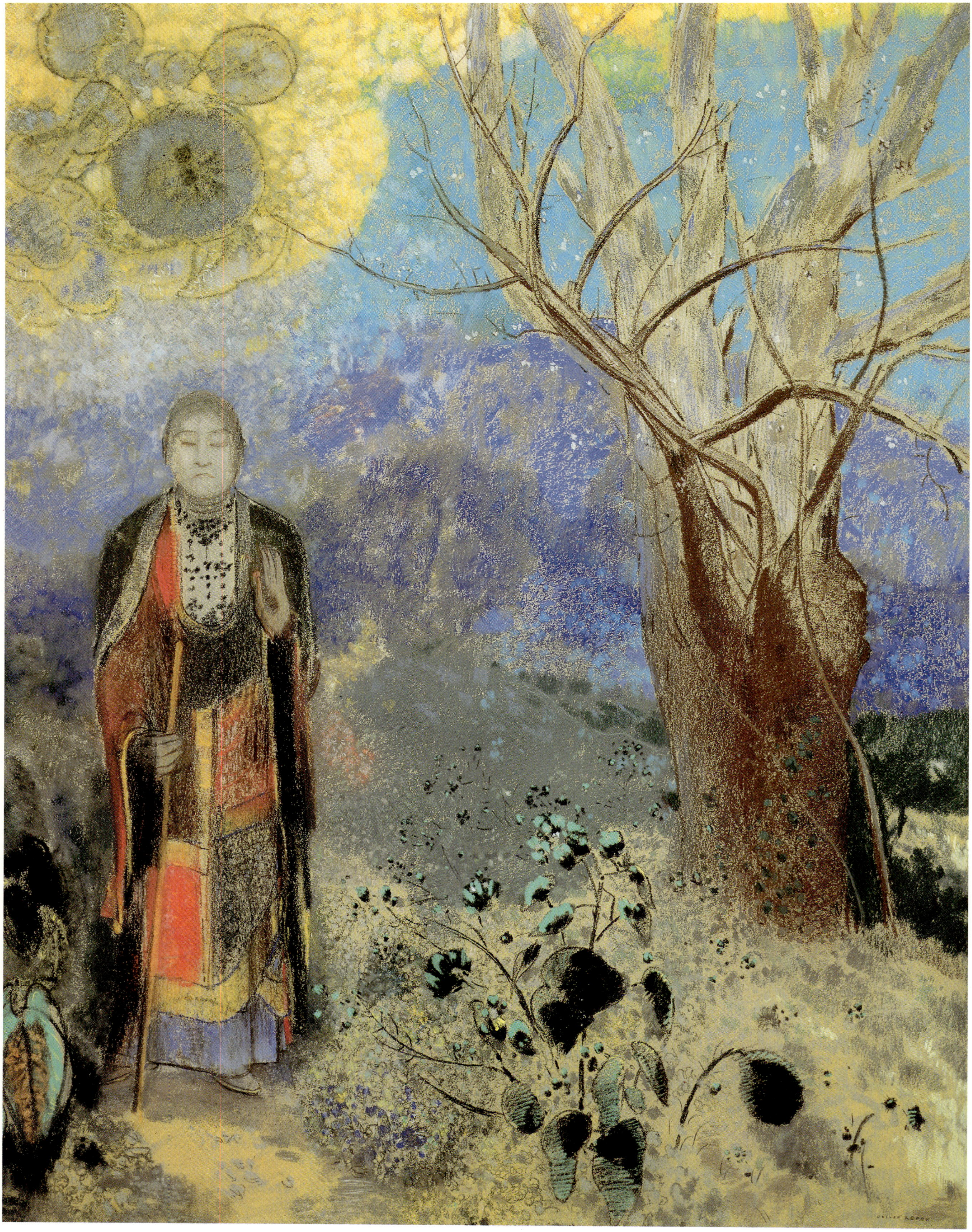

107 Piet Mondrian
Fishing Boat Leaving Harbor
c. 1900
Watercolor and charcoal, 62 x 100 cm
Musée d'Orsay, Paris

108 Giuseppe Pellizza da Volpedo
The Sun
1904
Oil on canvas, 150 x 150 cm
Galleria Nazionale d'Arte Moderna, Rome

109 James Ensor
Skeleton Painter
1896
Oil on wood, 37.5 x 45.5 cm
Koninklijk Museum voor Schone Kunsten, Antwerp

110 Claude Monet
Water Lilies
1906
Oil on canvas, 87.6 x 92.7 cm
Art Institute of Chicago (Mr. and Mrs. Martin A. Ryerson Collection), Chicago

111 Frantisek Kupka
Water or *Woman Bathing*
1906–9
Oil on canvas, 63 x 80 cm
Musée National d'Art Moderne, Paris

112 Odilon Redon
The Buddha
c. 1905
Pastel, 90 x 73 cm
Musée d'Orsay, Paris

SCULPTURE

SCULPTURE UNDER THE SECOND EMPIRE (1852–70)

"Never was Phidias better understood, nor Michelangelo more loved. But whatever may have been said, to understand is not to equal, and enthusiasm is not the same thing as potential" (Mantz 1859, 184). "But how, alas, is one to set about rejuvenating an art that was sublime in Egypt, perfect among the Greeks, impressive in ancient Rome, thrilling in the hands of Puget, full of feeling when David's was the hand on the chisel, a roaring success in Barye's bronzes? Who is going to find a vein still unworked at the bottom of this mine that seems exhausted and yet is inexhaustible? That is the thought preoccupying our sculptors, that is what disturbs them" (Blanc 1866, 62). "What the sculpture of today lacks is the accent of modernity" (Mantz 1869, 363).

Such judgments highlighted the need for a revival but that revival was slow in coming because sculptors were so knowledgeable about the past. Sculpture under the Second Empire was indeed chiefly a matter of "neo" this and "neo" that.

NEOCLASSICISM

Defined during the first quarter of the nineteenth century, Neoclassicism continued until the century was well advanced. In France, circumstances were very much in its favor. The Second Empire, keen to assert its descent from the First, took up the style that had enjoyed the patronage of the latter, and Neoclassicism was the natural choice for the many monuments to Napoleon erected during his nephew's reign. Pierre-Charles Simart (1806–1857) had drawn on allegory and antiquity for the bas-reliefs that he designed for the emperor's tomb in the Hôtel des Invalides (1846–53), while in 1859 Eugène Guillaume (1822–1905) quite naturally used classical dress (the first time this had been done on a major statue) for the *Napoleon* that he carved for the atrium of Prince Napoleon's Maison Pompéienne in the Avenue Montaigne, Paris (now demolished). The political power of Neoclassicism asserted itself in 1863, when the frock-coated "Little Corporal" that Charles-Émile Seurre (1798–1858) had set on top of the Colonne Vendôme in 1833 was replaced by a Napoleon portrayed as a Roman emperor by Augustin Dumont (1801–1884), which claimed to be a reconstruction of the first statue (by Antoine-Denis Chaudet, 1763–1810) torn down in 1814. In the following year, despite the fact that the statue in question was contemporaneous with Guillaume's, this "antique disguise" was roundly condemned (Thoré 1864, 144) when the large *Napoleon on Horseback* (*Napoléon équestre*, 1859, plaster, destroyed) made by Auguste Clésinger (1814–1883) for the Louvre's Cour Napoléon was exhibited outside the Palais de l'Industrie. Nevertheless, it retained its popularity, and it was again as a Roman emperor, modeled on the equestrian *Marcus Aurelius* in the Campidoglio in Rome, that Antoine-Louis Barye (1796–1875), for example, represented Napoleon in the *Monument to the Bonaparte Brothers* in Ajaccio (1865).

Encouraged by the government (albeit not to the exclusion of other forms of expression), Neoclassicism also enjoyed the backing of the Académie des Beaux-Arts, which was responsible for the École des Beaux-Arts in Paris and the Académie de France in Rome and which turned out to be very much narrower in its predilections. To be successful, an artist needed to win the Prix de Rome. He studied for this under teachers who were themselves former winners of the prize and members of the Institut de France, and it took him to the Villa Medici in Rome, where the supervision of the Académie des Beaux-Arts still made itself felt through the system of submissions and reports. Students were continually urged to study antiquity as the "source and timeless example of great art" in such a way as to imbue themselves with it. What the Institute feared most of all was the temptation that might emanate from contemporary Italy. Thus Eugène Guillaume, who went on to amass every possible reward and distinction (member of the Institut de France in 1862, principal of the École des Beaux-Arts in 1863, director of the Académie des Beaux-Arts in 1878, professor at the Collège de France in 1882, director of the Académie de France in Rome in 1891, elected to the Académie Française in 1899 for his books on art), was clearly a model student. His first submission, the *Cenotaph of the Gracchi* (*Cénotaphe des Gracques*, plaster, submission of 1847; bronze, Musée d'Orsay, Paris), was based on a type of funerary monument common under the Roman Republic and in the early years of the Empire, and throughout the time he spent in Rome he remained faithful to the inspiration of antiquity. His final-year figure *Reaper* (*Faucheur*, 1849, plaster; bronze, Musée d'Orsay, Paris) is more than simply an image of labor: this is a nude study inspired by an antique model, the *Borghese Gladiator* (Louvre). Like him, Eugène Lequesne (1815–1887) was incapable of getting away from classical form. The only Gallic things about his nude seated figure of *Camulogenus* (*Camulogène*, 1872, marble, Musée des Beaux-Arts, Lille) are the mustache and the hairstyle; the old chief who fiercely defended Lutetia during Caesar's seventh campaign in Gaul is presented as a middle-aged man meditating philosophically on his defeat.

This combination of the weight of tradition with favorable political circumstances gave Neoclassicism the appearance of the official style under the Second Empire, and at the 1867 Exposition Universelle the two big medals went to two artists who represented Neoclassicism in its strictest form. They were Guillaume, the very symbol of an official sculptor during the second half of the nineteenth century, and Jean-Joseph Perraud (1819–1876), a more attractive character whom Auguste Rodin admired and whose works, even at their most Classical, afford a glimpse of Romantic anguish.

Neoclassicism was well represented in the Salons and, because of its solemnity, it was the preferred style for official buildings—which was natural enough when it came to designing law courts, for example, but rather more surprising in the case of the Gare du Nord in Paris. Undoubtedly, Neoclassicism did offer certain advantages: "Where would statuary be without the gods and heroes of mythology furnishing it with plausible pretexts for the nudes and drapery it so needs?" (Benoist 1928, 35). That was indeed what Neoclassicism meant: idealized nudes, antique drapery, a balanced composition with no hint of passion, all executed in marble, which was considered the most noble of materials. But not everyone agreed. The fact was that Neoclassicism seemed ill-adapted to the modern world.

One of the first questions raised was that of the nude. Few sculptors, in fact, were able, like Auguste Ottin (1811–1890), to find a subject to justify it in the contemporary world. The idea for his *Modern Wrestling, The Hip Throw* (*La Lutte moderne, le coup de hanche*, fig. 481) came from two famous wrestlers who staged bouts in Paris in 1859, the "hip throw" being one of the best-known throws in hand-to-hand combat, a sport in which "full nudity is obligatory, enabling one to study form," as the artist noted in his *Mémoires* (Archives du Louvre). However, to anyone who has not read Ottin's *Mémoires*, the obvious conclusion is that this is simply a modern version of the famous antique statue in Florence known as *The Athletes*. Realism might already have been entrenched in painting and literature, but in sculpture (apart from portrait sculpture) there could be no question of it yet. So when Charles-Alphonse-Achille Gumery (1827–1871) showed his *Harvester* (*Moissonneur*, plaster, destroyed) at the 1859 Salon, the work was nothing other than a study of the nude. The same could be said for Simart's *Ruzzica Player* (*Joueur de ruzzica*, 1837, plaster, Musée des Beaux-Arts, Troyes), ostensibly inspired by a game that the artist had seen played beneath the walls of Rome, or Guillaume's *Reaper*. Like Paul Mantz and Henri Delaborde, who both regarded it as one of the finest figures in the exhibition, Maxime Du Camp did not deny that Gumery's *Harvester* had qualities, but for him it raised the problem of the nude *per se*, which he denounced in the name of realism: "I realize that, up to a point, the nude is the fundamental law of sculpture, but even so one must be able to apply that law without outrageously offending common sense; or else it must be admitted that the hair constitutes the costume and the tool the occupation . . . Because antiquity often depicted its gods in the nude, people imagine rather over-simply that they imitate the ancients when they bestow such nudity on a reaper in the act of sharpening his scythe . . . In God's name, why not take away the hat, the scythe, the goatskin, and the sharpening-stone; why not put the figure in a bathing suit and, since it absolutely has to be a nude, call it: *Reaper Learning to Swim*" (Du Camp 1859, 184, 185). Jules Vallès went further: "But you know full well that the weather in Paris is rainy and cold, that the poor get their rags drenched and are chilled to the bone, their feet frozen; and you know full well that a man playing a pipe in a fig leaf, not even wearing underclothes, would be arrested . . . So why sculpt people in the nude?" (Vallès 1868).

Not everyone took that view. Jules Cavelier (1814–1894), in his *Penelope*—included in the 1849 Salon but first shown in 1842 under the title *Greek Woman Asleep* (*Femme grecque endormie*)—played with the drapery and the picturesque details of chair, basket, and jewelry and the work was a huge success (fig. 113). The duke de Luynes bought the piece for his Dampierre château, but Cavelier retained the reproduction rights, and his contract with Ferdinand Barbedienne, who offered the figure in a choice of six sizes, earned him more than eight times the value of the marble (10,000 francs). Indeed, the *Penelope* became so widespread that in 1862 it formed the object of a puzzle in an illustrated journal (*Le Monde illustré*).

While still ranking antiquity above everything, more advanced spirits such as Castagnary, Théophile Thoré, Théophile Gautier, and Maxime Du Camp denounced the absurdity of seeking to imitate it and the sterility to which such imitation must inevitably lead. Thus when Léon Lagrange suggested as axiomatic that "pagan antiquity, which raised the art of sculpture to such heights, will forever remain an excellent source of inspiration for sculptors" (Lagrange 1861, 167), Du Camp retorted: "The process is a very simple one: you take the head of Antinoüs, the pectorals of Germanicus, and the legs of Bacchus, and with these bits and pieces you make a statue of a man; female statues are obtained in the same fashion: the Venus de Milo supplies the face, Polyhymnia loans her draperies, Diana of Ephesus provides the movement and the remainder" (Du Camp 1857, 166).

Lagrange was one of a group of critics who could not find high enough praise for the *Virgil* sculpted by Gabriel-Jules Thomas (1824–1905), *Agrippina Bearing the Ashes of Germanicus* (*Agrippine portant les cendres de Germanicus*, 1859–61, marble, Mont-Valérien Fort) by Jacques-Léonard Maillet (1823–1895), and Cavelier's *Cornelia, Mother of the Gracchi* (*Cornélie, mère des gracques*, fig. 457) at the 1861 Salon, and for Perraud's *Education of Bacchus* (*Éducation de Bacchus*, 1857–63, marble, Musée des Beaux-Arts, Lons-le-Saunier) at the 1863 Salon, or for *Mercury* (*Mercure*, 1864, bronze, École des Beaux-Arts, Paris) by the late Jean-Louis Brian (1805–1864), which was presented in the following year and which provided, for these traditionalists, incontrovertible proof of the "degree of beauty [that] can be attained by the art of sculpture reduced to its classic elements, the study of nature and of antiquity" (Lagrange 1864, 32). All these works (most of which were immediately acquired by the state) were distinguished by a certain serenity or at least a balance that sets off their formal qualities. "Excellent work . . . faultless arrangement . . . conscientious execution," and "masterly execution . . . nature refined by taste . . . studied and imitated with wonderful care . . . a most exalted talent" were some of the phrases that Thoré used about Cavelier's *Cornelia* (Thoré 1861, 166) and Du Camp about Perraud's *Education of Bacchus* (Du Camp 1863, 910, 911). However, Thoré criticized *Cornelia* for not producing "any moral or practical impression. The piece lacks enthusiasm, fire . . . communicative life, personality, character." Perraud's *Faun*, Du Camp wrote, "smacks too much of study of the model and a precoccupation with antiquity; it lacks that indefinable quality of the personal and distinctive that confers an ineradicable cachet on works of art; in a word, it lacks that divine flame, inspiration." As for the *Mercury*, although for Thoré it had "the appeal that the sketches of a master generally possess" (Thoré 1864, 149), it was criticized for holding the attention only "by its regularity of form and the rightness of its proportions"—in other words, it gave the appearance of being "a materialistic work, without significance and without impact, conceived purely from the standpoint of formal equilibrium" (Castagnary 1864, 127). If *Cornelia* was a work that one forgot as soon as it was out of one's sight, and if the *Faun*, which "if disfigured . . . could easily pass for an antique masterpiece" (Gautier 1857, 2:183), left one cold, what was the reason? It was certainly not a lack of talent. Rather, it had to do with the fact "that the sculptors of antiquity believed in fauns and we do not any more. For us, a faun is a model . . . viewed through our recollections of such and such a statue, bas-relief, or medallion" (Du Camp 1863, 911). As David d'Angers said of Simart, "antiquity is a field that quickly becomes sterile if one does not, while reaping it, add some inspiration of one's own" (Jouin 1878, 2:175).

Modern Allegory

For contemporaries, a revival of sculpture might occur through representation "of the passions, sufferings, virtues, and vices of our time. Whereas for more than eighty years now [sculptors] have been going round and round in the same circle without being able to escape from it, incessantly doing and redoing what had already been done before them; they seek no inspiration in themselves, they seek it only in their memories. What they lack is imagination and reflection. They neither see nor understand that in our age, an age so peculiarly rich in discoveries, a new allegory (i.e., statue) is born every day" (Du Camp 1863, 910). Jules Vallès went further: "Never has it occurred to them to tear their subject matter from the entrails of modern life, never have they dug deep into the heap of passions teeming around them; in statuary there are two or three poses, two or three folds, two or three facial expressions, and two or three noses that our sculptors have been using for centuries!"

Granted, as early as 1857 Louis-Joseph Lebœuf (?–1870), "a revolutionary . . . who boldly disregarded the whole procession of mythology to tackle large human figures" (Cantrel 1863, 1930), did take an initial step by exhibiting a figure of *Labor* (*Travail*, plaster, whereabouts unknown) that was much appreciated by forward-looking critics. "He represents it as it is . . . in its true form as a sturdy, fearless young man. He stands there bare-chested, broad, breathing deeply, his shoulders muscular, his arms pronounced, leaning on an anvil and holding in his hand the heavy blacksmith's hammer" (Du Camp 1857, 167). Lebœuf's *Labor* may have had something to do with the dream of a *Monument to Labor* (*Monument au travail*) that Thoré conceived at the 1865 Salon in front of *Plowman* (*Laboureur*, plaster, Musée Crozatier, Le Puy) by Charles Capellaro (1826–1899) and *Sower* (*Semeur*, bronze, destroyed) by Henri Chapu (1833–1891), "again men of ancient times who originate from mythology, a group of farmers in smocks, that sort of *sagum* worn by our ancestors, which hangs as satisfyingly as the Roman tunic; and to accompany them the plow and all the tools of agriculture, large and small . . . Could not industry, like agriculture, inspire statuary with some more modern ideas? What fine monuments might be erected in train stations, harbors, docks, markets, and public squares to give expression to the power of labor and the conquests of the mind in contrast to war and superstition! Maybe it will come" (Thoré 1865, 263). Certainly, some thirty or forty years later, the idea occurred to such sculptors as Rodin, Aimé-Jules Dalou, and Constantin Meunier, though it did not, at least in their lifetimes, get beyond the planning stage.

But under the Second Empire there was no question, as yet, of any monument to labor, and if the locomotive, for instance, did make several appearances in the carved decoration of the Louvre, it was always slipped in discreetly, as an attribute.

However, critics like Thoré and Du Camp were to find an answer to their aspirations in a work that seemed to them the very incarnation of modern man. This was Perraud's *Despair* (*Désespoir*, fig. 470), which was unanimously admired in plaster at the 1861 Salon and then in marble at the 1869 Salon (Musée d'Orsay, Paris). The piece struck them as a "giant step" in the evolution of sculpture. This figure, seated on the ground, according to a well-established convention, is intended to be an allegory of the tragic condition of human existence. He expresses the situation of Perraud himself, as revealed on numerous occasions by his friend and biographer, the sculptor Max Claudet: "Perraud's whole existence can be summed up in the two words work and pain. Despair is the story of my life, he used to say" (Claudet 1877, 129). But the figure is without any accessories, and allows the viewer complete freedom of interpretation, as witness the three titles it bore successively. In 1861 it was accompanied only by a line from a lament by Petrarch on the death of Laura: *Ahi! null'altro che pianto al mondo dura*; in 1869 it was exhibited as *Despair*; finally, in 1877 Claudet called it *Orpheus*. "Such indecision . . . is indicative of the dissipation . . . of the precise meanings traditionally attached to a title, character, or story; it illustrates an aspect of thinking about figure sculpture for which, henceforth, only historical information is attached that, as it dwindles, becomes charged with personal and poetic meanings of substantially increased importance" (Jacques de Caso 1987, 610). This was how *Despair* (for that was the title that prevailed) went against the rules of Neoclassicism, which set out to be precise and descriptive; for example, the plain *Male Figure* (*Figure d'Homme*, plaster, whereabouts unknown) exhibited in 1837 by Eugène-André Oudiné (1810–1857) became a *Gladiator* (*Gladiateur*) when in 1865 it reappeared in marble (whereabouts unknown). In terms of form, however, *Despair* retains an academic perfection that irritated the very people who most admired the allegorical resonance of the figure and prompted Castagnary to make this extraordinary suggestion (prophetic, if one thinks of Rodin): "Shall I say that this exceptional statue has one capital fault? Why not . . . The head is wrong. It is vulgar, trivial, poorly constructed, and poorly attached; moreover, it is useless. Yes, useless . . . If we imagine the figure without that unfortunate appendage, is its conception in any way diminished? Does it not rather gain in strength and intensity? Do not the torso, arms, and legs say what they have to say more effectively?" (Castagnary 1869).

The Neo-Greeks

Around the hardcore of Neoclassical artists, who included Guillaume, Perraud, Thomas, Maillet, Cavelier, and Élias Robert (1821–1874), there were a number of artists who did not pass through the Académie de France in Rome but were likewise alive to the advantages of Neoclassicism, though they did not practice it exclusively. Not only was it capable of supplying a wealth of subject matter, antiquity also offered a way of giving graceful expression to themes that might have been situated in a quite different period. The Salons included a large number of such figures, which were often referred to as "néo-grecques" (neo-Greek). After Cavelier's *Penelope* (*Pénélope*, 1842–49, fig. 113), which could be regarded as an early example of the genre, *Woman Spinning* (*Fileuse*) by Mathurin Moreau (1822–1912) enjoyed particular success. The piece was praised by critics of such opposing schools as Du Camp, for whom it was one of the only works worth saving from the shipwreck of sculpture, and the more measured Delaborde, who saw it as the acme of contemporary taste: "Pretty is undoubtedly the word for this work, in which one should look neither for elevation of thought nor for vigor of execution but in which one will find neither affectation of style nor a gracefulness frankly borrowed from elsewhere . . . A discreet eclecticism . . . ingeniously reconciling the demands of today's taste and certain traditions that, if not of sterner stuff, are at least more pure" (Delaborde 1859, 524).

We admire the grace of the spinner's movements, the "archaeological" accuracy of her tall wicker basket, and the elegance of the drapery. One of the advantages of Neoclassicism was that it permitted this kind of flattering arrangement of dress. If the artist preferred the nude, antiquity could also furnish the pretext. Few sculptors did as Emmanuel Fremiet (1824–1910) did with his *Pan with Bear Cubs* (*Pan et Oursons*, fig. 120) group, which was to take a humorous look at what Thoré called "good old mythology." Mythology was usually no more than an excuse—one which the artist did not always even seek to make plausible: "Why *Ariadne* [1862, marble, Invalides, Paris]?" asks Émile Chatrousse before the figure sculpted by Aimé Millet (1819–1891), "Because it is always . . . *mythology or death*. And anyway it looks so good, a Greek name on the bottom of a statue! That would be enough to give the piece style, if it lacked it. Besides, this particular figure has none of the traditions or resonance of mythology . . . [but] could be regarded as a carefully chosen type of modern beauty . . . As for the emotion and color of Ariadne—any human feeling, in fact—I detect little here; the pose does not suggest them. The face is weeping, certainly, but in so calm and graceful a fashion as to foreshadow Ariadne consoled" (Chatrousse 1862, 124). It was not so much for depth of emotion that artists turned to antiquity now, but more as a pretext for portraying the nude—which following Clésinger they sought to make as sensual as possible. Faced with *Golden-Haired Venus* (1859–62, marble, Château de Compiègne) by Charles-Auguste Arnaud (1825–1883) or *Bacchante* (fig. 466) by Albert-Ernest Carrier-Belleuse (1824–1887), certain critics railed against these "nymphs, [these] bacchantes, [these] Venuses . . . [who] now assume the most violent postures, indulging in the most unnatural contortions to place before the viewer's eyes precisely what he doubtless has no wish to see" (Du Camp 1863, 907, 908). They denounced the "enervating and unhealthy influence" that had spread from painting to sculpture—and that led Du Camp to condemn this type of nude for excessive realism, as he had condemned the Neoclassical nude for lack of justification. But most people liked what they saw. They marveled at the model depicted in *Bacchante*, which was one of the big hits of the 1863 Salon, with the ripeness of her body emphasized by her contorted pose and with her luxuriant hair (a feature that Baudelaire and Courbet had turned into a symbol of eroticism). But without going so far as the ever-extreme Du Camp, many regretted the fact that she presented an "accidental" type rather than "eternal beauty": "I could have wished for greater elevation and a happier choice of model; the feet are clumsy and the hands lack nobility. You will say in reply that a bacchante is not a duchess. No doubt, but those feet do rather spoil the statue for me" (Yriarte 1863, 47). But clearly the most common Neoclassical standpoint was still the one expressed wrily in the following words: "His bacchante is made of flesh . . . However, this naturalistic quality has its down side: all the accidents of reality will never match up to a timeless art whose very essence is to generalize and to elevate form to the ideal type subsuming all ephemeral variations." What better definition of Neoclassicism could there be than the one implicit in this comment by Thoré (Thoré 1863, 432)?

Neoclassicism Outside France: "Made in Rome"

If in France it evolved in a quite specific way, elsewhere (notably Russia, the United States, Scandinavia, Great Britain, and Germany) Neoclassicism remained linked to Italy. Significantly, most marble statues bear the inscription "made in Rome." The situation changed, however, under the Second Empire, and by the end of that period it was no longer Rome that drew artists but Paris. They then abandoned Neoclassicism in favor of a more modern eclecticism or realism. For his *First Pose* (*Première Pose*, fig. 477), for example, the American Edward Roberts (1843–1900) drew his inspiration directly from *Waking Up* (*Réveil*) by Jules Franceschi (1825–1893), which he had undoubtedly seen at the 1873 Salon (fig. 479).

In Italy, the years 1850 to 1860 saw the passing of the first generation of the followers of Antonio Canova (1757–1822) and Bertel Thorwaldsen (1768/1770–1844). One of them, Pietro Tenerani (1789–1869), a pupil and principal collaborator of Thorwaldsen, disappeared after completing the grandiose *Monument to Pius VIII* (fig. 491) in Saint Peter's (1853–66) in the severe style he had learned from his master. Neoclassicism maintained its dominance until the end of the century and found masterly expression in the new basilica of S. Paolo Fuori le Mura in Rome, which was consecrated in 1854 (the first church having been destroyed by fire in 1823). Among the many sculptures that decorate it, one of the most interesting is the font (1860, fig. 490) by another of Thorwaldsen's pupils, Pietro Galli (1804–1877). The restoration was completed by the addition of a splendid four-bayed portico, begun in 1892 by Guglielmo Calderini, in the center of which stands a monumental figure of *St. Paul* (figs. 488, 489) by Giuseppe Obici (1807–1878). Obici also sculpted the *Virgin* that tops the *Column of the Immaculate Conception* (*Colonna dell'Immacolata Concezióne*) in the Piazza di Spagna (1856).

The Canovian tradition survived in Scipione Tadolini (1822–1892), whose father had worked with the great man. Tadolini's *Eve After Sinning* (*Eva dopo il peccato*, about 1850, plaster, Museo di Roma) and his graceful and melancholy *Greek Slave* (*Schiava greca*, fig. 474) enjoyed considerable success, with some forty replicas being executed of each one. This kind of distribution by means of large numbers of marble replicas was typical of Italy (in France it would be done through an edition in bronze).

In the Scandinavian countries, Neoclassicism remained a potent presence, notably in Denmark, where Thorwaldsen's influence was of course still very strong. Among other manifestations of that presence were some ten major friezes executed at intervals down the century, starting with the Alexander frieze that Thorwaldsen made for the Palazzo del Quirinale in Rome (1812). These were commissioned by the state to decorate churches and palaces. Christiansborg Palace in Copenhagen, for example, received the friezes of *Ragnarok* (1825) by Hermann Ernst Freund (1786–1840), *Ceres and Bacchus* (1835–1841) by Hermann Vilhelm Bissen (1798–1868), and *The Marriage of Alexander and Roxana* (1842–1864) by Jens Adolph Jerichau (1816–1883); destroyed by fire in 1884, these works were restored by pupils. In later years there were also private patrons such as Ottilia Jacobsen, who commissioned the *Valhalla* frieze (1886) by Stephan Abel Sinding (1846–1922) for the Ny Carlsberg Glyptotek.

In fact, the Neoclassical tradition persisted in Denmark into the early years of the twentieth century, when (about 1905) Carl and Ottilia Jacobsen were portrayed as a Roman couple by Carl Aarsleff (1852–1918) on the rear of the Glyptotek that they had founded. However, it was modified by numerous external contributions. Bissen, for example, who was seen as Thorwaldsen's most direct heir, was not impervious to naturalism. His *Woman Bathing* (1858–60, marble, Ny Carlsberg Glyptotek, Copenhagen) is a case in point, with her distinctly Danish features and meditative aspect, so different from the cold serenity of Neoclassicism. Like the Romantics in France, Bissen also accommodated the early history of his own country in his work (*Absalom*, bronze, facade of Copenhagen City Hall). Moreover, he was the first Danish sculptor to be affected by the realism of contemporary history, winning the 1848 competition for a monument to commemorate the Battle of Fredericia with the figure of an ordinary Danish soldier, which the jury preferred to Jerichau's *Thor*. Twenty years younger than Bissen, Jerichau was the other great representative of Danish Neoclassicism in the mid-nineteenth century. Like Bissen, he spent a long time in Rome. Yet in 1845–46 he executed a *Panther Hunt* (marble, Ny Carlsberg Glyptotek, Copenhagen) to show that he was capable of tackling modern subjects (although still in a very Neoclassical manner). In his later works, many of whose subjects in fact avoided the history and mythology of the ancient world, he yielded to a lyricism that was not without sensuality—as had already been apparent in certain scenes of the *Marriage of Alexander and Roxana*.

In Sweden, Johann Peter Molin (1814–1873) was also torn between a Neoclassical training and Romantic inclinations as a result of a stay in Paris from 1858. It is impossible not to think of Ottin's *Hip Throw* in connection with the *Knife Fight* (fig. 482) that Molin executed in Paris in 1858–59 and showed in the 1862 Salon. The work combines celebration of the athletic nude with an anecdotal content redolent of extreme violence, the two fighters being roped together and thus obliged to fight to the death. The bas-reliefs on the base compound the horror of the spectacle, since they make clear that this contest is over a woman.

In the United States, as in France, Neoclassicism benefited from the political situation: it helped to bolster the regime by suggesting kinship between it and the Roman Republic of antiquity. Encouraged by the example of Horatio Greenough (1805–1852), the first American to practice sculpture professionally and also the first to take up residence in Italy, two generations of artists settled first in Florence, to which they were attracted by Lorenzo Bartolini, and subsequently, after Bartolini's death, in Rome. They included Chauncey Bradely Ives (1810–1894), Hiram Powers (1805–1873), and Thomas Crawford (?–1857), followed soon after by William Henry Rinehart (1825–1874), William Wetmore Story (1819–1895), Randolph Rogers (1825–1892), and Harriet Hosmer (1830–1908), all from either Philadelphia or Boston (the two cities that vied with each other for the title of the "Athens of America"). Ives, having arrived in Florence in 1844, left in 1851 for Rome, where he died. His *Pandora*, sculpted soon after his arrival in Rome, was an immediate success (fig. 458). The subject was a popular one among an Anglo-Saxon public with a tendency to moralize, suggesting as it did the presence, behind an appearance of innocent beauty, of a mind cursed with curiosity. The piece testifies to its author's admiration for Canova and is frequently compared to the famous *Greek Slave* by Powers (1844, marble, Yale University Art Gallery, New Haven). *Pandora* was to be reproduced many times, nineteen at least life-sized or half life-sized marbles having been manufactured by 1891. A more sought-after work than any of these, however, was *Nydia* by Rogers. Also executed in Rome, the piece was inspired by Bulwer Lytton's novel, *The Last Days of Pompeii*. The sentimental response unfailingly evoked in viewers by this blind girl shown fleeing the volcano made the work so successful that Rogers was obliged to set up almost a replica industry.

Hiram Powers sought to step up his production by designing not only sophisticated tools but also machines capable of manufacturing them. He executed graceful figures with exquisite modeling that remained in thrall to the Neoclassical ideal even where the subject hardly lent itself to such treatment. John Quincy Adams Ward (1830–1910) used native models for his *Indian Hunter* (bronze, many copies) as early as 1860, whereas the figure with the Greek profile that Powers made ten years later, *Last of the Tribe*, is far more suggestive of Diana, despite her hairstyle and her picturesque short skirt, than of an Indian maid (fig. 476).

The situation in Britain during the 1850s was rather particular. The country's principal sculptor, John Gibson (1790–1866), also spent most of his time in Rome, where he devoted himself to a kind of sculpture that was deeply influenced by Thorwaldsen. In a specially designed temple at the 1862 International Exhibition he showed the *Venus* (fig. 453) that testifies not only to his admiration for Greek art but also to the close attention he paid to anatomy and modeling. The figure is lightly stained because like many of his contemporaries he was interested in Greek polychromy. Gibson's absence from his native land hastened the decline of Neoclassicism, and the British sculpture of the period is essentially represented by two monuments: the *Wellington Monument* in St. Paul's Cathedral, sculpted by Alfred Stevens (1817–1875) and owing its inspiration to Michelangelo and Rome (see p. 206), and the *Albert Memorial* (1863–72) in Hyde Park, which was executed by a series of sculptors under the supervision of the architect Sir George Gilbert Scott, in what was regarded as the national style, namely Neo-Gothic.

The German Reinhold Begas (1831–1911), a pupil of Gottfried Schadow and Christian Rauch, initially adhered to a graceful Neoclassicism (fig. 485), exemplified by his *Cupid and Psyche* group (1854–57, marble, Skulpturengalerie, Staatliche Museen, Berlin). However, in 1856 he went to Italy, where he discovered the work of Michelangelo and Gianlorenzo Bernini. He also formed a friendship with Böcklin, whose way of interpreting mythology made a great impression on him. His style underwent a change, and from then on what he was admired for was "life in action," the kind of movement that he captured in the two groups he showed at the 1878 Exposition Universelle, *The Rape of the Sabines* (bronze) and *Mercury and Psyche* (marble), while the Neptune Fountain that he made for Berlin in 1886 is a free interpretation of the Fountain of the Rivers in Rome. However, his name is still chiefly associated with the imposing *William II Monument* (1892–97, bronze, Berlin, destroyed), a job he was requested to do by William II himself, despite the fact that the 1889 competition had been won by Adolf von Hildebrand (1847–1921). Mainly remarkable for the number of sculptures that it comprised, the *William II Monument* looked like a failure from the outset.

THE LAST ROMANTICS

Under the Second Empire, Auguste Préault (1809–1879) was seen as the principal representative of a heroic era that lived on in him (and others) at a time when the Romantic battle was already over. He had his share of official commissions, but even if he did take a somewhat unconventional approach to *Jupiter* and *Juno* (1867–70, stone, grounds of the Château de Fontainebleau), wreathing them in flowing drapery in the two decorative groups that he designed for Fontainebleau, this was not the sort of work in which he expressed his true personality. He preferred relief to sculpture in the round. In fact, it was not until 1876 that the state commissioned a bronze version of *Ophelia* (*Ophélie*, fig. 114), a work he had sculpted spontaneously more than thirty years before. It is unfortunate that commissions for official buildings, together with a series of portrait medallions, account for the greater part of Préault's surviving work.

Years of struggle, in literature as well as in the field of the plastic arts, had done their work and the importance of Préault was now acknowledged: "He believes that sculpture must be concerned with modern emotion; he believes that marble and bronze are capable of expressing human pain . . . How could his works fail to produce a remarkable impression on so many skillful polishers of marble who never thought that sculpture could express a feeling and contain a sigh" (Mantz 1863, 56). However, freedom of expression was still not granted to him, and any lack of anatomical correctness (one of the reproaches most frequently leveled at the Romantics) was painstakingly noted. For Préault, who once wrote on a portrait of Delacroix the words "I am not for the finite, I am for the infinite" (Cabinet des Dessins, Louvre, Paris) and who had little time for restraint, distortion was often a way of reinforcing the almost invariably tragic message of the work. He had used it as early as 1834 in *Slaughter* (*Tuerie*, bronze, Musée des Beaux-Arts, Chartres), and in 1863 he pushed the method to extremes in a relief entitled *Hecuba* (*Hécube*), which has since disappeared: "He has treated the human form like an ornamental motif, he has sculpted a thing rather than a person, and in distancing himself so arbitrarily from reality and from life he has missed the drama that could not exist where man is not" (Mantz 1863, 56). The confusion of different elements including water, hair, drapery, and aquatic plants that had featured earlier in *Ophelia* here becomes a tendency toward decorative abstraction that prefigures Symbolism.

Of the big names of Romanticism, Antonin Moine (1796–1849) committed suicide, Henri de Triqueti (1804–1874) quietened down, and Antoine-Louis Barye won general approval for his realistic vision of the world of animals. When Barye exhibited his *Jaguar Devouring a Hare* (*Jaguar dévorant un lièvre*, bronze, Louvre, Paris) at the 1852 Salon, the Goncourt brothers saw it as "one of those imitations [of living nature] beyond which sculpture cannot go" (Goncourt brothers 1852, 124). However, in his sixties he revealed a classical disposition that found expression in the four groups he produced to commission for the Denon and Richelieu wings of the

Louvre. True to the academic rules, their balanced volumes are arranged in pyramids, though the contrasting organization of the figures and the way in which they are looking in opposite directions retain a certain dynamic quality, inherited from Romanticism, that makes these works genuinely three-dimensional groups, capable of being viewed from several directions rather than only from the front, as is nearly always the case.

Violence and Combat

Romanticism and its excesses might have passed away spontaneously, but they had left a taste for extravagant expression and violence. Besides, certain subjects almost cried out for such treatment. For *The Pythia of Delphi* (*Pythie de Delphes*, 1869, marble, Narbonne), the usually quiet Charles-Arthur Bourgeois (1838–1886) borrowed the powerfully raised arm and the shout from François Rude's *Marseillaise*. On the other hand, nothing linked Marcello (1836–1879; real name Adèle d'Affry, duchess of Castiglione-Colonna) to Neoclassicism, so it was not surprising that she should have chosen to portray her *Pythia* (1870, bronze; the piece was to stand in the Paris Opéra) "in a trance." The horrified critic of the *Gazette des Beaux-Arts* used the occasion to repeat his eulogy of classical serenity: sculpture, he said, "is not made for melodrama, and it is almost sacrilege to rig out in a Greek name a nightmare from the year one thousand" (Ménard 1870, 64). Like Bourgeois, Auguste Ottin fluctuated between classical inspiration and Romantic temptation. This was the result of his stay at the Villa Medici, during which he had found the constraints of student life the harder to bear for the fact that he had arrived in Rome aged over thirty-five and married (which in principle was forbidden and involved him in endless complications). And if the figures of the Médicis Fountain in the Luxembourg Gardens appear more academic than Marcello's *Pythia*, Ottin used their disproportion to suggest the primitive violence of Polyphemus as in his jealousy he prepares to drop a rock on the idyllic group of Acis and Galatea below.

But it was in the representation of the animal world that this violence chiefly manifested itself. After Barye, Auguste-Nicolas Cain (1821–1894) again evoked the cruelty of that world in 1882 in the groups placed on either side of the Castiglione staircase in the Tuileries Gardens: *Lion and Lioness Fighting Over a Boar* (*Lion et Lionne se disputant un sanglier*, fig. 547) and *Rhinoceros Attacked by a Tiger* (*Rhinocéros attaqué par un tigre*, 1882, bronze). Combat between men and animals was also to provide a source of inspiration for sculptors, perhaps taking a more tragic turn than in Barye's hunting scenes because now it was a question of the former being set upon by the latter. At the 1846 Salon, Ottin showed an *Indian Hunter Surprised by a Boa* (*Chasseur indien surpris par un boa*, plaster; bronze, 1855, grounds of the Château de Fontainebleau) that was no more pronounced in its exoticism than the *Indian Girl Tying a Strip of Cloth Decorated with Shells around one Leg* (*Jeune indienne ajustant à une de ses jambes une bandelette ornée de coquillages*) by François-Joseph Bosio (1768–1845) exhibited in the previous Salon (marble, Musée Calvet, Avignon). However, thanks to a humorous description of the work that the artist made to a friend, one senses in Ottin's piece all the accumulated irreverence toward the ancient world, as symbolized in this case by the *Laocoön* in the Vatican Museum, though in plastic terms the reference is hardly clear: "This is an Indian hunter sporting his birthday suit save for a strip of cloth binding his hair . . . Surprised by a wicked boa . . . the horse passes out . . . and the offended hunter fires an arrow down the boa's enormous gullet. The whole thing daubs up a treat; it's a bit like the Marly horses only better" (1845, Archives du Louvre; the reference is to a group of statues by Guillaume Coustou originally made for the Château de Marly).

Such combats between men and animals (the animal standing for a hostile nature) remained in favor until the end of the century. However, special mention should be made of Auguste Clésinger, who went back to mythology for his *Infant Hercules Suffocating the Snakes of Envy* (*Hercule enfant étouffant les serpents de l'envie*, 1856, bronze reduction, Musée d'Orsay, Paris) dedicated to the imperial prince. The artist was quite frank about his objective: he wished to attract the favor of Napoleon III. As in the classical model (Uffizi, Florence), the strength and healthiness of the young Hercules reassure us as to the outcome of this struggle provoked by the jealousy of Juno: Hercules will succeed without unnecessary gesticulation, simply by the power of his gaze and the strength of his fist. With Frederic Leighton (1830–1896), a painter whose famous *Athlete Struggling with a Python* (fig. 480) is his only monumental sculpture, the combat is once again more equal, even if the body of his athlete (who, contrary to the classical rules, never loses his anonymity) suggests unusual physical strength. On the other hand, *Gilliat and the Octopus* (*Gilliat et la pieuvre*, 1890, marble, Villeurbanne) by Joseph Carlier (1849–1927), inspired by the celebrated underwater battle described by Victor Hugo in his novel *Les Travailleurs de la mer* (1866), takes us into a more Romantic universe where the triumph of man is not assured. Gabriel-Jules Thomas, with *Stone-Age Man* (*L'Homme de l'âge de pierre*, 1894, plaster, Musée Paul Dubois-Alfred Boucher, Nogent-sur-Seine), another figure locked in combat with a snake, harks back to the *Laocoön*, still the great model.

As early as 1850 Emmanuel Fremiet had modeled a *Fight Between a Bear and a Man* or *Bear and Retiarius* (*Combat d'ours et d'homme* or *Ours et Rétiaire*, plaster, disappeared), which was the starting point of studies he was to pursue for almost half a century. In 1859 he caused a stir with his *Female Gorilla Carrying off a Negress* (*Gorille femelle emportant une négresse*, plaster), a new edition of which was produced in 1887. Thanks to the support of Count de Nieuwerkerke, the piece was shown behind a curtain, which guaranteed instant celebrity, but it was later destroyed by malicious hands. "There existed [the artist himself explained] a noble art—representation of the human figure—and an art that was not noble—representation of animals. Between the two there was certainly room, it is true, for an intermediate art, a mixed formula, combat between animal and man, and it was this genre that I adopted with *Retiarius Suffocated by a Bear* (*Rétiaire étouffé par un ours*) in order to alienate neither the Institut nor the jury. But I had the misfortune to proceed to the gorilla. At a time when the rumor was beginning to spread that men and apes were brothers, it was certainly a daring thing to do, and what made my attempt worse was that, the gorilla being the ugliest of all the apes, the comparison was not flattering to man. To compound the temerity, this gorilla was carrying off a young woman. Of course, the fact that the young woman was a negress might have been seen as excusing the gorilla. Not a bit of it: rising up in unanimous disapproval, the jury gravely announced that such a work was an offence against morality and remorselessly excluded it from the Salon" (Thiébault-Sisson January 3, 1896). Apart from the incongruity of the subject, which was further underlined by the almost lifelike treatment of the fur, surely the scandal was partly due to the fact that the triumphant animal had supplanted man, who was thus demoted to the much more modest position that he occupies in nature? In 1887, ideas having moved on, the second version of the group won the artist a *médaille d'honneur*, and in 1895 Fremiet reached a pinnacle of ferocity by exhibiting an *Orangutan Throttling a Borneo Savage* (*Orang-Outan étranglant un sauvage de Bornéo*, marble, Museum d'Histoire Naturelle, Paris).

But the world of animals also interested sculptors for its own sake. With Pierre-Jules Mène (1810–1879), a narrative developed around the sculptural composition. Sculptors such as Cain, Alfred Jacquemart (1824–1896), and Fremiet strove for maximum realism, showing animals life-sized and in their habitual attitudes, with no attempt to conceal the potentially horrifying aspect of certain scenes (Jacquemart, *Lion Sniffing a Corpse* [*Lion reniflant un cadavre*], 1852, bronze, Jardin des Plantes, Paris; Fremiet, *Slaughter of a Percheron* [*Abattage d'un cheval percheron*], 1852–53, bronze, whereabouts unknown). This familiar world was enormously successful with the bourgeoisie. Fremiet's *Wounded Dog* (*Chien blessé*, 1850, bronze, Musée d'Orsay, Paris), for instance, was immediately acquired by the state for the Musée du Luxembourg and became the artist's best-known group even within his lifetime; as late as 1910–12 it was among the works most often reproduced.

Literary Inspiration

Often defined in Baudelaire's phrase as "a manner of feeling" (Baudelaire 1961, 879), Romanticism set great store by inspiration. Consequently, literary subjects were held in particularly high esteem. In the front rank of such subjects were those drawn from Dante, followed by subjects drawn from Shakespeare. Ever since it was written in the early fourteenth century, the *Divine Comedy* had enjoyed extraordinary favor in the field of the plastic arts. Romanticism breathed new vigor into it, delighting particularly in the association between Virgil and Dante. It saw the former as the very embodiment of the elegaic poet, in contrast to the somber, tormented genius of the latter. Conversely, Neoclassical artists favored exclusively the Latin poet (*Virgil* by Gabriel-Jules Thomas, 1861, fig. 119). At the 1853 Salon, for example, Préault showed two colossal medallions representing *Dante* and *Virgil* (bronze, Musée d'Orsay, Paris). Dante is modeled vigorously with a distinctive profile inspired by the celebrated (though occasionally disputed) fifteenth-century bust in the Museo e Gallerie Nazionali di Capodimonte, Naples, while Virgil receives an image of male beauty somewhat reminiscent of the bust of *Lamartine* by David d'Angers (the hairstyle is similar, with parallel locks). But it was clearly with Dante, and particularly with the Dante of the *Inferno*, that Préault felt an affinity. In his bedroom he had a copy by Courbet of Delacroix's *Dante and Virgil in Hell* (*Dante et Virgile aux Enfers*), a scene he had himself treated in sculpture. The tangle of the damned with their excessively elongated bodies looks forward to the milling swarms of Rodin's *Gates of Hell* (*La Porte de l'Enfer*, 1880–1917, fig. 129).

The two poets again appeared side by side some years later, first in a double bust by Triqueti (1861, bronze, Museum of Fine Arts, Boston), more classical in conception, then as full-length statues in the onyx staircase of the Hôtel de la Païva (*Virgil* by Barrias, fig. 254, and *Dante* by Aubé, 1865, marble, fig. 117). But the fortunes of Dante proved more durable: the plaster model (exhibited in 1879) of the statue that Jean-Paul Aubé (1837–1916) had erected in front of the Collège de France was to make further successful appearances at the Expositions Universelles of 1889 and 1900, and reductions of it (in three dimensions) were produced in large numbers.

The admiration that the Romantics felt for Dante (on a par with that aroused by Michelangelo) also extended to Beatrice, of whom Joseph Fabisch (1812–1886) modeled a graceful if hardly distinctive image under the Second Empire (fig. 118). However, she stood for too pure a love to hold the interest of Romantic artists for long.

From Antoine Étex (1808–1888) to Rodin (who was to make it the subject of his *Gates of Hell*), they were more attracted by the condemnation inherent in a forbidden love such as that of Paolo and Francesca. But the character around whom all the fantasies and fears of late Romanticism crystallized most effectively during the second half of the century was that of Ugolino, as drawn from canto XXXIII of the *Inferno.* For his final work produced at the Villa Medici, Jean-Baptiste Carpeaux (1827–1875), who in 1852 asked his friend Louis Dutouquet "Is the word *malheur* [misfortune] marked on my brow?" (Clément-Carpeaux 1934, 1:33), selected from this episode the crucial moment when Ugolino, condemned to die of starvation, is about to give in to the temptation (which will send him to hell) of eating his children and grandchildren as, on the point of dying themselves, they beg him to (fig. 528). The horror of this moment is captured in the tension of Ugolino's body, which is all angles in contrast to the abandonment of the children. Like Jean-Jacques Feuchère's *Satan,* one of the most characteristic works of Romanticism, shown at the 1834 Salon, Ugolino has his fingers in his mouth and one foot set nervously on the other. Carpeaux managed to express what are still human feelings pushed to the extreme, following Dante's text to the letter: "As soon as a little ray made its way into the prison and I discerned in four faces my own look, I bit both hands for grief; and they thinking I did it from a desire to eat, rose up suddenly and said: 'Father, it will be far less pain for us if thou eat of us.'" On the other hand, in the small terra-cotta sketch which he made in 1863 (Musée d'Orsay, Paris) he moved on to the next stage, namely a bestiality that no longer has anything human about it. Again, the work is a direct illustration of Dante's text: "He [Ugolino] sank his teeth into the wretched skull [of the archbishop], crunching it up as a dog crunches bones." What we see of Ugolino as he crouches over his prey are mainly the teeth, which are indicated by deep knife cuts made with the freedom that a sketch permits. Auguste Rodin (1840–1917) was also pursued by the character of Ugolino, whom he took as his subject in numerous drawings and in two sculpted groups. Of the first, possibly only a torso survives, while the second, executed in 1882 for *The Gates of Hell* (fig. 129), reappeared in 1906 in a larger version (plaster, indefinite loan from the Musée Rodin, Musée d'Orsay, Paris).

After Dante, the writers of most interest to sculptors were William Shakespeare, the pre-Romantics Goethe, Bernardin de Saint-Pierre, and André Chénier, and, among the moderns, François-René Chateaubriand, Alfred de Vigny, and Alphonse de Lamartine. But similar subjects could give rise to very different interpretations, and Préault's wonderful *Ophelia* (*Ophélie,* fig. 114), all flowing lines like a decorative motif, was succeeded by the more sensual figure of Myrto, *The Tarantine Girl* (*La Jeune Tarentine,* fig. 472), whom Alexandre Schoenewerk (1820–1885) depicted washed up by the tide. Another sculptor, Joseph-Michel-Ange Pollet (1814–1870), found a marvelously Romantic subject in Vigny's poem *Éloa, ou la sœur des anges* (1823): to avenge himself for the curse he had received, Lucifer, the beautiful rebel angel in whom the Romantic artist saw the symbol of his own destiny, attracted the attention of the angel of compassion, Eloha, and dragged her down with him (fig. 487). The tense figure of Lucifer has very much the tormented character one might expect, but the group as a whole, which is mainly reminiscent of Baroque abductions, highlights the dichotomy between form and background that was one of the problems of Romantic sculpture.

In countries less affected by Romanticism, it was through literature that the Neoclassical tradition came under attack. In Italy, Goethe inspired Alfonso Balzico (1820/25–1901) to sculpt a charming *Margarete* (fig. 500), whose picturesque quality is in fact carefully studied. British sculptors, while their predilection was for subjects drawn from their national literature (Shakespeare), were also open to foreign sources. The Pre-Raphaelites in particular helped to popularize Dante, and Alexander Munro (1825–1871), for instance, a member of the Brotherhood who had close ties with Rossetti, executed a small group entitled *Paolo and Francesca* (1851, marble, Wallington Hall).

NEO-MEDIEVAL AND RELIGIOUS SCULPTURE

Viollet-le-Duc and the French Restoration

Thanks to the Commission des Monuments Historiques set up in 1837 and such figures as the writer Prosper Mérimée and the architect Eugène Viollet-le-Duc, the two decades of the Second Empire coincided with the beginning of some major restoration campaigns. However, one of the most celebrated of these, the restoration of the Château de Pierrefonds, constitutes a rather special case by virtue of its extensiveness, apparently the direct result of a decision by the new emperor. Napoleon III instigated basic repairs to the dungeon and towers as early as 1857, but in 1862, as part of the same intellectual and political movement (namely to ensure that there was no break between the imperial dynasty and the regimes that had preceded it) that was to prompt him to set up the Musée des Antiquités Nationales at Saint-Germain-en-Laye in the following year, he decided to turn it into a new place of residence as luxurious as the others. The unusually large number of sculptures commissioned to decorate it allowed Viollet-le-Duc, who supervised the site very closely, to give free rein to his imagination—a faculty, however, that had always been rooted in a deep knowledge of fifteenth-century art. The result, both internally and externally, was a fantastical world (occasionally verging on the surreal) drawn from medieval bestiaries or the portals of cathedrals. But Viollet-le-Duc showed unparalleled imagination in disguising his borrowings. The Cheminée des Preuses (1864–65) in the great hall of the château offers a good example. In an initial sketch, the figure of the Amazon queen Hippolyte is directly inspired by one of the Virtues of Strasbourg Cathedral. In the final drawing given to the sculptor Louis-Auguste Gaudran (1827–1894) for execution, she has been subtly modified: a breastplate replaces the tunic, the crown bristles with fleurons, and the whole rhythm of the figure is different.

One of the largest fields open to restoration was offered by the churches destroyed in the Revolution. From the cathedral of Notre-Dame-de-Paris to the church at Vézelay and from Laon to Clermont-Ferrand and Toulouse, Viollet-le-Duc restored both architecture and decoration or reconstructed them using similar elements. It is this latter activity that, at least so far as sculpture is concerned, constitutes one of the most disputed aspects of Viollet-le-Duc's work. As at Pierrefonds, he had a team of sculptors working around him. They included Geoffroy-Dechaume (real name Adolphe-Victor Geoffroy; 1816–1892), Michel-Pascal (real name François Michel, 1810–1882), and François-Antoine Zoegger (1829–1885), and their role was essentially to execute his designs, just like the "image-carvers" of medieval times who "collaborated directly on the work under the direction of the master" (Viollet-le-Duc, *Dictionnaire raisonné de l'architecture française du Xe au XVe siècle*, 1854–68). When the tympanum of the central portal of Clermont-Ferrand Cathedral was reproduced in the August 15, 1874 issue of *L'Art pour tous*, the caption stated that, while the sculpture was the work of Zoegger, the design was by Viollet-le-Duc, who had been commissioned to complete and enlarge the cathedral. The gable of the facade terminates in a tree of Jesse dominated by a figure of the Virgin, also by Zoegger, that replaced a sixteenth-century figure knocked down in 1793. The Virgin was executed in embossed copper (which has the advantage of lightness) by the firm of Monduit at the request of Viollet-le-Duc, who liked the work they had done on other sites, which included Notre-Dame, the Sainte-Chapelle, and Saint-Denis. It was Monduit's successors, Gaget et Gauthier, who were to make the hammered-copper version of the *Statue of Liberty* (after Frédéric-Auguste Bartholdi, 1834–1904), measuring 46 meters in height and inaugurated on October 28, 1886, that stands at the entrance to New York Harbor (fig. 2), and the 6.7-meter-high *St. Michael* (from a model by Emmanuel Fremiet) for the spire of Mont-Saint-Michel (1897).

Viollet-le-Duc adopted a rigorous approach to his restoration work. However, on the facades of Parisian churches, where many sculptures were put back under the Second Empire, the execution of such statues sometimes appears more whimsical. Certainly, Gabriel-Jules Thomas took the trouble to impart an element of mannerism to his *Stoning of St. Stephen* for the church of Saint-Étienne-du-Mont (fig. 643), just as Théodore-Charles Gruyère (1814–1885) drew on the eighteenth century for his relief depicting the *Virgin Giving the Rosary to St. Dominic* (1867, stone) for the church of Saint-Thomas-d'Aquin in Paris. However, with the restoration of the facade of the church of Saint-Paul-Saint-Louis there was a deliberate change of meaning. The church's link with the Jesuits disappeared in favor of elements of a more local nature: around the clock, brought from the neighboring parish church to replace the monogram of Christ back in 1806, *St. Catherine* and *St. Aura* (commemorating two local monasteries) took the places of *St. Ignatius* and *St. Francis Xavier*. Only *St. Louis* (1860, stone) was retained, though the static quality of Eugène Lequesne's figure, like that of *St. Aura* (1860, stone) by Antoine Étex, contrasts with the Baroque context of the facade; *St. Catherine* (1862, stone, a lively piece by Préault) fits in better here.

In addition to the restorations, the expansion of cities made it necessary to build new churches. After the still Neoclassical buildings of the previous period (Notre-Dame-de-Lorette, Saint-Vincent-de-Paul), the Second Empire preferred the neo-Roman or Neo-Gothic styles. Sainte-Clotilde (1845–57) was the first of these churches, which harked back to a period of particularly fervent faith. Of the sculptures covering the facades of these churches, some are better adapted than others to their architectural surroundings. Former Prix de Rome laureates often found it more difficult than sculptors trained on the Notre-Dame site to recapture the spirit of the Middle Ages. On Sainte-Clotilde, while Auguste Ottin (*St. Gontran, St. Scholastic,* and *St. Benoît,* 1854, stone) or Louis Lequesne (*St. Cloud,* 1851, stone) appear to have been discharging a somewhat tedious duty, Alexis-Hippolyte Fromanger (1805–1890; *St. Rémy* and *St. Maur,* 1854, stone) and Geoffroy-Dechaume (*St. Clovis* and *St. Clotilde,* 1854, stone) show a concern for archaeological verisimilitude. Victor-Edmond Leharivel-Durocher (1816–1878) went further, finding a quality of gentleness and "serious grace" for his much admired figures of *St. Geneviève* and *St. Théodeschilde* (1864, stone) on the right-hand portal.

Not all former Prix de Rome winners were hostile to the medieval style, but such contact with pre-Renaissance Italian art as their time in Italy had enabled them to enjoy often led them to prefer the Quattrocento or the early Renaissance as their source of inspiration. Such was the case with Charles-Alphonse-Achille Gumery, who harnessed that period's qualities of clarity and grace for his relief of *The Annunciation* (*L'Annonciation,* 1859–61, stone) for the tympanum of the Rue de l'Annonciation door of the church of Notre-Dame-de-Grâce in Paris. Another example is the *Christ Between Two Angels and the Four Evangelists* (1853, stone) that Eugène-André Oudiné carved for the church at Gennevilliers (fig. 462).

Except where a desire for homogeneity compelled them to adopt a particular style (for Notre-Dame, Michel-Pascal executed a reredos that "will dupe the archaeologists of the future" [Mantz 1863, 55]), artists generally enjoyed greater freedom in the interior decoration of churches. This was an area that under the Second Empire saw a large number of commissions for frescoes, paintings, and sculptures. "The commission is the death of art . . . It is an impertinence by Patronage against Genius or a kindness by Stupidity toward Insipidity," protested Barbey d'Aurevilly ("Salon de 1872," 1886, 253), condemning the dullness of religious works, which he put down to a lack of faith and instruction on the part of the artists. He was not entirely wrong, yet there is no denying the quality of certain pieces, which were perhaps all the more inspired for being more visible on top of an altar than high up on a facade. Étex in *Ecce Homo* (Saint-Eustache) and Auguste Clésinger in his *Pietà* (Saint-Sulpice), to take two examples in Paris, gave free rein to a lyricism that was particularly expressive, in both pieces, in the drapery of the angels (figs. 459, 460). Delacroix, who was often hard on Clésinger, rightly acknowledged that his group showed "an understanding of the grace of line such as is extremely rare" (Delacroix 1980, 215).

The Cult of the Virgin

In 1854 Pius IX proclaimed the dogma of the Immaculate Conception. A column set up in the Piazza di Spagna in Rome commemorated the event (1856), while France, blessed with appearances of the Virgin at Lourdes (1858), placed itself under her protection. Anne Pingeot was able to find some twenty monumental *Virgins* erected under the Second Empire alone (Pingeot 1986, 208–13), the most famous being *Our Lady of France* (*Notre-Dame-de-France,* fig. 519), made with the proceeds of a national subscription (214,649 francs), to which in 1856 Napoleon III added the gift of 100,000 kilograms of iron melted down from the 213 cannons captured at Sebastopol. The figure was erected on a residual volcanic hill, the Rocher des Dons, at Le Puy, and the effigy at its feet is that of Monsignor Morlhon, "promoter" of the statue. The sculptor was Jean-Marie Bonnassieux (1810–1892), whom Henri Lacordaire saw as "the hope of Christian art" and whose long career was indeed punctuated with a large number of works inspired by religion, notably a *Sacred Heart* that, in reproduction, made the family wealthy. However, although Bonnassieux devoted a book to his *Douze Statues de la Vierge* (1879), it was not him but Fabisch who was given the job of sculpting the *Virgin of Lourdes* (*Vierge de Lourdes,* 1864) from the description given by Bernadette Soubirous.

The Franco-Prussian war of 1870 provided a fresh occasion for appealing to the intercession of the Virgin. The *Virgin* of Clermont-Ferrand Cathedral (fig. 518) formed part of a program of works begun in 1867, but it was also linked to the political situation by a "Vow of the city and diocese of Clermont," solemnly pronounced in the cathedral on December 15, 1870, invoking the protection of the Virgin for "the sons of the Auvergne absent from their homes in the service of France," as well as for their territory (the Auvergne, not France).

The revival of the cult of the Virgin also gave rise to complete decorative schemes. Chapels dedicated to her were now added to older churches. Sometimes their decoration recalled the principal episodes in Mary's life; sometimes it illustrated the litanies of the Blessed Virgin. In the church of Saint-Philippe-du-Roule in Paris, it was the latter that provided the theme for a mural cycle painted by Claudius Jacquand (1857), while in Sées (Orne *département*) they also provided Leharivel-Durocher with his subjects for the bas-reliefs that adorn the apse of the Chapelle de l'Immaculée Conception (1863). Designed as "prayers in stone" and colored (against the artist's wishes) in a way that impairs their mystical significance, the reliefs form part of a decorative scheme that seeks to demonstrate the dogma.

THE NEO-FLORENTINES: MICHELANGELO AND THE RENAISSANCE

For scholars of the Académie de France in Rome as well as for those who made the trip to Italy at their own expense, Naples and Florence were the country's two main poles of attraction, apart from Rome itself. But whereas in Naples it was as much the Museo Archeologico Nazionale and the excavations of Pompeii and Herculaneum as the picturesque quality of the city and its people that interested them, in Florence they discovered the Renaissance. As they usually stopped off in Florence on the way to Rome, they saw the city with fresh eyes and their admiration was all the greater.

In the middle years of the century, scholars at the Académie de France had rather forgotten about the road to Tuscany. They resumed the habit of going there to work after Paul Dubois (1829–1905), who spent from 1859 to 1863 in Italy at his own expense, and Henri Chapu and Alexandre Falguière (1831–1900), Prix de Rome winners in 1855 and 1859, had made it fashionable once more. "Concern for the new sought outside the avenues of academia is clearly high on the list of priorities for M. Paul Dubois. Well . . . what could be more new than what has been forgotten? In this respect, a trip to Italy is full of revelations" (Mantz 1865, 34). Visitors to the 1863 Salon were surprised to discover the plaster versions of *St. John the Baptist* (*Saint-Jean-Baptiste*, bronze, 1864, Musée d'Orsay, Paris) and *Narcissus* (*Narcisse*, fig. 469), in which they did not see the usual Neoclassical models but were confronted with studies from the life, closely observed without seeking to be realist. To confirm his sources, Dubois also submitted a pencil study based on Sebastiano del Piombo and another based on Leonardo da Vinci. Critics could not praise the works too highly. Some particularly liked the way in which, though drawing his inspiration from the Florentine statuary of the Quattrocento, the artist had primarily "looked for beauty": *Narcissus* they found remarkable for its purity and harmony of form, while *St. John the Baptist* was described as "a perfect work of rare character and distinction" (Thoré 1864, 148). Others highlighted the presence of "thought, that rare quality" and were delighted to find at last in *St. John the Baptist* (which may have been suggested to Dubois by Donatello's figure) "a modern subject, that is to say one for which antiquity affords no model; consequently, it is a subject apt to attract a bold spirit who understands that the sculpture of our day no longer meets the needs that used to justify its existence" (Du Camp 1863, 909). The reception accorded the two works by public and critics was confirmed by an official commission to carve *Narcissus* in marble for the Louvre's Cour Carrée and subsequently to produce a replica, also in marble, for the Musée du Luxembourg, where it joined the small bronze *St. John the Baptist* placed there in 1866. The state did not reserve all its favors for advocates of Neoclassicism.

Two years later *The Florentine Singer* (which the artist's notebooks allow us to relate to figures by Benozzo Gozzoli, Pinturricchio, and Lorenzo da Viterbo) earned Dubois the *médaille d'honneur* at the 1865 Salon (fig. 121). Highly representative, both in terms of its refined and pleasing appearance and in terms of the culture to which it refers, of a whole school of Second Empire sculpture, this was undoubtedly also one of the best-known works of the period: not until 1953 was notice of termination served on the reproduction contract (in six sizes) with Barbedienne.

Similar sophistication and the same admiration for the Florentine or French Renaissance characterize all Paul Dubois's works, which includes the *Monument to General de Lamoricière* in Nantes Cathedral (1865–79), and equestrian statues of the *High Constable de Montmorency* in Chantilly (*Connétable de Montmorency*, 1886, bronze) and *Joan of Arc* in front of Reims Cathedral (*Jeanne d'Arc*, 1889–95, bronze). His initial success continued undiminished, not only in France but also abroad, where he was acknowledged to be in the front rank. For example, he is one of the two sculptors portrayed full-length on the facade of the Ny Carlsberg Glyptotek in Copenhagen.

Dubois, Chapu, and Falguière make up the core of what one might call the neo-Florentines. As early as 1857 the flowing drapery of Chapu's *Christ with Angels* (*Christ aux anges*, fig. 461) showed the close attention he had paid to fifteenth-century Florentine art, while the nervous quality of Falguière's *Winner of the Cockfight* (*Vainqueur au combat de coq*, fig. 465) derives from the fact that the artist was clearly inspired by Giambologna's *Mercury* (*Mercurio*), a bronze copy of which graces the loggia of the Villa Medici in Rome. After them, Eugène Delaplanche (1836–1891), Louis-Ernest Barrias (1841–1905), Antonin Mercié (1845–1916), Tony-Noël (1845–1909, real name Edme-Anthony-Paul Noel), and André-Joseph Allar (1845–1926), the winners of the Prix de Rome in 1864, 1865, 1868 (Mercié and Tony-Noël), and 1870, "became persuaded that the fifteenth century was not as Gothic as had been made out and that people like Donatello, Verrocchio, Mino da Fiesole, Rossellino, and other barbarians had seen pretty clearly into the human soul. In the wake of this surprising discovery, the ideal underwent a change. Sculpture came back to life. Cortot was abandoned, and even M. Lemaire [who made the pediment of the church of the Madeleine in Paris] was betrayed. *The Florentine Singer* and *St. John the Baptist* by M. Paul Dubois made that infidelity explicit, and since then the students of the Académie de Rome have nearly all tended to become Tuscans" (Mantz 1872, 58). A traditionalist critic but an admirer of the Italian Renaissance, Paul Mantz wrote those words about the 1872 Salon, which included the model for Mercié's *David* (1872, bronze, Musée d'Orsay, Paris), which was much influenced by Donatello, *Death* by Tony-Noël (*Morte*, 1870, plaster, Musée Vivinel, Compiègne), a piece imbued with "Florentine feeling," and two busts by Charles Degeorge (1837–1888), a *Florentine Girl* and a *Venetian Youth of the Fifteenth Century* (*Jeune Vénitien du XV*e *siècle*, 1872, bronze, whereabouts unknown). However, the Académie des Beaux-Arts was worried to see the influence of the Renaissance prevailing over that of antiquity, and when Mercié submitted a relief entitled *Wolf, Mother, and Child* (*La Loup, la Mère et l'Enfant*, 1872, plaster, whereabouts unknown; edition in bronze), although it acknowledged the work's "clever design as well as the taste and delicacy of the execution," it took the opportunity—informally, of course—to condemn the artist's predilection for the Renaissance masters and to warn him that, "without giving him greater individuality, [this risked] diverting him from the professed goal of sculpture, that is to say the grandeur of which his choice has deprived him" (*Rapports sur les Envois de 1872*).

The Institut's warning had little effect on the neo-Florentines, who on returning to France kept faith with the ideal of their years in Rome. Their Florentine sources were then supplemented by the influence of the French Renaissance—as witness, for example, Chapu's *Youth* (*Jeunesse*), a figure with particularly elegant drapery made for the *Monument to Henri Regnault and Pupils who Laid Down their Lives for their Country* (*Monument à Henri Regnault et aux élèves morts pour la patrie*, 1875, marble, École des Beaux-Arts, Paris).

The interest of the younger generation was not confined to Quattrocento Florence: Michelangelo ("my revered master," Carpeaux called him) inspired passionate admiration among them, remaining their ultimate point of reference. "It's as fine as Michelangelo's slave in the Louvre," Bonnat was to exclaim on seeing the *Jaguar Devouring a Hare* (*Jaguar dévorant le lièvre*, 1850, bronze, Louvre, Paris) by Barye (Bonnat 1889, 381). Visiting Michelangelo's house (the Casa Buonarroti) in January 1837, Bonnassieux carried off a thread torn "with veneration" from the master's chair. This boundless reverence is also visible in their works. One thinks, for example, of *Andromeda* (*Andromède*, 1859, marble, whereabouts unknown) by Jules Franceschi, in which Théophile Gautier recognized figures from the Medici Chapel: like Michelangelo, Franceschi had "exaggerated his muscles, made his shapes protrude, and strained his lines, yet he lacked the supreme skill and savage beauty that distinguish his model" (1859). Ten years later, Delaplanche drew on the same source for his *Eve after Sinning* (*Ève après le péché*, fig. 471), designed at the Villa Medici in 1868 at the same time as Barrias was working on an *Oath of Spartacus* (*Serment de Spartacus*), in which the body of the dying slave echoes Michelangelo's *Entombment* in Florence Cathedral.

And many more examples might be cited, both in France and abroad, where one of the most spectacular proofs of the influence of Michelangelo is offered by the two allegorical groups of the *Wellington Memorial* in St. Paul's Cathedral, London: *Truth and Falsehood* and *Courage and Cowardice* (fig. 484). The monument, which was only completed in 1912, is designed along the lines of a Renaissance tomb as a triumphal arch shielding a recumbent figure and crowned by an equestrian statue. It is the work of Alfred Stevens (1817–1875), an artist gifted in many fields, including poetry and music, who had spent nine years in Italy (1833–42). But if these allegorical groups, situated on an intermediate level, refer to Michelangelo in the seated figures of the Virtues (recalling the Sibyls of the Sistine Chapel), the way in which they are shown crushing the Vices and the design of certain details (the figure of *Courage*, for example) testify to an effort of renewal and a strength that were remarkable in a still very traditionalist Great Britain.

ECLECTICISM: MONUMENTAL DECORATION

"Carve a statue! But for whom, for what? A marble or bronze statue does not go in a drawing room. And, having carved the statue, whom is one to sell it to? Anyway, it all costs big money: marble, assistants, the founder . . . By its very nature, sculpture is a social art, intended for public squares, public monuments. Added to which, in aristocratic societies, there are large country houses and wealthy residences . . . Sad to have to depend on the state or a handful of millionaires for one's work and one's livelihood when the main feature of modern civilization is, on the contrary, an irresistible trend toward emancipation through work and intelligence!" (Thoré 1870, 169, 170).

If the Second Empire looks to have been a golden age for sculpture, it is because urbanism and the economy were enjoying a boom. Quite apart from the international exhibitions (1855, 1867, 1889, and 1900), redesigned cities sprouted scores of new buildings, the decoration of which provided large numbers of artists with a living. The Louvre's Cour Napoléon alone employed not only thousands of workmen but more than 335 sculptors between 1853 and 1857. Their newly rich customers, whether corporate bodies or private individuals, were concerned about only one thing: appearance. A building's decoration must simultaneously suggest its function and proclaim the wealth of its occupant or occupants. The most extreme example was that of the caryatids that Leharivel-Durocher made in 1868 for a building belonging to some brothers called Saint: they represented their four patron saints.

Major building projects were completed with astonishing rapidity as a result of a division of labor between statue carvers, ornamental sculptors, and assistants. A commission was carried out in several stages, each sanctioned by a management inspection and a payment on account. The first stage was execution of a "sketch," which was frequently altered at the request of the architect or the inspector of fine arts. For example, the Musée d'Orsay has some thirty sketches of the Opéra in Paris, some of them modeled inside maquettes of the architectural element in which they were to be sited (doors, fireplaces, pediments, etc.). A number of the models are very different from the finished work, such as the *Torchères* (fig. 473) sketched by Albert-Ernest Carrier-Belleuse or the first project for Jean-Baptiste Carpeaux's group for the facade, which the architect Charles Garnier thought unacceptable because "for everyone who saw [it], the impression was the same: that of a group representing Adam and Eve being advised by the devil" (Garnier 1878–81, 433). The next stage was execution of the model in clay. This was done very carefully since the result was to be cast in bronze and molten metal reproduces every tiny detail. Carpeaux, for example, made a full-sized model of his *Four Corners of the World* group (1867–73, Observatory Fountain, Paris, fig. 499). For execution in stone or marble, a smaller model (half, one-third, or one-quarter the size of the final piece) sufficed. Enlargement (using a calliper system) was done by assistants working in situ, with the artist checking for accuracy and occasionally carving some parts himself: "When shall I be in the fortunate position of making only my models and supervising the execution of my marbles?" complained the young Ottin at the Villa Medici (April 13, 1840, Archives du Louvre). Carpeaux, however, shared with his assistants Armand and Bernaërts the work of carving *Dance* (*La Danse*, fig. 123) from a half-sized model now in the Musée d'Orsay.

Neoclassicism remained in favor, not surprisingly, for law courts (Paris, Marseille, and Amiens, for example), rather more so for a commodities exchange (Marseille) or train stations. The facade of the Gare du Nord in Paris (1867) is decorated on two levels with allegorical figures representing the European capitals (above) and French cities (below) served by the network. At the Gare d'Austerlitz, that same year, a locomotive put in a timid appearance behind Élias Robert's still very classical *Industry* (*Industrie*), though it was not until the end of the century, principally at the Gare de Lyon, that the entire decorative scheme was designed as a homage to trade and industry.

The facade of the Palais de Justice in Place Dauphine, Paris, was remodeled between 1859 and 1868 under the supervision of Joseph-Louis Duc (1802–1879). It was decorated with six allegorical figures (*Wisdom* and *Truth*, *Equity* and *Strength*, fig. 486, and *Punishment* and *Protection*) by Augustin Dumont, Jean-Louis-Nicolas Jaley (1802–1866), and François Jouffroy (1806–1882) respectively. It was the norm, as has been said, to practice maximum division of labor, but because the individual artist's personality tended to take second place to the overall style, the result was not as heterogeneous as might have been feared. Thus while Jaley showed evidence of a certain sentimentality in his Salon figures, such as *Memory of Pompeii* (*Souvenir de Pompéi*, 1853, marble, Musée des Beaux-Arts, Troyes), his *Equity* and *Strength*, recognizable only by their attributes, were as stern and inexpressive as *Wisdom* and *Truth* by Dumont, a sculptor who had always resisted the influence of the various currents undermining Neoclassicism. Moreover, the architect was there, supervising, and indeed there are clear differences between Jaley's sketches (recently acquired by the Musée d'Orsay) and the final figures, notably in the dress of *Strength*, whose bare chest was presumably judged too frivolous.

In 1874 Eugène Guillaume was commissioned to produce for the newly rebuilt (1873) Galerie Saint-Louis in the Palais de Justice a statue of *St. Louis* to replace the old one. Although he did his best to make a faithful portrait of the king and give him a period image, the classical principles of equilibrium around a central axis, frontality, and above all clarity of subject matter (the oak tree beneath which Louis IX dispensed justice is a giveaway) are fully respected. Even for the polychromy, both antique and medieval sources can be quoted. In fact, the discovery that antique sculpture was colored had been an incitement to sculptors to paint their work since the 1830s. One of the most spectacular pieces in this respect was the reconstruction by Pierre-Charles Simart for the duke de Luynes of Phidias's chryselephantine *Athena* at the Parthenon. Simart's work was shown at the 1855 Exposition Universelle.

The Palais de Justice is a good illustration of the maxim that "you can't overdo repetition." Effigies of *Plenty, Prudence, Justice,* and *Strength* had been chosen to decorate the so-called Cour de Mai facade on the Boulevard du Palais as early as 1780. In 1866, the Quai de l'Horloge facade (Cour de Cassation) was given, above the four figures by Eugène Lequesne (*Wisdom, Justice, Innocence,* and *Strength*), a pediment by Louis-Léon Cugnot (1835–1894). Like those of Guillaume in Marseille (1862) and Justin-Chrysostome Sanson (1833–1910) in Amiens (1873), Cugnot's pediment represents *The Law Protecting the Innocent and Punishing the Guilty* (*La Loi protégeant l'innocent et punissant le coupable*). The last facade (on the Quai des Orfèvres) was built between 1911 and 1914, with the niches between the windows containing four further figures: *Truth* (*Vérité,* by Henri Lombard, 1855–1929), *Clemency* (*Clémence,* by Jules Coutan, 1848–1939), *Law* (*Droit,* by André-Joseph Allar), and *Eloquence* (*Éloquence,* by Raoul Verlet, 1857–1923). Now, however, poses and costumes contributed as much to the definition of such figures as did attributes: the nude figure of *Truth* holds her mirror up high; the toga-clad *Eloquence* stretches out an arm to emphasize a point of oratory; finally, *Clemency,* a quieter version of Coutan's famous *Armed Peace* of 1886 (*Paix armée,* bronze, Parc Montsouris, Paris), is shown giving a reassuringly protective gesture.

The Palais de Justice, construction and decoration of which went on for more than a century, offers a good example of the persistence of Neoclassicism. In such artists as Allar and Coutan, who were born in 1845 and 1848 and won the Prix de Rome in 1869 and 1871 respectively, it was pushed back by the influence of the Renaissance, which in turn disappeared from the works of Lombard and Verlet, born a decade later.

The Renaissance influence appeared in monumental decoration even under the Second Empire. For public buildings, however, except where (as in the Louvre) it was imposed by the architecture itself, it took second place to Neoclassicism. This was partly a question of generations: on the Opéra in Paris, for example, the four principal facade groups were commissioned from four artists then at the peak of their careers, namely Guillaume, Perraud, Jouffroy, and Cavelier (later replaced by Carpeaux), who had been born in 1822, 1819, 1806, and 1814 respectively; the four isolated figures, on the other hand, were made by slightly younger artists, Eugène-Antoine Aizelin (1821–1902), Henri Chapu, Paul Dubois, and Alexandre Falguière, men with ties to the neo-Florentines.

At the Louvre, the hierarchy was less clear-cut, the decorative scheme having been borrowed religiously from the old Louvre. In keeping with the model provided by the reliefs of Jean Goujon (1510–about 1566), the Renaissance style was *de rigueur* for the graceful figures in relatively low relief accompanying the bull's eye windows of the Cour Carrée; and these in turn soon spawned the allegories of *Painting* and *Sculpture* by Auguste Debay (1804–1865) that flank the round dormers of the École des Beaux-Arts (1861, stone). For the Cour Napoléon, a vast building project supervised by Ludovico Tullius Joachim Visconti and subsequently by Lefuel and completed with astonishing speed (1852–57), former Prix de Rome winners (with the exception of the elderly Barye) and future members of the Institut shared the task of decorating the nine pavilions, the exuberance of which was in some contrast to the sober Neoclassicism. However, that exuberance is more the result of an accumulation of decorative elements from a wide variety of sources, justifying the aggressive hostility shown by Étex to such "monuments made like Harlequin's clothing" (*Essai d'une revue synthéthique sur l'Exposition universelle de 1855*). The entrances on the river side are decorated with two allegories by Jouffroy, who was unable, so far as the spirits are concerned, to shake off the principles in which he had been trained. In contrast (and perhaps by way of compensation), the decoration of the base draws the eye with its superabundance of elements (putti, garlands, etc.) arranged around prows of ships. As for the two main wings, the Pavillon Denon and Pavillon Richelieu, four pairs of caryatids, very much inspired by the ones Jacques Sarrazin (1588–1660) had made for the Pavillon de l'Horloge (fig. 309), support pediments made up of central groups. These are unsurprising works by Simart and Francisque Duret (1804–1865), although the former's contribution is notable for some particularly graceful female allegories standing out against a low-relief background comprising objects suggestive of the sciences, commerce (a locomotive), the arts, and so on. The difference in depth of the entablature emphasizes the levels of composition. It was for these wings that Barye executed the four groups *Peace, War, Strength,* and *Order* (*Paix, Guerre, Force, Ordre*)—badly worn today, alas, like all the decoration here, although the one-third-sized maquettes (Musée d'Orsay, Paris) have fortunately survived.

In 1861 the Pavillon de Flore, which was threatening to collapse, was demolished and rebuilt. For the two facades, Lefuel appealed in 1863 to Cavelier and Carpeaux. For the top of the facade (because the figures were no longer contained within the pediment but had escaped to sit on top of it), Carpeaux, with his Italian memories still fresh in his mind, modeled a group inspired by the Medici Chapel in Florence. *Imperial France Lighting the World and Protecting Agriculture and Science* (*La France impériale éclairant le monde et protégeant l'agriculture et la science*) echoes the tripartite composition of the tomb of Giuliano de' Medici by Michelangelo and even directly evokes the figure of the duke shown seated between *Day* and *Night*. Attentive to detail, as his initial training at the free drawing school known as the Petite École had taught him, he drew the eagles in the Paris botanical gardens, the Jardin des Plantes, over and over again; in fact, one of them was to provide the throne for imperial France. A bas-relief beneath the pediment represents *Flora* (*Flore*). Carpeaux originally imagined her recumbent, in the style of Germain Pilon's *Diana* (*Diane*) at the Château d'Anet, but on his return from a trip to Belgium in July 1863 the goddess found herself endowed with a rather fuller figure and a very Flemish *joie de vivre*. She kneels on one knee and spreads her arms to strew flowers over the putti gathered nearby. When the model was exhibited in 1866 (thanks to the personal intervention of Napoleon III, Carpeaux kept the commission despite his slowness in carrying it out), its very vitality came as a shock. There was even some concern that this might prevent it from blending into the architecture.

At the time, Carpeaux was excitedly searching for the composition for his *Dance* (fig. 123) for the Opéra. The architect, Charles Garnier, a friend and fellow student at the Petite École and later at the Villa Medici in Rome, had arranged for Carpeaux to produce the group in place of Cavelier, who was too busy elsewhere. "I am in a state of high delight," Carpeaux wrote to another friend, the architect Dutouquet, on December 25, 1863, "for I have just been chosen by Garnier to perform one of the finest tasks involved in the Opéra. I have been asked to make one of the large bas-reliefs on the facade in the spirit of the Arc de Triomphe or the culmination of the monument" (Cabinet des Estampes, Bibliothèque Nationale, Paris). The official commission did not come through until 1865, but ever since Garnier had first got in touch with him Carpeaux had been thinking about his subject, as witness his sketches for *Lyric Drama and Light Comedy* (*Le Drame Lyrique et la Comédie légère*) in the Musée d'Orsay. It seems to have been Garnier himself who suggested the final composition: "A lighthearted round dance with an inspiring genius at its center" (Garnier 1878–81, 433). By 1866 the group was gradually coming together: "I was filled with wonder," Garnier wrote, "at the vigor of his composition and the thrilling modeling of his clay figures. In fact I said to myself: So be it! If the monument suffers slightly from my sculptor's exuberance, that will be only a minor misfortune" (Garnier 1978–81, 435). Carpeaux added more and more figures: the half-sized model that he sent for casting in January 1868 included no fewer than nine, rather than the three required!

When the facade of the Opéra was unveiled in July 1869, *Dance* caused a scandal. This time the emperor's position was no longer so secure and Carpeaux could not count on his support. The sculptor Charles-Alphonse-Achille Gumery was asked to supply another group, and only the war of 1870 prevented this from being installed. In the number of its figures, their powerful nudity, and their movement, *Dance* did indeed form a striking contrast to the other three groups, *Lyric Drama* (*Le Drame lyrique*) by Perraud, *Instrumental Music* (*La Musique instrumentale*) by Guillaume, and *Harmony* (*L'Harmonie*) by Jouffroy, which were all quietly organized around the dominant figure of an inspiring genius, flanked on either side by three other figures. "These three compositions furnish incontrovertible proof, alas, of the mediocrity of the geniuses attached to the School. MM. Perraud, Jouffroy, and Guillaume, incapable of producing anything bad, produced something mediocre, which is worse! As a result, their groups look as if the only reason they have been placed there is the better to highlight M. Carpeaux's *Dance* by serving as a foil to it" (Vermersch 1869).

The Opéra was inaugurated in 1875, yet it is often regarded as the very symbol of the Second Empire (swept away by the events of 1870). Under the firm direction of Garnier, its decorative scheme took the idea of blending to the extreme, using a mixture of artists, styles, and subjects (whose only point in common was a link of some kind with the building, from effigies of composers to some representation of the activities the building would house, the trades involved in its construction, or the qualities required by the architect). If the decoration as a whole harks back mainly to the Renaissance and the seventeenth century, Garnier was obliged, so far as the larger sculptures were concerned, to call upon artists who were in the public eye and who therefore practiced Neoclassicism. However, for the interior at least, he sought to ensure that their works would harmonize with the richness and cheerful atmosphere of the whole. Fearful, for example, that the "pure chisel" of Gabriel-Jules Thomas would give him "two frozen fortresses of white marble," he asked the sculptor for some "Bernini in bad taste" (Garnier 1878–81, 358–59). What he got, for the entrance to the auditorium, were two caryatids, *Drama* and *Music* (*Le Drame* and *La Musique*, fig. 122), that, although severe in style, were executed in polychrome marble and bronze. In the areas of decorative and functional sculpture Garnier had a freer hand, and he commissioned Carrier-Belleuse to produce two torchères for the staircase (fig. 473). One of the most productive artists of the period—"God gave him a chisel on every finger," Schoenewerk used to say (Salmson 1892, 75)—Carrier-Belleuse had little time for academic principles but rather appeared to be the heir to the French decorative tradition: "Like the masters of whom he is fond (Caffieri, Puget, Coustou, Houdon, Pigalle, etc.), he has energy and spirit" (Baudelaire 1961, 1093). However, what the graceful female figures of his torchères recall most of all is the Renaissance style of Fontainebleau.

Before reaching their peak in Garnier's Opéra, it was in the interior decoration particularly of private residences that these qualities of opulence, color, and gaiety had been in evidence. Having obtained a couple of commissions to study the physical characteristics of different populations (in Algeria in 1856 and in Greece in 1858), Charles Cordier (1827–1905) discovered the enormous variety of different types of marble. He was the first to take advantage of the North African quarries that had been well known in antiquity and that colonization had brought back into use. The ten busts he submitted to the 1857 Salon on his return from Algeria included two in bronze and onyx, *Arab from El Aghuat Wearing a Burnous* (*Arabe d'El Aghouat en burnous*) and *Negro from the Sudan* (*Nègre du Soudan*, Musée d'Orsay, Paris), and the fine black-marble bust of *Priestess of the Bean Feast* (*Prêtresse de la fête des Fèves*, 1857, Musée de l'Homme, Paris), the coloring of which lends tension and drama to the subject. He encountered immediate success. The emperor and empress were delighted and purchased several pieces. The painter Stanislas Lami involved him in the work of decorating the Château de Ferrières by commissioning him to produce *Atlantes* and *Caryatids* in bronze and onyx for the gallery of the large Italian room (1862). These exotic figures with their feather and turban headdresses contrast with the white-marble statues, some still Neoclassical in style, others more picturesque, such as Schoenewerk's *Florentine Warrior* (*Guerrier florentin*, 1865), that occupy the niches at first-story level. The same mixture of styles and the same warm-toned polychromy are found in the Hôtel de la Païva, the sole survivor of the luxurious private houses that once lined the Champs-Élysées in Paris (figs. 254, 311, 313–15). Nevertheless, under the supervision of the architect Pierre Manguin, it was the art of the Renaissance that prevailed—more sumptuous with Dalou for the decoration of the dining room, more elegant with Carrier-Belleuse in the bedroom (about 1865–66).

Eclecticism spread very quickly beyond Paris as building projects were launched throughout the provinces. Valenciennes, for example, where Carpeaux had been born, asked its native son to sculpt a *Town of Valenciennes Defending its Ramparts* (*Ville de Valenciennes défendant ses remparts*, fig. 529), for the City Hall, part of the facade of which was being restored. From being the main element of a large relief, the piece eventually found itself standing alone above the pediment. This followed a protracted struggle with the architect, as we know from the proceedings of the committee: "The Town of Valenciennes, which has only this building, cannot sacrifice it to the whim of a sculptor who is permanently disposed to do something different from that which he is asked to do . . . It needs to be thoroughly brought home to M. Carpeaux that a monument is not composed for an inscription or a sculpture but rather the sculpture for the monument." Indeed, to adapt the piece to the peculiar shape of the pediment Carpeaux had had to get rid of first the enemy soldiers and then the "ordinary . . . insignificant accessories [that should have] come together to suggest the presence of a large army." So everything had to be said in the pose, which, unchanged from the initial sketches (except for being reversed), gained in expressiveness from the fact that the figure was so pared down: leaning forward in a vigorously defensive posture, like the *Marseillaise* on the Arc de Triomphe, Carpeaux's *Town of Valenciennes* acknowledges its debt to Rude.

The charming theater in Angers, inaugurated in 1871, was one of the first buildings to follow the model proposed by the Opéra. The neo-Renaissance prevailed almost everywhere, but the grandiose composition of the water tower of the Palais de Longchamps in Marseille (1869) already gave a hint of the neo-Baroque spirit that was to come (even if Cavelier's figures are still very restrained). It is apparent in Falguière's *Triumph of the Revolution* (*Triomphe de la révolution*), the quadriga that was placed on top of the Arc de Triomphe in 1882 (plaster, destroyed; sketch, wax, Musée d'Orsay, Paris), the group representing *The Saône and its Tributaries* (*La Saône et ses affluents*, beaten lead, 1887–89, Lyon) by Frédéric-Auguste Bartholdi, Coutan's Illuminated Fountain (Fontaine Lumineuse) at the 1889 Exposition Universelle, and the Fountain of Titan (Fontaine du Titan, 1892, Béziers) by Jean-Antoine Injalbert (1845–1933), culminating in the complex that Paris built for the 1900 Exposition Universelle, consisting of the Grand Palais, the Petit Palais, and the Pont Alexandre III.

Outside France

If Neoclassicism held out where it was sustained by special circumstances (in Athens, for example, where major architectural projects harking back to ancient Greece were realized under the influence of the Bavarian Wittelsbach dynasty), eclecticism spread rapidly outward from France, notably thanks to the fact that French sculptors received commissions from far and near, usually for public monuments. As early as 1855, for example, Louis Rochet (1813–1878) took part in an open competition for the erection of a monument in Rio de Janeiro to commemorate Pedro I, emperor of Brazil. He won, and the monument was inaugurated in 1862, having first been shown at the 1861 Salon. There were rather fewer commissions in the field of decorative sculpture, one being the groups that Célestin-Anatole Calmels (1822–1906) made for the triumphal arch in Lisbon's Praça do Comércio (fig. 495). However, following the war of 1870 and the events surrounding the Commune, a number of sculptors left Paris to seek refuge in London or Brussels, where their services were called upon for such building work as was in progress. Brussels, for example, was building its Bourse (completed in 1874), which was very "Second Empire" in spirit with a wealth of decoration playing every possible variation on the theme of commerce and industry. The principal elements (the pediment, *Belgium as Patron of Commerce and Industry*) and the three groups crowning the central portion of the facade (*Belgium Schooling the Spirits in the Development of Commerce and Industry* flanked by *Transport on Land* and *Transport by Sea*), all the work of the Belgian Jacques Jaquet (1830–1898), still belong to a mature Neoclassicism. However, the frieze running round the building is rather different in style. The work of Carrier-Belleuse (then living in Brussels) and Rodin (who had also left Paris), together with two Belgian sculptors, Jules Dillens (1849–1904) and Antoine van Rasbourg (1831–1902), it illustrates the same subject but this time with the aid of successive groups of chubby, lively putti wielding the attributes of the arts and crafts responsible for Belgium's wealth (notably mining, ironwork, distilling, commerce, the textile trade, the wine trade, and weaving).

Begun at the same time but not completed until 1893, Philadelphia's City Hall offers an even more glaring example of the influence of France (fig. 323). Just as in the Louvre, the richly decorated upper part of the facades stands out against high roofs. The decoration, however, bears witness to a certain effort to adapt to the American continent in that the caryatids on one facade are dressed in Native-American style, while a bison's head provides the central motif of the pediment. French influence continued to make itself felt up until the end of the century. Frederick William MacMonnies (1863–1937) went to live in Paris following the World's Columbian Exposition in 1893 to produce the works that he had been commissioned to make for Prospect Park, Brooklyn (the models for which were in fact shown at the 1900 Exposition Universelle): two groups of horses (bronze, 1898), which look like direct descendants of the famous works that Guillaume Coustou made in 1745 for the Château de Marly, and the decoration of the Soldiers' and Sailors' Arch (fig. 492). The facade of the latter monument bears two high reliefs, *Army* and *Navy* (1901, stone), of which the first might almost be seen as a neo-Baroque interpretation of Rude's *Marseillaise* on the Arc de Triomphe in Paris. The triumphalism of such decoration was by no means unique, recurring as it did in an even more assertive form in Madison Square, New York, where the Dewey Triumphal Arch (1899, destroyed) was preceded by columns on bases that were decorated with victories.

Vienna also offers work in a very similar spirit (the Danube Fountain, 1869, by Johann Meixner [1819–1872]). In Austria, however (as in Flanders and Italy, other countries with a Baroque tradition), the neo-Baroque trend soon prevailed, and the overthrown Titans of the groups *Land Power* (fig. 497) and *Sea Power* that Edmund von Hellmer (1850–1935) and Rudolf Weyr (1847–1914) made about 1895–97 for the facade of the Hofburg in Vienna are quite as splendid as those of Rome's Trevi Fountain (1732–51).

THE CULT OF THE GREAT: FROM CEMETERY TO GALLERY

"There's an element of disgrace in being known mainly by people who do not understand you. Having a big reputation is a kind of disgrace," Degas noted in about 1880. The opinion he was expressing was a highly personal one, for the nineteenth century made a veritable cult of the great man or woman.

In sculpture, the principal manifestation of that cult was the vast quantity of effigies of contemporaries or earlier figures produced everywhere at this time, culminating in the erection of public monuments or the manufacture of sets of great men or women. For a long time such monuments conformed to a single design: a full-length statue set on a pedestal decorated with bas-reliefs and/or allegorical figures. For the 1864 competition for a monument to commemorate the defense of Paris at the Clichy tollgate in 1814, Carpeaux had the idea of using the tollgate itself as a pedestal, with the detached figure of Marshal Moncey, hero of the fighting, at the top and the Allies climbing up one side and the French attempting to repel them on the other, both armies forming meandering lines to create that swirling effect for which he had a real predilection. However, the disconcerted jury preferred to grant the commission to the architect Edmond Guillaume (1826–1894) and the sculptor Amédé-Donatien Doublemard, whose project was very much more traditional in conception.

The growth of cemeteries (those "archives of humanity," as David d'Angers called them) was another consequence of the cult of great men or women. Indeed, the success of the cemeteries that France decided to create in 1804 rested on the opportunity they offered for prolonging someone's memory in a society in which true death was being forgotten. However modest his station, every deceased person became a "great man" for his immediate circle, and the same idea ran through the inscriptions and sculpted decoration that served to recall his past life. The trend became more and more pronounced as the years went on and while, in the first half of the century, many monuments reflected sentiments of a private nature, after 1850 their decoration referred more to the deceased's public life. The relief that Paul Cabet (1815–1876) made for his wife's tomb (1866, bronze, Montparnasse Cemetery, Paris), showing a female figure swathed in voluminous drapery, holding her head in her hands, is probably one of the last manifestations of a theme that had once been extremely popular, namely the grief experienced by the survivor at the loss of a husband, wife, or child. In the same cemetery, *Mourning* (*Deuil*) by Jules Coutan, a fine Baroque-inspired figure (1890, marble), seems highly conventional by comparison.

Apart from a few decorative elements and except where it was a question of a sculptor's family, such expressions of grief were to disappear almost entirely from funerary monuments. Instead, it became customary to highlight the qualities and great deeds of the deceased, usually combined with a portrait. For instance, following the death of Visconti in 1853, the architect of the Louvre, a recumbent statue of the man by Victor-Edmond Leharivel-Durocher (1859, marble, Père-Lachaise Cemetery, Paris) portraying him in the robes of an academician was installed to his greater glory. It was set atop a sarcophagus decorated with a view of the new Louvre in bas-relief. His father, the archaeologist Ennio Quirino Visconti, who died in 1818, had received no more than a stele simply adorned with a funerary crown beneath a bust of the deceased. Funerary sculpture was in fact becoming increasingly descriptive. Allegory was often used, as in *Fame* with a marine trophy for Admiral Bruat (*La Gloire*, 1857, marble, Père-Lachaise Cemetery, Paris) by Hippolyte Maindron (1801–1884), or *Architecture* (1893, marble, Père-Lachaise Cemetery, Paris) by Louis-Ernest Barrias for the tomb of the architect Antoine-Gaéten Guérinot. There was, however, a growing preference for narrative bas-relief recalling precise details of the deceased's life, such as the three scenes set in the workshop of the caster Crozatier (about 1855, bronze, Père-Lachaise Cemetery, Paris) by Astyanax-Scaevola Bosio (1793–1876?). On the more important monuments, however, this kind of relief was replaced by a statue of the deceased seen in action—or caught at the moment of death, if that was what made him famous. Thus Auguste Debay showed Monsignor Affre expiring on the barricades (1848–60, marble, Notre-Dame, Paris), while Aimé-Jules Dalou (1838–1902) showed Victor Noir, the young journalist killed by Prince Pierre Bonaparte in January 1870, stretched out stiffly on the ground. Here, the body's modern dress, depicted in meticulous detail, takes on a particuler importance, emphasizing the absurdity of such a death (1890, bronze, Père-Lachaise Cemetery, Paris). *Anatole de La Forge* by Barrias, on the other hand, brandishing his saber, appears to be leading the inhabitants of Saint-Quentin, the city he had so bravely defended against the invading Prussians in 1870, as we are reminded by the sign bearing that name behind the statue (1893, bronze, Père-Lachaise Cemetery, Paris).

Much frequented yet enclosed within walls, the cemetery provided a semipublic space where it was possible to pay homage to those who, despite the mounting statue mania of the second half of the century, failed to find such homage in the main square, either because of the modest nature of their careers or because of political circumstances. From David d'Angers to Falguière and from Géricault to Ingres and Jules Lefebvre, author of the famous *Truth* (*Vérité*) shown at the 1870 Salon, a substantial number of artists were commemorated in this way, usually by their pupils, who in one way or another used the monument to recall the master's major works. Some of those artists received a second monument, either in the city of their birth or somewhere that was peculiarly marked by their memory (*Ingres* in Montauban, 1868–72; *Perraud* in Lons-le-Saunier, 1880). Not many sculptors received such double attention—it was more common, at the turn of the century, for writers. Shortly after his recumbent figure of Alexandre Dumas *fils* (1897, marble, Montmartre Cemetery, Paris), Charles-René de Paul de Saint-Marceaux (1845–1915) also honored the writer with a public monument, later erected in the Place Malesherbes in Paris (1906, stone).

Painters and sculptors make up for it in the institutions with which they are associated. The bust of David d'Angers (1861, marble), by Armand Toussaint (1806–1862), was commissioned directly for the museum of his native city, and that of Puvis de Chavannes (1890–92, marble) for the Musée de Picardie in Amiens, the staircase of which is decorated with large compositions by the artist. And in 1896 the plaster version was sent to Lyon, where Puvis was born and whose museum had also received murals painted by him. A monument to Ingres by Eugène Guillaume (1871, marble) with a substructure decorated with portraits of two of his favorite pupils, Flandrin and Simart, was installed in the École des Beaux-Arts in Paris.

Some famous artists formed part of series. These were particularly popular in the nineteenth century and were associated with the idea of the pantheon or capitol that cropped up throughout the century. In 1820, at the instigation of Canova (who was no doubt inspired both by the famous collection of self-portraits in the Vasari corridor connecting the Uffizi and the Palazzo Pitti in Florence and by the example of Count d'Angiviller at the Louvre), the collection of busts of famous men, including a number of artists, formerly housed in the Pantheon had been transferred to the Capitol in Rome. The much visited Promoteca Capitolina was set up at the time when certain churches in Rome (San Luigi dei Francesi) or Florence (Santa Croce) were emerging as favored burial places for anyone who had (or had had, because numerous monuments were erected retrospectively) any claim to fame, particularly in the field of art. It is typical of the nineteenth century on more than one count, reflecting not only its fondness for history and for sets of things but also its interest in human physiognomy. That interest, which stemmed partly from the studies of phrenology made by Franz Joseph Gall and Johann Kaspar Lavater, was to govern the gallery of famous contemporaries that David d'Angers undertook on his own account, as well as the rows of busts lining the corridors of the Théâtre Français, the Bibliothèque Nationale, and the Opéra in Paris (figs. 132, 133).

Series of this kind appeared everywhere, not just in Europe but also in the United States. Sometimes they invoked the blessing of the past for a public building. For example, in London about 1850, a set of twenty-two statues of members of Parliament was made for the new Houses of Parliament. At other times (as had been the case with the Galerie des Lyonnais Célèbres in Lyon put together at the beginning of the nineteenth century and installed in the Palais Saint-Pierre in 1835), they constituted veritable rolls of honor. In Washington, D.C., the Capitol's National Hall of Statuary assembled the statues of politically famous men (two for each state), while in Manchester, England, the Sculpture Hall of the Town Hall, begun in 1868, exhibited the busts of those citizens who had contributed most to the city's prosperity. Paris already had a well-established tradition: Count d'Angiviller had begun commissioning statues of famous men for the Grande Galerie of the Louvre in 1776, and under the July Monarchy (1830–48) a number of series had been undertaken (Famous Women at the Palais du Luxembourg, Historical Galleries at Versailles). Indeed, it was in Paris that the principle found its highest expression. An initial set (executed in 1853–57) of eighty-six famous men, the youngest of whom was Houdon (died 1828), was placed above the peristyle of the Louvre's Cour Napoléon, giving France the image of a learned, scholarly, peace-loving country. Under the Third Republic (from 1870), this was echoed by the 108 statues (1879–83) erected on the Hôtel de Ville, succeeding those that had adorned the previous building (from 1849). Something like a quarter of the people commemorated at the Louvre reappear here, complemented by almost contemporary figures (*Viollet-le-Duc*, died 1879). Anyone not born in Paris was excluded, with the sole exception of Dominique de Cortone, the architect of the first Hôtel de Ville.

Generally, such series were confined to architectural decoration, as is the case with the frieze of famous artists from antiquity to the nineteenth century that runs round the *Albert Memorial* in London's Hyde Park (1861–76), but they soon commanded a larger space. There is a very important example in the Square du Petit-Sablon in Brussels, to where the group of the *Counts of Egmond and Hoorne* (*Comtes d'Egmont et de Hoorn*, 1864, bronze) by Charles-Auguste Fraikin (1817–1893) was moved in 1879 from its original site in the Grand'Place, where the aristocrats had been beheaded for political reasons in 1568. Ten marble statues of men who had been famous locally in the sixteenth century were placed around the square while the outer balustrade received forty-eight statuettes representing the guilds of that time. The whole arrangement was inaugurated in 1890.

However "legible" such historical figures were (the painter with his palette, the sculptor with his mallet, the writer with his pen, each wearing the costume of his day and usually having his name inscribed beside him), their presence does not appear to have been sufficiently demonstrative when it came to clarifying the function of a building. Consequently, they are nearly always accompanied by allegorical figures. Museums are a good example of this (a number of buildings specially designed to house existing collections were in fact built in the period after

1850). Whether it was the Musée de Picardie in Amiens (1854–66) or the museum and library in Grenoble (1863–72), their decorative schemes conformed to the same rules, juxtaposing allegorical figures (*History, Archaeology, Painting,* and *Sculpture* in Amiens; *Painting, Architecture, Sculpture, Poetry, Science,* and *History* in Grenoble) and medallions portraying famous men (national figures in Grenoble: *Lesueur, Corneille, Pierre Lescot, Jean Goujon, Descartes,* and *Montesquieu;* local heroes in Amiens: *Parmentier, St. Médard, St. Ouen, Robert de Luzarches, Maurice Quentin de La Tour*). In Amiens, however, the central part is also decorated with portrait medallions depicting *Raphael* and *Michelangelo*—an association that recurs frequently. In fact, the same principles governed the sculptural decoration of new museums springing up all over Europe at that time. On Vienna's Kunsthistorisches Museum (1872–81), for example, statues of such historical figures as *Rudolph of Habsburg* and *Charlemagne,* allegorical reliefs representing the centers of European art, and allegorical figures—*Goldwork* and *Architecture* by Karl Kundmann (1838–1919), *Painting* by Edmund von Hellmer, and *Sculpture* by Johannes Benk (1844–1903)—fill every free space on the vast facade. At the turn of the century, allegory even prevailed over history (the Grand Palais and Petit Palais in Paris, built for the 1900 Exposition Universelle; the Musée des Beaux-Arts in Nantes, 1893–1900; the Musée Bargoin in Clermont-Ferrand, 1903).

In stark contrast to this lack of invention is the facade of the Ny Carlsberg Glyptotek in Copenhagen (fig. 289), opened in 1897 to show the collections of Carl Jacobsen. Jacobsen was particularly interested in contemporary French sculpture, of which thanks to him the Glyptotek possesses a large collection, and the facade of the building is conceived as an act of homage to the masters he so admired. Instead of Michelangelo, Raphael, or Jean Goujon, the figures who appear there are those he regarded as the most important contemporaries: Carpeaux, Falguière, Rodin, and Meunier, three Frenchmen and a Belgian (1903–5, bronze busts), are followed by four Danes, Hermann Vilhelm Bissen, Hermann Ernst Freund, Johannes Wiedewelt, and Theobald Stein (1923–25, bronze busts). The first place, however, is reserved for Paul Dubois (1902, bronze), by Raoul Larche (1860–1912). Dubois is portrayed full-length, like the statue of Jens Adolph Jerichau which joined him twenty years later. Similarly, inside the museum the ceiling of one of the sculpture rooms is decorated with two reliefs, one representing the tomb of General Lamoricière in Nantes Cathedral and the other depicting the facade of the École des Beaux-Arts in Paris—that is to say the institution, much admired by foreigners, of which Dubois had been appointed director in 1878 and where most sculptors trained, and what was regarded at the time as one of the principal contemporary works of sculpture. Jacobsen's choice was perhaps one we would not make today, but what more powerful testimony could there be to the acknowledged supremacy of French sculpture during this period?

REALISM

Through its third dimension, sculpture comes close to the real—to the point where it is capable of serving as a substitute for a person or thing. This is why Baudelaire regarded it as an art that was close to nature, understood by primitive peoples and peasants (*Salon de 1846*). As in all ages, it is the eye that creates the work, and the way a work is seen changes according to period and subject. In the nineteenth century, the industrial age brought a new society to power. In the West, that society was shaped by Greece and Rome. Its culture, in terms of the plastic arts, was unsure of itself—hence all the revival movements, which revealed the bookish nature and defensive tastes of the new commissioning class. Yet among the latter there were those who wanted a new art for a new civilization. That new art was a return to the kind of realism that had known periods of favor in all ages, notably in sculpture. One thinks of certain Egyptian or Roman faces, the recumbent figures on certain Renaissance tombs, certain seventeenth- and eighteenth-century effigies. Incidentally, it is interesting to note that the art of portraiture has always been a mainstay of this trend, for reasons that are easily understood: the most faithful likeness was required as a stand-in for the actual person, a stand-in that (people believed) was assured of immortality, thanks to the permanence of the materials used.

Such a mirror was sought after by people who were not ashamed of what they were. Sculptures of this kind were also used to make oneself understood by the greatest number. The ruling powers in every country were adept at using sculpted images for this purpose. It was easier where there was a monarch. In France, for example, under the Second Empire, statues of Napoleon III and (in even greater numbers) of "uncle" Napoleon I were erected in every corner of France (not forgetting Corsica) to proclaim in a double salvo, as it were, the legitimacy of the regime. In Britain and the Commonwealth, gigantic monuments were occasionally set up to honor Queen Victoria. The town of Metz, which after the Franco-Prussian war of 1870 became German, soon had its equestrian statues of *William II, Prince Carl Frederick,* and *Frederick III* by Ferdinand von Miller (1842–1929) of Munich. In 1918 those statues were torn down, but the bases were kept. A *Poilu* (French soldier) was installed on the one that had formerly belonged to *William II,* while a *Monument to Déroulède* took the place of *Frederick III.* Equestrian statues of *Victor Emmanuel II* (fig. 493) and statues of *Garibaldi* shared the squares of Italian cities between them. In republics, allegories of power might take the place of monarchs but tributes to rulers were not forgotten, the only difference being that they became posthumous. Where the circumstances of a death permitted, they might achieve substantial numbers and dimensions. For example, the unexpected death (during the night of December 31, 1882) of Léon Gambetta, one of the founders of the Third Republic and defender of the national territory, and the assassination (in Lyon in 1894) of the French president Sadi Carnot were marked by the erection of monuments as imposing as they were numerous. Realistic portraiture was obligatory in every case; the setting, on the other hand, readily accommodated Neoclassical drapery under the Second Empire and neo-Baroque exuberance under the Third Republic.

Historical Realism

Historical realism made it possible to satisfy both the need for realism and the taste for the picturesque that history provided. What the cinema was later to develop in its historical reconstructions was achieved by the sculptors of the nineteenth century, brought up as they were on the past. Eugène Guillaume abandoned Roman antiquity for once, turning to the Middle Ages. His *St. Louis,* commissioned by architect Joseph-Louis Duc in 1874 for the Palais de Justice in Paris, shows the thirteenth-century French king Louis IX dispensing justice beneath his oak tree at Vincennes. Executed in stone, the statue was painted by Charles Lameire, since according to Guillaume: "Coloring or painting . . . is an operation that the sculptor must never lose sight of, because in the good old days statues were always painted" (Shedd 1988, 51–60). This realistically medievalist reconstruction was based on the seal of St. Louis, dating from 1250, the statuette in the Musée de Cluny, the engraving of the reliquary bust commissioned by Philip the Fair, statues in Reims and Mainneville (Eure *département*), and the ivory throne of Dagobert preserved in the Cabinet des Médailles in the Bibliothèque Nationale. It was a great deal of trouble to go to, considering that Duc had demolished the thirteenth-century Galerie Saint-Louis to make room for the new Cour de Cassation. A hundred years later, in January 1975, a bomb was thrown at the statue as a protest against "state justice." Although the plaster model shown at the 1878 Exposition Universelle had been kept in the Hôpital Saint-Louis waxworks museum, unfortunately it was not used for the remake (it can hardly be called a restoration).

Marc Antokolsky (1842–1902) was a Russian sculptor with French connections. He was represented at the Exposition Universelle in Paris in 1867, won the *médaille d'honneur* in 1878 and the *grand prix* in 1900, and was a corresponding member of the Académie. His work was reproduced in bronze by the firms of Barbedienne and Thiebaut and in stoneware by Émile Muller. Portraitist to the Russian court, Antokolsky also modeled retrospective figures such as the 3-meter-high statue of *Peter the Great* for Petrodvorets (1881). Ten years earlier he had produced *Ivan the Terrible*, a large bronze now in St. Petersburg's Russian Museum that truly does inspire terror with its impression of great force. The former ruler, Peter the Great, was the man who modernized Russia. Taking the title of Czar in 1547, he unleashed a campaign of repression against the aristocracy in 1560 and in 1581 killed his eldest son in a fit of rage. The statue portrays him racked by pathological mistrust, his right hand tensed on the chair, his left hand clasping a rosary; the impression given is of some twentieth-century imam.

In place of the throne occupied by such rulers the artist might use a horse. Fremiet, who was an animal sculptor, was thus able to combine his talents. The pawing horse and its rider, *Stephen the Great*, are no doubt exactly what his Romanian subscribers wanted: a picturesque design complete in every detail, an apparition from the past that anyone might "recognize." The statue was exhibited at the 1882 Salon in Paris before being erected in Iasi in Romania, where it stands to this day.

The 1880s brought many examples of this kind of historical realism. In Bamberg, Germany, the wife of Emperor Henry II, *Cunegond*, sculpted by Ferdinand von Miller in 1880, joins *King Max Joseph, Emperor Henry II* (fig. 496), *Bishop St. Otto*, and *King Conrad III* to form a circle round the figure of *Maximilian*, while Annaberg has a portrayal of *Barbara Uttmann* (1885), who in 1561 first introduced the bobbin for lacemaking. The latter statue, by Robert Henze (1827–1906), is didactic in nature, illustrating how a public monument adds a visual complement to a general process of schooling: the clothes indicate the period, while the gesture reveals the purpose of the homage (in this case, a scrap of lace made using the spindle).

Historical realism was also used to glorify the trades in an anonymous way, as in the delicate decorative scheme of the Square du Petit-Sablon in Brussels, where forty-eight sixteenth-century guilds are illustrated by half-life-sized figures executed by twenty-three sculptors in 1882 to designs by Xavier Mellery (1845–1921). For example, Jean Cuypers (1844–1897) modeled a youth carrying a pipe over his shoulder and a pair of bellows slung from his belt to represent the tinsmiths' and plumbers' guild.

Two heroes, both cut down in their youth, have statues at opposite ends of Europe. In the West, there is *Henri de la Rochejaquelein* by Falguière (fig. 516), commemorating the Vendéan leader who died at the age of twenty-two, a statue that was commissioned for St. Aubin, in the Vendée. The bronze was melted down during the Occupation to recover the nonferrous metals, but the plaster that had been exhibited at the 1895 Salon is still in the Musée des Augustins in Toulouse, thanks to a gift by the sculptor's widow. In the East, in the town of Pushkin, Pushkin the father of modern Russian literature, who was killed in 1837 at the age of thirty-seven in a duel with a French émigré, was portrayed in 1899 by Robert Bach (1859–1933) as a dreamy student (the subscribers had asked for him thus), head-in-hand on a bench. Both effigies set out to be as accurate as possible, in the clothing as well as in the way in which the pose seeks to indicate the character of the model.

Also in the 1890s, two strongly contrasting women had statues erected to them. For Copenhagen's Roseborg Park, Christian Gottlieb Bissen (1836–1913) made a statue of *Queen Maria Carolina* that reproduces every detail of the motionless sovereign's clothing. In Paris, Louis-Ernest Barrias's *Maria Deraisme*, a brilliant public speaker, is caught in full flow as she leans on the back of a chair. Unveiled in 1898 in the Square des Épinettes in Paris, the statue used 658 kilograms of bronze and was also melted down during the Occupation. A fresh statue was erected on the socle in 1983, since the plaster model had been kept by the City of Paris and another cast could be made. To save money, this time the chair was omitted.

Historical realism was also capable of reproducing events. These might be of a generic nature, such as *Saturnalia* (*Les Saturnales*, 1888–99) by Ernest Biondi (1855–1917), which looks forward to the films of Federico Fellini, or they might be real events such as the *Wreck of the "Vengeur"* (*Naufrage du Vengeur*), a French vessel of the Revolutionary navy that, during a battle with the British, scuppered herself rather than surrender (1794). To commemorate the heroism of her sailors, who had thrown themselves into the sea crying "Long live the Republic," the Convention government decreed that a model of the ship should be suspended in the entrance of the Panthéon. Three-quarters of a century later, the young Third Republic commissioned two illustrations for major sites.

On the *Monument to the Republic* by the Morice brothers (Léopold, 1846–1920, was the sculptor and Charles the architect) that was installed in the Place de la République in Paris after a competition organized in 1879 by the City of Paris (which at the time was further to the left politically than the national government), this heroic deed occupies one of the twelve reliefs relating the most striking events in the life of the First Republic. The scene is midway between death on the barricades and *The Raft of the Medusa*.

In the Panthéon in Paris, which was rededicated "To great men" following the death of the national poet, Victor Hugo, in 1885, a number of monumental sculptural projects were planned to mark the definitive appropriation of this originally ecclesiastical monument. Three successive waves of commissions were to fill the immense interior, but curiously, due to the slowness of their execution, the saints ordered under the conservative Marshal

Mac-Mahon arrived under the radical republican regime that succeeded him, and the grandiose compositions commissioned by the republicans were completed at a time when the public taste was once again for simplicity. Ernest Dubois (1863–1931), who was not afraid to work on a grand scale, exhibited the plaster version of his high relief of the *Vengeur*, which had been commissioned in 1908, at the 1909 Salon des Artistes Français, but it was not until 1927 that the marble (executed in Italy between 1911 and 1916) was placed in situ against the great southwest pillar. The mast of the vessel allows a composition on several levels, with each character playing his role, frozen by history in a moment of time.

Constantin Isenberg (1859–1911) drew on similar resources in his *Monument to the Torpedo Boat "Stereguchi,"* a vessel that sank in heroic circumstances during the Russo-Japanese war. He captured that moment of drama in bronze in 1903, and strollers in St. Petersburg have been able to relive it ever since.

Allegorical Realism

Sculpture offered the straight-laced nineteenth century a way of exhibiting female nudity clad only in a title. Forging a link between Romanticism and realism, Auguste Clésinger's *Woman Bitten by a Snake* (*Femme piquée par un serpent*, fig. 115) provoked outrage at the 1847 Salon. The scandal was largely orchestrated by Théophile Gautier, who informed the whole of Paris (not such an enormous task) that the sculpture was based on a cast taken from the life. And what a life! The model was in fact Apollonie Sabatier, the "Guardian Angel, Muse, and Madonna" of Baudelaire who was "at home" to the literary elite on Sundays at her Rue Frochot home. Only the face is Neoclassical in its impassivity: the very fleshy body twists in the grip of a passion for which the tiny snake curled around the wrist is supposed to be responsible.

Another snake (a big one this time) is involved in the statue of *Salammbô* (fig. 550) by Maurice-Désiré Ferrary (1852–1904), exhibited in the center of a rotunda at the Lady Lever Art Gallery, near Liverpool in England, a museum which stands like a temple in the middle of a model village built by a soap magnate. Drawn from Flaubert's Carthaginian novel of the same name, Ferrary's polychrome statue appeals to the viewer's worst instincts.

But the true role of allegory in the nineteenth century was to act as a foil. Nothing sets off a great man better than a woman at his side, preferably with no clothes on. This kind of unrealistic association of highly realistic elements would scarcely be conceivable nowadays. Yet in the Galerie des Illustres in the Toulouse Capitole, *Pierre de Fermat*, the mathematician, is being consulted by a woman whose pose shows off her figure to great advantage. The cloud on which she is seated is extended by drapery that links bust and allegory together. Pierre de Fermat seems for his part quite interested in the lady—his "genius," according to Théophile Barrau (1848–1913), who made the group in 1898. Quite the opposite happens at Tréguier on the north coast of Brittany, where Jean Boucher (1870–1939) reverses the poses. This time it is *Renan* who is sitting on a bench with a draped *Minerva* behind him waving a bay twig in his direction. In Catholic Brittany, there were no hostile demonstrations when this provocative monument was unveiled in 1903, thanks to the torrential rain beating down on the crowd. While Minerva belongs to the repertoire of Symbolism, Renan is as real as could be. Indeed, the group might be entitled "Spirit and Matter."

Portraits

In a portrait without attributes or allegories, spirit and matter must both be present, defining each other—quite a job for the artist, though one he often had to do in order to earn a living. "Painters end up in portraiture as poets end up in journalism," wrote Robert de la Sizeranne (Sizeranne 1902, 2:5), and the same goes for sculptors. The role of the customer awarding the commission was as Rodin described it to Paul Gsell: "By a curious and inevitable law, a person who commissions an image of himself will seek desperately to obstruct the talent of the artist he has chosen. It is most unusual for a man to see himself as he is, and even if he does know himself he will not like an artist portraying him in all honesty" (Rodin 1951, 104).

The freedom of the artist was not great, even if he did not have the ambitions of David d'Angers, who believed that "the sole task of sculpture is to achieve the apotheosis of the soul" (Bruel 1958, 1:398). In the century of photography and the triumph of the bourgeoisie, Baudelaire's definition in his *Salon de 1846*—"a portrait is a model complicated by an artist"—was less often confirmed than the kind of realistic mimicry that was required. However, the artist was not quite as dispensable as that. The bust of *Auguste Vacquerie*, with his distinctive physical appearance, differs in the treatments of Dalou and Carriès (figs. 502, 507). Dalou's version (Musée Victor Hugo,

Villequier) is all expressive realism: "Irony and passion, the verve of the polemicist and the religiosity of the writer who, in his way, is a believer, this spirited, precise bronze sums up all that is most intimate in the man. The lips are as if pursed in scorn while the eyes bestow a blessing" (Hamel 1887, 2:50). The Carriès bust, although begun at *Le Rappel*, the paper that Vacquerie was editor of in 1884, was not exhibited until the Salon of the Société Nationale des Beaux-Arts of 1892. Today it stands in the Théâtre de l'Odéan in Paris. A more meditative, smoother portrait (cut off below in that curious manner that the caster Pierre Bingen managed to achieve), the work belongs to Art Nouveau. *Elisabetta di Sassonia, Duchess of Genoa* (fig. 511), as portrayed half-length by Pietro Canonica (1869–1959) in 1898, is thoroughly Italian in her pose (the decorated shelf on which her arms rest is like a distant echo of a Florentine bust), while *Mr. and Mrs. Jacobsen*, sculpted in 1904–6 by Ludvig Brandstrup (1861–1935) for the Ny Carlsberg Glyptotek in Copenhagen, resemble a solid Nordic married couple (fig. 514).

In another double portrait, of the novelist William Dean Howells and his daughter Mildred, by the American sculptor Augustus Saint-Gaudens (1848–1907), the attitude of the figures is frozen. Though the scene purports to be realistic in its setting of everyday furniture and dress, it departs from realism in the elongated treatment of certain reliefs and the fixed look that the daughter is directing at her father, who is looking up at her from his newspaper. The names of the figures above their portraits reinforce the horizontals, harking back to certain fifteenth-century compositions.

Zola wrote in *L'Événement illustré* on June 16, 1868: "Naturalistic sculptors will be the masters of tomorrow." The prediction turned out to be true. In his novel *L'Œuvre*, written in 1885–86, he gave the character of Mahoudeau the sculptor the features of his childhood friend Philippe Solari (1840–1906). Accompanied by Cézanne, Zola and Solari had roamed the countryside around Aix-en-Provence in their youth. Despite their friendship, Solari's portrait of *Cézanne* is not as successful as it might have been. The curious head juts forward in a rather unnatural way (fig. 509).

In contrast to this simplified face, in *Queen María Cristina de Habsburgo with Prince Alfonso* (the future King Alfonso XIII of Spain) the sculptor Venancio Vallmitjana i Barbany (1826–1919) created a portrait icon (fig. 505). The finery, jewelry, laces, and ribbons, coupled with the majesty of the living throne represented by the seated mother, her two arms forming a mandorla around the child, together form a graceful propaganda image. This is the imaginary realism of the sentimental weeklies—the opposite of what one expects under the heading of realism.

The recumbent figure of *Victor Noir* is a good example. Victor Noir was a journalist who, having gone to see Prince Pierre Bonaparte to arrange a duel, was killed by his host in the latter's drawing room on January 10, 1870. On March 21, the demonstrations that had accompanied Noir's funeral notwithstanding, the Prince was acquitted. Following the fall of the Second Empire later that year, a public subscription to some extent rectified the denial of justice by making it possible to erect a monument to Victor Noir in Père-Lachaise Cemetery. The sculptor Dalou, a fervent Republican, sculpted the figure for free, and it was cast in bronze by Pierre Bingen in 1890. The result was a portrait conveying all the brutality of the murder: the young man lies on the floor in his calling clothes, his coat and jacket still open (he has not had time to button them, though he has pulled on his gloves already), his top hat at his feet, where it has fallen. From the youthful face to the ankle boots with toes splayed, the whole figure cries out against an act of brutal aggression toward an unarmed man. Realism was here harnessed in the cause of republicanism. The monument was unveiled on July 15, 1891.

The Realism of Everyday Life

First writers, then painters began to look around them. Sculptors were slower. As late as 1868 Jules Vallès could still thunder: "The time is past for serene gods, and men have something better to do than worry about their beauty . . . She died long ago, did Greece, that mother of masterpieces! And three thousand years later it's about time we let her go! . . . I want us to consign martyrs and heroes to the devil, I want a return to simplicity" (Vallès 1975, 1058–60). Not easy for an art dedicated to eternity. Henry Jouin, writing in 1883, feared "the naturalism [that] bothers quite a few of us nowadays" and that looked like producing "works conceived in a total absence of thought." In support of his fears, he quoted Diderot: "We paint whatever we like: sculpture—strict, solemn, chaste—selects," and David d'Angers: "Sculpture is a religion . . . When it stoops to the portrayal of family life, I feel I am watching a priest dance."

On the other side, there was Zola's "Tell all in order to know all" (Zola 1982, 178), because the artist was still the person who extends our world thanks to his superior sensitivity coupled with his skill in communicating. There was Jules Renard, who gave a definition of realism in his *Journal* on October 28, 1901: "Yes, I create fresh truth. Without my way of seeing it, it would remain a dead thing. The fact is, observation is invention" (Renard 1984, 674). There was Joris-Karl Huysmans: "All modern life needs examining" (Huysmans 1975, 123). And there was Edmond de Goncourt, in the preface, written on October 15, 1881, to his novel *La Faustin*: "*Human documents.* This phrase, much mocked at the moment, I reclaim as my own. I see it as the form of words providing the best and most significant definition of the new way of working represented by the school that has succeeded Romanticism: the human document school."

When Aimé-Jules Dalou modeled his *Embroideress* (*Brodeuse*) in the last year of the Second Empire, he needed only to look at his wife in her camisole (fig. 127). The pose is just right, the dress familiar. This is not a Greek woman any longer or a Roman woman, as in Mathurin Moreau's *Woman Spinning* (*Fileuse*, fig. 467) or the *Woman Winding Thread* (*Dévideuse*) sculpted by Jean-Jules Salmson (1823–1902); this is a Parisian, seen at home. The large plaster version no longer exists, but a sketch bears witness to Dalou's new way of looking at the world. The sculpture is housed in the Musée du Petit Palais in Paris (gift of Mr. Dreyfus) with the Dalou Collection, which the City of Paris acquired on the sculptor's death.

What an advance on Eugène Delaplanche! His *Maternal Education* (*Éducation maternelle*), shown in plaster at the 1873 Salon and marble two years later, sets out to mirror everyday life, but the result is rather studied. Illiteracy was a major problem in rural France. Here a pseudo-countrywoman, shown barefoot, is teaching her daughter to read. She has the powerful appearance of one of Michelangelo's Sibyls. Her laced bodice is reminiscent of that of Chapu's *Joan of Arc* (1870). The gesture of her right arm, placed about her daughter's shoulders, is no longer rounded on the marble version erected in the Square Samuel-Rousseau in Paris, facing the church of Sainte-Clotilde. Jules Castagnary was full of praise, likening the plaster to a genre painting and the marble to a historical painting "elevating by its style the familiarity of the subject and demonstrating, by the rightness of its attitudes and by the moral unity of the group, what advantage a contemplative mind might draw from the humblest social realities" (Castagnary 1892, 2:191).

For Émile Chatrousse (1829–1896), the opposite happened when he executed his 1876 *Parisian Woman* in marble (*Parisienne*, fig. 504). According to Huysmans, "the effort was a failure; the cold material, appropriate for the symbolic nude and the rigid tubular folds of the antique peplum, froze the smart stylishness of the Parisian Woman" (Huysmans 1883, 228). No such reproach could be leveled at Juan Roig i Soler (1819–?) for his *Woman with Parasol* on the fountain in the Parc de la Ciutadella in Barcelona (1884). *Knitting* by Thomas Eakins (1844–1916) is equally composed, but the prosaic title avoids any suggestion of a classical Fate figure here. *Knitting* is one of his first independent sculptures, the others having been done in preparation for paintings. This time it was the other way around: the relief was inspired by a watercolor of 1877. Commissioned in 1882 for a mantelpiece, the sculpture was never in fact installed. The folded leaf of the table and the cat hiding under the chair emphasize the intimacy of the scene.

A realistic subject treated in a new way is *Conversation* (*Causeuses*) by Camille Claudel (1864–1943), which shows four women leaning together and chatting (fig. 151). The piece certainly offers a slice of everyday life, the only difference being that the figures are nude. The fact that it is executed in green onyx compounds the improbability of the scene. Claudel was one of those rare artists who took an interest in trivia. In a letter written to her brother Paul in 1893 or 1894, she drew and described some of her projects (Société des Manuscrits et Autographes Français, Paris). They included *The Confidence* (*La Confidence*, "three characters eavesdrop on a fourth behind a screen"), *Grace* (*Bénédicité*, "very small figures around a large table, listening to grace before a meal"), *Sunday* (*Dimanche*, "three fellows in new blouses, etc., perched on a very high cart leaving for church") and, most poignant of all, *Sin* (*La Faute*, "a girl squatting on a bench weeping, her parents watching her nonplussed"). Except for the first composition, these are all untraceable. However, *Deep Thought* (*La Profonde Pensée*, a young woman kneeling at a hearth) and *Fireside Dream* (*Le Rêve au coin du feu*) have been known to exist since 1898 and 1900 respectively.

Ernest Nivet (1871–1948), whom we shall come across again in the next section, was another sculptor who worked this seam. He met Camille Claudel in Rodin's studio in 1891. Also there was François Pompon (1855–1933), a sculptor's assistant all his life, who did small subjects from the life (his father, his mother, Mother Cachereux, animals, all the models that cost him nothing) while carving stone for others, such as Rodin, Jean Dampt, Carlier, Mercié, Sarah Bernhardt, and particularly Saint-Marceaux. Pompon's *Pensive Countrywoman* (*Paysanne pensive*, fig. 539), her arms resting heavily on her stomach, is reduced to essentials. The woman's . Pompon's strength was to observe and simplify. He was sixty-seven before he had his first personal success.

Regional Realism

Every reserve of every provincial museum in France reveals its unknown local artist. Not that Jean Baffier (1851–1929) was unknown, but his Parisian career did not prevent him from putting down roots in the central province of Berry. This geographical withdrawal went hand-in-hand with a return to the past. The large chimneypiece *For Celtic Tradition* (*Pour la tradition celtique*) that he showed at the 1898 Salon of the Société Nationale des Beaux-Arts (where Rodin exhibited his *Balzac*, fig. 540, and *The Kiss*) is a curious work. It is Renaissance in its structure and modeling but is decorated with nineteenth-century Berry countryfolk. He revived the medieval tradition of *Months*, showing the work of the countryside, such as pruning the vines, sowing, and slaughtering the pig. Two porters in clogs support the entablature, which illustrates the story of wine-making from the basket of grapes being emptied into the vat to the hooping of the barrel. The bonneted old woman who forms a console in the center recalls the bust of *Mother Baffier*. The small figures use trompe l'oeil effects like the characters in the Bourges house of Jacques Cœur (chief financier to Charles VII and one of Bourges's most famous sons), which date from the fifteenth century. On the left-hand cant, a rustic stripped to the waist supports the corner with his back while treading grapes with his feet; in the window recess below, a young man declares his love to a girl. On the right, a peasant woman in a hat, hands on hips, serves as caryatid; beneath her, a young couple admire their child. The animals and fruits of the frieze are taken from the herbals and bestiary of the late Middle Ages and early Renaissance. This is indeed a return to the past. The figures at the sides suggest a rustic existence redolent of simple happiness; all the others are subject to an "architectural" oppression that well expresses the true hardship of rural life.

For his *Family Soup Tureen with Plate of Meat* (*Soupière familiale avec plat à viande*), Baffier imagined apron-clad butchers bearing a tureen of wholly unoriginal shape, which adds to the effect of the difference of scale. The viewer's attention is drawn to the butchers, shown toiling effortlessly. The scene resembles a fairy tale—or one of the legends collected in *Nos Géants d'Auterfoès* (Our giants of yore), an anthology that Baffier published in 1920.

Ernest Nivet, who returned to nearby Châteauroux following a period spent in Rodin's studio in Paris, also devoted himself to scenes of the Berry countryside. The small format of his *Garment Menders* (*Ravaudeuses*) is reminiscent of certain works by Camille Claudel and Pompon. We rediscover the genre scenes that the sculptor Pierre-Adrien Graillon and his sons César-Adrien and Félix-Adrien-Henri had been illustrating in Dieppe back in the first half of the nineteenth century.

Provincial realism found its way into such illustrated weeklies as *L'Illustration*, which in July 1880 devoted a full page to fishing. It can be inferred that a public that "demanded" such images was also prepared to find them in art. A quarter of a century later (in 1906), the same enthusiasm on the part of the public even reached Rome. The first-year submission by Jean-Baptiste Larrivé (1875–1928), a bas-relief entitled *Fishermen* (*Les Pêcheurs*), caused Auguste Paris (1880–1915) to describe himself as "much impressed by this search for *realism* that seems to be all the rage at the moment at the Villa Medici."

For *Joselito "el Gallo,"* the monument in Seville Cemetery to a bullfighter killed at the age of twenty-five, Benlliure y Gill (1862–1947) used the funeral procession with its weeping women in local costume (not a fringe nor piece of embroidery is missing), children, and men carrying the ornate coffin on which the body of the young hero rests. Carved in white marble (as is his pillow), the *torero* exudes a brightness and calm that contrast sharply with the dark-bronze masses of the crowd that swirls at his feet, forming his socle.

Industrial Realism

The great revolution had arrived. Indeed, the adjective "industrial" sums up much of this second half of the nineteenth century. The technological revolution was accompanied by a rise in the power of its protagonists, namely bosses and workers. In the same year (1884), in France, the law granted freedom to trade unions and Zola began his novel *Germinal*. At the 1900 Exposition Universelle, Hungary devoted a substantial section to mining and metallurgy.

Before anyone thought of monuments to labor to honor the new god, artists had turned their attention to the poverty that labor had created. Achile d'Orsi (1845–1929) used the very title of his *Proximus tuus* ("Your neighbor"), a piece that was cast in Naples in 1880 and exhibited in Venice in 1881, to hurl a challenge at the viewer. Vincenzo Vela (1820–1891) evoked the epic achievement of the St. Gotthard Tunnel only by the tragic procession of his *Victims of Labor* (*Le Vittime del lavoro,* 1882). Two workers bear their comrade on a stretcher, accompanied by two more men carrying lamps. The details are as authentic and numerous as possible: heavy boots, bowed heads, smoke from the lamp of the one who is shown leaning the opposite way from the other three in order to identify the victim.

Another procession is portrayed in *Return from the Mine* by Constantin Meunier (1831–1905). The drawings and sculptures exhibited simultaneously in his Brussels house (opened as a museum in 1939) help us to understand the fascination that Belgium's "Black Country" held for a man who was enough of a mystic to spend long periods in the Trappist monastery at Westmalle, yet enough of an atheist to believe only in man. Meunier is still a relatively little-known artist. He was admired by the members of the avant-garde (Gustave Geffroy, Mirbeau, Georges Clemenceau) when he exhibited at the Paris Salons and in private galleries such as Bing's L'Art Nouveau. Yet at the same time he is seen as a forerunner of Soviet Realism, which is not as contradictory as it appears.

Meunier's workers are heroes (hence the admiration of the avant-garde), tall, stripped to the waist to display their muscles (hence the approval of the "people's democracies"), rather than puny from malnutrition or deformed by labor, as in the real world of the nineteenth century.

Dalou went down the same road. The hundred or so sketches taken from the life that he was to use for his *Monument to Labor* (*Monument au travail*) represent people who do strenuous work (a roadbuilder, a sower, a paver) but yet are "forces," whether in action or still, like the *Large Peasant* (*Grand Paysan*). "I have resolved to start work without further delay on the monument I have been dreaming of since 1889, a monument to glorify working men. The subject is in the air; it is of our time and will one day be treated by someone else, *I must fix a date*. This is the future, the religion destined to replace the mythologies of the past," wrote Dalou on April 28, 1897 (Dreyfous 1903, 248–49). It was apparently during the inauguration ceremony for the bronzed plaster model of his *Triumph of the Republic* (*Triomphe de la République*, fig. 130) in Paris's Place de la Nation on September 22, 1889 when Dalou, convinced people had been deprived of their rights to the advantage of officials, first had his idea. He had sculpted statues of workers on a monumental scale before, but the workers there were used as foils, like the *Blacksmith* (*Forgeron*) shown pushing the chariot of the Republic and already depicted on the 1879 competition maquette (Musée du Petit Palais, Paris), or like the *Peasant* (*Paysan*) at the foot of the *Boussingault Monument* inaugurated at the Conservatoire des Arts et Métiers in 1895.

None of the original sculptors—Meunier, Dalou, Rodin, Charles van der Stappen (1843–1910), and Henri Bouchard (1875–1960)—completed their monuments to labor (Schmoll gen. Eisenwerth 1965, 175–216).

Alexandre Charpentier (1856–1909) composed his *Bakers* (*Les Boulangers*, 1897, fig. 149) relief geometrically, as can be seen from the terra-cotta sketch. The glazed bricks round off static volumes, as if the sculptor had sought to emulate the impassivity of *The Archers of Darius* (about 500 B.C., Louvre). Set up in the Place Saint-Germain-des-Près before being moved to the Square Scipion, this example of polychrome sculpture is not unique. Also in Paris, there were Jean-Camille Formigé's relief medallions for the Palais des Beaux-Arts, left over from the 1889 Exposition Universelle and now displayed in the Square Paul-Langevin, the glazed-stoneware *Monumental Portico* made for the Sèvres pavilion at the 1900 Exposition Universelle (architect Charles-Auguste Risler, sculptor Jules Coutan), now in the Square Félix-Desruelles, and finally the Grand Palais frieze, *Art Through the Ages* (*L'Art à travers les âges*) by Joseph Blanc, based on cartoons by Édouard Fournier (1900). The present whereabouts of the *Frieze of Labor* (*Frise du travail*) by Anatole Guillot (1865–1911), two arched high reliefs executed in stoneware by Émile Muller for the entrance of the 1900 Exposition Universelle, are unknown.

One trophy to the glory of industrial realism, the Arc de Triomphe erected in Clermont-Ferrand for the entry of Napoleon III in 1862, complete with gear wheels and flywheels, has a later pendant, as it were, in a humble Russian tomb in the Alexander Nevski Monastery in St. Petersburg.

Animal Realism

Animals were portrayed accurately to satisfy the customer's taste for realism. Whether that customer was an animal-lover or a hunter, what he or she wanted most of all was a good likeness. Barye, however, lifted animal art above the level of genre sculpture. To accuracy, he added the violent story of life in the wild, developing combats on a monumental scale (see above, "The Last Romantics"). Auguste-Nicolas Cain continued Barye's work. Visitors might be surprised to find themselves facing a bronze rhinoceros or crocodile in the Tuileries Gardens in Paris, but it was in order to achieve this effect that each animal had to look as real as possible. Such "natural" decoration was much in demand for new parks. Notable examples were produced by Fremiet at Schloss Neudeck in Upper Silesia, the last domain of the notorious marquise de Païva and her husband, Count Guido Henckel von Donnersmarck (Zgorniak 1989, 46–52), Pierre-Louis Rouillard (1820–1881) in the grounds of the Beylerbeyi Palace in Istanbul (fig. 548), and Georges Gardet (1863–1939) on the Hennessy estate in Cognac, where an imitation of reality was sought by siting a group of bronzes in the middle of a pond (fig. 549).

Alongside such monumental commissions, small-format animal art developed as a result of the growing number of potential customers among the newly wealthy middle classes coupled with the relative modesty of their domestic arrangements. These small bronzes, designed to stand on mantelpieces and chests of drawers, provided a regular income for the bronze casters whose numbers likewise increased during the second half of the century. Artists occasionally produced their own editions, examples being Barye, Fremiet, and Mène, the father-in-law of Cain. Mène found a virtually limitless market for his genre statuettes, most of which depicted horses.

Others, such as Paul Wayland Bartlett (1865–1925), with his *Brazilian Frog* (1894, fig. 147), approached the modeling of animals using the resources of symbolism. Others, guided by the technique of stone-cutting, rediscovered the simplicity of solid form, as François Pompon did when he sculpted his *Mole* (*Taupe*, 1908, fig. 148). Observation remained the most important quality for animal sculptors, which is why they are included here under "Realism."

IMPRESSIONISM

The technique of sculpture hardly seems to lend itself to what we call "Impressionism," if that movement consists in an artist representing his time through the medium of his immediate sensations. "Permanent" materials necessitate the involvement of assistants in rough-hewing marble or casting bronze—prolonged hard work that may seem out of proportion to a subject which simply sets out to represent everyday life. When he is working in a nonresistant material, however, the sculptor has no intermediaries, whether molding a flexible medium (damp clay, soft wax, or wet plaster) or carving in softwood, his hands are able to respond to impulses from his brain and to transcribe immediate impressions. Eighteenth-century sculptors had already been aware of this in their sketches. Impressionism in sculpture is thus associated with the idea of speed, as permitted by a ductile material.

Following the long period of resistance to change that was Neoclassicism, one sculptor who embraced the new trend was Jean-Baptiste Carpeaux. The tension that bursts from his drawings and paintings permeates his clay sketches. His thumbprints create holes, shadows, and protruberances where light shifts and dances. Like Carrier-Belleuse, he set up a special workshop to reproduce his work. Interestingly, the models he chose for editions included some sketches, which demonstrates that there was a market for such "unfinished" works. The rehabilitation of the art of the eighteenth century, notably by the Goncourt brothers, had something to do with this. Among the unfinished models of which Carpeaux chose to produce editions were versions of *The Chinaman* (*Le Chinois*) and the *Mater dolorosa*, and the sketch for *Dance* (*La Danse*), the group he composed for the facade of the Opéra in Paris.

In 1860, Carpeaux had the idea of presenting his native town of Valenciennes with a monument to another of that town's famous sons, *Watteau* (1684–1721). He worked on the monument for the rest of his life but died before it was finished (fig. 530). The sketch of the frail painter, modeled in delicate touches in a slightly twisted pose, matches the definition of Impressionism as regards the technique used if not as regards the subject. Ernest-Eugène Hiolle (1834–1886) completed the fountain-monument, which was unveiled in 1884, but the enlarged version loses the immediacy of sensation present in the sketch. The bronze of the *Watteau* sketch was cast only in 1928, at the instigation of the sculptor's daughter, Louise Clément-Carpeaux.

Sculptures by Painters

Carpeaux, the precursor, was a sculptor who also painted. But when we come to look at Impressionist sculpture itself, we think of the painters who also sculpted. Foremost among them was Honoré Daumier (1808–1879), whose *Ratapoil* of 1850, modeled from the life with accusatory perspicacity, constituted a protest against the growing power of Louis-Napoleon Bonaparte.

Other painters had a variety of motives for turning to sculpture. First, some were interested in all forms of expression. One thinks in this connection of what Gauguin wrote in a letter to Camille Pissarro, probably in 1882: "The mania for sculpture is definitely growing. Degas is apparently sculpting horses and you do cows; you ask me for information about metal models, but my poor friend I know no more about this than you. I just fix something up to suit myself as best I can and nearly always badly. I think a more convenient way for you, though, would be to buy some of that narrow tin tubing they sell for pneumatic bells. You twist it the way you want and it holds pretty steady with much less flexibility than wire" (Thompson 1983, 25–28).

As a young man, Degas may have written from Italy to Pierre Cornu: "I often wonder whether to be a painter or a sculptor. I don't mind telling you, I'm very confused" (Borel 1949). Degas had two friends who may have led him in the direction of sculpture: Joseph Cuvelier, killed in 1870, several of whose equestrian statuettes survive, such as the one of *Baude* in the Musée des Beaux-Arts, Lille (wax shown at the 1869 Salon), and above all Albert Bartholomé (1848–1928), whom he got to know during the 1880s. Bartholomé was a painter, but the death of his wife Périe de Fleury in 1887 plunged him into such despair that he refused to touch his brushes again. Degas suggested that he erect a tomb for his late wife, which is how Bartholomé became a sculptor, and in particular a funerary sculptor (Burollet 1986). Degas himself had been modeling since the late 1860s. Having hesitated between the two techniques at the beginning of his career, he now made a choice. As he explained to the critic François Thiébault-Sisson in 1897 (*Le Temps*, May 23, 1921):

> I realized that to achieve . . . an accuracy so perfect that it gives the feeling of being alive, it is necessary to resort to three dimensions . . . because approximation is not acceptable . . . The truth is something you will achieve only with the aid of modeling, because modeling imposes a

> discipline on the artist that forces him to notice every single thing that matters . . . More than ever I feel the need to convey my impressions of form in sculpture . . . I sum it all up in a piece that, though tiny, is solidly grounded and does not lie.
> In fact, you're a sculptor as much as a painter, maybe more.
> Never! It's only for my own satisfaction that I've modeled animals and people in wax, not as a rest from painting or drawing but in order to make my paintings and drawings more expressive, to give them more fire, more life. They're exercises to get me going.

Degas may have modeled mostly for himself, but there was one exception: *The Little Fourteen-Year-Old Dancer* (*La Petite Danseuse de quatorze ans*, fig. 534) promised for the fifth Impressionist exhibition in 1880 but not exhibited until the following year. This half-life-sized figure, modeled in wax but also using factory-bought doll's hair, a tarlatan tutu, and ballet shoes, caused a considerable stir. Some people were alarmed by her: "Fearsome because she hasn't a thought in her head, with brute impudence thrusting forward her face or rather her little snout, and that's the word for it, too, because this poor little girl has the makings of a rat. Why is she so ugly? . . . Probably M. Degas is a moralist . . . he's plucked this flower of early deprivation from the espaliers of the theater and is showing us how it has withered prematurely. The intellectual result is achieved, the members of the public allowed in to gaze on this wax creation are initially dumbfounded, then one hears the bourgeois fathers exclaiming: 'Heaven forfend that my daughter should ever become a dancer!'" (Mantz, *Le Temps*, April 23, 1881).

Others were thrilled. Nina de Villard, the companion of Charles Cros (brother of the sculptor Henri Cros), wrote in *Le Courrier du soir* on April 23, 1881: "I experienced one of the most violent artistic impressions of my life in front of that statuette; for a long time I had been dreaming of such a thing."

Joris-Karl Huysmans understood the figure's importance immediately (Huysmans 1883, 226–27):

> At a stroke, M. Degas has toppled the traditions of sculpture just as he has long been shaking the conventions of painting.
>
> In taking up again the method of the old Spanish masters, M. Degas has instantly, by the originality of his talent, made it very special, very modern . . .
>
> The painted head, slightly thrown back, chin in the air, mouth half-open in the sickly, gray-brown face, drawn and old before its time, the hands clasped behind the back, the flat chest under a tight-fitting white bodice, its fabric molded in wax, the legs planted combatively, marvelous legs, wise with those exercises, sinewed and twisted, topped, as it were pavilioned by the chiffon of the skirts, the straight neck, ringed with a ribbon of the *Mérite agricole*, the hair falling to the shoulder and using, in the bun decorated with the same ribbon as the beck, real fiber—there she is, this dancer who comes alive as one looks at her as if she is about to step off her base.
>
> Simultaneously sophisticated and barbaric with her hard-working costume and her colored areas of palpitating flesh, crisscrossed with muscle, this statuette is the only truly modern experiment I know of in sculpture.

Finally, Nina de Villard again: "Around me, people were saying: it's a doll—how difficult to get people to look, without getting angry, at something they haven't seen before . . . But let the artist take heart: the work so misunderstood today will perhaps one day stand in a museum, viewed with respect as the earliest formulation of a new kind of art."

An American woman who saw it as such was Louisine Havemeyer, who tried unsuccessfully to buy it with the aid of Mary Cassatt (1861). Even so, the United States is today the home of Degas's waxes, which were acquired by Paul Mellon in 1955, of the first series of casts made posthumously (series "A," acquired by Louisine Havemeyer in 1921 and left by her to New York's Metropolitan Museum of Art in 1929), and of the series of models discovered in 1976 and now the property of the Norton Simon Museum in Pasadena. The heirs and the caster, A. A. Hebrard, allowed France to acquire series "P" in 1930, and Paul Mellon gave the country four waxes in 1956 and a fifth in 1992. The whole collection is now displayed at the Musée d'Orsay (see Anne Pingeot, *Degas Sculptures*, 1991).

Ought the bronzes ever to have been cast? Sculpture was a private thing for Degas. When the dealer Ambroise Vollard asked him to have bronzes made from his wax models, Degas answered (Vollard 1924, 112–13):

> "It's too much of a responsibility, leaving something behind one in bronze, a material made for eternity!"
>
> One day, he told me about a *Dancer* who was in her twentieth transformation: "This time I've got her. Another couple of quick sessions, and Hebrard (that was the name of the caster) can come."
>
> Next day, I found the dancer had returned to being a ball of wax. Seeing my amazement:

"You're thinking mainly of what it was worth, Vollard, but you could have given me a hatful of diamonds and I shouldn't have had the same delight as I had in demolishing it for the pleasure of starting all over again."

When Degas died in 1917, Joseph Durand-Ruel (the eldest son of Paul Durand-Ruel, one of the greatest Impressionist dealers) made an inventory of the artist's studio. "When I made the inventory of Degas's possessions, I found about 150 pieces scattered over his three floors in every possible place. Most of them were in pieces, some almost reduced to dust. We put apart all those that we thought might be seen, which was about one hundred, and we made an inventory of them. Out of these about thirty are valueless: thirty badly broken up and very sketchy; the remaining thirty are quite fine. They can be cast in bronze" (*New York Tribune*, October 19, 1919). That raises the question of posthumous casting. On the one hand, it gives durability to works that may be fragile and friable; also, increasing their number makes them more widely known. On the other hand, one is exceeding Degas's wishes, since all his life he refused to cast his sculptures in any permanent material. Yet he is no longer there to experience "the pleasure of starting all over again." Wax models are not made to last. The caster Albino Palazzolo (1883–1973; see below), tracked down by Jean Adhémar, explained: "He made his own armatures, using anything that came to hand, rags, corks, glasses, brush handles, a doll's bath-tub . . . it all held together so poorly, disaster seemed inevitable . . . And as with his paintings, he liked coming back to them much later . . . which ended up destroying everything" (Jean Adhémar, November 1955, 35–36, 70).

Degas's heirs gave Albert Bartholomé the job of repairing the sculptures. Given the distance that separates a piece by Degas from a piece by Bartholomé, it is impossible not to admire the scrupulousness with which the latter restored his friend's waxes. After World War I, bronze editions were cast. That the original waxes were preserved was due to the skill of the aforementioned Palazzolo, whom the caster A. A. Hebrard, having taken him on in 1903 at the age of twenty, rapidly promoted to the position of manager of his factory. Palazzolo first made a wax copy, from which he was then able to cast a bronze master model for each of the seventy-two models preserved. Twenty proofs marked A to T, a HER.D series and a HER series for the heirs and the caster, multiplied by the seventy-two original models, would give a total of 1,584 bronzes. In fact there are more, the foundry having cast several extra proofs and many forgeries having been recast since.

The *Nude Study for the Little 14-Year-Old Dancer*, which according to Marie van Goethem was begun in 1878, highlights the conflicting tensions involved in classical ballet.

Paul Valéry made an interesting link between Degas's dancers and another of the artist's favorite subjects: "No animal has so much of the dancer . . . as a thoroughbred" (Valéry 1960, 2:1190–91). Thanks to his *Horse Standing* (*Cheval arrêté*, fig. 533), we are able to follow the work process Degas used. The wax has been X-rayed by the research laboratory of the Musées de France, showing the twisted-metal armatures and even revealing the presence of a cork inside the animal's head. Degas was not a trained sculptor and made use of everything as only an artist knows how. It is possible to go on to examine the surface of the wax and compare it with that of the bronze.

Degas's *Horse and Rider* (*Cheval et Jockey*) is a study of double movement, with the animal's neck apparently foreshortened by the effect of speed. The statuette was probably made from the photographs of Eadweard Muybridge, published in "Animal Locomotion, An Electro-Photographic Investigation of Consecutive Phases of Animal Movement" in 1887 but known about earlier. By breaking down movements imperceptible to the eye, as the Frenchmen Étienne Marey was doing about the same time, such photographs served to expand human perceptions.

All these subjects, like the following, might have been dealt with under "The Realism of Everyday Life." But what Degas added was more important than the subject. *The Bath* (*Le Tub*), for example, which he sculpted in 1889, is not so much a genre scene (a woman at her toilet) as the insertion of a flexed body inside a circle (fig. 126). As a result of this assemblage of real objects (a doll's bath, a scrap of sponge, a piece of cloth that Degas gathered and painted), a curious sensation emanates from this piece, a different sensation from that conveyed by the female torsos that Rodin modeled on antique vases. *The Masseuse* (*La Masseuse*), which dates from about 1895, is ostensibly a genre scene, but the concessions to the couch and the costume of the masseuse take nothing away from the volumes and the different movements, to which everything else is subordinated. Like Proust, Degas transfigures the familiar world. Both add something of themselves to what they portray.

The sculptures of Pierre-Auguste Renoir (1841–1919) are very different. Renoir took up the technique late, though he would liked to have done so earlier—that much is clear from some of his canvases, as Maillol pointed out: "Consider Renoir's [painted] nudes: what you have is sculpture. No need to look further!" The only works that Renoir executed himself are the medallion and bust of his last son Claude, called *Coco*.

Again, the dealer Ambroise Vollard was the man behind these sculptures. Where he had failed with Degas, with Renoir he was successful. The painter was seventy-three, his hands crippled with rheumatism. But nothing stopped Vollard. He made available to Renoir two young sculptors: Richard Guino (1890–1973), an assistant of Maillol, whose job it was to execute the master's ideas, and Louis Morel. The resulting sculptures raise the question of the creation of works of art through intermediaries. Using a stick, Renoir would show Guino what he wanted. A good technician, quick on the uptake, Guino had a great admiration for Renoir, who "released him from his state of perpetual hesitancy" (Haesaerts 1947, 18). When Renoir's wife Aline Charigot died during the war (in which two of her sons had been wounded), the painter wrote to Guino: "July 23, 1916 . . . please come and see me at Essoyes as soon as possible. I have a study showing my wife, seated. I'd like you to make a bust in modeling clay based on the painting. I'm counting on you friend. Renoir." Using the 1885 painting of Madame Renoir and her eldest son Pierre, Guino modeled the bust that was placed on the grave in Essoyes. The painted mortar in the Musée d'Orsay is a successful example of polychrome sculpture (fig. 136).

The *Little Blacksmith* (*Le Petit Forgeron*, 1916–17) belongs more to Mediterranean mythology than to the forges of the Le Nain brothers. The figure has "the upturned nose, prominent upper lip, open mouth, and receding chin [of] all his characters" (Haesaerts 1947, 20). It was his enlargement—already done for his companion figure, the *Large Washerwoman* (*La Grande Laveuse*)—that marked the end of the collaboration of Guino and Renoir on December 27, 1918.

The line of Impressionist sculptures by painters also includes *Lady Out Walking* (*La Dame en promenade*) or *The Little Parisienne* (*La Petite Parisienne*) that Gauguin carved in tropical bay in 1880 (associated with Baudelaire's poem "A une passante," which ends: "O you whom I could have loved, O you who knew it"), the delicate nudes of Pierre Bonnard, and the mighty strokes of inspiration of Pablo Picasso, who in his early sculptures, such as the *Madman* (*Le Fou*, 1905), was content to model in facets.

The Sculpture Theorist of Impressionism

Medardo Rosso (1858–1928) was an artist who went beyond Milanese realism to bring a new vision to sculpture. He first visited Paris in 1884, settled there permanently in 1889, and in 1902 took French nationality. In his compositions, in which he sought to merge the subject with the surrounding air, he restricted the viewer to a single viewpoint. His late-flowering Impressionism had a great influence on contemporary artists, though not on the prevailing taste. His *Evening, Impression of a Street. Woman Wearing a Veil* (1893), though purchased on the orders of Georges Clemenceau, the French prime minister in 1907, and allocated to the Musée du Luxembourg, never reached its destination. After spending twenty-four years in the reserve, it was eventually allocated to the Musée des Beaux-Arts in Lyon. These often yellowish waxes, molded with a plaster core, were incomprehensible to someone like Dujardin-Beaumetz, for example, who held the post of undersecretary of state at the department of fine arts for seven years (1905–12).

After a friendship that went so far as an exchange of works in 1893—the *"Petit Palais" Torso* (*Torse dit du Petit Palais*) for *Woman Laughing* (*La Rieuse*)—and after an enthusiastic letter that Rodin wrote to Rosso on January 17, 1894 ("You have given me immense pleasure; the moment I saw your studio, I was crazy with admiration for you"), the two artists fell out. Rosso accused Rodin of plagiarism: *Balzac* (1891–98, fig. 540), he claimed, was inspired by his own *Bookmaker* (1894, fig. 537) or by the figure on the left in *Conversation in a Garden* (*Conversation dans un jardin*, 1894). While there is a certain similarity between these leaning figures, it is a tricky matter comparing a statuette with a monumental statue, because the problems change as the scale increases. Rosso, however, generally worked in small formats, as can be seen from the photograph *Street Impression. Paris at Night* in the Museo Medardo Rosso in Barzio (Claris 1902, 103). Rodin grasped the possibilities of this new departure on the grounds that "fortune favors only the well-prepared." In the resultant stormy relationship between Rodin and Rosso, Léonce Bénédite, the curator of the Musée du Luxembourg, sided with Rodin. That is why Rosso is so poorly represented in the Musée d'Orsay, heir to the Luxembourg's collections. It is an unfortunate outcome for a crucially important artist, who set out his theories to Claris in 1902, giving a fine definition of Impressionist sculpture in the process: "I believe that a work can only be executed by the person who conceived it. The important thing for me in art is to make people forget the material. By summing up the impressions received, the sculptor must communicate everything that struck his own sensibility, in order that, looking at his work, the viewer experiences in its entirety the emotion that he felt in observing nature . . . Baudelaire would simply have told the artist: 'Make me come alive.'"

The Followers of Medardo Rosso

The figure of *Marshal Ney* by Giuseppe Grandi (1843–1894) seems closer to Daumier's *Ratapoil* than any impression of Rosso's. Paul Trubetskoy (1866–1938), on the other hand, took in all the latter's discoveries. Raffaelli extolled his "magnificent pieces of Impressionist sculpture, by which I mean sculpture in which life is more important than precise form, in which overall appearance is more important than detail, and in which harmony flows from the intensity of the impression conveyed rather than any painstaking, laborious composition" (Claris, 1902, 89–90). Trubetskoy's *Tolstoy Riding "Frenzy"* (dated Moscow, 1899, fig. 145) was exhibited in Paris, along with fifteen other works, in the Russian section of the 1900 Exposition Universelle. Bénédite purchased it for the Musée du Luxembourg. A photograph of the sculptor and his subject was published a year after the great Russian writer's death. Trubetskoy embarked on a career in international high society and executed numerous portraits capturing the pace and elegance of that world. The Museo del Paesaggio in Verbania Pallanza, restored for the Trubetskoy exhibition in 1990, has a large number of the models he executed in Russia, France, and the United States.

Rembrandt Bugatti (1884–1916), in some of his portraits and especially in his statuettes of animals, added a certain vivacity of expression to great subtlety of modeling. However, his sculptures in the round represent a move away from the Impressionism of Rosso.

SYMBOLISM

As the nineteenth century drew to a close, poets and musicians juggled what they referred to as "correspondences." Sculptors, being caught up in matter, needed their inspiration: literature and music. Two "Symbolist doors" illustrate the use they made of them: Rodin's *Gates of Hell* (1880–1917, fig. 129), was inspired by Dante's *Divine Comedy* and Baudelaire's *Les Fleurs du Mal* (The flowers of evil), while the *Parsifal Manuscript Door* (*La Porte du manuscrit de Parsifal*, 1889–94) that Princess de Scey-Montbéliard commissioned from Carriès was intended for the entrance of a "Wagner sanctuary."

The voyage through hell that Dante imagined on Good Friday 1300, with Virgil as his guide, represents a descent into a kind of giant crater. The nine circles become smaller and smaller in proportion as the damned who inhabit them are undergoing punishment for graver and graver sins. Dante, who was the first great poet to write in a vernacular language (in his case, fourteenth-century Italian), describes as a painter or sculptor would. It is easy to understand the fascination he held for nineteenth-century artists. However, it was not Dante's geometrical world that attracted Rodin but the unforgettable protagonists that he created in his distilled verse: Paolo and Francesca, Ugolino, the ghastly metamorphoses of the two Florentine villains, and so on. In hell, actions serve no purpose; they are simply actions. The hundreds of figures that Rodin modeled on different scales float against an indistinct background—is it mud, steam, or ice? There is no plane in the *Gates*. The damned rise, descend, emerge from and plunge into depths of nowhere. The only fixed point is the poet, occupying the place of God in the Last Judgment. Behind him on the lintel, which is the only part comprising figures on the same scale, including the only skeleton and the only horned devil, an initial infernal selection process appears to be going on. On the doors themselves and on the jambs, the composition is freer. Rodin tells us why: "I have revived the methods used by the artists of the Renaissance, that mixture of figures, some in bas-relief, others sculpted in the round, to obtain the beauty of pale shadows that gives such softness" (letter to Judith Cladel, about 1899). The statement contradicts the Symbolist idea in that the sculptor is here confessing a purely plastic intention. This is why twentieth-century sculpture begins with Rodin. Yet because the meaning of the work was still all-important to him, he was the greatest sculptor of the nineteenth century. In Rodin, the two centuries meet; he concludes the one while heralding the other.

In 1887, Paul Gallimard gave the sculptor his original copy of *Les Fleurs du Mal* for him to illustrate. For a long time, Rodin lived in the company of Baudelaire's "cursed" poems. "Baudelaire had gone farther; he had descended to the bottom of the fathomless mine, set out down abandoned or forgotten galleries, eventually penetrating those regions of the mind where the monstrous vegetation of thought spreads its tentacles" (Huysmans 1884, 189). When Rodin sketched in pen in the margins or tailpieces the ideas that occurred to him, they were some of the figures of his *Gates*. The inspiration of Baudelaire shines through the damned souls wandering aimlessly amid his ruined architecture. The volume, bound by Marius Michel and decorated with a skull and a thistle incised and worked in mosaic in the leather, was purchased by the Musée Rodin in 1931.

"How much thought, how many days of exhausting study there are here! All life passed before my mind's eye as I studied this work . . . Look at those lovers, condemned to eternal punishment; they gave me the inspiration to portray love in the different phases and positions in which it appears in our imagination. I am talking about passion," Rodin told W. G. C. Byvanck (Byvanck 1892, 8). Judith Cladel is more explicit when, speculating on the true subject of the *Gates*, she suggests: "One vast carnal poem, a labor of lovers who desire, possess, and devour each other . . . this phase of extraordinary production naturally coincided with the high point of his existence, under the influence of the passions of Love . . . in which he found an echo of his thinking" (Cladel 1950, 144).

Though the commission dates from 1880, it was not until 1883 that Rodin met his great love, Camille Claudel. Mathias Morhardt, who knew them both, quoted this confidence of Rodin's in 1898, after the break-up: "The delight of being always understood, of having one's expectations always exceeded, was . . . one of the great joys of his life."

"The body, after all, knows as much as the mind." Paul Claudel used these words in 1951 to explain his sister's sculptures, but they apply equally to the figures of the *Gates of Hell* by the man he vilified in his 1905 pamphlet, "Rodin, ou l'homme de génie" (Rodin or the man of genius).

When Léon Daudet dubbed Rodin "the Michelangelo of *Les Fleurs du Mal*" (*Ère nouvelle*, 1935), he was no doubt thinking of the damned in the *Last Judgment* in the Sistine Chapel. Baudelaire's quatrain in "Les Phares" fits both the fresco and the *Gates*: "Michelangelo, no-man's land where one sees Hercules / And Christs together, and, rising stark upright, / Powerful phantoms who, in the twilight, / Rend their winding-sheets and stretch their fingers out."

Jean Carriès (1855–1894), who grew up in a Lyon orphanage, arrived in Paris in 1873. Like Rodin, he failed to gain entry to the École des Beaux-Arts. Self-taught, he exhibited at the Salon from 1875, and by 1882 was presenting his *Have-nots, Suicides, Derelicts* (*Déshérités, Désespérés, Épaves*) at the Cercle des Arts Libéraux in the Rue Vivienne in Paris ("It was literary people who thought up the names," Carriès said). He became interested in patinas and made the acquaintance of the caster Pierre Bingen, who reinstated the lost-wax process of casting and did his finest work for Carriès. Always fascinated by materials, at the 1878 Exposition Universelle Carriès discovered Japanese ceramics. He subsequently became a potter in order to rediscover the secrets of stoneware glazes.

Winnaretta Singer (1865–1943), the "sewing-machine heiress" who was married to Prince de Scey-Montbéliard from 1887 to 1892 before becoming the wife of Prince de Polignac in 1893, acquired the manuscript score of Wagner's opera *Parsifal* and wanted to construct a reliquary in which to exhibit it. The American painter John Singer Sargent, having seen an exhibition of the work of Carriès in 1889, spoke enthusiastically about it to the princess, with the result that Carriès received the commission. Eugène Grasset, who had taken French nationality in 1891, designed a "Renaissance" structure, a surbased arch and a pier, which Carriès decided to decorate in glazed stoneware. Masks of Japanese and Chinese inspiration are arranged in a quincunx on the left, separated by a zigzag ribbon on the right, while curious beasts form the disturbing entourage of the frail figure of *The Damsel* (*La Damoiselle*), who is placed beneath a sort of canopy that is actually the mouth of a monster. She occupies the place of the thinker on the *Gates of Hell*. Does she symbolize the folly of purity, the struggle against self and redemption, like *Parsifal*?

The work was never finished because of a disagreement between the person who had commissioned it, Princess de Scey-Montbéliard, and the artist, who wrote on August 25, 1890: "My work has taken everything . . . that woman will really have the flesh off my back when she has what I've done." In the end he gave up: "I've worked for thirty-four months non-stop for the modest sum of 46,000 francs, which does not even cover the costs of tools and materials that I've had to pay out, not to mention my time and my expensive ceramic experiments . . . I could do you something quickly for your money. I'd rather return it to you" (Alexandre 1895, 166). All that survives of the whole episode are the plaster model and a few stoneware tiles kept at the Musée du Petit Palais in Paris, to which the Carriès Collection was donated by Georges Hoentschel in 1904. The large model (height 5.75 meters, length 8.20 meters) cast in 1890–91 was demolished in 1936 to make room for an exhibition of Italian art.

Carriès had a more developed "medieval" spirit than Rodin. He also had a "regional" side that Rodin lacked. And he was more interested in surface than in structure. But both men enjoyed the approbation of writers and the backing of important figures in society. And although one died at thirty-nine and the other lived to the age of seventy-seven, they both made a major contribution to Symbolism.

Though it is not a door, the relief by Pierre Roche (real name Fernand Massignon, 1855–1922) entitled *Deliverance* (*Délivrance*, 1905-11) suggests a rite of passage (fig. 533). The Russo-Japanese war of 1904 gave him four visions—*Pride Lust, Anger,* and *Avarice* (*L'Orgueil, L'Envie, La Colère, L'Avarice*)—that he dedicated to the victims. He modeled these deadly sins responsible for conflicts, added the last three, arranged them all as a triumphal arch, and in the middle placed the head of a young woman with her severed hands over her ears. The inscription on the base gives us the meaning: "Speak no evil, see no evil, hear no evil." Presented in plaster at the Salon of the Société Nationale des Beaux-Arts in 1905, the relief featured in lead at the 1911 Salon; it is kept in Roubaix (École Nationale Supérieure des Industries Textiles). Roche was a friend of Joris-Karl Huysmans, a bust of whom he showed at the 1898 Salon of the Société Nationale des Beaux-Arts. The writer's conversion following a satanist phase in 1891 was the talk of literary and artistic Paris. The *Seven Works of Divine Mercy* (*Les Sept Œuvres de Miséricorde*, 1910 Salon of the Société Nationale des Beaux-Arts) that Pierre Roche composed in bas-relief formed a companion piece to his *Deliverance* and belonged to the same current flowing from Symbolism to mysticism.

The love of materials that Huysmans extolled in his novel *À rebours* (*Against the Grain*) in 1884 ("Besides, des Esseintes saw artifice as the distinctive mark of man's genius. As he used to say, nature has had its day") was something of which Roche sought to explore the subtleties in his "gypsographie et églomisations," his ceramic tiles, and his works in lead. Théodore Rivière (1857–1912) added inlays of precious stones to the delicacies of chryselephantine statuary. His *Salammbô and Mâtho*, exhibited at the Salon of the Société des Artistes Français in 1895, was inspired by Flaubert's Carthaginian novel *Salammbô* (1862):

> Suddenly wracked with sobs, he sank to a crouch: "Oh, forgive me! I am a wretch, viler than scorpions, baser than the mire and the dust! A moment ago, as you spoke to me, your breath passed over my face and my delight in it was that of a dying man, lying prostrate to drink at the water's edge. Tread on me: let me but smell your feet! Curse me: let me but hear your voice! Do not leave! Have pity! I love you! I love you!"
>
> He was on his knees on the ground before her; he had passed both arms about her waist, his head was flung back, his hands roamed; the golden disks dangling from his ears gleamed against his sunburnt neck; huge tears welled up in his eyes like silver globes; caressingly, he sighed, murmuring vague words that were lighter than a breeze, sweeter than a kiss.
>
> Salammbô felt herself invaded by a feebleness in which she lost all awareness of self.

Earlier, Flaubert had described Mâtho's arms, "on which veins crisscrossed like ivy along the branches of a tree." Rivière's setting follows the text closely. Pierre Bingen cast the bronze, which stands out against the whiteness of the ivory representing Salammbô's skin. A turquoise hangs from the other pieces of gold jewelry.

The success of a work can be measured by the number of firms reproducing it and the number of editions. Such was the impact of Rivière's piece that, following the Salon, the Sèvres factory made biscuit versions in two sizes and Susse produced bronzes, also in two sizes, either patinated or gilt.

Lamia by Sir George Frampton (1860–1929) plays with the contrasts between bronze, ivory, and opal to even greater symbolic if not literary effect. Keats's poem, published in 1820, tells of the moment when the sorceress with the body of a serpent and the head of a woman, transformed by Mercury into a beautiful girl, is about to marry Lycius, the young man whom she loves; the eyes of Lycius's old teacher see through her, however, revealing the nature of her power, which instantly fades away. She turns back into a serpent. Lamia symbolizes beauty, Lycius emotion, and the old teacher reason. Emotion comprehends beauty, but reason dissects and destroys. The work, which dates from 1899–1900, was exhibited at the Royal Academy of Arts in London in 1900 and is held there still (Read 1989, no. 193).

Between 1899 and 1902, Max Klinger (1857–1920) composed his great *Beethoven Monument* (Museum der Bildenden Künste, Leipzig, fig. 554). A painter and above all an outstanding etcher, Klinger here turned to sculpture. To achieve a *Gesamtkunstwerk* (total artwork), he utilized polychromy. The nature of each stone lends meaning to the work. The white, black, and purple marbles, alabaster, bronze, and ivory used in the sculpture reconstitute an idea Klinger had while playing the piano one evening in Paris in 1885. The *Beethoven Monument* was exhibited at the fourteenth Sezession exhibition in Vienna (1902), along with works by Klimt, Hoffmann, and Alfred Boehm (1861–1927).

It was not a story taken from literature but a piece of actual experience that Camille Claudel depicted in *Middle Age* (*L'Âge mûr*). The first model of this group of three figures showed a man leaning back toward the kneeling girl, who held him back with both hands, while on the other side of this oblique axis the old woman threatened the girl. That was in 1894. Five years later, the model exhibited at the 1899 Salon of the Société Nationale des Beaux-Arts showed the end of the struggle: where before the axis leaned toward the right, toward the girl, now it leans toward the left. The girl has lost the struggle. This time her hands are open, grasping only emptiness. The man's hand eludes her. The old woman draws her conquest away on a wave, her drapery billowing in the wind. Where are they going? To death, no doubt. Yet the artist who gave expression to her pain in this way was to suffer a death worse than theirs: for the last thirty years of her life, from 1913 to 1943, her family had her locked away in a lunatic asylum (see *L'Âge mûr de Camille Claudel*, 1988). Perhaps Huysmans was right when he wrote: "Pain is a result of education" (*À rebours*, 1884, 98).

Antidotes to the ravages of the passions were offered by the Belgian sculptor Georges Minne, who modeled "boys spiritualized to the point of starvation" (Jullian, August 1969, 34), such as those depicted in *Solidarity* (fig. 252). This group, which sprang from a project for the *Volders Monument*, was shown in plaster at the Libre Esthétique in Brussels in 1898. The writers Émile Verhaeren (1855–1916) and Maurice Maeterlinck (1862–1949) influenced the work of Minne in the 1890s, after Rodin had left his stamp on it. It was the latter who, in composing his *Three Shades* (*Trois Ombres*) from the figure of *Adam*, had shown how to replicate figures. Minne multiplied them in his Fountain with Kneeling Figures (commissioned by Henry van de Velde for Karl Ernst Osthaus, 1898, Folkwang Museum, Essen), shown at the Viennese Sezession in 1900.

The American painter John Singer Sargent made one foray into sculpture in the bas-reliefs that formed part of his commission for the Boston Public Library (1895–1903). *Redemption* shows *Adam* and *Eve* attached to the cross, their task being to collect in a chalice the blood from Christ's nailed hands. In 1899 Singer was in Paris, consulting a compatriot, the sculptor Augustus Saint-Gaudens, on the subject of casting. In 1901, he exhibited the *Crucifix* at the Royal Academy of Arts in London, before the piece was installed in Boston in 1903. The serpent wound round Christ's feet and the pelican with its three chicks filling the lower quatrefoil of the cross complete the bold symbolic scheme of the piece.

When Rodin showed *The Hand of God* (*La Main de Dieu*) modeling the first man and the first woman in a single impression from a block of matter (1902), he was likening the creation practiced by the artist to that of God (fig. 521). The twist of the woman's neck is the same as on the allegorical figure on the tomb of Giuliano de Medici in Florence. Once again, Baudelaire may be the link ("L'Idéal," *Les Fleurs du Mal*, 1857): "Or you, great Night, daughter of Michelangelo / Calmly displaying in your unusual pose, / Those charms shaped for the Titans' kisses."

Such portraits evoke more than they show. Albert Bartholomé drew his inspiration from Japanese no masks to represent *Tadamasa Hayashi* (1853–1906; fig. 135). Hayashi had come to Paris for the 1878 Exposition Universelle as interpreter to Captain Wakai. In 1883 he opened a Japanese art shop that became extremely popular with European and American art lovers. Through him, more than 200,000 Japanese prints reached France, while his own collection of Western art was in turn to influence the art of Japan. He did translations for Edmond de Goncourt, who published *Utamaro* in 1891 and *Hokusai* in 1896, and wrote the following portrait in the March 25, 1895 issue of *Le Journal*: "Oh, the turgescences on Hayashi's yellow brow as he gives birth to this translation, and the little cries that punctuate his reading of the text as he works on his French, and his funny, screwed-up face" (Edmond de Goncourt 1956, 4:766).

Edgar Poe by Henry de Groux (1866–1930)—two creative artists admired by Claude Debussy. Believing the Belgian Symbolist painter and sculptor de Groux to have been dead for five years, Arsène Alexandre had organized a retrospective for him at the 1911 Salon d'Automne. "This exhibition is wonderful!" Debussy wrote to his friend Robert Godet on December 18, 1911, "A Napoleon leading the retreat from Russia that is more profoundly chilling than all the piles of snow, suggesting all the bitterness of the coming decline. A Tolstoy in bronze, substantial, seeming to stride toward a meeting with Fate, far more handsome than Rodin's skillful mutilations! A portrait of Wagner with the face of a cynical old magician sitting on a secret. All that, so many images, shapes that haunt you incessantly. I saw H. de Groux there, hardly changed at all. Still that look of a brilliant clown, and all the world's dreams in his eyes" (Debussy 1942, 128). Nearly seven years earlier, on January 4, 1904, Jules Renard had already noted this superb riposte in his diary: "People had passed the hat round for the painter de Groux, who hadn't a cent left. He took the money with the words: 'I'm going to amaze you with my ingratitude.'"

Like Poe, *Paul Verlaine* (1844–1896) relied heavily on alcohol (fig. 510). The bust by Rodo (1863–1913; real name Auguste de Niederhäusern) conveys the anxiety of the wizard of "transpositions," whom he had met in Paris in 1866. From the wax medallion shown at the Salon of the Société des Artistes Français in 1889 to the monument in the Luxembourg Gardens in Paris that was put up by public subscription and inaugurated on May 28, 1911, Rodo exhibited at least seventeen portraits of Verlaine or fragments of the monument. Verlaine for his part wrote a poem, published in his *Dédicaces* in 1894, about "this bust that represents me." The model exhibited at the 1899 Salon of the Société Nationale des Beaux-Arts sets out to be a total work of art, a typical "Symbolist monument." From the stem of the base three allegories emerge and from the top the bust of the poet. "There were three souls in Verlaine," Rodo told Henry Bourgerel, "a religious soul, a sensual soul, and the soul of a child, full of memories and secrets" (Lapaire 1996, 149). But trying to "do a Rodin" was not enough. Despite Rodo's extensive correspondence with his older contemporary (sixty letters preserved in the archives of the Musée Rodin in Paris), he was unable to make his monument express what he had captured in the sketch for the bust now in the Musée Bourdelle.

Antonin Dvorak (fig. 508) by Josef Maratka (1874–1937) resembles Rodo's *Verlaine* in its expression of anxiety. The Czech sculptor made this bust after a period spent in Rodin's studio from 1901 to 1904.

In 1886 Rodin began modeling a portrait of Camille Claudel in traditional costume. When his assistant Victor Peter, executing the work in marble, reached the collar, Rodin made him stop: the head emerging from the block offered the contrast, as in Michelangelo, of a finished section imprisoned in the rough-hewn stone. This triumph of sculpture was exhibited as it was at the Salon of the Société Nationale des Beaux-Arts in 1895, entitled *Head*. Only later did it receive its Symbolist title of *Thought Emerging from Matter*, then simply *Thought* (*La Pensée*, fig. 152), the present title of this portrait of someone who was to lose her mind. Camille Claudel's face emerging from the block of marble is like the face that Odilon Redon showed emerging from the sea in his painting *Eyes Closed* (*Yeux clos*, 1890), or from the earth in the lithograph.

Émile Derré (1867–1938), a sculptor with a concern for justice, showed *Goodness* (*La Bonté*), a statue of Louise Michel, at the 1905 Salon d'Automne, following it up in 1906 (shortly after her death) with a bronze bust of the anarchist teacher sentenced to deportation after the failure of the Commune. "Some friends of the famous citizen, notably M. Ernest Vaughan, warden of the Quinze-Vingts [a Paris hospice for blind paupers and beggars], who was formerly exiled with her, had the idea for this act of homage and are going to ask the City of Paris for a site." A base was provisionally erected in the Place Constantin-Pecqueur in Montmartre, inscribed with the words: "To Louise Michel (1836–1905). Goodness incarnate: knew only poverty and prison." Was it a subscription raised among local workers that made it possible to execute the bronze exhibited at the 1906 Salon of the Société Nationale des

Beaux-Arts? Though the group was reproduced on postcards, its whereabouts are unknown, nor is there any record of its unveiling. The *Monument to Louise Michel* may have remained more symbolic even than planned.

To finish this overview, let us look at two masterpieces that were dominated by their meaning. *Silence* by Augustus Saint-Gaudens, made for the Adams Memorial in Rock Creek Cemetery, Washington, D.C., owes as much to the writer Henry Adams as to the sculptor. Adams's wife committed suicide in 1885. The writer commissioned her tomb after a trip to Japan, where he had discovered Buddhism. The allegory he wanted had to suggest "the acceptance, intellectually of the inevitable." Having attended the posing of a draped model in late 1886, he refused to see the work before its completion, though he followed its progress from wherever he was on his travels. He wrote to his brother from Australia on August 3, 1891: "I can't help still looking forward with a little dread to my own first sight of it, not because I doubt that his artistic rendering of an idea must be better than my conception of the idea, but because the two could hardly be the same, and what is his in it might to me seem to mix badly with the image that had been in my mind" (Scheyer summer 1956, 178–98). However, Adams did communicate his idea to Saint-Gaudens, who wrote in his notes: "Adams-Buddha—mental repose—calm of thought in contrast with the violence or force found in nature." Seated on a rock, the amply draped figure bears no inscription, at the request of Adams. Like a sphinx, it questions all who approach. "The interest of the figure was not in its meaning, but in the response of the observer" (*The Education of Henry Adams, an Autobiography*, 1924, 329)—hence the requirement for anonymity, the refusal to give it a name.

Another sphinx is Rodin's *Balzac* (1898, fig. 540). In the 1880s, Rodin had begun removing parts of the bodies of his statues to give more meaning to the rest; in portraying the author of the novel sequence *La Comédie humaine*, he concealed the entire body. The figure has no arms, even; only the head emerges from the top of this menhir symbolizing creation. This is the starting point of twentieth-century sculpture. Indeed, it was because it was so far ahead of its time that the monument, commissioned from Rodin in 1891 by the Société des Gens de Lettres at the suggestion of its chairman Émile Zola, was rejected by the society in 1898: "The Committee . . . has the regretful duty to protest against the sketch shown at the Salon by M. Rodin, in which it declines to acknowledge the statue of Balzac" (meeting of May 9, 1898, when Zola was no longer chairman). Rodin, who was never to see his *Balzac* in bronze, kept the plaster in his Meudon garden, where Jacques-Ernest Bulloz and Edward Steichen both photographed it. In his exhibition at the Alma Pavilion in 1900, he gave the plaster *Balzac* the place of honor, as does the Musée d'Orsay. The first casting was made in 1930 for Antwerp (Middleheim Museum). On July 1, 1939, Maillol and Charles Despiau unveiled the bronze erected in the Boulevard Raspail in Paris.

"I seek silence and night to weep" (Corneille, *Le Cid*). Émile-Antoine Bourdelle (1861–1929) gave us an allegory of that *Night* (1900–4), a figure derived from Michelangelo. It is a kind of grotesque mask with which to enter the new century, hiding its face so that we see only the eyes (fig. 153).

ART NOUVEAU

About the turn of the century, the twists and turns of thought became meandering lines, then meandering lines became an end in themselves. Whether or not such works were imbued with symbolism, they are lumped together here by virtue of that triumph of line.

In 1884 Rodin made a portrait of *Luisa Lynch de Morla Vicuña*, wife of the Chilean ambassador to Paris (fig. 137). In conversation with the artist (Rodin 1912, 248), Paul Gsell alluded to this marble, which was purchased by the state at the 1888 Salon: "There is a female bust in the Musée du Luxembourg, possibly the finest you've ever done, leaning forward irresolutely, as if her mind were in the grip of giddiness from plunging into the abyss of dream."

Symbolism has not been abandoned. The Art Nouveau element in this questioning portrait comes out in the movement of the hair, the oval of the fur coat, the bunch of flowers that accompany this "new attitude resulting from the inimitable twist of the neck, the way the face is thrust forward" (Geffroy 1893, 101). Jean Escoula carved the bust and Pierre Cornu the flowers.

"I had seen your female head in the Musée du Luxembourg. I had gone to it because it summoned me from a great distance. I did not see it, I felt it—and since that day I have striven ceaselessly toward the source you represent," Bourdelle wrote to Rodin in 1906 (Musée Rodin archives). Art Nouveau was of potential fascination for the future propagators of a return to architectural sculpture. The off-balance construction of *Madame Vicuña* was not repeated in *The Actress* (*L'Actrice*, fig. 138) by Paul-François Berthoud (1870–1939). The important thing here is ornamentation. The marble and bronze version of this bust was shown at the Salon of the Société des Artistes Français in 1902. Is the patinated plaster left to the museums of Clermont-Ferrand the one that was to be exhibited at the 1930 Salon d'Automne as a "terra cotta"? The way the space is divided up by the convolutions of ribbons and locks of hair is typical of Art Nouveau. In the allegory of *Music* (*Hubda*) by Joseph Vaclav Myslbek (1848–1922) it is a tree and its branches that provide the necessary curves, as if the young woman were wrapped in a harp. Agathon Léonard (1841–1923; real name Agathon Léonard van Weydeveldt) took line and wind to their logical conclusion in his *Scarf Dance* (*Jeu de l'écharpe*, fig. 241). The models shown at the Salon of the Société Nationale des Beaux-Arts in 1897 ("ten maquettes . . . project for the decoration of a dance hall") were acquired by the Sèvres factory, which in 1900 exhibited the fifteen pieces in biscuit porcelain, making up a table centerpiece: twelve dancers, a flute player, and two torchbearers. Sèvres produced biscuit editions (contract renewed in 1914, 1920, and 1953), and the firm of Susse produced bronzes, sometimes embellished with ivory and silver. For Léonce Bénédite, curator of the Musée du Luxembourg, Léonard was one of "those invaluable artists who, by combining sculpture with goldwork, jewelry, and curios, have rejuvenated it, shifted its function, and given it a direct outlet in the life of today" (Bénédite June 1904, 440).

This goldwork aspect of Art Nouveau also appears in *Pandora* (1890, fig. 551) by Harry Bates (1850–1899). The viewer's interest, like Pandora's own, is concentrated on the ivory and bronze box. Her desire to know the contents of the casket is communicated by the inclined head. Pandora's imagination encompasses it like her rounded arms.

Jean Dampt's *Domestic Peace* (*Paix du foyer*) appeals to the same curiosity but inversely, as it were. "All man's unhappiness stems from one thing, which is his inability to remain at rest in one room" (Pascal 1670). Dampt lets us into that room. In it sits a woman, with a cat on her lap and a dog beside her. She is bare-shouldered and has flowers in her hair; in her hand she holds an olive branch. Against a dense pattern of leaves behind the figure, the legend proclaims: "PAIX AU FOYER." Every kind of symbolism can be read into this work, including the anti-feminist leitmotiv! The work (which combines walnut, ivory, jade, and enameling) illustrates the passage from the Gothic style to Art Nouveau. Shown in the decorative arts section of the 1900 Exposition Universelle, it had been commissioned by the Union Centrale des Arts Décoratifs two years earlier.

Another example of the "Gothic-Art Nouveau" line of descent is the decorative scheme of the church of Saint-Jean-de-Montmartre in Paris by the architect Anatole de Baudot. In the entrance porch and on the front of the high altar are reliefs (1897–1904) by Pierre Roche. The frames are medieval, the figures Art Nouveau. Outside, background and form merge in the angel figures. In the middle, *St. John* emerges from the molding to threaten the snake seen winding around his wrist. All these reliefs respect the "law of the frame."

In contrast to such coiled forms are the shredded volumes modeled by Victor Prouvé (1858–1943) for his *Private Monument for "Poèmes barbares"* (*Monument intime pour les Poèmes barbares*, a volume of poems written by Leconte de Lisle, fig. 143). The wolf, the eagle, and the branches like frozen waves are more eloquent through their twisting and turning than the literary rebus.

Art Nouveau, which inspired major decorative schemes for facades and interiors, also had its monumental sculpture, such as the *Shaftesbury Memorial* (1886–93) by Alfred Gilbert (1854–1934). This work, unveiled in

London's Piccadilly Circus on June 29, 1893, was erected by public subscription in memory of the philanthropist Anthony Ashley Cooper, seventh earl of Shaftesbury (1801–1885). Rather than portraying the man, Gilbert chose to place an allegory of *Eros* (or rather *Anteros*, "mutual love") on top of a fountain symbolizing love of humanity. The winged figure, cast in aluminum, stands on one foot on a bronze octagon on which fish and putti surge in sinuous volumes. "For new thoughts, let us fashion antique verses," wrote the eighteenth-century French poet André Chenier. Here we have the opposite: a Renaissance fountain translated into *fin de siècle* English.

Gilbert's masterpiece, the *Tomb of the Eldest Son of the Prince of Wales, the Duke of Clarence* (fig. 140), took more than thirty years to complete in the chapel of Windsor Castle (1892–1928). The surround of the sarcophagus is enormously inventive. At the deceased's head kneels an angel reminiscent of the one Marie d'Orléans placed on the mausoleum of her brother the duke d'Orléans in Neuilly, near Paris. The angel is neither raising empty hands nor lifting his face to the sky, as in the Neuilly chapel; rather, with head bowed toward the deceased, he reaches out to place above him a crown of cities and laurels—a heavenly Jerusalem, perhaps? The railings around the tomb heighten the mystery. A kind of Tree of Jesse, they bear the patron saints of the family like poisonous flowers springing from volutes of pairs of angels. There is nothing natural in any of these shapes, nothing pure, nothing calm, except for the ivory faces of *St. George* (1895), *St. Michael* (1899–1900), the *Virgin Mary*, and *St. Elizabeth of Hungary* (1899)—the first figures made—whose resignation contrasts with the profusion of the lines of the sumptuous garments that constitute what are the most highly developed creations of a new iconography (see also Beattie 1983; Dorment 1986; Blühm 1996–97).

EXPRESSIONISM

Expressionism did not find its definition in sculpture. Nevertheless, this term can be applied in a general way to the expression of certain extravagant feelings highlighted by particular attitudes, gestures, and faces. This trend, which received its name in the last years of the nineteenth century and the early years of the twentieth, had been around for a long time in the final flare-ups or gradual decay of styles as they reached their end. Romantic literature made great use of it, for example, as witness *Meg Merrilies Furies* (fig. 543), taken from a novel by Walter Scott. The work of the young American sculptor Edward Thaxter (1857–1887), it represents a character in the famous Scottish historical novelist's *Guy Mannering* (1815), a stage version of which was produced in Boston in 1872 and 1873. The figure of the old gypsy is intended to inspire fear in the manner of a Gorgon. Thaxter's marble reproduces every detail of the screaming face, the wild hair, and the hand clutching the shoulder.

The *T'Serclaes Memorial* by Jules Dillens (1849–1904), which was commissioned in 1898 for the arches of the Maison de l'Étoile in the Grand'Place in Brussels, comprises a number of registers in which the exploits of the alderman of Brussels, Everard T'Serclaes, who drove foreign soldiers from the city in 1356 but who was murdered in 1388, are recounted in three reliefs. In the center of this "shrine treated like a large piece of jewelry" (Potvin 1913), the mutilated body of T'Serclaes, whose tongue was torn out, is shown half-emerging from the shroud at what for passers-by is eye level. The artist seeks to stir feelings by juxtaposing illustrations of his subject's earthly glory in small-format tableaux with the final state of his body, which is shown life-sized. Among earlier examples, the two-story tombs of the kings of France in the abbey church of Saint-Denis show *Louis XII* and *Francis I* kneeling in court dress above their prone, worm-eaten corpses. These recumbent effigies, together with that made by Ligier Richier for the *Monument to the Heart of René de Châlon* in Bar-le-Duc, are enduring "Expressionist" masterpieces of the Renaissance. So it is not surprising that, despite the country's preference for moderation and symmetry, France should in the second half of the nineteenth century have produced a great Expressionist sculptor who was also a lover of cathedrals: Auguste Rodin.

One of Rodin's most striking works is *The Burghers of Calais* (*Bourgeois de Calais*, commissioned 1884, plaster model exhibited 1889, bronze monument unveiled 1895, fig. 131), commemorating the burghers of the town who sacrificed themselves to King Edward III in 1347 in order to raise the siege of the town. The movements of the figures vividly express their sense of despair at their imminent death. Rodin's achievement was described by Rainer Maria Rilke, the Austrian poet who worked as Rodin's secretary from September 1905 to May 1906 (Rilke 1966, 1:423, 424):

> He saw how those men set out; he felt how each one of them re-experienced the whole of his past life, how each one, heavy with his own past, stood waiting, ready to bear it out of the ancient city. Six men appeared before him, all dissimilar . . . each in his own way had taken his decision and was living this last hour . . . with his soul, suffering it with his body, which clung to life. And then he stopped seeing even the forms. Suddenly, in his memory, gestures appeared, gestures of refusal, leave-taking, renunciation. Many, many gestures. He collected them. He gave form to them all. They flowed into his mind out of the abundance of his experience. It was as if, in his memory, a hundred heroes had stood up, eager to be sacrificed. And he took all hundred, and made of them six heroes. He shaped them naked, each self-contained in all the eloquence of his trembling body. Superhuman in scale: in their resolution, life-sized.
>
> He created the old man with dangling, limp-jointed arms; and he gave him a slow, leaden step, the worn-out step of the elderly, and an expression of weariness running down his face into his very beard.
>
> He created the man carrying the key. In him there are still many years of life, and all now compressed into this sudden final hour. He can scarcely bear it. His lips are pinched, his hands grip the key tightly. He has lit the fire of his strength and it is burning up in him, in his stubborn determination.
>
> He created the man who is holding his bowed head in his hands as if to collect himself, seeking one more moment alone.
>
> He created the two brothers, one still looking back while the other bows his head in a gesture of resolution and submission, as if already offering it to the executioner.
>
> And he created the empty gesture of the man who "goes through life alone." The "passer-by," Gustave Geffroy called him. The man had started walking, but has turned back one more time, not toward the city, not toward those who are weeping, not toward his companions. He has turned back toward himself. His right arm is raised, flexed, irresolute: his hand is open, releasing something, as one might give a bird its freedom.

Some of the studies for the monument are more Expressionist than the final monument itself. Rodin worked on the figures separately, making them nude at first, then clothed. He linked them to others or mutilated them to make them even more expressive. For example, it was a nude *Pierre de Wissant* (to use one of the names attributed to the "burghers" in 1944 by Georges Grappe, one of the first curators of the Musée Rodin), headless and with no hands, who greeted visitors beneath the rotunda of the Alma Pavilion that Rodin built for his private exhibition in 1900.

The *Torso of Clotho* by Camille Claudel (*Torse de Clotho*, 1893) does not have the abundant hair that makes her the Parca who weaves our fate, nor the actors of the complex group *Middle Age*, in which she plays the role of the victorious crone. It is simply a study of an emaciated woman whom modesty forbids from showing nude.

That was also the year (1893) when Bourdelle went to work in Rodin's studio. He was very much under the spell of his master when, following a competition in 1895, he was commissioned to produce a *Monument to the Defenders and Combatants of Tarn-et-Garonne 1870–71* (*Monument aux défenseurs et combattants du Tarn-et-Garonne 1870–71*) for the city of Montauban in southwest France. An epic Romanticism inflames this composition. Bourdelle worked up a number of figures that he did not use in the final group, such as the "three faces springing from an Inferno of which Dante and Virgil had no conception, namely Fear, Suffering, and Death" (*Le Corps en morceaux*, exhibition catalog, 1990).

It may seem inappropriate to include *Edward Jenner Inoculating His Own Son with Vaccine* (*Edoardo che inocula il vaccino al proprio figlio*, 1873) by the Italian sculptor Giulio Monteverde (1837–1917) and *Barbarian Mother Bearing the Body of Her Dead Son Away from the Battlefield* by the Norwegian Stephan Abel Sinding under the heading "Expressionism." Yet in both groups relations between parent and child achieve a level of vehemence that goes well beyond the proprieties of "drawing room sculpture." There is almost a ferocity in the way the scientist uses his son to verify his discovery, although the work certainly belongs to the category of historical realism. The group was a huge success at the 1873 International Exhibition in Vienna, and at the 1878 Exposition Universelle in Paris a *médaille d'honneur* went to the marble version (Palazzo Bianco, Genoa). Sinding's group in the Ny Carlsberg Glyptotek in Copenhagen echoed the supple nude anatomy of the dead soldier that Mercié had perched atop his *Gloria victis* (fig. 125). Sinding's piece, however, does not offer a Renaissance-inspired allegory with wings unfurled but a rustic and coarsely clad mother, with muscular arms, moving away, head flung back and stomach thrust forward, the better to carry the body of her son, which she holds in both arms. The eye for detail (the lacing of the bodice, the weapons on the terrace) and the perfection of the young man belong to "official" sculpture. But the interplay of oblique lines and weights is a problem of sculpture, one long studied by those who have tackled the Pietà theme, which Sinding has here reexamined. The marble was carved in Rome in 1883.

The same balance in imbalance was sought by van der Stappen in *Ompdrailles-le-Tombeau-des-Lutteurs* (1892), a piece inspired by a novel written by the French provincial author Léon Cladel (fig. 483). The character called Arribial is arched backward, with his left leg forward (like Sinding's *Barbarian Mother*), supporting the body of his friend Ompdrailles, who has just been killed. Arribial's intention is to show the body of his companion to the crowd. The dead man, like some Christ being taken down from the cross, dangles with arms outstretched. There is a suggestion here of Michelangelo's *Pietà* in Florence Cathedral. The opposing movements of the live figure and the corpse create enormous tension. The group was erected in the Avenue Louise in Brussels.

In 1896, Georges Minne (1866–1941) used the return of *The Prodigal Son* (*L'Enfant prodigue*, fig. 526) to portray the violence of a father's love. He clasps his son to him, wrenching him off the ground and leaning back, the better to feel his son's weight on his chest. The strength of the father's emotion dictates the form of the piece. The vertical of equilibrium passes through the old man's heart. Minne liked to harness movement to spiritual ends. He gathered a circle of artists around him at Laethem-Saint-Martin, which became something of a center of Expressionism.

For Bernhardt Hoetger (1874–1949), who went to live in France in 1900, the fashionable preoccupation with the sordid side of life (which the French called *misérabilisme*) attracted his interest. His *Blind Man* (*Aveugle*) has his head thrown back to rest on the shoulder of a bent female figure. A smaller version of the plaster group exhibited at the Salon of the Société des Artistes Français in 1901 was produced by Eugène Blot, Camille Claudel's publisher, who in 1905 showed the two artists at his gallery simultaneously.

Carl Millès (1875–1955), in his *Struggle for Existence* (*Lutte pour la vie*, 1903, fig. 524), shows two men running with their arms out, vying for first place. *At the Finish* (*Au but*) by Alfred Boucher (1850–1934), erected in the Luxembourg Gardens in 1890 but melted down during the Occupation of Paris, represented a race between three young men. The fragmentary nature of the Millès piece, which concentrates on the exhaustion expressed on the faces and the desperately outstretched arms, the hand of one trying to hold back the other's arm, gives precedence to signification rather than expressing the virtuosity of the mingled limbs of the runners, as in Boucher's work. Millès, who lived in poverty in Paris from 1897 to 1904, also produced *misérabiliste* statuettes at the time, which are in contrast to the voluptuous, monumental statues from his hand exhibited in museums in the United States (he took American citizenship in 1945) and in the Milles Gården (his foundation in Sweden).

In 1906, returning to a Baroque setting, Henri Cordier (1853–1926), who was the son of Charles Cordier, the "ethnographic" sculptor of the Second Empire, represented *Doubt* (*Le Doute*). A naked man, seated on a rock beside an open book that bears the words "the New Testament of Our Lord Jesus Christ," listens to another man, who appears to be counseling him with an alarming look and smile on his face and who can only be a devil. The work, which stands in the Santa Fe Gardens in Buenos Aires, took five years to complete. It is chiefly remarkable for the evil but attractive face of the one instilling doubt, who is reminiscent of the portraits by Franz Xaver Messerschmidt (1736–1783) in Vienna's Lower Belvedere Palace. In the wake of this commission, Henri Cordier went to Argentina and to Montevideo in Uruguay, where he executed various monumental works in the years preceding World War I.

The *Troll Who Can Smell Christian Blood* (1896, fig. 141) by Niels Hansen Jacobsen (1861–1941), in the gardens of Copenhagen's Ny Carlsberg Glyptotek, is clearly out hunting. His body resembles a rough-barked tree, and he bends low to catch the scent. Many tales and legends of the north were created in an atmosphere that seemed to anticipate Expressionism. Without going so far, Charles Perrault's *Contes de ma mère l'oye* (1697; *Tales of Mother Goose*) used an "Expressionist" repertoire that Gustave Doré was able to exploit in his 1862 illustrations.

When the Russian Seraphin Sudbinin (1867–1944) modeled his *Horrible* (1906, fig. 512), a bronze head in the Russian Museum in St. Petersburg, he bore witness to how the devil always hides behind charming (and disturbing) features. The expression is concentrated in the eyes.

The Poison of the Borgias (*Le Poison des Borgia*, fig. 253) by Albert Miserey (1862–1938) also sets out to frighten the viewer, employing considerable resources to do so. The plaster model in the Musée de Bernay measures more than 2 meters in height and conveys a paroxysm of pain; it makes Puget's *Milo of Croton* (1672–82) appear restrained by comparison. The work was awarded a third-class medal at the Salon of the Société des Artistes Français in 1894.

There is less extravagance but more expressiveness in the half-life-sized composition *The Slave* (*Le Serf*, 1900–8, fig. 146), which Henri Matisse (1869–1954) began in 1900. Matisse was actually critical of the "very great sculptor [Rodin] who has given us some wonderful pieces . . . but for [whom] a composition is simply a grouping of pieces . . . the result of which is a certain confusion of expression" (*La Grande Revue*, 1908, 731–45). Nevertheless, he was fascinated by the master, who in fact failed to recognize Matisse's worth. "He told me I had a 'fluent touch,' which is not true. He suggested I do some 'niggling' drawings and show him. I never went back" (Escholier 1956, 161–62). It did not stop him using Rodin's model, old Pignatelli, the farmer from the Abruzzi region of Italy who had posed for *St. John the Baptist*, *Eustache de Saint-Pierre* [one of the *Burghers of Calais*], and *Ugolino*. His name was now Bevilaqua. Surely Matisse and he must have swapped reminiscences during the many posing sessions? A photograph taken in Matisse's studio about 1904 shows the plaster model of *The Slave* with arms. Did they break off by accident or were they removed deliberately? It hardly matters, since the artist chose not to replace them but to show two stumps. Or were there complete arms on the plaster exhibited at the Galerie Druet in 1906? Certainly they were missing from the bronze that Matisse presented to the Salon d'Automne in 1908. Matisse also echoed the Rodin of *Man Walking* (*L'Homme qui marche*) in his modeling, with its use of hollows and bumps, and in the way he mutilated his work to intensify its expressiveness (see *Le Corps en morceaux*, exhibition catalog, 1990, chapter 13). The fact that *The Slave* has no arms is not so much a symbol of his unfree status, more a successful structural solution. The title is nevertheless extremely important, for it incites the viewer to dwell longer on the work in order to understand (or imagine) its message.

PRIMITIVISM

As art historians have shown us, styles have an infancy, a classical period, a period of brilliance, and a period of decline. Cycles are thus perpetually recurring. So it comes as no surprise that the avant-garde of the late nineteenth and early twentieth centuries, with its rich historical awareness, should have found a fresh source of energy in the so-called "primitive" arts. Artists who were driven by a need for a revival tapped a new power of expression here. Since "we see in things only what we know" (Auguste Villiers de l'Isle-Adam), the avant-garde saw primitive objects as works of art rather than as documents of ethnography.

Those admirers were also reacting against the kind of technical virtuosity that, while it could do anything, no longer knew what to say. But although such admiration was opposed to industrial progress, it nevertheless owed industrial progress a debt of gratitude for making possible the international exhibitions that brought non-Western civilizations to the attention of a wider audience.

Gauguin, who spent eight years of his childhood in Peru and whose mother and tutor both collected pre-Columbian pottery, never gave up hoping to travel overseas again ("to flee, far away, simply flee," as Mallarmé had dreamt in 1865). "You have to remember there are two characters in me, the Indian and the sensitive plant. The sensitive plant has gone, leaving the Indian to walk firmly in a straight line," the artist wrote to his wife in February 1888 (Gauguin 1946, 126), and to his friend Charles Morice he wrote in April 1903: "I'm a savage. And civilized people sense it: for the only thing in my works that is surprising or disconcerting is this 'savage-despite-myself.' That is what makes them unique" (Gauguin 1946, 319).

Having become "synonymous with a geographical Romanticism that has not yet lost its savor . . . a symbol of rejection of the stifling superfluities of the hot-house civilization of Europe in favor of a return to that more natural way of life of which Rousseau is the generally accepted advocate" (Goldwater 1966, 75), Gauguin fused his life and his art, but under the watchful eye of Paris. "You will always find true nourishment in the primitive arts, in the arts of mature civilization, I am sure of it" (Guérin 1927, 20). And if Gauguin chose only the flat, decorative aspects of the "primitive," the strongest influence nevertheless remained that of "mature" civilization: Ingres, Puvis de Chavannes, Manet, Degas, Cézanne (Rubin 1984, 179).

What is true as regards painting is less so as regards sculpture: "The origins of sculpture are lost in the mists of time; it is thus an art of the Caribbean . . . Indeed, we find all peoples very skillfully carving fetishes long before turning to painting, which is an art of deep thought, the very enjoyment of which calls for a special initiation" (Baudelaire, *Salon de 1846*). In the late nineteenth century, in the West, such "initiation" would seem to be of less use for Salon painting than for a Gauguin relief. An important nuance is that primitive art is nowadays defined as "art without writing," whereas Gauguin reserved a key role for the inscription on his "categorical imperatives" (Roquebert 1986).

Be Amorous, You Will Be Happy (*Soyez amoureuses, vous serez heureuses*, fig. 128) expresses great confusion. Writing from Le Pouldu in Brittany on September 1, 1889, Gauguin asked his friend Schuffenecker for "a panel of lime wood (size of a 30 canvas, about 15 centimeters thick). It's for a sculpture I intend to do here in between. I'd need it as soon as possible." Then he was announcing to Émile Bernard: "I've also done a large 30 panel in sculpture to be executed later in wood, *when I have the money* to buy the wood . . . It's also the best and strangest thing I've done in sculpture. Gauguin (as a monster) holding the hand of a woman who is resisting, saying to her: Be amorous, you will be happy. The fox is an Indian symbol for depravity, then small figures in the interstices. The wood will be painted." In October, he told Schuffenecker: "Next month I'll be sending off to Paris [a wooden sculpture] that I'm quite pleased with. Anyway, you'll see it. The countess has promised me to get Minister Rouvier to buy it. Were that to happen, it would be viewed advantageously" (Rouvier had married Noémie Cadiot, alias Claude Vignon, who also sculpted, if rather differently).

Sure enough, in November 1889 Gauguin informed Schuffenecker: "I've just dispatched my carved wooden panel to Paris; it'll be with Goupil in a fortnight or so. Let's hope it'll sell better than painting." A further letter to Schuffenecker on November 16 said: "Go and see the sculpture at van Gogh's; it'll be arriving any day now" (Theo van Gogh, Vincent's brother, managed the Paris branch of the Goupil art gallery). And finally, to Émile Bernard: "I'm glad you've seen the sculpture, which you've understood; no one, apparently, understands it. Why understand?"

And yet the subject is a key element in the composition, though neither love nor happiness actually illustrates it. According to Christopher Gray, the panel reflects the conflict that Gauguin was undergoing. On the left is a mulatto woman, wide-eyed with fear, her left hand with its wedding ring appearing to prevent her right hand from surrendering to the seducer. Halfway up on the right is a woman crouching, an image of fear who also appears on the Death figure in the Gauguin painting *Life and Death* (*La Vie et la mort*, 1889, Mahmoud Khalil Museum, Cairo), itself inspired by the Peruvian mummy in the Musée de l'Homme in Paris. The flowering tree between the two women symbolizes fertility. Apart from the fox, who alone looks out at the viewer, the other living figures are wrapped up in their own emotions, like the damned on Rodin's *Gates of Hell.* Two branches descending obliquely from the title form borders separating the upper corners. Hands pass behind both. In the right-hand corner, Gauguin is represented "as a monster," thumb in mouth as in the *Tobacco Jar* in the Musée d'Orsay. Above this "rejected, desperate child," to use Gray's words, does the face of the sleeping savage represent Gauguin's dormant second self?

A year later, in September 1890, the artist wrote to Émile Bernard from Le Pouldu: "I've managed to produce another carved panel, the matching piece to the first, *'Be mysterious,'* which I'm happy with, in fact I don't think I've *ever* done anything like it" (Gauguin 1946, 203). It is almost the same size (slightly smaller). Is it perhaps from the same lime panel, which Gauguin sawed in half and this time used sideways? A diagonal creates a "syncopated" space (Roquebert 1986, 398). Plants fill the lower right-hand section, figures the upper left. In the top right-hand corner, a luminous face framed by its hair and the foliage, which form what is almost a halo around it, presents its left profile and one eye looking outward. This has been seen as the sun or moon with masculine features. On the left, a figure shrouded in hair appears almost to emerge from the wood. For Françoise Cachin, this is "a sickly, malevolent Breton girl whose gesture resembles a warning as much as a prayer" (Cachin 1988–89, 199) and who is not unrelated to a Breton calvary figure. A nude back links the two faces. "If there are some wonderful backs in the history of world sculpture, they are usually the versos of works sculpted in the round and not the principal feature of the composition" (Roquebert 1986, 398). This back, one of the finest in all nineteenth-century art, anticipates Gauguin's Tahitian women. This, remember, was before Gauguin's first trip to Tahiti, of which "the myth was indeed born here in old Europe" (Cachin 1988–89, 159). Gauguin, it seems, went halfway round the world in search of what he already had inside him.

The plant forms (almost plain at the bottom, becoming more complex higher up) have been compared to those in a Japanese woodcut reproduced in *Le Japon artistique,* which Bing published in April 1889.

If *Be Amorous* is bitter and ironic, *Be Mysterious* (*Soyez mystérieuses*), as Albert Aurier pointed out, gives expression to Gauguin's belief in the final triumph of the spirit (Aurier 1891, 155–65). Beyond the symbols, which are open to a wide range of interpretations, the technique of Gauguin's reliefs breaks down space to a greater extent than any of his paintings. "Don't paint from the life, art is an abstraction," said the man who paved the way for Picasso, as is glaringly obvious from the fifth panel of *The House of Enjoyment* (*La Maison du jouir,* 1902), which the Musée d'Orsay acquired in 1990 to complete the entrance of Gauguin's last house in the Marquesas.

An equally stark but also symbolic work is *Isis* by the "Nabi sculptor" Georges Lacombe (1868–1916), which was shown at the Salon des Indépendants in 1895.

"Nature is a temple, in which living pillars / Sometimes utter a babel of words; / Man traverses it through forests of symbols, / That watch him with knowing eyes." The beginning of Baudelaire's poem "Correspondances" (*Les Fleurs du Mal*) seems to describe this avenue of trees, the roots of which come out of the ground to form the hair of a female figure whose breasts are the source of a red river. Isis worship forms part of the occult tradition reinstated by the Rosicrucians, who held their first exhibition at Durand-Ruel's gallery in Paris in 1892. This piece would be at the opposite end of the scale from Primitivism if the way the wood is carved, respecting the original shape of the log, and the roughness of the chiseling did not prevail over the symbolism of the five-petaled flowers and the skull pressed into the ground by the huge right foot of the mother-woman, who has her closed eyes.

These few examples reveal the ambiguity of the beginnings of Primitivism (some have even talked of a "Romantic Primitivism"), before it was taken up by the Fauves and by the artists of Die Brücke and Der Blaue Reiter in the twentieth century. However, at the Salon of Les XX in Brussels in 1891, when Gauguin exhibited his two reliefs, *Be Amorous* and *Be Mysterious,* he was dubbed a "minus habens" and a "Congolese sculptor." In other words, contemporaries were well aware of the radical break being made by the man Varnedoe called "the Primitive of modern primitivism" (Rubin 1984, 179). The shock had still not been absorbed in 1943. When Lucien Vollard donated seven Gauguins in that year, they were placed on the books of the Musée de France d'Outre-mer. Not until 1971 were they presented to the Jeu de Paume, before finally, in 1986, being allocated to the Musée d'Orsay.

THE RETURN TO STYLE

It was before 1890 that the work of Adolf von Hildebrand (1847–1921) marked a return to Classicism in Germany. France did not follow suit until after 1900, at a time when, in Germany, the first generation influenced by Hildebrand—notably Louis Tuaillon (1862–1919) and Franz von Stück (1863–1928)—was giving way to such artists as Georg Kolbe (1877–1947), Ernst Barlach (1870–1938), and Wilhelm Lehmbruck (1881–1919), in whom the search for expression was more important than classical form. Hildebrand's *Standing Youth* (*Stehender Mann*, 1877–84, marble, Nationalgalerie, Berlin) and *Bowls Player* (*Kugelspieler*, fig. 535) do indeed, like *Standing Bather* (*Baigneuse*, fig. 536) and *Mediterranean* (*Méditerranée*, fig. 154) by the Frenchman Aristide Maillol (1861–1944), reveal a new desire for greater formal simplicity. "The perfect work of art," wrote Gide (incidentally providing a perfect definition of this reaction), "will be the one . . . in which the most contrasting and apparently contradictory qualities: vigor and gentleness, discipline and grace, logic and lack of restraint, precision and poetry—breathe so easily as to appear natural and not at all surprising. Which means that the first thing the artist must give up is any desire to astonish contemporaries" (Gide 1924, 38).

This return to style, as it has been called, must not be confused with a revival of Neoclassicism, even if Hildebrand did get there by way of a highly personal study of antique sculpture during an extended stay in Florence, where he settled in 1873 and where he spent over twenty years. The French sculptors Maillol, Bourdelle, Pompon, and Joseph Bernard (1866–1931) put up a particularly lively defense against Neoclassicism, rejecting the traditional teaching dispensed by the École des Beaux-Arts. "The story of anyone arriving in Paris to pursue an artistic career is not a funny one, Maillol used to say. The poor fellow falls into the School as one might fall down a well. He'll not find the truth there—that's just it: the truth is outside!" (Cladel 1937, 34). Nevertheless, the reference to classical antiquity is very present in their works, if only through the titles: "Maillol loved museums," Léon Werth recalled. "We do not know which museum. We cannot name Maillol's masters, his advisers, his familiars . . . Simply that his spirit lingered near them" (Werth 1913, 66, 67). In addition to a certain detachment from the live model, what characterized these artists was indeed a desire to rediscover the qualities of clarity and balance (of which antiquity remained the supreme model) in order to reinvest sculpture with sincerity, strength, and poetry.

For Hildebrand, as for Maillol, beauty resided in the harmony of movements made without passion, by a body in full control of itself. This conception led to the suppression of the subject, as Gide understood so well in the case of *Mediterranean*: "She is beautiful; she means nothing; this is a silent work. I believe one would have to go back a long way to find so complete a disregard of any preoccupation other than the simple manifestation of beauty" (Gide 1905, 476). Consequently they were able to concentrate on a specific viewpoint and simplify their poses: there was no twisting, no limbs running in parallel, which would impair the clarity of the composition, but rather quite distinct elements. The same desire for simplification is evident in the treatment of surfaces, of which nothing spoils the regularity: "I have got rid of the hollows that cast shadows," Brancusi was to say (Geist 1968, 157).

Hildebrand gave an account of his theories in *Das Problem der Form*. Published in 1893, the book was immediately influential, at least in Germany. Meanwhile, Hildebrand himself had been exhibiting regularly in Paris for several years. The 1900 Exposition Universelle in that city included Tuaillon's *Amazon* (*Amazone*, fig. 142) and a number of small bronzes by Stück: *Amazon* (*Amazone*), *Wounded Centaur* (*Verwundeter Kentaur*), and *Athlete* (*Kugelstemmender Athlet*). They could be seen as a link between the group of German sculptors and the group of Frenchmen, although it was more a personal development helped by outside circumstances that led Maillol, Bourdelle, Bernard, and even Bernhardt Hoetger, having passed the age of forty, to regard sculpture with a fresh eye. It was in fact the threat of blindness that forced Maillol to give up the painting and weaving to which he had devoted himself hitherto. Bourdelle and Bernard were likewise struck by serious illness, which prevented them from working at their sculpture for a while. Maillol, who revealed himself as a sculptor on the occasion of an exhibition at Vollard's gallery in 1902, turned at the same time toward wood carving, which he abandoned before long, as well as toward modeling. In his *Women Bathing* (*Baigneuses*, about 1900), the original material can be sensed even through the bronze cast. Wood is particularly recognizable thanks to the way he used irregularities in the original block to create the rangy, slightly stiff silhouettes and emphatic gestures.

Bourdelle worked for Rodin from 1893, the two men being united by ties of mutual esteem. As we have seen, *Monument to the Defenders and Combatants of Tarn-et-Garonne 1870–71* in Montauban displays the expressive Romanticism characteristic of Bourdelle's youthful work. It is particularly evident in the studies which were executed in connection with the monument but were not used in the final version, such as *Screaming Faces* (*Figures hurlantes*, fig. 545). Already, however, one senses a desire for greater rigor and a certain formal simplification. These qualities can be seen, for example, in the figure of *France* and in the *Large Warrior* (*Grand Guerrier*), whose power rests on lines that, although contrasting, are few in number. However, it was not until the great works of the early years of the new century (*Head of Apollo*, 1900–9, bronze, and *Heracles the Archer*, 1909, bronze, both in the Musée d'Orsay,

Paris) that this discipline took full hold of Bourdelle's work. *Pallas*, which dates from 1905, still belongs to a transitional period: the head, which is very obviously a contemporary portrait, is in stark contrast to the torso whose lines are so straight they suggest a column.

A similar development marked the work of Hoetger, who trained in Düsseldorf but lived in Paris from 1900 to 1907. After 1903 his style became less agitated and more geometrical, moving in the direction of monumentality. Rodin admired him: "[He] has found the path I was looking for; if I was not an old man I should take it myself, that path toward the monumental, which is the only proper one" (Hoetger 1977). As in the work of Joseph Bernard, this deliberately smooth, simplified form concealed an attraction for Symbolism. This is also evident in the titles given to the heads that both artists executed in the tradition (one is almost tempted to say) of the "expressive heads" that constituted one of the oldest competitions run by the École des Beaux-Arts. Hoetger's *Flight of Thought* (*Gedankenflug*) differs from Bernard's *Effort Toward Nature* chiefly in the manner of its creation: the former is modeled, while the latter is the product of direct carving. The latter process, which Bernard reinstated, consisted in tackling a block of hard material (wood or stone) directly and drawing a form from it in response to the prompting of the material itself. It is in that operation, "in which the proper thing is to remove a minimal volume of matter in order to uncover a presence that is guessed at more than projected, like a secret of eternal beauty hidden in the compact obscurity of a block of stone [or piece of wood], that the creative adventure lies" (Fumet 1978, 103).

This renewal of sculpture was to be of particular importance in terms of the relations between sculpture and architecture, relations that had previously been dominated by the desire to work on an ever larger and more spectacular scale. Hildebrand, reaffirming the close tie that should unite the two, redefined the bas-relief, which is the most obvious manifestation of that tie. Contained within two planes, that of the background and that of the surface, to which the figures adhere as much as possible, composition must be simple and clear in order to be easily intelligible (*Archery Lesson, Archers and Amazons*, triptych, 1887–88, plaster, Wallraf-Richartz Museum, Cologne). In the early years of the twentieth century, with the total perfection of Maillol's *Desire* (*Désir*, 1907, lead, Musée d'Orsay, Paris), with Bernard's *Dance* (*Danse*, 1912–13, marble, Musée d'Orsay, Paris), and above all Bourdelle's reliefs on the Théâtre des Champs-Élysées in Paris (1913), new requirements emerged. It was important to fill all the available space and to emphasize the opacity and density of the wall the sculptures decorated. Consequently, the wall simply appeared, "in specific places and in an orderly fashion, to be alive with human figures while retaining its surface and quality of light as a wall" (Bourdelle; see *1913, Le Théâtre des Champs-Élysées*, 1987).

113 Jules Cavelier
Penelope
1849 Salon
Marble, height 127 cm
Château, Dampierre

114 Auguste Préault
Ophelia
1876 Salon
Bronze, 75 x 200 cm
Musée d'Orsay, Paris

115 Auguste Clésinger
Woman Bitten by a Snake
1847
Marble, 56 x 180 cm
Musée d'Orsay, Paris

116 Auguste Ottin
Polyphemus
1852–63
Bronze, height 280 cm
Acis and Galatea
1859
Marble, height 115 cm
Medici Fountain, Luxembourg Gardens, Paris

117 Louis-Léon Cugnot
Petrarch
1865
Marble
Hôtel de la Païva, Paris

118 Joseph Fabisch
Beatrice
1855 Exposition Universelle
Marble, height 183 cm
Musée des Beaux-Arts, Lyon

119 Gabriel-Jules Thomas
Virgil
1861
Marble, height 185 cm
Musée d'Orsay, Paris

120 Emmanuel Fremiet
Pan with Bear Cubs
1867 Salon
Marble, 82 x 182 cm
Musée d'Orsay, Paris

121 Paul Dubois
Florentine Singer
1865
Silver-plated bronze, height 155 cm
Musée d'Orsay, Paris

122 Gabriel-Jules Thomas
Drama and *Music*
1873
Polychrome marble and bronze, height 260 cm
Stalls entrance, Opéra, Paris

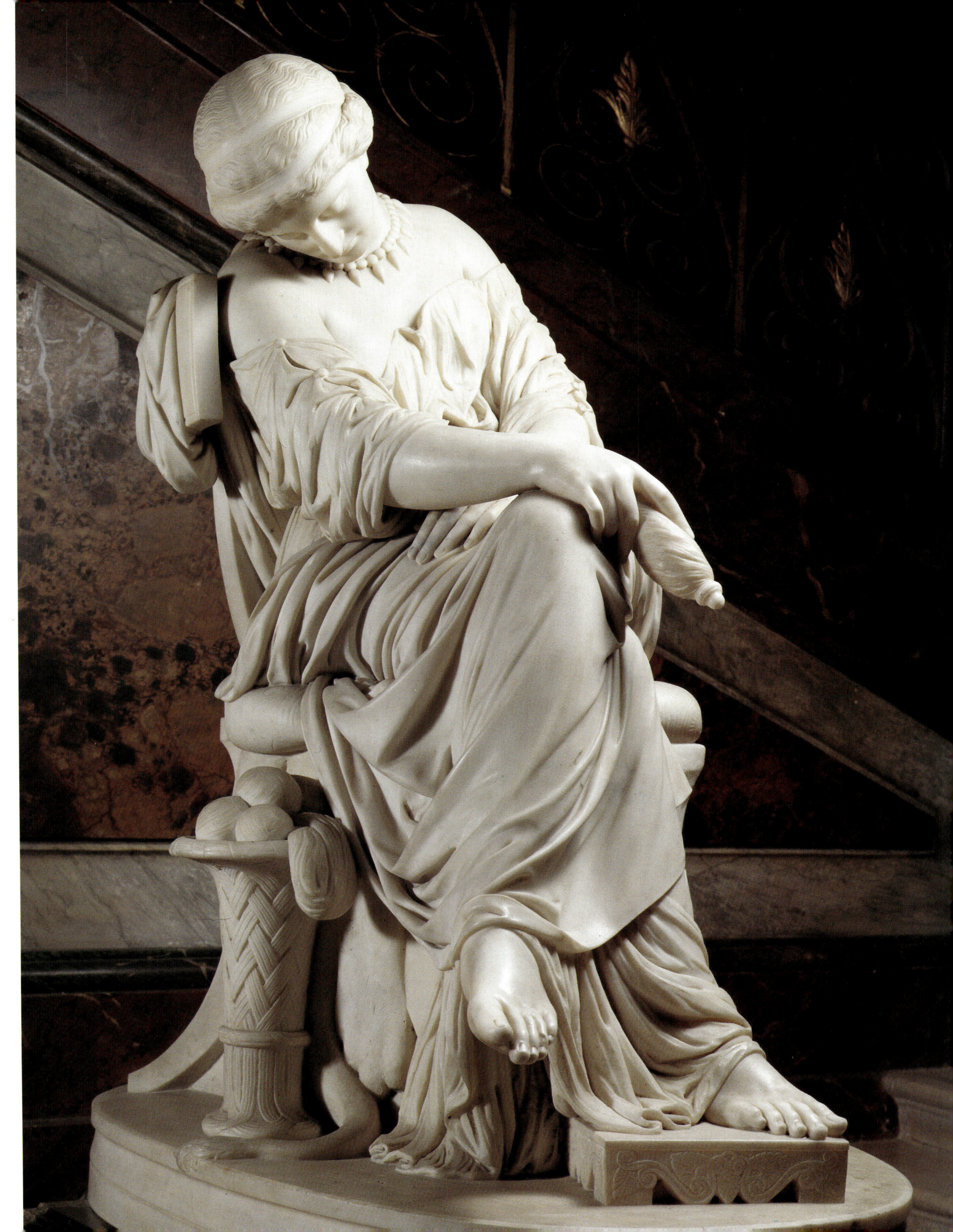

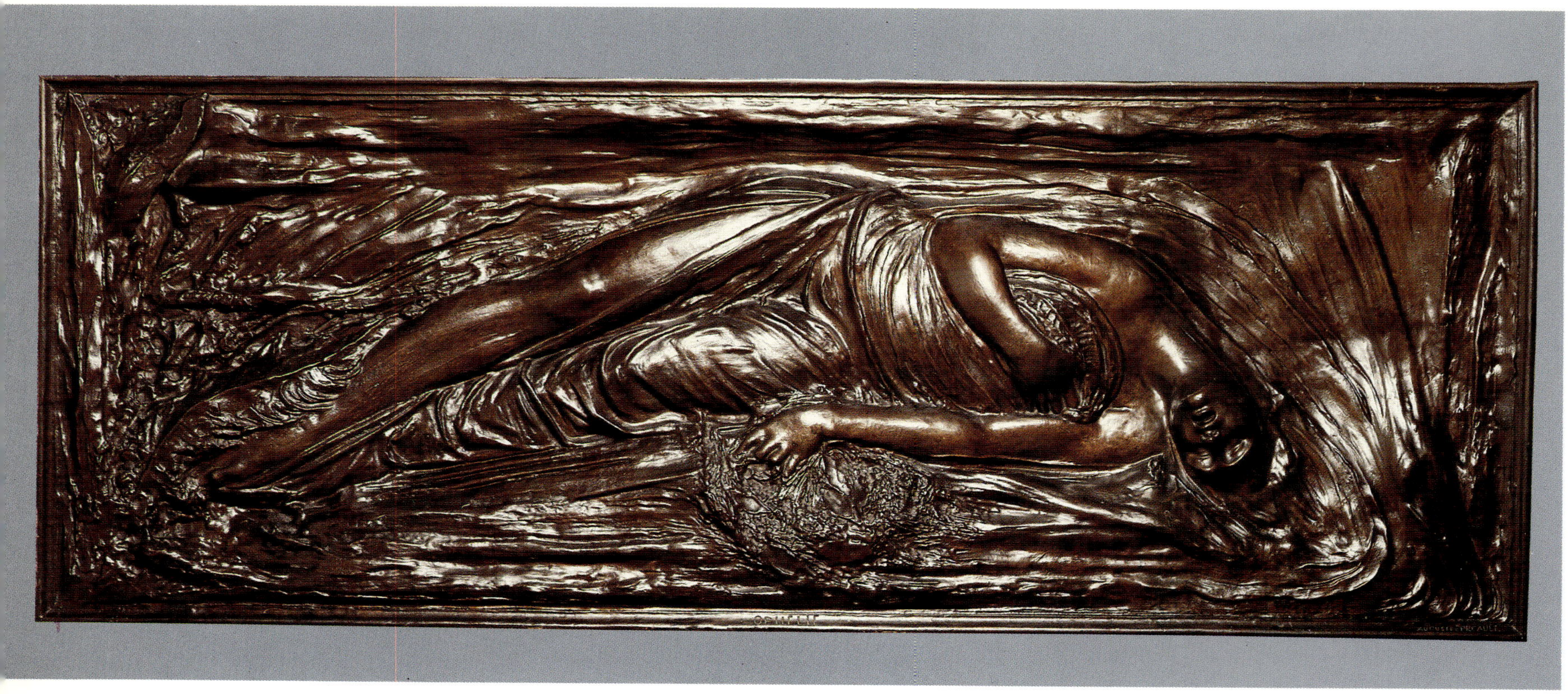

114

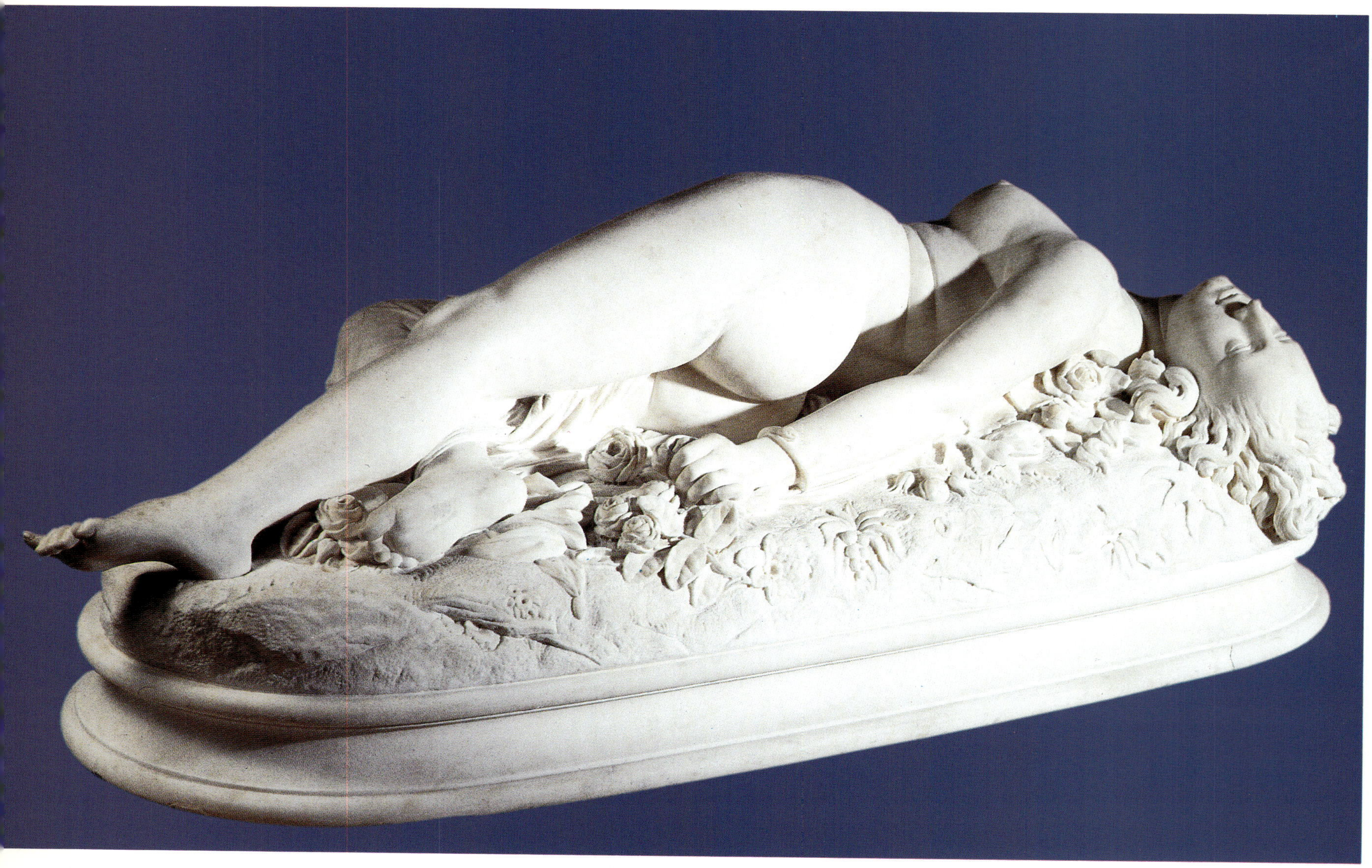

115

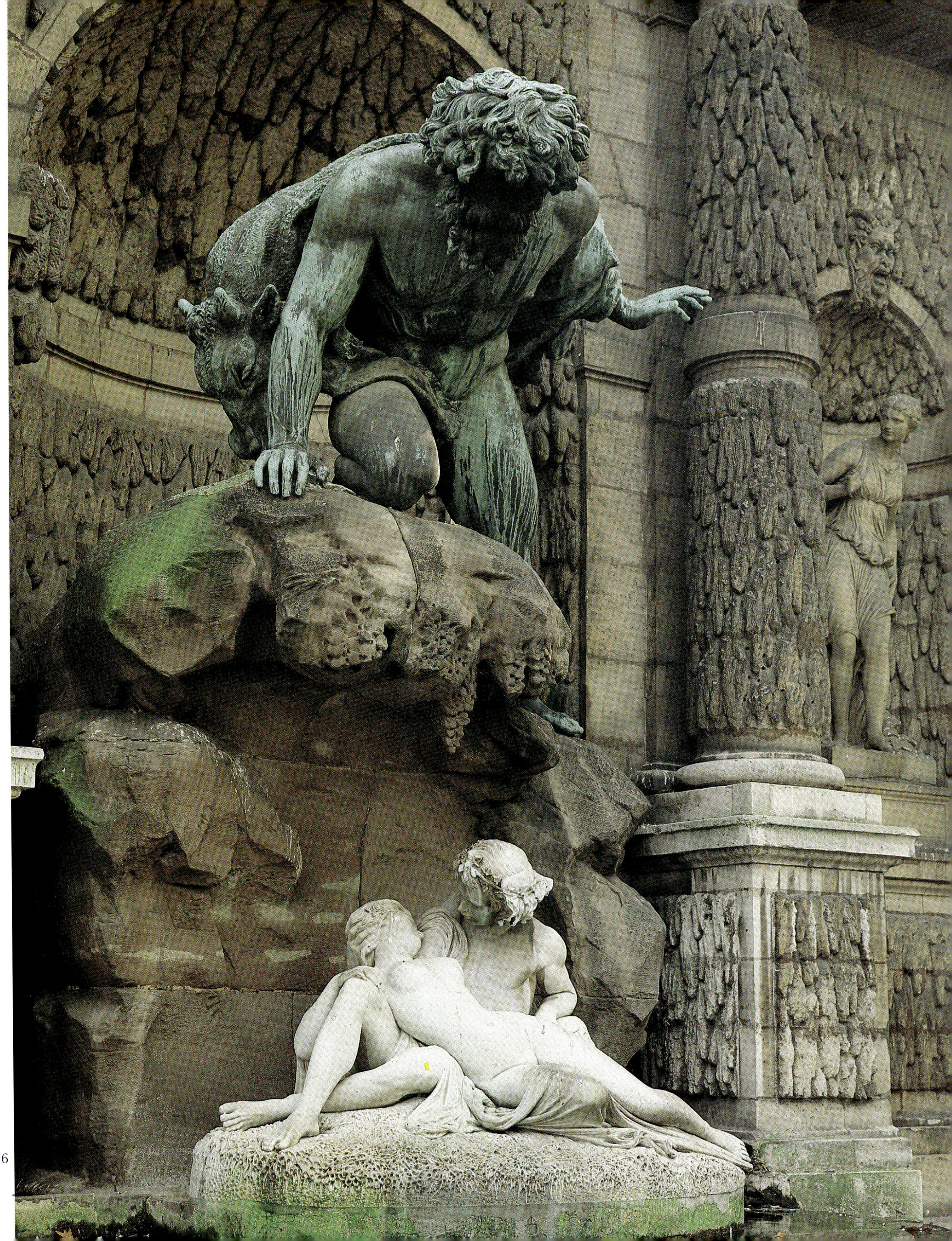

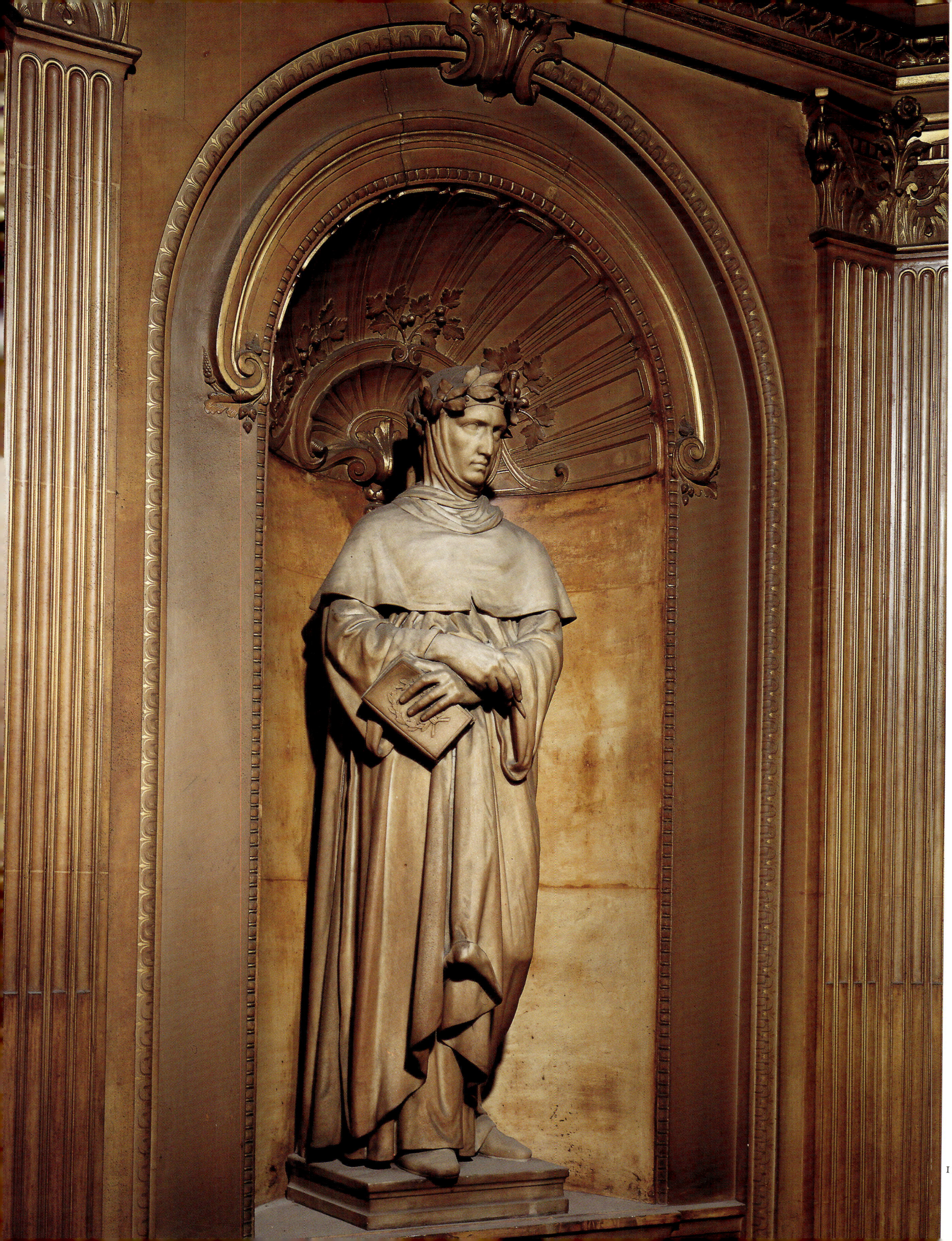

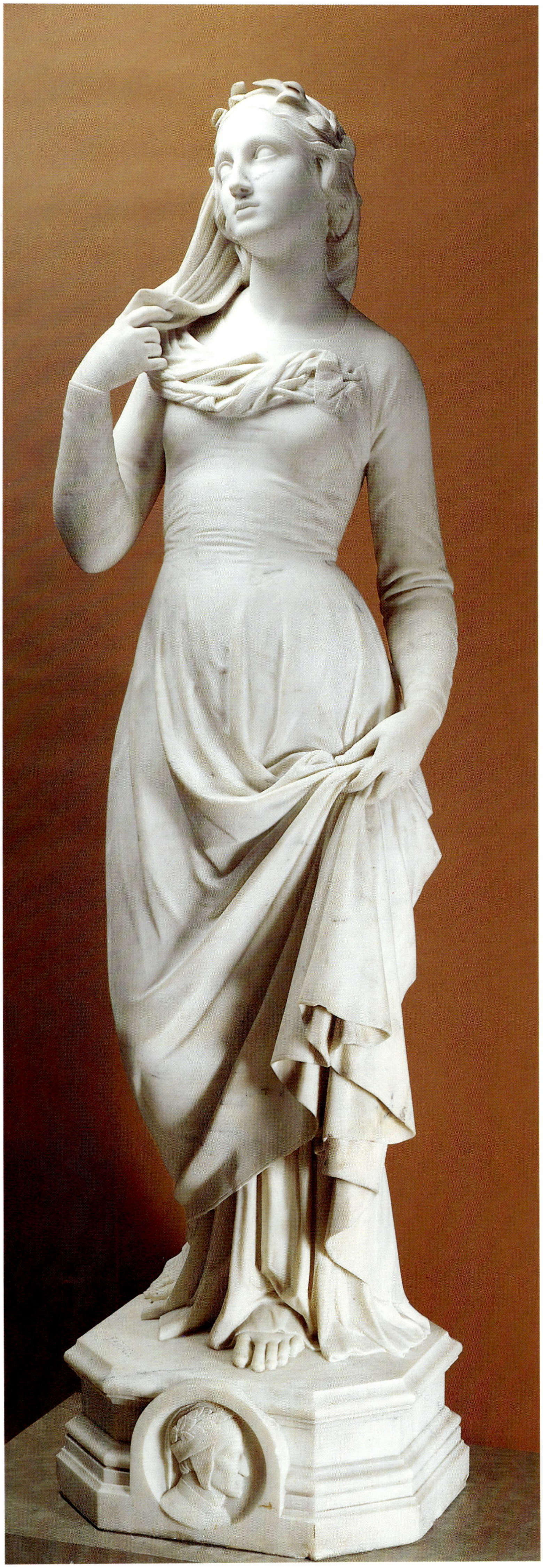

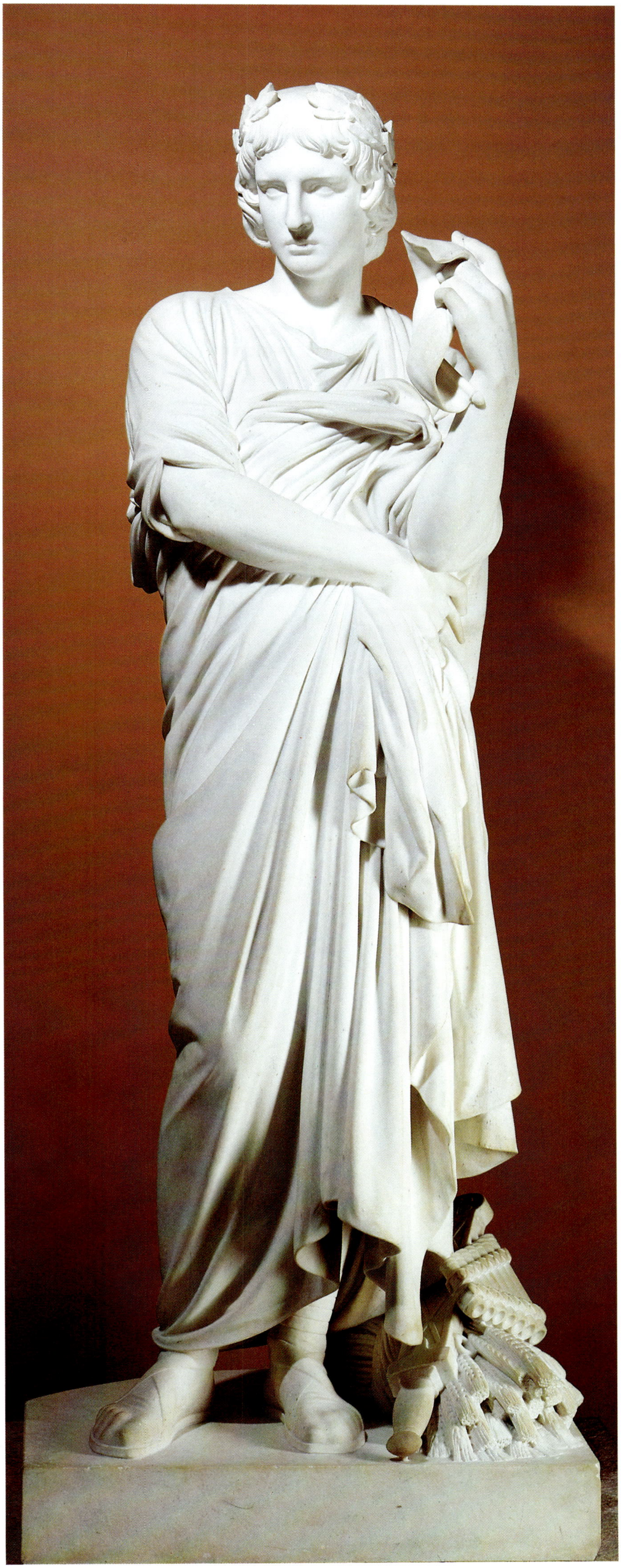

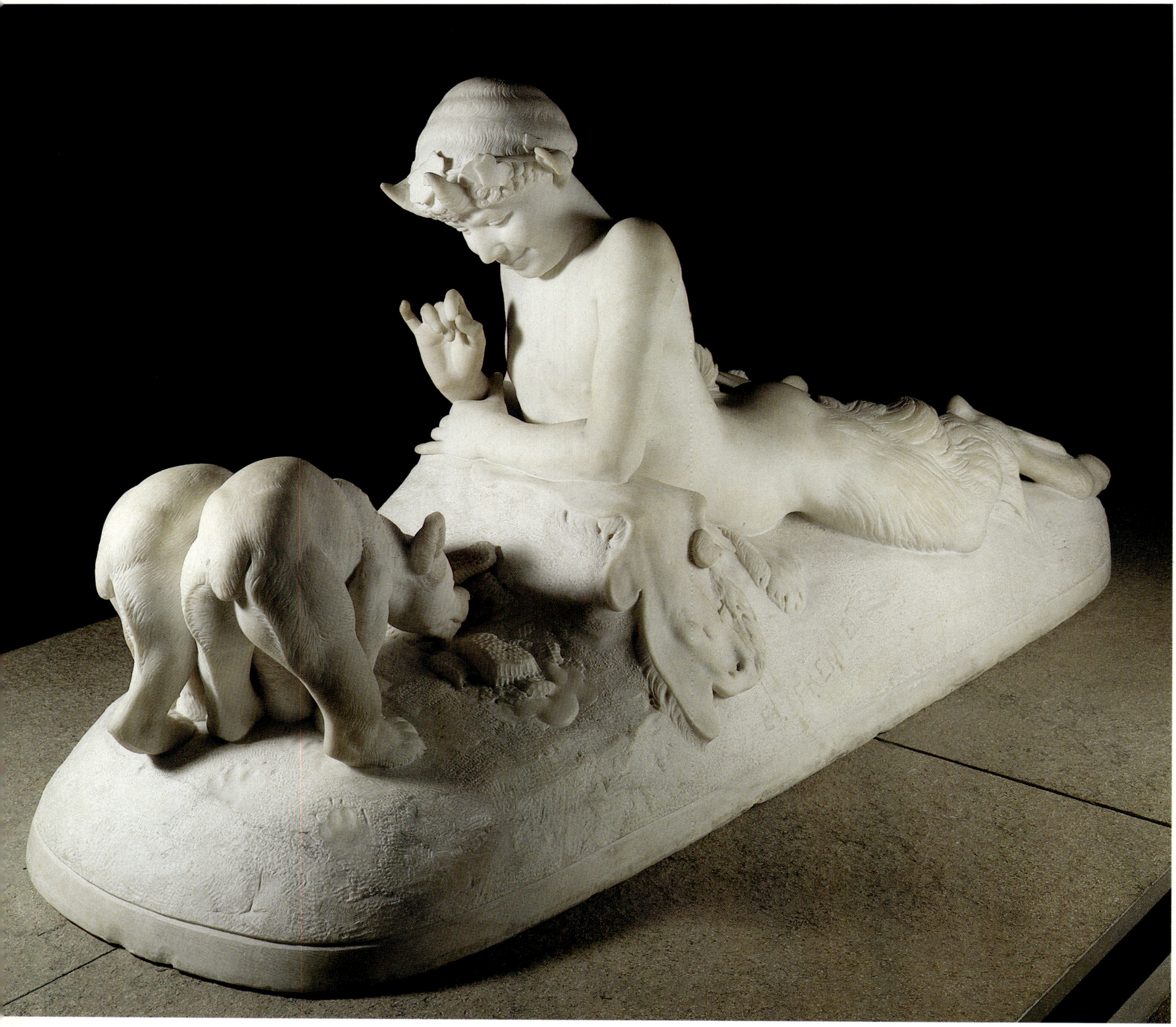

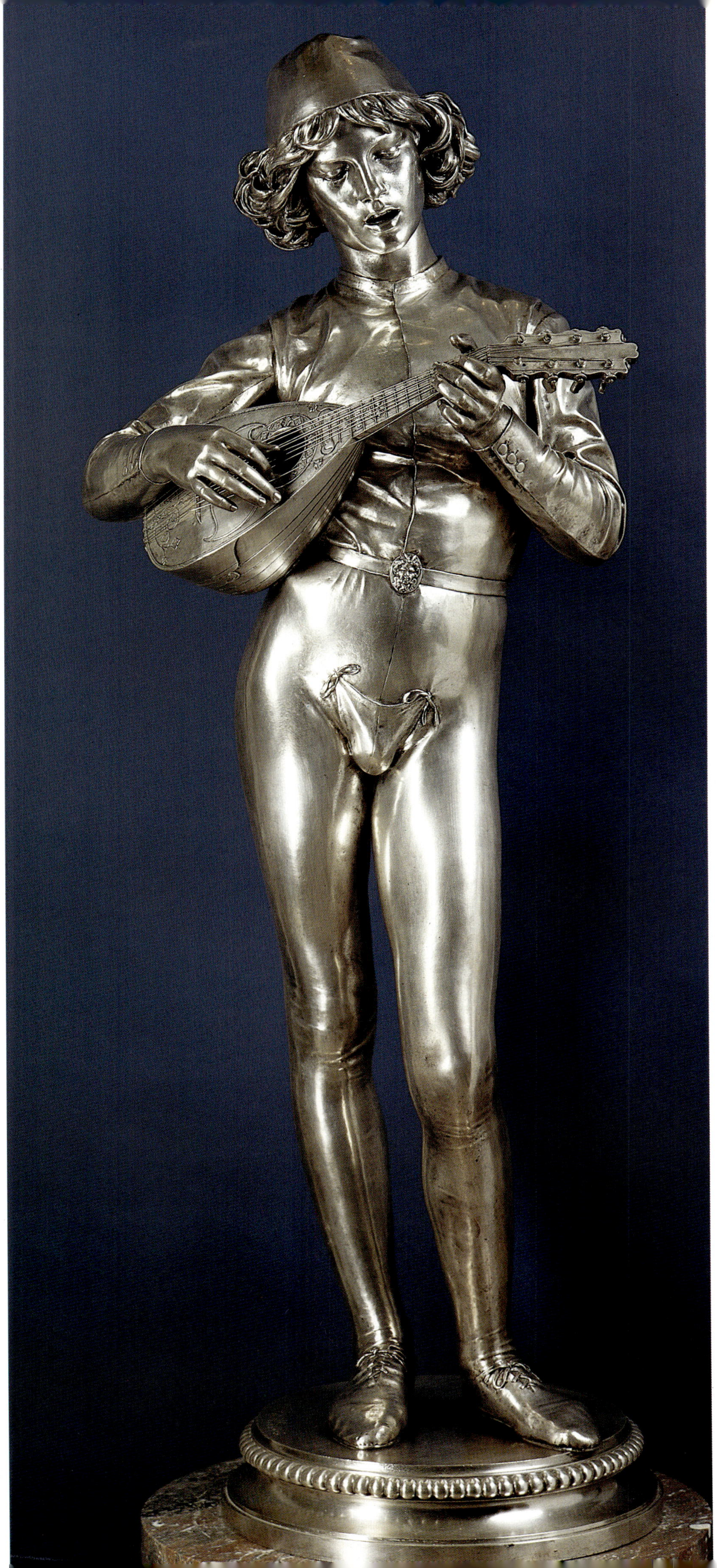

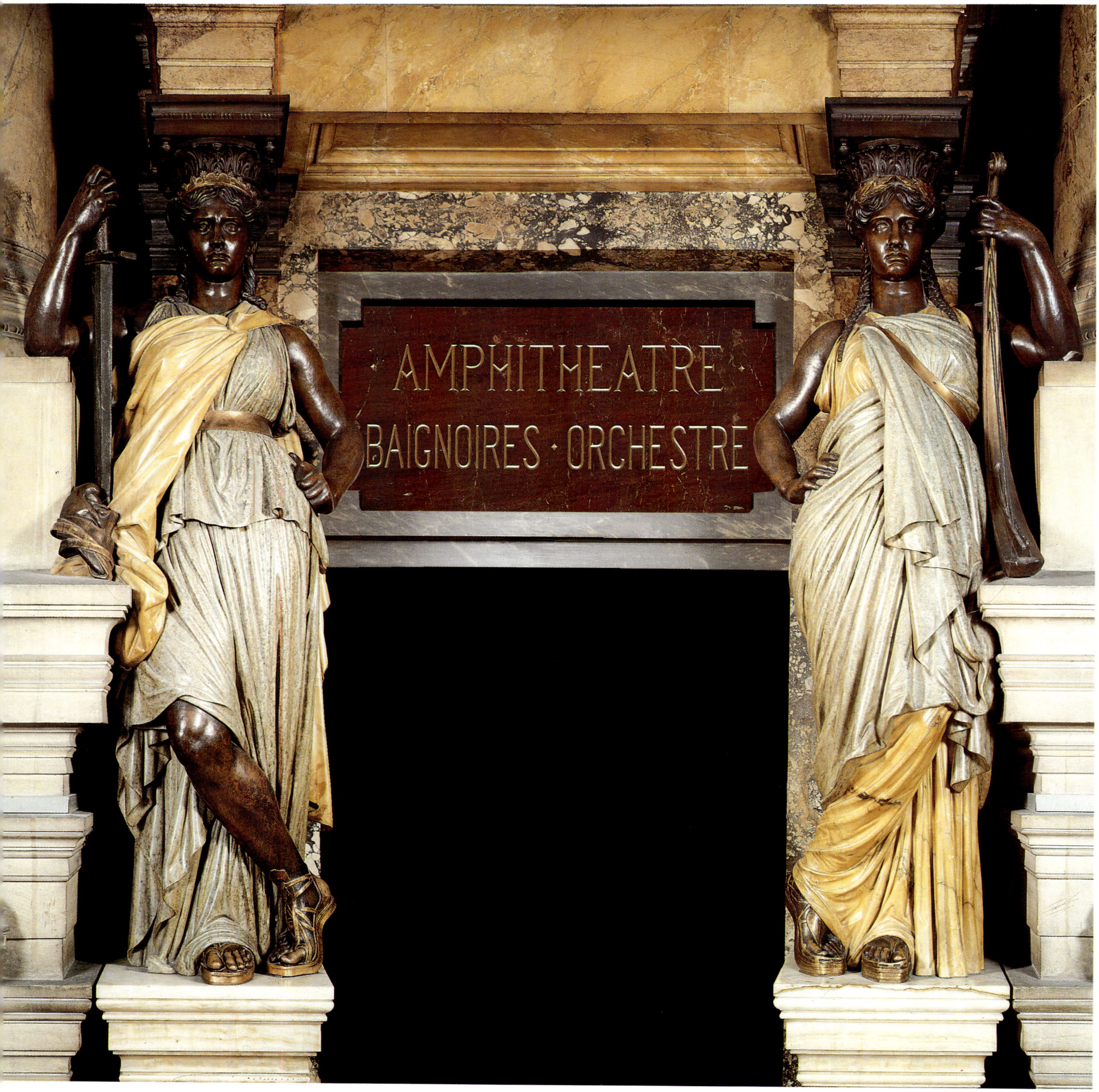

→ 123

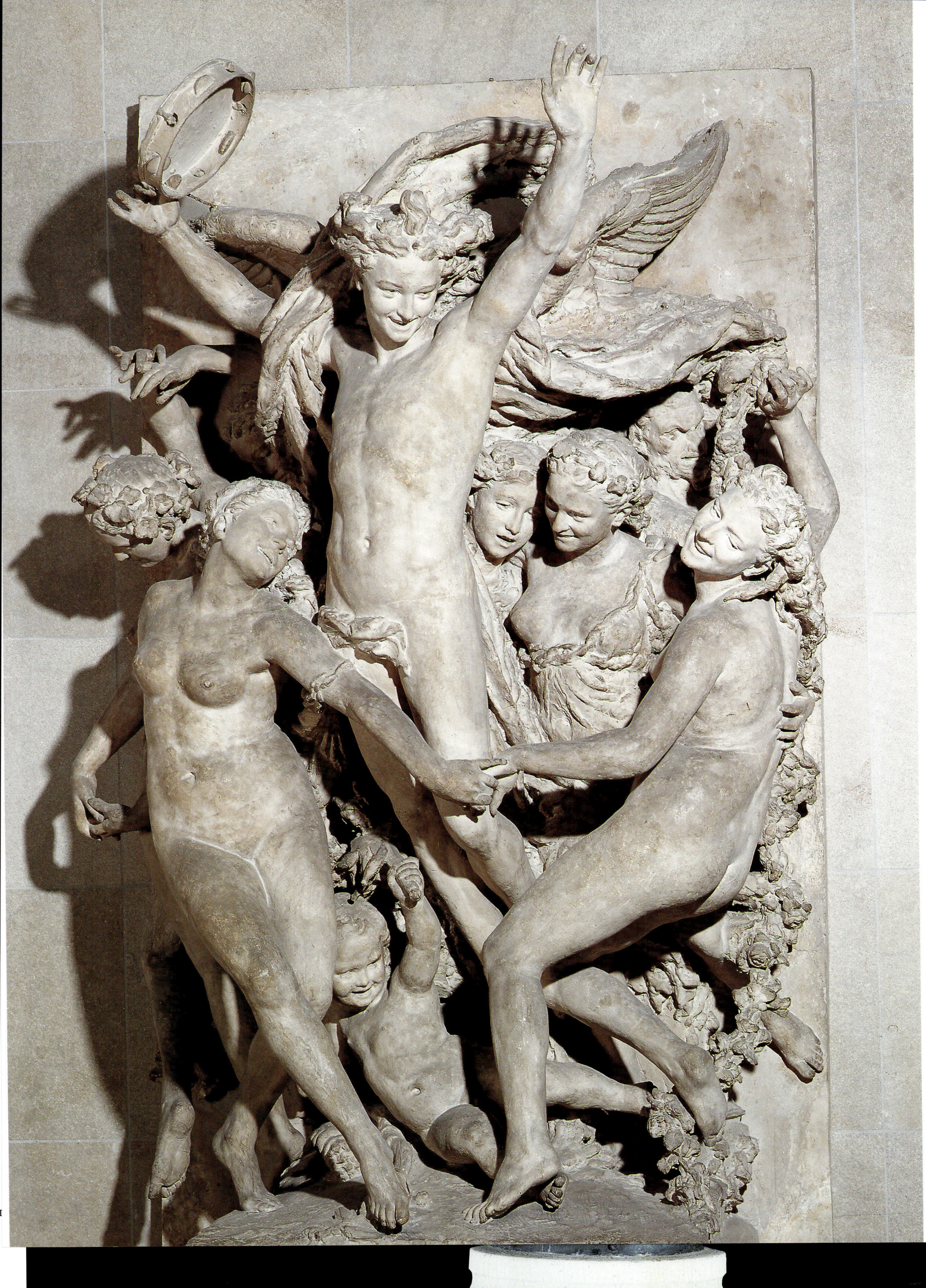

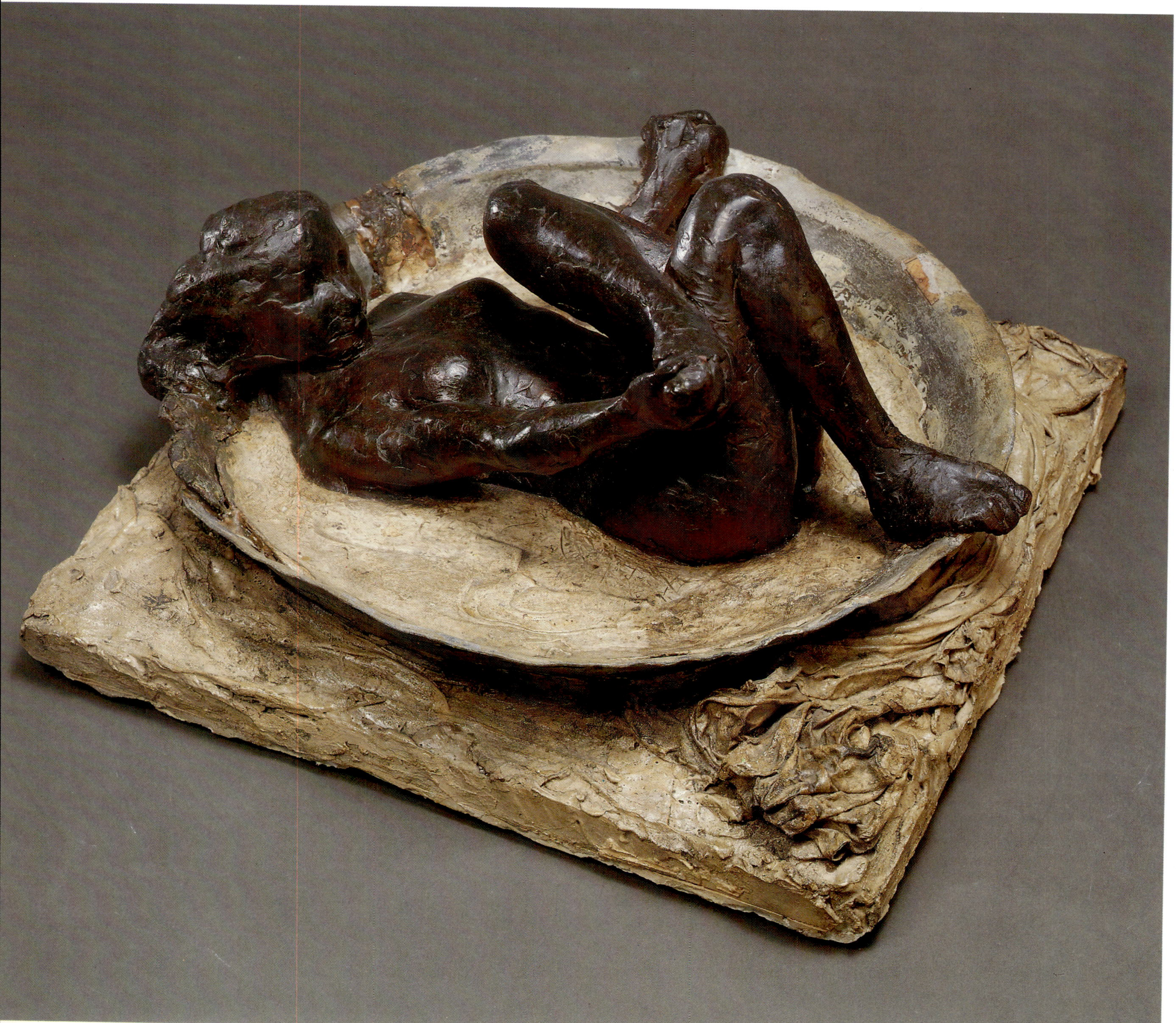

127

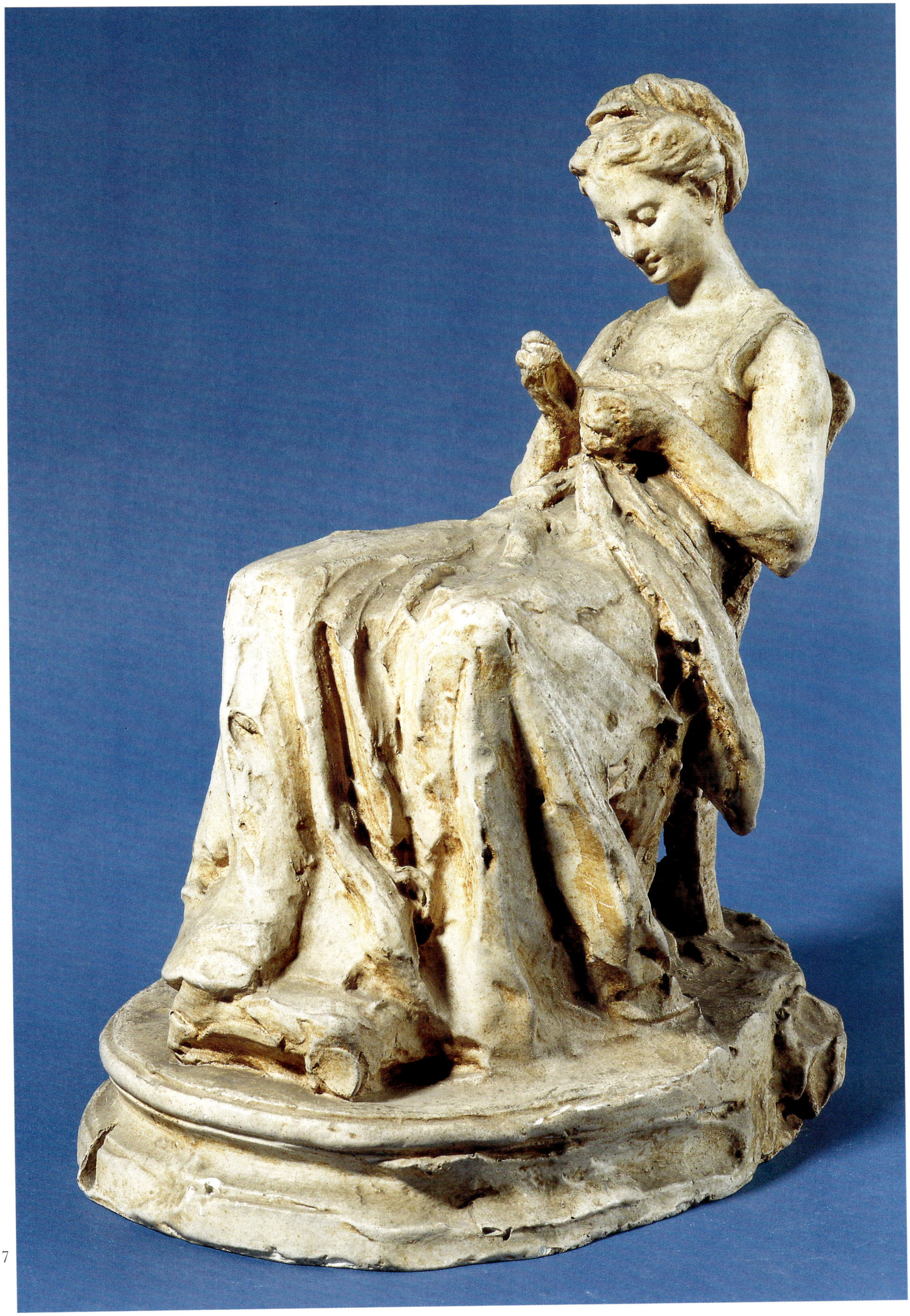

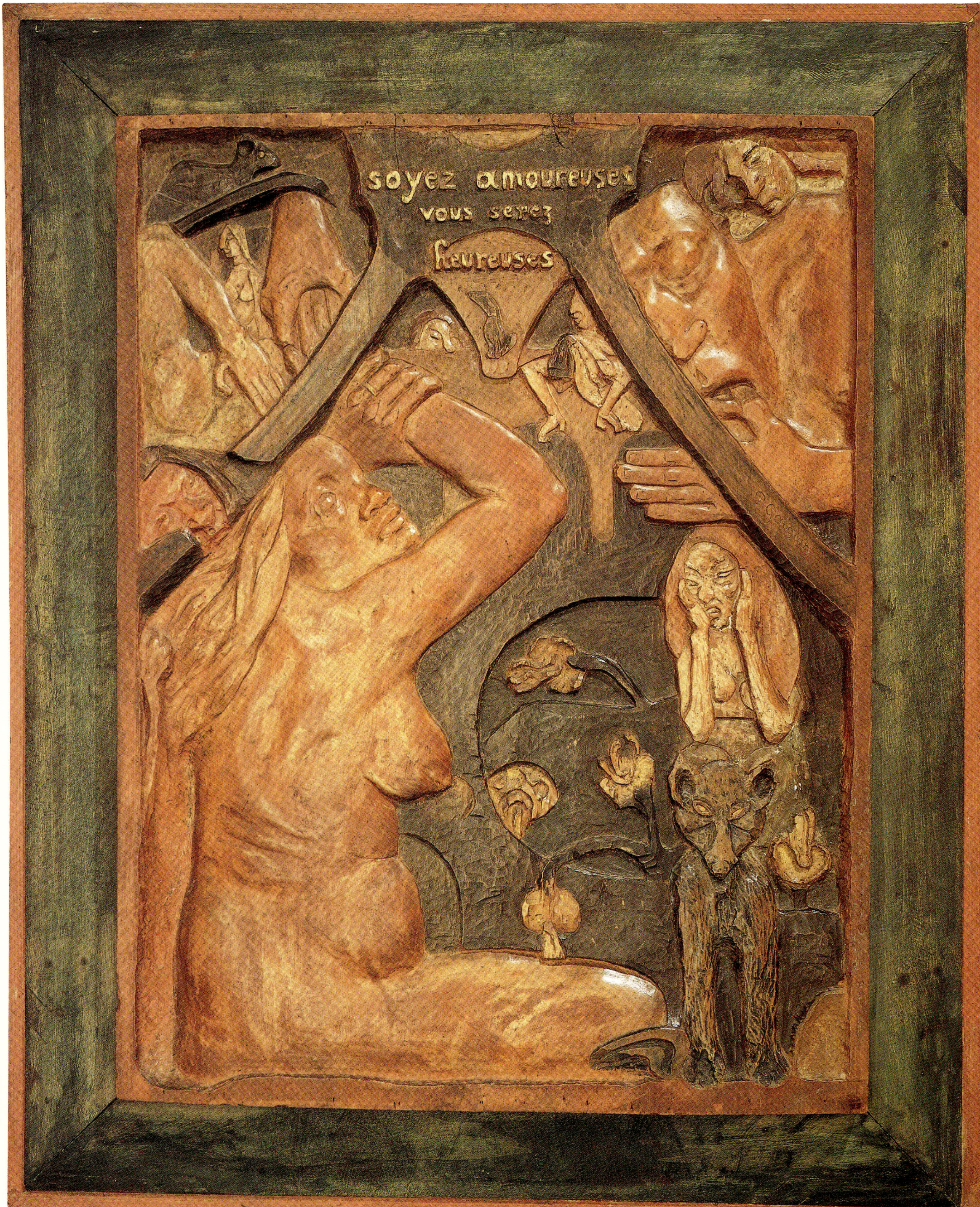
soyez amoureuses
vous serez
heureuses

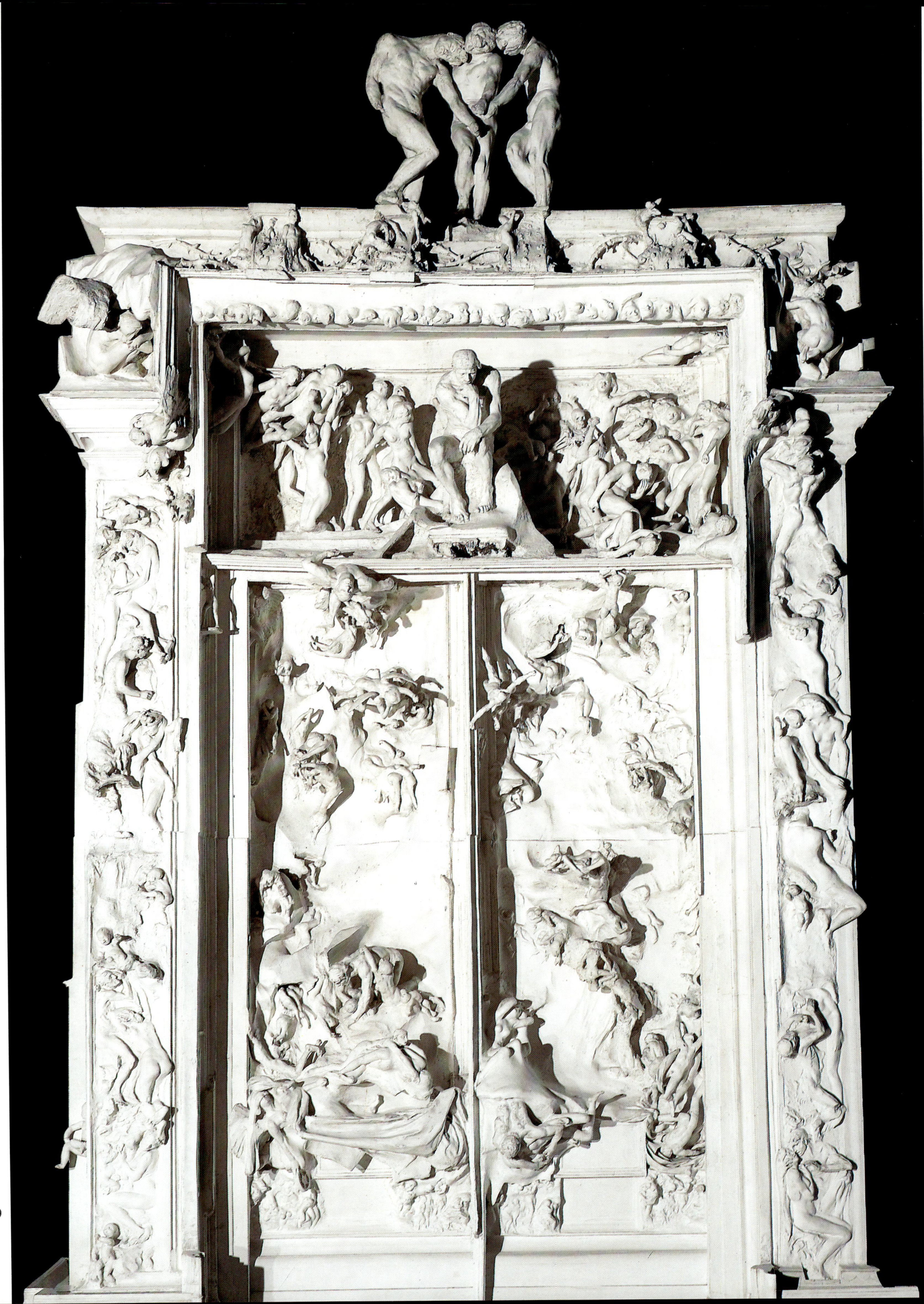

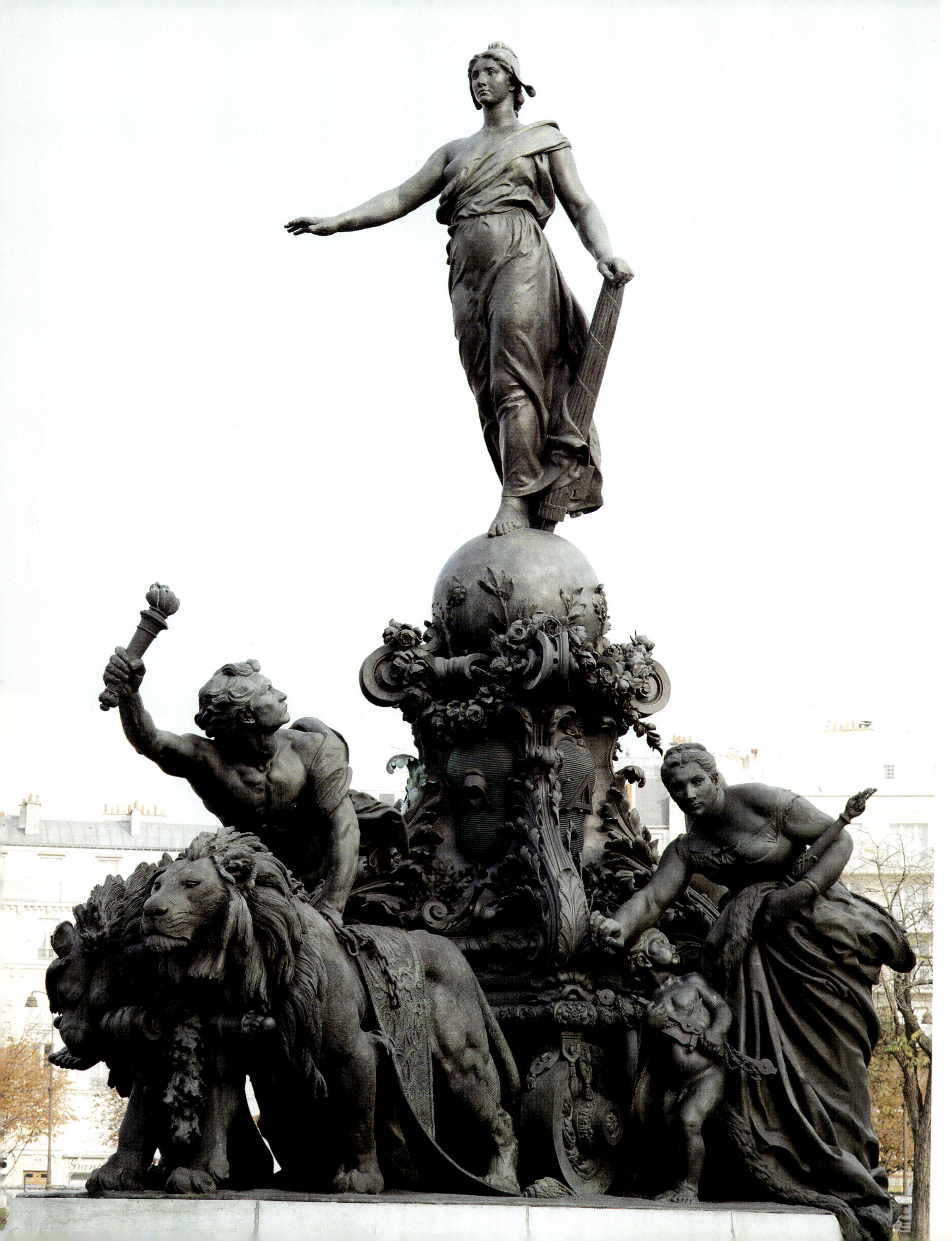

123 Jean-Baptiste Carpeaux
Dance
1868
Original plaster, height 232 cm
Musée d'Orsay, Paris

124 Jean-Baptiste Carpeaux
Sketch for the Marshal Moncey Monument
1864
Original plaster, height 167 cm
Petit Palais, Paris

125 Antonin Mercié
Gloria victis
1872–75
Bronze, height 311 cm
Petit Palais, Paris

126 Edgar Degas
The Bath
1888–89
Plaster, wax, fabric, and metal, 44 x 45 cm
National Gallery of Art (Mellon Collection), Washington, D.C.

127 Jules Dalou
Embroideress
1870
Plaster, 28 x 16 cm
Petit Palais, Paris

128 Paul Gauguin
Be Amorous, You Will Be Happy
1889
Wood, height 97 cm
Museum of Fine Arts, Boston

129 Auguste Rodin
The Gates of Hell
1880–1917
Original plaster, height 520 cm
Musée d'Orsay (indefinite loan from the Musée Rodin), Paris

130 Jules Dalou
Triumph of the Republic
1879–99
Bronze, height 12 m
Place de la Nation, Paris

131 Auguste Rodin
The Burghers of Calais
1884–95
Bronze, 231 x 245 x 200 cm
Place de l'Hôtel-de-Ville, Calais

132 Henri Chapu
Alexandre Dumas Père
1876 Salon
Marble, height 103 cm
Comédie-Française, Paris

133 Jean-Baptiste Carpeaux
Alexandre Dumas Fils
1873 Salon
Marble, height approx. 81 cm
Comédie-Française, Paris

134 Auguste Rodin
Bellona
1879 (competition for bust of The Republic)
Bronze, height 102 cm
Musée d'Orsay, Paris

135 Albert Bartholomé
Tadamasa Hayashi
1892
Bronze, height 25.5 cm
Musée d'Orsay, Paris

136 Pierre-Auguste Renoir
Madame Renoir
1916
Polychrome mortar, height 82.4 cm
Musée d'Orsay, Paris

137 Auguste Rodin
Louise Lynch de Morla Vicuña
1884
Marble, height 56.9 cm
Musée d'Orsay, Paris

138 Paul-François Berthoud
The Actress
1902
Stained plaster, 54 x 75 cm
Musée Bargoin, Clermont-Ferrand

139 Jules Dillens
T'Serclaes Memorial
1898
Bronze
Place de l'Hôtel-de-Ville, Brussels

140 Alfred Gilbert
Tomb of the Eldest Son of the Prince of Wales, the Duke of Clarence (detail)
1892–1928
Bronze and ivory, length approx. 4 m
Albert Memorial Chapel, Windsor Castle

141 Niels Hansen Jacobsen
The Troll Who Can Smell Christian Blood
1896
Bronze
Ny Carlsberg Glyptotek, Copenhagen

142 Louis Tuaillon
Amazon
1895
Bronze, height 268 cm
Nationalgalerie, Berlin

143 Victor Prouvé
Private Monument for "Poèmes barbares"
Bronze, height 118 cm
Musée de l'École de Nancy, Nancy

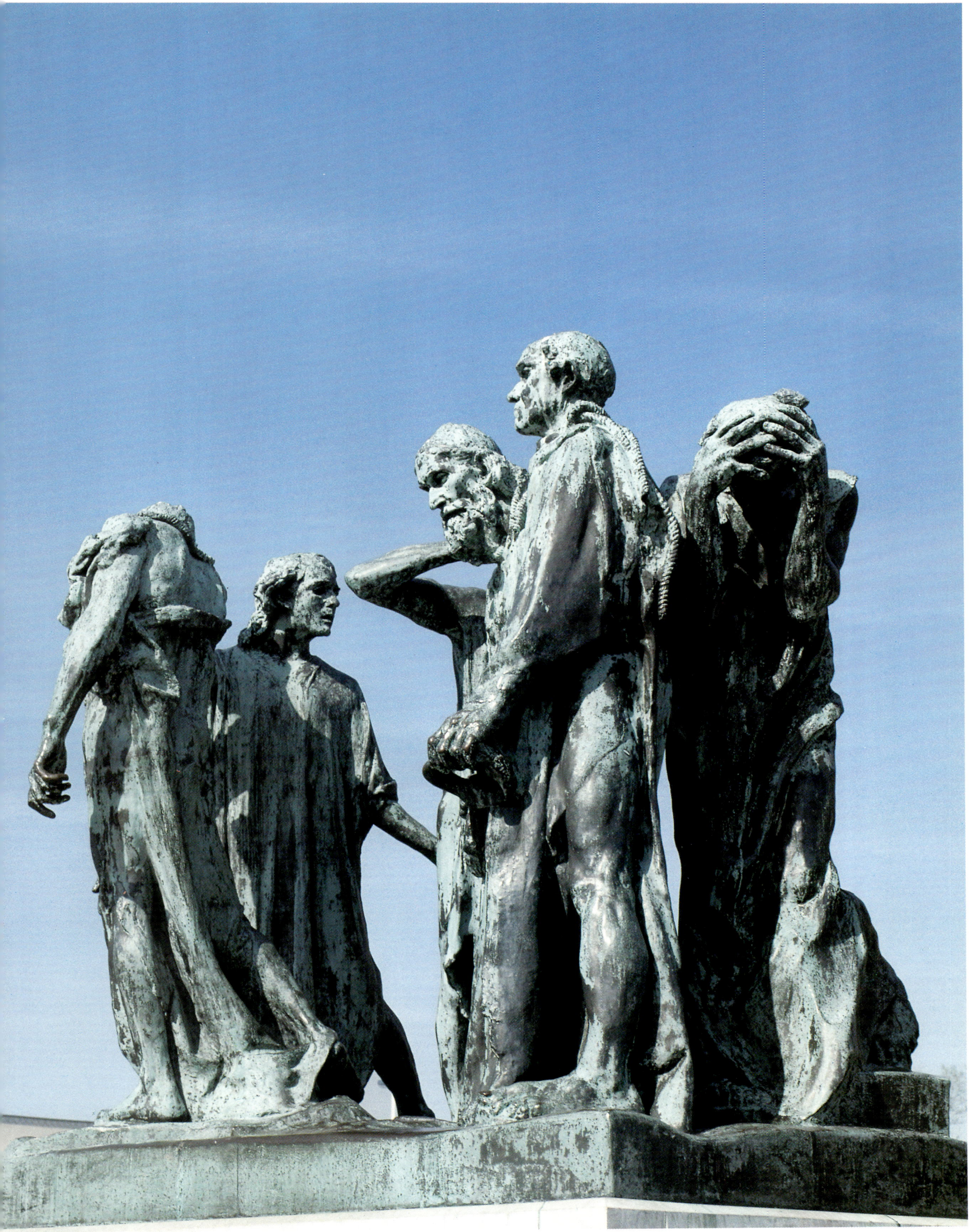

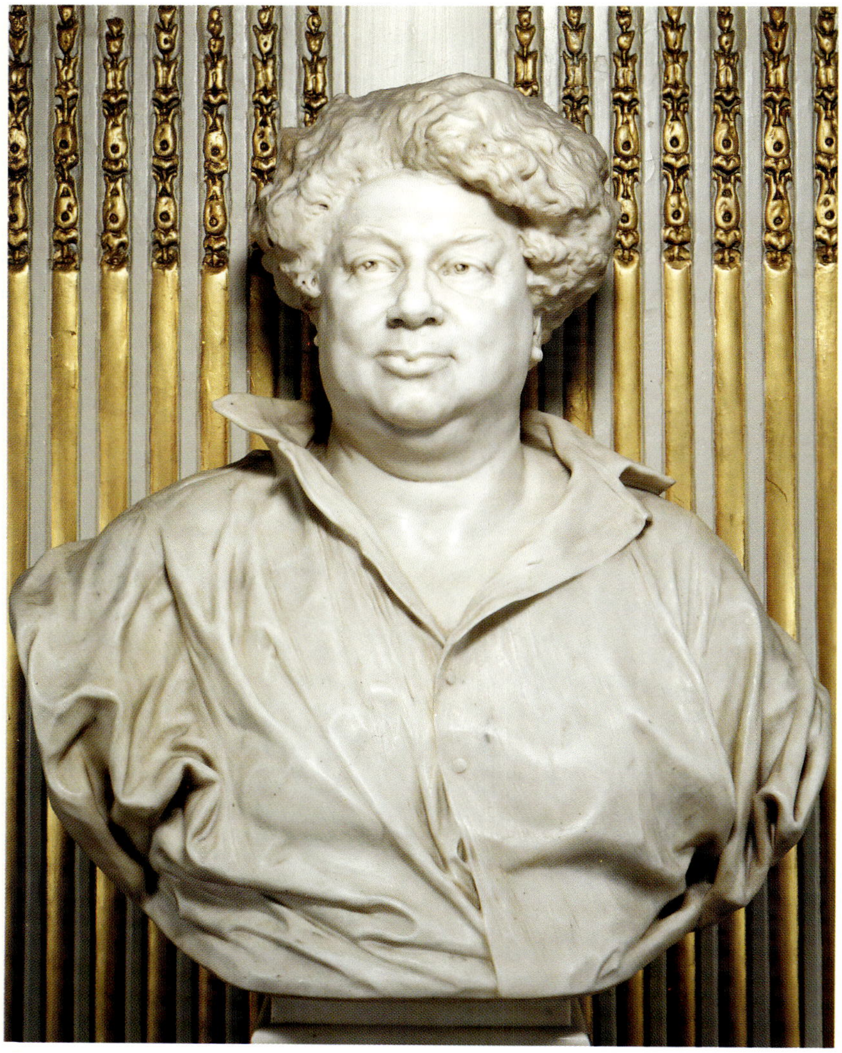

132

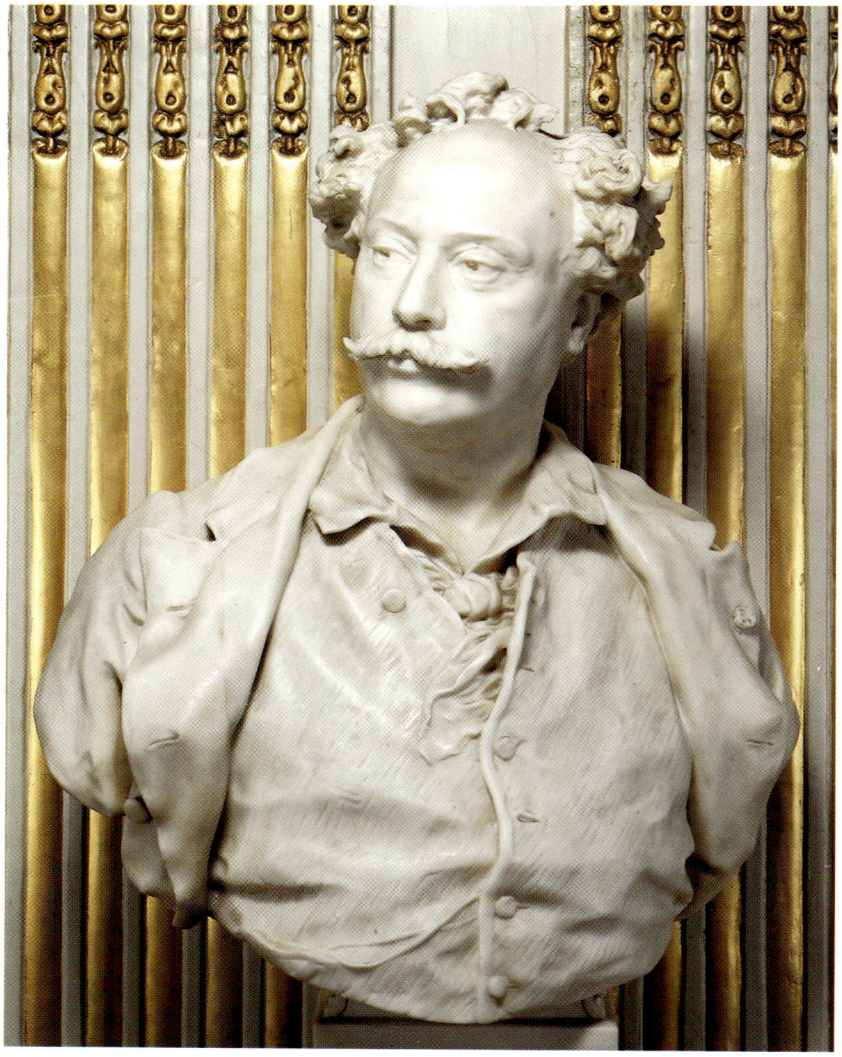

133

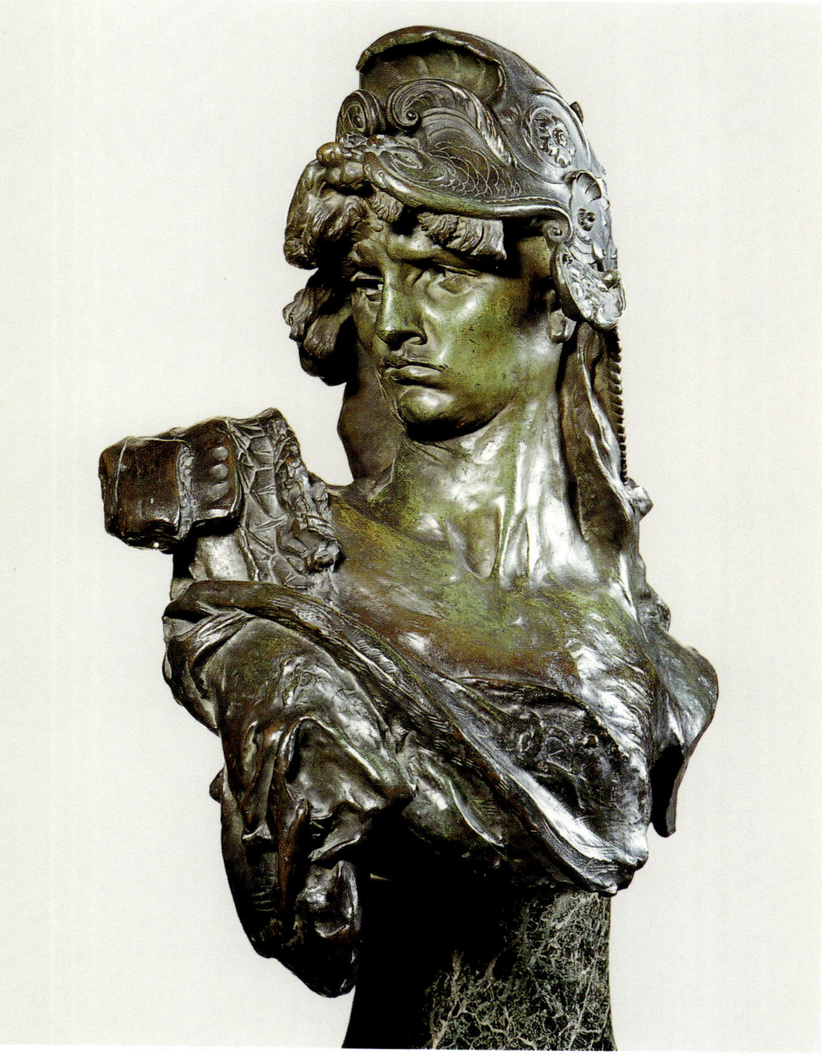

134

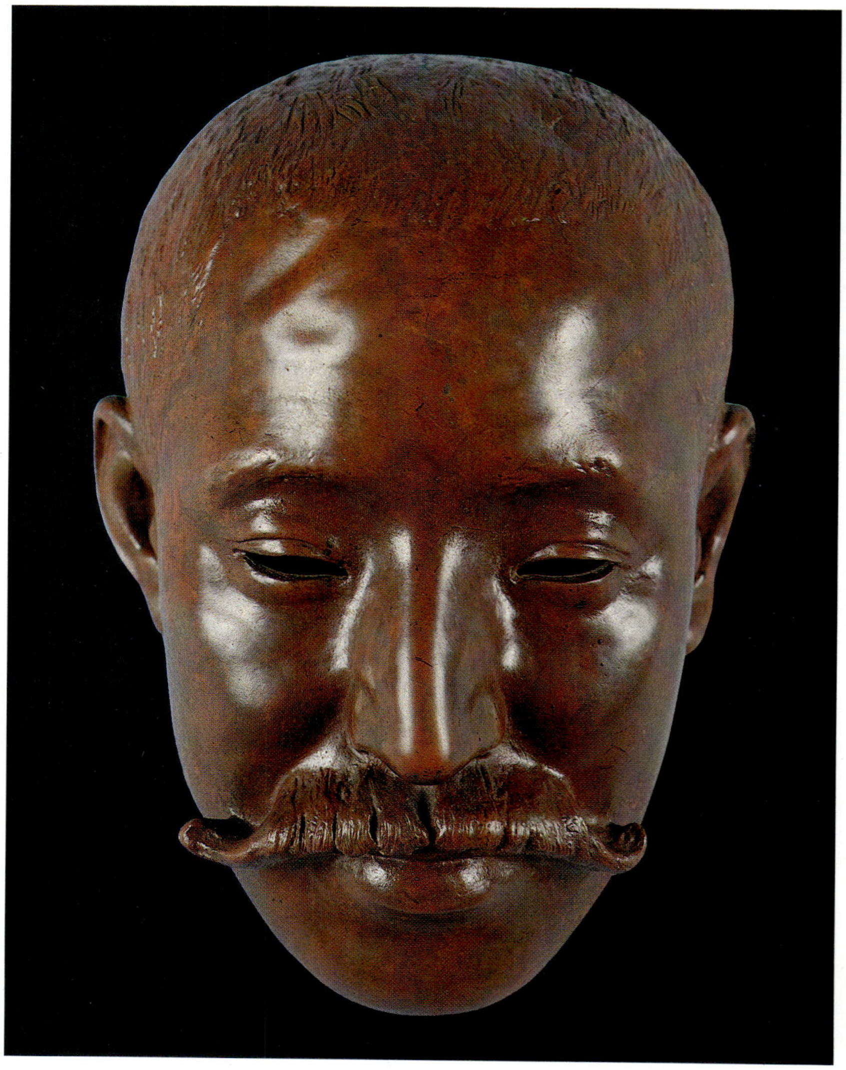

135

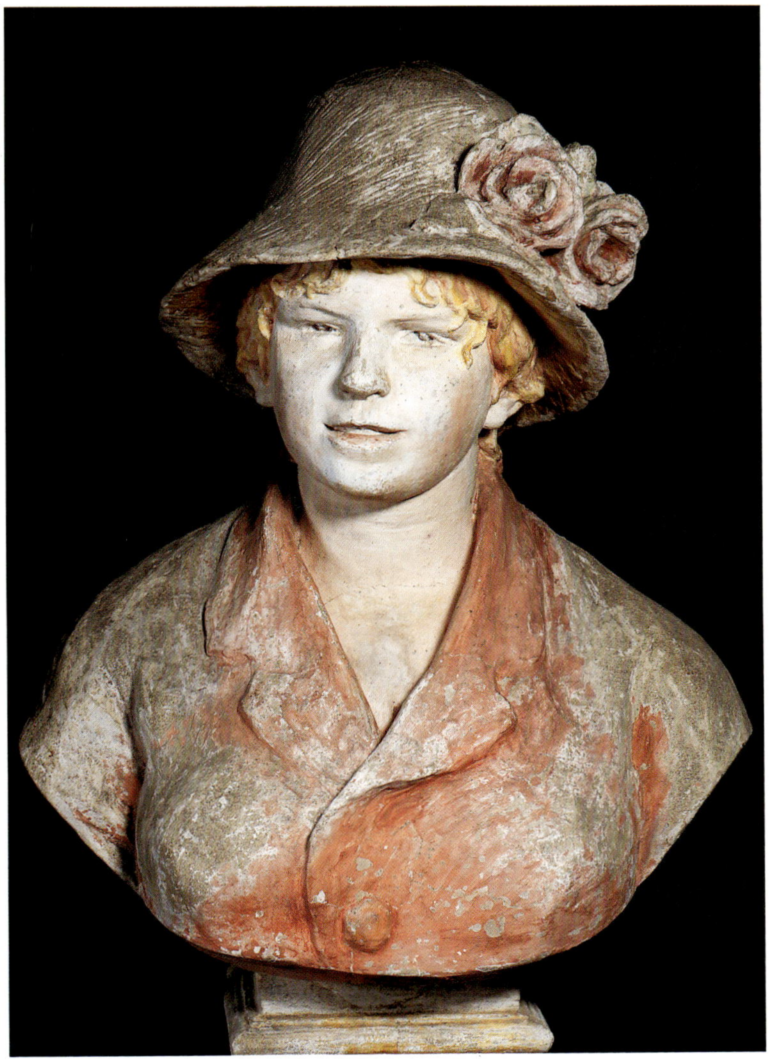

136

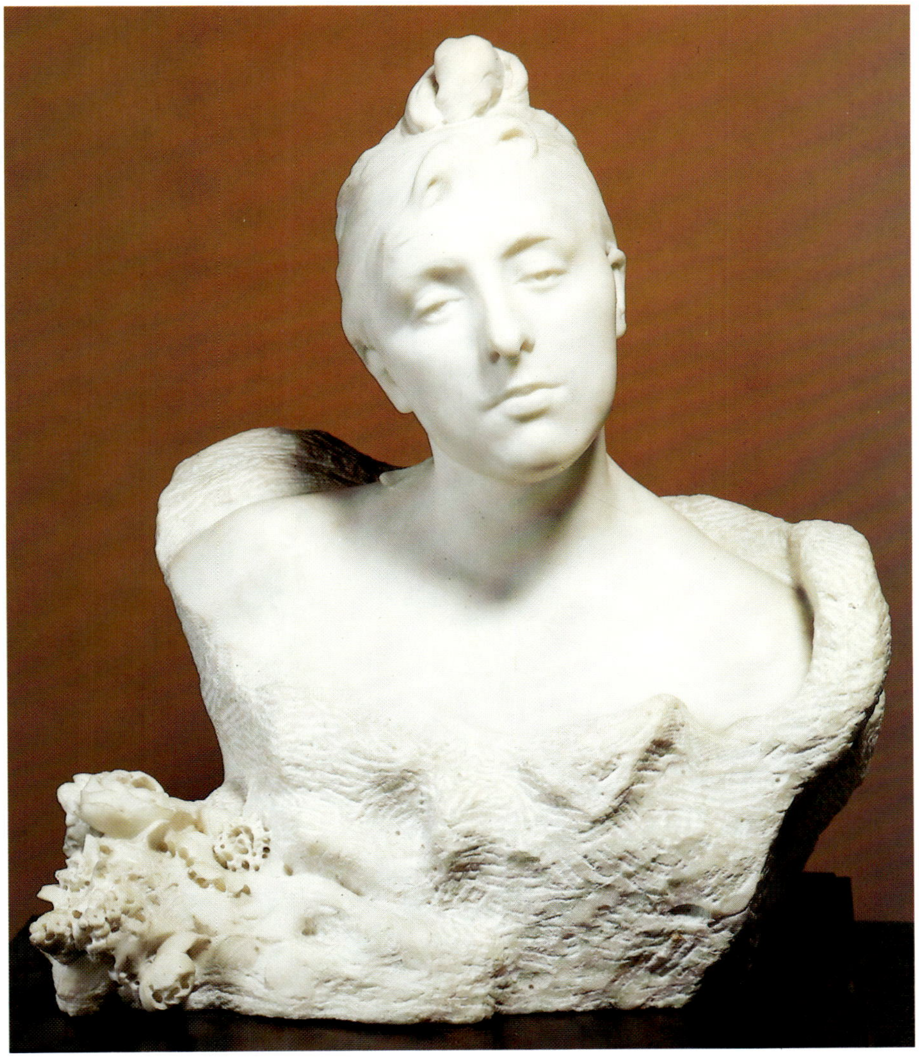

137

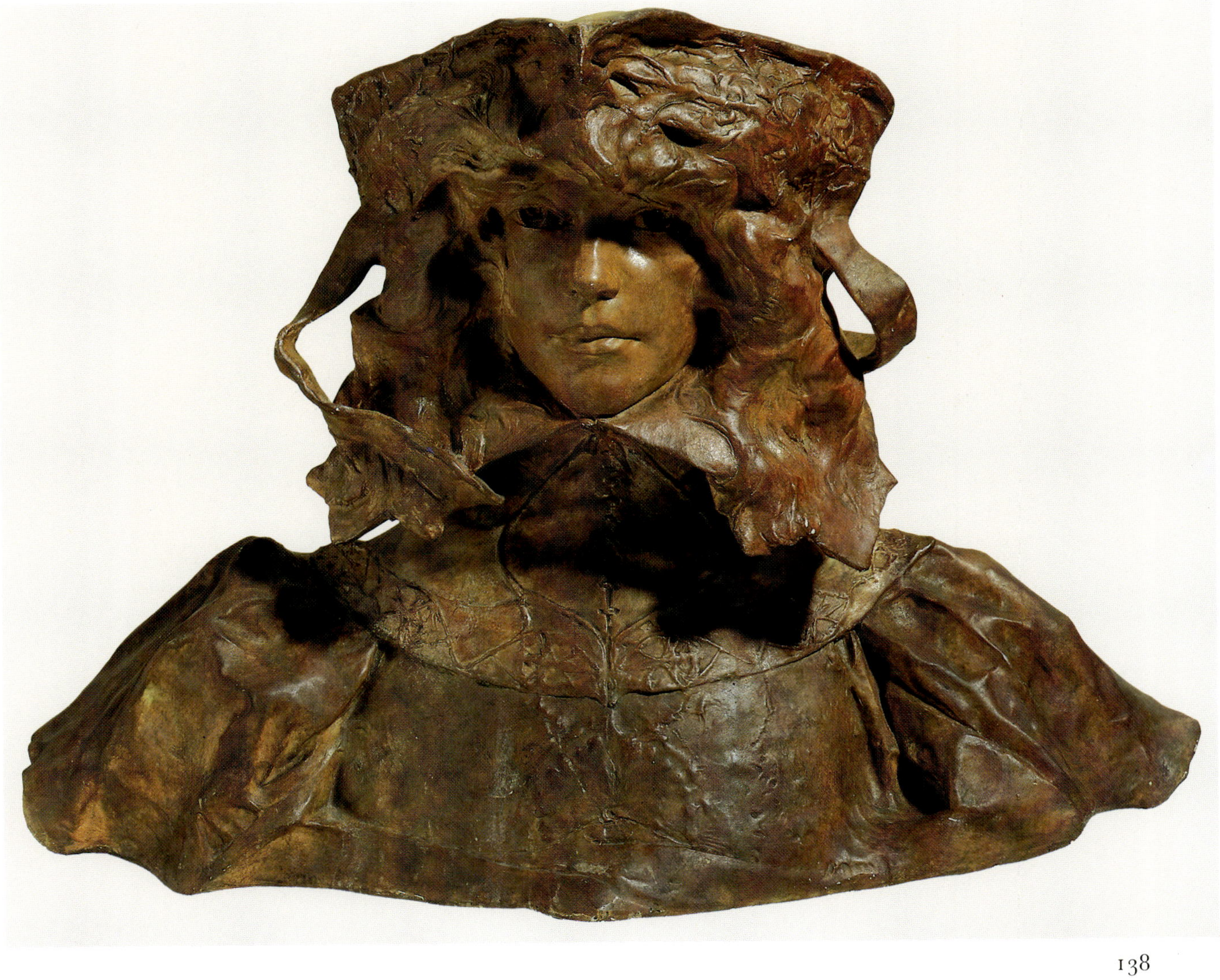

138

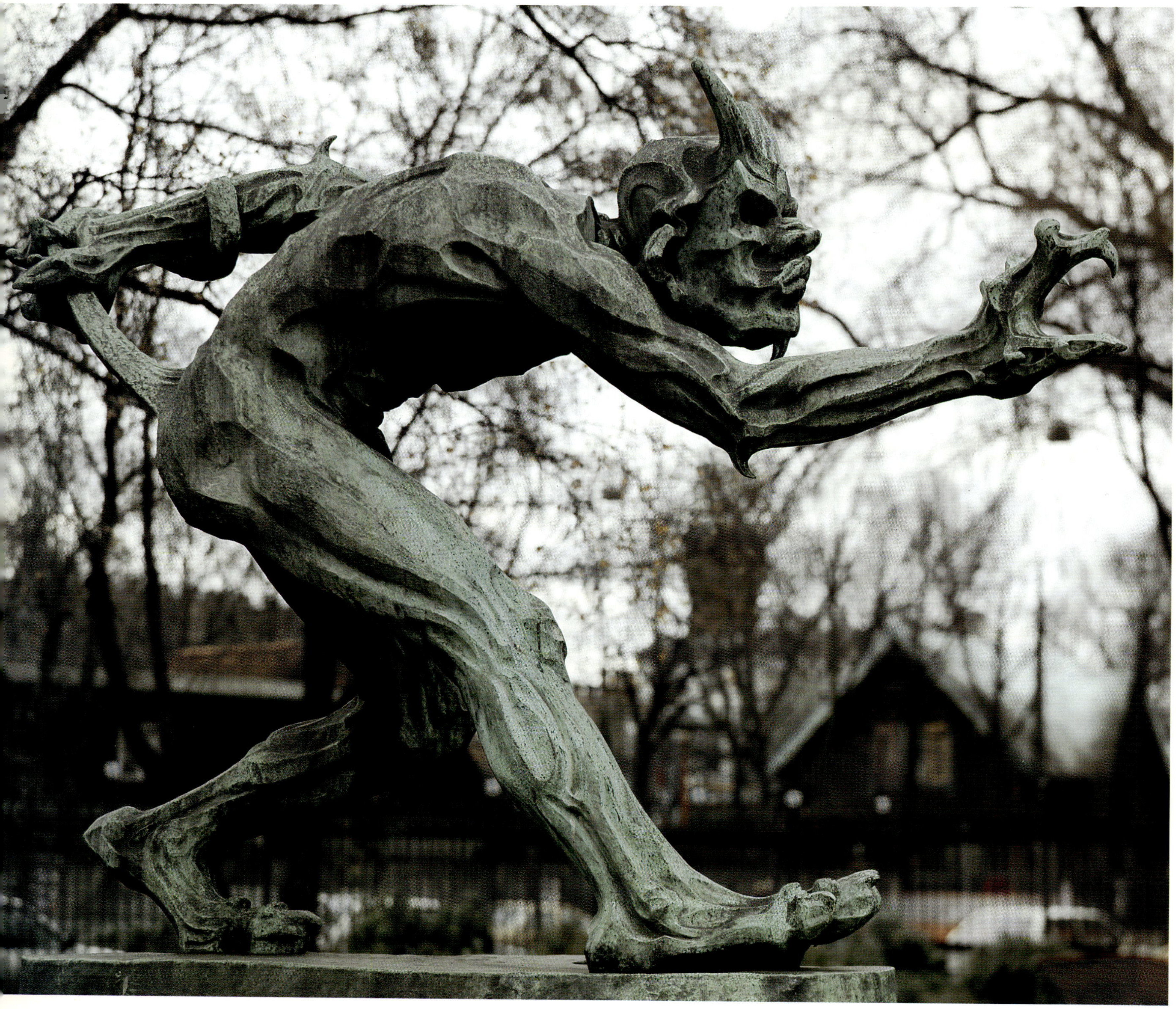

141

→ 142

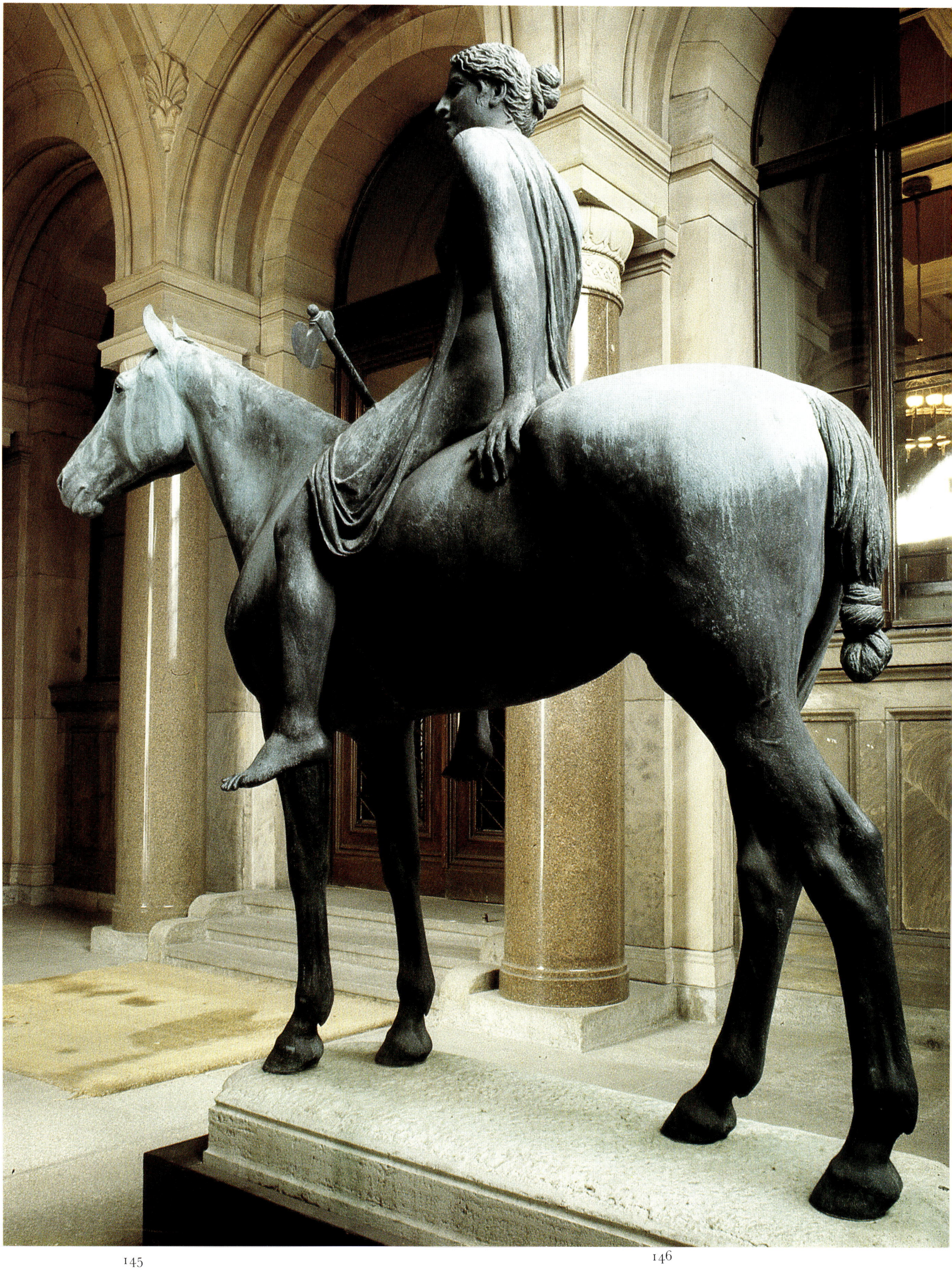

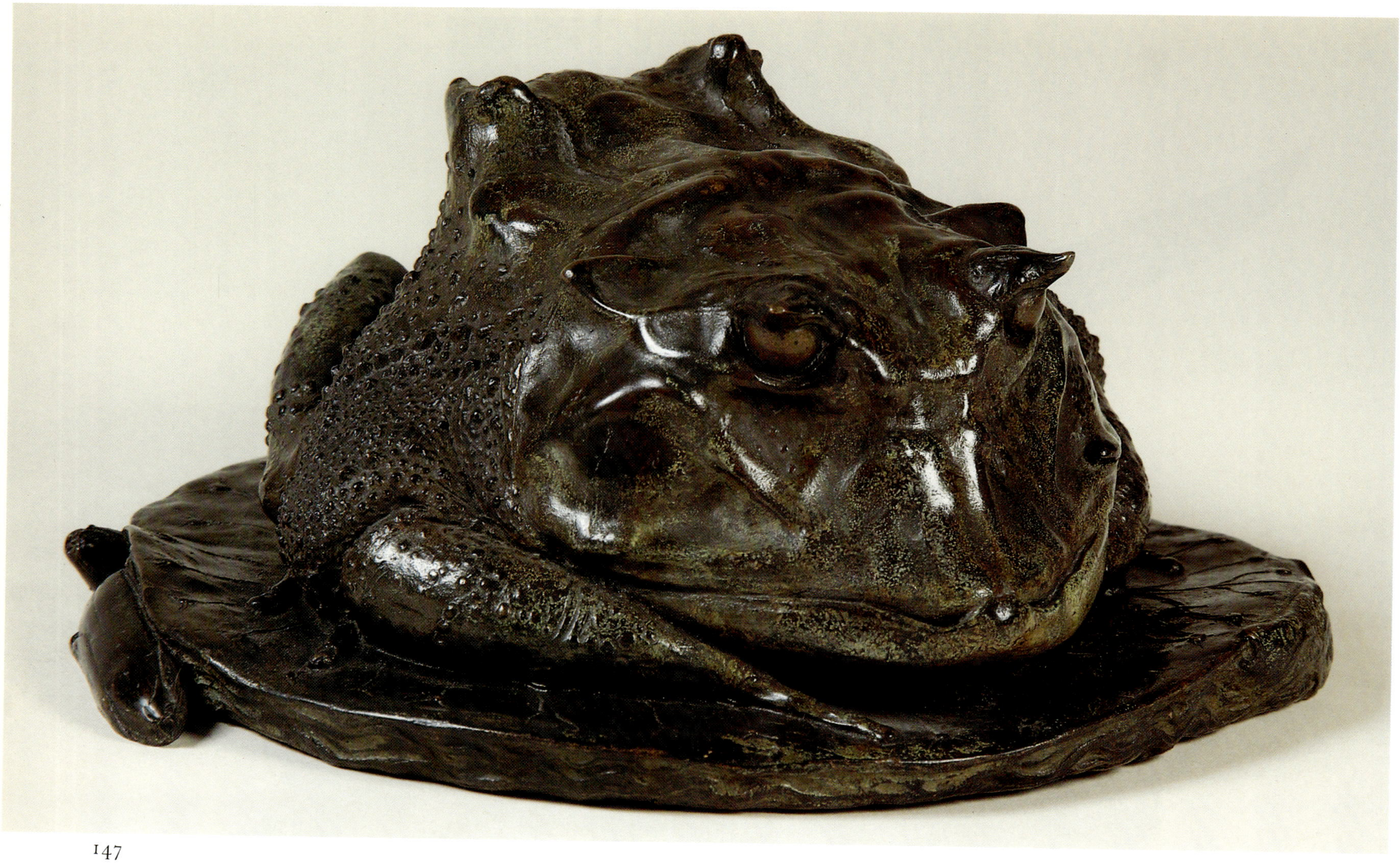

147

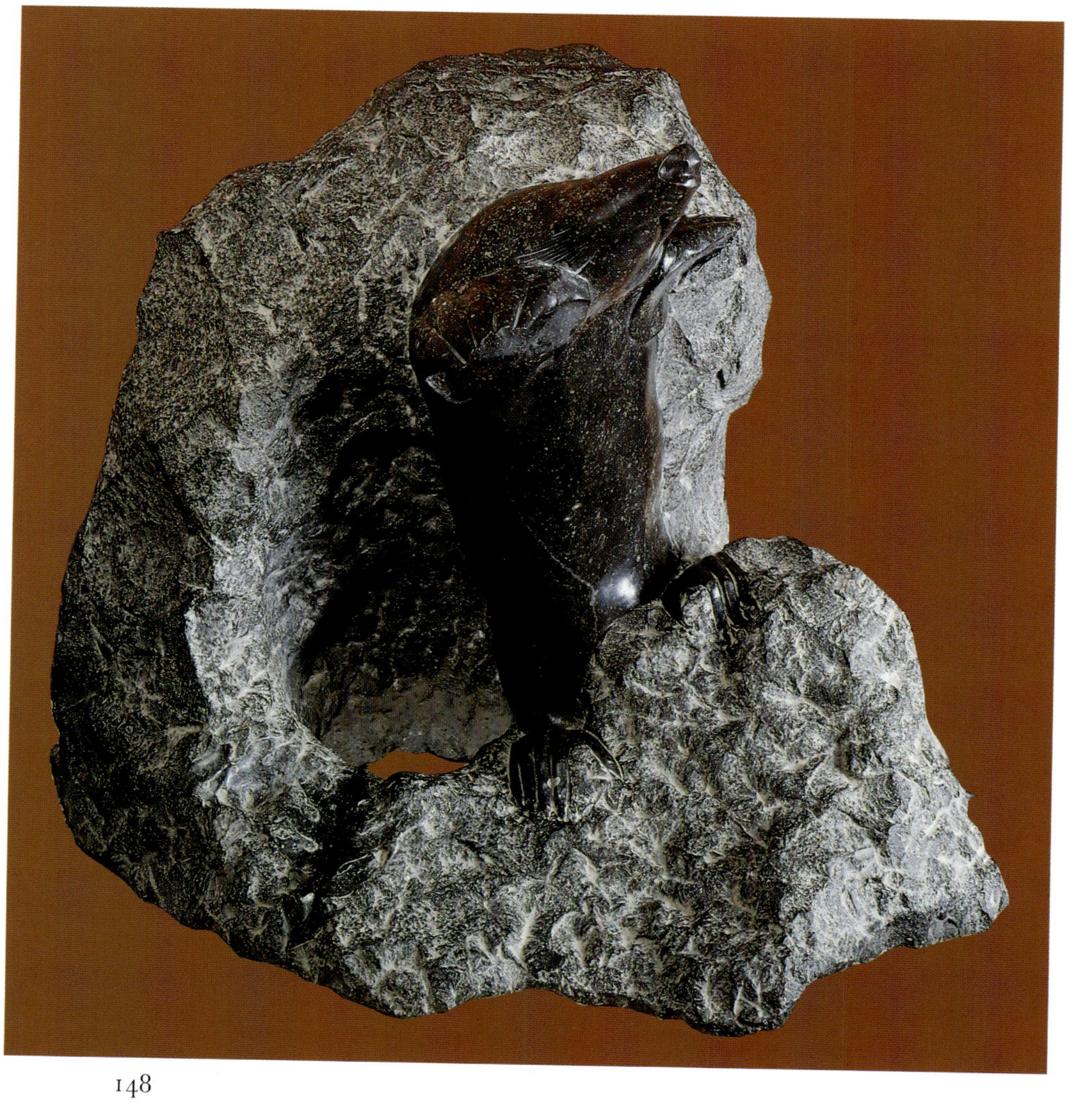

148

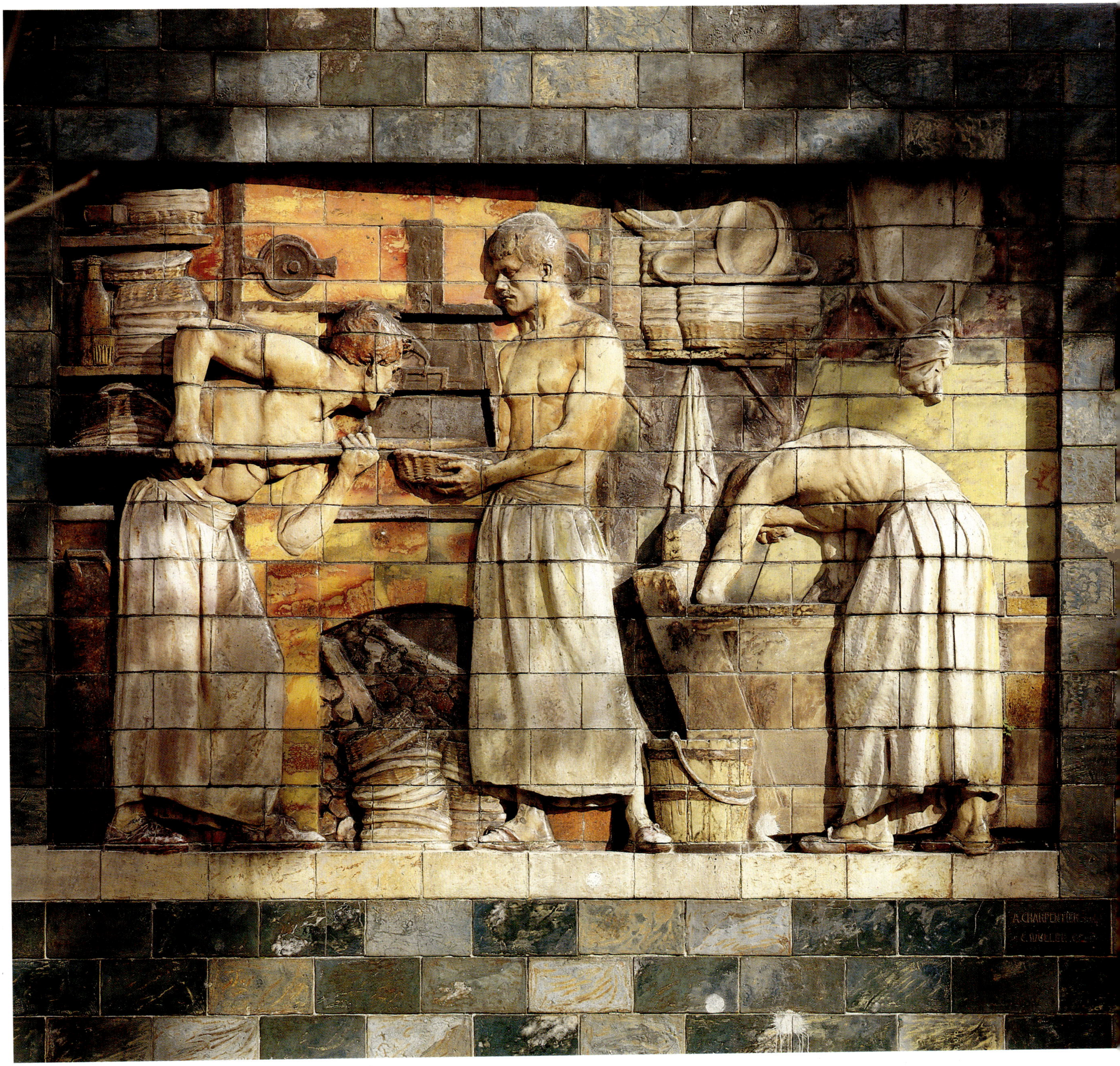
A. CHARPENTIER

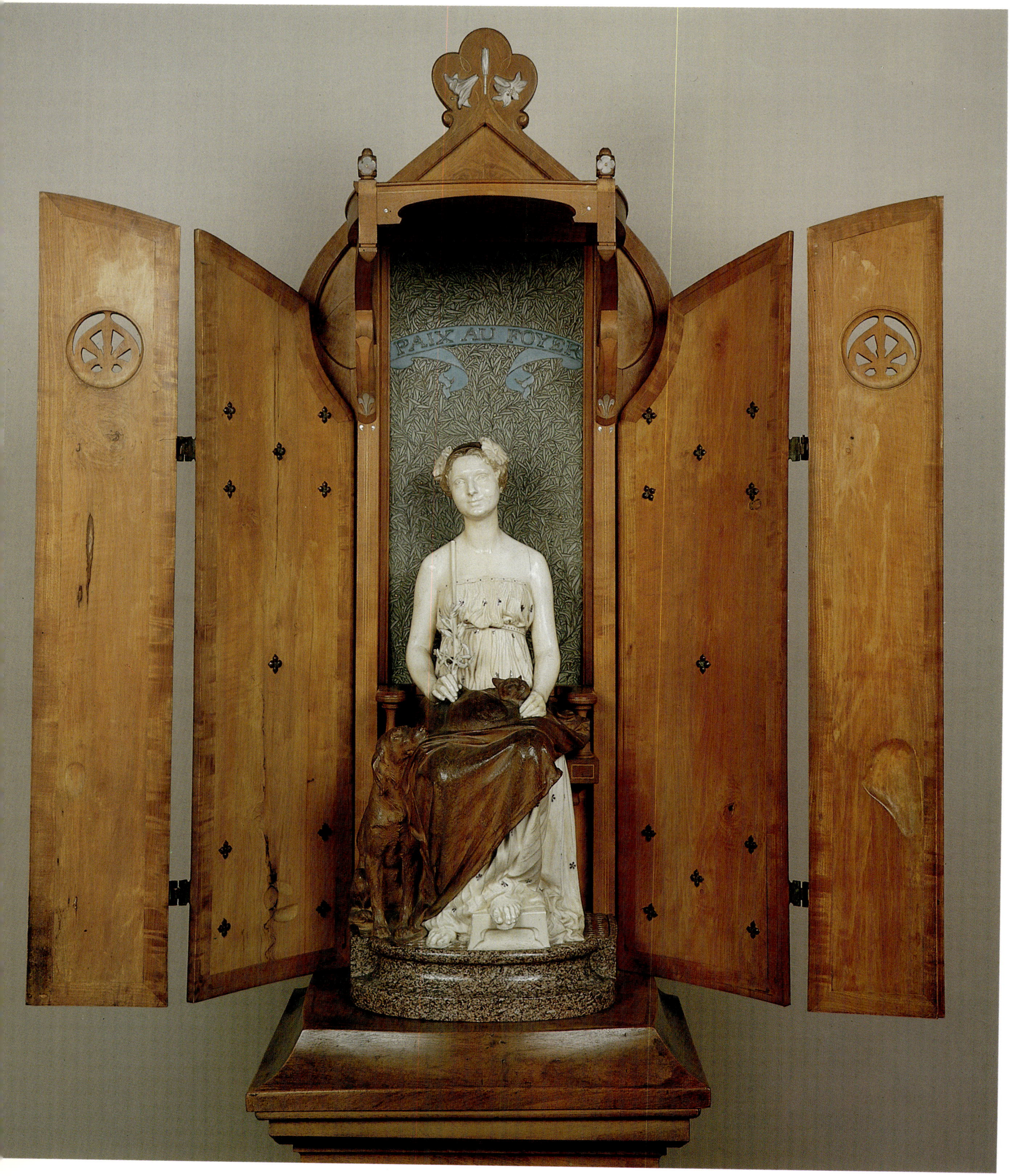
PAIX AU FOYER

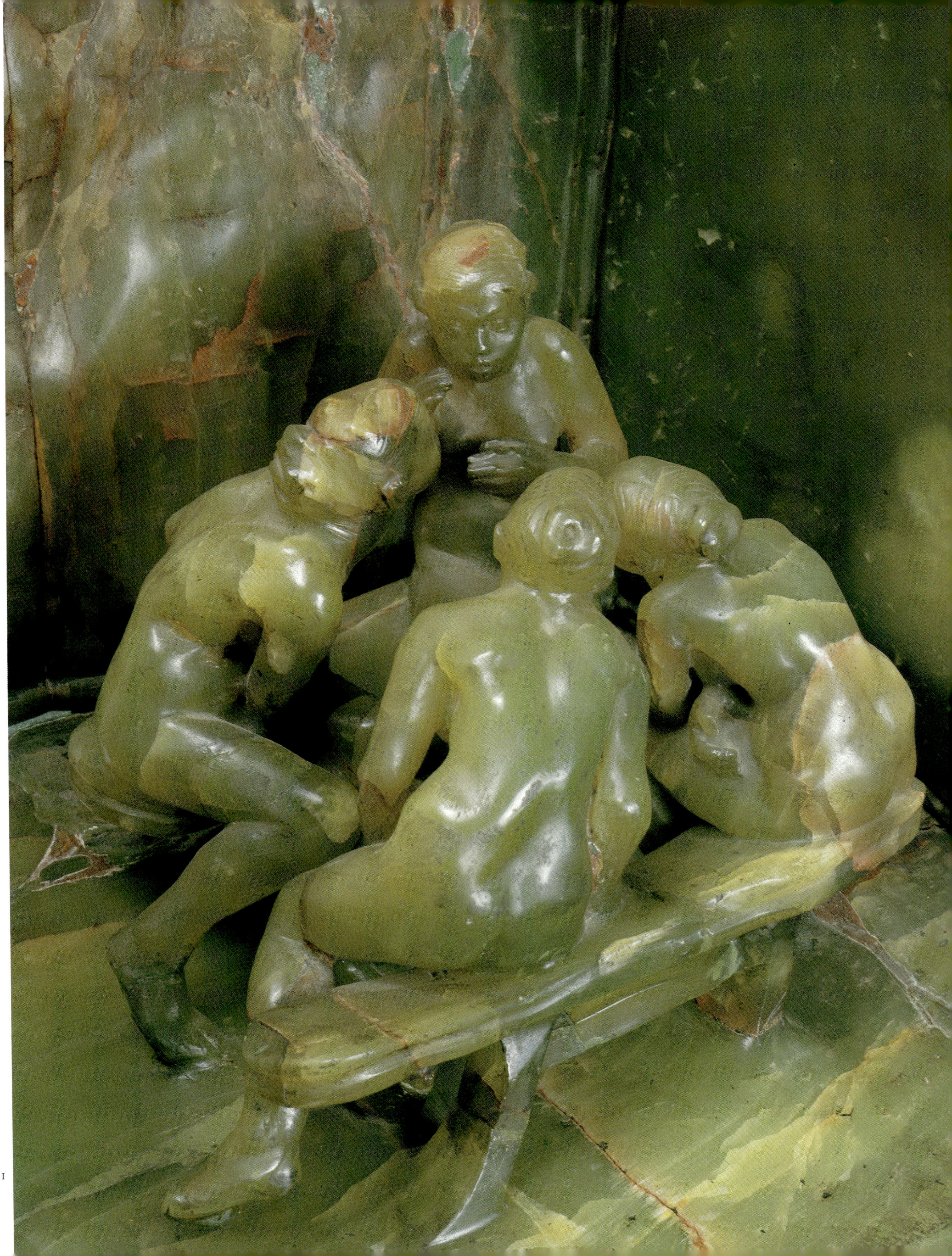

51

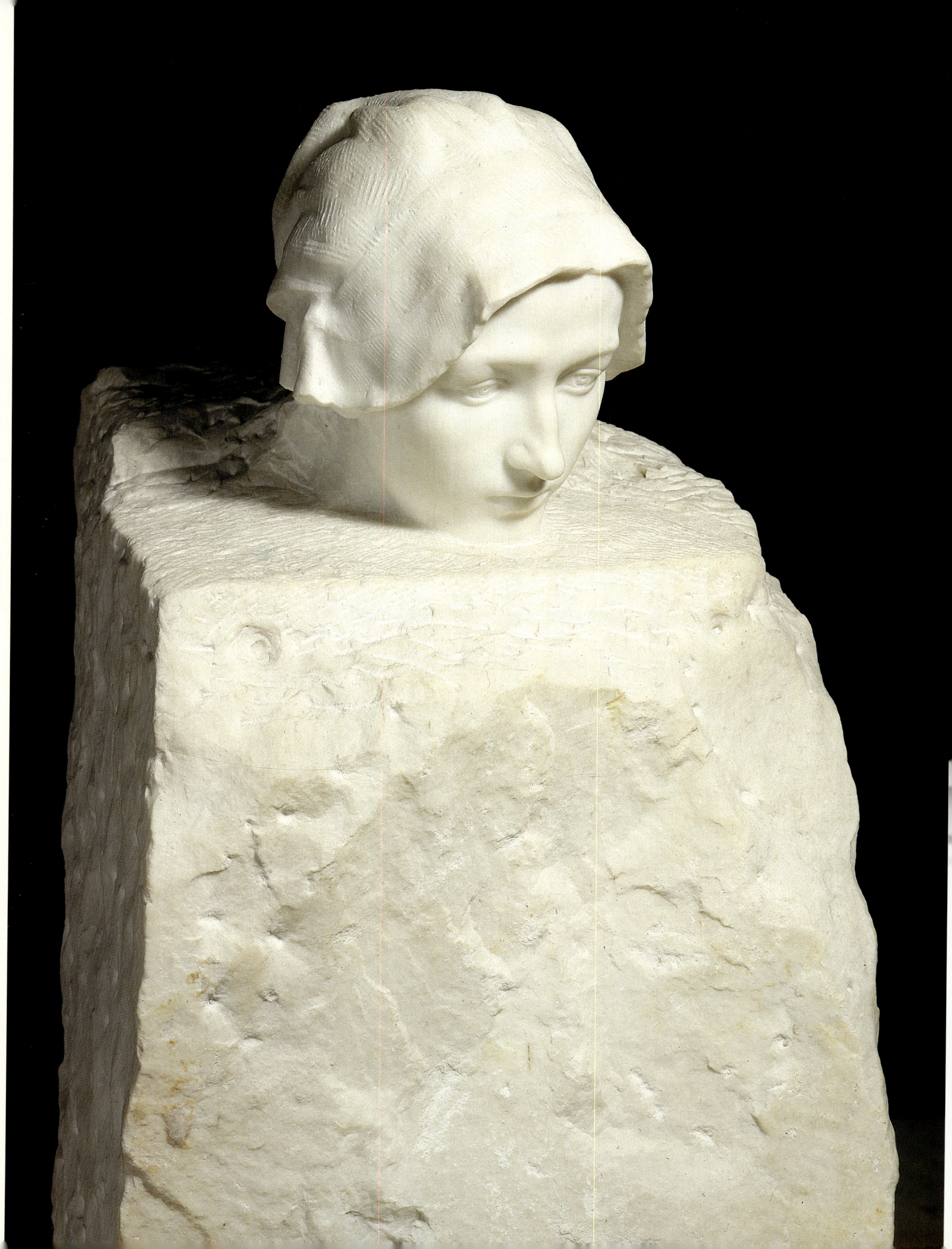

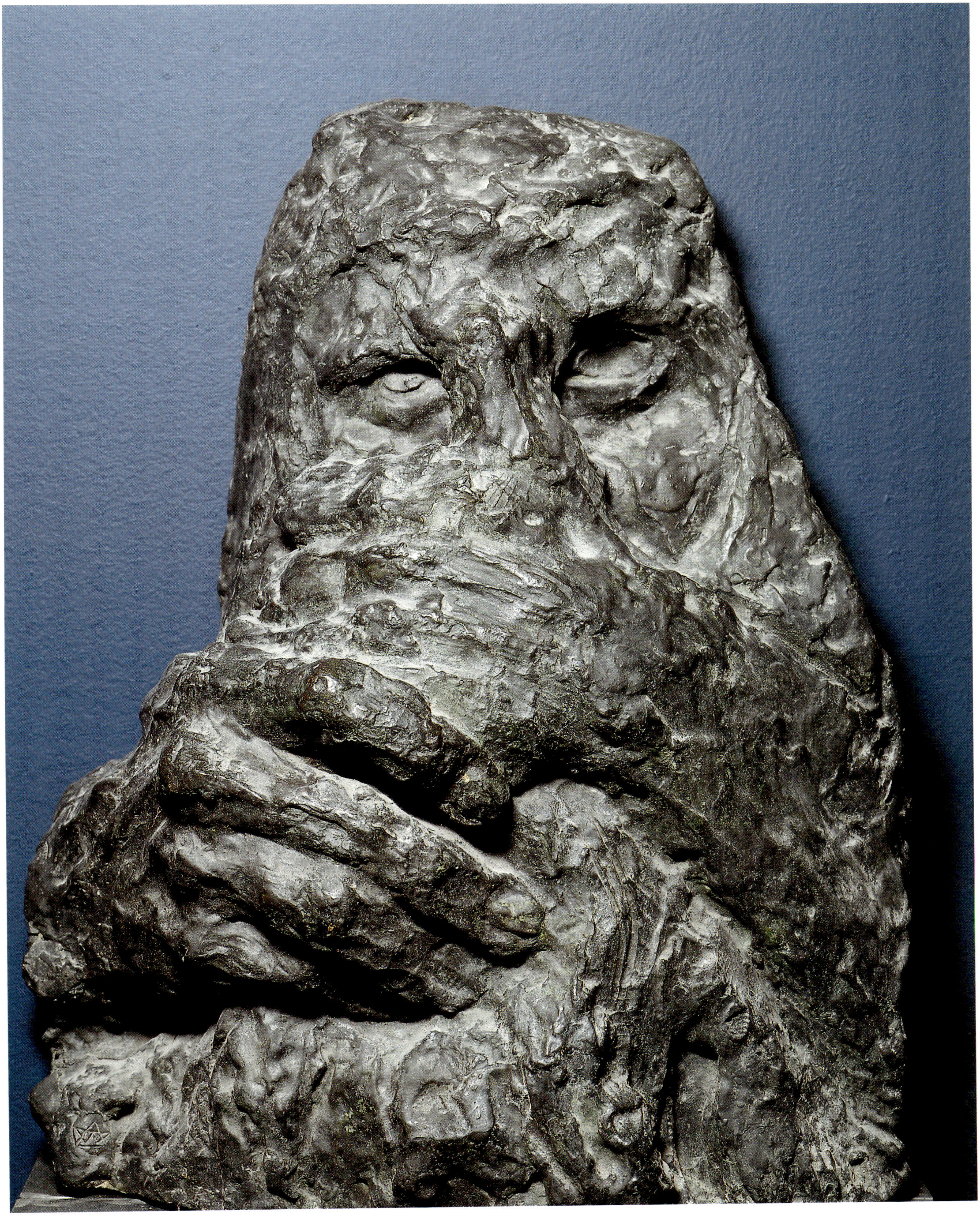

153

← 152

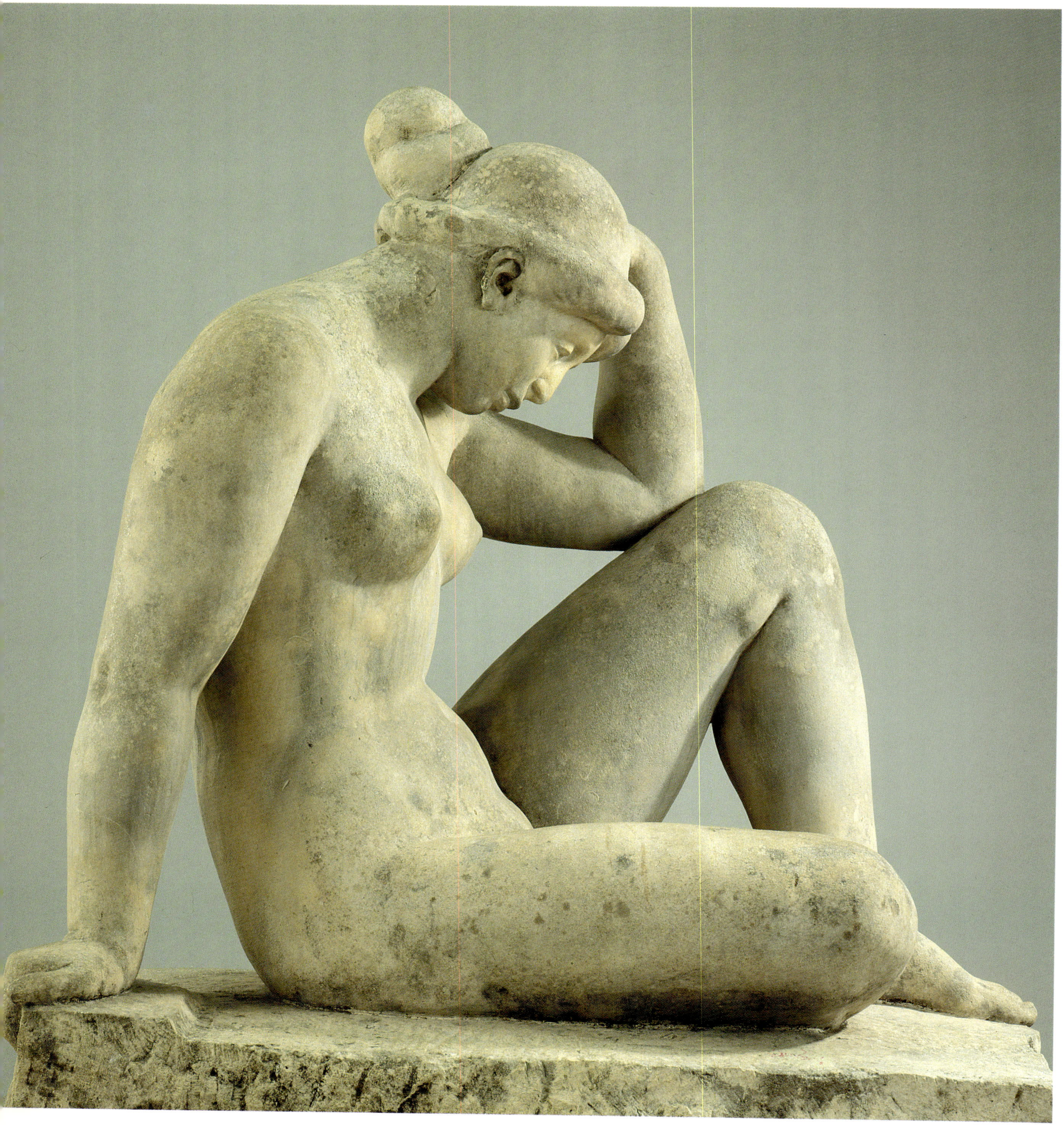

144 Théodore Rivière
Salammbô and Matho
1895 Salon of the Société des Artistes Français
Bronze, gold, ivory, and turquoise, height 40 cm
Musée d'Orsay, Paris

145 Prince Paul Trubetskoy
Tolstoy Riding "Frenzy"
1899
Bronze, height 50.2 cm
Musée d'Orsay, Paris

146 Henri Matisse
The Slave
1900–after 1908
Bronze, height 92 cm
Musée Matisse, Le Cateau-Cambrésis

147 Paul Wayland Bartlett
Brazilian Frog
1894
Bronze, 11 x 26 cm
Musée d'Orsay, Paris

148 François Pompon
Mole
1908
Black marble, height 46 cm
Musée François Pompon, Saulieu

149 Alexandre Charpentier
The Bakers
1897
Glazed earthenware (E. Muller)
Square Scipion, Paris

150 Jean Dampt
Domestic Peace
1900
Ivory, wood, and enamel, height 50 cm
Musée des Arts Décoratifs, Paris

151 Camille Claudel
Conversation
1897 Salon of the Société Nationale des Beaux-Arts
Onyx, height 45 cm
Musée Rodin, Paris

152 Auguste Rodin
Thought (portrait of Camille Claudel)
1886–89
Marble, height 74 cm
Musée d'Orsay, Paris

153 Émile-Antoine Bourdelle
Night
1904
Bronze, height 61 cm
Musée Bourdelle, Paris

154 Aristide Maillol
Mediterranean
1905–6
Stone, height 114 cm
O. Reinhart Foundation, Winterthur

PHOTOGRAPHY

THE INVENTION OF PHOTOGRAPHY (1816–41)

Among the necessary preliminary tools, as it were, the most important was the development, in seventeenth-century Italy, of the camera obscura, which landscapists and *vedutisti* used until the nineteenth century to define their subjects. This ancestor of the photographic camera had undergone many improvements by the end of the eighteenth century and already pointed the way toward a kind of photographic framing of the image. In terms of the chemistry involved, the sensitivity of silver salts to light (already known about in the sixteenth century) was corroborated by the experiments of Thomas Wedgwood at the beginning of the nineteenth century, when he managed to record unfixed silhouettes on paper.

Joseph-Nicéphore Niépce (1765–1833) set out to reproduce a "viewpoint" from nature, having previously been interested in the direct, automatic reproduction of engraving (heliogravure). As early as 1816, using a camera obscura he had made himself, he obtained several unfixed images with reversed values (negatives), and in 1821, by employing a light-sensitive substance known as bitumen of Judea, he successfully captured a positive image on a metal plate. Combining his two parallel avenues of research, he subsequently tried to use line engraving and lithography to obtain printed plates reproducing photographic images. In 1827, Niépce wrote a paper at Kew about his discovery, which he then delivered to London's Royal Society, but he failed either to sell the discovery or to exploit it commercially.

Louis-Jacques-Mandé Daguerre (1787–1851), a painter, scene painter, and pioneer of the diorama, heard about Niépce's work and suggested they collaborate. The two men got together at the end of 1829 with a view to perfecting the process, and they had begun exchanging the results of their respective experiments when Niépce died suddenly. Daguerre went on to direct his research along a different path. Niépce's method required several hours' exposure to light for the image to make an impression inside a camera obscura, Daguerre, however, suspected that some sort of impression was made immediately, even if it was not visible to the naked eye (latent image); it needed only to be revealed chemically. After substituting iodine for bitumen of Judea as the sensitizing agent, about 1835 he contrived to render the image visible with the aid of mercury vapor. The invention, operational by 1837, underwent a further improvement in 1839 through the use of sodium thiosulfate as fixing agent, as discovered by John Frederick William Herschel (1792–1871). It was disclosed by François Arago (1786–1853) on the occasion of a historic joint session of the Académie des Sciences and the Académie des Beaux-Arts on August 19, 1839, and at Arago's suggestion the government of Louis-Philippe paid financial compensation to Daguerre and Isidore Niépce in order that it might be exploited without restriction—in other words, made available to the whole world. However, the French invention was challenged by British scientist and humanist William Fox Talbot (1800–1877), who achieved remarkable results by a different route.

Talbot had begun his research in 1834, initially perfecting the process of "photogenic drawing," which consisted in exposing to sunlight a flat object (leaf, plant, piece of lace) placed on a sheet of paper that had been sensitized with silver chloride; the paper then received a negative impression of the object. But his attempts to expose sensitized paper inside a camera obscura remained unsatisfactory until, in January 1841, Talbot also discovered the principle of the latent image, which needed developing to render it visible. In the following month he patented the "calotype photographic process." He sought to commercialize his process by setting up a studio in Reading in 1843. Run by his assistant Nicolaas Henneman, the studio was intended to produce photographic images. Talbot conceived the idea of publishing a book, *The Pencil of Nature*, to demonstrate the quality of his invention applied to different motifs: the urban landscape, architecture, sculpture, genre scenes, still life, botanical subjects, facsimiles, and so on. Illustrated with twenty-four plates in the form of original prints stuck in, the work was published by subscription and appeared in installments from 1844 to 1846. Talbot's invention may not have enjoyed the same resounding success as that of Daguerre, but in reality it held out far greater promise for the future. The use of the photographic negative made multiple prints possible, permitting the widespread circulation of images. Printing on paper was soon found to be preferable to Daguerre's single plate on copper covered with polished silver, with its consequent mirror effect.

A third key figure in the invention of photography was Hippolyte Bayard (1801–1887), a self-taught civil servant at the French ministry of finance who perfected a process of his own involving direct positive printing onto paper. Spurred on by an initial announcement concerning Daguerre's invention, which Arago made to the Académie des Sciences on January 7, 1839, Bayard set to work immediately. In the same month he produced a number of "photogenic drawings," and by the end of March he was turning out marvelous camera obscura prints. Despite reservations on Arago's part (the great scientist was by then too committed to supporting Daguerre), on June 24, 1839 Bayard showed some thirty architectural views and still lifes at a charity gala, which was picked up by the press. Three months after the official revelation of the Daguerre process, the Académie des Beaux-Arts nevertheless drew attention to the superiority of the paper print over the metal plate. Bayard derived no benefit from his invention, and eventually, in 1842, he adopted Talbot's negative/positive process.

The so-called "daguerreotype" was an instant success, and its use spread rapidly throughout the world, particularly in the United States. The precision engineering of the silvered plate, which made even the tiniest details legible, fascinated public and artists alike. The technique was especially suited to portraiture, creating an immediate demand, much to the detriment of miniaturists and engravers. But while portraits accounted for most of their production, daguerreotypists practiced virtually all genres, particularly landscape (both rural and urban), architecture, the nude, the genre scene, and the still life. Before long, amateur daguerreotypists were leaving to explore distant lands: from France, Joseph-Philibert Girault de Prangey (1804–1892) visited Greece and the East, Jules Itier (1802–1877) traveled in Egypt and China, and Baron Jean-Baptiste-Louis Gros (1793–1870) went on diplomatic missions to Bogotá and Athens. A book entitled *Excursions daguerriennes* used the technique to illustrate many locations visited by these early photographic explorers. Relatively long exposure times required the subject to be motionless, but certain portraitists (such as Albert Sands Southworth [1811–1894] and Josiah Johnson Hawes [1808–1901], for example, who were active in Boston in the 1840s) attempted to give a feeling of greater veracity by simulating not actual movement but a certain mobility on the part of their subjects. Although the daguerreotype gave rise to some remarkable images, it could only be reproduced by interpretative engraving or heliogravure (still in its infancy). As the mirror effect made it hard to read and the gray tones were found to be rather dull, it was rapidly abandoned (about 1850 in France, slightly later in the United States) in favor of Talbot's process involving paper. This had meanwhile undergone considerable improvement, due notably to the work of Désiré Blanquart-Évrard (1802–1872), who introduced it into France in 1847.

PIONEERS AND PRIMITIVES IN GREAT BRITAIN THE CALOTYPE ERA AND THE INTRODUCTION OF COLLODION

The process of pulling a paper print from a negative of the same material involved some loss of precision compared with the daguerreotype, but the motif was more powerfully conveyed by the interplay of values, which allowed a more schematic way of seeing. The granulation of the paper that the sunlight had to penetrate in order to print the sensitized sheet also gave the different textures of that motif a more homogeneous character, the subtlety of which was not unrelated to certain techniques used in the graphic arts. The search for greater veracity in conveying the reality of the visible world very soon led technicians to devise new processes, such as the glass plate and the use of wet collodion to bind the emulsion, invented by the Briton Frederick Scott Archer (1813–1857) in 1851. The transparency of glass gave greater precision to the motif, the values of which were rendered with greater veracity than a paper support allowed. The collodion process gained ground in Britain and France during the 1850s, and by about 1860 it was in general use.

In the important series of pictures he produced while perfecting and developing his process, Talbot showed himself to be a remarkable artist. All these inventors (Bayard in particular), in experimenting visually with a new means of expression, soon discovered its specific qualities in terms of framing, different ways of approaching the subject, indicating contours, and so on. Talbot's favorite location for his photographic trials was his Lacock Abbey estate near London, but it was not long before he was capturing urban views in London, Oxford, Cambridge, and subsequently (in 1845) in Rouen and Paris, where he had gone to publicize his work. He was also a lyrical landscapist, and in 1846 he published a second book, *Sun Pictures of Scotland.* Following Talbot, a series of photographers took up his process, including the Reverend George W. Bridges, who experimented with it in Italy, Greece, and Palestine in 1846, and the Reverend Calvert Richard Jones, who worked in Malta and Italy in the same year and went on to capture picturesque views in Wales, England, and Ireland.

One of the most remarkable productions of the paper-negative era in Britain arose out of a collaboration between two Scottish artists, the painter David Octavius Hill (1802–1870) and the photographer Robert Adamson (1821–1848). It was with a view to doing the groundwork for a vast painting depicting *The First Assembly of the* monumental still lifes that, if they often remain in thrall to Chardin, demonstrate the subtlety of analysis of textures that the paper negative was capable of conveying in the hands of a true artist.

Charles Nègre (1820–1880), who studied under Ingres and Delaroche, began to practice photography in close conjunction with his painting. After producing a number of splendid nudes in his studio, he turned his attention to the genre scene and the small tradesmen of Paris in the early 1850s (fig. 159). In this he showed extraordinary inventiveness, either simulating or actually taking snapshots (*Market Scene at Hôtel de Ville Port*, fig. 160). In 1852, working in his native south of France, Nègre began recording locations and monuments for a huge publication, only part of which actually appeared. In 1857–59, this time using collodion, he completed a photographic report on *The Imperial Home at Vincennes*, a first in its field, combining architectural views with indoor scenes showing the workers wounded on the building sites of the Empire and the work of the institution's staff. Charles Nègre spent some time developing a photomechanical process making it possible to produce a larger number of fade-resistant prints of a photographic image—one of the major preoccupations of photography in the 1850s. His "heliographic damascening" process was based on the principles of line engraving and he used it to produce his monumental Chartres Cathedral pictures to illustrate the *Monographie* by Jean-Baptiste Lassus (1857). However, in the competition organized by the duke of Luynes (1867) it was passed over in favor of the "photo-lithography" process devised by Alphonse Poitevin (1819–1882).

Édouard-Denis Baldus (1813–about 1890) gave up painting in order to concentrate on photography at the very beginning of the 1850s. As a member of the 1851 Mission Héliographique, for which he covered Burgundy and the south of France, he conveyed a monumental vision of architecture that impressed contemporary critics. He spent 1852 working in Paris and northern France. In 1854 he photographed some Romantic landscapes in the Auvergne (fig. 162), and in 1855 he was commissioned to produce a railroad album on the occasion of the opening of the Paris-Boulogne line (fig. 161). Baldus thus inaugurated a key genre in nineteenth-century photography (Louis-Auguste [1814–1876] and Auguste-Rosalie [1826–1900] Bisson and H. Albert Collard also distinguished themselves in this field) devoted to the architecture of engineers and the transformation of the industrial landscape. This was some twenty years before the Impressionist painters tackled such subjects—in what was actually a less radical manner. In 1856, Baldus was commissioned by the government of Napoleon III to record the ravages caused by the flooding of the Rhône. This was a new kind of assignment, which the artist treated in vast images designed to form panoramas with all the epic force of history painting. It was partly with the aid of the collodion process that Baldus fulfilled another commission relating to the construction of Lefuel's new Louvre (1855–58), the decorative elements of which he recorded in images that lent them an almost prodigious quality. A final railroad album devoted to the south of France (1859), also using collodion, rounded off Baldus's creative period. His art, marked by its breadth and a taste for abstraction, was in some respects closest to the aesthetics of the American landscape.

Scientists played a major part in the development of photographic techniques, of course, but they also had a substantial role in terms of the expression of sensibility. The chemist Victor Regnault (1810–1878), manager of the Sèvres porcelain factory, was a highly original portraitist, creating likenesses of his family and friends in which he established a link between figure and scientific object. His marvelously peaceful views of the banks of the Seine (1853–54), his pictures of the factory (blending picturesque views with industrial architecture, fig. 166), and the series he devoted to the Parc de Saint-Cloud were excellently served by the paper-negative technique of which he was a master. Louis Robert (1810–1882), a friend of Regnault who also practiced his art at Sèvres, was an equally accomplished portraitist and demonstrated a similar lyricism in his large landscapes of the Parc de Saint-Cloud and Versailles.

Travel and in particular archaeological expeditions accounted for much of the primitive photography of the 1850s. We have a remarkable example in the interest that Victor Hugo showed in photography from his Jersey exile (Hugo refused to live in France under the Second Empire) and the publication project he conceived relating to the Channel Islands. This was intended to be an original blend of poems, prose pieces, drawings, and photographs, and was the reason for setting up the Jersey studio run by Charles Hugo and August Vacquerie (figs. 164, 165). A modern transposition of the Romantic travel book (the writer imagined a new edition of his 1842 book *Rhin* illustrated with photographs by his son Charles), for a variety of economic and political reasons the Channel Islands book never saw the light of day, but it did give birth to several hundred images, including landscapes and architectural views, that were conceived by the poet himself and that should be viewed in conjunction with the poems of *Les Contemplations*, written about the same time. The project also produced an important series of portraits of the poet as exiled, combatant demiurge (directed by Hugo himself), members of his family, fellow exiles, and various banned persons. Intrigued by photography for a while, by its chiaroscuro possibilities and breadth of values, Hugo used it in various ways to develop his graphic oeuvre.

Countless travelers from a range of professions made skillful use of the paper-negative process to document different types of work. Pierre Tremaux took a series of photographs between 1847 and 1854 for a book on Sudan, giving a lithographic interpretation of the country (fig. 171). Eugène Piot worked in Greece and Italy in the early 1850s, while from 1849 Frédéric de Flacheron, a Frenchmen living in Rome, studied the ancient and modern monuments of the city and its surroundings. Alexis de Lagrange reproduced locations and monuments of India in 1849, Joseph Vigier traveled in the Pyrenees in 1853, Léon Gérard looked at medieval German towns in 1857, and in 1859 Gustave Viaud, brother of novelist Pierre Loti, took photographs in Tahiti. However, for reasons that had to do with the way archaeology was developing at the time, the two countries that occasioned most of the major photographic missions of the 1850s were Egypt and Palestine.

It was in order to give backing to the erroneous theories of archaeologist F. de Saulcy on the Solomonic origins of the precinct walls of the Temple of Jerusalem that a part-time archaeologist named Auguste Salzmann took up photography in 1854 (fig. 189). He then embarked on a vast campaign to identify the main Jewish, Islamic, and Christian sites and monuments of the Holy City, the results of which were published in 1856. Scouring Jerusalem in the same state of careless abandon as Chateaubriand had enjoyed fifty years earlier, Salzmann took a large number of general views and close-ups. These are among the most vibrant studies of motifs that photography had yet produced. In them, the eye of the artist complements the scientific preoccupations of the archaeologist to give us pictures of astonishing modernity that are nevertheless imbued with an atmosphere of dream and spirituality.

Egypt formed the object of many expeditions of a more or less scientific nature. The writer Maxime Du Camp (1822–1894) spent the years 1849 to 1851 there in the company of Gustave Flaubert. There were also the works of engineer Félix Teynard (1817–1892; fig. 173) in 1851, archaeologist John B. Greene (1832–1856; fig. 172), who gave us the most lyrical vision of the country's archaeological sites and produced many pictures of an abstract nature (1853–54), and Egyptologist Théodule Devéria (1831–1871; fig. 168), son of engraver Achille Devéria, who devoted most of his attention to the objects of the Memphis Serapeum (1859–60). Much of this work was published by Désiré Blanquart-Évrard, who, having developed a technique for speeding up the making of prints, opened a photographic printing works in Loos-les-Lille in 1851. Between then and 1855, Blanquart-Évrard published a large number of albums in the form of original prints, thus providing an outlet for the work of photographers.

The genre scene and the nude, categories that traditionally belonged to painting, were taken up by certain photographers, sometimes working for painters. As early as 1847, Humbert de Molard used the staff of his Normandy estate to create scenes from country life that, while realistic in character, were informed by the spirit of the genre scene. Le Secq and Le Gray both made tentative efforts here, while Nègre, in addition to his Paris street scenes, studied the *pifferari* (Italian flute-players) who passed through the capital and (when he made his report on the south of France) the inhabitants of Provence wearing local costume. Émile Pec's (1816–?) marvelous *Young Woman at Prayer* has something of the same quality of a figure in a setting (fig. 163). Julien Vallou-de-Villeneuve (1795–1856), a Romantic illustrator in the 1820s, turned to photography in the 1850s and produced numerous Italianate or Eastern-inspired genre scenes, portraits of Comédie-Française actors in the same vein, and a series of female nudes combining sensuality with solidity of construction. These were known to Gustave Courbet, who used one for his picture *The Painter's Studio* (fig. 562). In fact, it was precisely in order to replace the study of models or to avoid plagiarizing engravings that Eugène Delacroix became interested in nude photography in the early 1850s, getting Eugène Durieu (1800–1874) to make nude studies of men and women, from which he occasionally drew later (when not working directly from the life alongside the photographer).

The wet collodion process marked a temporary plateau in the development of techniques, as if the better to take possession of the forms of the visible world. For a while the process remained craft-based, but new techniques began to emerge. One of these was the albumen print, which replaced the various salt papers of the early years of photography, paving the way for an industrialization of the medium that was to be accomplished partly at the expense of visual creativity.

It was the use of albumen paper that spawned the great Parisian portrait studios, foremost among which was that of Nadar (real name Gaspard-Félix Tournachon, 1820–1910). Nadar was a product of a Romantic, bohemian environment. It was through the caricatures that he had been drawing for various papers since the 1840s that he was moved to take up photography. In 1853, he published an initial *Panthéon*, a vast lithograph incorporating a series of caricature portraits of contemporary writers, and in the following year he took his first photographic portraits, some of which he used for a new version of his *Panthéon*, including pictures of artists and musicians (1858). Some of the biggest names in literature and art passed through the tiny photographic studio in the Rue Saint-Lazare where Nadar exercised his craft, and most of them he received as friends, some even as intimates (figs. 156, 178). Encouraged by this success, in 1860 Nadar moved to a larger studio at 35, Boulevard des Capucines (Le Gray had a studio in the same building), where the first Impressionist exhibition would be held fourteen years later (1874). Production became more and more commercial as time went on, and Nadar's grand manner became bogged down in academicism. However, since this was just what his increasingly bourgeois clientele was looking for, the studio continued to operate into the 1930s under Paul Nadar, to whom from 1874 his father had given more and more production responsibility. What chiefly characterizes a Nadar portrait from the photographer's most creative period is a remarkable restraint, which not only brings out the personality and private nature of his model, but also captures their moral character. Nadar's work dispensed with both the natural setting of the amateur calotypist and the artificial, overdecorated setting of the professional studio. He preferred neutral backgrounds which concentrate attention on the model. The use during the Rue Saint-Lazare period of salt-paper prints, robust in their rendition of tone but slightly blurred when it came to producing and utilizing differently handled lights, gave the models a delicacy which enabled Nadar's work to escape the excessive "verism" that so offended Baudelaire in the photographic portrait. Apart from his individual portraits, Nadar also worked in collaboration with his brother Adrien Tournachon (1825–1903)—who was also gifted with a marvelous personal vision but who had a weaker personality—to produce a series of "expressive faces" with the mime Deburau (1854–55). Previously, he had collaborated with the Boulogne neurologist Guillaume Duchenne on his work on human physiognomy. Nadar was also responsible for a number of technical innovations. In 1861, he photographed the catacombs and sewers of Paris by electric light, and he also took a number of aerial photographs from the gondola of a balloon.

In contrast to the pared-down style of Nadar's portraits, that of Adam-Salomon (1811–1881) in the 1860s was more decorative. Adam-Salomon, a sculptor who had turned to photography, was influenced by Franz Hanfstaengl (1804–1877), photographer to the Bavarian royal family. In this transposition of the aristocratic portrait as practiced by such artists as van Dyck and Lawrence, elegant accessories were used to set off figures in elaborate compositions. Such pictures were very favorably received by the critics, as well as by middle-class people.

One of the largest bodies of work in French photography of the 1860s stemmed from a commission received by Charles Marville (1816–about 1879), a photographer who had already made a name for himself in the calotype period with poetic images of the banks of the Rhine, published by Blanquart-Évrard. Marville was requested by the City of Paris to document the old quarters that were doomed to disappear as a result of Haussmann's major urban renewal of Paris (fig. 169). In this enormous task Marville showed himself to be a master of the *veduta*, producing splendid compositions that are clearly and powerfully articulated. The spirit of realism in these documentary pictures, which is enhanced by the use of collodion and the albumen print, is nevertheless tempered by a softness of lighting that imbues them with a delicate poetry. In the series devoted to new street furniture, Marville had a way of isolating the object by means of a frontal approach free of any apparent subjectivity, managing in this way to set off these new forms powerfully by placing them in the context of a monumental vision. A similar spirit of modernity informs many of the pictures that Hyacinthe-César Delmaet (1828–1862) and Louis-Émile Durandelle (1839–1917) were commissioned by architect Charles Garnier to take of the construction of the new Opéra.

The photography of geographical and archaeological exploration was taken further by the work of an intrepid traveler called Désiré Charnay (1828–1915), who began by studying the cities and ruins of Mexico between 1857 and 1859. His pictures, which are given a fantastical quality by the luxuriance of the vegetation of hitherto virgin locations, were published in 1863 with a text by Viollet-le-Duc. By then Charnay was operating in Madagascar as part of France's colonial effort, producing more fine studies of tropical vegetation, as well as marvelous individual and group portraits of the island's different ethnic groups. It was in the same field of ethnographic reporting that sailor Paul-Émile Miot (1827–1900) distinguished himself with some sensitive portraits of Native Americans from the Micmac tribe (Arthur de Gobineau used these in his 1859 account of a journey to Newfoundland). Later on, in Tahiti and the Marquesas Islands (1869–70), his pictures of indigenous people captured the same qualities of majestic grace and melancholy as Paul Gauguin was to interpret twenty years later.

In the field of the still life, shortly before 1864 Charles Aubry (1811–1877) did a series of plant studies for drawing schools that put forward a new aesthetic approach to the photographic still life (fig. 190). By using extreme close-ups (which subjected shapes and textures to intense scrutiny), bold framing (sometimes cutting the motif off abruptly and doing astonishing things with solids and empty spaces), and often violent lighting, Aubry offered plastic solutions that were devoid of any painterly connotation, solutions that would be developed by some twentieth-century photographers. However, Aubry's pictures met with nothing like the fame enjoyed by Adolphe Braun's (1812–1877) "hunting trophies" in the late 1860s. An academic transposition of the paintings of such artists as Jean-Baptiste Oudry and François Desportes, these huge decorative plates, designed to adorn the walls of ceremonial dining rooms, are nevertheless fascinating to our eyes by virtue of their meticulous rendition of textures.

GREAT BRITAIN: HOBBY PHOTOGRAPHERS AND THE PICTORIAL MODEL (1855–80)

Lewis Carroll (fig. 194), Julia Margaret Cameron (figs. 187, 188, 193, 195), and Lady Hawarden (fig. 186) dominated British photography in the years following the age of the pioneers. They provided the most admirable examples of a lyricism that was peculiar to the sensibility of the Victorian era. Their work, innocent of any documentary intention, largely centered on representing the female figure, which they captured with an astonishing degree of plasticity in poses that owed much to religious and theatrical convention.

Completely forgotten until its rediscovery by Helmut Gernsheim shortly after World War II, the work of Lewis Carroll (real name Charles Dodgson, 1832–1898) would be of the very first importance even if it had not sprung from the imagination of a man the whole world knows as a writer of genius. That fact, of course, lends an additional dimension to an oeuvre that does indeed bear genuine comparison with the man's literary achievement. Carroll's diary is evidence of how important a part of his life was the practice of photography between 1855 and 1880. While he produced some fine portraits of adults, such as those of Rossetti and his family, Millais, and Southey, his true world was that of childhood, and more especially that of little girls, which he conveyed with a disturbingly poetic clarity, often using very bold framings. Some of his portraits of little girls were attempts to capture truthfully attitude and gesture; many of them have a theatrical quality, with the models dressed up and placed in scenic poses. At other times, the models are lying down with their eyes closed, immersed in sleep or reverie (recurrent themes in Carroll's work). Obsessional in many respects, the photographic work of Lewis Carroll constitutes a remarkable example, in the nineteenth century, of the use of photography to give expression to a fantasy world.

Julia Margaret Cameron (1815–1879) discovered photography quite late in life when, in 1863, her family gave her a camera obscura. She threw herself into her new hobby, and in the sixteen years remaining to her she virtually turned the medium upside down. Her art, which was highly literary, looked back to the past in some ways but with a stylistic conception and a boldness of framing that also looked forward to cinematography. Above all, she was a splendid portraitist, with her solemn likenesses of such figures as Tennyson, Browning, Carlyle, Watts, Holman Hunt, Woolner, Joachim, and Herschel. Most of these portraits are half-length, with the faces emerging powerfully. Some are more blurred than others, but all are bathed in a light (occasionally chiaroscuro) that blends marvelously with the collodion material. Cameron's portraits of women and children and, above all, her groups of figures usually involve a religious allegory of some kind, whether classical or Christian, but here too her framings are extraordinarily innovative. In this respect, her illustrations for *Idylls of the King and Other Poems* by Tennyson are masterpieces in a field that would seem scarcely to be the province of photography, namely fiction and legend. Cameron's photography is not unrelated spiritually to Pre-Raphaelite painting, though its greater concentration of style and her use of the blurred image differ from the brotherhood's very precise manner. Her true references came from fifteenth- and sixteenth-century Italian art, in particular Raphael, and to a lesser degree Michelangelo. Her genius as an artist lay in this cultivation of the sublime, which firmly turned its back on modern life but which she nevertheless employed revolutionary photographic means to re-create.

The world of Lady Clementina Maude Hawarden (1822–1865) was even narrower than Lewis Carroll's, being virtually confined to portraying her daughters, and their emergence into womanhood. In these variations on a single theme, we find figures treated with a magisterial feeling for light. Hawarden likewise draws us into the world of fiction and theatricality, though her poses are often excuses for visual effects rather than illustrations of allegories (to which, unlike Cameron, she provides no clues). An apologia for female grace, intense emotion, and sensuality, her work is sometimes tinged with a discreet eroticism.

Mention should also be made here of a practice that was not uncommon among hobby photographers in Victorian society: that of keeping personal albums containing collaged fragments of photographs combined with drawings or watercolors. Anticipating the type of collage practiced by the Surrealists, the burlesque poetry of such assemblages is evidence of the feeling for nonsense so dear to that society.

British professional photography of a documentary nature saw an extension of distant explorations with the activities of Francis Frith (1822–1898), who worked in Egypt in 1858 before he started publishing topographic images taken by his fellow photographers in Europe, India, and the East. Robert MacPherson (1811–1872) displayed an unusual lyricism in his photographs. These were studies of Italian cities, and in particular the monuments of ancient and modern Rome, and the landscapes of the Roman Campagna. The Scot Thomas Annan

(1828–1888) was commissioned by the authorities in Glasgow to make a record (like Marville's in Paris) prior to the destruction of the old quarters of the city (1868–77), which he did with remarkable formal rigor.

Finally, there were two other professional photographers at this time, whose work is of particular interest. Both had a painterly conception of photography and both enjoyed enormous fame in their day. Their work demonstrates how photography moved toward Pictorialism at the end of the century and provides an important indication of popular taste.

Oscar Gustav Rejlander (1813–1875), who was of Swedish origin, studied painting in Rome and settled in England as a portraitist in 1840. He became interested in photography in 1852 and in 1857 he exhibited a huge composition combining thirty negatives. *The Two Paths of Life*, a moralizing pastiche of painting, was purchased by Queen Victoria and made the artist famous. Rejlander experimented with different types of combinations of images, notably superposition of negatives (another major innovation that prefigured the investigations of the Surrealists). Although as a photographer of portraits and genre scenes, Rejlander stuck to the painterly model and pursued a moral purpose, he occasionally demonstrated real sensitivity. In fact, this ambiguous artist was responsible for some delightful surprises: the double portrait of Mr. and Miss Constable (1866), for example, could be a still from an American movie of the 1940s, and a work such as *The Dream* (1860) is striking today for the modernity of its pre-psychoanalysis image and the freedom of its erotic allusions (fig. 176).

Henry Peach Robinson (1830–1901), who also trained as a painter and studied literature, opened a portrait studio in 1857. In the following year he produced *Fading Away* (fig. 177), the preliminary version of which (accompanied by lines from Shakespeare's *Twelfth Night*) is bathed in a fine chiaroscuro, while for the final version (this time illustrating a poem by Shelley) he combined five negatives to place the girl in the bosom of her weeping family. In 1861 Robinson exhibited *The Lady of Shalott* (fig. 184), which illustrates a Tennyson poem and was largely inspired by Millais's painting *Ophelia* (1852, fig. 17). He went on working in this way until the end of the century, producing rustic landscapes and interiors with figures that were also, for the most part, the product of combinations of images. These genre scenes are excessively graceful and composed too cleverly. They are imbued with phony naivety and stuffed with anecdote, yet they earned Robinson enormous popularity and won him many medals. His book *Pictorial Effect in Photography*, first published in 1869, went through ten editions in Britain and eventually appeared in a French translation (1885). He undoubtedly influenced an initial wave of French Pictorialism, which was dominated by an identical conception of the genre scene. Robinson, however, cannot be regarded as the sole father of Pictorialism: Peter Henry Emerson was equally important, and his work and theoretical writings possessed a quite different dimension.

THE RISE OF AMERICAN PHOTOGRAPHY (1860–80)

Two historical events helped photography in America to develop rapidly, both as art and as a form of documentary. These were the Civil War and the conquest of the West.

Civil War Photography (1861–65)

Mathew Brady (1823–1896), who headed the largest photographic studio in the country at the time, played a pioneering role in setting up the photographic campaign that accompanied this war. In 1860 he photographed Lincoln and then his investiture as president of the United States in Washington, D.C. In the following year his studios covered the first military expedition of the Union army, culminating in the Battle of Bull Run. Brady also purchased pictures by independent photographers, eventually accumulating some five thousand images of the war, which he exhibited or sold to the collecting public or to newspapers under his own name, though only rarely were they his own pictures. In fact, he was more an agency head and commissioning agent than a hands-on practitioner. Among the many photographers whose service Brady was clever enough to secure for his campaign, three names stand out: Alexander Gardner, Timothy O'Sullivan, and George Barnard. Alexander Gardner (1821–1882) was regarded in his day as "the greatest artist" among the Civil War photographers. Spotting his mastery of the technique of the glass negative using wet collodion (ideal for the making and mass distribution of such reports), which was just beginning to take hold in the United States, Brady put him in charge of his Washington, D.C., studio in 1858, so that Gardner was led quite naturally to follow the opening battles of the war. Fed up with receiving no official recognition for what was his own work, Gardner left Brady's employ and in 1862 enlisted with the Army of the Potomac as its photographer, opening his own gallery in Washington, D.C., in the following year. Out of a total of 3,000 pictures, of which he had taken about 150 himself, Gardner selected 100 plates printed by himself and published them as a portfolio in 1866. He called it *The Photographic Sketchbook of the War.* When he left Brady, he had taken Brady's best photographers with him, including Timothy O'Sullivan (1840–1882), a New Yorker of Irish descent (fig. 191). Between them, they gave their coverage of the Civil War a determinedly modern character that was in stark contrast to Fenton's grand but more static, more painterly interpretation of the Crimean War. The scenes of day-to-day army life in the camps look much more as if they were photographed in real-life situations, with a greater concern to capture the decisive, historical moment. Many have a "snapshot" feel to the framing that would not have displeased Degas, for example. Gardner also took some of the most striking pictures of Lincoln, his face lined with care, and others, no less poignant, of the men who had plotted to assassinate the president (the latter were also photographed in 1865, while they were awaiting execution). Deeply involved in that fratricidal conflict, Gardner and O'Sullivan adopted what was then the very new approach of stressing the ghastliness rather than the triumphal aspect of war, including large numbers of shots like O'Sullivan's *A Harvest of Death,* taken after the Battle of Gettysburg (1863). This concern for truth, which we find fascinating, was not popular at the time. After the war especially, Brady had a great deal of trouble persuading Congress to buy his pictures. People wanted to forget. George N. Barnard (1819–1902), whom both Brady and Gardner had employed, published his own portfolio in 1866. Entitled *Photographic Views of Sherman's Campaign,* this marked a very convincing return to the mythic, heroic character of major accounts of battles. His grand compositions are distinguished by a remarkable depth of field. In fact, the newspapers of the day were careful to draw attention to the aesthetic qualities of these pictures detailing the destruction visited on the Southern states.

The Exploration of the West

Between 1867 and 1875, a large number of government-backed missions were detailed to make a census of the new territories of the West, recently annexed by the Union. Although undeniably a response to economic and even military concerns, such expeditions were also inspired by disinterested scientific curiosity, notably in regard to geology. There was often also an almost mystical desire to celebrate the nature and soil of America, fostered by the writings of three great authors who represented the idealistic side of this young country: Ralph Waldo Emerson, Henry Thoreau, and Walt Whitman. The rapid development of landscape painting from about 1850 through the work of artists such as Albert Bierstadt and Thomas Moran was an initial expression of this. When such artists accompanied photographers on geographical expeditions, occasionally taking photographs themselves, they were looking for virgin locations. The photographers followed their example.

The landscapists of the West had artistic ambitions far loftier than the production of the stereoscopic views that appeared as early as 1850 in the eastern part of the country. Carleton E. Watkins (1829–1916) was originally from the east coast but had moved to San Francisco in 1851, where he was soon joined by many other photographers. In 1861 he decided to record the most interesting locations and tree species in the Yosemite Valley, which had been discovered in 1856. No doubt taking his inspiration from the great views of Egypt captured with the same technique (wet collodion on glass) by Briton Francis Frith in 1857, Watkins became the first American to work with these quite large negatives, which were of course ideal for such imposing landscapes (they soon came to be dubbed "mammoth"). His plates caused a sensation. The pictures Watkins took are permeated by a Romantic feeling for the sublime not unrelated to the American landscape painting of the era, though they give an incontrovertibly photographic version of such art, distinguished by a masterly treatment of space and atmosphere. These qualities improved further over the years, and in 1866 Watkins returned to Yosemite, this time on a geological expedition to the valley, which in 1864 Congress had decided to turn into a national park. The first director of the park was Josiah D. Witney, a great admirer of Watkins. In 1867 the photographer's Yosemite views were exhibited in Paris as part of the 1867 Exposition Universelle, and in 1868 Whitney published (in a limited edition of 250 copies, distributed among various top politicians and sold to members of the public) *The Yosemite Book*, containing fifty plates by Watkins. No less remarkable are Watkins's views of Oregon, which he visited that same year in the company of painter William Keith, and his photographs of the Californian coast. For the latter, he tackled highly picturesque subjects with great inventiveness.

This was also one of the principal qualities of Timothy O'Sullivan, a photographer who was misunderstood by contemporaries but is now regarded as the most modern of this whole school (fig. 191). It was O'Sullivan that the young geologist Clarence King (a great Watkins fan) asked to accompany him as the official photographer on the U.S. Geological Survey of the 40th Parallel, between the Sierra Nevada and the Rockies. Financed by the War Department, the expedition lasted from 1867 to 1869. In 1871–73, O'Sullivan signed up for another geological expedition west of the 100th meridian (a particularly difficult route that involved, among other things, crossing Death Valley). This expedition was headed by Lieutenant George M. Wheeler, whose objectives were primarily of a military order. Nevertheless, he left O'Sullivan free to organize his work as he saw fit. It is impossible not to admire the patience and brilliance with which, in these two assignments, the photographer contrived to be the first to bring out the harsh beauty and sheer telluric power contained in those hostile desert places, the ingenuity with which he fitted each composition into the horizontal frame of his viewfinder, and his great economy of graphic means. Another notable aspect of O'Sullivan's work was the way in which he would highlight certain everyday details—something which later came to typify a particular kind of modern American art.

Andrew Joseph Russell (1830–1902), who like O'Sullivan worked for Gardner during the Civil War, was also misunderstood in his day. His pictures of the construction of new railroads show in a similar way that the constraints of an objective, precise photographic vision could, in a true artist, engender aesthetic originality.

Eadweard J. Muybridge (1830–1904) deliberately set out to rival Watkins. In 1867 and 1872 he took some fifty large photographs of Yosemite Valley. These remarkable shots, more stylized and pictorial in conception than those of Watkins, were the product of certain tricks of technique, such as using a mask to correct effects of light in the viewfinder, and employing two negatives, one for the clouds, the other for the landscape. These landscapes, with their dramatic chiaroscuro effects and occasionally vertiginous viewpoints, somewhat unjustly eclipsed those of Watkins. They also drew particular comment at the 1873 international exhibition in Vienna, where the work of O'Sullivan, for example, went unnoticed.

Likewise attracted by the landscape of the West, William Henry Jackson (1843–1942) began working for himself, following the line of the Union Pacific railroad. He subsequently signed up (as a volunteer, at first) with the geological and geographic expedition that F. V. Hayden led into Wyoming and Colorado between 1870 and 1873. This enabled him to improve both his technique and his conception of landscape, partly through contact with such painters as Sanford Robinson Gifford and Thomas Moran, who were also members of the expedition. It was during this expedition that he took his imposing views of the geysers and hot springs of Wyoming. We have Jackson to thank for some very interesting studies of Native Americans living in the caves of Canyon de Chelly in 1875 (O'Sullivan took some superb photographs of the same caves at about the same time) as well as of the Hopi tribe in their pueblos. Jackson subsequently settled in Denver in 1879 and returned to the kind of commercial photography he had done originally.

The heroic era of the first major exploratory expeditions was over, an era when photographers, despite needing to perform some dangerous physical exploits, were free to follow their own inspiration without having to worry about selling their work. In future, if they did not want to go bankrupt (which is what happened to Watkins), photographers would have to take account of popular taste, and the public was more interested in reproductions of spectacularly picturesque locations that were already famous.

In the eastern United States, the tradition of reports on the railroads or series covering great natural sights in the form of portfolios of outsize plates was to continue until the end of the century. Two notable exponents were William Hermann Rau (1855–1920) of Philadelphia, who from 1890 was associated with the Pennsylvania Railroad Company, and George Barker, who produced a famous series on the Niagara Falls about 1888. We can also include in the context of the exploration of the landscape of North America the huge and imposing views of Stanley Park, a natural park near Vancouver, taken about 1888 by the Scottish studio of William MacFarlane Notman and Sons of Montreal. One of these served as a model for a painting by Bierstadt entitled *Hunting Scene.*

As for ethnographic studies, particularly of Native Americans, these were to receive a major boost at the turn of the century. The ambitions of Los Angeles librarian Adam Clark Vroman (1856–1916) were infinitely more modest than those of Edward Sheriff Curtis (1868–1952), but the photographs he took between 1895 and 1904, some of which were published in volume form, reveal a remarkable sincerity and sense of composition. Curtis used platinum prints, which are distinguished by an intense luminosity coupled with exquisite delicacy. Vroman's vision looks much more modern to our eyes than that of Curtis, who studied the native civilization of North America at the turn of the century for a sumptuous publication funded by Pierpont Y. Morgan. Although Curtis took a more Pictorialist approach, the grandeur of this project is undeniable.

COMMERCIAL AND SCIENTIFIC PHOTOGRAPHY (1870–80)

The development of photography in these years did not favor artistic creation. Photographers very soon realized that they could not live by their art, and they tried to organize themselves into commercial studios, increasingly taking account of what the public wanted. Gone was the era of the great "primitives," men and women who were deeply involved in their work and prepared their negatives and made their prints like craftsmen. Technical progress, which during these years accelerated in all directions, also contributed to the industrialization of photography and the standardization of materials. Wet collodion negatives were replaced about 1872–74 by dry collodion plates—and about 1880 by plates using silver-bromide gelatin, which were sold ready for use. Prints on albumen paper, which already represented a major step toward uniformity in comparison with prints on salt paper, were between 1867 and 1880 replaced in their turn by papers for positive prints that were again preprepared, ready to use.

However, this simplification of techniques also had its advantages. Although the photographer capable of tackling all genres became a thing of the past, in certain sectors, where demand was assured and where photographers were required to exercise ingenuity, some remarkable work was done. The photography of civil engineering, which had always been encouraged in France by such official institutions as the École Nationale des Ponts and received a boost from the celebration of this type of architecture at the time of the 1889 Exposition Universelle, remained at a consistently high level. In medicine, too, where photography was practiced by such doctors as Paul Régnard, Désiré-Magloire Bourneville (1840–1909), and Albert Londe (1858–1917), some astonishing results were achieved, as in the study of hysteria carried out by Professor Jean-Martin Charcot (1825–1893) at La Salpêtrière Hospital in Paris, which produced some exciting, highly theatrical images. Progress in the field of the snapshot produced a veritable explosion of social reportage in every country, from Britain and France to Poland and Russia. But nowhere do we find more accomplished examples than in the studies undertaken by two American photographers of the turn of the century, Jacob Riis and Lewis Hine. Although they were the product of a systematic approach, their pictures nevertheless display marvelous sensitivity. Jacob August Riis (1849–1914) began as a reporter for the New York Police Department, assigned to the city's Lower East Side. Using a flashbulb (invented in Germany in 1887), he investigated the slum tenements in the neighborhood, inhabited by Jewish, Italian, Chinese, and African-American communities, or occupied by gangsters or criminals (fig. 207). Riis published some of the resulting pictures in his book *How the Other Half Lives* (1890). No less striking are the pictures taken some years later by Lewis Wickes Hine (1874–1940). Hine first turned his attention to the thousands of poor immigrants disembarking at New York's Ellis Island in 1905. He photographed not only their arrival, but also the wretched housing and miserable jobs they were offered. From 1907, the National Child Labor Committee employed Hine to investigate the exploitation of children in factories.

About 1867–68, by extending physicist Antoine Becquerel's research into the solar spectrum, Charles Cros (1842–1888) and Louis Ducos du Hauron (1837–1920) succeeded independently in achieving color photography, using the principle of three-color selection. But it was mainly through the process known as "autochrome," invented in 1904 by the brothers Auguste (1865–1954) and Louis (1864–1948) Lumière and marketed in the form of direct positive plates. As a result of this invention, color photography came to be widely practiced by large numbers of photography enthusiasts at the turn of the century. Some of those enthusiasts became known by joining painting societies and having their autochromes exhibited in public. In France, one of the most outstanding was a collector of Impressionist and Post-Impressionist paintings by the name of Antonin Personnaz (1854–1936), who produced some very fine landscapes largely inspired by the kinds of painting he championed. Others who should be mentioned were the Austrian Heinrich Kühn, a master of the still life, and, in the United States, Alfred Stieglitz, Edward Steichen, and Alvin Langdon Coburn, who preferred to use the process for portraits (see pp. 297–98).

In the photographic exhibitions of the day, the results of these many inventions of photography were proudly hung alongside commercial photography, for exhibitors only had to pay in order to be able to take part. A system of medals rewarded the wonders of photographic technology. Back in the early 1850s, photographers had fought hard to have their pictures exhibited not as industrial products, as happened in the context of international exhibitions; they wanted a separate annual or biennial *salon d'art.* In 1859 they got their way with the creation of the Salon Photographique in the Palais de l'Industrie, near the fine arts exhibition. Paradoxically, however, once the new institution had been created (and had been reviewed by Philippe Burty in *La Gazette des Beaux-Arts* of that same year), aesthetic criticism of photography disappeared from the specialist press, which began to concentrate increasingly on problems of technique and practical application. It was to prevent photography from being swallowed up in this way by science, commerce, and industry that a number of amateur photographers rebelled. They were keen to put the accent back on the photographer's vision. Taking full advantage of the technical advances that had been made in photography, they wanted to go further and restore the notion of photographic creation.

PHOTOGRAPHING THE INSTANTANEOUS

Even before the techniques had been perfected making it possible to freeze movement, photographers had contrived in certain works to create that illusion. But it was in the commercial stereoscopic view that the earliest examples of truly instantaneous photography occurred. These were pictures taken from a very high viewpoint, showing the movements of crowds on the Paris boulevards. Using a lens with a very short focal length enabled photographers to make a clear record with a sufficiently brief exposure time to capture movement, but this could only be done on a very small surface, with the object photographed very far away. Tiny silhouettes of passers-by and carriages were enlarged under a magnifying glass and reproduced in British, French, and American journals to enable people to study these attitudes taken from the life and, so it seemed, of a naturalness never before observed. In particular, they gave the painters and art critics of the naturalistic movement something to think about. These pictures of boulevards teeming with figures, which were published in their thousands by such specialists as the Frenchman Hippolyte Jouvin, the American Edward Anthony, and the Scot George Washington Wilson, bring to mind Edmond Duranty's book *La Nouvelle Peinture* (1876), in which the author set out very precisely what was required of the painter of modern life: "We no longer separate the figure from the background of the interior or the background of the street; it never appears to us, in life, against neutral, empty, vague backgrounds."

Some photographers were keen to pursue these investigations into movement to their logical conclusion. The Polish photographer Ottomar Antschütz (1846–1907), using a purpose-built camera, took some amazing sequences in 1884 of the flight of swans, which artists collected. Antschütz then photographed human movement. But Eadweard Muybridge had not only got there before him (having constructed one of the first automatic shutters in 1869); he went a lot further.

Muybridge began studying the trotting and galloping of horses in 1872, when railroad magnate Leland Stanford hired him to prove that a trotting horse had all four feet off the ground at the same time. His investigations came to fruition in 1877. Using first one, then a dozen, then twenty-four flashlight cameras whose shutters were progressively triggered as the horse advanced, Muybridge was able to photograph the various positions of the animal's legs as it trotted or galloped. He subsequently made a similar study of a man walking. The resulting pictures, published in *The Scientific American* in October 1878 and afterward in the French journal *La Nature,* caused a sensation. In the following year the painter Thomas Eakins (no mean photographer himself) painted *A May Morning in the Park,* a work that was directly inspired by these discoveries, and invited Muybridge to come and lecture at the Pennsylvania Academy of Arts. As a result, Muybridge obtained funding from the university that enabled him to continue his work. By this time he had replaced the collodion negative (capable only of representing silhouettes) by gelatin-bromide plates, which revealed all the details of bodies and their musculature. In 1887 Muybridge published eleven portfolios of something like eight hundred superb plates using a photomechanical process known as collotype. Entitled *Animal Locomotion* and *Human Locomotion,* these portfolios analyzed the movements of all kinds of animals, as well as humans, both male and female, photographed performing various activities, some sporting, some not. Not only scientists but large numbers of painters in the United States, Britain, France, and Germany had subscribed to these publications. Muybridge was invited to France in 1881 and subsequently to Britain to present his discoveries to artists, all of whom (from Degas to Meissonier) drew inspiration from them. Avant-garde artists, however (Symbolists in particular), were careful to keep their distance from such scientific discoveries, which, for all that they stated the objective truth, were not necessarily more expressive in artistic terms. That was what Rodin felt, too, although the sculptor had subscribed to Muybridge's publications.

In order to re-create animal movements in temporal sequence—and thus prove that his breakdown of them was accurate—Muybridge developed in 1800 the zoopraxiscope or zoogiroscope, a rotating cylinder on which the photographs were mounted. This device created the illusion of moving pictures and was thus a predecessor of motion pictures, invented by Thomas Edison (1847–1931), with his Kinetophonograph (1889), and the brothers Auguste (1865–1954) and Louis (1864–1948) Lumière with their *cinématographe* (1895).

The work of French scientist Étienne-Jules Marey (1830–1904) had provided the intermediate stage that paved the way for cinema. Extending Muybridge's early investigations, in 1882 Marey had built his chrono-photographic rifle, which made it possible to reconstitute, on a single plate, a series of successive movements that he could then model in three dimensions by means of sculpture (figs. 197, 198). However, what Marey particularly set out to study was the principle of movement itself. By dressing his models (whom he photographed against a black background) in black body-suits, with only a white line and white dots indicating the skeleton and joints, he obtained abstract graphic configurations that were to have considerable impact in the years about 1910. Marcel Duchamp and the Italian Futurists later elevated the very notions of speed and movement into symbols of their art.

AMATEUR PHOTOGRAPHY FROM 1880

As we have seen, the early discoveries of truly instantaneous photography primarily benefited painters such as Degas and Caillebotte, but this influence was short-lived. In photography, on the other hand, the snapshot was to enjoy a long history, even if photographers were slower to exploit it artistically than the painters had been. The first nonscientific photographers to explore its artistic potential in the final years of the nineteenth century were amateurs.

In the 1880s, increasing technical simplification and the fact that cameras were becoming ever lighter and more portable brought the practice of photography within virtually everyone's reach. Undoubtedly the most revolutionary invention was George Eastman's Kodak camera, developed between 1883 and 1889. This handheld appliance was soon available ready-loaded with negatives on industrially manufactured flexible film that cut exposure times to one-fiftieth of a second. Amateur photographers everywhere began recording their own everyday lives, featuring family and friends. Preserved at George Eastman House in Rochester are some striking examples of photographs taken by unknown amateurs using Kodak cameras about 1889. In these pictures, the ephemeral grace of movement is suggested with a confidence reminiscent of the paintings Degas was producing in the 1870s; indeed one might almost, in this connection, speak of a veritable snapshot style. Yet for all that, such pictures are fairly rare from this period. What emerges from any study of this mass of photographic material is the perception that amateurs were not in fact very good at taking snapshots; if their prints do occasionally have a poignant quality, it is for other reasons. In fact it was among painters and writers (who likewise took up the new and fashionable plaything and who were naturally preoccupied with problems of style and expression) that the most successful snapshots are to be found in the 1890s—successful, that is, from an aesthetic point of view. What distinguishes them is the way the viewer is introduced into the very heart of the scene, created by means of an asymmetrical composition, with figures cropped in close-up, and occasionally deliberate blurring. Count Giuseppe Primoli (1851–1927) was the first in this field, and most of his snapshots, from as early as 1888, are remarkable for their bold framing, liveliness, and humor. He photographed not only the famous (Edgar Degas emerging from a urinal, the actress Réjane strolling along a Paris street [1889], Annie Oakley on her trained mount in Rome [1895]), but also anonymous circus acrobats and ordinary folk in the streets of Italian towns. Exhibiting at the Photo-club de Paris in 1895, Primoli stressed his artistic aspirations. Even in the case of a painter such as George Hendrik Breitner, who was not particularly avant-garde, the street scenes he took around him in Rotterdam or Amsterdam or the shots he took in his studio, featuring models or cats, are bursting with life and energy. Breitner practiced photography in parallel to his work as a painter (he took more than 2,500 photographs), regarding it as an equally creative activity. Toulouse-Lautrec set up numerous self-portraits, appearing in disguise in most of them; his friends Maurice Guibert and Maurice Joyant did the actual photography and printing. These are bold, amusing images, full of self-mockery.

The photographs that the Nabis Bonnard and Vuillard produced assiduously for more than a decade have similar qualities to their painting, in particular the same original approach to composition and the same dancing grace in the depiction of figures. In his illustrations for Ambroise Vollard (*Parallèlement* and *Daphnis et Chloé*), Bonnard repeated literally certain highly poetic nudes of his companion Marthe and himself (fig. 204). Like Vuillard, although to a lesser extent, he also drew directly on his photographs for his paintings.

The photographs taken by Degas (better known because of the texts that the artist himself and his circle devoted to them) are a slightly different case. Degas only started practicing photography regularly in 1895, well after he had created his most "photographic" style in painting, and furthermore he did not use the latest equipment. What particularly interested Degas was recording interiors composed in the manner of nocturnes and photographed by artificial light. The theme attracted him over and over again and is reminiscent of some of his paintings (*Rape*, for example) or his monotype series. Meanwhile, he continued to study the movements of dancers and of women at their toilet, and some of the photographs of this type (among the most striking, in fact) clearly provided inspiration for certain late canvases and pastels.

The recently rediscovered photographic work of the Japanese-influenced wood engraver Henri Rivière (1864–1951) is of great interest (fig. 209). Rivière put together various series (on life in the Montmartre district of Paris or on Breton peasants) that were directly related to his illustrations for the Chat Noir shadow theater of his own invention. Indeed, one particular series from 1889, devoted to the construction of the Eiffel Tower, then nearing completion, is so boldly radical in its framing that, with its confusion of subject and style, it stands comparison with the work of Alexander Rodchenko, for example. From 1900 the painter Alfons Mucha (1860–1939) took photographs of models intended to serve as sketches for his paintings. Photographed in exotically decorated interiors, these pictures are not true snapshots, but the framings used and the graceful poses of the women re-create the decorative curves typifical of Art Nouveau. Another draftsman and lithographer who drew inspiration from his own photographs for his graphic output was the German Heinrich Zille (1858–1929; fig. 206). Zille, who worked mainly outdoors, was as interested in the curves of the dynamic silhouettes of a group of boys tumbling down a slope as he was in the graffiti scrawled on a fence (figs. 222, 223). The writer Émile Zola, who loved to repeat "We only see properly what we photograph," took four thousand photographs from 1899, covering a wide range of subjects. Many of the pictures featuring the 1900 Exposition Universelle in Paris or the streets of Rome, where he lived while writing a book about the Italian capital, are related to Impressionism, which he had so effectively championed. Another body of work deserving a place in this rapid survey is that of Jacques-Henri Lartigue (1894–1986), an amateur painter and snapshot photographer of genius. Lartigue was also unusually precocious—some of the family scenes taken when he was eight years old are already impeccably stylish. There were many other artists and writers who, at the turn of the century, took a passionate if passing interest in this mechanical art. These included Edvard Munch and August Strindberg, whose striking examples of instantaneous photography evoke the dark, tormented minds of the men who took them.

THE PICTORIALIST MOVEMENT IN EUROPE AND THE UNITED STATES

Photographic technique was now reaching maturity, so it was natural that attention should turn to content, namely the photographer's vision. Also, the size of the public that photography now reached was to lend fresh weight to the preoccupations of a new breed of amateur.

The recognition of photography benefited greatly from changes taking place at that time in the organization of artistic life—notably, in France, with the rejection of the Académie des Beaux-Arts and its hierarchy in favor of a fusion of the arts embracing painting, sculpture, architecture, and decoration. It was no accident that painters who were interested in photography also practiced poster art, wood engraving, and embroidery. The fact was, the mechanical arts were no longer regarded as inferior. Following the example of painters and decorative artists, Pictorialist photographers in Europe and the United States proceeded to come together in free associations or clubs destined to take over from official bodies in championing the cause of art photography.

The movement began in Great Britain, the cradle of non-documentary, non-commercial art photography. Peter Henry Emerson (1856–1936) is today regarded as one of the fathers of Pictorialism, even though, because of his uncompromising nature and his indifference to honors, he was not intimately involved in the official development of the movement he had inspired. A doctor by training, Emerson decided to give up his medical career shortly after acquiring his first camera in 1880. From then on he devoted himself to photography. From the outset, he associated with a group of English naturalistic painters, spending ten years with painter Thomas Frederick Goodall, sharing the life of the peasants and fishermen of East Anglia. He published the resulting pictures in a dozen publications, in which the text was seen as complementing the photographs rather than vice versa. Strictly speaking, however, this was not reportage so much as an act of homage, the kind of tribute that painter Jean-François Millet (of whom Emerson was a great admirer) had paid to the people of the French countryside. Like his hero, Emerson contrived to invest his subjects' movements and rituals with a quality of timeless, monumental gravity. His first and quite brilliant work, *Life and Landscape of the Norfolk Broads*, appeared in 1886. It was illustrated with forty original prints made by Emerson or under his supervision. These were made on platinum paper, a new, sophisticated, and highly stable printing process that enabled Emerson to obtain the kind of low contrast, transparent shadow, and subtle gradation of values that he saw as essential if nature was not to be traduced. The printing of an edition of about three hundred copies involved so much work that in future Emerson employed heliogravure from original negatives (a technique that would also be favored by the Pictorialist photographers, who were keen that their elitist art should nevertheless receive wide distribution). *Marsh Leaves*, which was published in 1895 and represents the summit of Emerson's art, marks a development. Here his peasants have given way to a series of rural landscapes, and naturalism has been replaced by a kind of Impressionistic poetry (Emerson also admired the painting of Monet) that occasionally verges on the abstract, influenced as it was by Japanese art. Emerson's interest in Whistler had been growing steadily since 1887, and he also acknowledged the influence of an exhibition of prints by Hokusai. Emerson's work was widely distributed abroad and was accorded a major retrospective in London (1900). He wrote an important book (*Naturalistic Photography*, 1889) setting out his views, but it was through his photographs that he exerted most influence.

In professing his debt to painters from Corot to Whistler while fiercely defending the integrity of the technique of photography, in encouraging the use of platinum paper or heliogravure, and especially in recommending a method of focusing that was neither too sharp nor too detailed (according to him, it corresponded to the natural vision of the eye), Emerson laid down the broad principles of the Pictorialist movement. A sworn enemy of any kind of photographic manipulation other than chemical, Emerson represented the purist wing of Pictorialism, which was in turn to give birth to the "modern" photography of the twentieth century.

It was not in London but in Vienna, in 1891, that a great admirer of Emerson, Baron Alfred von Liebig, organized the first exhibition of photographs where the works were selected by a jury of six painters and sculptors (600 were chosen out of 4,000 submitted). Two years later, the British Linked Ring Brotherhood, a breakaway movement from the Photograph Society that had formed in 1892 around Henry Peach Robinson and Emerson emulator George Davison (1854–1930), started annual exhibitions, which they called salons and which obeyed the same principle of selection. For the journal *The Studio*, this was the sign that the battle for recognition of photography as a means of artistic expression had finally been won. Also in 1893, the director of the Hamburg Kunsthalle inaugurated an exhibition of photographic portraits from which commercial likenesses, composed according to conventional formulas, were excluded. In the following year, Robert Demachy (1859–1936) opened the first "Exhibition of Photographic Art" at Durand-Ruel's gallery in Paris, with a jury comprising four painters, a sculptor, an engraver, an art critic, and a national inspector of fine arts. In the United

States, the city of Philadelphia played a pioneering role in establishing the Pictorialist movement. Between 1884 and 1894, exhibitions organized on the British model but international in character were held annually in New York, Philadelphia, and Boston, bringing together the work of both professional and amateur photographers. In 1898, the Philadelphia Fine Arts Academy, working in conjunction with the city's Photographic Society, held its first annual exhibition devoted to Pictorialist photography (300 were shown from 1,500 submitted). The city of Chicago then organized its own exhibition along the same lines.

Alfred Stieglitz (1884–1946) personally took up the baton from 1899, when he became president of the Camera Club of New York, which grew in part out of the Society for Amateur Photographers, founded in 1884. It was also Stieglitz who created the Photo-Secession group in 1903 to encourage the emergence of an American Pictorialist school.

All these societies produced catalogs and journals lavishly illustrated with photogravures or halftones. There was *Photogramms of the Year,* an organ of the Linked Ring Brotherhood, and the particularly sumptuous and sophisticated publications of the Photo-club de Paris, *La Revue de photographie, L'Art photographique* (cover design by Alfons Mucha), and *Esthétique de la photographie.* America had *Camera Notes,* a short-lived journal with a cover inspired by the decorative art of William Morris, and above all Alfred Stieglitz's *Camera Work* (1903–17), the most perfect, most complete, and most avant-garde journal of them all. All these publications contained lengthy debates about the various aesthetic conceptions of the art of photography and how it related to the other arts, either by photographers themselves, such as George Davison, Frederick Evans (1853–1943), Robert Demachy, Alfred Stieglitz, and Edward Steichen, or by such art critics as the Frenchman Robert de la Sizeranne and the American Charles Caffin. The latter contributed to *Camera Work* with the Bostonian Sadakichi Hartmann (he was Japanese on his mother's side), a great connoisseur of Impressionist and Symbolist art, and Japanese prints.

Pictorialism was an international movement. Although Pictorialists all shared the same basic beliefs (never to commercialize their work and to shun trivial reality and documentary preoccupations), each country had its distinguishing characteristics. On the whole, European photographers, with the exception of Britons, tended to use markedly pictorial techniques, treating photographic prints like original graphic prints. Such techniques were based on the use of products of organic origin, such as gum bichromate or oily inks on two-color gelatin. The Pictorialists enjoyed experimenting with all kinds of recipes, occasionally combining different processes.

French Pictorialists used those techniques in a particularly delicate way, as can be seen in the work of Robert Demachy (fig. 214) and Constant Puyo (1857–1933). Demachy, who came from a wealthy banking family, was a man of enormous culture and a highly respected figure in European Pictorialism. In his portraits and animated scenes, he often showed himself to be an excellent interpreter of the painting of Degas, while his landscapes, which are full of light and atmosphere, pay tribute to French Impressionism. He was not afraid to introduce factories into them, and his 1904 homage to Turner entitled *Speed* captures the first automobiles.

Constant Puyo was also an excellent technician with an undoubted gift for landscape, but the pictures that made him famous, filled with beautiful models in fancy dress, are of mediocre inspiration as well as being treated with a precision that stifles any kind of poetic impulse. Like other photographers, Demachy and Puyo worked from snapshots, which they enlarged. Those of Puyo, particularly his panoramas, often have a freshness that makes them preferable to the final prints.

The pictures of Viennese photographers are characterized by a heavily Pictorialist technique. The most remarkable of these photographers were Hugo Henneberg (1863–1918), Hans Watzek (1848–1903), and above all Heinrich Kühn (1866–1944), who together formed the Kleeblatt or Trifolium group, and the Germans Theodor (1863–1943) and Oskar (1871–1937) Hofmeister. They favored large formats (over 1 meter, occasionally) and landscape, either rustic in character, evoking the realism of earlier decades, or frankly Romantic. Kühn, who was closely associated with the Viennese Sezession, and particularly with the architect Hoffmann (who designed his house in Innsbruck), proved to be the most avant-garde (figs. 215, 220). His superb technique undoubtedly became less heavy through contact with such photographers as Clarence White, resulting in a number of intensely luminous prints. Kühn remained a great Pictorialist until the 1920s, and in his portraits, landscapes, and perfectly composed still lifes he managed, without ever aping painting, to achieve a harmonious integration of all the artistic developments of recent decades, from the influence of Japanese art and crafts to that of Cézanne.

In the English-speaking world, the combined influence of the art of Whistler and that of Japan, being less superficial than in other countries, benefited photography as an art form. Critics of the period, notably A. J. Anderson and Sadakichi Hartmann, often drew a link between photography and Japanese painting as being two modes of expression in black and white. They stressed all that Japanese graphic art might contribute to the vision of photographers, with its elliptical approach, achieved in photography through the soft-focus effect. The most outstanding British Pictorialist was surely Frederick Henry Evans (1853–1943). Originally a bookseller, Evans was a great friend of Aubrey Beardsley, whose *Morte Darthur* illustrations he published, and George Bernard Shaw, who fiercely defended the kind of photographic purism that Evans represented (fig. 210). Of all the Pictorialists who employed the soft-focus effect, Evans was the one whose vision remained most precise, though without this ever impairing his profound lyricism, either in his landscapes or in the splendid series he did on British and French Gothic architecture, of which he was an inspired eulogist. The purity of his art was further enhanced by the magnificent quality of his platinum prints and the meticulous care he took over mounting them. Given the job of presenting the exhibitions of the Linked Ring, which he joined in 1900, Evans became famous for the elegance and restraint he showed on such occasions, inspired by the example of Japanese artists and of Whistler, who also sought to achieve harmony between the work, its frame, and the decorative scheme within which it was displayed. Another representative of pure photography was Baron Adolf de Meyer (1868–1946), whose cosmopolitan lifestyle did not prevent him from becoming a remarkable photographer (fig. 218). Meyer's masterly treatment of light, his predilection for shimmering textures, and his sense of decorum and artifice were to enable him to create (at the same time as Steichen) and excel at the new genre of fashion photography.

The vitality of the Pictorialist movement in the United States is probably explained by the fact that its adherents felt they were involved in the creation of a national art in the same way as the painters and sculptors with whom they now felt able to compete. While also imbued indirectly with European Impressionism and Symbolism, they were better able to assimilate the influence of those movements, the effect of which was consequently more liberating than constraining. Although it would be a gross exaggeration to attribute the successful development of American Pictorialism entirely to Alfred Stieglitz, he was nonetheless one of the leading figures (figs. 212, 217). The son of a wealthy industrialist of German extraction who had settled in New Jersey, Stieglitz was a typical amateur in the best sense of the term. He never needed to earn his living, and in 1883 he decided to devote himself to photography. He trained in Germany, where he had attended a chemistry course taught by Hermann Wilhelm Vogel. It was to Vogel he owed his impeccable technique, which he was able to build on further when he took over the management of a printing works on his return to the United States in 1891. Stieglitz thus received the best possible background for his future activities as editor of three journals devoted to art photography. Having exhibited successfully in all the major European shows, which enabled him to follow the early developments of Pictorialism, Stieglitz was able to fulfill his dream of promoting and establishing the movement in America by maintaining it at a very high level. The most important achievement of Stieglitz was that he made *Camera Work* not just a purely photographic publication but a genuine art journal, thus ensuring that it, and therefore art photography itself, would prosper in the United States. From 1908 the journal devoted increasing space to the work of Rodin, Monet, Cézanne, Matisse, Picasso, and Brancusi, whom Stieglitz and Edward Steichen were the first to introduce to America, in advance of the ground-breaking 1911 Armory Show. *Camera Work* helped to promote recent American painting, which it covered extensively. A great talent-spotter, Stieglitz was also a very great photographer. He immediately established himself as a practitioner of pure photography, although he also, particularly at the beginning, gave support to those who went in for a more painterly style of photography. His great subject was the street, which he treated sometimes with delicate intimism, at others in a grandly symbolic manner intended to glorify the rise of modern America and the power of New York as it built more and more skyscrapers. His famous *Steerage* of 1907, showing part of a ship packed with immigrants, already marked a return to the disenchantments of real life, which the Pictorialists had always sought to shun; it looked forward instead to the postwar rise of modern photography.

Edward Steichen (1879–1973) came from a modest family that had settled in Milwaukee. Having trained as an artist, in 1899 he was still hesitating between photography and painting when his prints attracted attention at the annual exhibition in Philadelphia. Frequent trips to Europe from 1900, coupled with his knowledge of European avant-garde artistic circles, enabled him to play an advisory role within the Photo-Secession group. Steichen's earliest photographs include some marvelous nocturnes taken in the forests around Milwaukee. From Europe, where he had gone to meet Rodin, he brought back a series of portraits of the sculptor, as well as shots of his *Balzac* statue, also taken at night, and pictures of all the great artists, writers, and musicians he had encountered, from Monet and Watts to Maurice Maeterlinck and Richard Strauss (fig. 201). Steichen's brilliant use of such techniques as gum bichromate and carbon printing showed greater respect for the photographic image than was common among Europeans, and his works stand out for the breadth and sovereign ease of their composition (fig. 205).

In contrast to both Steichen and Stieglitz, Clarence Hudson White (1871–1925), who took up photography in 1893 and founded the Newark Camera Club in 1898, represents the sentimental side of American Pictorialism (fig. 203). However, his extraordinary feeling for light and a kind of poetry that is at once knowing and naive enabled him to avoid the pitfalls of mawkishness and pastiche, arousing genuine emotion. Both in spirit and in his choice of intimist and vaguely Symbolist subjects, White evokes simultaneously the art of the Pre-Raphaelites, Whistler, and the Nabis.

Less of an artist than White (with whom she was closely associated), although equally precocious, was fellow American Gertrude Käsebier (1852–1934). Käsebier was the most remarkable female representative of a movement that included many women. Käsebier's work, which was much admired by contemporaries, is wholly identified with Pictorialism. It consists mainly of portraits (including several of Native Americans) and mother-and-child groups full of religious symbolism.

Alvin Langdon Coburn (1880–1966), one of the youngest American Pictorialists of the turn-of-the-century period (he later took British nationality), was also one of the most original. His close-up portraits show the influence of Julia Margaret Cameron, whom *Camera Work*, in an attempt to establish a history of art photography, published as being one of the precursors of Pictorialism, along with Hill and Adamson. Following Cameron's example, in 1913 Coburn was to publish a series of portraits of great figures of his day, *Men of Mark*. But above all he succeeded better than anyone else in absorbing the lesson of Japanese art. This comes through in the magnificent series devoted to the city of *London* in 1905 (still inspired by Whistler), in his *Clouds* series (1911), and in the extraordinary *The Octopus, New York* of 1912, a high-angle shot of a well-known New York plaza, transformed into an abstract, decorative diagram. In 1916, having moved to England, he was introduced into the Vorticist group by Ezra Pound and published his first abstract or semi-abstract photographs, taken with the aid of a kaleidoscope and known as vortographs.

The major retrospective organized at the Albright Knox Art Gallery in Buffalo in 1910 marked the official recognition of art photography, but at the same time sounded the death knell of Pictorialism, the sources of inspiration of which were beginning to dry up. The journal *Camera Work* folded in 1916 and the following year saw the publication of work by a young photographer, Paul Strand (1890–1976), that heralded the new current of twentieth-century photography. *Blind*, an enormously powerful portrait of a blind beggar in New York, marked a break: here was a return to stark reality, evident in the mercilessly sharp focus that this time accompanied the close-up. As for Strand's obviously Cubist-influenced still lifes and abstract cityscapes, they were likewise typical of a formalism that was to have a long history in modern and contemporary photography.

Ultimately, the lesson of Pictorialism might well be that creative photography is as likely to degenerate when it cuts itself off from other forms of the medium, such as scientific and documentary work, as it is when it is too closely associated with them. Nevertheless, the movement marked an important step in the recognition of art photography and reinforced the role played in creative photography by the imagination and vision of the photographer.

OUTSIDE PICTORIALISM

The work of someone like Lewis Wickes Hine, who was contemporary with the Pictorialists, showed that it was still possible to be creative while practicing documentary photography (fig. 211). Alfred Stieglitz never wished to meet him, but Hine paid close attention to the activities of the Photo-Secession group and the group's exhibitions at the Little Galleries of the Photo-Secession, 291 Fifth Avenue, New York. He often took his pupils along, one of whom was Paul Strand.

The work that a French photographer was producing about the same time provides an even more magisterial demonstration that, in photography, documentary recording and art are not mutually exclusive (figs. 213, 219). Eugène Atget (1857–1927) came to photography relatively late (in 1890), having first sought to teach himself painting and after a brief flirtation with theater. He started in Paris, photographing architecture or nature with the idea of supplying painters, decorators, and illustrators with studies to work from. But by 1897 he was already launched on his great project of documenting the old quarters of Paris that he knew were shortly going to be either demolished or at least radically transformed. Atget organized his work in a highly systematic way over the years, assembling series on particular groups of buildings (city walls, courtyards, private houses, churches) or decorative details (staircases, fireplaces, door knockers). Though basically interested in the past, Atget nevertheless had the idea early on of photographing those aspects of modern life he knew to be transitory in their present form: fairs, small traders, café and shop fronts. Nor did he confine his attention to Paris but worked in its suburbs, too, from Versailles to Sceaux, whose parks he revisited on several occasions toward the end of his life for purely artistic reasons. Although he went on taking photographs until 1927, Atget should be seen as the last great photographer of the nineteenth century, both for his technique, which was very traditional for the time, and for the way he deliberately kept his distance from the avant-garde. What made Atget an artist was his originality and strength of vision, which he defended fiercely while working for private clients (who ranged from Édouard Detaille and Luc-Olivier Merson to Utrillo, Kisling, Braque, Man Ray, Derain, and Delaunay). After 1898, he also worked for public collections, which regularly purchased sets of prints from him and in 1920 bought five thousand negatives. Very occasionally Atget accepted commissions—initially from the City of Paris and in 1921 an unusual one on prostitutes from painter André Dignimont. It was the remarkable clarity of his eye that earned him the respect of the Surrealists, who published his photographs in their journals, as well as that of visionary critic Walter Benjamin. In fact, Atget's study of Paris went even further than that made by Charles Marville in the 1860s, for Atget had a unique gift for spotting the curious charm of those very ordinary and apparently minor details that, quite as much as its great monuments, make up the atmosphere of a city: dead-end streets, corsetry workshops, hairdressing salons, shop fronts where the individual panes offer the kind of patchwork of reflections that Atget was fond of capturing. As the last heir of the nineteenth-century photographic tradition, Atget was also to be a key source of inspiration for many of the twentieth century's great photographers.

155 Anonymous American
Portrait of Edgar Allan Poe
November 1848
Daguerreotype (quarter-plate)
American Antiquarian Society, Worcester, Mass.

156 Nadar (real name, Félix Tournachon)
Portrait of Charles Baudelaire
c. 1855
Print on salt paper from a collodion glass negative,
24 x 17.5 cm
Musée d'Orsay, Paris

157 David Octavius Hill and Robert Adamson
Sophie Finlaw, Annie Farney, and Brownie the Dog
c. 1845
Print on salt paper from a paper negative,
19.5 x 15.2 cm
Musée d'Orsay, Paris

158 Macaire brothers
Ship about to get under way in the port of Le Havre
c. 1851
Daguerreotype (half-plate)
Bibliothèque Nationale de France (Department of Prints and Photography), Paris

159 Charles Nègre
Chimney Sweeps on the Quai Bourbon, Paris
1851
Modern print from original paper negative,
16.8 x 20 cm
Musée d'Orsay, Paris

160 Charles Nègre
Paris, Market Scene at Hôtel de Ville Port
1851
Print on salt paper from a paper negative,
14.7 x 19.9 cm
Private collection, Paris

161 Édouard Baldus
Amiens Station
c. 1855
Print on salt paper from a paper negative,
32 x 64 cm
Musée d'Orsay, Paris

162 Édouard Baldus
Cliffs in the Auvergne
1854
Modern print from original paper negative,
34.9 x 45.1 cm
Private collection, Paris

163 Émile Pec
Young Woman at Prayer
c. 1853
Print on salt paper from a paper negative,
26 x 19 cm
Private collection, Paris

164 Charles Hugo
Exile's Rock, Jersey
Summer 1853
Print on salt paper from a collodion glass negative,
22.5 x 18.2 cm
Musée d'Orsay, Paris

165 Charles Hugo
Victor Hugo on Rocks at St. Helier, Jersey
Summer 1853
Print on salt paper from a collodion glass negative,
15.4 x 21.6 cm
Musée d'Orsay, Paris

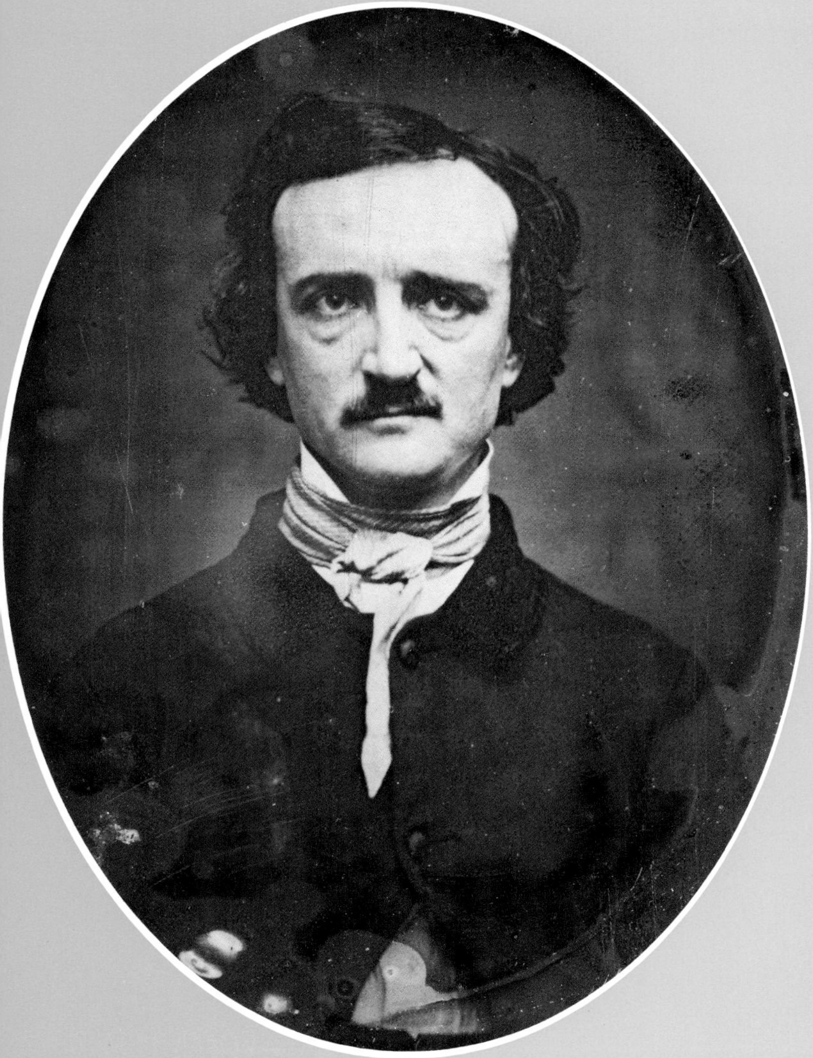

155

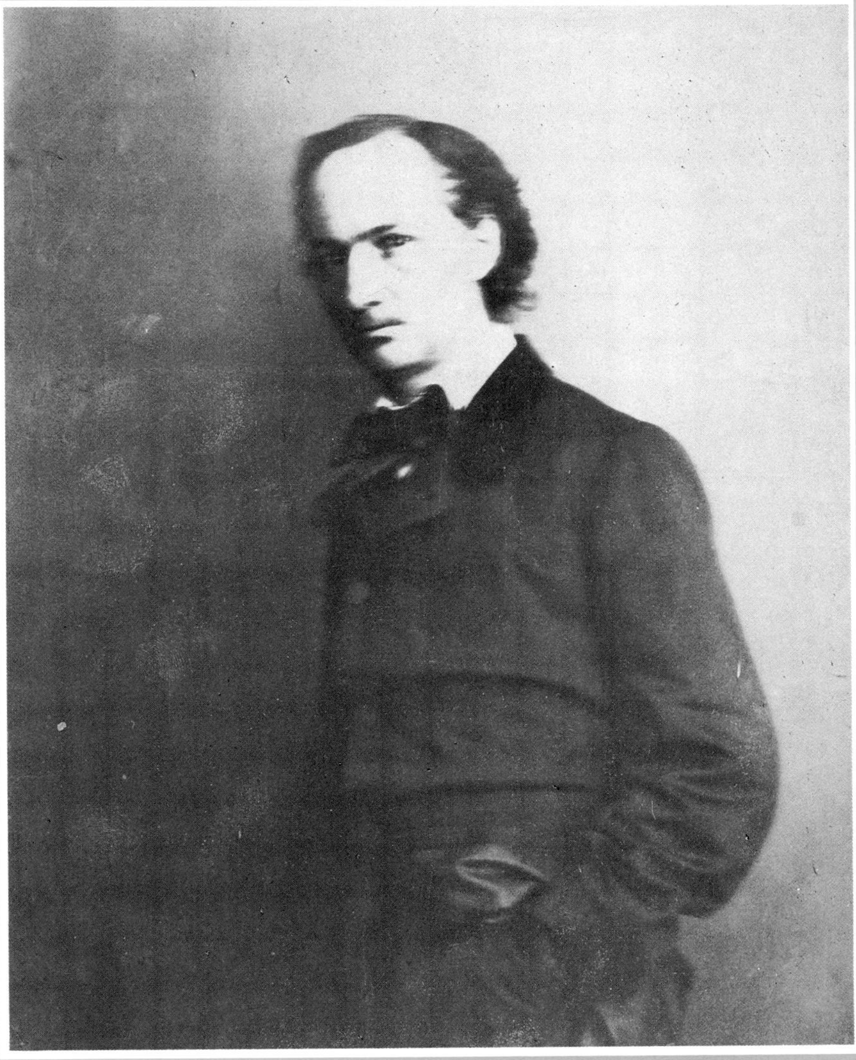

156

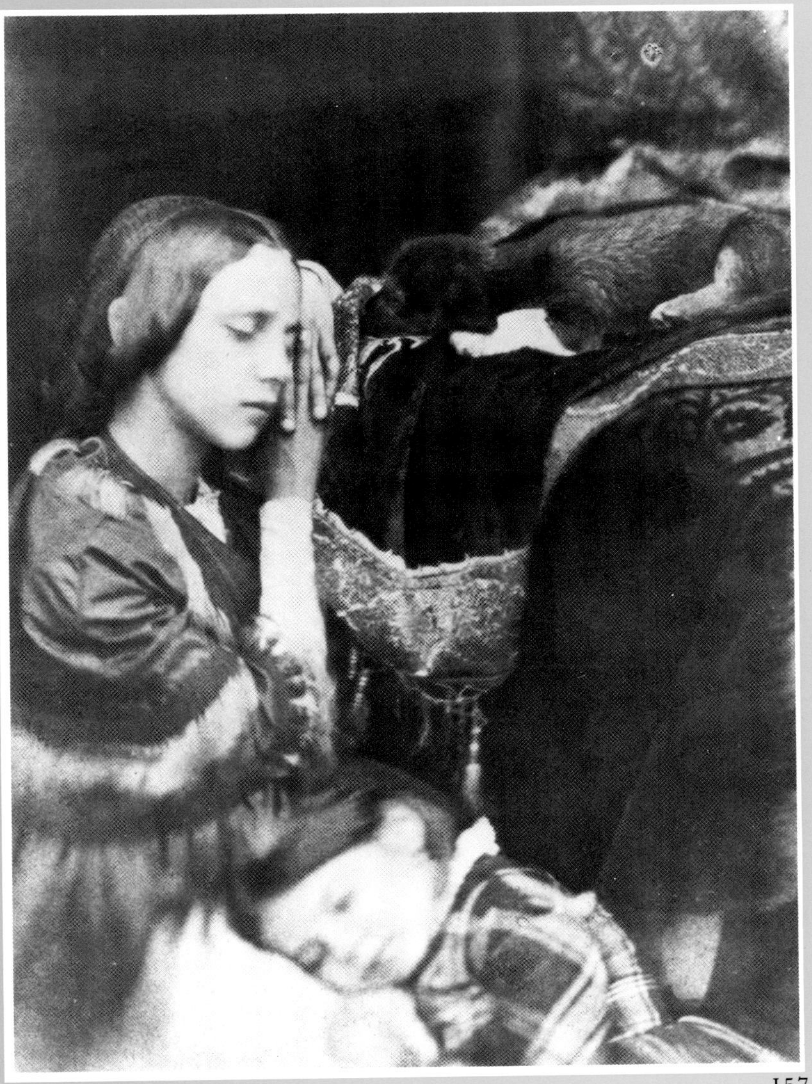

157

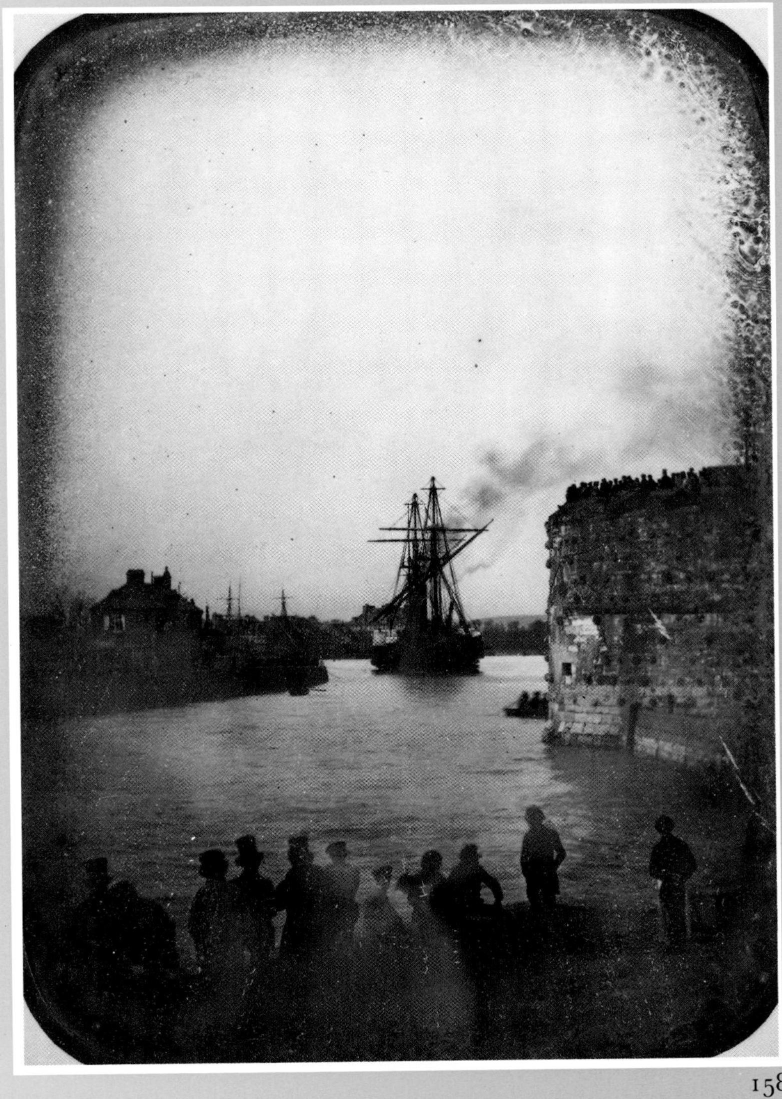

158

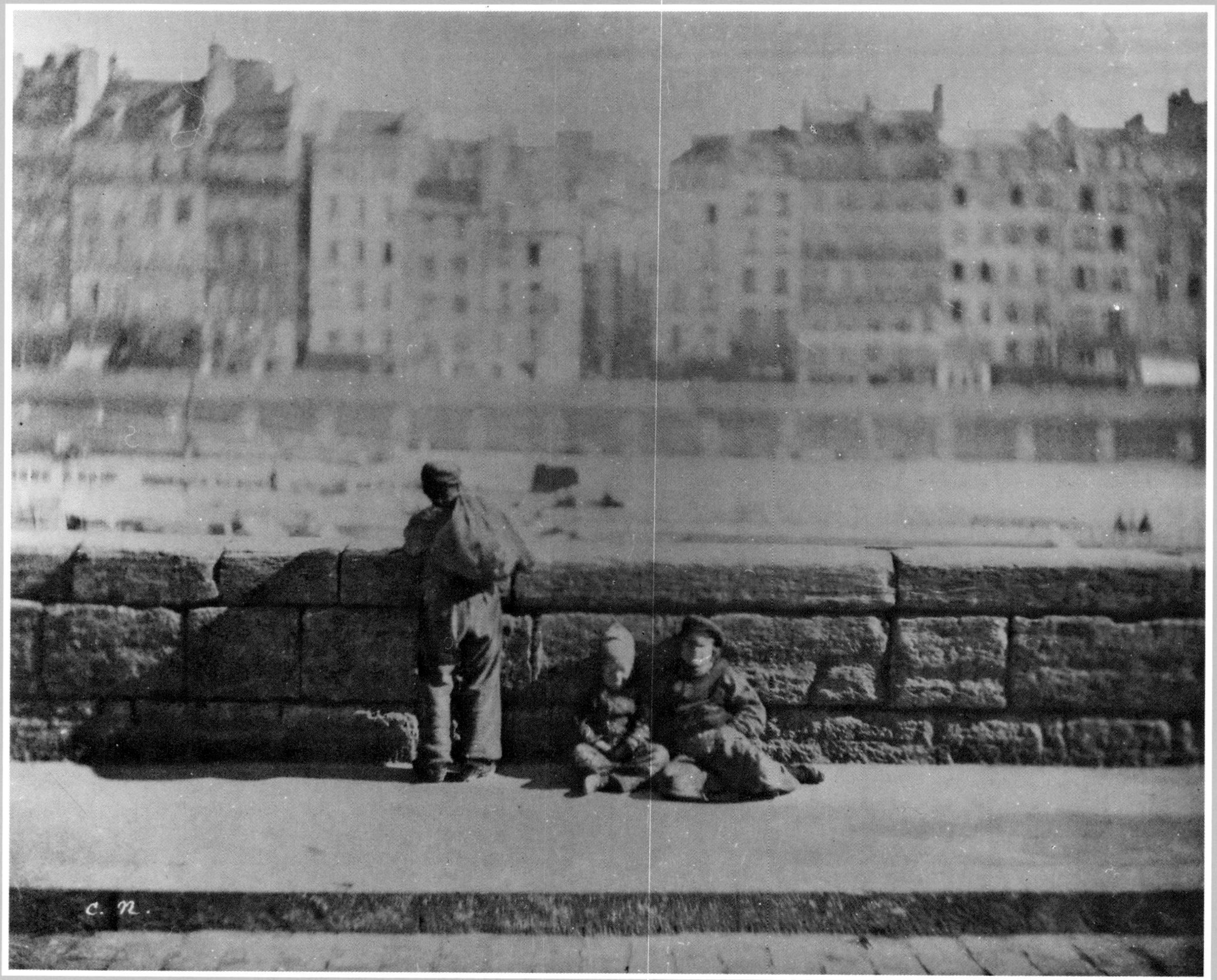

159

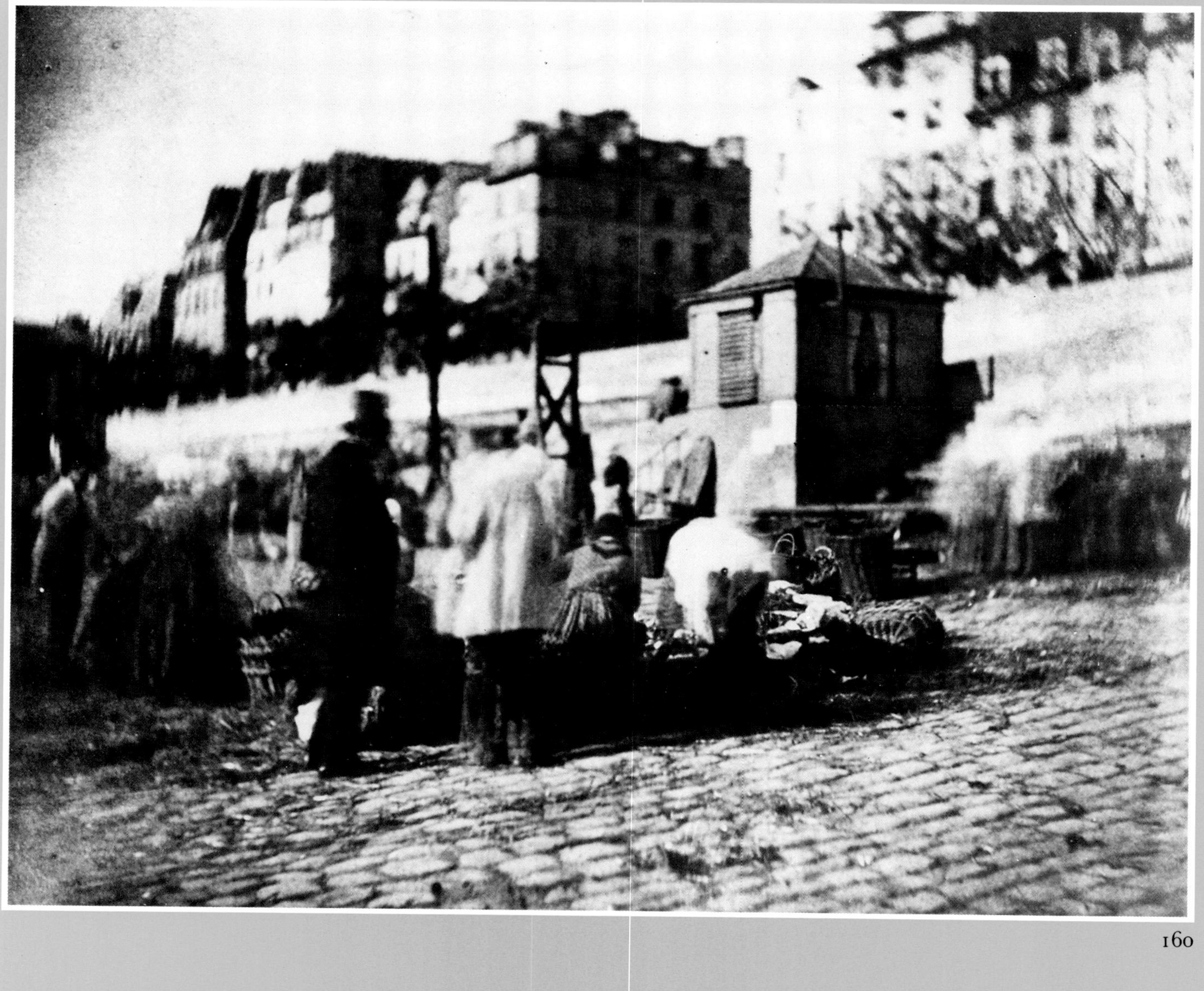

160

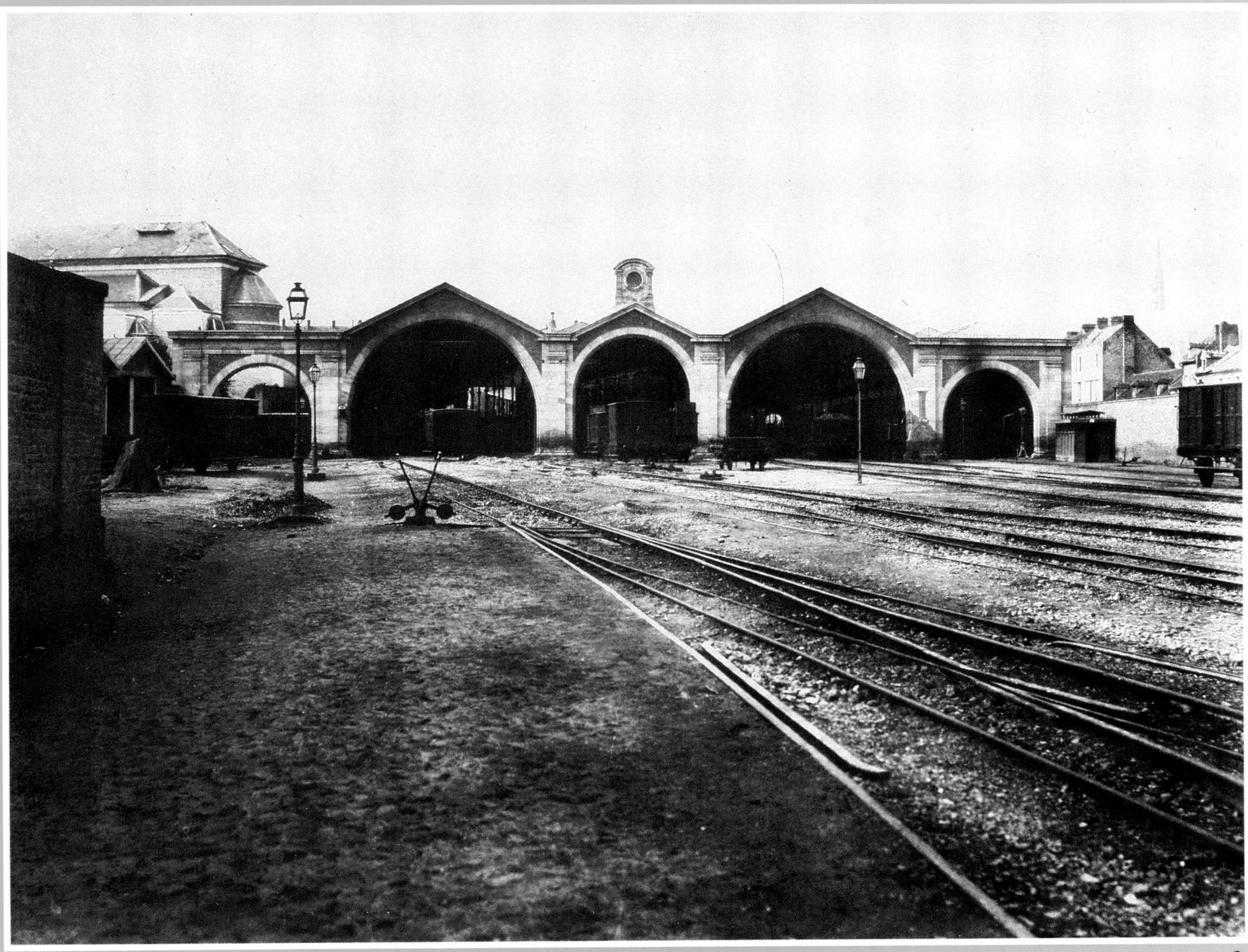

161

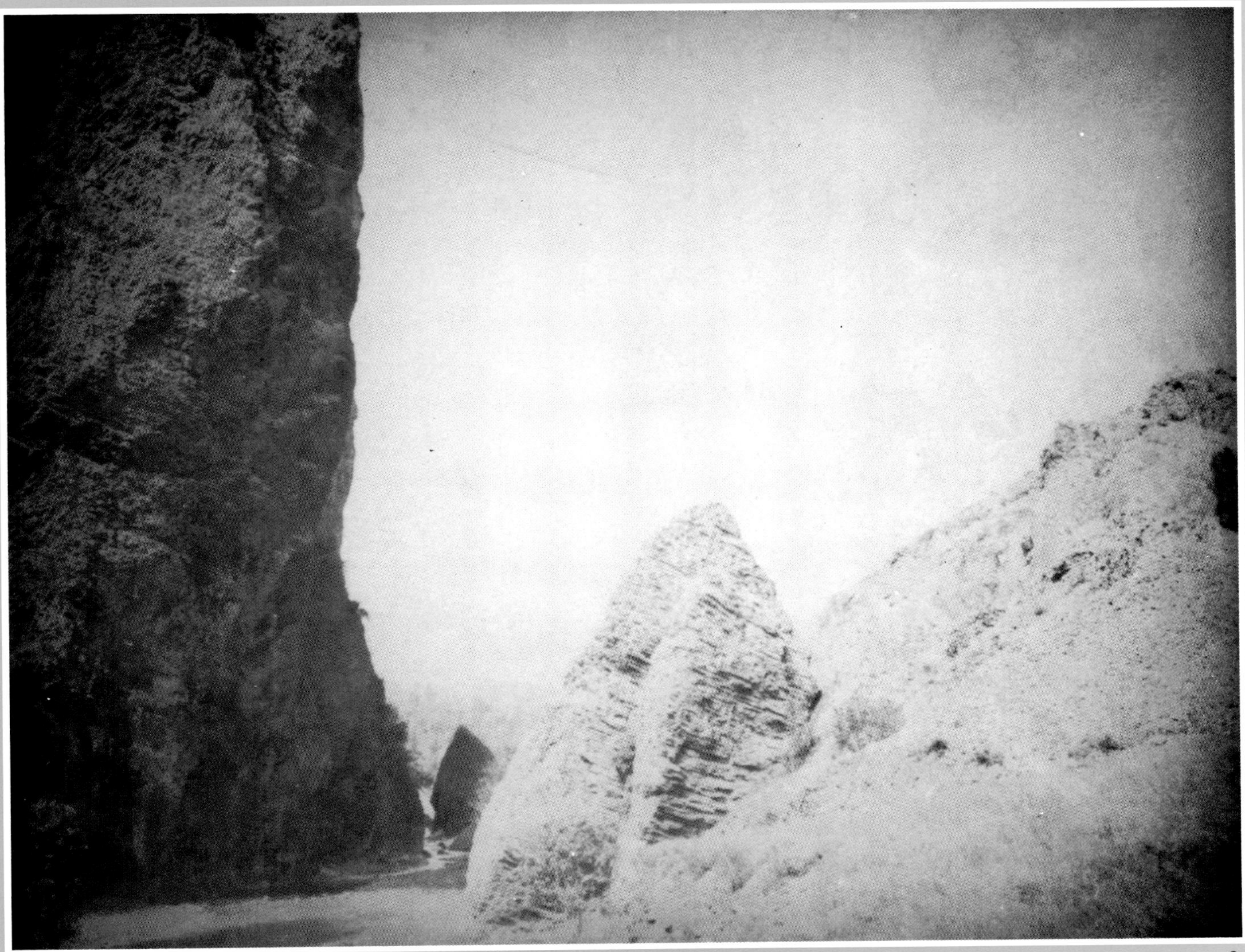

162

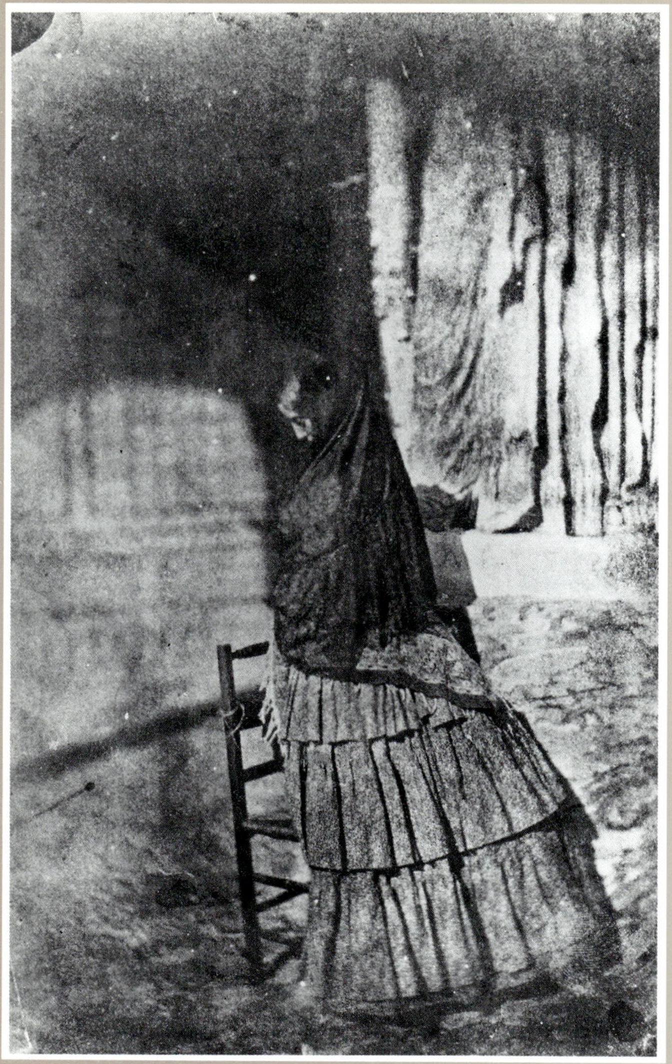

163

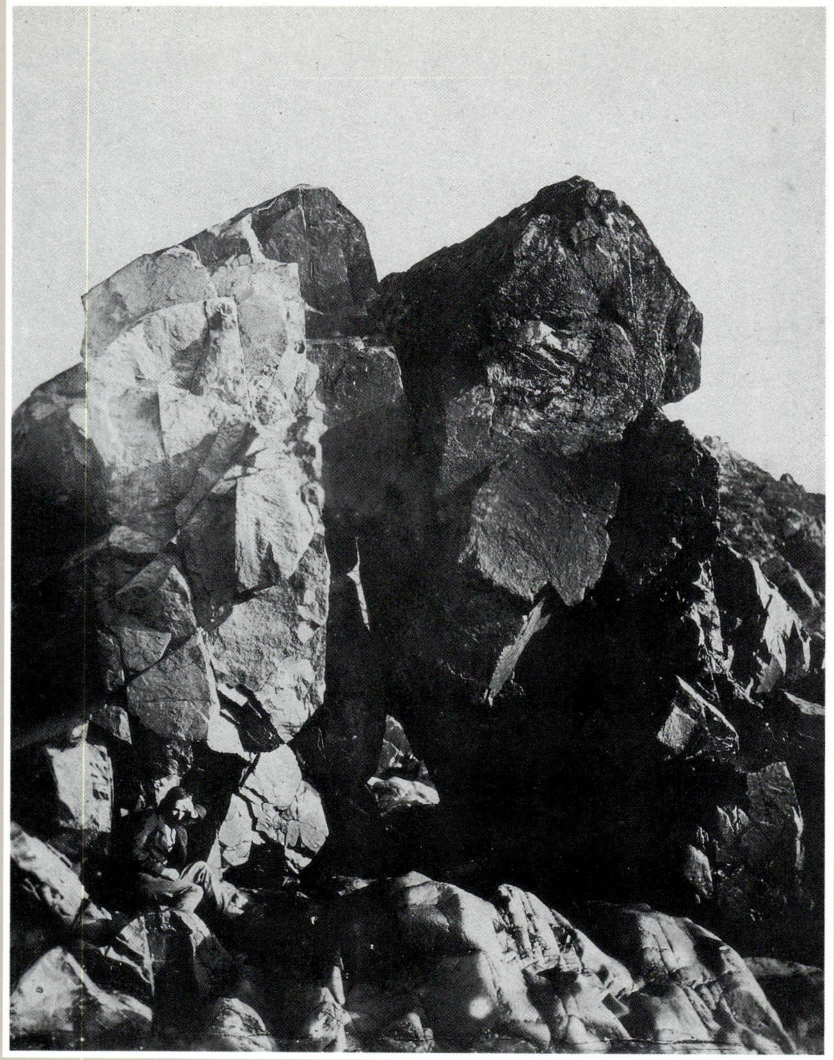

164

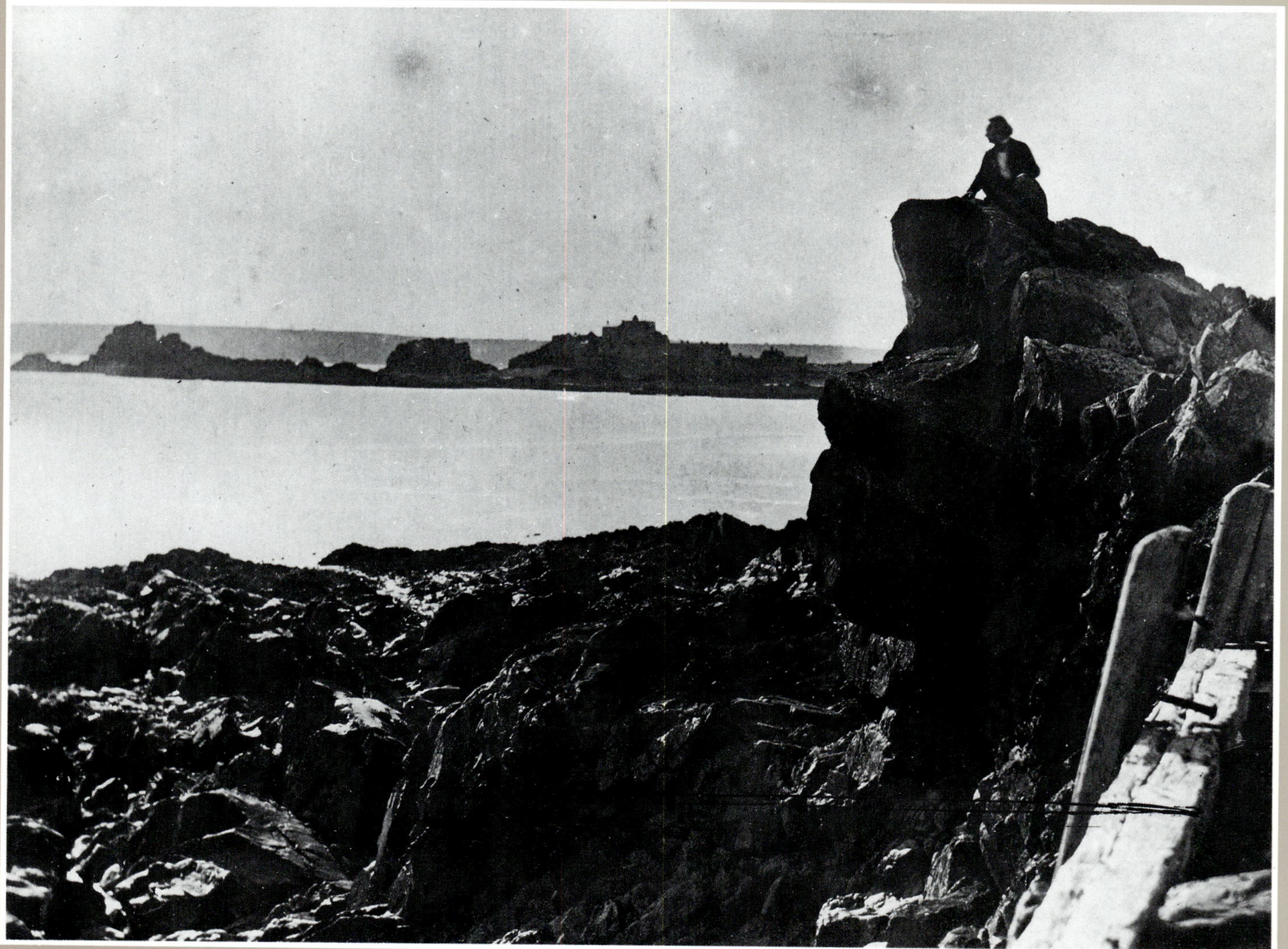

165

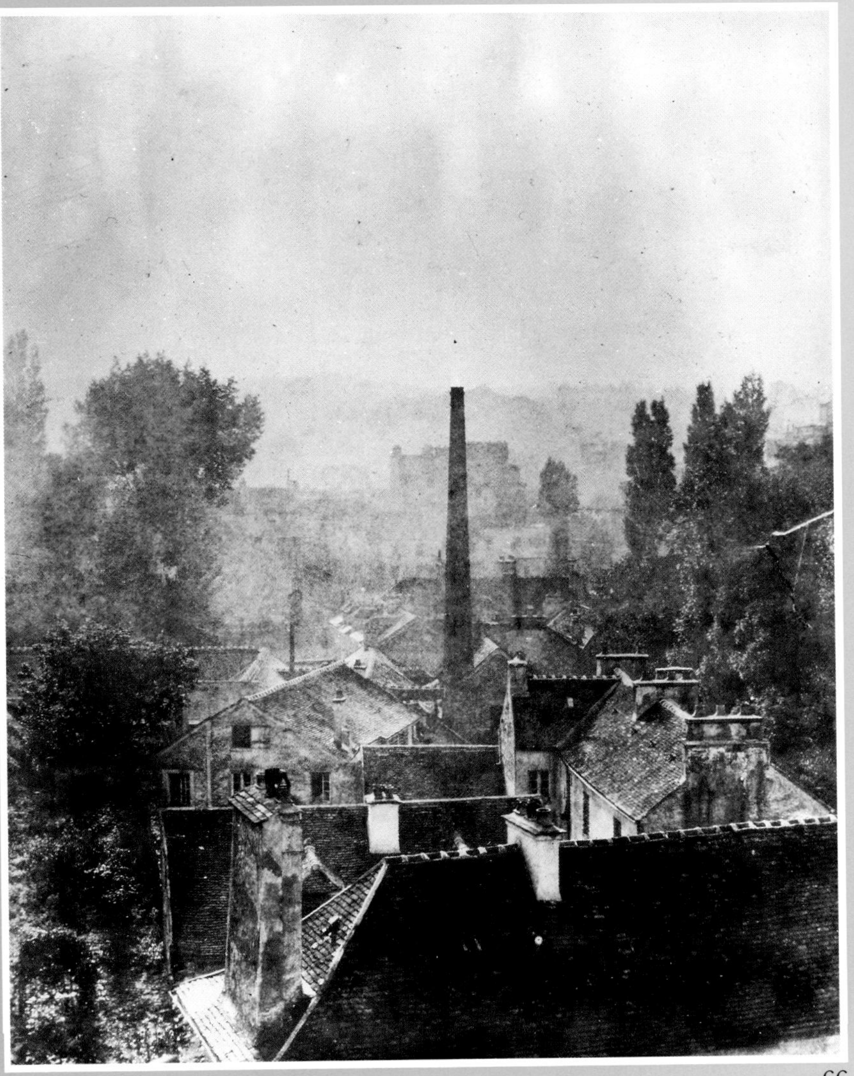

166

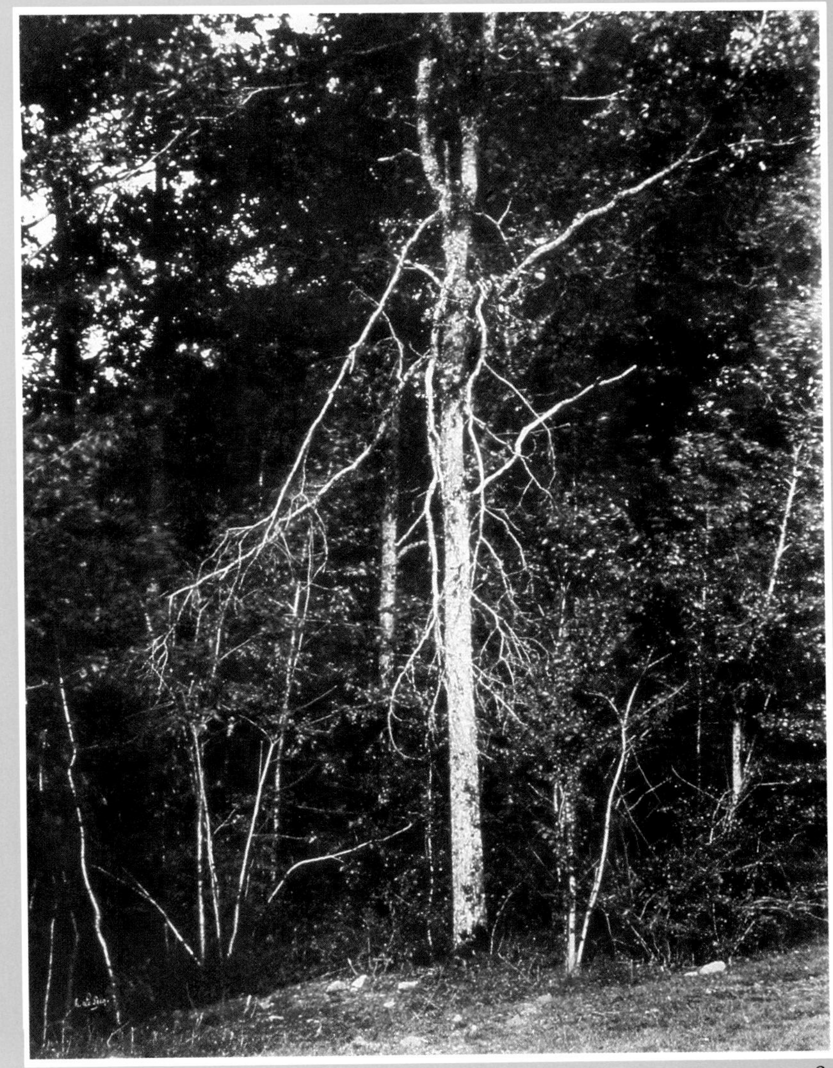

167

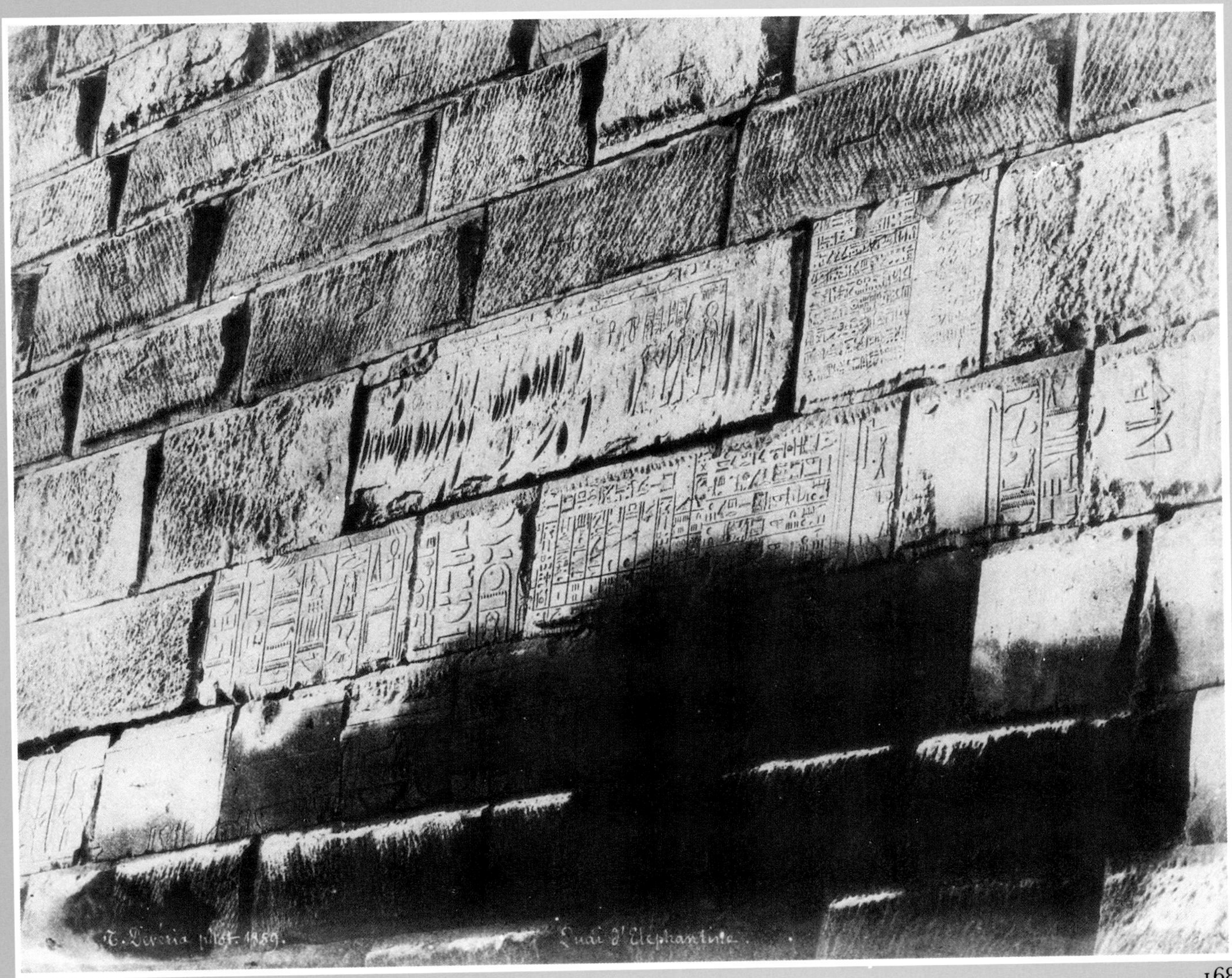

168

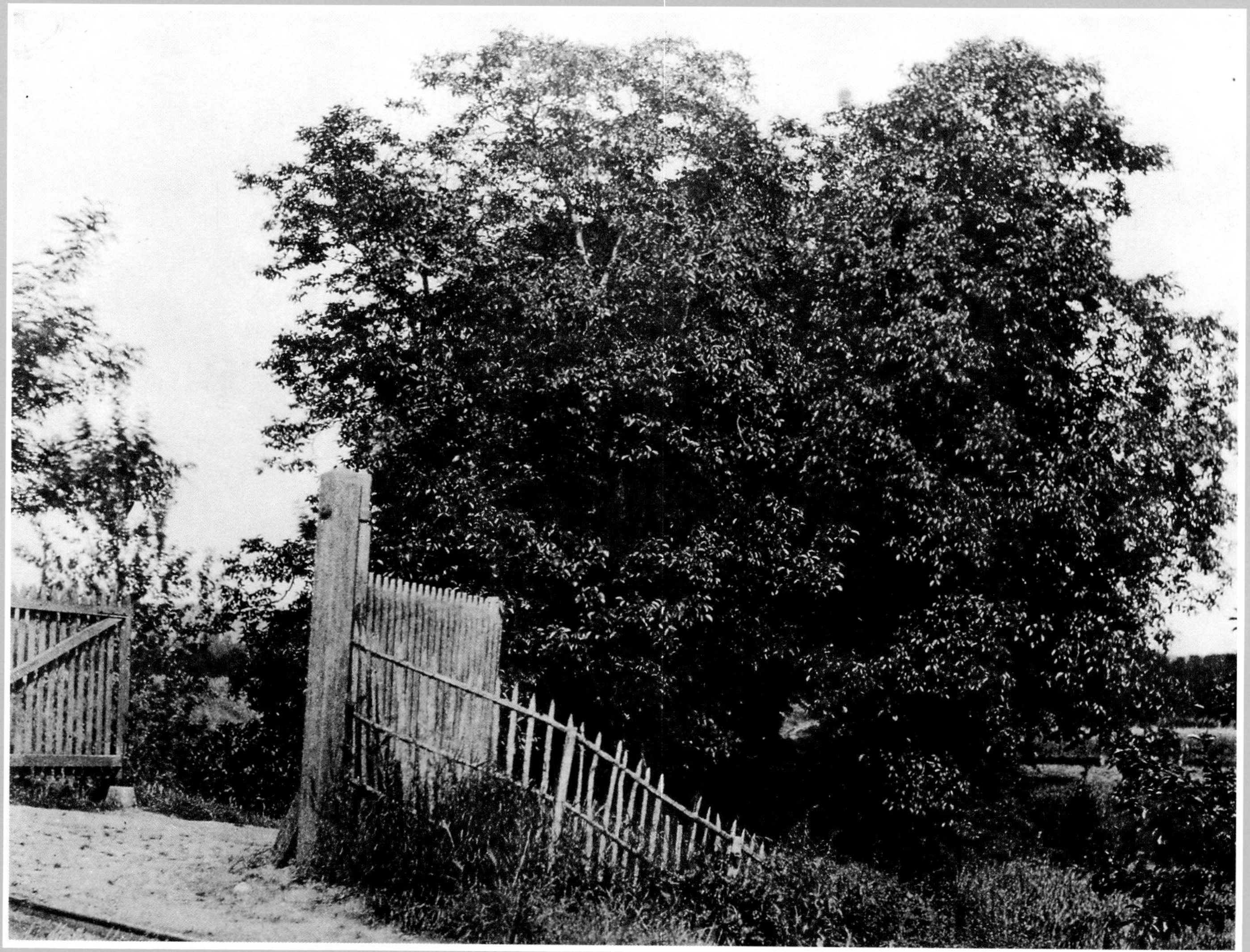

169

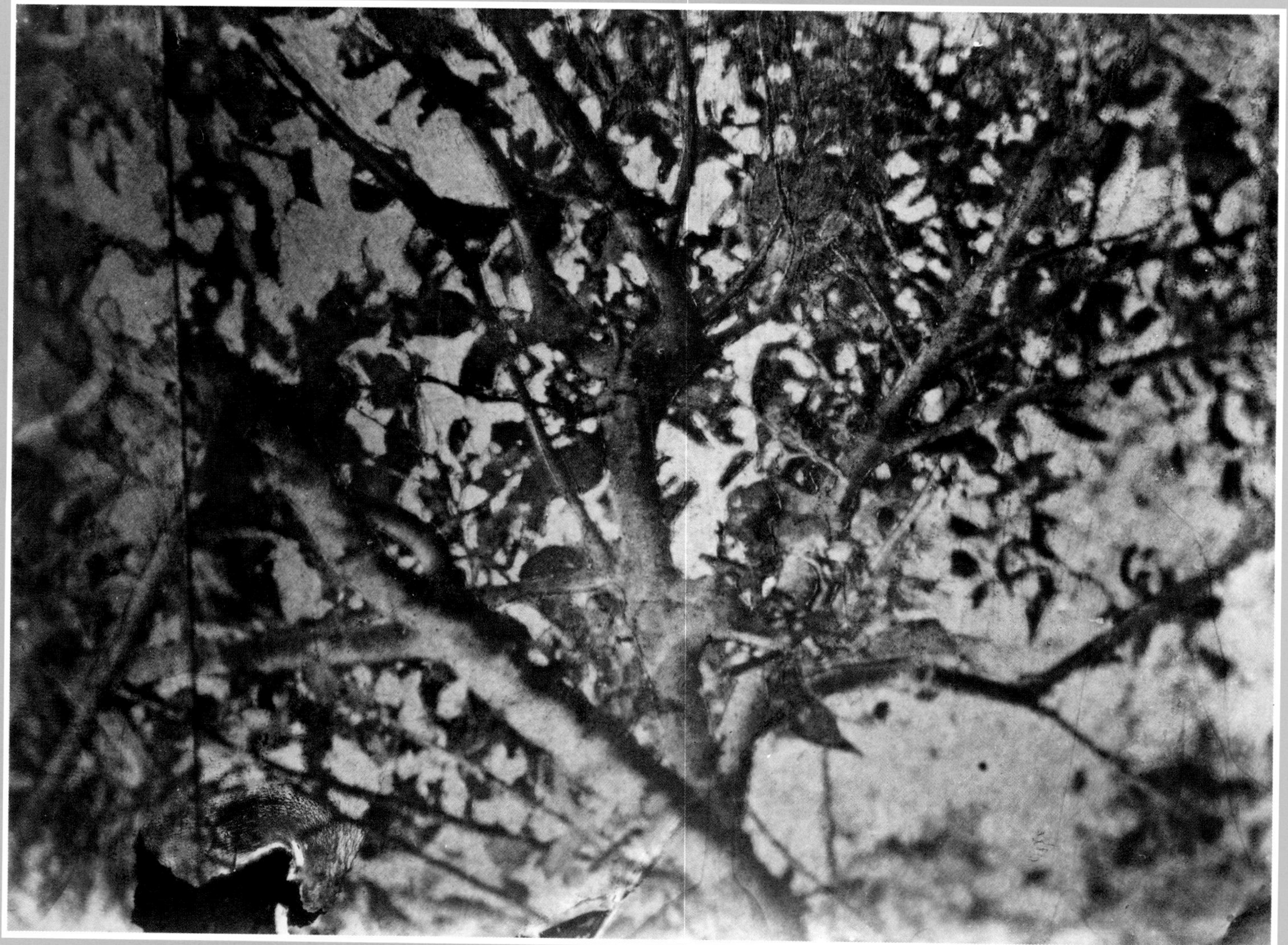

170

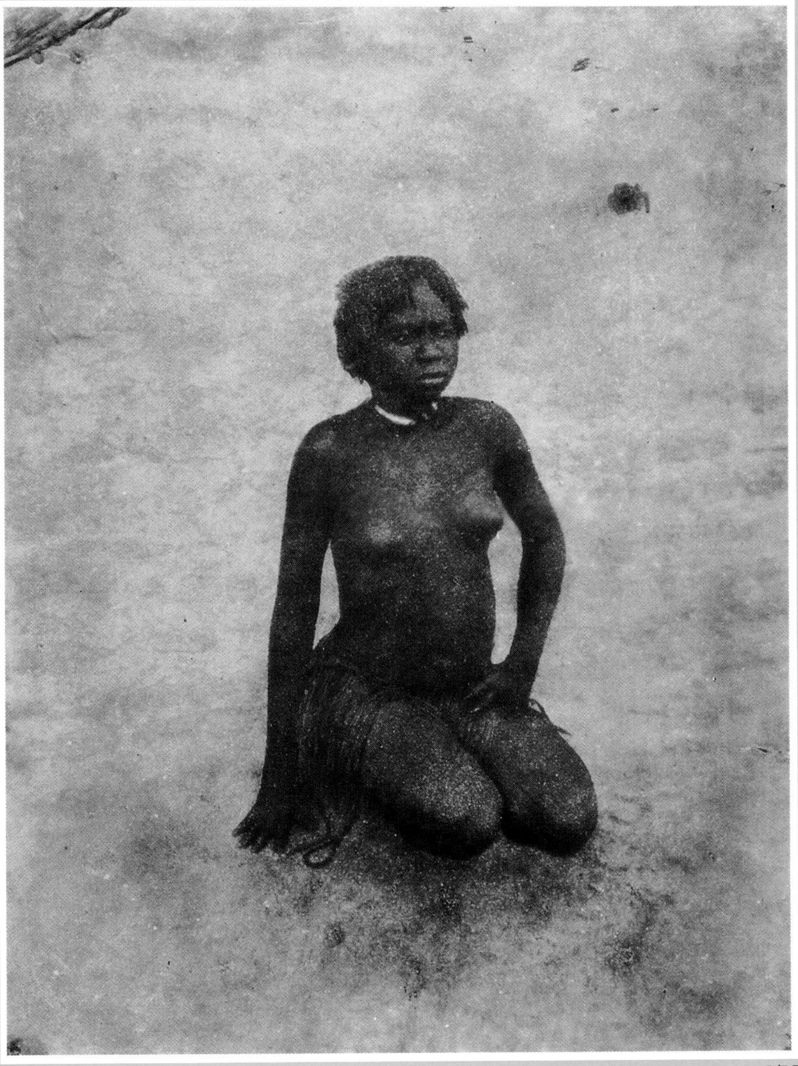
171

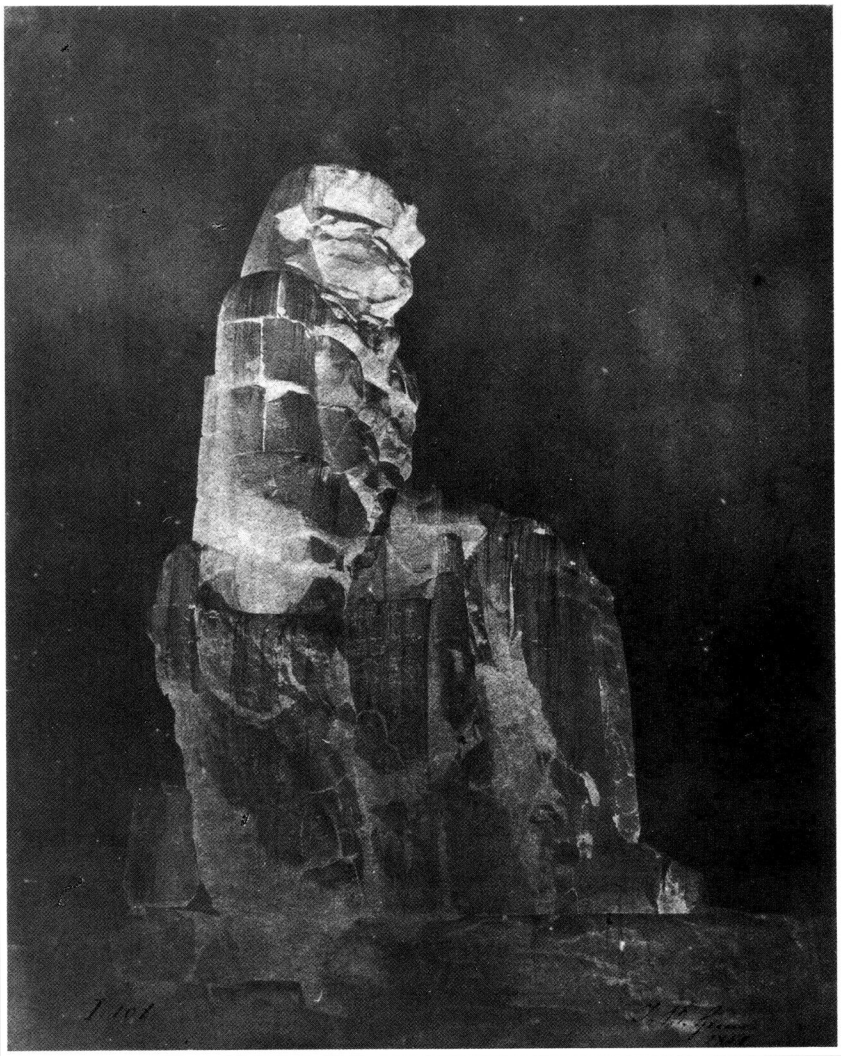
172

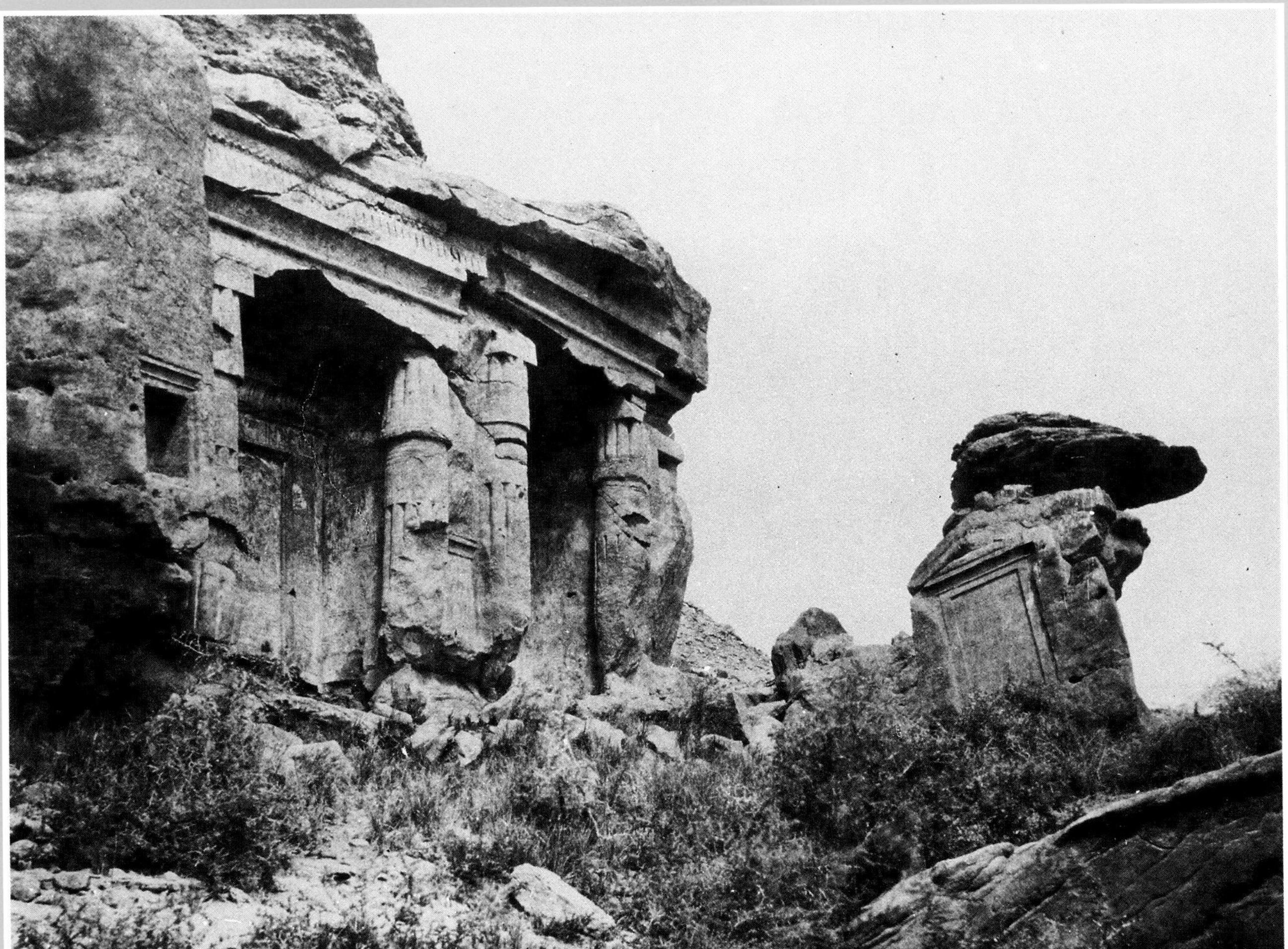
173

174

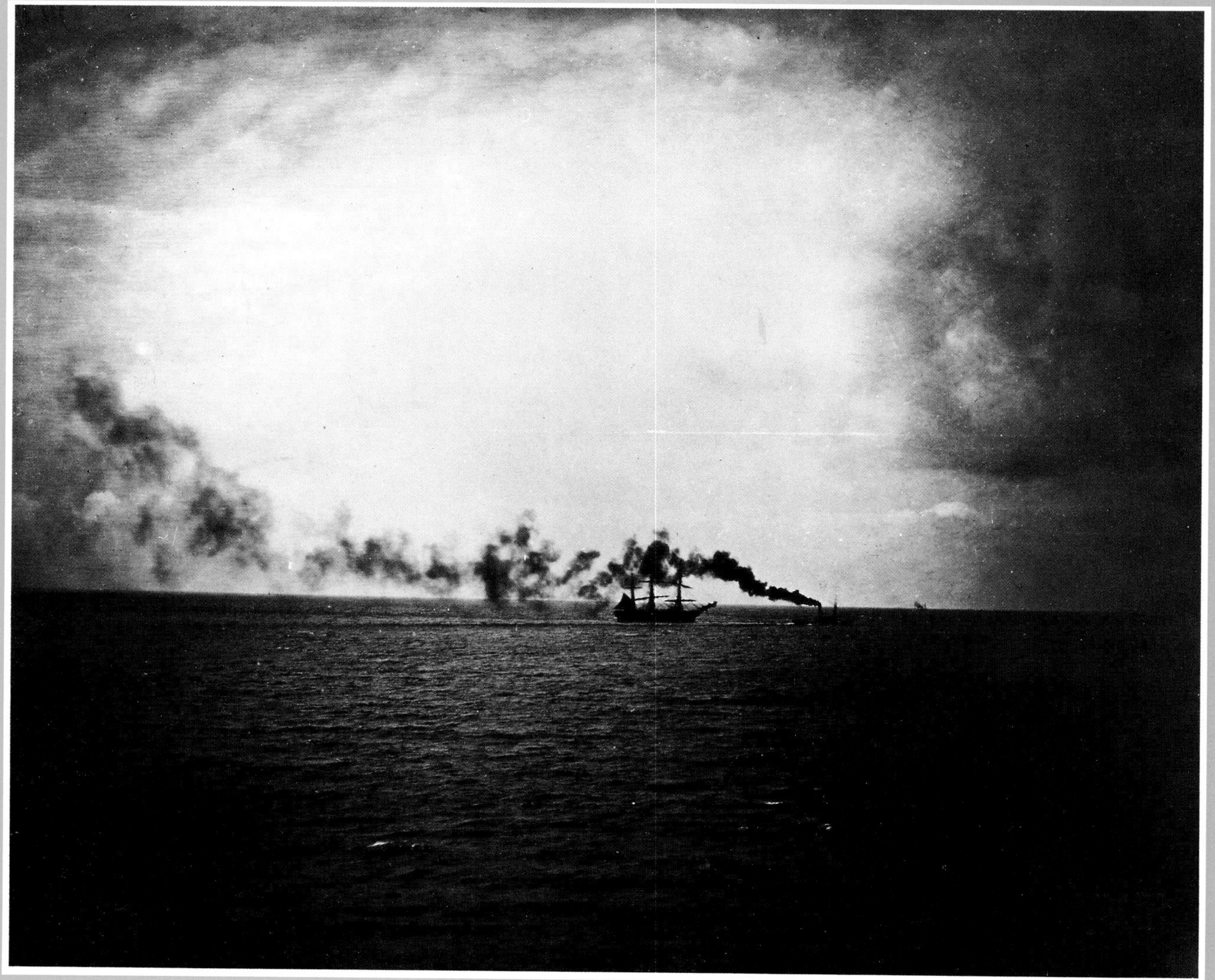

175

166 Victor Regnault
Sèvres, the Factory
1853
Print on salt paper from a paper negative,
43 x 34 cm
Musée d'Orsay (indefinite loan from the Manufacture Nationale de Sèvres), Paris

167 Henri Le Secq
Dead Tree in Forest
1852–54
Print on salt paper from a paper negative,
50.6 x 37.9 cm
Bibliothèque des Arts Décoratifs, Paris

168 Théodule Devéria
Egypt, Elephantine Quay
1859
Print on albumen paper from a paper negative,
22 x 27.8 cm
Musée d'Orsay, Paris

169 Charles Marville
The Open Gate (plate by Blanquart-Évrard for *Études photographiques,* first series, no. 19)
c. 1853
From a paper negative, 16 x 20.8 cm
Bibliothèque Nationale de France (Department of Prints and Photography), Paris

170 Attributed to Pierre-Charles Simart
Branches of a Tree
c. 1856
Enlarged print on salt paper from a collodion glass negative, 32.2 x 43.3 cm
Private collection, Paris

171 Pierre Tremaux
Young Nuba Woman
1847–54
Print on salt paper from a paper negative,
25.4 x 19.5 cm
Bibliothèque Nationale de France (Department of Prints and Photography), Paris

172 John B. Greene
Thebes, Colossus
1854
Paper negative, 30.3 x 22.5 cm
Musée d'Orsay, Paris

173 Félix Teynard
Egypt, Djebel Selseleh (Silsili), Architectural Stelai Carved in Quarries (plate 78 from the album *Égypte et Nubie...*)
1851
Print on salt paper from a paper negative,
23.5 x 30.4 cm
Musée d'Orsay, Paris

174 Gustave Le Gray
Maneuvers at Châlons Camp
1857
Print on albumen paper from a collodion glass negative, 28.2 x 36.6 cm
Bibliothèque Nationale de France (Department of Prints and Photography), Paris

175 Gustave Le Gray
The Steamship
1857
Print on albumen paper from a collodion glass negative, 32 x 41.3 cm
Musée d'Orsay, Paris

176 Oscar Gustav Rejlander
The Dream
1860
Print on albumen paper from a collodion glass negative, 14 x 19.6 cm
International Museum of Photography at George Eastman House, Rochester, N.Y.

177 Henry Peach Robinson
Fading Away
1857
Print on albumen paper from a collodion glass negative, 17.8 x 24.1 cm
Royal Photographic Society, Bath

178 Adam-Salomon (real name, Anthony Samuel)
Portrait of Franz Liszt
May–June 1861
Print on salt paper from a collodion glass negative, 24.2 x 18.7 cm
Musée d'Orsay, Paris

179 Nadar (real name, Félix Tournachon)
Portrait of Charles Baudelaire
c. 1855
Print on salt paper from a collodion glass negative, 21 x 16.3 cm
Private collection, Paris

180 Roger Fenton
"The Long Walk"
1860
Print on albumen paper from a collodion glass negative, 30.6 x 43.3 cm
Royal Photographic Society, Bath

181 Henri Le Secq
Flying Buttresses, Notre-Dame Cathedral, Paris
1851
Print on salt paper from a paper negative, 17.5 x 21.8 cm
Bibliothèque des Arts Décoratifs, Paris

182 Albert Collard
Bridge
c. 1860
Print on albumen paper from a collodion glass negative, 29.2 x 49.9 cm
Musée Carnavalet, Paris

183 Henri Voland
Half-reclining Nude
c. 1861
Print on albumen paper from a collodion glass negative, 13.8 x 28 cm
Bibliothèque Nationale de France (Department of Prints and Photography), Paris

184 Henry Peach Robinson
"The Lady of Shalott"
1860–61
Print on albumen paper from two collodion glass negatives, 31.8 x 52.1 cm
Royal Photographic Society, Bath

185 Roger Fenton
"A Memento of Furness Abbey"
1860
Print on albumen paper from a collodion glass negative, 15.2 x 12.7 cm
Royal Photographic Society, Bath

186 Lady Hawarden
Clementina Maude Posing by a Window
1862–63
Print on albumen paper from a collodion glass negative, 15.2 x 12.7 cm
Victoria and Albert Museum, London

187 Julia Margaret Cameron
"The South-West Wind"
1864
Print on albumen paper from a collodion glass negative, diameter 20.4 cm
The J. Paul Getty Museum, Malibu

188 Julia Margaret Cameron
The Five Wise Virgins
1864
Print on albumen paper from a collodion glass negative, 25.4 x 20 cm
The J. Paul Getty Museum, Malibu

189 Auguste Salzmann
Jewish molding forming jamb of one of the Roman gates in the Temple Precinct, Jerusalem
1854
Print on salt paper from a paper negative, 32.8 x 22.5 cm
Musée d'Orsay, Paris

190 Charles Aubry
Thistle Studies
c. 1865
Print on albumen paper from a collodion glass negative, 37.4 x 26.6 cm
Musée d'Orsay (indefinite loan from the Mobilier National), Paris

191 Timothy O'Sullivan
A Harvest of Death, Gettysburg, Pennsylvania (plate 36 of Gardner's *Photographic Sketchbook of the War*, 1865–66)
July 1863
Print on albumen paper from a collodion glass negative, 17.2 x 22.4 cm
New York Public Library, New York

192 Adolphe Dallemagne
Portrait of Édouard Manet
c. 1866
Print on albumen paper from a collodion glass negative, 20 x 12.5 cm
Bibliothèque Nationale de France (Department of Prints and Photography), Paris

193 Julia Margaret Cameron
"Maud" (plate illustrating Tennyson's poem)
c. 1867
Carbon print from a collodion glass negative, 32.3 x 26.5 cm
Musée d'Orsay, Paris

194 Lewis Carroll (real name, Charles Dodgson)
The Painter John Everett Millais with his Wife and Daughters
July 21, 1865
Print on albumen paper from a collodion glass negative, 11.5 x 8.5 cm
Humanity Research Center (Gernsheim Collection), University of Texas, Austin

195 Julia Margaret Cameron
The Whisper of the Muse
April 1865
Print on albumen paper from a collodion glass negative
26.1 x 21.5 cm
The J. Paul Getty Museum, Malibu

196 Eadweard Muybridge (real name, Edward Muggeridge)
Greyhound Running (plate from *Animal Locomotion*)
c. 1881
Print on matte silvered paper, sepia toned, from a collodion glass negative, 18 x 24 cm (whole sheet)
Musée Marey, Beaune

197 Jules Marey
Heron Flying—Viewed from the Front (enlarged motion analysis)
Print on silvered paper, 14.5 x 22 cm
Musée Marey, Beaune

198 Jules Marey
Human Locomotion—Jumping on the Spot with Feet Together (geometrical motion analysis)
1884
Modern contact print from original gelatin-bromide plate, 8.5 x 3 cm
Collège de France, Paris

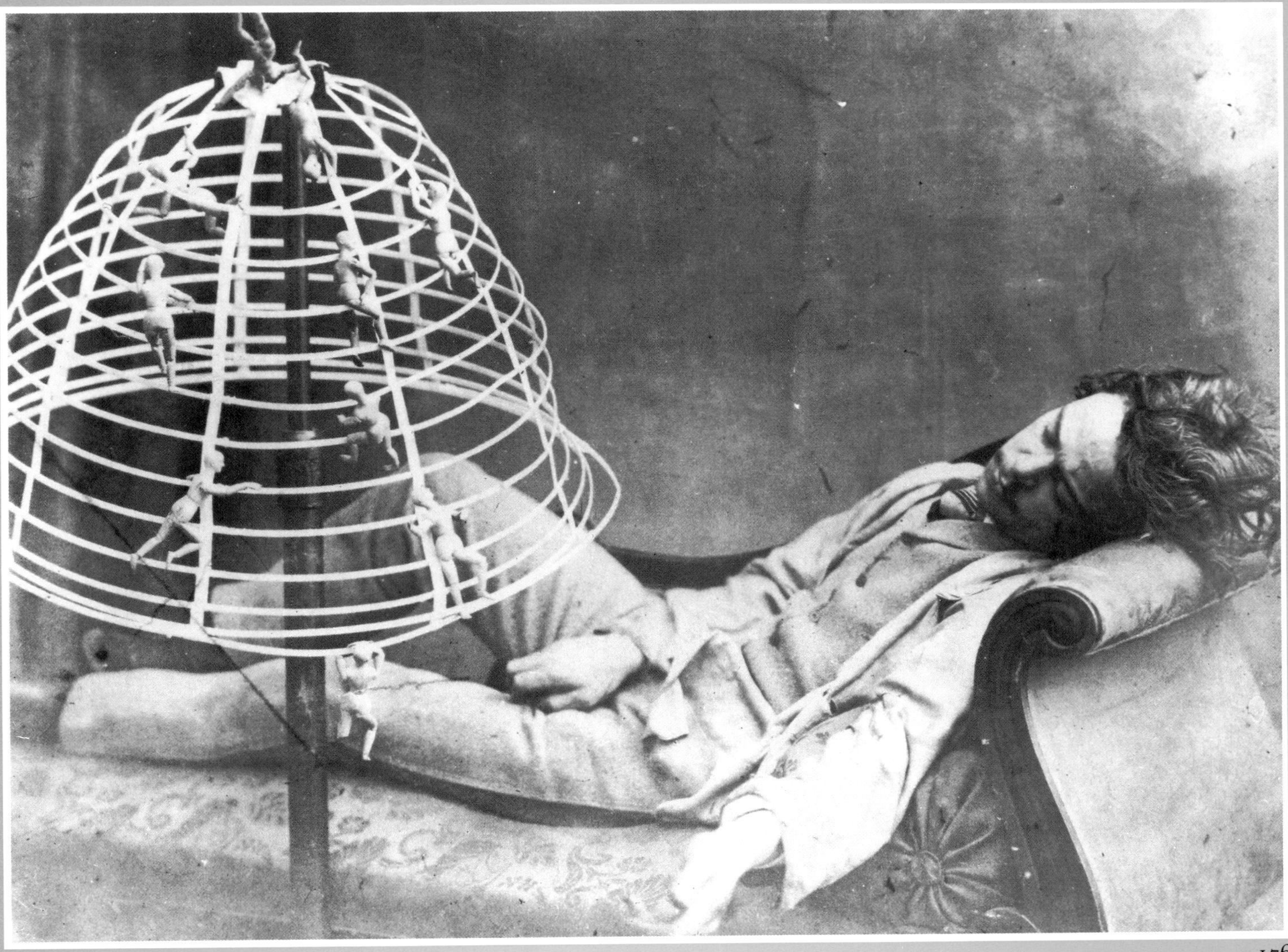

176

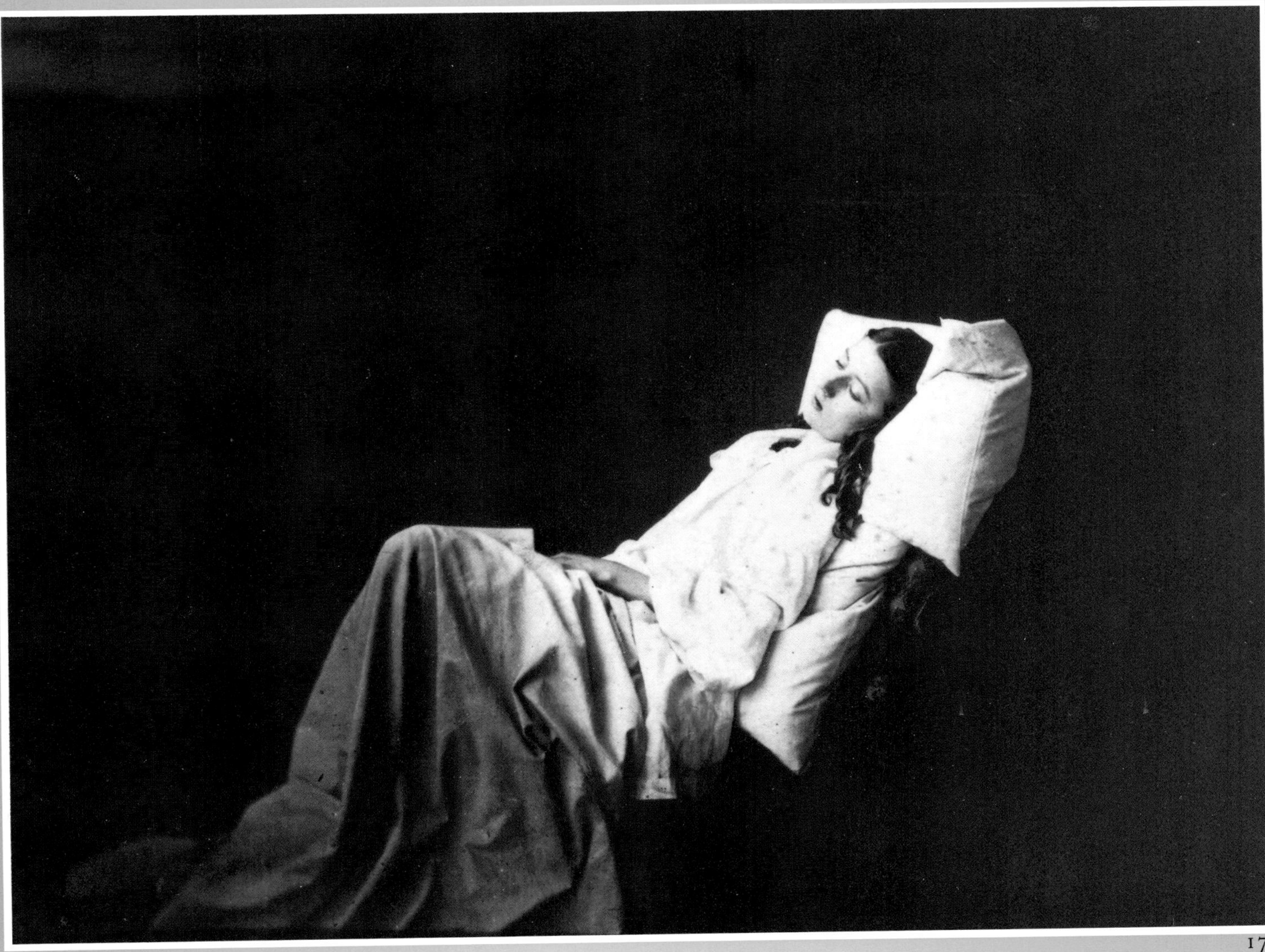

177

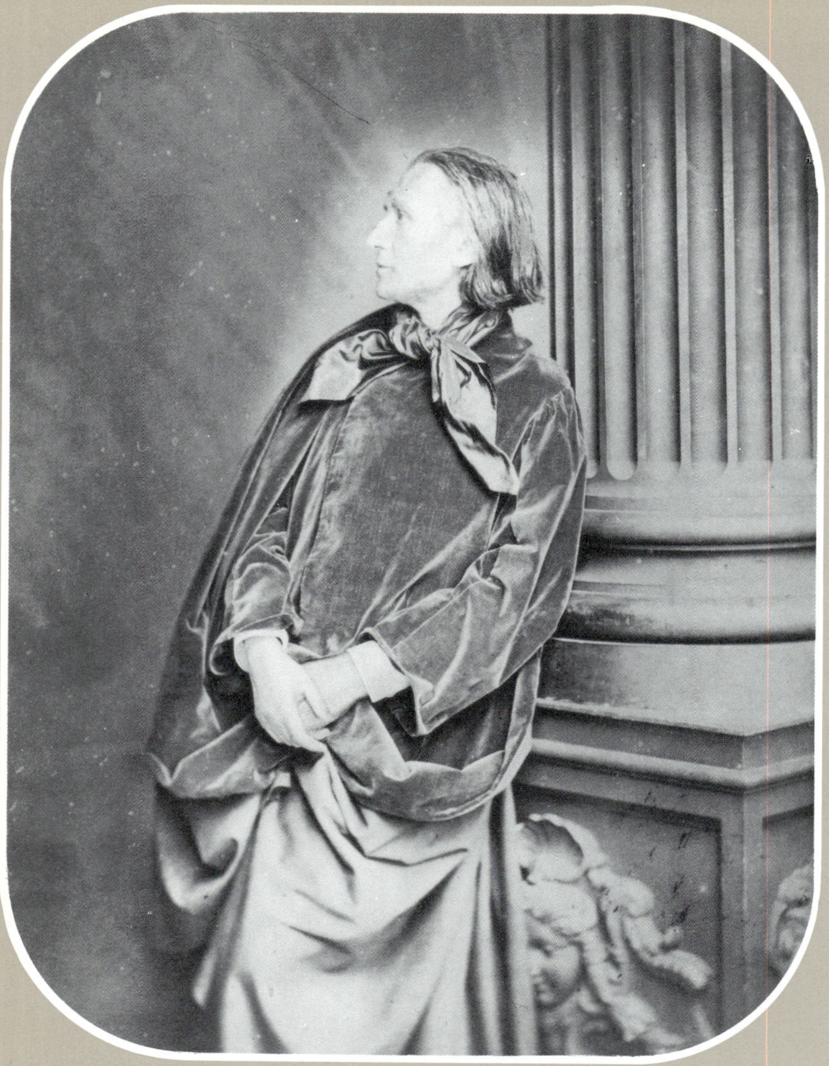

178

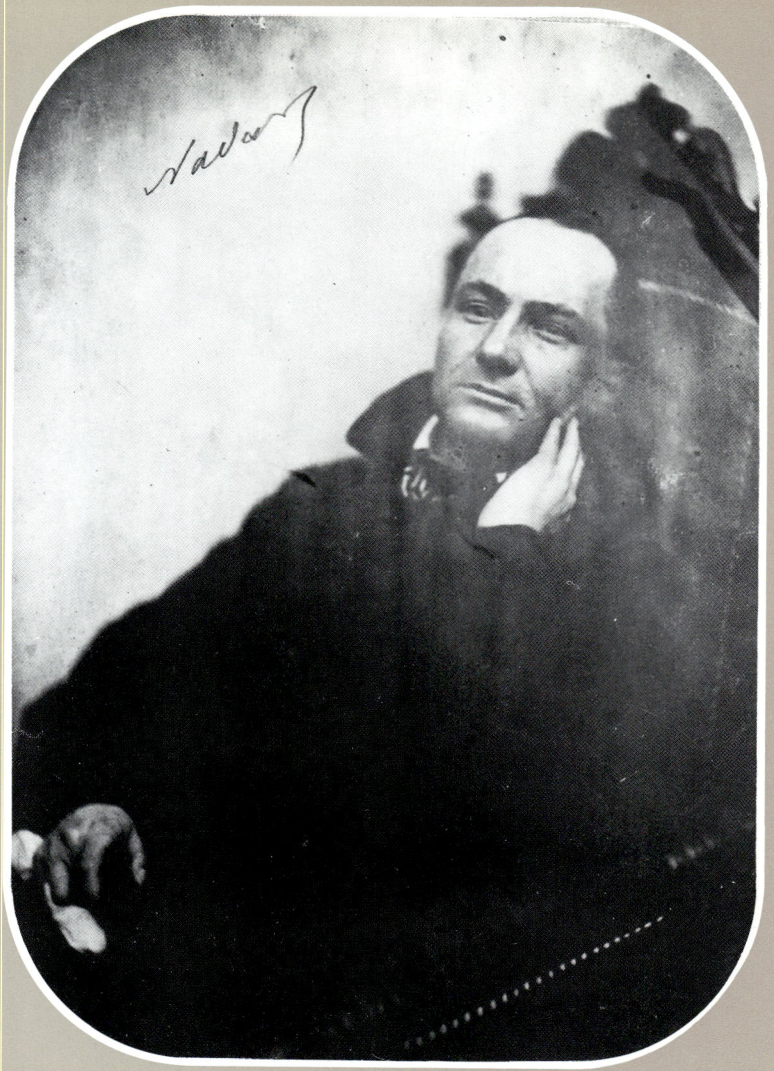

179

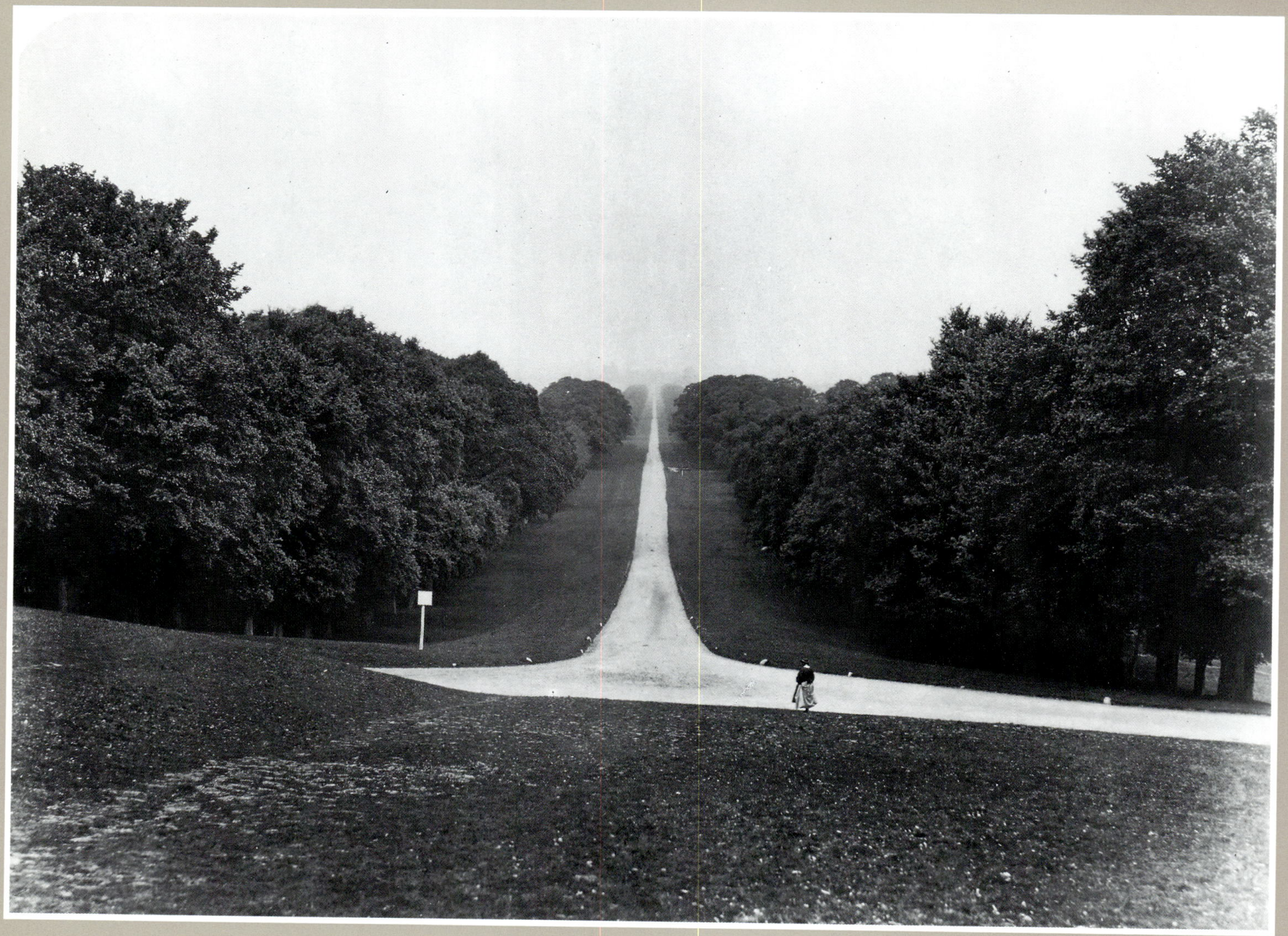

180

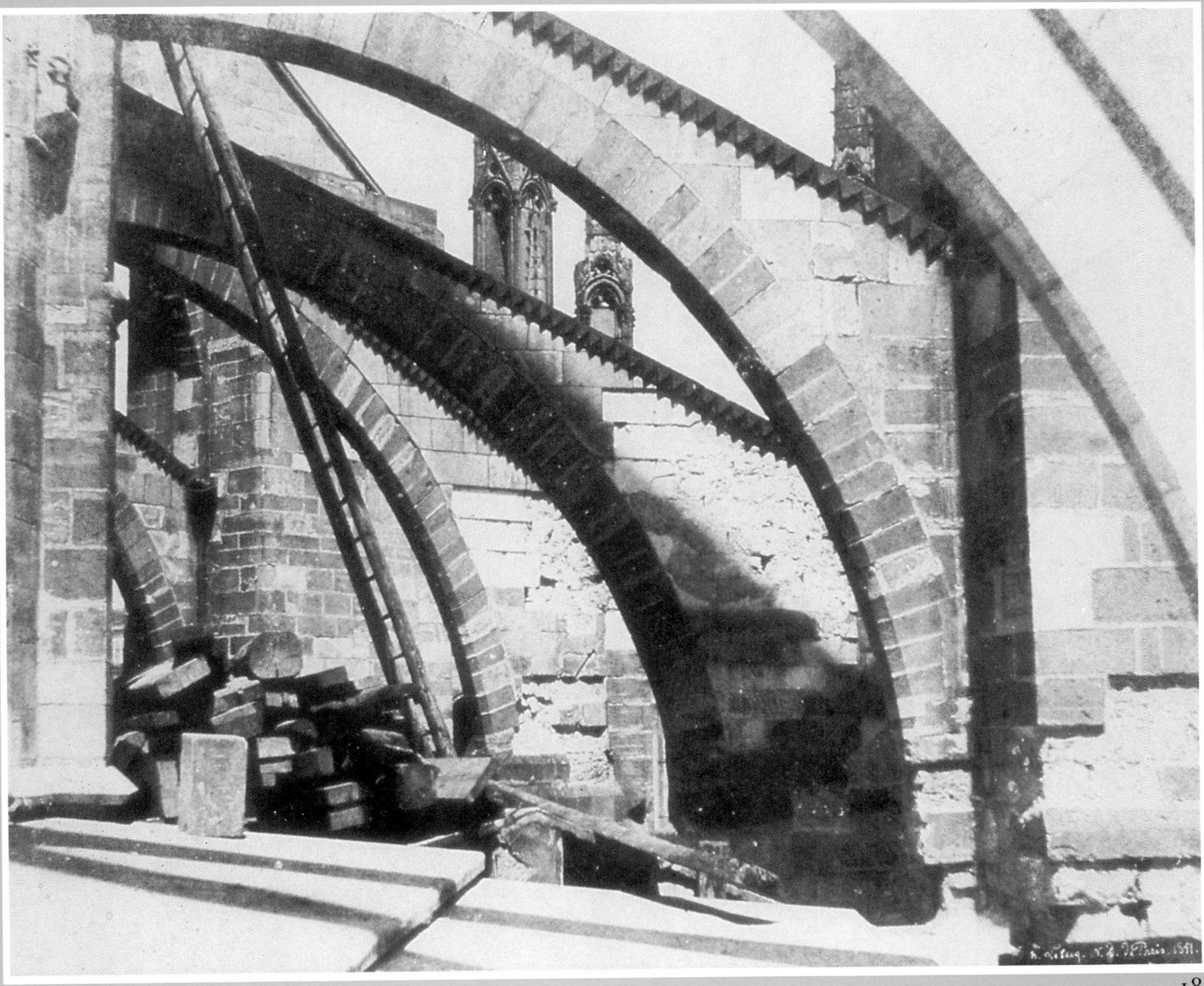

181

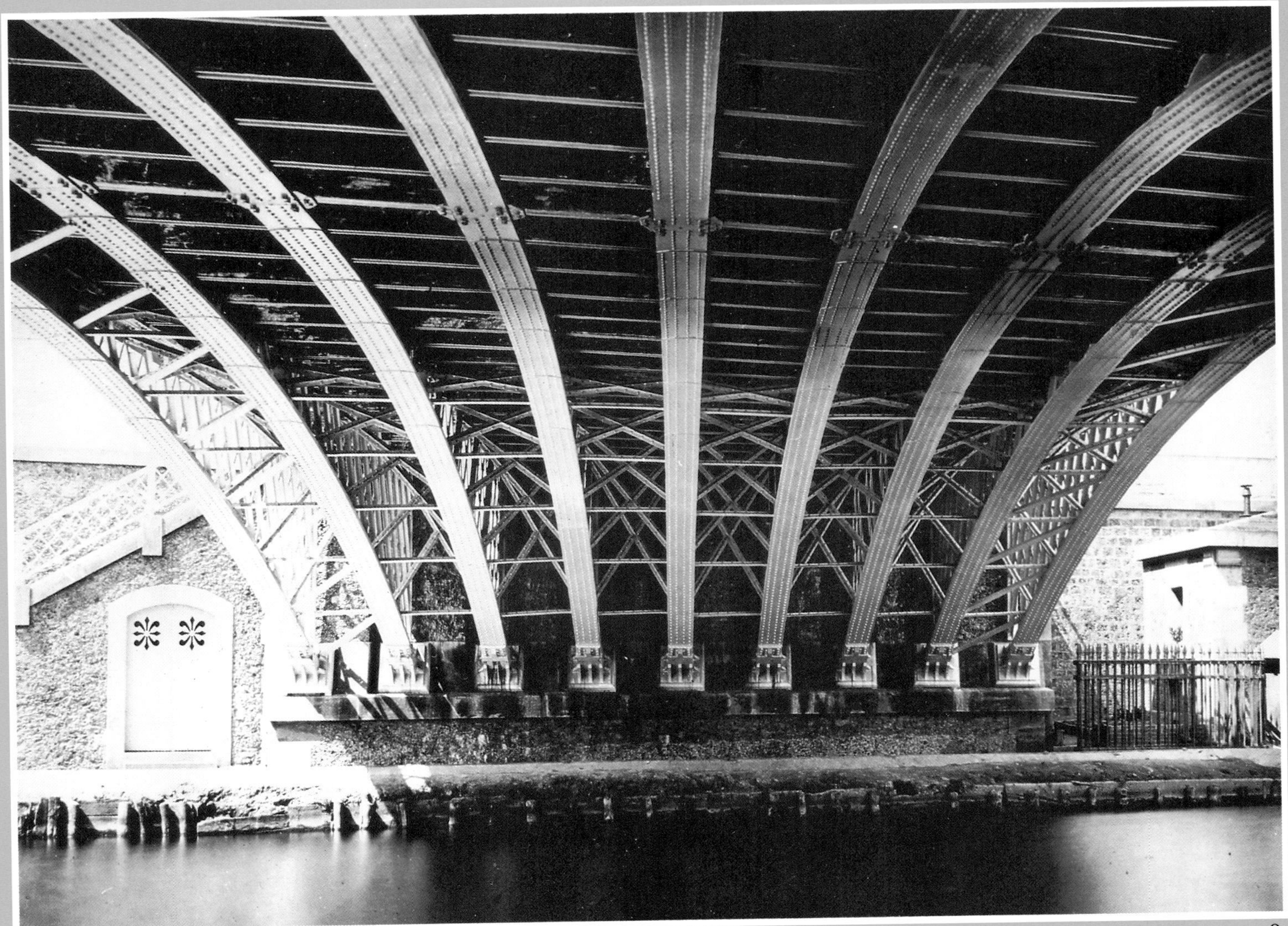

182

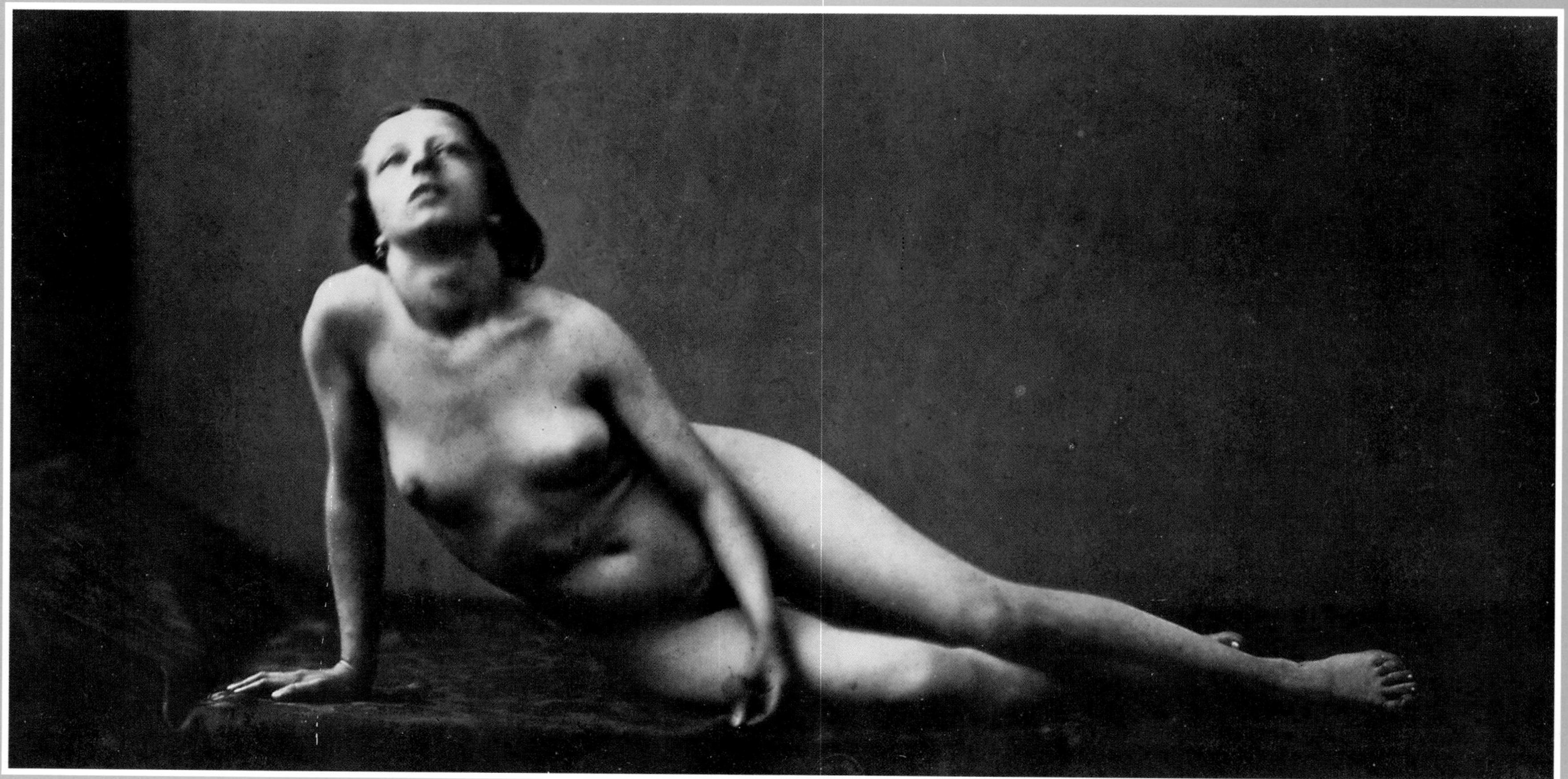

183

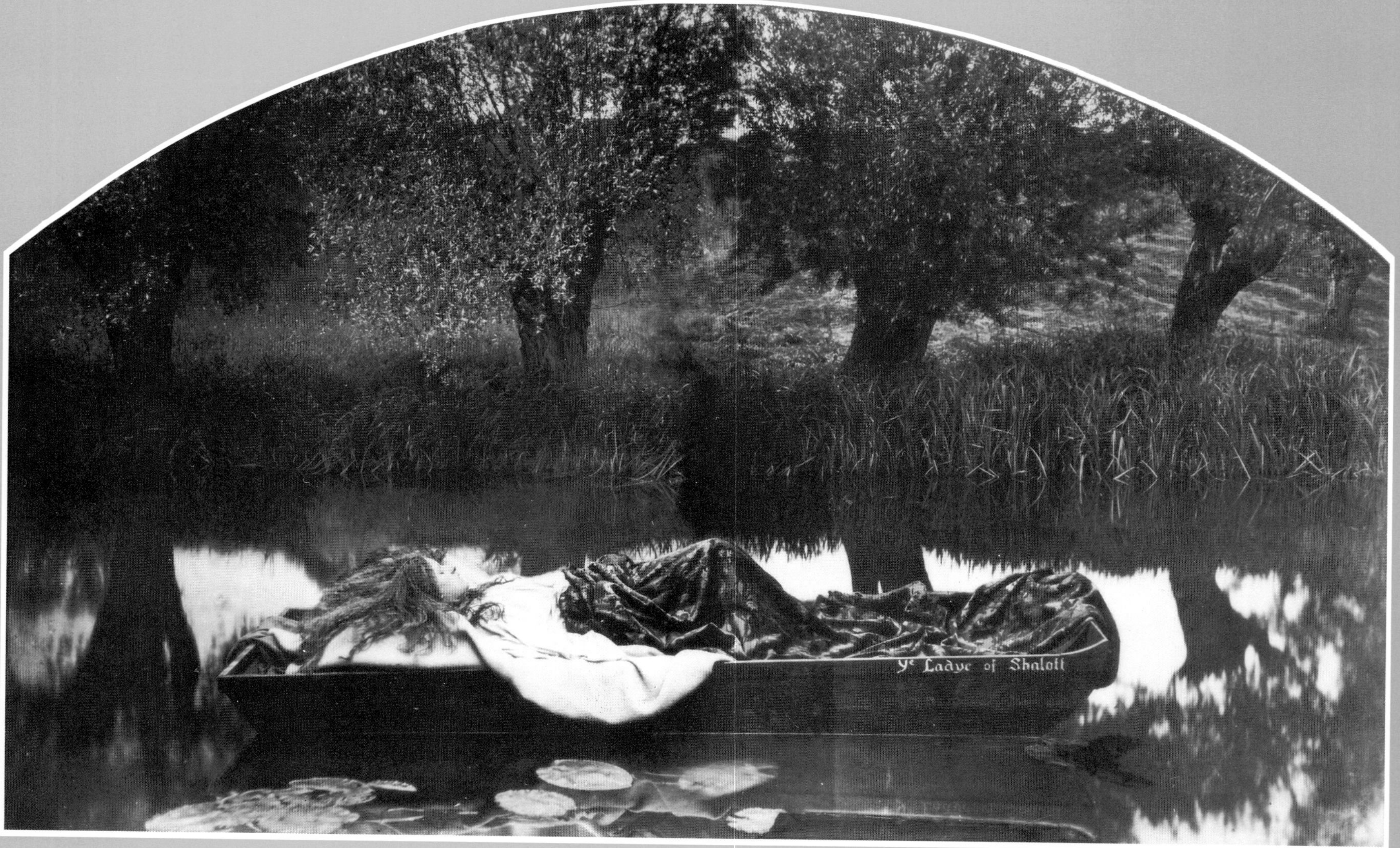

184

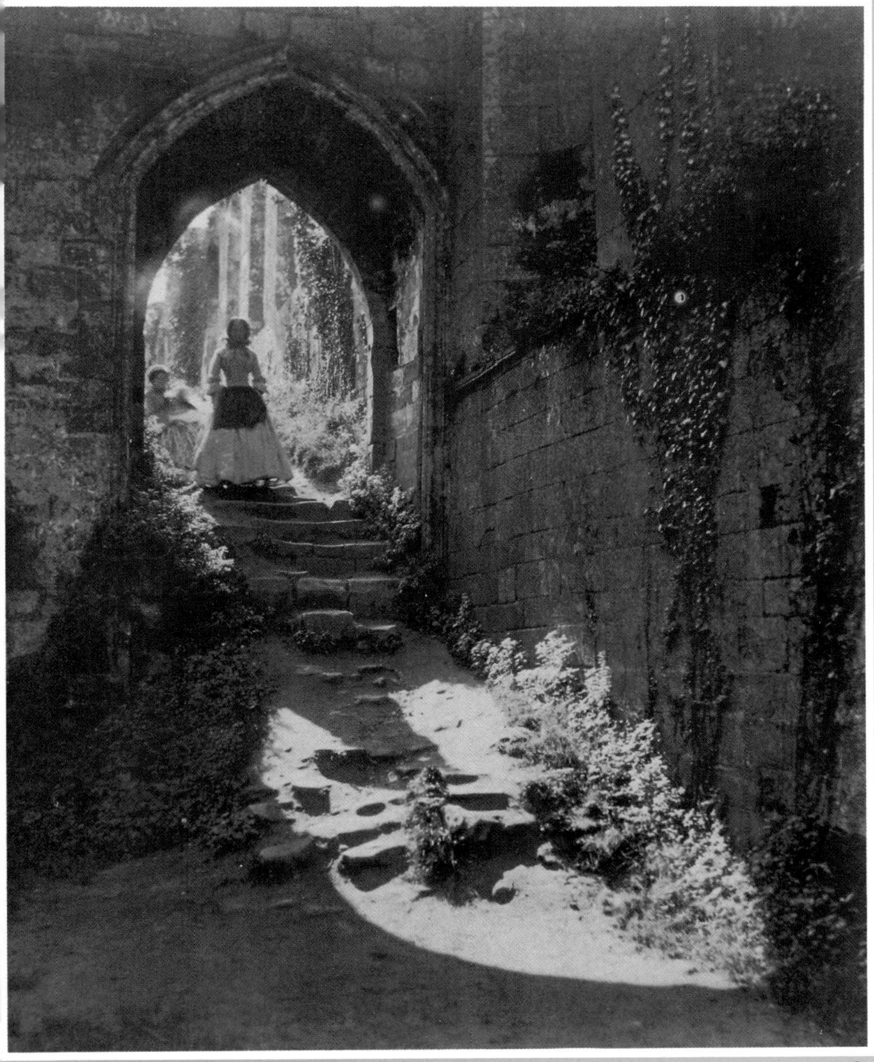

185

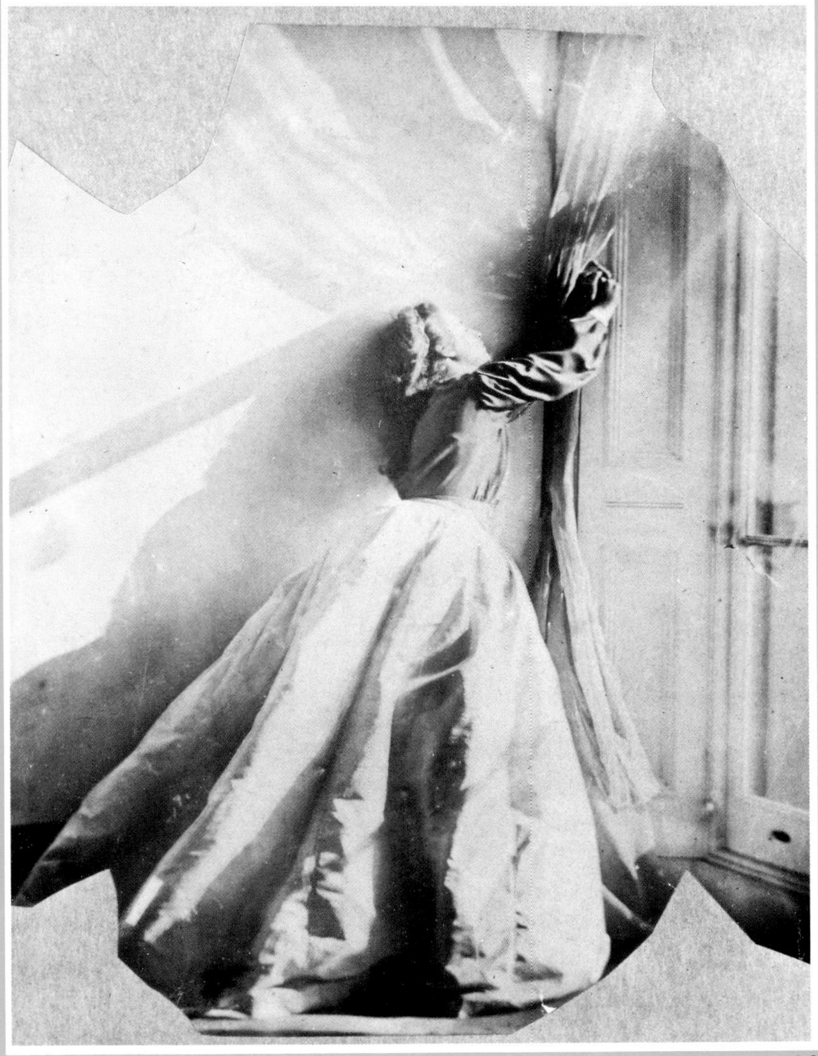

186

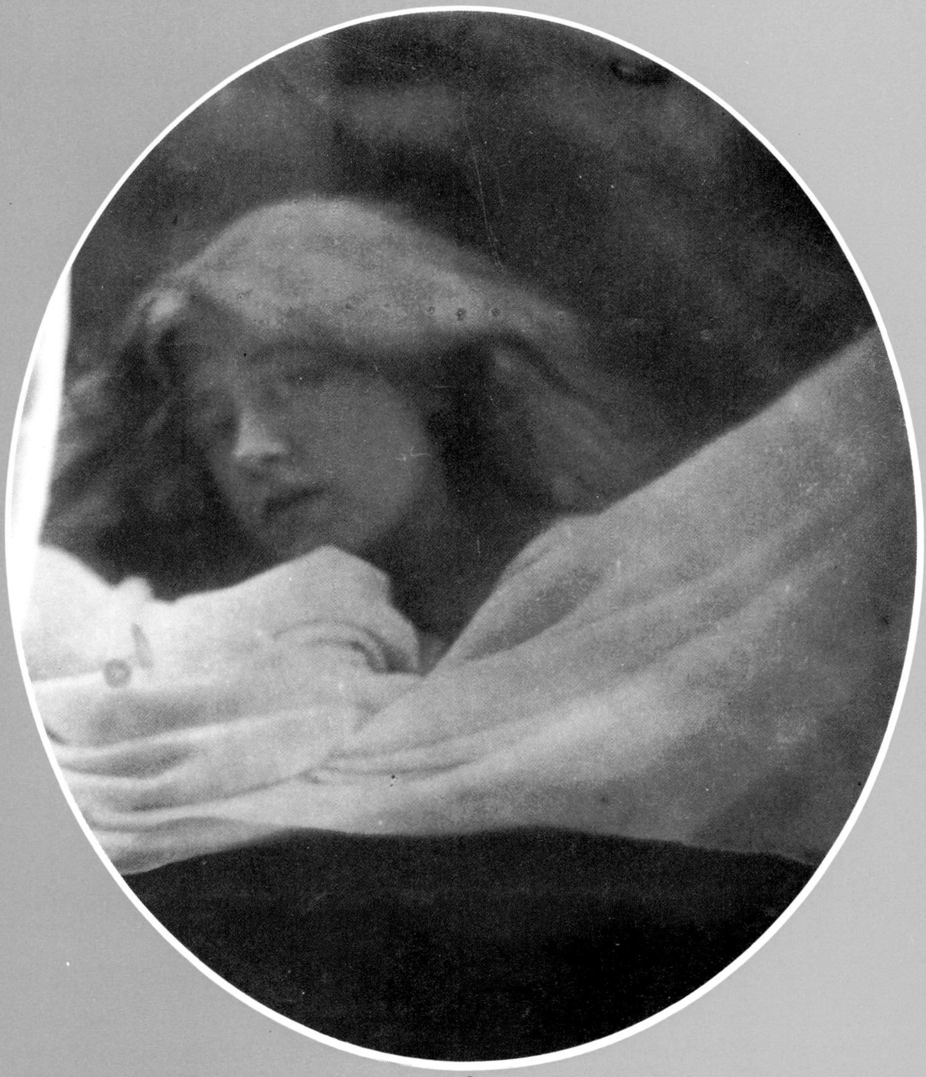

187

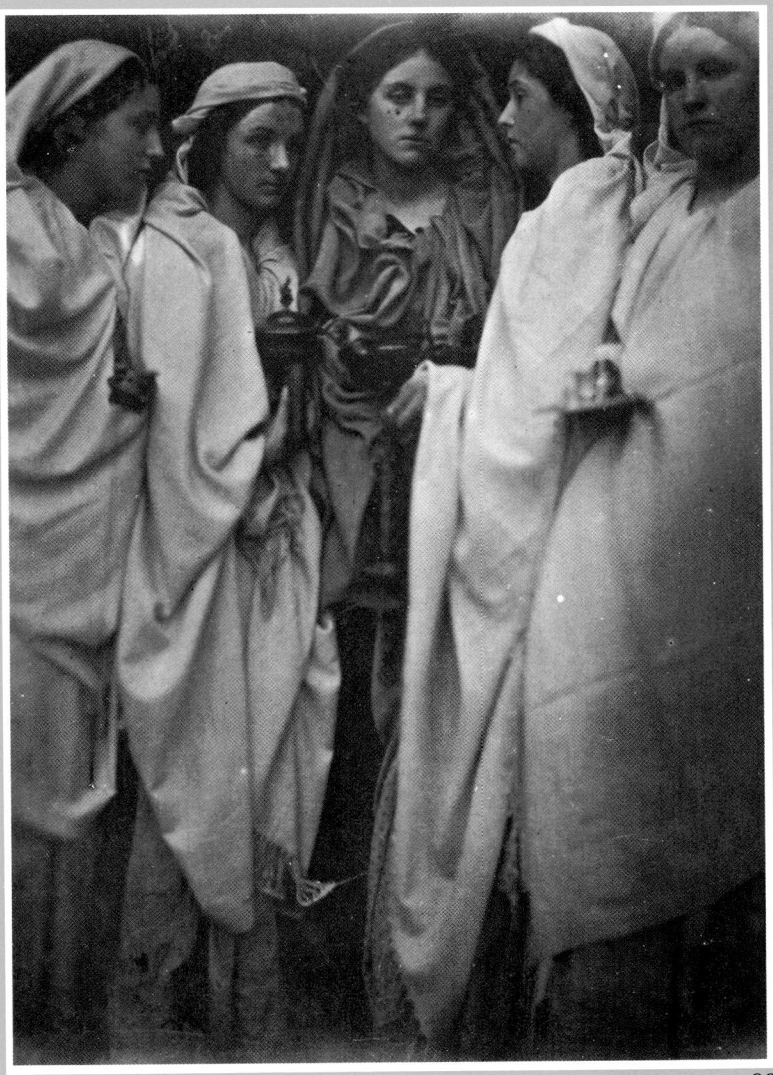

188

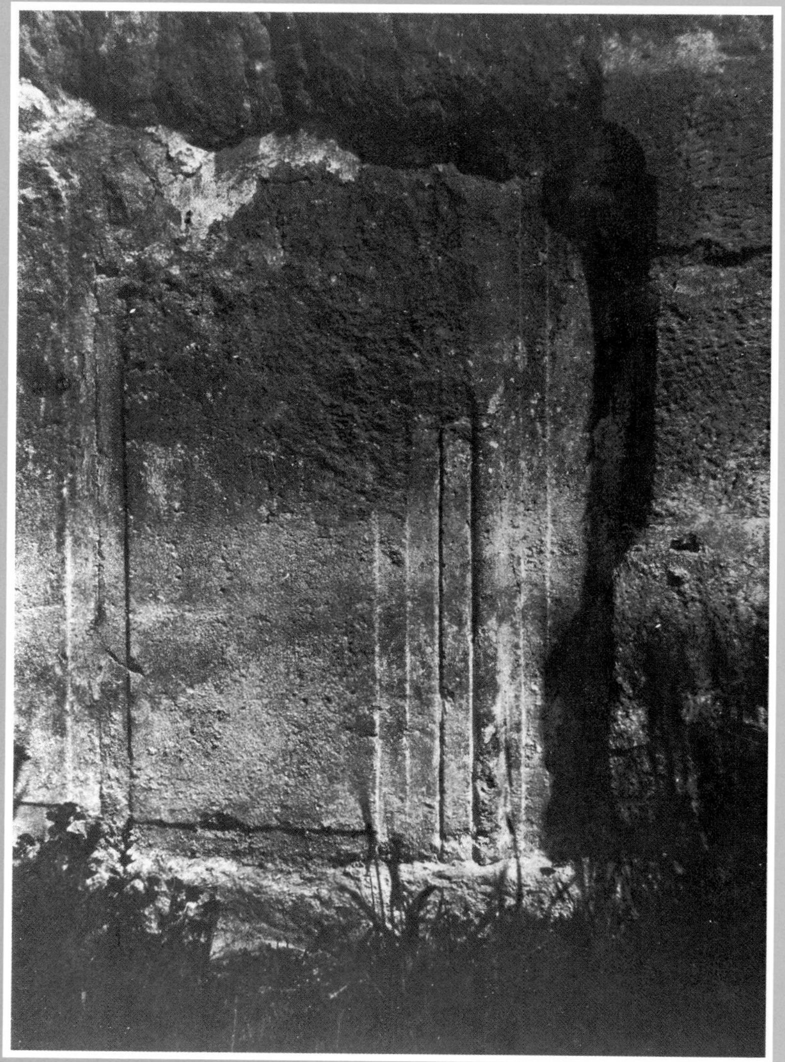

189

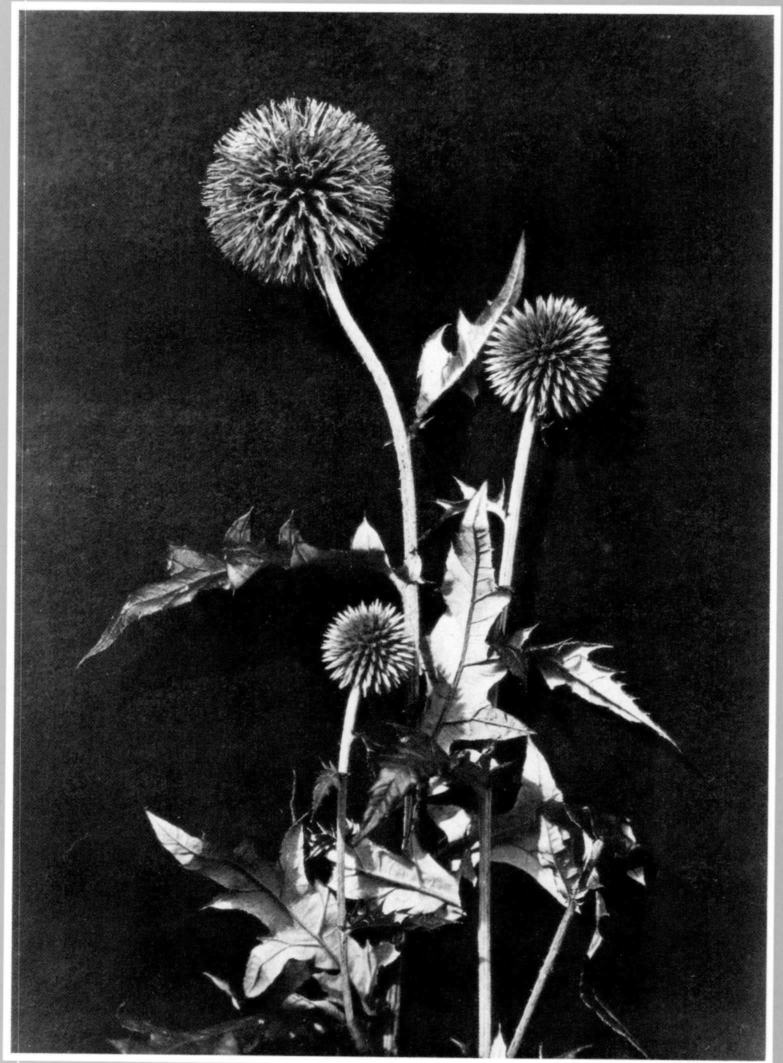

190

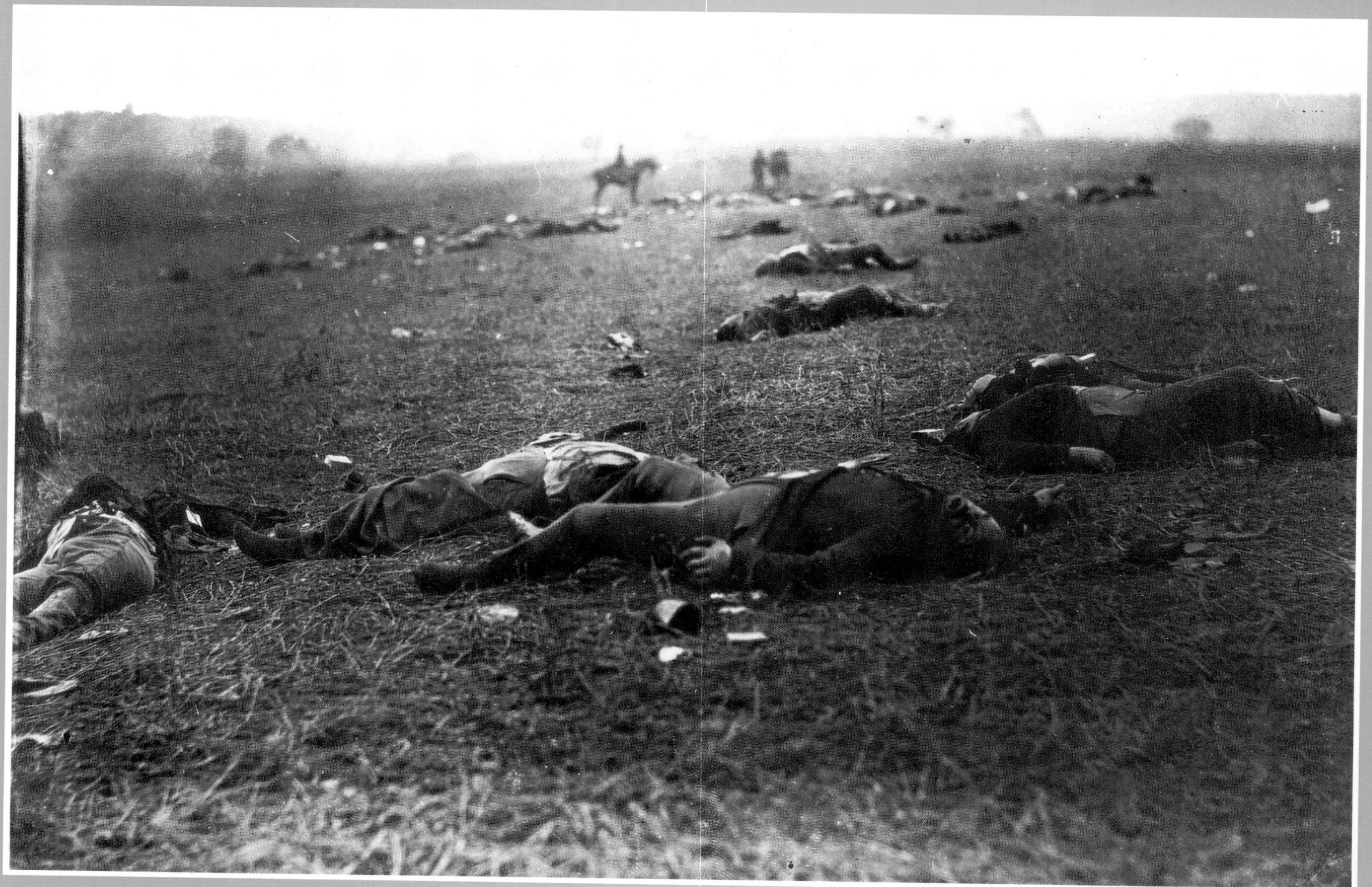

191

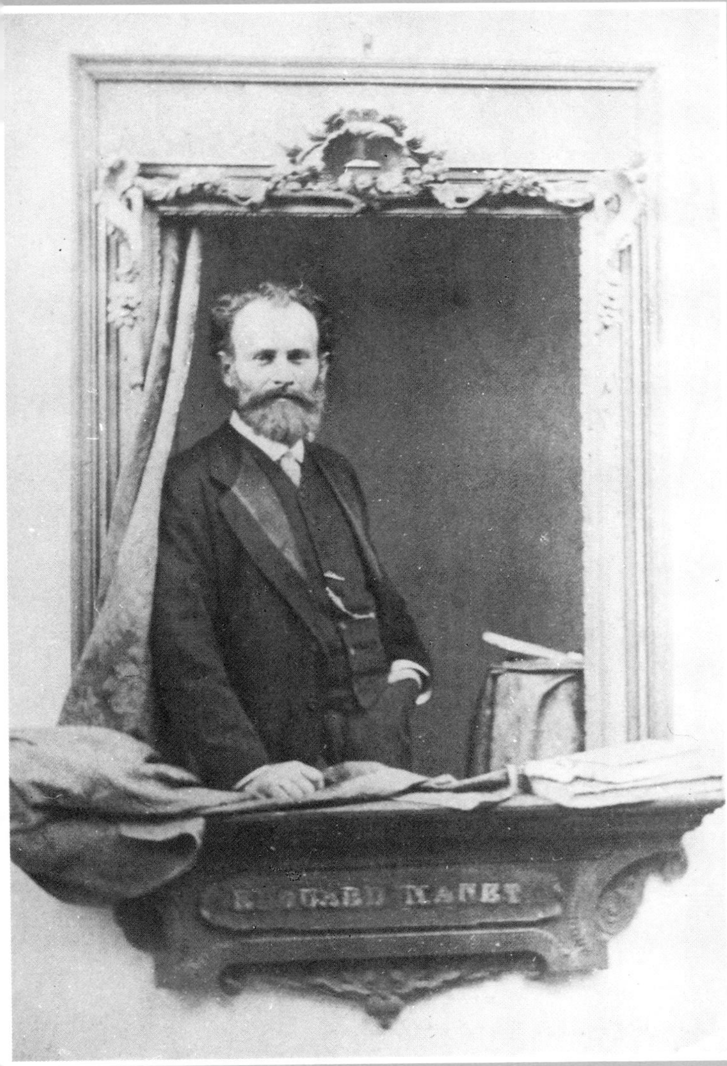

192

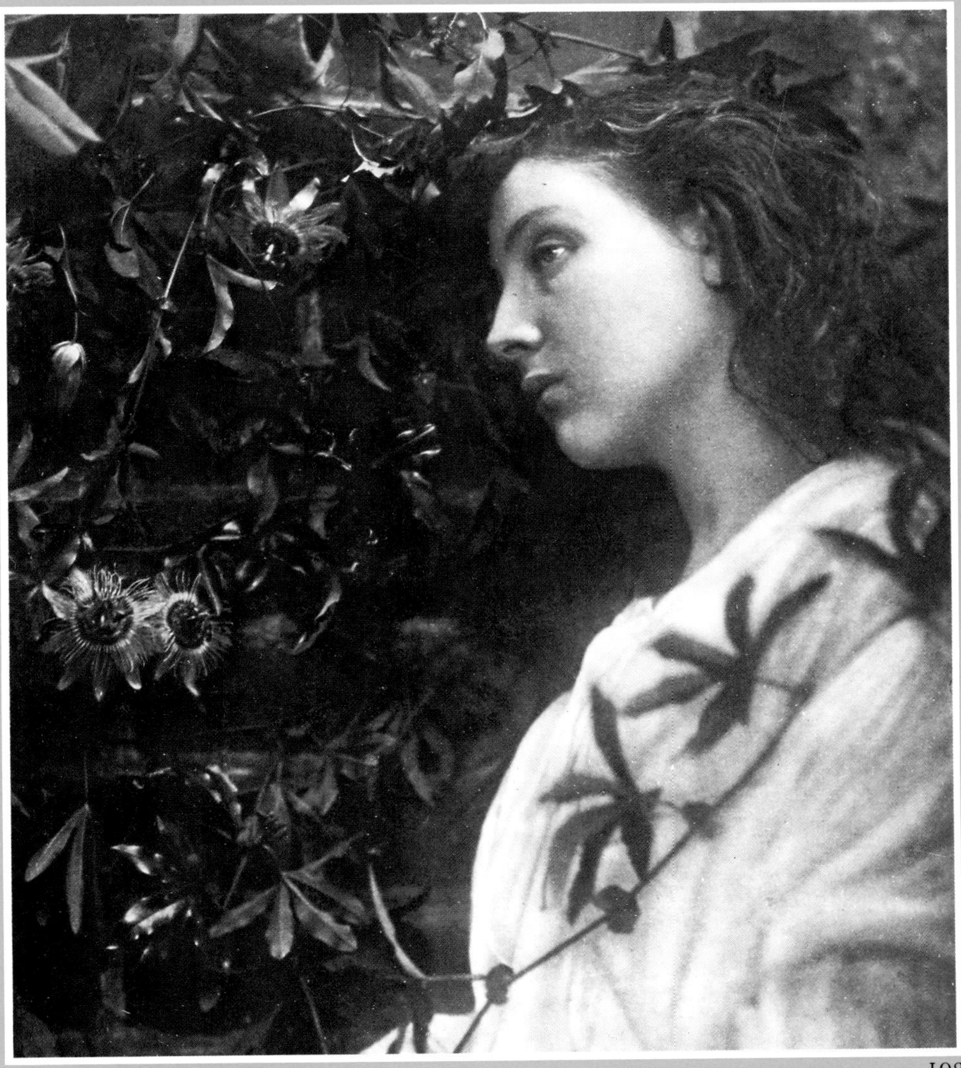

193

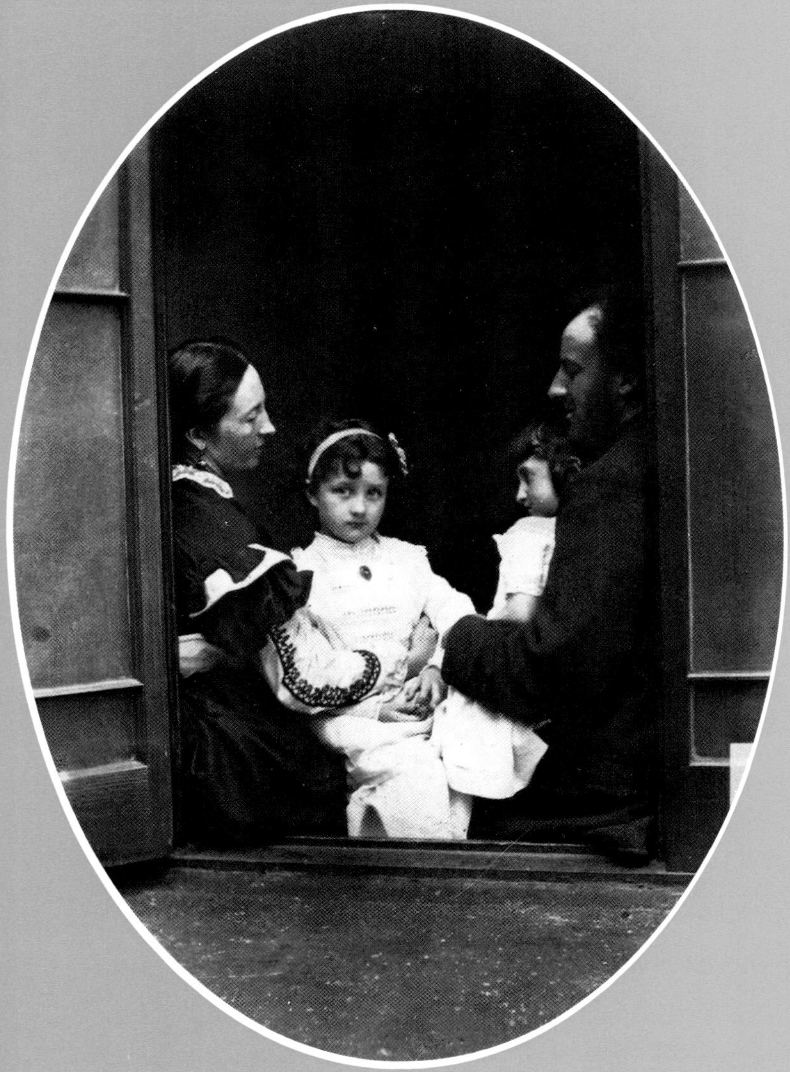

194

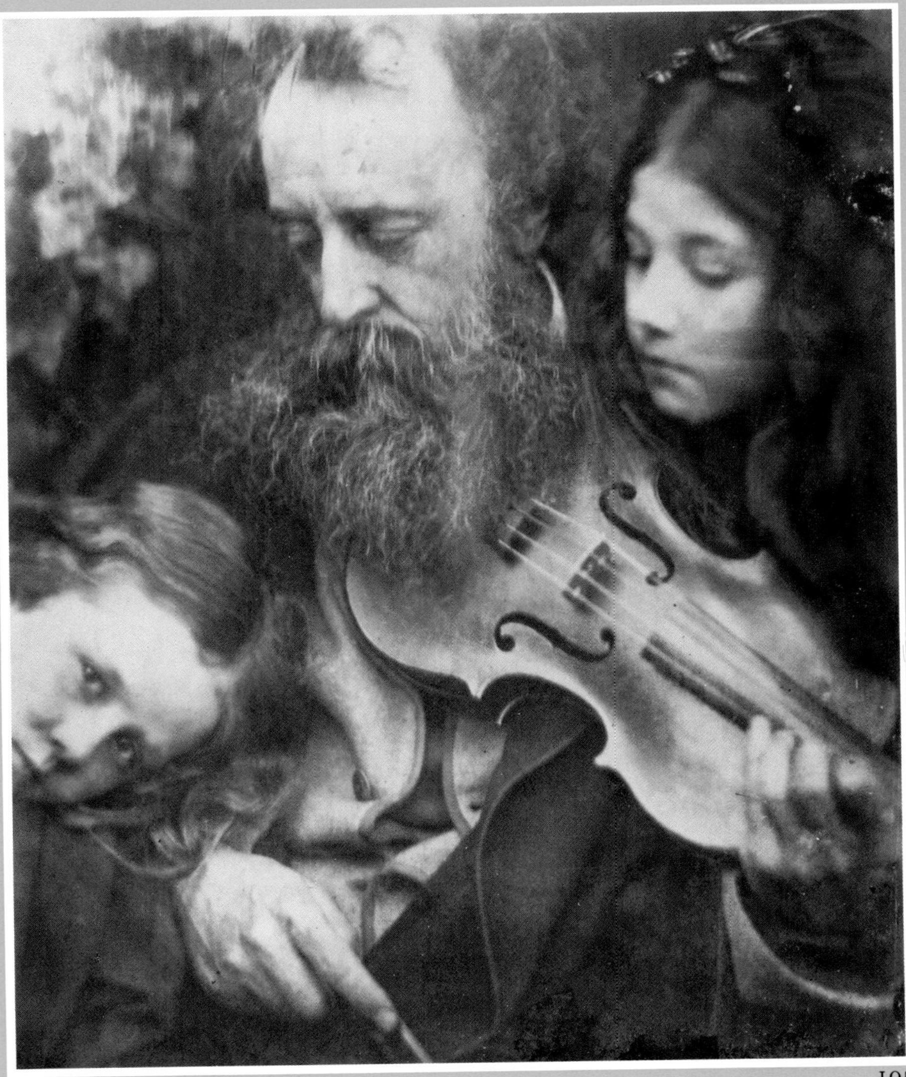

195

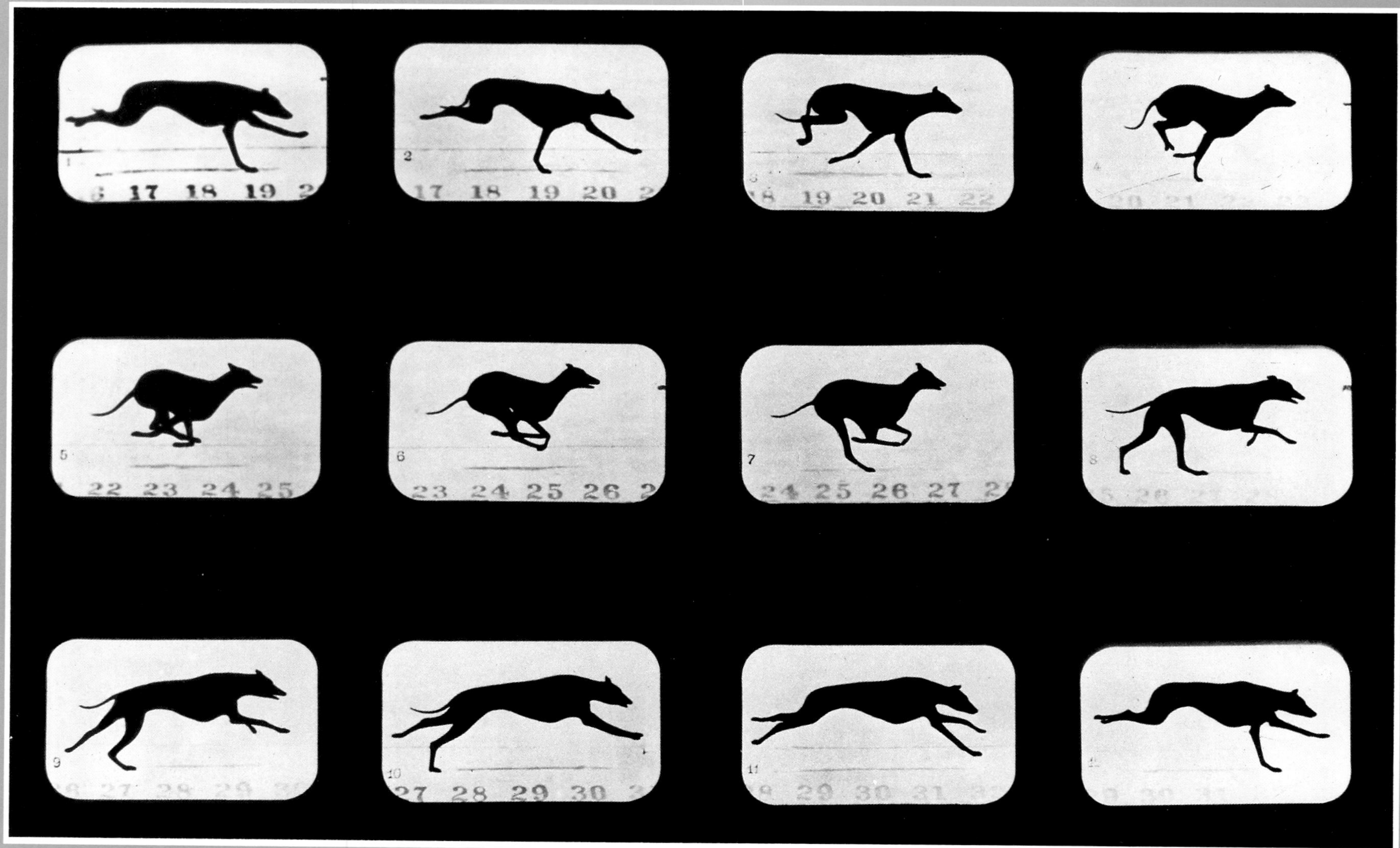
17 18 19
17 18 19 20
19 20 21 22
22 23 24 25
23 24 25 26
24 25 26 27
27 28 29 30
29 30 31

196

197

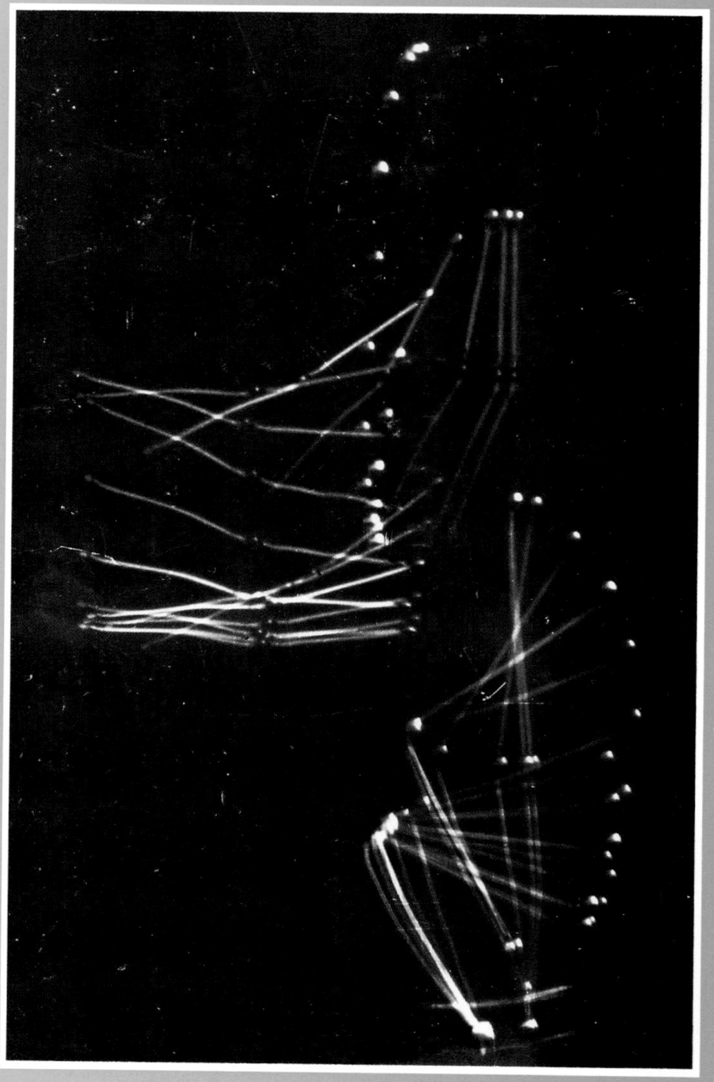

198

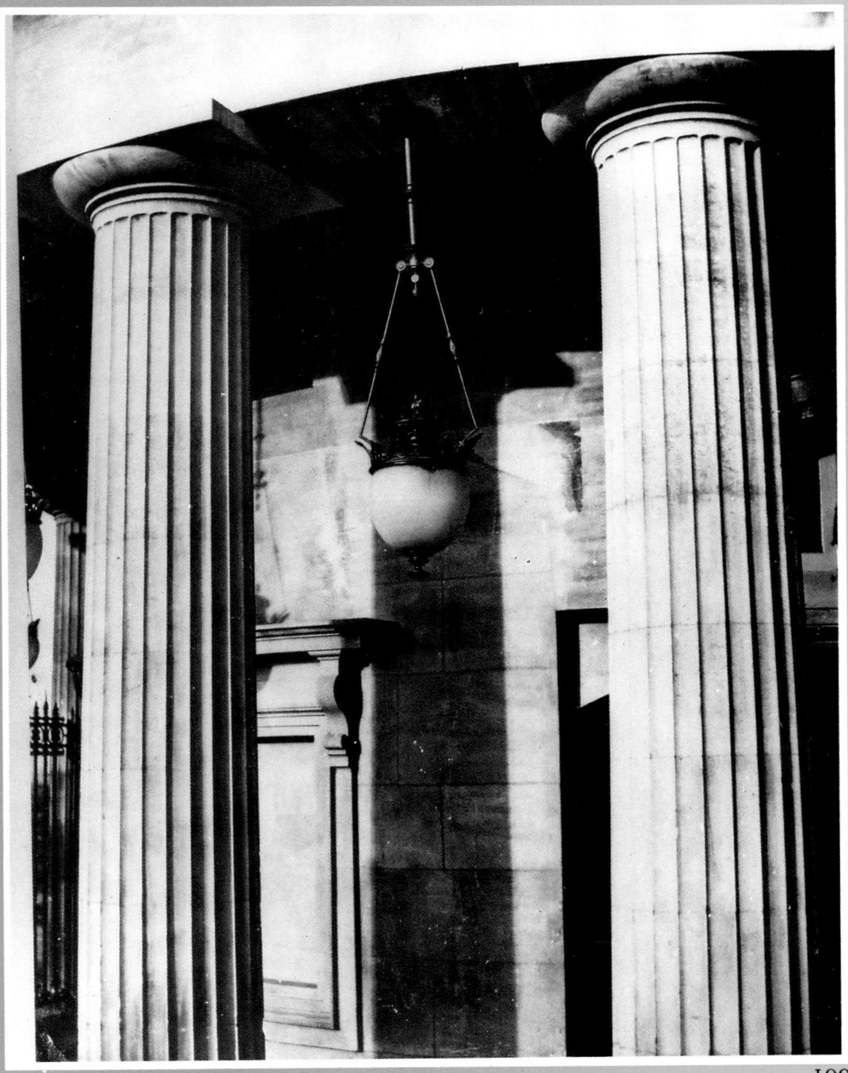

199

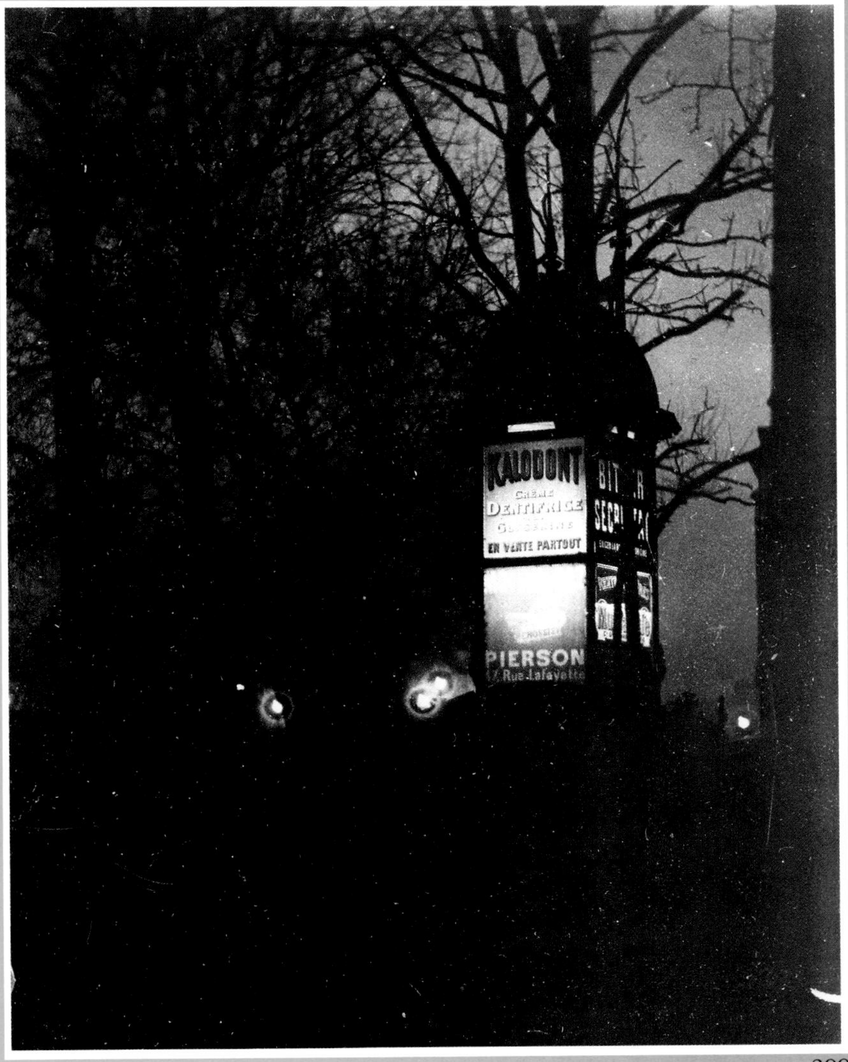

200

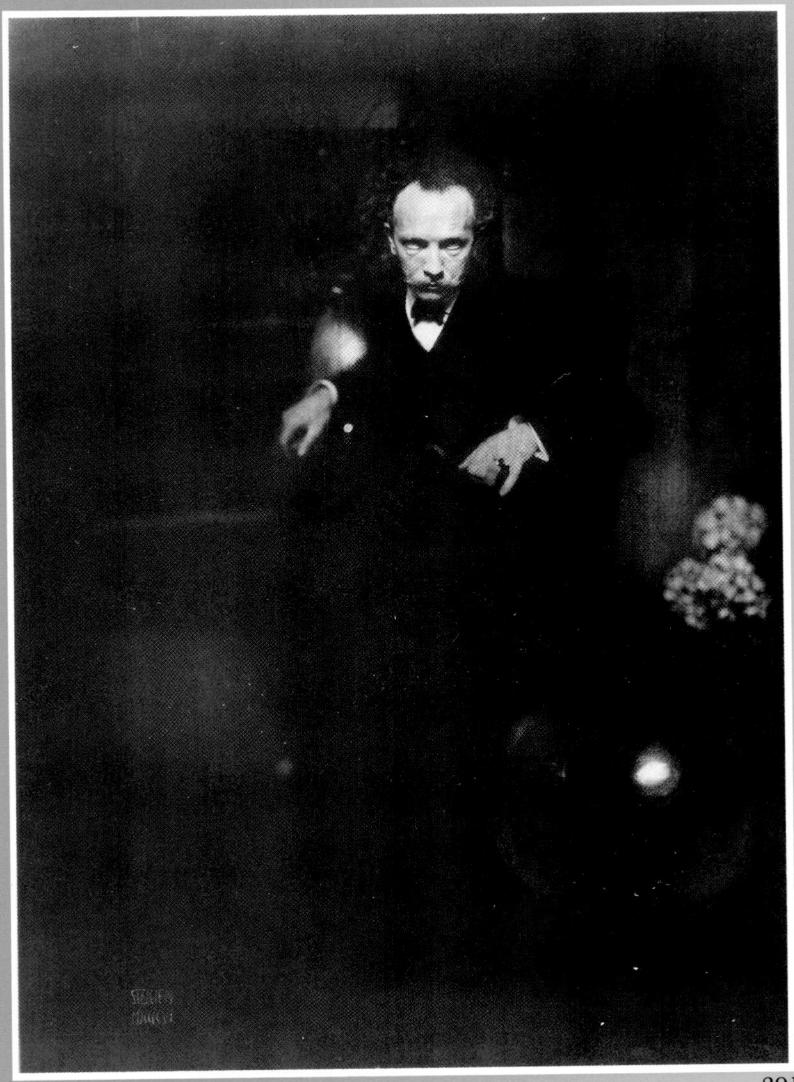

201

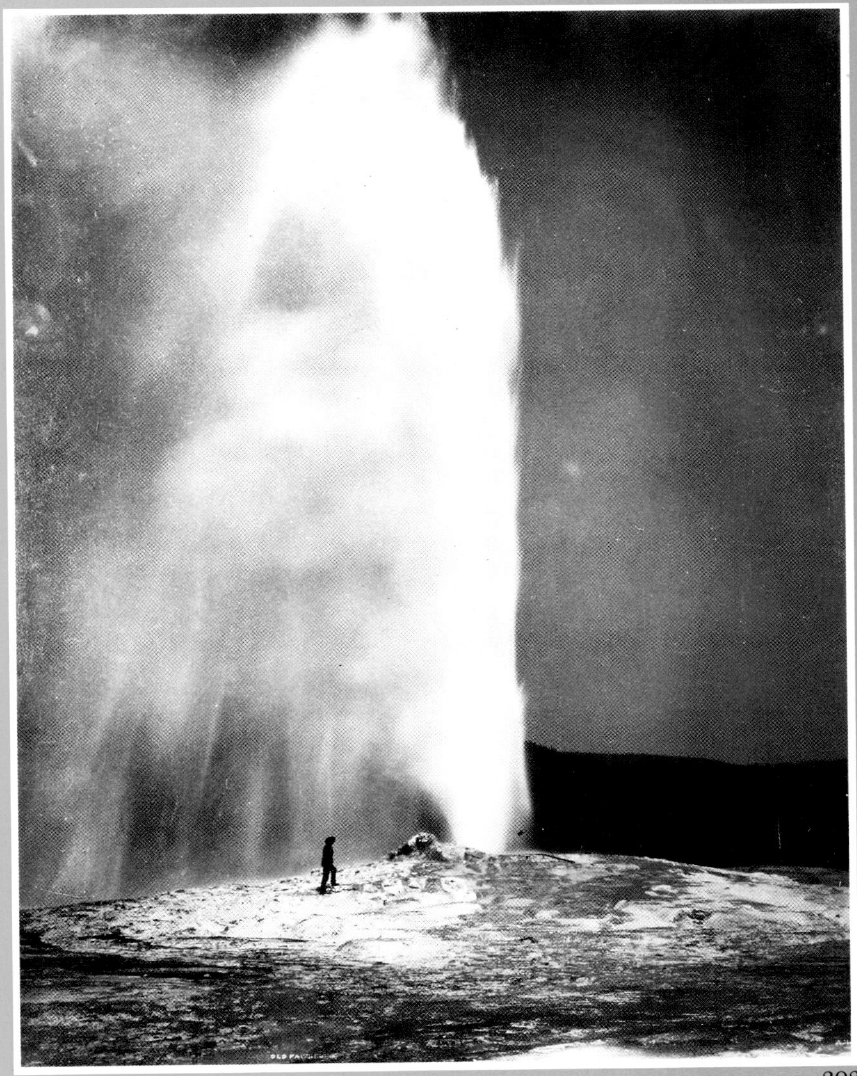

202

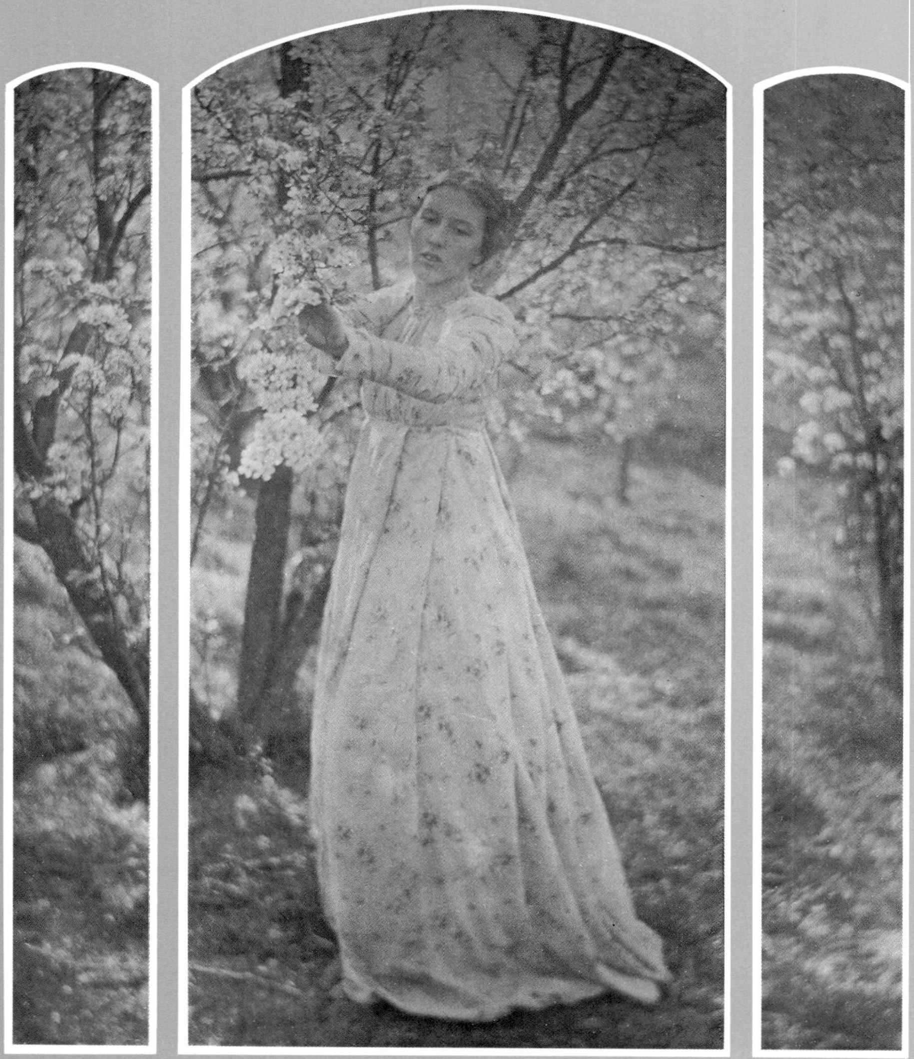

203

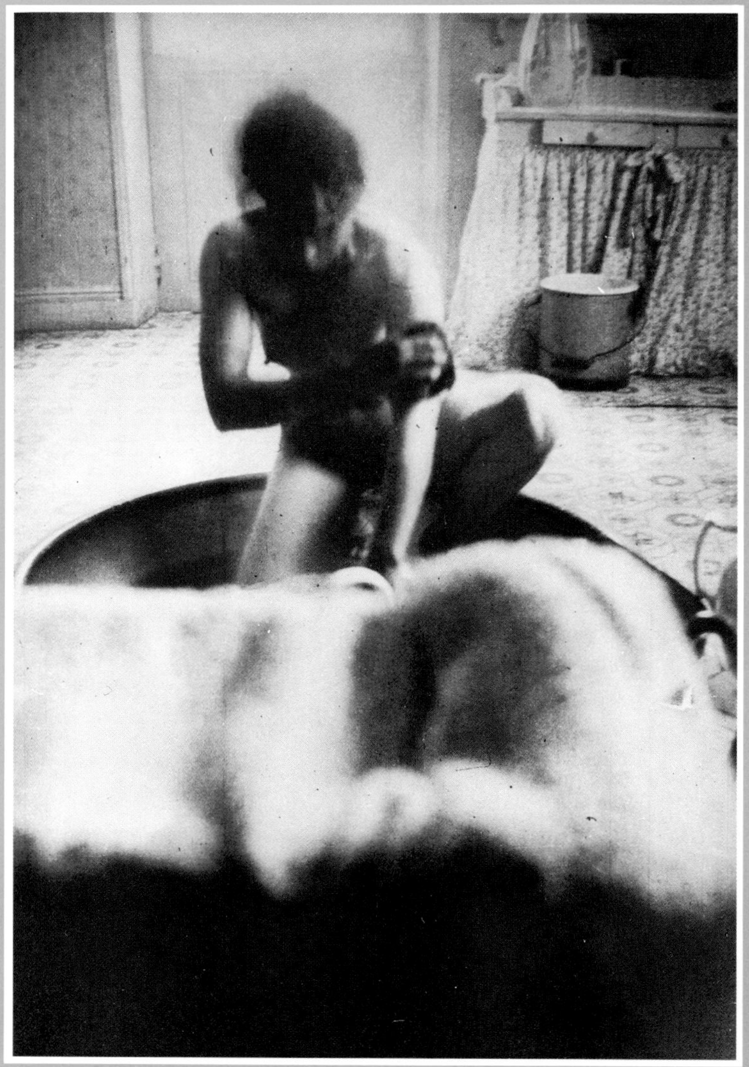

204

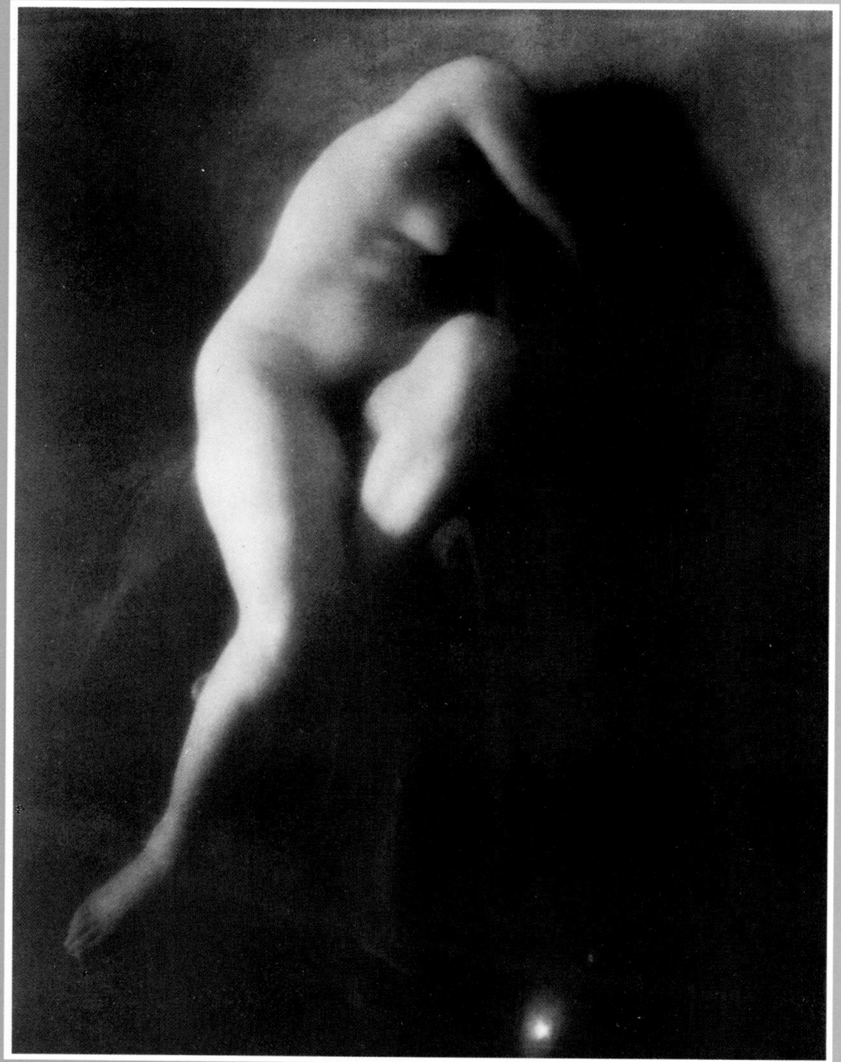

205

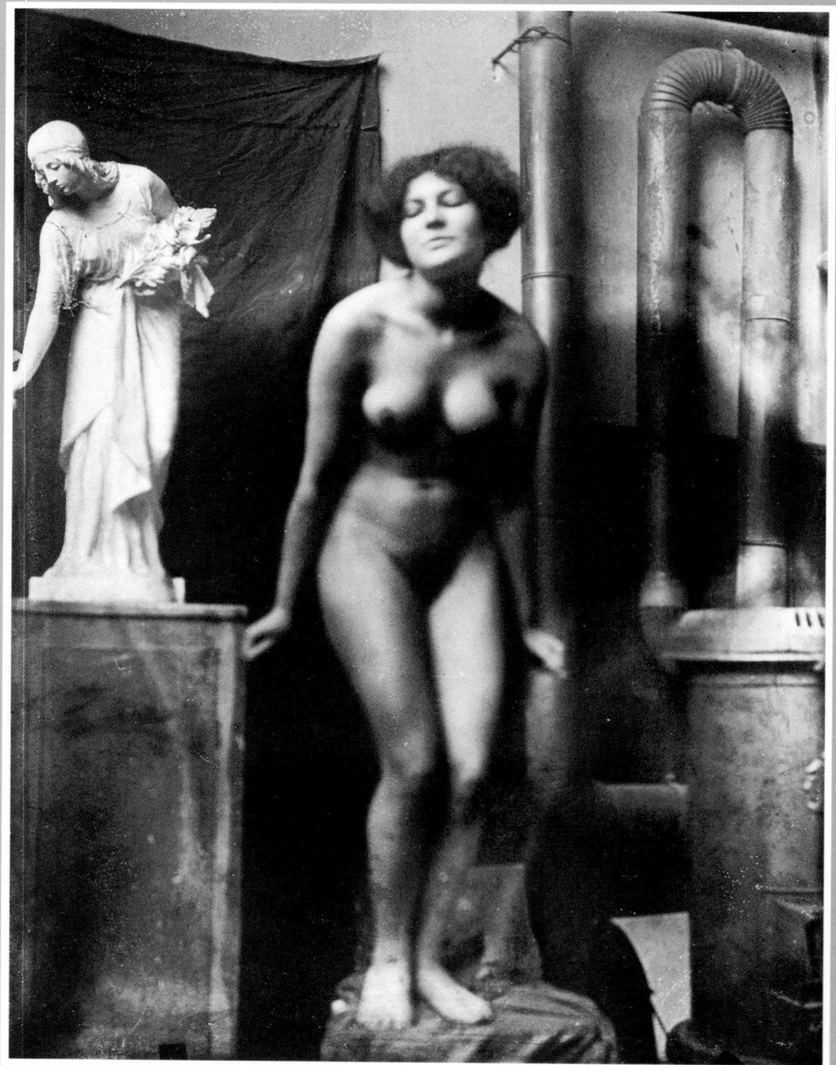

206

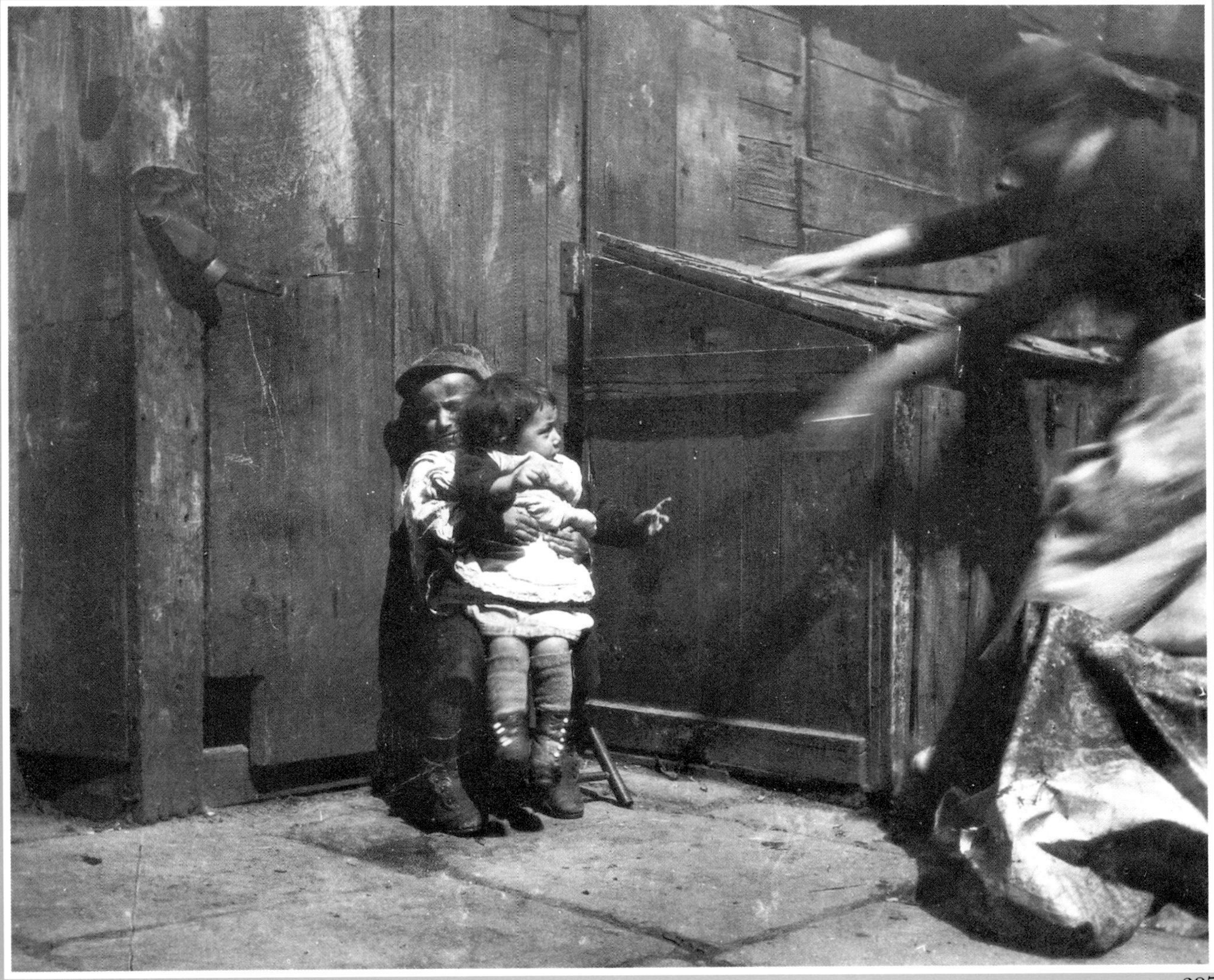

207

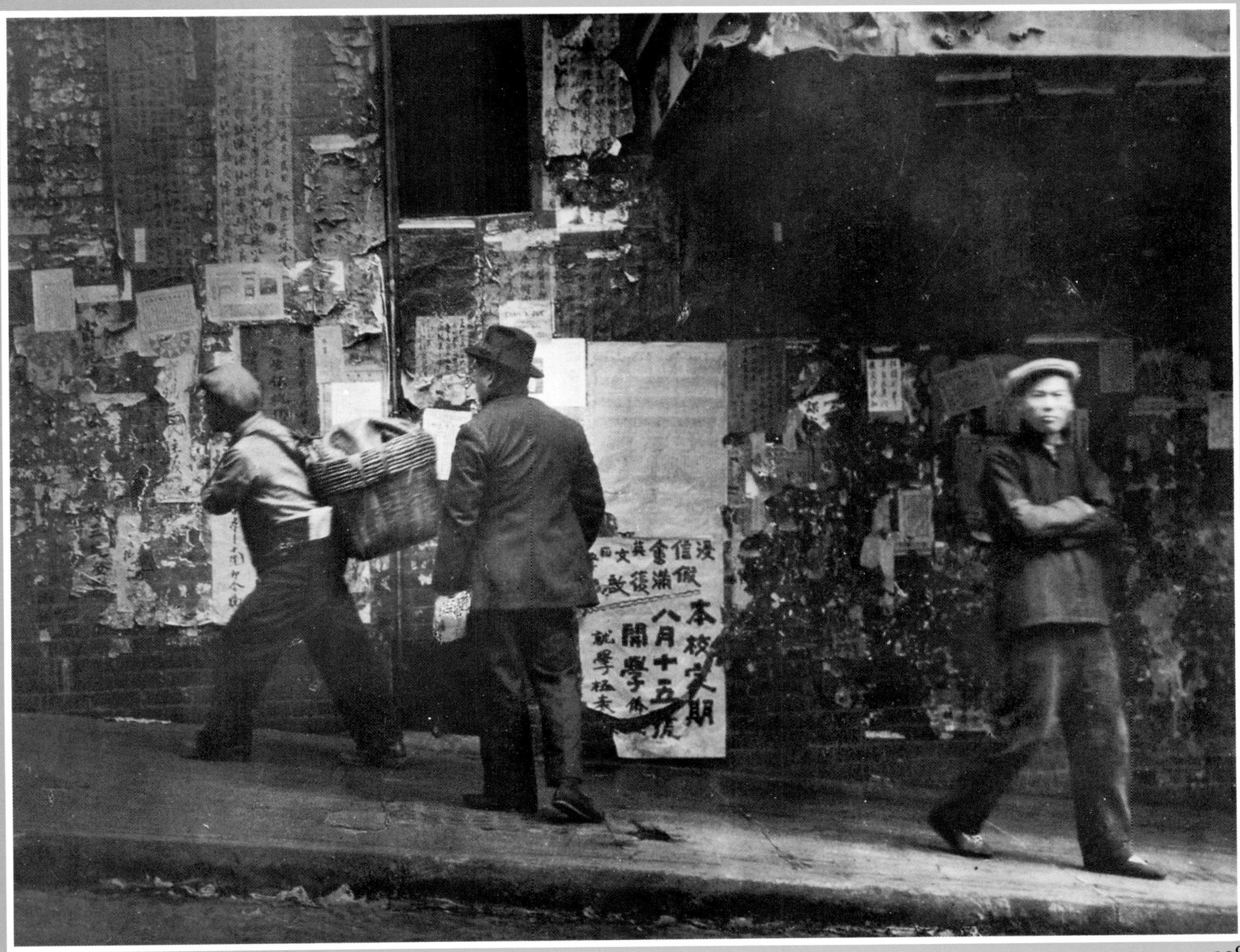

208

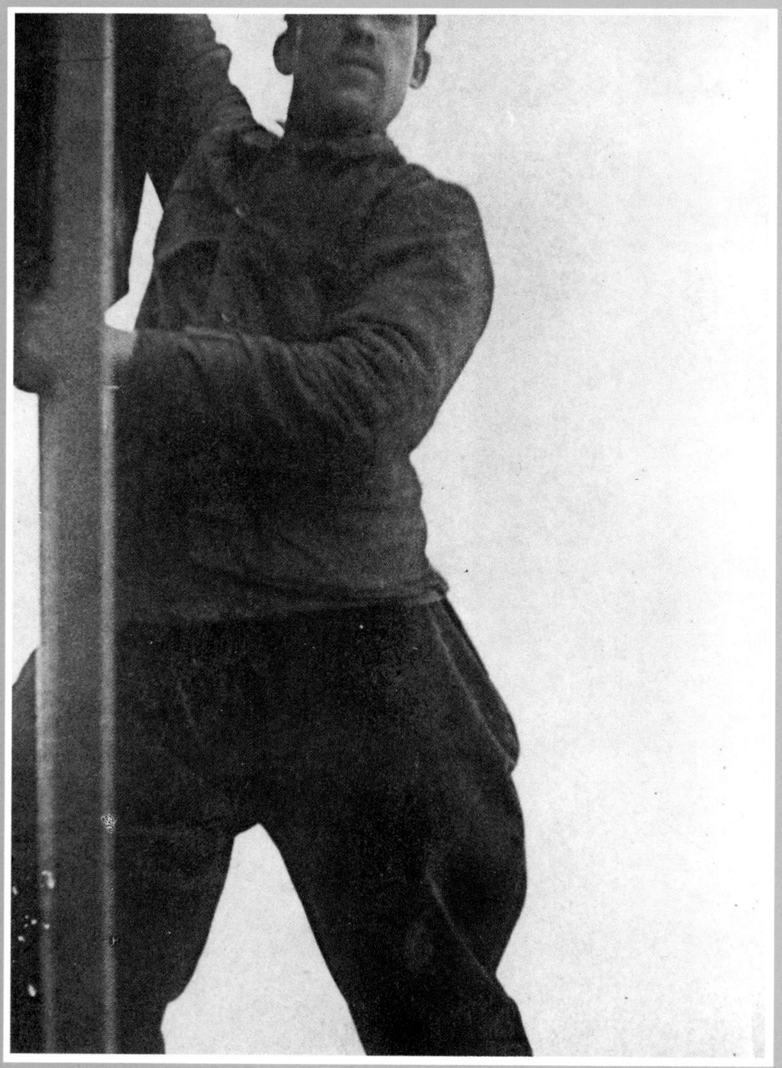

209

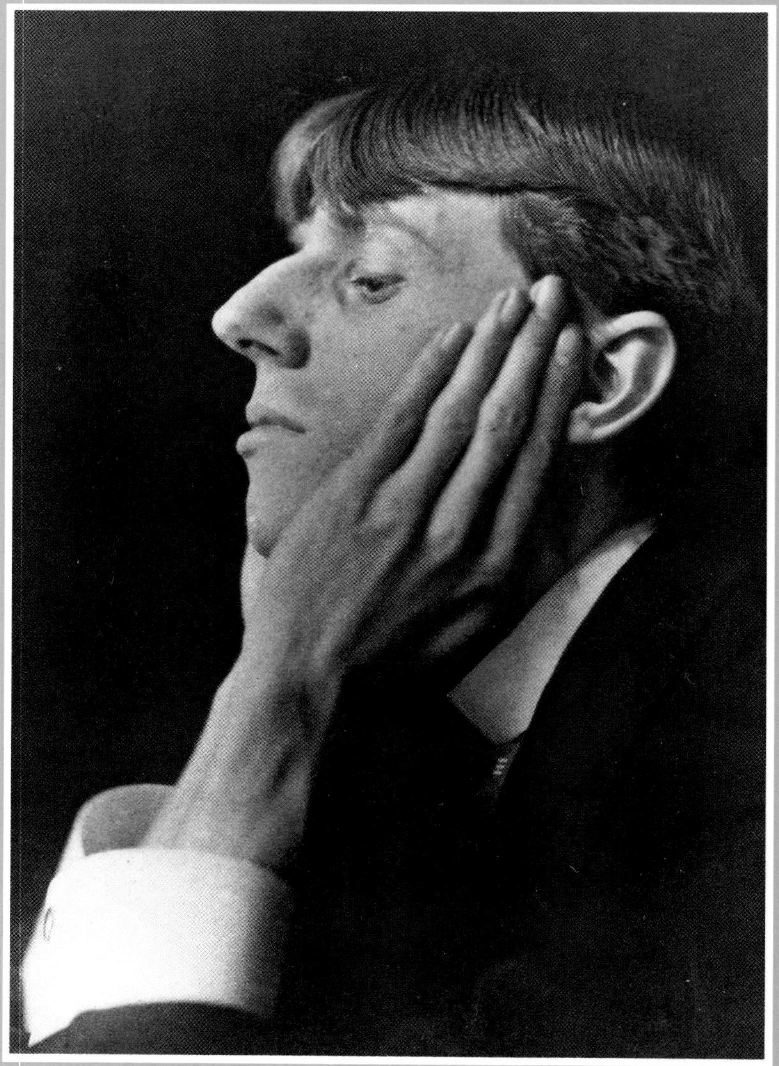

210

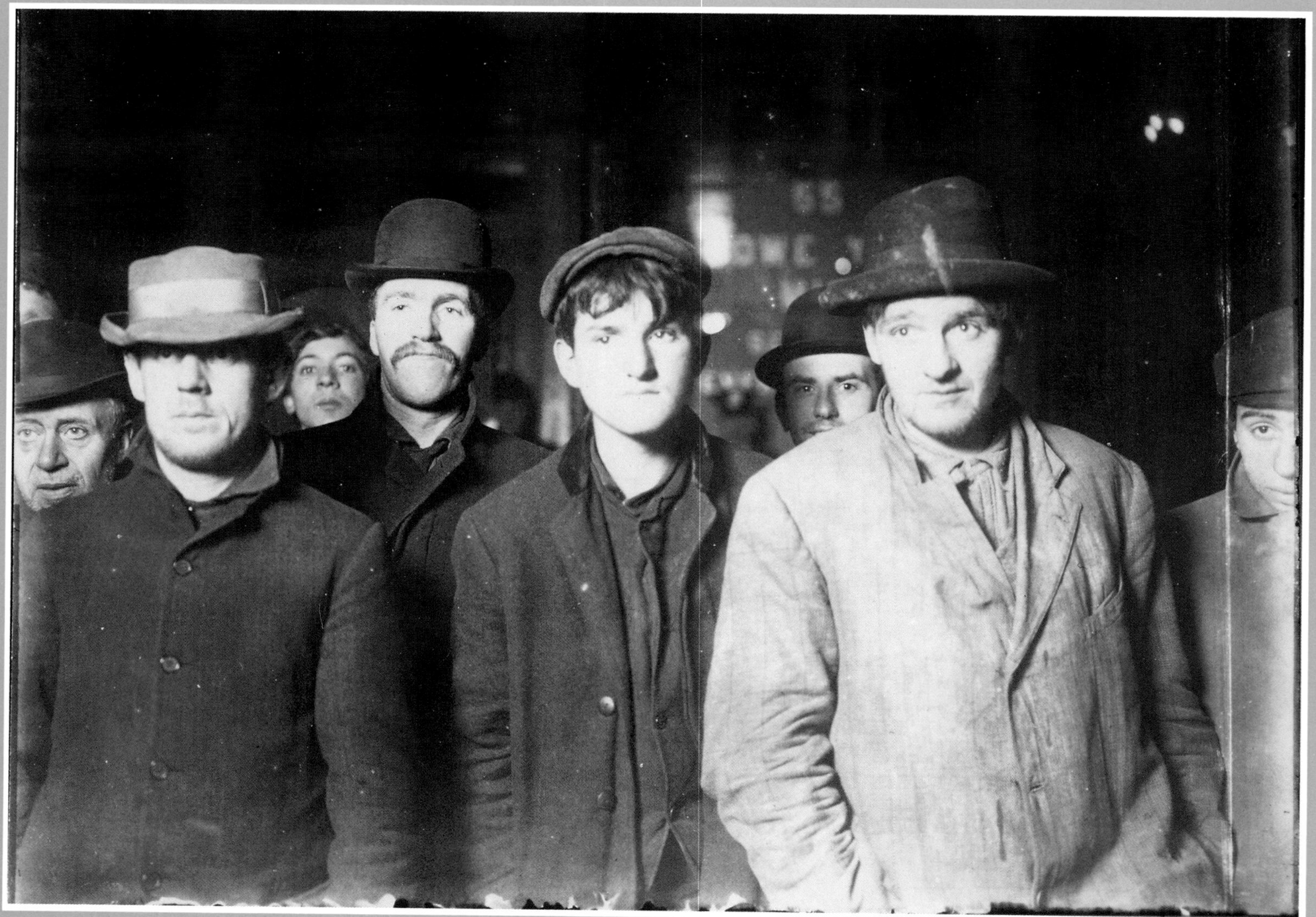

211

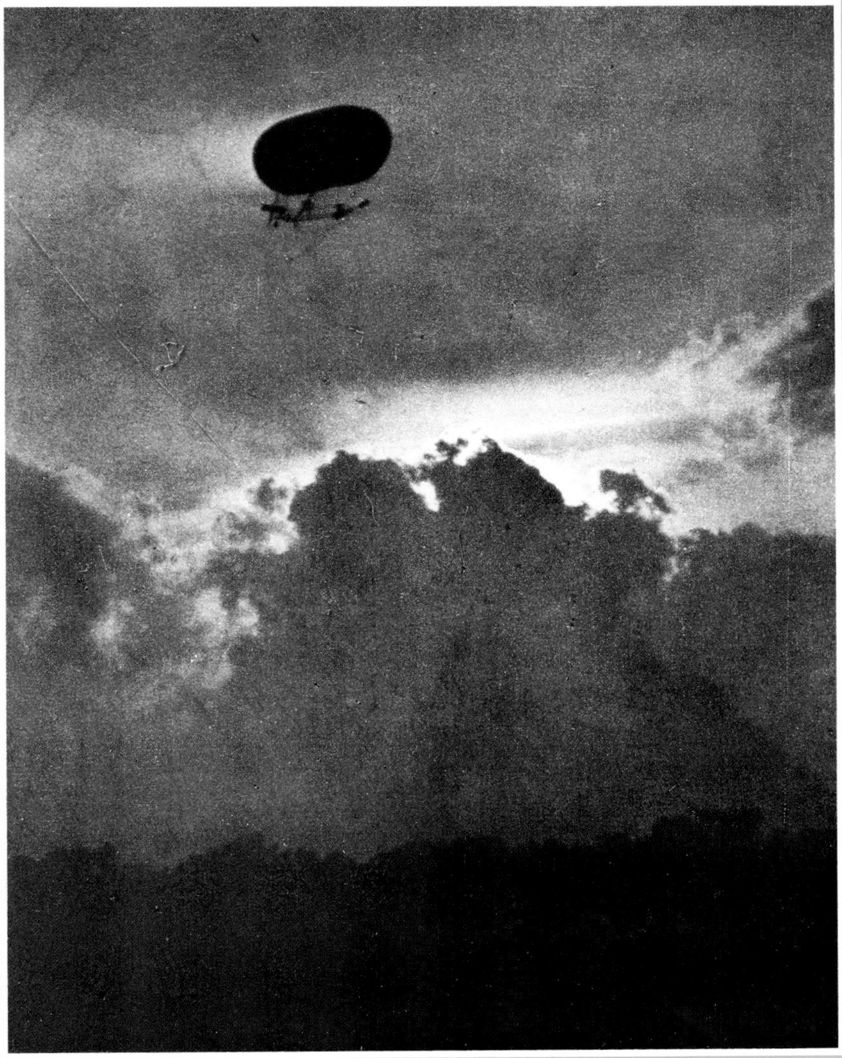

212

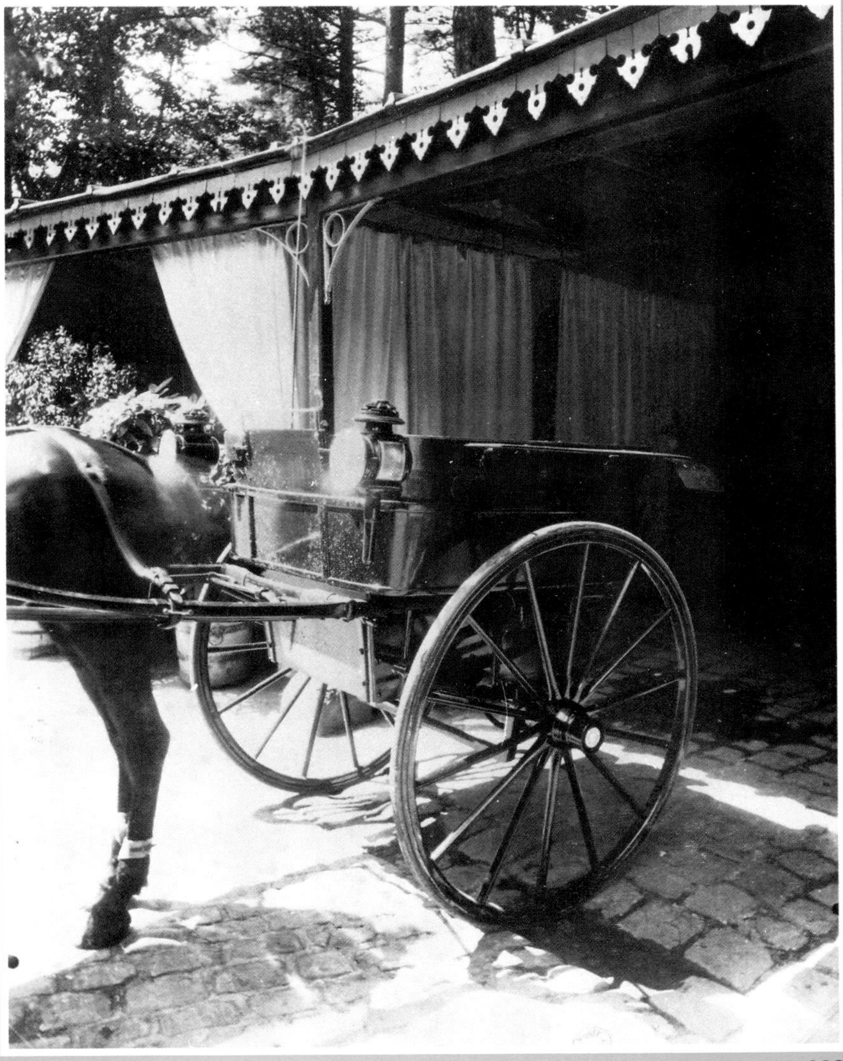

213

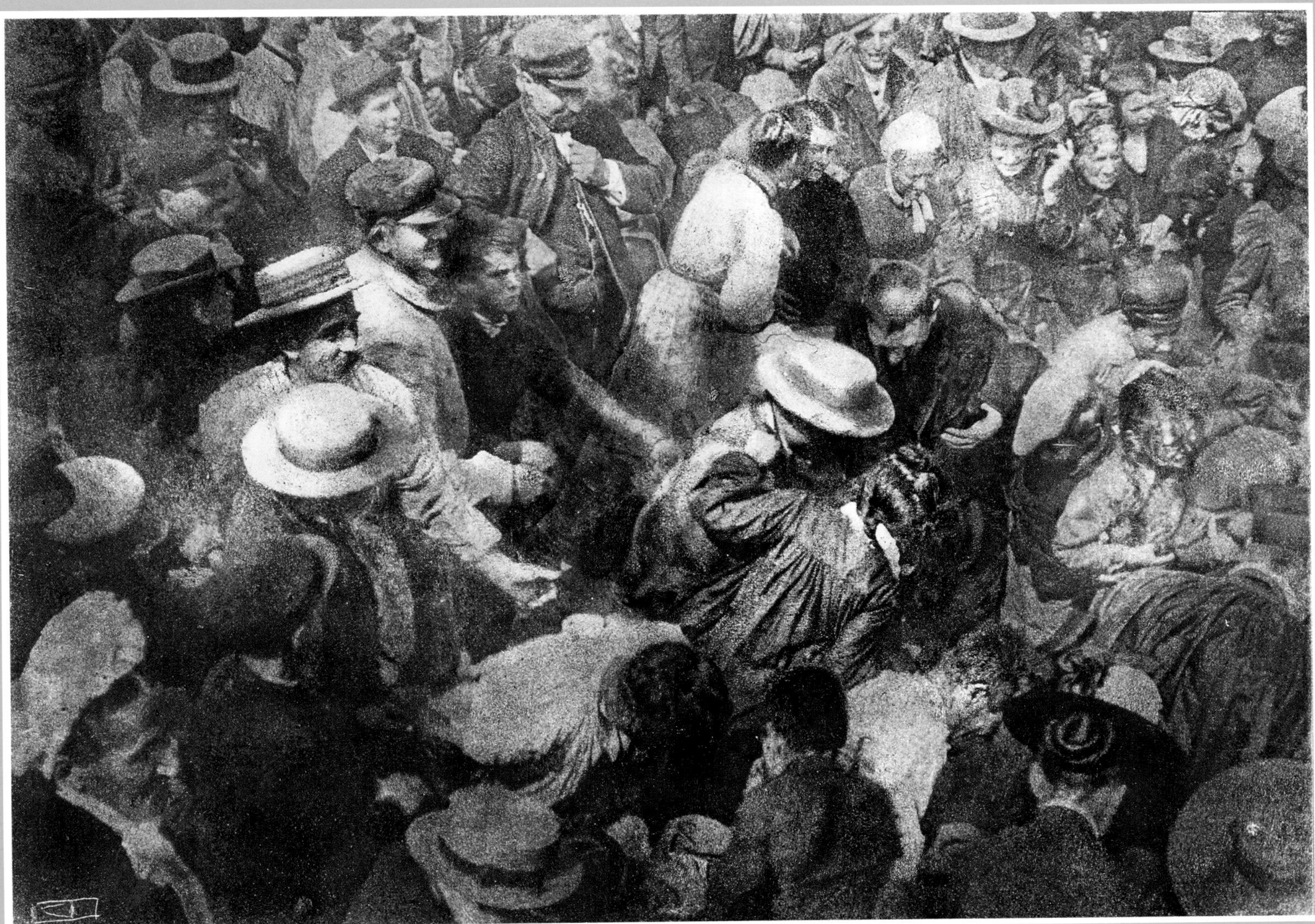

214

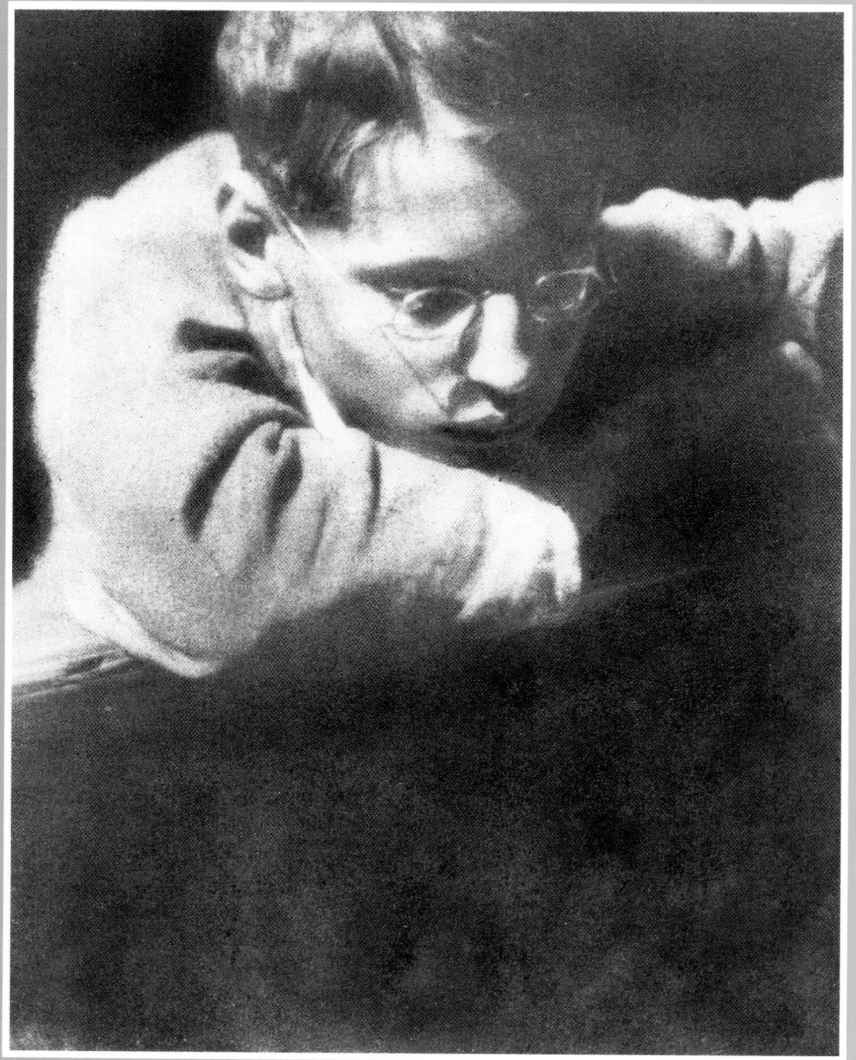
215

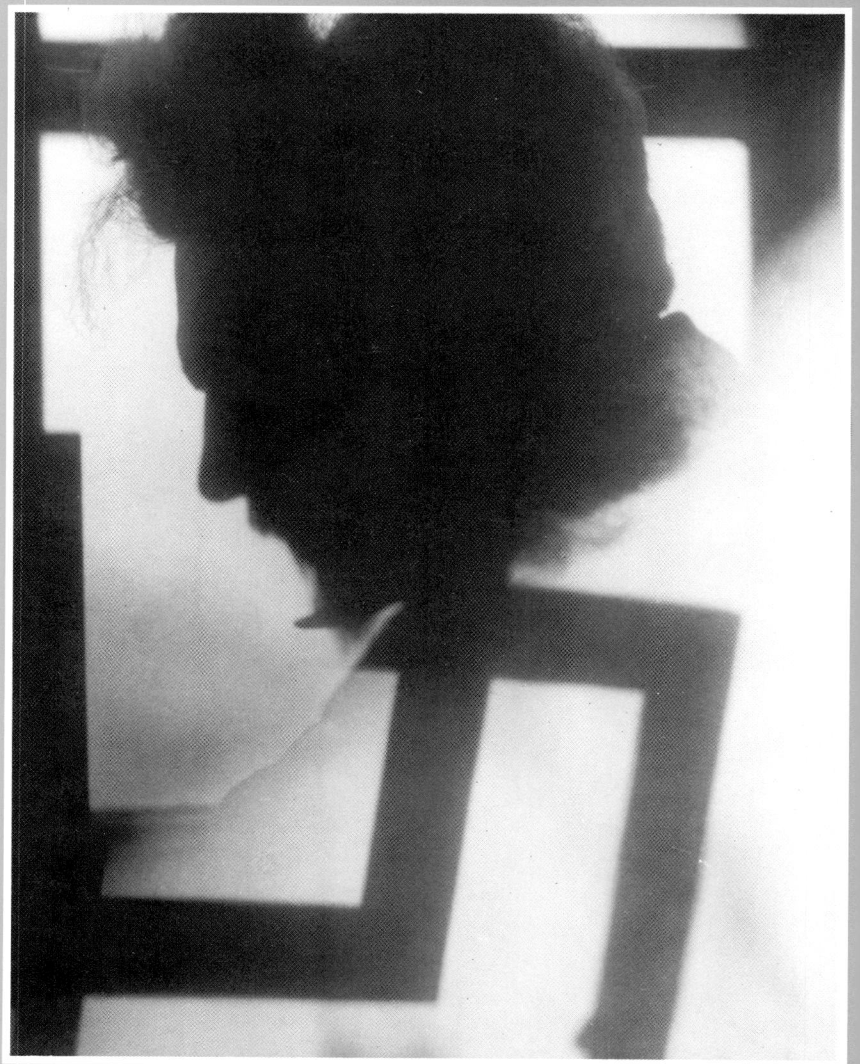
216

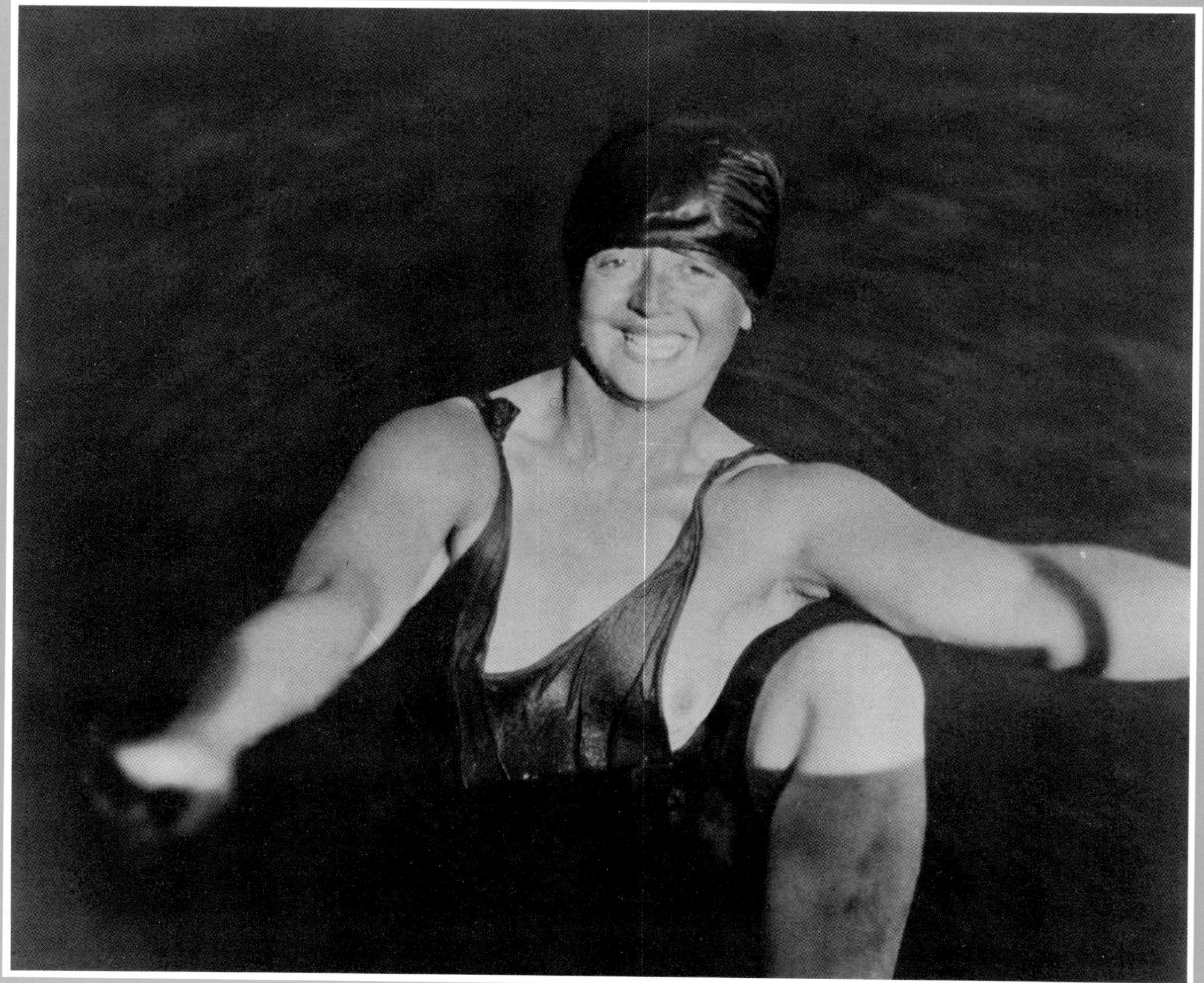
217

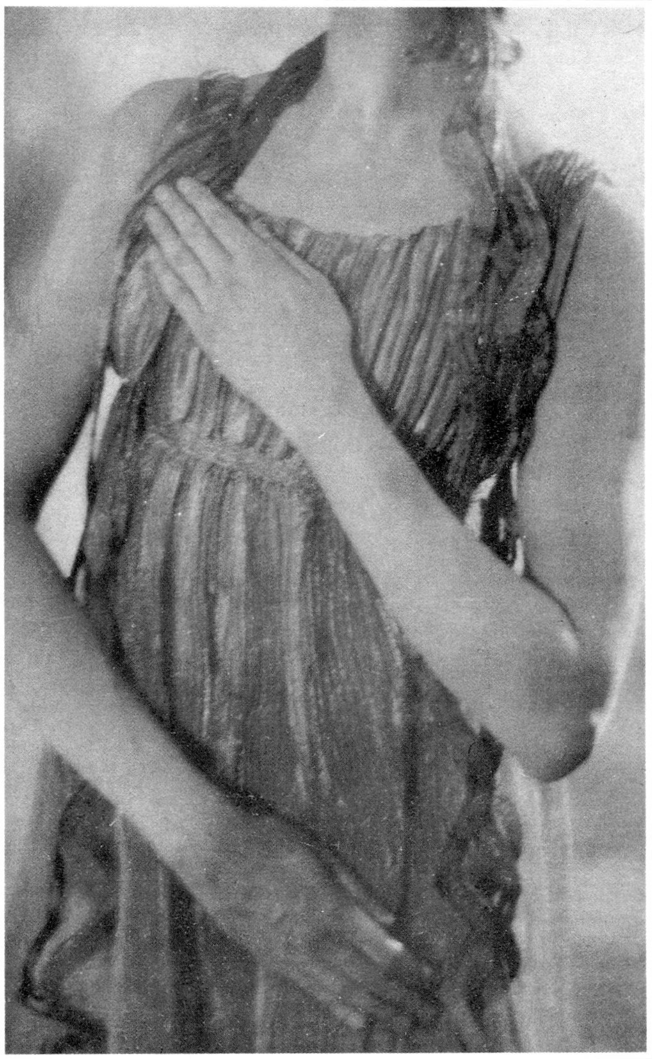

218

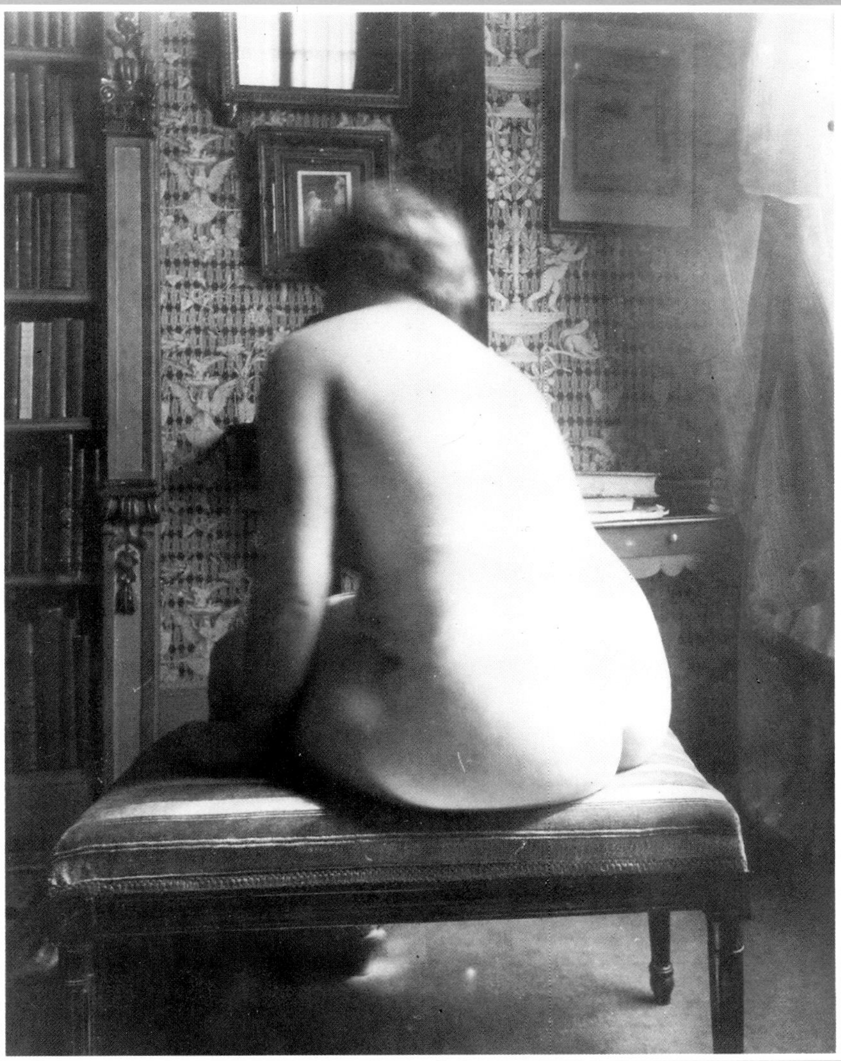

219

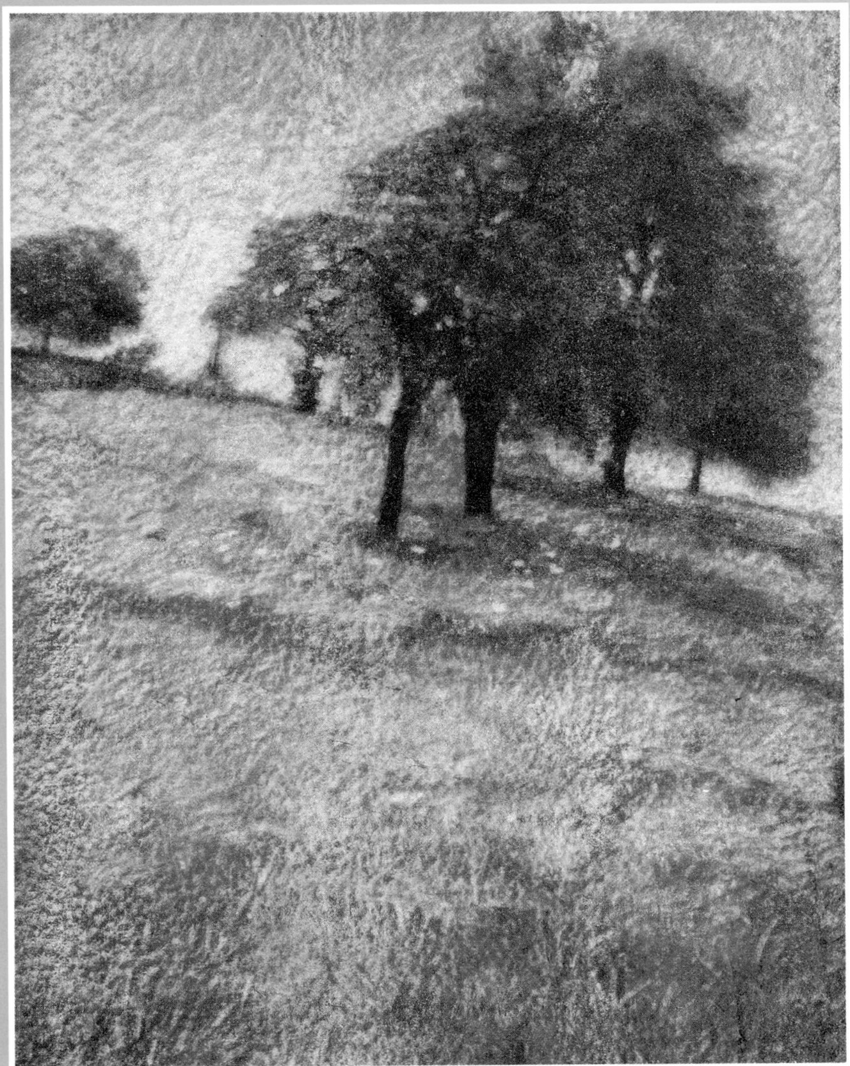

220

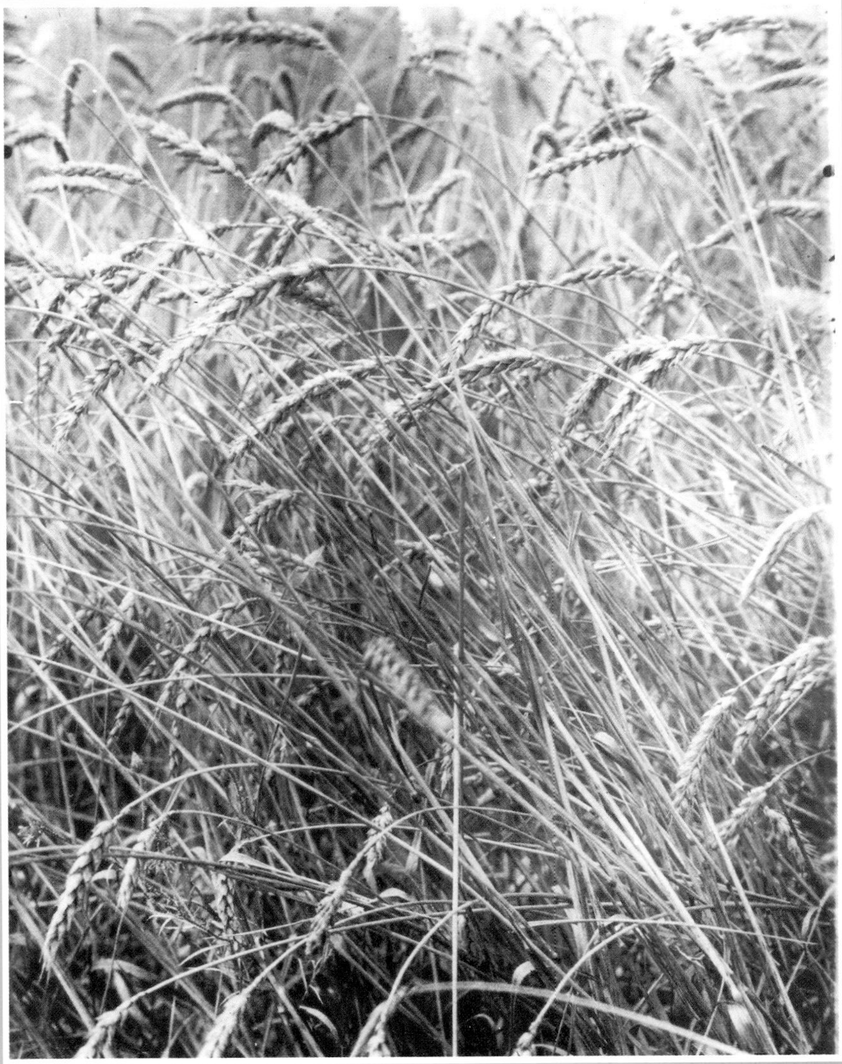

221

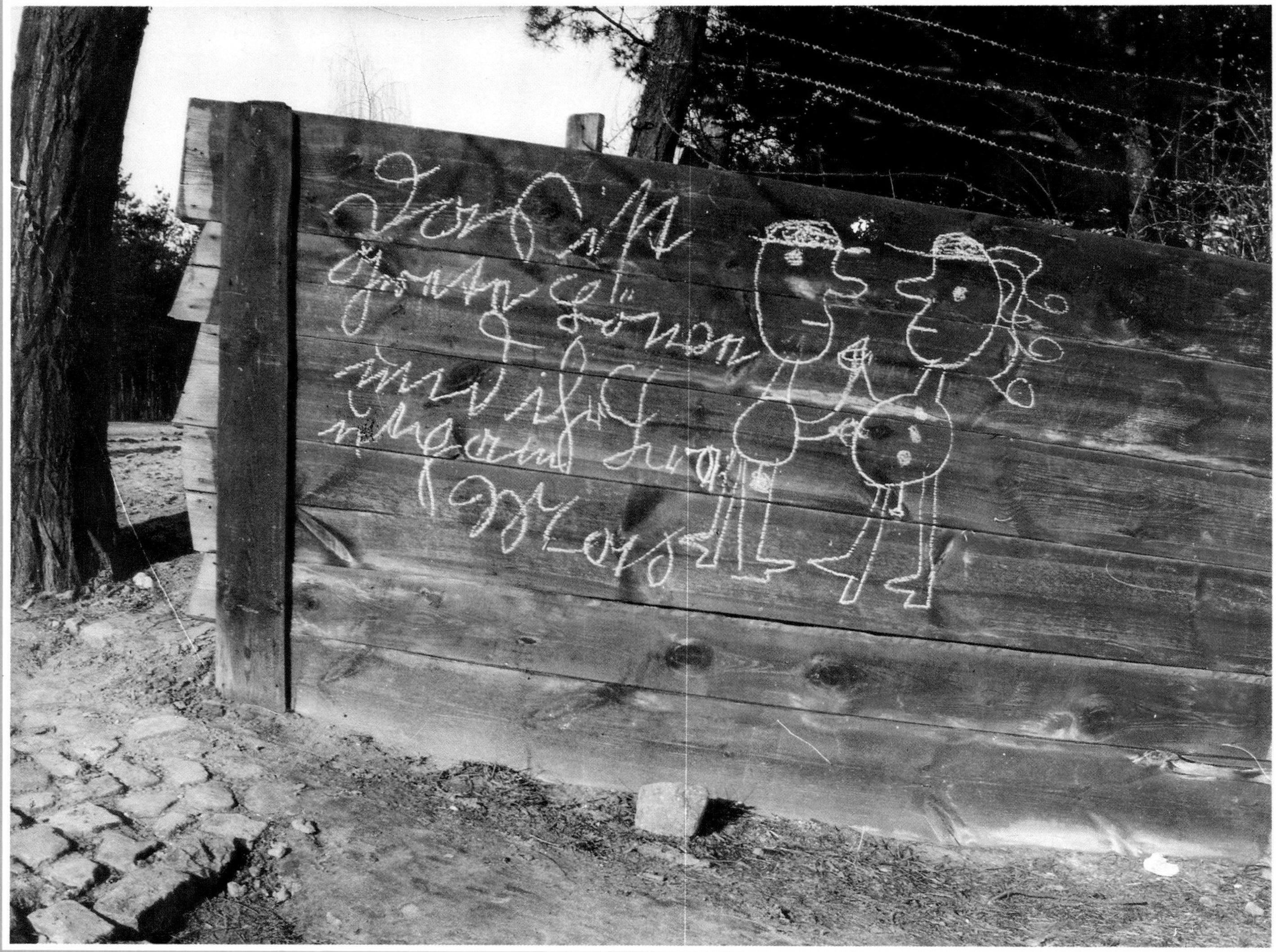

222

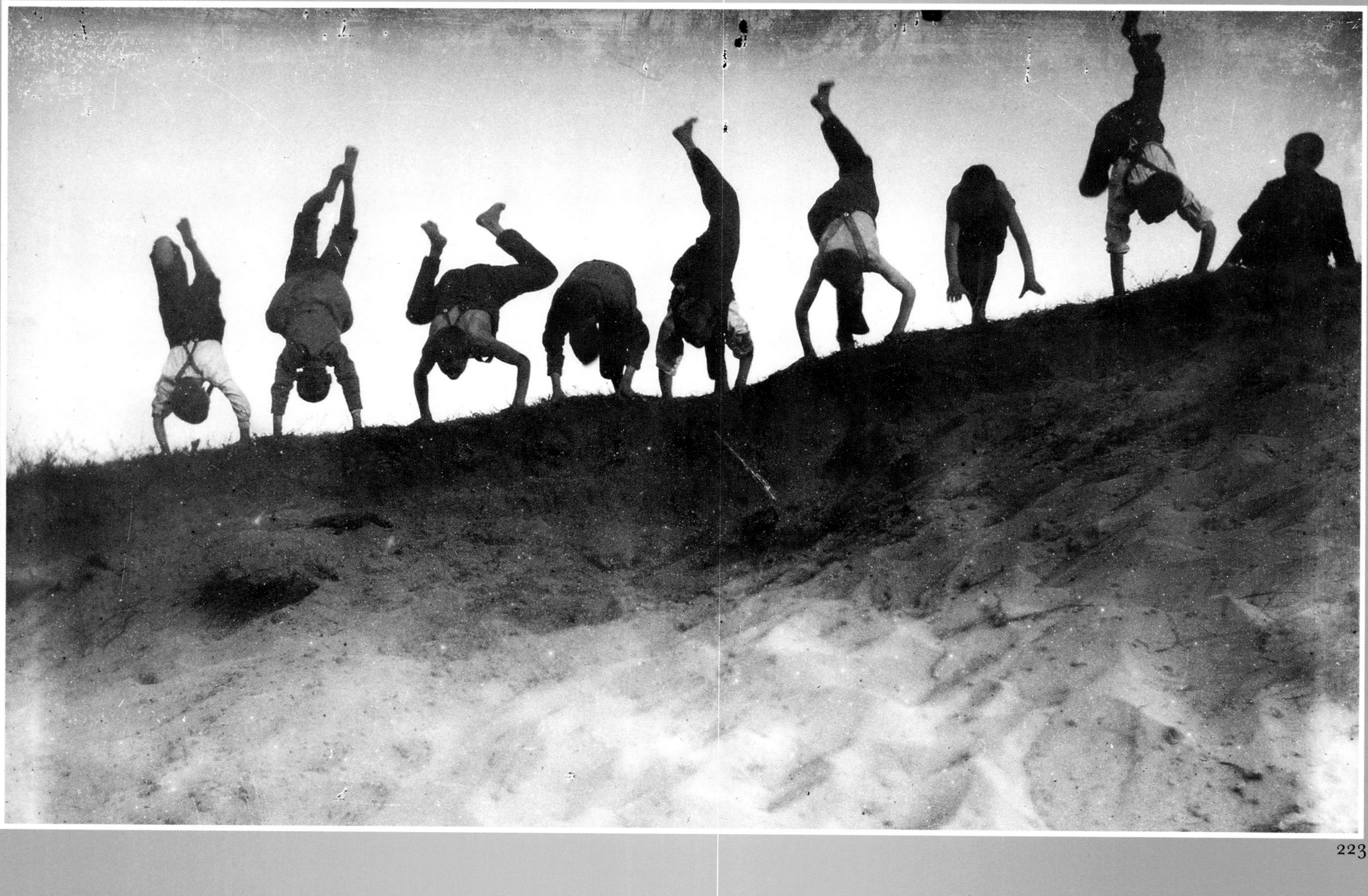

223

199 Charles Marville
Streetlamp Hanging between two Columns, Parc Monceau
c. 1870
Print on albumen paper, 35 x 25 cm
Bibliothèque Historique de la Ville de Paris, Paris

200 Gabriel Loppé
Morris Column in Paris at Night
c. 1900
Print on albumen paper from a gelatin-bromide glass negative, 18 x 13 cm
Musée d'Orsay, Paris

201 Edward Steichen
The Composer Richard Strauss
1904–6
Enlarged print on paper prepared with carbon and gelatin, 46.7 x 32.7 cm
Metropolitan Museum of Art (Stieglitz Collection), New York

202 William H. Jackson
Old Faithful Geyser, Yellowstone, USA
1872–80
Contact print on albumen paper from a collodion glass negative, 51.5 x 41.2 cm
Musée d'Orsay, Paris

203 Clarence H. White
Spring
1898
Print on platinum paper in the form of a triptych, 41 x 20.7 cm (middle panel), 38.2 x 6 cm (side panels)
Museum of Modern Art (Lily Auchincloss Fund), New York

204 Pierre Bonnard
Marthe in the Bath
c. 1908–12
Original contact print from original negative on flexible film, 7.8 x 5.5 cm
Musée d'Orsay, Paris

205 Edward Steichen
In Memoriam
1904
Print on paper prepared with bichromate gum, 47.6 x 36 cm
Private collection, Paris

206 Heinrich Zille
Nude in the Studio
c. 1900–2
Modern contact print from original negative plate, 12 x 9 cm
Berlinische Galerie, Museum für Moderne Kunst, Berlin

207 Jacob A. Riis
"Minding the Baby . . . A Whirlwind Scene, Gotham Court, New York" (taken from life at Gotham Court, New York)
c. 1889
Print on silvered paper from a glass negative, 12.7 x 17.7 cm
Museum of Modern Art (courtesy of the Museum of the City of New York), New York

208 Arnold Genthe
Chinatown, San Francisco
c. 1905
Print on gelatin-silver bromide paper, 23.1 x 32.6 cm
Art Institute of Chicago, Chicago

209 Henri Rivière
Workman on the site of the Eiffel Tower
1889
Print on matte silvered paper, 12 x 9 cm
Musée d'Orsay, Paris

210 Frederick Evans
Aubrey Beardsley
1894
Print on platinum-prepared paper, 15 x 10 cm
Musée d'Orsay, Paris

211 Lewis W. Hine
"Bowery Mission Bread Line, Midnight, Cold, Snowy"
1906
Print on silvered paper, 12.6 x 17.6 cm
International Museum of Photography at George Eastman House, Rochester, N.Y.

212 Alfred Stieglitz
A Dirigible
Camera Work, October 1911, no. 36, plate VIII
Heliogravure from original negative, 17.9 x 18 cm
Musée d'Orsay, Paris

213 Eugène Atget
Carriage in the Bois de Boulogne (from the series *La Voiture à Paris*)
1910
Contact print on albumen paper, 22 x 17.8 cm
Musée Carnavalet, Paris

214 Robert Demachy
The crowd
1910
Enlarged print on paper prepared with bichromate gum, 15.8 x 22.8 cm
Metropolitan Museum of Art, New York

215 Heinrich Kühn
The Artist's Son Walter
1917
Oil transfer on Japan paper, 29.5 x 23.5 cm
Musée d'Orsay, Paris

216 Alvin L. Coburn
Ezra Pound (vortograph)
1917
Print on silvered paper
International Museum of Photography at George Eastman House, Rochester, N.Y.

217 Alfred Stieglitz
Ellen Morton at Lake George
1915
Print on silvered paper, 18.2 x 22.5 cm
Werner Bokelberg Collection, Hamburg

218 Baron Adolf de Meyer
"Prélude à l'après-midi d'un faune," a nymph (detail; plate 16 of the album)
1912–14
Collotype impression on Japan paper, 23.1 x 14.4 cm
Musée d'Orsay, Paris

219 Eugène Atget
Nude in a Room, Viewed from Behind (Prostitute)
c. 1921
Contact print on albumen paper, 22.5 x 17.5 cm
Musée d'Orsay, Paris

220 Heinrich Kühn
"Landschaft mit Bäumen" [Landscape with trees]
c. 1900
Print on paper prepared with bichromate gum, 38 x 28.4 cm
Museum Folkwang, Essen

221 Eugène Atget
Wheat
Before 1912
Print on arrowroot paper, 22 x 17.4 cm
Private collection, Paris

222 Heinrich Zille
"Kinderzeichnung auf Bretterzaun" [Child's drawing on board fence]
c. 1900
Modern print from original negative plate, 9 x 12 cm
Berlinische Galerie, Berlin

223 Heinrich Zille
"Acht Jungen üben Handstand" [Eight boys practicing handstands]
c. 1900
Modern print from original negative plate, 9 x 12 cm
Berlinische Galerie, Berlin

THE DECORATIVE ARTS

ART AND INDUSTRY
(1851–89)

How can art, "encouraged by an increased number of artists and buyers of luxury goods to become industrial," be reconciled with industry, "encouraged by public taste and manufacturing progress to become artistic"? In his voluminous report that records the lessons to be drawn from the Great Exhibition in London's Crystal Palace, the Count de Laborde, denouncing the headlong rush into the abyss following unbridled industrialization, became the fervent defender of an alliance between art and industry. "It is with art that we can destroy materialism."

The history of the decorative arts in the second half of the nineteenth century is essentially that of the "arts applied to industry" and the considerable effort made to reconcile the two. The crucial historical fact behind this development was industrialization, which, although well under way in the first half of the century, had made immense strides during the Second Empire. The unbridled enthusiasm, the outlandish audacity that were to characterize the earliest international exhibitions went hand in hand with a sense of unease, due to an upheaval in production methods and an inescapable retrenchment back to tried and tested values. The international exhibitions, those vast department stores devoted to the omnipotence of industry which were to succeed one another regularly from 1851 to 1900, bore witness to the unceasing struggle waged by decorative artists, who, confronted by the demands of industrial society, were forever forced to adapt their creations to the profound transformations that gripped the world.

Industry it was that contributed to an unprecedented propagation of even the most cosmopolitan stylistic trends. As early as the beginning of the 1850s, the growth of mass production led to the adoption throughout the whole of the civilized world of a certain eclecticism, which conformed to the dominant taste and vested interests of the times. "There are no more frontiers. One has now to take the masses into account, the mass of consumers, the mass of producers, and be ready to witness the spread of a certain level of uniformity over the world's art and industry" (Laborde).

The Mirage of Industrialization

It is difficult to imagine today how fascinated people were by the industrial mechanization brought about by the development of new technologies. Indeed, some believed that only the machine, by surpassing any kind of handiwork, could attain absolute perfection. Among the throng of inventions that saw the light of day during the nineteenth century—the number of patents lodged by these inventors belonging to the unsung history of the time was vast—the list of improvements to machine tools appears endless.

Two discoveries made prior to the Second Empire clearly illustrate the considerable developments in mechanical reproduction techniques: electroplating and reduction. Invented by Moritz Hermann von Jacobi in 1837, electroplating could be applied in a host of ways, from the battery silvering of modest tableware to the reproduction of monumental sculpture. "Electroplating is in fact one of those modern-looking and faultlessly accurate processes that enable reproduction of all and everything equally well" (Burty 1869, 529–46). At the same time, thanks to mechanical reduction methods invented concurrently by Achille Colas and Frédéric Sauvage, sculpture could be reduced in size at will, marketed in any number of different sizes, and thus could make an entrance into any middle-class interior.

Mechanization of form and ornament spread to every area: series of decorative elements molded in cast iron, earthenware, staff, or carton-pierre replaced wrought iron, stone, stucco, and carved wood. Molding techniques allowed major crystal glassworks to perform astonishing feats: the sumptuous pieces of furniture, gigantic fountains, and even entire edifices built in perfect crystal speak volumes for their mastery.

Elsewhere, improvements in printing—on paper, fabric, ceramic, glass, wood, and metal—opened up new possibilities for mass-producing novel types of goods. Photography and photoengraving also attracted the attention of decorators: sculptor, ornamenter, and inventor, Henry Dufresne was to patent a process which, using photographic printing, could reproduce delicate damascened patterns (1856–59). Amid the profusion of research, in addition to lasting and worthwhile discoveries which were to render reasonably priced and continuous production more feasible, there were isolated and highly disconcerting attempts to go beyond craft methods by using artificial materials.

The triumph of mechanization was no foregone conclusion, however. Throughout the Second Empire, the struggle to make the new manufacturing processes cost-effective remained in the balance. To satisfy a growing demand, company managers continued organizing work on a piecemeal basis, still allotting a large share to artisan practices, while technological improvements only gradually filtered through. It was the coexistence of manual and mechanized working methods, time-honored methods complementing new-found technologies, that remained the norm for all sectors of production at the time.

Demarcation became the rule. As early as the eighteenth century, artists such as the English china manufacturer Josiah Wedgwood, the German-born cabinetmaker David Roentgen, and the French silversmiths François-Thomas Germain and Robert Auguste had found themselves at the helm of what amounted to business concerns. In the following century, this phenomenon accelerated, giving rise to controversy concerning the nature of artistic property. Overseeing a host of collaborators and contractors, a major jeweler and silversmith such as François-Désiré Froment-Meurice acted like a kind of conductor: "If M. Froment-Meurice signs his elegant chatelaines, fasteners, and saltcellars with his name, other men in the trade know full well that his works as a silversmith were neither designed nor executed by him. He supplied the metal and bought others' handiwork" (Gustave Planche).

This fragmentation of the various stages of manufacturing went hand in hand with an unprecedented growth in the number of factories. At the Exposition Universelle of 1867, the firm of Parisian cabinetmakers Racault Krieger proudly presented a model showing how the tiny workshop founded by Antoine Krieger had swollen into a sizable company with five hundred workers beneath one roof. The stores opened by various firms in many towns, despite competition from department stores, served as outlets for the very latest models. Sales were greatly boosted by the issuing of manufacturers' illustrated catalogs, which proposed an ever-growing range to their customers.

How could the ruling classes have possibly resisted the spell of industrialization when countless new techniques allowed for the modestly priced imitation of the rarest and most noble materials and the infinite—yet entirely faithful—reproduction of the most elaborate forms, ensuring, without any pang of conscience and with a considerable saving in time, that low-cost manufacturing became available to all?

This almost religious belief in industrial production was not without its pitfalls, however: it was likely to make people content to go for the easy option and was to lead, inescapably, down a blind alley where ersatz materials were used simply to fake the work of the artisan.

"The superfluous does not, whatever one might say, take precedence over what is necessary. In the place of diamond, glass; in the place of velvet, paper; in the place of bronze, plaster; in the place of marble, cardboard; in the place of silver, tin; and in the place of gold, whatever one comes up with, no matter! It is the outside that glitters and not the inside; and do we not have Art, that Prometheus who stole the spark of fire from Olympus? At least anything art creates might endure" (Luchet, *Le Monde illustré*, 1862).

Toward an Alliance Between Art and Industry

In the hard-fought contest of strength over the fate of the industrial arts, the main players were England and France. Housed in vast halls dedicated to the worship of the machine, industry was to triumph in the international exhibitions—those held in London, in 1851, 1862, and 1871, countered with equal success by those held in Paris in the years 1855, 1867, and 1878.

Such unprecedented commercial successes, however, did little to disguise a disturbing state of affairs which had already come to the fore in the earlier purely national industrial shows (particularly in France and Germany). Indeed, the cul-de-sac down which the decorative art industries were traveling became still more glaring on the international stage. Such comparisons between the Western nations themselves and, in addition, between West and East, was just what was required to break free from the dictatorship of industry and call into question the rampant manufacturing culture that had grown up around intensive mechanization.

Once this unease came to the fore, one exhibition emulated another and there was a sudden realization of what was happening. In England, as in France, lessons were soon being drawn. In London, Henry Cole was the first to lead the ground swell of reform. He was to give fresh impetus to the London School of Design, which had been moribund since 1837, headed the Felix Summerly Art Manufactures intended to promote cooperation between fine art and mechanized manufacturing, and organized competitions under the aegis of the Society for the Encouragement of the Arts, Manufactures and Commerce. In his *Journal of Design and Manufactures*, issued between 1849 and 1852, Cole denounced the dearth of principle in industrial design. As a result of his vigorous encouragement, the teaching of industrial design was to grow appreciably. By 1860, there were no less than 85,000 students matriculating in eighty schools.

Cole himself considered the establishment of the first applied arts museum in the West as the most important of all these efforts. At first temporarily housed in Marlborough House, in Pall Mall, the South Kensington Museum, built on land purchased by profits made from the Great Exhibition, opened its doors to the public in 1857. Cole himself was the museum's first director.

Simultaneously, in France, attempts to unify the arts and industry were under way. The Count de Laborde, in his copious report published in 1856, stressed at length the need to reform arts education and recommended creating a large-scale model manufactory. "As far as industry is concerned, future progress depends on artists of the highest standard turning to industry and intelligent industrialists becoming artists. Intimate collaboration between inspiration and hard work, close cooperation between the imagination of the inventor and the hand of the executant—a cooperation which can alone calm the ardor of the spirit and ennoble, elevate the use of the tool; a cooperation which will above all conserve in its rightful proportion everything industry must owe to art and what art must do for industry."

The search for a blueprint also led to attempts to extend the teaching methods which held sway in the fine arts schools to the new world of industry. The notion of "the fine arts as applied to industry" which had already appeared in the 1830s became pervasive under the Second Empire.

In France, the Société d'Art Industriel, founded in 1845, had already taken on the task of raising the training and design levels in industry. Ten years later, it was replaced by the Société pour l'Encouragement et le Développement de l'Art Industriel en France, becoming, in 1858, the Société du Progrès de l'Art Industriel, only to take on its final shape in 1863 as the Union Centrale des Beaux-Arts. This association—instigated by the private sector—launched a major program of exhibitions (the earliest were held in 1861, 1863, 1865, and 1869), lectures, and publications. Though in France it had been preceded in this by the Lyon Chambre de Commerce, which had already founded a museum of applied arts in 1858, the Union's own museum and library were inaugurated in 1864.

Hard on the heels of the example of South Kensington, museums of the applied arts spread to other European cities, including Vienna (1864), Berlin, and Hamburg. In Henry Cole's view, these musuems constituted nothing less than antidotes to brutality and vice, fulfilling an educational role: the artworks, ancient and modern, that they were to acquire opened up a vast field of study to designers and workers in the field alike. The establishment of a retrospective museum during the 1867 Exposition Universelle was a similar response to the need to enlighten the industrial classes, "so as to make the comparison between those things produced by man in different times and by different peoples easier and to provide for manufacturers every kind of model for imitating" (Ducuing 1868).

The ambition to set down a range of universal aesthetic principles based on a thoroughgoing knowledge of every civilization found expression in a proliferation of treatises on ornament. A masterpiece of chromolithographic printing, Owen Jones's monumental *Grammar of Ornament* (1856), translated into French and German and many times reprinted, enjoyed prodigious success. In a wide-ranging study that went farther than any previous collection, Jones, from the systematic analysis of all the ornaments he listed, claimed to have extracted no less than thirty-seven rules for decoration.

In Germany, Gottfried Semper's publications, notably *Der Stil in den technischen und tektonischen Künsten* (Style in the technical and tectonic arts, 1860–6), and in France, Albert-Charles-Auguste Racinet's *L'Ornement polychrome* (1869), were also moving toward an aesthetics of rationalization and were to provide a burgeoning industry with superior models.

The defense of a much vaunted ideal union of the beautiful and the useful was greeted with approbation in the numerous illustrated reviews covering the international exhibitions, and in the new art journals, particularly *Art Journal* in England (from 1849), and *L'Art au XIXe siècle* (from 1856) and *La Gazette des Beaux-Arts* in France (from 1859).

For artistic creativity, too, the growth in mass production opened up new vistas. The considerable surge in demand for elaborate ornaments—the possession of large quantities of which showed one had "arrived" in social terms—was in fact a direct consequence of the Industrial Revolution. It was ornament which could elevate the mass-produced object now it was affordable to the majority. A phenomenon of sheer numbers replaced the handiwork that had formerly endowed a piece with its own uniqueness: increasingly, models were being reproduced that had been specifically envisaged for reproduction. The ease with which an object might be reproduced soon became one of the foremost characteristics of the industrial age.

As a "redemptive force," art had to provide industry with prototypes that might be produced in any material whatever, thereby enabling the popularization of the image of the artwork and making a contribution to the enlightenment of the working classes. "It is not the rich piece, the work that is demanding to execute which has most to gain from taking the most original and best works by our artists as a model: it is rather at the cheaper end, in mass-market industry, whose outlets are legion—just as their manufacturing methods, aided by reproductive processes, are inexhaustible" (Laborde).

To come to grips with this, the heads of industry were compelled to co-opt the assistance of eminent artists, past masters in the laws of composition and modeling. "An artist of the first order . . . will always remain for the industrialist a source of an enduring reputation and even of secure profits" (Mérimée 1862, 247–62). On the occasion of the international exhibitions of 1851 and 1855, Richard Redgrave, artistic director of the Department of Practical Art in London, attributed the unquestioned superiority of the French imperial manufactories explicitly to the constellation of excellent painters, sculptors, and designers that they employed.

In a trend enthusiastically seconded by private business, artistic projects were encouraged to become collaborative. One of the finest successes of this type was the sumptuous wallpaper decoration showing the Garden of Armida, an extraordinary example of artistic cooperation of which the manufacturer, Frenchman Jules Desfossé, was justly proud: "By associating my own work as an industrialist," he stated in 1855, "with illustrious names in the fine arts such as MM. Couture, Clésinger, and Muller, I am conscious of having opened up new paths for progress and having as of old married industry to art from which it derives a goodly part of its splendor."

At that time, benefiting particularly from the exodus occasioned by the 1848 revolution, the great English manufactures had no hesitation in recruiting French artists in an effort to improve their prestige. The renown of Elkington & Company was much furthered, first from 1848 to 1861, by the arrival of the silversmith Antoine Vechte (1799–1868), followed by the ornamental sculptors Antoine Willms (1823–1899)—appointed "chief artist" of the firm—and Léonard Morel-Ladeuil (1820–1888), from 1859 onward. In the field of ceramics, Léon Arnoux (1816–1902) took over at the firm of Minton's in 1849, collaborating there until his death. He brought over fellow Frenchmen, such as Émile Jeanneret and Albert-Ernest Carrier-Belleuse (1824–1887). "They go off for one or two years and put their shoulders to the English wheel which gets from them all it needs to sustain its ceramics and furniture-making. Carrier has engendered more cupids and nymphs than there are people in a fair-sized county town" (Falize 1878).

By the mid-century, some fruitful joint ventures between makers and artists had thus been set up. These included architects for household and ecclesiastical furnishings; painters for ceramic or enamel painting, and stained-glass and wallpaper design; sculptors for furniture, architectural bronzework, goldwork, and again ceramics; and "industrial designers" who worked in every technique. If the most prominent artists—and in France these were Gérôme and Couture, Clésinger and Fremiet—only rarely ventured to enlist their talents in the service of industry, others kept up close and long-lasting ties with various manufacturers and even took over at the head of the art departments of certain firms. One of the greatest European silver houses, Christofle et Cie, owed much of its international success to brilliant contributions from artists. "We know the artists they have on their books. It is enough to cite the names of the sculptors, A. Gumery, J. Klagmann, Mathurin Moreau, Carrier-Belleuse, Eudes and Rouillard; and the architect, Rossigneux, the draftsman, Émile Reiber" (*Le Monde illustré*, 1873).

The Reign of Eclecticism

Although there were undeniably some splendid achievements, were not people perhaps—through a desire to elevate industrial manufacturing by endowing it with an artistic dimension—deviating from the desired goal: the union of the beautiful and the useful?

In all the theories of artistic renewal that were then being aired, one can clearly perceive all the complexity of a period undergoing radical transformation. Ambivalence is everywhere and confusion, patent. The striving, as Henry Cole had instructed, to learn to see, and to see by comparing; the conviction that they were furthering a renaissance in the decorative arts through the study and imitation of the masterpieces of earlier times under the auspices of specialized museums-cum-art schools; the provision of a vast selection of motifs (though in two dimensions and devoid of any context) in their treatises on ornament; the use of learned artists impregnated in the fine arts tradition—all this effort amounted, for the most part, to simply obeying and propagating everywhere the same irresistible need to shelter behind a familiar stockpile of historical styles.

Historicism was not a nineteenth-century innovation—it is a phenomenon inherent in every period that looks for its roots in the past. At the end of the eighteenth century and at the onset of the nineteenth, for example, the imitation of time-honored styles and the attractions of the Orient made for magnificent creations which were, however, confined to the whim of some enlightened prince or art-lover. In England, the tastes of a passionate connoisseur such as William Beckford—ranging as they did over classical antiquity, the Gothic, the Renaissance, the Baroque, and even the Middle Ages and the Far East—heralded the mania for archaeology characteristic of later generations.

All Romantic Europe delved with fervor into its medieval ancestors and set off in quest of evidence of its history. It is therefore hardly astonishing to see eclecticism as an enshrined—though much resented—law by the 1840s. "Our century does not have its own shape. We have failed to mark with the stamp of our own time either our homes, or gardens, or anything at all . . . We have something from every century, save our own—something which has never before been seen at any other period" (Alfred de Musset 1836).

From 1840 to 1890 and even beyond, Western culture itself was buried beneath eclecticism, carried along on a violent surge in industrialization and the commercial boom brought with it. It was a subtle, many-headed movement, whose succeeding waves would ebb with the passing fashion only to return once more in a different guise.

This singularly widespread and long-lasting phenomenon appears still more surprising since it seemed as though conditions were ripe for the birth of a new type of art: an expanding technological base, a well-qualified and abundant workforce directed by a business-minded bourgeoisie keen to give palpable proof of its power, and economic prosperity which international conflicts such as the Franco-Prussian war of 1870 did little to sap. These proved to be illusory. In truth, the new inventions in mechanics were not yet fully under control. While the working man was slowly becoming aware of his identity, the middle classes were scarcely constituting a unified political, economic, and social force. Development in artistic creativity mirrors all the daring, the hesitations, the contradictions, and the escapism, born of the divergent interests that lay deep within the ruling class.

In spite of much fervent celebration of industrial progress, "an insurmountable barrier of sentimental prejudice" (S. Guiedon) inhibited these generations from being able to accept the beauty of forms simplified by machine and led inevitably to the mass-produced object being made to resemble some overwrought piece from an earlier period.

Eclecticism, as a style escapist in both time and space, was a cosmopolitan trend, at once reassuring in its references to antiquity or to European history (references which would gladden a middle class in search of its roots as well as an aristocracy with a nostalgia for the regimes of the past) and seductive in its borrowings from Eastern civilizations that flattered the colonial ambitions of Western society. In such a society, "the life-giving domain of the private individual is in conflict with his workplace . . . At his counter, the private individual takes account of the real; at home, he demands that his illusions be entertained . . . For the private individual, his home represents the universe. There he gathers together the far-off and the past. His drawing room is a box at the theater of the world" (Walter Benjamin).

Eclecticism sated the bourgeoisie's need for ostentation; it was a class that loved to exhibit its wealth and believed in a fair day's work—to which mechanical tools would give a perfect finish—and that preferred something solid, something brand new created especially for it, rather than to surround itself with the vestiges of past generations. Artists—convinced that they possessed a higher knowledge which was far more extensive than anything their predecessors might have imagined—delved freely into the world of ornament and selected at will the one most appropriate to the matter in hand.

One of the first and most spectacular creations marking the onset of eclecticism in France was the monumental dressing table for the duchess of Parma (fig. 232). Commissioned from the goldsmith Froment-Meurice in 1845, it was only finished by 1851, just in time to appear in pride of place at the Great Exhibition of that year. Designed by the architect Félix Duban (1797–1870) and the ornamenter Michel Liénard (1810–?), garnished with ronde-bosse figures and painted in enamel after models by Feuchère and Geoffroy-Dechaume, this piece—whose stagy sumptuousness concealed a cast-iron armature—mixed reminiscences from the Middle Ages, the Renaissance, Islamic art, and the Baroque.

At the 1855 Exposition Universelle, this ambition to outdo earlier periods, sustained by the proud assurance that stems from the impression of boundless knowledge, was still more in evidence. Parisian cabinetmakers, whose bold strokes had already been noted in London (most notably in a gigantic carved sideboard by the firm of Fourdinois), did their utmost to show off their skill. "Our makers have all, or almost all, wandered into the pitfalls of the sublime . . . they have aimed for effect, and the abundance of ornament sometimes only served to mask the poverty of line of the whole . . . If we had to list every single piece, every combination that played a role in the decoration of just a few of these enormous bookcases-cum-dressers, we would be forced to have recourse to a large encyclopedia. Every period, every country, the whole of nature, with its three kingdoms, every biblical, mythological theme . . . combined seem to conspire to see who can distract the attention of the onlooker to its advantage" (*Rapports* 1855).

Porcelain manufacturers also joined the fray. At Limoges the firm of Jouhanneaud et Dubois brought in artists such as Constant Sévin and Alexandre Schoenewerk, whose allegorical compositions were veritable tours de force (fig. 229). Twelve years later, Philippe Burty was to lambast this propensity for allegory, also commonplace in the production of commemorative silver, whose "overall shape is as if consumed by a crowd all twisting backward, bumping into and embracing one another from base to summit."

In those years of unchecked inventiveness, by aiming too high, the best intentions often led to overloaded and confused compositions. It was a great temptation to be content to simply extend tried and tested schemas so as to lavish on them a host of symbols and ornaments which bore the ponderous hallmarks of a past all too revered. Was not all this learned culture—tacked on with greater or lesser discernment—finally a way of simply making "the old, brand new" (Fourdinois)?

Regretting, as did so many of his contemporaries, the passing of a "single-mindedness of purpose which was the rule in former times," the jeweler Eugène Fontenay (1823–1887) saw this vast and excessive erudition as being at the root of the disconcerting mishmash of elements—a mishmash that reflected the hesitancy of artists powerless to shake themselves free of tradition. "These styles, all combined, have become our heritage, a fateful heritage . . . which, like a new cloak of Nessus, eats us to the marrow."

Such backward-looking disorder, such a *horror vacui*—typified by those hushed interiors where the decorator or wallpaper designer has everywhere left his mark—are the reflection of an uncertain world where the arts, still unsure of themselves, made a stand against the belligerence of industry and the prosperity of commerce. Rarely has there been a period more critical of itself. As can be seen from the various reports on the industrial fairs, the attempts to unify the arts and industry got bogged down in the imitation of the art of earlier times and ended in failure.

Eclecticism—an unloved son—left people with a bitter taste of collective guilt. "Today, modern art has at its disposal only hackneyed ideas and formulas that no longer have anything to do with its needs. From this comes the restlessness, the vagueness, the dissolution, the ease with which one moves from one extreme to the other, an eclecticism and cosmopolitanism, a journey through every possible world, going from the Byzantine to the daguerreotype, from recherché mannerism to willful brutality. It is clear that something must be done—but what?" (Gautier 1853). Such severe and often unjust commentaries give the unhappy impression that the critics, who were also hypnotized by the whirl of styles, could not perceive or understand the forceful originality of their time.

Against a pessimistic backdrop of dire warnings and of exhortations to develop a novel style, Fontenay, fortified by experience earned during a long career and by a love of history, was one of the few to take up the defense of his colleagues. "Contemporary manufacturers," he stated in 1887, admittedly rather late in the day, "that are always being reproached for having no individual character, have made a hundred times more effort than those before them when—down a well-tilled furrow—they simply followed the well-defined and undefinable march of their styles."

Never before had so much research been undertaken nor so many inventions devised. If there is one certainty, at least as far as the first thirty years of the eclectic adventure are concerned, it is the constant desire to innovate, not only in the use of new materials and techniques, but also in composition and decoration. The love of archaeology that united all these artists was equaled only by the extraordinary facility with which they knew how to amalgamate the sources selected: through daring juxtapositions and a continual exercise in transposition, they sought no less than a complete reworking of the forms they had assimilated.

The Quest for Stylistic Unity

Oddly, it is precisely what gives the creations of the period their originality—the intermingling of the various styles and diverse transpositions of materials—that is often stigmatized by the critics of the time as ignorance of the laws of decoration. In the name of a principle of stylistic unity, it was required that each style employed be faithfully respected.

Such was the remonstration made by Mérimée to the exhibitors in London in 1862. In preference "to strange amalgams of different styles thrown together haphazardly that indicate on the part of their authors only a dearth of ideas and faulty reasoning . . . to the ill-considered use of a material in place of another," he would rather a purportedly exact imitation "of a carved cabinet that one might take for the work of an eighteenth-century Venetian cabinetmaker [or] another that might have been made for Mme. du Barry."

Whether for an object or piece of furniture, whether for the decoration and the furnishing of a single room or the complete fitting of an entire house or château, unity of design in keeping with the style adopted was the order of the day. Supervision of the work—entrusted directly to an expert in interior decoration (usually a cabinetmaker-cum-decorator), to a sculptor, or, better still, to an architect—guaranteed the desired cohesion. Such stipulations amused the author Edmond About at the 1868 Salon at the expense of a certain "Charles Rossigneux, jack-of-all-trades architect, who builds the house, decorates the apartment, plans the furniture, sketches out the stained glass, has the crockery, crystal, silverware, and even Madame's jewelry done to his designs, this improbable artist seems almost ridiculous today since he has not wanted to confine himself to a single specialism, having them all."

The Hôtel de la Païva on the Champs-Élysées in Paris, built between 1856 and 1866 and designed by Pierre Manguin, remains (though its furniture has since been dispersed) the perfect example of a similarly ambitious decorative project, though it is more indicative of the society pretensions of she who commissioned it than of any real desire for aesthetic perfection. A veritable clerk of works, surrounded by a constellation of painters (Baudry, Barrias, Eugène Thirion, Henri-Pierre Picou, Émile Lévy, Joseph-Victor Ranvier) and sculptors (Carrier-Belleuse, Dalou, Eugène Legrain, Delaplanche, Émile Picault), Manguin also turned to the best craftsmen (the cabinetmaker, Antoine Kneib, the bronzesmith, Barbedienne, the silversmith, Christofle, the ceramicist Théodore Deck, the silk manufacturers, Lamy et Giraud and Tassinari et Chatel) to achieve an opulent ensemble in a "modernized Renaissance style." The requirement for a unified overall plan, however, did not entail a slavish imitation of the Renaissance. On the contrary, the creativity of the artists collaborating on this prestigious venture is apparent in everything they did, as can be seen today in the models for the furnishing fabrics, which have fortunately been preserved, and in the few pieces of furniture that have been identified, which include the magnificent console tables for the drawing room.

Classicism Lives On

The Western world remained in the thrall of doctrines derived from classical antiquity. Among the bewildering confusion offered by the various arts, classicism appeared to many as an essential safety net. The application of the type of teaching provided at the École des Beaux-Arts to industry, the advances made in archaeology, and the creation of extensive collections all helped to elevate the Greco-Roman heritage to a level of prestige that it had not known since the fall of the Napoleonic empire. Throughout all its various guises, whether successive or contemporaneous, be it neo-Greek or neo-Pompeian, neo-Florentine or neo-Henri II, neo-Louis XIV or neo-Louis XVI, one finds the same quest for an unchanging ideal. Well might Burty in 1869 thunder against the "Latin yoke that chafes at our necks . . . having aped the Roman style like the Italians, like the Valois, like Louis XIV and the entire eighteenth century, we'll one day descend into using the Empire style that everyone knows so well." Yet his taunts did little to undermine the confidence of the devotees of the classical school.

The Neo-Greek or Neo-Pompeian Style

"Greek art is the refined spirit of the ancient societies, the studied grace of the inhabitants of the city, combined with a child's innocence, with the simplicity of the toiler in the fields. It is a new sense which, once it takes grip of us, once it is incorporated into our natures . . . follows us in all things, surfaces through all our ideas." In writing these heartfelt lines in 1856, Laborde could already have rejoiced to see his fulsome principles being adopted by Parisian manufacturers. In reality, conjoining elements inspired by Greek, Etruscan, Roman and Byzantine, and even Egyptian antiquity, "neo-Greek" or "neo-Pompeian" taste was already entrenched in France by the 1850s, as in the Pompeian villa (fig. 280) built by Alfred-Nicolas Normand (1812–1890) for Prince Napoleon (1856–58).

By the 1867 Exposition Universelle, this trend for the antique had swollen to disquieting proportions. "There is a certain Etrusco-Greek style that is strangely overused; it pops up everywhere, in friezes and on antefixes, on cornices in apartments, on furniture and on subjects for clocks or in bronze" (*Rapports*, 1867). Léon Marchand made a gigantic bronze and marble chimneypiece after a design by Eugène Piat, but more in keeping with the prevailing infatuation was the furniture by Charles-Guillaume Diehl, the bronzework by Barbedienne (fig. 373), Georges Servant, and Henri Houdebine, the goldwork by Christofle and Alexandre Gueyton, Fontenay's jewelry, and the Sèvres porcelain (fig. 378). One of the remarkable successes of a fruitful collaboration between the draftsman Brandely, the sculptor Fremiet, and the cabinetmaker and bronzesmith Guillemin, the spectacular furniture presented by Diehl—even if it did not win the unanimous support of a jury bewildered by its boldness—remained nonetheless the strongest creation that French cabinetmaking had produced for some time.

England seems to have been less susceptible to this type of archaeological erudition. The cosmopolitan varnish of the neo-Greek style never truly took root there and only two first-rank artists, Owen Jones and Christopher Dresser, genuinely incorporated Greek art into their work. Significantly, the most striking pieces were made by a Frenchman, Marc-Louis-Emanuel Solon (1835–1913), who executed for Minton's some elegant decoration on *pâte-sur-pâte* porcelain, or were made for export, such as the sumptuous furniture designed about 1884 by Alma-Tadema for a music room in New York (fig. 403). The United States was more receptive to French influences and warmly welcomed such endeavors. From the use of rigid shapes and machine-cut surfaces, the Americans extracted a "Greco-Oriental" and faintly Renaissance style all their own, to which the name of the Pullman luxury car is still linked. In Germany, only Prussia remained loyal to Karl Friedrich Schinkel's passion for the antique, the *Berliner Stil* soon becoming one of Neoclassicism's final retrenchments.

The Renaissance: an Unbroken Line

Rather than distant antiquity, the more accessible Renaissance embodied the archetypal ideals of harmony and beauty, and its prestige was still intact in the nineteenth century. The archetype was still more alluring since the new generations saw it as a time of splendid triumph for historicism: it was in returning to the Greco-Roman traditions that the Renaissance was able to create its many masterpieces. "The marvels of the Renaissance are surely enduring proof that the free and intelligent study of the antique is the best way of getting our specific national genius to bear fruit" (*Rapports*, 1873).

Timidly initiated early in the century by a few English and German architects, the neo-Renaissance trend gained ground from the 1840s onward and continued, independently of fashion, until the 1880s. The erstwhile enthusiasm of the Romantics—with their occasionally wayward grasp of the facts—gave way to in-depth study of European art of the fifteenth and sixteenth centuries. By the middle of the century, the arts of the Renaissance—now better documented and more widely known (thanks notably to Jacob Burckhardt's *Die Kultur der Renaissance in Italien* of 1860)—had become an inexhaustible source of replenishment for the architect, sculptor, and draftsman alike.

The devotees of the application of the fine arts to industry saw in the example left by these "marvelous man-gods" the confirmation of all their ideas and efforts: "How great artists might collaborate on an industrial project has never been understood better than in the sixteenth century" (Mérimée 1862). This obligatory profusion of references to one of the most fertile periods in Western art spread all the more easily throughout Europe since each country could itself summon up memories of a resplendent past. It is therefore no surprise that the neo-Renaissance movement extended from the Italian Quattrocento to the beginning of the Dutch seventeenth century.

In Italy, sculptors and cabinetmakers from Siena, Florence, Milan, and Rome—such as Barbetti, Luigi Frullini, Brambilla e Annoni, Giovanni Battista Gatti—freely took their inspiration from the many treasures the peninsula holds and attained extraordinary virtuosity in furniture featuring a host of minute details in bas-relief, engraved ivory inlay, and *pietre dure*. Their proverbial skill earned them important commissions for decoration—Barbetti at the Palazzo Saracini in Siena and for Leopold de Rothschild in England, and Frullini in the United States, where he obtained the commission to fit out the dining room and the library of Château-sur-Mer (1877–78) in Newport. Meanwhile, the arts of majolica and glasswork were enjoying a new lease of life at Gubbio, Doccia, and Murano.

In France, the "drones" described by Honoré de Balzac in the 1830s, "bent over the treasures in the Cabinet des Estampes and trying to make something new from an adroit pastiche," left a wealth of collections and anthologies of ornament designed for manufacturers. The draftsmen of the nineteenth century delved deep into this bottomless world of rinceaux, arabesques, grotesques, and allegorical figures that the *petits maîtres* of the sixteenth had engraved. The candor of Feuchère's or Liénard's neo-Renaissance soon gave way, however, to the severe and often portentous erudition of Sévin and Claudius Popelin. Spurred on by wood-, metal-, and terracotta carvers, furniture and objets d'art alike became covered in figurines. This systematic use of statuary that mechanical reduction facilitated culminated in the "strange misuse" that Burty, once more, was not slow in pointing out: "I have seen in bronze—or fake bronze—Michelangelo's slaves, writhing under the idealized weight of defeat and not beneath any real burden, transformed into torchères and supporting upon their athletic shoulders . . . a carcel lamp."

In middle-class homes, the Henri II style could easily be adapted to the dining room, the study, or even the bedroom. The richness of these pieces, carved out of solid wood—generally walnut—lies in the abundance of their decoration. Closer to the seventeenth century, a number of valuable pieces in ebony or ebonized pearwood, decorated with *pietre dure*, painted enamels, and silvered or gold-leafed bronzes speak of a less austere taste, characterized by colorful ornamentation. Similarly, in silver and jewelry, the techniques of repoussé, enameling, and niello, and a taste for mounted gemstones returned to favor thanks to the Renaissance example.

It was at the 1878 Exposition Universelle that the neo-Renaissance style staged one final flourish. Among the contributions most remarked on was Henri-Auguste Fourdinois's monumental door garnished with painted enamel and bronze low-reliefs—the fruit of a joint enterprise with the architect, Paul Sédille, the painter, Hippolyte Rousselle, and the sculptor, Allar. The jeweler Fontenay also returned to the Renaissance with a perfume burner that is a masterpiece of refinement which prefigures Peter Carl Fabergé's famous eggs (fig. 382).

In England, the most disparate sources—from the Italian, German, and French Renaissance—were amalgamated with national styles, be they Tudor, Elizabethan, or Jacobean. The preeminent role of certain French artists, notably Morel-Ladeuil and Carrier-Belleuse, comes to the fore in a number of commemorative pieces which bear the hallmarks of international eclecticism. Termed "Old English," the plans for interiors published by Bruce J. Talbert in his *Examples of Ancient & Modern Furniture, Metal Work, Tapestries, Decoration, etc.* (1876), are more in the tradition of Jacobean furniture.

Vienna, from deep within the German-speaking lands, was one of the main artistic centers promoting a return to the architectural language of the Italian Quattrocento. At first sensitive to Italian influences as promulgated by the architect Gottfried Semper, following its unification Germany itself forged a specific style based on northern European art of the sixteenth and seventeenth centuries. The movement dominated the applied arts as unified under the roof of the Münchner Verein zur Ausbildung der Gewerke in 1876. This choice broached no exceptions and cast aside the indecision of eclecticism, being considered by nationalists as the only style capable of giving voice to the true Germanic character. Publications such as *Das Deutsche Zimmer der Renaissance* (Hirth 1880) presented collections of furniture adapting the "modern German Renaissance" to the various rooms in a middle-class residence.

Descendants of the Art of Versailles: Neo-Louis XIV and Neo-Louis XVI

In France at least, as Henri Clouzot so rightly stressed, "the Second Empire style (taking it from 1840) . . . is a far more unified extension than is commonly imagined of the styles of the seventeenth and eighteenth centuries." Brought back into favor under Louis-Philippe, the art of Versailles belonged to history certainly, but not to a distant one. The Parisian furnishings and precious objects of the preceding century gradually acquired the status of collectors' items. At first restricted to a small circle of knowledgeable art-lovers centered around the Goncourt brothers, the taste for the eighteenth century was then adopted by patrons from the worlds of finance and industry. During the "retrospective museum" organized by the Union Centrale in 1865, Lord Hertford had already gathered together a few of the masterpieces of French cabinetmaking and bronzework that today have pride of place in the Wallace Collection in London.

Earlier still, at the 1855 Exposition Universelle, Joseph Cremer, in a spirit of naive invention, had attempted to imitate the marquetry of André-Charles Boulle by using a paste poured into a design obtained through electroplating, while Maison Monbro, with the industrial enameler Achille Legost, had already felt it had surpassed the great cabinetmaker with chased polychrome enamel based on medieval examples but treated in an Oriental style. It is enough to scrutinize the finest French and English furniture pieces shown at the 1867 Exposition Universelle to see the extent to which the traditions of the joiner-cabinetmakers of the eighteenth century had lost nothing of their vigor. Even pieces that were purportedly "Renaissance" are often much indebted to the Louis XIII, XIV, or XVI styles. An unquestionable masterpiece, the prodigious ebony and pearwood cabinet by Fourdinois—inlaid throughout thanks to a newly developed process using woods such as box and limewood—is a virtuoso piece which defies categorization and demonstrates great knowledge of allegory and classical ornament (fig. 384). Is it in the Renaissance style? Its overall layout reminds one rather of the ebony cabinets from the middle of the seventeenth century. Also, are not the low-relief figures redolent of the decoration on certain Neoclassical monuments? The intertwining lacework, with its delicate naturalism—of a fineness "that would put a gem engraver to shame" (Luchet 1867)—recalls rather the incomparable skill of the woodworkers or bronzesmiths of the reign of Louis XVI. The same complexity characterizes Louis-Auguste-Alfred Beurdeley's opulent ebony standing bookcase, "streaming with metals and gemstones" (Luchet), and whose Renaissance (but is it Renaissance?) carcass carries Pompeian decorations inspired by Louis XVI types.

Outside France, as well, the bright star of the art of Versailles was not on the wane. Decorator Charles Sechan, for the grandiose furnishing of the Dolma Batce Palace on the shores of the Bosporus, imagined a pomp worthy of the seventeenth century. The sultan's chamber must be "a most sumptuous room in the bombastic Louis XIV style, very like . . . the bedroom of the Grand Roi at Versailles, with a pretty cornice with consoles as in the Galerie d'Apollon . . . with a mantelpiece . . . such as one finds in Lepautre or Daniel Marot." The decor à la Jean Bérain also appeared on the faience and cut crystal.

Better adapted to middle-class interiors than the solemn Louis XIV style, the Louis XVI style—or Adam style in England—remained much in vogue in polite society. "It is comfortable, delicate and does not clutter up our modern, narrow and poky interiors" (Burty 1869).

In Paris, the Empress Eugénie, whose admiration for Queen Marie-Antoinette was notorious, set the tone, though it was more for sentiment than aesthetic reasons that she was led to ferret out the remains of the waning Ancien Régime. The bouquets and flower garlands painted directly on the white porcelain top of a Sèvres gueridon that she was to offer as a gift to the duchess of Hamilton in 1853 are a tribute—on a large scale and with greater realism—to the master decorators of the final third of the eighteenth century. At the Tuileries, her ceremonial halls—in green, pink, and blue—as redecorated by Lefuel, far from being slavish copies, are on the contrary skillful variants combining rocaille with the flowery style of Louis XVI.

This tasteful vogue spread to all the decorative arts. One of the high points of the style is a dressing table of positively regal richness—mahogany, lapis lazuli, and jasper, bronze and silver gilded in two shades—which was to become one of the main attractions of the Christofle stand at the 1867 Exposition Universelle. Built in the manner of Adam Weisweiler by Émile Reiber, who turned to Carrier-Belleuse and Chéret for the sculpture, this valuable piece revealed the artistic aspirations of the Parisian silversmiths. "Riesener the divine is outclassed, the metal-engraver Gouthière outdone" (Luchet 1867).

Picturesque Styles: Rocaille and Chinoiserie

One of the earliest breaches opened in the Neoclassical fortress was the reappearance of a picturesque and exotic Rococo in England in the 1820s. Thirty years later, in Vienna, Paris, London, and New York, the rocaille style had regained all its lost ground.

Alone among all the old styles newly in vogue, the Louis XV disobeyed classicism's rigid lines. Its ample, winning forms were admirably designed for the arts of conversation, for relaxation and rest. In accordance with the rules governing the life of a society watchful of its well-being, the swelling, padded lines of its chairs invaded contemporary salons: *confidents* and *indiscrets* (two or three seats joined back-to-back), poufs and *crapauds* (small, low armchairs) were in perfect harmony with the requirements of the period.

By the time of the Great Exhibition in London in 1851, Léon de Laborde was congratulating Italy on being the only "privileged country" to let the Rococo style pass by, and was not averse to a jibe at the expense of those "people whose whole apartment is a boudoir," where there teem "stuffed pieces of furniture which have lost all shape and padded mattresses with scooped-out backs to laze upon." Nevertheless, in the case of the German-born New York cabinetmaker John Henry Belter, the "rocaille" chair escapes the dictates of the upholsterers. The mastery he acquired in laminated wood—for which he lodged several patents between 1847 to 1860—allowed him to marry, in a surprisingly free manner, undulating forms to unbridled naturalism.

Rococo's image remains linked to the fanciful world of chinoiserie and Japanesery revived in the 1860s by the international commercial boom and the lure offered by the international exhibitions. Firms such as Giroux, Viardot, and Sormani in Paris kept the taste for exotic lacquer and marquetry alive, often adorned in what was a new departure with cloisonné enamel and engraved crystal. In what was termed "style japonais," Édouard Lièvre's furniture adapted shapes and emblems of the Far East to the luxurious traditions of French cabinetmaking (fig. 227). As in the eighteenth century, the great china factories continued to draw their inspiration from China and Japan, but with greater freedom than previously. Japanning and cloisonné, notably by English makers such as Minton's and the Worcester Porcelain Company, culminated in works of impressive decorative power.

The dying embers of the art of Versailles in Germany, the castles of Louis II of Bavaria, Linderhof (fig. 265) and Herrenchiemsee, present a picture of an aggravated and phantasmagorical Rococo which heralded the new vogue for the style consecrated by the 1888 Munich Exhibition of Applied Arts.

The following year in Paris, the rocaille style still appeared the dominant characteristic of French entries. Far removed from the bold strokes of the mid-century, eclecticism then withered into a swollen, ragged Rococo. Compared with Zwiener's pieces weighed down by bronzes, Émile Gallé's creations—particularly his vitrine designed in an entirely Louis XV style—have a charming naturalistic freshness, preludes to a new dawn (fig. 394).

The Break with Classicism: Neo-Gothic

The rediscovery by the West of its medieval past—which amounted to the very first artistic revolution of the nineteenth century—put into question more than four centuries spent under the sway of classicism. Alone among European countries, however, Victorian England succeeded in extracting from the language of the Gothic a fresh approach to arts and crafts which thus gave it its fullest expression.

The moralizing crusade that Ruskin's spiritualist writings inspired against the dehumanizing side effects of unregulated industrialization gave rise to a movement whose amplitude rapidly went beyond the sentimental fascination of the Romantics with medieval art. This root and branch movement owed its strength and its cohesiveness to the conviction of those architects and Pre-Raphaelite painters who became its most zealous proponents. The most enthusiastic encouragement came from the architect and theoretician Augustus Welby Northmore Pugin (1812–1852), to whom England owed its foremost success at the Great Exhibition, the Mediaeval Court. But, beyond the many cultural references, Pugin's adherence to the laws of Gothic art carried with it above all a defense of functionalist principles: a clear and honest structure, in the respect given to each particular material. For twenty years under Pugin's impetus, there was a proliferation of furniture and architectural elements, such as ceramic facings and stained glass, of rigorous construction and geometrical stylization.

Within this austere atmosphere, William Burges's (1827–1881) colorful decors and furnishings jar considerably (fig. 387). Closer to the circle of William Morris and the Pre-Raphaelites, Burges was nonetheless the only artist who managed to turn the Victorian dream of a return to the Middle Ages into a reality. At Cardiff Castle (from 1868), in his own Tower House, or in his pieces of painted furniture (from 1858, aided by artists such as Burne-Jones, Rossetti, and Simeon Solomon) one finds the same rich vein of chromatic inventiveness.

Remaining confined to an enthusiastic minority, and never gaining the total commitment of English manufacturers, the Gothic Revival was nonetheless the strongest innovative trend until the early 1870s. This new idiom, as popularized by Bruce Talbert in his *Gothic Forms Applied to Furniture* (1868) and by Charles L. Eastlake in his *Hints on Household Taste* (published in 1868 and reprinted seven times before 1886), was to exercise a considerable influence on American artists.

In secular decoration on mainland Europe, the use of a medieval vocabulary became less widespread. In France, neo-Gothic Troubadour furniture had all but vanished. In 1851, Laborde, a fervent advocate of Greek art, did not hesitate to declare that there was "not a single furniture manufacturer who would dare to make a chair with cross-bars and lancets. I have seen . . . the Jury at the London Exhibition refuse the last Gothic-cathedral style carriage-clock." There were traces surviving in carved furniture by Mazaroz-Ribaillier or in some silverwork by Froment-Meurice and Frédéric-Jules Rudolphi (and, later on, by Lucien Falize), but the Middle Ages only became significantly attractive in the context of an exceptional commission, as in the restoration of the Château de Roquetaillade overseen by Viollet-le-Duc and his pupil Louis Duthoit (decoration executed from 1869 onward). In German-speaking lands, the Alt Deutsch style remained vigorous in the middle of the century. Inspired by the Late Gothic, the huge carved bookcase by the Viennese maker Carl Leistler was the most ambitious piece in the style to be exhibited in the Crystal Palace. Much later, the passion of King Louis II for Wagner gave rise to the grandiose and bewitching decoration of the castle at Neuschwanstein (1868–81, fig. 266).

Medieval styles were still regarded as the ones best adapted to Christian subjects. The main thrust of the course of nineteenth-century religious art was to revive within the Catholic Church the unity it had known at the time of the Gothic cathedrals. Both the Ecclesiological Society in London and the Christliche Kunstverein in Cologne were determined to promote the making of ecclesiastical objects that conformed to thirteenth-century models, while in France, Adolphe-Napoléon Didron (1806–1867), in his *Annales archéologiques*, naturally enough advocated a return to the century of Saint Louis, stating that the contemporary church must be "carved, painted and furnished in accordance with the demands of that same period."

In the second half of the nineteenth century, it was ecclesiastical silver, under the influence of architecture, rather than its secular counterpart—all too often pulled in contradictory directions—that experienced a period of impressive richness. In this industrial period, firms such as Poussielgue-Rusand (fig. 388) and Armand-Calliat were able to reproduce to order a considerable selection of models in their catalogs, resulting in some of the finest creations of industrial art of the century.

Going Against the Grain of Industrialization: the Rebirth of Handicraft

In their striving to correct an imbalance within the field of artistic creativity, French and English theoreticians and architects alike distilled from their analytical studies of the masterpieces of the medieval era a steadfast conviction in the need to acknowledge the place of the artisan in interpretation and know-how. Ruskin himself considered as the most important chapter of his book *The Stones of Venice* (1851–53) to be just that section describing the nature of Gothic architecture in terms of its implications for the freedom of the craftsman. Ruskin's nostalgic ideal denouncing the enslavement of man by machine and Viollet-le-Duc's far-sighted analysis in his very influential *Dictionnaire raisonné du mobilier français de l'époche carlovingienne à la Renaissance* (1858–75) were, in England, to find expression in some satisfying pieces by Burges, and also in the splendid career of William Morris (fig. 264).

In France, the rehabilitation of craft was due rather to the inquisitiveness and persistence of a number of independent artists who took their cue from the Renaissance or from the East. There followed a veritable "rebirth of the arts of the earth" and, more generally, of all the crafts using fire. Jean-Claude Ziegler's (1804–1856) salt-glazed stoneware, Charles-Jean Avisseau's (1795–1861) rustic pottery in the manner of the sixteenth-century ceramicist Bernard Palissy, Théodore Deck's (1823–1891) Renaissance, Hispano-Moorish, or Persian faience, Philippe-Joseph Brocard's (1867–1890) enameled blown glassware, and Claudius Popelin's painted glazes all attest to the gathering momentum of this movement of artisan-artists as the years progressed. They all shared a love of fine workmanship and rejected the demarcation of labor that industrial manufacture necessarily brings with it. A Parisian cabinetmaker such as Auguste-Hippolyte Sauvrezy was the very epitome of the artist-cum-practitioner. He was a learned all-rounder (his library contained three hundred volumes, including all the salient works of ancient and modern decorative art), able to devise his own models as well as to follow their execution through to the finishing stage.

Generally, the study of the ancients—be they Greeks, Etruscans, Byzantines, or craftsmen of the twelfth and thirteenth or fifteenth and sixteenth centuries—gave a new lease of life to a host of long-lost techniques. In jewelry there was the rebirth of granulation, filigree, niello, cameo, intaglio, damascening, and repoussé. In ceramics and metalwork there resurfaced all the varieties of enamel on glass, pottery, and metal, filigree and jasper glass, and glossy majolica.

Manufacturers who continued to place emphasis on handiwork had much to gain from this marvelous renaissance. In spite of considerable success in the industrial sphere, however, the fond dream of an alliance between art and industry which so marked the years between 1850 and 1860 foundered as the gap between the industrial arts and craft creation widened. In fact the craft renaissance sounded the death knell for all those brave new hopes that had been born in the wake of the Great Exhibition of 1851.

The Appeal of Nature: Illusion and Stylization

The constant imitation of earlier styles was not the only temptation for industrial artists and craftsmen. There was also direct imitation of nature herself. Both these tendencies were the result of a deep-rooted pictorial taste in Europe. The industrial artist and craftsman alike, with the supreme confidence conferred by the improvements in mechanical reproduction and the newly recovered mastery of craft techniques, thought to transcribe nature with almost photographic accuracy. At the mid-century, quite distinct from the repertory of styles already acquired, a naturalist trend was to flourish in wood carving, marquetry, painting on porcelain, relief decoration of ceramics and metal, painted wallpapers, and furnishing fabrics. Rigid in its craving for precision, this return to the portrayal of nature was all too ready to wallow in trompe l'oeil effects. The floral marquetry in porcelain by Julien-Nicolas Rivart at the 1855 Exposition Universelle provides an example of this virtuoso illusionism. Often anecdotal, occasionally invasively exuberant and alarmingly flawless, this obsession was put to its most original use in objects whose very form was borrowed from flora or fauna, attaining singular ornamental power in the luxuriant vegetation appearing on large-scale wallpapers, such as Desfossé's *Le Jardin d'Armide*. Eclecticism in its many facets was susceptible to the fascination with trompe l'oeil, as evident in the Hellenistic decor of the goldwork composed by Sévin for Barbedienne, for instance, or the meticulous carved wood sculptures by Frullini from Florence and the Fannière brothers' engraved silver finishes (fig. 393).

With his customary clairvoyance, Laborde was one of the first to denounce the illusionist tendency for its attempts to "introduce realism into decoration." Laborde imagined his ideal industrial artist as a "man of taste who has studied all the potential of the decorative arts that had been developed in other periods—such as antiquity and the Middle Ages—as well as in other lands—for instance the East and China—and who, combining these allusions with an unremitting study of nature in the precise feel for its conventional imitation could come up with novel effects that would be all the more worthy of admiration since they are within the grasp of the richest makers . . . as well as in that of the [most] modest." This same ideal was simultaneously defended by the major English and French theoreticians to be associated with reforms in the teaching of drawing. From Pugin (in *Floriated Ornament*, 1849), to Dresser (*Botany as Adapted to the Arts and Art Manufactures*, 1857–58), from Viollet-le-Duc to Ruprich-Robert (*Flore ornamentale*, 1866), there is the same desire to create, through a rigorous stylization of nature, the long-awaited new style. It was this expectation that would be fulfilled by William Morris in England and by Émile Gallé in France.

An Eastern Heritage

For some time, Europe had been amenable to Middle Eastern influences and had been glad to incorporate the whimsical world of exoticism into the gamut of its styles. Yet, for all that, the vast coming together of people from various parts of the world at the international exhibitions provided an opportunity for an abrupt confrontation between the Western world, spurred by its ongoing economic growth and an East that appeared to exist outside time. Within the turmoil created by these huge fairs, it was the East that embodied "an art as old as time, unchanging, unmoving, ceaselessly repeating itself, yet full of youth, of sap, of charm, of novelty . . . an art so magnificent that it imparts a regal splendor to everything" (Laborde). Could it be that the rapid development of Western civilization had brought with it a deterioration in aesthetic standards? All the principles, all the unity and truth, as Owen Jones put it, had vanished into the mayhem left by industry—to be kept alive in the Orient alone.

The international exhibitions were thus to set the stage for some salutary heart-searching. It is "to these peoples whose immobility seems to throw down a derisive challenge to all our machinery to whom we must . . . turn for the secret of the true decorative art" (*Rapports*, 1867). In the ever growing number of treatises of decoration, the fantasy of former times gives way to the examination and systematic analysis of Eastern ornament, first through comparison with other sources of styles and then through veritable archaeological anthologies.

Through a study of the infinite variety of Moorish, Persian, and Indian motifs—which ran from the strictest geometricism to a lively and informal naturalism—the devotees of the classical school, as much as those nostalgic for the Middle Ages, were conscious of renewing contact with a lost tradition. In the science of ornamental arrangement and color combinations, it was to the Orient that one had to look to find "that feeling for antiquity, that is to say the feeling for a noble simplicity which is also a feeling for nature" (Laborde). It was in the Orient too that the Frenchman Viollet-le-Duc and the Englishman Burges alike recognized traces of the craft guilds of the Middle Ages. "In the present day, the arts of the Middle Ages have long since disappeared from Europe, and are only to be found in the Orient. Here in England, we can only obtain medieval objects manufactured for us with effort and difficulty, whereas in the Egypt, Syria and Japan, you can purchase them in the bazaars" (Burges 1862).

The Discovery of Japanese Art

Within the vast array of decorative arts, Japanese art was not in truth a discovery of the nineteenth century. In the eighteenth, collectors had vied with each other for Japanese porcelain and lacquer, which had also been much imitated. Japan only truly began to lay bare her artistic treasures from 1858, the year in which commercial treaties with the Western powers were signed. The Japanese entries in the exhibitions of 1862 and 1867 were a sensation. The enthusiasm of painters for Japanese prints was swiftly echoed by that of dealers-cum-publishers and craftsmen, as well as industrial barons and designers. The movement owed much to the passionate advocacy of a number of first-rate artists—Bracquemond (fig. 392) and Reiber in Paris, Edward Godwin and Dresser in London, and Edward Chandler Moore in New York, among others—who succeeded in giving fresh impetus to the renewal of decorative techniques. Far from being limited to the art of the print, the knowledge of Japan was gradually honed and extended to the most varied materials, such as stencils, woven fabrics, lacquer, ivory, cloisonné enamel, polychrome metals, and ceramics. Discovered slightly later, the stoneware vessels of the ancient tea ceremonies were exhibited at Philadelphia in 1876 and Paris in 1878, where their "primitive" appearance was received with surprise.

Japanism was first and foremost the source for a wide-eyed and enraptured vision of nature. "Cranes coursing through an azure sky, carps mirrored in green waters, tits making the frail reeds bend, butterflies searching for peach-trees in blossom, the moon slipping past the hanging twiglet of a birch, an open fan, a rosy fruit, a blooming peony" (Burty 1869). Japanism also lay at the origin of a new approach to craftsmanship, which brought with it respect for materials and an acceptance of the accidents implicit in technique, and which above all was to confer on the commonest, most ordinary object, all the qualities of a work of art.

Espoused by the very best manufacturers and spreading widely throughout Europe and the United States alike, Japanism became the most important wellspring for new ideas during the 1870s and 1880s. In France, motifs taken from Japanese prints met with uninterrupted success, ranging from the printed and colored faience table service (1866) or the engraved enameled glass vases brought out by Eugène Rousseau (from 1875?) to porcelain by Haviland and faience by Manufacture J. Vieillard & Cie. More eclectic, Deck and Gallé mixed allusions to both East and West in their works, the former in brightly colored faience, the latter in polychrome relief earthenware and ornamental glasswork. Remaining more faithful to a Japanese aesthetic, Jean-Charles Cazin opted for the tempered tones of stoneware. Silversmiths and jewelers strove to extract from Japanese craft the secret of such consummate skill. As early as 1867, Christofle and Falize were to pit their wits in an effort to obtain the colored patina and cloisonné enamels of the Japanese. From the 1880s onward, the interest in ancient Japan brought with it greater sobriety. In Gallé's crystal glass, in Ernest Chaplet's underglaze porcelain and Christofle's forged metal, the decoration became muted into a discreet symbolism or else dissolved away completely leaving the material to stand alone.

England, less rooted in eclecticism, was still more welcoming to art from Japan. The English artist, however, opted for geometrical form and repetitive motifs which tended to the abstract more than poetical naturalism. Furniture, fabrics, wallpapers, cast-iron mantelpieces designed by Edward William Godwin (1835–1888), Lewis F. Day (1845–1910), and Thomas Jeckyll (1827–1881), gold and silver or earthenware brought out in plentiful quantities by the larger manufacturers, such as Elkington, Minton's, and Worcester, were to give rise to an Anglo-Japanese style that accentuated formal structure and restricted ornament to rigorous stylization. Christopher Dresser, a botanist, brilliant theoretician, and prolific industrial designer, was the first European designer to spend any length of time in Japan, whence he returned with observations of real value (*Japan, Its Architecture, Art and Art Manufactures*, 1882).

Japanese arts and crafts were likewise behind some of the greatest achievements of American decorators and craftsmen, such as furniture made by Herter Brothers, for example, with its refined marquetry and carved decoration evocative of Japanese stencil work, enhanced by a bold simplicity, or pieces made from hammered, patinated, and inlaid silver by Louis Comfort Tiffany which took naturalism to the point of abstraction.

The English Example: William Morris and his Followers

It was in Victorian England, during the 1860s, that an individual style was forged—a style which, though discarding neither the heritage of the past nor the Oriental contribution, managed to break free from the stranglehold of eclecticism. Here was a new style which no longer sought to identify with an established style.

The remarkable career of William Morris (1834–1896) encapsulates this unparalleled success. He was at one and the same time instigator, creator, and executant. A writer, theoretician, poet, and Socialist activist, he was also an artist-glassmaker, weaver, and printer, turning his hand to painting, decoration, and design. He sensed "that for the true artist, nothing can be left to chance or remain unfamiliar, passionately interested in art's humblest and highest manifestations alike, finally, with a wealth of talent, genius, knowledge, and skills, as only the greatest masters of the past ever possessed" (Lahor 1894).

Morris's position lay halfway between the visceral hostility tainted with sterile nostalgia of a Ruskin in his loathing of the machine in its role as yet another source of man's subjugation and the pragmatism of reformers such as Henry Cole, who wished to influence industrial manufacture through the betterment of artistic education. Only Morris was able to achieve the delicate balance which was to coalesce all the hopes of the period and above all put them into practice. He showed his wholehearted commitment to creativity as early as 1861 in opening a firm which amounted to a veritable laboratory for ideas as well as a production outlet, proposing his services as architect, decorator, and manufacturer. All the intelligence of his system as it unfolded over the years—reaching its culmination in the premises set up in Merton Abbey, Surrey, in 1881—lay in a rare flexibility as regards both design and realization. As Walter Crane suggested, the great advantage and the charm of Morris's method was that it could encompass both splendor and simplicity.

Morris was never to depart from the guidelines bequeathed by the Gothic Revival: close ties between artist and craftsman; respect for the individuality of the craftworker within a unified field of work; a desire for straightforwardness and honesty; and finally an inspiration that was taken from nature. Yet Morris was also to investigate other sources that led him back to the Italian Renaissance, to Persia, and even to the Indies. "I recall him speaking with as much enthusiasm and warmth about Beauvais cathedral, which he esteemed the most miraculous of all, as about a marvelous Persian rug that bedecked [his] dining room" (Mourey 1896).

Morris exerted such a profound influence not so much because of his self-righteous Socialist doctrines, or his work as a decorator (his naturalistic style progressed considerably as its inspiration evolved), but rather because of his exemplary position as artist, exponent, and entrepreneur. His success in practice—his firm was to continue as a going concern for eighty years—can also be attributed to its organization, which relied on collective responsibility (George Wardle in 1897 went as far as to compare it to one huge playground for adults). Morris's attitude with regard to the machine was also crucial. It was more subtle than is generally supposed, and his love for handiwork did in no way prevent him from using the appropriate mechanical techniques that large-scale manufacture (specifically of wallpaper and printed chintz) rendered unavoidable. The achievements of the enterprise owed much to the regular collaboration of architects such as Philip Webb (1831–1915), painters such as Burne-Jones (fig. 386)—from whom the woven tapestries at Merton Abbey derive the richness of their figurative elements—potters such as William de Morgan (1832–1917; fig. 264), and industrial designers such as William Arthur Smith Benson.

Although he had only received brief training in George Edmond Street's practice, Morris believed firmly in the central role of the architect in the creation of the modern home, "with all the appliances fit for carrying on a dignified and happy life" (Morris, *The Lesser Arts of Life*, 1882, 185). The preeminence of the role played by the architect in decoration had been a tradition accepted since antiquity, and it was this which gives the English style of the period its vigor and freshness. It was in the main artists adept in the laws of architecture who, in the England of the 1880s, gathered into associations with interior decorators and craftsmen—the earliest being the Century Guild founded by Arthur H. Mackmurdo (1851–1942) in 1882—so as to follow the path opened up by Morris.

The complex nature of the Victorian era itself is, however, encapsulated in the inability of the Arts and Crafts movement to continue where Morris left off. Forever torn between the age-old dream of craftsmanship built around the guilds and the need to bend to the imperatives of the industrial world, it was the younger generation of English artists themselves who made it impossible to bring to total fruition earlier ideas that had been forged in such a brilliant manner.

Industrial Art and the Birth of Functionalism

"Who will create, who dreams of creating everyday, simple, no-nonsense furniture that owes nothing to anyone, and which could serve as well for our children—what revolution in our lives is needed to bring it about?" Such modern furniture did in fact exist in Europe, and had done for about twenty years previously, but Burty, in this yet another victim of the prejudices of his time, was unable to recognize it.

In 1871, an industry providing furniture in steamed bentwood was already in full swing, thanks to the German-Austrian Michael Thonet (1796–1871). To date the total number of manufactured units produced by the firm of Gebrüder Thonet since its foundation has reached four million (fig. 405). As early as 1842, the year in which he moved to Vienna, Thonet lodged patents—in France particularly—covering methods of bending wood into "every conceivable shape." Fifteen years later, Thonet had established his first factory in Moravia and had thus progressed to genuine mass production. His extraordinary success is an exemplary illustration of the shift from craftwork to industry and the introduction of forms developed on the factory floor. Somewhat too functional, these practical pieces of furniture bereft of all ornament at first only made a tentative entrance into middle-class homes. About 1880, to satisfy demand from private customers, Thonet even had to reintroduce historicist shapes.

In the United States, meanwhile, improvements in the manufacture of furniture reached their apogee between 1860 and 1880. Fold-away and adjustable patented furniture, such as pull-down beds and walk-in wardrobe-bedrooms, often lost nothing of their traditional stamp. With the German-born manufacturer Georg Jakob Hunzinger, however, form and inventiveness joined forces: his seating furniture in turned maplewood with steel struts and sprung rockers, which met with considerable success, derived its effectiveness in aesthetic terms from the successful combination of mass-production technology and contemporary lifestyle (fig. 407).

England, then at the height of her economic growth, was at the same time a country rich in industrial designers. The Victorian artists prepared without too many misgivings to put their creativity to work for the benefit of industry were, however, few and far between. It was Christopher Dresser who probably best grasped the beauty that can arise from a close collaboration between machine technology and materials. Fired with enthusiasm for scientific progress, he provided around fifty manufactories with countless designs over a period of more than forty years. The silver cutlery set with an astonishing "futurist" geometrical design that he patented and produced on a large scale as early as 1880 was a forerunner of the creations of twentieth-century *Maschinestil* and remains living proof of his motto: "Truth, Beauty and Strength" (fig. 423).

ART NOUVEAU

Definition, Principles, and Trends

In the history of forms, Art Nouveau—in terms of its theories and decrees—appears as the first telltale sign of a shift toward a radically new stylistic departure. The decisiveness of the break was equaled only, however, by its brevity, since the most prominent examples of Art Nouveau date from a period which lasted only ten years (from 1895 to about 1905). After that time, and up until World War I, its themes and motifs continued to become bastardized in products of often mediocre quality, as a new form of rationalism gained ground, which, though derived from Art Nouveau's own theories, rejected its idiom based on dynamism and organic life.

Within each of the many branches of activity exercised by decorative artists, developments did not simultaneously attain an identical level. At an early juncture, for example, ceramicists were to put to good use the lessons learnt from the Far East, in particular from Japan. The rebirth of ceramics in the period between the Paris Expositions Universelles of 1878 and 1889 was certainly the clearest harbinger of the onset of Art Nouveau's maturity. On the other hand, furniture design attained this stage only much later, and found it hard to abandon historical cloning. There were also geographical discrepancies. At the onset of the 1890s, France, with Émile Gallé and Hector Guimard (1867–1942), and Belgium, with Paul Hankar (1859–1901) and Victor Horta (1861–1947) were producing brilliant creations, but it was only during the twilight years of the century that Charles Rennie Mackintosh (1868–1928) in Glasgow, and Josef Hoffmann (1870–1956) and Otto Wagner (1841–1918) in Vienna were to design the earliest Art Nouveau ensembles of a more geometrical nature.

The period had a preference for terms such as "art moderne" or "Modern Style." The range of names employed itself conveys in a significant way the international nature of Art Nouveau and its rejection of historical styles. If Belgium adopted the French term "Art Nouveau" and if the Netherlands translated it literally into "Nieuwe Kunst," Germany opted instead for the notion of all-conquering vitality in forging the denomination, "Jugendstil," derived from the Munich journal *Jugend* founded in 1896. This last choice reminds us of the extent to which Art Nouveau was linked to those art periodicals which sprung up at the end of the century, giving vent to the ever-growing concerns that the search for a truly contemporary style aroused—a preoccupation that some indeed were to consider overstated. In Austria, the names used emphasized a willingness to break with the historical and passeist viewpoint: the term "Sezessionstil" originated with the group of Viennese avant-garde painters and sculptors founded in 1897 under the banner of the "Wiener Sezession." (These artists had in turn borrowed the name adopted in 1892 in Munich by a faction opposed to the system of selection employed in official exhibitions.) As this terminology was being adopted, nicknames also appeared: in France, terms such as *style anguille* (eel style), *style nouille* (noodle style), *style os de mouton* (mutton-bone style), and *style rastaquouère* (money-bags tyle) were used. A few particularly violent brickbats were to become famous. For instance, the critic and novelist Octave Mirbeau, though an effective combatant in the defense of modern art, was to note how "everything turns, wrenches, overturns; everything rolls up, rolls in and then rolls out before all of a sudden collapsing, no-one knowing why or how . . . The furniture looks as if it has been drinking and seems to act as an invitation to the very worst acrobatic excesses" (*La 628–E8*, 1907, 328).

The origins of Art Nouveau lie in a number of factors: in a wish, often voiced from the end of the 1850s, to create a living space which could cater for the needs of contemporary life; in the search for emancipation, and in the quest for innovation that, in the last third of the century, acted as a spur to all decorative artists, aided and abetted by a host of theoreticians and thinkers. Art Nouveau was also a result of the struggle dating from the 1850s to abolish the distinction between "major" and "minor" arts in favor of a principle of the unity of the arts. Actions such as this originated in a particular way of seeing art's economic and social role, according to which art was no longer a luxury or whim for some rich, idle, or dilettantish individual. For the devotees of the unity of the arts, the need for beauty was linked to an urge to create a state of well-being to which all could aspire, each according to their different means but to which all would have an equal right. Hence, a large number of artists who started out in the "major" arts, in their eagerness to make the world a better place, did not hesitate to abandon, temporarily at least, their erstwhile activity—be it painting or sculpture—and devote their talents to the renewal of the "domestic" arts. Henry van de Velde (1863–1957), Richard Riemerschmid (1868–1957), and Peter Behrens (1858–1940) are cases in point. Les Cinq, for instance, a Parisian group that in December 1896 held a first exhibition "of useful, everyday objects of general utility that are also works of art" (preface to the catalog), comprised a painter, Félix Aubert (1866–1940), three sculptors, Alexandre Charpentier (1856–1909), Jean Dampt (1854–1945), and Henry Nocq (1862–?), and an architect, Charles Plumet (1861–1928).

Although inherited in large measure from Morris's Arts and Crafts movement, the notion of a group of creative people pooling their talents for the purposes of developing a harmonious style was also characteristic of Art Nouveau. The Vereinigten Werkstätten für Kunst und Handwerk (Associated workshops for art and handicraft, Munich, 1897), the Darmstädter Kunstlerkolonie (The Darmstadt artists' colony, 1898), and the Wiener Werkstätte (The Viennese workshops, 1903) all explicitly declared their descendance from the English prototype.

The program of the artists' colony on the Mathildenhöhe in Darmstadt, which aimed at creating *Gesamtkunstwerke* (total artworks) where art and life, the artist and the craftsman, the house and its interior decor would be as one, was shaped by the ideas imported from England. The colony's mentor, Ernest Louis, the grand duke of Hesse-Darmstadt, had been exposed to the theories and products of the Arts and Crafts movement during his education. There are marked similarities between the ideals and aims expressed in the *Arbeitsprogramm* drawn up by Josef Hoffmann and Koloman Moser and the theoretical writings of William Morris, notably the desire to turn the home into an aesthetic environment and a belief in the beneficial influence of beautiful objects. Among the leaders of Art Nouveau only Émile Gallé failed to acknowledge a debt to Morris or Ruskin. Naturally, he was susceptible to Ruskin's fond dream of seeing art objects produced in a spirit of joy and love, as well as to Morris's humanitarian philosophy, but his was a resolutely modern outlook. As an experienced manufacturer, fully aware of the problems entailed by the union of art and industry, as an industrialist whose ambition was to create a modern and rational concern as much by the use of tools as by its organization, Gallé found Ruskin's theories inadequate and condemned them as outdated. Ruskin, in his rejection of ugliness, had in the same breath denounced progress and any moves toward modernity. Morris, too, in the thrall of the medieval ideal of the cathedral, was incapable of shaking off the legends of an idealized Gothic society, believing that the revolution he championed could be brought about and vouchsafed only by reference to the past. Unlike Morris, who bemoaned the passing of yesteryear, Art Nouveau accepted the modern, and wanted, as far as was possible, to make the contemporary world a better place by dint of modern scientific means.

It was science that would allow the artist to set aside the notion of the unique masterpiece and turn to creating "models of beauty," which, reproduced industrially, could take their place in every home. It was in this respect that the progressive ambition which extolled "art for all" met economic considerations head-on. All those who espoused the aesthetic principles of the Arts and Crafts movement inherited these contradictions. Numbering among these was the desire to provide people with art and to reeducate their taste, while at the same time only being able to supply works that were beyond the financial means of the masses. Morris showed himself to be so uncompromising as to the quality of his materials and the finish of his pieces that his products were of necessity confined to the affluent. This paradox attained its zenith in the case of van de Velde, who never ceased from promulgating a dream of rebuilding society through the arts and yet who started out by providing a shelter from that very society for his wife and himself in building and equipping the Bloemenwerf House. Only on exceptional occasions, it must be said, did van de Velde bend to the requirements of mass production. This is borne out by his altercations with the Deutscher Werkbund, a veritable pact of alliance passed in 1907 between art and industry of which he had been a founder member and by dint of which twelve artists of the first rank (including Behrens and Riemerschmid) had committed themselves to channeling their energies into safeguarding the aesthetic quality of mass-produced things.

For others, social progress lead to a positive plan of action. France and Belgium both saw the growth of a number of workers' groups, which were to hold congresses. In the yearly salons—from 1900 on particularly—"workers' furniture" made an appearance, while the Belgian Gustave Serrurier-Bovy (1858–1910) dedicated the major, and perhaps best, part of his career to creating "social furniture." As his price list proves, Serrurier's products were certainly cheap, and he also tried to ensure that the householder shared in the work by providing two types—curtains and stencils—that the occupants themselves could execute. The fact that this was all to end in failure in no way detracts from the sincerity of Serrurier's intentions. For Gallé, as for Louis Majorelle (1859–1926), "social art" resulted above all from the application on an industrial and commercial scale of research of a technical and artistic nature which, however, remained extremely costly and could only be undertaken thanks to considerable financial support. Gallé and Majorelle both attempted to solve the problem and reach a balance through the provision of two ranges, one "rich" and the other "ordinary." Nonetheless, as soon as reproductions were obtained from a "good" model and adapted to various materials and decorated using less costly techniques, the risk of mimicking arose and products manufactured in large quantities became simply a pale imitation of more costly creations which remain the only preserve of true art.

Both in the case of the everyday and of the exceptional, all concerned followed an identical avenue of research, leading to the unity of the art object. As Art Nouveau saw it, structure and decoration should be one and the same, and both should express function. The overriding ambition of Art Nouveau was to put an end to the dualism between structure and externals, for the most part with reference to the natural and medieval approach expounded by Viollet-le-Duc.

In the area of the decorative arts, special mention must be made of Eugène Grasset (1845–1917), who, in "L'Art Nouveau," a lecture given at the Union Centrale des Arts Décoratifs in 1897, endorsed the relationship between form, function, and materials, and decreed that any program of research would have to take account of Viollet-le-Duc.

France

After Grasset had delivered his lecture, he was considered by the Parisian artistic milieu prepared to acknowledge the existence of "practitioners of industrial art" as the epitome of the "modern" artist for whom the arts formed a single whole. The artist's inventiveness had penetrated every domain and found an outlet in many different guises. As a poster and wallpaper designer, as an illustrator, cabinetmaker, and craftsman in wrought iron or enamel, Grasset had turned his hand to every branch of the decorative arts. His explorations were undertaken in a rationalist approach which owed much to Viollet-le-Duc's teachings. "The pattern book we should be consulting is Nature," Grasset declared in 1896 (Nocq 1896, 13).

At no time did Grasset lose sight of the demands imposed by the techniques he employed. His projects for stained glass indicate a thorough knowledge of specific processes, from pane-cutting to leading the cames. Specifically designed for vitreous materials, his cartoons could be transferred without modification by the master glassmaker Félix Gaudin (1851–1930), for Grasset knew how to organize color and surface relationships as they were affected by light, and how to scale the subjects in accordance with the spectator's viewing distance. In the area of nonreligious stained glass, his most consummate success is without doubt the window entitled *Spring* (*Le Printemps*, 1894, fig. 253). The features and outlines of the female figures represented in this allegory are borrowed from a type dear to Grasset which present traits in common with Pre-Raphaelite models. On the other hand, the flight of swallows and the apple blossom betray their Japanese origins, also noticeable in the way space is organized into overlapping planes set with valleys. This rather bland iconography resurfaces in numerous later decorative compositions, among them hangings that were to meet with considerable success at the 1900 Exposition Universelle, *La Fête du printemps* (Musée de l'École de Nancy, Nancy).

With the construction and fitting of a block of rented apartments, the Castel Béranger (16 Rue La Fontaine, Paris, 1894–98), Hector Guimard found ample opportunity to display his talents as a master of all trades and to make his mark as an avant-garde *décorateur* (figs. 269, 300). He made designs for everything, directing all aspects of the work, from the masonry and the sculpture to the tiniest ornamental detail in the apartments. At that time, Guimard's sinuous line was also to be found in panels made out of Lincrusta-Walton, a contemporary material halfway between papier-mâché and linoleum, employed as wainscoting and in wallpapers printed by Le Mardelé (fig. 446). Their design was based on the swaying motion of standing stalks, little motifs stirred into a life all of their own, and seals redolent of Japanese *tsubas* (sheaths for swords). As for the ever-present stained-glass window, Guimard did not think of it as a visual obstruction, but rather as a light source. In general, he would frame a pane of plate-glass with discreet patterns in transparent blue, green, yellow, and pink glass, using lead for graphics with an incisive line. Although stained glass, wallpapers, ironwork, and the mantelpieces in Bigot stoneware were supplied to the tenants, other elements, such as the furniture, were optional extras. The most important pieces of furniture shown in the luxurious album dedicated to the Castel Béranger were indeed executed, but in only one or a very few versions. As none of the occupants of the building wanted to own any of the furniture, Guimard found himself obliged to offer it to others. From the outset then, the distribution of the new *style Guimard* was a problem. The furniture from the Castel Béranger and other pieces that were to follow up until the years 1902–3 bear witness to the rationalist training of Guimard, who was an artist who considered nature solely from the point of view of its structural implications. This rationalist training, however, had been imparted to someone of a fiery temperament: the starting point, the inflection, and the tailing off of each of his long, thin, and supple lines are all marked by a vigorous knot of abstract motifs. From 1902–3 onward, however, Guimard's furniture gained in body. The composition was no longer based on the provocative play of line, but the understated opposition between filled and empty spaces. Increasingly, outlines billowed out, and the artist devoted ever greater space to sculpture. Finally, Guimard the architect managed to apply all his subtlety and refinement to the equipping of a town house he built for himself in 1909 on Avenue Mozart in Paris.

Such close ties between architecture and interior fittings remained the exception rather than the rule in Paris, where Art Nouveau found expression above all in furniture and objets d'art. In a significant turn of events, the overall conception of the Siegfried Bing pavilion built for the 1900 Exposition Universelle was entrusted to a decorator, Georges de Feure (1868–1944). The decoration and fitting of the antechamber, dining room, and bedroom were carried out by Eugène Gaillard (1862–1933; fig. 414). In spite of the use throughout of curvilinear forms, in the furniture a balance was maintained between rigorous design and simplicity of construction. The drawing room had been laid out by Édouard Colonna (1862–1948), a man of radically different temperament. Robustness was here replaced by a softer line, whose sole aim would appear to have been a desire for slenderness and elegance. The carved wood is more discreet, taking its shape from a simple and pliable type of molding which extends the whole length of the framework. The citron wood harmonized with the minor keys of the yellows and greens of the wall hangings and rugs, which were designed by the same hand. As for de Feure, he also designed hangings for the walls of the washroom and the boudoir. The decoration was derived from flowers, though it was highly stylized and the flora remained vague. Here, muted tones and ingeniously handled arabesques conveyed an impression of innovation. However, these fabrics owed a great deal to Javanese batiks that the Dutch-born de Feure knew well. Similar patterns were to adorn the gilt wooden furniture of the boudoir, which constitutes one of the most obvious attempts to rekindle the tradition of Parisian elegance.

A decision of equal import was taken by the jeweler Georges Fouquet (1862–1953) when he entrusted the refurbishment of his shop on Rue Royale not to an architect, but to painter-decorator Alfons Mucha (1860–1939), who had designed the Fouquet stand at the 1900 Exposition Universelle. In this case, though, the rational and practical approach was set aside; instead there was a profusion of motifs that evoked subterranean, aquatic, and vegetal worlds, or else glorified the supremacy of the peacock.

It was this same bird that was to provide René Lalique (1850–1945), whose reputation about 1895 was growing, with numerous pretexts for combinations of marvelous, and even sometimes fantastic, forms (fig. 246). He ran the gamut of every part of the peacock, from the head crowned with its crest, to the feet and the eye markings on its plumage, and analyzed and employed each of these elements according to its expressive potential, going so far as to juxtapose them with female figures. The faces and bodies of these women, veiled or unclad, occupied a preponderant place in Lalique's jewelry designs. These bold and voluptuous forms did not surface in the jewelry Grasset designed for the Maison Vever. Their subjects are just as expressive and as symbolically charged as Lalique's, but their structure is tighter. The clashing colors, the deliberate crudeness of their facture, and the use of cabochon stones in place of the more usual cut gems endow them with a barbaric appearance. The craving for color that jewelers had at the time is clearly evident in Art Nouveau jewelry. Extensive use was made of both translucent and opaque enamels, and the enameler's art made such strides at the turn of the century that jewelers were provided with a miraculous palette. In Eugène Feuillâtre (1870–1916) and Fernand Thesmar (1843–1912), France possessed a pair of virtuosi in cloisonné and translucent enamel work. Moreover, both were endowed with a fine sense of how to accord form and ornament. The same can be said of the work of silversmith Ernest Cardeilhac (1851–1904). With the assistance of a first-rate draftsman, Lucien Bonvallet (1861–1919), he was to produce perfectly assembled pieces of novel inventiveness. The plant ornaments, though conserving the spontaneous and natural grace of their models, were tempered by stylized and repeated motifs.

Efforts to renew the art of ceramics had already proved their mettle at the 1889 Exposition Universelle, though the focus of attention was more on materials than on forms. Hence Ernest Chaplet (1835–1903), working in Choisy-le-Roi after 1889, focused all his talents on a study of glazes prepared from oxides which could make porcelain take on various colors depending on the composition of the air in the kiln. He obtained a whole range of more or less purplish reds, turquoise blues, celadons, and whites. By exploiting what had previously been considered as a shortcoming in firing, Chaplet was able to create original and surprising effects, such as a veined red flecked with white. His material later became denser, reminiscent of stoneware by Auguste Delaherche (1857–1940). The forms employed by Delaherche were always simple, though some models took their inspiration from the natural world. The potter only accorded a secondary role to the hazards of firing; the incisions, gadroons, and ribs he applied to his pieces not only served as decoration, but also as channels for the poured glaze to produce the desired effect. In spite of the premature death of Jean Carriès (1855–1894), who had left Paris in 1888 to devote his life to the fire demon in the very heart of the Puisaye in the Nièvre *département*, the making of artistic stoneware was to continue in Saint-Amand with, in particular, the works, sturdy yet precious, of Émile Grittel (1870–1953) and Paul Jeannerey (1862–1920).

Objets d'art, after a long struggle, were finally admitted first to the Société Nationale des Beaux-Arts, in 1891, and then to the Société d'Art Français in 1895. The most striking thing is the individualist nature of the work, there being no joint efforts. The absence of group work is one of the central traits of Parisian Art Nouveau. The Groupe des Cinq, which formed in 1896, and later became the Groupe des Six, and then Art dans Tout, is the exception that proves the rule. Sculptors who had turned to the decorative arts, Alexandre Charpentier and Jean Dampt exerted a dominant influence. They had been preceded in their rehabilitation of the "domestic arts" by their colleague Rupert Carabin (1862–1932) who, in his bookcase executed in 1890, had produced a ground-breaking piece of work (fig. 413). From 1889 to 1914, he exercised his skill as a sculptor as much in the creation of furniture and objets d'art as in sculpture proper. Charpentier was a more sober character and for him it was the overall line that remained of prime concern. The hand of the sculptor does betray itself in the low-reliefs that adorn the decorative woodwork in certain of his pieces and in the gilt bronze plaques, ornamented with nude and draped female figures, that brighten others, but neither in any way detracts from the rhythm or elegance of the furniture itself. It is in the modeling that the sculptural approach is apparent. His armoire designed to contain instruments for a quartet together with its accompanying music stands surely ranks as one of the most convincing creations of Art Nouveau furniture.

Charpentier's "musical" cupboard was exactly contemporaneous with the foundation of the École de Nancy, which dated from 1901. The latter was not a wholly new association in the sense that it extended something that had already been set up on the occasion of the Exposition d'Art Décoratif in the Lorraine in 1894. The École de Nancy nevertheless differed in that it was established in a less optimistic atmosphere than the 1894 group. It was born, in fact, of Émile Gallé's concern about the power and vitality of the creations from abroad on show at the 1900 Exposition Universelle. The prime intention was therefore to build up a climate of understanding, though the artistic credo holding that nature was the unique and inexhaustible source of renewal for the decorative arts also found an affirmation there, or, to be more precise, a reaffirmation. If the year 1894 appears as a crucial one in the history of the Lorraine movement's influence, it was equally true for Gallé, who at last acquired a glassworks of his own in Nancy itself. This newly installed plant removed all the complications caused by the distance between Nancy and Meysenthal, where Gallé's furnaces had been. Gallé's creativity in the areas of glass, wood, and pottery (although since the beginning of the 1890s, the latter no longer occupied much of the artist's creative energy) was now to be found under one roof in Nancy. In Gallé's estimation, the scientific study of nature was indispensable. Its real role, however, was not to enrich some treasury of models—"the most precise naturalistic work fails to move us because it lacks a human soul" (Gallé 1900, 8)—but rather to provide a key to conveying the subtlest abstractions capable of enlivening a work of art.

By applying his naturalistic concepts to furniture—one of his last writings, *Le Mobilier contemporain orné d'après la nature* (1900), was at once a last will and testament and a profession of faith—Gallé devised solutions that were both novel and individual. The most typical and also most famous pieces are those built up from umbels (1894–1903). The ribs that appear on the furniture are taken from the striated and fluted stalks of the hogweed, while the tops sit upon braces derived from the plant petioles, the flowers themselves lending their ragged edges to cornices and chair backs (fig. 394). Animal forms were also plundered and pressed into service in this new approach to furniture. Fauna lies at the origin of Gallé's last works. The Vitrine aux Libellules (Dragonfly Vitrine, Musée d'Orsay, Paris) and the Aube et Crépuscule (Dawn and Twilight) bed, finished in 1904, were commissioned by the magistrate Henry Hirsch. The vast starry sky, the return of the flock, and the sphinx's wings on the back of the headboard are so many unsurpassed demonstrations of Gallé's use of marquetry, enriched here and there by the shimmering surfaces of mother-of-pearl and glass.

It was in glass, however, that Gallé's extreme sensitivity to the beauties and quirks of nature found expression. The artist, in an effort to conjure up a range of effects, combined etching and enameling with the inclusion of particles of metal and with special preparations of oxides blended during fusion (figs. 238, 240). Above all, he was to overlay layers of glass. In 1898, he took out two patents, one for *marqueterie de verre* (glass marquetry), the other for glass patina. These technical advances were, however, not meant as an end in themselves. His techniques and his research served only to convey the imagination and the thought of the glassmaker. Subject and materials interpenetrate, dissolve into one another and form an indivisible whole. Through this extraordinary union, glass could be composed into a world unlike any other. Even when limited to a single motif, nature nonetheless appeared to invade the entire surface of a vase. There was never any question of simply applying the decoration to the vessel; each dragonfly, cicada, orchid, primrose, or pine branch forms a single body with the sides. By dint of its abundance and thanks to the variety of colors and effects used, the marine world is shown indubitably as the place where life first burgeoned.

The naturalistic character of Gallé's furniture offered an original way of escaping from the ponderousness of pastiche. Two other creative talents were to follow in his footsteps: Eugène Vallin (1856–1922) and Louis Majorelle. Unlike Gallé, they both reaped the benefit of a solid training as cabinetmakers.

From 1881—the year in which Vallin took over at the head of his uncle's ecclesiastical furnishing business—commissions for work flooded in. His initial forays into secular furniture, however, did not begin until 1894. The door that Vallin designed three years later for his own house on the Boulevard Lobau in Paris is a clear symbol of his adoption of Gallé's ideas. Such naturalistic proliferation—as in the decorative umbels, for instance—remains an exception in the artist's oeuvre, which quickly evolved, abandoning the meticulous rendering of plants but retaining from his study of the botanical world allusions of an architectural nature. Within the space of a few years, Vallin had excised from his work all evocations of the plant world, which for him were redundant. Ornament was entrusted solely to the wandering line itself, but the vigor, the supple curves, and the skillful inserts are all still redolent of the growing plant. Completed in 1904, the decoration and furnishing of a dining room commissioned by the financier Charles Masson (Vallin only worked to commission and eschewed large-scale manufacturing) epitomizes his robust and sober art, with its convoluted curves and lively vertical lines, which give structure priority over decorative features (fig. 252).

When Louis Majorelle inherited the family business on the death of his father in 1879, he pursued his craft of lacquer decoration and vernis Martin applied to furniture in a Louis XV or XVI style. In 1894, he sent to the Exposition d'Art Décoratif in the Lorraine a large marquetry natural-color wood table—something of a special case in his work at this time—christened The Spring (La Source). The design was by Jacques Gruber (1870–1936), who at this time was employed by the firm of Daum Frères in Nancy. On the marquetry top appears a young woman with torrents of loose hair, the decoration of the legs and feet being borrowed from aquatic fauna and flora. The strongly naturalistic feel of the whole and the use of marquetry and unstained woods were influenced by Gallé's Rhine table, one of the highlights of the Exposition Universelle of 1889. But Majorelle was not slow in reducing his use of natural elements in both the structure and the decoration of his pieces. By as early as 1900, his furniture was becoming increasingly rigorous in its build: the less ornate ribs now allude to plants only in their nervous, supple line. Whenever the representation of nature turns precise and concrete, it is confined to certain specific areas—such as pediments, fronts, or corners—and is conveyed by wood carving or chased gilt bronze. The bronze elements, such as knobs and lock-plates, play a very specific role in the piece's construction and design, inflecting the curves and accentuating their suppleness, stressing the outlines of the supporting members, stiles, and rails. Their sinewy flight thus lightens the elements in the sturdy build of the piece that might have been ponderous. In conjunction with the use of luxurious imported woods—Cuban mahogany, courbaril, snakewood—it is his metalwork that makes Majorelle seem the very paragon of contemporary "modern" French furniture making in its opulent and ornamented incarnation.

Gallé's very presence, his striking success, and the strength of his convictions in the on-going struggle for the unity of the arts acted as catalysts for others. The existence of a craft community that was appreciative of, and totally familiar with, fine materials also furthered moves in that direction. One who issued from just such a background, Victor Prouvé (1856–1943), was to become its veritable champion. A student of the Salon painter Cabanel, Prouvé, talented in many areas and uncommonly skillful, became an exponent of the most varied techniques. However successful and interesting the cartoons he provided for Gallé and Majorelle might be, they can nonetheless only be considered as the work of a collaborator. Of quite another order was his contribution to artistic bookbinding. In this area he was to become both master and overseer—like his friend, Camille Martin (1861–1898), who trained as a painter but was just as familiar with the problems posed by applied art. Their entry in the Société Nationale des Beaux-Arts was perhaps the most important event of the Paris show. Instead of using the punch, which only permitted the application of small pieces of leather, the artists from Nancy used pyrography. Henceforth, goatskin quilting could be ringed with a vigorous, elastic line and the leather cut-outs became wider, adding force to their large-scale compositions. The use of a hot tool for finishing made it possible to give greater emphasis to the modeling of each motif. So as to achieve total concordance between the subject of the text and the decorative theme, Prouvé and Martin decided to dispense with the rules governing the division of the surfaces and the use of margins and ribs, rules which for them made it harder to achieve this harmony between content and binding. After a few halting steps, they obtained striking effects with bindings whose decoration stretched without a break over both front and back cover. Their *Salammbô*, for example, successfully evokes the barbaric splendors of Flaubert's Carthage (fig. 245). Camille Martin's temperament appears to have been very different. He found inspiration in nature, which he conveyed with both delicacy and poetry (fig. 244). Martin sought the decorative essence of his models and, observant artist as he was, he knew how to distill from every plant he scrutinized its usefulness as ornament.

Prouvé, that master of a dozen crafts, also contributed to the arts of jewelry, embroidery, and leather work, as well as to the highly specialized industry of furniture fabrics which had been developed by another young interior decorator, Charles Fridich (1876–1962). He had devised a way of decorating plush by using acid, a technique which allowed the production of an infinite number of tones—plain or gradated, iridescent or shimmering, blended or pure. In his more luxurious creations, he frequently used contrasting materials, such as silk and hide.

In common with Victor Prouvé, Jacques Gruber, likewise a painter by trade (he had been a pupil of the Symbolist Gustave Moreau), made his mark in various branches of artistic life in Nancy, such as pyrography and cabinetmaking. Gradually, stained glass gained the upper hand over his other preoccupations as a "modern" *décorateur.* His work as a master glassmaker did not derive from a particular tradition, although he had gained experience of working with vitreous materials during his time at Daum and subsequently through his habit of inlaying engraved glass elements, frequently decorated with landscapes of the Vosges, into his furniture and tabletops. Before he had his own workshop, Gruber entrusted the execution of his cartoons to men of the trade such as Charles Gauvillé, who made the large stained-glass window at the Crédit Lyonnais bank (1901–2). In 1904, Gruber finally had a workshop, and the commissions—of a purely secular nature—poured in. The essential principle guiding Gruber's art lies in the rejection of the identification of stained glass with painting. Paint appears but in two guises—grisaille used to highlight certain details and silver stain, which, applied on glass with a relief, sparkles in an extraordinary way. The main effects were obtained by abutting or overlaying glass stained throughout, by acid engraving, and by the use of "American" glass. Gruber combined all these processes with remarkable skill, creating a subtle, lively, ever-changing material with novel effects.

Gruber's collaboration with Daum, although it only lasted from 1893 to 1895, was a fruitful one for the firm. The glassworks found in Gruber an exceptionally well-trained decorative designer. For the most part, Gruber designed decorative schemes that included human figures, especially female, though he also, in a tribute to the flora of the Lorraine, incorporated plants into his designs. Daum owed its success to the flawless and efficient industrialization of its manufacturing processes. It was not that it invested time and money in research of a technical or artistic nature; rather, it exploited and made financially viable time-honored tricks of the trade used in conjunction with an ornamental repertoire that was in tune with the taste of the day. It was above all in the area of lighting fixtures—where Majorelle was instrumental in designing bases and standards in bronze or wrought iron—that Daum displayed an understanding of the needs of the period.

Belgium

At the end of the nineteenth century, the city of Brussels played a key role as both a marketplace and a forum for ideas. It was a rich and liberal-minded city which benefited in addition from a growing population that brought in its wake a noticeable increase in building work. This background of expansion enhanced the city's receptivity to forms that were at the cutting edge of avant-garde thought and art. One of the men orchestrating this was the lawyer, Octave Maus (1856–1919), leader of the avant-garde, founder of the journal *L'Art moderne* in 1881, and the driving force behind first the group Les XX (1884–1893), and then of Libre Esthétique (1894–1914), whose exhibitions, concerts, and lectures amounted to a series of "campaigns."

The period was dominated by four eminent individuals whose work was connected to architecture. Paul Hankar and Victor Horta were architects through and through in both training and career. Gustave Serrurier-Bovy abandoned his architectural studies at the Liège Académie des Beaux-Arts in 1884 in order to open a furnishings and decorations store in the same town. As for Henry van de Velde, he gave up painting completely in 1883 so as to devote himself to the building and furnishing of the Bloemenwerf House, his private residence.

Within the oeuvre of Victor Horta it is impossible to draw a clear distinction between architecture and interior decoration, just as it is nonsensical to try to study a single piece outside the context for which it was originally conceived. Rejecting any element that failed to harmonize with the architecture, Horta was determined to be responsible for furbishing the entire interior, down to the smallest detail. The corollary of this was that his activity as a furniture designer and decorator was limited to buildings which he himself had designed. Horta's work as an interior designer is characterized above all by the use of asymmetry and by a certain dynamism of line. Unlike that of Guimard or van de Velde, Horta's line is unpredictable. It is not drawn from a single curve, but made up of a cluster which, propelled by a rotary movement, can fuse or burst out in different directions. In his quest for increased dynamic effect, Horta never closed the curve; he left it open, endowing it with the famous whiplash appearance. Furniture, carpets, stained-glass windows, flooring, and wall and ceiling decorations all obey identical rules. In the dining room of the Hôtel Solvay, for instance, the extraordinary centrifugal motion of the chandelier is echoed in the spiral marquetry of the parquet and the swirling carpets. The mantelpiece in the drawing room in the Van Eetvelde House (1895) is one of Horta's finest creations. Each element—fireguard, crooks, tongs, poker—was thought out in meticulous detail with respect to the overall plan and is subjected to a single dynamic rhythm. Only through sculpture can such undulations take on solid form. This explains why he chose a precious mahogany imported from the Congo whose fiber is continuous and whose veins are hardly visible. In some cases, as in the furniture he designed for the Aubecq House (1902–4), Horta chose another solution and opted for American ash, whose sinuous veining accentuates the sensation of movement.

Horta's work was that of a sculptor with a passion for relief and for curves. Hankar, on the other hand, favored planar surfaces and a graphic element. His effects were obtained not by ornament but by line alone. Hankar always managed to display a sense of lightness even in his most involved creations, such as the showcase he designed to house Wolfers' contribution to the Exhibition of Applied Arts in Turin of 1902, where the decoration appears to be clambering up the piece as if to take it by storm. Even in his earliest furniture projects, such as the stools for the Peeters pharmacy (1896), built on a square plan and fitted with tapering legs connected by a turned crosspiece and embellished with a braided leather roundel and large buttons, the sources of Hankar's art are obvious: the Gothic rationalism taught by Viollet-le-Duc and Japanese design. The final stage of this refined yet rigorous art is reached in the furniture designed in 1899 for the Villa Wolfers at La Hulpe, executed in light oak and dark mahogany. The construction of the seats emphasized those oblique elements dear to Viollet-le-Duc. They have elegant forward-thrusting joints and braced crosspieces, while the infill for the seat and the back consists of leather straps (fig. 410).

Profoundly affected by the discovery of the works of Morris and Mackmurdo during a stay in London in 1884, Serrurier-Bovy applied for and obtained a franchise from Liberty's. A few years later, he established his own firm and presented work at the salons of the Libre Esthétique in 1894 and 1895 (fig. 412). It met with resounding success, especially the 1895 Artisan Bedroom, which was accompanied by a brochure wherein the author expressed his desire to produce furniture of high quality characterized by "honesty" of construction and intended for wider distribution. Stylistically speaking, Serrurier-Bovy's early suites in Hungarian oak with turned legs and hollow backs are in the popular tradition of country furniture, though with allusions to the principles of the Arts and Crafts movement. On the Artisan chairs, however, there appear curved and lightly undulating lines—in the stretchers running round the legs or the armrests terminating in a "whiplash"—that herald his creations of the years 1898 to 1901. This furniture is characterized by greater elasticity of line, the pieces opening up into broad convex or concave curves. The wood he chose was exotic, warm-hued, and silky-smooth mahogany imported from the Congo. There followed a period of consolidation which began in 1901 with a visit to the artists' colony at Darmstadt, after which the designer began to show more of a predilection for rectilinear shapes and abstract ornaments, while the materials could either be luxurious or simple. The components of the piece are held together by visible screws, which, together with a few stencil drawings and the occasional inlay, comprise the decoration. The purity of the forms used now gave the furniture an avant-garde look.

At the age of thirty, Henry van de Velde, following an encounter with William Morris and the Arts and Crafts movement, suddenly decided to abandon painting. The work which marks van de Velde's decision to devote himself to the applied arts is a wall hanging made of appliqué tacked onto the fabric combined with embroidery, entitled *La Veillée des Anges* (*Angels Keep Watch*, fig. 447). The influence of Gauguin and of cloisonné work is clearly apparent, though the piece also constitutes an Art Nouveau prototype in its undulating rhythms, in the play of curve and counter-curve, and in its abstract tendency. The continuity of line and the dynamicism of the curves both anticipate van de Velde's famous "dynamographic" line, as he termed it. Nonetheless, certain furniture pieces intended for the Bloemenwerf House present outlines which are tough and taut, with surfaces and structures which a gentle bowing or the sweep of a segment of a circle hardly succeed in softening. The dining room seats with protruding roundels amount to an incisive analysis of the function of both this type of furniture and its assembly. The armchairs, which, like the rest of the seating furniture, were to be reused later in numerous interiors furnished by van de Velde, are more elegant but without, however, detracting in the slightest from the fusion between construction and ornament. The backs curve deeply inward and, though the armrests, connected to the uprights by convex tenon joints, open outward, the overall line of the chair is a totally closed one. The large desk he presented at the 1899 Sezession exhibition in Munich represent the high point of the artist's work and exemplifies his creative approach (fig. 251). Van de Velde here achieved the perfect synthesis of construction and ornament, with the dynamic lines arranged in such a way as to form a single enveloping whole.

In 1898 and 1900, van de Velde, in his role as apostle of industrial art, had founded two factories, the Société van de Velde pour les Arts d'Industrie at Uccle near Brussels and its Berlin offshoot, the Henry van de Velde Kunstwerkstätten. The long-awaited collaboration of art and industry was not achieved in either premises, however, since the workshops only produced a number of beautiful and costly objects brought out in a handful of copies at most. What van de Velde really appreciated, in each of the varied spheres he worked in, was craft—the single piece polished and repolished, on which he could leave his mark. We will here confine ourselves to two very different domains: bookbinding and fashion. His first binding project dated from as early as 1893 and was intended for Édouard Fournier's book, *L'Art de la reliure en France*. This design, heavily influenced by the English, presents a number of stylized tulips executed by Paul Claessens (1861–1939), who, in agreement with van de Velde, was to employ traditional techniques alone: irons and punches, and inlay morocco. The most striking feature is the absence of any relationship between the text within and the ornament on the cover. The design is abstract and covers the total surface from front board to back, featuring bright tones which accentuate the monumentality of the sinuous, intertwined motifs. Between 1895 and 1900 van de Velde also designed a dozen or so dresses for his wife, Maria Sèthe, that were intended to be worn privately. The fabrics for these generously cut dresses, with their deep pleats and fine embroidery, were unicolor and the sleeves bouffant; sometimes there appears the hint of a train. Such was their simplicity and unceremoniousness that Toulouse-Lautrec, invited to dine one night at the Bloemenwerf House, was under the impression that his hostess had received him in a dressing gown. It would have been a dressing gown the color of crushed strawberries to match the egg yolks and the red beans served on dishes of violet and green. Rarely could the unity of the arts have attained such heights.

Keen to promote his colonial policy and make his subjects aware of all the treasures that the Congo might offer, King Léopold II entrusted a number of artists with the finest of the elephant tusks that had begun to arrive in the main ivory market in Antwerp in 1892. The earliest results of his generosity were presented at the international exhibition held in the same city in 1894. Three years later, at the international exhibition in Brussels, there was a presentation of some truly "modern" art made using ivory. It was to be all the more "modern" since the halls and showcases of the Congo Pavilion—built at Tervueren—had been designed by Hankar, Serrurier-Bovy, van de Velde, and Horta. One of the most successful figures of the exhibition was Philippe Wolfers (1858–1929), a silversmith, jeweler, and sculptor who had been the most adept at using ivory in conjunction with other valuable materials (fig. 421). His themes centered on woman as idol or else on the struggle between the forces of good and evil. Strongly influenced by René Lalique, Wolfers was less original in the field of jewelry design, though his compositions, which display a splendid consistency of inspiration, number among the most convincing. He combined swans and water lilies, herons and eels, as well as—in a threefold invocation of the night—bats, owls, and opium poppies. What is more, he strove to use the materials he saw as most appropriate, his owls and bats, for example, being carved from dark-hued amethysts. Wolfers, a stranger to the art of stained glass, was nonetheless to play a part in its renewal through his work with the Val Saint-Lambert crystal-glass factories.

The 1897 Tervueren exhibition also served to consecrate another artistic talent, Hélène de Rudder (1870–?), known as the "Belgian embroiderer," who, having obtained the commission to decorate the main hall in the Congo Pavilion, presented eight striking panels that range from a startlingly Manichean viewpoint, on the one side, embracing civilization, religion, marriage, and freedom with, on the other, barbarism, fetishism, polygamy, and slavery (fig. 449). To make her monumental compositions, she superimposed different materials on a background, dispensing with a border. De Rudder was careful to choose the silks, satins, and brocades—some of them old—most appropriate to the cartoon executed. After first cutting out the shapes, she would then size them together, stitching them to a silk or moire ground fabric, while the contours and details were picked out in embroidery. Such a technique has, however, the inconvenience of fragility and by 1900 the artist was forced to return to the more traditional petit point.

Holland

In Holland, as early as the end of the 1870s, an atmosphere conducive to a renaissance of the decorative arts was already developing. The effects of the alarm sounded by the architect J. de Kruyff following the lamentable Exhibition of Applied Arts that was held in Amsterdam in 1877 were soon felt. A Museum of Applied Arts was founded in Haarlem, which was soon joined by a school, and the creation in Amsterdam itself of the Rijksschool voor Kunstniverheid (National School of Decorative Art), in which the architect Petrus Josephus Cuypers (1827–1921) was appointed to teach. From his studio were to emerge some of the central figures in Dutch Art Nouveau, Carel Adolph Lion Cachet (1864–1945), Theodor Willem Nieuwenhuis (1866–1951), and Gerrit Willem Dijsselhof (1866–1924). In 1895 the latter two, together with the metal engraver Frans Zwollo (1872–1945; fig. 431) and the sculptor Mendes da Costa (1863–1939), founded the society Labor et Ars, which had a dual purpose: to free the decorative arts from tradition and from academicism, and to improve the relationship between art and crafts. Simultaneously, the country was opened up to the influence of England through the translation in 1884 of the writings of Lewis Day (*Everyday Art*, 1882) and, in 1896, of Walter Crane (*Claims of Decorative Art*, 1894).

In this area, however, it was Belgium that played the role of mediator. Periodicals such as *La Société nouvelle*, *L'Art nouveau*, and *Van Nu en Straks*, as well as the group Les XX, had made Morris's ideas their own and van de Velde had certainly forged strong links between the two countries. Indeed, it was at his instigation that in 1896 the painter Johan Thorn Prikker (1862–1932) undertook his first creations in batik – a technique characteristic of Dutch Art Nouveau which found a valuable source of inspiration in the fabric designs of its colonies in Java. He was able to produce and market these designs the following year for the accounts of Lion Cachet and Dijsselhof, who were the first to take an interest in the potential opened up by this type of dyeing. Dijsselhof's masterpiece, a surgery for the Amsterdam house of a doctor Van Hoorn, today rebuilt in the Gemeentemuseum in The Hague, has walls adorned with sumptuous textiles featuring bird and flower motifs whose sources are obvious (fig. 451). Not only was it van de Velde who prompted Thorn Prikker to turn to the decorative arts, but he also greatly influenced his friend's work. The furniture he designed for the Arts and Crafts House in The Hague, to which he was appointed artistic director in 1898, bears witness to Thorn Prikker's admiration for van de Velde's fluid line, though, for all their gracefulness, they perhaps lack the strength of the Belgian's.

There is nothing redolent of Belgium in the products that emerged from the workshops of Van Wisselingh & Co. in Amsterdam, which manufactured the models dreamt up by Nieuwenhuis, Lion Cachet, and Dijsselhof.

All these artists show signs of the time they spent with Cuypers. Nieuwenhuis, though he remained above all an illustrator sensitive to the weirdness of the octopus and the peacock, produced soberly and solidly shaped furniture which often makes one forget their lavishness, the result of an occasionally excessive use of ornament. His pieces are decorated with panels with carved or inlaid plant motifs in a wood contrasting with that of the structure. The seats were for the most part upholstered in floral-patterned batik. With Lion Cachet, some pieces have an Oriental appearance and happily employ valuable import woods such as ebony. The decoration, whether carved, inlaid, or cut into the leather, is similarly rich and unfolds like a suite of whimsical variations on the theme of the plumage of the lyrebird or peacock. The most restrained, yet also the most ponderous, of the three was Dijsselhof, whose most exuberant works were his wall coverings.

Another of Amsterdam's furnishing and decoration institutions, T Binnenhuis (The Interior), founded in 1900, took a more severe approach. Affiliated to this store were a number of workshops assigned to execute its projects, run by Willem Hocker, Jacob van den Bosch, and Hendrik Petrus Berlage (1856–1934). At the end of 1901, however, several artists, unhappy with the financial management of T Binnenhuis, decided to leave. The silversmith Jan Eisenloeffel (1876–1957) was the driving force behind this dissident group, from which emerged a rival organization, De Woning (The House), in 1902. The lion's share of sales at T Binnenhuis were accounted for by furniture made by Berlage, who had set himself up in Amsterdam as an independent architect in 1889. One of his architectural works, the Beurs (Amsterdam Stock Exchange, 1898–1903), represents a turning point in the history of modern Dutch architecture. His furniture, in which construction is emphasized to an extraordinary degree, is indeed that of an architect. The lines, born of a yearning to embody the strictest functionalism, are solid but taut, decoration being provided by structural elements and concentrated for the most part on the fixing of the stretchers and legs. Straight lines and right angles—everything is based on a single idea (perhaps derived in part from Japanese furniture): the structure is a frame in which to insert flat surfaces.

Jan Eisenloeffel was the most important figure in the rebirth of the arts of metalwork. From 1898 to 1910, he was to create countless models for tea or coffee services, for kettles, jardinieres, lamps, chandeliers, inkstands, and biscuit tins, the majority being executed in base metals such as copper or brass. These models were designed to be manufactured mechanically, their mass production made feasible by an embossing technique, handles and pourers being riveted on by hand. Spurred on by similar work in Vienna, Eisenloeffel left his surfaces smooth and unadorned, limiting the decoration to a few geometrical patterns.

The work of Frans Zwollo was quite different, remaining that of a traditional metal engraver with a deep love of a craft he had learnt in Amsterdam with Bonebalilier and in Brussels with Wolfers. His approach was elaborate and precise and his plant-inspired ornamental repertoire was conveyed by a supple play of lines drawn on hammered surfaces.

From the strictly chronological point of view, the earliest Nieuwe Kunst productions in Holland are to be found in the field of ceramics. These were linked to the career of Theodorus Colenbrander (1841–1930), who, following studies in architecture, took up the position of artistic director at the Rozenburg manufacture in The Hague, founded in 1883. For five years, from 1884 to 1889, he worked ceaselessly to create totally original decorative schemes, some of which did not shrink from the weird. The motifs were borrowed from nature as seen through the Orient, before being treated in an almost abstract manner to emphasize the pure scarlet tones of the enamels (fig. 433). Colenbrander was also to apply this type of decoration to his cartoon for the knot-pile carpets he designed from 1895 onward for the Amersfoort manufacture. After Colenbrander departed, Rozenburg was to maintain its reputation through porcelain christened "eggshell" due to its delicacy and fragility. This had been developed about 1899 under the auspices of its director Jan Jurriaan Kok (1861–1919), a former student at the polytechnic school in Delft. This new material met with resounding success at the 1900 Exposition Universelle in Paris. Jurriaan Kok's designs were occasionally eccentric yet always elegant, characterized by a highly personal combination of round and angular outlines. As for the decoration, this was provided by excellent painters such as Schellink (1876–1958) and van Rossum. The naturalistic decors, borrowed from both the plant and animal kingdoms, are further evidence of the positive influence at the end of the nineteenth century of the civilizations of Indonesia on the industrious Netherlands.

Germany

Germany was slow to wake from her dreamy neo-Renaissance and neo-Rococo slumber of the past. Without notice, however, a wind of change started to blow through the land. In January 1896 in Munich, there appeared the first issue of the weekly periodical *Jugend*, devoted to all the phenomena of "modern art and life." Next year there followed—much in the vein of the British journal *Studio—Deutsche Kunst und Dekoration*, under the direction of the Darmstadt publisher Alexander Koch. This publication soon made its mark as the most eloquent promoter of new artistic trends. Also in 1897 were founded in Munich the Vereinigten Werkstätten für Kunst und Handwerk, which had emerged from the Gesellschaft für Kunst im Handwerk that had been set up the previous year. In 1898, there then appeared the Dresdener Werkstätten für Handwerkkunst which had the avowed aim of mass production. By the following year, in the small south German town of Darmstadt, the Kunstlerkolonie began to take shape. Under the tutelage of the grand duke of Hesse-Darmstadt, Ernest Louis, the colony became a center of the avant-garde, pooling some of the foremost creative talents of the time. The Darmstadt example spurred other towns to further the applied arts and resolutely modern-minded decorative art schools were born in Weimar, Karlsruhe, and Stuttgart. Finally, in 1900, Henry van de Velde, whose participation in the Dresden Exhibition of Applied Arts 1897 had stirred up such enthusiasm, set up business in Berlin under the aegis of his new friends and patrons, Eberhard von Bodenhausen and Count Harry Kessler. Most striking—and one of the specific characteristics of Jugendstil—is the absence of any style peculiar to Darmstadt, Munich, Dresden, or Stuttgart. Hence, working side by side with cofounders of the Vereinigten Werkstätten in Munich, such as Hermann Obrist (1862–1927), Bernhard Pankok (1872–1943), Richard Riemerschmid (1868–1957), and Bruno Paul (1874–1968), were independent artists such as Otto Eckmann (1865–1902), August Endell (1871–1925), and Peter Behrens (1868–1940). Some of these artists, however, were subsequently to depart from Munich: Behrens for Darmstadt, Riemerschmid for Nuremberg, and Pankok for Stuttgart.

At no point did German furniture seek to conceal its construction. The clear lines emphasize the importance of build and a concern for functionality, since German furniture was intended primarily to be practical. The planes are crisply, but not dryly, divided and juxtaposed with rigor, without either relief or modeling to enliven them. Carving and marquetry, when they do occur, are strictly limited to flat surfaces and never affect the structure. It is the veining of the fine woods used, which Riemerschmid, in particular, exploited in a most sensitive fashion, that provides the bulk of the decoration. Pankok, with his truly anthropomorphic creations—the seats have shoulders, arms, hands, and knees—and with his fluttering marquetry, was an exception. Elsewhere, sinuous linear rhythm is eliminated and ousted by constructions made exclusively from straight lines. Joseph Maria Olbrich's (1867–1908) first pieces in Darmstadt still have bowed outlines and a few carved flower motifs, but the ones he produced in 1902–3 for the new ducal palace are entirely geometrical, both in terms of construction and ornament. Opulence in execution remains the rule, however, the preferred materials being red maple, marquetry in rare woods, and metal inlay. On the other hand, any hunt for evidence of delicacy or preciousness in Behren's work would be fruitless, even in his earliest projects. Finally, it is important to stress that furniture, in the work of all these men, was always conceived with respect to an overall plan: because of the constant search for oneness, the quest for a unified decor, no piece was designed in isolation.

The meandering line that was rejected in furniture nonetheless played a part in the elaboration of more than one Jugendstil masterpiece. Some of the earliest work in Munich, such as the embroidery that emerged from the workshop opened by Obrist in 1894, is characterized by just such a line. In April 1896, an exhibition of thirty-five embroidery patterns designed by Obrist and executed by Berthe Ruchet attracted the attention of critics from abroad, who saw in it the genesis of a new type of applied art (fig. 452). These nature studies of stalks, flowers, and leaves are linked together by geometrical motifs that also retain something of a naturalistic appearance. They are shot through with a tumultuous movement evocative of tongues of fire, the lashes of a bullwhip, or the crashing waves in Japanese prints.

A still more glaring debt to the Far East was owed by Otto Eckmann (1865–1902). An associate of Justus Brinckamm, the enlightened curator of the Hamburg Museum für Kunst und Gewerbe, Eckmann was able to study the Japanese print collections at his leisure, taking from them inspiration for sketches, not only for vignettes for the reviews *Pan* and *Jugend*, but also for tiles, textiles, and ceramics. His love of the plant world was to flourish in pieces made for the workshops of Josef Zimmermann and Otto Schulz, such as candleholders or lighting, and vase mounts. Though these were condemned by some as being excessively Mannerist, this did not deter the grand duke of Hesse-Darmstadt Ernest Louis from appointing him to refurbish his study in the palace at Darmstadt.

The graceful and flighty lines of Eckmann's work in wrought iron are reminiscent of the panes of stained glass mounted on tall shafts that Siegfried Bing showed to connoisseurs at the opening of his gallery in Paris at the end of 1895. Their maker, Karl Koepping (1848–1914), had gained much from his dual training as a painter and chemist. In his work, it is the floral motifs that engender form, and the elegant and fragile end result turns his glass objects into showpieces rather than household items.

The young multitalented artists in Darmstadt were interested in tableware and drew up numerous designs, above all for cutlery. In Bruckmann & Söhne of Heilbronn and M. J. Rückert in Mainz, Olbrich, Christiansen, and Behrens were to find industrialists of an audacious spirit (figs. 422, 425).

In the area of table chinaware, no truly novel forms or decorative schemes appeared before 1895. In the space of a few years, however, a handful of artists transformed tableware decoration. In this they were aided by the development of underglaze painting, which rendered the colors obtained permanent. Such colors, however, could only be painted edge-to-edge, which meant applying them over large surfaces to the exclusion of close detail. Adalbert Niemeyer (1867–1932), Hermann Gradl (1883–?), and Rudolf Sieck (1877–1957) at the Nymphenburg manufacture, Adolph Flad (1881–1937) and Willy Stancke at the Königliche Porzellan-Manufaktur in Berlin, and the Hentschel brothers Konrad (fig. 243), Rudolf (1869–1951), and Julius (1872–1907) in Meissen were to relinquish all suggestion of the third dimension, composing flat designs with floral, animal, or geometrical motifs arranged in accordance with a "modern" rhythm.

Another revival—and one which was to prove highly successful – was to affect pewterware, an art practiced as much by the large manufactories as by smaller workshops. Kayserzinn, for example, was to be found at all the major international shows and, possessing branches in every capital, was able in 1910 to produce a catalog of more than eight hundred models for table services and bibelots. The firms of Lüdenscheid, Gerhadi and Co., and Edward Hueck called on Olbrich, Behrens, and Paul Haustein (1880–1944), enabling the Darmstadt Kunstlerkolonie to make known the results of its research in a material which in Germany met with a succcess that it experienced nowhere else.

One art which gave rise to particularly attractive artefacts was weaving. The founding of the Scherrebeck Kunstwebschule was the earliest repercussion abroad of the Scandinavian tapestry renaissance. A desire to raise the level of what had been a rural craft led Friedrich Denken, Brinckamm's assistant, together with Pastor Jakobsen, to found this school of art weaving, inaugurated on February 18, 1896. Though the school had to declare itself bankrupt in April 1903, in the space of seven years it had nonetheless had time to produce works that count among the best examples of Jugendstil, thanks in the main to Denken who was able to secure the collaboration of some valuable allies—Eckmann, Hans Christiansen (1866–1945), Alfred Mohrbutter (1867–1916), Otto Ubbelohde (1856–1922), and Heinrich Vogeler (1872–1942)—who designed cartoons specifically to be woven at Scherrebeck. The wool shorn from sheep reared on site was spun in the school's workshops then colored using solely vegetable dyes. Weaving was performed on traditional high-warp looms by skilled hands that had to take each thread of wool and entwine it between the lengths of warp. Moreover, as the wool strands were crocheted together, the reverse side of the tapestry was flawless too, creating a double-sided piece. Vogeler's contribution was particularly intriguing. A stalwart champion of the unity of the arts, he had already produced a number of designs for furniture and other household items. In his cartoons there unfurled a world of legend from which, thanks to the intimate association of the strange and the everyday, there emerged an inimitable and poetic flavor. In the spatial arrangement, the absence of perspective, and the economy of means and coloring, his compositions testify to the dual impact of the Japanese print and folk art.

Great Britain

England—a country openly hostile to developments on mainland Europe—was to an extent freed from the shackles of historicism thanks to the effects of the aesthetic declarations of the Arts and Crafts movement. Art Nouveau appeared, from a stylistic point of view at least, to be their natural outcome. Furniture was still built along the same simple principles of construction, in which straight verticals were preponderant. The woods chosen were light in color, and when furniture was painted or lacquered, pale tints were once again in evidence. Though carving was rejected, materials like pewter, mother-of-pearl, and repoussé leather on the other hand played a crucial role in decoration. The key distinction between turn-of-the-century decorative art and that of the Arts and Crafts movement, however, was the acceptance—particularly on the part of two of the most important creative artists of the time, Charles Francis Annesley Voysey (1857–1941) and Charles Robert Ashbee (1863–1942)—of machining.

Before starting out in furniture or in architecture—his earliest commission, a house in Bishops Ichington, dates from 1888—Voysey had first and foremost devoted his time to designing textiles and wallpapers, an activity he was never to abandon (fig. 445). Although Voysey had condemned European Art Nouveau on a number of occasions, his textile and wallpaper creations undoubtedly have common traits with what was being produced in Belgium and in the Netherlands particularly. Voysey only addressed himself seriously to the question of furniture design from the 1890s, his best work dating from after 1895. For Voysey, the preeminent quality of a piece of furniture lay in its simplicity, but that simplicity should have nothing Spartan about it. Elegance and beauty for Voysey could only be expressed through carefully thought-out designs and proportions, while the fact that they might be executed in a common wood—oak for the most part—should have no deleterious effects. Voysey's furniture always has certain salient characteristics: octagonal-sectioned ribs sometimes verging on the emaciated, slightly bowed-in outlines, and corners highlighted by the simplest of moldings. For his designs in worked metal, the artist accorded an increasing role to panels and strap hinges.

Ashbee's name will forever be linked to the Guild of Handicraft, founded in 1888, for which he was the main driving force (fig. 429). Unlike that of Voysey and Ernest Gimson (1864–1919), where formal purity was synonymous with refinement, the furniture produced by the Guild, for which until 1900 Ashbee alone was responsible, has an almost banal simplicity. It was not until the architect Mackay Hugh Baillie Scott (1865–1945) entrusted the Guild with executing the furniture he had been commissioned to design by the grand duke of Hesse-Darmstadt in 1897, that more elaborate and sophisticated forms were created. On the other hand, designs for silverware, where the elegant interplay of line was to reach a peak about 1900, were from the outset marked by a highly individual grace and lightness. They are distinctive for their frequent use of semiprecious stones, placed with a sure and refined sense of taste, as can be seen in the pieces designed by Ashbee.

The creations of Albert Gilbert (1854–1934) were quite different. He trained as a sculptor, jeweler, and silversmith, and his work harks back to prestigious Italian Renaissance examples (fig. 418). Though he would have denied it, some of his jewelry pieces, however, are imbued with an Art Nouveau rhythm. This is the case in the pendant and chain presented by Gilbert to the Royal Institute of Painters in Watercolour on the occasion of his election to that society.

The lion's share of the fabric and wallpaper designs Voysey executed were brought out by Liberty & Co. Arthur Lasenby Liberty (1843–1917), an astute businessman, had sensed the need to shake off the excessive refinement of the Aesthetic Movement. For this reason, he surrounded himself with a team of talented designers, in particular Archibald Knox (1864–1933), with the intention of arriving at a new type of home environment. Strongly influenced by the functionalist theories of Dresser, Knox and Liberty were to produce an extensive range of boxes, dishes, vases, ink bottles, chandeliers, and clocks. Their forms were always built up from simple geometric volumes, such as cubes, cylinders, cones, squares, oblongs, or pyramids (fig. 419). Although the motifs are taken from the plant world, the ornamentation is the result of geometrical stylization in harmony with the basic shape chosen. Among the more important characteristics of Liberty's silver- and pewterware are the total absence in the decoration of the human figure, and the use of semiprecious stones and enamel combined with repoussé metalwork. As for furniture, the firm did not have a furniture workshop until 1905—it was Leonard F. Wyburg, head of an interior decoration agency since 1883, who was essentially responsible for the majority of the designs brought out by Liberty. Straight lines, squares, and circles were the main constituents of Wyburg's designs, which were made primarily from oak and walnut, though mahogany was also used. Discreet use was made of marquetry, limited to a single floral motif, frieze, or similar design across the tops of seat backs, on the pediments of wardrobes, and on other items of dressing room furniture. Another form of decoration used was copper repoussé work on both doorknobs and lock-plates.

In England, however, nothing attained the refinement and sophistication of the interiors designed by Charles Rennie Mackintosh (1868–1928), and it was to the Glasgow group, with Mackintosh, his wife Margaret Macdonald (1865–1933), together with Herbert MacNair (1868–1955) and his wife, Frances Macdonald (1874–1921), that it fell to make a *Gesamtkunstwerk* of the British home. Their most important creations date from the period between 1895 and 1905 (fig. 272). Mackintosh's early furniture, prior to 1895, belonged to the Arts and Crafts tradition, though it was also evocative of Voysey's work. Well proportioned, solidly built, they are for the most part made of oak, embellished with metal adornments centered around the hinges, lock-plates, and handles. In 1896, probably through the intermediary of Francis H. Newbery, director of the Glasgow School of Art, Mackintosh met Kate Cranston, the owner of four of the city's tea rooms, and soon found himself being offered the decoration of the walls for one of them, George Walton (1867–1933) designing the furniture. At the Argylle Tea Rooms in the following year, however, the roles were to be reversed, and it was Walton who did the walls, while Mackintosh designed furniture which broke totally with the Arts and Crafts heritage. The dining room chairs have the strangely proportioned elongated backs that were to become one of the hallmarks of Mackintosh's work.

Mackintosh's style remained largely unchanged until 1900. The refurbishment of his own apartment at 120 Mains Street, in preparation for his wedding to Margaret Macdonald in August 1900, that he designed throughout down to the tiniest detail—cutlery, tongs, curtains, and bedding included—was an opportunity for Mackintosh to display his notion of a "modern" interior more freely. Two color harmonies were employed: white for the living room and bedrooms, and black for the corridors and dining room. Its great originality resides in the fact that the walls, ceilings, and floors were bereft of all decoration with the exception, in a few isolated places, of stenciled ornaments in the pale tones of pinks, greens, grays, and silver. The white muslin curtains were embroidered by Margaret Macdonald herself with uncomplicated geometrical motifs. In this connection it should be recalled that the Glasgow School of Art had set up an embroidery class of its own in 1894, run by Jessie R. Newbery, from which there emerged a considerable number of designs for clothes and interior decoration which have all the traits of the "Glasgow style."

Elegant and sophisticated, the apartment at 120 Mains Street was also something of a showroom for Mackintosh himself. During the summer of 1900, he sent reproductions of it to Carl Moll, president of the Vienna Sezession, as well as to the eighth Sezession exhibition, together with a set of designs which combined existing works with others specifically designed for the show. Mackintosh's showpiece exerted a considerable influence over Viennese artists, not only on young designers, but also on Gustav Klimt, who, when he came to design his Beethoven frieze in 1903, harked back to the plaster panels originally conceived for the Ingram Street Tea Rooms. After 1900, Mackintosh's goals merged with those of the Viennese. An increased use of geometrical motifs in Viennese decoration, in particular the one built up from four squares, owes something to the work of Mackintosh. Unlike the Viennese, who were to overexploit the decorative potential of the square, Mackintosh, between 1901 and 1903, pursued his chosen task of trying to integrate ornament of an organic type into increasingly geometric forms. At this time, the role of his wife, Margaret Macdonald, became crucial, particularly in the Rose Boudoir conceived for the 1902 Exhibition of Applied Arts in Turin, the Wärndorfer Music Salon, and the Willow Tea Rooms (1901–4). Margaret Macdonald's predilection for Arthurian legend and the works of the Belgian Symbolist playwright Maurice Maeterlinck were to surface in wall decoration as well as the embellishments added to furniture. Conveyed by a refined harmony of white, gray, pearl, black, pink, and mauve, her designs encouraged Mackintosh himself to break with the robust and aggressive side of his early interiors. He was to abandon assembling in panels, and was no longer preoccupied—in the name of the principle of "honesty" in construction—with emphasizing the raw state of his materials. If the furniture he created from this time was generally lacquered, this was not only because he wanted it to harmonize with the surrounding environment, but also, and above all, because he wished to conceal its construction (fig. 250). Rarely had the unity of an interior attained such an elevated artistic plane.

Austro–Hungary

Though the revelation brought by Mackintosh was clearly a decisive factor in the dazzling expansion of the decorative arts in Vienna, it fails to explain everything. For one, the influence exerted by Anglo-Saxon creations was not confined to the Glasgow School. It is important to recall the size of the British participation (fifty-two works by Ashbee for only thirty-three by Mackintosh) in the eighth Sezession exhibition that opened in autumn 1900. Important were Adolf Loos's (1870–1933) frequent stays in the United States from 1893 onward. There he observed with interest the products of the American Arts and Crafts movement—particularly the furniture by Gustav Stickley—that came up with functional solutions Vienna had not yet arrived at. On the other hand, in the empire itself, the search for a sobriety adapted to contemporary life was facilitated by the down-to-earth examples of the Biedermeier style. It was also furthered by the teaching of Otto Wagner (1841–1918), holder since 1894 of the chair in architecture at the Vienna Akademie der Bildenden Kunst, who impressed upon his students the need to adhere to the sacrosanct principles of Art Nouveau (fig. 409). It is to Wagner that the credit must go for having created, in 1898–99, the first "modern" Viennese furniture, thus blazing the trail for fifty years of modernism. This furniture, destined for his apartment at 3, Köstlergasse, was followed with incontrovertible logic by two seminal creations: the telegraph office of the *Die Zeit* newspaper (1901–2) and the Post Office Savings Bank (Postsparkasse, 1904–6). Using bentwood, Wagner designed chairs on a square section that were brought out by the firm of Kohn in more or less elaborate versions. At the Post Office Savings Bank, mahogany and brass were confined to the manager's office, whereas dark beechwood and aluminum were employed in the other offices, the stools intended for the main hall being in beechwood, aluminum, and drilled plywood, and varnished in a dark brown. For the shelving, Wagner used aluminum nails as decorative elements to highlight and signal the structure, ornament here being solely the end result of a construction method. These models, numbering among the purest designs in Vienna, met with no success, however, unlike the traditional bistro chairs in turned wood.

Just as Wagner was designing the furniture for his apartment, Adolf Loos was presenting a brilliant demonstration of what he meant by "utilitarian art" in building the Café Museum, where the rejection of all decorative compromise in an espousal of sober and rationalist formulas earned it the nickname "Café Nihilismus." For the bentwood seats, produced once more by Kohn, Loos elected to use an ellipsoid, thus permitting a shell at once light yet solid. Never joining the Sezession group, Loos was something of a solitary creator, aided by support from rich traders and a well-heeled intelligentsia. He made his name first of all as an interior designer, furnishing a total of nearly forty apartments between 1901 and 1911. Unlike the artists of the Sezession, the Belgians, the Germans, and the Glasgow School, he renounced "total art" and averred that a house should never be completely finished. He therefore had no hesitation in introducing into the apartment he fitted out between 1900 and 1903 for Gustav and Maria Turnowsky on Wohllebengasse, traditional chairs (such as chaise longues and wing chairs) covered in Biedermeier fabrics (striped pink silk with little floral motifs) and a model for a standard brass bedstead. By dint of its simplicity and authenticity, however, the furniture for the Turnowskys is still "modern." With the exception of some fluted beading that emphasizes the structure of the various pieces, ornament was banned. There was no varnish or marquetry. Only the nobility of the materials themselves counted: dark-hued mahogany for Gustav Turnowsky's bedroom and, for Maria's room, blondish maple, plaques of yellow copper, and gray-blue marble. Such functionalism is not, however, synonymous with austerity, because by using wood paneling, arranged in a repetitive rhythm, with mirrors and panes of beveled glass, Loos engineered optical effects and obtained a very subtle impression of fragmentation and multiplication.

In total opposition to Loos's approach, the earliest pieces (prior to 1900) of furniture by Josef Hoffmann betray affinities with those of Olbrich. They are decorated with floral motifs and have vibrant surfaces, the result of his technique of assembling cut-out elements of varying shapes. The furniture presented at the 1900 Sezession exhibition, on the other hand, marks the onset of an evolution toward geometrical abstraction and the rejection of ornament. From 1903, the furniture Hoffmann designed to commission was of rigorously cubic or parallelepiped volumes.

Like Hoffmann, Koloman Moser (1868–1918), who exhibited his earliest furniture designs at the eighth Sezession exhibition, favored clarity and rigor. His work developed toward increasing spatial organization and geometrical abstraction (fig. 249). The predominance of the straight line and flat surface, the choice of common woods, the use of copper plaques with a light relief in repoussé are all derived from the Arts and Crafts movement. The Mackintosh effect can be detected in Moser's predilection for tripartite compositions accentuating the verticals, in his frequent recourse to a strongly protruding border turned in at right angles running around the central volume, and by the decorative use of vertical metal plaques adorned with symbolic figures. What was inimitable with Moser, however, was his capacity to exploit empty space, his uncommonly subtle manner of arranging straight lines and curves on the surface. A painter by training, he had the ideas of a painter: often a gold frame borders the main body of the piece, and frequently a finely drawn motif enlivens and links the various volumes to each other, providing a striking contrast with the smooth surface of the wood.

The creation of the Wiener Werkstätte, made possible thanks to the financial support of the industrialist Fritz Wärndorfer, took place on May 19, 1903. For three years (Moser left at the end of 1906 following a disagreement over its management), the theoretician Hoffmann and the ever-inventive Moser were to collaborate closely (figs. 247, 440). The activities of the workshops spread to the most varied domains: ceramics and stained glass, silverware and sheet-metal work, jewelry and dress design, fabrics, wallpapers, leatherwork, and furniture. As Hoffmann had already foreseen in the journal *Der Architekt* (1897), the time had come when wallpaper, ceiling painting, furniture, and household items would be ordered not from a supplier but from an artist. As to production proper, it was entrusted either to manufacturers—Bakalowitz for stained glass, Böck for ceramics, Backhausen for textiles—or else to artisans such as the cabinetmaker Wenzell Hollmann. The leap to mechanization was not to be made, however, and the activity of the Wiener Werkstätte evolved no further than that of a costly craft industry. The technical perfection and the consummate mastery of materials demanded by Hoffmann and Moser were expensive. The pleasure of dispensing with the superfluous does not necessarily entail an economy drive. Nonetheless, if one concurs with Hoffmann and Moser that ornament only acquires a role when the objects so decorated are put to use, then a functional aesthetics was indeed forged.

In Hungary, a country reduced to the status of a province of the Austrian empire, the search for a new style was inextricably linked to the furthering of a national style based on the rediscovery of folk art. In the realm of the decorative arts, this nationalist current was derived from research undertaken by the linguist József Huzka and had much to gain from the foundation in Budapest of a Museum of Applied Arts.

Magyar nationalism was strikingly expressed by the pavilion erected at the international exhibition in Milan in 1906, designed by the architect Géza Maroti-Rintel (1875–1941). Its interior decoration had been assigned to Odön Farago (1869–1945) and Ede Thoroczkai Wigand (1870–1945). Wigand, whose earliest sketches for furniture had been markedly influenced by the sober forms and lines of English and Viennese examples, was finally to adopt the craft techniques of folk art and decorative schemas inspired by the traditional arts of the Siculi.

Quite another case is represented by Farago, who had already displayed the nationalistic vein of his artistic vision at the 1900 Exposition Universelle in Paris, where the Hungarian entry had escaped from Austrian control and become the object of a special presentation.

The contribution of painters to the new departure in Hungarian decorative arts was paramount. Following advice from Maillol and the Nabis, József Rippl-Rónai (1861–1927), who worked in Paris from 1892 to 1902, executed cartoons for tapestries, fire screens, and sketches for glass that he was to send to his first exhibition in Hungary in 1898. Once back in his native land, Rippl-Rónai executed, among other things, a dining room for Count Tivadar Andrássy and produced pottery designs for the Zsolnay manufactory (fig. 432). Remaining at home, the painter János Vaszary (1867–1938) had played a role in the renaissance of tapestry, having cartoons with peasant themes made by the Németelemer handloom weavers, who used the techniques employed at Scherrebeck. In 1902, the Németelemer workshops were transferred to Gödöllö, where there soon formed an artists' colony presided over by Aladár Körosföi Kriesěh (1862–1920) and Sándor Nagy (1868–1950), who had both been trained in Paris at the Julian studios (fig. 450). Glass production for its part was much influenced by examples from abroad. Istvan Sovanka (1858–?) abandoned wood carving to begin work at the Zay-Ugroí glassworks, where he made vases which, following Gallé, present layers of cased glass and acid-etched decoration, comprised for the most part of floral motifs or birds. In 1885, Miksa Roth (1860–1944) opened a stained-glass workshop from which emerged glass mosaics and Tiffany-style windows based on cartoons by Rippl-Rónai, Nagy, and Wigand.

In spite of the success that Hungary was to encounter in Paris in 1900, in Milan in 1906, and in Turin in 1911 (events in which political well-wishing played its part), only one product became widely distributed abroad: ceramics from the firm of Zsolnay at Pécs. It is true that the *faience fine* of Vilmos Zsolnay (1829–1900) had already attracted attention at the international exhibitions at Vienna (1873) and Paris (1878). But in 1893, with the aid of the chemist Vince Wartha, Zsolnay perfected eosine enameling, from which he developed a remarkable series of luster glazes applied to silica china. The firm employed the services of artists of caliber on a permanent basis, such as the modeler Sandór Apâti Abt and the painter Lajos Mack, or, less regularly, Rippl-Rónai. This enabled the manufacturer's products to rival, as far as iridescence was concerned, those of Tiffany or Clément Massier.

Decorative arts in the regions which were later to form the Czech and Slovak republics also experienced a new lease of life. This was linked to two Prague institutions: the School of Decorative Arts founded in 1885 and the Polytechnic Institute. It fell to two students of a professor at the latter institution, the architect Josef Zitek (1832–1909), to break with the then dominant neo-Renaissance and neo-Baroque styles: Jan Koula (1855–1919) and Josef Fanta (1856–1954). Together, they produced the group of pieces sent by the Prague Chamber of Commerce and Industry to Paris in 1900. Much of the furniture that adorned the vast office had been designed by Fanta and Koula. The simplicity of the light-colored woods presented an interesting contrast with the abundant ornaments, including bronze plaques, enamel inlay, chased and repoussé copper, as well as embroidered silk panels whose motifs took their cue from folk art. The seating by Jan Kastner (1860–1912) was also derived from peasant art, but only in respect of the basic shape: the female mask with the long lank hair who stares out from the backs of the chairs bears witness to Viennese influence (fig. 406). The second ensemble presented at the Paris Exposition Universelle had been completed under the direction of an architect who was still in his twenties, Jan Kotěra (1871–1923), a former student of Otto Wagner's and, since 1898, professor of architecture at the Prague School of Decorative Arts. As a furniture designer Kotěra was patently influenced by his master: the forms are massive and angular while the decoration is for the most part provided by geometrical or stylized floral motifs, executed in marquetry.

The School of Decorative Arts at Prague swiftly made its mark as a flourishing center for ceramics and metalwork. The former benefited from the teaching of the modeler Celda Klouček (1855–1921). He taught his students how to work with enamel stoneware, producing rounded, closed forms with a more or less stylized plant-inspired decoration featuring female mascarons, which would be incised or applied in light relief. This attractive body of work is quite distinct from that produced by the Amphora porcelain manufactory, founded at Trnovany by Alfred Stellmacher. His son, Eduard, who succeeded him in 1892, was responsible for a fine series of large vases of elegant and slender form, supple outline, and bright color, whose decors mostly combine flowers with female figures. The task of overseeing the jewelry workshop fell to Emanuel Nóvak (1866–1918). From 1907 on, instruction in jewelry-making techniques was given by Josef Ladislav Némec (1871–1934), a former student at the school and the owner of a workshop created by his father in 1872. Némec's own jewelry, characterized by vigorously modeled floral motifs, is of great quality (fig. 424).

In addition to these individuals, several other manufacturers were following innovative paths, either in terms of form and decoration or of materials. The celebrated Bohemian glassworks, though they too felt the influence of Gallé and Tiffany, continued to practice the techniques that had made them famous and distinctive. Plants in southern Bohemia, such as the Johann Loetz-Witwe glassworks at Klásterský Mlýn, founded back in

1840, began producing iridescent glass adorned with fillets applied during reheating. The master glassworkers of the north, rich in a centuries-old tradition in cut crystal, etching, and painting, now applied "modern" decoration. As for the Nový Svět glassworks, owned by the counts Harrasch since 1704, it was to channel all its expertise into the production of supple and elegant floral decoration: its plain glass with inset colored pieces and the services decorated with dynamic etched lines inspired by those of van de Velde number among the most interesting creations of the period.

Scandinavia

Scandinavia occupies a special place in the history of Art Nouveau. This was because the artistic forms that developed there arose out of a single tradition. Art evolved while remaining faithful to its heritage. The "Dragon" or "Viking" style, whose roots lie in the strong interest shown at the beginning of the century in Norse mythology, was the primary source of the new turn the decorative arts were to take in Scandinavia.

Each country was to come up with its own particular brand of the "Dragon" style. If in Sweden, where it was cultivated solely by a small group in Stockholm, it never really took off, in Norway, on the contrary, it became an essential weapon in the struggle for national identity. The Viking decoration borrowed from the ships and other objects excavated as early as 1867 was preeminently adapted for use in metalwork. Cream jugs, teapots, sugar bowls, and dishes were to be fitted with feet and grips in the form of dragon talons and heads. The firms of Tostrup and Andersen in Christiana were the first to interpret this style. In Finland, as in Norway, the "Viking" style was an expression of nationalism, a sentiment all the more vigorous since end-of-century Finland was riven with uprisings fueled by growing oppression at the hands of Russia. The untamed forests of Karelia—where the *Kalevala* (Land of heroes), the national oral epic, had been born—acted as a magnet to artists in their quest for traditional motifs. Among the earliest figures to undertake such a pilgrimage were the painter Akseli Gallén-Kallela (1865–1931) in 1890 and the Swede Louis Sparre (1863–1964). The artists built and furnished their living quarters themselves. At the Exposition Universelle of 1900, the Finnish Pavilion, designed by Eliel Saarinen (1873–1950) among others, created a ground swell of sympathy among Europeans and demonstrated brilliantly that Finland possessed a culture quite distinct from Russia's. The execution of the interior had been assigned to Iris, the society founded in 1897 by Sparre that possessed its own carpentry shop and ceramics workshop at Borga. The wood paneling, furniture, wall hangings, and fabric had been designed by Gallén-Kallela (fig. 411), while the ceramics were the work of the Belgian potter Alfred William Finch (1863–1930), head of the Borga workshop.

In 1874, at the instigation of Sophie de Adlesparre and in an effort to prevent the centuries-old rural art of tapestry making from vanishing in Sweden forever, the association Handarbetets Vänner (Friends of Handicraft) was set up. The association produced a mass of chair covers, mostly adorned with heraldic coats-of-arms, together with larger tapestries, which, however, attained neither the intensity nor the imaginativeness of their Norwegian counterparts. The latter showed no attempt at naturalism, but were rather a powerful effort at stylization on a grand scale. For Norwegian artists, a highly detailed naturalistic design was of no value and their techniques were necessarily the servant of this approach. Rather than dyeing the wool in countless colors, only three or four were employed in addition to the natural tones, resulting in increased energy and purity. Two individuals and two institutions of the first rank stand out in the art of Norwegian tapestry making: Gerhard Munthe (1849–1929) and Frida Hansen (1855–1931); and Det Norske Billedvoereri (Norwegian Tapestry Union) at Christiana and the Nordenfjeldske Kunstindustrimuseum at Trondheim, a school of weaving linked to the Museum of Decorative Arts. The director of the latter was Augusta Christensen, who propounded a particular working method: at the weaving stage, the wool was blended in a number of tones from a similar range of colors so as to produce the desired color scheme without recourse to a vast range of tints. Subjects, especially in the work of Frida Hansen, were for the most part taken from the royal sagas (fig. 1). Norwegian carpets and tapestries aroused considerable interest in Paris in 1900, as did the furniture. Here a determined effort had been made to devise new forms without departing from ancestral architectonic elements. Onto simple, roughly made frameworks, John Borgersen carved unconstrained, broad, rich motifs suggestive of waves, ship's cables, and sea monsters. Christian Knag (1855–1922) from Bergen was more a colorist and his sober furniture includes some of the most valuable examples of polychrome design.

The great Danish porcelain factories were meanwhile continuing their unflagging activity. Under the leadership of Philipp Schou (1858–1922), assisted by his artistic director Arnold Krogh (1856–1931), the Royal Copenhagen Factory specialized in blue underglaze work, the vibrant white of the porcelain serving as a ready-made ground, while the blue and green veering to gray took on subtle nuances depending on the number of coats. The landscapes and flowers impart a sensation of freshness with an essentially Nordic feel. Production at Bing and Grøndhal was totally transformed with the arrival of the painter Jens Ferdinand Willumsen (1863–1958) as artistic director, a post that he was to occupy from 1897 to 1900 (fig. 438). Conscious of the need to differentiate his output from that of the Royal Copenhagen, Willumsen opted to abandon *grand feu* colors as practiced by Royal Copenhagen and instead put greater emphasis on the natural whiteness of the porcelain. This Copenhagen-born style then spread to Sweden, through the intermediary of Alf Wallander (1862–1914)—who is also known for his work in other branches of decorative art, notably pewter (fig. 434). Wallander had been appointed artistic director of the Rörstrand factory at Lidköping in 1895. He created proliferating floral patterns painted in an original and fantastical manner with light tones over darker, or else modeled in very shallow relief. With consummate skill, he allowed the opium poppies, narcissi, orchids, seaweed, and kelp to surge forth from the sides of vases while avoiding any unpleasant sensation of their being somehow stuck on. The art of Thorvald Bindesbøll (1846–1908) lies at the antipodes of such delicate refinement. One of the most innovative of Scandinavian artists, he was an architect by training, but his name became associated with the most varied techniques: ceramics, cabinetmaking, silver, and bookbinding. His highly personal style is informed by a dynamic calligraphy that tends toward abstraction.

Spain

In Spain, Art Nouveau flourished exclusively in Barcelona, where it became closely linked with nationalism. When, in 1890, the architect Lluís Domènech i Montaner (1850–1923) installed a craft workshop in the restaurant erected for the city's 1888 international exhibition, he intended to offer a forum for artisans practicing traditional techniques, some of which were in danger of falling into oblivion. The craftsmen, however, were not recruited from Catalonia alone: Domènech and Antoni Gaudí traveled as far as the region of Valencia in the hunt for the surviving practitioners of traditional pottery. There were two other notable events that were indicative of how the decorative arts were returning to favor, both of which occurred in 1903: the foundation of the movement Foment de las Artas Decoratives with the aim of promoting industrial art, and the publication of an article by the cabinetmaker Joan Busquets i Jané (1874–1949) in the review *Joventut*. Jané's article sought to distinguish between industrial arts that produce objects without taking into account their surroundings, and a decor that is conceived for a specific locale and is in total harmony with the architecture. In such a context, it is hardly surprising that furniture designs by architects figure among the most influential works of Catalan Art Nouveau and that the movement's vitality finds its fullest expression in the works of Gaudí, Domènech, and Josep Puig i Cadafalch (1867–1957).

Personality also had its part to play. Gaudí's creations, for example, seem to give voice to an overwrought sense of individuality. The furniture he designed for the Palau Güell, comprising a chaise longue and a still weirder dressing table, break totally with all that had been produced until that time. The first is striking for the staggering contrast between the comfortable padded upholstery so dear to the period—but which here is redolent of a snake uncoiling—and the wrought-iron framework, which is imbued with a distinctive rhythm. In the second example, the distinctively askew mirror destroys all hope of symmetry, while the feet are undeniably redolent of those of an animal on the move. The seats and armchairs planned for the Casa Calvet (1898–1903) and for the Casa Battlò (1906) represent the zenith of Gaudí's career as a furniture designer. Unlike his contemporaries, whose rethinking of seating furniture tended to concentrate on aspects of ornament, the Catalan designer would totally overhaul the whole notion of the chair. The base and the back, slightly bowed to hug the body, appear independent of the structures supporting them. The arms of the easy chairs, meanwhile, open welcomingly wide, inviting one to relax, the down-swept ends of the armrests offering a place for the hands to repose. The material chosen (rubor wood in this instance) was not flexible enough and some sections consist of small pieces fitted into each other in an effort to preserve rhythm of line. These works are so taut with inner tension that they can only be compared to sculpture. As for decoration, it consists of drill-holes or incisions suggestive of plant forms. The pews of the Colonia Güell Church at Santa Coloma de Cervelló (1898–1915) seem less weighty, since the spaces left unfilled play as important a role as the wrought-iron structure running tightly round the soberly modeled wooden sections. These gravity-defying benches accord perfectly with the impression of solemnity the chapel was intended to convey and their "functionalism" can only attain complete expression in the half-light of the sanctuary.

From the works of Gaspar Homar i Mezquida (1870–1953), a pupil of Francesc Vidali who had been born into a cabinetmaking family but who founded his own business in 1893, there emanates on the other hand an urbanity altogether more in keeping with the easy-going image normally conveyed by the art of the 1900s. This is true of the works for which he was solely responsible at least, since he was not averse to putting his talents as a craftsman at the service of architects such as Puig i Cadafalch, the author of the neo-Gothic furniture at the Casa Amatller (about 1900). Homar's most significant work remains the interior decoration of Lleo Morera's house, built in 1904 (fig. 415). Homar had a liking for multipurpose furniture, whose broad flat surfaces serve as a base for marquetry figures designed by the painter Josep Pey i Farriol (1875–1956). The latter was also to provide decoration of a similar nature—showing female figures gliding over a floral background—for the ceramicist Antoni Serra (1869–1932), a painter himself who had heeded the call of the potter's art, in his case porcelain decorated in *grand feu* colors.

The work of Alejandro de Riquer i Inglada (1856–1920), whose background was also in the visual arts, serves as an illustration of the links that were established between graphic art and interior design. The 1888 international exhibition offered him an opportunity to tackle architectural drawing. He subsequently pursued this with some success, producing work of quality, notably his plan for the circle tier for the Teatre del Liceu in Barcelona. Whenever the occasion presented itself, he would produce designs, sending remarkable examples of bookbinding to the 1900 Exposition Universelle in Paris. Imbued with a subtle Japanese influence, these are among the Catalan works which are nearest to the kind of Art Nouveau found on the other side of the Pyrenees, as is the jewelry of Lluis Masriera (1872–1952), a member of the third generation of an important family of jewelers (fig. 417). In 1900, after he had seen designs by Lalique, Fouquet, and Vever in Paris, his work moved in the direction of Art Nouveau. Decoration showing plants, animals, and female figures predominate, though not at the expense of more traditional iconography (particularly of a religious nature).

Italy

Modernity and originality, as the Italians imagined them on the occasion of the Exhibition of Applied Arts in Turin in 1902, were inspired by examples from abroad. The prototype of the Stile Floreale house presented by Agostino Lauro (1861–1924) can only be understood in relation to its antecedant, the Bing pavilion at the 1900 Exposition Universelle. Vittorio Valabrega, whose manufacture switched from producing eclectic pieces to a more "modern" style in 1898, was also to opt for the Franco-Belgian line, whereas Alberto Issel, an enthusiast for nonexotic woods such as oak, proposed rectilinear furniture based on the work of the Arts and Crafts movement and Mackintosh. English and Scottish examples also lie behind the work of Giacomo Cometti (1863–1938) from Turin, a sculptor by training, who abandoned his earlier vocation to turn to creating low-cost household furniture. In Carlo Zen (1851–1918), the absorption of foreign influences is also discernible. The Milanese Eugenio Quarti (1867–1931), whose work is similar, designed one-off luxury pieces.

Ernesto Basile (1857–1932), Sicily's most prominent figure, had a much stronger personality. Before adopting the vocabulary of Scottish and Sezession artists, to which he added a touch of the picturesque, he had been receptive to the sobriety and functional character of the interiors designed by van de Velde and Serrurier-Bovy. He was lucky enough to find a peerless executant of his sketches in the Golia-Ducrot factory at Palermo and was thus able to bring out a series of remarkably homogeneous ensembles. In 1901, with the dining room he designed at the Villa Igea in Palermo, he became the leading Italian interior designer of his time. Moreover, he managed to surround himself with a competent team of collaborators with a sure sense of the decorative, such as the painter Neapolitan Ettore de Maria Bergler (1851–1938), who designed vast floral allegories.

In Italy, efforts at renewal were concentrated for the most part on furniture making. Other areas, however, were attacked with equal success, two being stained glass and wrought iron, where Giovanni Beltrami (1860–1926) and Alessandro Mazzucottelli (1865–1938) produced work of note. Beltrami set up his workshop in Milan in 1892, producing a large and varied body of stained glass based on cartoons of his own or by his collaborators, Continotti, Zuccaro, and Buffa, the latter being responsible for the introduction of Art Nouveau into the production of the Società Ceramica Richard-Ginori (fig. 439). As for the self-taught Mazzucottelli, he was as unaffected by Ruskin's theories and Morris's work as by van de Velde's "whiplash" line. Instinct was his sole guide and it led him, during the years 1898 to 1907, to completely transform naturalistic iconography—be it images from the plant or animal worlds or motifs of an academic kind—into a body of imagery both lively and unconstrained.

The name of Carlo Bugatti (1856–1940), even if his work cannot be regarded as an expression of Art Nouveau but rather that of a loner, should not be ignored, since his was indubitably the strongest personality in Italian decorative art of the period. His explorations led to the creation of an entirely original genre—what might be called the "Bugatti style." His work, which draws on Orientalism, is instantly recognizable and is quite distinct from that of his colleagues. His exotic vein of fantasy, all colonnettes and consoles, silk fringes, hammered metal plaques, and parchment stretched as on a drum, was to evolve toward increased geometricism and greater austerity, characterized by a recurrent use of circles and ovals. His last style is exemplified gloriously by the little drawing room that he designed for the Turin exhibition. Faced with this decor of a disconcerting novelty yet unparalleled modernism (including chairs not dissimilar to the type of molded plastic seats that would be produced fifty years later), the queen of Italy is supposed to have exclaimed: "These pieces are in the Moorish style!" "Your Majesty is mistaken," replied Bugatti. "This style is all mine."

United States

It would not have been possible to detect even a hint of Art Nouveau in the American section of the gigantic World's Columbian Exposition in Chicago in 1893. Naturally, a few pieces among those sent by Tiffany & Co., such as the Magnolia vase (fig. 234), the Viking punch bowl (The Museum of Modern Art, New York), or the series of jewelry objects—flasks, bonbonnières, purses, and mirrors—involve plantlike ornaments in which certain details are arranged in a pattern and according to a rhythm close to the intertwined motifs of Art Nouveau. More noticeable, however, is its strength or solidity of form, and the often excessive wealth of material combinations and of technical display, which were primarily intended to demonstrate the vitality of an American nation sweeping all before it.

Gustav Stickley (1858–1942) was the first to show a clear willingness to forge a new American style. In 1900, the Gustav Stickley Company became the Craftsman Workshops and the following year Stickley set up a mouthpiece by founding the review, *The Craftsman.* Stickley used exclusively oak, stressing framework and construction by emphasizing the type of joint he preferred: the dovetail. Decoration is provided by the veining and by the deliberately exposed joints, though, from 1903, in the models sketched by Harvey Ellis, the occasional metal element or carved panel enlivens the austerity of their unadorned surfaces.

The work of the brothers Greene, Charles Sumner (1868–1957) and Henry Mather (1870–1954) in Pasadena displays greater elegance in terms of formal design and greater refinement in the development of the decoration. The furniture from their workshops was primarily intended for the houses they themselves built. Made from mahogany or ebony, inlaid with mother-of-pearl, copper, or tin, it reveals a strong Japanese influence.

Much the same can be said of the furniture of Frank Lloyd Wright (1867–1959), once he had thrown off the influence of Louis Sullivan. Wright worked in Sullivan's architectural firm from 1887 to 1893, absorbing many of its director's decorative schemas. In 1892 he opened his own practice and his designs evolved rapidly toward a straight-line geometry which is not far removed from the work of Stickley. The chairs he designed for the Husser House (1899), Ward W. Willits House (1901), Dana-Thomas House, (1902), and Barton House (1904) are characterized by high backs with narrow vertical struts that continue down beyond the seat base, while horizontal bars link the legs. The lines emphasize the architectonic character of the chairs, which were all conceived for a specific space designed by the architect himself.

Ceramics found itself rather more under European ascendancy. Two manufactures came to the fore, however, and were to meet with great success in the Old World: the Rookwood Pottery (fig. 435), founded in 1880 in Cincinnati by Maria Longworth Nichols (1849–1932), and the Grueby Faience Company, established the same year in Massachusetts by William Henry Grueby (1867–1925). The former created a style known as Standard Rookwood, comprising warm-toned pieces, adorned with flowers obtained by the use of colored barbotines applied on the bare paste and covered with enamels. Rookwood also achieved total mastery in underglaze painting, with decorations derived essentially from the plant world. Occasionally, however, the fineness and delicacy of the decoration could degenerate into a nondescript miniaturism. Grueby's art is of a more masculine stamp. Like French ceramicists, Grueby was interested in matte or semimatte glazes in muted tones. His green, known as "Grueby green," was to be much vaunted.

The art of the furnace also produced its own Art Nouveau master in the person of Louis Comfort Tiffany (1848–1933; figs. 436, 443). Not only did Tiffany produce a highly personal body of artistic work, but he also exerted considerable influence on glass production back in Europe. In his desire to endow large-scale windows with all the splendor of jewelry, Tiffany abandoned painted and engraved colored glass, and, aided by a team of knowledgeable chemists, went on to perfect new formulas that allowed rich and novel effects in color, iridescence, and opalescence, as well as variations in texture. Tiffany used this material, which in Europe was termed "American" glass, to create stained-glass windows for Bing (who had met him during a tour of America in 1892) after cartoons provided by Toulouse-Lautrec, Besnard, and the Nabis, contributing to the growing international reputation of Bing's Art Nouveau. "American" glass, later used in glass roofing, was to find another, highly profitable application in lighting. In 1893, Tiffany, still in his factory at Corona, in Queens, New York City, developed yet another new material which he called Favrile glass, whose opal and matte iridescence was obtained by vapor from molten metal. The decoration—suggestive in its shimmering of meandering rivers, scudding clouds, feathers, and floral motifs—was built up by spraying onto the incandescent material particles of a glass of different type and color, which a second firing incorporated into the body, later to be shaped by the glass-blower.

The successful outcome, in aesthetic terms, of an Art Nouveau object or piece of furniture depends on a harmony between structure and ornament. If the ornament appears neither stuck nor plastered on, then the artist's triumph is complete. If, on the other hand, it has been gratuitously thrown together, then he has concocted a mishmash and the piece falls into irretrievable ugliness. Nothing is worse than Art Nouveau when its dynamism droops, a common result of the sort of commercially debased articles that swamped Europe. It was such failures, such balletic ugliness, that Mirbeau lambasted so ferociously. A successful piece springs solely from the quality of the rhythm, from a unity of beat or thrust.

In spite of all the common traits—a desire to proclaim their independence from the models of the past, a faith in the possibility of creating forms and decor suited to modern life—the different idioms of Art Nouveau remained quite distinct. Its methods can also appear contradictory depending on the place where a piece was made, the historical or cultural context, or for reasons of personal sensibility. It is no longer possible to concur with Pierre Francastel's distinction (*Art et technique aux XIXe et XXe siècles*) between two major trends corresponding in essence to a "vegetal" tendency and a "rationalist" one. More subtle is the distinction made by Stephen Tschudi Madsen (*Sources of Art Nouveau*), still based on a supposed antagonism between curved and straight lines, delineating four types of approach: a highly dynamic, abstract, and structural conception found in the Franco-Belgian regions; an approach derived from the plant world and placing the accent on organic growth, as represented by the École de Nancy; the linear, surface-orientated conception of the Mackintosh group; and the geometrical, constructive conception common to Germany and Austria. More frequently, however, the currents coexist, overlapping in an artist's career and even combining in a single work. For all the deceptive unity of the term, Art Nouveau was not an integral movement and there was nothing linear about its development. It was no more a stepping stone on an inexorable ascent to the Bauhaus than the final stage of an elegant and distillate eclecticism. Fueled by its own internal inconsistencies, Art Nouveau was truly one of the most significant products of that complex reality that was the end of the nineteenth century.

224 Maison Fourdinois in collaboration with Paul Sédille (architect), André-Joseph Allar (sculptor), and Hippolyte Rousselle (enameler)
Monumental Door
1878
Oak, walnut, marble, and bronze, with ebony, boxwood, and kingwood marquetry, and painted enamel, 4.80 x 2.80 m
Musée d'Orsay, Paris

225 Maison Lamy et Giraud in collaboration with Pierre Manguin (architect)
Velvet panel for the Hôtel de la Païva
1865
Three-ply velvet, 156 x 75 cm
Maison Prelle, Lyon and Paris

226 Maison Monbro in collaboration with Achille Legost
Side cabinet
1855
Ebony, marble, gilt and enameled bronze
132 x 86 x 45 cm
Musée d'Orsay Paris

227 Édouard Lièvre in collaboration with Édouard Detaille
Cabinet on stand
1877
Rosewood, ebony, gilt bronze, and chased iron
210 x 110 x 57 cm
Musée d'Orsay, Paris

228 Maison Beurdeley
Bookcase
c. 1867
Ebony, gilt bronze, lapis lazuli, jasper, and marble
290 x 220 x 65 cm
Private collection

229 Manufacture Jouhanneaud et Dubois in collaboration with Sévin and Schoenewerk (sculptors)
Figural ewer
1855
Porcelain biscuit
101 x 49 x 37 cm
Musée d'Orsay, Paris

230 Philippe-Joseph Brocard
Vase
1867
Stained blown glass, painted and enamel-painted decoration, height 415 cm, diameter 205 cm
Musée d'Orsay, Paris

231 Manufacture Barbizet
Tazza supported by a sphinx
c. 1855–65
Enamel-painted *faience fine*, 174 x 60 x 50 cm
Musée d'Orsay, Paris

232 Maison Froment-Meurice, in collaboration with Duban (architect), Feuchère and Geoffroy-Dechaume (sculptors), and Liénard (ornamenter)
Dressing table looking-glass
1847
Partially gilt and enameled silver, enamel-painted copper, and garnets, 130 x 92 x 504 cm
Musée d'Orsay, Paris

233 Maison Froment-Meurice, in collaboration with Duban (architect), Feuchère and Geoffroy-Dechaume (sculptors), and Liénard (ornamenter)
Jewelry casket
c. 1847
Partially gilt silver, enamel-painted copper, emeralds, and garnets, 426 x 358 x 275 cm
Musée d'Orsay, Paris

234 Tiffany & Co.
Magnolia vase
1893
Silver band repoussé, gold, enamel, and opal, height 87.5 cm
Metropolitan Museum of Art, New York. Gift of Mrs. Winthrop Atwell

235 François-Eugène Rousseau in collaboration with Maison Appert Frères
Bamboo vase
c. 1875–78
Tinted, engraved glass, enamel and gilt decoration, 28.3 x 7.9 cm
Musée d'Orsay, Paris

236 Jean-Charles Cazin
Cylindrical vase
c. 1873–75
Glazed stoneware, height 242 cm, diameter 112 cm
Musée National de Céramique, Sèvres

237 Émile Gallé
Vine snail
1884
Blown glass, engraved and enamel decoration, 28.4 x 18.4 cm
Musée des Arts Décoratifs, Paris

238 Émile Gallé
The Pines of Ravenna
1903
Triple-cased engraved crystal, 20 x 18 cm
Musée de l'École de Nancy, Nancy

239 Laurent Bouvier
Vase
c. 1900
Glazed stoneware with engraved decoration, 47 x 13 cm
Musée des Arts Décoratifs, Paris

240 Émile Gallé
The Pines of Ravenna
1903
Triple-cased engraved crystal, 20 x 18 cm
Musée de l'École de Nancy, Nancy

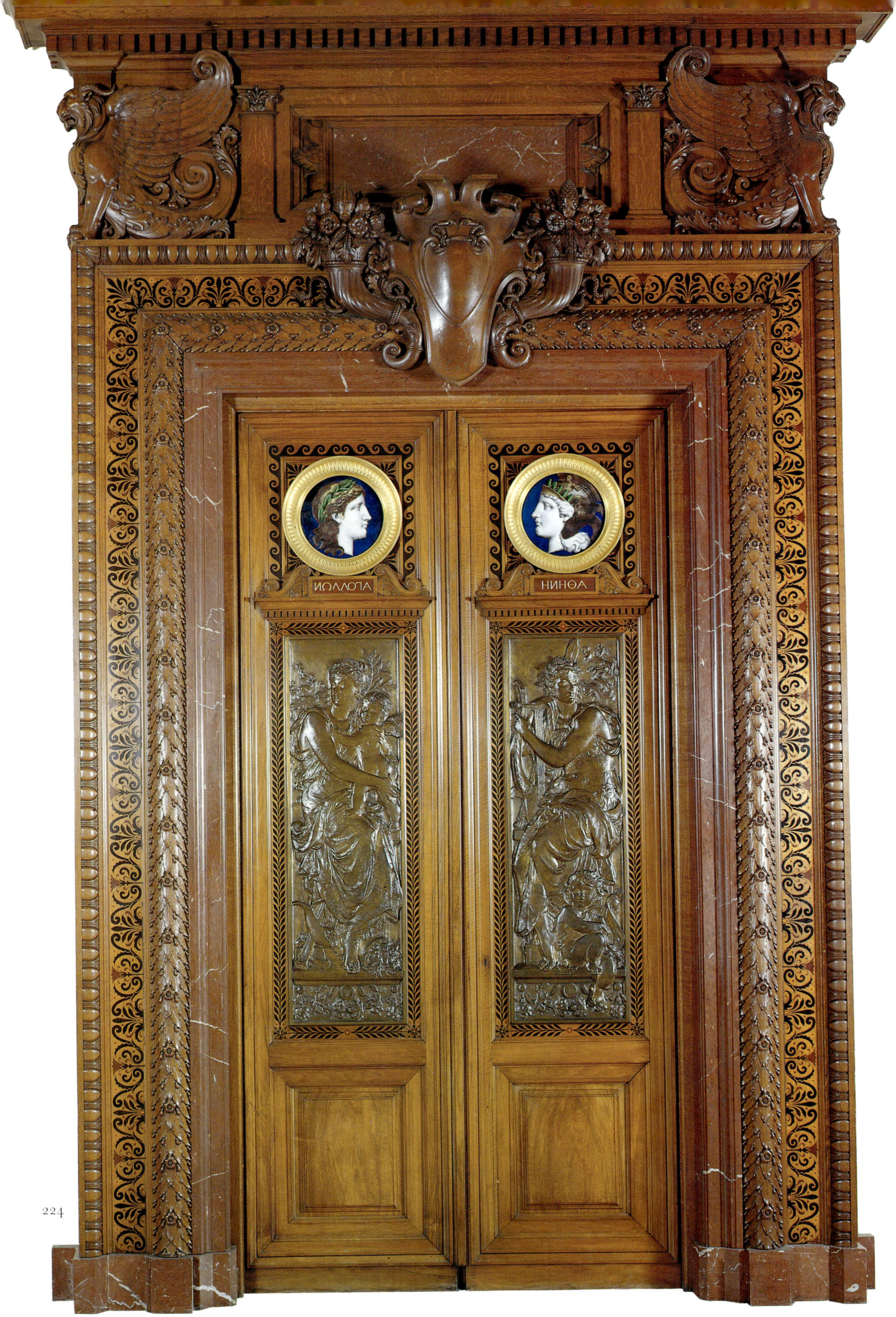
ΑΠΟΛΛΩΝ
ΑΘΗΝΗ

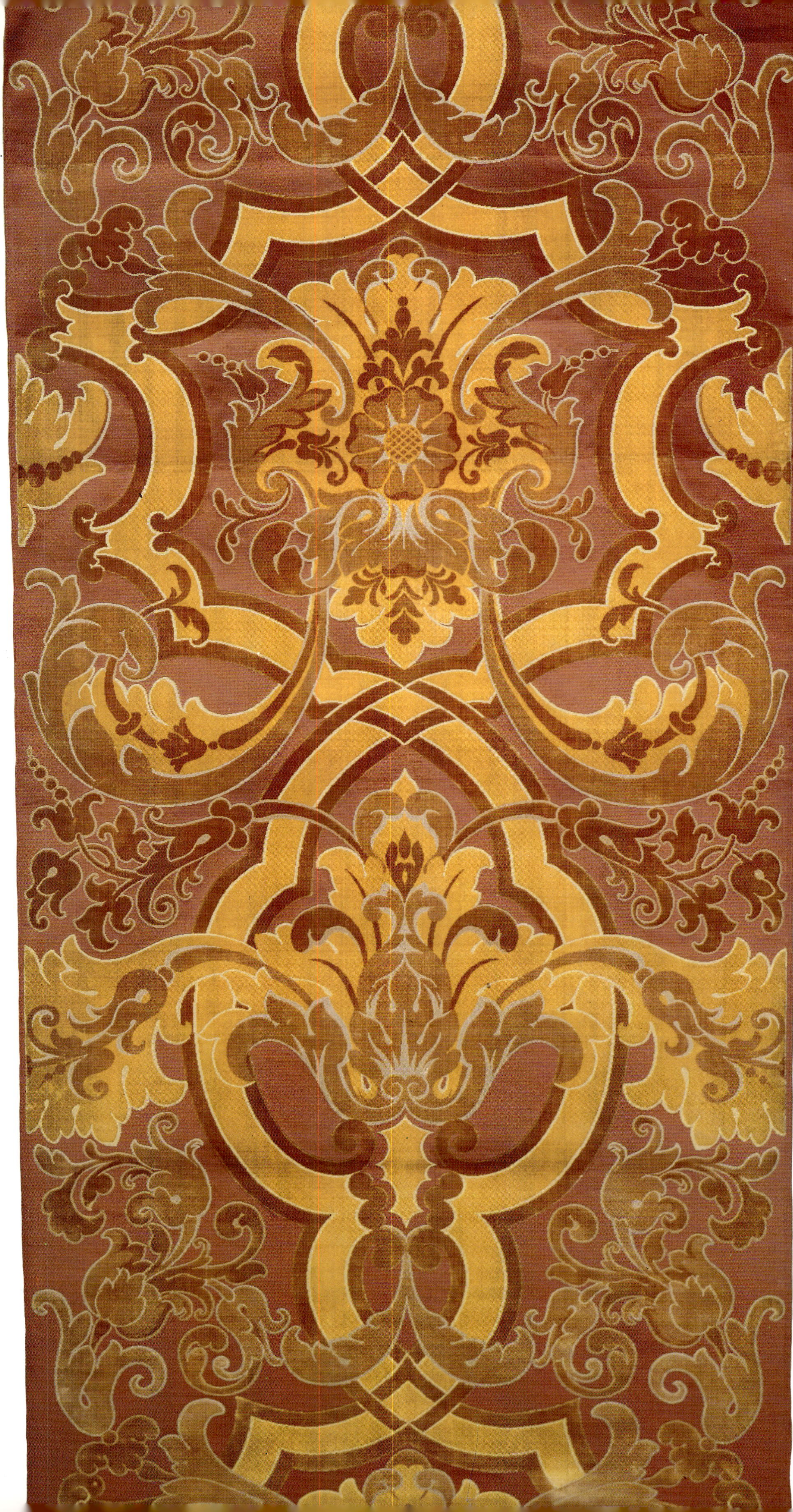

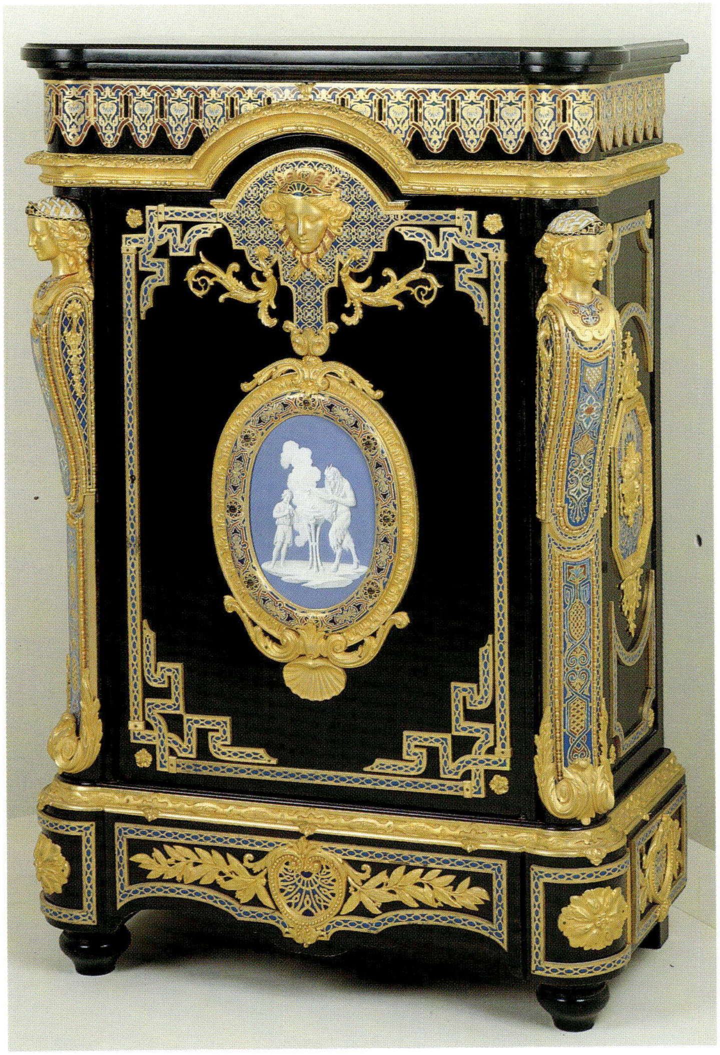

226

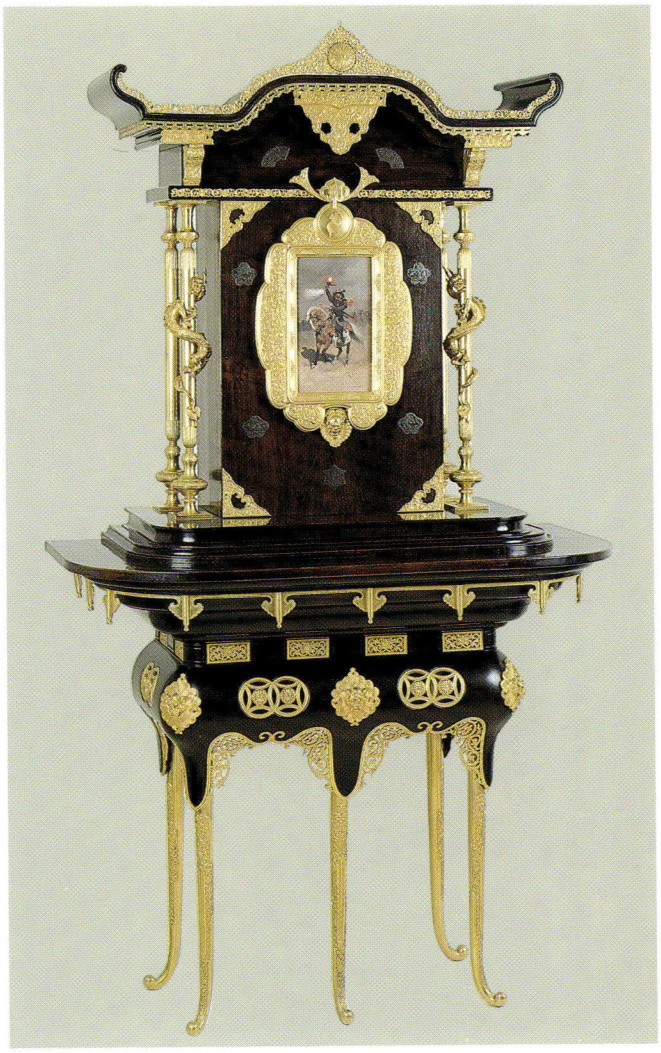

227

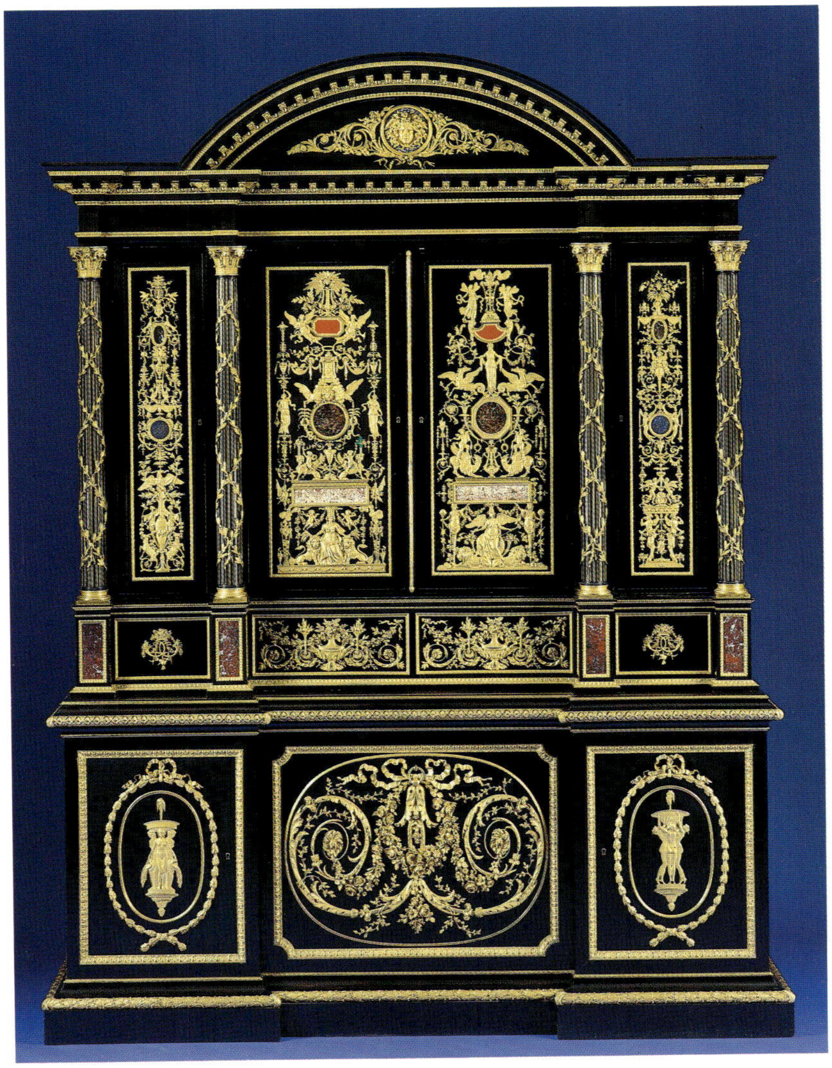

228

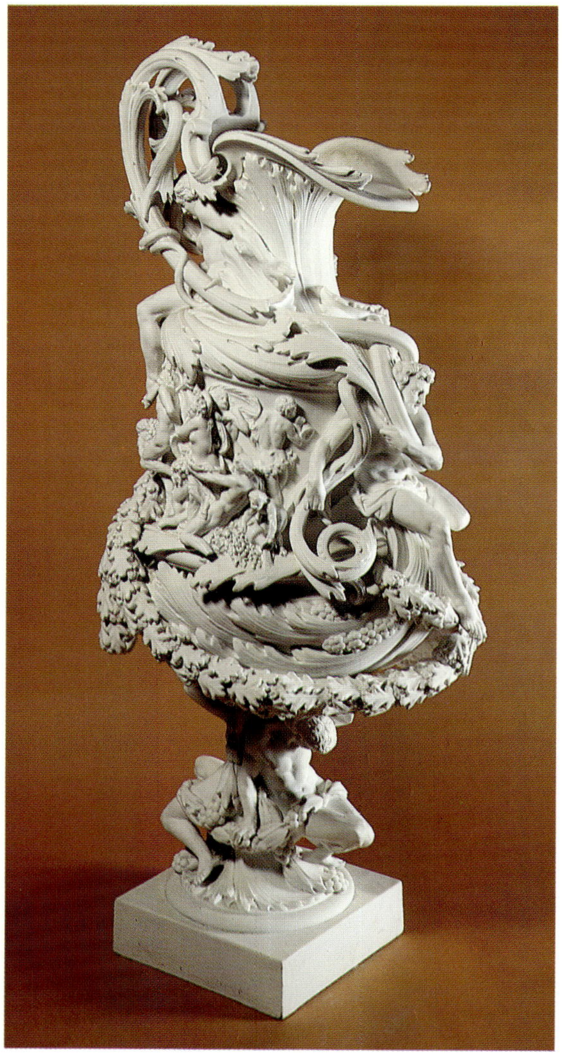

229

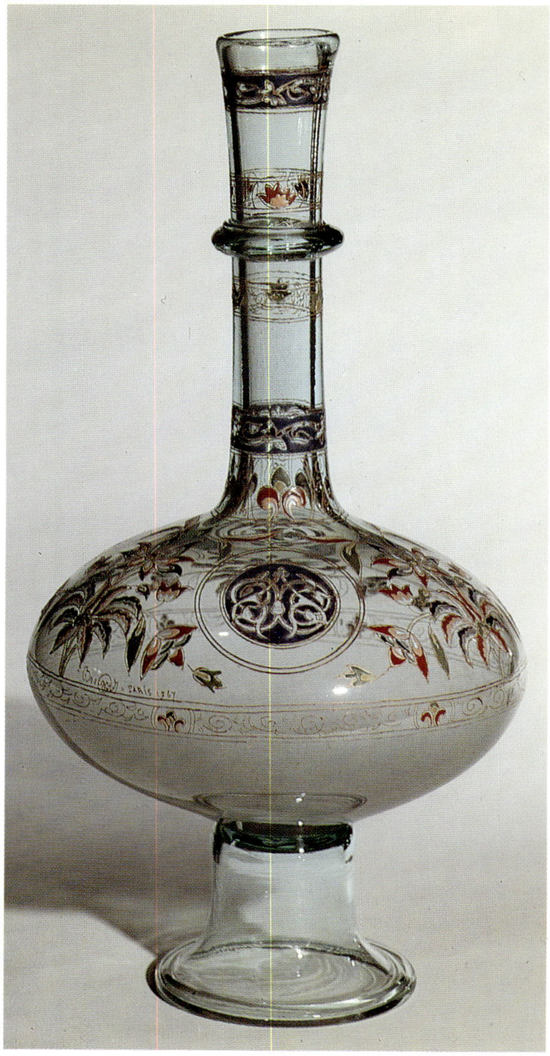

230

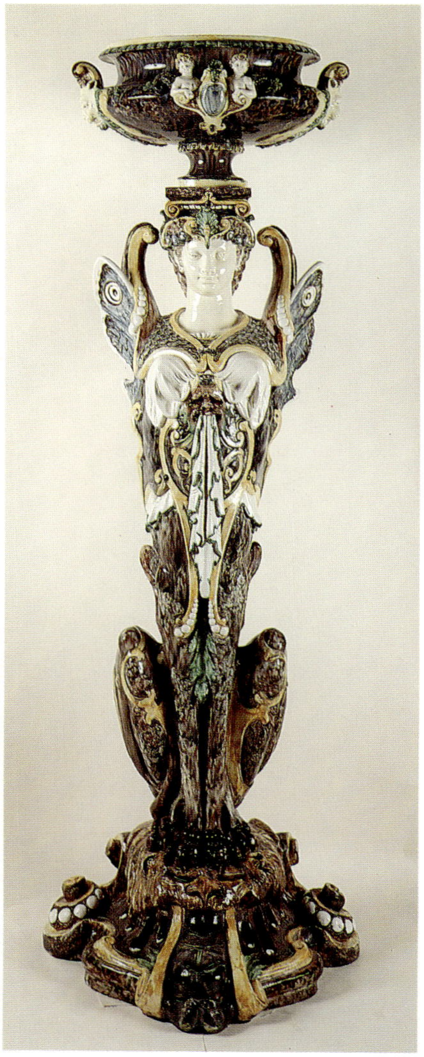

231

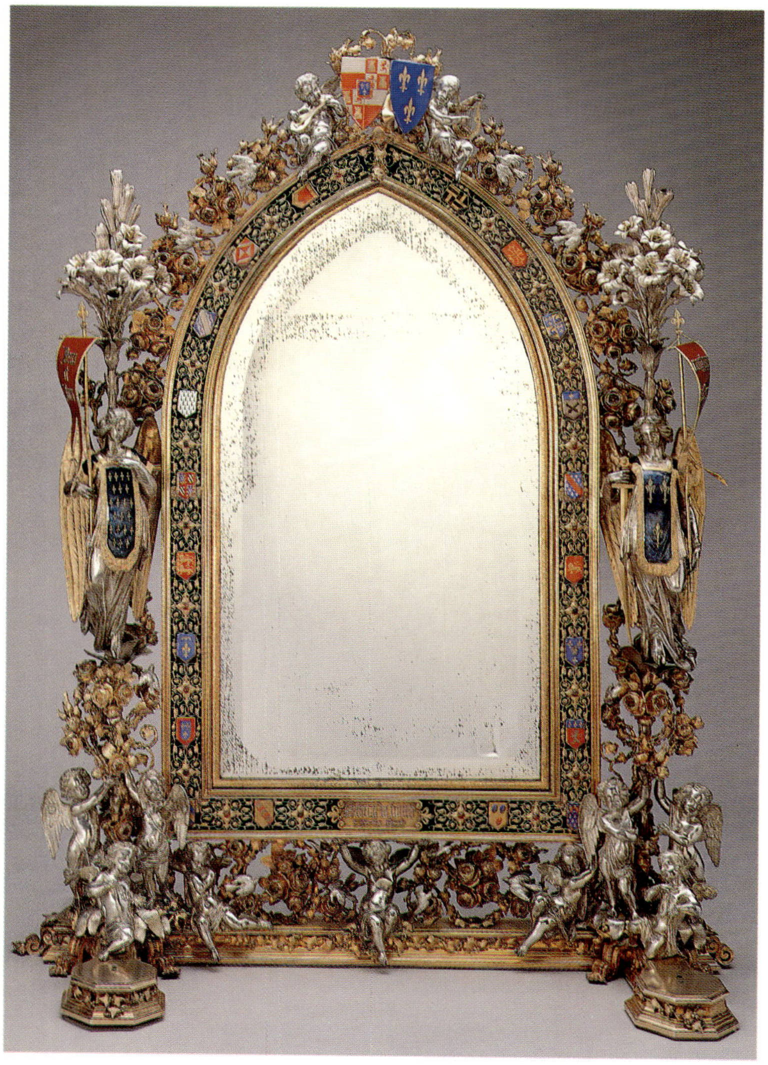

232

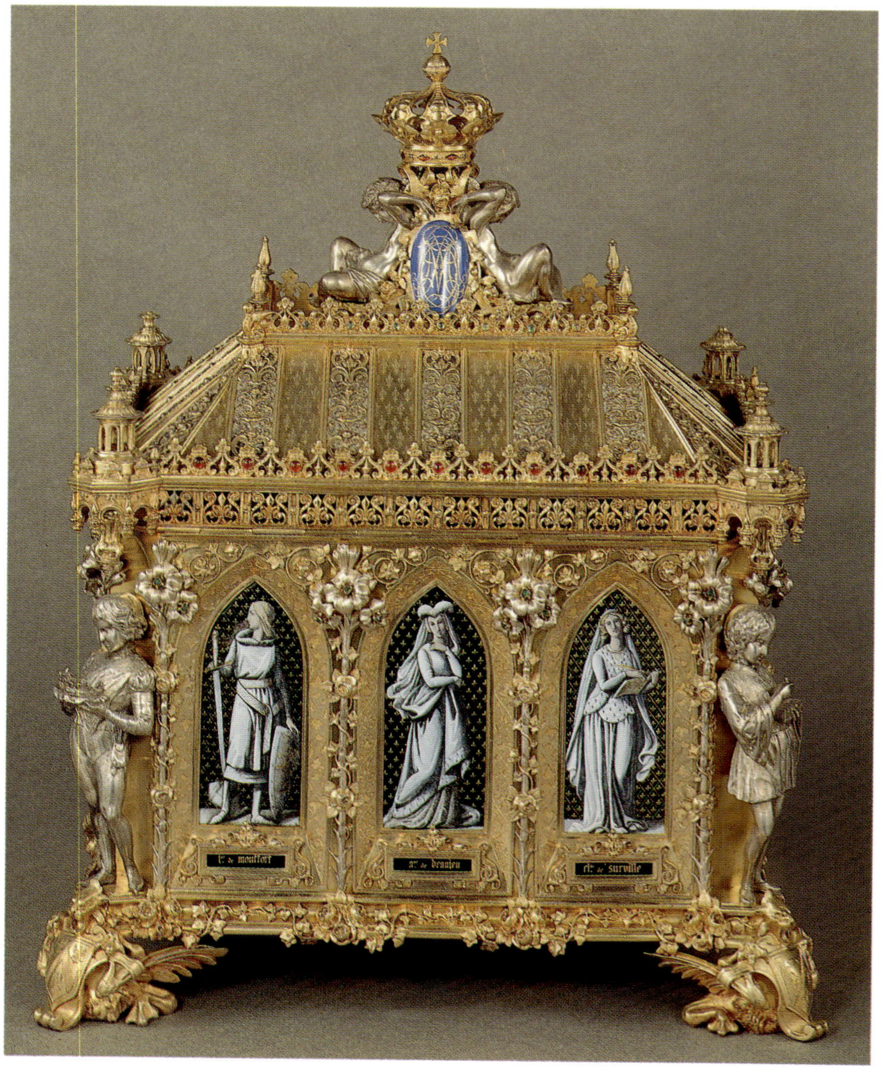

233

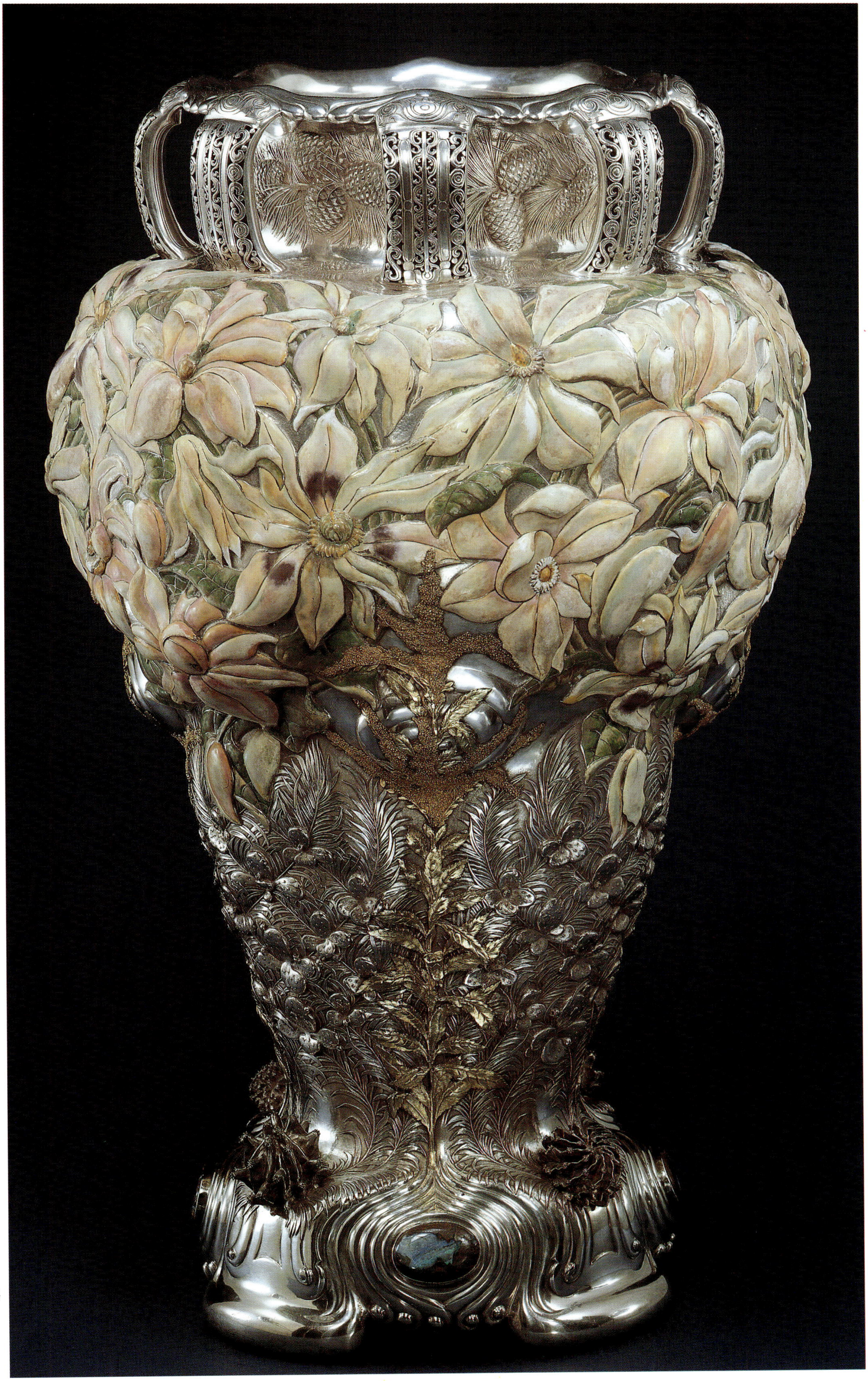

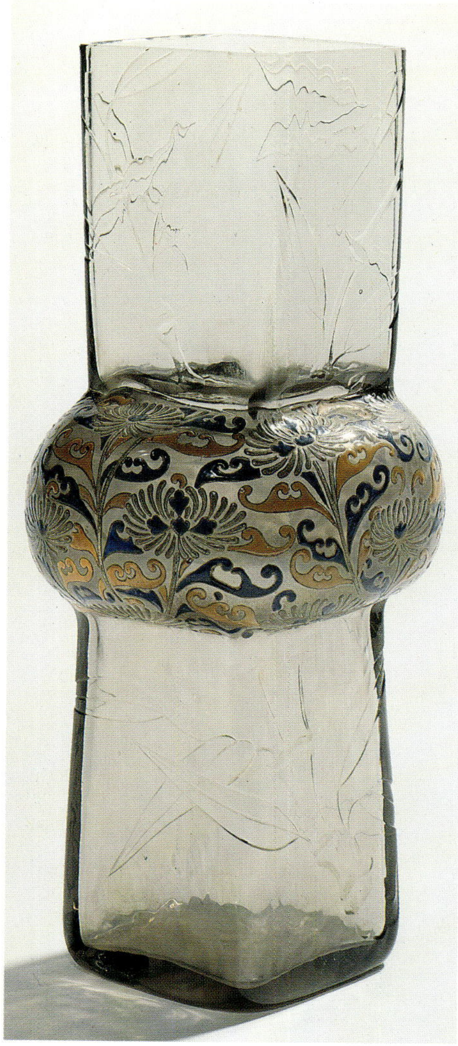
235

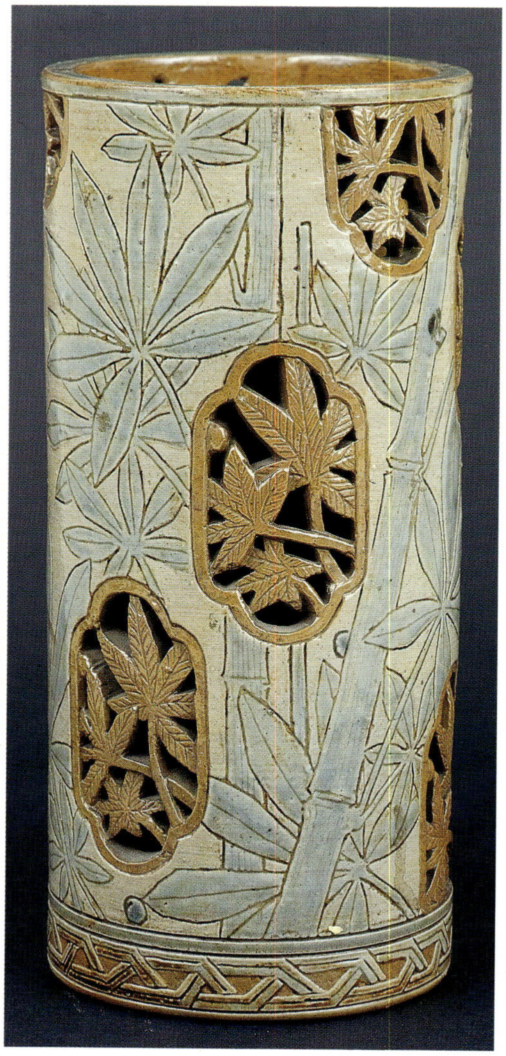
236

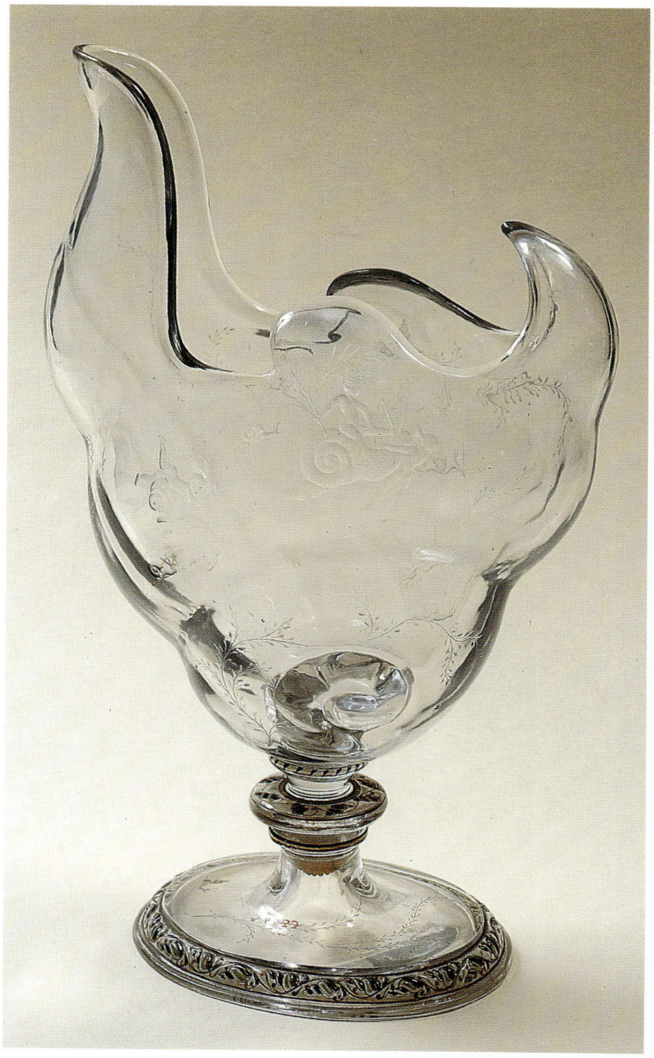
237

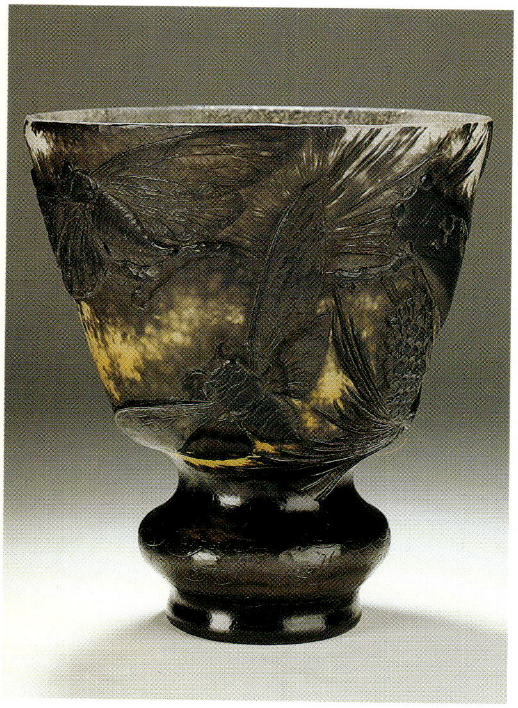
238

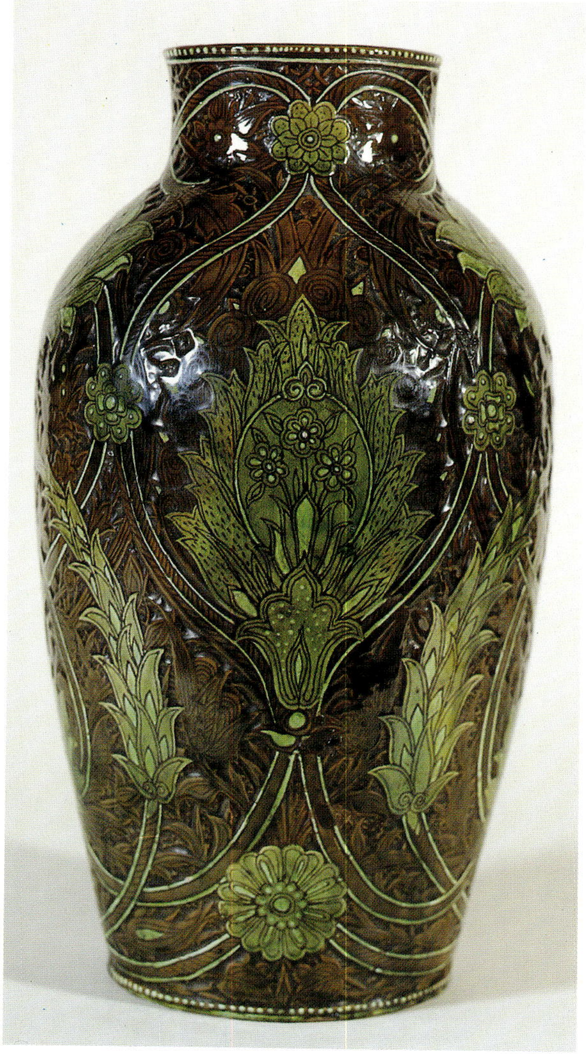
239

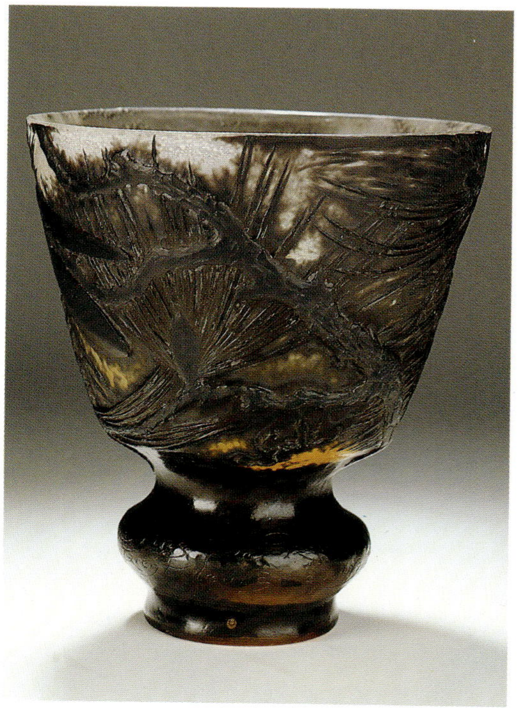
240

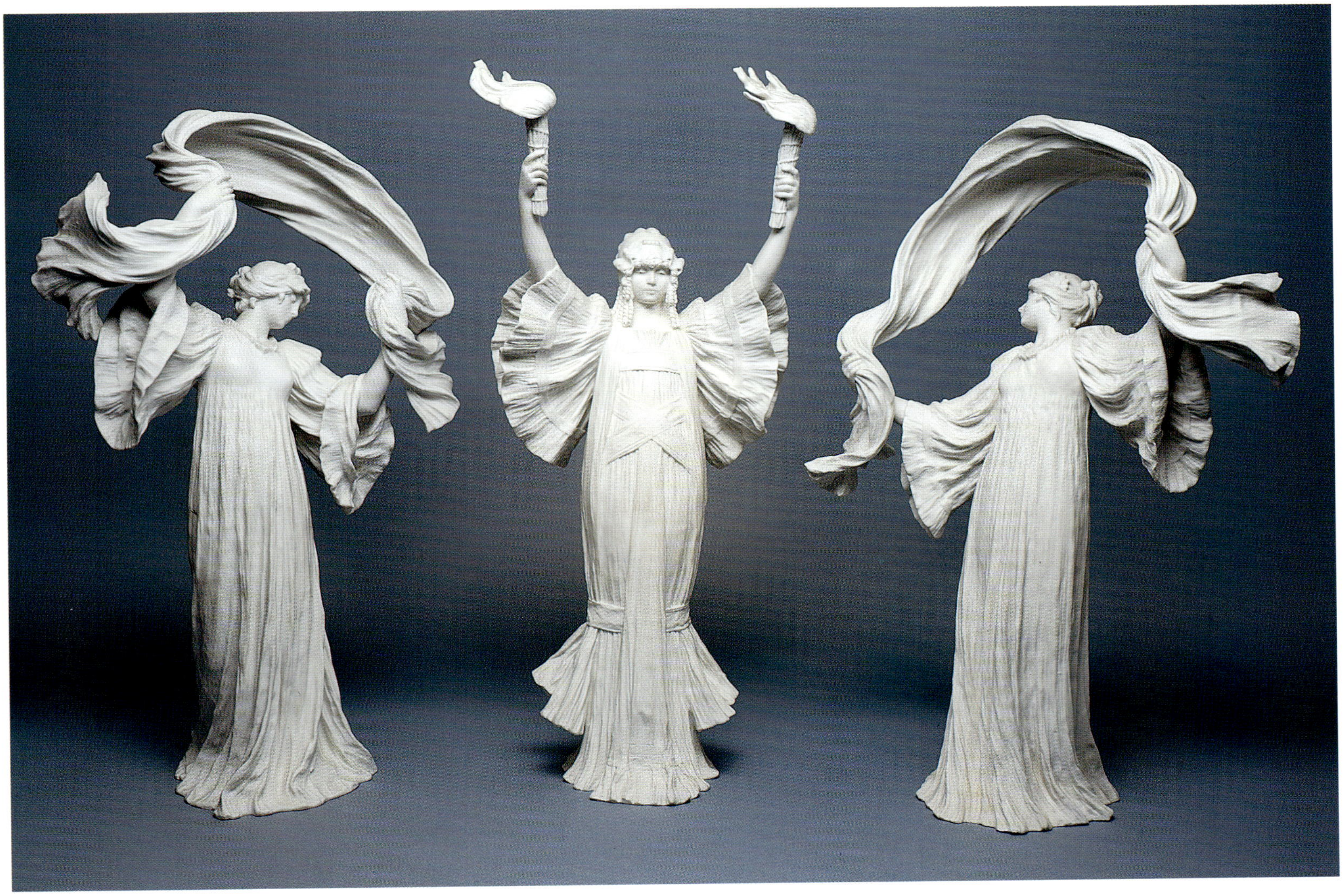

241

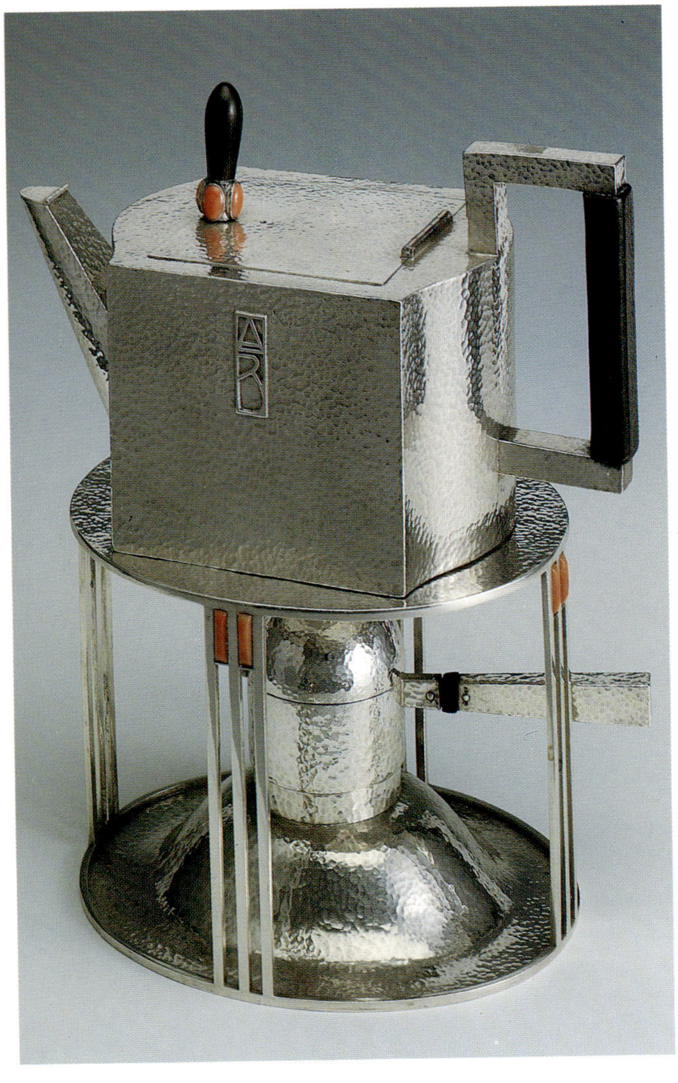

242

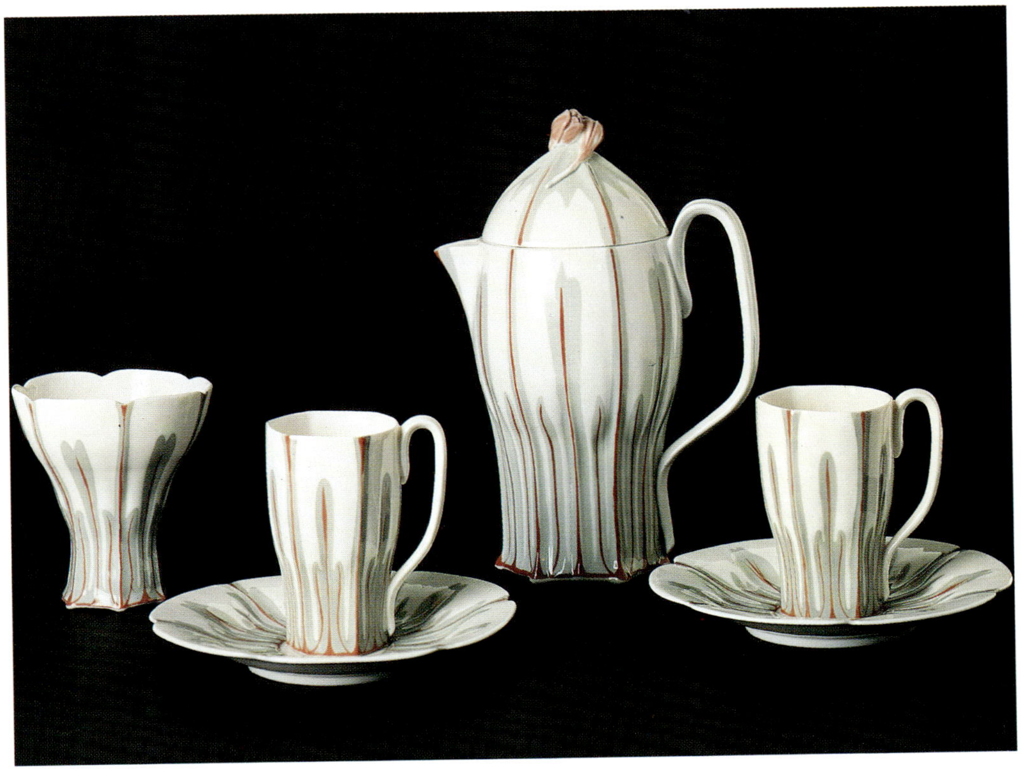

243

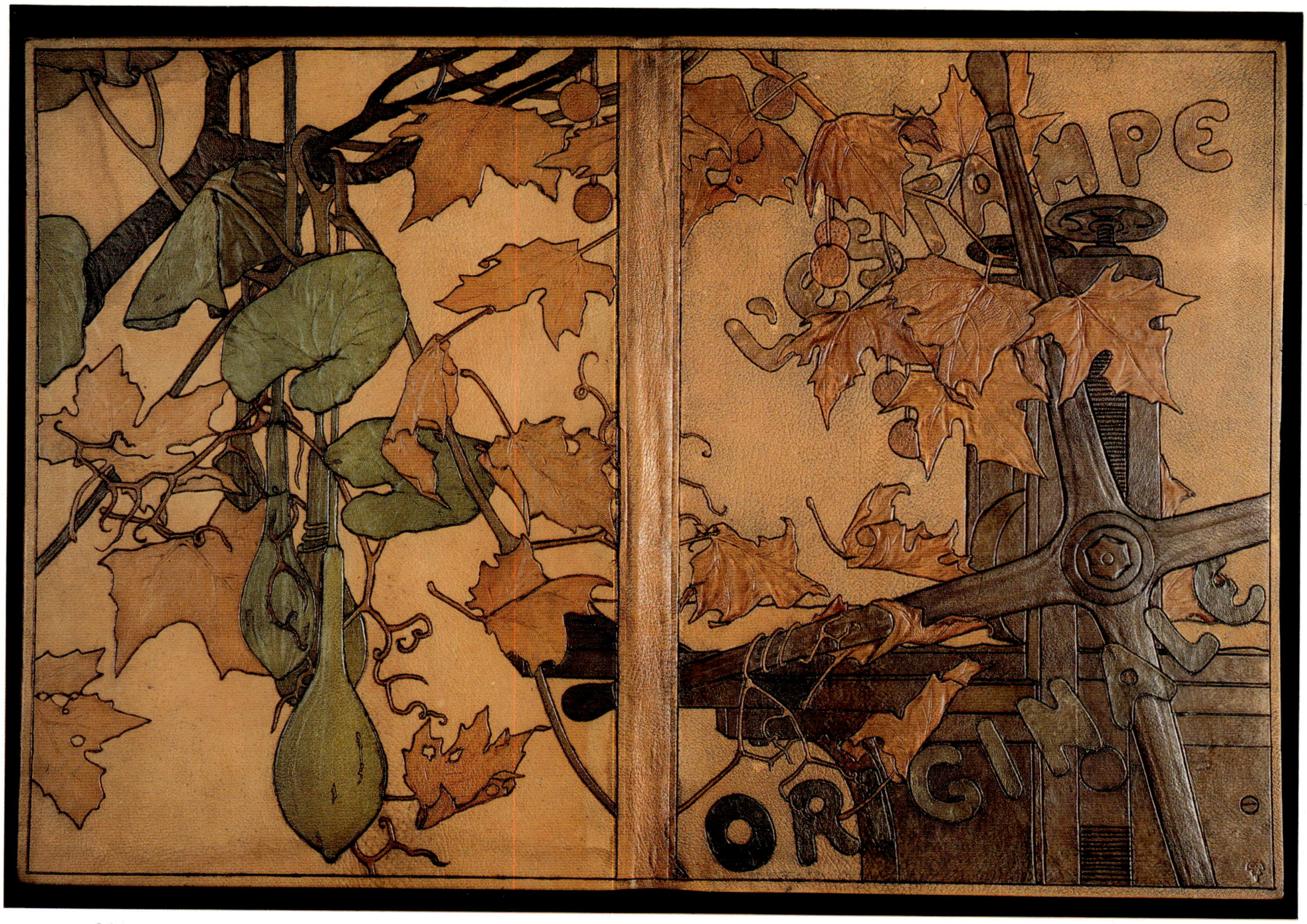

244

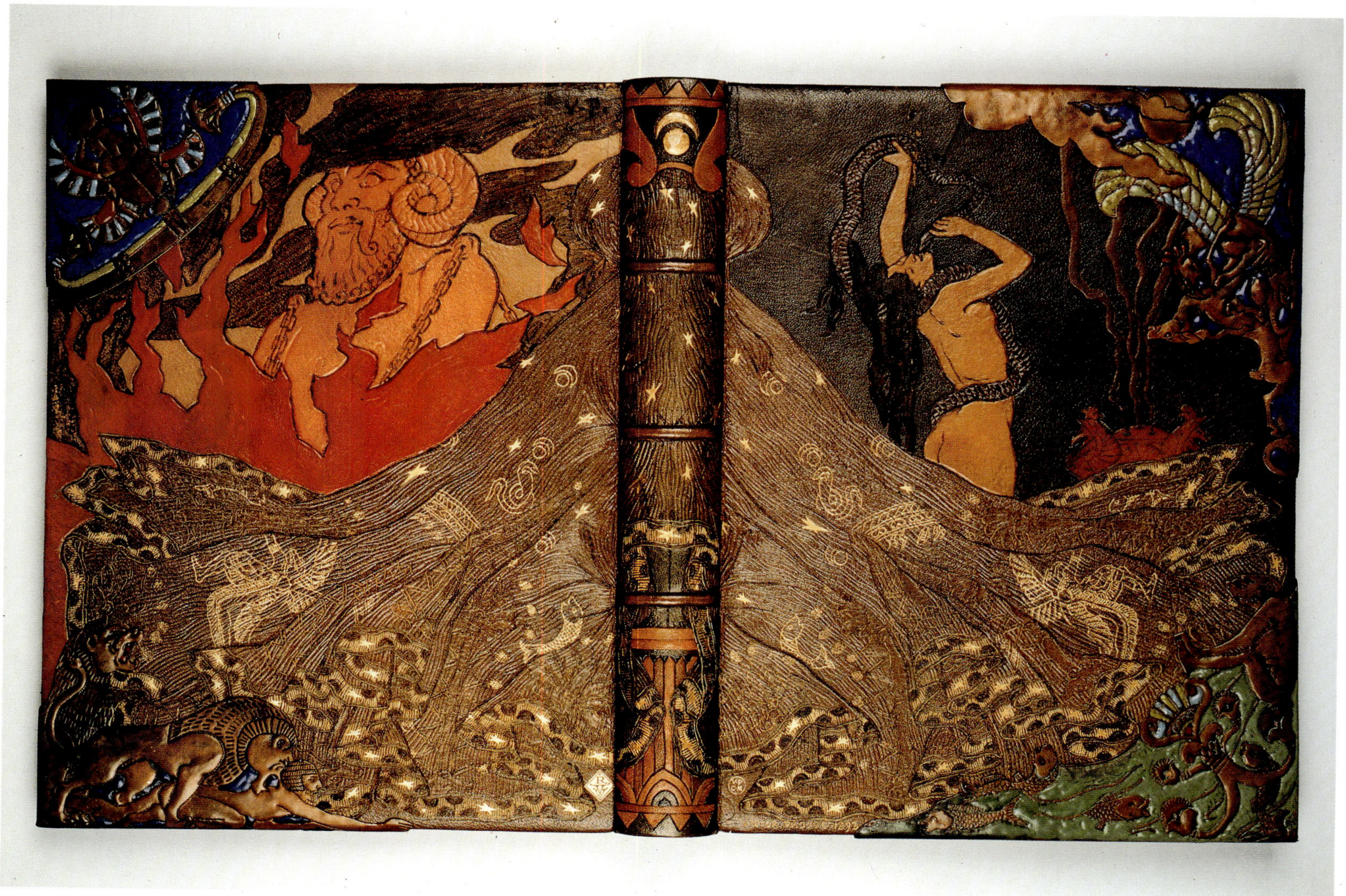

245

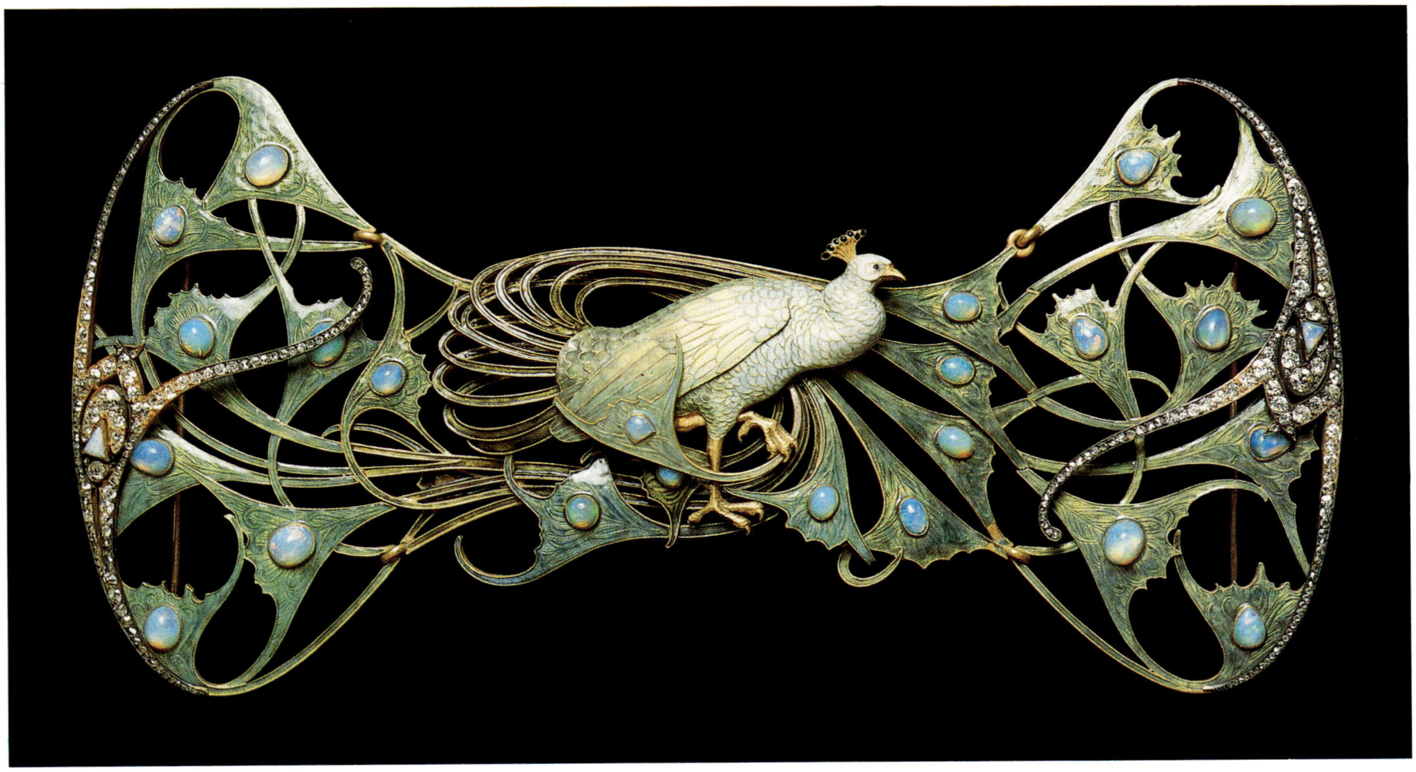

246

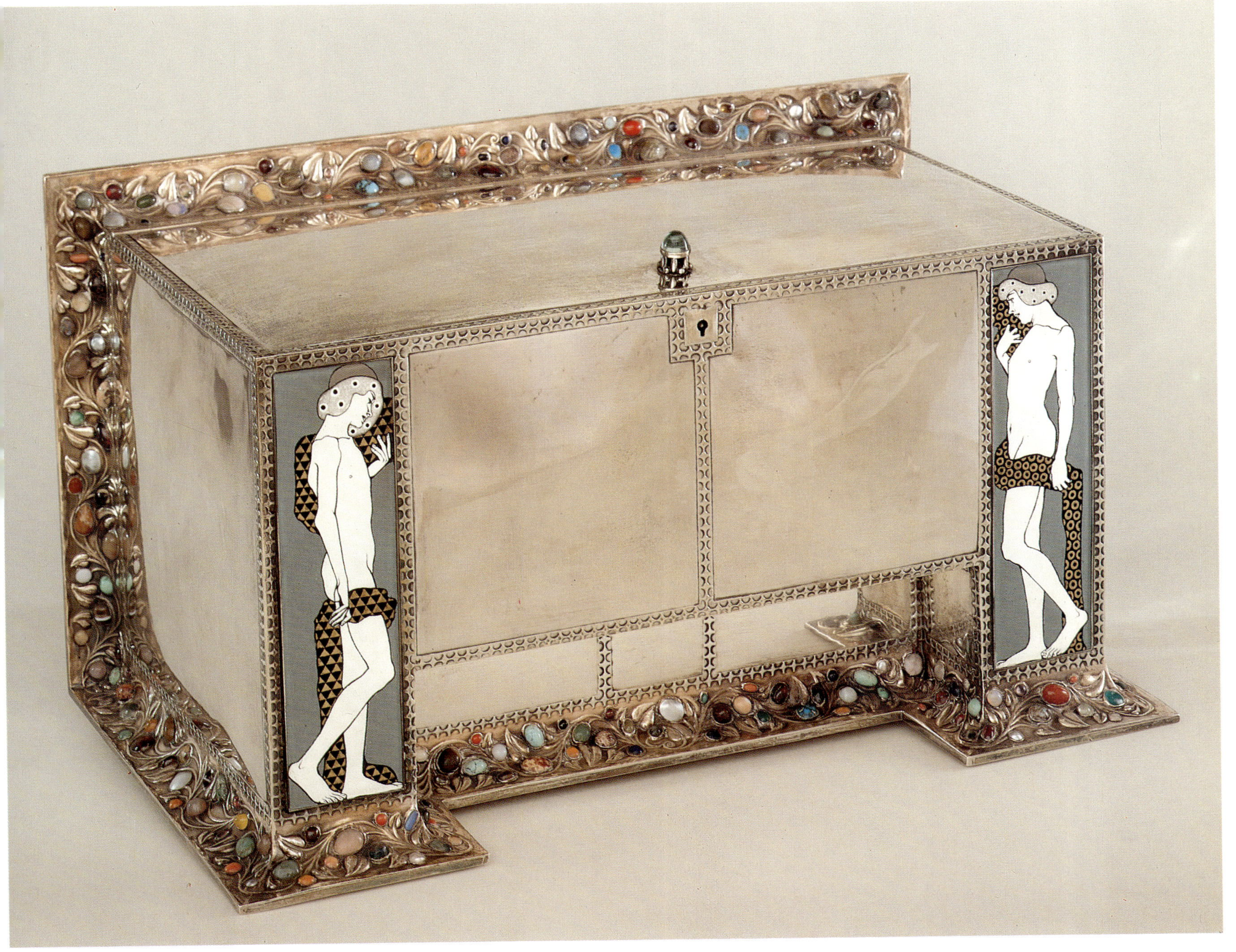

247

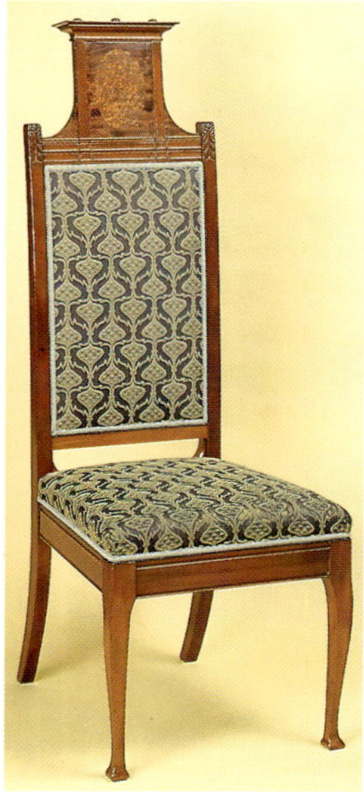
248

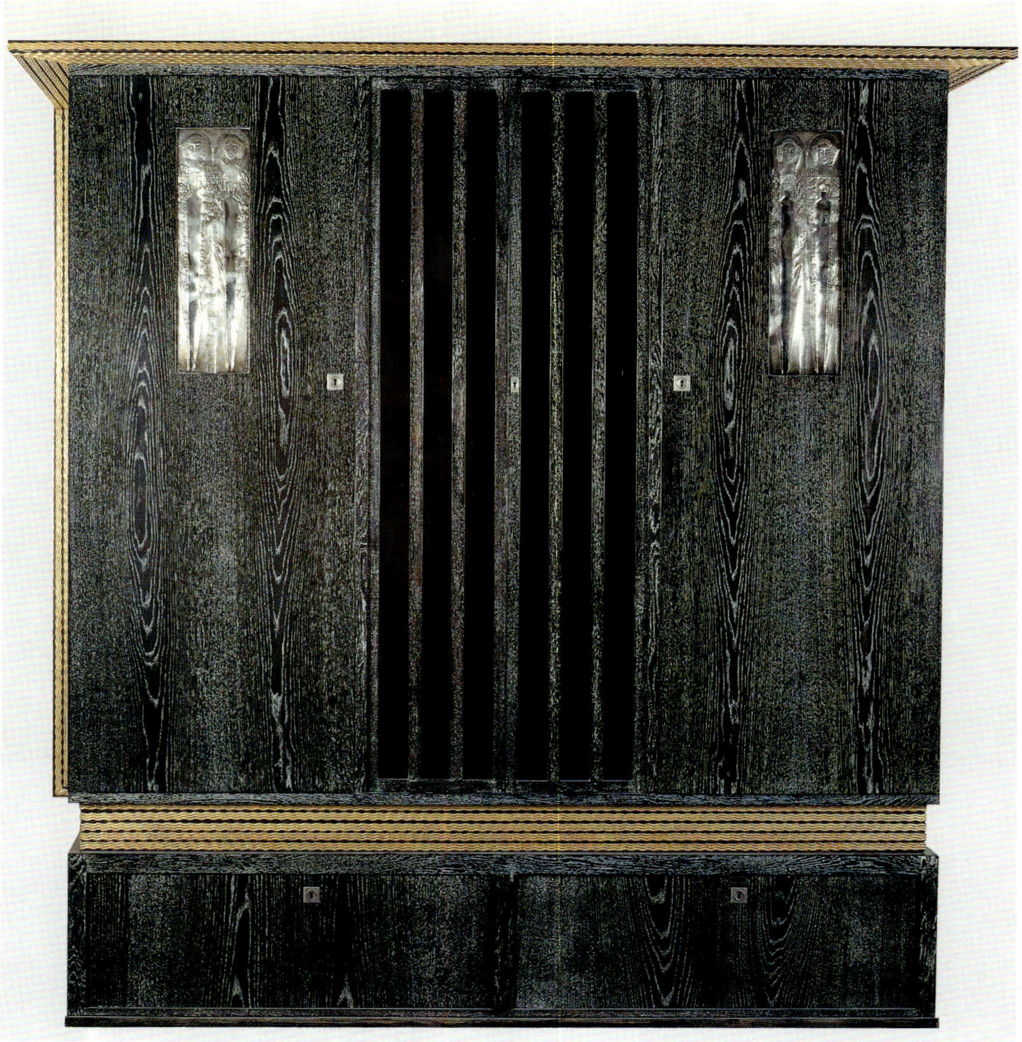
249

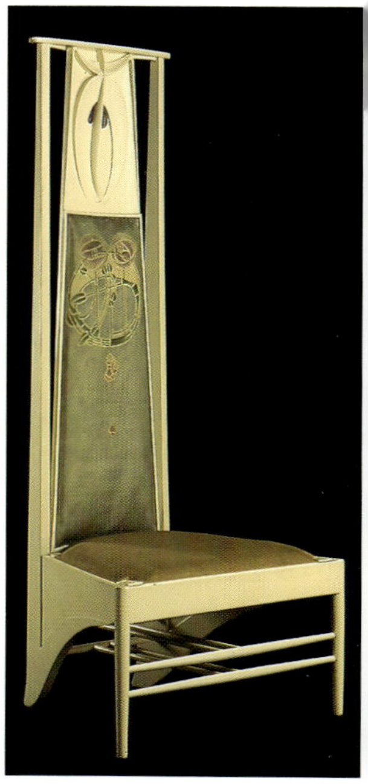
250

251

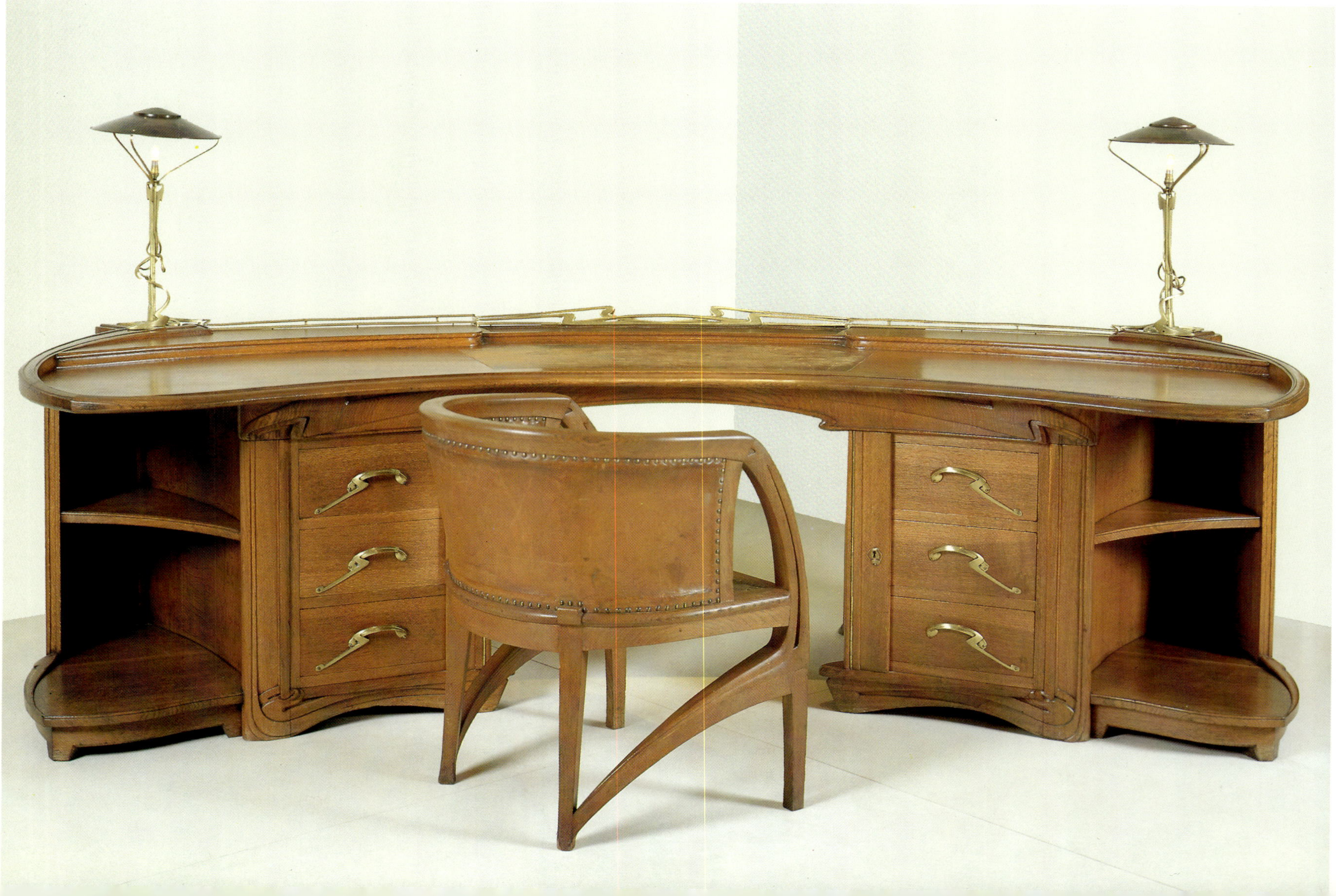

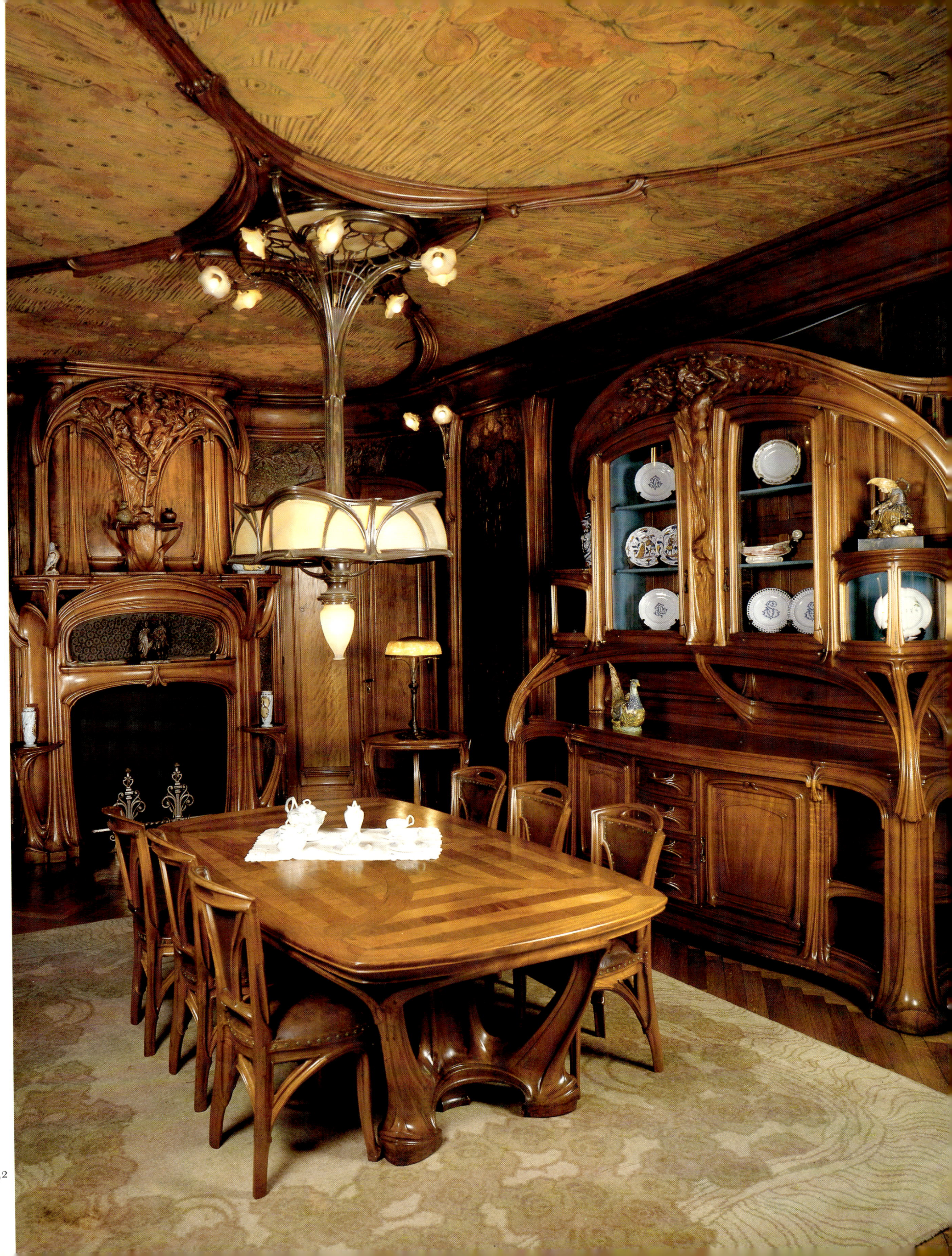

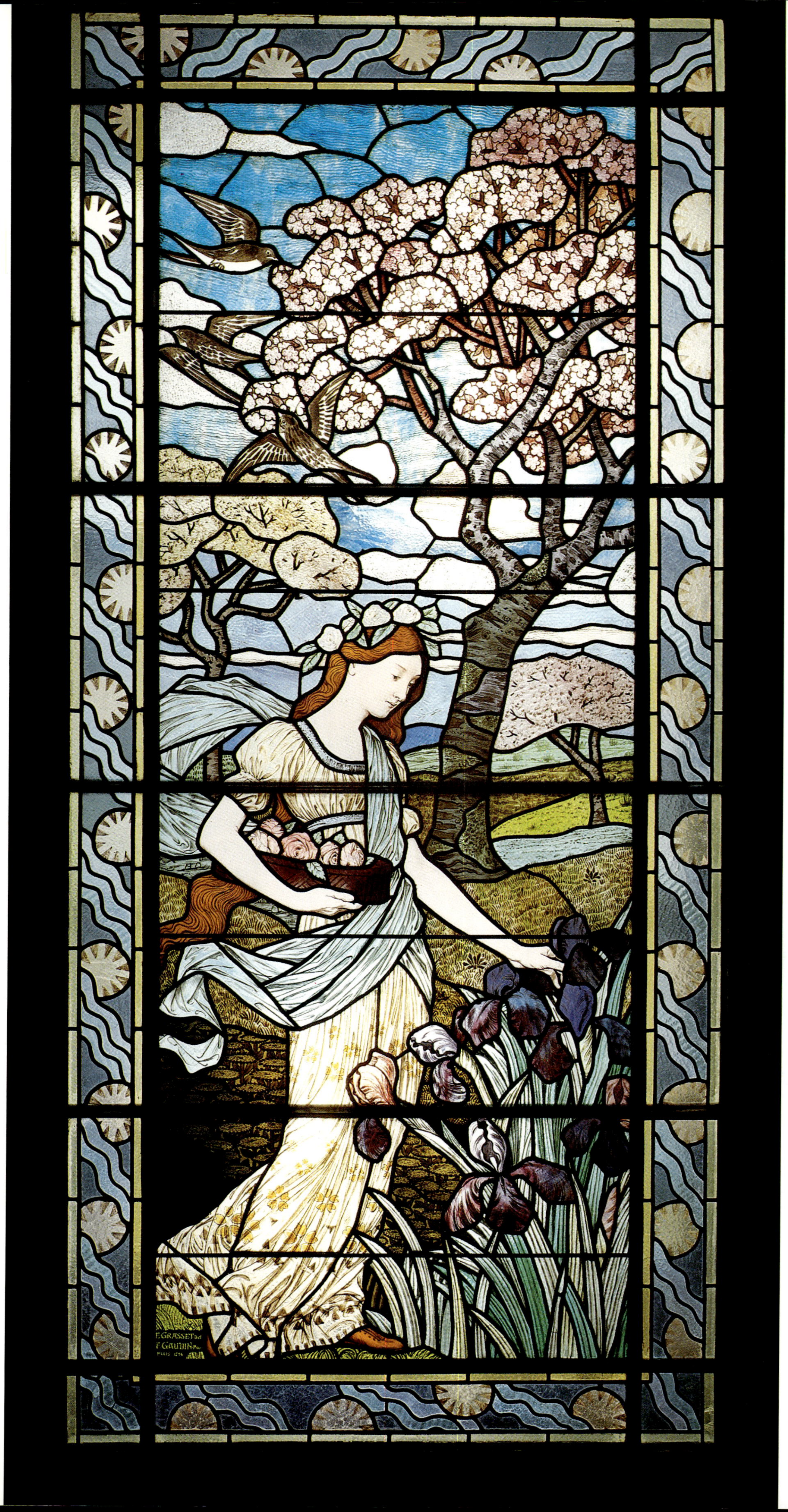
E.GRASSET del
F.GAUDIN
PARIS

241 Agathon Léonard
Scarf Dance
1900
Biscuit, 61 cm
Musée National de Céramique, Sèvres

242 Josef Hoffmann and the Wiener Werkstätte
Teapot and burner
1904
Hammered silver, coral, and ebony, teapot: 11 cm,
burner: 8.5 cm, diameter 13 cm
Österreichisches Museum für Angewandte Kunst,
Vienna

243 Konrad Hentschel and Sächsische Porzellan, Meissen
Manufaktur
Pieces of the Crocus service
1902
Porcelain, underglaze *grand feu* decoration
Württembergisches Landesmuseum, Stuttgart

244 Camille Martin
Portfolio for *L'estampe originale*
1894
Inlaid morocco, pokerwork, height of each cover:
62 cm
Musée de l'École de Nancy, Nancy

245 Victor Prouvé and Camille Martin
Binding for *Salammbô* by Gustave Flaubert
1893
Inlaid morocco, with gilt fillets, pokerwork,
and champlevé enamel, height of each cover: 42 cm
Musée de l'École de Nancy, Nancy

246 René Lalique
Corset ornament
c. 1898–1900
Gold, enamel, opals, and brilliants, 92 x 19 cm
Fundação Calouste Gulbenkian, Lisbon

247 Koloman Moser and the Wiener Werkstätte
Casket
c. 1905
Banded silver, enamel, and semiprecious stones,
236 x 424 x 244 cm
Österreichisches Museum für Angewandte Kunst,
Vienna

248 Arthur Heygate Mackmurdo
Chair
1886
Mahogany, original upholstery, wool, and silk,
height: 127 cm
Musée d'Orsay, Paris

249 Koloman Moser and the Wiener Werkstätte
Music cupboard
c. 1904
Oak treated with white-lead and black varnish, gilt
wood, repoussé silvered metal, and white metal,
height: 199 cm
Musée d'Orsay, Paris

250 Charles Rennie Mackintosh
Chair
International Exhibition of Applied Arts, Turin, 1902
Oak painted white, original upholstery, height: 152 cm
Glasgow University, Glasgow

251 Henry van de Velde
Large desk and fauteuil
Sezessions Austellung, Munich, 1899
Oak, gilt bronze, copper, and leather
Desk: 128 x 268 x 122.2 cm
Musée d'Orsay, Paris

252 Eugène Vallin and Victor Prouvé
Dining room for Charles Masson
1904
Mahogany, stained and painted repoussé leather
Musée de l'École de Nancy, Nancy

253 Eugène Grasset and Félix Gaudin
Spring
1894
Stained-glass window, 294 x 132 cm
Musée des Arts Décoratifs, Paris

ARCHITECTURE

URBANISM:
THE BIRTH OF THE MODERN CAPITAL CITY

The Example of Paris

The 1848 revolution and the instability of the Second Republic led to the election of Louis-Napoleon Bonaparte, prince president in 1848, and then, in 1852, emperor, with the title Napoleon III. During his reign (1852–70), France grew wealthier and Paris acquired the shape of a capital city it possesses today. Once on the throne, the emperor, keen to tackle poverty and unemployment, to counter outbreaks of rioting (made easier by narrow, winding streets), to improve hygiene, and to eradicate the terrible epidemics of typhus and cholera, wasted no time in setting about modernizing Paris. During his trips to America and the time he spent living in London, he had discovered the beauty of broad avenues and parks, and had seen how life could be improved through running water, gas lighting, and less congested traffic. Furthermore, the emperor was determined to improve the lot of those most wretched in society, the working classes. Already, in 1844, he had published a pamphlet entitled *Extinction du paupérisme* (The eradication of poverty) and had espoused Saint-Simon's collectivist ideals.

Keen to link himself with the memory of Napoleon I, Napoleon III took up where his uncle's projects had left off. He completed the Louvre in a historical synthesis of the styles (figs. 308–310), under the guidance of the architects Ludovico Tullius Joachim Visconti (1791–1853) and Hector Lefuel (1810–1880). At that time, the Louvre was still cluttered with shacks: "It is difficult now to picture what the Carrousel and the area around the Louvre resembled at that time, with its bric-a-brac sellers, its dentists working in all weathers, its thimbleriggers obstructing the unpaved square, all mire and dust" (Du Camp 1882, 25). Initially Visconti, followed, from 1853, by Lefuel, built a wing parallel to the gallery on the side facing the river, linking the Louvre to the Tuileries on the Rue de Rivoli, thereby realizing a dream long ago entertained by Louis XIV. In order to disguise the discrepancy in axis between the Tuileries and Jacques Lemercier's (1585–1654) Pavillon de l'Horloge, the architects doubled the facades between the Cour Carrée and the Place du Carrousel and laid out garden squares, thus rectifying the perspective. Vast and solemn domed pavilions, taking their inspiration from Lemercier's, broke the monotony of these lengthy wings that Lefuel adorned with balustrades, sculptures, low reliefs, and columns. From 1863 to 1868, Lefuel also reconstructed the wing connecting the entrance gates of the Carrousel to the Pavillon de Flore, which were decorated by Jean-Baptiste Carpeaux.

Vilified by his contemporaries, who spoke of vulgarity and excess, Lefuel nonetheless exhibited a fertile imagination, considerable skill in the handling of ornaments, and a fine sense of how to balance masses and blocks, which bears out the opinion of Louis Hautecœur: "Lefuel was a decorator, one who remains an architect" (Hautecœur 1957, 7:177).

The fire in the Tuileries during the 1871 Commune put paid to one of the largest building sites of the second half of the nineteenth century, and it was Lefuel who, through the restoration of the damaged areas, was to give the Louvre its present-day face.

If Paris was undergoing a transformation, it was all due to the imperial will. Town planning was thus to be an affair of state, that is, from 1851, building work was decided by decree, with no previous consultation and without parliamentary debate. June 23, 1853 saw the appointment of a new prefect of the Seine *département*, Baron Georges-Eugène Haussmann (1809–1891), who was to put the emperor's policy into practice, assisted by an expeditious architectural bureau headed by Victor Baltard (1805–1874) and comprising Joseph-Louis Duc (1802–1879), Théodore Ballu (1817–1887), Antoine-Nicolas Bailly (1810–1892), Jacques Gilbert (1795–1874), and Gabriel Davioud (1832–1881), who was made responsible for fountains.

Napoleon III totally remodeled the city, annexing outlying *communes* and creating present-day Paris with its twenty administrative *arrondissements* (1859), each one provided with its own town hall and churches (fig. 282). Once a precise plan of the city had been drawn up, three successive networks of roads ensured that the various neighborhoods were each linked, made access to the main stations less onerous, and permitted the creation of a major administrative center (the Louvre and the Île de la Cité) and the introduction of parks and squares. In an operation lasting from 1855 to 1858, the initial necessity was to pierce two wide thoroughfares north-south and east-west through Paris. This is the great intersection formed by the meeting point of the Rue de Rivoli, that opens a route from west to east (from the Place de l'Étoile to the Bastille), with the Boulevard de Sébastopol—extending into the Boulevard Saint-Michel—that bisects the capital north-south through the Île de la Cité. This work entailed leveling part of the medieval town, and churches, monasteries, avenues, and the slum-infested streets bordering the Seine were razed to the ground. Room was now available for the central law court, the Palais de Justice, built in a classical style by Duc, a commercial and bankruptcy court, the Tribunal de Commerce, Renaissance style crossed with Baroque elements by Bailly, a new general hospital, the Hôtel-Dieu, by Gilbert and Arthur-Nicolas Diet (1827–1890), as well as for the barracks designed to maintain the capital's internal security. It was this Paris, put on the wheel and disemboweled, that was described by Zola: "'Look down there, over by the Halles [the market area], they have cut Paris into four'. . . And with his hand spread out, open and sharp-edged as a cutlass, he made a movement of separating the city into four parts. 'You mean the Rue de Rivoli and the new boulevard they're building,' said his wife. 'Yes, the great transept of Paris, as they call it. They're clearing away the buildings around the Louvre and the Hôtel de Ville; that's mere child's play! . . . When the first network is finished, then the fun will begin. The second network will pierce the city in every direction, so as to connect the suburbs with the first . . . Look, just follow my hand a moment. From the Boulevard du Temple to the Barrière du Trône, that's one cutting; then on this side another, from the Madeleine to the Plaine Monceau . . . Paris slashed with saber cuts, its veins opened, giving sustenence for a hundred thousand diggers and bricklayers'" (Zola 1871, 1:389; 1957, 76).

The second grid extended the city toward the west, while a third, laid out between 1867 and 1879, regularized the area around Charles Garnier's (1825–1898) new opera house and transformed the eighteenth, twentieth, and thirteenth *arrondissements*, expelling the industrial plants so as to make way for housing. On the left bank, the Boulevard Saint-Germain was opened, whereas on the right, the old boulevards were widened and enhanced by a "fine row of trees, a wide asphalt sidewalk for pedestrians and two long avenues of monumental houses."

Opening the boulevards brought with it the destruction of numerous theaters. Haussmann was to have them rebuilt in the city center, near the Hôtel de Ville: the city's opera house on the Place du Châtelet, together with the theater of the Cirque Impérial (now the Théâtre du Châtelet) constructed by Davioud, and the Théâtre de la Gaieté by Alphonse Cuzin on the Square des Arts et Métiers. Others, such as the Vaudeville by Auguste-Joseph Magne (1816–1885), were built out on the boulevards. Almost all were in the Italian Renaissance style, with ground-floor arcades and first-floor loggias, and were occasionally surrounded by buildings with colossal orders. They were in keeping with Haussmann's directives: "To make of the new theaters monuments worthy of the French capital; to build them solidly and to decorate them richly; to provide them with wide and accessible entrances; with vast well-lit, well-ventilated halls so the audience can walk around at its ease and pass its time there enjoyably; and finally to exploit the progress of modern industry to render our theaters alluring and comfortable" (Haussmann 1891, 2:291).

Haussmann joined forces with two exceptional figures, the engineers François-Eugène Belgrand (1810–1878) and Adolphe Alphand (1817–1891). Thanks to the unfailing efforts of Belgrand, the newly appointed head of the water board, by 1870 most dwellings were supplied with spring water at ground-floor level and a model sewage system, to be copied the world over, was in place in less than a decade. Paris was also to be peppered with fountains designed by Davioud, the finest example being the Observatory Fountain with the group of the *Four Corners of the World* (1874, fig. 499), sculpted by Jean-Baptiste Carpeaux.

In an effort to provide Parisians with walks on which to promenade and also so as to purify the air, Napoleon III made Alphand responsible for the creation of more garden squares and parks: the Bois de Boulogne to the west, the Bois de Vincennes to the east for the working class, Parc Monceau in the northwest, and the Parc des Buttes-Chaumont in the northeast. All had the same winding lanes, a rather "English" atmosphere, perfectly adapted to the relief, particularly in the case of the Buttes-Chaumont, which was laid out over a former quarry.

To fulfill the needs of the up-and-coming bourgeoisie, streets were lined with luxurious and often uniform-looking blocks. Characterized by wide facades with sculptures, wrought-iron balconies, and double-doored carriage entrances, they were strictly regulated as to their breadth, and the number of their stories, windows, doors, and projections. The interior decor was opulent in the extreme. "The vestibule and stairway were of an aggressive luxury. Downstairs, a female figure, a sort of Neapolitan covered in gilt, carried an amphora from which emerged three gas jets adorned with frosted globes. Panels of mock marble, white and fringed with pink, rose regularly in a round cage, whereas the cast-iron banister rail with mahogany, imitated old silver with outpourings of gold leaves. A red carpet, fitted with copper rods, covered the stairs" (Zola 1882, 31). It was the height of fashion to build one's private mansion on one of the plots sold by the brothers Péreire in the northwest quarter near the Parc Monceau, where the new middle-class business people—such as the chocolate-maker, Émile Menier—were to congregate. As for the mansion on the Avenue des Champs-Élysées built—in the kind of Franco-Italian style prevalent for such *hôtels particuliers*—by Pierre Manguin (1815–1869) for the celebrated courtesan, the marquise de Païva, with its extraordinary stairway in onyx, its mantelpieces carved by Dalou and its ceilings by Baudry, it beggars description (figs. 254, 311, 313–15).

Owing to the high cost of renting and the uniformity of building plans that encouraged the adoption of similar lifestyles, social classes that formerly lived cheek-by-jowl were to begin to move apart, leading to the growth of wholly working-class areas in the thirteenth, fourteenth, nineteenth, and twentieth *arrondissements.* A surge in population, combined with the influx of hordes of people from the countryside attracted by work on the vast building sites, gave rise to the construction of model estates, designed to resolve the problem of lower-class housing. This was the case in the Cité Napoléon, built in 1850 by Gabriel Veugny at the instigation of the emperor himself and comprising more than one hundred and eighty houses (fig. 319). Projects in the private sector initiated by the captains of industry enabled the setting up of similar estates in Tours, Marseille, and Mulhouse. The model estate built for the Menier business at Noisiel (in the *département* of Seine-et-Marne) still survives today. The only truly successful example was, however, the "Familistère" or "Palais Social," constructed between 1859 and 1879 by Jean-Baptiste-André Godin (1817–1888) at Guise (near Laon). The former journeyman and metalworker designed, with the minimum of funds, modern living quarters more comfortable than some Parisian apartment buildings, with hot water, garbage chutes, and air conditioning. Comprising three interconnecting blocks built round three inner glazed courtyards, the Familistère encouraged community living, while respecting the right of each to privacy.

The Third Republic was to complete a number of Haussmann's plans, as well as reconstructing the Hôtel de Ville burnt down in 1871, which the architects Ballu and Édouard Deperthes (1833–1898), constrained by the burden of history, were to restore to its former Renaissance self, though not before weighing it down further under ornaments and sculptures.

The central charge leveled at Haussmann was that he destroyed old Paris in a way that, it is true, was sometimes over-systematic. But his merit lies in having set down an overall plan whose vision was one of grandeur and boldness. "Baron Haussmann made yawning holes in Paris, lancing her shamelessly. It seemed as though Paris could never survive Haussmann's surgery. But today, surely Paris lives by what that bold and courageous man did? His means? From the shovel, pickaxe, cart, trowel, and wheelbarrow—those childish weapons that every people possesses—to the newest machinery. What Haussmann managed to do is truly admirable" (Le Corbusier 1925, 149).

The French Provinces

From 1853 to 1864 the prefect of Lyon, C. Marius Vaïsse, oversaw works that extended and beautified the city in a way that can be compared to Haussmann's in Paris. Much the same can be said of Lille and Rennes in the north and Montpellier, Toulon, and Marseille in the south. The growth of the summer vacation and the fashion for spa cures encouraged the building of new infrastructures and the development of centers such as Vichy and Vittel, the creation of the winter holiday town at Arcachon (by the brothers Péreire), and of Cabourg, in Calvados, northwest France, and the seaside town of Deauville on the Channel.

Europe

On the rest of the continent, many major cities were reorganized, notably Brussels, under its mayor Jules Anspach, and in Italy, Naples, Turin, and Florence. Proclaimed as the country's capital in 1870, Rome extended spectacularly along two new eastbound arteries, the Via Venti Settembre and the Via Nazionale, laid out in 1871 and embellished during the following fifteen years with monumental public buildings such as the Palazzo delle Belle Arti by Pio Piacentini (1846–1928) or the Banca d'Italia by Gaetano Koch (1849–1910). The colossal construction that dominated the city, however, was the monument erected in 1885 to Victor Emmanuel II by Giuseppe Saconi (1854–1905), which was not completed until 1922.

Vienna and the Ringstrasse

"The Parisian who arrives in Vienna imagining that M. Haussmann can never be equaled far less surpassed, not for the quality but for the sheer quantity of new buildings, is strangely surprised when he travels round the city on the Ring (corresponding to our boulevard) and sees nothing but new houses—and one might add nothing but elegant houses, if sometimes rather massive" (Casati, 1869).

Vienna had hardly stirred during the first half of the nineteenth century and Francis Joseph, acceding to the throne in 1848, grew determined to vie with Napoleon III's Paris. In 1857, the emperor decided to level the ring of fortifications that still ran round the city, organizing a competition for the redevelopment of the newly cleared site. The competition for the plan of the Ringstrasse in 1858 was won by Ludwig Förster (1797–1863); the execution of his project, that was to be modified constantly, would, however, extend over a thirty-year period (fig. 286). On either side of the new wide and airy avenues there sprung up the great mass of the city's public buildings—the opera house, museums, the new city hall, parliament buildings, the university, as well as stations, banks, grand hotels, and vast housing developments.

These monuments crib from every style: "Around the same square and at the same time, and for the public services of the same inhabitants, there was seen to rise: a pseudo-Greek parliament, a pseudo-Gothic city hall, and a pseudo-Renaissance university" (Sédille 1884, 134). With its richly colored exterior, the Parliament (1873–83), erected by a connoisseur of Greek archaeology, the Dane Theophil von Hansen (1813–1891), is the last construction of true grandeur in the style. Friedrich von Schmidt (1825–1891), the "Viollet-le-Duc of Vienna," who had worked on the restoration and completion of Cologne Cathedral, designed a City Hall (1872–83) that was inspired by thirteenth- and fourteenth-century Gothic, the same style in which Heinrich von Frestel (1828–1883) was to execute the Votivkirche. The Italian Renaissance made its appearance with the two museums built by Gottfried Semper (1803–1879) and Karl von Hasenauer (1833–1894; fig. 287), whereas the Burgtheater (1874–88) designed by the same two architects, situated opposite the City Hall, seems, with its bowed facade, almost neo-Baroque. The Staatsoper (1861–69), designed by Eduard van der Nüll (1812–1868) and Eduard August Siccard von Siccardsburg (1813–1868), is perhaps one of the most original monuments on the Ringstrasse.

Lining the Ringstrasse there rose apartment blocks and houses that competed with each other as to architectural and decorative effect. Unlike the sobriety of Haussmann's Paris, "in Vienna the architect is permitted to impart movement to his facades with fore-parts, projecting columns, corbeled loggias, wide balconies, or else to enhance their outline by raised pavilions, exaggerated pediments, and gables, or by turrets, cupolas, and roofs whose perimeters need not conform to regulations, and in general by anything that contributes to its adornment and thus embellishes the public thoroughfare" (Sédille 1884, 126). Once again, it was the Renaissance that was the inspiration for form and decoration in these dwellings, which were constructed in cement-faced bricks and decorated with motifs in multicolored terra cotta.

The Ringstrasse allowed the old town to be incorporated into the modern city's transport network without, as had been the case in Paris, severing or destroying the urban fabric. The quality of the open spaces—and the number and size of parks and garden squares—as well as the monumentality of the architecture proclaimed the rebirth of the Austrian capital.

The New World

In the South American republics, fired by the example of France, new towns soon mushroomed. La Plata (Argentina), dating from 1882, and Belo Horizonte (Brazil) created at the end of the century were disposed in a grid plan crisscrossed by wide thoroughfares at right-angles, ringed by circular boulevards and adorned by numerous public buildings. Brazil already possessed a fine tradition of Neoclassical architecture, initiated by Frenchman Auguste-Henri-Victor Grandjean de Montigny (1776–1850), who had arrived in Rio de Janeiro in 1816. In Mexico City in 1860, under the influence of Haussmann, Emperor Maximilian opened the Paseo del Emperador (now Paseo de la Reforma), an imitation of the Champs-Élysées. The École des Beaux-Arts in Paris continued to exert a powerful influence well into the 1910s.

Chicago

Unregulated town planning and construction in Chicago were the underlying reasons for the terrible fire that ravaged the city in 1871. Paradoxically, this catastrophe led to a rebuilding program undertaken over two years by American, German, French, and English architects and to the growth of the Chicago School, thanks to which the skyscraper was to attain its finest expression.

Although a host of architectural projects had been drawn up since 1890 in anticipation of the World's Columbian Exhibition of 1893, nobody had thought of a development plan for Chicago. It was Daniel Burnham (1846–1912) who, in 1897, presented his great project for turning Chicago into a city to rival Paris. Twelve years later, in 1909, after many experiments and numerous journeys through Europe, Burnham exhibited in the Art Institute of Chicago his Plan of Chicago that had been in gestation over a period of thirty years. This plan—that Burnham soon published—was intended to regulate the metropolis's disorganized growth and to set out a coherent grid of streets and arteries, to create green spaces, new public buildings, and railroad facilities in keeping with Chicago's extraordinary commercial expansion, as well as to modernize the port services.

Burnham demonstrated his exceptional talents of organization during the 1893 exhibition, where he already made explicit his admiration for Haussmann by stressing the central axis, the alignment of the cornices, and the employment of ashlar stone. He gathered round him a team of architects who were quite at home in the classical idiom, such as Richard Morris Hunt (1827–1895) and Charles McKim (1847–1909). "Among great cities, Paris has reached the highest stage of development, and the method of its attainment affords lesson for all other cities . . . The task that Haussmann accomplished in Paris corresponds with the work which must be done for Chicago" (Burnham and Bennett 1909, 14 and 18).

This unequivocal declaration makes clear Burnham's idea: to renovate Chicago's urban landscape and make the inhabitants aware of the need for an organized overall development plan. Nonetheless, if Burnham indeed applied the basic rules of organization learnt from the example of Paris, he also exploited Chicago's splendid site on the shores of Lake Michigan and created a project unique in the history of town planning. In his Plan of Chicago, thanks to the dazzling and evocative drawings of Jules Guérin, an American trained at the École des Beaux-Arts in Paris, the visionary Burnham managed to conjure up a dream city, a "Paris on the lake" on an American scale, that his associate Edward H. Bennett was to build in the space of twenty years.

ECLECTICISM

In France, during the reign of Louis-Philippe, the bourgeoisie was to rise to the highest positions in society, becoming supreme in the economic and political life of the country under Napoleon III. Uncertain in its tastes, searching for both legitimacy and roots, it fell back on tried and tested values, delving into the artistic heritage of the past in a mix of the most varied styles and materials. Nostalgia for yesteryear affected painters and writers alike, from Walter Scott and Chateaubriand to Alexandre Dumas and Victor Hugo. As early as the first years of the nineteenth century, the landscape was being peppered with Gothic manors and churches, and Renaissance-style town houses and dwellings, to be followed later by buildings and interiors in the Louis XIII and Louis XIV manners. "Apartments were turned into catalogs of pastiche: Henri II dining rooms, Louis XIII antechambers, Louis XIV drawing rooms, Louis XV boudoirs, Louis XVI bedrooms, Empire studies all seemed a prerequisite for any woman of the world, for any unscrupulous female keen to match [the demimondaine] la Païva. Town and city halls were Renaissance or Louis XIII, barracks Louis XIV, town houses Louis XV or Louis XVI" (Hautecœur, quoted in Dagon 1975, 114). And these manifestations were not the only ones: voyages of exploration, colonialism, and the international exhibitions all broadened horizons. Picturesque, exotic, highly colored styles were all being discovered for the first time, as were the arts of Japan, which lie at the fountainhead of modernity.

It was also a period in which ancient monuments were being rediscovered, first through drawings, then through engravings and publications. The role assumed by the *Voyages pittoresques et romantiques dans l'ancienne France* published by Nodier and Taylor from 1818 to 1850 appears paramount in this connection. Archaeological collections, historical studies, and travelers' accounts sprung up everywhere, making artistic sources from far-flung locations generally available, while architects crisscrossed country after country, bringing to light many famed monuments: Pascal Coste visited Egypt and Persia, Owen Jones and Jules Goury unveiled the wonders of Grenada, Jules Bourgoin examined the components of Arabian art, while Léon Parvillée gave a new lease of life to enameled ceramics in his study *Architecture et décoration turques au XVe siècle.*

Numerous restoration programs imprinted on every architect a thorough grasp of the construction techniques, structures, and decors of past centuries. If some were only to absorb the forms, the outer shells, then others showed extraordinary brio in grappling with the various idioms, thereby forging a genuine Second Empire style. There even emerged a number of truly exceptional minds who undertook a more structured study of the monuments from which they hoped to derive the principles of a modern architecture.

Eclectic Classicism

Right up to the end of the century, antique forms and decoration conserved both their vigor and purity. Certain buildings, such as thermal baths, favored the use of this language, while it can hardly have been a surprise to have observed, rising over the Athens of 1874, a Greek-style Zappeion (or exhibition hall), whose large circular court made from a Doric portal decorated in polychromy was one of the most successful creations of its type. It was built by François-Jean-Florimond Boulanger (1807–1875) and Theophil von Hansen, a specialist in ancient Greece, who, as we have seen, worked in Vienna. Russia, with its strong Neoclassical tradition, continued erecting museums or houses in the style until the 1910s.

In France, the role played by Jacques-Ignace Hittorff (1792–1867) in the rediscovery of the Pompeian style and of the polychrome antique was preponderant. He was, above all, the first to apply such ideas to actual buildings, using polychromy to reinforce, highlight, and enhance his architecture. He sparked a scandal by adorning the facade of the church of Saint-Vincent-de-Paul in Paris in mosaic-like fashion with enameled lava-stone slabs (a shocked Haussmann had them taken down). The architect, however, did have the Cirque Impérial (Cirque d'Hiver; fig. 317) painted in bright colors in 1852. Pompeii and antiquity also breathed again in the "folly" on the Avenue Montaigne commissioned in 1856–58 by the emperor's cousin Prince Jérôme Napoleon from the architect Alfred-Nicolas Normand (1812–1890; fig. 280). For this house, intended to lodge the prince's collections and receive those writers and artists the prince liked to gather round him, Normand used a vast number of replicas executed in situ to recreate the decoration of Pompeii, adding furnishings after pieces conserved in the Museo e Gallerie Nazionali di Capodimonte in Naples; the influential critic and poet

Théophile Gautier was to set his short stories *Arria Marcella* and *Jettatura* in Pompeii. The building was demolished in 1891 and survives only through Normand's plans and Gustave Boulanger's painting, *The Rehearsal of the Flute Player* (*La Répétition du joueur de flûte*).

Polychromy was to become prevalent in architecture and soon spread to apartment buildings and factories alike, before reaching its apotheosis in Charles Garnier's Opéra in Paris and in the creations of Art Nouveau. Pompeian motifs meanwhile were to provide the finishing touches to Second Empire decor.

Italian sixteenth-century classicism remained an influential model. In Paris, Félix Duban with his work for the École des Beaux-Arts and at the Hôtel Pourtalès on Rue Tronchet, as well as Henri Labrouste in the Bibliothèque Sainte-Geneviève, used elements of the idiom with finesse and sobriety. The same is the case in the 1888 Ny Carlsberg Glyptotek in Copenhagen, an Italianizing building designed by Jens Vilhelm Dahlerup (1837–1907), which is enlivened by a polychrome ensemble of red bricks and black marble columns (fig. 289). A further example is the Berlin Kunstgewerbemuseum (Museum of Applied Arts, 1877–88), by Martin Gropius (1824–1909) and Heino Schmieden (1835–?), which successfully kept alive the exceedingly subtle Hellenizing tradition of Karl Friedrich Schinkel. In the United States, too, a refined and consummately self-aware Renaissance spirit was in the air. For the Public Library at Boston (fig. 322), Charles McKim, William Rutherford Mead, and Howard Judson White (1853–1906) drew their inspiration from Labrouste's Bibliothèque Sainte-Geneviève. The monumental scale, the sparse but totally appropriate detailing, and the interior decoration realized by Pierre Puvis de Chavannes (fig. 721), John Singer Sargent, and the sculptor Augustus Saint-Gaudens make the library into a highly felicitous construction.

In the war of styles that opposed classicists and Gothicists, when it came to public buildings it was still difficult to escape from exteriors laid out in the Renaissance style. This George Gilbert Scott (1811–1878) was to learn through bitter experience when, having presented his Gothic designs for the Foreign Office in London, he was told that he should present a Renaissance design. Consequently, Scott "bought some costly books on Italian architecture and set vigorously to work to rub up" his rusty knowledge. The Ministry, built between 1868 and 1873, had a Victorian Renaissance feel. In Paris, Théodore Ballu designed an Église de la Trinité (1861) which was influenced by the Italian and French Renaissance in a style termed "society" and employing "fake" materials such as stucco, imitation marble, and even, for the vault, pasteboard. National movements also came to the fore in Germany, where a vogue for the Renaissance developed characterized by gabled houses built of dark-red brick and adorned with stonework. This was also the case in turn-of-the-century Scandinavia, notably in the Copenhagen City Hall by Martin Nyrop (1849–1921), while at Viborg Hack Kampmann (1856–1920) built a library inspired by that of Labrouste. In Stockholm, Isak Gustav Clason (1856–1936) constructed the Nordiska Museet (1889–1907) in a Nordic Renaissance style more subtle and more refined than that prevalent in Germany.

Artists, however, quickly began to opt for the more sculptural classicism of the seventeenth century over the sixteenth-century Italian Renaissance. For example, at Dresden in 1871, Semper, in his more sober reconstruction of the opera house (1838–41), accentuated the effects, increased the number of orders, juxtaposed roofs, and, in the organization of the interior and the disposition of the volumes, sought to vie with the clarity of Garnier's Paris Opéra. The new Louvre by Visconti and Lefuel had an international impact (figs. 308–10), and the characteristics of seventeenth-century French classicism as reinterpreted by these two architects were to surface on every type of building, from banks and factories to suburban villas. The arrangement of the orders and the balance of the volumes at the Louvre, as illustrated by the large pavilions in the center and to the sides crowned by mansard roofs pitched in straight, concave, or convex lines, reverberated through the architecture of Great Britain, the United States, and Latin America. Hence, as early as 1862, Gridley J. F. Bryant (1816–1899) and Arthur D. Gilman (1821–1882) chose the mansard roof for the City Hall in Boston, while Alfred B. Mullet, in his State, War and Navy Department Building (1871–75), Washington, D.C., produced the finest extant example of the Second Empire manner.

In Britain, the roofs of the great hotels, such as the Grosvenor, were capped with mansards. There exist, however, two unique examples of supremely Second Empire dwellings: Barnard Castle (1869–75) in County Durham by Jules-Auguste Pellechet (1829–1903), and Waddesdon Manor in Buckinghamshire designed by Georges-Hippolyte Destailleur (1822–1893). A return to the Queen Anne style emerges in one of Richard Norman Shaw's (1831–1912) most attractive works, Old Swan House, Chelsea (1876), where he employed modern construction processes.

In Cologne, Julius Raschdorf (1823–1914) designed a high school and a theater (1870–72; destroyed), both in a blatantly French character, complete with mansards. This architect, however, is most often remembered for his neo-Baroque works, since this was the predominant style in Germany in the 1890s.

A highly condensed version of classical vocabulary, together with the influence of Louis XIV's Louvre and its colonnade, are also to be found in the most colossal and most striking eclectic monument ever erected. Dominating the city, the central law courts of Brussels, the Palais de Justice (1861–63), designed by Joseph Poelaert (1817–1879), with its "Babylonian colonnades" and its grandiose vestibules and staircases, its massive dome and "its enormous cornice, one kilometer long," stands in affirmation of the overweening pride of the final years of the nineteenth century. Indeed, as the mayor Jules Anspach was to declare: "The city is committed to one sixth; I want this sixth to cost it as dear as possible so that the law courts are worthy of their purpose and the city where they will be erected" (quoted in Mignot 1983, 160). In London, Shaw reused this classical language at a very late juncture in the colonnade of the Piccadilly Hotel, which was otherwise topped by a high gable with neo-Baroque scrolls.

Quite apart from the vogue for the new Louvre, dreamland châteaus were also to be born of royal nostalgia: standing high above dizzying chasms or encircled by gardens and cascades set in a refined landscape above which they towered, such castles derived as much from national legend as from French classicism. The fantastic castle at Neuschwanstein by Eduard Riedel (1813–1885) and Georg von Dollmann (1830–1895), for example, pays worshipful homage to Wagner and his Nordic myths. Planned by 1868 but only executed from 1878 onward, Herrenchiemsee parrots Versailles, while Linderhof (1870–86) fell in with the waxing neo-Baroque fashion. This movement is illustrated in Germany by Berlin Cathedral (Berliner Dom), as well as by the stiflingly monumental Reichstag by Paul Wallot (1842–1912). In spite of the growing importance of the city even prior to its being proclaimed capital of the Reich in 1871, successive German emperors failed to turn it into a significant example of nineteenth-century town planning, though in the twentieth century it was to be the home of renewal, modernity, and originality.

The Middle Ages

Though the fascination for the Middle Ages had already begun by the end of the eighteenth century under the influence of the Romantic movement, it was during the 1820s that the Romanesque and Gothic styles started to impose themselves.

It was in Great Britain that Gothic first returned to favor. Initially under the impetus of the Catholic movement, promoted by the journal *The Ecclesiologist,* Gothic gained further ground thanks to the contribution of Augustus Welby Northmore Pugin (1812–1852). In 1836 he was appointed to decorate the Palace of Westminster (Houses of Parliament) in London, designed in a Gothic style by Charles Barry. Pugin also brought out two important publications: *Contrasts* (1836) that presents views of the same town in 1440 and 1840, stressing the ugliness of the industrial city and the perfection, refinement, and logic of Gothic, and *Apology for the Present Revival of Christian Architecture in England* (1843), in which he expatiated on the theme of Gothic as the Christian style *par excellence,* approaching Viollet-le-Duc's position in his contention that architectural beauty derives solely from the adaptation of form to function. This brilliant theoretician dreamt of an architecture that might be the fruit of a marriage between art, craft, and technology, and was thus a forerunner of the experiments of the as yet unborn Arts and Crafts movement. Pugin also built some fine churches and designed furniture. In the latter, which is characterized by the use of simple forms, he made no attempt to conceal the methods used to assemble it.

Pugin's ideas were taken up and extended by John Ruskin (1818–1900), who laid stress, in his seminal *Seven Lamps of Architecture* of 1849, on the necessity of a homogeneous style, the antithesis of eclecticism, and proclaimed his detestation of the machine, which he deemed incapable of any beauty. He was close to Viollet-le-Duc in his censure of all deceit in architecture—deceit with regard to internal structure and the true nature of materials, so often covered over by paintings, and with regard to the quality of decoration, that should never be molded or machine-made. Ruskin departed from the Frenchman's line, however, in his empathic and moral reading of the Middle Ages. This spiritual dimension—close to that of Louis-Auguste Boileau (1812–1896)—conflicts with Viollet-le-Duc's profound rationalism. Unlike Viollet-le-Duc, both Ruskin and Pugin, rising up against the industry, technology, and society of their own time, were to extract "moral" value from medieval architecture.

English neo-Gothic became dominant on the international scene in the 1850s. George Gilbert Scott obtained the commission for the Nikolaikirche in Hamburg (1845–63), while Henry Clutton (1819–1893) and William Burges (1827–1881) won the competition for Notre-Dame-de-la-Treille in Lille, in which George Edmund Street (1824–1881) came second, though ultimately none of them was to design the church, for which the French Gothic enthusiast Jean-Baptiste Lassus also presented a plan. English-style Gothic churches were erected in Athens, Istanbul, on the Côte d'Azur in France, in the United States, and in Canada—everywhere in fact with an established Anglican community.

High Victorian Gothic splits into two phases. The first was characterized by the use of color. Polychrome buildings were erected with red and black brick on the exterior as well as within. The finest example is William

Butterfield's (1814–1900) All Saints Church, Margaret Street, in London (1850–53), built in the heart of a working-class district. In his St. James-the-Less (1860–61), Vauxhall Bridge Road, London, Street was vying with Butterfield. Meanwhile, Scott, who owned the largest practice of the time, designed one of the tallest Gothic buildings in the world, the Midland Grand Hotel. Scott was also responsible for the period's benchmark neo-Gothic work, the Albert Memorial (1863–61) in Hyde Park, which Scott himself believed to be his most eminent piece. Built to commemorate the death of Albert, the prince consort, Scott's idea "was to erect a kind of ciborium" encrusted with precious metals and enamel. Granite, marble, polished serpentine in various colors, and gilt bronze contrast with the white marble sculptures that lead the eye up to John Henry Foley's statue of the seated prince (1876) placed beneath a vaulted baldachino covered in a garishly colored glass mosaic.

Ruskin, in constant contact with these artists, was to exert considerable sway over them. *The Stones of Venice* (1851), in which he advocates the study of Italian Gothic, provided confirmation for these architects of their ideas about the use of color. In 1868, Street, who had published his *Brick and Marble Architecture of the Middle Ages in Italy* in 1855, designed London's Royal Courts of Justice in a Gothic style smacking somewhat of thirteenth-century French models. Thanks to Ruskin, the Irish architects Thomas Deane (1792–1871) and Benjamin Woodward (1815–1861) presented a Venetian Gothic design for the University Museum in Oxford, the most interesting aspect of which is the extensive court roofed by a heavily articulated structure in glass and iron of the kind Ruskin loathed (fig. 331).

By the onset of the 1860s, there had began a second, more severe phase linked to the ideas propounded by the architects of the Arts and Crafts movement, Edward William Godwin (1835–1886), Philip Webb (1831–1915), and William Burges. A calm and regular overall plan combined with a sense of medieval craftsmanship characterized the works of these artists, and Godwin's earliest offerings, the town halls of Northampton (1861–64) and Congleton (1864–67), are of the highest quality. For the painter Whistler, Godwin concocted one of the most original facades of the decade, composed entirely of white-painted bricks with the windows and doors arranged asymmetrically. It displayed a knowledge of and a taste for the arts of Japan that heralded a movement of architectural renewal yet to come (fig. 288).

Other countries continued, rather late in the day, to build in the Gothic style, with examples such as the Parliament of Ottawa (1861–67) and the Munich Rathaus (city hall, 1867–74). One of the last and most successful of these constructions appeared in Budapest: Imre Steidl's (1839–1902) Országház (Parliament, 1882–1903) on the banks of the Danube. This building's harmonious volumes, variety of roofing, and delicate detailing are a delight to the eye (fig. 321).

In the Netherlands, Petrus Josephus Hubertus Cuypers (1827–1921), Holland's counterpart to Viollet-le-Duc, carried out a lot of restoration work on Gothic churches, erecting in addition a number of his own. His most celebrated works, which rank among the most important of the nineteenth century, are the Rijksmuseum (1877–85) and Amsterdam's main train station (1881–89). These are close to German and Scandinavian Renaissance models, yet with a lighter touch.

In France, meanwhile, enthusiasm for the Middle Ages was supported by such erudite historians as Arcisse de Caumont (1801–1873), who published an *Essai sur l'architecture du Moyen Age* as early as 1823, and by archaeologists such as Adolphe-Napoléon Didron (1806–1867), who founded the *Annales archéologiques* in 1841. Restoration work was also an opportunity to gain appreciation of medieval building. The Inspection des Monuments Historiques was set up in 1830 and the Comité des Monuments Historiques followed in 1837, the architecture enthusiast and author of *Carmen*, Prosper Mérimée, being appointed *inspecteur général*. The rekindling of the Catholic faith, the choice of a religious building style, and the weariness felt by a growing number of architects with the classical vocabulary led them to turn to one of the finest periods of Christian art, the Middle Ages. Jean-Michel Leniaud has rightly stressed the thorough-going revolution represented by "the arrival of the Middle Ages onto an entirely classical cultural scene, an entrance that can be compared to that of Japan prior to Impressionism and tribal art prior to Cubism" (Leniaud 1980, 3). The fact that the logic of Gothic construction was demonstrable, that its sources lay in Gallic soil, and that—unlike Greco-Roman monuments—it suited the French climate ensured that it carried the day. Naturally, many architects did little but ransack its forms, but exceptional talents, such as Jean-Baptiste Lassus (1807–1857) and Eugène-Emmanuel Viollet-le-Duc (1814–1879), were to put the spirit of Gothic above its outward forms. Viollet-le-Duc, pushing the analysis of Gothic still further, went on to derive from it the logical rules that were to govern the architecture of the future.

Romanesque art also had its champions. In 1845 in Nîmes, Charles-Auguste Questel (1807–1888) built the first neo-Romanesque church, Saint-Paul, but between 1840 and 1860 few others were erected. Théodore Ballu employed the style at Saint-Ambroise, Paris (1865) and Léon Ginain (1825–1898) took inspiration from it in his Notre-Dame-des-Champs, Paris (1867–75). Romanesque, which was occasionally affected by borrowings from the Orient, or from Italy or Sicily, also harked back to provincial French schools. Léon Vaudoyer (1803–1872), for example, appointed architect for the cathedral of Marseille in 1850, drew up a structured plan incorporating

Byzantine domes that referred—in its alternating multicolored courses—both to Italy and to the Romanesque school of the Auvergne. He built Sainte-Marie-Majeure above a terrace supported by arcades, thus proclaiming the Eastern roots of the city to those approaching it from the sea (fig. 327). In 1865, still in Marseille, and in a similar vein, Henri Espérandieu (1829–1874) designed Notre-Dame-de-la-Garde (1865). This Romanesque-cum-Byzantine style culminated in the creations of Paul Abadie (1812–1884), notably the Sacré-Coeur in Paris. The Assemblée Nationale decreed the construction of the basilica in 1873 (erected by national pledges of subscription and called the Église du Voeu Nationale), the foundation stone being laid in 1875. It was largely complete before the end of the century under the direction of Lucien Magne (1849–1916), but the interior as it was finally to appear dates from 1910. This pilgrimage church marries elements from the East and Venice and also from one of the Romanesque churches Abadie himself restored, Saint-Front at Périgueux. Although it was strongly inspired by archaeological models, it has to be said that the white outline with its crop of domes high on the hill of Montmartre does provide Paris with a fitting crown.

In his design for the basilica Notre-Dame de Fourvière, whose colossal mass dominates the city of Lyon, Pierre Bossan (1814–1888) exhibited a more personal style (fig. 326). "Bossan held that architecture should above all seek unity, strike a dominant—but that it should also engineer contrasts and rise to a crescendo, the upper parts of a building being made the most ornate" (Hautecœur 1957, 218–19). Recesses, arcades, galleries, polygonal towers with Oriental-style battlements, pediments adorned with reliefs on a golden ground, an interior scintillating with reflections of gold, copper, and marble all show Bossan's taste (one he shared with Garnier at the Opéra) for the picturesque and for a vivid polychromy that make Fourvière into a building apart, which, unlike the Sacré-Coeur, was never imitated.

"Forests were the first temples to the Divine and it was from forests that men took their formative notions of architecture. This art thus was to vary according to climate . . . The forests of the Gauls passed in turn into the temples of our forefathers, and our oak woods conserved their sacred origins. These vaults chiseled into leaves that shoulder the walls and end suddenly like broken tree trunks, the freshness of the vaults, the obscurity of the sanctuary, the dark aisles, the secret passages, the squat doors—everything in the Gothic church retraces our mazelike woods, everything makes one sense the religious awe, the mysteries and the divine." From Chateaubriand's brand of Romanticism there arose the idea of a Gothic originating in France, peculiar to its climate, and whose logic of construction its architects were soon to demonstrate. If many recalled the forms of the style and nothing else, Jean-Baptiste Lassus made rational use of it, never losing sight, however, of its poetry and mystery, and exploiting in his interiors both perspective and light. The authoritative restorer at both the Sainte-Chapelle and Notre-Dame in Paris, he was to emerge triumphant from the "battle of the Gothic" with his Saint-Nicolas in Nantes, before confirming his victory in the Sacré-Coeur at Moulins and in the church of Saint-Jean-Baptiste at Belleville (1834–50). The regularity of plan, the drive for simplicity, the elements gleaned from the cathedrals of the first half of the thirteenth century (his favorite being Chartres) occasionally make for a somewhat dry Gothic. An advocate of the total unity of the arts—the motto he chose during the competition for Notre-Dame-de-la-Treille was "Eclecticism is the scourge of art"—Lassus also designed the ecclesiastical furniture, goldwork, decorative ironwork, and liturgical ornaments for his churches and remains the artist who best managed to reconcile history, mysticism, and reason.

Viollet-le-Duc and Rationalism

A complex and rounded personality, a man of the world, Viollet-le-Duc was without question the most famous and most controversial architect of the century. Vehemently opposed to the training given at the École des Beaux-Arts and to the type of architecture furthered by the Grand Prix de Rome, he rose up against the dominant eclecticism of the period and strove to establish the rule of reason over the construction, decoration, and restoration of ancient monuments.

In contradistinction to Ruskin, who rejected restoration and advocated in its place the mere maintenance of ruins, Viollet-le-Duc was to hammer out a method and a theory. Crisscrossing France, he made endless drawings, classifying styles, types, and categories. He then progressed—prior to any decision—to trying to grasp the construction, the balance, and the logic of how the building to be safeguarded actually functioned, as well as its originality and artistic merit. The same methods were applied to the restoration of sculpture—drawings and the making of an impression or mold, followed by the removal of the damaged elements, which were later reproduced in fresh stone. The earliest of these restoration projects—a masterstroke for a young man of only twenty-six—was the church of the Madeleine at Vézelay, while the enormous site of Notre-Dame in Paris was to occupy him from 1843 to 1867. In addition, he worked at Amiens, Beaune, Carcassonne, and many others places.

The most astonishing of these restoration-cum-building projects remains the Château de Pierrefonds, near Compiègne in northern France (fig. 257). In addition to completing the parts of the château already begun—primarily the exterior—Viollet-le-Duc also applied his extraordinary formal imagination to the painted and carved decoration, taken from the world of plants as well as from a fantastical and humorous bestiary. Monsters concealed the water spouts, scurried across the paneling in the hall in the keep, and snaked over the Gothic-inspired furniture which the architect also designed. In the interior decoration Viollet-le-Duc made extensive use of color, which for him was not only a way of underlining structure and form, but was also, like light, a way of modeling space. This exceptional understanding of medieval culture also found expression in his dictionaries: the *Dictionnaire raisonné du mobilier français de l'époque carlovingienne à nos jours* (1858–74) and the *Dictionnaire raisonné de l'architecture française du XIe au XVIe siècle* (1854–68), which earned Ruskin's rueful remark: "I should have been the one to write such a book." Every architect delved into this work and extracted things worthy of reflection up to the time of Frank Lloyd Wright, who wrote in his autobiography that at the time of his training he believed that the *Dictionnaire raisonné* was the only intelligent book of architecture, the one which, in spite of the example of other architects, had encouraged him to keep faith with the art. In 1863, the *Entretiens sur l'architecture* ratified Viollet-le-Duc's position as a precursor who made constant appeal to logic and placed spirit above form. "Any form whose rationale it is impossible to explain can never be beautiful" (Viollet-le-Duc 1863, 1:304). A form is only beautiful when it corresponds to its function, and, since needs evolve with civilization and technology, forms as well as decoration must conform to the demands of programs and materials. Moreover, decoration is not something distinct from structure but is in fact an expression of it, drawing exclusively on a vocabulary of natural forms, both flora and fauna. This is surely the equivalent of Louis Henry Sullivan's celebrated phrase some fifty years later: "Form follows function."

Viollet-le-Duc, who loathed symmetry and pastiche, proposed that the study of yesterday's works be a search for its spirit. "Taste is respect for truth . . . To possess taste is to love truth, to know how to express it simply, to reject exaggeration which is always a sham . . . Make form into a vehicle for an idea, and you will prove to be an artist of taste." The builder of churches (Saint-Denis-de-l'Estrée, Aillant-sur-Tholon), of modest châteaus, and of Paris apartment blocks expended all his energy on adhering to the program, on dealing with practical details and blending the historical references so dear to his heart in an original way.

Several of Viollet-le-Duc's disciples, such as Joseph Vaudremer (1829–1914), sought to apply his principles. Vaudremer's Saint-Pierre at Montrouge (1864–70) is built in a style which blends Romanesque and paleo-Christian elements and has considerable structural finesse and highly simplified detailing. The Santé prison (1865–85, fig. 296) owes much to his teacher, Gilbert. This building, in keeping with all his secular edifices, notably the Lycée Buffon in Paris, has a simple and functional plan. Vaudremer's work influenced Henry Hobson Richardson (1838–1886), who was to forge a massive and muscular style using Romanesque forms (Trinity Church, Boston).

A similar rationalism appears in the work of Anatole de Baudot (1834–1915), notably his Lycée Victor Hugo in Paris and the Lycée Lakanal at nearby Sceaux. This theoretician, however, in defending his rationalist and functionalist ideas, stirred up such a wave of hostility that few commissions came his way. His great work, the church of Saint-Jean de Montmartre, was the first to use reinforced cement, which he left exposed. Viollet-le-Duc's rationalist theories were later developed by Jules Guadet (1834–1880) in his important work *Éléments d'architecture.*

The "Beaux-Arts" Style

If Viollet-le-Duc, for one, refused to study at the École des Beaux-Arts, exclaiming that "the school is a mold for turning out architects and they are practically all the same when they leave it," this was not an opinion shared by the foreign students who came in droves from 1850 onward to learn how to draw up a large-scale plan, to arrange architectural masses, to employ the architectural idioms of the past, and to master the techniques of draftsmanship. In 1846, Richard Morris Hunt became the first American to matriculate at the school, joining the studio of Lefuel, who, in 1854, entrusted him with certain tasks on the site of the new Louvre. Once back in the United States, Hunt became a most influential architect, exhibiting a preference in the numerous houses he designed for the late Gothic or the early French Renaissance style typical of the Loire châteaus. Henry Hobson Richardson, a student of Jules André (1819–1890), worked in conjunction with Théodore Labrouste on the Ivry asylum in the Seine *département* (1799–1885), while Louis Henry Sullivan, William Augustus Ottis (1855–1929), Edward H. Bennett (1874–1954), and William Holabird were also to make their way to Paris to study. The studios of Victor Laloux (1850–1937) and Léon Ginain were also particularly popular. Moreover, the

Massachusetts Institute of Technology in Boston (1865) and Columbia University, New York, the first two architecture schools in the United States, both opened by William Ware (1832–1915), were modeled on the École des Beaux-Arts. This influence also extended to Latin America, where the role of French architects was preeminent.

One of the most astonishing and richest countries in terms of palatial buildings was Turkey. Devastated by a fire in 1870, Istanbul issued an appeal to France. In 1873 Haussmann, accompanied by a team of architects and engineers, made his way to Turkey. Architects of every nationality assisted in the rebuilding of the city, but the architectural landscape was dominated by a single family, the Balyans. Nikogos Balyan (1826–1866), former student of Henri Labrouste, an architect, engineer, and talented interior decorator, in collaboration with his father Karabet Balyan (1800–1886), erected the majority of the most impressive buildings in Istanbul. Their best-known works are the palaces situated on the shores of the Bosporus: Dolma Batce (1844–56, fig. 320) on the European side, a mix of Renaissance and Baroque design, transformed by an Ottoman atmosphere and scale; Beylerbeyi, all white marble; and Göksu (1856) on the Asian shore. The most celebrated official French artists were employed in their interior decoration.

In 1861, the competition for the commission to rebuild the new Paris opera house was won by Charles Garnier, the epitome of the Beaux-Arts student, only thirty-six years old and at the time unknown (fig. 312). Empress Eugénie voiced her disappointment at the elimination of her personal favorite, Viollet-le-Duc, and her observations at the presentation of Garnier's plans are recorded. "What style is that? It's no style at all. It's not Greek, it's not Louis XV, it's not Louis XVI." "No," replied Garnier, "those styles have had their time. This is Napoleon III, and yet you complain." The foundation stone was laid in 1862 and the facades raised in 1867, but, the war having interrupted building work, the Opéra was only inaugurated on January 5, 1875. This extensive building site formed part of Haussmann's urban plan. He had decided on a location for the opera house as early as 1858, but Garnier was to spurn the architectural characteristics of the period, favoring the curved over the straight line, the picturesque over the regular, and ornamental exuberance over austerity. He composed a sonorous polychromy of marble and porphyry in green and pink, making the bronzes glimmer and the copper dome sparkle. It all contrasted strongly with the sober gray of Haussmann's great blocks (fig. 122). Situated in the heart of a business quarter near the main railroad stations and traffic arteries, the Opéra seems to correspond well to Théophile Gautier's description: "A worldly cathedral to civilization."

The masterly plan of the Opéra is rational and perfectly clear, even to someone simply walking past, owing to the composition and staggered placing of the masses and to the interplay between the roofs (fig. 283). Other qualities of the building include the harmonious relationship between the different parts, combined with the scale and generosity of the interior space. Garnier deliberately chose to lay out the auditorium in an undemonstrative manner so as not to distract the audience from listening to the music. He concentrated his efforts on the foyer and staircase, surrounding the dazzled spectator with a grandiose space. The Opéra was also one of the finest examples of a synthesis of the arts, since Garnier, keen to integrate all spheres of creativity, supervised the schemes of the painters, sculptors, stuccoists, and mosaicists. He was at once heir to a tradition of theater architecture and the harbinger of a new style.

In 1878, Garnier was commissioned to build a new theater for the casino of Monte Carlo. This building, like all his designs—the casino and baths at Vittel, the Cercle de la Librairie in Paris, his villas in Bordhigera—has a monumental quality, a feeling for color and the sweeping gesture, and the same rationality he had put to such good use in the Paris Opéra. These qualities inspired one of his Hungarian pupils, Reszó Lajos Ray (1845–1899), in his design for the Szent Lukash Hotel in Budapest. Garnier's style had its adepts and the Opéra swiftly became the model to follow. The same terraced roof can be seen in the theater by Alphonse Gosset (1835–1914) in Reims, and certain aspects of the overall design and decoration are evident in the Cristobal Colon Theater in Buenos Aires, although the latter was in the Renaissance style. A theater was built in Rio de Janeiro which amounted to a tribute to Charles Garnier.

But who could hope to equal Garnier's facility, assurance, and rationality, or the Romanticism, the colorful dream, the strange and poetical character of the Paris Opéra?

ARCHITECTURE IN METAL

"Architecture is an art on which science and technology can have direct and significant effects, since it owes to them its very existence and so much of its expressive means." This observation by the architect and engineer Léonce Reynaud (1803–1880), designer of the first Gare du Nord in Paris, seems particularly appropriate to architecture in metal, which attained its apogee during the second half of the nineteenth century. Metal had already been put to architectural use in preceding centuries, but only to a limited extent, since iron ore had at that time to be smelted over charcoal before being hand-worked at the forge. Due to the technological progress brought about by the Industrial Revolution, which had begun in mid-eighteenth-century Great Britain, the price of metal was soon competing with that of wood. Metal was to find its place in three main manifestations. The first of these was cast iron, produced by the process of coke smelting developed in 1709. Cast iron was brittle and ruptured under traction, but it was discovered to be a perfect material for supports since it was sixty times more resistant than limestone. It was thus employed for colonettes and posts, while molded it could serve as an important element in decoration. The second major use of metal was in the form of wrought iron, a form of iron with a very low carbon content. Wrought iron became the preferred material for frames and bridges since its tensile strength is ten times that of timber and twenty times that of stone. Finally, there was the "metal of the future," steel, which only came into use at the end of the nineteenth century because it remained costly, even after Sir Henry Bessemer had contrived a converter capable of producing it in sufficient quantities in 1856.

For architects, however, the essential quality of metal was its incombustibility, the dangers linked to the heat conductance and torsion of the material being appreciated only later. Hence, as early as 1778, the wooden framework and roof timbers of the Salon Carré in the Louvre were replaced by iron. Then, in 1811, following a fire, the dome of the former wheat market (the Bourse du Commerce) was replaced by one in cast iron. Metal was occasionally pressed into service for restoration work: the new roof members of Chartres Cathedral were in iron faced in copper, while Rouen Cathedral's spire was built of openwork cast iron.

Covered Spaces

"The most basic characteristic of modern architecture is its large surface area. No civilization has demanded more than ours the covering of such vast spaces" (Viollet-le-Duc 1872, 2:110). Remaining in the background during the first years of the century, metal soon soared in popularity, thanks not only to technological progress but also because the onset of trade on an international scale brought the need for architecture that could satisfy the new demand for urban railroad stations, covered markets and halls, stores, monumental glazed roofs, exhibition centers, and factories—all constructions that shared a common need for ever vaster, unemcumbered, and unrestricted spaces, with few supporting members. Metal was flexible, strong, and resistant, yet it was also light, requiring fewer supports and less substantial foundations. In addition, it permitted greater transparency. In short, it was the perfect solution to the problem. Combined with advances in glassmaking, which allowed larger surfaces to be obtained, the use of metal gave rise to ever vaster covered areas, the apotheosis being reached with the international exhibitions.

The "Poetry of Railroad Stations"

"This year, Monet has exhibited some superb station interiors. There one can hear the rumbling of the trains steaming in, one can see the clouds of smoke belching out beneath the vast hangers," wrote Émile Zola in 1877, contemplating the series of seven canvases Monet devoted to the Gare Saint-Lazare in Paris (1841–42) designed by Alfred Armand (1805–1888) and the engineer Eugène Flachat (1802–1893). The railroad system grew rapidly and the tidal wave of passengers and merchandise created a need for ever larger stations. Engineers and architects were required to devise trusses of ever greater span that did not require ties, so as to keep the space as uncluttered as possible. To this need was added the desire to integrate stations into the urban space: in London, Lewis Cubitt's (1799–1883) idea was to stress the industrial mission of Kings Cross Station (1851–52), while, fifteen years later in 1868, the engineer William H. Barlow for St. Pancras threw up from ground level a series of drop arches, covering in a single span 73 meters—a feat that was to remain unequaled until 1889. Gilbert Scott was to clad this superb nave in Italianizing neo-Gothic stonework of great fluency, which housed the Midland Grand Hotel. French architects meanwhile proclaimed the presence of their stations by the great arc of the glazed roof, as François-Alexandre Duquesney (1790–1849) was to do at the Gare de l'Est in Paris, whose central rose window is flanked by a pair of porticoes. For the Gare du Nord, rebuilt from 1861 to 1864, Jacques-Ignace Hittorff chose a triple nave borne by two files of cast-iron colonettes echoed in the facade by three glazed arches of decreasing size underscored by Ionic pilasters and surmounted by a pediment and statues. It was a design that provoked criticism from the rationalists, not least from Anatole de Baudot, who lamented the sight of "a new work, a creation of the nineteenth century, presenting itself in a classical guise." Stations increased in size, leading to notable technological advances. Frankfurt Station (1885–87) by Johann W. Schwedler, for example, was a forerunner of the Galerie des Machines at the 1889 Exposition Universelle, with its arches descending at the base to hinged joints at the exact point where the stress is transmitted. Stations also became increasingly palatial, borrowing their overall design from the thermae of antiquity. In the Gare d'Orsay, built for the 1900 Exposition Universelle and designed by Victor Laloux (1850–1937), this is clearly the case, though the trend developed in an even more spectacular way in America (Pennsylvania Station, New York, 1906).

It was extremely rare for architects to choose to build stations that actually emphasized their iron-and-glass structure, though this is precisely what Gustave Eiffel (1832–1923) did at the West Station in Budapest (1875–77): "This station is particularly noteworthy in that it represents one of the first examples of blending metal and stonework and in that the decorative elements are formed in the main by leaving the metal parts exposed" (Eiffel, *Biographie industrielle et scientifique,* 1923).

"Metal Babylon"

On August 4, 1845, the task of rebuilding the country's covered markets—one that had already been tabled in the time of Napoleon I—was delegated to Victor Baltard, assisted by Félix Callet (1791–1855) and the engineer César Joly. His plans were submitted by June 1848, but it was only in 1851 that the prince president was to lay the foundation stone for Paris's central market halls, the Halles (fig. 297). A controversy flared up as soon as the projects were published, since the architects had proposed building in stone. The emperor, impressed by the iron-built nave of the Gare Saint-Lazare (1841–42)—a 40-meter span without uprights, a feat that nobody, not even the English, had achieved—was a fervent champion of metal and of the plans presented by a much misunderstood talent, Hector Horeau (1801–1872). On June 22, 1853, Napoleon III called a halt to work on the first stone-built pavilion to which Parisians had given the derisive nickname of the "Fort de la Halle" (in allusion to its thickset appearance reminiscent both of a fortress and of the muscular Parisian costermongers called *forts des halles*). He voiced his opinion to Haussmann: "I need huge umbrellas, nothing more," and passed him some rough sketches of what was required. Haussmann recounts in his *Mémoires* how difficult it was to persuade Baltard, a "hardened classicist" who was opposed to using metal. It took sixteen years to finish the Halles, which comprised two groups of pavilions set around a wide transverse road and separated by byways crisscrossing the road, all covered by high roofs with tall gables. Taken down in 1973, all that remains of this "cast-iron giant" is a pavilion reerected at Nogent-sur-Marne and the descriptions by Zola: "The shadows, dozing in the crevices of the roof, exaggerated the forest of pillars, multiplied to infinity the delicate ribs and fillets of the structure, the fretted balconies, the transparent jalousies. And there, high up above this town, and far into the shadows, was springing a rich vegetation, a fine flowering, a monstruous jungle of metal, whose stalks and stems rising in twisted patterns and branches forcing into knots and clusters covered an entire world with the light and sable leafage of an age-old forest . . . It looked like the outlines of houses and palaces that overlapped, a metal Babylon of Hindu lightness, crisscrossed by hanging terraces, aerial corridors, flying bridges thrown over the void" (Zola 1873, 621 *et seq.*; 1958, 26 *et seq.*).

Universally admired, becoming a model for architecture worldwide, the Halles were the occasion for Viollet-le-Duc to see his rationalist theories borne out: "I would refer in the first place to the Halles Centrales in Paris that unhesitatingly proclaim the function allotted to such grand constructions. I am of the firm belief that if all our monuments were erected with such total respect for the needs and habits of the population, if they were as readily to adopt the same means of construction, they would have a character specific to our own time, and, what is more, they would be endowed with a form both beautiful and rational" (Viollet-le-Duc 1872, 1:323). Baltard was, however, to show himself far less innovative at Saint-Augustin in Paris (1860–71), whose entirely metal skeleton was wrapped in a stonework envelope with hints of the Romanesque style (fig. 255).

Arcades and Department Stores

In a desire to put commerce as it were "in the limelight," to present their products in the best possible conditions and—through a multiplicity of attractions—to lure in the customer, tradesmen began congregating in bright and cheerful galleries soon to be known as arcades, which were to meet with a wave of popularity in the first half of the century. About 1840, the number in Paris alone had reached around one hundred, but their growth was blocked by Haussmann's road-building projects and the opening of the *grands boulevards.* The few that were built in France swelled still more in size. The Passage Pommeraye in Nantes, designed by Hippolyte Durand-Gasselin, was composed of two stories of galleries richly decorated with brightly colored columns and allegorical statues. In Brussels, the Galerie Saint-Hubert by Jean-Pierre Cluysenaer (1811–1880) remains one of the largest and best maintained. While in 1867 Hector Horeau dreamt of roofing the boulevards of Paris, in Milan, between 1865 and 1877, Giuseppe Mengoni (1829–1877) was realizing a genuine covered avenue, the Galleria Vittorio-Emanuele, which entailed enlarging the Piazza del Duomo and straightening the Piazza della Scala. Laid out in the shape of a Latin cross set around an octagonal central rotunda, its impressive dimensions, its ostentatious luxury, its vast portal in the form of a triumphal arch all commanded admiration. Its influence was apparent in the Galleria Umberto I in Naples, as well as at the Kaisergalerie in Berlin (destroyed). At Genoa, the Galleria Mazzini (1871) surpassed in size every European arcade erected in the first half of the century. In Moscow, the GUM galleries (State Department Store) by Aleksandr Pomerantsev and R. I. Klein were a compromise between covered passageway, Eastern bazaar, and department store (1888–93).

Department stores developed at much the same time, though independently, in the United States and in Paris. One of the first, Au Bon Marché, opened in 1852 in Paris, and was to become the supreme model of the genre. Founded by Aristide Boucicaut, it was to expand in 1869 and again between 1872 and 1874, under the direction of Louis-Charles Boileau (1837–1914), employing a metal framework supplied by the firms of Armand Moisant and Gustave Eiffel. Émile Zola took this store as his inspiration for the novel *Au bonheur des dames,* published in 1883, describing it as a "cathedral to modern trade, solid and light, built for a horde of women customers," clear and well lit, crisscrossed by narrow footbridges. Following La Belle Jardinière (1866) and La Samaritaine (1869), it was Paul Sédille's (1836–1900) new Printemps, rebuilt in 1881 after the first store had burnt down in 1865, which, with its light-well extending from the ground level up to the roof, was long to remain the prototype, exhibiting for the first time a non-load-bearing wall, a stone envelope on which nothing bore down, the load being supported by the metal construction alone. Polychrome marbles, enamelware, and richly ornamented stained-glass windows added to the dazzling opulence of the building. Le Printemps became the model to which all Parisian, provincial French (Nouvelles Galeries, Bordeaux, 1893), and European stores were to adhere.

Greenhouses

Greenhouses, those veritable "gardens under glass," were soon to do away with their outer stonework shell once and for all. First appearing in Great Britain about 1815, they remained much in vogue during the Second Empire and were used to enhance even private town houses and middle-class homes. The great glasshouses of the Museum d'Histoire Naturelle in Paris, designed in 1833 by Charles Rohault de Fleury (1801–1875), established a blueprint for all iron-framed greenhouses, from the conservatories created by Horeau in Lyon and in the capital (both destroyed) to the constructions erected from 1898 onward by Jean-Camille Formigé (1845–1927) for the *fleuriste municipal* at Auteuil near Paris. The finest example occurs at the botanical gardens at Laeken, designed by Alphonse Balat (1818–1895) in 1875, which possesses Europe's largest glass rotunda (fig. 328). A place for promenading and entertainment, the glasshouse soon also became a new stage for social life—one that was totally transparent and had all the luminosity of the open air.

The creations born of engineering seemed to provide a means of escape, a way out from the stylistic impasse of the end of the century. Since in metal everything seemed possible, some people proclaimed the demise of construction in stone. The extraordinary pavilions that rose in the very middle of the international exhibitions were hardly likely to dampen such positivistic enthusiasm, this firm belief in progress that would bring with it a life of beauty and freedom. Nor would such structures undermine the desire to forge an alliance between art and industry, a dream sustained by all the expressions of Art Nouveau.

The International Exhibitions

The idea of a peaceful international forum for comparing trade, industry, and the fine arts originated in the 1840s and was realized in 1851 with the Great Exhibition in London. An international competition was held for the commission to build a hall designed to house the products "of all nations." Some 245 plans were received, two attracting the jury's attention in particular, one by Hector Horeau and the other by Richard Turner (1798–1881), a specialist in greenhouses and the designer of the Palm House at Kew Gardens with Decimus Burton. The committee, however, decided to develop the project by Joseph Paxton (1803–1865), who had earlier made his name as the designer of the iron and glass conservatory at Chatsworth. Paxton conceived a gigantic oblong pavilion in cast iron and glass measuring 563 by 124 meters. It was flat-ceilinged, save for the transepts round which the galleries were arranged. These were covered with semicircular vaults so that space might be made for a few of Hyde Park's great trees. Thanks to the standardizing and prefabrication of all the structural elements and ornaments, the building was erected in a mere six months. Owen Jones (1809–1874), specialist in polychrome and familiar with Eugène Chevreul's recent discovery of simultaneous chromatic contrast, opted for white and blue for the exterior, while the interior was laid out in the three primary colors: yellow for the curved surfaces, blue for the trussed girders, and red for the joists supporting the glass roof, separated by areas left white. The Crystal Palace was a monument of great novelty and symbolic value by dint of its transparency, its grandiose dimensions, and the modernity of its construction. It stimulated numerous more or less successful imitations, such as the Glasplast in Munich (1854; destroyed) or the New York Crystal Palace (burnt down in the 1858 fire), built in 1853 in a mediocre Orientalizing style. Paxton's Crystal Palace, rebuilt at Sydenham Hill between 1852 and 1854, was gutted by fire in 1936. Fortunately, photographs, drawings, and paintings such as Pissarro's canvas of 1870 give an idea of what it looked like.

The first Exposition Universelle to be held in Paris took place in 1855. The aim was to erect a monumental construction built to last. The Palais de l'Industrie, located at the lower end of the Champs-Élysées, by the architect Jean-Michel Viel (1796–1863) and the engineer Alexis Barrault (1812–1867), combined somewhat lamely a triple nave in metal with a 48-meter span (compared with 22 meters at the Crystal Palace) and a stone facade with triumphal entrances. Until its destruction to make way for the Grand and Petit Palais built for the 1900 exhibition (fig. 267), the Palais de l'Industrie was the site of the Salon des Beaux-Arts. The 1867 exhibition was a celebration of the power of the Second Empire. An oval-plan edifice formed by seven concentric galleries was built to house the products of both industry and art. It was designed by the engineer Jean-Baptiste Krantz (1817–1899) with the assistance of the architect Léopold Hardy (1829–1894). The 1878 exhibition asserted France's attempts to recover from the defeat of the Franco-Prussian war and was a defining moment for architecture in cast iron and glass. Also, it was the first time ceramic decoration had been employed on such a large scale. The galleries, arranged in a rectangle 300 meters wide by 725 meters deep, covered the entirety of the Champ-de-Mars.

The high point of architecture in iron dates from 1889 with the 300-meter Eiffel Tower, designed by Gustave Eiffel (figs. 292, 293), and the Galerie des Machines (actually named the Palais des Machines), designed by the architect Ferdinand Dutert (1845–1906) and the engineer Victor Contamin (1840–1898). The latter developed trusses capable of spanning the 110.60 meters without struts or ties, articulated at the base and summit, allowing for a flexible and balanced response to the stresses and strains involved. The novelist Joris-Karl Huysmans was to describe this exhibition hall for industrial machinery in his anthology of art criticism, *Certains* (1889): "The interior of the *palais* is indeed superb. Picture a colossal gallery, wider than any ever seen before, higher than the tallest nave, a gallery surging upward from a cluster of arch ribs, describing something like a pointed semicircular arch, like an overblown rib vault, with its famous apexes meeting beneath an unbounded sky of glass . . . The room borrows its form from Gothic art, but has been burst open, inflated in size, unhinged—impossible to achieve in stone and so original with the calyxlike bases of its great arches . . . It is to be acknowledged that, from an artistic point of view, the gallery constitutes the most admirable creation ever attempted by metallurgy" (Huysmans 1889, 179–80). In 1900, there followed the splendid enclosed space of the Grand Palais. Designed to house the Salon des Beaux-Arts, it also served as a space for automobile exhibitions, agricultural show stands, and horse shows. It is framed by an imposing Neoclassical facade 20 meters high and 240 meters long, decorated with mosaics, sculptures, and reliefs. The Galerie des Machines, destroyed in 1910, also fired the imagination of the sculptor Raymond Duchamp-Villon: "Thus it was that nobody knew nor dared to defend against speculation a work that was all power and boldness, that shouted loud and clear the glory of steel in a fantastic hall: the Galerie des Machines. Built for the 1889 Exhibition, its memory colors our earliest impressions of social life and I can still clearly see in the clarity of the immense nave the hallucinatory motion of the traveling crane above the whirling flywheels, the reptilian belts, among all the screeching, the whistles and sirens, surging up from the black holes made of disks, pyramids, and cubes" (Duchamp-Villon, "L'architecture et le fer," November 1913).

Bridges

Ever since the first cast-iron structure erected over the Severn River at Coalbrookdale in Shropshire, in 1777, which looked like a stone humpback bridge jointed like wood with mortises and tenons, Great Britain had stolen a march in bridge-building. The engineer Thomas Telford (1757–1834) built large bridges suspended by iron chains, such as the Menai Bridge in Wales (1819–24). This system was perfected in the United States, where John Augustus Roebling (1806–1869) built a spectacular construction suspended high above Niagara Falls from cables, to be followed by the great Brooklyn Bridge (1883), completed by his son Washington Augustus Roebling (1837–1926). Arched bridges were to lead both to the finest (such as those of Gustave Eiffel) and most bizarre examples. The latter include a bridge at Hamburg (1868–72), which consists of two undulating lines that crossed over at each pylon, and the Forth Bridge over the Firth of Forth near Edinburgh (1882–90), by Benjamin Baker and John Fowler. The construction techniques utilized in these increasingly sophisticated bridges yielded discoveries that served both for the great pavilions at the international exhibitions and the development of skyscrapers.

Gustave Eiffel, a Magician in Iron

Eiffel, though no pioneer in the use of metal, greatly furthered its development, exploiting its lightness, simplicity, strength, and monumentality. It was of course the 300-meter tower, the climax of the 1889 Exposition Universelle, that made him famous (figs. 292, 293). In 1867, he set up his own business, the Société des Établissements Eiffel at Levallois-Perret, northwest of Paris, receiving commissions for numerous metal bridges and for metal frameworks for buildings at the exhibition of 1878, for the Bon Marché department store, for the large glass roof of the Crédit Lyonnais, and for the *Statue of Liberty*, sculpted by Bartholdi (fig. 2).

The business's bread and butter, however, were the bridges that could be dismantled and transported, a stock of which was always held at Levallois. They were used the world over, from Bolivia to Cochinchina, and the brochure brought out by the company in 1884 boasts of their advantages: "All the components of these bridges are exceptionally lightweight, as much due to the system used as to the choice of metal, in this case exclusively steel. Transportation presents no difficulty whatever the road surface as ordinary vehicles may be used. Installation is extremely easy and can be performed by workmen from the locality without any special skills. Permanent siting is also an easy task, no special framework being required. The bridge is assembled on one bank and, by using a pierhead supplied by the firm of Eiffel, the bridge once built is pushed across the river to its permanent site."

The earliest prestigious work following the great viaducts of the river Sioule was the Maria Pia Bridge (1875–77) across the river Douro at Porto (fig. 329). Eiffel had to overcome many difficulties: a depth of 20 meters, fierce and frequent rises in level, rapid, swirling currents, and soil so unstable that it made lowering piles into the riverbed unfeasible. With his engineers, he designed an arched bridge whose central 160-meter span had no intervening supporting member. The perfect execution of this construction together with its formal beauty induced the board of the Ponts et Chaussées (the French state bureau responsible for public civil engineering projects) to entrust Eiffel with the building of the Garabit Viaduct in southern France (1880–84), which crosses the valley of the river Truyère at a height of 122 meters. It was designed by the engineers Émile Nougier and Maurice Koechlin (1856–1946), the duo who later built the Eiffel Tower, together with architect Stephen Sauvestre (1847–?).

The idea for erecting a colossal tower first arose in Great Britain. In 1853, the engineer Richard Trevithick (1771–1833) proposed raising a decorated openwork cast-iron column 1,000 feet high, but his premature death put an end to the project. In the United States, the engineers Clarke and Reeves dreamt of a 304-meter high tower for the Centennial Exhibition in Philadelphia (1876), while the obelisk of the Washington Monument in Washington, D.C., rose to a height of 169 meters. In Turin, Alessandro Antonelli constructed a stone edifice of 163 meters, known as the Mole Antonelliana (1863). The first drawing for the Eiffel Tower was made by Maurice Koechlin in 1884. He sketched a 300-meter pylon, which, transformed by Sauvestre, was to become the tower that everyone knows. The almost mathematical erection of this enormous piece of Meccano generated great controversy. A petition was signed by illustrious artists, such as the composer Gounod, Garnier, the playwright Victorien Sardou, Léon Bonnat, the Salon painters Meissonier, Bouguereau, and Gérôme, the poets Sully Prudhomme and Leconte de Lisle, and the writer Guy de Maupassant, lambasting "a dizzyingly ridiculous tower soaring over Paris like some gigantic black factory chimney, crushing beneath its barbarous mass Notre-Dame, the

Sainte-Chapelle, the Tour Saint-Jacques, the Louvre, the dome of the Invalides, the Arc de Triomphe, all our monuments humiliated, all our architecture belittled, all will vanish into this stupefying daydream."

Painters (Seurat and Henri Rousseau, followed by Robert Delaunay), photographers (Louis-Émile Durandelle and Pierre Petit), illustrators, and engravers (Henri Rivière) were to discover the tower's modernity so strongly felt by Duchamp-Villon: "Living its strange life, animated by an imperceptible swaying—erect in the sunshine, withdrawing under a gray sky—the Tower, glorious and sonorous, has resisted the elements as it has resisted men. Today, it impresses itself on us, indispensable, and we no longer need all its statistical records to be able to admire it. This masterpiece of mathematical energy has, above and beyond its rational conception, noble origins in the subconscious domain of beauty. It is greater than a figure or a number, since it incorporates an element of that profound life to which our mind must yield if it is to seek emotion in the arts of statuary or architecture" (Duchamp-Villon 1913).

Metal and Rationalism

"In architecture," Viollet-le-Duc declared, "there are two ways to be true. One must be true to one's program and to one's construction methods. Being true to the program means fulfilling to the letter and in all simplicity the conditions imposed by necessity; being true to the construction methods means employing materials in accordance with their qualities and their properties" (Viollet-le-Duc 1872, 1:45). If, through his *Entretiens sur l'architecture,* Viollet-le-Duc proved himself to be the true pioneer of modern architecture (fig. 294), he had no immediate successors. His theories were applied later by architects such as Frank Lloyd Wright, Hendrik Petrus Berlage, Otto Wagner, Auguste Perret, and Le Corbusier.

Some of the ideas he favored for the use of iron were, however, put into practice sooner. Plate 36 of the *Entretiens,* for example, proposed an iron-faced facade in a transposition of the timber-faced houses of the Middle Ages (fig. 261). Only the skeleton is load-bearing, the wall being mere infill—an audacious stroke for a private house. In 1871, Jules Saulnier (1817–1881) utilized the same process for the construction of the first skeleton building, the Menier chocolate factory at Noisiel-sur-Marne, in which an iron frame was filled in with colored brickwork (fig. 333). This is the system from which the American skyscraper was born, and elsewhere Viollet-le-Duc advocated large buildings with metal skeletons and stone cladding such as the ones that would be constructed in Chicago in the 1890s. Hector Guimard employed Viollet-le-Duc's system of oblique load-bearing cast-iron pillars for the school of the Sacré-Coeur in 1895, while Ernest Lheureux (1827–1898) interpreted it more freely in supports for the glazed roof frame at the Law School Library in 1897 (demolished; fig. 291). As to the repertory of nature-based ornamentation—mostly derived from the plant world—as stipulated either by Viollet-le-Duc himself in his dictionaries or by pupils, such as Victor-Marie-Charles Ruprich-Robert (1820–1887) in his *Flore ornamentale,* its heirs are to be found in the work of Eugène Grasset, Victor Horta, and Louis Sullivan.

Another rationalist, Henri Labrouste (1801–1875)—one who combined the talents of an engineer and those of an architect—was the winner of the prestigious Grand Prix de Rome at the age of only twenty-three. At the Bibliothèque Sainte-Geneviève in Paris, he was to use—for the first time in a public building—a cast- and wrought-iron skeleton from foundations to rafters, thereby countering the risk of fire and providing for the maximum number of readers. This delicate and elegant breed of architecture was to be best realized in the reading room of the Bibliothèque Nationale in Paris (1857–68), a vast rectangular space topped by nine radiant white glazed earthenware cupolas borne by tall cast-iron columns (fig. 262). The stack room, located near the reading room itself, is eminently rational; intended for the storage of 900,000 books, it comprises four stories and a basement built entirely in iron covered by a glazed roof that allows the sunlight to penetrate through the latticework floors.

In 1853, for the church of Saint-Eugène in Paris, Louis-Auguste Boileau employed wrought and cast iron in a systematic fashion for the first time (fig. 260). Through the inventive use of Gothic forms, Boileau succeeded in giving an impression of amplitude, multiplying the perspectives, using very slender cast-iron columns directly inspired by those in the refectory at Saint-Martin-des-Champs, a suburb of Morlaix in Brittany. Nevertheless, Boileau was castigated by Viollet-le-Duc: "As for the diagonal ribs, the Gothic columns cast in iron, the mullions indented in the medieval manner, these are puerilities in rather poor taste; the forms that suit some materials do not suit all indiscriminately" (quoted in Foucart 1969, 63). Boileau was above all a theoretician who dreamt of arriving at a universal style capable of expressing the very essence of Christianity through a fusion of all the forms of architecture judged high in spiritual content so as to forge a "synthetic cathedral" that would raise Gothic art to its perfection. In the Sagrada Família church in Barcelona, Antoni Gaudí was to take inspiration from the extraordinary system of lighting that Boileau proposed.

Hector Horeau, who endured years of official opposition to his rationalist approach, lies at the wellspring of many early examples of metal architecture. For example, his key idea—a structure covering a vast multipurpose space, providing maximum visibility and using as few load-bearing elements as possible (fig. 284)—originally dates from 1835. When he presented a design along these lines in the competition for the Great Exhibition, it was awarded first prize, although it was Paxton who was finally entrusted with the building. Hittorff's Gare du Nord also adopted the idea of a triple aisle that Horeau had devised at that time. As early as 1835, Horeau had advocated building two large iron pavilions on either side of the Champs-Élysées for exhibitions of industry and art, something that would indeed come to pass in 1900. For the architect, however, the cruelest blow was the sidelining of his bold and rational project for the Halles in Paris. "Horeau wanted to build the Halles in iron and brick, cover them over in surbased arches without tie-beams, butressed by monumental columns supporting the double slope of the roof. This was thus a forerunner of the Galerie des Machines by Dutert" (Hautecœur 1957, 308). Another of Horeau's inventions was a house that would be fireproof, comfortable, extendable, durable, and even "dismantlable, portable, and wheel-borne." This idea materialized, in part at least, in the United States—a newer and less artistically prejudiced country.

Apartment Blocks and Skyscrapers

The United States was soon to make a specialty out of load-bearing cast-iron facades that one could select from luxurious catalogs. Delivered in separate pieces, these facades were used to build the frontier cities of the American West and Australia. In New York, James Bogardus (1800–1874) erected a five-story factory in which iron columns were substituted for the masonry of the external walls. Although Minneapolis, New York, and Chicago all lay claim to being the place where the skyscraper was invented, it was unquestionably in Chicago that it was given its finest and purest expression. The city had already become a major commercial center before the outbreak of the great fire of 1871. The massive and urgent need for business premises meant that the construction methods employed in bridge-building were used, often with results that were deplorable from an aesthetic point of view. The Chicago School was a reaction to this. It comprised a group of architects which included Henry Hobson Richardson, Daniel Burnham, John Welborn Root (1850–1911), William Holabird, and Martin Roche, as well as Louis Henry Sullivan.

In the early stages, these architects followed traditional paths, with masonry walls supporting the load, as in the Marshall Field Wholesale Store and Warehouse (1885–87; destroyed in 1930) by Richardson, which was for long to remain a prototype for office building, or Burnham and Root's Monadnock Building (1889–91), brick-built throughout. The earliest skyskrapers were appearing at this time: the New York Tribune Building (1872–75) by Richard Morris Hunt and the nine-story Chicago Home Insurance Building (fig. 263) by William Le Baron Jenney (1832–1907). In 1887, Burnham and Root erected the Rookery, whose metal frame was built up directly from ground-level and which, with its splendid glazed interior courtyard and its flights of escalators, soon became famous.

But it was dangerous to erect tall structures in stone, as their foundations were liable to collapse under the weight. Now steel was to make anything possible. Jenney made the first experiments with a steel skeleton in the Second Leiter Building (1889). Its success was overwhelming, and the Chicago skyline was soon studded with ever taller towers, built in ever quicker time, reflections of the power and imagination of the industrialists, bankers, and businessmen who commissioned them.

THE INTERNATIONAL EXHIBITIONS

Glorifications of the triumphs of industry, displays of prestige and pride, a source of architectural experimentation and fantasy, journeys of discovery since they unveiled worlds as yet undreamt—the international exhibitions were born of a desire to compare products and production methods from all the modern states and give a fillip to competition. Until 1851 only exhibitions on a national scale had taken place; the first in Paris on the Champ-de-Mars in 1798 had been intended to give a spur to French manufacturing and "thereby wield a fateful blow to English industry." From 1801 to 1849, these shows were regularly held in the courtyard of the Louvre, on the Place de la Concorde, or on the Champs-Élysées and lasted from a week for the first to six months for the last, a length of time that was to become the norm for the international exhibitions.

The earliest duels were contested between France and Great Britain, between London (1851, 1862) and Paris (1855 and 1867, and then 1878, 1889, and 1900). Vienna (1873), Amsterdam (1883), Belgium (1885, 1897, 1905, 1910), the United States (1876, 1893, 1904, 1915), and, later, Italy (1916) were to add still greater richness and diversity to these periodic conventions. While France, Great Britain, and Austria chose their capitals, this was not always the case in Belgium (Brussels, but also Antwerp and Liège), the United States (Philadelphia, Chicago, St. Louis), and Italy (Milan). Finally, the French exhibitions were a state affair, while Great Britain and the United States lent toward private funding.

Initially small-scale affairs centered around a single great complex (Crystal Palace, 1851, Palais de l'Industrie [fig. 258] and the Galerie des Machines, 1855), from 1867 the exhibitions were increasingly transformed into cities of the ephemeral, which, whenever they were located in the city center, seemed to be in total contradiction with it. The Great Exhibition took place in London's Hyde Park and in 1873 the exhibition was held in Vienna's Prater, but in Paris the problem of where to hold them resurfaced on each successive occasion. It was Viollet-le-Duc's observation in 1878 that eventually clinched the argument: "We should not forget that, though the exhibitions attract their fair share of the idle, the inquisitive, and of wealthy foreigners with time on their hands, [in France] they are also highly popular affairs and have become a valuable object of study that our craftsmen, our workmen should be able to visit for long and often enough, without wasting time traveling and without being forced to spend large sums." From 1867, the exhibitions began to spill over into the Champ-de-Mars, the esplanades in front of the Invalides, the Trocadéro, part of the Champs-Élysées, as well as on both banks of the Seine between the Trocadéro and the Place de la Concorde, covering anything from 40 acres in 1855 to 333 acres in 1900. The large *palais* were designed to correspond logically to the way the products were displayed. The one erected in 1867—which was built out of modern materials such as iron, cast iron, and glass—consisted of seven concentric rings each housing produce from a single specific area, while each segment enabled a sampling of the produce of any one nation. Some of these halls were built to last, as in the case of the Palais de l'Industrie, which was replaced in 1900 by the Grand and Petit Palais exhibition spaces, and of the 1878 Trocadéro (by Gabriel Davioud and Jules Bourdais [1835–1915]), designed to house a vast theater space in addition to art shows. This building aroused astonishment: "Imagine, on a piece of raised ground, the enormous architectural paradox of the Palais du Trocadéro, with a dome taller that Saint Peter's, flanked by two towers that resemble bell-towers, minarets, or lighthouses, with its vast belly and its long, graceful wings, with its one hundred Grecian columns, its Moorish pavilions and Byzantine arches, decorated and painted like some Indian palace, from which pours down a torrent of water in the midst of a ring of gilt statues" (Amicis 1880, 34). Davioud's design for the Trocadéro was influenced by the Palais de Longchamp in Marseille, designed by Espérandieu. The Eiffel Tower survives from the 1889 exhibition, while 1900 bequeathed to Paris one of the city's treasures, the Grand Palais by Henri Deglane (1855–1931), Albert Thomas (1847–1907), and Louis Louvet (1860–1936), the Petit Palais by Charles Girault (1851–1932), and the Pont Alexandre III, built by the engineers Louis-Jean Résal (1854–1919) and Amédée Alby (1862–1942) with the architects Marie-Joseph Cassien-Bernard (1848–1926) and Gaston Cousin (1859–1901), and decorated by Dalou and Gardet.

In addition to such large-scale works there burgeoned, deep in the Trocadéro gardens or beneath the leafy groves of the esplanade of the Invalides, everywhere there was space in fact, the most exotic, picturesque, colorful constructions, living anthology pieces of architecture and ornament.

The exhibitions, formerly earnest and didactic affairs, in 1851 and 1855 welcomed participants from farther afield that presented architecture and produce from the colonies. This tended to turn them into a "geography fairyland," into an "ecumenical city" built in the heart of the modern city. There was an immense contrast, for example, between the Rue des Nations in 1878—in which each country was represented by a facade characteristic of its golden age, and where polychromy and primitive architecture were juxtaposed with examples of extreme refinement, full of ornate and teeming detail—and Haussmann's drab and sober streets. It was "as if the comparison had been deliberately engineered to show off each architectonic style, to bring out its individual face, by placing side by side those peoples least like each other, so that the juxtaposition would accentuate still more the distinctive characteristics of their art. Next to Italy was placed Japan. After the United States came Sweden; Denmark's neighbor was Greece; Portugal lay next to the Netherlands and Central America to Morocco" (Blanc 1878, 51).

It is this quality which reappears in the extraordinary story of the village of forty houses Charles Garnier erected at the foot of the Eiffel Tower in 1889. "The true fantasist that he is, M. Garnier has placed regions where we fry right next to countries where we freeze. Here, in the shade of palm trees, Arab and Sudanese dwellings; there, recognizable by their characteristic roofs, the houses of the Japanese and the Chinese who, as members of ancient civilizations, must be pained at such close contact with the crude shelters of the Laplanders, the Eskimos, African savages, and Redskins" (Jourdain 1889, 370). The most enduring memory was of the originality, the newness of unsuspected architectural forms and of an intense use of color. At Chicago, in 1893, there was a striking contrast between the exhibition's "white town," pure product of the Beaux-Arts style, and the architecture of the "real" city, with its streets crossing at 90 degrees, its commercial buildings, and its skyscrapers in iron, steel, and glass.

Newly conquered countries were a source of both astonishment and delight. In 1889, along the esplanade of the Invalides, was displayed a dreamworld Orient: the pagoda of Angkor, whose sculptures were to attract the attention of Gauguin; the Cochinchina pavilion, which drew all eyes by its "most capricious lines and the strongest colors," all greens, reds and yellows; the Palace of Annam and Tonkin with its pointed roofs containing the cast of the great Buddha of Hanoi; and the "Pagoda of Great Tranquillity." Next to these civilizations of extreme refinement were the contrasting Senegalese villages of Senegal, Alforou, Pahouin, and Loango, with their buildings in unbaked earth, decorated in potent, violent motifs.

Many of the foreign pavilions were designed by French architects and were intended to provide an image of the power and wealth of the countries concerned. The 1889 exhibition was marked by the unusual participation of the republics of Latin America, particularly Argentina's iron and glass pavilion by Albert Ballu (1849–1939). "Its opulent and multicolored decoration, with the iron and gilt cast iron brightened by the brilliancy of the polychrome faience, the shine of the mosaics, and the shimmer of the colored-glass cabochons, gave it the look of some gargantuan piece of jewelry. In the evening, on all four sides, electricity lit nine hundred luminous dots, and like precious stones that flame beneath the glare of the chandelier, the blazing cabochons hung their red, green, and blue glints over the hundreds of frets on the openwork balconies" (Georget 1889, 2:222). The palace could be dismantled and it was shipped to Buenos Aires, where it remained until its demolition in 1933.

These confrontations were occasionally fruitful in new departures. In 1867, Léon Parvillée, who had been involved in restoring the great monuments of the Ottoman empire, erected on the Champ-de-Mars a reduced-scale model of the green mosque at Bursa, baths, and a small Bosporus pavilion—a copy of the old pleasure houses that lined the banks of the strait, adorned with paintings, stained glass, and glazed bricks. "We owe it to M. Léon Parvillée to have brought over to France those fine glazed bricks whose secret had until then remained in the East and that will finish by replacing the stucco that we have so overused" (Saint-Félix 1867, 28). These glazed bricks were a triumph at the Palais des Beaux-Arts in 1878, and also in the halls built by Jean-Camille Formigé in 1889, and they gradually invaded private houses and apartment blocks. The splendor of this multicolored decoration in conjunction with iron was to stir up much lively controversy. In 1889, Gauguin upheld the use of iron alone: "Iron, iron, and again iron! Why, next to coarse, severe iron, flimsy materials like scarcely fired earth; why, next to these geometrical lines of a new character, such an antiquated stockpile of ornaments? With colors as somber as the material itself, then you would have an imposing structure evocative of melting metal" ("Notes sur l'art à l'Exposition Universelle," *Le Moderniste illustré*, July 4, 1889).

The discovery of Japan struck English architects and designers with the force of a revelation as early as 1862. Godwin was the first to decorate his house according to Japanese principles, while Thomas Jeckyll (1827–1881), for the Centennial Exhibition of 1876 in Philadelphia, devised a most astonishing cast-iron pavilion, commissioned and executed by the firm of Barnard, Bisthop and Barnard. It took the form of a Japanese temple with very delicate bird and flower motifs, while the grille surrounding the pavilion was comprised of massive cast-iron sunflowers. Such patterns were also adopted for use in the home: birds and flowers decorated chimney surrounds and the sunflower was featured on andirons: produced out of cast iron and marketed by the same firm of Barnard, Bisthop and Barnard, these elements soon found their way into houses all over Europe and the United States.

The Japanese house in Philadelphia was of immediate inspiration to McKim, Mead, and White, who transformed the interior space in Victor Newcomb's house at Elberon, New Jersey, opening up the central volume without partitions. As for Frank Lloyd Wright, he was struck by the Hooden pavilion in 1893, a mock-up of the Phoenix Hall at Uji, near Kyoto. This low horizontal timber structure was undecorated. The open interior space, featuring partition screens, had a significant impact on the architect's work.

Series of architectural samples were also displayed, such as the workers' housing regularly presented by major industrial concerns, or as in Stanislas Ferrand's famous 3,000-franc house exhibited in 1867. The pavilion of the City of Paris in 1878 presented maquettes of its own most recent projects, while in 1889 the accent was placed on the progress made in public health, with two life-size mock-ups, one representing a hygienic and the other an unhygienic dwelling.

There were also buildings aimed at entertainment, however, and the 1878 exhibition, which had none, was a failure. In Paris in 1900, Alexandre Marcel (1860–1928) built a most amusing "round-the-world trip" that gave one the impression—thanks to Louis Dumoulin's paintings—of embarking at Marseille for a voyage through Greece, Turkey, Syria, Egypt, Ceylon, Angkor, China, and Japan, and whose exterior was a digest of various architectural styles. While visiting the exhibition, King Léopold II of Belgium commissioned from Alexandre Marcel the Chinese pavilion and the Japanese tower that remain to this day in the park at Laeken. On a more serious level, the king was also to commission both the Arc de Triomphe in the Parc du Cinquantenaire in Brussels (fig. 494) and the Congo Pavilion at Tervueren from Charles Girault.

At the heart of the last great Paris exhibition in 1900, on the threshold of the new century, amid the great halls that were palpable evidence of a particular accent resulting from the extraordinary osmosis of a multitude of styles, especially Eastern ones, a wind of change was blowing. As in Chicago in 1893—where critics and architects alike had been greatly struck by Louis Henry Sullivan's Transportation Building and its orientalizing, colorful, powerful, and novel decoration—in 1900 it was the animated surface of the facade of Loie Fuller's theater by Henri Sauvage (1873–1932) and the sculptor Pierre Roche that drew the notices: "It seems as if the undulating lines of the theater's structure have been determined by the artistic dancer's billowing yet miraculously solidified dress." The blue pavilion, designed by René Dulong with an interior by Gustave Serrurier-Bovy, was hailed as a "genuinely modern restaurant," with "bright, comfortable rooms in which every detail, right down to the newly decorated plates, has been carefully calculated, and where the exposed timber structure puts the accent on the somewhat countrified and ephemeral air of the building most agreeably."

But the most individual, startling, and "modern" pavilion was the one Eliel Saarinen (1873–1950) designed for his country, Finland. Though he still showed an attachment to the art of his country, Saarinen here presented a forward-looking piece drawing on the work of Henry Hobson Richardson and the sober decoration of the Glasgow School.

When the exhibition closed, there was a lingering nostalgia for these strong and diverse forms of architecture, for these different worlds set side by side, for "humanity from beyond a dream, with its playhouses and dances, its palaces and princes, its temples and its gods."

ART NOUVEAU ARCHITECTURE (1890–1914)

Given that the term Art Nouveau covers the applied arts in general, as well as painting and sculpture in relation to the decorative arts, the choice of what should be included in the field of architecture is inevitably subjective. If the notion of Art Nouveau is more inclusive than Impressionism or Cubism, it is not as all-embracing as the Baroque, Neoclassicism, or Symbolism. The temptation to amalgamate is a strong one, but this would lead to simplification and would be deceptive. This is especially true of the period in question, which was astonishingly short and impressively rich in terms of the numerous "schools" and geographical areas concerned, from the United States to the Czech and Slovak republics. Adolf Loos and Jules Lavirotte, for example, were contemporaries who had nothing in common in their theories or in their practice. Moreover, an era of neglect stretching over more than fifty years (from 1918 to 1968, at least) has not only prevented the objective study of modernity in the tumultuous *fin de siècle* period, but has also clouded the issue by causing the disappearance of many key works.

The foremost characteristic of Art Nouveau is thus its very diversity. Each country was, more than ever, fervently attached to its national identity, even to its regional idiosyncrasies, and frontiers became less permeable. Even if cultures evolved in directions so similar that they appear on occasion to be kith and kin, reverting to historic, "local" material in each particular place allowed for some extraordinarily idiosyncratic artistic expressions that had no equivalents elsewhere. Western civilization, under pressure from political upheaval and the shake-up of the social hierarchy that industrialization had brought about, was in the process of fragmenting. If each nation did indeed exhibit signs of innovation, it was almost always accompanied by protests that it had not purloined it from its neighbor. Art Nouveau, "new art" (or "new arts" to be more accurate), is characterized by the sheer number of its factions. Indeed, the differences between these various factions have seemed to be the salient characteristic of the "style," which thus takes on, from Chicago to Prague, a certain unity—so reassuring for historians—that it never in truth possessed. Nonetheless, it is also as well to point out the existence of occasionally airtight artistic borders that often had nothing to do with geography. For example, the English journal *The Studio,* so receptive to innovations from Germany and Austria, was particularly uncommunicative about French and Belgian art, while the French press was equally unforthcoming on Anglo-Saxon and Austrian architecture.

It might thus be feasible to sketch out some cultural groupings characterized by their affinities—the Latins to one side and the northern Europeans (including Austria) to the other—something easily comprehensible in terms of the shared roots of the different national heritages that served as benchmarks for the new modernity. However, it is important to remember that the barriers were harder to cross than might be supposed, often even within one and the same country. For example, Madrid's few modernist buildings owe nothing to the great artistic center of Barcelona. The creations of Turin, Florence, and Palermo have little relationship with each other beyond the chronological; Antwerp was no more Brussels than London was Glasgow; and, while Nancy in the northeast is in the Lorraine region, Strasbourg is German. The individualism of each particular artistic group is sometimes undiluted. For example, in Nancy it would appear that nobody was aware of the construction of the nearby Château de Chamblay by Horta or that Guimard was developing his vast oeuvre of cast-iron art at the Saint-Dizier foundry not far away on the Marne.

In fact, this sometimes excessive tendency to draw distinct zones of influence and interrelationships is often simply a reflection of the irritation felt by the historian when faced with such disparity. Since they are not glaringly obvious, the origins of Art Nouveau architecture have been the subject of some debate. It is worthwhile recalling the extent to which the nineteenth century was a historicist, scientific, almost backward-looking period. The years of the Second Empire had already provided a foretaste, with the nostalgic return to the Middle Ages and a new receptivity to unfamiliar cultures (as with the interest in Japanese arts and crafts), together with eclecticism—the formal synthesis of the styles of the preceding three centuries. In truth, Art Nouveau did little more than follow a path opened up by previous decades. This period, more than any other, was one of synthesis. But, just as earlier architects had been too respectful of their models—the castles built by Louis II of Bavaria are the most blatant example (figs. 265, 266)—Art Nouveau architects plundered what they could from the past, reinterpreting it in terms of new aesthetic goals, often adding a dose of humor. It is here, perhaps, that one can discern the origins of the postwar distrust of "styles," of the progressive abandonment of imitation, and of the virulent and complete debunking of that *art 1900* (as Art Nouveau is sometimes referred to in France), which had used "styles" in a manner verging on caricature.

It is necessary, however, at the outset to relativize the historical significance of Art Nouveau in architecture. It was always an art practiced by a small minority of artists and for twenty years the omnipotence of academicism hardly wavered. The imposing Palais de Justice in Brussels, designed by Joseph Poelaert, still looks down on Horta's little town houses with all the disdain of a monument built for all eternity. It was Horta's Maison du Peuple that was pulled down in 1964–65, after all, not the law courts. The number of Art Nouveau structures in the various capitals was modest in comparison with the numerous eclectic buildings being built and many of the former would have been regarded at the time as artistic eyesores. Tradition was always well able to look after itself and, by making a hue and cry, prevented too many outpourings of what seemed in its opinion to be heretical modernity.

Art Nouveau, in spite of its obvious achievements, was never anything more than a strictly limited fashion. Although some international influence was exerted, although there were some texts—and a few important professions of faith that amounted to codes of practice—the movement, swayed by its various regional strands and by the personality of each individual architect, and devoid of any unity whatsoever, could never put itself forward as a style or a school in any meaningful sense of the term. It was a trend rather than a new artistic order, a curio whose ephemeral character could be foreseen from the fact that the fortunes of the upper middle classes (and architecture, unlike most other arts, cannot survive without a clientele), the class which imposed its taste, were not in general in the modernist camp, at least in the majority of countries.

The immediate roots of Art Nouveau are twofold. They appear to have played a preponderant role in two basic categories that can be distinguished: Arts and Crafts among the Germans and Anglo-Saxons, and Viollet-le-Duc among the Latins, including France. Splitting the world into two in this way is of necessity arbitrary and may appear simplistic, but it must be acknowledged that the practice of the guilds, schools, and groupings of every kind, of which the Arts and Crafts movement is the prototype, was more prevalent in Great Britain, the United States, Germany, and Austria, whereas Latin countries have tended to offer extraordinary examples of individualism. Catalan modernism does not have the character of an artistic school because the links between Gaudí and his collaborators, as between Horta and his, are those of a head of studio with his assistants. The works executed by the latter are too often stamped with the master's influence, even when there is no blatant plagiarism. This empire of a strong personality over a sizable proportion of the architects of modernity probably accounts at least partially for Barcelona and Brussels appearing as sites of considerable unity, as places where Art Nouveau seems to have developed in accordance with a blueprint that never existed. In Latin countries, the only exception is the École de Nancy, though the school's complete designation also includes the words "Alliance Provinciale des Industries d'Art" (Provincial Alliance of Art Industries), thereby clearly proclaiming the predominant status of the decorative arts within the group. Moreover, it is much more through the works of Gallé and Majorelle than through those of their architect friends that the École de Nancy has since gained its worldwide fame. It is significant, though unnerving, to observe that the Villa Majorelle, probably the most celebrated Art Nouveau house in the capital of Lorraine is the work of a Parisian, Henri Sauvage.

It seems thus unworkable in our eyes—even if some mental trickery might enable one to engineer certain comparisons—to include Vienna and Paris in one and the same analysis, even if ideas circulated more freely than contemporary newspapers would have us believe. Evolution did not always move in the same direction: if Art Nouveau does indeed exist, it is rather to be contrasted with the Sezession, the two terms having a distinct history and different posterity.

Latins Against Northern Europeans

The Latin group can be identified primarily by the influence exerted upon it by the theoretical works of Viollet-le-Duc, the *Dictionnaire raisonné de l'architecture française* (1854–68) and, above all, the *Entretiens sur l'architecture* (1863–72), which was both a polemic text intended to speed up reform in architectural training in France and the written version of a famous lecture series which a notorious round of heckling had prevented Viollet-le-Duc from giving. This influence was purely theoretical and ideological, Viollet-le-Duc's oeuvre as a creative architect being considerably smaller than his work as a restorer. If his texts lean heavily on Gothic forms, it is because he could see in them a kind of perfection in architectural thought, where form, function, and materials joined forces with impeccable logic. The originality of his ideas resides in a complete acceptance of the contemporary period, which is in marked contrast to the representatives of the Arts and Crafts movement and their theoretician John Ruskin, who was nonetheless an admirer of Viollet-le-Duc. Viollet-le-Duc provided demonstrations of his ideas in the form of drawings accompanying the *Entretiens* (often far more convincing than the text), notably concerning the use of metal, the modern structural material *par excellence* for which his proposals were aesthetically extremely inventive.

The enthusiastic acceptance or rejection Viollet-le-Duc aroused could serve as a frontier between Art Nouveau and the Sezession. Spain, France, and Belgium warmly welcomed his legacy, seeing it as a way of regenerating architecture without totally jettisoning the formal vocabulary of the past. But in Italy, where modernism made its appearance noticeably later, the divergence is far more clear-cut between Turin—which forged close links of every kind with Austria—and the remainder of the peninsula. Owing to their own history and culture, artistic centers such as The Hague and Munich were far more receptive to ideas emerging from Paris and Brussels than were Berlin or Amsterdam. Overall, Anglo-Saxon countries saw in Viollet-le-Duc little more than a standard-bearer of the Gothic Revival, and thus put up the stubbornest resistance to Art Nouveau. Certain American architects such as Louis Sullivan, however, were attentive to the rationalist and modernizing message of the brilliant restorer of Pierrefonds. Such differences are in fact theoretical and one should curb the urge to lay down rigid aesthetic borders, as they do not really exist. Little effort is required to see in modern works in Vienna up to 1899 a patent kinship with art in the Latin countries, whether in the blocks of the Linke Wienzeile and the Wagner Stadtbahn (fig. 277), or in Hoffmann's early creations and even Olbrich's Sezession building (fig. 276), where the sinuous line and floral decoration has not yet acquired the strict geometrical forms characteristic of the thoroughbred Sezessionist style. The break would be still more complete when each artistic center had gained an awareness of the work of the others, a process in which comparisons afforded by the numerous international exhibitions played a fundamental role. If the 1900 Exposition Universelle was disappointing on the architectural front, it nonetheless provided an opportunity to admire the wide range of interior fixtures and fittings and to put an end to the split between Latins and northern Europeans, which, if it existed in the realm of ideas, was not yet the case in reality.

THREE ARCHITECTS AND THEIR CITIES

Gaudí in Barcelona

The first great Art Nouveau architect was undeniably Antoni Gaudí i Cornet (1852–1926). Was he a one-off? An isolated figure or a prophet? At the outset one should note that his early significant works—the Casa Vicens in Barcelona and the Capricio at Comillas, both built in 1883–85—already show a complete mastery of his particular style and that at a time when no other architect was producing anything in the same vein. The comparison often drawn between his creations and the Palais Idéal (Hauterives, in the Drôme, France) by the "Facteur" Cheval (real name Ferdinand Cheval, 1836–1924) is not an arbitrary one, as it attempts to come to terms with an originality and an isolation whose unnerving precociousness is somewhat awkward. Gaudí's work was so reluctant to leave its local Barcelona setting that it is difficult to fully grasp. The architect did indeed exhibit a few pieces of furniture at the Exposition Universelle in Paris in 1889, but his appearance made no greater stir than when he participated in the Salon of the Société Nationale des Beaux-Arts in 1910 in what almost amounted to a retrospective, centered around a polychrome mock-up of the Sagrada Família. His name was given in the catalog as Antoni Gaudé, thereby revealing the full extent of ignorance surrounding both the architect and his work.

From certain points of view, however, the case of Gaudí is not far removed from those of Horta and Guimard, in particular with respect to the appearance of an enlightened patron, Count Eusebi Güell i Bacigalupi, without whom Gaudí's work would probably have developed more cautiously, or would even have been forced into compromise. Thanks to the favorable conditions provided by Barcelona at that particular time, Gaudí's work developed in a singular fashion. Catalan Art Nouveau—or *modernisme*—appeared within the context of the *Renaixença*, which asserted the grandeur of Catalonia in the face of the rest of Spain. The economic power of the region legitimized its claim not only to autonomy in the linguistic and political spheres, but also to a right to cultural specificity expressed as much through literature as painting. This was the reason for the almost systematic rejection of anything coming from Madrid, Barcelona showing instead a far greater interest in art from France, Great Britain, and Austria. The city was open to European modernism from all countries, but, closed in on itself, few of its own creations would have repercussions beyond its confines.

Two other architects joined Gaudí in forming the triumvirate of Catalan modernism, each possessing his own identifiable personality, vocabulary, and style. Nevertheless, all three can be recognized by the crucial influence a reading of Viollet-le-Duc's theories had on their work and above all by an attachment to their native region. In this last connection, it was Lluís Domènech i Montaner (1850–1923) who showed the most commitment, following a political career which paralleled his activities as an architect. It is hardly surprising that his most significant works include three monumental designs, of which two, at least, profess a passionate regionalism: the café-restaurant that he built for the 1888 international exhibition where ceramic fulfilled a preponderant ornamental role, and the Palau de la Música Catalana concert hall (1905–8, fig. 363), whose very name and decorative opulence served as a manifesto for Barcelona modernism, underscored by its iron and brickwork. The Hospital de la Santa Creu i de Sant Pau (1902–10) is a large-scale complex made up of pavilions, pleasantly colored and richly decorated, organized on the lines of a city within the city. Once again, bright ceramic tiles were used to decorate the turrets and towers.

The third figure of this trio, Josep Puig i Cadafalch (1867–1956), was chiefly involved in the construction of private houses and residential blocks. More strongly influenced by the neo-Gothic aspects of rationalism than Domenech, and acting as much as a local architectural historian as a creative artist, it was almost impossible for him to build otherwise than as a distinguished medievalist. His most famous works, the Casa Marti (1896) and above all the Casa Amattler (1900), suffer from over-lavish decoration, amusing enough, but sometimes slapdash and anachronistic. The facade of the Casa Amattler, in particular, is topped in the manner of a Flemish medieval house, an astonishing effect indeed, but one which hardly bears comparison with Gaudí's neighboring Casa Batllò. An affection for traditional Catalan values finds equally consistent expression in the work of Gaudí himself, notably in the widespread use of wall ceramic, in the religiosity of his idiom—crosses and inscriptions even figure on civil buildings—and in the quotations from Gothic art.

There are a host of arguments for excluding from the Art Nouveau corpus Gaudí's early works, whose glaring precocity makes them historically so unwieldy. The Casa Vicens, indeed, has no peer whatsoever at the beginning of the 1880s. Picturesque, violently colorful thanks to the ceramic tiles made by the owner (the house is a sort of tiling manufacturer's showcase), the building, which is situated in the middle of a dull little street, makes one look twice. The architect's complex and synthetic cast of mind is already discernible: the singularity of each interior space, visibly expressed by facade plans making much use of set-backs; the upper reaches of the construction, already prey to a typically Gaudíesque exuberance; the amalgamation of several decorative styles that marked the history of Catalonia, principally Moorish and medieval; and above all Gaudí's pronounced taste for the polychrome ceramics characteristic of the new Hispano-Moorish style which exerted an influence on every *modernista* architect, although, being prevalent all over Spain, it was often looked on with suspicion.

The Casa Vicens was an affirmation of the business prowess of the client. For Gaudí, like Horta and Guimard, took pleasure in depicting some of his clients' personality traits in his works, thereby rendering them unique in style as well as aim. For example, the flat and austere Baroque frontage of the Casa Calvet (1896–1904), concealing a dark and over-decorated little stairwell, is the antithesis of that of the Casa Batllò (1904–6)—a remodeling and refurbishment of an existing building—which is bony, lively, and highly colored, opening into an almost plain vestibule and a light-well of great simplicity. In both cases, the owners were drapers, however, and the houses, which were built near each other and one shortly after the other, share the same urban constraints; the requirements of each patron, however, led the architect to propose, within the context of fundamentally similar specifications, totally different projects. This was even the case in the furniture Gaudí designed for each house: that for the Casa Battlò is characterized by exceptionally pure lines, whereas in Casa Calvet it tends toward the quaint and the complicated. The artist's major works are to be found elsewhere, among the buildings produced for Count Güell (another convert to the textile industry and recently ennobled): the Casa Milá and the church of the Sagrada Família.

Gaudí found in Güell a true Maecenas, both attentive and receptive. Everything on which they were to collaborate bears the stamp of the same liberty of invention which even today remains unsurpassed. First—in something of a warm-up gallop—Gaudí built the Güell stables (1884–87), a picturesque group of little pavilions connected by a strange railing comprising in part an immense open-jawed dragon constructed from industrial waste products. The functional symbolism of this bizarre composition is not devoid of religious superstition. Viollet-le-Duc's ideas on the function of decoration were rarely taken so literally nor applied so early in the *fin de siècle* period. The Palau Güell (1886–91) was to follow shortly after (fig. 307). The palace's frontage is austere, but the complexity of the wrought-iron decoration of the ground-floor gates—where the owner's initials appear in the midst of tense interlacing lines—anticipates closely the stalklike banisters of the staircase at Victor Horta's Hôtel Tassel (1893), often cited as the earliest clear occurrence of Art Nouveau. The interior is of particular interest. Arranged on different levels, it contains unlit and enclosed spaces intended to provide protection from the heat of the sun. The central hall is covered by a dome comparable to that of a church. Each column is original in design. The roof is punctuated by numerous quaint chimney stacks.

The Parc Güell (1900–14), in its present unfinished state, does not resemble the garden city it was supposed to be and is now only a pleasant place to go for a walk (figs. 278, 362). The only buildings to be completed—and which constituted in fact merely the most indispensable preparatory improvements—are today, in the absence of the houses that were planned, aimless constructions all too easily compared to fairground attractions. The ideas underpinning the Parc Güell were in fact more serious than they might at first appear. Gaudí, by solving the construction problems as he encountered them, devised the most astonishing expressive and decorative effects, such as his viaducts-cum-walkways in molded concrete perpends bonded like stonework and his celebrated ceramic bench surmounting a monumental portal, the columns of which function as a reservoir for drinking water.

Yet it is in the Colonia Güell Church (1898–1915), intended for a housing project in the suburbs of Barcelona, that Gaudí should have realized his most perfect work. The death of its patron in 1918 prevented the architect from advancing beyond the monumental crypt, the distillation of a whole oeuvre dedicated to the mineral, inorganic world, perhaps even to the disquiet of untamed forms. The columns, inside and out, lean slightly following an ingenious and complicated schema, both expressive and unnerving, serving at one and the same time as structure and as a constituent element of the decoration.

The Sagrada Família (1884–1926) is perhaps Gaudí's best-known work. It was certainly the longest in construction, since it was begun in the 1880s and was unfinished when he died. The building as a whole labors considerably under its Catholic symbolism and an excessive extravagance of decoration. But the four potent towers are the virtuoso masterpiece by an architect who was both a believer and a poet.

The Casa Milá (1906–10), known as La Pedrera (the "stone quarry" or "rock pile") due to its amorphous appearance and the coarse treatment of the bare concrete surface, was Gaudí's final creation (figs. 279, 304, 361). As in every one of his works, the extraordinarily early date of construction derails all commentary, since the architect, while remaining his own man, once more devised something with few parallels in his earlier projects and above all in the architectural practice of the time. Only the dedication to the Virgin on the top floor and the ceramic decoration of the weird chimney stacks that pepper the roof walkways remind one of the sporadic durable traits of his paradoxical style.

Gaudí worked with numerous collaborators, the most talented of whom were Francesc Berenguer i Mestres (1866–1914) and, even more so, Josep Maria Jujol i Gibert (1879–1949), responsible for the astonishing ceramic mosaic creations in the Parc Güell and at the Casas Batllò and Milá. Their own work remains, however, entirely tributary of Gaudí's influence. To the first is often attributed the Bogedas Güell (1889–90) at Garaf, which would be proof enough of a fine talent were it not more reasonable to ascribe them to Gaudí himself. We owe to the second a number of edifices at San Joan Despi, including the Casa Negre (1913–16) and the Torre de la Creu (1916), though these amusing stylistic exercises were little more than pastiches of works by Gaudí.

It should not be thought that Barcelona's "modern" architects all possessed the originality of Puig, Domènech, or Gaudí. A large proportion—many of whom are little known—left works in the Catalan capital that could be assimilated, due to their somewhat facile floral decoration that reappears all over Europe, to "international Art Nouveau." It is in Madrid, rather, that an ambitious and original work of this type can be found: the vast town house at 4 Calle Fernando VI, designed by Jose Grases y Riera. With its monumental sculpture, massive balconies, and impressive corner rotunda, it is the masterpiece of Madrid Art Nouveau. It was published in France in the *Monographies de bâtiments modernes* (no. 228), accompanied by a commentary that underlined the exceptional place of the building in the context of the architect's oeuvre as a whole. For all that, the heavy, Baroque-style edifice illustrates all that separated Catalan *modernisme* from the few exercises undertaken in the Spanish capital.

Horta in Brussels

Brussels enjoyed conditions that were as favorable as those in Barcelona for the appearance of an architectural revolution, particularly since its history, its geographical location, and its Franco-Flemish culture made looking inward impossible. As a national entity, the country of Belgium was recent; it was building up its small empire of colonies and, in its ever-expanding cities, workers' movements were more solidly organized than anywhere else. In the realm of the visual arts too, the group Les XX, followed by the Salon de la Libre Esthétique, had contributed greatly to putting Brussels on the avant-garde map, and no other city was better suited to playing a pioneering role.

The French influence had already long ensured the rapid assimilation of rationalism and a widespread use of metal, as illustrated by Balat's superb glasshouses at Laeken. Simultaneously, there arose an eclecticism similar to that in Paris, as demonstrated by the king's invitation to Charles Girault, the architect of the Petit Palais in Paris, to come and build in Brussels. Art Nouveau, however, did not remain as isolated as it was in Barcelona, nor was it as virulently combated as it was in Paris. Victor Horta (1861–1947) did not encounter the same impediments to recognition as others did elsewhere, even if his notoriety opened on a scandalous note with the aedicule built in 1889 in the Parc du Cinquantenaire to house Jef Lambeaux's relief, *Human Passions* (*Passions humaines*), the sculptures for which were judged at the time to be insufficiently clad. The edifice was a modest one, but it already reveals a practice that would continue throughout Horta's long career: the contribution of sometimes mediocre artists in the decoration of his buildings.

It was not until 1893 and the construction of the Hôtels Autrique and Tassel that the earliest examples of a totally personal architecture emerged, both in terms of spatial arrangement and a truly modern decorative approach. His clients, like many of their successors, formed part of the entourage of Brussels freemasonry (it seems highly likely that Horta was a mason himself), similar in their progressive, even socialist, ideas, and in belonging to a middle-class milieu of intellectuals and industrialists who had made their money quickly. Horta was also one of their number: financial constraints aside, his own house scarcely differs in spirit from those he designed for Baron van Eetvelde or Armand Solvay.

The Tassel family house is generally considered to be the first Art Nouveau building and its originality soon gave rise to commentaries stating just this point of view. Bearing in mind that Catalan modernism was at this time largely unknown, this perfectly realized work can indeed lay claim to being the first masterpiece of a style that was still in the process of gestation. Through the undisguised use of almost plain metal girders on the exterior, the load-bearing structure of the central span of bays is made unequivocal. On a facade as sober as those he would design later in his career, Horta somewhat provocatively displayed the intrinsic beauty of iron, its crucial function in the construction, emphasizing still more the importance of metal by giving it a key decorative role. More than any other architect, Horta drew plans that were carefully thought out in respect of the potential of each site, which in Brussels were generally narrow and deep. Here, everything is organized around a single staircase which links all the floors and all the volumes, a formula upon which for many years Horta was to compose subtle and ingenious variations. The recent renovation of this luminous stairwell has restored to its original state the luxuriant decor painted on its walls, the celebrated stalks (preferred to flowers) that Horta turned into a decorative formula, unfurling like creepers over more than one story. Its ornamental unity derives essentially from the repetition of motifs which share the same simplicity, suppleness, and nervous tension on mosaics, ironwork, and stained glass.

It was above all at the Hôtel Solvay (figs. 353, 354), begun in 1894, then in the Van Eetvelde (1895, fig. 275) and Horta (1898) houses, that, continuing in this vein, the architect attained heights he was never to equal in his career as a designer of interiors. This is especially true of the first of these, created for an industrialist who had made his wealth in chemical products. Appearing from the exterior like a sizable house of sobriety and elegance, it is, within, a veritable palace, brightly colored and richly furnished, the architect having been given complete creative freedom. He even designed a piano in bronze and crystal glass, which sadly has since disappeared. Horta's modernism is clearly evident in the highly functional planning of space, the frequent and unashamed use of exposed metal columns, even on the upper floors, and the plentiful ornamentation, remarkable for the dizzying virtuosity of its inlaid paneling in different woods. The central staircase remains the most striking space, a shade too showy in its luxury perhaps, but perfectly homogeneous, amounting to a portrait of its owner.

It is no coincidence that Horta—a master of the perfect synthesis between home and homeowner—spent most of his career in Brussels, where rental apartment blocks were few and far between. Baron van Eetvelde, a high-level court official with interests in Congo timber, provided Horta with the opportunity of building a house distinctly more restrained and of a less outgoing elegance than Solvay's. Horta's own financial means, meanwhile, induced him to build for himself a lively if functional dwelling. The house he designed in 1899 for Octave Aubecq, a particularly austere gentleman, has the most remarkable facade of all and a magnificent ground plan, although the interior is surprisingly bourgeois.

The finest creation of Horta's whole career was the Maison du Peuple (1895), which was stupidly destroyed in 1964–65. Built as the headquarters of the Belgian Socialist party (Société Coopérative Ouvrière de Bruxelles), it served various purposes. In addition to its political function, it also served as a shopping center (with butcher's, grocer's, and stores) and place of entertainment (café, theater space). The majority of Belgium's Maisons du Peuple displayed the same determination to proclaim the strength of the workers' movement, its role, and its place in the country's future by dint of a resolutely modern architectural style. The one in Antwerp (1898) by Jan van Asperen is a notable example. Horta, lest there be any ambiguity as to the building's function, came down firmly in favor of bricks and iron—supremely humble materials—exhibited as plainly as possible. Never before had architecture attained such rationalism; even the theater had no decoration other than seats and balconies. The Maison's purpose coincided with the architect's own ideas on truth and probity. By 1964–65, the architect had unfortunately dropped out of fashion and many arguments of an aesthetic as well as functional nature were trotted out to justify the destruction of a masterpiece that at the time it was built had gained unanimous plaudits. In fact, the very vehemence of the arguments put forward merely emphasized the intrinsic importance of both building and architect.

Such fierce press campaigns were never waged when the works of Paul Hankar (1859–1901) began to be pulled down one by one. The catalog of this major Belgian Art Nouveau artist, who died prematurely, is today reduced to a handful of buildings. Some miraculously preserved and seminal works luckily allow one to admire the extent of his radical rejection of historicism. If Horta remains in many respects a bourgeois and somehow Baroque architect, Hankar's corpus is much closer to medieval models, and was destined for a less well-heeled clientele, the majority of whom were artists themselves. In 1893, the same year as Horta's Hôtel Tassel, Hankar was to build for himself his earliest significant domestic building, at 71 Rue Defacqz, whose unassuming nature did not prevent its becoming known and being frequently published. Many highly original elements here make their first appearance, such as the asymmetry of the facade, in which each volume, each bay, and each floor asserts its independence. The influence of Japanese art on Hankar was more obvious in the Zeghers House on Avenue Louise (1894; destroyed). Here the circular windows that proved so attractive in the Ciamberlani House (1897) and in the Bartholomé workshop-house (1898; destroyed) appeared for the first time. This house also displayed superb draftsmanship typical of his work in metal, less elegant and decorative than Horta's, but often more innovative and never repetitious. The experience Hankar gained in shopfitting—as can still be seen at the Niguet Store (1899), at 13 Rue Royale—allowed him to score a notable success at the Colonial Exhibition at Tervueren in 1898 with Japanese-style designs made exclusively in wood.

The modern architects and artists of Brussels were all to gather around either Horta or Hankar. The first attracted architects of a bourgeois cast, whose innovations formed part of an unbroken tradition. This was the case with Paul Saintenoy (1862–1952), for instance, whose house at 81 Avenue Louise (1898) is a perfect example of a fine stone-built construction complete with cornices and balconies featuring whiplash ironwork in the Horta style. It is quite unlike his Old England Store (1899, fig. 347), where the metal elements are reminiscent of the leaning columns borrowed from Viollet-le-Duc by Guimard in his 1895 school of the Sacré-Coeur. The same can be said of Paul Vizzavona (1881–1956), whose time spent in Horta's practice shows through in buildings that are often blatant pastiches of the master, and of Jules Brunfaut (1852–1942). The latter's Art Nouveau career is practically confined to a single building, the Hôtel Hamon (1903), exceptional in its whiteness (more Italian than Belgian), but in which certain Horta mannerisms can be seen, especially in the balconies and window lintels.

The case of Gustave Strauven (1878–1919) is quite different again. Draftsman to Horta from 1896 to 1898, during the master's most creative period, in his own work he displayed an astonishing imagination—halfway between dream and nightmare—in which every style seems to come together in the creation of some curious piece of jewelry. The houses at 85 Boulevard Clovis (1901), at 9 Rue Paul de Jaer (1902), and above all at 11 Square Ambiorix (1903, fig. 348) suggest close links with the Parisian Jules Lavirotte. However, these oddities remained curiosities on the Brussels scene, and Strauven left no disciples.

Generally speaking, Hankar's idiom made more impact in Brussels than Horta's, because its modernity was conveyed by a more immediately comprehensible geometry (similar to that found in the furnishings of Gustave Serrurier-Bovy of the same period; fig. 412). There are numerous houses—if not entire streets—adorned with taut, superbly drafted ironwork, with circular windows and brick walls decorated with sgraffito. Homes of this kind were designed by Léon Delune, Alphonse Boelens, and, in particular, Antoine Pompe (1873–1980), whose talent was far from being confined to Art Nouveau, and Paul Cauchie (1875–1952), who trained as a painter. Only one house can be attributed with certainty to Cauchie: the one he designed for himself at 5 Rue des Francs (1905), where the rigorously laid out arrangement of the apertures combines with the large-scale painted decoration to create one of the finest Art Nouveau facades in Brussels (fig. 351).

Ernest Blérot (1870–1957) was an unusual figure. Capable of designing superb mansion houses on the wealthier streets of the capital, such as his own (sadly destroyed) at 1 Rue Vilain XIII (1901–8), he also completed various working-class housing projects (Rue de Belle-Vue, 1898–99; Rue Vanderschrick, 1900–1). Each followed a basic design, which he varied through the imaginative use of ironwork, color, form, and the positioning of apertures and projecting blocks. Blérot can seem like a brilliant amateur, since his art is often left to the whims of an unpredictable imagination to the detriment of any rigor whatsoever, though certain practices—such as frames with moldings made up of totally alien elements—enabled him to successfully avoid inconsequentiality. Blérot's career is equally impossible to pin down, for he gradually abandoned architecture after the war to take up the design of automobile prototypes.

In spite of the very different personalities of these architects and the conflict some felt between their design of bourgeois architecture and their urge to create decent working-class homes, Brussels Art Nouveau possesses real unity. One cannot speak here of a school, but rather of shared practices—the narrow-fronted town house, blue stone, sgraffito—and of the joint influence of Horta and Hankar on their generation. This might explain why Henry van de Velde (1863–1957) did not belong in what was to him an alien environment. The first house by this self-taught, complex personality—the celebrated Bloemenwerf House built for his own use (figs. 303, 350)—dates from 1895. The work does not take its inspiration from French rationalism, but rather from modern Anglo-Saxon movements, which makes it, in its abstinence from decoration, a most exceptional dwelling in a Belgian context. It soon became notorious, being visited not only by Siegfried Bing, who invited the architect to exhibit in his Art Nouveau gallery in Paris, but above all by Germans, such as the art critic Julius Meier-Graefe, who made a great contribution to the artist's international fame.

In fact, the greater part of van de Velde's Belgian career was as an interior decorator and as a creator of furniture and other objects (figs. 251, 447). Competing with Horta—who had established himself in the building world earlier and more successfully than van de Velde—he never managed to make his mark as an architect. The ill-fated commercial ventures of his workshops induced him to accept an invitation from Count Kessler to go to Germany (fig. 341). His departure can be seen, rather than as a sign of failure for the man, as a boon for an artist whose ideas, totally at odds with those of his compatriots, could never have reached their full expression elsewhere than in a German-speaking country. His art belongs in truth to the history of the Sezession.

The construction in Brussels of the Palais Stoclet by Josef Hoffmann in 1903 can be considered as sounding the death knell for Belgian Art Nouveau (fig. 345). The only wholly luxurious construction which was not eclectic in all Brussels, the Palais Stoclet represents in a way the kind of prestigious building that van de Velde was only able to build abroad.

Guimard in Paris

The third center for Art Nouveau in the Latin countries was Paris, although, due to the size of the city, the overpowering preponderance of eclecticism (the eternal reference to "styles" that formed the fundamental principle of training at the École des Beaux-Arts), and the singular individualism of the French, the capital is far from providing the most homogeneous example. These factors are important for appreciating how difficult it was for such modernity to gain a foothold in Paris and the opposition it immediately stirred up, which often pushed artists into packing up and leaving for a breath of fresh air in some distant province. Though it is true that in Brussels and Barcelona architects also had a weakness for certain quarters of the city, in the French capital geographic borders seemed still more clear-cut. Social barriers too were more absolute than elsewhere: the aristocracy and the *grande bourgeoisie* had long been in the habit of adorning their ponderous and luxurious mansions with eighteenth-century objets d'art. In Paris more than anywhere else, Art Nouveau was to be the preferred choice for wealthy traders and for the more adventurous members of the lower-middle class.

It was people belonging to these groups who made up the clientele of Hector Guimard (1867–1942). His first houses were pleasantly imaginative designs in tough *meulière* stone and brick, in which one can discern little more than a certain savoir-faire, while the school of the Sacré-Coeur (1895) goes as far as pastiching Viollet-le-Duc since it almost copies a design for a covered market published in the *Entretiens sur l'architecture.* As for the initial state of the Castel Béranger, at 14 Rue La Fontaine (figs. 269, 300), commissioned by Mme. Fournier, a widow desirous of making a capital investment, at the beginning of 1896 it was scarcely more than a large almost commonplace pile of neo-Gothic inspiration, merely as picturesque as Guimard's previous works.

For the young architect, the acquisition of a travel grant resulting from the 1894 Salon was to be what is commonly termed a "conversion on the road to Damascus," in the sense that, unlike the winners of the Prix de Rome who went south, he used the fund to journey to Great Britain, Holland, and Belgium. In Brussels in 1895, Guimard met Paul Hankar and, more crucially, Victor Horta. How he became acquainted with architects who were as unknown as he was at the time and who introduced him to them remains a mystery to this day. Proof of it exists, however; Guimard made a watercolor of Hankar's house on Rue Defacqz and waxed lyrical about Horta's Hôtel Tassel, which, on his return to Paris, he attempted to make better known. It is true that the French architect himself made much of his meeting with Horta—whom he termed his "master"—while the transformations in the decor at Castel Béranger (completed between the end of 1895 and the beginning of 1897), undertaken thanks to the understanding of his client, do indeed bear witness to a radical shift in the Guimard vocabulary. It might be better, however, to keep this "illumination" in perspective and see it more simply as the revelation of the architect's latent creative potential. For Castel Béranger, as we know it today, and in spite of the length of time over which it was built and all the changes wrought in the decoration in its final stages, possesses a singular unity. If some of the ironwork in particular does indeed recall Horta, Guimard went well beyond imitation, attaining true stylistic originality, especially in one of the elements he designed late on in the project: the remarkable iron gate for the entrance hall.

It is too frequently forgotten that this building is not a palatial abode intended to satisfy a single family but a conglomerate of lodgings to be let at very reasonable rents. The savings made on the structural work allowed for the design of numerous original models of everything, including ironwork, furniture, stained glass, mantelpieces, the fountain in the inner courtyard, the residents' mailboxes, and an incredible gas oven. The architect's pencil baulked at nothing; nothing escaped his control. Criticized for the sinewy abstraction of his highly personalized motifs, Guimard retorted, not without humor, that nobody was forced to live in the building.

Guimard advertised the building widely. Conveniently for him, the City of Paris awarded it a prize in its first competition for facades. An exhibition, a lecture, and the publication of a deluxe volume made Castel Béranger famous overnight and allowed the architect to extend his customer base considerably. In particular, it earned him the commission for the gigantic Salle Humbert de Romans (1897–1901), an exceptionally functionalist and costly music and educational complex of great quality which was unfortunately demolished soon after, due to its unsuitable location in an outlying district. He also designed an important series of villas in the Parisian suburbs and on the Normandy coast (1898–1905), where his quest for unity led him to dispense with the idea of the facade altogether.

The Castel Henriette at Sèvres (1899–1900, fig. 356), the Castel Val at Auvers-sur-Oise (1903), and the Castel Orgeval (1904–5) at Villemoisson-sur-Orge are some of the milestones in Guimard's quest for architectural coherence through a sculptural approach. His art is celebratory and expansive, but striking in its rejection of the prettified ornamentation of the period. His work was not without its symbolic content, notably in a very personal adaptation of northern Gothic in the Coilliot House (1898–1900) at Lille and of Norman half-timbering in the Villa La Bluette (1899) at Hermanville, where pebbles and shells were used as building materials and in the decoration. The acme of his rationalist approach, however, is provided by the structures he designed for the entrances to Parisian Métro stations (fig. 368). The need to produce a series of entrances which would be visible and identifiable from a distance without cluttering up the urban space led the architect to design slender cast-iron posts clasping large plaques inscribed with some highly original graphics. Only the Bastille and the Place de l'Étoile stations offer points of comparison with the monumental and princely edifices Otto Wagner provided for the Vienna subway. Guimard's exemplary creations did not meet with approbation, however, critics seeing them as an assault on good taste—even the green paint he employed was censured for its "Germanism"—and over time the subway company commissioned new models from other architects.

This failure can also be seen as an exasperated reaction to Guimard's penchant for naive self-publicity. Having proclaimed himself in 1900 an "art architect," he introduced a "style Guimard" label in 1903, but his numerous efforts were never enough to break the conspiracy of silence that was to surround his work. Nonetheless, after a long period of crisis during which his activity was limited almost entirely to commissions from his chief client, Léon Nozal (a house at Cabourg, a factory at Saint-Denis in the Paris region, and a mansion on the fashionable Rue Ranelagh; all demolished), his abstract and violent imagination became more temperate. Guimard found a fresh energy in his new, less agitated, more classical and refined manner, as can be seen in the town house he built for himself at 122 Avenue Mozart (1909–12, fig. 298), the blocks in Rue Agar (1909–11), and the Hôtel Mazzara (1910–11), as well as in the furniture he designed for these buildings. Yet, in this period of renewal and creativity, nothing could induce him to jettison functionalist aesthetic principles and unitary ideas, which he summarized laconically in three words: logic, harmony, and feeling. But this last phase in his work met with no reaction, and it left no legacy.

Guimard's early career singled him out as the key representative of a modernity issuing directly from Viollet-le-Duc's work. Léon Bénouville (1860–1903) and Charles Plumet (1861–1928) were the brilliant heirs of rationalism's neo-Gothic strand, notably in the houses they built next door to each other on the Rue Tocqueville in Paris (1897). Bénouville was to die prematurely, however, while Plumet soon reverted to a career of inoffensive classicism. His apartment block at 50 Avenue Victor-Hugo (1901, fig. 365)—held up at the time as a paragon of the acceptable face of innovation and worthy of emulation—was to earn its author unwavering popularity. It was perhaps this success that led Plumet to turn out variations on the same schemas, such as the top-floor loggia with arcade that he was to use as his signature—even to the point of pastiching his own work of 1901 at number 39 of the same avenue in 1912.

Faced with this Gothic strain, and Plumet illustrates how short-lived it was because he turned to a more classicizing manner, Art Nouveau in Paris was distinguished by a kind of disheveled Baroque, which caused criticism to be focused on some more or less oozing and ornamental cream puffs. As long as it remained locked away in theaters, concert halls, and restaurants (Maxim's [fig. 342], Lucas Carton), a certain exuberance was all very well, but in the street it became indecent. One should not ignore this playful, even risqué side to Art Nouveau; it is one of its many facets. Not everything was rationalist and abstract, nor even always brilliant—far from it. The period could also display fantasy, opulence, and stability, even in its outlandishness. Some Parisian apartment blocks have since become famous, such as Wagon's on the Place Félix-Faure (fig. 366), or Auscher's (1866–1932) on the Rue de Rennes. However, it was Jules Lavirotte (1864–1929) and Xavier Schoellkopf (1870–1911) who were to build with great brio the most startling of the capital's fantasies. The former, after a few essays of a halfhearted boldness, displayed his talents with three edifices built in quick succession in a block on a single site: a private town house at 12 Rue Sédilot (1899), with combined hints of an overblown Louis XV and the recent example of the front door at the Castel Béranger (fig. 269); the building at 3 Square Rapp (1899–1900), a piecemeal work in which large-scale architectural ceramic first enters the fray; and finally, the famous block at 29 Avenue Rapp (1900–1, figs. 268, 301). This last, a masterpiece of asymmetry and decorative imagination, presents a facade wholly in flambé sandstone in which each level appears to have been treated independently of the others. Its erotic suggestiveness is obvious, particularly in the decoration for the entrance door, which is as phallic as the ground-floor plan. The building was nonetheless awarded a prize in the Paris facade competition (Lavirotte being the only architect to win the competition three times), but nothing in the jury's report hints at the scarcely veiled allusions of the decor, the commentary contenting itself with praising the self-cleaning, hardwearing, and pleasantly colored ceramic cladding. The author of the report did, however, venture to suggest that the architect's ideas were not to be imitated.

The orange-branch pattern of the cladding on the mansion house at 34 Avenue de Wagram (1904) is a pure poetical fantasy (fig. 369). The size of the windows and the shape of the balconies hark back to the entertaining anarchy of earlier frontages by Lavirotte, but this was the last time that the architect was to amuse himself so flamboyantly. His later works belong to a more orderly, almost ordinary artist (23 Avenue de Messine and 6 Rue de Messine, 1906–7). His later work was nondescript.

As for Schoellkopf, he came to the attention of the critics through several highly individual edifices that could make him appear, *mutatis mutandis*, as a kind of French Gaudí. The large house at 4 Avenue d'Iéna (1898), the house built for the cabaret singer Yvette Guilbert on Boulevard Berthier (1900, fig. 299), and the block at 29 Boulevard de Courcelles (1902)—only this last has survived intact—are the main works of a hardly prolific, but imaginative, baroque, and disquieting artist. Unfortunately, the architect does not seem to have been able to acquire a clientele prepared to support him and his later works—in particular on Rue d'Alésia—are closer to standard eclecticism.

Parisian Art Nouveau suffered from an evident lack of cohesion. Its shortcomings were exemplified by the popularism of a few short-lived artistic associations with titles like L'art dans Tout (Art in Everything), L'art pour Tous (Art for Everyone), and L'art à l'École (Art at School). Some questionable wedding-cake confections—at heart rather academic in spirit—had done their worst to discredit even abroad a fashion that was referred to with distrust. From out of the midst of this improbable decorative mishmash a few works worth defending did emerge, such as the fine apartment block with metal piers on Rue Boursault (1901) by Jules Simonet (1826–1896), a few works by François-Adolphe Bocage, such as 6 Rue de Hanovre (1908), 40 Rue Boileau (1907–8) by Joachim Richard (1869–after 1948), and 9 Rue Claude-Chahu (1903) by Charles Klein (1873–?). In all of these constructions ceramics play a key role. Finest of all, perhaps, were the "reasonably priced hygienic apartment blocks" of Henri Sauvage (1873–1932) on Rue Danville, Rue Sévéro, and Rue de la Chine. Frantz Jourdain (1847–1935), more of a theoretician and a polemicist than a wholly convincing architect, exerted his authority and used much ink in defense of modern artists. The department store La Samaritaine (1905–7), built for Gabriel Cognacq, could have helped to carry the flag, but this commercial building—a function which somewhat neutralized its role as a manifesto—appeared too late to exert much influence on the development of Art Nouveau. The same can be said of the startling church of Saint-Jean-de-Montmartre by Anatole de Baudot (completed 1905), constructed entirely in concrete, and the wholly metal commercial block erected on Rue Réaumur (1903–5) by Georges Chedanne (1861–1940), who was nevertheless a winner of the Prix de Rome. Such works, often unique in the catalogs of their creators, ultimately represent brilliant exceptions.

SEASIDE RESORTS, SPA TOWNS, STRASBOURG, AND NANCY

Barcelona, Brussels, and Paris were not the sole representatives of Catalan, Belgian, and French Art Nouveau. Not only did artists from these capitals find themselves drawn to exercise their talents beyond their habitual geographical limits, but there also existed secondary centers in their own right. Antwerp Art Nouveau, for instance, of a most individual Flemish cast, is far more coherent than it might appear, and is not limited to the famous shipowner's house with its prow emerging out of one corner.

The case of France is in this respect exemplary. The profusion of artistic centers was due above all to the capital's cultural influence, rather than the country's role at the heart of Latin Art Nouveau. This influence was transmitted by Art Nouveau's wealthy Parisian clients, who migrated to fashionable seaside resorts (in Normandy and the Basque country, and on the Côte d'Azur) or to spa towns such as Vichy. Its influence was extended by the organs of a specialized press that offered to each and every provincial architect models of an obviously Parisian cachet. Several cities, it is true, remained impervious to these innovations, either because local practices went against the exhibitionism of Art Nouveau—this was the case in Lyon, where interior decoration mattered more than the decoration of facades—or because of the density of their city planning. This last point is clearly illustrated by the case of Bordeaux in the southwest, where there exists but a single important work in the entire inner city: the Hôtel Frugès (the same Frugès who was to later commission the Pessac housing estate from Le Corbusier) at 63 Place des Martyrs-de-la-Résistance. Even though its architect, Pierre Ferret (1887–1965), was from Bordeaux, the architectural ceramicists (Gentil and Bourdet) and the metal craftsmen (Émile Robert and Edgar Brandt) were from Paris. The Parisian École des Beaux-Arts on Rue Bonaparte thus had, almost in spite of itself, a part to play in the dissemination of Art Nouveau, for it was there that the French architectural elite was formed: Achille Proy at Le Puy-en-Velay, southern central France, and Louis Duthoit (designer of the luxurious Bouctot-Vagniez House, 36 Rue des Otages, 1908–12) in the northern city of Amiens—the only significant Art Nouveau architects in those places—are two instances among many.

The case of Vichy is an example of Parisian hegemony, since nearly all those involved, from the architects Charles Le Coeur (1830–1906) and Charles Letrosne (1868–1939) to the ceramicist Alexandre Bigot (1862–1927) and the painter Alphonse Osbert (1857–1939), had for the most part practiced in the capital. The same applies to nearly all the other spa towns that underwent development at this time, but also to the great hotels on the Côte d'Azur, Édouard Niermans's Négresco (1913) in Nice for instance being a perfect, if academic, example. Such conventional eclecticism, intended to please aristocratic visitors from all over the globe, is evidence of the opportunism of its architect, who had been an Art Nouveau pioneer back in Paris—particularly in the famous brasseries, Pousset and Mollard.

The Normandy coast and the northern *département* of the Côtes-du-Nord constituted something of a paradise for the *folies* of the 1900s. Guimard, assured of success at the hands of his *nouveau riche* clientele, came to build three villas in the area. But it is not in the already aristocratic resorts such as Deauville and Trouville that one can find the most salient examples of seaside architecture colored by Art Nouveau, but rather places like Cabourg, Mers-les-Bains, Fécamp, and Le Havre (fig. 359). Even there, "Parisians" outnumbered the rest: William Cargill (1864–1945) and Édouard Choupaÿ pursued fruitful careers in the region around Le Havre, but their training had been in the capital and the best part of their output remains Parisian. At the less sought-after coastal resort of Mers-les-Bains, houses of an almost vernacular appearance are distinguished by their ornate painted-timber decoration. Here we meet once more with Édouard Niermans, now at the peak of his powers, as well as with Théodore Bourgeois (1858–1930), an architect who worked in the Paris region and author of the amusing Bon Abri at 7 Rue Boucher-de-Perthes. The Art Nouveau of seaside resorts also presents some intriguing architectural curiosities, such as the famous drugstore at Douvres-la-Délivrande (fig. 358), and Éden-Roc by another Parisian, Georges Massa, a mixed-style manor house perched quaintly on a rocky outcrop over the Golfe-Juan. All this is symptomatic of a great deal of imagination, as are the various restaurants and other public buildings which provided the main focus for the new fashion in the provinces (the Alhambra restaurant and the Opéra brasserie in Rouen, the Cigale restaurant in Nantes and the Élysée-Palace theater in Vichy).

In addition to these often isolated constructions, which do little more than prove the incompleteness of the fashion's success, two towns stand out on more serious counts, and for reasons that almost have more to do with politics than art: Nancy and Strasbourg. The main consequence of France's defeat in the 1870 Franco-Prussian war was her loss of Alsace and Lorraine. If Nancy remained French at the frontier of a Germany that had annexed a sizable proportion of her region, during the heyday of Art Nouveau Strasbourg lay entirely in the hands of the empire. This factor goes a long way toward explaining the Germanic character of much modern architecture in the capital of Alsace, as represented by architects who were either German or had studied in Germany.

Two of the city's most talented architects were Edmund Berninger (1856–1926) and Gustave Krafft (1861–1927). The former, born in Thuringia, had trained in England, Holland, France, and Italy; the latter was from Strasbourg, and was educated in Stuttgart and Paris. Their German roots might have motivated them to become architects in the German style, but their work displays an ingenious synthesis of Belgian Art Nouveau and influences from Nancy and Paris. Their earliest house in Strasbourg, 76 Allée de la Robertsau (1900), is a grand and elegant Italian-style villa. The store on the Place Broglie (1901, fig. 334), on the other hand, recalls Saintenoy's Old England Store in Brussels (fig. 347), Horta's whiplash lines, and Louis Bonnier's (1857–1946) entrance to Siegfried Bing's Art Nouveau store. The buildings of Lutke and Backes (1866–1931), more massive than those of Berninger and Krafft, are certainly more typical of Strasbourg architecture in the 1900s. At 56 Allée de la Robertsau (1902), at 1 and 3 Avenue Sellenick, and at 22 Avenue Général-de-Castelnau, the Germanic character of the buildings is lighter than in Metz and less ponderous than in Mannheim, but also shows the influence of Latin Art Nouveau. In truth, the Alsatian capital has always been graced with constructions evocative of other areas, but marked by a highly individual touch.

As for Nancy, the town possessed a unity of style that even Paris did not attain. So recurrent are the motifs (for the most part borrowed from the flora of the region) and so frequently do the names of the same craftsmen appear—notably Wolff and Vautrin for sculpture, and the ever-present Jacques Gruber for stained glass (fig. 444)—that one might at a glance attribute all the Art Nouveau houses to the same architect. In fact, Nancy's modernity was concentrated in a handful of architects only, Émile André (1871–1933), Henri Gutton (1874–1963), Joseph Hornecker (1873–1942), and Lucien Weissenburger (1860–1929) being the most inventive among them. The architectural unity derives in the main from the well-known École de Nancy, which in some sense gave coherence to the city's modernity, though the term itself applies more to the decorative arts—furniture and glass—than to architecture. Nonetheless, through professional or personal ties between creative artists, the unifying principles behind the École de Nancy eventually rubbed off on architects too. Evidence for this is found in the repetition of the same local plants on vases and inlaid tables, and, even more so, in the influence of the Gothic and Japanese styles that characterize art in Nancy. The edifices built by André and by Weissenburger are absolutely typical in this respect—with their pinnacles and tall, narrow windows, they have a strong sense of the vertical. Regionalism is visible everywhere, even the Cross of Lorraine—at the time pregnant with political significance—appears on Weissenburger's own residence at 1 Boulevard Charles-V (1904), while there are pine cones on the front door at 92–92 bis Quai Claude-le-Lorrain (Émile André, 1903, fig. 360). Such medieval references can be seen as a way of emphasizing attachment to the culture of France, where Gothic art had attained unsurpassed heights. There are other clues: the export of products from Nancy to the capital, the presence of Parisian ceramicists in the town (Alexandre Bigot, followed by Gentil and Bourdet), the goodwill that the Paris press showed to work from the Lorraine, and finally the contribution made to the town's architecture by two Parisians, Sauvage and Jacques-René Hermant (1855–1930).

Sauvage's Villa Majorelle (1898–1901) marks the beginning of Art Nouveau architecture in Nancy (fig. 357). Though Art Nouveau was quick to flourish there in the decorative arts, until that time the only building that could be associated with the style—6 Boulevard Lobau (1896) by Eugène Vallin—is Art Nouveau uniquely by dint of its sculpture. The mystery of how Majorelle came to be acquainted with Sauvage, a virtually unknown young man from Paris, has not yet been resolved. What is sure is that the two artists were to be linked by bonds of true friendship, Sauvage executing a second house for Majorelle at Compiègne in 1908 and the facade of his Paris store at 126 Rue de Provence shortly before World War I. The villa at 1 Rue Louis-Majorelle in Nancy was a harmonious joint effort combining resident artists and Parisians: Majorelle himself, together with Prouvé and Gruber (and Weissenburger overseeing the local site work) on the one side, Bigot and Frantz Jourdain on the other. The outcome was a perfect artist's house, which asserts its modernity unambiguously and unashamedly, and whose function is proclaimed by the beautiful rose window on the second floor. The Parisian press aside, few commentaries on the building have come to light, but it seems likely that such a construction would have had an influence on local architects. Curiously, the major works of Émile André and Weissenburger appeared hard on the heels of its completion. In the case of André, this included the houses in the Saurupt Park—an ambitious and openly polemical housing scheme to which every major Nancy architect made some contribution—and 69 Avenue Foch (all 1902). Perhaps the most notable building by Weissenburger, whose earlier Royer printing works at 3 Rue de la Salpêtrière (1900) were not without coincidental kinship with Guimard's Coilliot House, was the elegant Hôtel Bergeret at 24 Rue Lionnois (1903–4).

The other Parisian masterpiece in Nancy is the Hôtel Luc, 25 Rue de Malzéville (1904), by Hermant. Its blend of classical harmony and Baroque detailing—consoles, columns, and ironwork—introduces a note of refinement. There is a hint of eclecticism, however, which was practically unknown to architects in Nancy, who at the time had only yielded to the influence of the Rococo of the Place Stanislas in a few interiors, such as Weissenburger's Excelsior restaurant (1910). The Hôtel Luc has its echoes in the work of Joseph Hornecker, such as 7 Rue Chanzy (1907) and his two houses in the Saurupt Park (1904 and 1905). These are among the few Art Nouveau buildings by this architect, whose largest project—of a backward-looking preciousness—was the reconstruction of the city's theater (1906–12).

ITALY

At an early date, Ernesto Basile (1857–1932) in Palermo was designing preeminently historicist houses, but his interiors, decorated more freely, reveal a more modern treatment (Villa Igea, 1899, fig. 343; Villino Florio, 1899–1903; fig. 306). In these works, however, Basile did not quite shake himself loose from the uncertainty and compromises that dogged every Italian architect. Indeed, in spite of such precocious forays, Art Nouveau was slow to appear in Italy.

Such reticence was partly due to political and economic problems, but also to the peninsula's constant distrust of art forms in which it had not had a hand in creating. If, at the 1902 Exhibition of Applied Arts in Turin, Italian modernism was revealed in the shape of the pavilions built by Raimondo D'Aronco (1857–1932), his imposing constructions bore the traces of his career in Turkey and of a Viennese influence that provoked immediate comment. With its rigorously emphasized structures and large number of metal elements in a decor of surprisingly modern geometricism, the design bore a heavy debt to Olbrich, although it sometimes descended into pastiche. Though unusual, D'Aronco's interiors did not quite manage to escape ponderousness and artificiality, particularly in the overblown ornamentation of the central rotunda.

Northern Italy, occupied for long periods by Austria, was closer in spirit to German-speaking peoples than to the French. Art Nouveau in Turin and Milan comprised a fanciful mix of Vienna-style modernism and the leaden academicism typical of Italy. The garrulous architecture of Pietro Fenoglio (1867–1927) from Turin too often sacrifices overall harmony to a wealth of pretty details. Built in 1902, the Fenoglio House and Villa Scott are, in spite of their eccentric over-decoration, serious works of architecture. In Milan, Giuseppe Sommaruga

(1867–1917) indulged in similar fusions of historicism and novelty. His chief work, the Palazzo Castiglioni (1903), is a severe-looking and luxurious residence characterized by a use of undressed stone and a heavy carved frieze.

In Florence and Rome, the natural imaginativeness of the south reasserts itself. In Florence, Giovanni Michaelazzi (1879–1920) was probably the most elegant representative of Italian Art Nouveau. His best-known works, Villino Giulio Lampredi (1910) and Villino Broggi-Caraceni (1911, fig. 273), are at once picturesque and rigorous, ingeniously painted yet without pointless ornamentation, using details of a refinement close to that of classic Guimard. His work is diametrically opposed to a type of architecture that appeared on the coast, the most curious example of which is Giuseppe Brega's (1877–1960) Villa Ruggeri (1902–7) at Pesaro, where lobster-shaped consoles and Corinthian columns are juxtaposed with pagoda-style roofs. Unfortunately, this diverting "folly" is nothing other than a superfluously theatrical joke, its interior layout not venturing beyond the commonplace.

It is interesting to note the nullifying effect of Rome on "Stile Liberty," as Art Nouveau is called in Italy, the city presenting no truly original work, not even by Basile, who was highly active in the area. Historicism reigned supreme, showing just how fragile modernism was on Italian soil. In this respect, the Turin exhibition of 1911 was particularly disillusioning, although it also coincided with a rise in nationalism and a rejection of all Austrian influence. This rejection appears in the *Manifesto dell'architettura futurista* by Antonio Sant'Elia (1888–1916), who proclaimed: "I combat and I scorn all the pseudo-architecture of the Austrian, Hungarian, German, and American avant-garde." The strange projects of this artist, who died without having built anything at all, nonetheless convey a genuine and profound admiration for the work of Otto Wagner and his school, adapted to a disturbingly imaginative and monumentally utopian style.

GREAT BRITAIN

It was in 1859 that the architect Philip Webb designed the famous Red House at Bexley Heath for the Pre-Raphaelite painter William Morris (fig. 271). The building uses a formal vocabulary derived directly from Gothic forms, but with a freedom in the layout, a deliberate use of humble materials—brick and tiles—and a thoughtful approach to the interior decoration quite unlike anything that had gone before. It is probably the earliest architectural manifestation of the Arts and Crafts aesthetic—although it is true that the modern English movement was more closely concerned with the decorative arts, as confirmed by the names of the guilds that Morris and his disciples set up, such as the Art Workers' Guild and the Home Arts and Industries Association. Architecture, however, an art like any other, could not be completely insulated from the theoretical and moral aspects of the Arts and Crafts movement, or its political, philosophical, and literary reflections, which had the side effect of curbing much of the imaginative freedom of many British architects.

End-of-century Victorian society was one of the most hidebound in Europe, and it showed a total distrust of anything coming from beyond its shores. The victorious Gothic renaissance of the time—the masterpiece of which is the Palace of Westminster (Houses of Parliament) in London—was simply the rediscovery of the Tudor and early Stuart periods, the golden age of English civilization, linked to a preoccupation with heritage conservation that was ahead of the times. That the artists of the Arts and Crafts movement managed to transform such a total obsession with the past into modernism was not the least of their talents. This was accompanied, however, by the almost systematic and occasionally virulent rejection of any work from continental Europe differing from theirs and by an unwavering, almost "archaeological" faith in craftwork and traditional materials. In a way, Arts and Crafts architecture developed in a context of total individualism, and it can hardly be an accident that it found such fertile ground in the realm of residential building, characterized by inflexibly simple and almost undecorated cottages, which were functional in plan and whose materials were supremely adapted to the environment.

This is brilliantly represented by the works of Edward Prior (1852–1932), William Richard Lethaby (1857–1931), and Charles Francis Annesley Voysey (1857–1941), theoretically minded architects strongly attached to the British vernacular style. The Barn built by Prior at Exmouth in 1897, with its large thatched roof reaching down to the ground, or The Orchard (Chorleywood, 1899), designed by Voysey for his own use, are the main examples. Practically absent from the larger cities, their works might have remained unpublicized were it not for the famous Arts and Crafts movement magazine, *The Studio*. They were involved in few public buildings—Prior and Lethaby's country churches can be regarded as a natural extension of their domestic architecture—and Voysey was to execute only one building of an industrial nature.

English Art Nouveau, in so far as it exists as defined in France or Belgium, must be sought out rather in the few buildings in which the Pre-Raphaelite aesthetic remained intact. These include Henry Wilson's (1864–1934) first project for the Ladbroke Grove Free Library in west London (1890), with its abundant plant decoration in the neo-Gothic style, or in his chapel in memory of George Frederick Watts (1896) at Compton in Surrey—whose decor draws on Celtic and Byzantine sources—and above all in the works of Charles Harrison Townsend (1851–1928). Although he had participated in the activities of the Art Workers' Guild, Townsend's work presents numerous links with that of his colleagues on the European continent. In his principal buildings—the Bishopsgate Institute (1894) in the City, the Horniman Museum in Dulwich (1896–1901), and the Whitechapel Art Gallery (1899–1901) in east London—much space is devoted to floral decoration and to allegorical compositions in mosaic. This taste for ornament, whose quaint diversity contained an element of eclecticism, made him into an isolated figure who was often vehemently opposed to the simplicity—which he termed ignorance—of Lethaby and Voysey.

If this last figure was to be hailed all over Europe, Mackay Hugh Baillie Scott (1865–1945) was no less renowned. Some of his plans were widely reproduced, such as his designs for a seaside house (1903). This is a skillful arrangement of closed spaces around a courtyard with painted interiors mimicking medieval models. Scott followed the same principle in the interior of the Haus eines Kunstfreundes (1901), designed for an international competition that he won ahead of Mackintosh. The outcome of this competition, in which awards were made to two British participants, demonstrated clearly the existence of links between German-speaking countries and Great Britain.

Charles Rennie Mackintosh (1868–1928) was the most important figure in Scottish architecture. His geographical isolation did not hinder him in any way from publicizing his work, which he did more successfully abroad than within the narrow circle of Glasgow cognoscenti—proof that his talent went far beyond the limits of parochial architecture. Though Mackintosh also converted to the English vernacular tradition, as shown by constructions such as the extremely simple Hill House (Helensburg, 1902–3), the artist is better known for the tearoom interiors he designed for Mrs. Cranston (fig. 272) and above all for the Glasgow School of Art (1897–1908, fig. 336). This building, which matured slowly over the years, is remarkable inside for its ingenious and varied solutions to the problems of movement and lighting. It is astonishingly simple outside, the doors and windows on each of its facades being laid out with infinite variety. As a member of "The Four" that included the Macdonald sisters—one of whom he married—Mackintosh attained celebrity through the vertical thrust of his compositions, his razor-sharp line, and the symbolic content of his ornamentation, which was similar in spirit to that of the Viennese Gustav Klimt and Koloman Moser. Mackintosh exhibited in Bing's Art Nouveau store in 1895, at the Munich Sezession in 1899, and then at the equivalent exhibition in Vienna (1900). This helped to extend his influence on European modernism—an influence he was never to have in his native land (indeed, the end of his career there is shrouded in obscurity). His impact abroad was such that Pascal Forthuny wrote in the 1902 *Revue des Arts décoratifs*: "It is now Glasgow rather than London that appears to be showing modern art its new direction."

THE MUNICH GROUP

The Arts and Crafts movement was naturally destined to meet with reactions on continental Europe. In architecture, such influence could hardly occur through buildings themselves—setting an English cottage in Saxony would be senseless—but rather through the existence of artists' associations motivated by parallel philosophies. The works of Hermann Muthesius (1861–1927) on English architecture, the fruit of study undertaken during an extended stay at the German embassy in London (1896–1903), played a vital role in advancing knowledge of the developments in Great Britain among German-speaking artists. In fact, the whole history of the Sezession movements in Germany and Austria was almost that of those groups that associated architecture and craft and whose logical outcome was the creation of the Bauhaus, the school established by Walter Gropius at Weimar in 1919. Events unfolded through a succession of important public exhibitions which were much less confidential than those that took place in Great Britain, and, above all, which were much more open to artists from abroad.

The Munich Sezession had been founded in 1892. The early impetus had come from painters such as Franz von Stück, but it was immediately taken up by seminal journals such as *Jugend, Kunst und Kunsthandwerk,* and *Dekorative Kunst,* thereby attracting a host of youthful artists to the Bavarian capital. But it was only in 1897, with the foundation of the Vereinigten Werkstätten für Kunst und Handwerk (Associated Workshops for Art and Handicraft), that the gathering of architects forming the Munich group gained its renown. These included August Endell (1871–1925), Richard Riemerschmid (1868–1957), Bernhard Pankok (1872–1943), and Peter Behrens (1868–1940). The first of their works was the famous Photoatelier Elvira (1897–98) by Endell, a photographic studio unfortunately since destroyed (fig. 339). The surviving pictures illustrate what was distinctive about the Munich artists, who had not yet shaken off all reference to the natural world in their decorative language. The frontage to the studio was a strange, piecemeal work, characterized by carved reliefs among which may be discerned waves, leaves, and shells in a Japanese arrangement not unlike the motifs on the celebrated fabrics by Hermann Obrist. Arbitrary in their scale, they unfurl artfully over a wall which is punctuated by a few irregularly positioned, but impeccably geometrical, apertures. Inside, the staircase—which resembled a loose caricature of the hall in Horta's Hôtel Tassel—was in the grip of the same anarchy of forms. In his later works, Endell often experienced considerable difficulty in integrating ornament into the overall composition, as at the Buntes Theater in Berlin (1901), whose marine-inspired decoration (featuring an animal frieze, alveolate ceiling, and lamps in the shape of coral), though visibly more of a piece, is symmetrical, spindly, and naive.

Riemerschmid and Pankok did much to make the Munich aesthetic more widely known, notably in the interiors designed for the Exposition Universelle of 1900 in Paris, the former with a room for an art-lover, whose paneling is strikingly reminiscent of Guimard's complicated graphics, and the latter with an equally refined bedroom, complete with alcove. A similar brand of aestheticism is found in Riemerschmid's sober and intimist decoration for the Munich Schauspielhaus and also in the Lange House at Tübingen by Pankok (both 1901). This supports the notion of affinities existing between the Munich group and contemporary French and Belgian artists, which might be explained by the more southerly character of Bavaria in comparison with the rest of Germany. These connections come to the surface in Behrens's early works, including his wood carvings, which were filled with symbolism, and his own house (1901, fig. 338). The latter—the only edifice on the Darmstadt Mathildenhöhe not built by Olbrich (fig. 340)—had facades decorated in ceramic. The vertical emphasis of these facades is almost neo-Gothic and led to condemnation in some quarters that they were too "French."

The Munich group was short-lived, with the artists soon being drawn to other locations by their activities: Riemerschmid divided his time between Nuremberg, Munich, and Cologne, and Pankok settled in Stuttgart in 1901. For his part, Behrens went to Darmstadt, Nuremberg, Düsseldorf, Vienna, and finally Berlin, where he constructed his famous AEG turbine factory (1908–9)—a building justly hailed as a model of functionalism but where his symbolism is tainted by an almost austere triumphalism. Behrens employed in his practice Gropius, Mies van der Rohe, and Le Corbusier, on whom he exerted a considerable influence. The break-up of the Munich artists furthered the dissemination of their ideas, in particular on the subject of industrial aesthetics. Riemerschmid and Pankok supplied furniture models for the Deutscher Werkbund (the former taking an active part in the association's foundation), while it was Behrens—in one of his many projects for AEG—who was responsible for designing the shape of today's electric light bulb.

THE VIENNA SEZESSION

The dynamism of architecture in Vienna at the turn of the century was probably unique in the world. The modern movement seems to have benefited from the advantageous context of a transitional period, during which the political and social situation in the Austro-Hungarian empire was split between grandeur and decadence. Above all, the movement received a sanction that was almost official. Its major representatives—Otto Wagner (1841–1918), Joseph Maria Olbrich (1867–1908), and Josef Hoffmann (1870–1956)—were masters on a scale that went far beyond the confines of their native land. Besides the links Austrians forged with artists abroad (evidence of which can be found in the British press, and in Italian and Central European architecture), their prestige even reached Brussels and Paris precisely at the time after 1903 when Latin Art Nouveau was undergoing a major crisis. The first article on Otto Wagner in French appeared in one of the first issues of the review *L'Architecte* in 1906, and it is no surprise that all the buildings studied date from before 1900.

Otto Wagner was a disconcerting and complex artist. If his career had been uninterrupted, he would certainly have proved the greatest eclectic architect in Vienna, as his work of the first thirty years of his life suggests. While his most ambitious plans drawn up in competition were never constructed (the Stock Exchange and Central Law Courts in Vienna, the cathedral and Reichstag in Berlin, Hamburg's City Hall, the Parliament in Budapest, and the Amsterdam Stock Exchange), a large number of Viennese apartment blocks display the historicism and variety of his inspiration (evidence of a measure of uncertainty with regard to questions of form). The earliest of these included the perfectly classic Villa Wagner (1886) and the transformation in 1900 of his pergola into a studio. The key date in Wagner's life was 1894, when he was appointed a member of the Vienna public transport commission and of the Danube river authority overseeing sluice-works. This gave him the chance to undertake important work as an engineer and to design stations for the Vienna subway system. Above all, however, that year saw him appointed professor of architecture at the Vienna Akademie. This was the germ for what was to become the "Wagnerschule," in which he demonstrated his extraordinary qualities as an educator, showing a tolerance and a faith in modernity that up until then he had had little chance of expressing in his own work. This activity also formed the basis for a theoretical work, *Moderne Architektur* (1895). The open-mindedness of his teaching was essential to his most important students: Olbrich, Hoffmann, Max Fabiani (1865–1962), Otto Schönthal (1878–1961), Josef Plecnik (1872–1957), and Jan Kotěra (1871–1923). In return, he was influenced by the first two of these and this led him to participate in the activities of the group that these students were to found with Gustav Klimt in 1897, the Sezession. The links between the Wagnerschule and the Sezession were limited to the members they shared, for the field of activity of the former—which supplied sympathizers to other groups, such as the more national and traditionalist Hagenbund—remained confined to architecture alone.

The Vienna Sezession's formative years were dominated by the personality of Olbrich, a veritable poet, whose symbolism is perfectly apparent in the few buildings from his short-lived Viennese period. His main works were: the interior of the Villa Friedmann (1898–99), in which he attained total unity between walls, apertures, and furniture, with a decor derived from plant motifs which is more stylized and less elaborate in the stairwell than in the bedroom; the Villa Bahr (1899–1900) at Ober-Sankt-Veit, near Vienna, where, in an extension of the long, steep-pitched roof, there appears a charming decor of fretwork trees, their trunks leaning as if under the weight of the whole house; exhibition installations for his Sezession building and the Vienna room presented at Paris in 1900, which combined all the various Mediterranean and even Oriental influences that appear in his work; and above all the famous Sezession exhibition building itself (1897–98, fig. 276). This edifice was built thanks to a grant of land on a plot near the Ringstrasse by the ministry of the interior, an action which was itself indicative of the rapid acknowledgment given the Sezessionist movement in official circles. In a treatment reminiscent of a new Greek temple, the almost mausoleum-like impression of this perfectly symmetrical palace is underscored by the absence of windows on the main facade and the use of decorative features incorporating owls and Gorgons, as well as an immense gilt-metal cupola comprising laurel leaves, which is symbolic and purely decorative.

In this very brief period, during which Olbrich only left Wagner's studio to quickly accept an invitation in 1898 from the grand duke of Hesse-Darmstadt to settle in Darmstadt, he had sufficient time to make an impact on modern Viennese architects, notably on the works of his master. The pupil's decorative symbolism resurfaces on the ornaments that Wagner designed after 1897 for the city's subway stations, especially those on the Karlsplatz (fig. 227) and at Schloßstrasse (which was reserved solely for imperial court use and was reminiscent of the Sezession building). The three contiguous buildings at 40 and 38 Linke Wienzeile and 3 Köstlergasse (1898–99) are the epitome of Viennese-style Jugendstil, the decoration becoming increasingly refined from one building to the next. The first of these—in which Olbrich is supposed to have had a hand—is nicknamed the Majolikahaus. It is characterized by its celebrated facade faced in tiles with a profusion of large pink-flowered branches (fig. 332) and its elegant communal areas with lift grilles decorated in plant motifs stylized to the point of abstraction. This building is echoed by Max Fabiani's masterpiece, the Portois & Fix office (1899–1900) at 59–61 Ungargasse, although there the pyrogranite tiles on the facade form an unrelenting geometric pattern in several colors. The second construction takes its inspiration more from the East, with sprigs of gilt leaves and female profiles in the medallions on its exterior decoration. The final building is of an exemplary sobriety far ahead of its time.

Olbrich's influence also surfaces in the early work of Josef Hoffmann, particularly in the decoration of the Apollo store (1899) and the hall for the Kunstgewerbeschule (where Hoffmann taught) at the 1900 Exposition Universelle, where even the plantlike, undulating line of his fellow student at the Wagnerschule makes an appearance. Olbrich's departure for Darmstadt allowed Hoffmann to take his place and assert his true, more sober style, where the decoration is often limited to geometric strips playing the exclusively functional role of emphasizing volumes or openings. The first four artists' houses on the Hohe Warte (1900–2)—reminiscent of the more ambitious and homogeneous project that Olbrich was instructed to undertake in Darmstadt—exemplify the great simplicity of Hoffmann's new manner, particularly evident in the open, light, and airy interiors, with their temperate geometrical strictness. The Austrians had become acquainted sooner than German artists with works from Britain—thanks in particular to the magazine *Kunst und Kunsthandwerk* (founded in 1898)—and this helps explain how Hoffmann's style evolved in the early years of the century. He gained confidence in his style through the affinities he observed in the work of Mackintosh, who had been invited on a number of occasions to the Sezession, even utilizing Mackintosh's furniture for several of his houses in the Hohe Warte. Hoffmann was able to adopt the simplicity of his colleague's geometrical patterns without, however, taking on the Scotsman's obvious symbolism. The transformation was a rapid one, and the synthesis Hoffmann devised between the British contribution and the classical tendencies derived from Otto Wagner soon led him to attain genuine purity, the earliest traces of which appear in the Purkersdorf Sanatorium (1903–5).

In 1903, Hoffmann founded the Wiener Werkstätte with Moser. The program, openly declaring affinities with the anti-industrial principles of the Arts and Crafts movement, was intended to give a new lease of life to Austrian craftwork. Two years later he left the Sezession, which he considered too academic, to set up a new group, the Kunstschau. Hoffmann began creating luxurious and monumental buildings, such as the Palais Stoclet, 281 Avenue de Tervueren, Brussels (1905–11, fig. 345), or the villas Ast (1909–11), Bernatzik (1912–13), and Skywa (1913–15) in Vienna, all of an astonishingly fresh classical sobriety. His exhibition pavilions for Rome (1911) and the Cologne Werkbund (1914) displayed—not without an unwarranted degree of grandiloquence—the splendor of Viennese architecture, all the while increasing Hoffmann's own international renown and making him appear as one of the direct ancestors of Art Deco.

Hoffmann's influence had a discernible impact on the formal development of Otto Wagner's works. In spite of his age, Wagner remained receptive to innovation. The interior of the Österreichisches Postsparkasse (Post Office Savings Bank, 1904–6, fig. 335) is of an exemplary functional simplicity, although the building's sober facades are topped by a clutter of symbolic statues. Contradictory tendencies are at play in Wagner's later works, notably the imposing and extremely classical church of the Steinhof Asylum (1905–7), on the one hand, and the sanatorium at the Wilhelminen Hospital (1910–13) or the second Villa Wagner (1912–13), on the other, where the architect goes so far as to plagiarize Hoffmann's own sober geometrical decors.

To list the buildings of all the other students of the Wagnerschule would be somewhat fastidious, although often—thanks to the highly flexible type of training they received—they possessed a personal style and produced a body of work of high quality. Otto Schönthal, for example, represents a playful even fantastical strand, all the more interesting for the scarcity of his works. The Vojczik House in Vienna (1901), with its colorful and composite Mediterranean look, epitomizes his oeuvre. The Zacherl Palace (1904–5) by Josef Plecnik is the high point of the Viennese period of this Czech architect, whose corpus lies at the crossroads of many different historical influences. With its plain, somber granite surfaces, recessed apertures, and austere carved decorative schemas, the Zacherl Palace is a strangely brutal monument. His compatriot Jan Kotéra benefited from his attendance at Wagner's studio to become, on his return to Prague, the major exponent of the modern movement in Czechoslovakia, where, through his teaching activities, he occupied a similar position to the one Wagner had occupied at the epicenter of the Wagnerschule. If his earliest building, the Peterka House in Prague (1899–1900), is too blatant in its quotations from Viennese Jugendstil, Kotéra's later works, which include the City Halls at Hradec (1903–4) and Prostejov (1905–7), quickly demonstrated his ability to adapt to the conditions prevailing in his native land.

Adolf Loos

The architect Adolf Loos (1870–1933) must be allotted a special place. A solitary figure who never belonged to the world of the Sezession, Loos in fact combated it unremittingly, to the point of refusing to be labeled as an "artist." Loos trained in the United States, and from his study of the Anglo-Saxon house he acquired the certitude that purity could only be born of the essentials: an original classicism devoid of all ornament—a practice he had termed, in a since famous aphorism, a "crime." His extreme position condemned him to a difficult life, and only a few of his numerous projects were built. From his prewar period, aside from a number of prophetic villas and interiors—among them, the celebrated American Bar (1908) with its severe marble-coffered ceiling—the most seminal is the block on the Michaelerplatz (1909–11, fig. 352) that the architect was compelled to defend publicly in a lecture. On a historic site just opposite the Hofburg, Loos erected walls of an unapologetic bareness on which only the color and texture of the materials were visible. While it is true that at that time no architect had ever gone so far, Loos also had to wait a long time before receiving even grudging recognition.

Olbrich and van de Velde in Germany

This was not a problem shared by Loos's two bugbears, against whom he launched his rejection of Art Nouveau: Olbrich and Henry van de Velde. For a number of years, the life stories of these two architects ran along similar lines: both were famous, yet both were voluntary exiles in Germany where they had settled in 1899, the former in Darmstadt, and the latter in Berlin, followed by Weimar. From Germany, they continued their work in considerable intellectual security, and were soon being employed by enlightened aristocrats, the press covering all the major work they were to undertake.

The project of Ernest Louis the grand duke of Hesse-Darmstadt to bring Olbrich and others to form an artists' colony in Darmstadt was not without precedent. Long open to the novel ideas he encountered during his travels, the grand duke had earlier given commissions to Ashbee and, above all, to Baillie Scott for his palace in Darmstadt. In a desire to revive traditional local industries, however, he had also made possible the creation of an ambitious miniature town. Standing like an Acropolis high over Darmstadt on the Mathildenhöhe, the Kunstlerkolonie was the work of Olbrich alone (fig. 340), with the exception of the house of Peter Behrens (fig. 338), which Behrens designed himself. One of Olbrich's most notable designs for the colony is the Ernst Ludwig Haus, a workshop whose entrance is signaled by a large arch flanked by two monumental sculptures by Ludwig Habich. Among the surrounding houses—which have unfortunately come down to us in various states of disrepair—the most significant are the Haus Olbrich, inspired by the houses of rural Germany, and the Grosses Glückert Haus that echoes, though this time in the form of wall decoration, the poetic trees of the Villa Bahr. The colony's great 1901 exhibition ensured success and publicity for all these buildings. The only structure then missing from the place as it is today was the Hochzeitsturm, construction of which began in 1905 to commemorate the prince's wedding (though the artist had been working on it for some time), and the accompanying exhibition buildings. The tower terminating in a hand symbolizing mariage—the five fingers being set with glazed tiles—was the salient work of Olbrich's symbolism.

Before settling in Berlin, Henry van de Velde had already worked in Germany. The success he had gained at the Dresden Exhibition of Applied Arts in 1897, the early commissions from Graf Kessler, and the support he received from Julius Meier-Graefe could but spur van de Velde to try his luck in that country. Germany welcomed him with open arms and from there he was to exert an influence abroad, specifically through the Leuring Villa at Scheveningen in the Netherlands and his plans for the Théâtre des Champs-Élysées in Paris (1910, fig. 367). Was he, however, in spite of the number of works he completed, really an architect, or barely more than an interior decorator? The contradictions of this artist and polemical theoretician, who was racked by doubt, allow for no easy answers. Van de Velde's spaces never possess the fluidity of Horta's and his art is on occasion better served by details in a piece of furniture or an illustration than by a whole building. His early Berlin works were interior fittings for stores, first for the Havana Tobacco Co. (1899–1900, fig. 341)—where the sumptuous detailing became bogged down in decorative profusion—and then Haby's barber shop (1900–1), where brass light fittings produced a unifying rhythm that was altogether calmer and more convincing. Although the emperor proved unappreciative, powerful Berlin circles proved more open to him. The Berlin period culminated in the brilliant interior of the Folkwang Museum at Hagen (1900–2), where Karl Ernst Osthaus was to create his own artistic colony, entrusting the bulk of its construction to the Dutchman J. L. M. Lauweriks. The museum represents a point of equilibrium halfway between van de Velde's early phase—elaborate and curvilinear—and the more unified and monumental works that were to follow during his stay in Weimar. He was called to Weimar by the grand duke of Saxe-Weimar to refurbish the museum and to build a theater and an applied arts school. This last, which opened in 1908, was based on the model of an English guild. Van de Velde conceived it as both a forum for creativity and a center for production. Here, industrialists and financiers met with craftsmen, and in this respect the school differed sharply from similar establishments in Britain. The practice represented another step along the path that was to lead to the Bauhaus, which replaced the school after the war. The principle also accorded with the spirit of the Deutscher Werkbund, founded in 1907 at the instigation of Muthesius, with Riemerschmid, Behrens, Olbrich, van de Velde, Pankok, and Hoffmann, where industrialists and artists joined forces to preserve a certain level of quality in mass production. For the 1914 Werkbund exhibition at Cologne, van de Velde built a theater, which, in spite of its brief existence, was his masterpiece. During the exhibition, however, the architect engaged in a notorious debate with Muthesius in defense of the right to individualism and against standardization.

THE NETHERLANDS

The modern movement appeared in the Netherlands at an early stage and permeated every area of artistic activity. The question as to whether modern Dutch architecture, influenced as much by Art Nouveau (especially in The Hague) as by the Arts and Crafts movement, was genuinely *sui generis* is an open one. It is significant to note that the works of the designer and architect Johannes Ludovicus Matheus Lauweriks (1864–1942), one of the most intriguing creative artists in the country—and the one most independent of eclecticism—were all built abroad, mostly in Germany. In Amsterdam, the majority of the outstanding creative talents at the beginning of the twentieth century were to be found in the entourage of Petrus Josephus Hubertus Cuypers (1827–1921). As well as Lauweriks, there was Willem Kromhout (1864–1940) and above all Hendrik Petrus Berlage (1856–1934). Through Cuypers, the key representative of the neo-Gothic movement in Holland and the celebrated designer of the Rijksmuseum and the central railway station, they were to absorb the spirit of Viollet-le-Duc, particularly his ideas on the integration of metal into modern architecture. This can best be seen in Berlage's masterwork, the Amsterdam Stock Exchange (1898–1903, fig. 337). This building is far from being entirely free of references to French railroad construction and medieval ecclesiastical architecture, but its appearance was nonetheless hailed as an event of international import.

The most interesting particularity of Dutch architects is that they often had the opportunity of working on large-scale projects, such as public buildings and industrial or office sites, and not merely for private clients. This helps explain how it was that Dutch Art Nouveau, more measured and calmer than elsewhere, survived until the arrival on the scene of more radical and progressive movements, such as the Amsterdam school and De Stijl.

UNITED STATES

The United States could have numbered among the most modern of the newer nations, particularly as the Chicago School, the most significant progressive movement in the country, had emerged in the wake of the great fire of 1871. The fire had leveled the city and imposed radical changes in construction methods, specifically the necessity of using brick as a fire-resistant material. Innovation was hardly facilitated, however, by American architects' attraction to European culture and their fascination with the École des Beaux-Arts in Paris (a fascination that earned the unimpeachably academic Victor Laloux a bewildering transatlantic heritage). A great number of Chicago's skyscrapers at the end of the nineteenth century were simply weird Gothic cathedrals dedicated to bureaucracy or industry. If the early works jointly built by the architects Dankmar Adler (1844–1900) and Louis Henry Sullivan (1856–1924) appear to have some precursory echoes of Art Nouveau as it was understood in Latin countries, eclecticism—together with a very American feeling for sheer size—was no less vital to the development of their stylistic language (fig. 344). This is perfectly illustrated by the famous Auditorium Building (1886–89), in which the auditorium proper seems more like some magnificent Oriental dream than a genuinely new work (fig. 324). The Wainwright Building in St. Louis (1890–91) featured, in the decoration around the cornice, the first promising-looking patterns of delicate arabesques, although strangely they are invisible from street level. If Sullivan did indeed formulate his celebrated maxim "Form follows function" to encapsulate the ideas of Viollet-le-Duc, it gives no clues as to the role of ornament, which is in his case at once Celtic, Oriental, and Art Nouveau. The novelty of his decoration, in which color plays a far from negligible part, was much vaunted at the World's Columbian Exhibition in Chicago in 1893, at which the two architects presented their Transportation Building. The edifice attracted all the more comment as the rest of the exhibition was generally disappointing in its slavish imitation of the architectural models of European eclecticism. After his break with Adler in 1895, Sullivan reached new heights in his work. His buildings were much less monumental yet possessed large and deliberately out-of-scale elements, with facades often left plain and severe. The outstanding examples are the Merchant's National Bank at Grinnell (1914), where the door is surmounted by a huge, finely worked rose window, and the Krause Music Store (1922), whose late date is indicative of the seamless stylistic continuity of Sullivan's career. The entrance of the Carson, Pirie, Scott & Co. Store (1899–1904), however, remains his masterpiece, with its luxuriant decoration melding with the sober structural elements.

From 1887 to 1893, Frank Lloyd Wright (1867–1959) had worked at Adler and Sullivan's agency, where he completed a large number of their private contracts. The time Wright spent there is clearly evident in his own early buildings, and particularly in the figurative friezes on certain houses, such as the Isidore Heller Residence (South Woodlawn, 1896), or in the flower-pattern earthenware tiles that he produced during the same period. His work was to develop in very different directions, however, notably toward a highly individual approach to both space and light. His liking for Japan (which he first visited in 1905) drew him to a simplicity that was uncompromising yet humane. It can be clearly seen in the pale-colored harmony of his furniture and his famous stained-glass windows, as well as in his ground plans—always arrived at through close consultation with the client. From the Joseph Husser Residence (Chicago, 1899) to the Unity Temple (Oak Park, 1904), with its subtle geometrical structure, the artist went on elaborating his distinctive horizontal architectural style. Wright was probably the most talented of the turn-of-the-century "Japanese-style" architects, as he only adopted a kind of Oriental spirit, never going so far as to quote directly or borrow wholesale, as in the Blacker (1907) and Gamble (1908) Houses by the brothers Greene—Charles (1868–1957) and Henry (1870–1954)—who were active in Pasadena on the West Coast. Their mainly wooden constructions successfully combined the Japanese tradition, which the architects had encountered at the World's Columbian Exhibition of 1893, with local forms. Their rejection of historicism was progressive and resulted eventually in the abandonment of all extraneous ornament, enabling them to concentrate their attention on what they considered most important: volume. Decoration became confined to stained glass, which became the only obvious link between their work and any customary definition of Art Nouveau.

The 1914 Werkbund exhibition in Cologne made clear the real reasons for Art Nouveau's demise: the obvious discrepancy between an individualist approach—that of Guimard or Gaudí—and the need to distribute artistic production through workshops or through industry proper, an area where the Germans and Austrians had been in the vanguard. The debate concerned the decorative arts as well as architecture in their close ties, and almost turned the argument back to the stage it had reached in the 1890s, when a generally bastardized Art Nouveau was not only on the point of becoming a historicist style, but also, worse still, a style of barren academicism. The convoluted story of the building of the Théâtre des Champs-Élysées (completed in Paris in 1913) demonstrates perfectly the battle of ideas and men that was being waged on the threshold of a new age between Henry van de Velde—whose design, typical of Berlin Art Nouveau, was an assertion of the artist's personality—and Auguste Perret (1874–1954), more of an engineer than an architect, who finished the theater in an almost paradoxical and exaggerated classicism. Perret's building on Rue Franklin (1903) and his garage on Rue de Ponthieu (1907) had opened the way for artist-cum-construction entrepreneurs thanks to a more unyielding adherence to volumes, materials, and functions than in the past, relegating decoration to its primary purposes. The terraced building Henri Sauvage was in the process of erecting on Rue Vavin in Paris—one that brought to an end a strange period of intellectual sterility for the artist—also belongs to the same spirit of unadorned functionalism. At last, architecture had managed to divorce itself from the falsehoods of the decorative. Whereas the great masters of Art Nouveau continued their life's work, all to a greater or lesser extent prey to hesitations and self-doubt, a new generation everywhere proclaimed victory for the "purist" ideas of the Germanic countries. Walter Gropius, in the factory he had constructed for the Cologne Werkbund, had already ushered in an era of stability and with it the triumph of glass and undecorated surfaces. It is hardly surprising that Le Corbusier, another outstanding representative of the age to come, could write in 1929 this disturbing summary of a period that might otherwise seem quite alien to him: "About 1900, a magnificent gesture: Art Nouveau. An old culture's togs are given a good shaking."

However, through its numerous shortcomings—particularly regarding its aspirations to being a truly popular art—the architecture of the late nineteenth century and the beginning of the twentieth shows that the "shaking" given to the "old culture" had been a painful one indeed.

254 Pierre Manguin
Onyx staircase
1865
With *Virgil* (left) by Louis-Ernest Barrias and *Dante* (right) by Jean-Paul Aubé
Hôtel de la Païva, Paris

255 Victor Baltard
Saint-Augustin Church, Paris (main facade, elevation)
Constructed 1860–71
Pen and black ink, watercolor and gold highlights, 601 x 422 cm
Musée d'Orsay, Paris

256 Alphonse Gosset
Reims Theater (main facade, elevation)
Theater constructed 1867–73
Pen and black ink, watercolor, white gouache highlights, 75 x 90.7 cm
Musée d'Orsay, Paris

257 Eugène-Emmanuel Viollet-le-Duc
Château de Pierrefonds (elevation)
1858
69.8 x 72.5 cm
Centre de Recherche des Monuments Historiques, Paris

258 Max Berthelin
Palais de l'Industrie, Paris (cross section)
1854
Pen and black ink, watercolor, 31.1 x 67.3 cm
Musée d'Orsay, Paris

259 Alphonse-Nicolas Crépinet
Project for the new Opéra, placed second after Charles Garnier's (perspective view)
1861
Lead pencil and watercolor, 50.6 x 68.9 cm
Musée d'Orsay, Paris

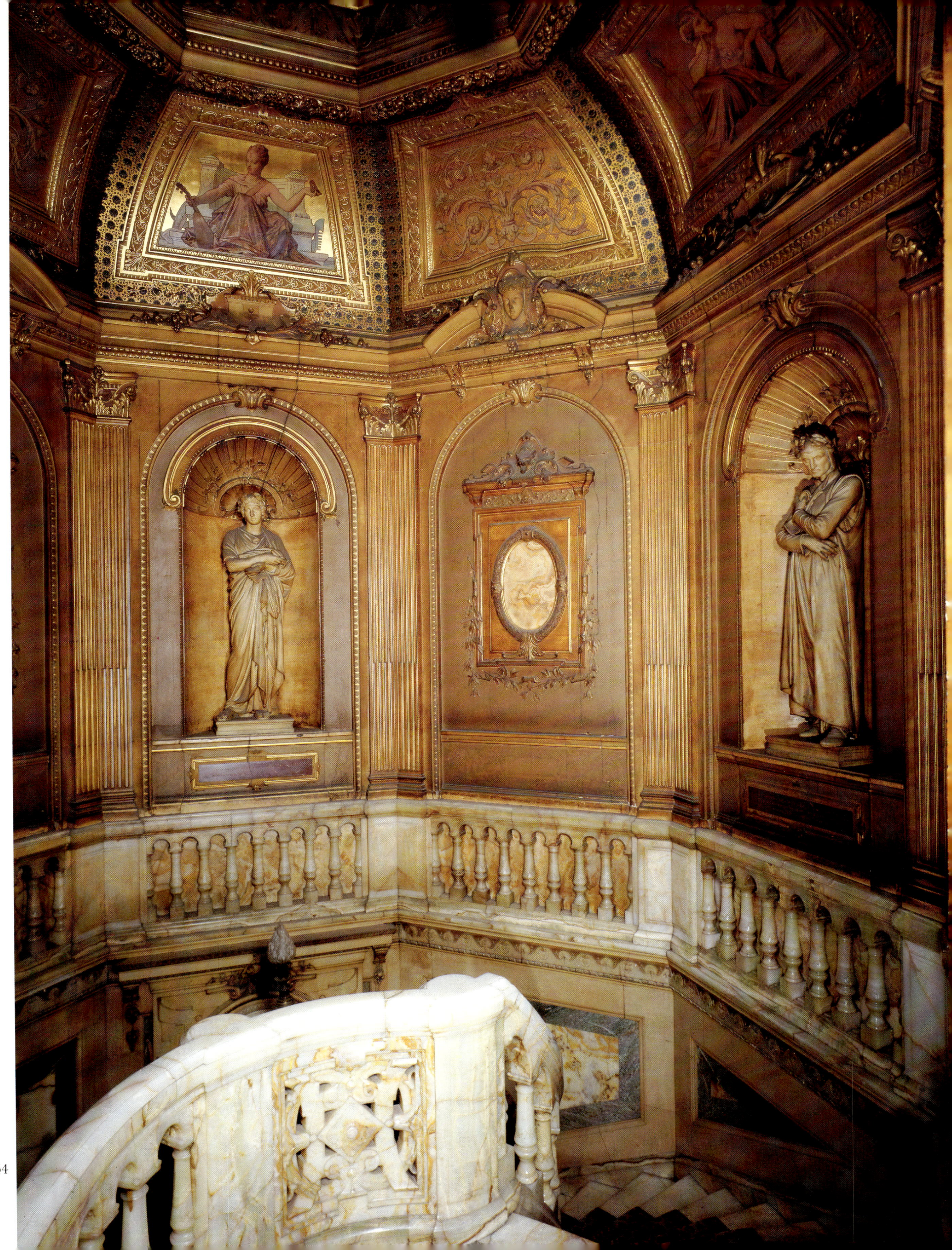

255

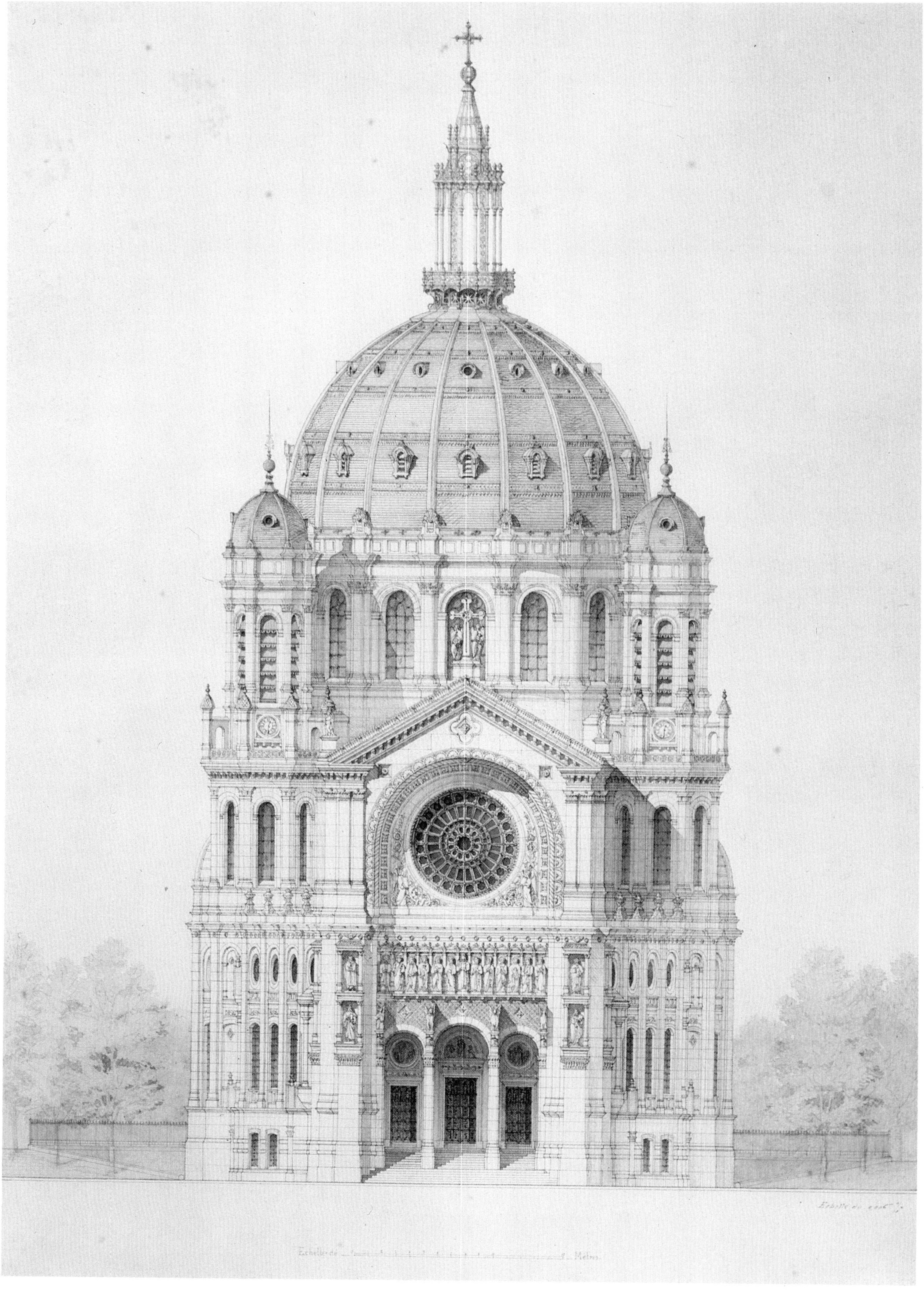

256

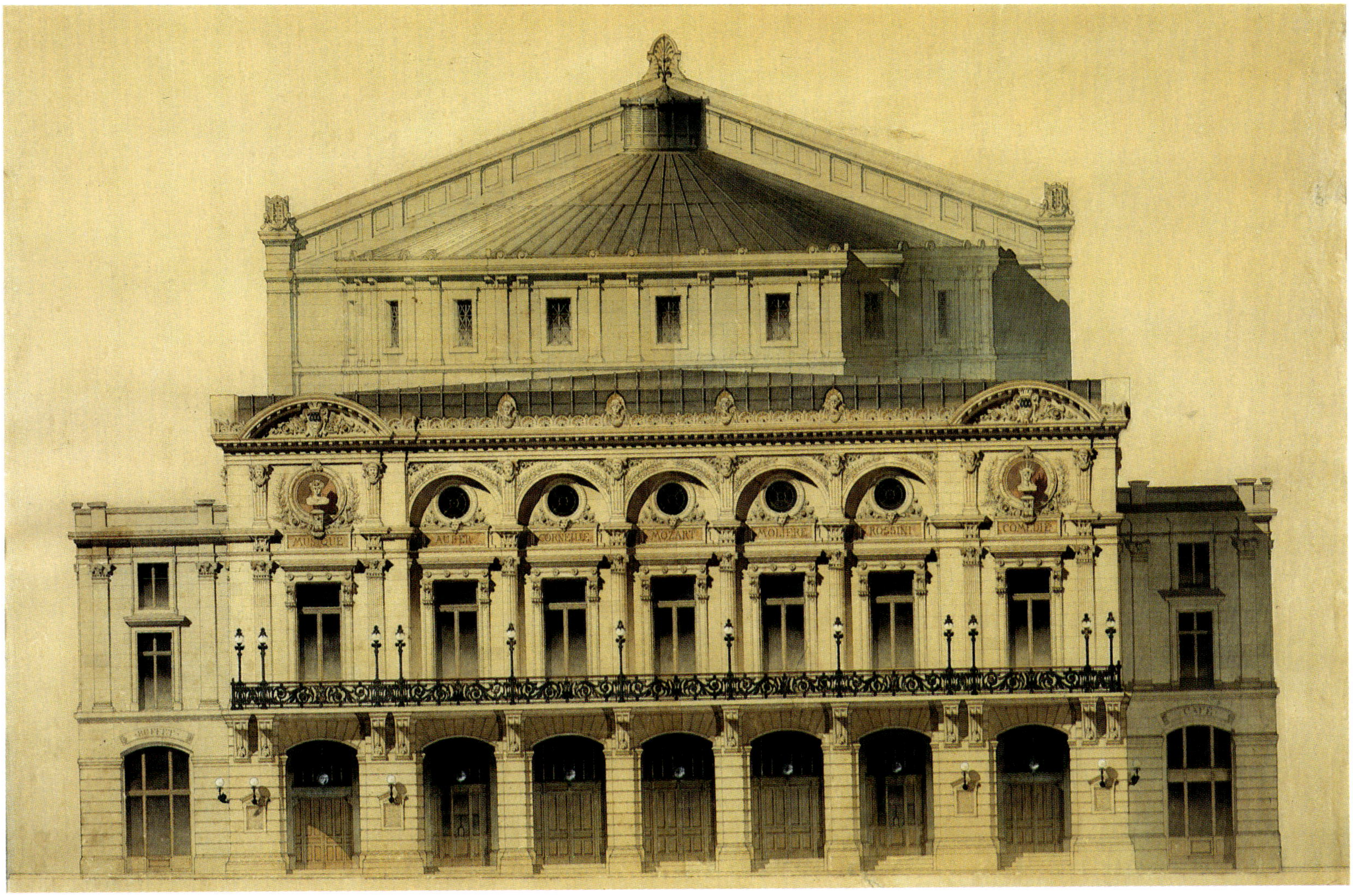

257

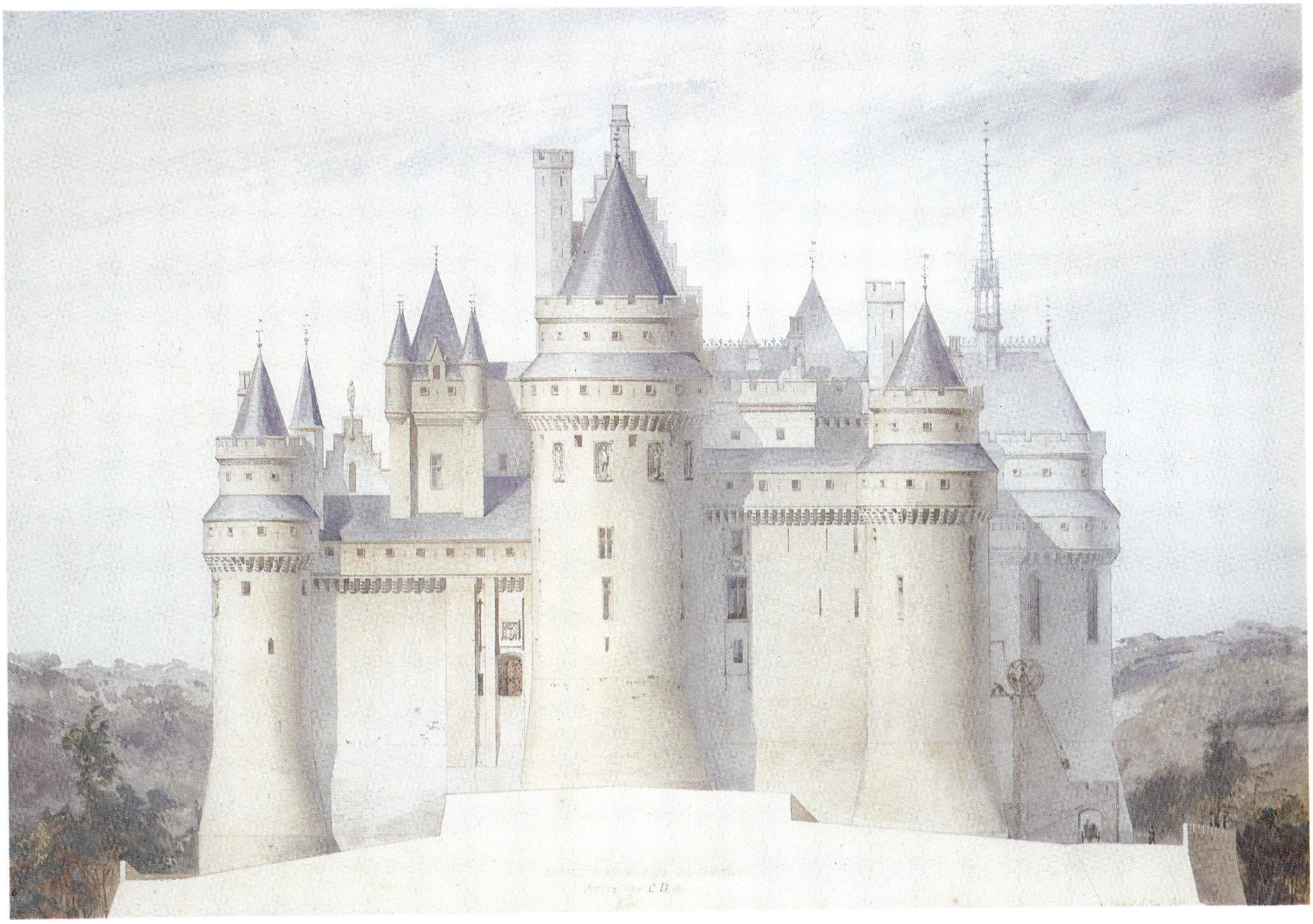

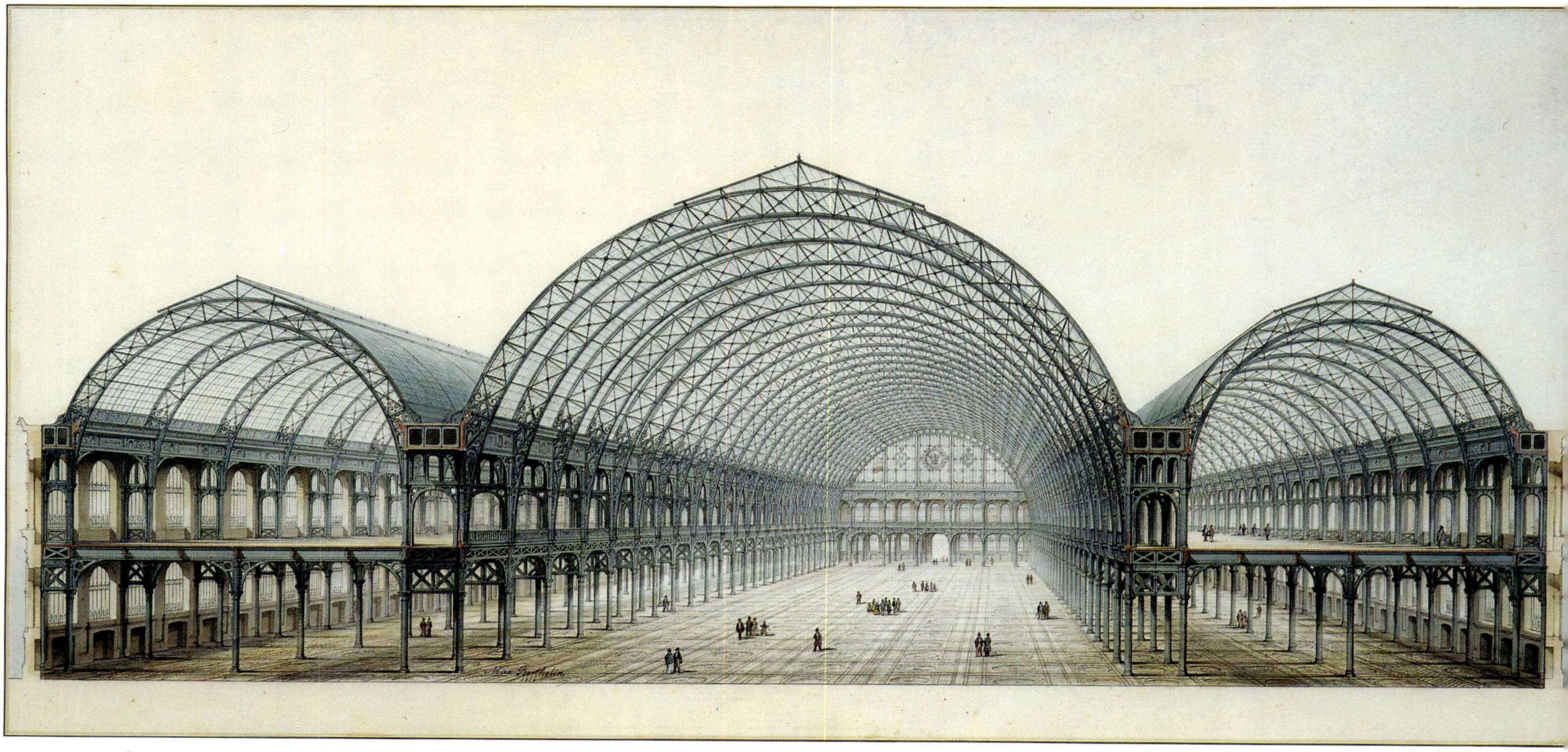

258

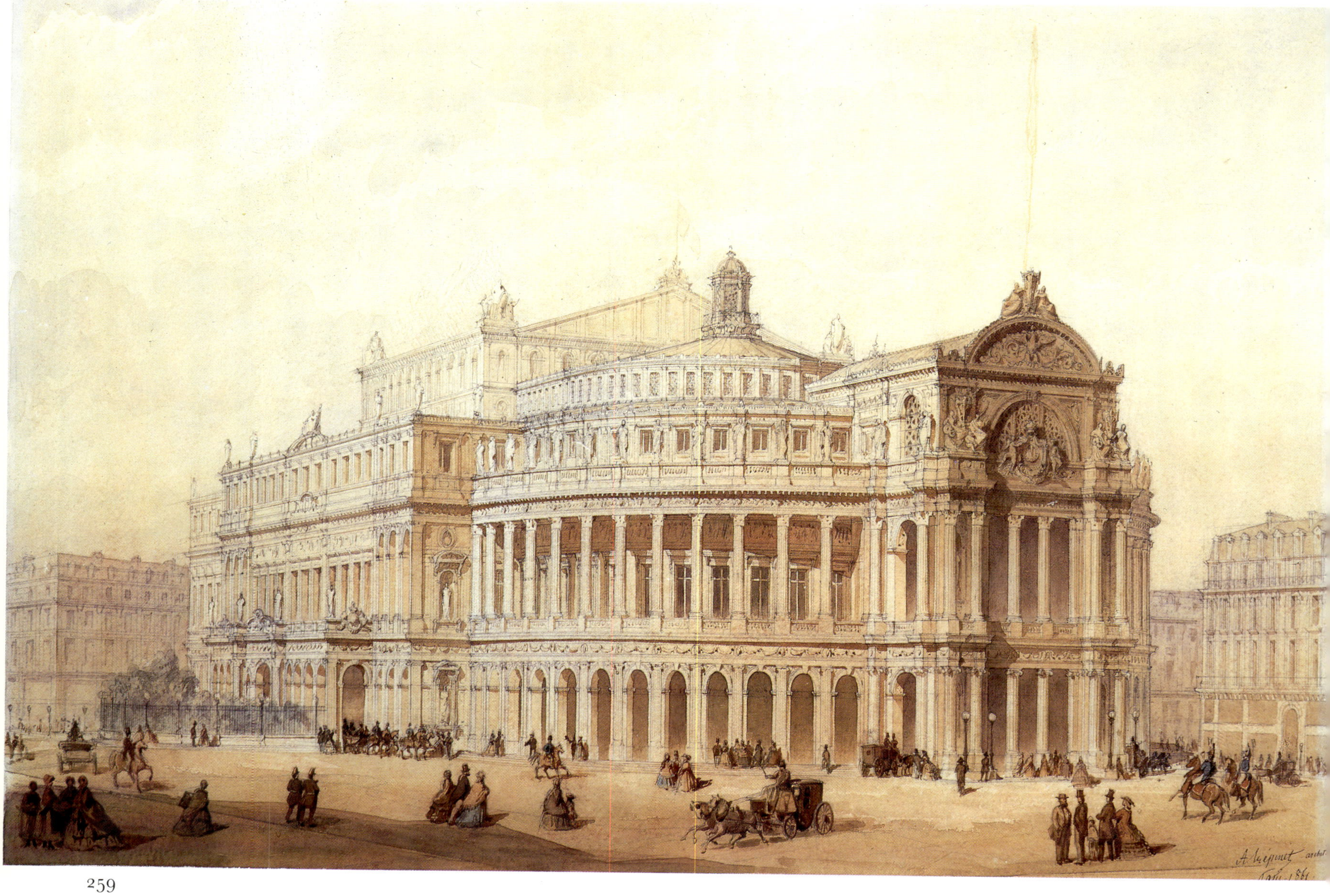

259

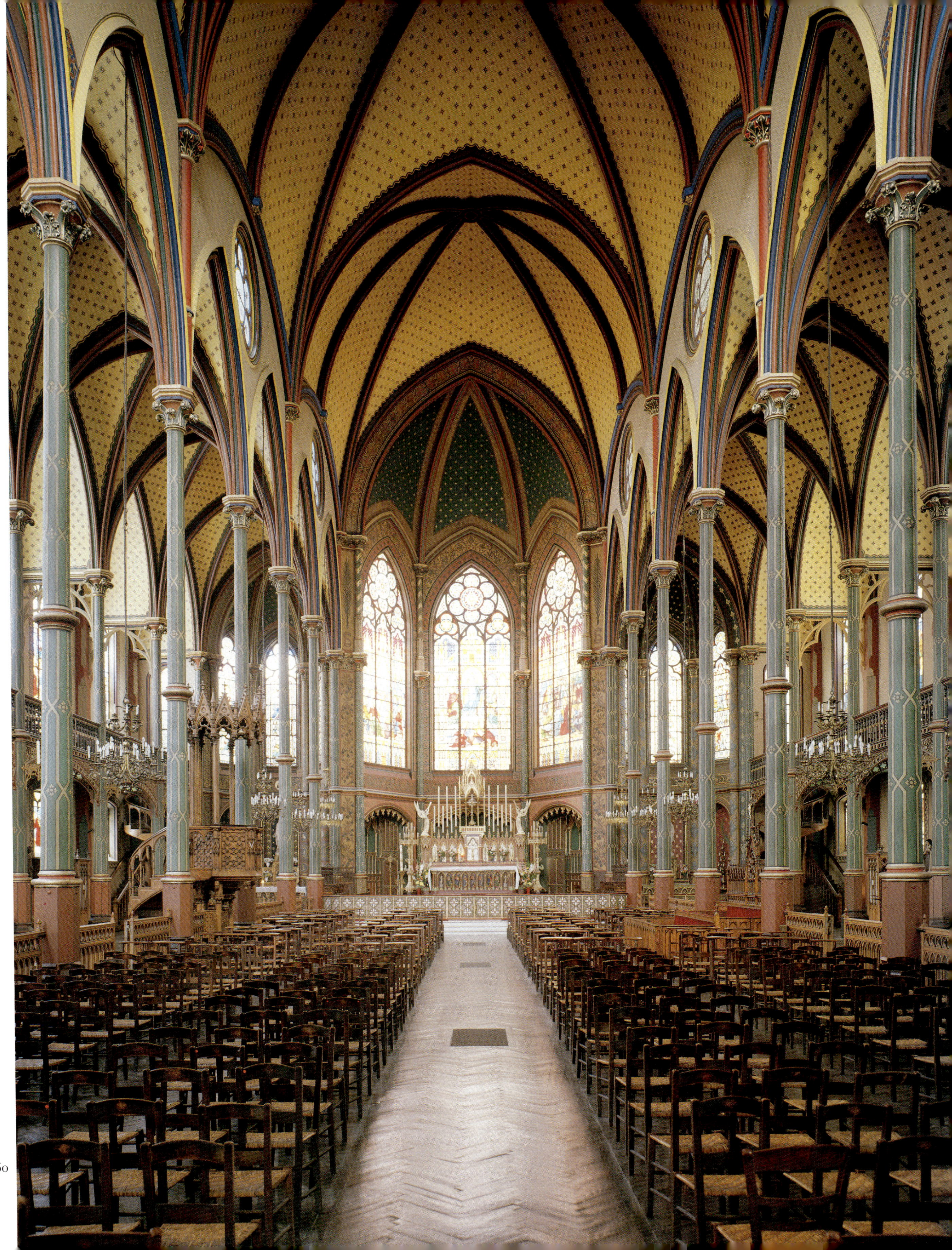

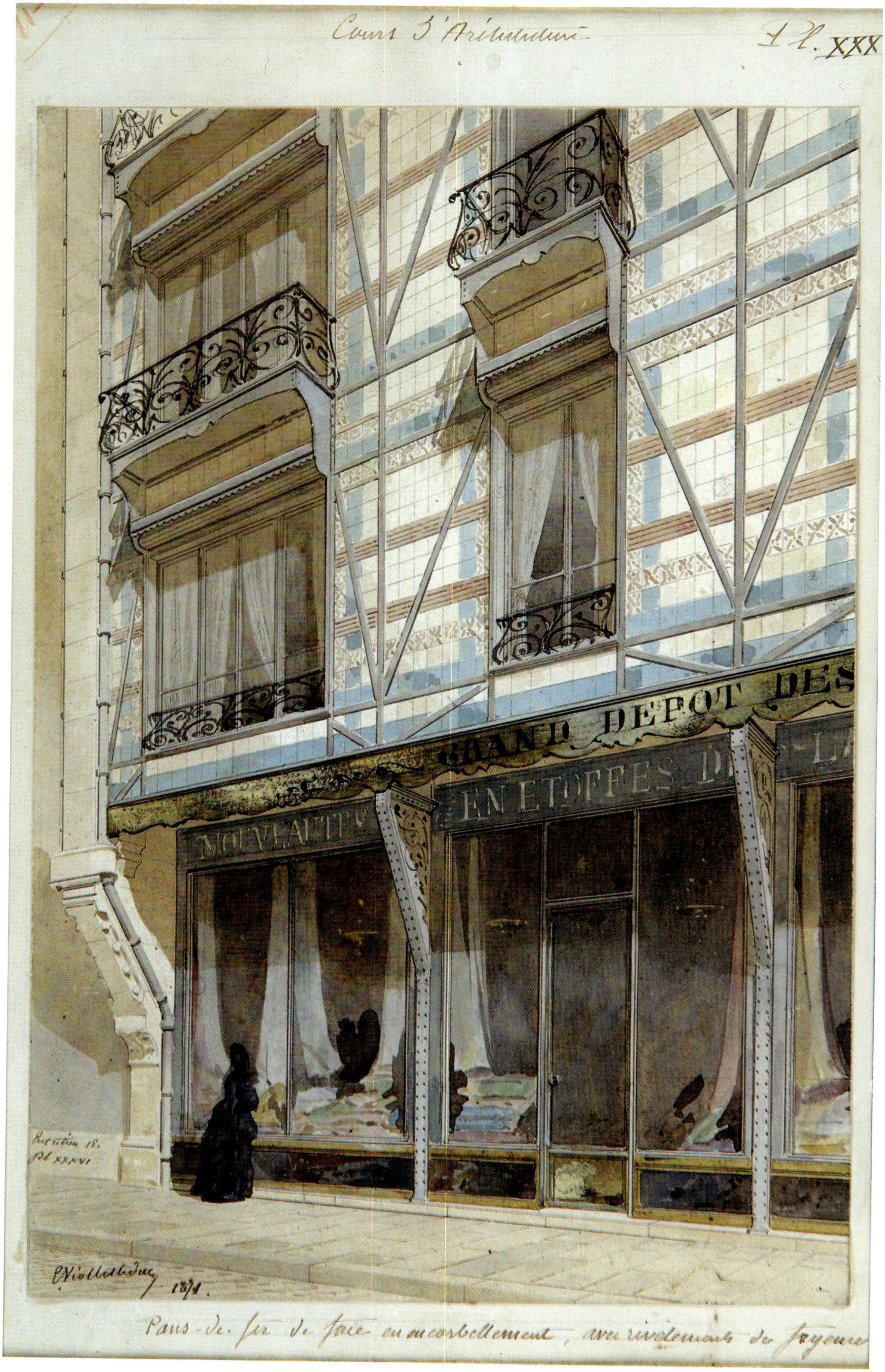
Cours d'Architecture
Pl. XXX
GRAND DEPOT DES
NOUVEAUTÉS
EN ETOFFES
Pans-de-fer de face en encorbellement, avec revêtements de faïence
1871

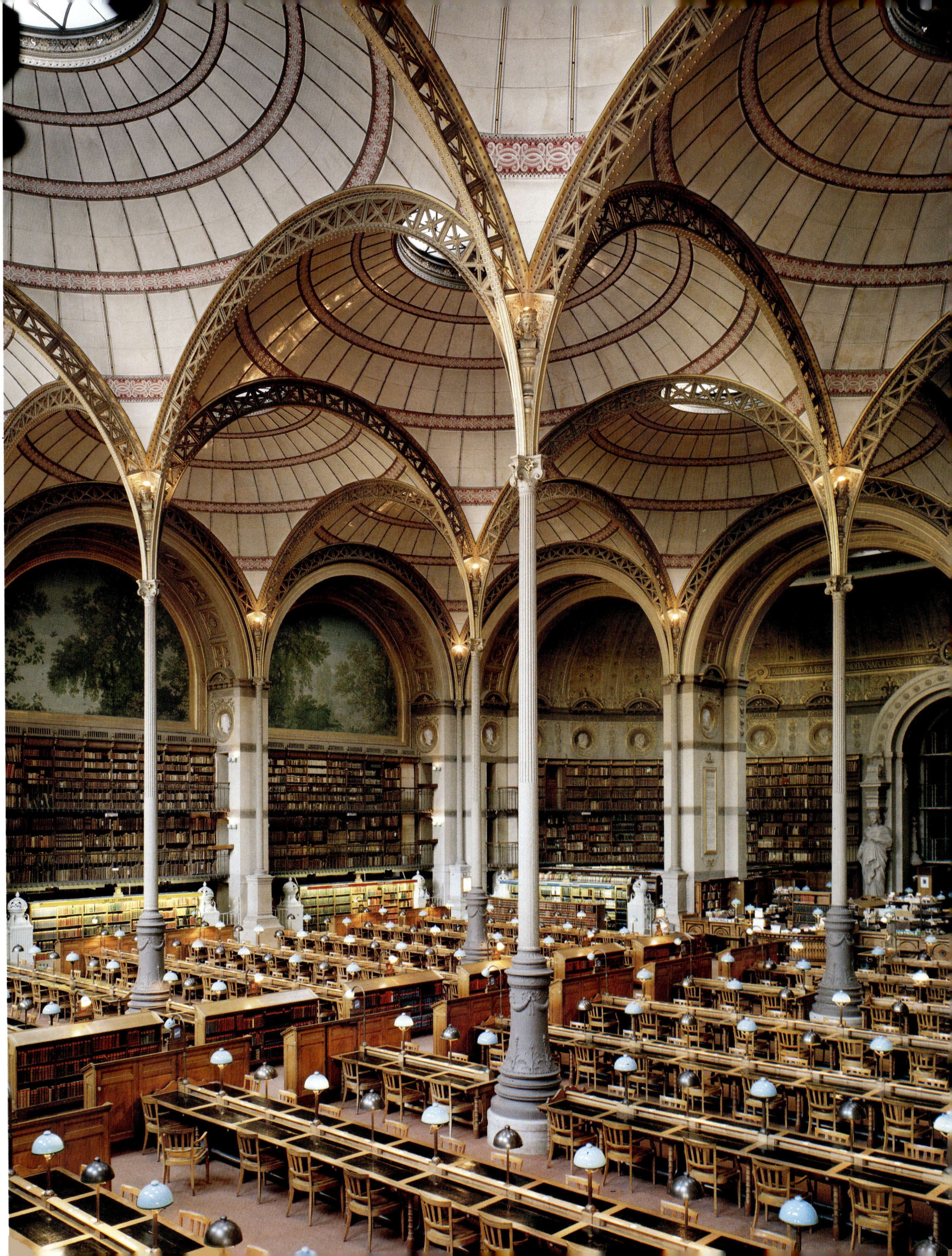

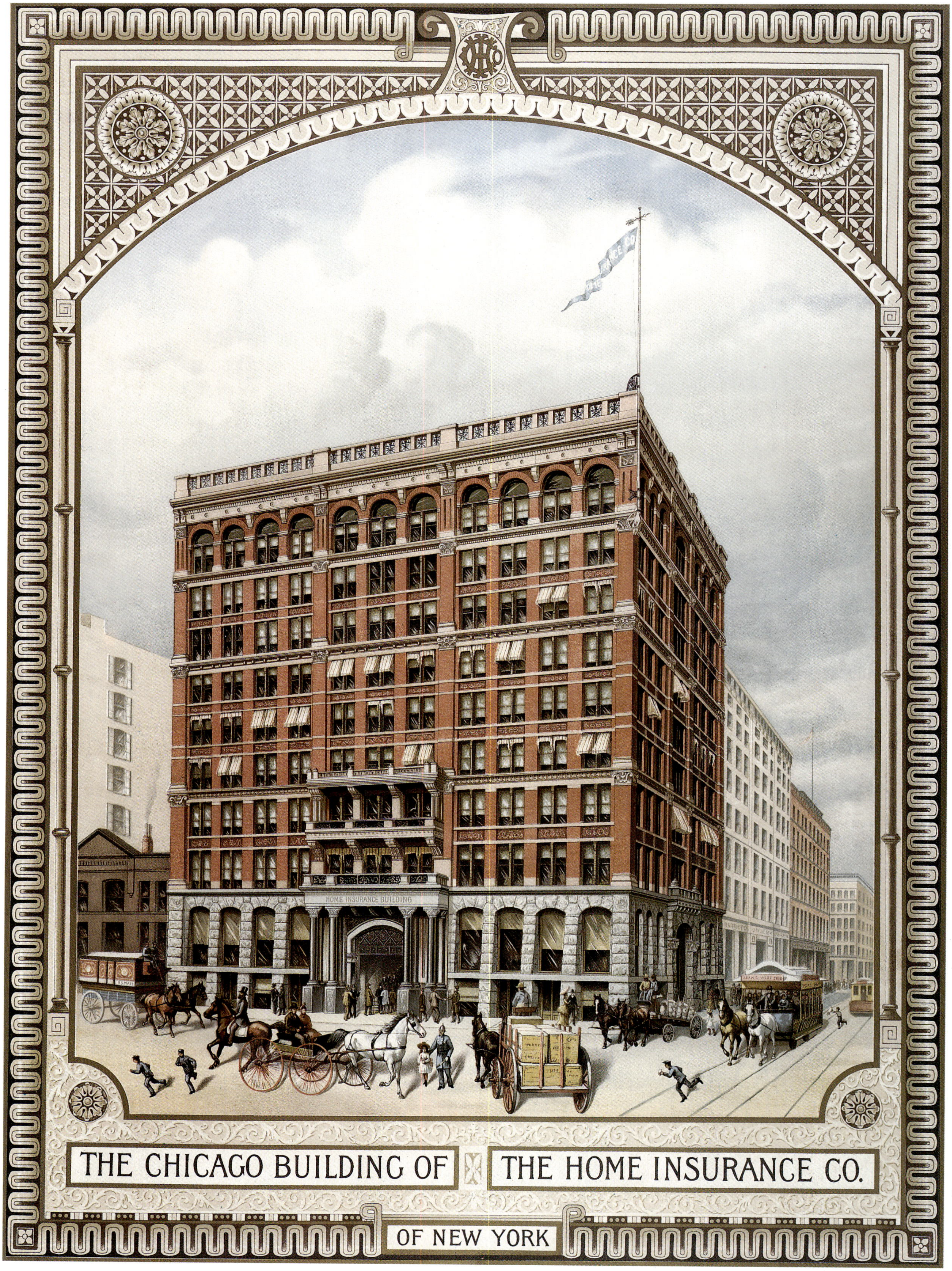
HOME INSURANCE BUILDING
THE CHICAGO BUILDING OF
THE HOME INSURANCE CO.
OF NEW YORK

260 Louis-Auguste Boileau
Saint-Eugène Church, Paris (interior)
1853–54

261 Eugène-Emmanuel Viollet-le-Duc
House with frontal iron frame faced with glazed earthenware
Plate 36 of *Entretiens sur l'architecture*
1871
Lead pencil, pen and black ink, watercolor
Private collection

262 Henri Labrouste
Reading room for printed books
1857–68
Bibliothèque Nationale, Paris

263 L. Prang and Co.
Poster for the Home Insurance Building (architect William Le Baron Jenney)
c. 1885–86
Deutsches Architekturmuseum, Frankfurt

264 William Morris in collaboration with William de Morgan
Panel of wall covering for Meubland Hall, Devon
c. 1876–76
Glazed earthernware tiling, 163 x 905 cm
Musée d'Orsay, Paris

265 Georg von Dollmann, Franz Seitz, Christian Jank, and Joseph de la Pai
Spiegelsaal
c. 1874–78
Schloss Linderhof, Bavaria

266 Eduard Riedel and Georg von Dollmann
Schloss Neuschwanstein
1869–86
Bavaria

267 General view of the 1900 Exposition Universelle, Paris
Engraving by G. Grivell
Musée d'Orsay (Collection Eiffel), Paris

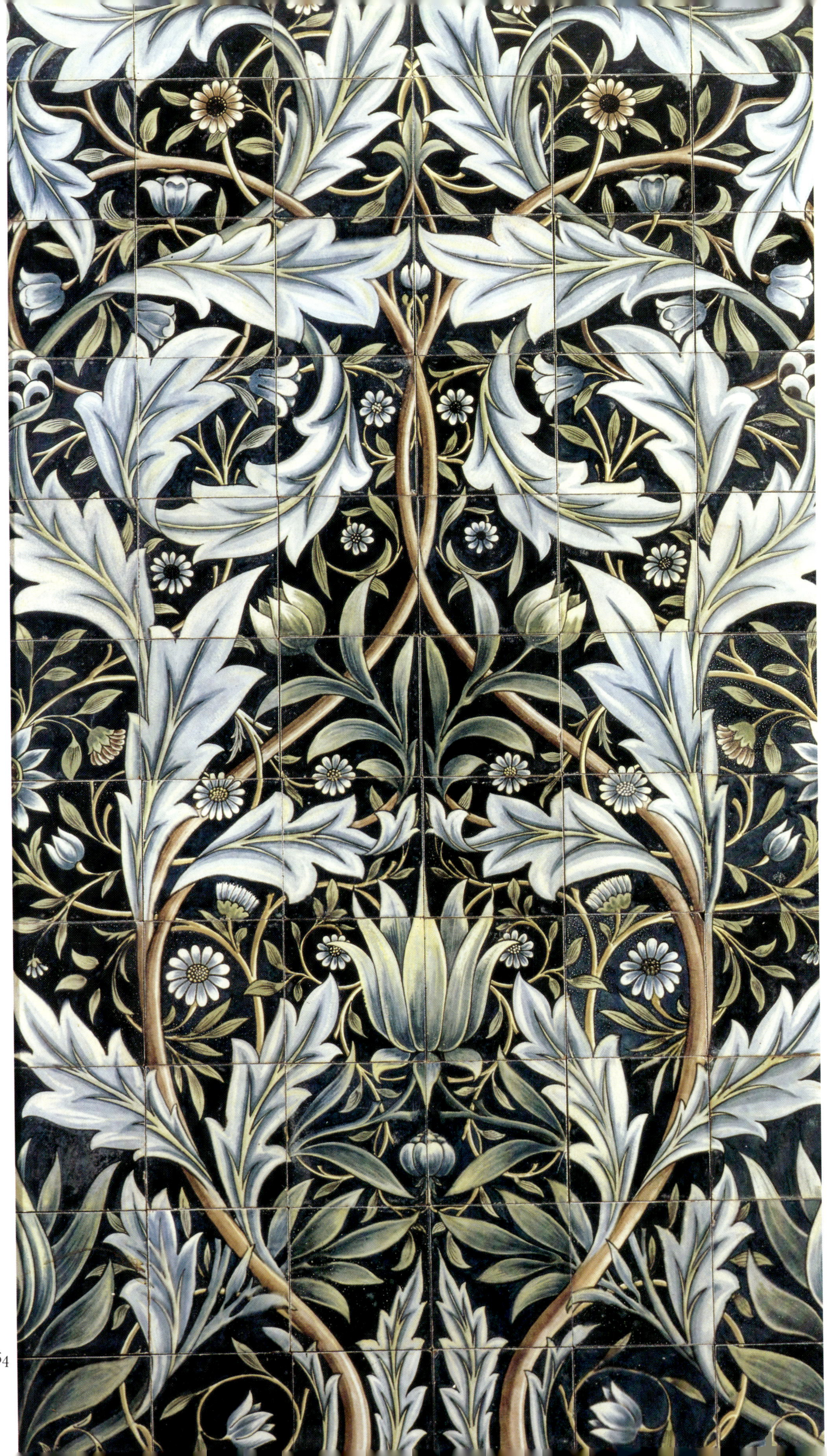

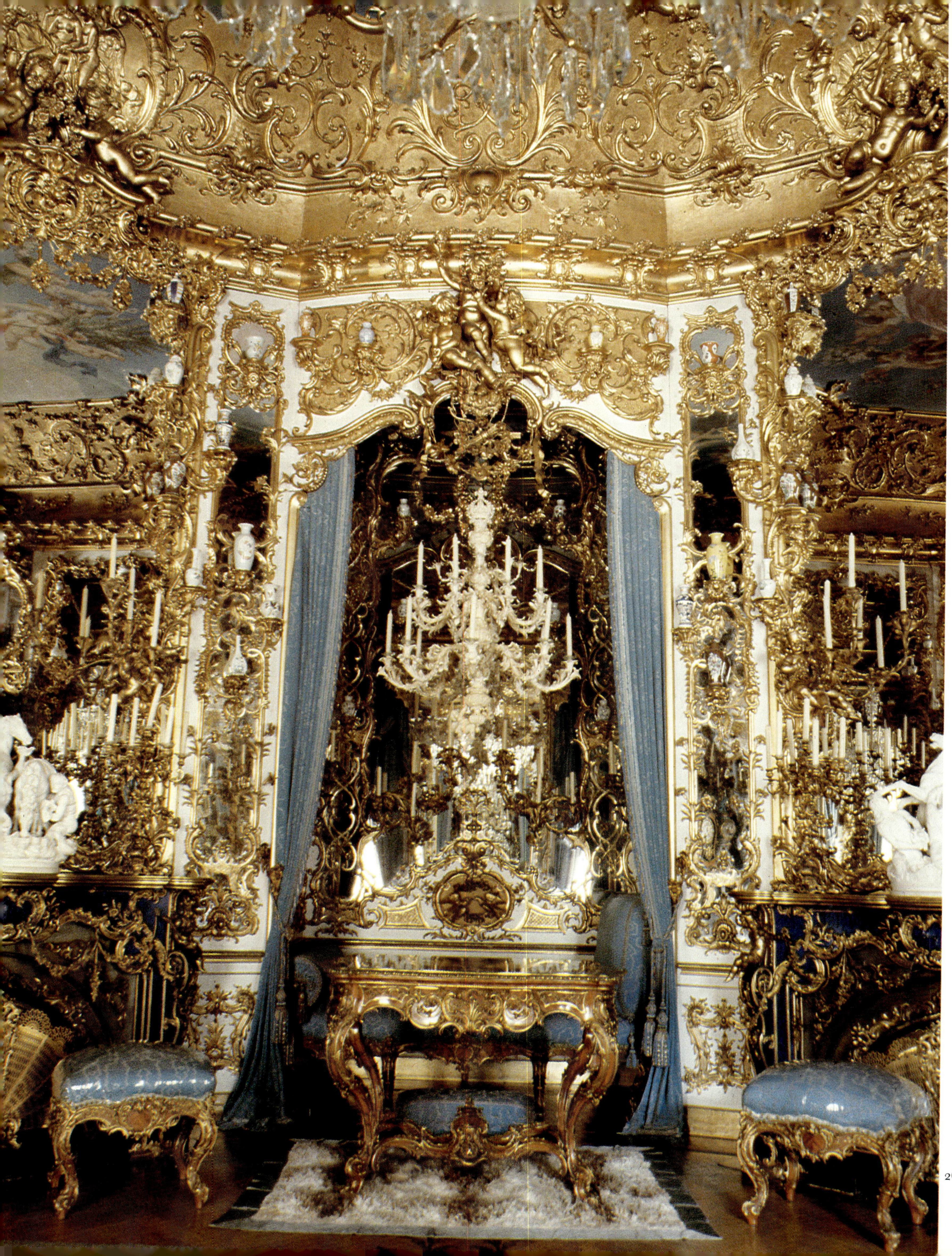

26

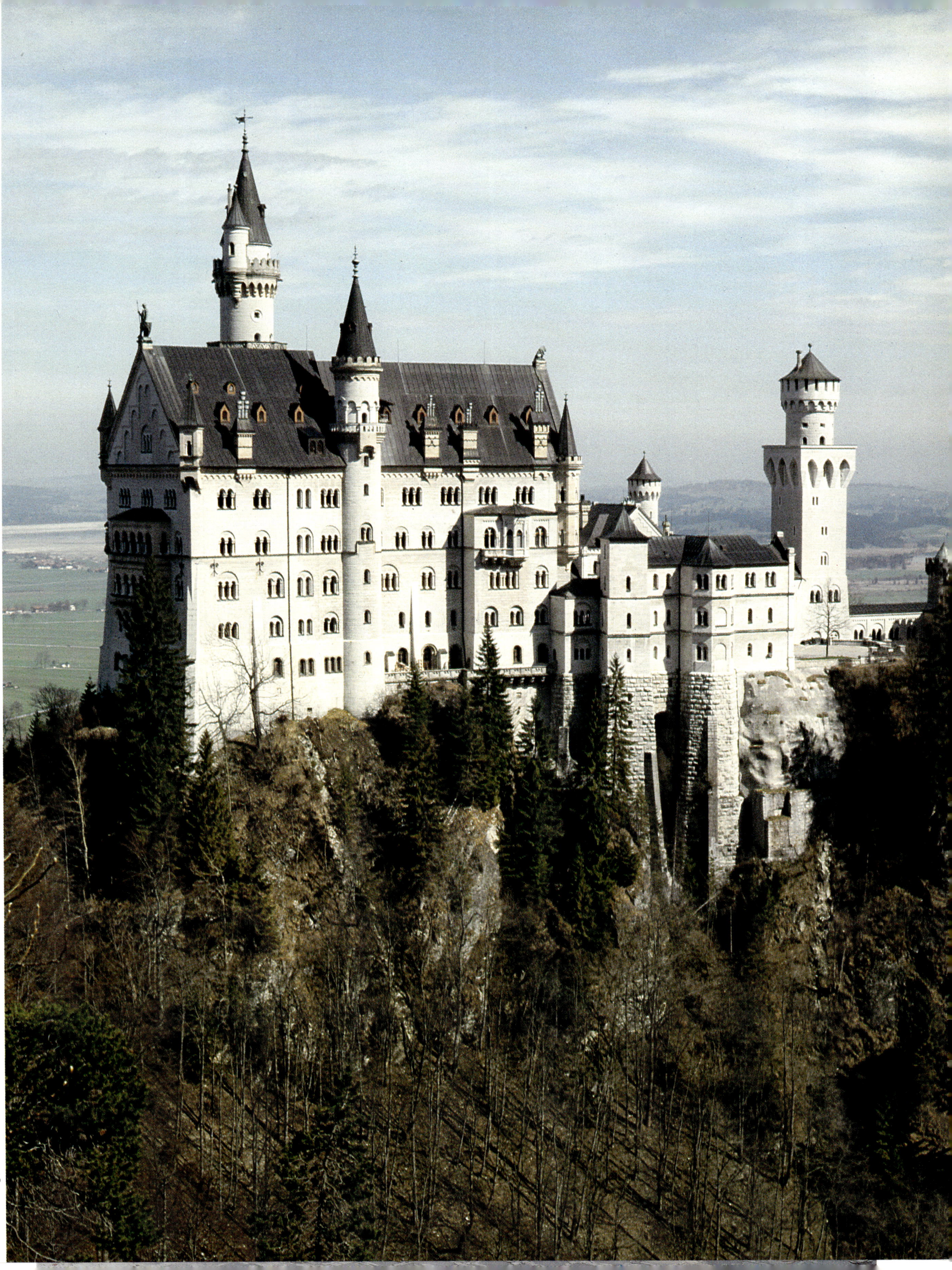

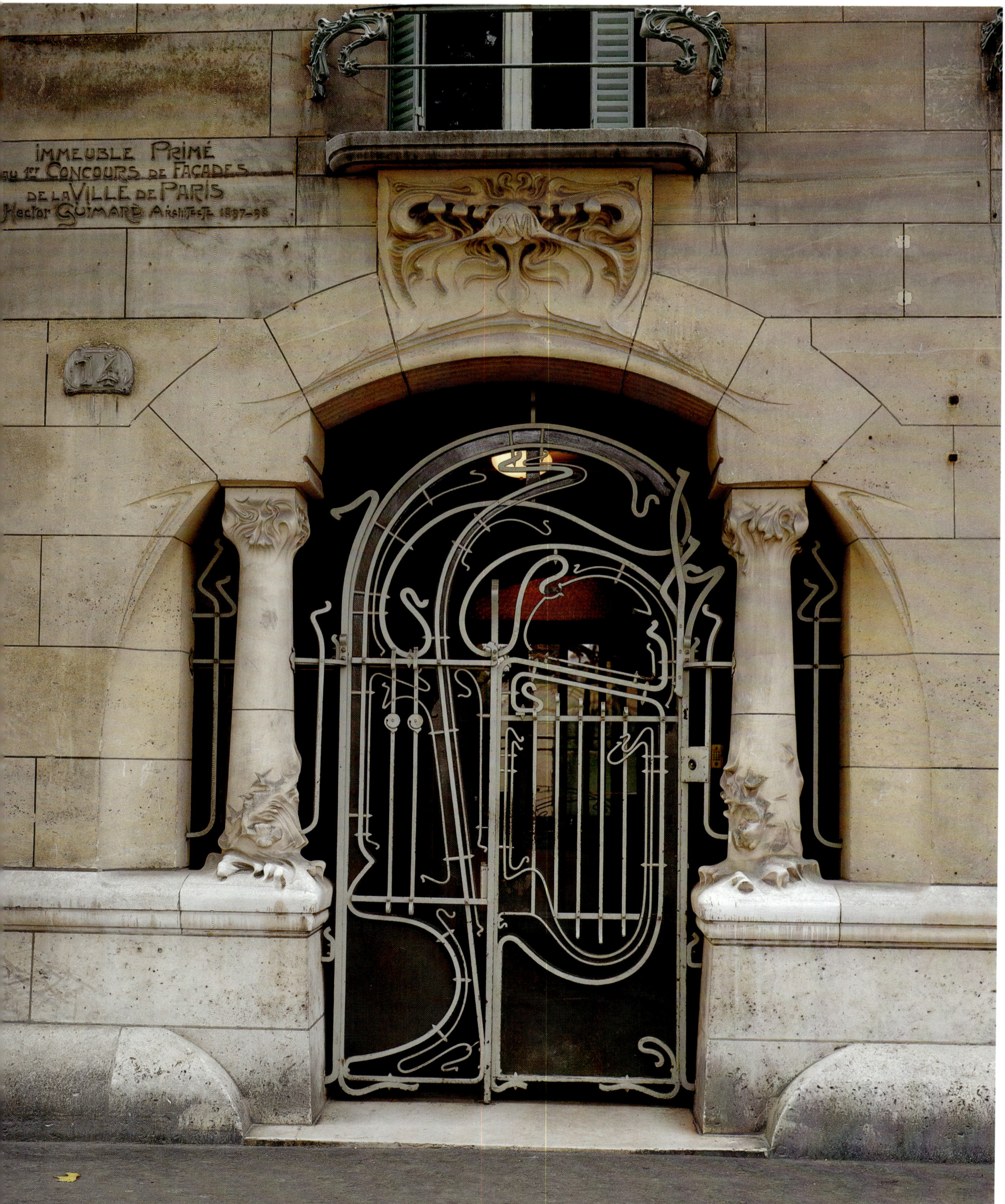
IMMEUBLE PRIMÉ
AU 1ER CONCOURS DE FAÇADES
DE LA VILLE DE PARIS
Hector GUIMARD Architecte 1897-98

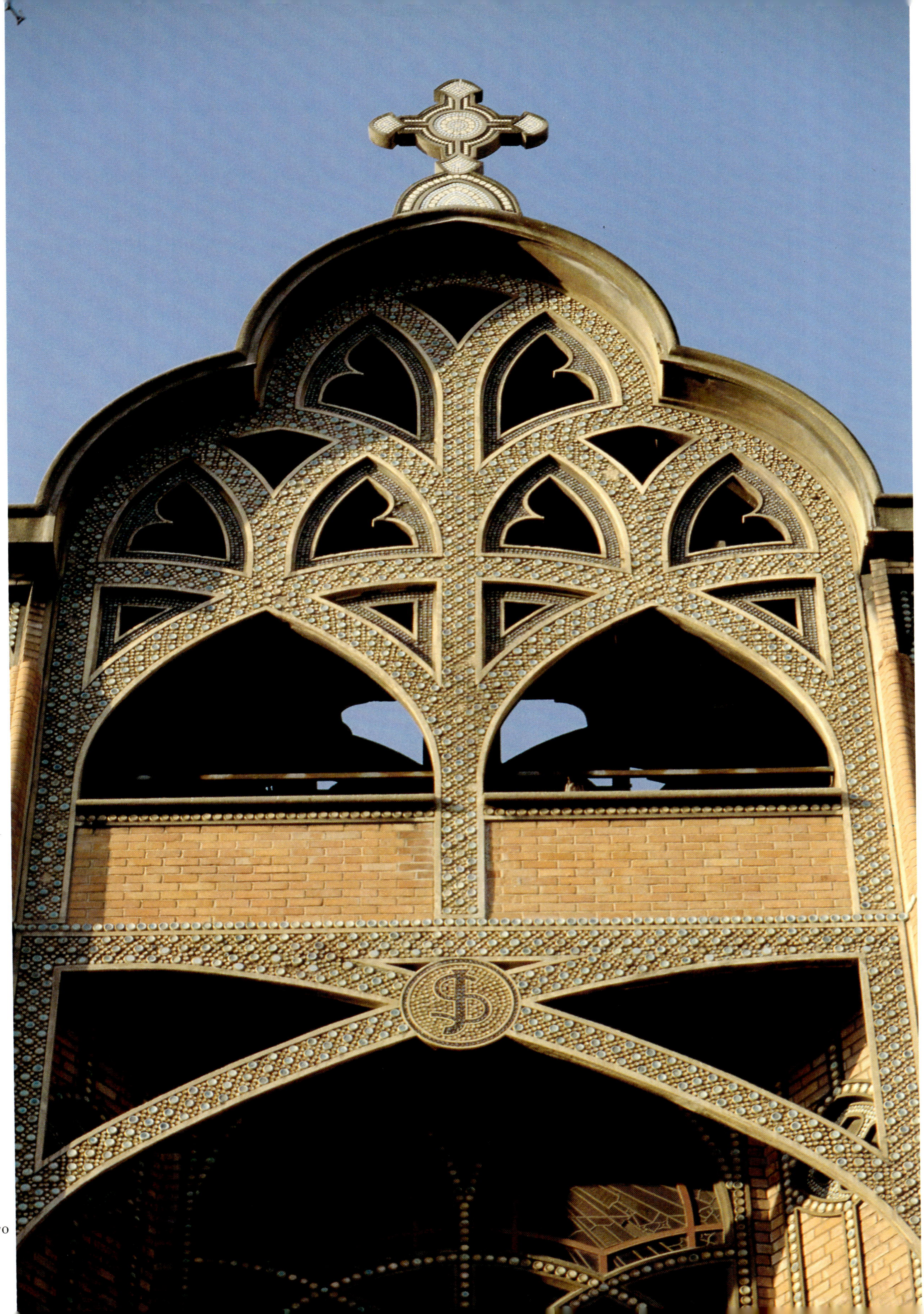

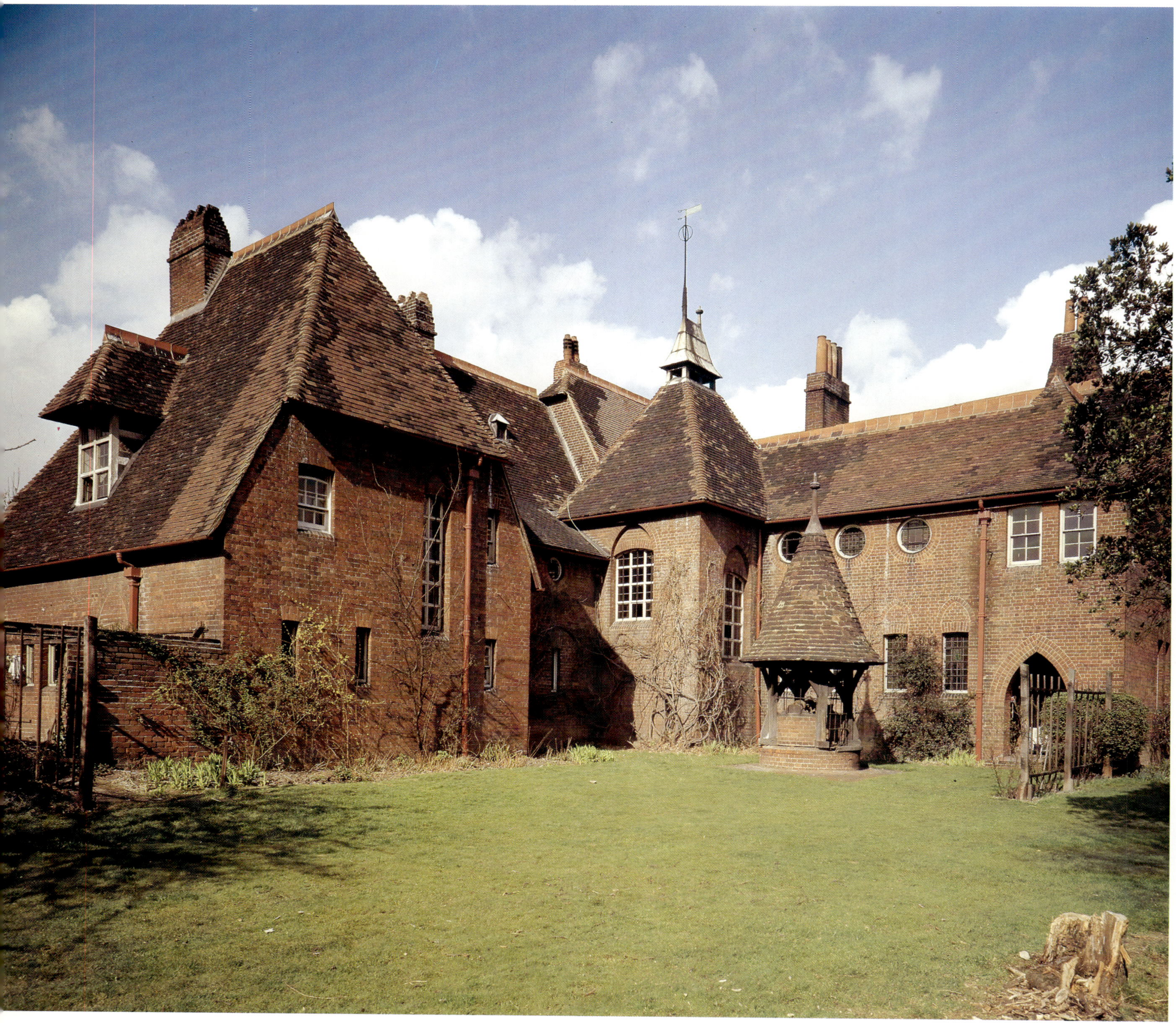

268 Jules Lavirotte
Building, 29 Avenue Rapp, Paris
Portal and front door (detail)
1900–1
Paris

269 Hector Guimard
Castel Béranger, 14 Rue La Fontaine, Paris
Entrance gate (detail)
1894–98
Paris

270 Anatole de Baudot
Church of Saint-Jean-de-Montmartre, Rue des Abbesses, Paris
Completed 1905
Paris

271 Philip Webb
The Red House
1859
Bexley Heath, Great Britain

272 Charles Rennie Mackintosh
Willow Tea Room
Door (detail)
1903
Glasgow

273 Giovanni Michelazzi
Villino Broggi-Caraceni
1911
Florence

274 Victor Horta
Hôtel Tassel
Interior
1893
Brussels

275 Victor Horta
Hôtel Van Eetvelde
Main hall
1895
Brussels

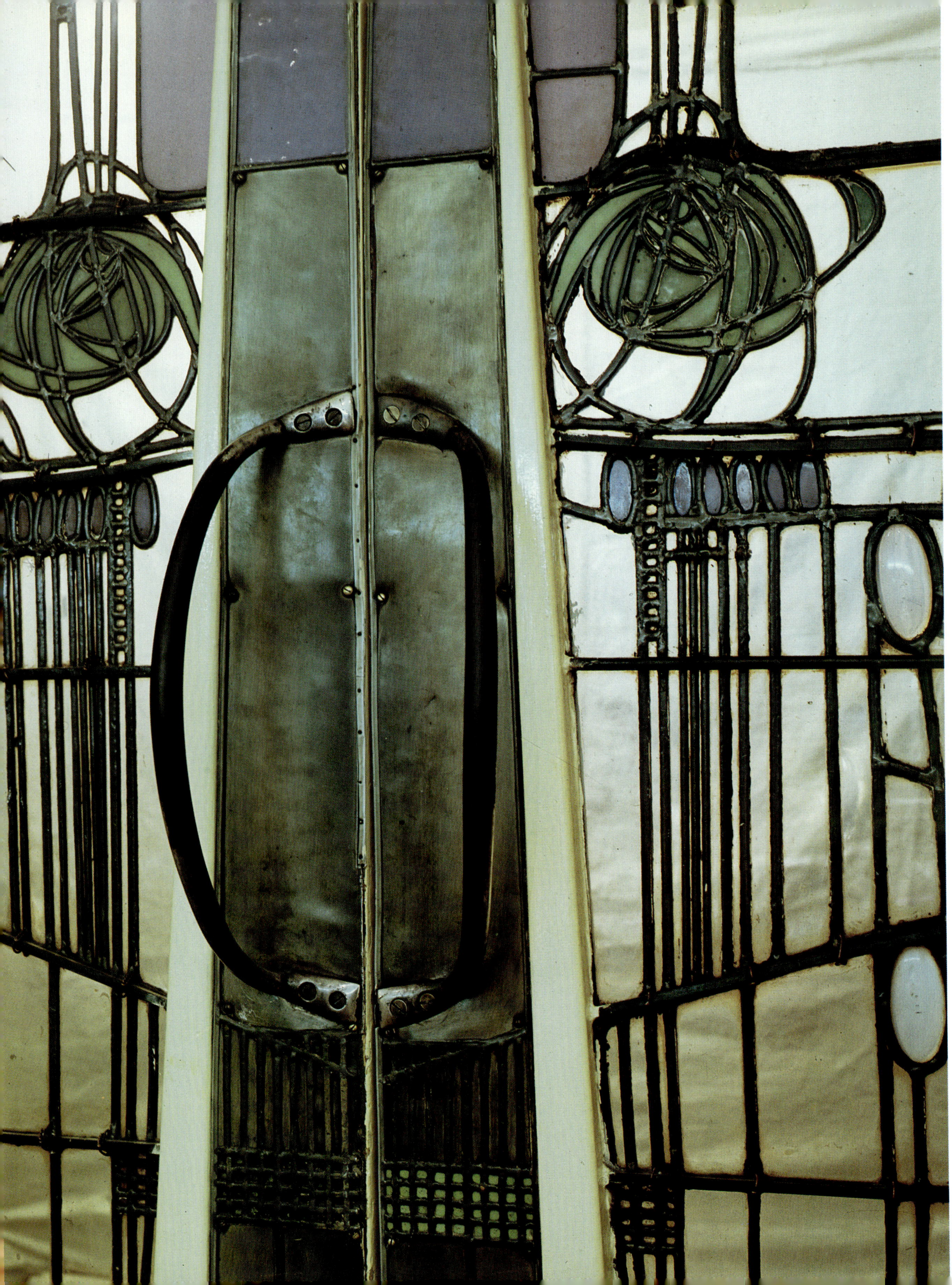

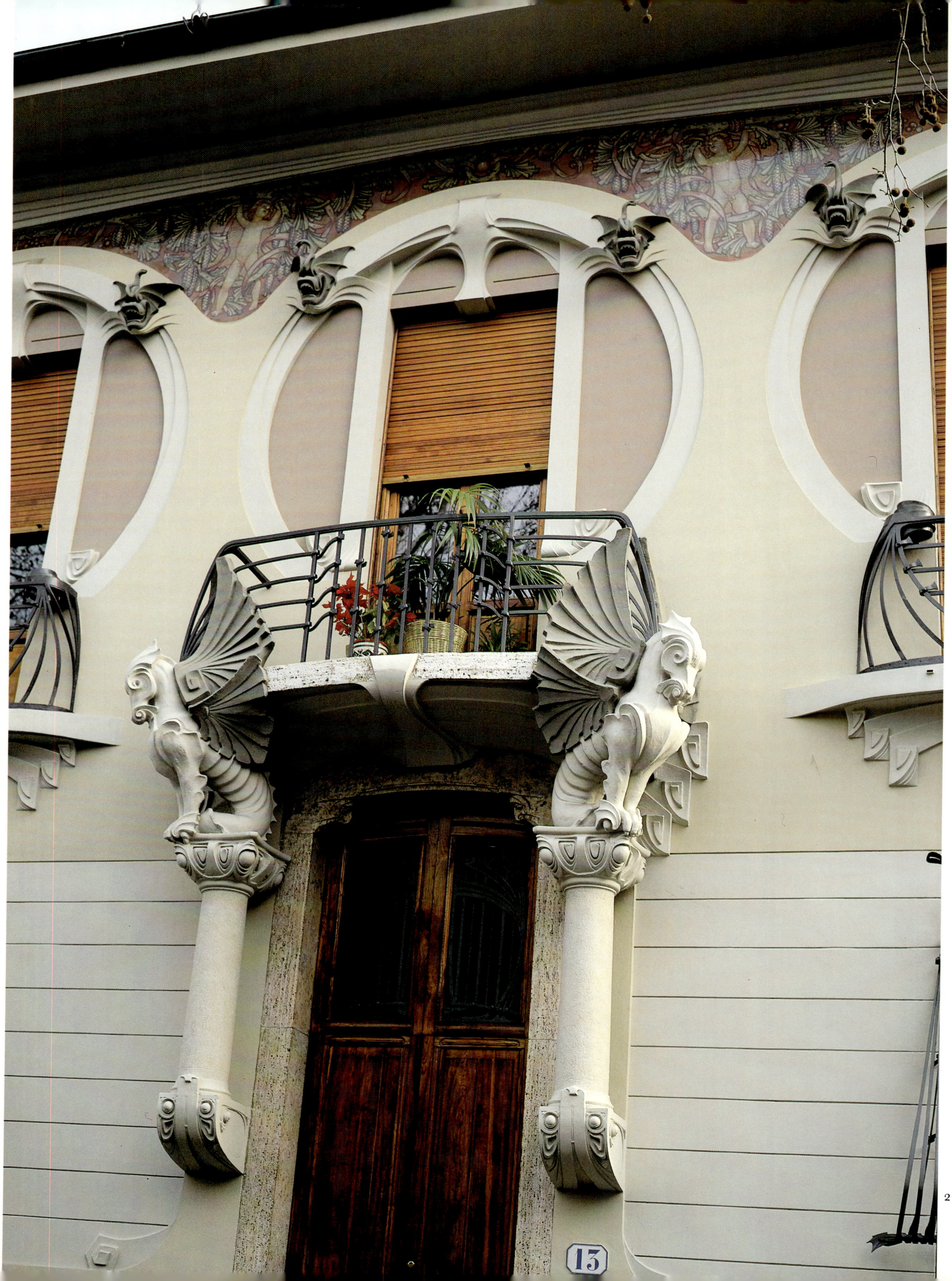

27

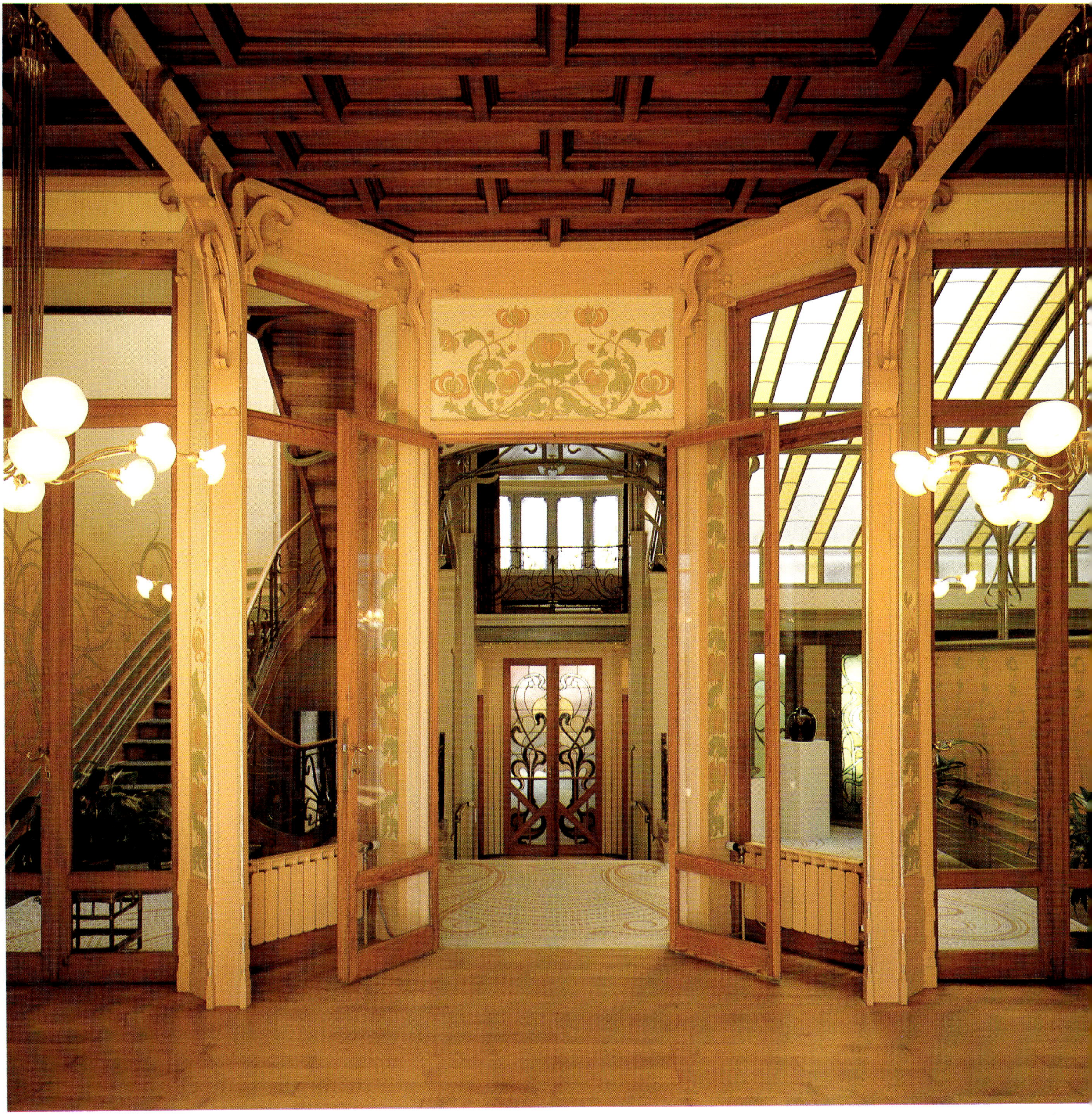

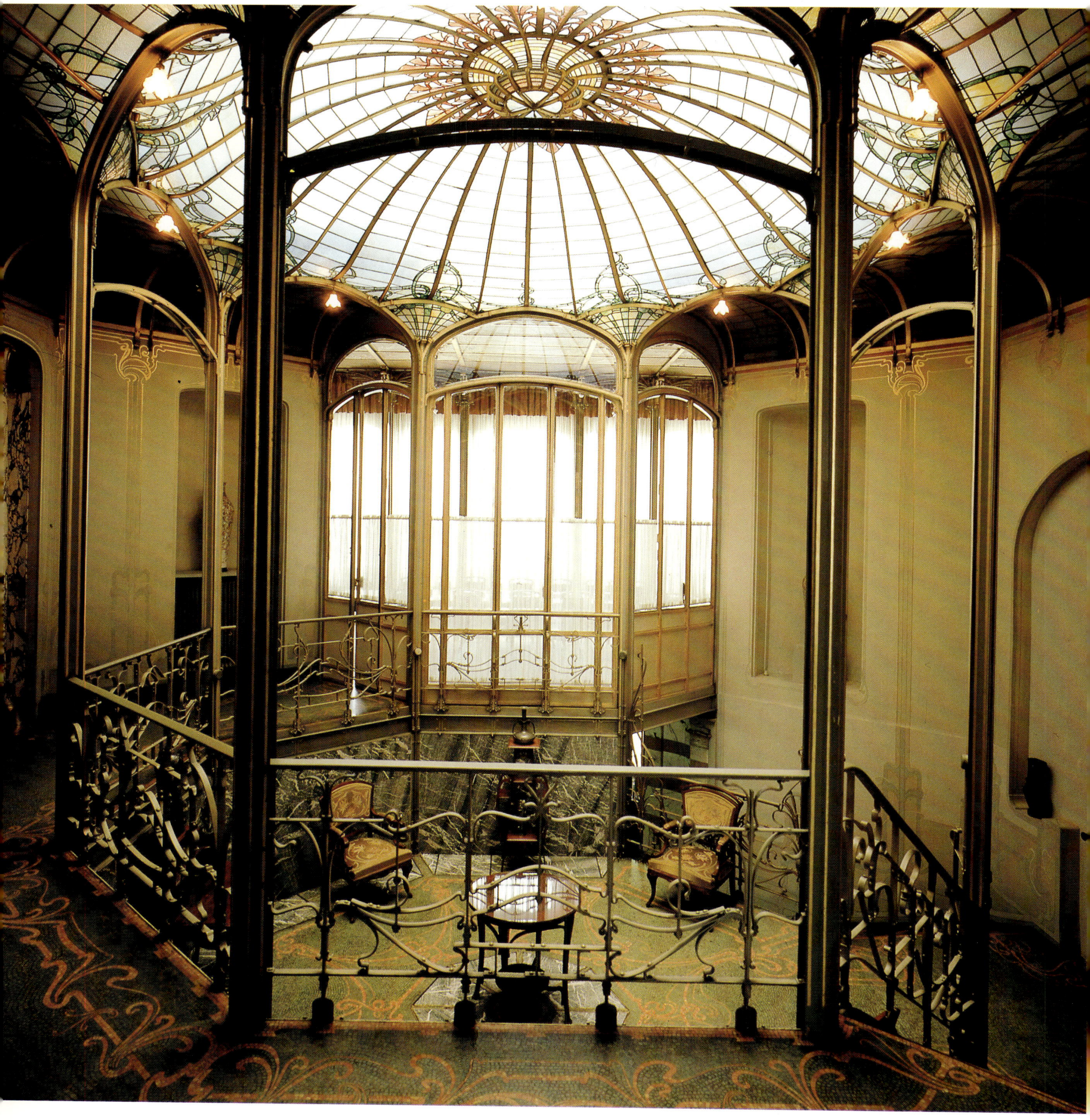

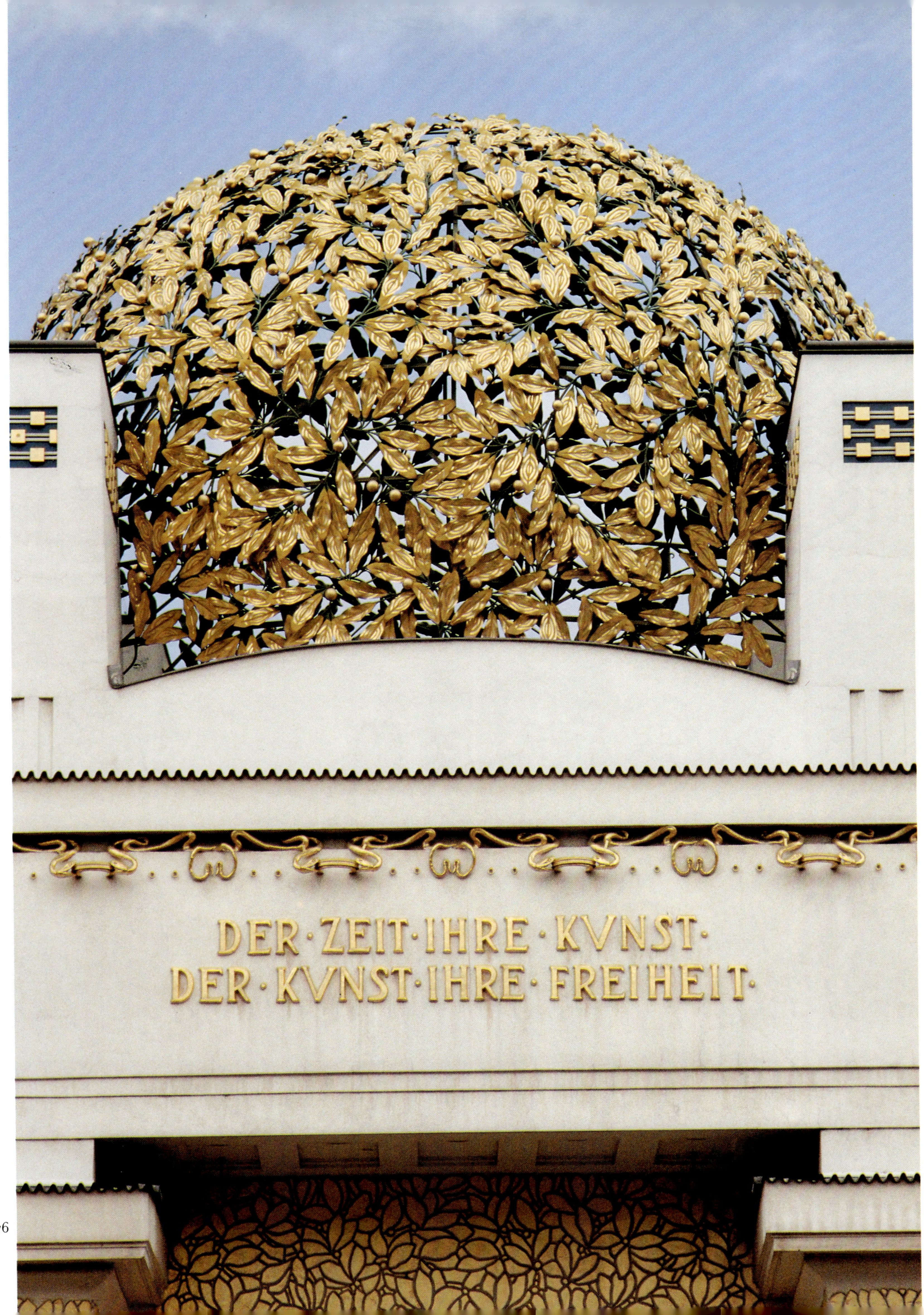
DER·ZEIT·IHRE·KVNST·
DER·KVNST·IHRE·FREIHEIT·

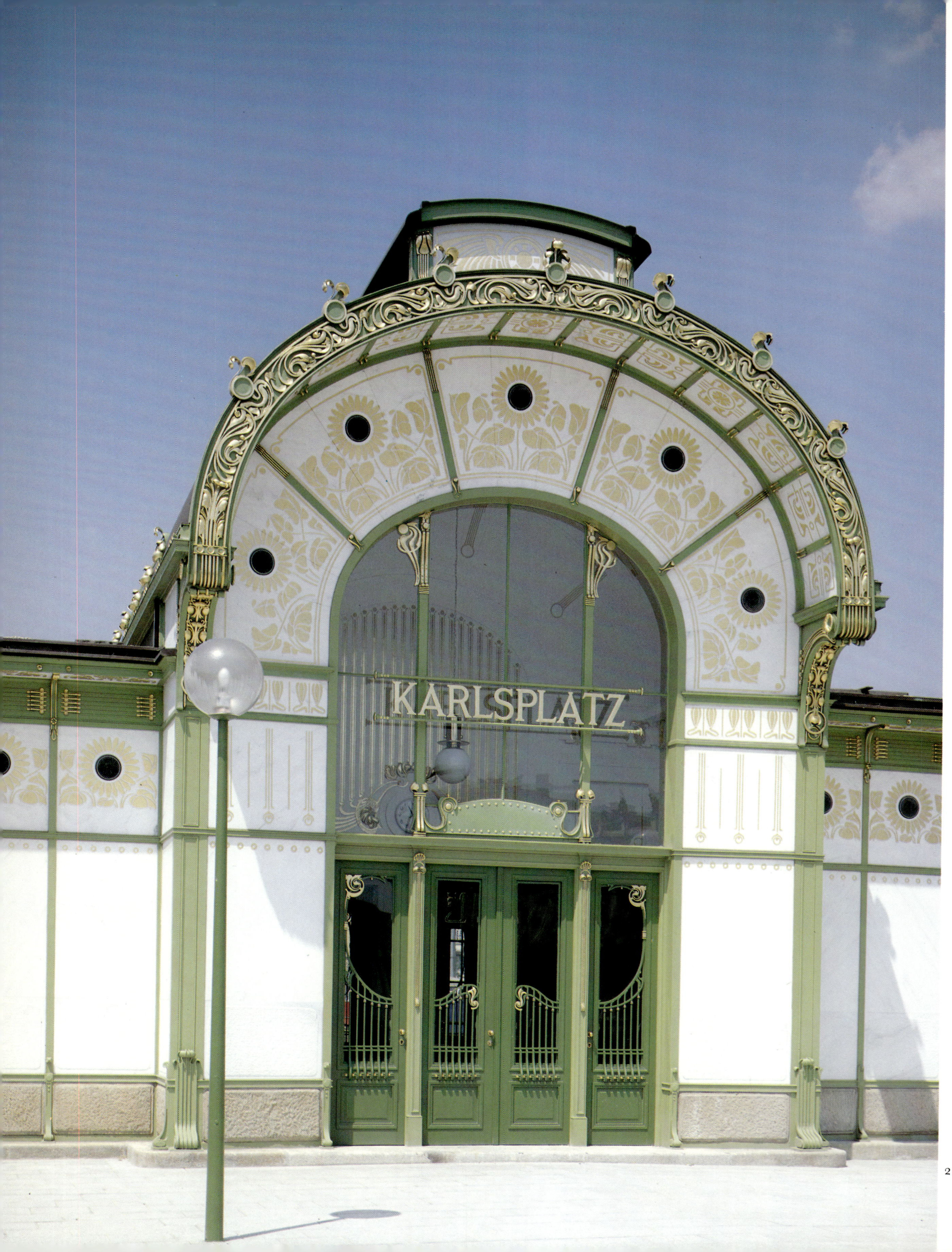
KARLSPLATZ

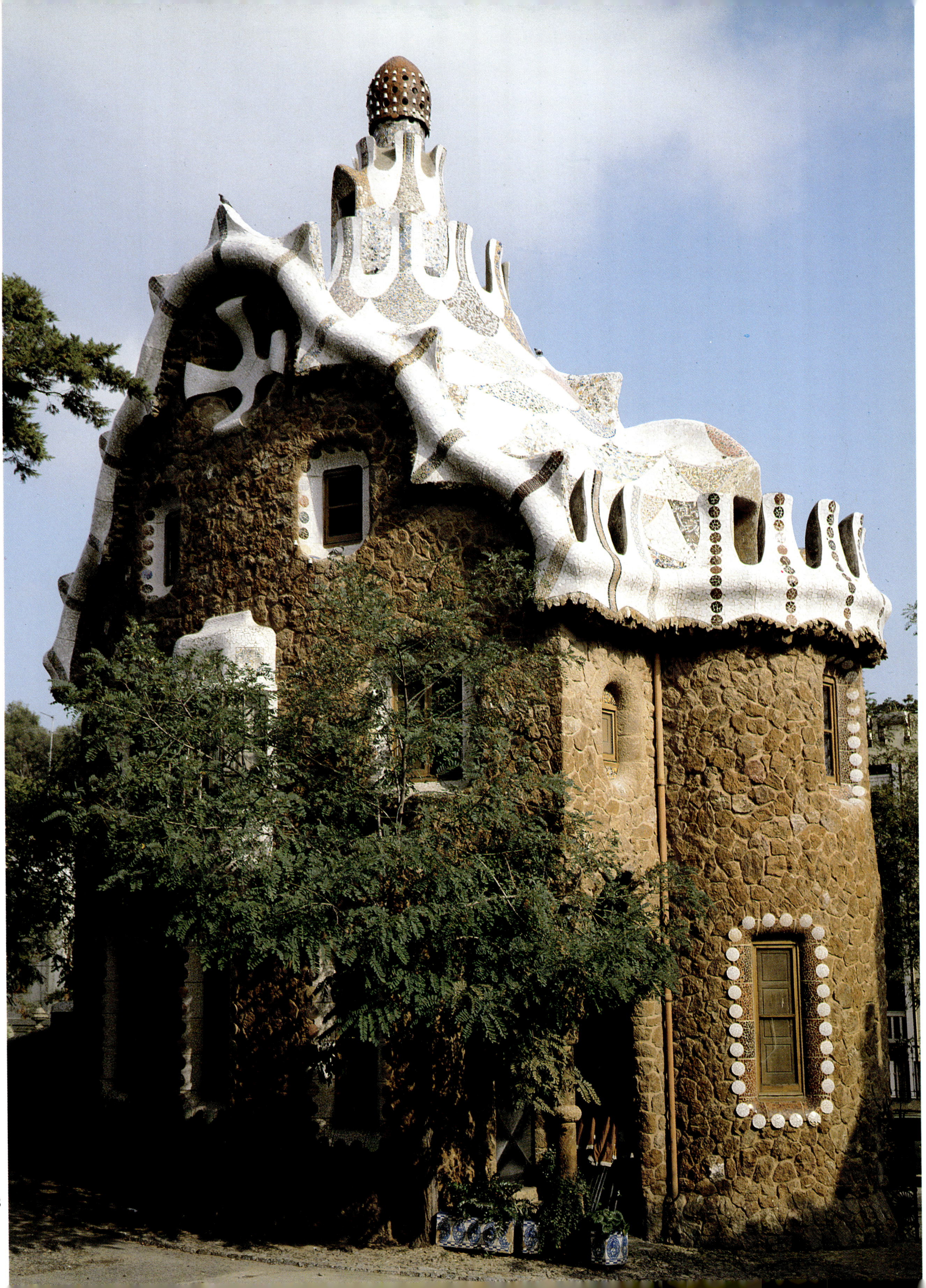

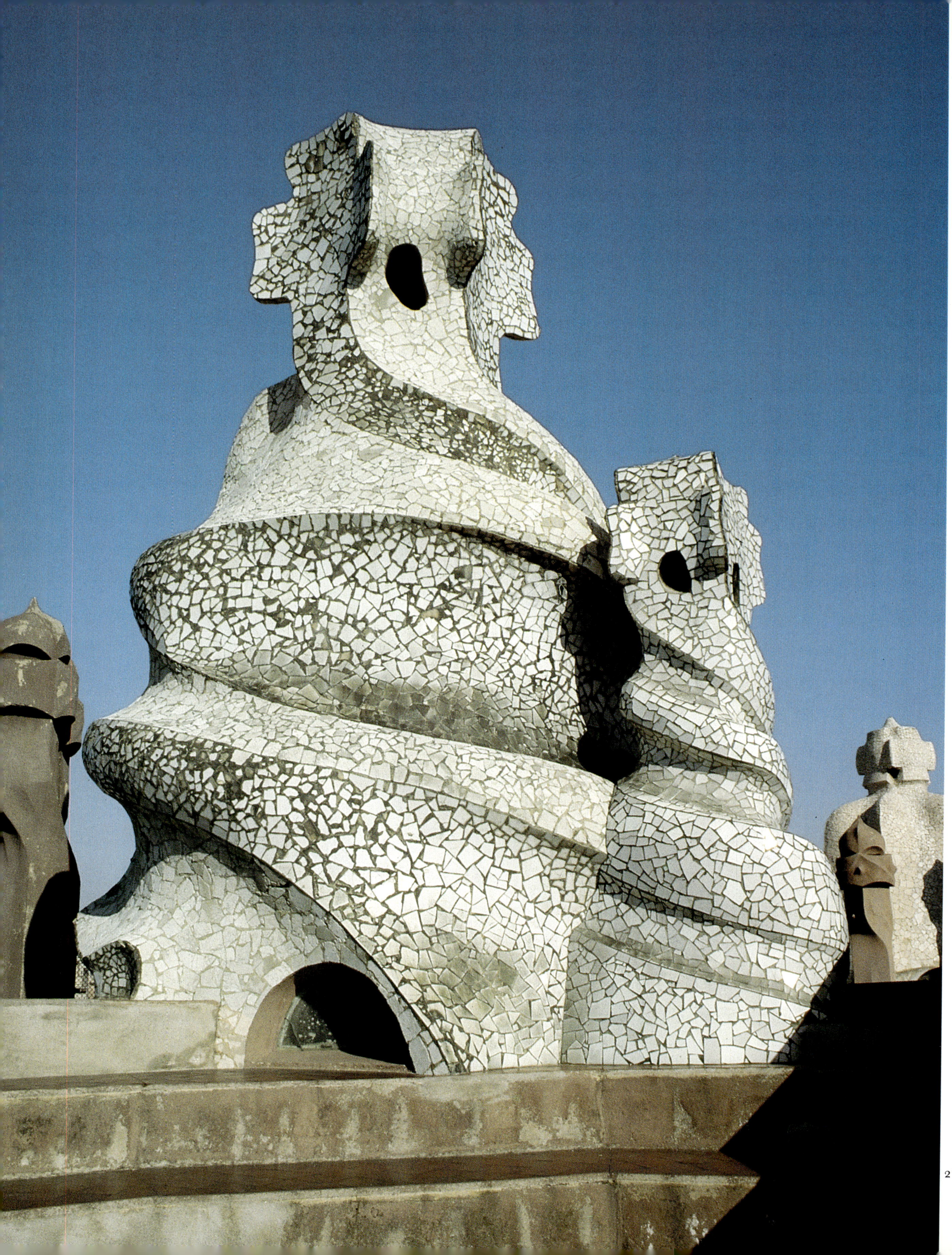

276 Joseph Maria Olbrich
Sezessionspalast
1897–98
Vienna

277 Otto Wagner
Karlsplatz subway entrance
After 1897
Vienna

278 Antoni Gaudí i Cornet
Parc Güell
Entrance pavilion
1900–14
Barcelona

279 Antoni Gaudí i Cornet
Chimney stacks, Casa Milá
1906–10
Barcelona

MAPS,
ARCHITECTURAL PROJECTS,
PLANS

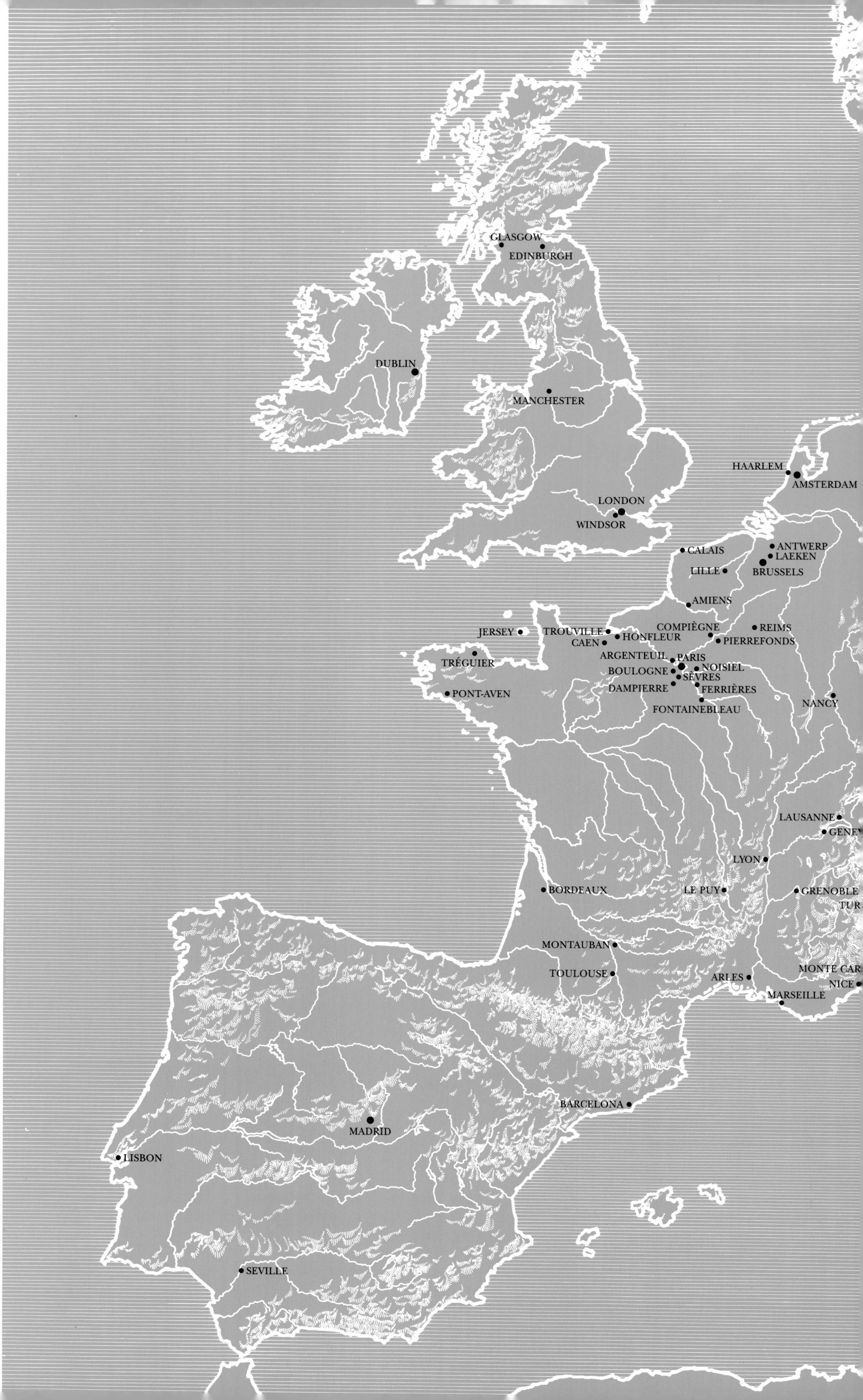
GLASGOW
EDINBURGH
DUBLIN
MANCHESTER
HAARLEM
AMSTERDAM
LONDON
WINDSOR
CALAIS
ANTWERP
LAEKEN
LILLE
BRUSSELS
AMIENS
JERSEY
TROUVILLE
CAEN
HONFLEUR
COMPIÈGNE
REIMS
PIERREFONDS
TRÉGUIER
ARGENTEUIL
PARIS
NOISIEL
BOULOGNE
SÈVRES
DAMPIERRE
FERRIÈRES
FONTAINEBLEAU
PONT-AVEN
NANCY
LAUSANNE
LYON
BORDEAUX
LE PUY
GRENOBLE
MONTAUBAN
TOULOUSE
ARLES
NICE
MARSEILLE
BARCELONA
MADRID
LISBON
SEVILLE

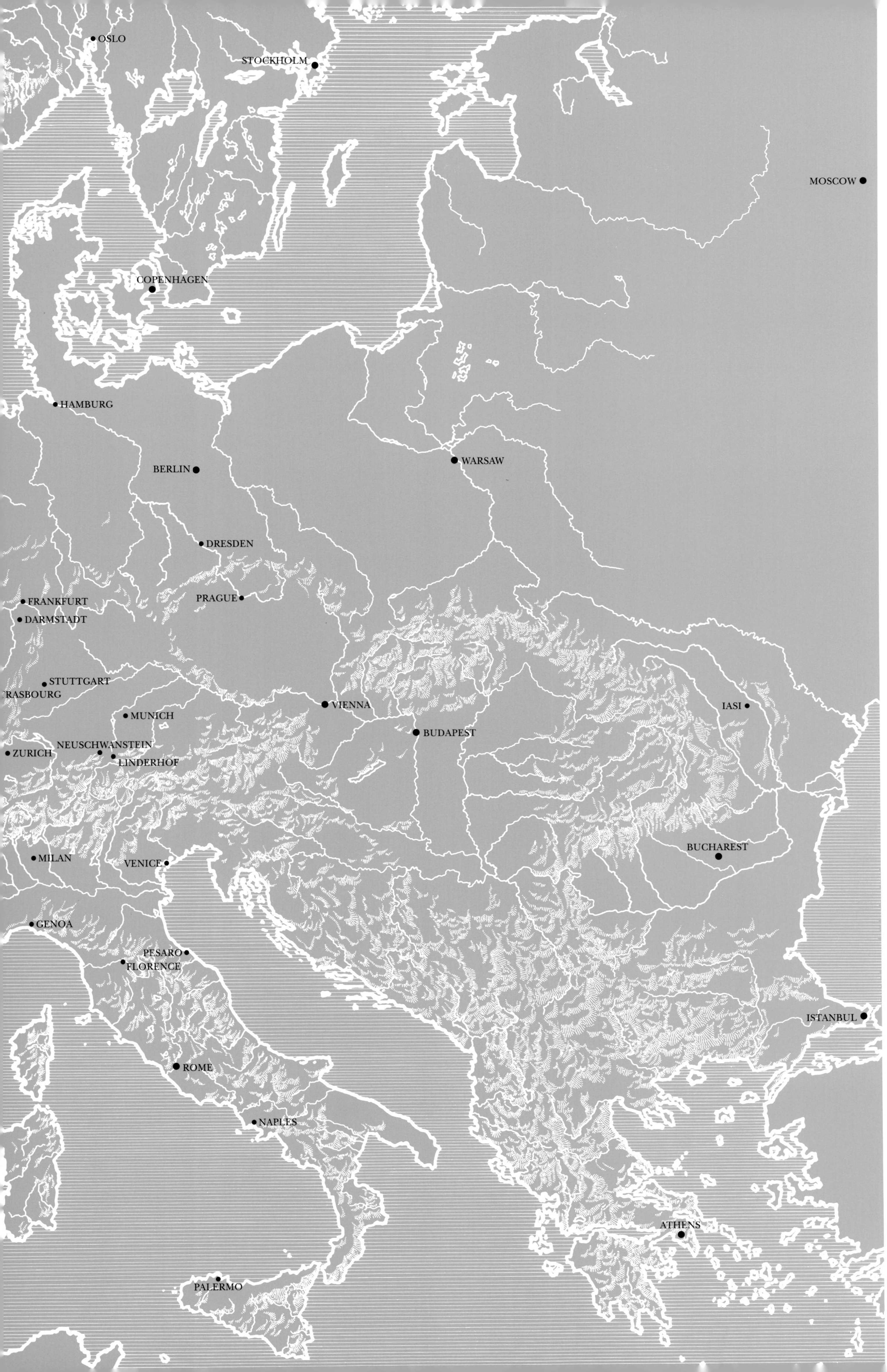

OSLO
STOCKHOLM
MOSCOW
COPENHAGEN
HAMBURG
BERLIN
WARSAW
DRESDEN
PRAGUE
FRANKFURT
DARMSTADT
STUTTGART
RASBOURG
MUNICH
VIENNA
IASI
BUDAPEST
ZURICH
NEUSCHWANSTEIN
LINDERHOF
BUCHAREST
MILAN
VENICE
GENOA
PESARO
FLORENCE
ISTANBUL
ROME
NAPLES
ATHENS
PALERMO

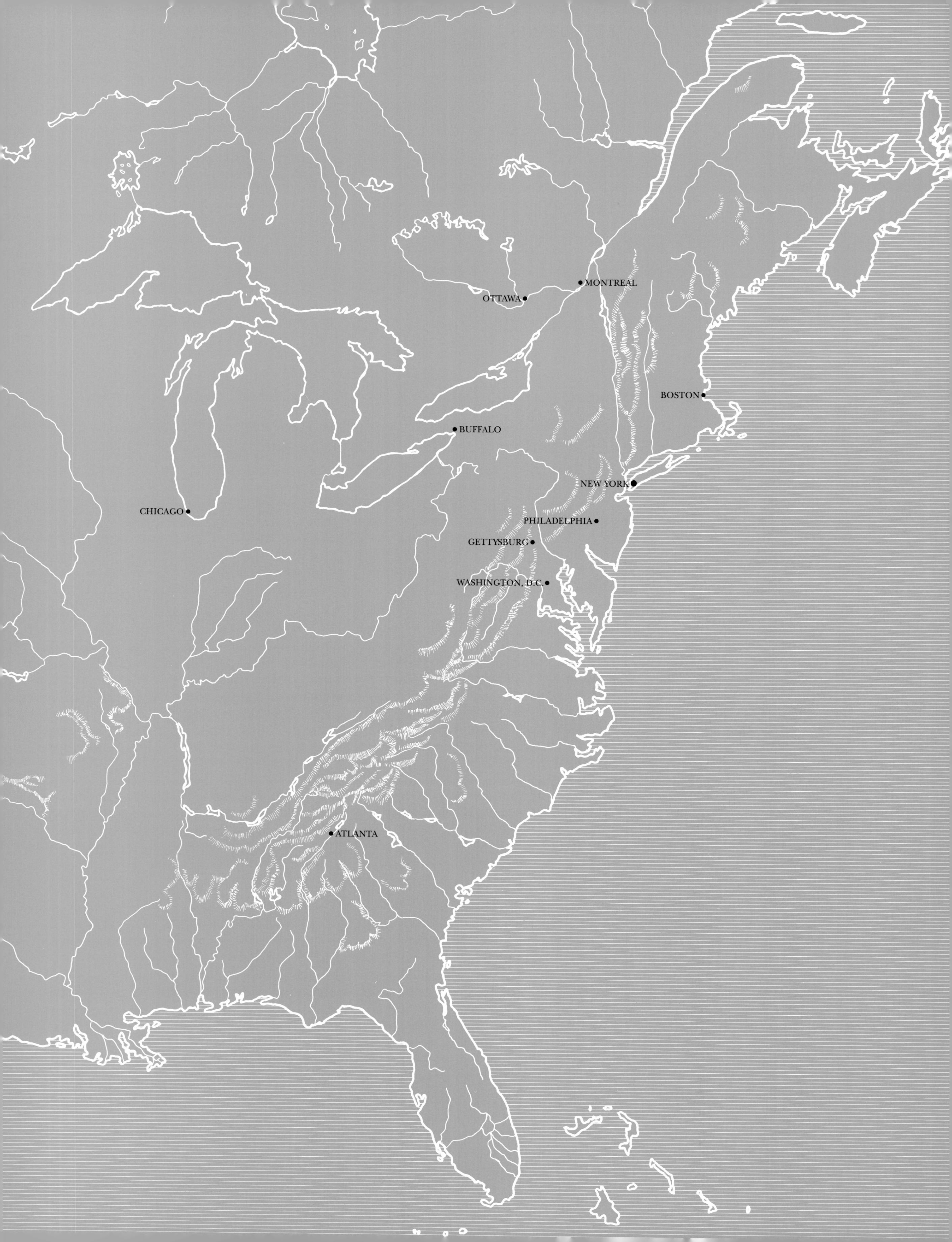
MONTREAL
OTTAWA
BOSTON
BUFFALO
NEW YORK
CHICAGO
PHILADELPHIA
GETTYSBURG
WASHINGTON, D.C.
ATLANTA

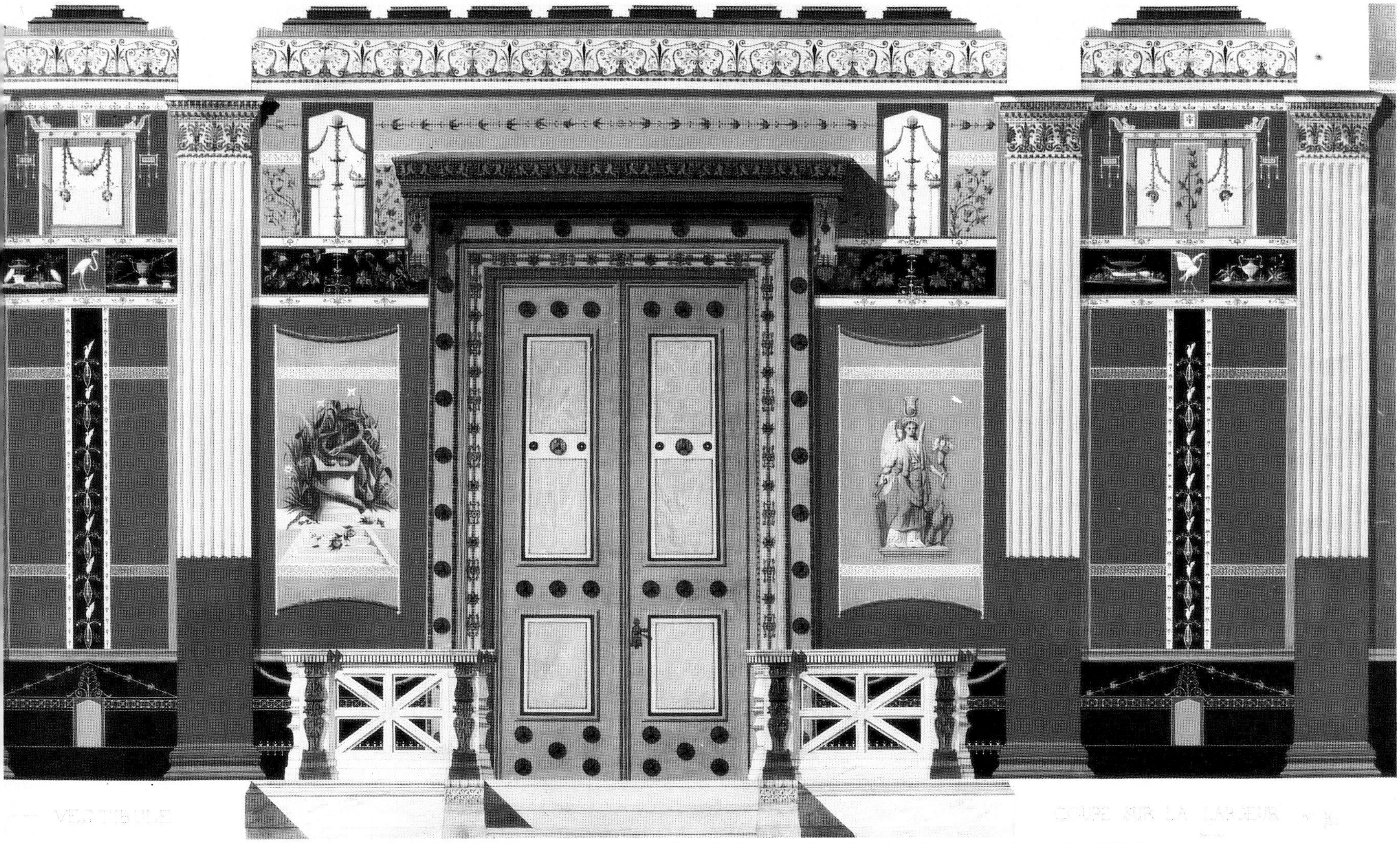

280. Alfred-Nicolas Normand. Vestibule in Prince Napoleon's Maison Pompéienne in the Avenue Montaigne, Paris (section across frontage). c. 1882. Watercolor

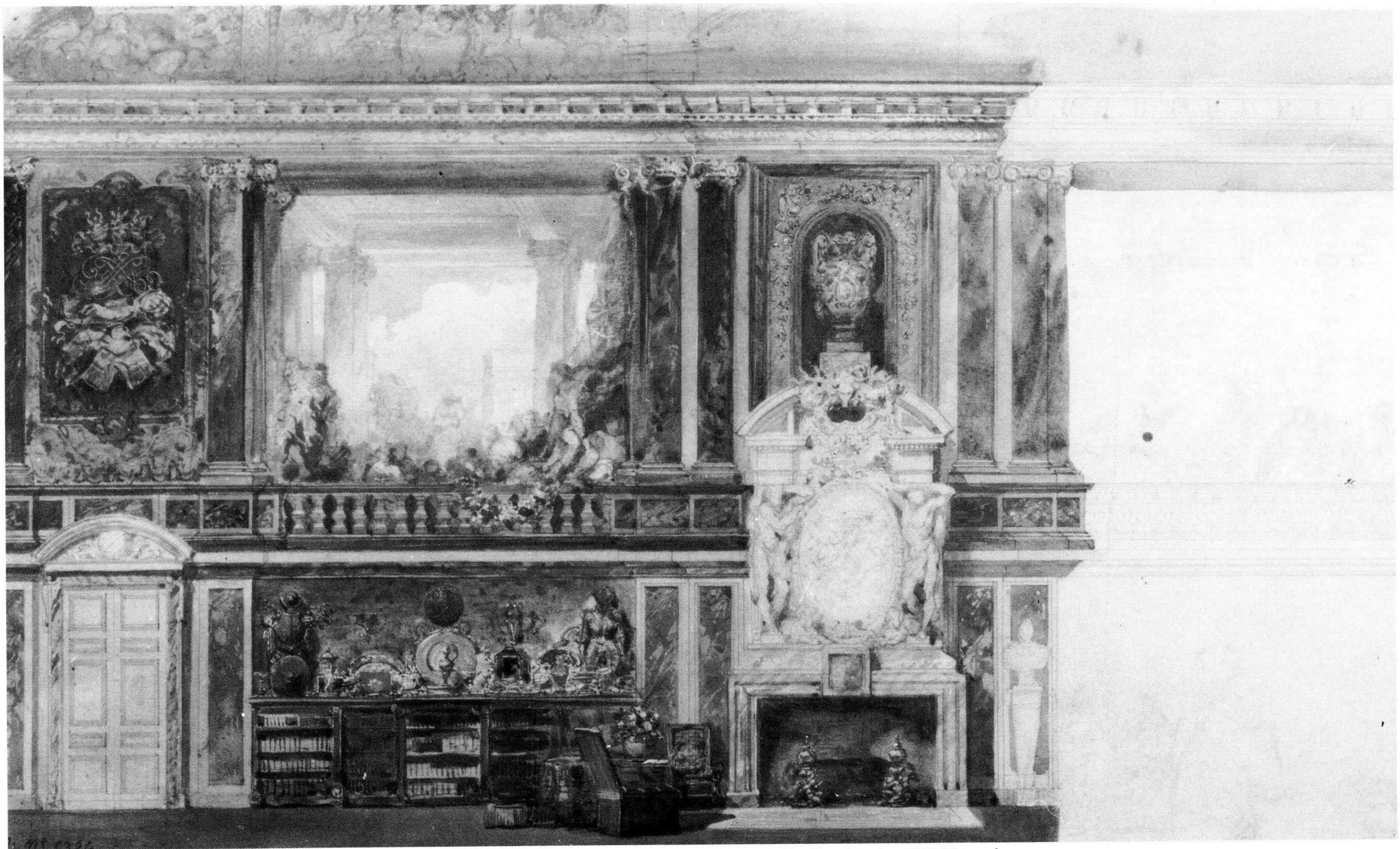

281. Eugène Lami. Decoration of the Great Hall, Château de Ferrières (plan). c. 1860. Watercolor

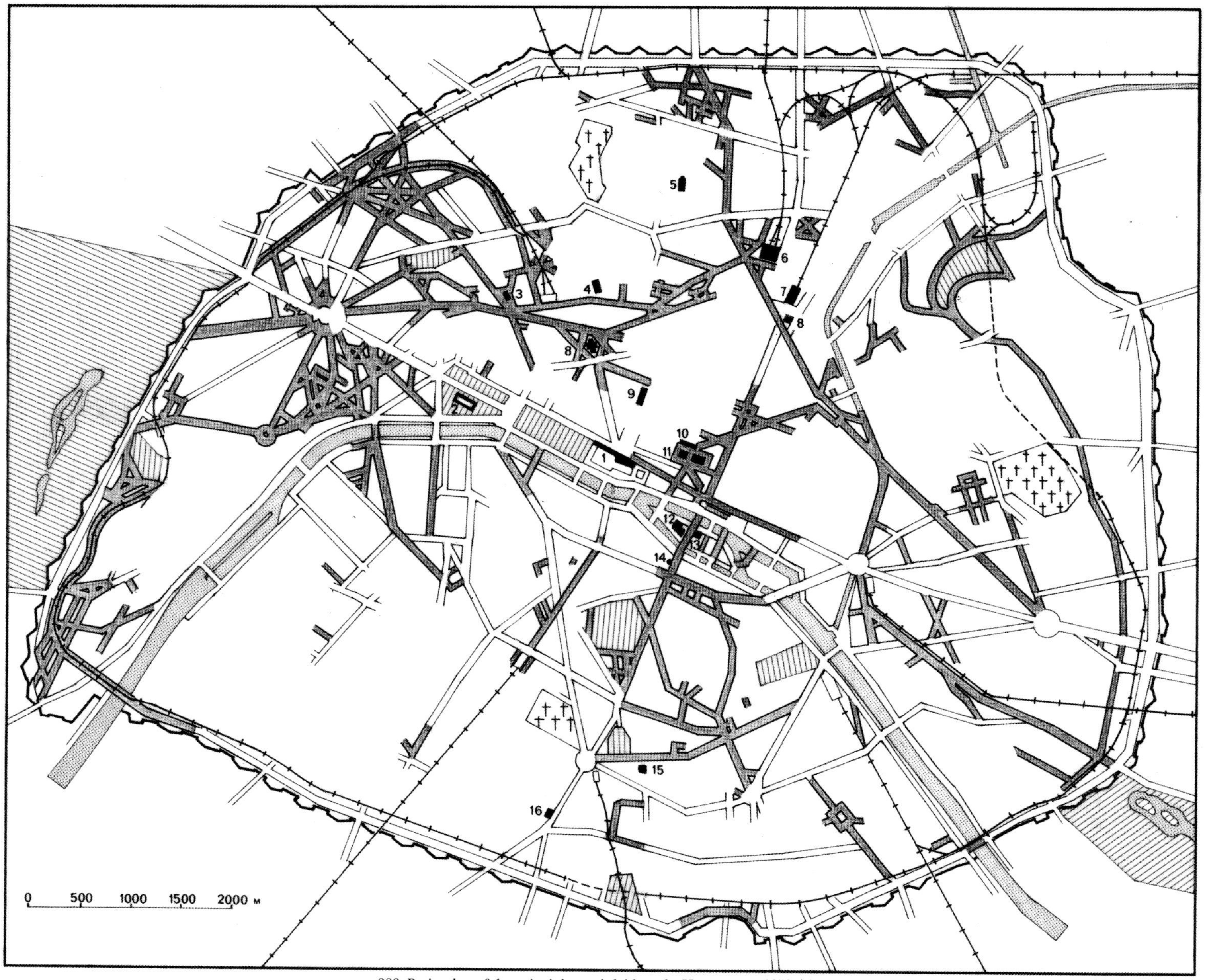

1 The Louvre
2 Palais de l'Industrie
3 Saint-Augustin Church
4 La Trinité
5 Basilique du Sacré-Coeur
6 Gare du Nord
7 Gare de l'Est
8 Saint-Laurent Church
9 Bibliothèque Nationale
10 Saint-Eustache Church
11 Les Halles (main covered market)
12 Palais de Justice (central law courts)
13 Tribunal de Commerce (commercial court)
14 Saint-Michel Fountain
15 La Santé (prison)
16 Saint-Pierre-de-Montrouge Church
(Drawing by Ferrante Ferranti after Poisson)

282. Paris, plan of the principle roads laid out by Haussmann. 1852–70

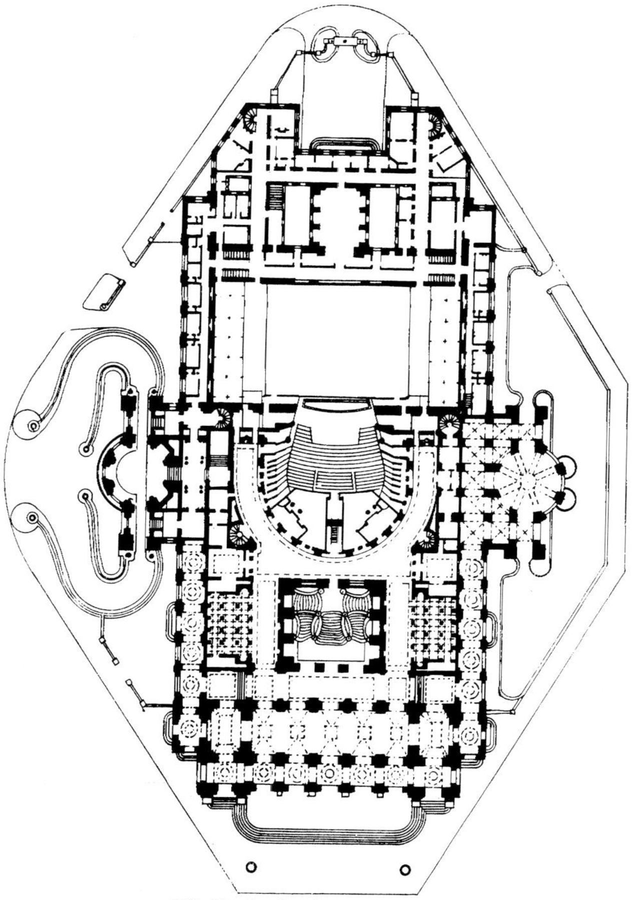

283. Charles Garnier. Paris Opéra (plan). 1861–75

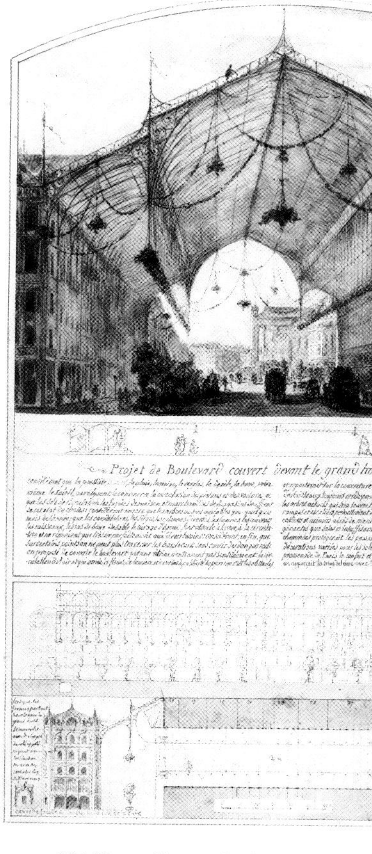

284. Hector Horeau. Project to roof the old boulevards. Ink and watercolor. 1866

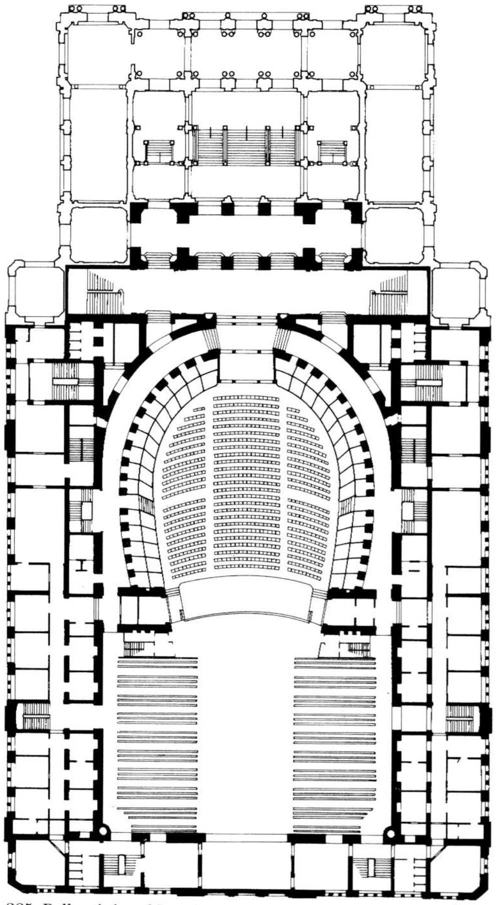

285. Pellegrini and Lavalle. Colon Theater at Buenos Aires (plan). Begun 1857

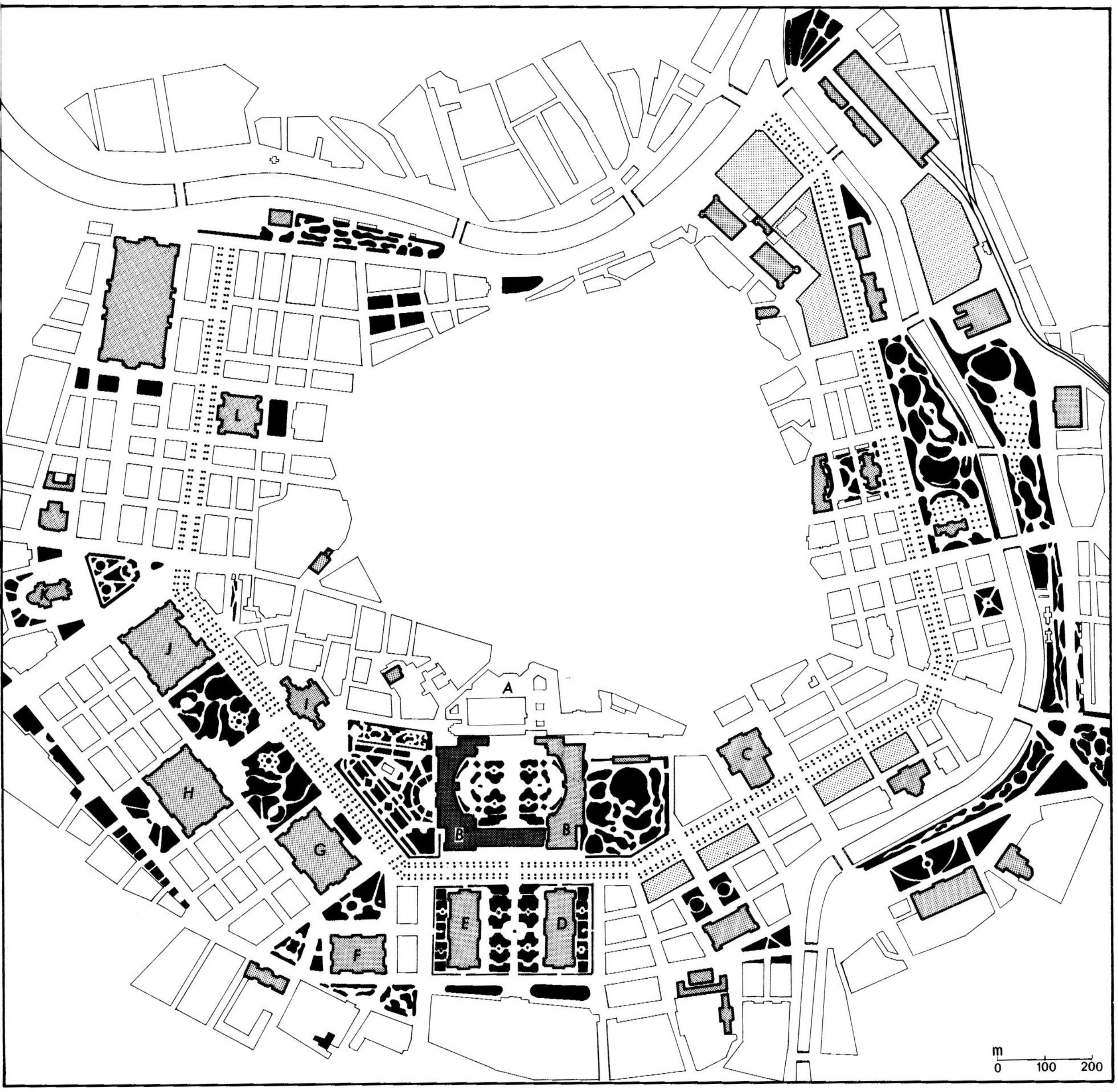

A, Alte Hofburg (old Imperial Palace)
B, Neue Hofburg (new Imperial Palace)
C, Staatsoper (opera house)
D, Kunsthistorisches Museum (Art History Museum)
E, Naturhistorisches Museum (Natural History Museum)
F, central law courts
G, Parliament
H, City Hall
I, Burgtheater (City Theater)
J, University
K, Votivkirche (Votive Church)
L, Börse (Stock Exchange)
(Drawing by Ferrante Ferranti after L. Benevolo)

286. Vienna, plan of the Ringstrasse. 1859–88

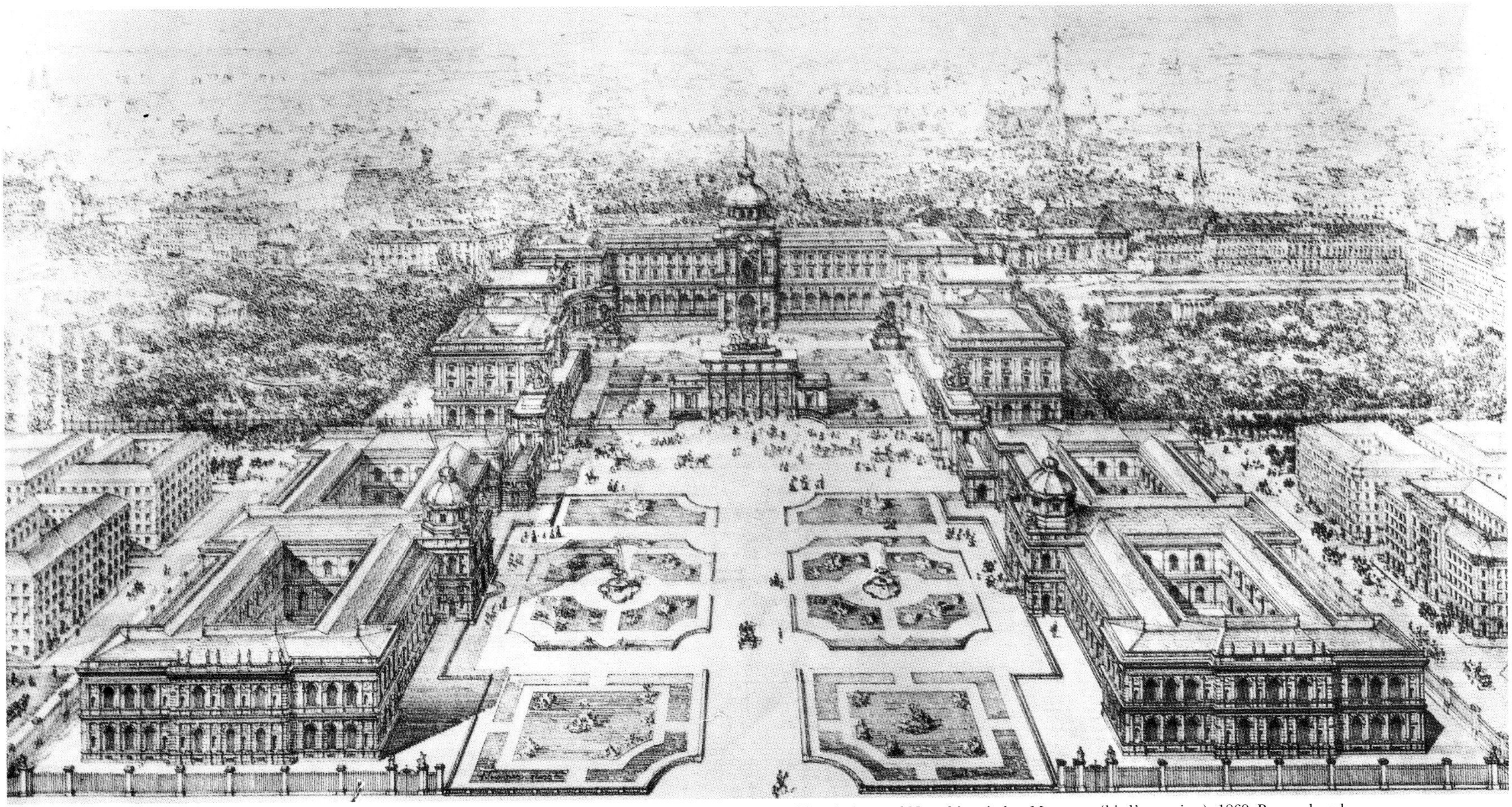

287. Gottfried Semper and Carl von Hasenauer. Project for joining the Hofburg to the Kunsthistorisches and Naturhistorisches Museums (bird's-eye view). 1869. Pen and wash

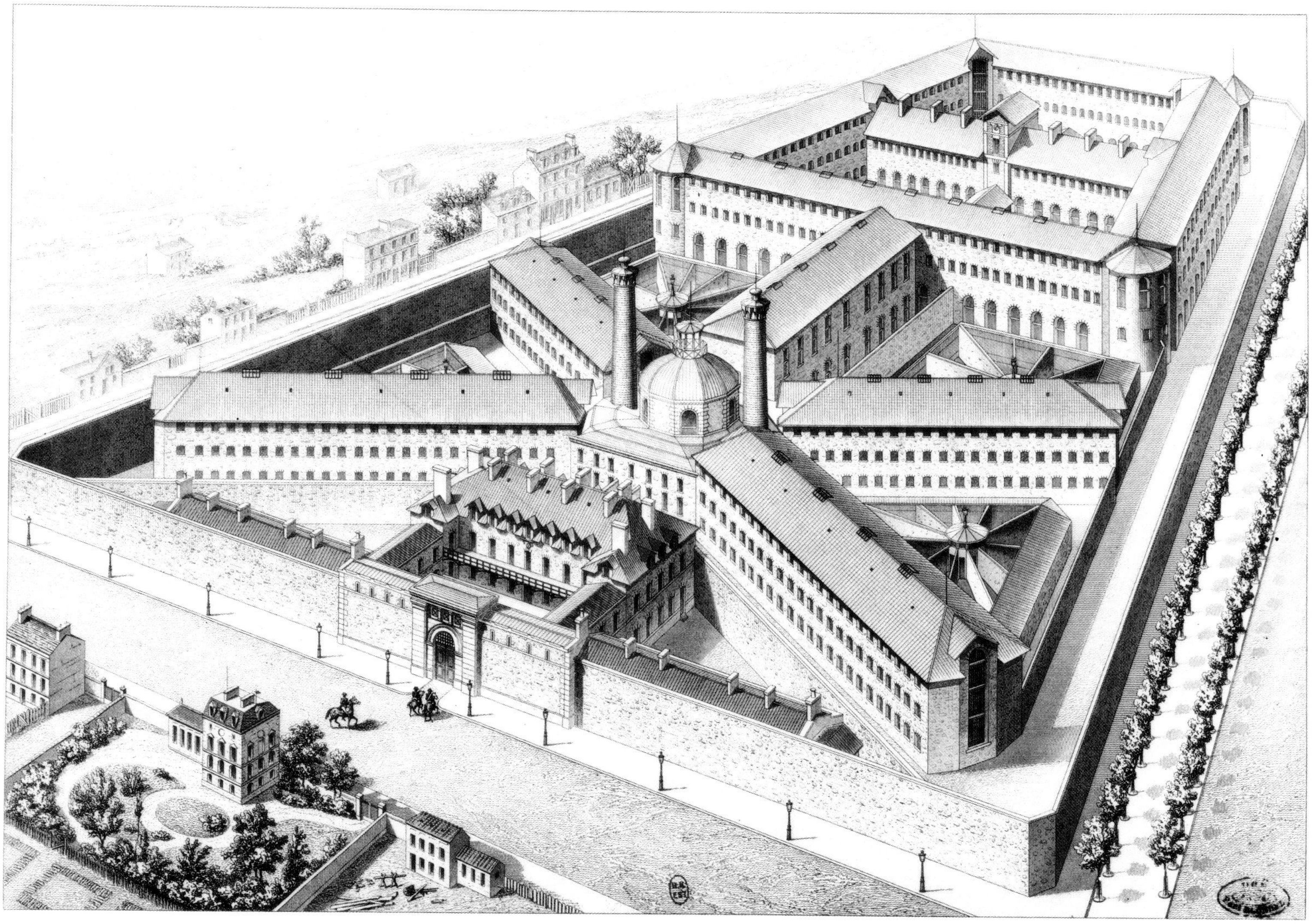

296. Joseph Vaudemer. Prison of La Santé, Paris. 1875

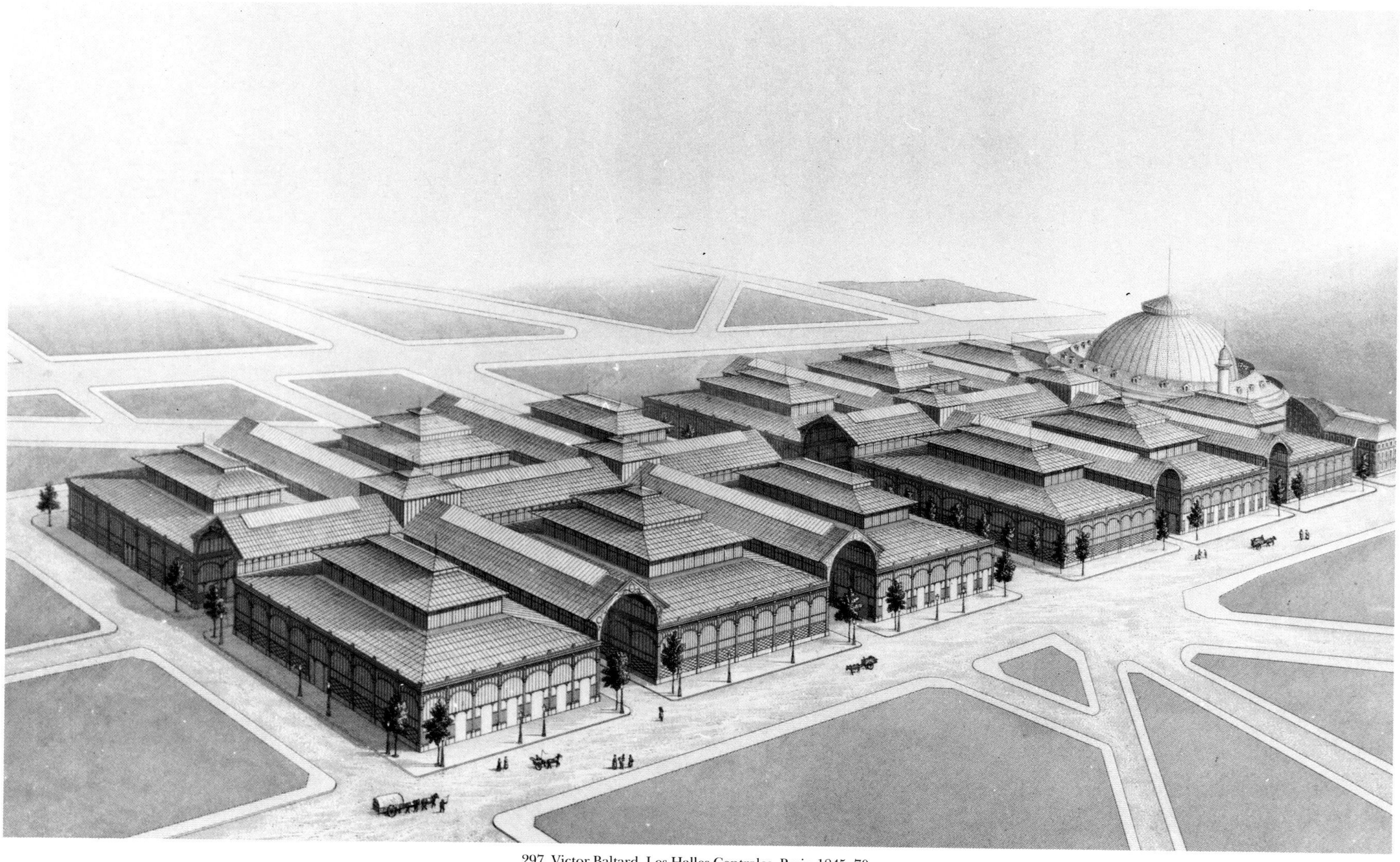

297. Victor Baltard. Les Halles Centrales, Paris. 1845–70

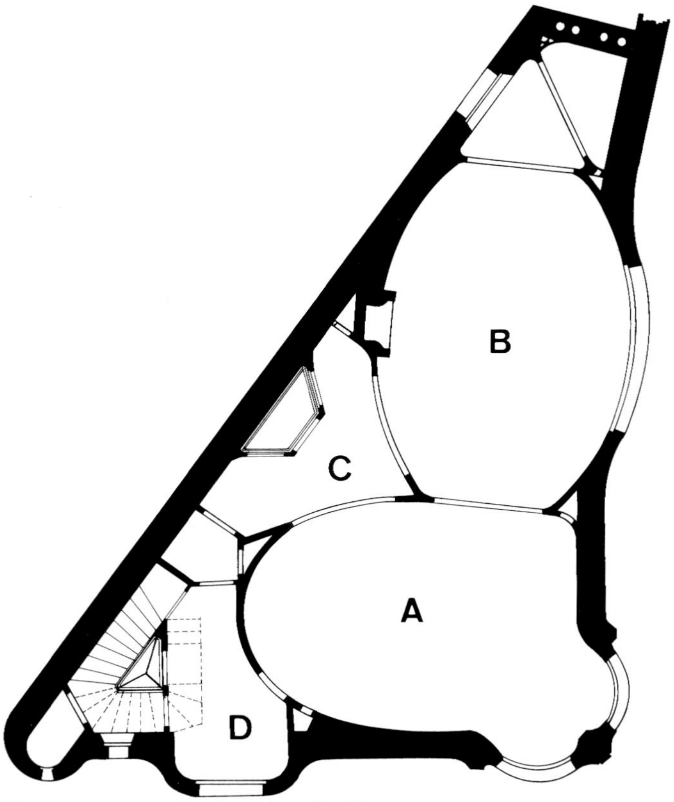

298. Hector Guimard. First floor of the Hôtel Guimard.
A, dining room; B, large drawing room; C, reception gallery; D, pantry

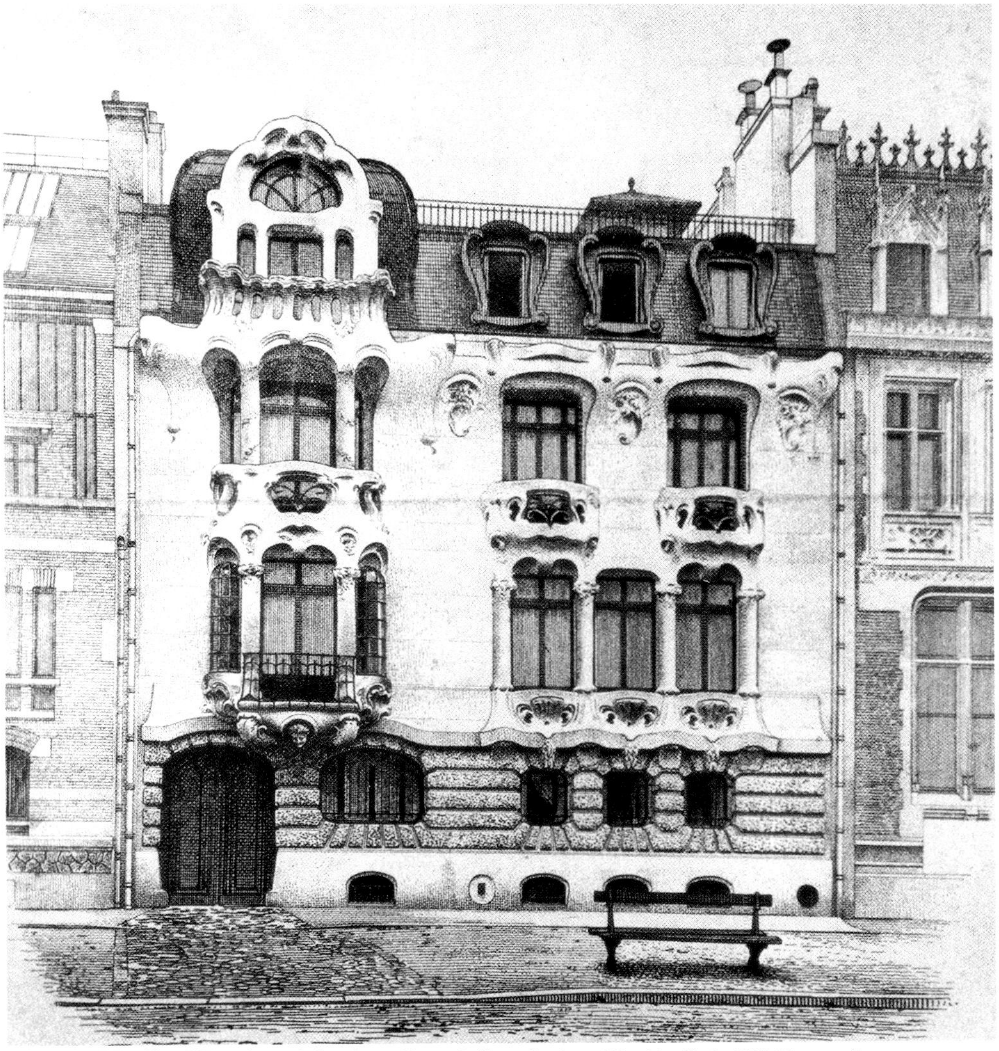

299. Xavier Schoellkopf. Town house belonging to Yvette Guilbert, Boulevard Berthier, Paris. 1900 (destroyed)

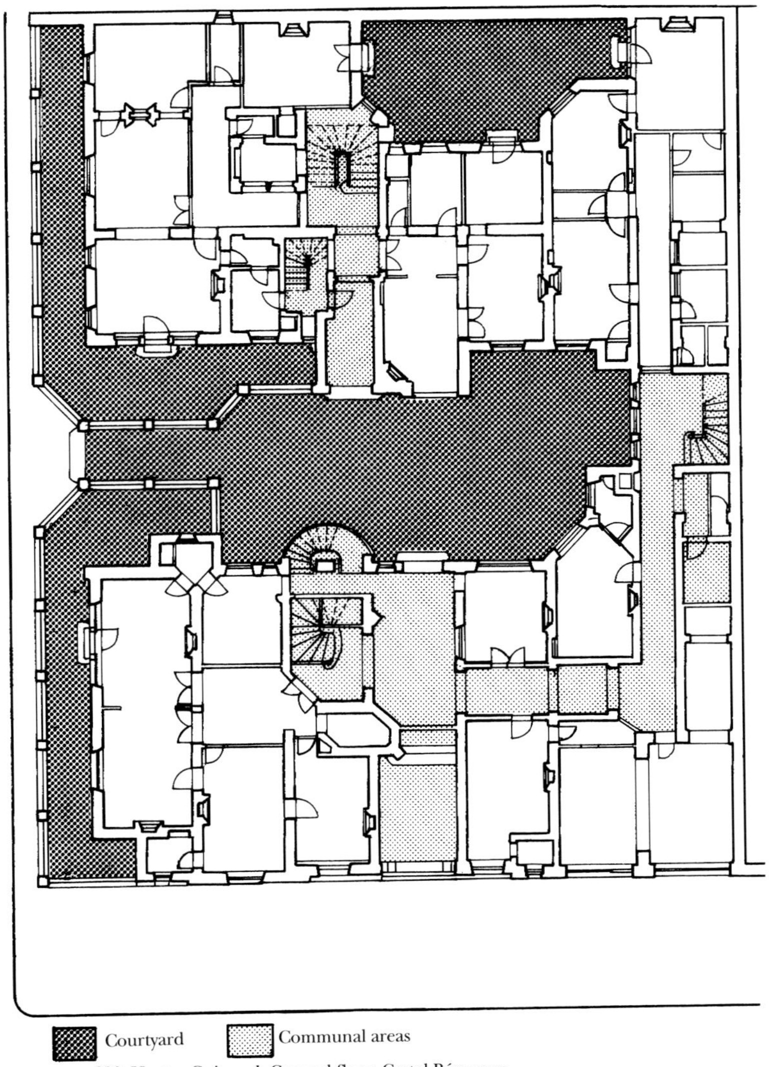

300. Hector Guimard. Ground floor, Castel Béranger, Rue La Fontaine, Paris (plan). 1894–98

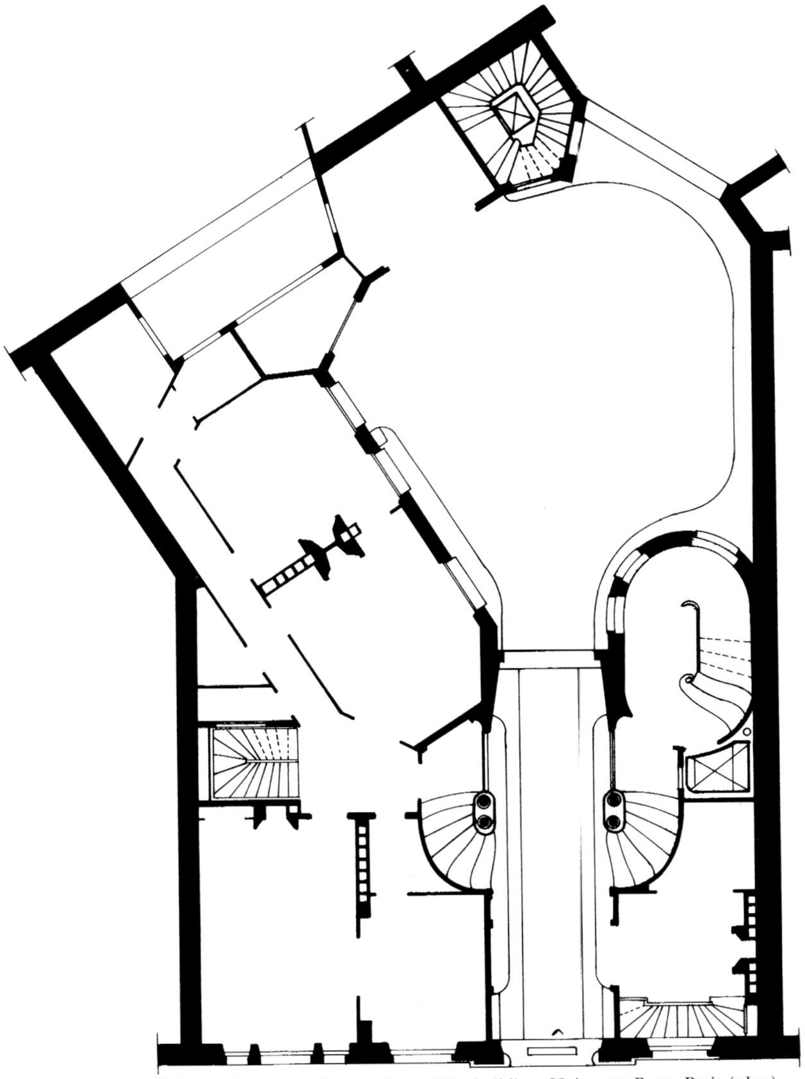

301. Jules Lavirotte. Ground floor of the building, 29 Avenue Rapp, Paris (plan). 1900–1. (Drawing by Ferrante Ferranti)

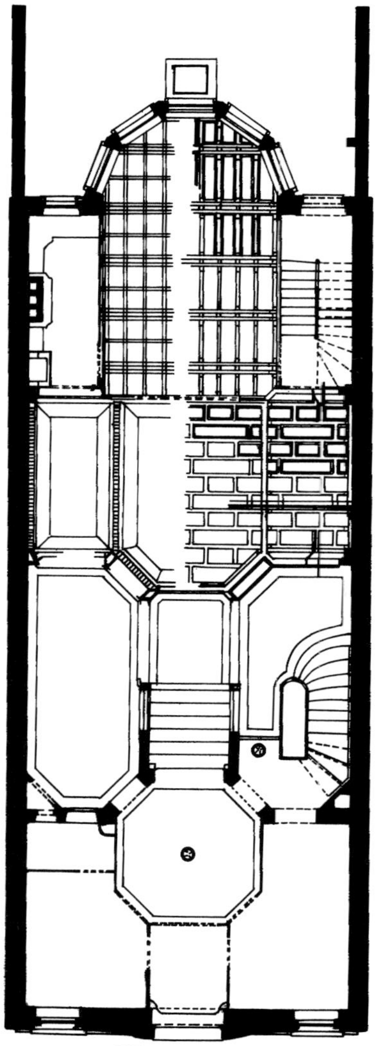

302. Victor Horta. Hôtel Tassel, Brussels (plan). 1893

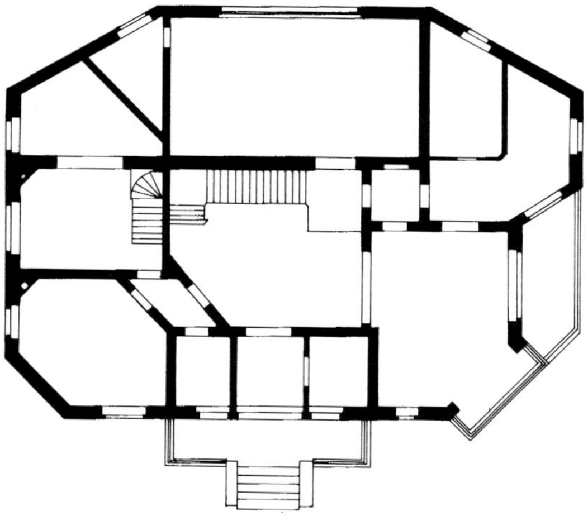

303. Henry van de Velde. Bloemenwerf House, Uccle (plan). 1895

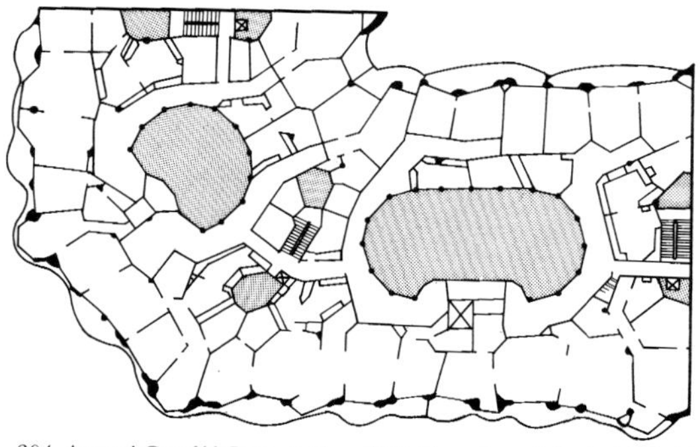

304. Antoni Gaudí i Cornet. Casa Milá, Barcelona (plan). 1905–10. (Drawing by Ferrante Ferranti)

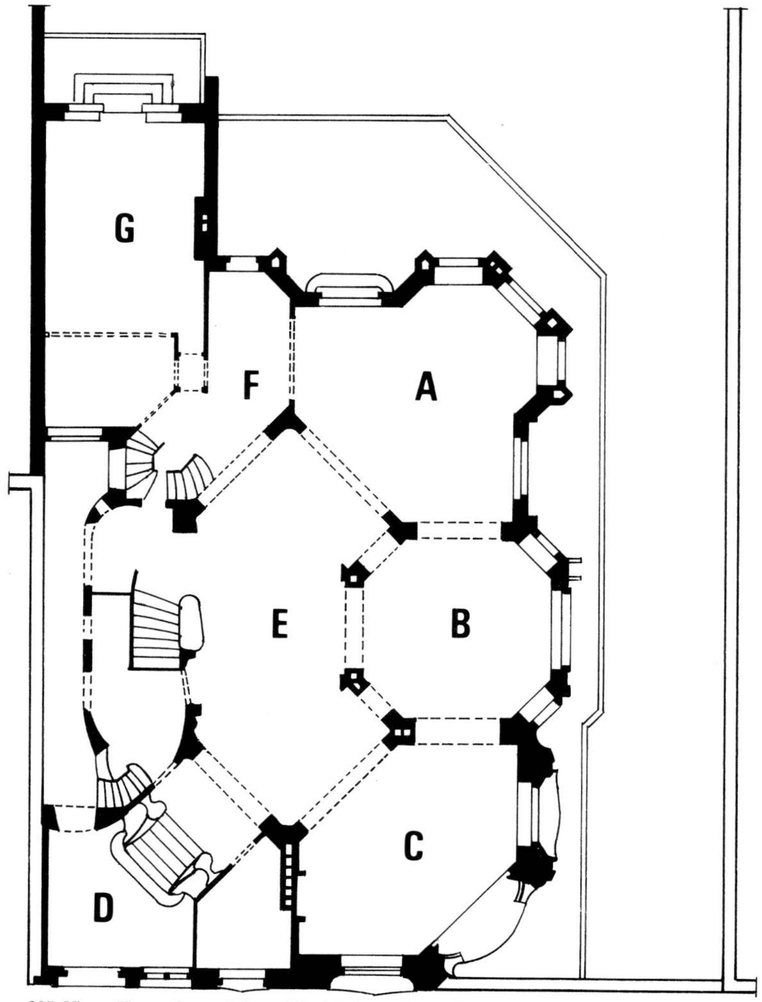

305. Victor Horta. Ground floor, Hôtel Aubecq, Brussels (plan). A, dining room; B, living room; C, gallery; D, vestibule; E, hall; F, pantry; G, kitchen

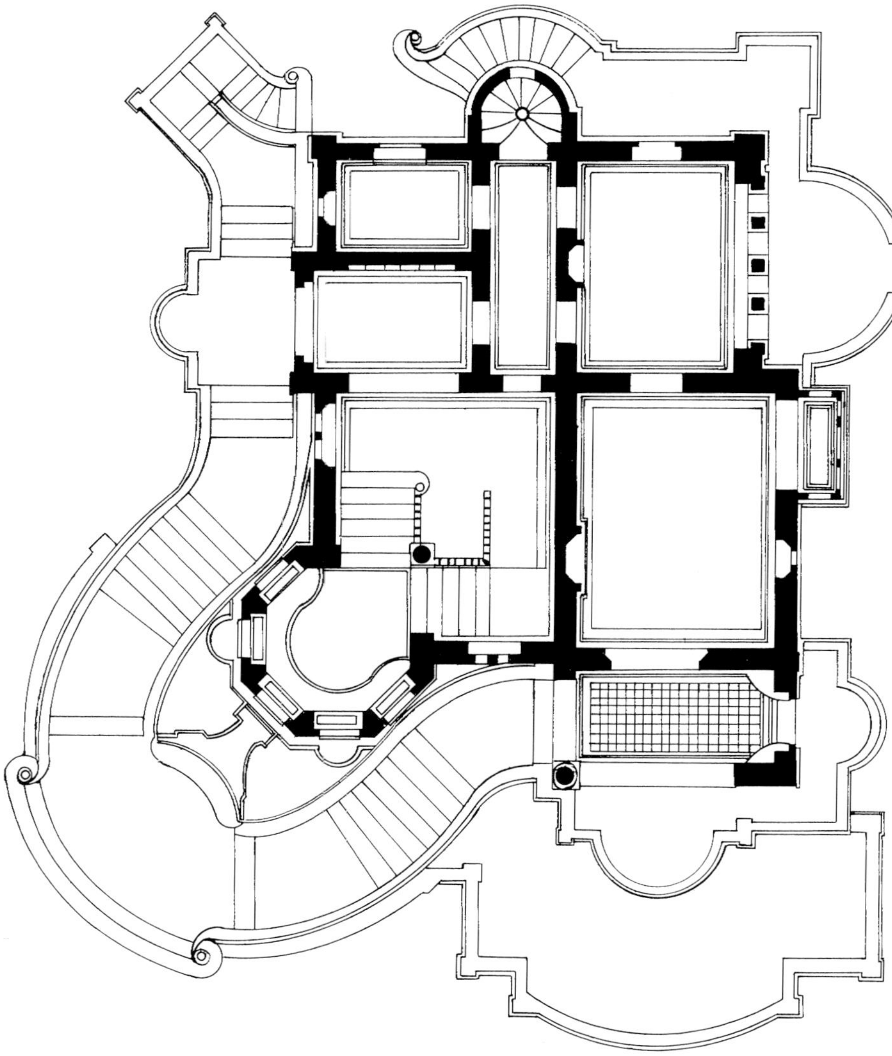

306. Ernesto Basile. Villino Florio, Palermo (plan). 1899–1903. (Drawing by Ferrante Ferranti after an original drawing)

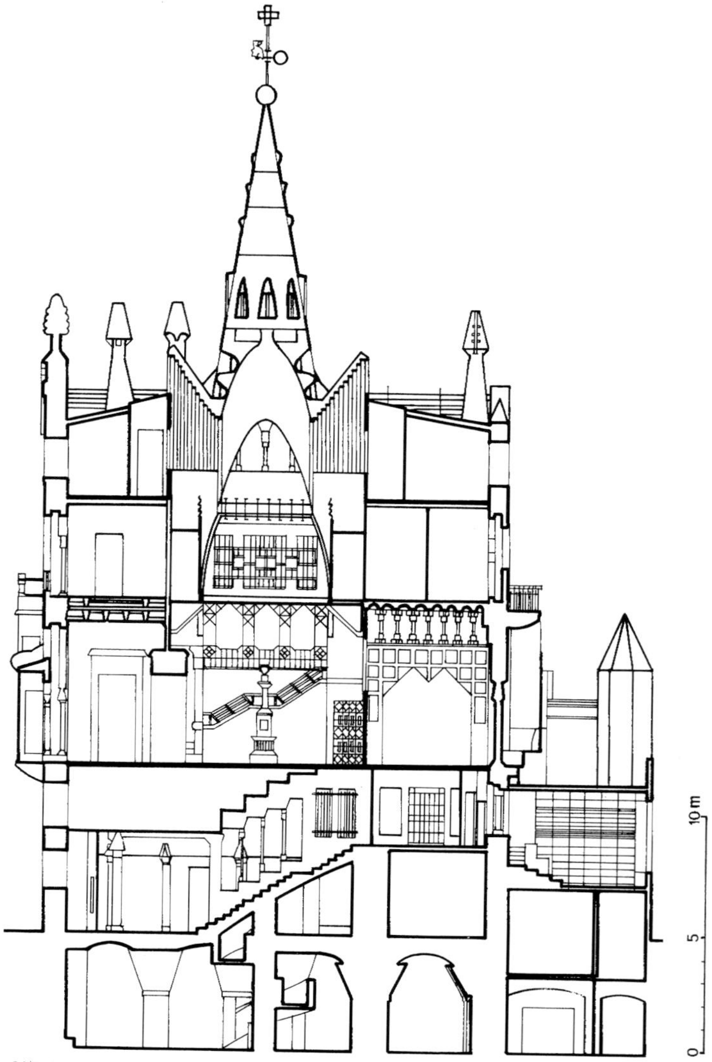

307. Antoni Gaudí i Cornet. Palau Güell, Barcelona (cross section). 1886–91. (Drawing by Ferrante Ferranti after an original drawing)

DOCUMENTATION

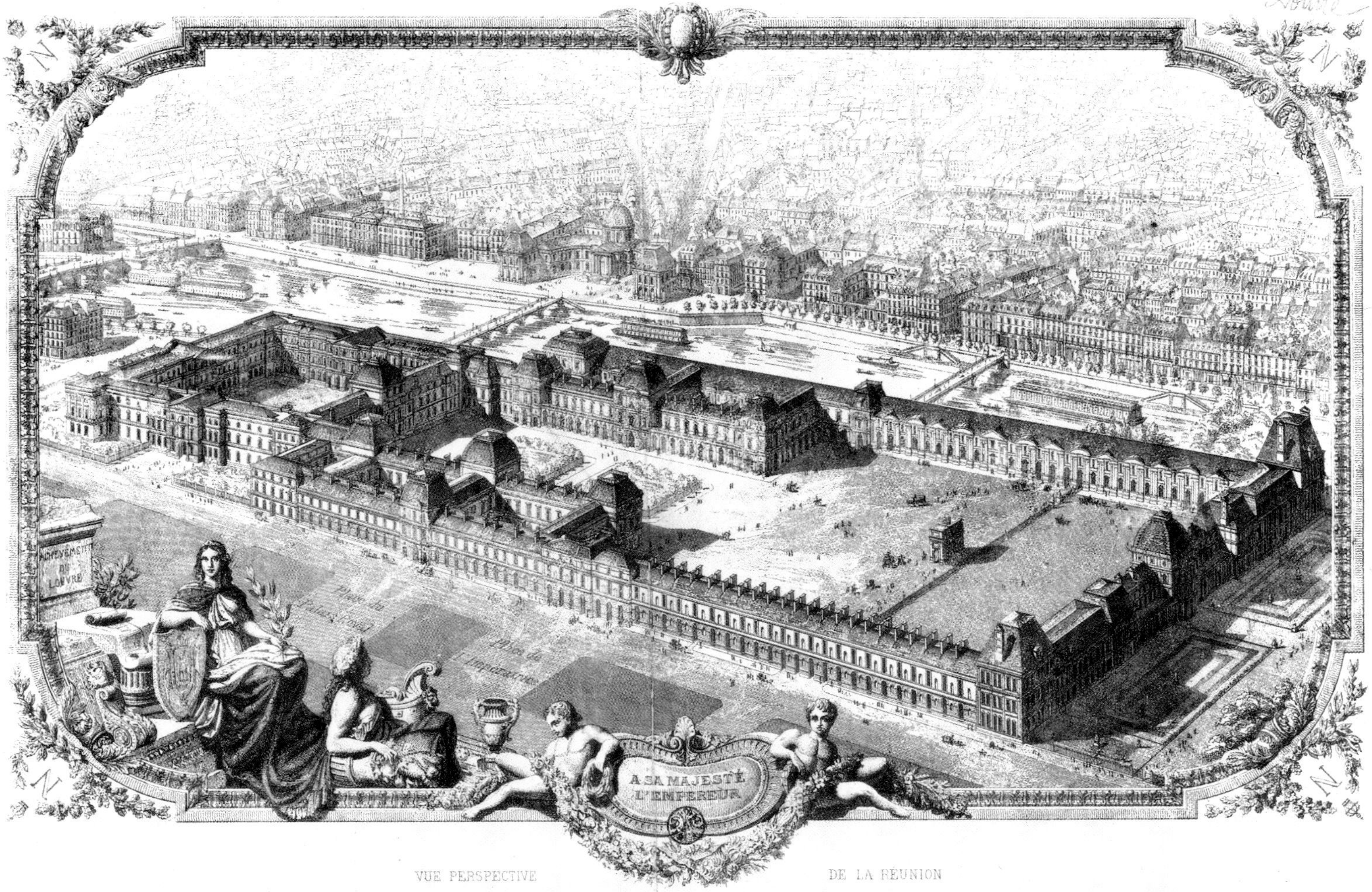

308. Perspective view of project to join the Louvre to the Tuileries Gardens. After the official plans by L. Visconti

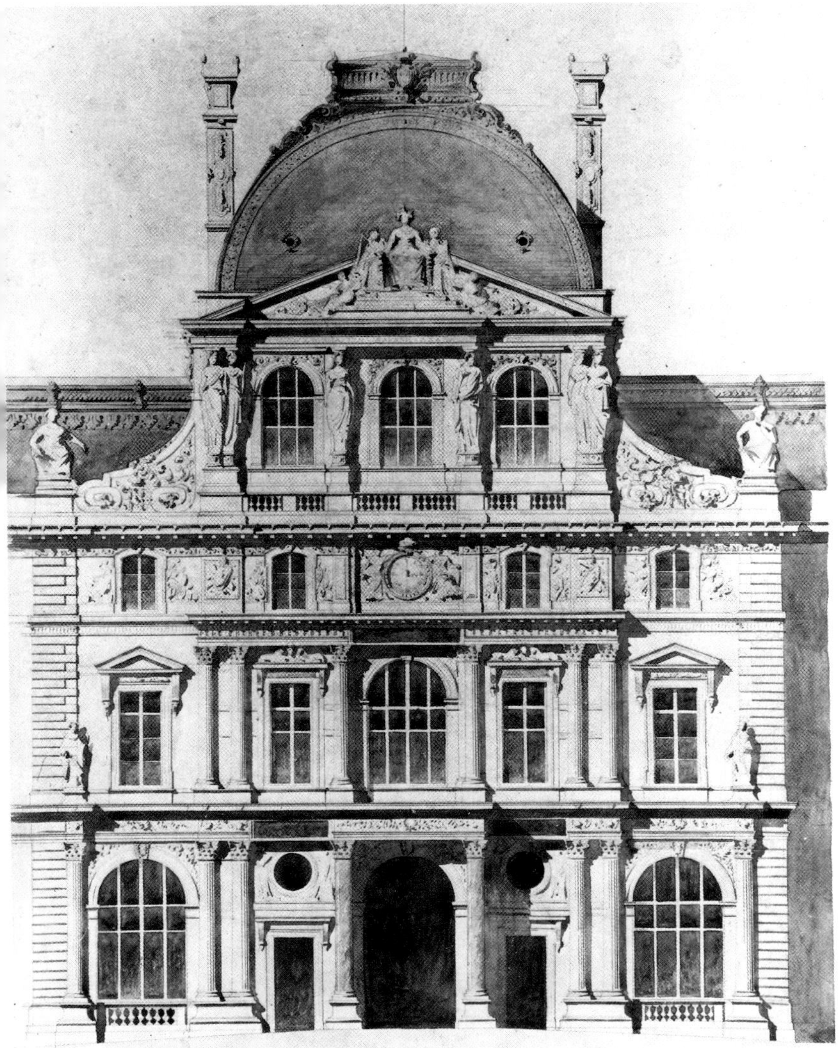

309. Hector Lefuel. New Louvre, Paris (west front elevation of the Pavillon de l'Horloge). c. 1854. Wash on tracing paper

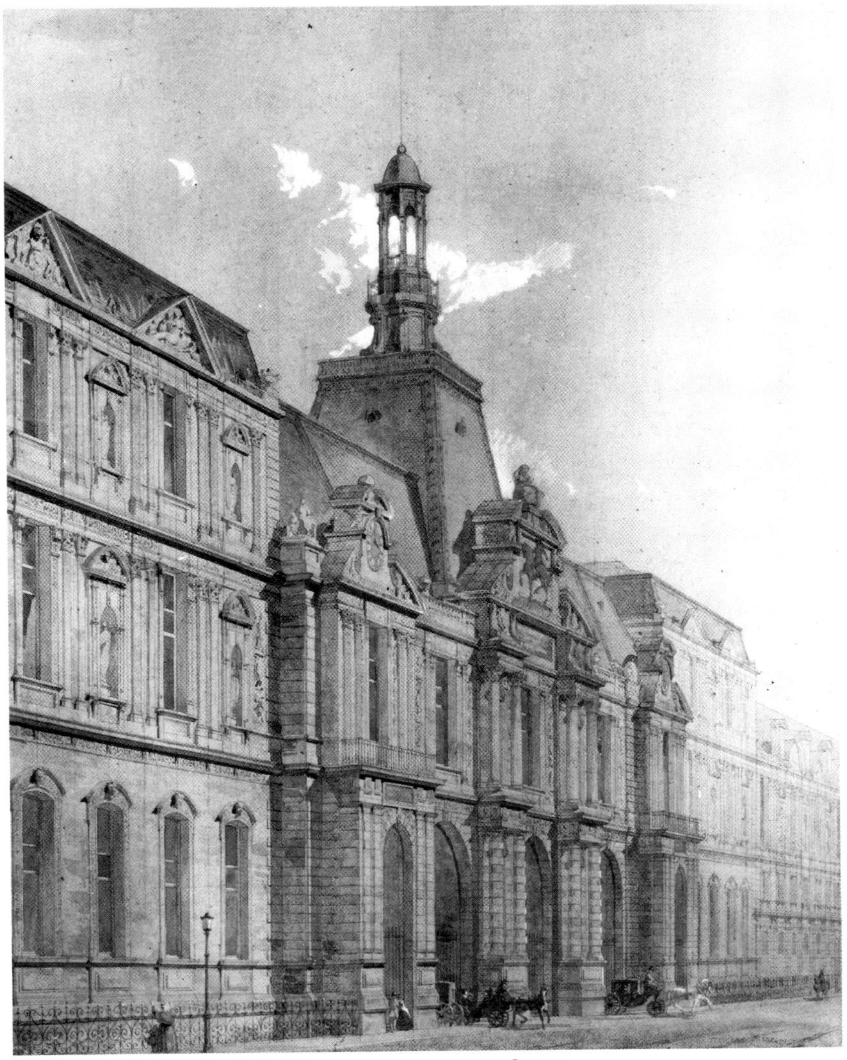

310. Hector Lefuel practice. Project for monumental gates, new Louvre

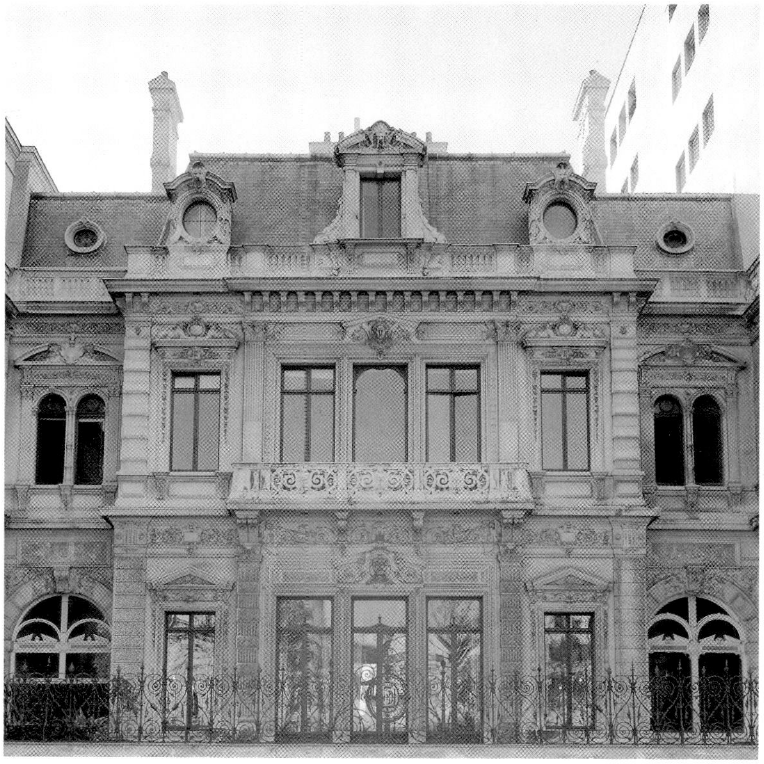

311. Pierre Manguin. Hôtel de la Païva, Paris (facade). 1856–68

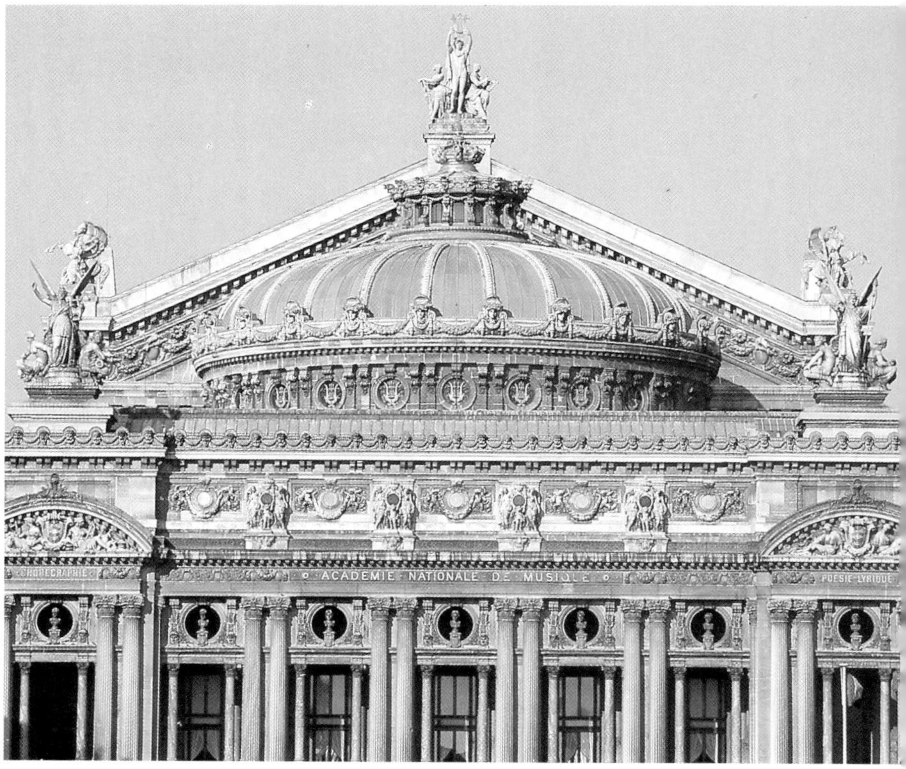

312. Charles Garnier. Paris Opéra (detail of the facade). 1861–75

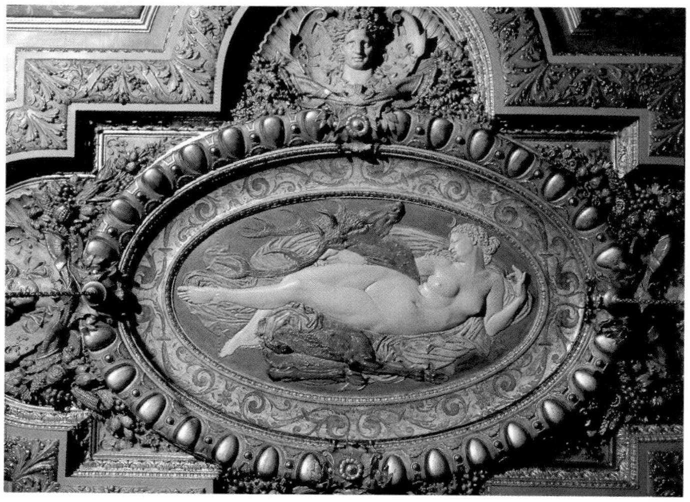

313. Jules Dalou. *Diana*. Dining room ceiling, Hôtel de la Païva, Paris. 1856–68

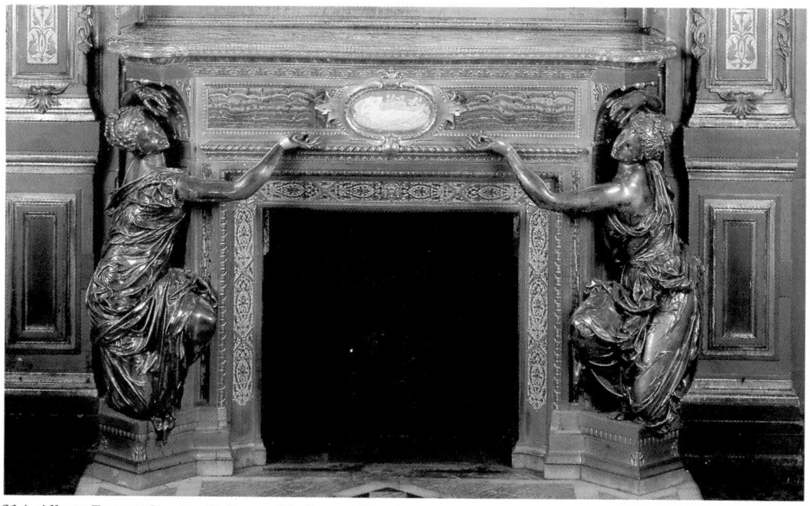

314. Albert-Ernest Carrier-Belleuse. Bedroom fireplace, Hôtel de la Païva, Paris. 1865

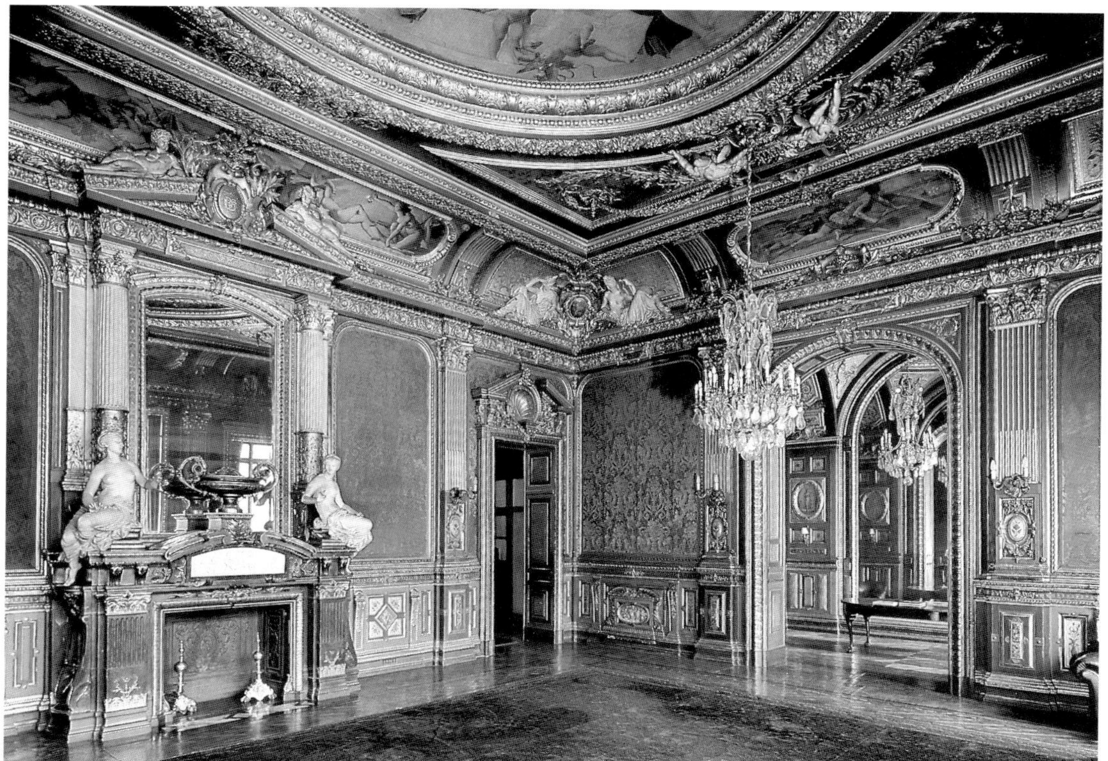

315. Great drawing room. Hôtel de la Païva, Paris. 1865. Ceiling painting *Day Pursuing Night* by Paul Baudry, and on the mantlepiece, *Harmony* and *Music*, marble, by Eugène Delaplanche

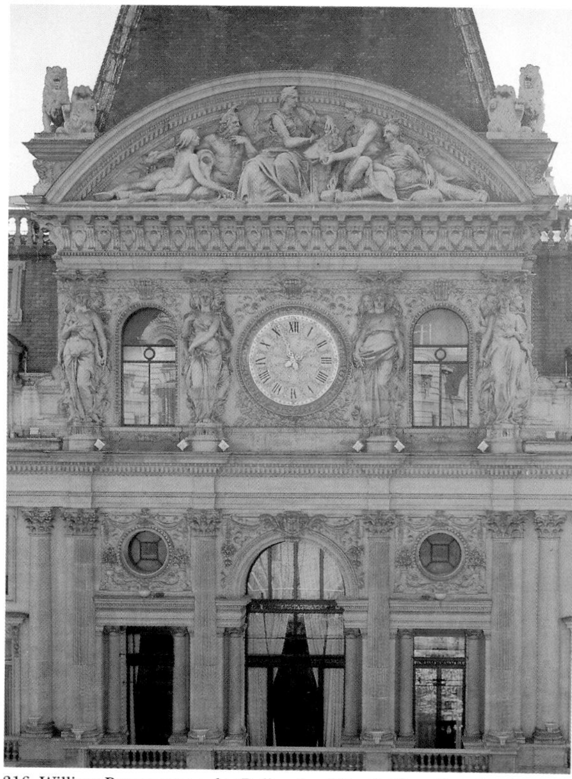

316. William Bouwens van der Boijen (architect), Henri Lombard, Édouard Pépin, Antonin Carles, and Désiré Ferrary *The Hours of the Day*. Crédit Lyonnais, Boulevard des Italiens, Paris. 1881

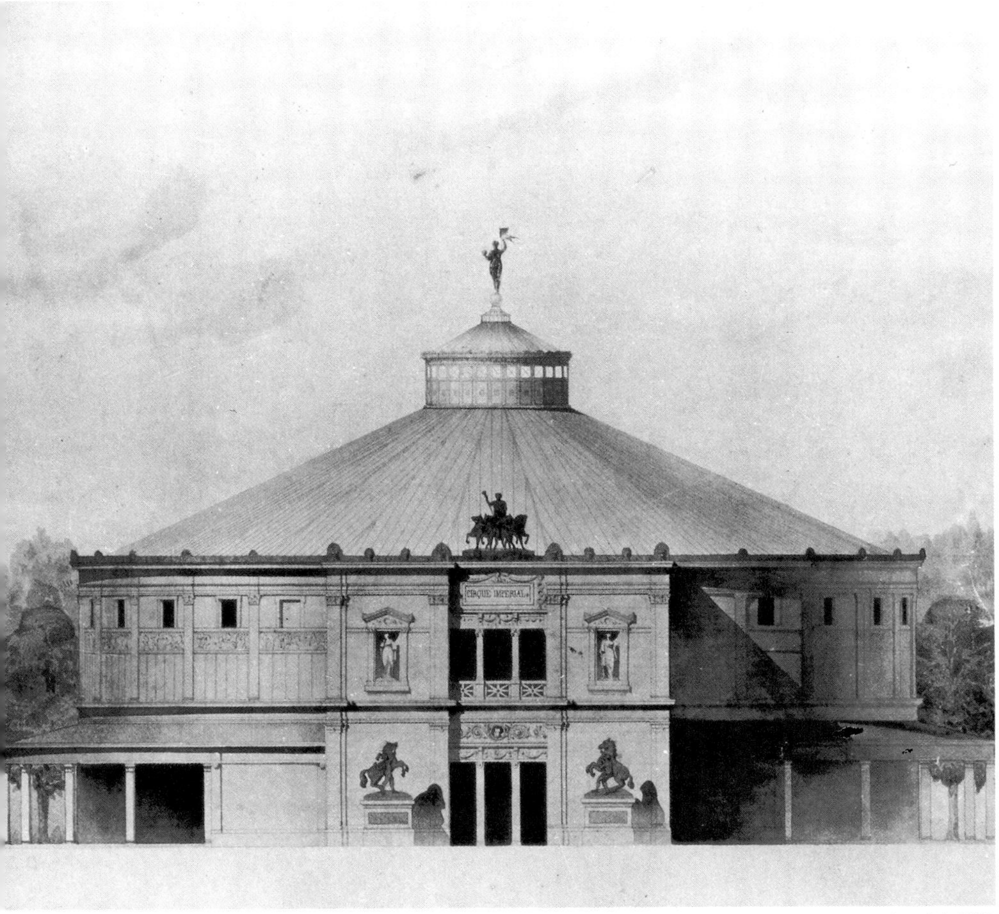

317. Jacques-Ignace Hittorff. Cirque Impérial, Paris (elevation of the main facade). 1862

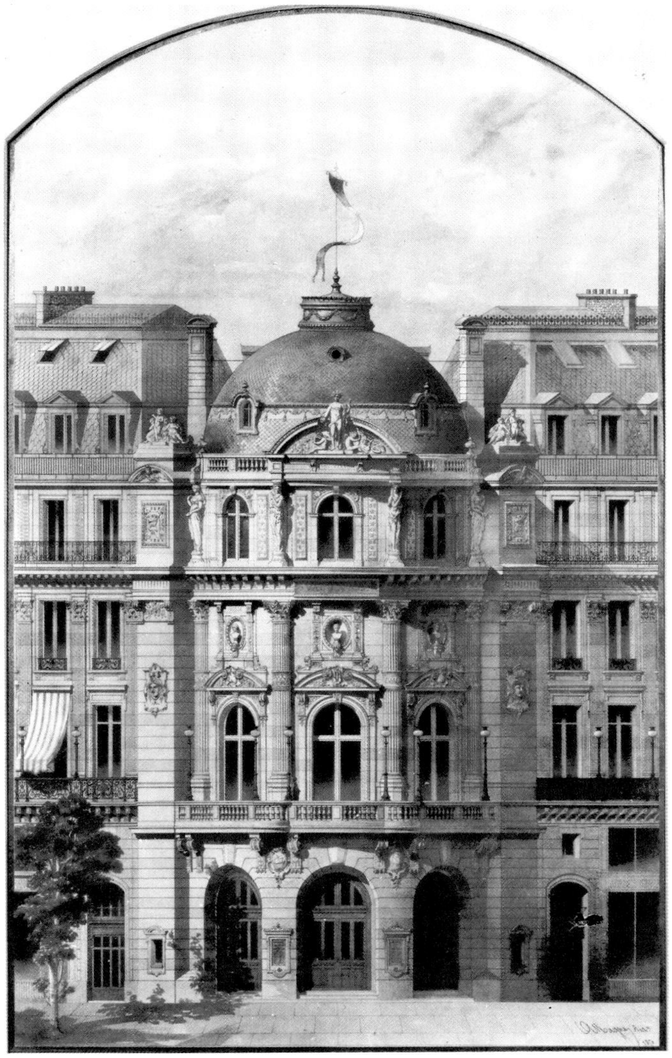

318. Auguste-Joseph Magne. Théâtre du Vaudeville, Paris (elevation of the main facade). 1866–69

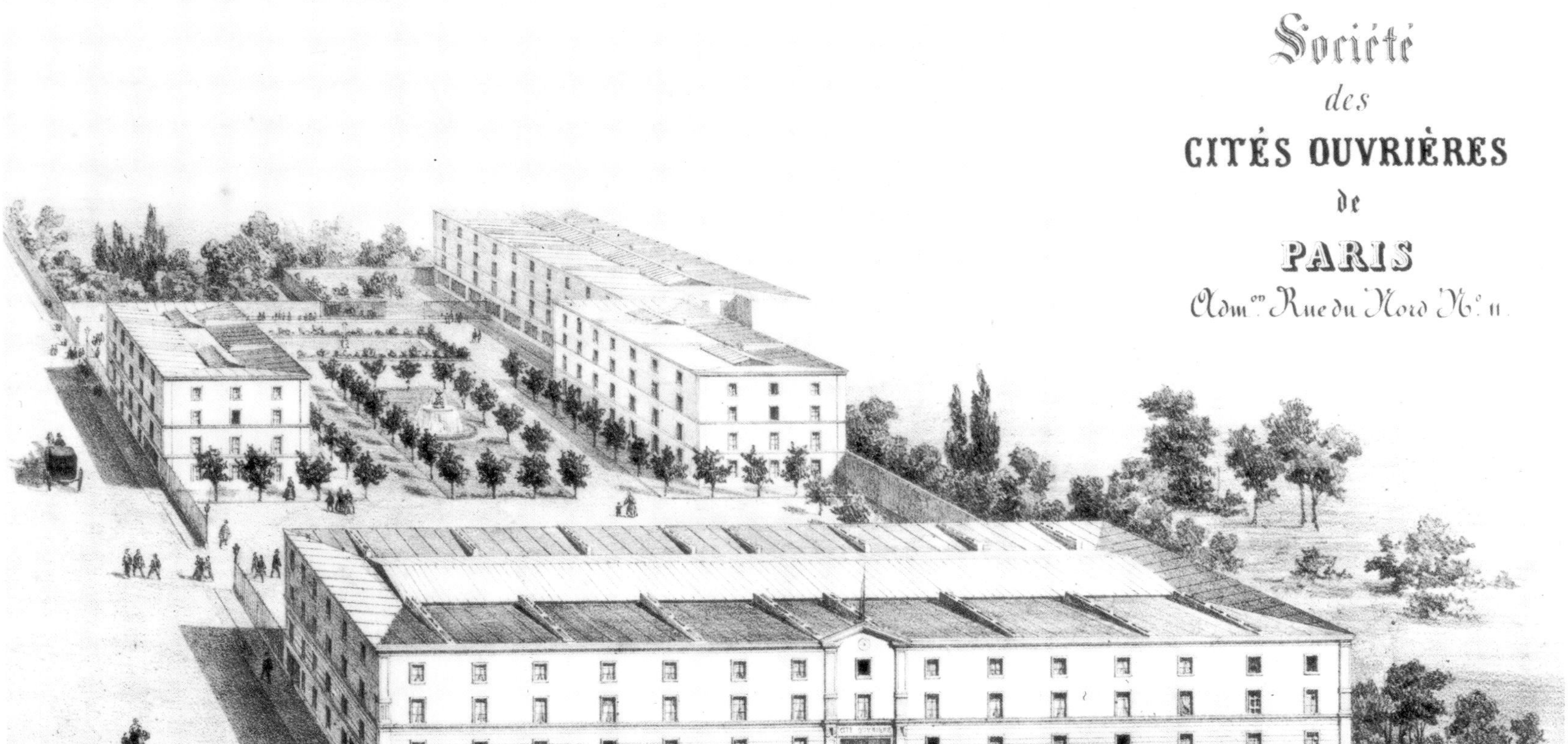

319. Gabriel Veugny. Cité Napoléon housing project, Rue Rochechouart, Paris (detail). 1849–54

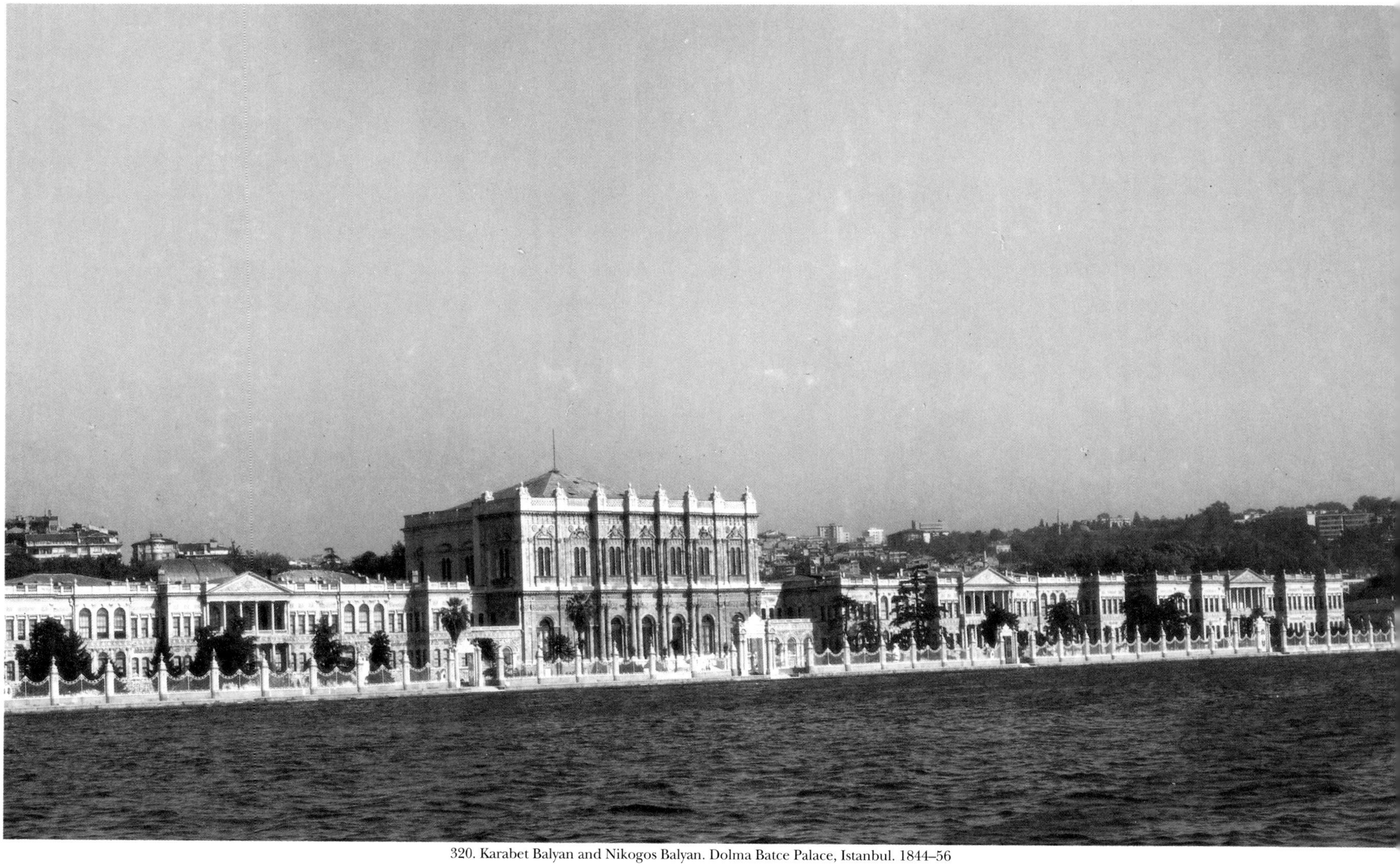

320. Karabet Balyan and Nikogos Balyan. Dolma Batce Palace, Istanbul. 1844–56

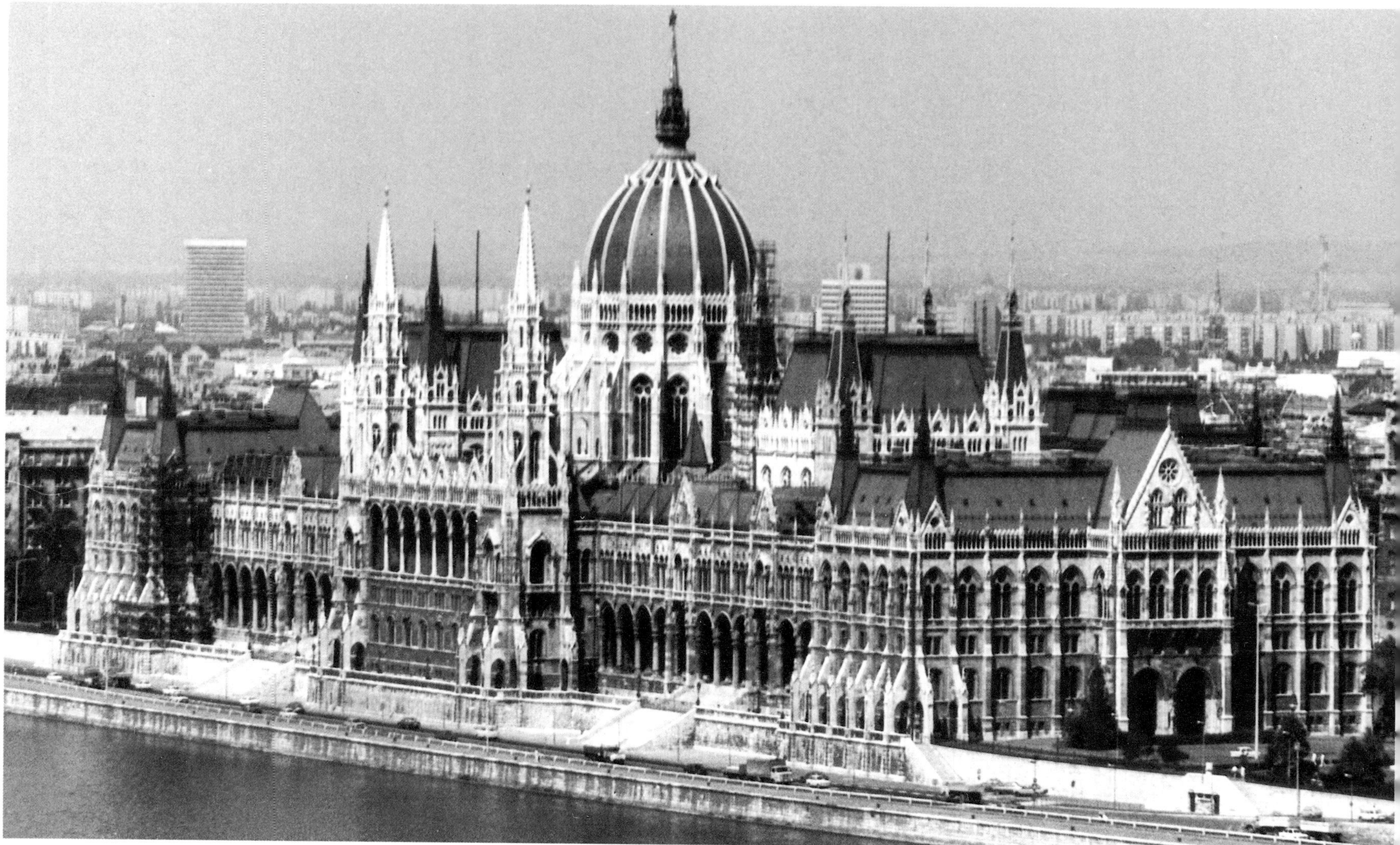

321. Imre Steidl. Országház (Hungarian Parliament Building), Budapest. 1882–1903

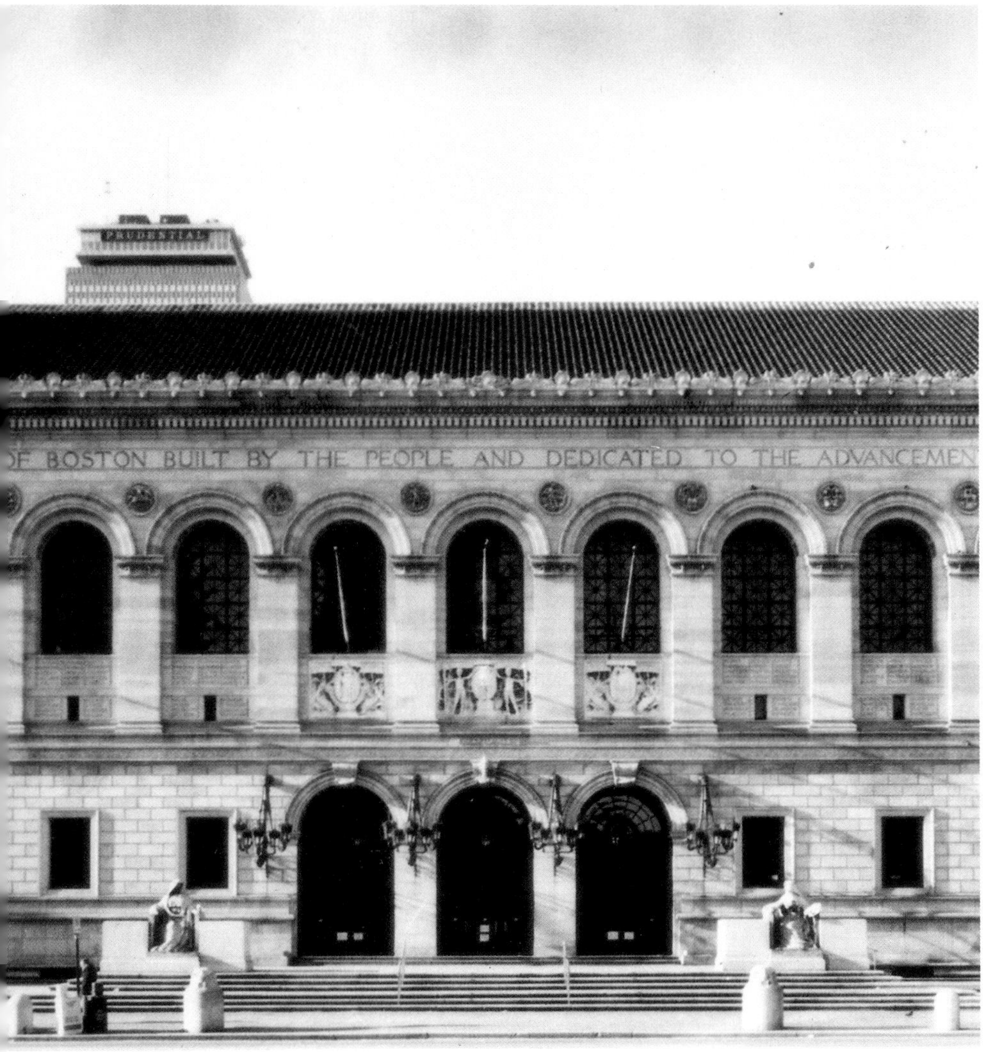

322. McKim, Mead and White. Public Library, Boston. 1882–92

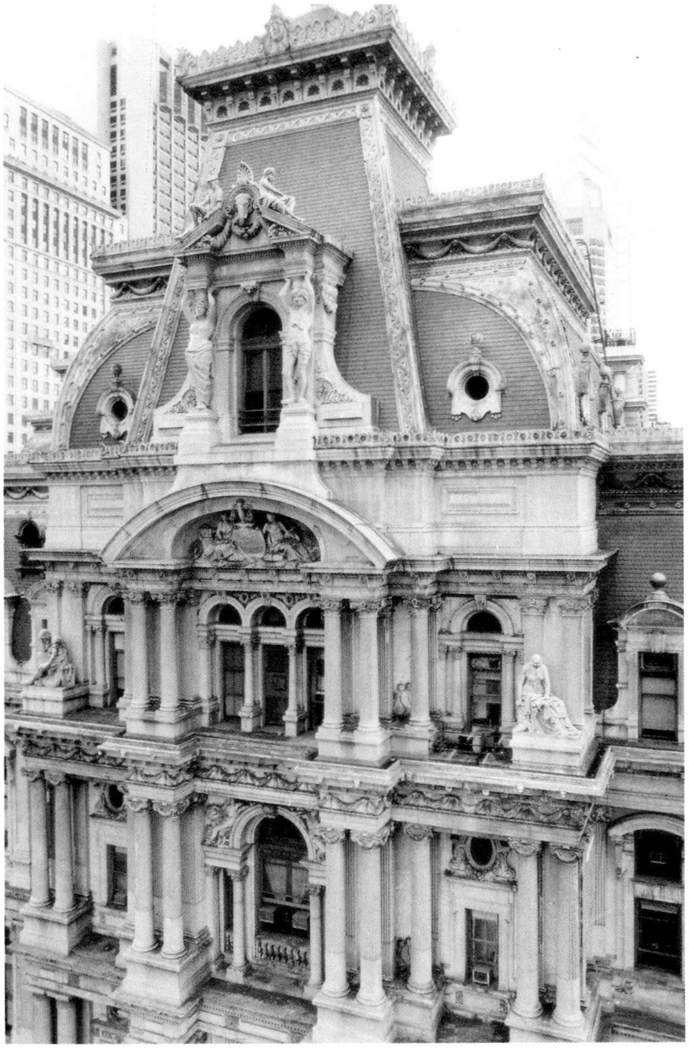

323. John MacArthur Jr. (architect), Alexander Milne Calder (sculptor). City Hall, Philadelphia (facade, upper section). 1868–93

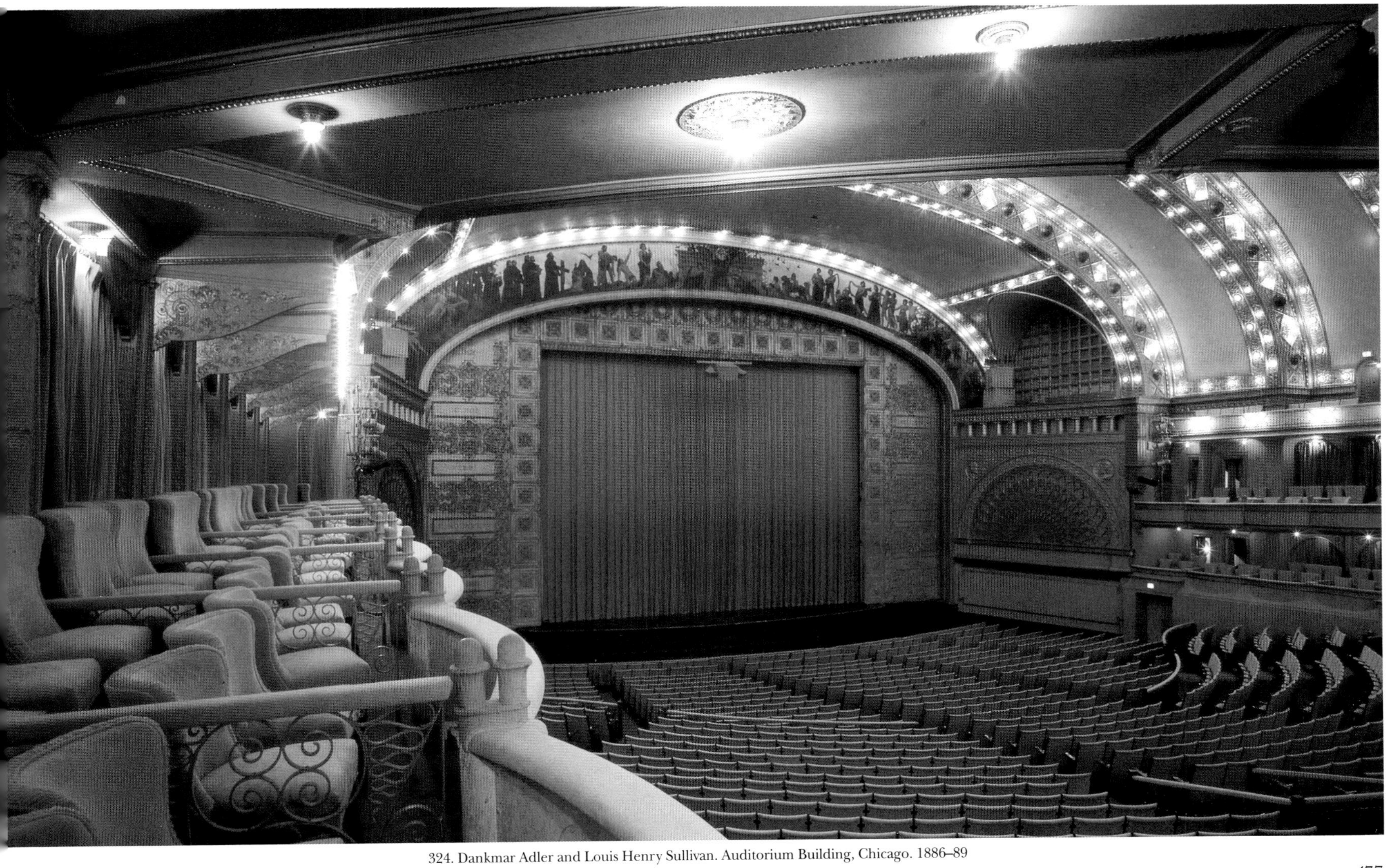

324. Dankmar Adler and Louis Henry Sullivan. Auditorium Building, Chicago. 1886–89

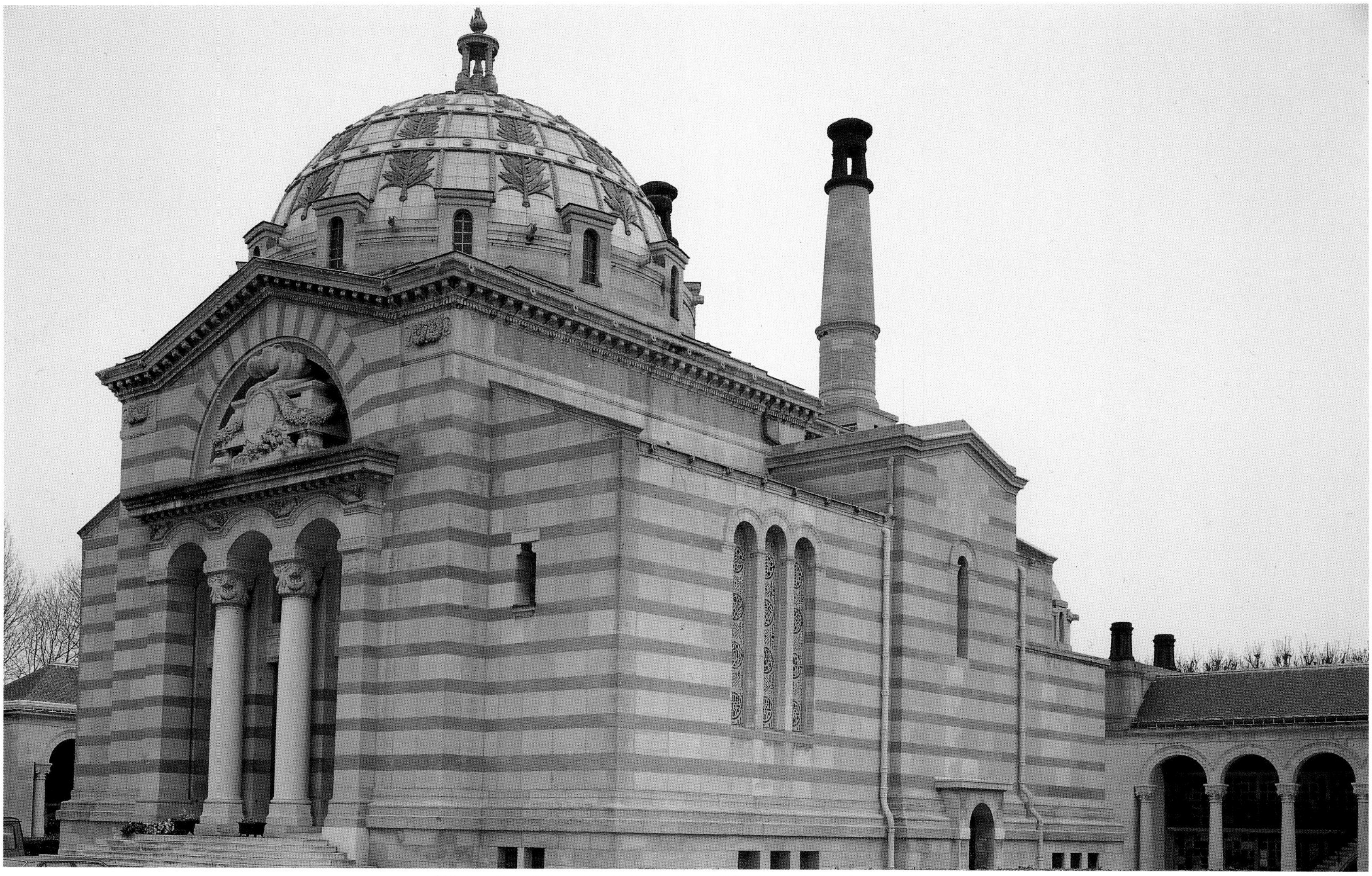

325. Jean-Camille Formigé. Columbarium. 1887. Père-Lachaise Cemetery, Paris

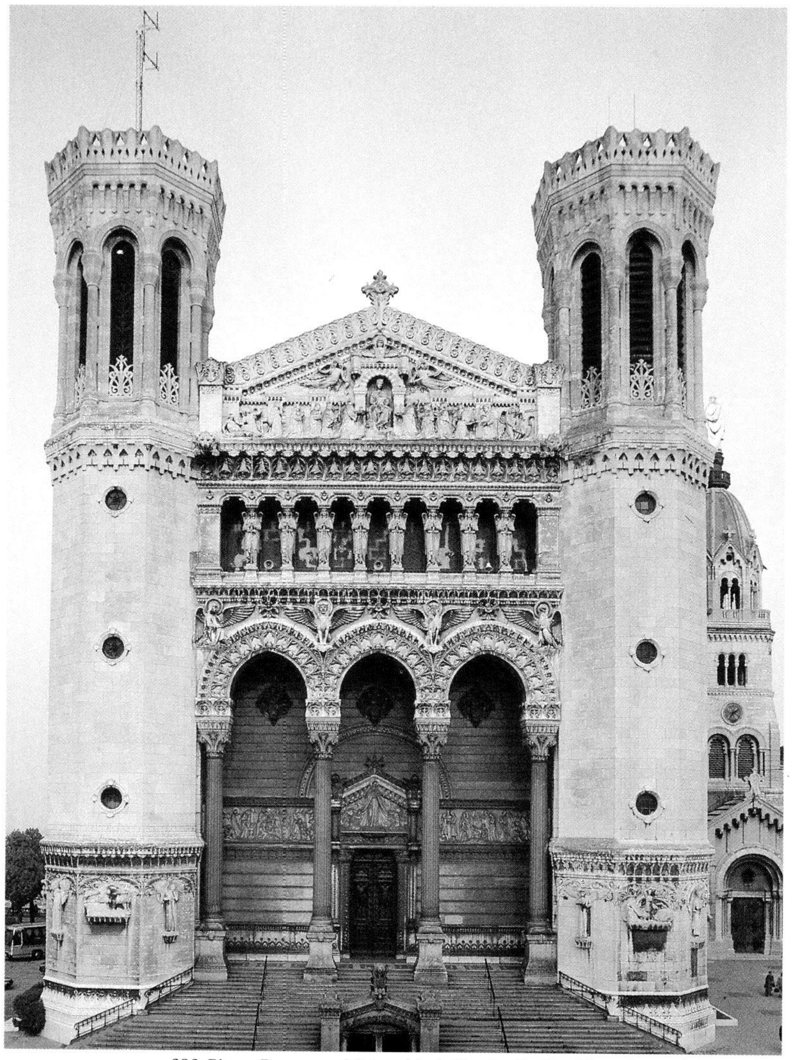

326. Pierre Bossan and Sainte-Marie Perrin. Basilica Notre-Dame de Fourvière, Lyon (main facade). 1872–1914

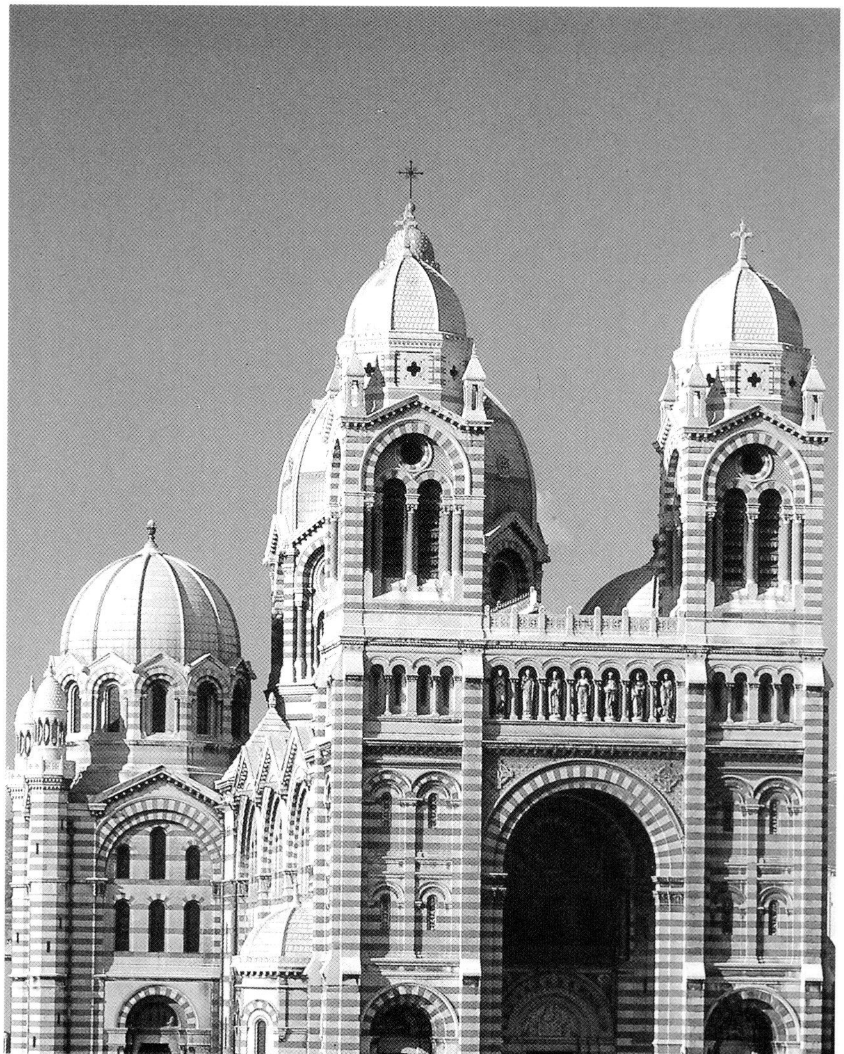

327. Léon Vaudoyer, then Henri Espérandieu, Henri-Antoine Revoil, and Alfred Vaudoyer. Cathedral Sainte-Marie-Majeure, Marseille. 1872–93

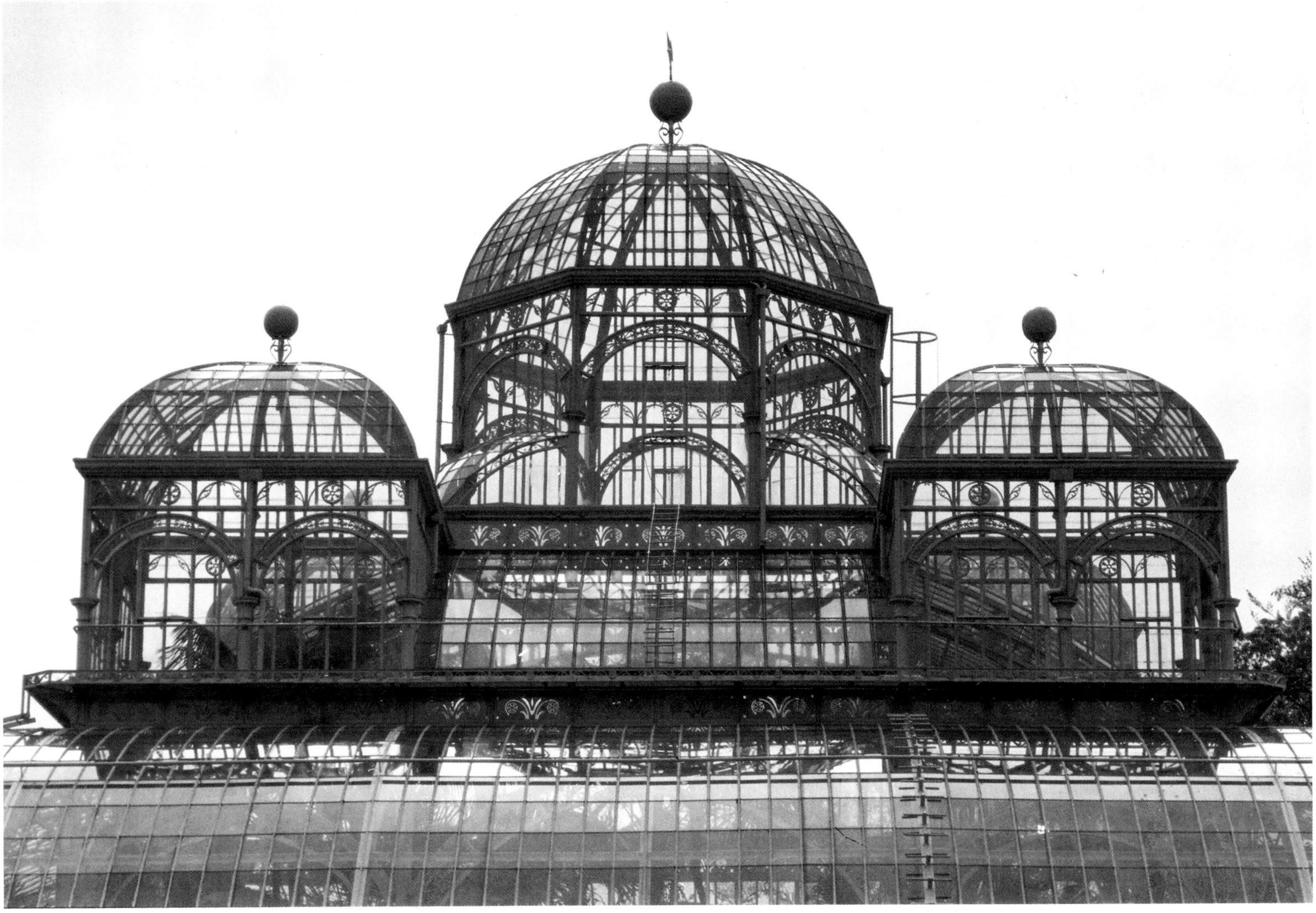

328. Alphonse Balat. Winter garden (detail), Royal Glasshouses at Laeken, Brussels. 1875–76

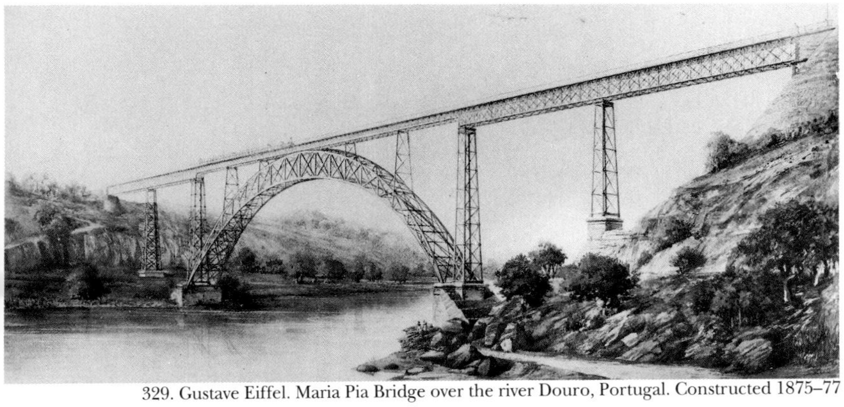

329. Gustave Eiffel. Maria Pia Bridge over the river Douro, Portugal. Constructed 1875–77

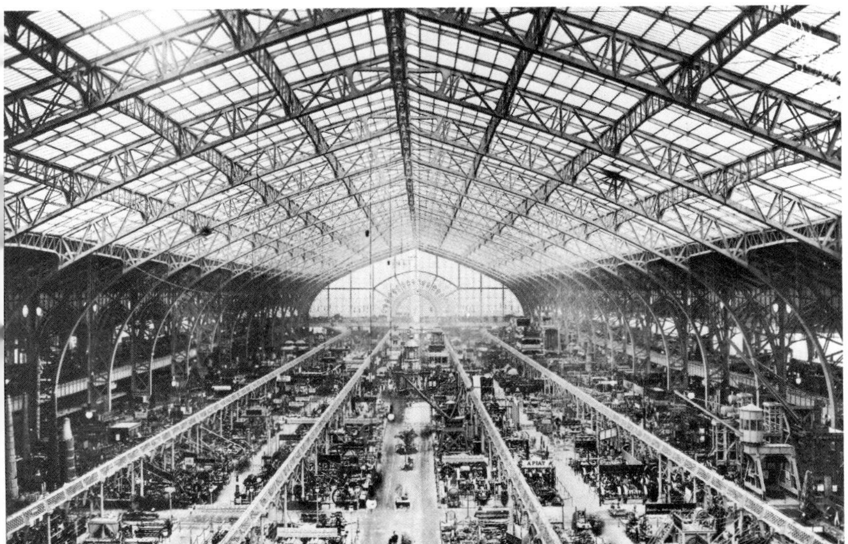

330. Ferdinand Dutert (architect) and Victor Contamin (engineer). Galerie des Machines, Paris (interior). 1889

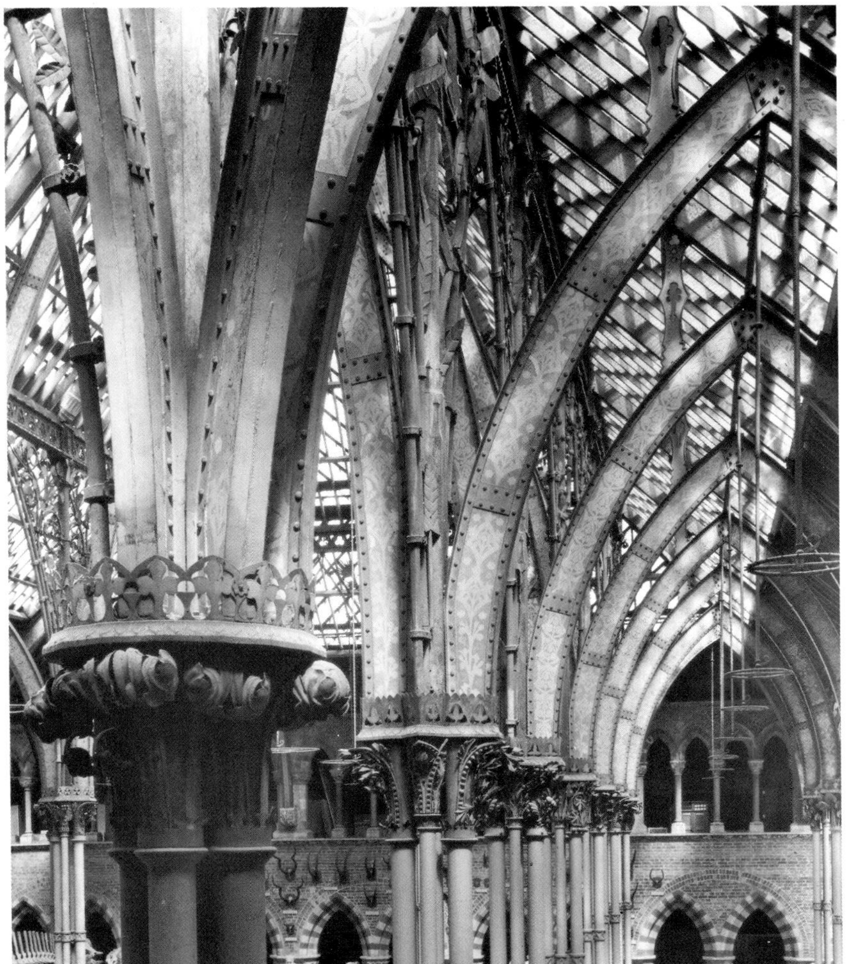

331. Thomas Deane and Benjamin Woodward. University Museum, Oxford (detail of arched iron braces and wrought-iron capitals). 1855–60

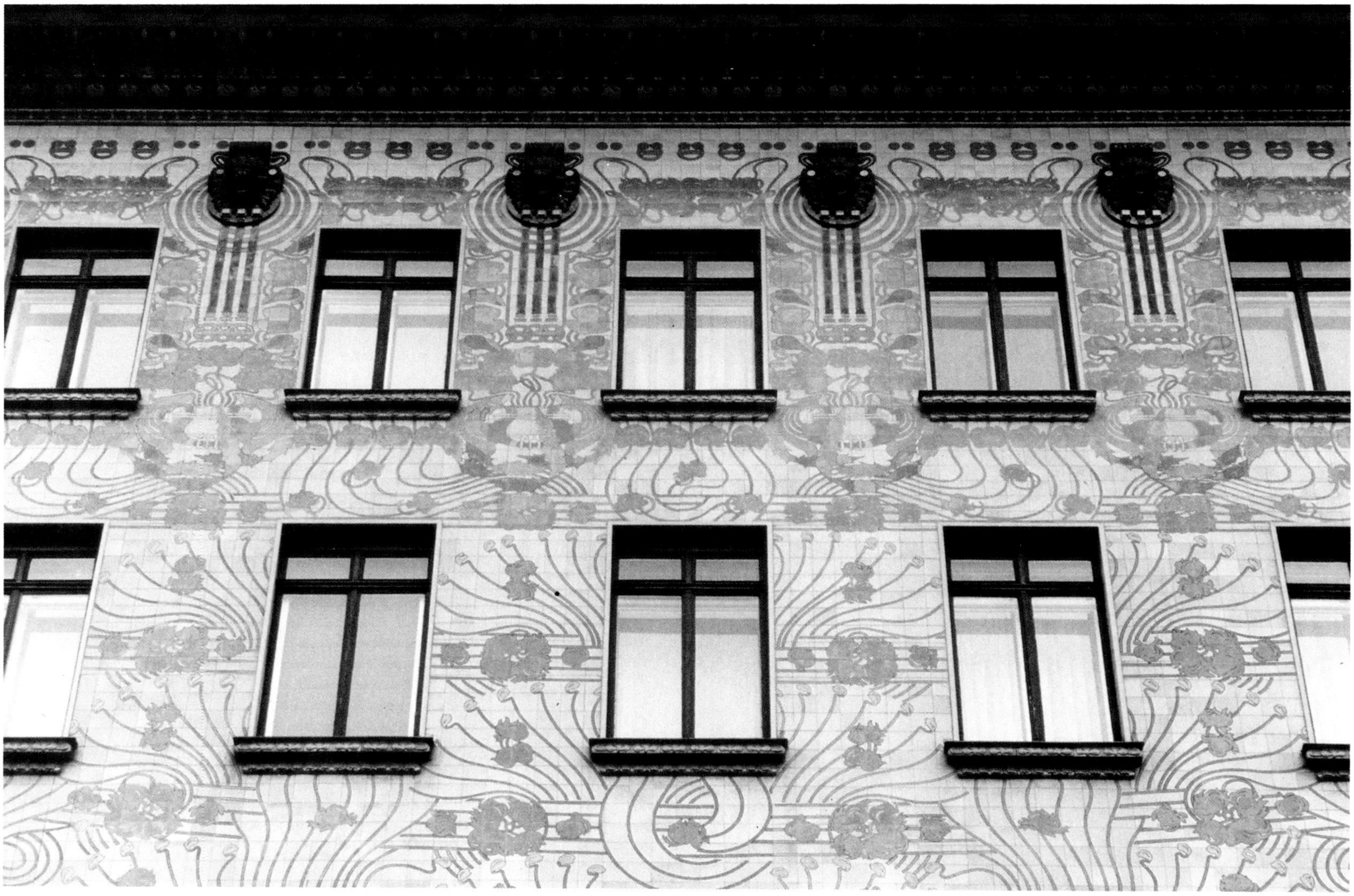

332. Otto Wagner. Majolikahaus, 40 Linke Wienzeile, Vienna. 1898–99

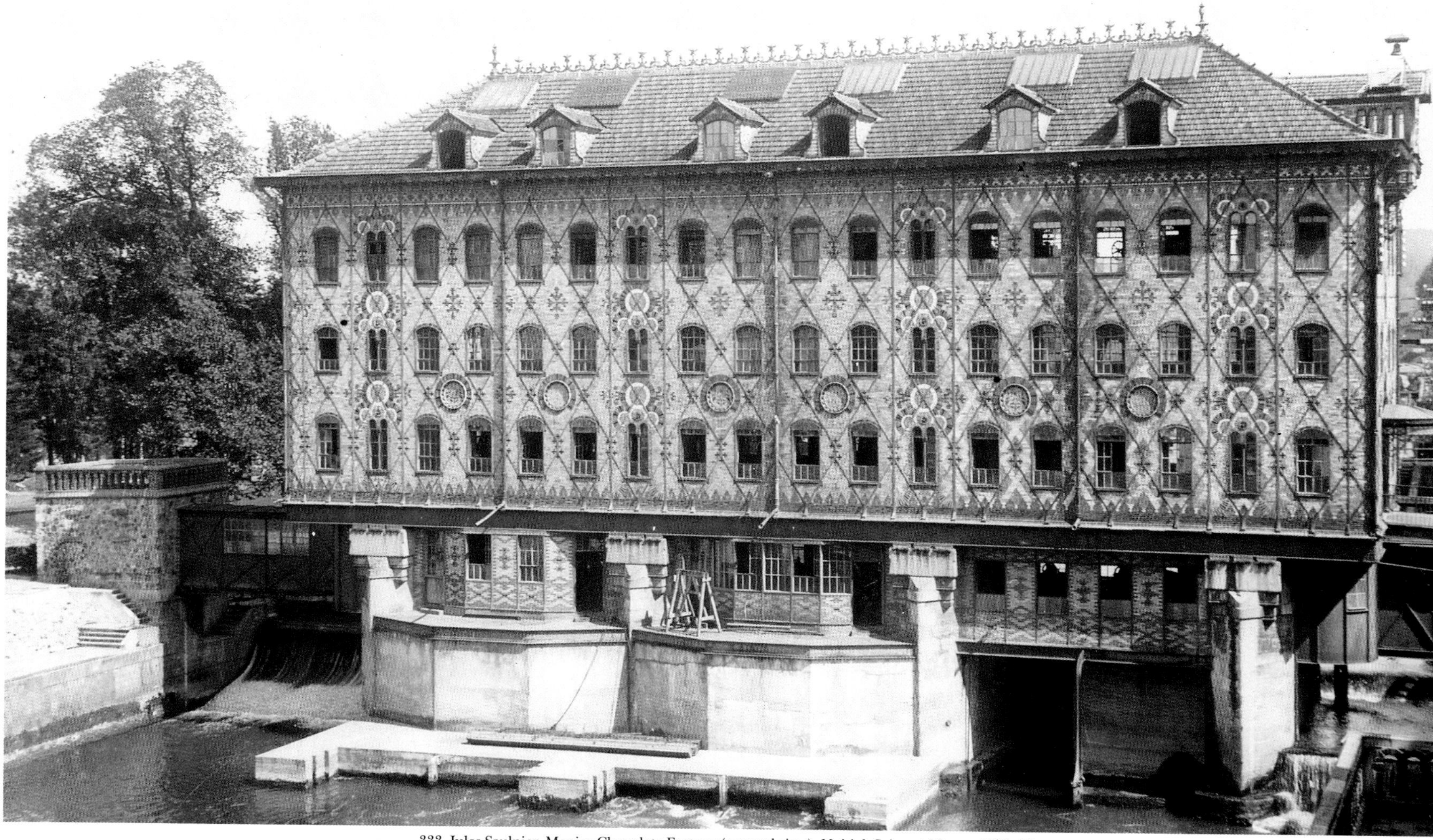

333. Jules Saulnier. Menier Chocolate Factory (general view), Noisiel, Seine-et-Marne. 1871–72

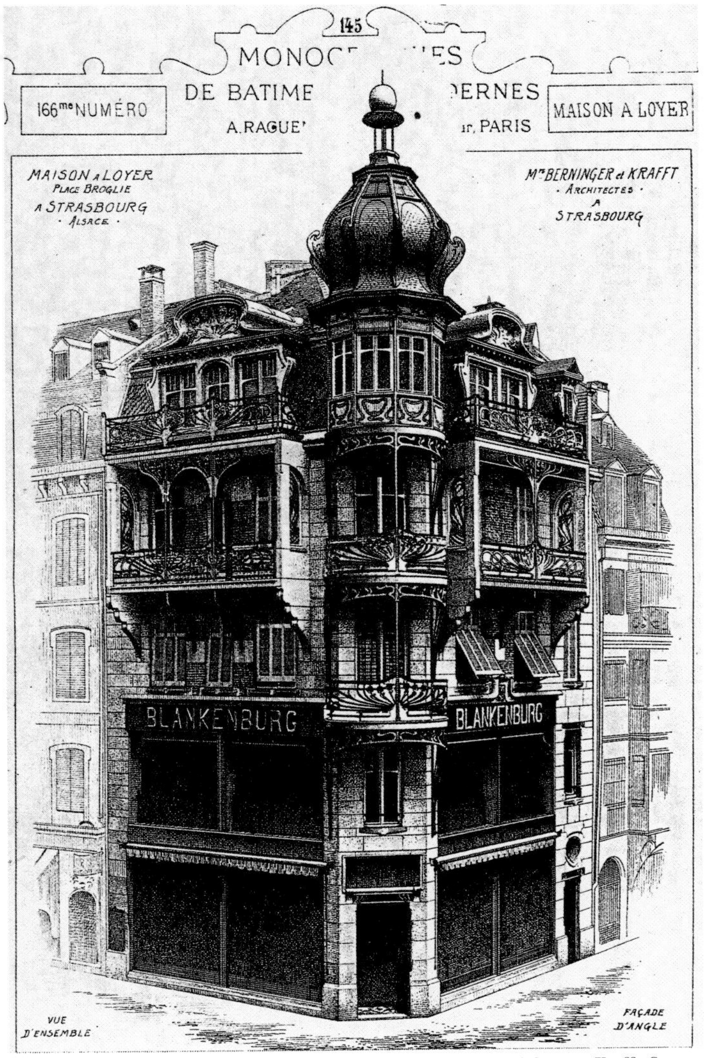

334. Edmund Berninger and Gustave Krafft. Store, Place Broglie, Strasbourg. 1901

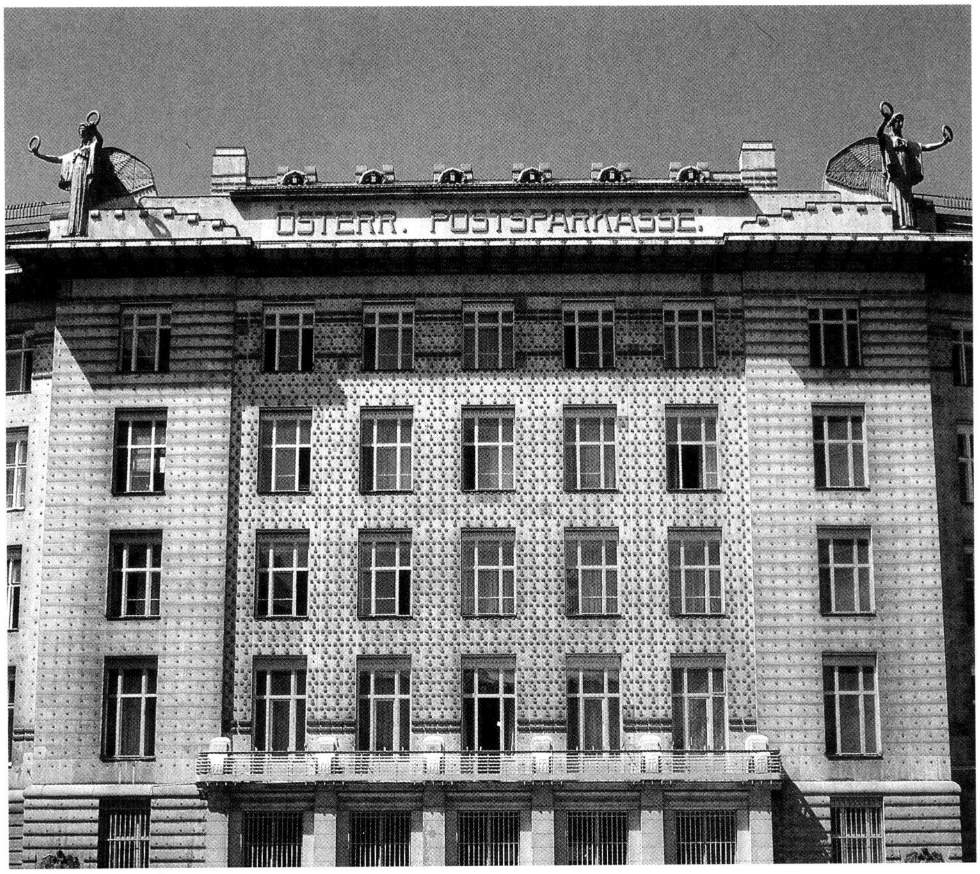

335. Otto Wagner. Österreichisches Postsparkasse, Vienna. 1904–6

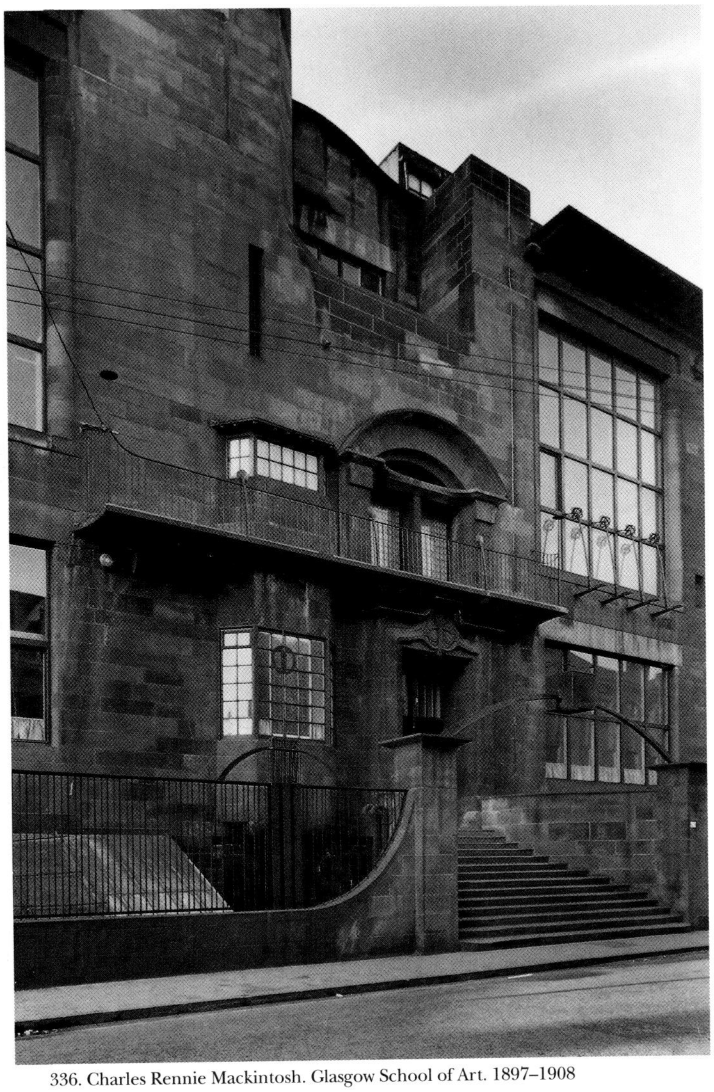

336. Charles Rennie Mackintosh. Glasgow School of Art. 1897–1908

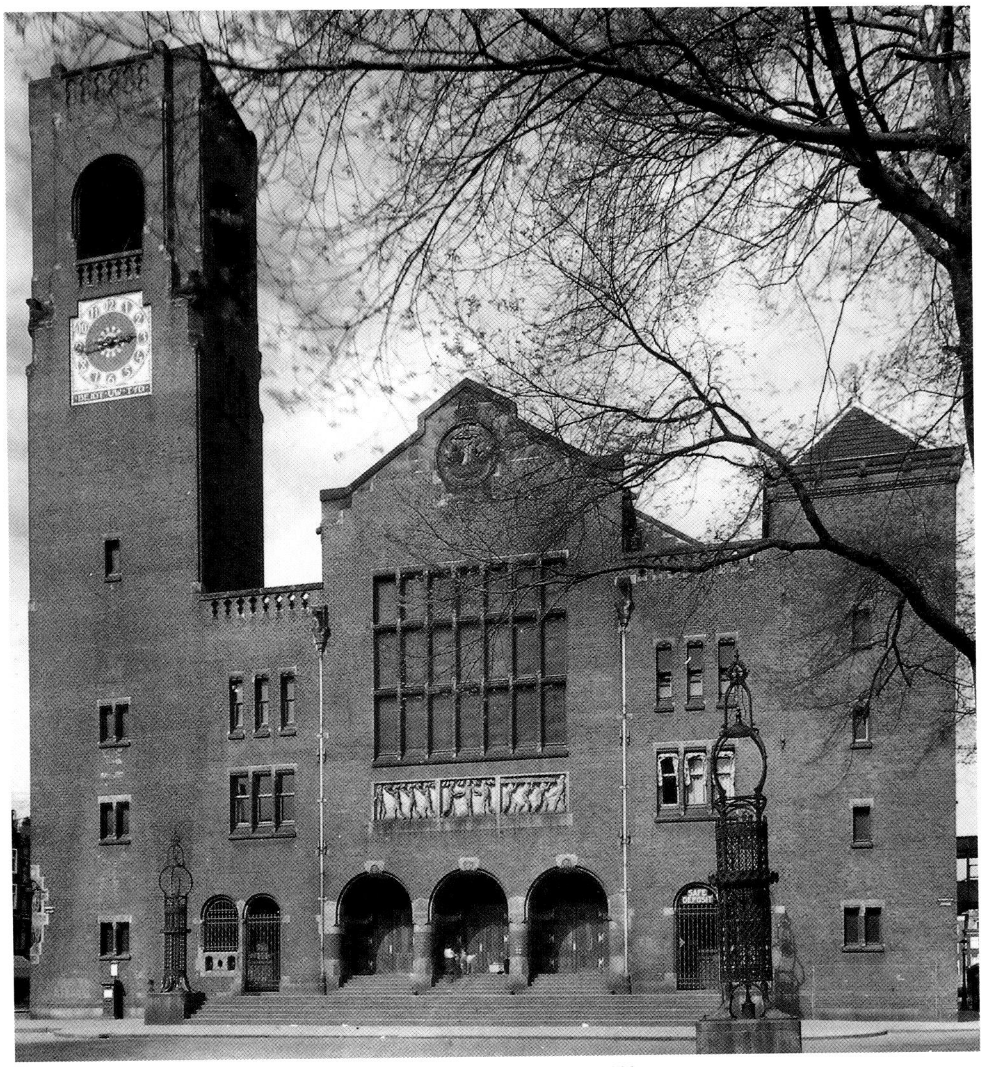

337. Hendrick Petrus Berlage. Beurs (Stock Exchange), Amsterdam. 1898–1903

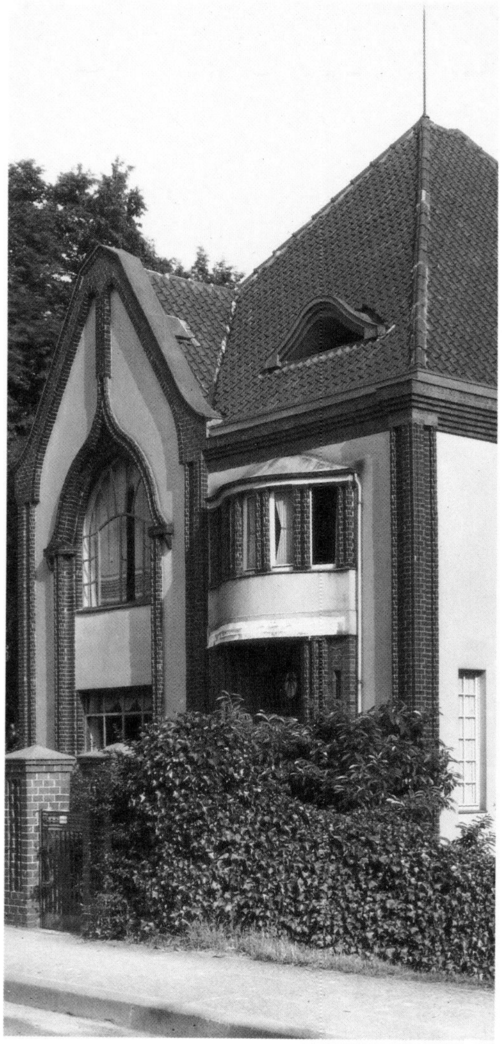

338. Peter Behrens. Behrens's House, Mathildenhöhe, Darmstadt. 1901

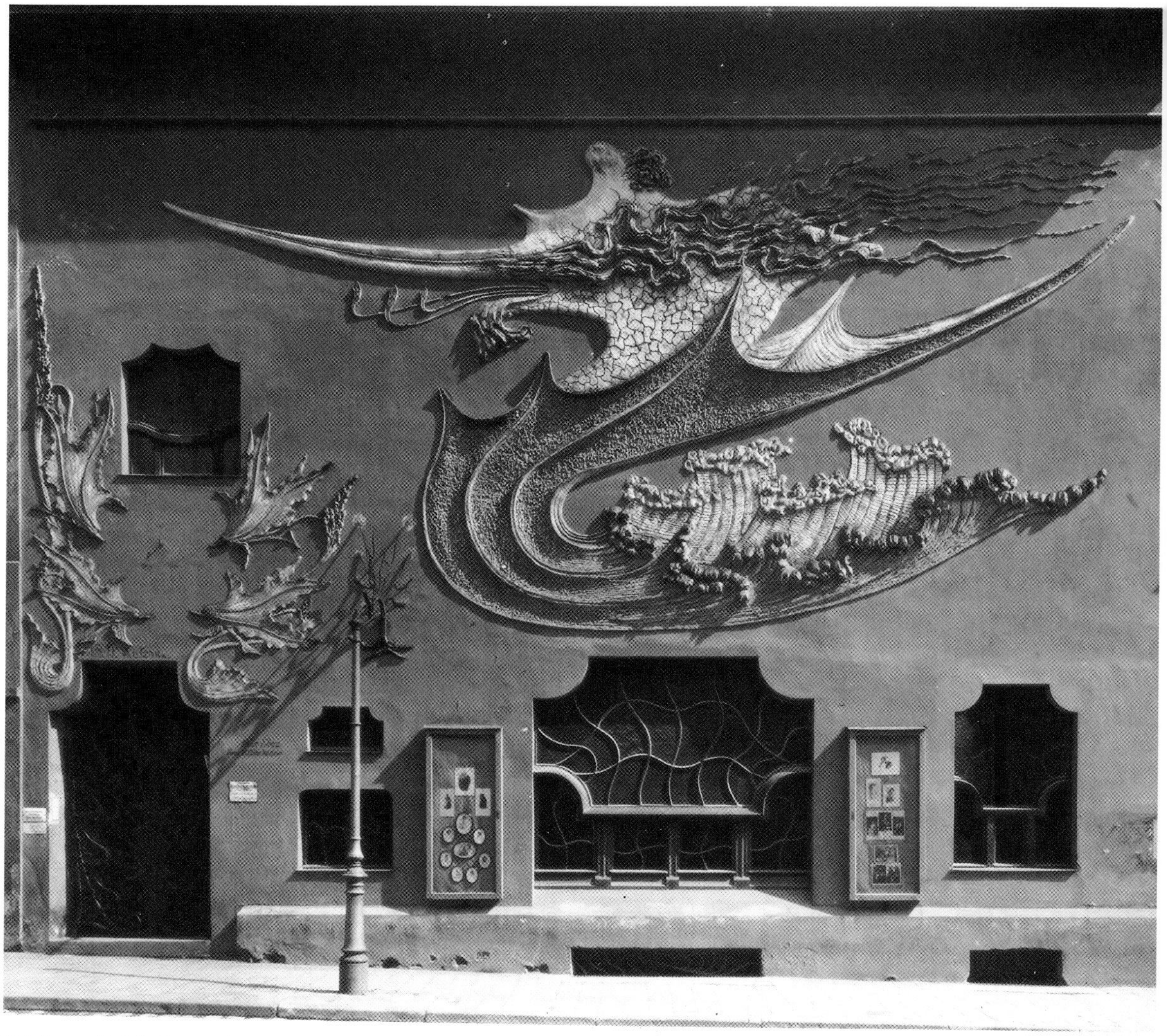

339. August Endell. Photoatelier Elvira, Munich. 1897–98 (destroyed)

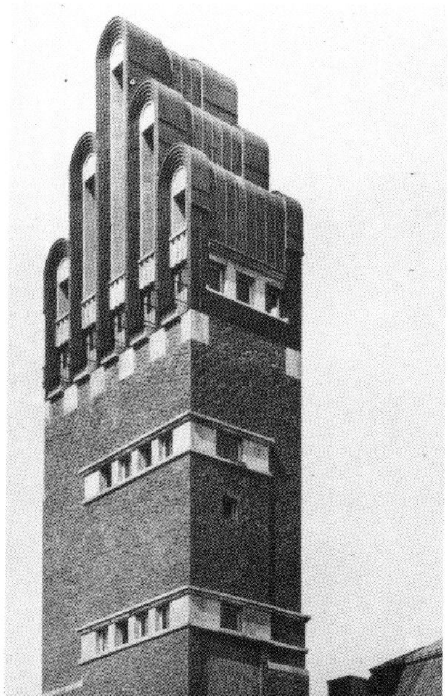

340. Joseph Maria Olbrich. Hochzeitsturm, Mathildenhöhe, Darmstadt. Built from 1905

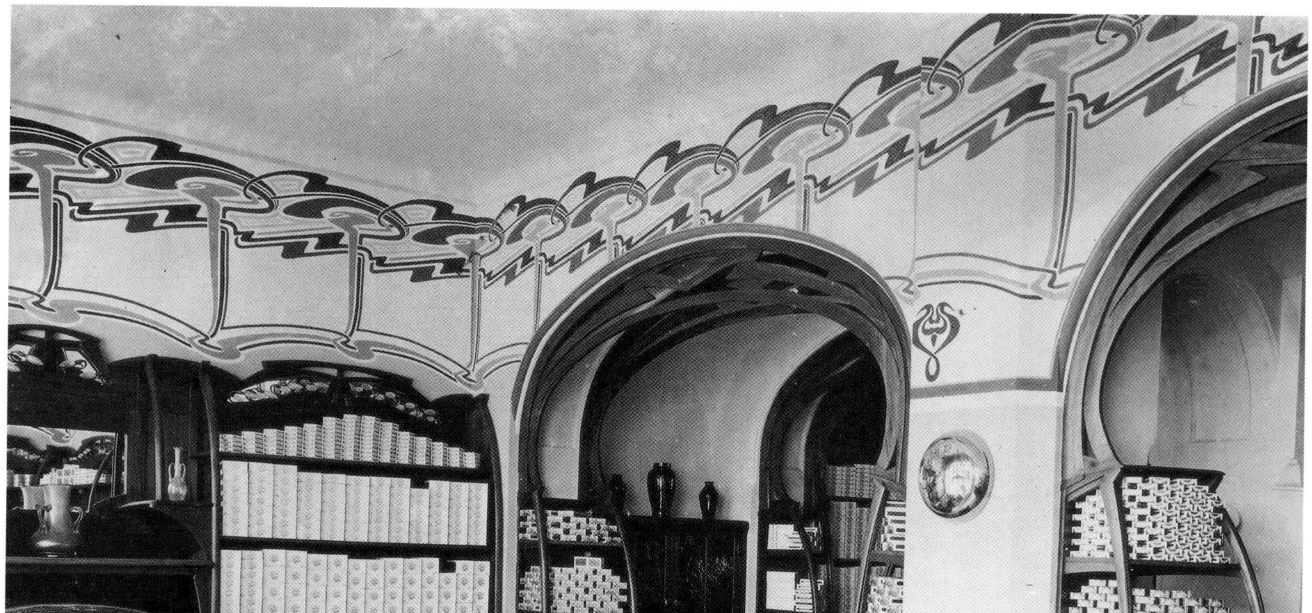

341. Henry van de Velde. Store for Havana Tobacco Co., Berlin. 1899–1900 (destroyed)

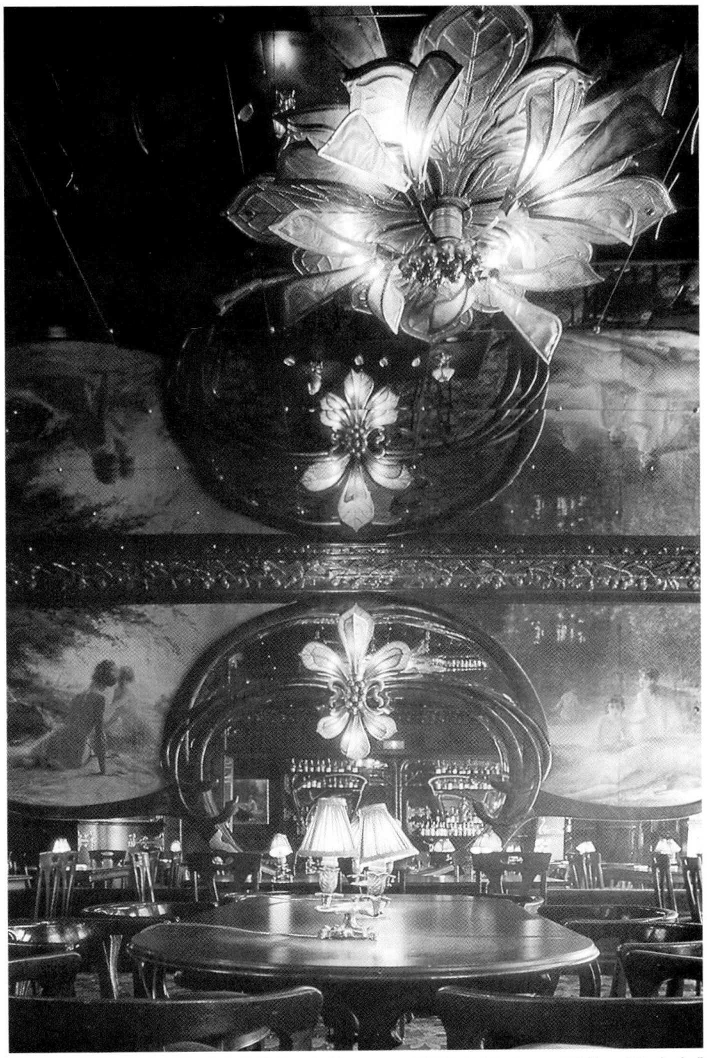

342. Louis Marnez and Trézel. Restaurant "Chez Maxim's," Rue Royale, Paris. 1899

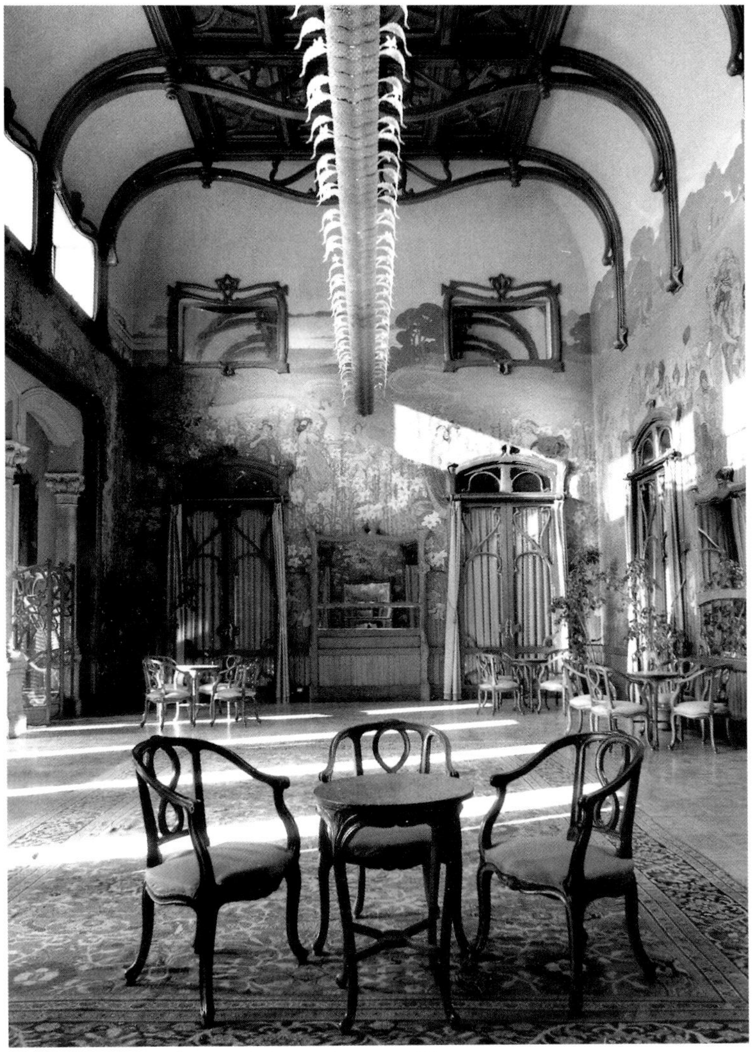

343. Ernesto Basile. Villa Igea, Palermo (interior). 1899

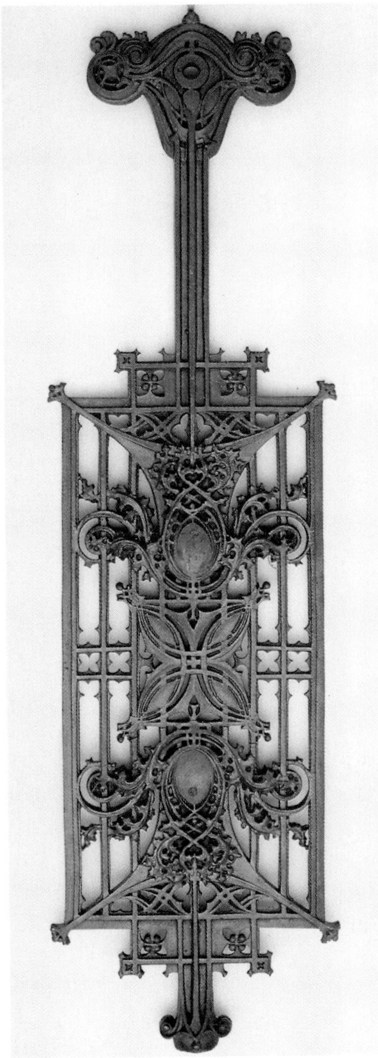

344. Louis Henry Sullivan. Carson, Pirie, Scott & Co. Store, Chicago (detail of decoration). 1899–1904

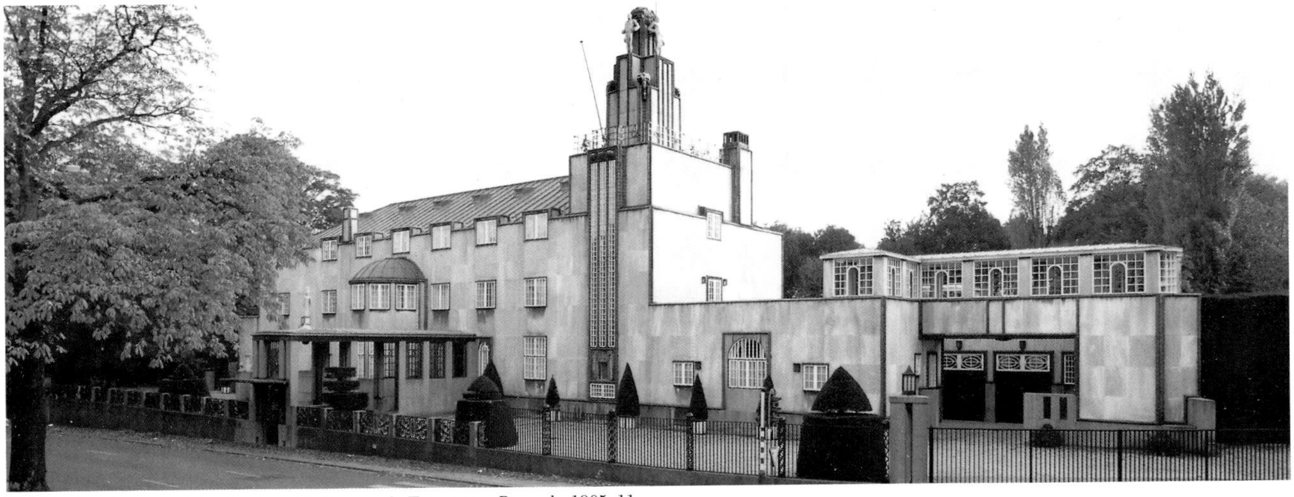

345. Josef Hoffmann. Palais Stoclet, 281 Avenue de Tervueren, Brussels. 1905–11

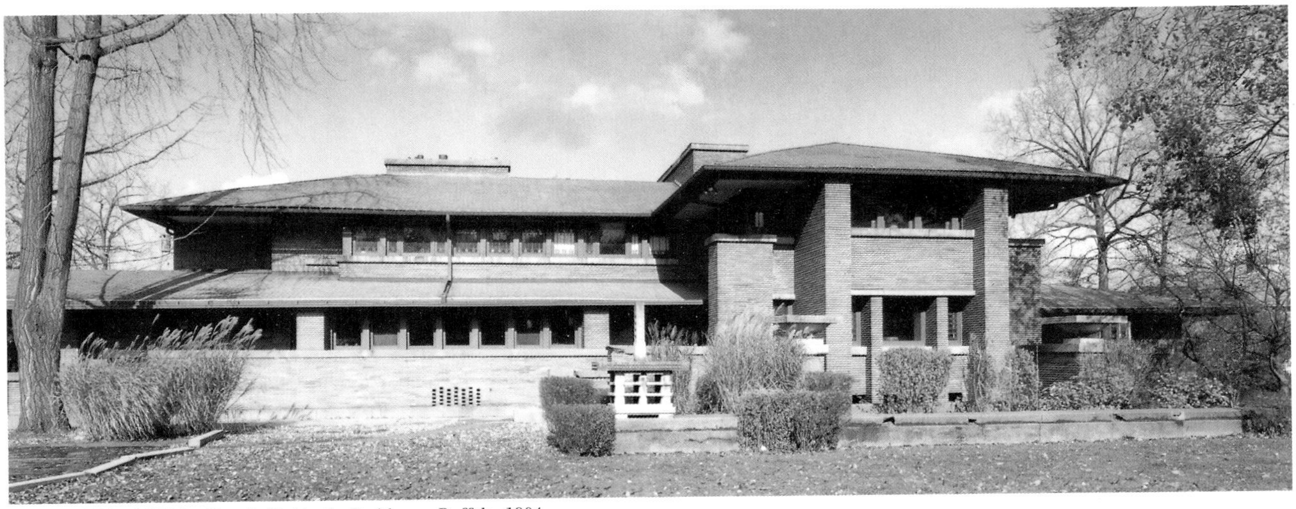

346. Frank Lloyd Wright. Darwin D. Martin Residence, Buffalo. 1904

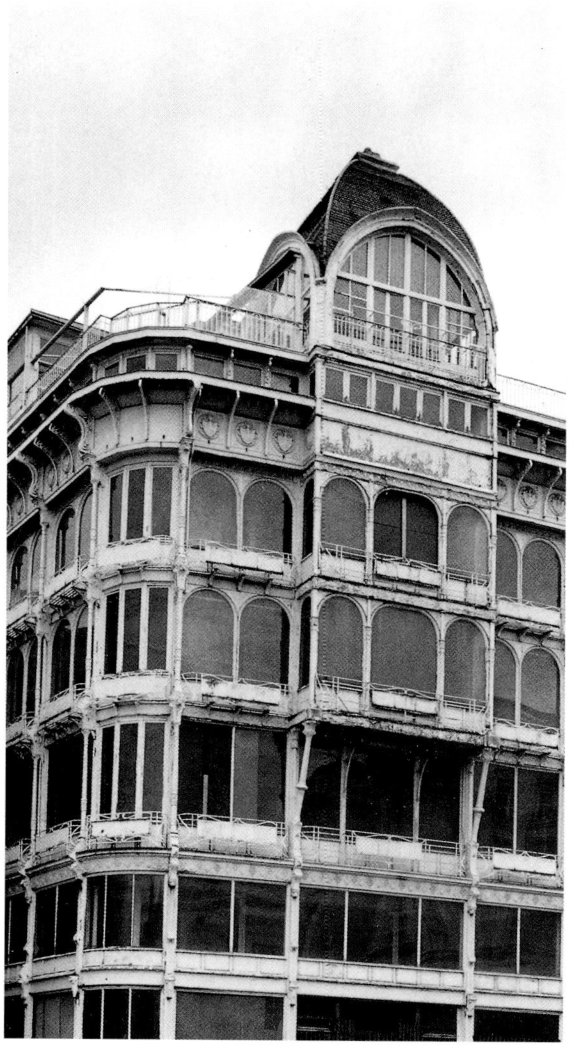

347. Paul Saintenoy. Old England Store, Brussels. 1899

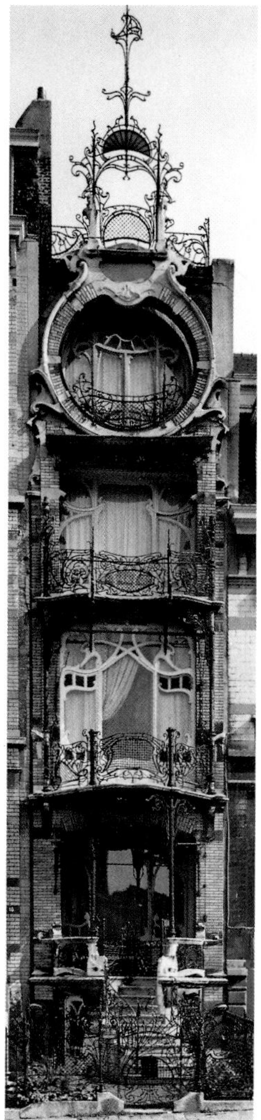

348. Gustave Strauven. 11 Square Ambiorix, Brussels. 1903

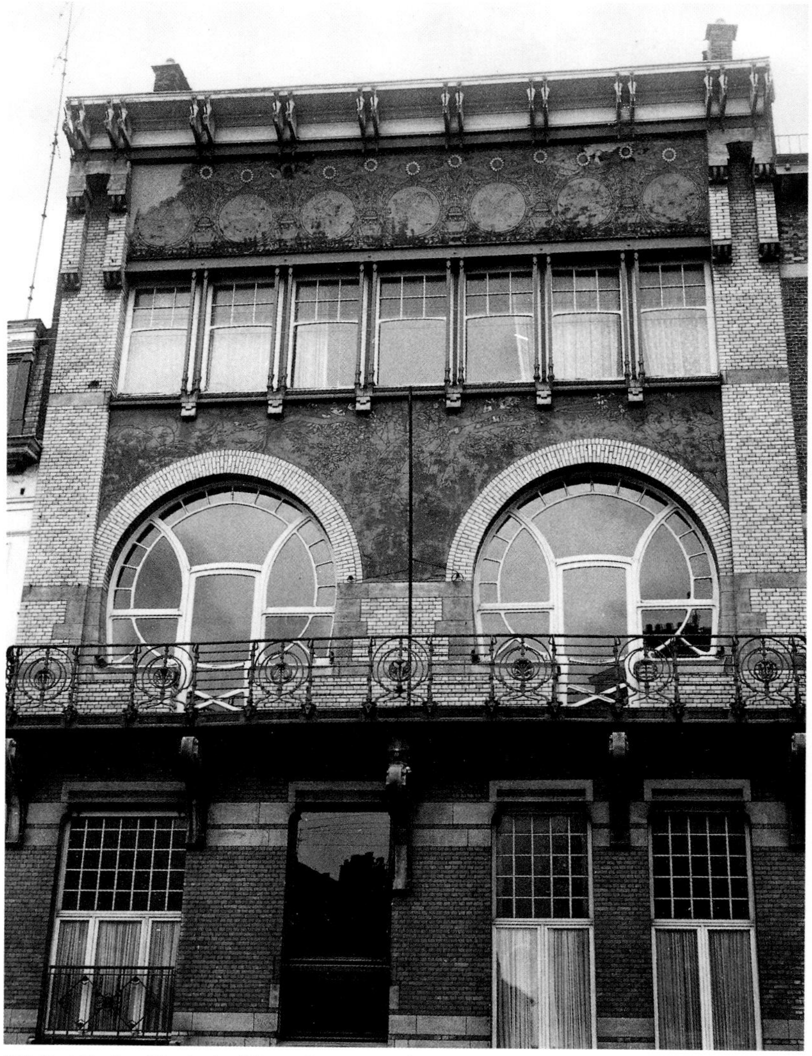

349. Paul Hankar. Ciamberlani House, Brussels. 1897

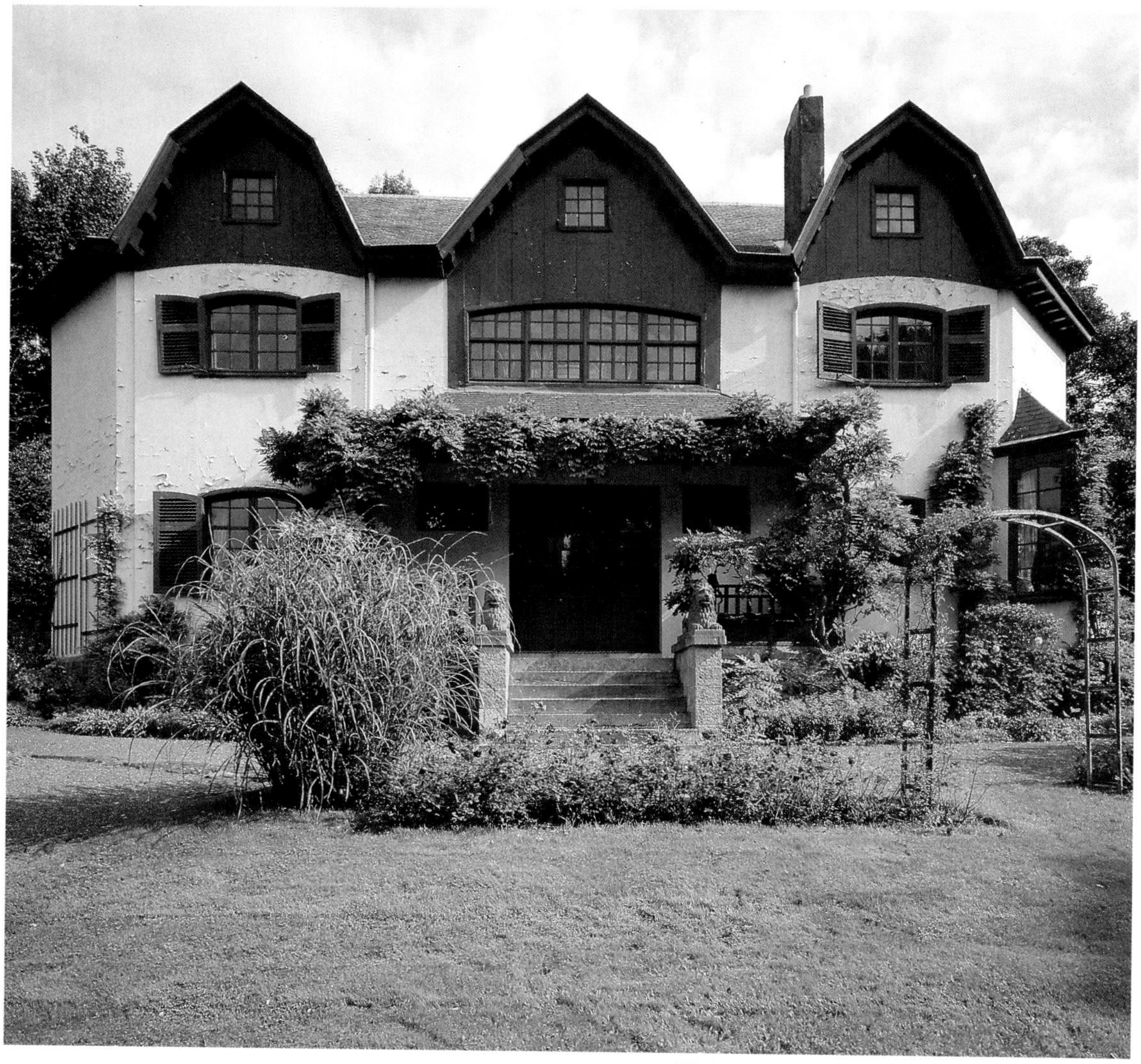

350. Henry van de Velde. Bloemenwerf House, Uccle. 1895

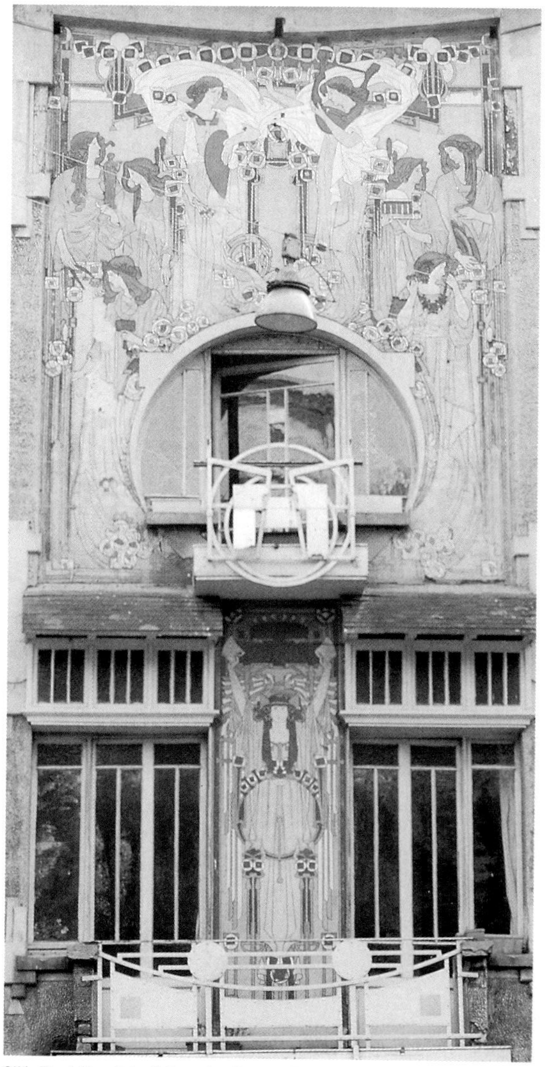

351. Paul Cauchie. 5 Rue des Francs, Brussels. 1905

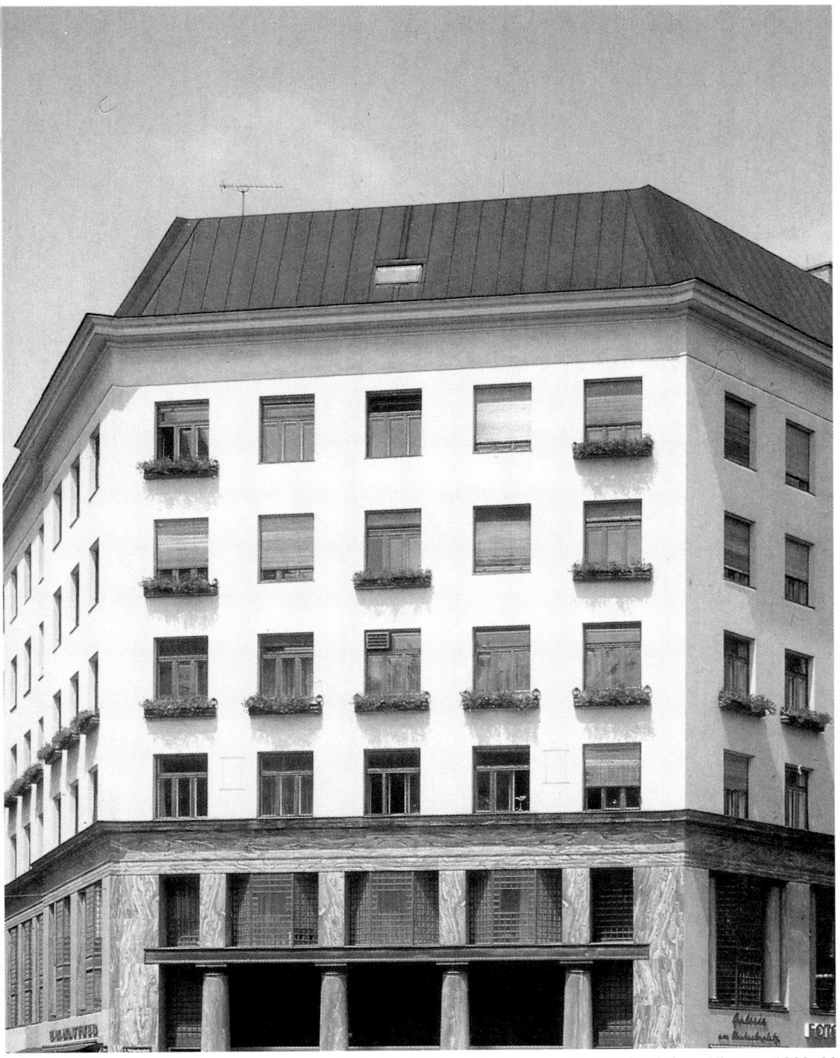

352. Adolf Loos. Building on the Michaelplatz, Vienna. 1909–11

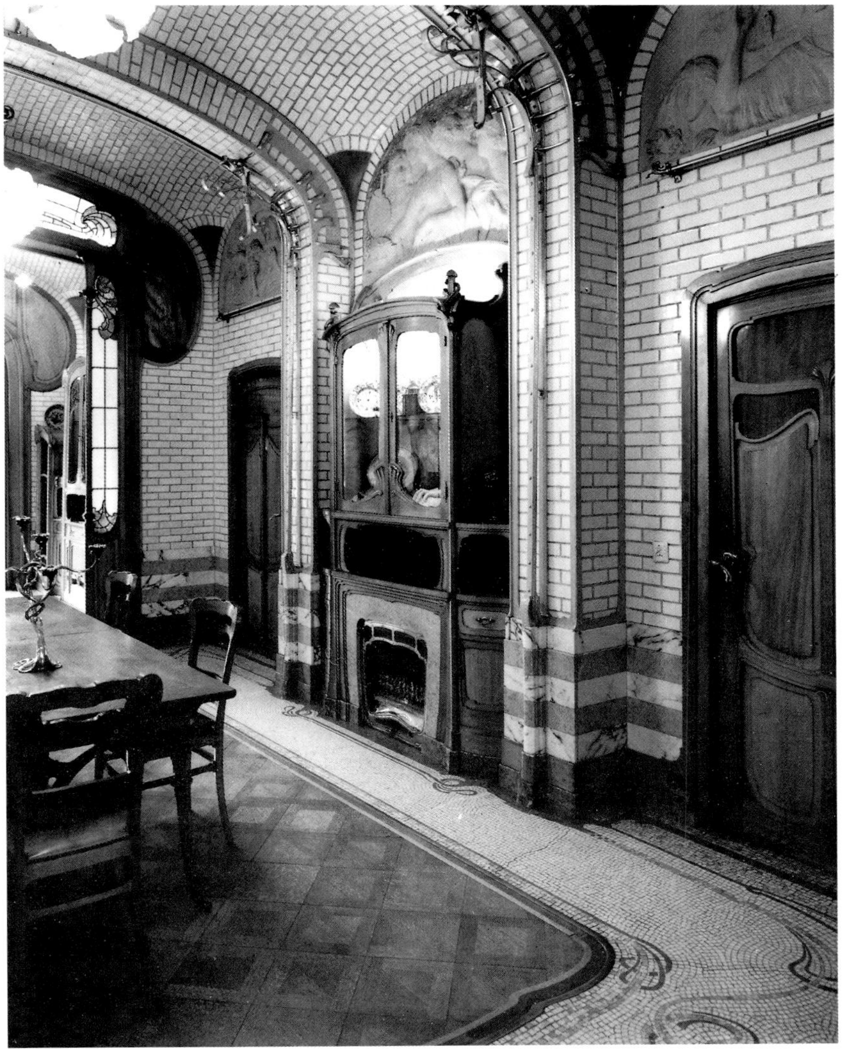

353. Victor Horta. Dining room, Hôtel Solvay, Rue Américaine, Brussels. 1898

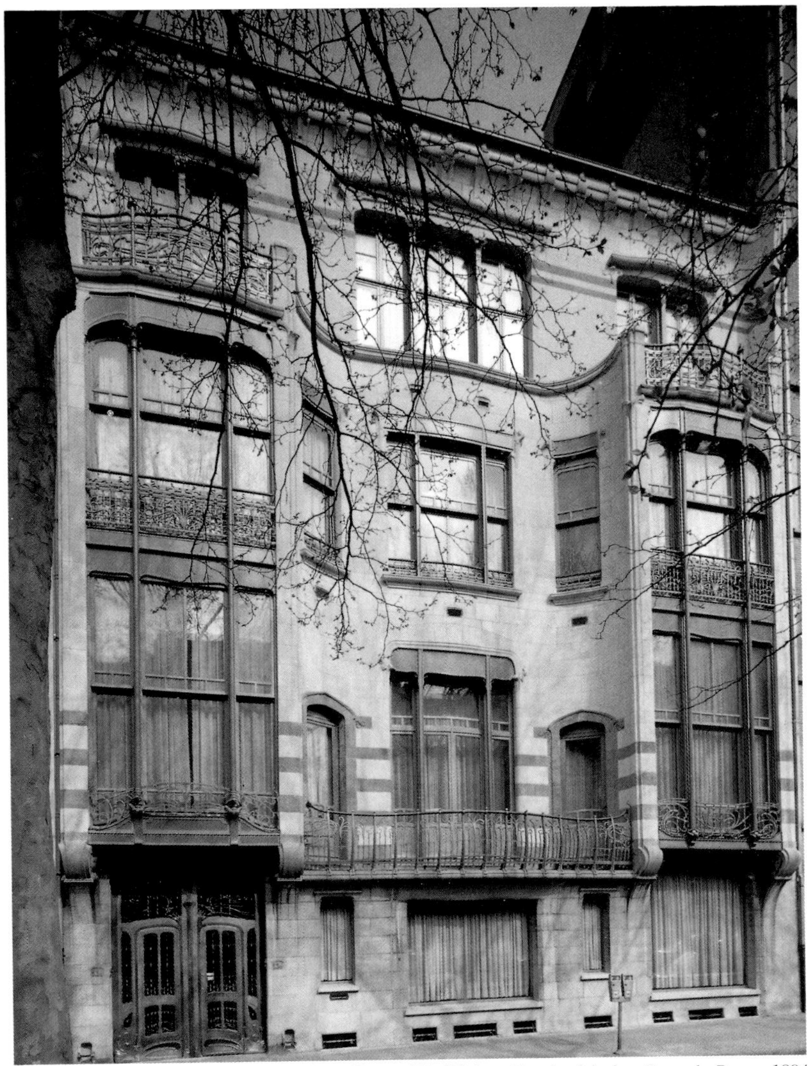

354. Victor Horta. Hôtel Solvay, Rue Américaine, Brussels. Begun 1894

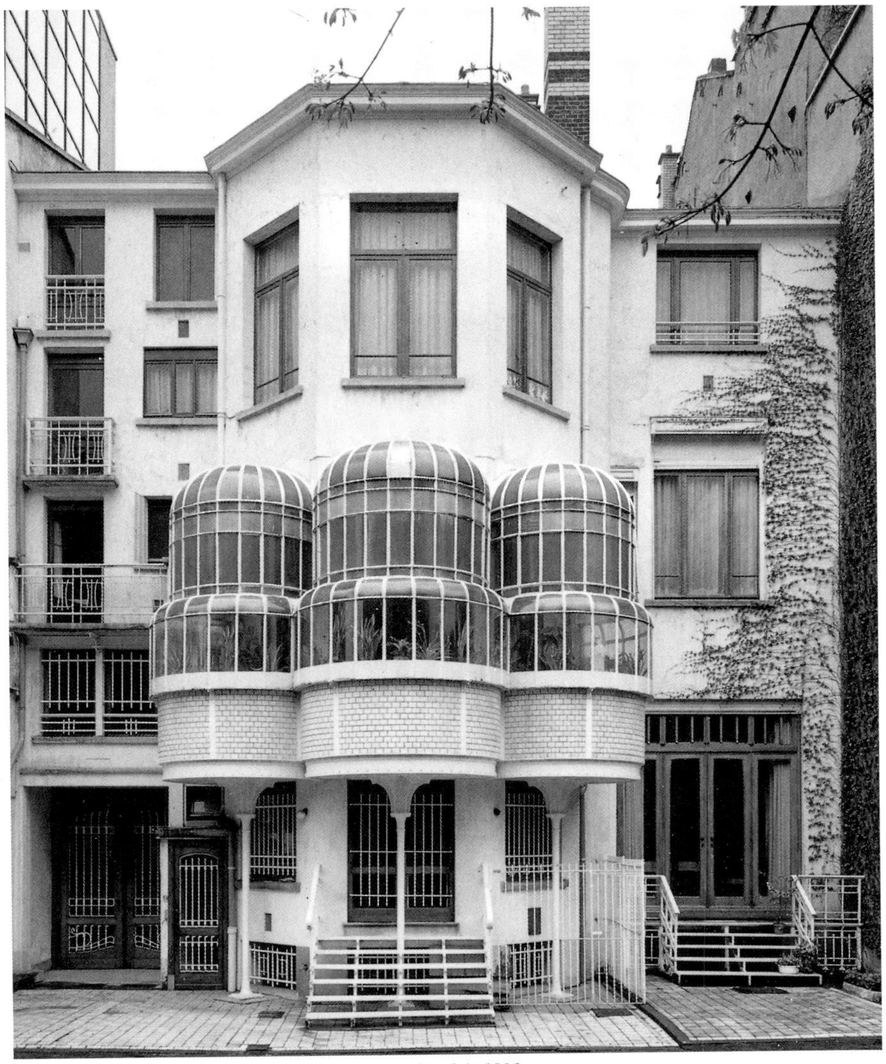

355. Victor Horta. Hôtel Max-Hallet, Brussels (rear facade). 1906

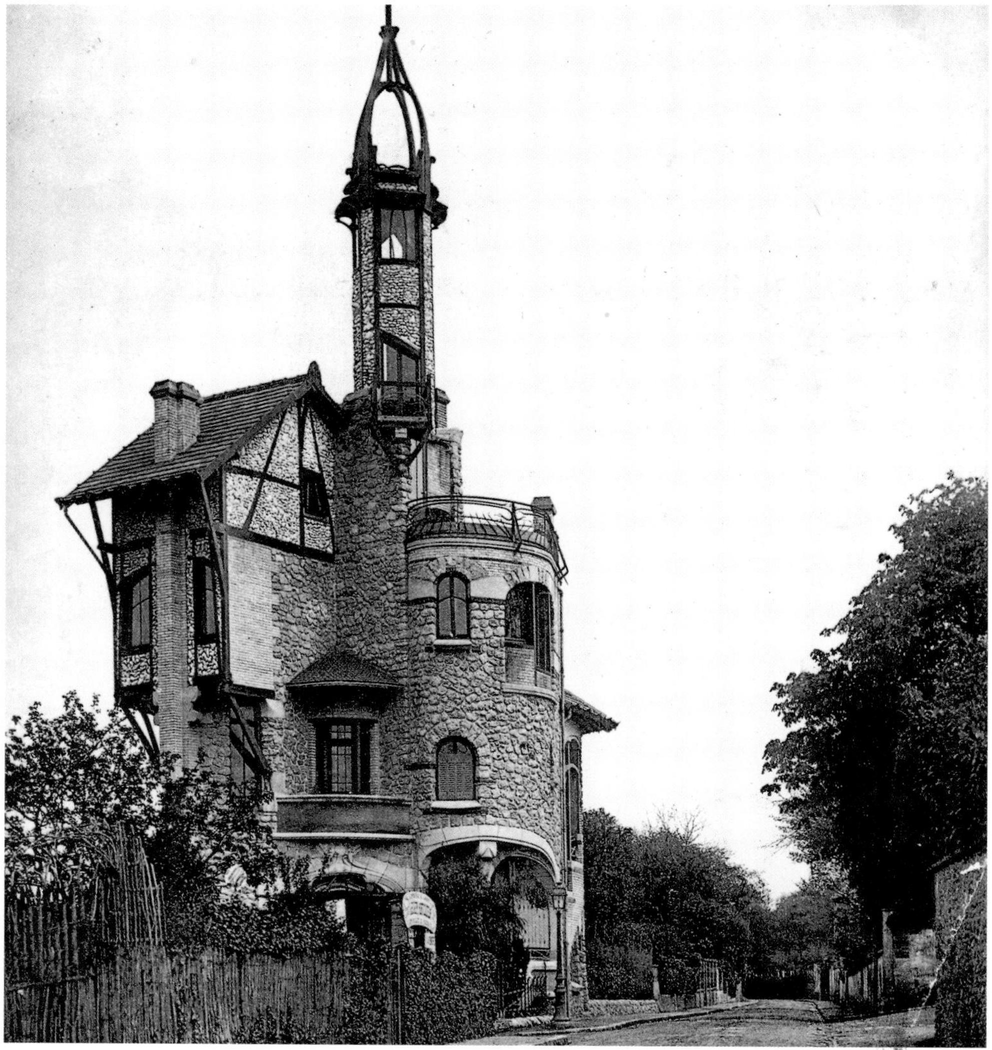

356. Hector Guimard. Castel Henriette, Sèvres. 1899–1900 (destroyed)

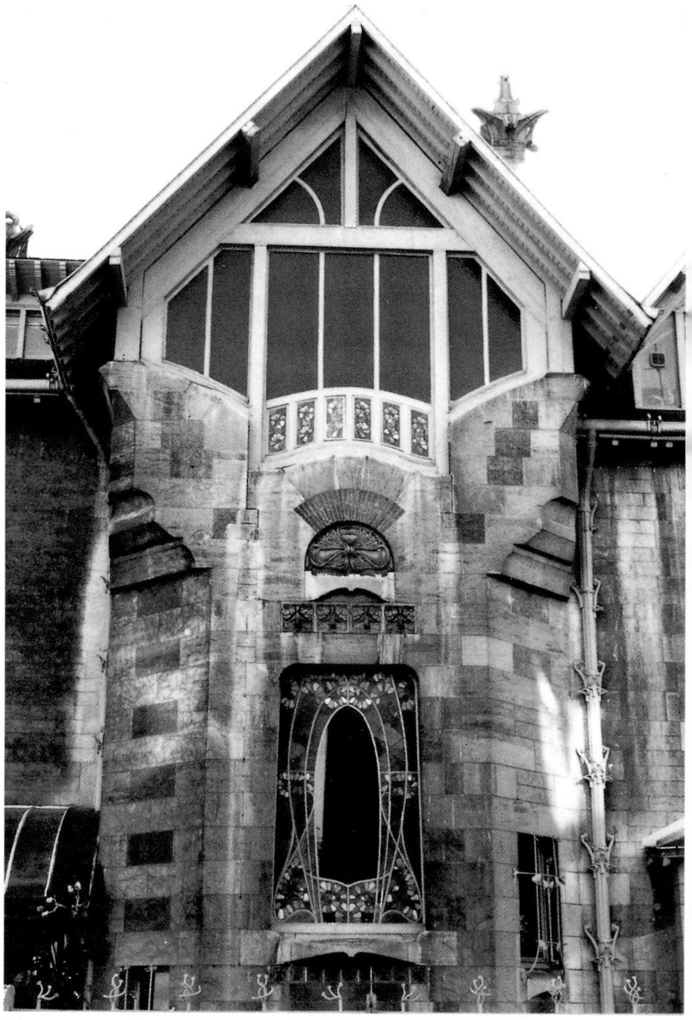

357. Henri Sauvage. Villa Majorelle,
1 Rue Louis-Majorelle, Nancy. 1898–1901

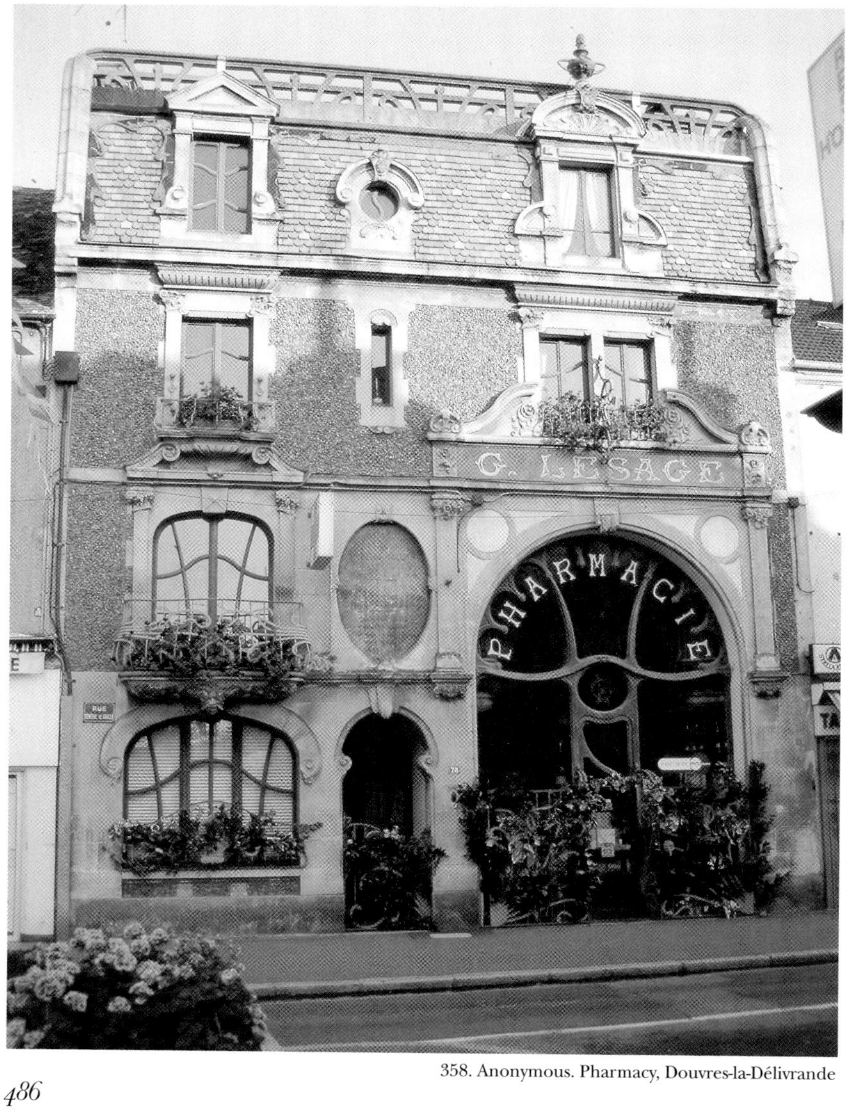

358. Anonymous. Pharmacy, Douvres-la-Délivrande

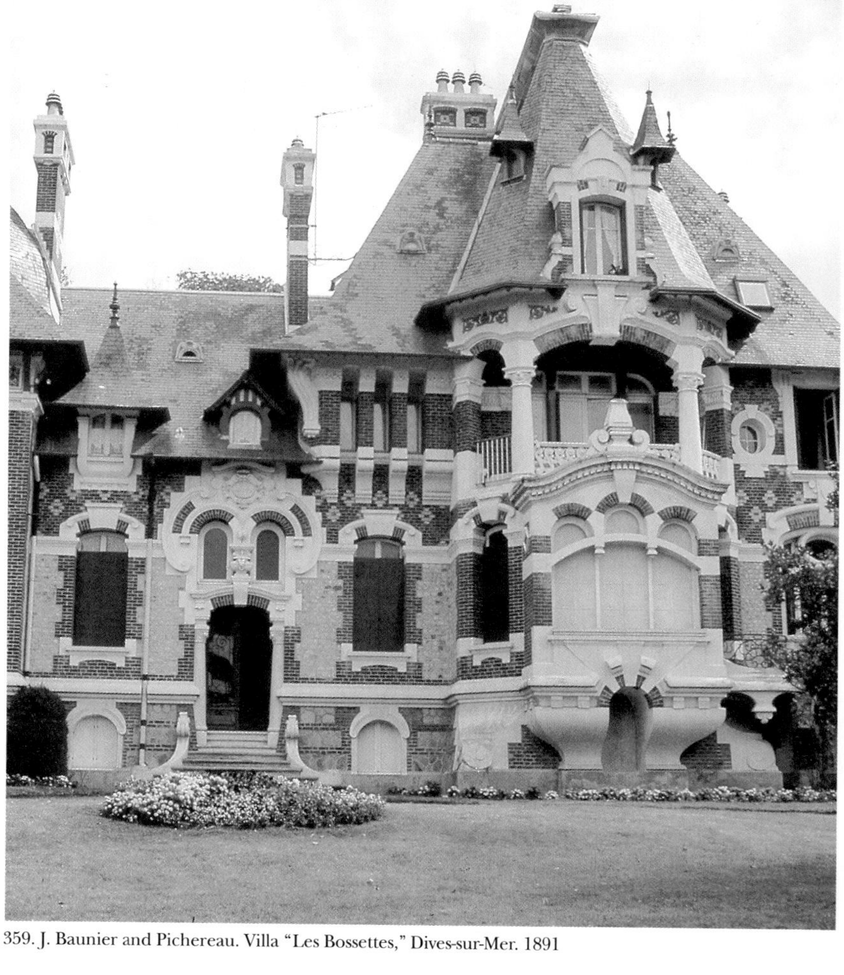

359. J. Baunier and Pichereau. Villa "Les Bossettes," Dives-sur-Mer. 1891

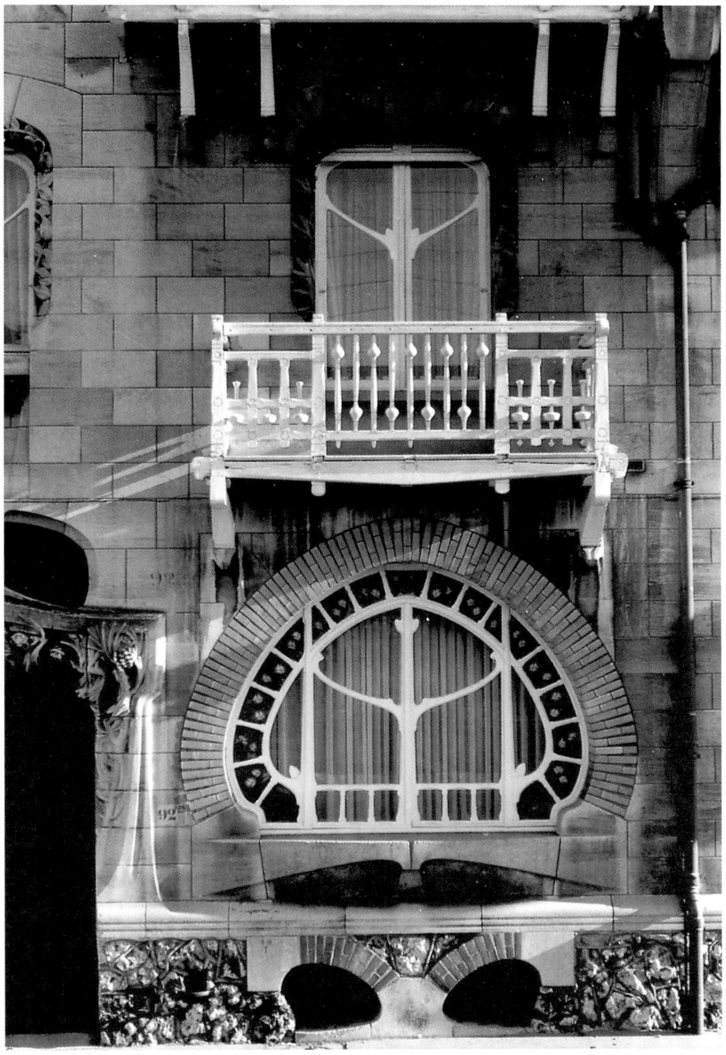

360. Émile André. Town house, 92–92 bis Quai Claude-le-Lorrain, Nancy. 1903

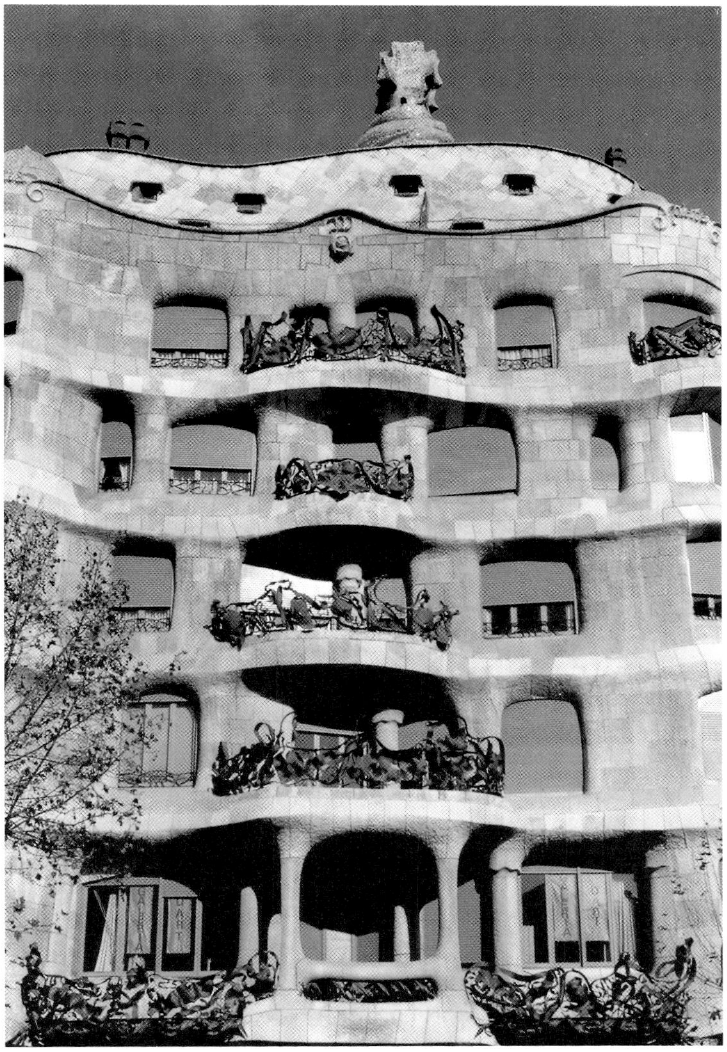

361. Antoni Gaudí i Cornet. Casa Milá, Barcelona. 1906–10

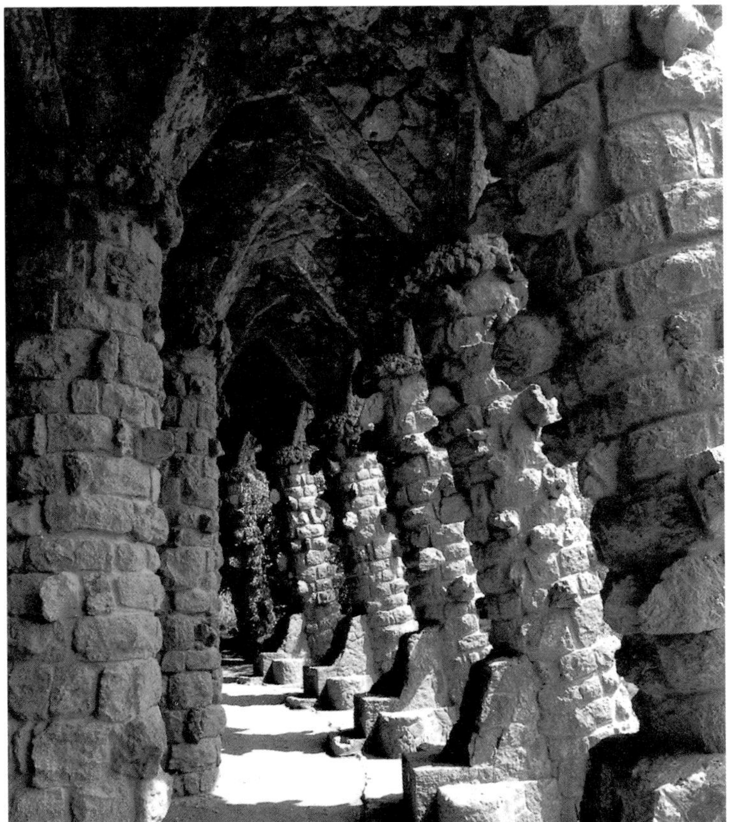

362. Antoni Gaudí i Cornet. Parc Güell (gallery walkway), Barcelona. 1900–14

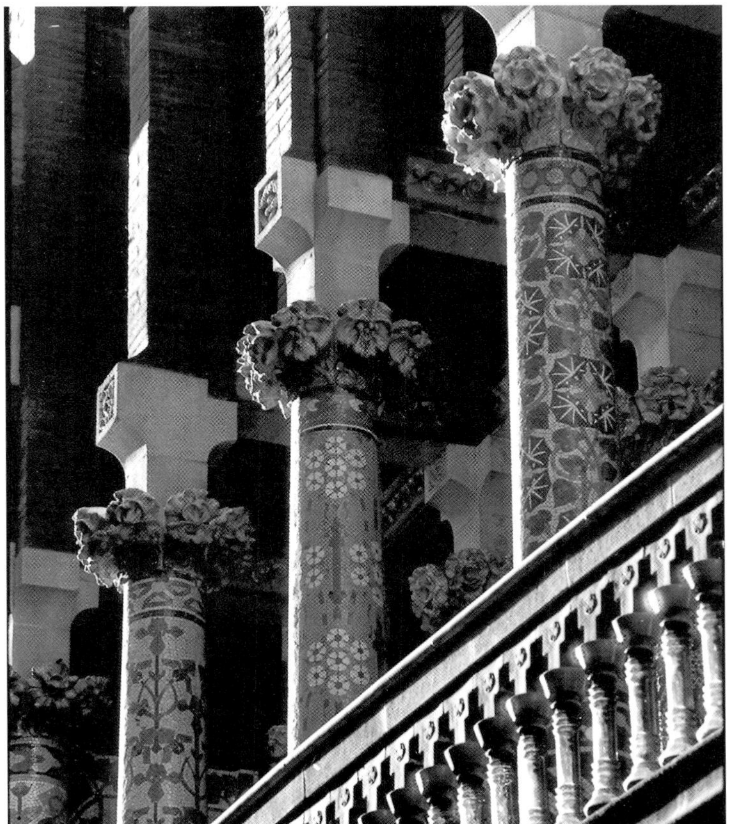

363. Lluís Domènech i Montaner. Palau de la Música Catalana (concert hall), Barcelona. 1905–8

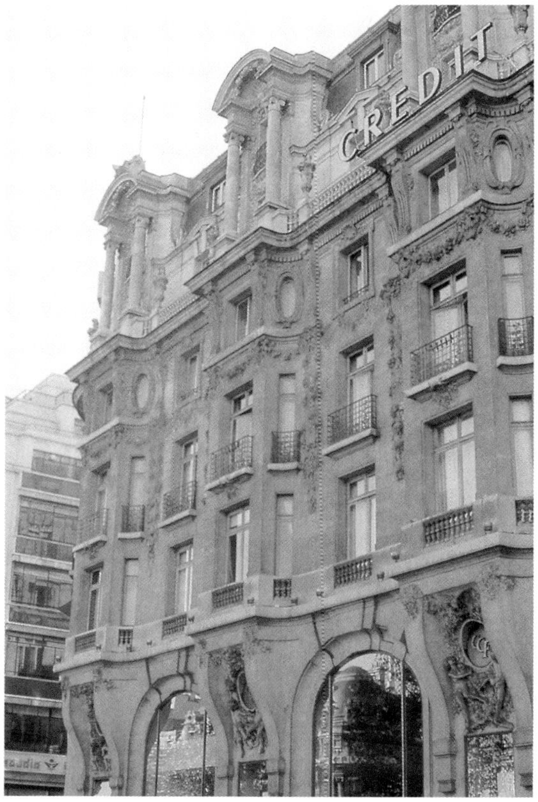

364. Georges Chedanne. Hôtel de Voyageurs, Avenue des Champs-Élysées, Paris. (Now the headquarters of the Crédit Commercial de France bank)

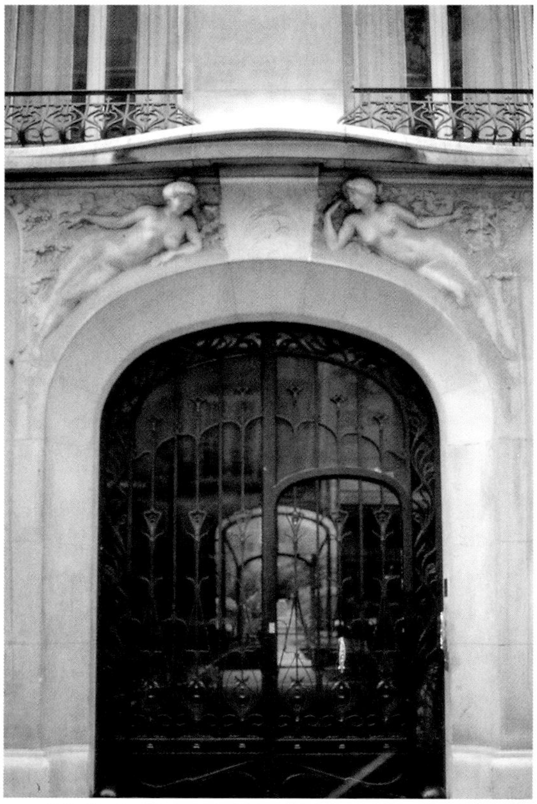

365. Charles Plumet. Building, 50 Avenue Victor-Hugo, Paris. 1901

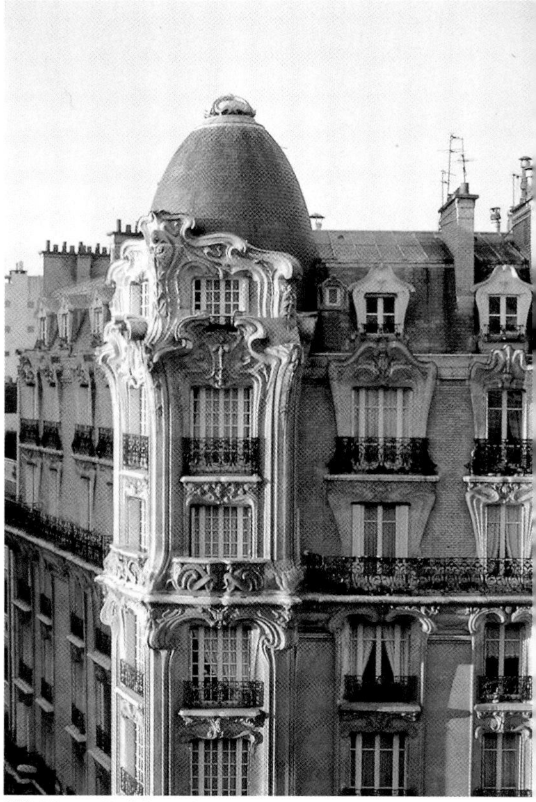

366. Wagon. Building, Place Félix-Faure, Paris

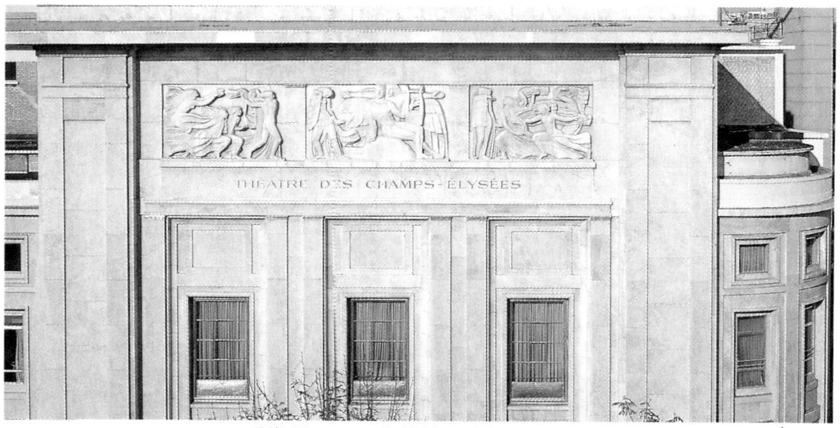

367. Henry van de Velde and Auguste Perret. Théâtre des Champs-Élysées, Paris. 1913

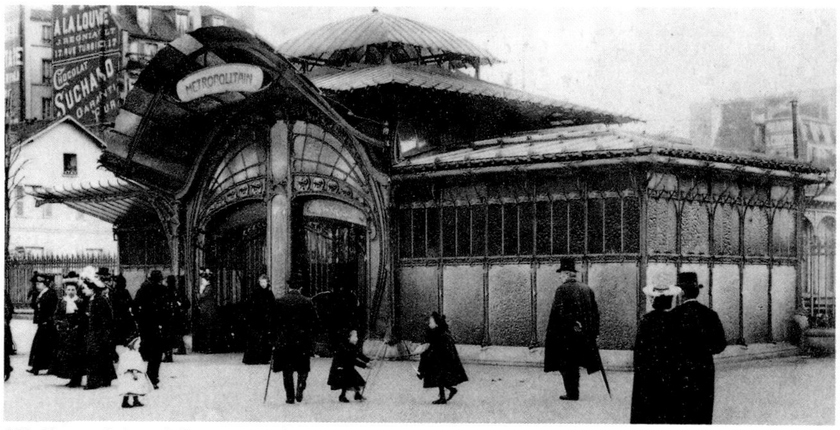

368. Hector Guimard. Entrance to the Métropolitain subway station Gare de la Bastille in Paris. 1900

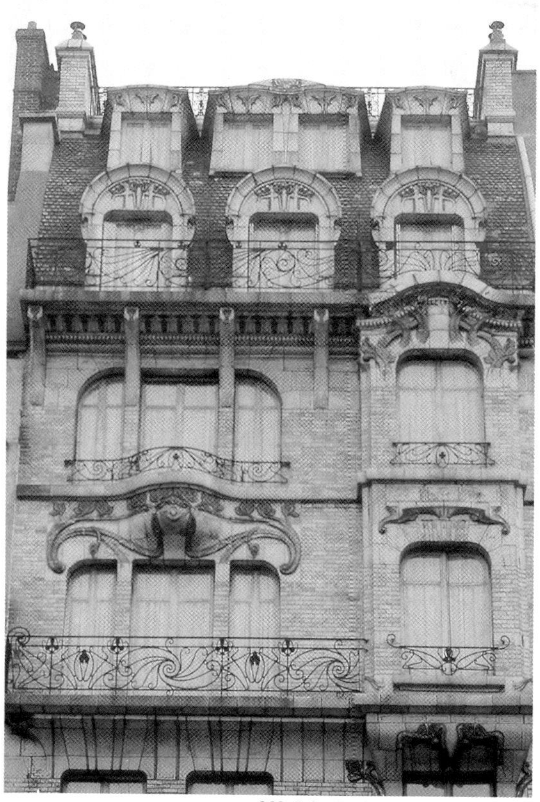

369. Jules Lavirotte. Ceramic Hôtel, 34 Avenue de Wagram, Paris. 1904

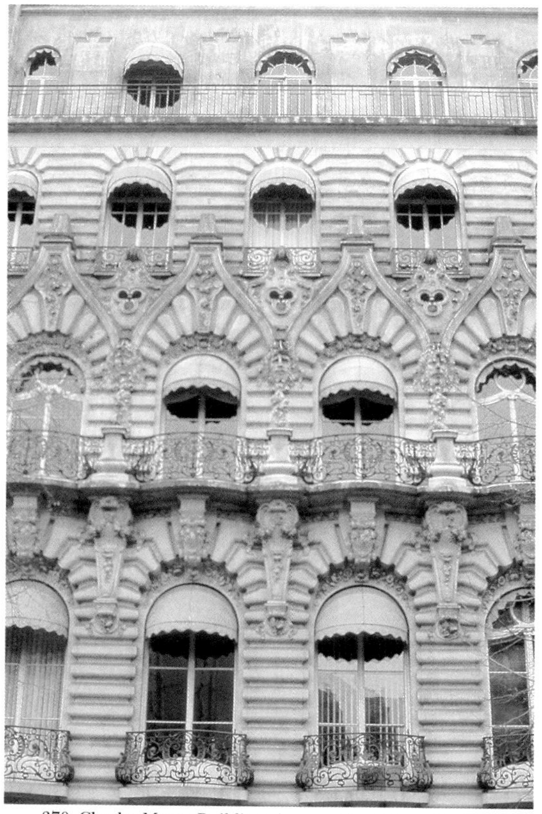

370. Charles Massa. Building, Avenue MacMahon, Paris

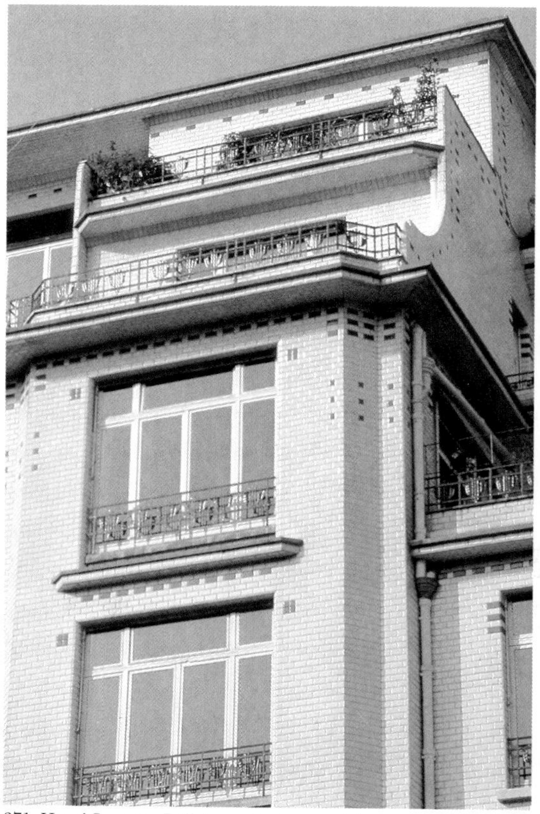

371. Henri Sauvage. Building with staggered frontage, 12 Rue Vavin, Paris. 1912–19

THE DECORATIVE ARTS

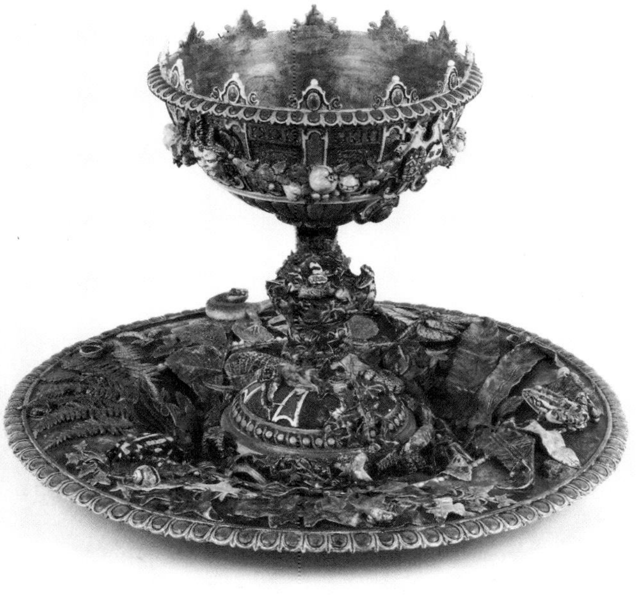

372. Charles-Jean Avisseau and Octave-Guillaume de Rochebrune. Footed bowl on dish. 1855. *Faience fine*

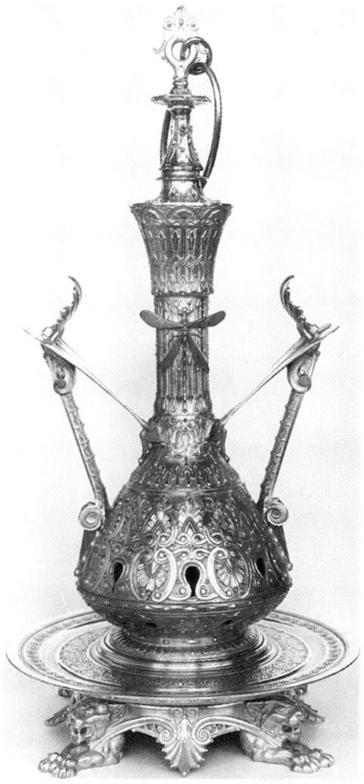

373. Barbedienne. Perfume-burner. 1855

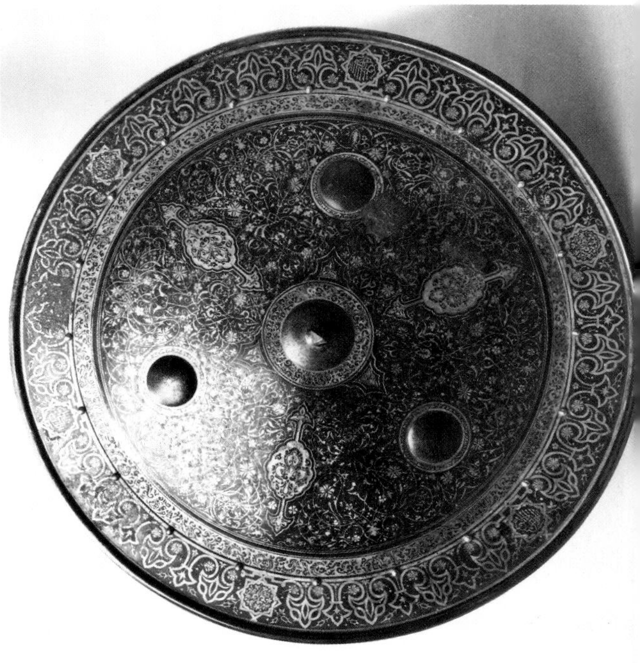

374. Alexandre Henry Dufresne de Saint-Léon. Shield. c. 1856–65. Patinated steel

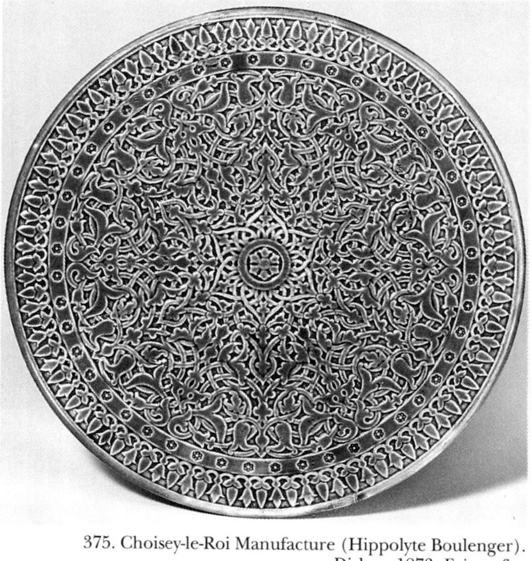

375. Choisey-le-Roi Manufacture (Hippolyte Boulenger). Dish. c. 1873. *Faience fine*

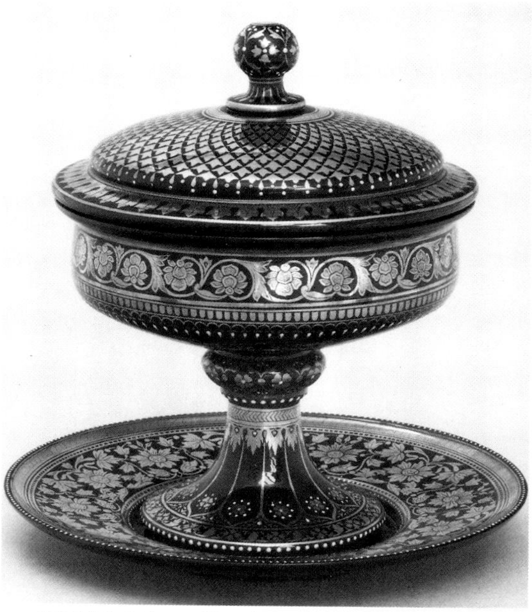

376. J. & L. Lobmeyr Manufacture. Lidded bowl and dish. c. 1873. Colored glass

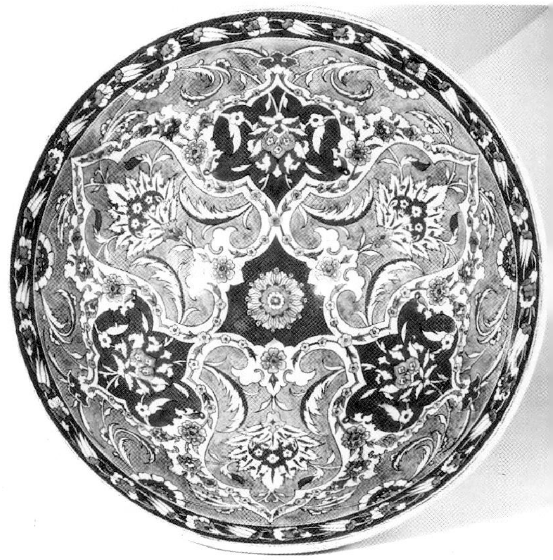

377. Théodore Deck. Bowl. 1867. Glazed faience

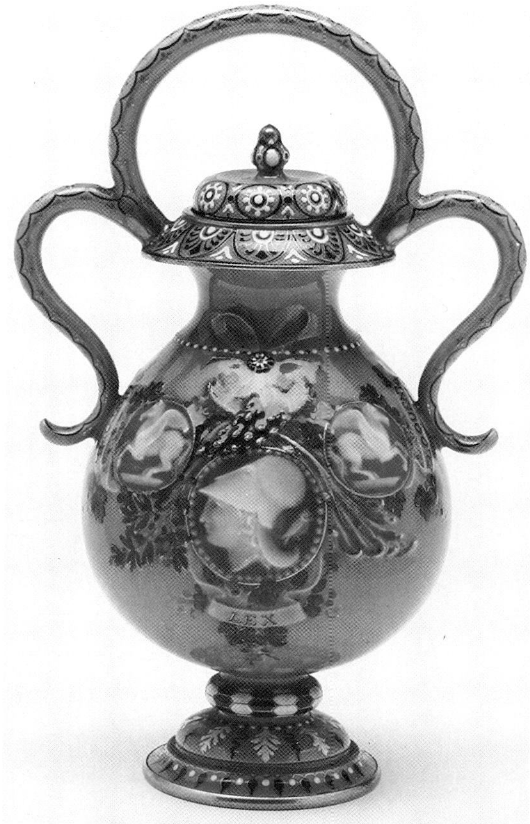

378. Manufacture de Sèvres, Gély. "Bijou" vase. 1871. Hard-paste porcelain

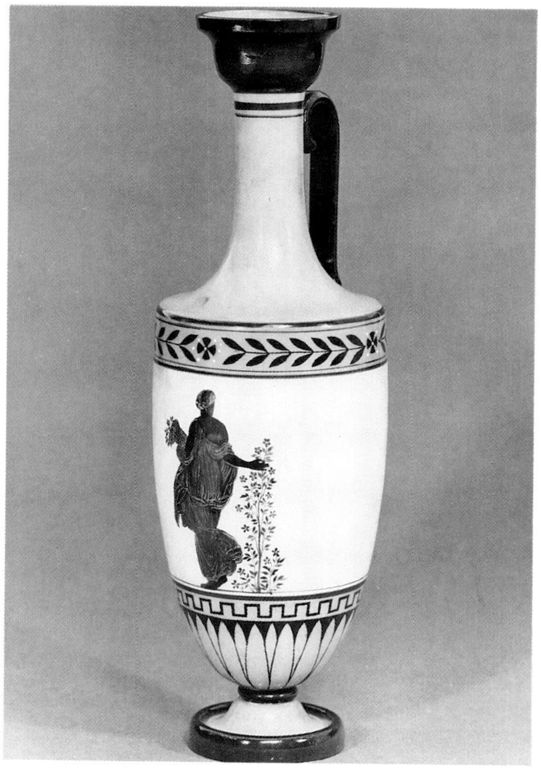

379. Wilhelm Hoffmann. Vase. c. 1873. Opaline with engraved and painted decoration

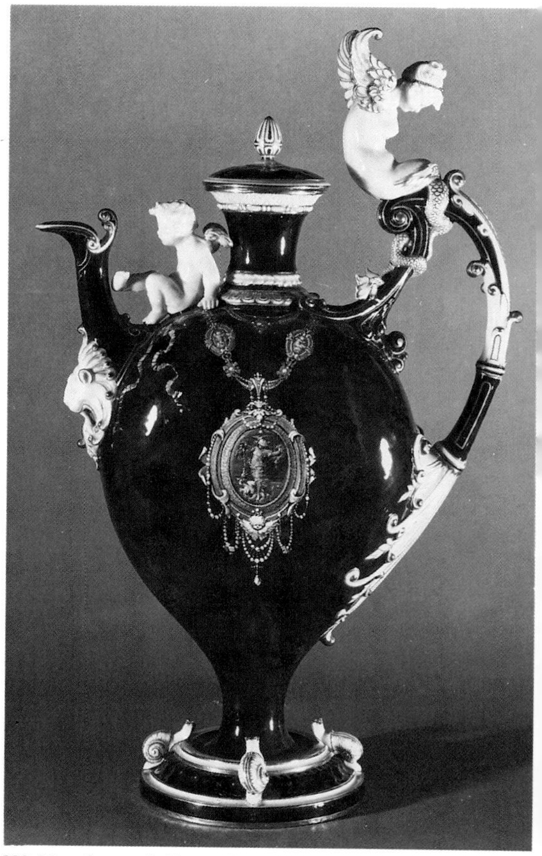

380. Manufacture de Sèvres, Carrier-Belleuse. "Buire de Blois" figural ewer. 1883. Hard-paste porcelain

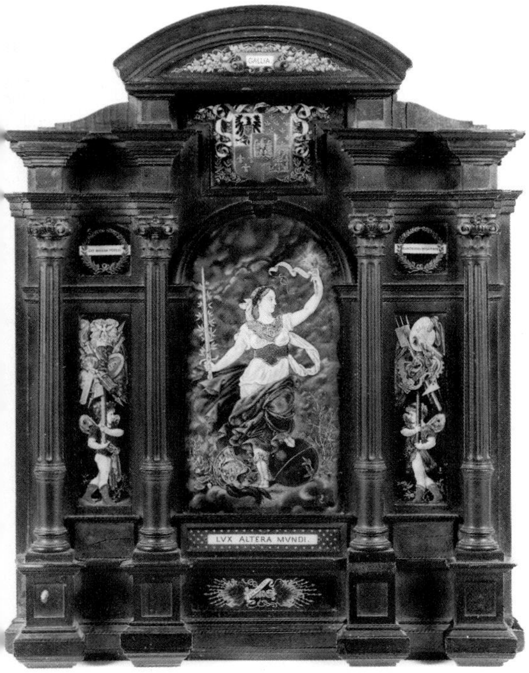

381. Claudius Popelin. "Gallia." 1867. Enamel-painted copper and ebonized pearwood

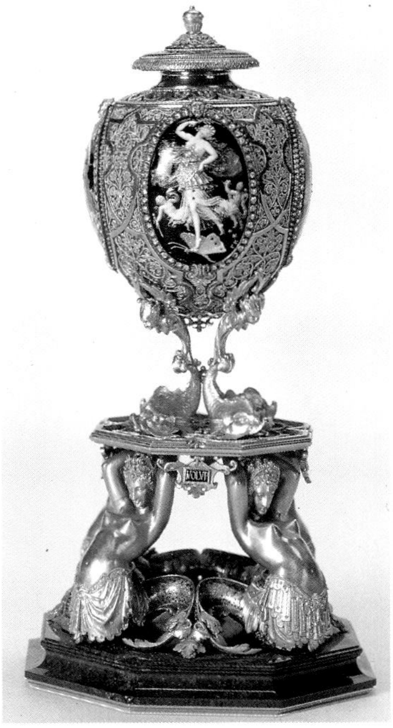

382. Fontenay, Richet (enameler). Perfume-burner. 1878. Gold, enamel, lapis lazuli, and diamonds

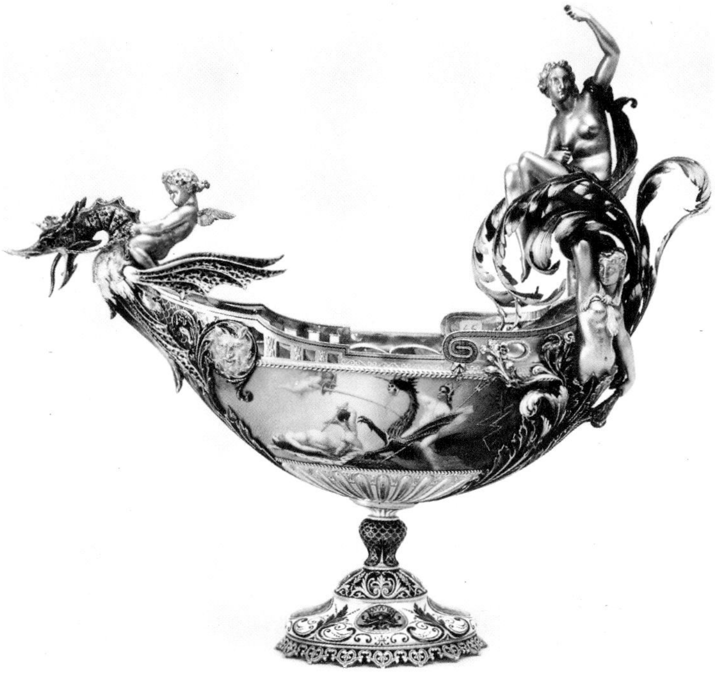

383. Charles Lepec. Nef. c. 1867. Enameled gold and gilt silver

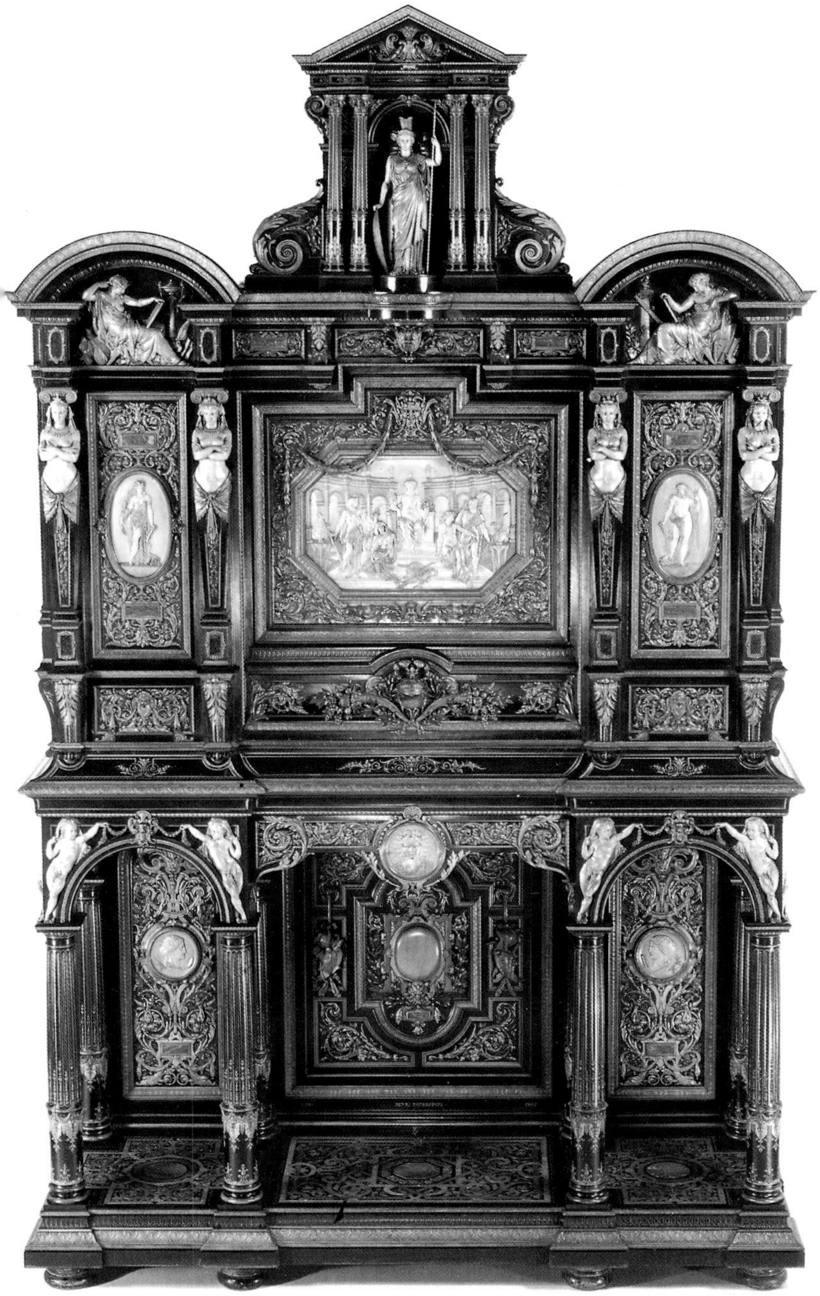

384. Maison Fourdinois. Cabinet. c. 1867. Ebony, boxwood, pearwood, lapis lazuli, jasper, and marble

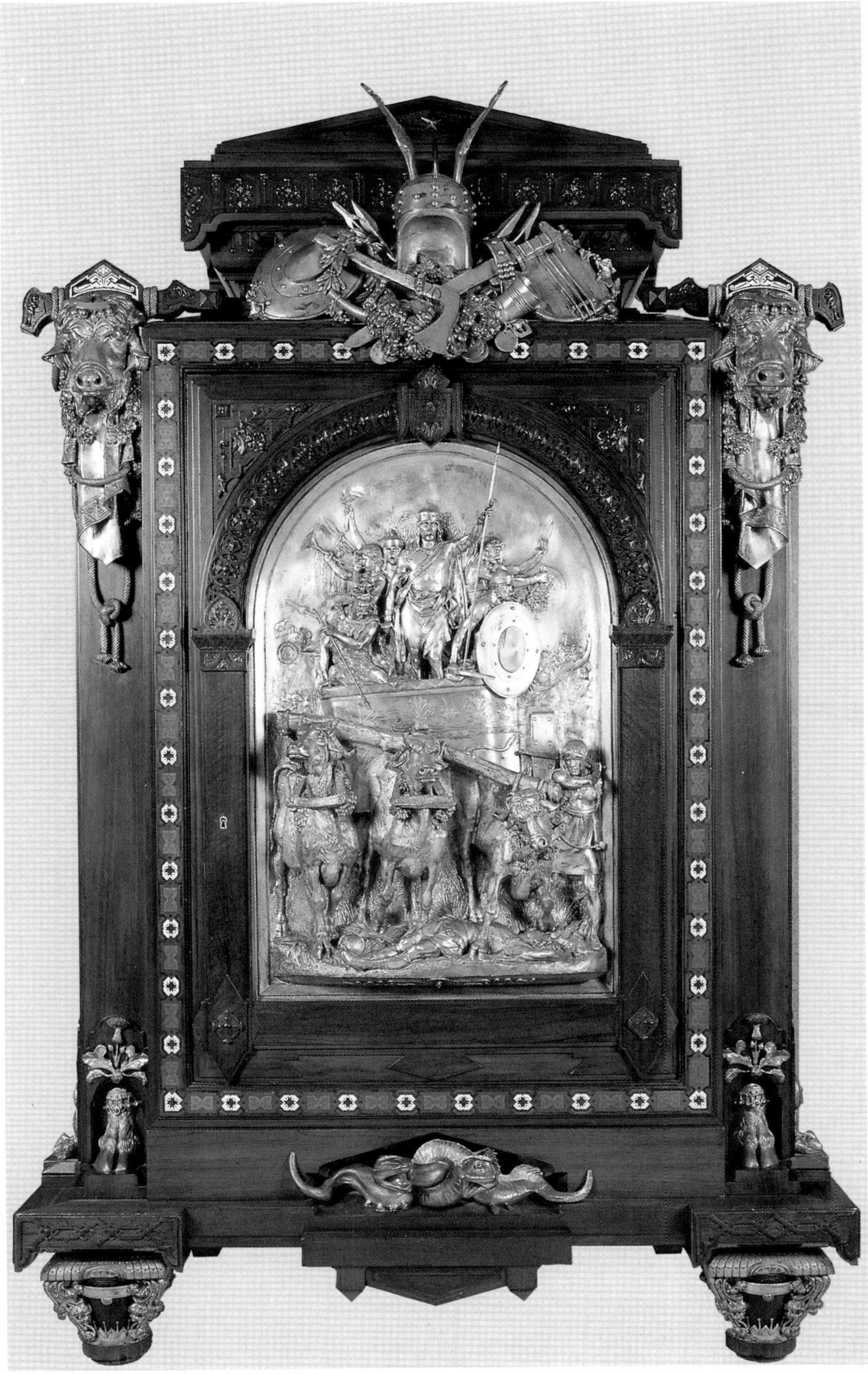

385. Diehl, Brandely, and Fremiet. Medal cabinet. 1867. Cedarwood, walnut inlay, ebony and ivory, silver-plated bronze and copper

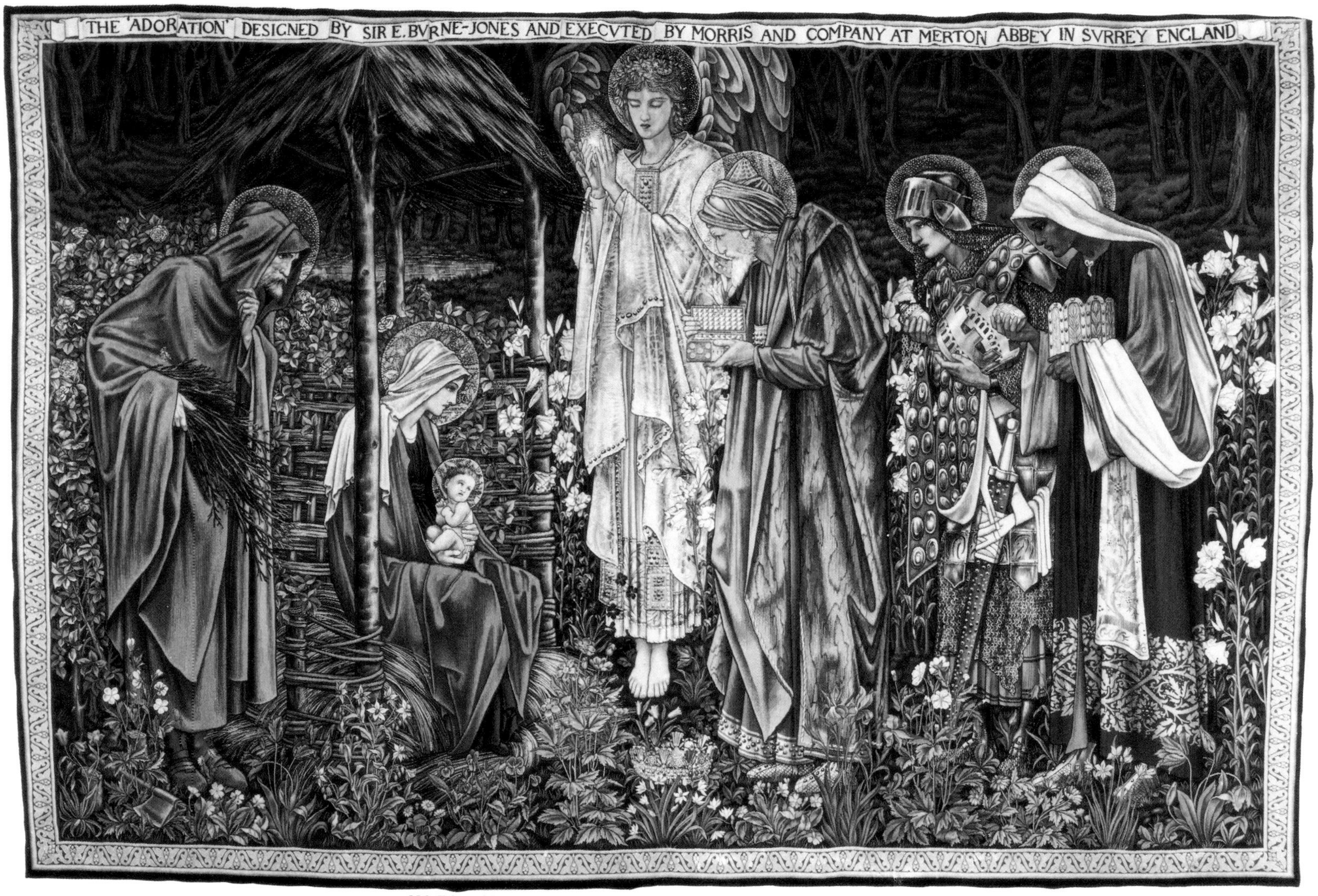

386. Edward Burne-Jones. *The Adoration of the Magi*. Cartoon painted c. 1888–90

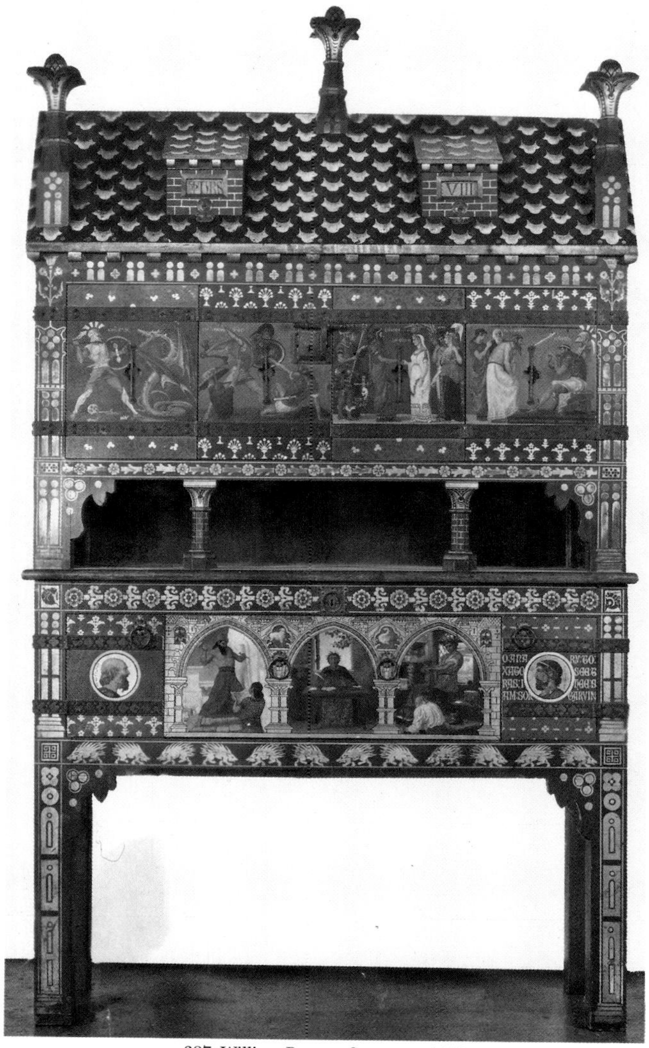

387. William Burges. Secretary. 1858. Painted and gilt wood

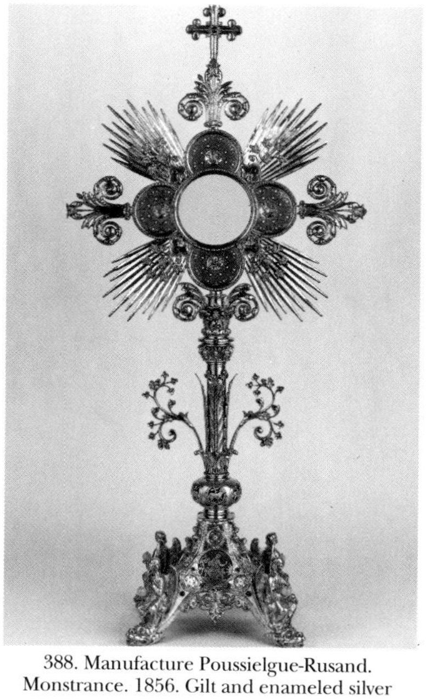

388. Manufacture Poussielgue-Rusand. Monstrance. 1856. Gilt and enameled silver

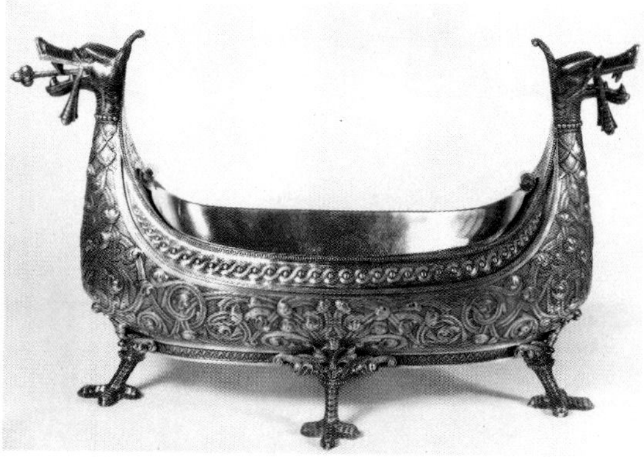

389. Torolf Prytz and J. Tostrup. Jardiniere. 1900. Chased and repoussé silver

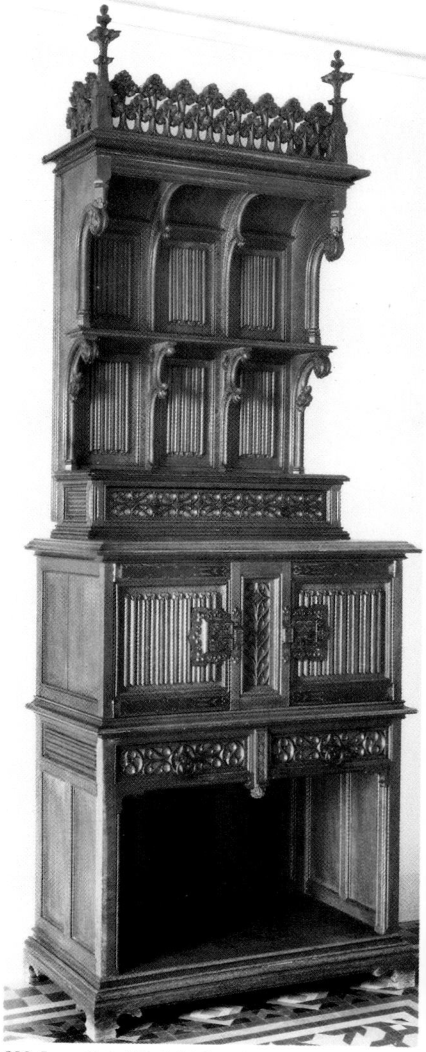

390. Josep Puig i Cadafalch and Gaspar Homar i Mezquida. Dresser from the Casa Amattler. c. 1900. Oak

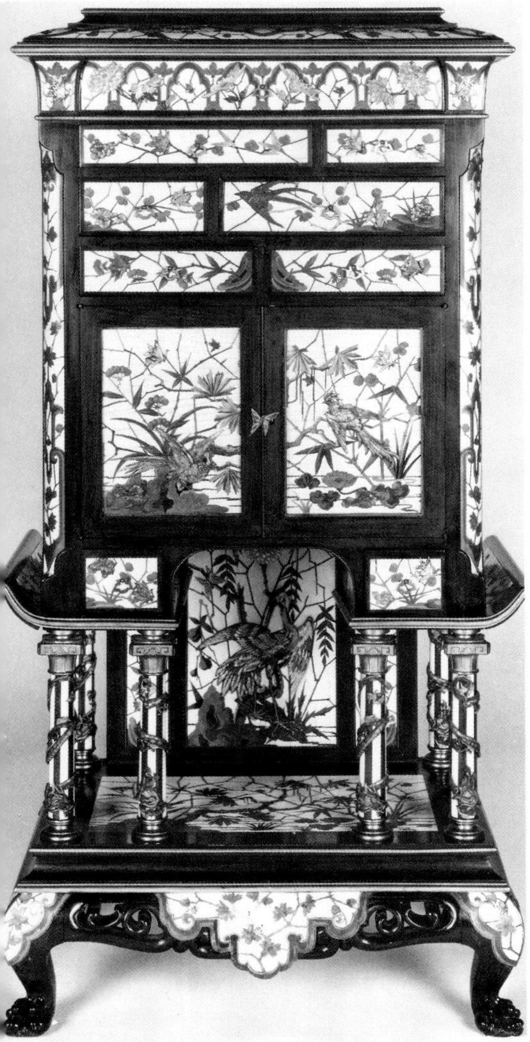

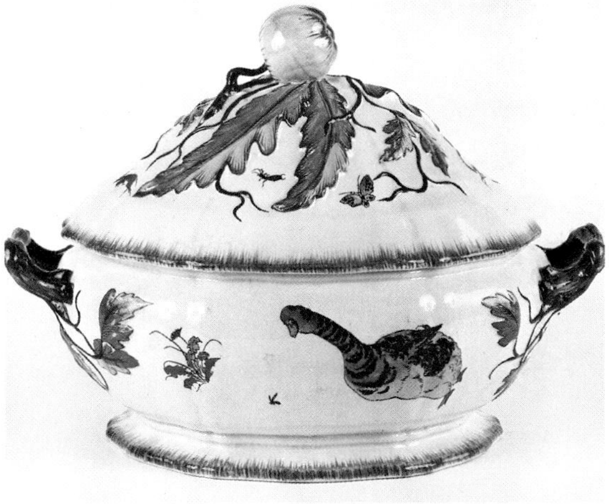

392. Manufacture Creil and Montereau, F. Bracquemond. Soup tureen. 1866. *Faience fine*

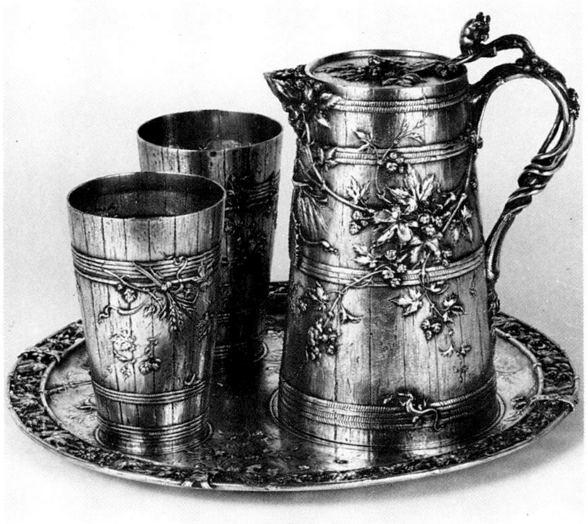

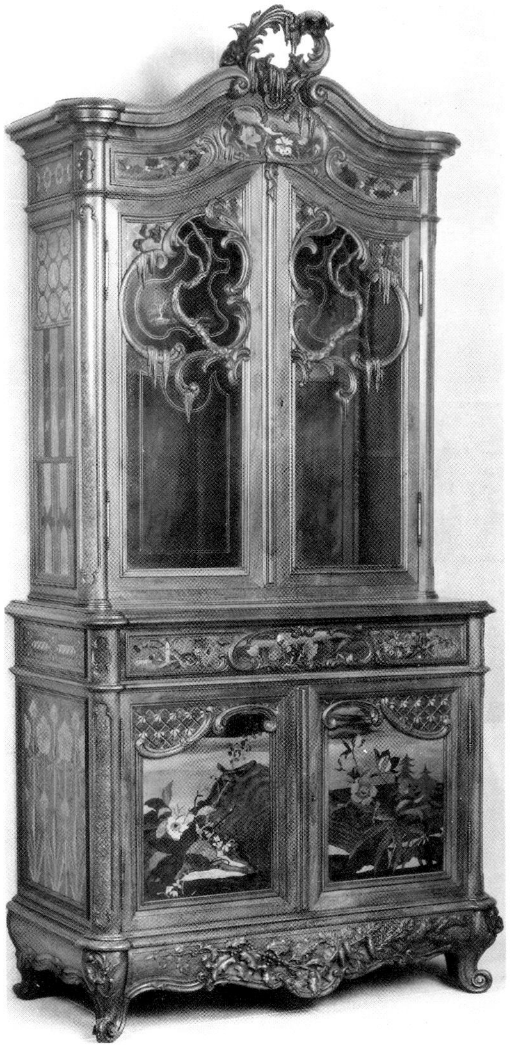

391. Veuve Ferdinand Duvinage (Maison A. Giroux). Cabinet. c. 1878. Rosewood, inlay of ivory, various woods and metals, patinated, silvered, and gilt bronze

393. Frères Fannière. Beer service. c. 1865. Chased and repoussé silver

394. Émile Gallé. "Winter Flora" glass-fronted cabinet. 1889. Walnut and Amboyna bur

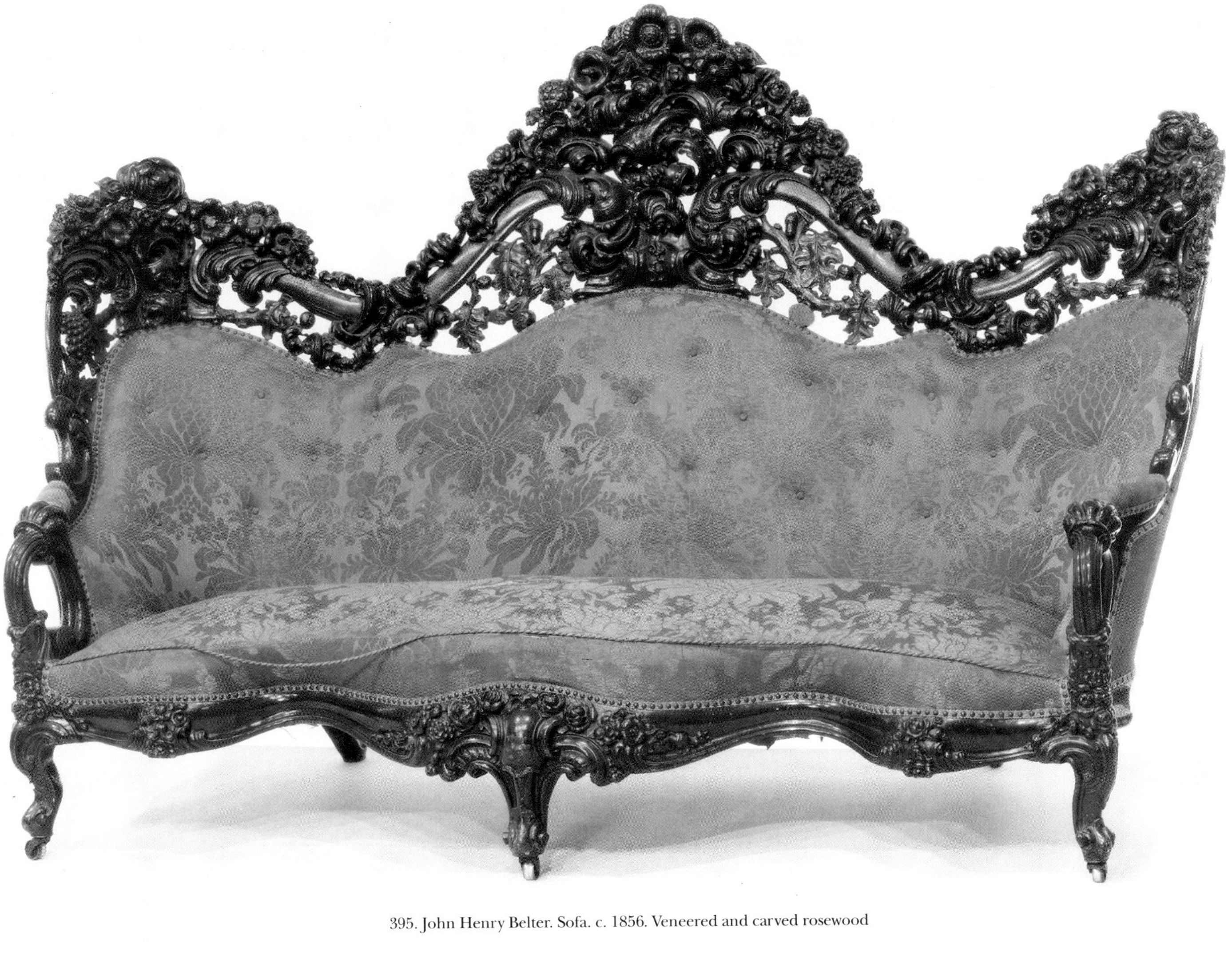

395. John Henry Belter. Sofa. c. 1856. Veneered and carved rosewood

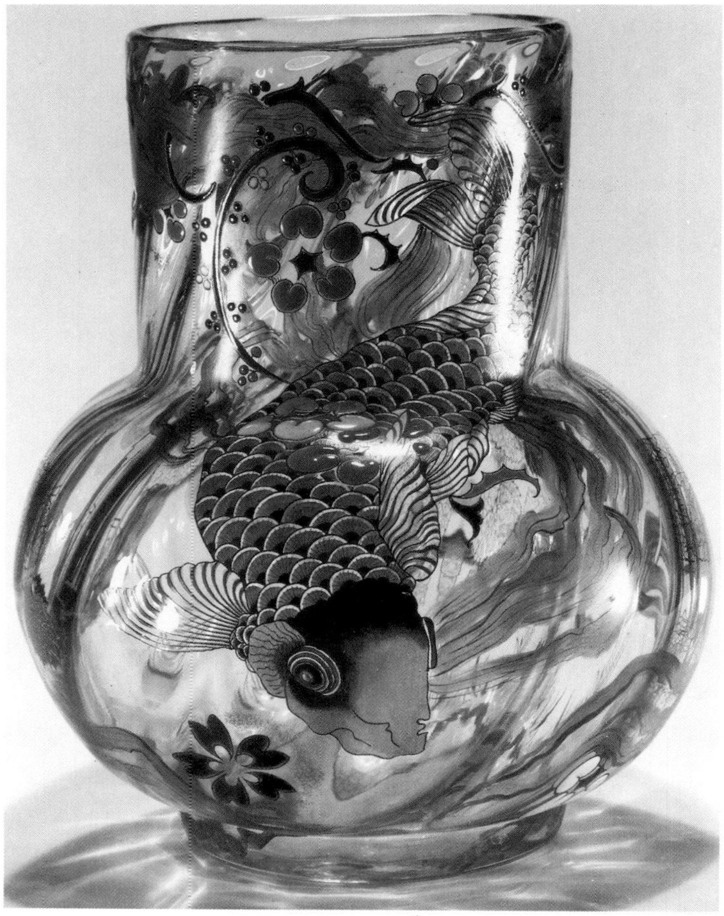

396. Émile Gallé. "Clair de Lune" vase. 1878. Blown glass, enamel-painted decoration

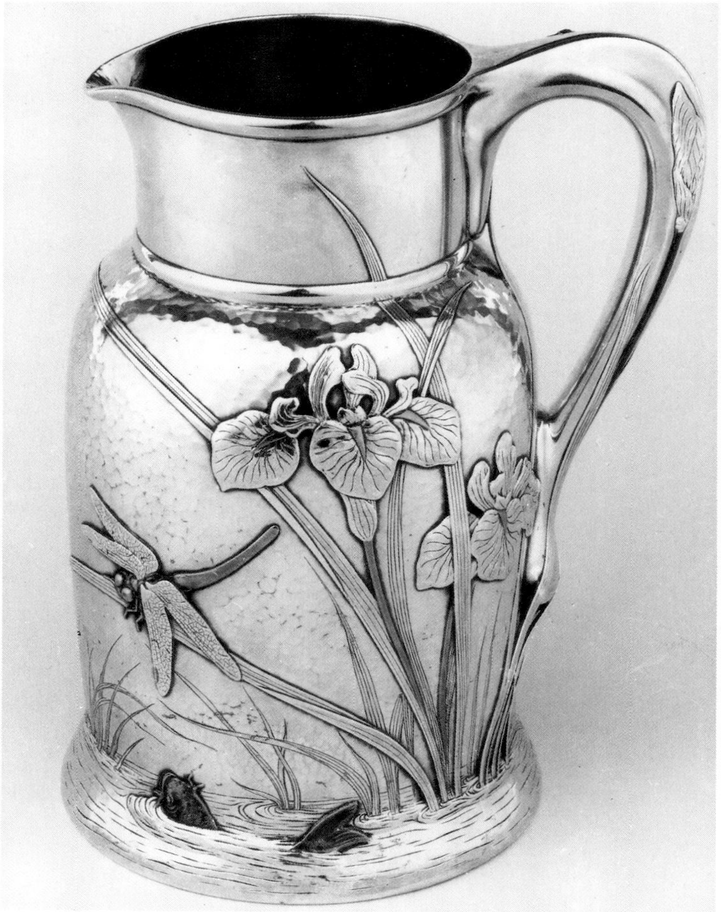

397. Tiffany & Co. under the direction of Edward Chandler Moore. Large jug. c. 1878. Hammered silver

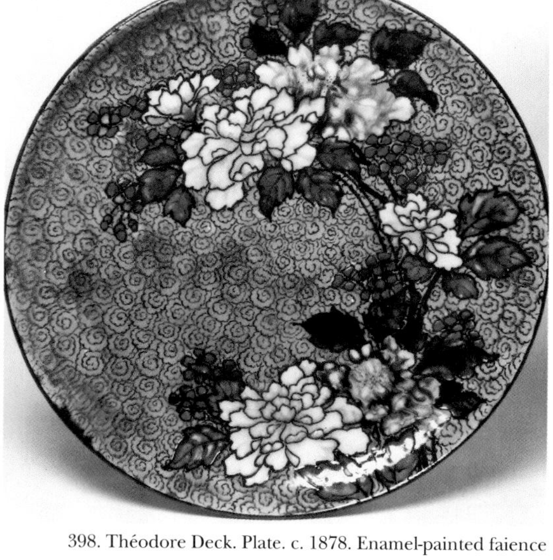

398. Théodore Deck. Plate. c. 1878. Enamel-painted faience

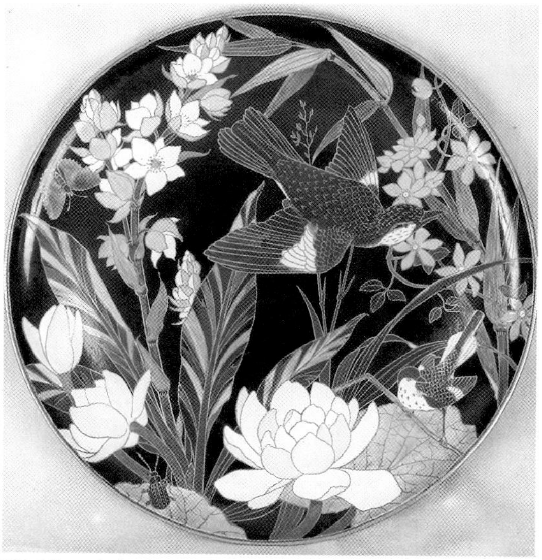

399. Minton's Art Pottery Studio. Plate. 1872. Enamel-painted faience

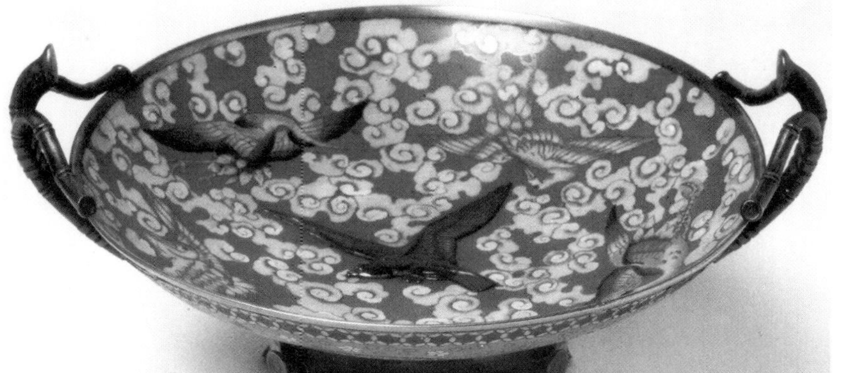

400. Elkington & Co. Ltd. Dish with handles. c. 1870–73. Enameled copper, silvered and anodized bronze

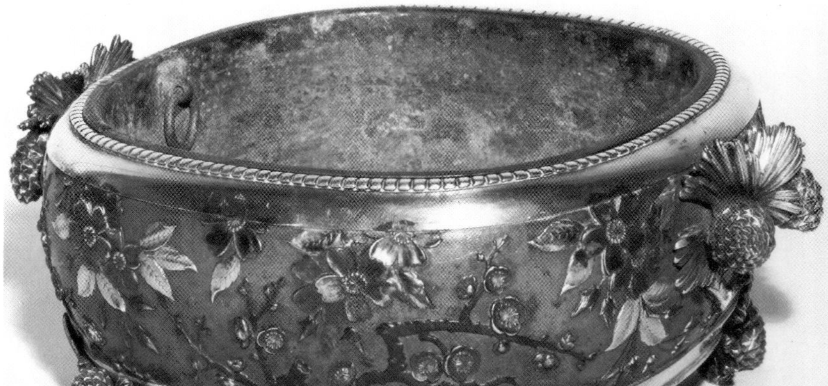

401. Manufacture Christofle under the direction of Émile Reiber. Jardiniere. c. 1878. Copper plate and bronze

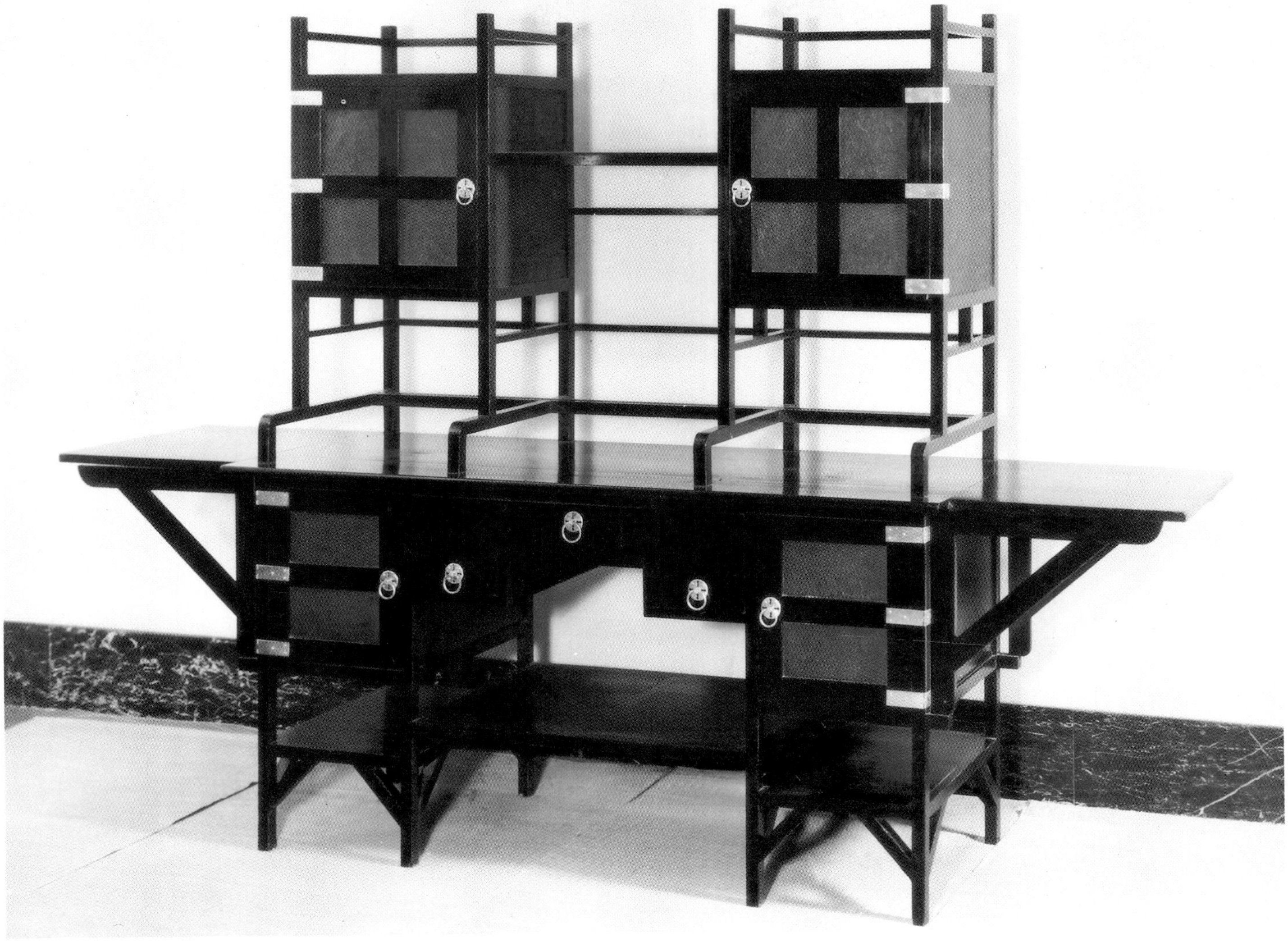

402. Edward William Godwin. Sideboard. c. 1877. Wood, black varnish, silvered metal, and printed paper

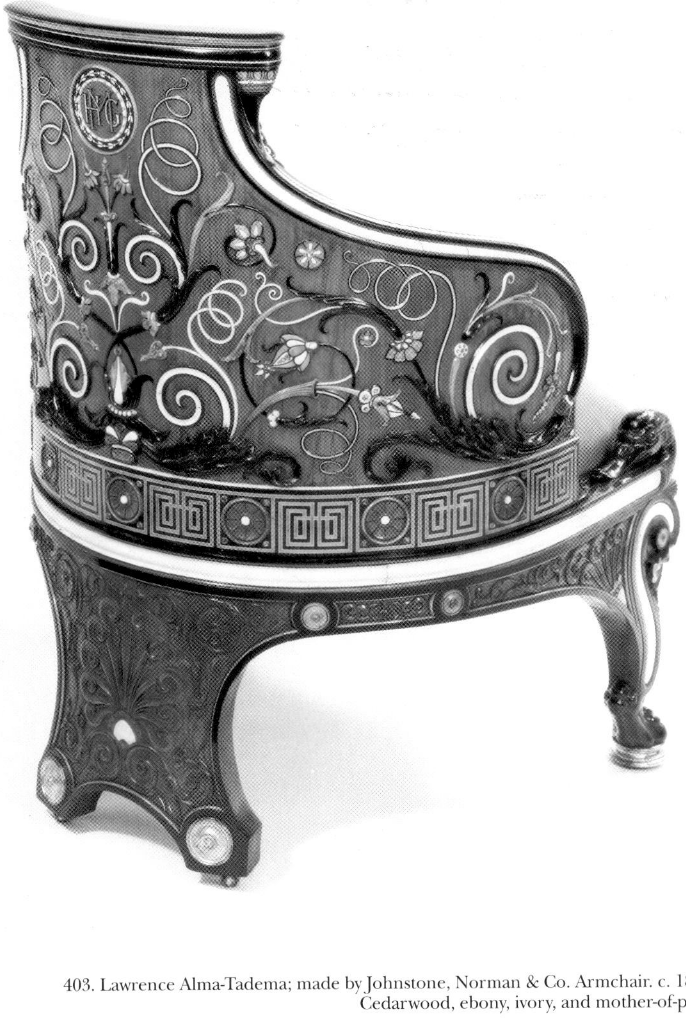

403. Lawrence Alma-Tadema; made by Johnstone, Norman & Co. Armchair. c. 1884. Cedarwood, ebony, ivory, and mother-of-pearl

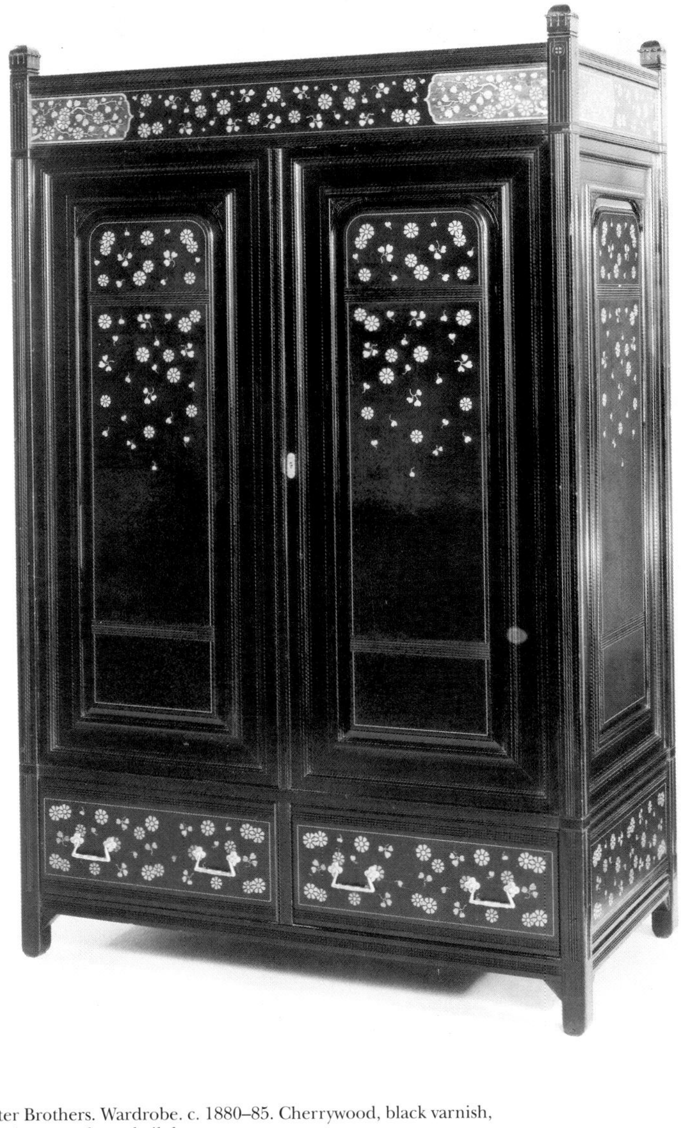

404. Herter Brothers. Wardrobe. c. 1880–85. Cherrywood, black varnish, inlay of various woods, and gilt bronze

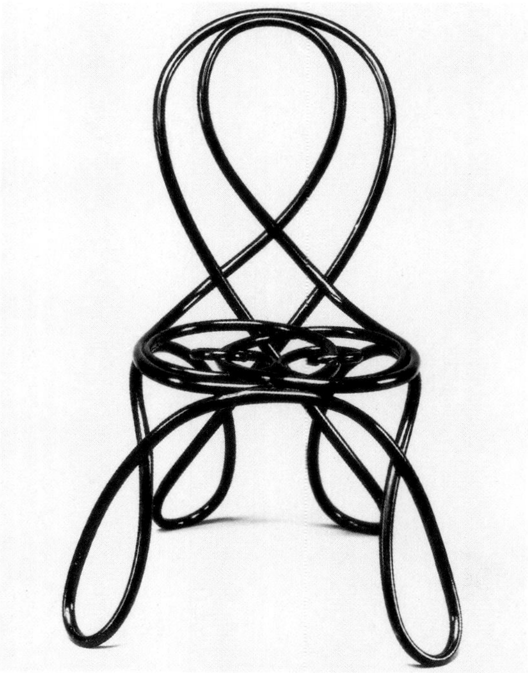

405. Gebrüder Thonet. Chair. 1867.
Bent beechwood

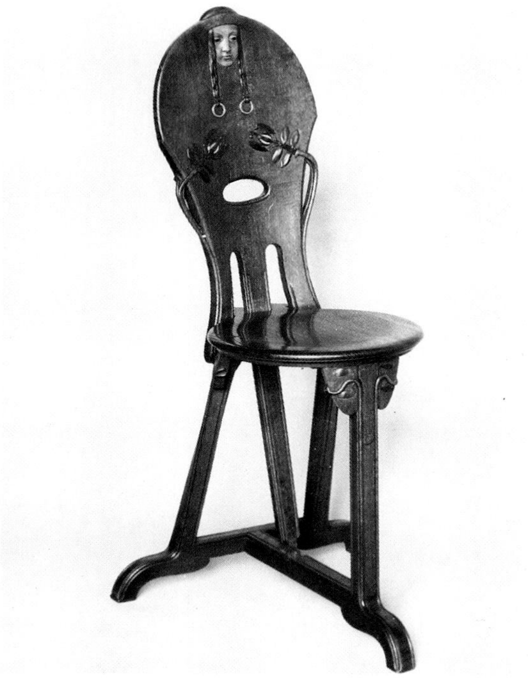

406. Jan Kastner. Chair. c. 1899–1900. Oak, walnut, maple, copper, and mother-of-pearl inlay

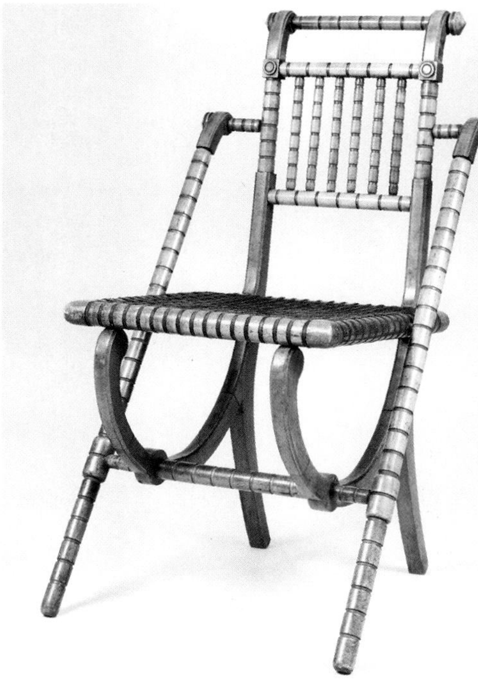

407. Georg Jakob Hunzinger. Chair. c. 1876.
Maple and steel

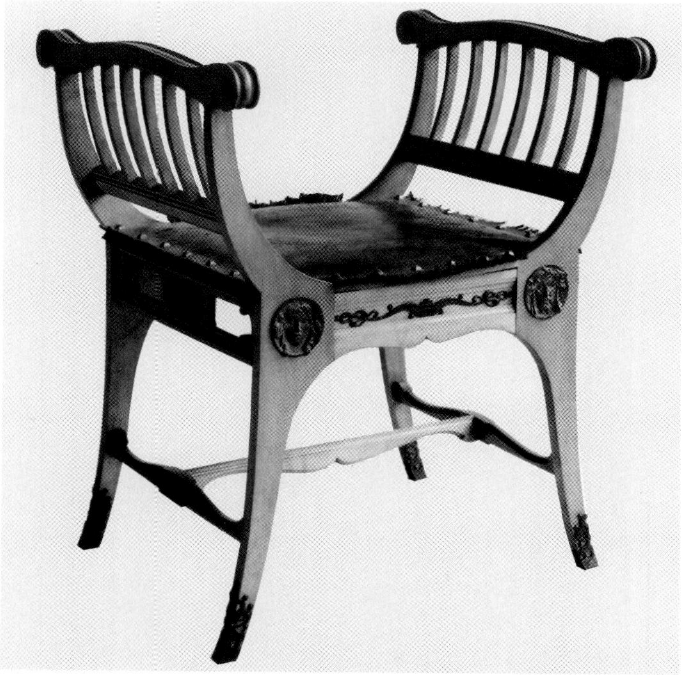

408. Josef Fanta and Jan Navrátíl. Armchair. 1900. Maple, chased and hammered copper, small bronze plaques

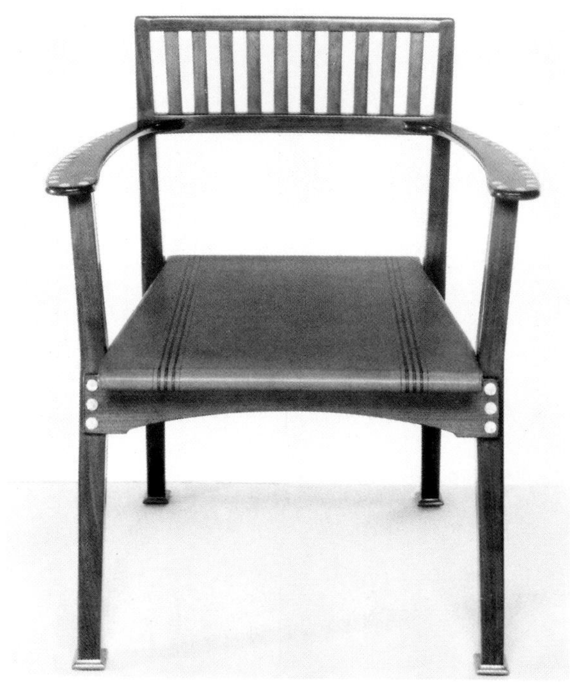

409. Otto Wagner. Armchair. 1900. Walnut, mother-of-pearl inlay, modern leather upholstery

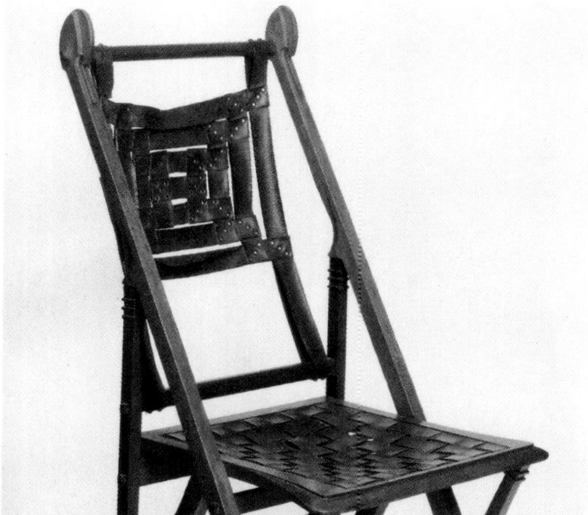

410. Paul Hankar. Chair. 1900.
Oak and leather

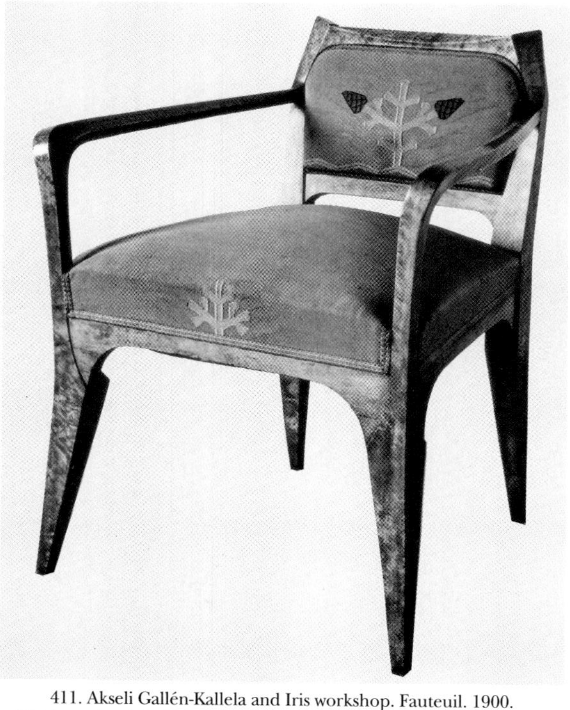

411. Akseli Gallén-Kallela and Iris workshop. Fauteuil. 1900.
Birchwood, original cloth upholstery with applied work embroidery

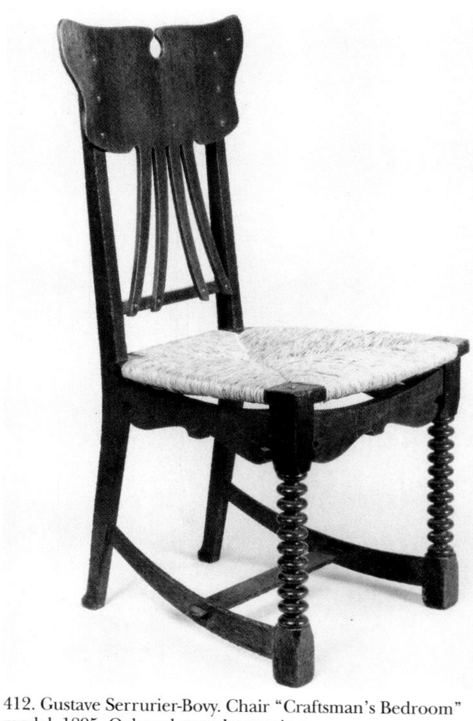

412. Gustave Serrurier-Bovy. Chair "Craftsman's Bedroom" model. 1895. Oak and straw-bottoming

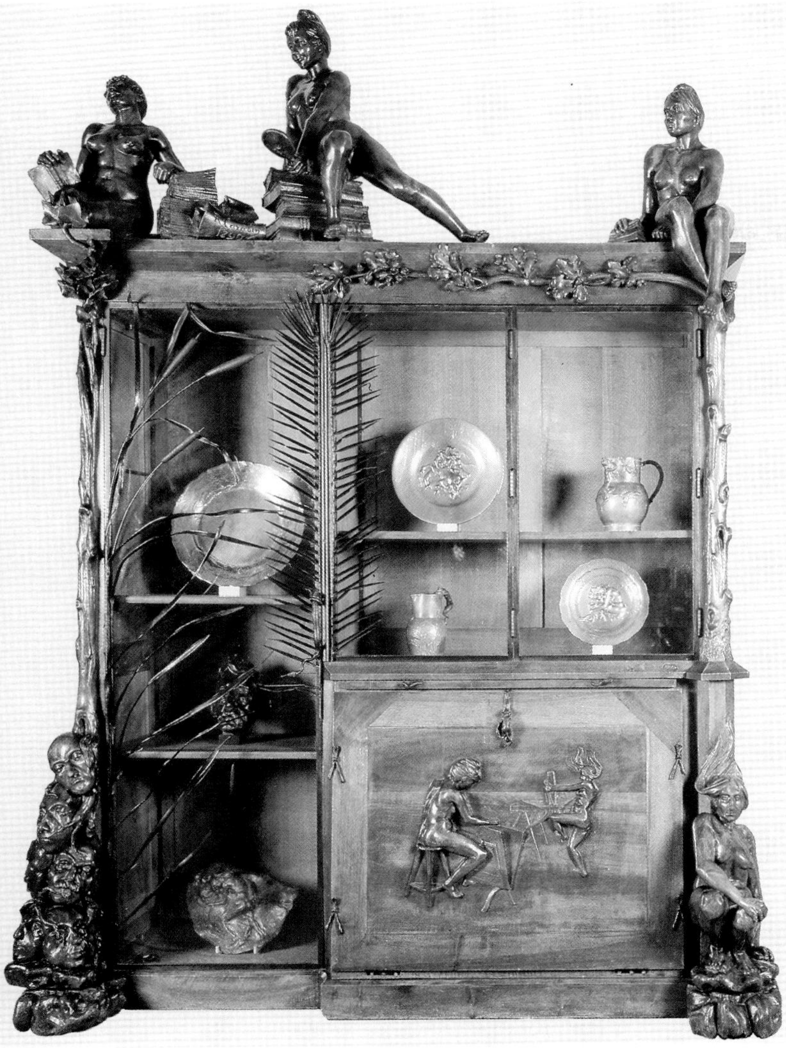

413. François-Rupert Carabin. Bookcase. 1890. Walnut and wrought iron

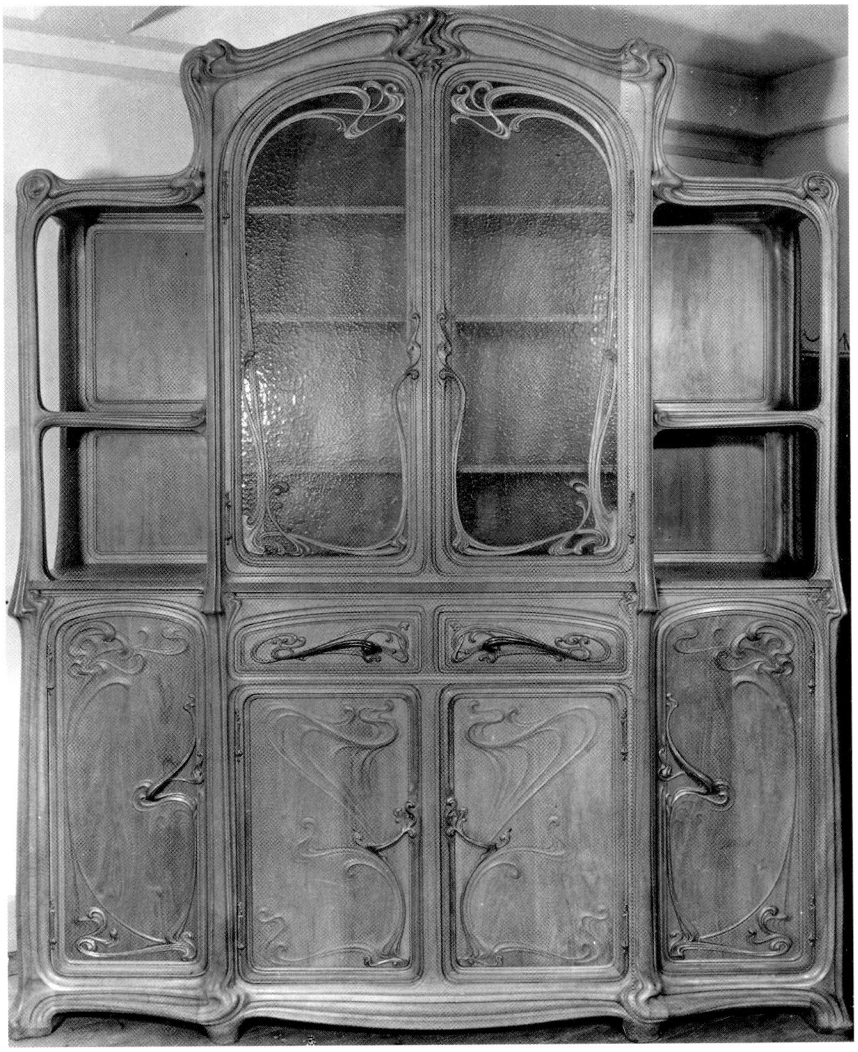

414. Eugène Gaillard. Sideboard. 1900. Walnut and copper

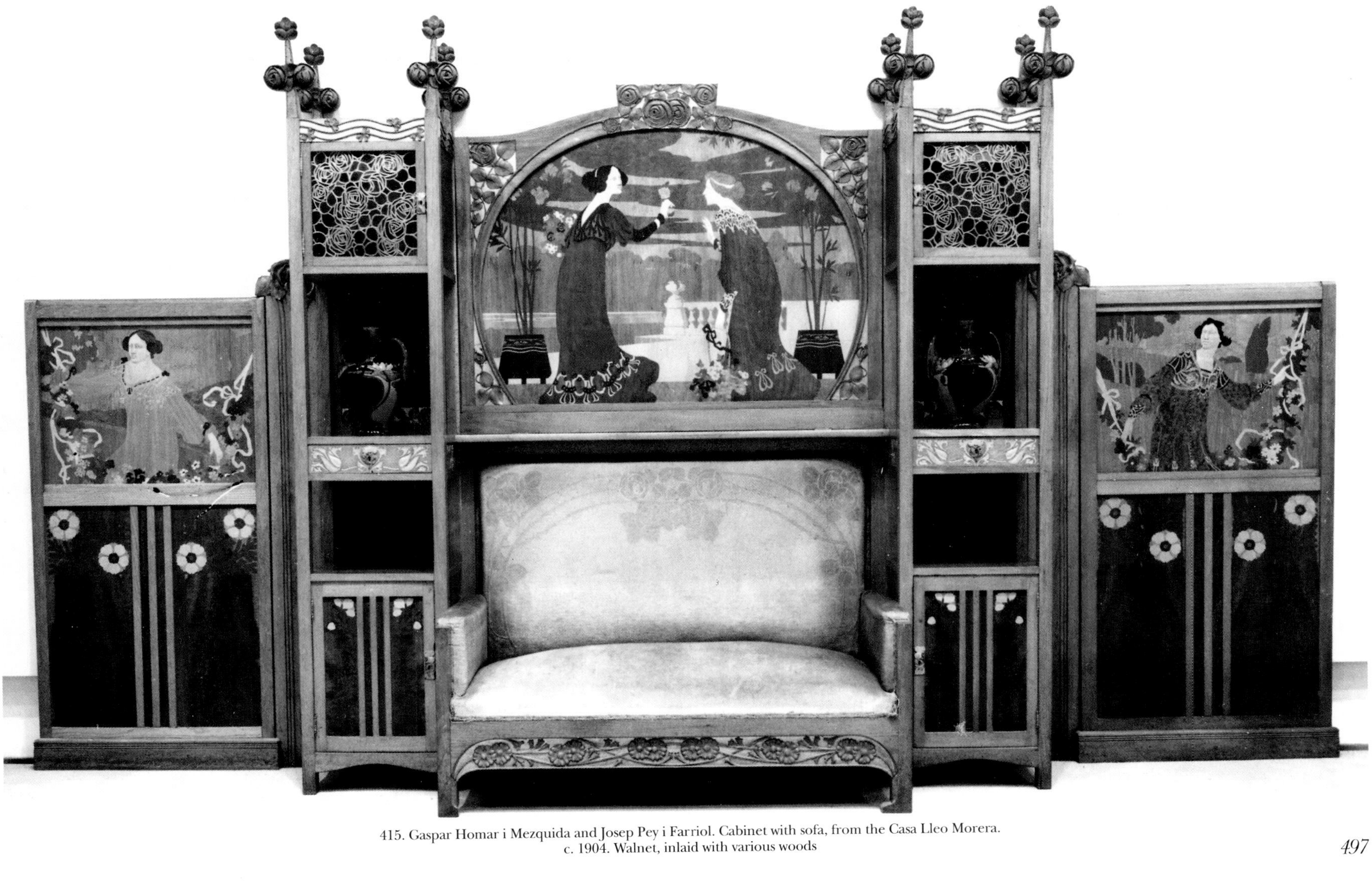

415. Gaspar Homar i Mezquida and Josep Pey i Farriol. Cabinet with sofa, from the Casa Lleo Morera. c. 1904. Walnet, inlaid with various woods

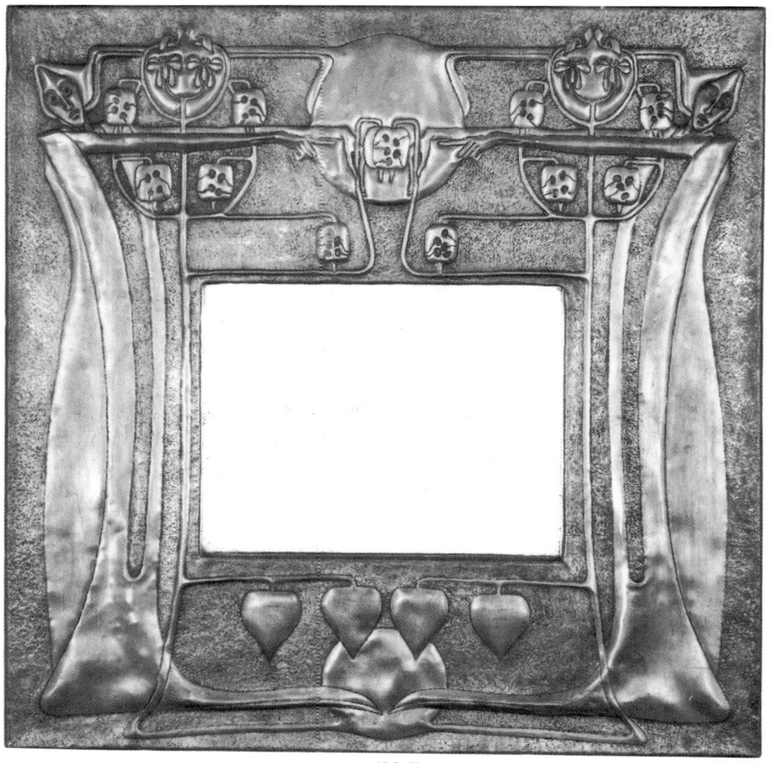

416. Frances Macdonald. "Honesty" mirror frame. c. 1896–97. Repoussé metal

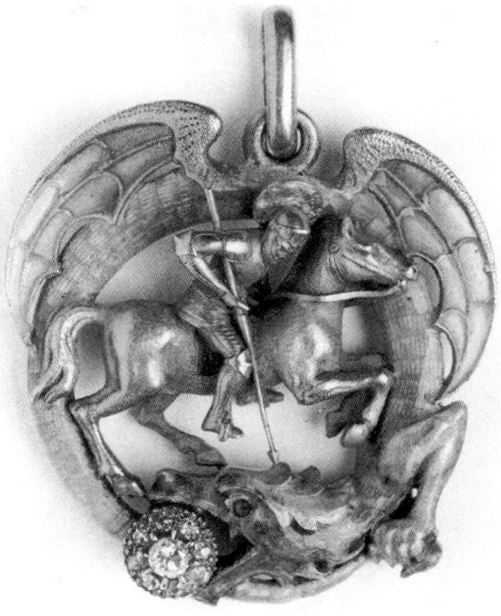

417. Lluis Masriera. "St. George" pendant. c. 1905. Gold, enamel, and diamonds

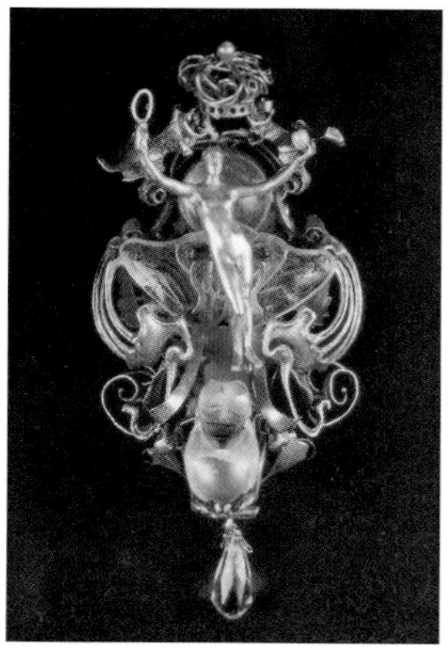

418. Alfred Gilbert. Pendant. 1891–97. Gilt silver, pearls, and crystal

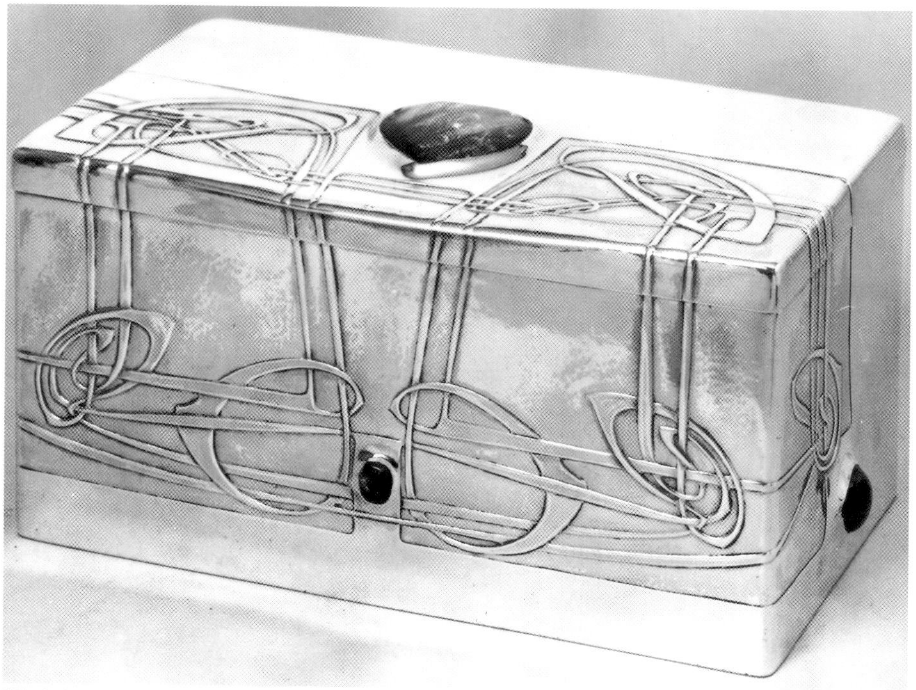

419. Archibald Knox and Liberty. Cigar box. 1903. Silver and opal on wood

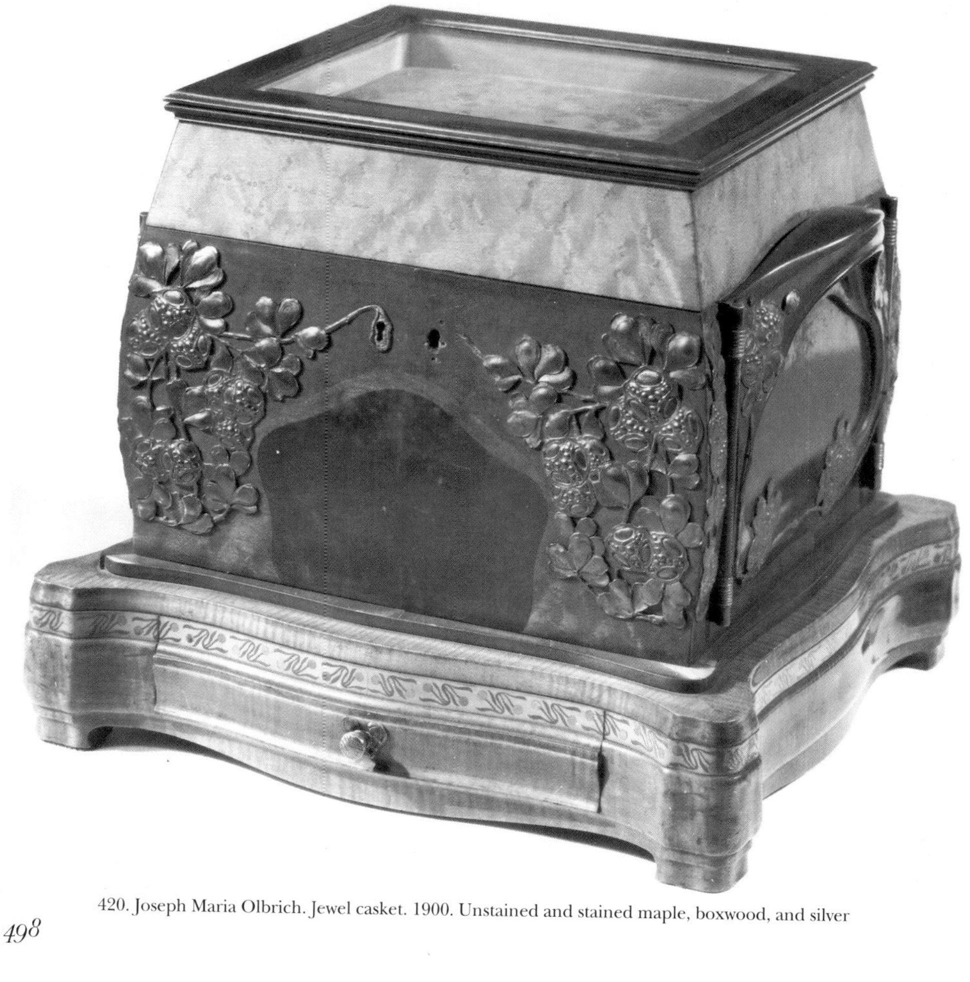

420. Joseph Maria Olbrich. Jewel casket. 1900. Unstained and stained maple, boxwood, and silver

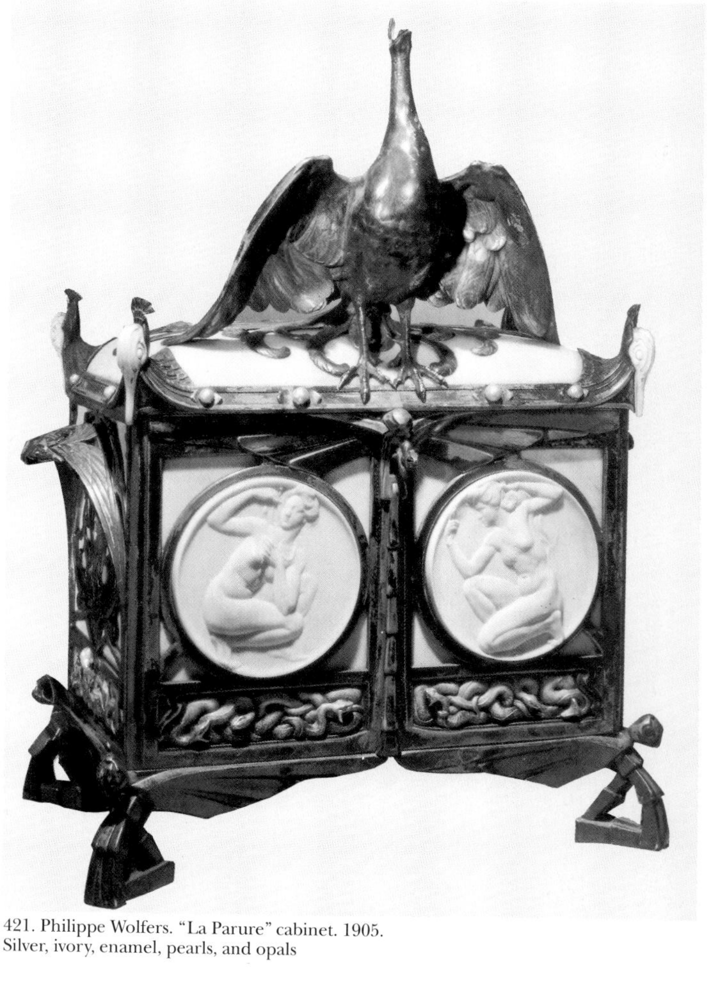

421. Philippe Wolfers. "La Parure" cabinet. 1905. Silver, ivory, enamel, pearls, and opals

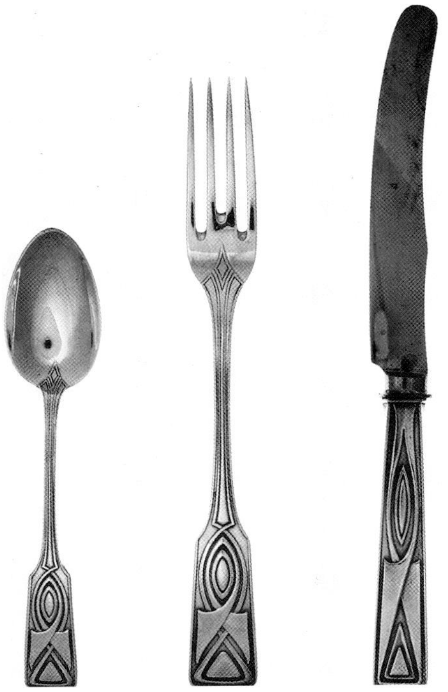

422. Peter Behrens and M. J. Rückert. Three-piece cutlery set. 1901. Chased silver

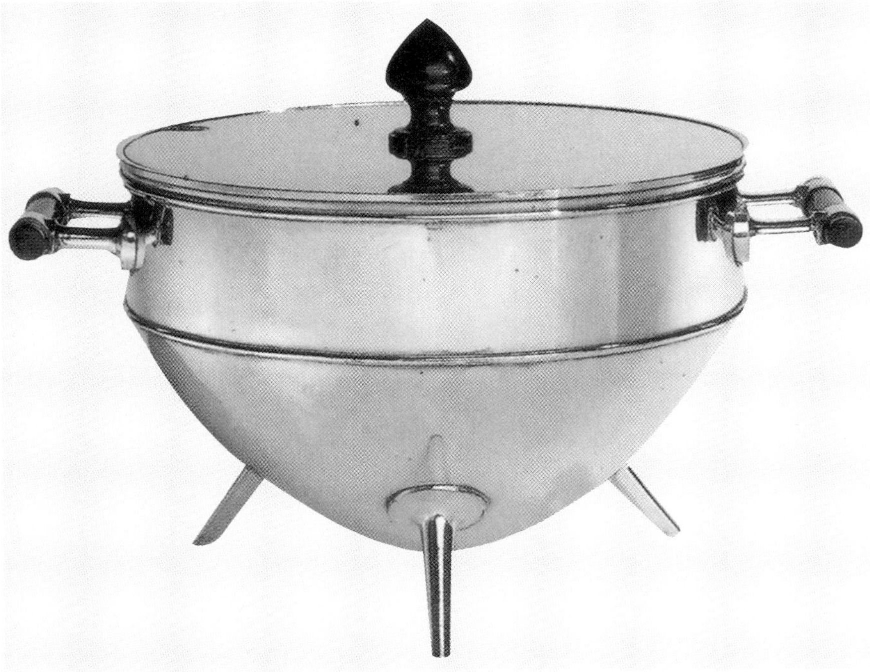

423. Christopher Dresser and J. W. Hukin & J. J. Heath. Soup tureen. Model patented 1880. Silvered metal and ebony

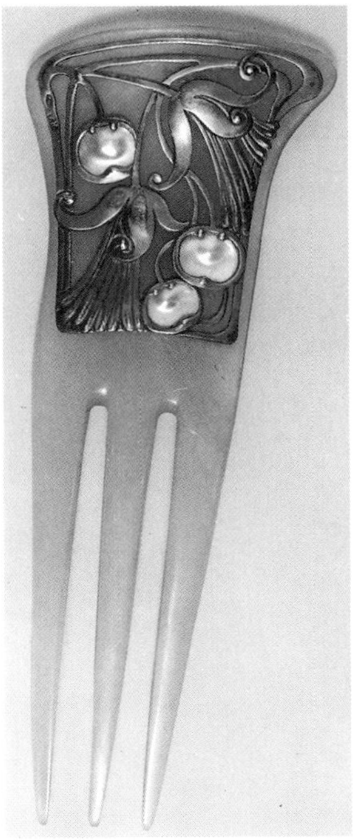

424. Josef Ladislav Némec. Dress comb. c. 1900. Gilt silver, horn, and mother-of-pearl

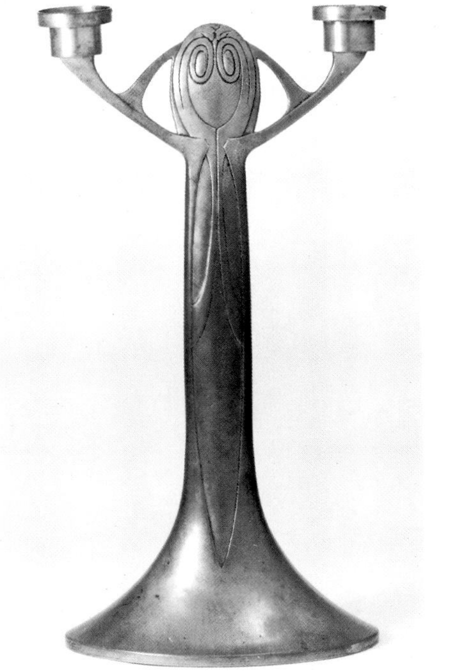

425. Joseph Maria Olbrich and Edward Hulek. Candlestick. c. 1902–3. Pewter

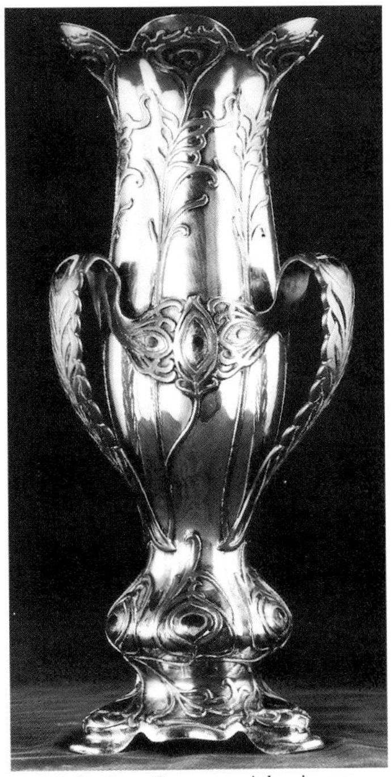

426. Gorham Company. Athenic vase. 1895–1900. Silver, copper, and enamel

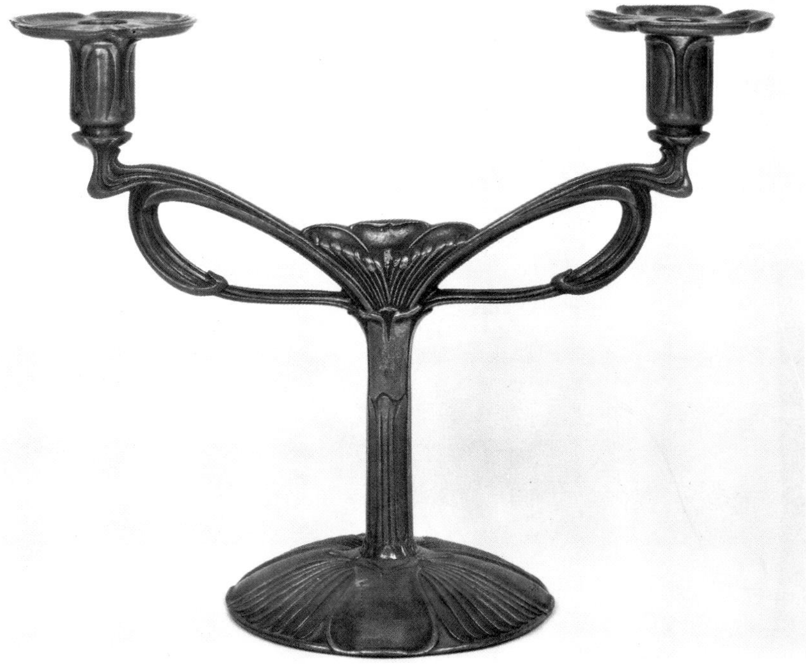

427. Georges de Feure. Candlestick. 1902. Silvered metal

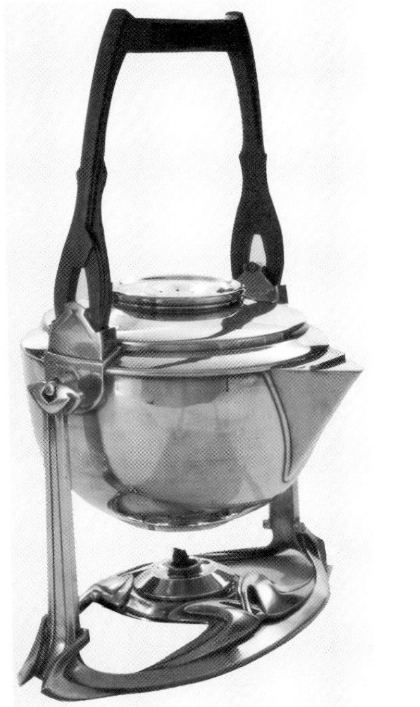

428. Henry van de Velde and Theodor Müller. Samovar. 1902. Silver

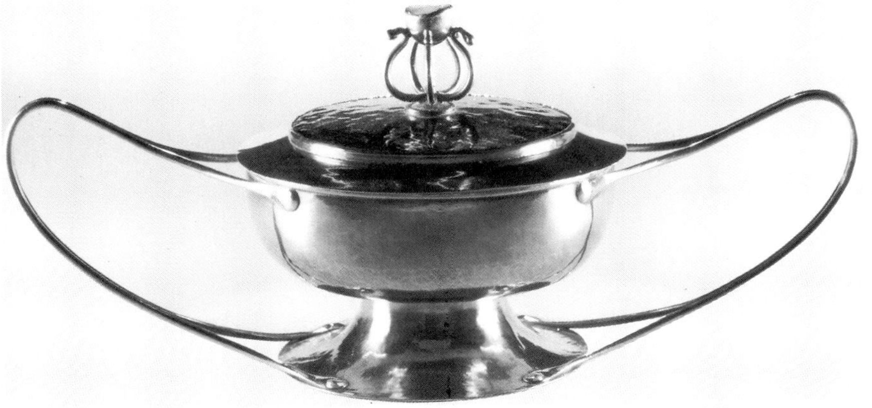

429. Charles Robert Ashbee and the Guild of Handicraft. Bowl with lid. 1902. Chased, repoussé, and enameled silver

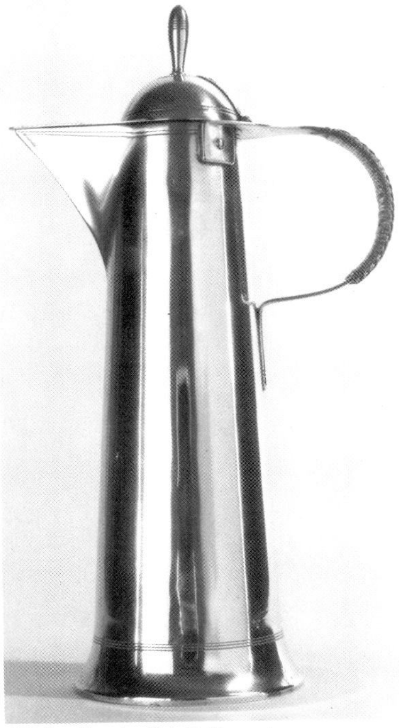

430. Jan Eisenloeffel. Coffee pot. c. 1902. Copper

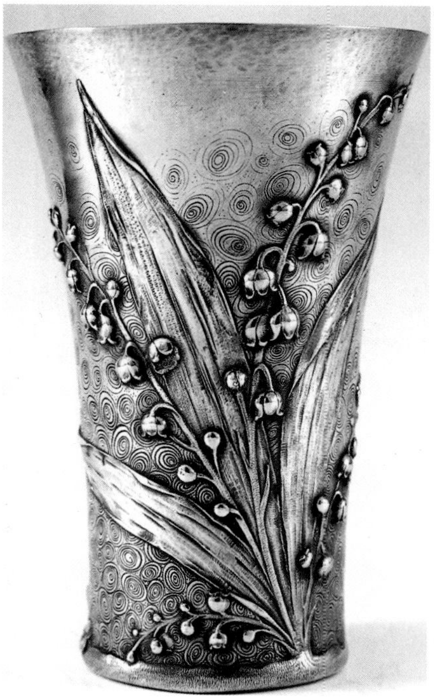
431. Frans Zwollo. Goblet. 1898. Chased, repoussé, and hammered silver

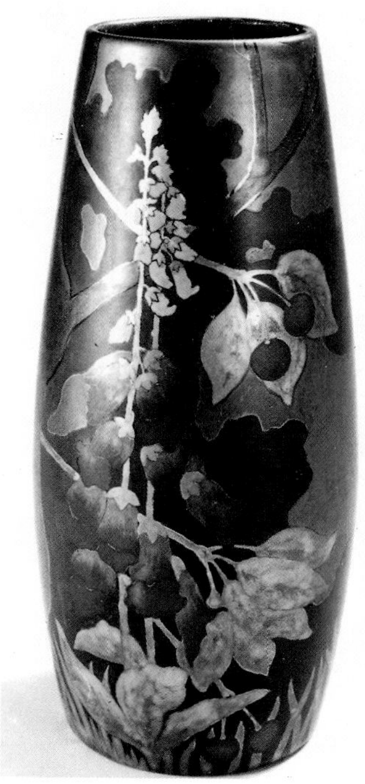
432. Zsolnay Manufacture. Vase. 1899. Lusterware

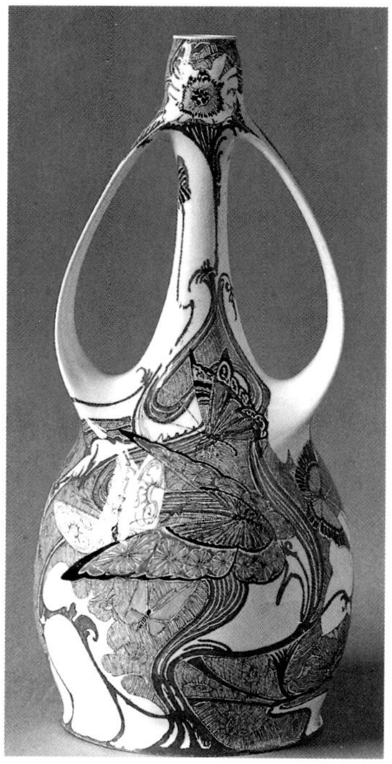
433. Rozenburg Manufacture. Vase. 1900. Porcelain, underglazed *petit feu* decoration

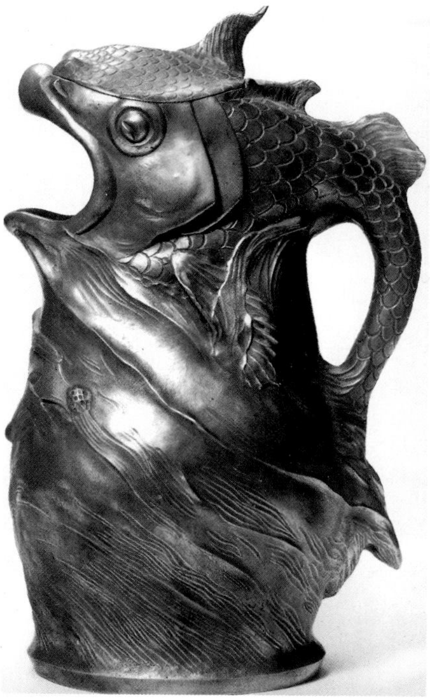
434. Alf Wallander and Schreuder & Olsson. Wine jug. 1899. Chased and repoussé pewter

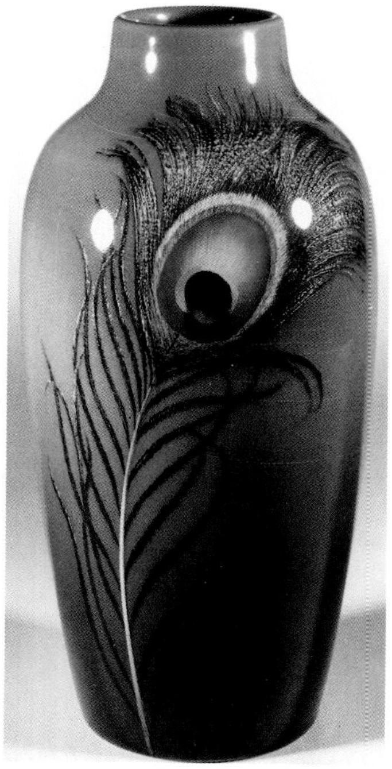
435. Rockwood Pottery. Vase. 1904. Faience with underglaze decoration

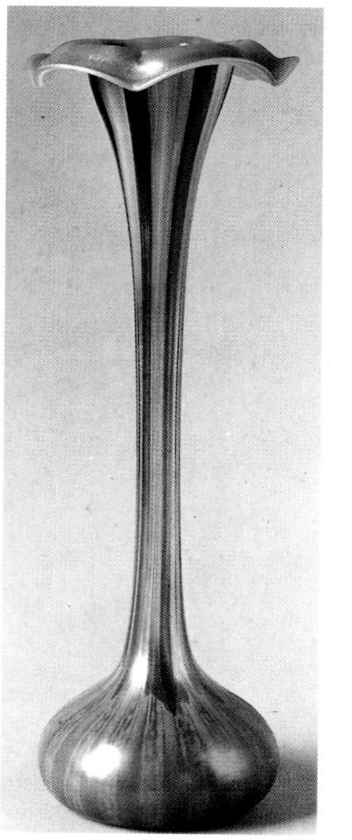
436. Louis Comfort Tiffany. Vase. 1900. Favrile glass

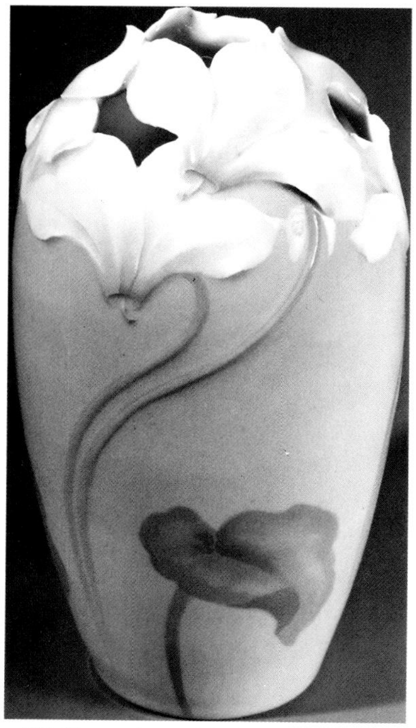
437. Rörstrand porcelain factory. Vase. 1897. Porcelain with underglazed *grand feu* decoration

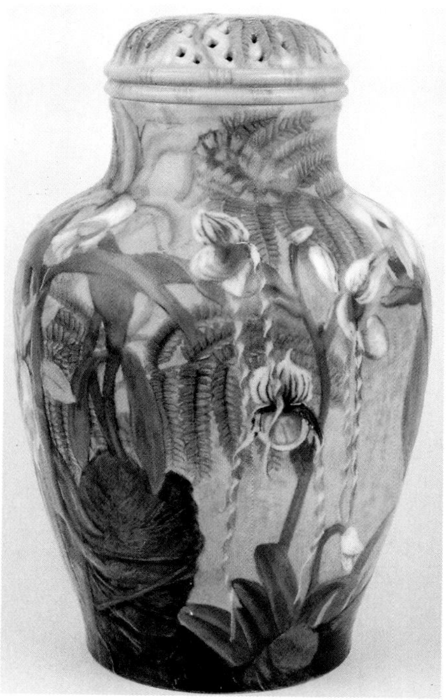
438. Bing and Grøndhal factory. Potpourri vase. c. 1898. Porcelain with underglazed *grand feu* decoration

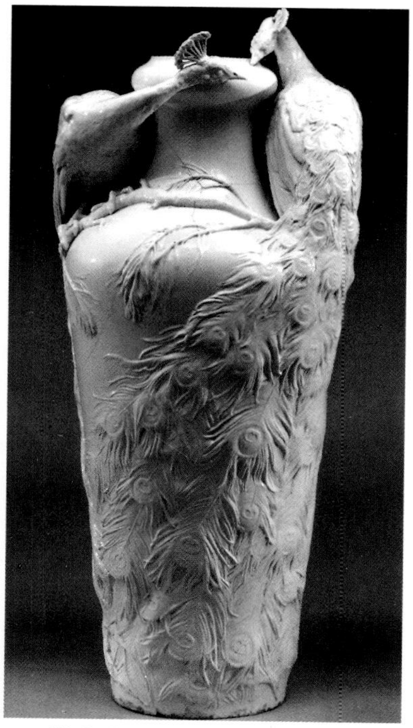
439. Società Ceramica Richard-Ginori. Vase. 1902. Hard-paste porcelain

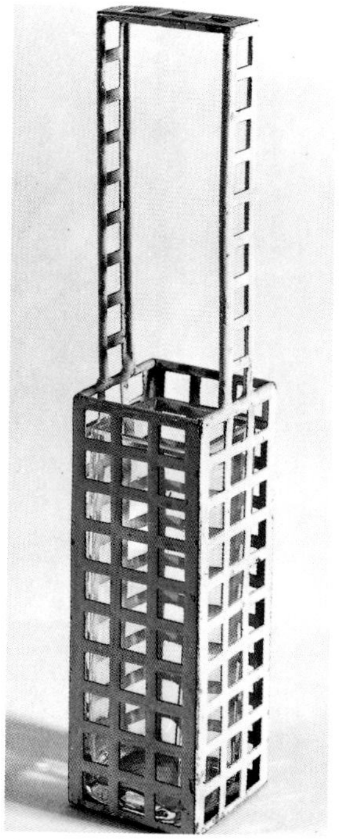
440. Josef Hoffmann and Wiener Werkstätte. Vase with handle. c. 1905. Perforated iron sheet, painted white

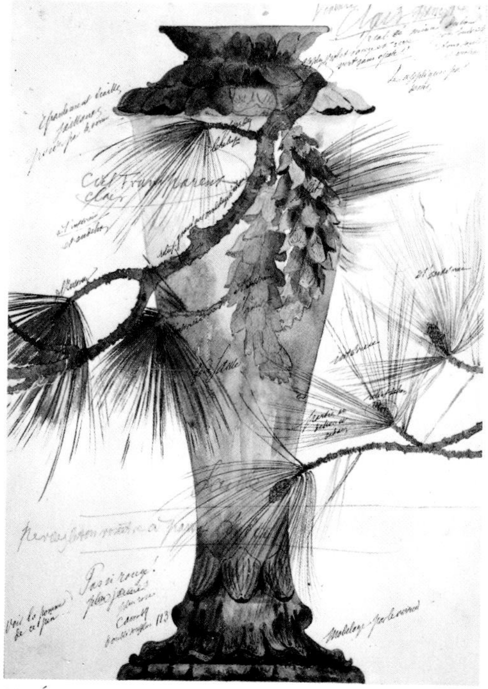
441. Émile Gallé. Model for crystal-glass vase decorated with pine branches. 1903. Watercolor and ink on paper

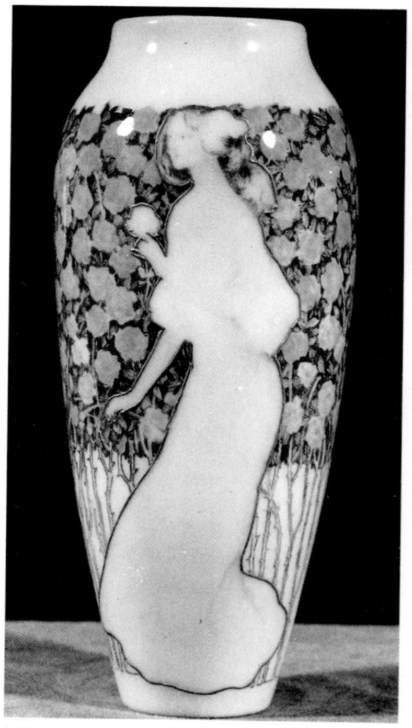
442. Josep Pey i Farriol and Antoni Serra. Vase. c. 1907. Porcelain with *grand feu* decoration

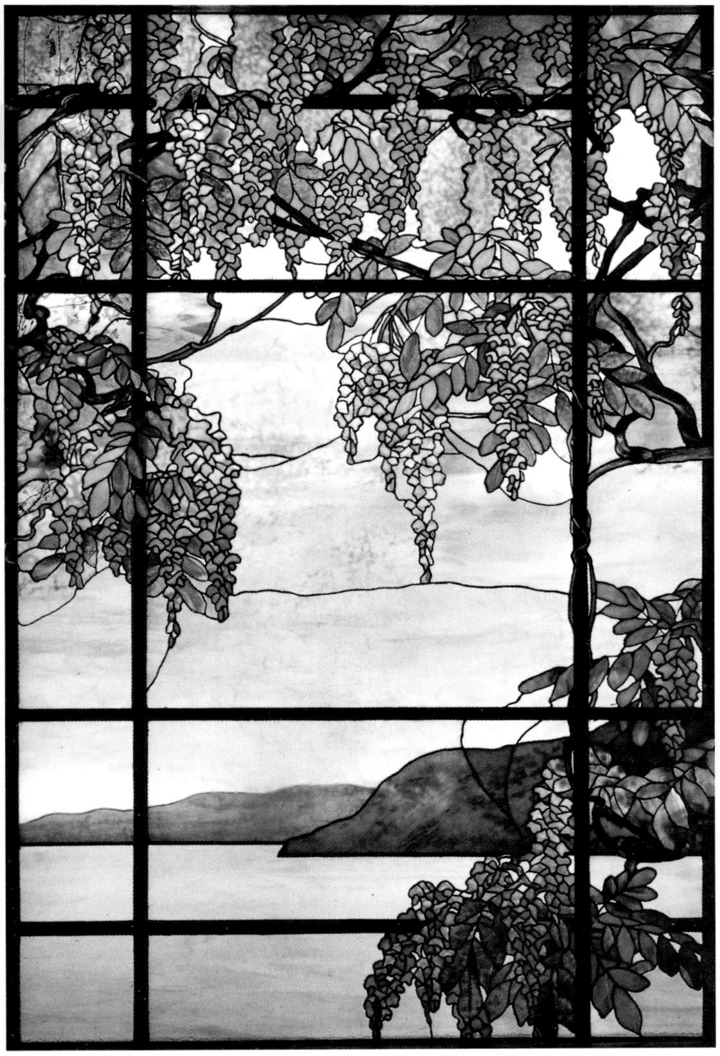

443. Louis Comfort Tiffany. View of Oyster Bay. c. 1905. Stained glass from the William Skinner Residence, New York

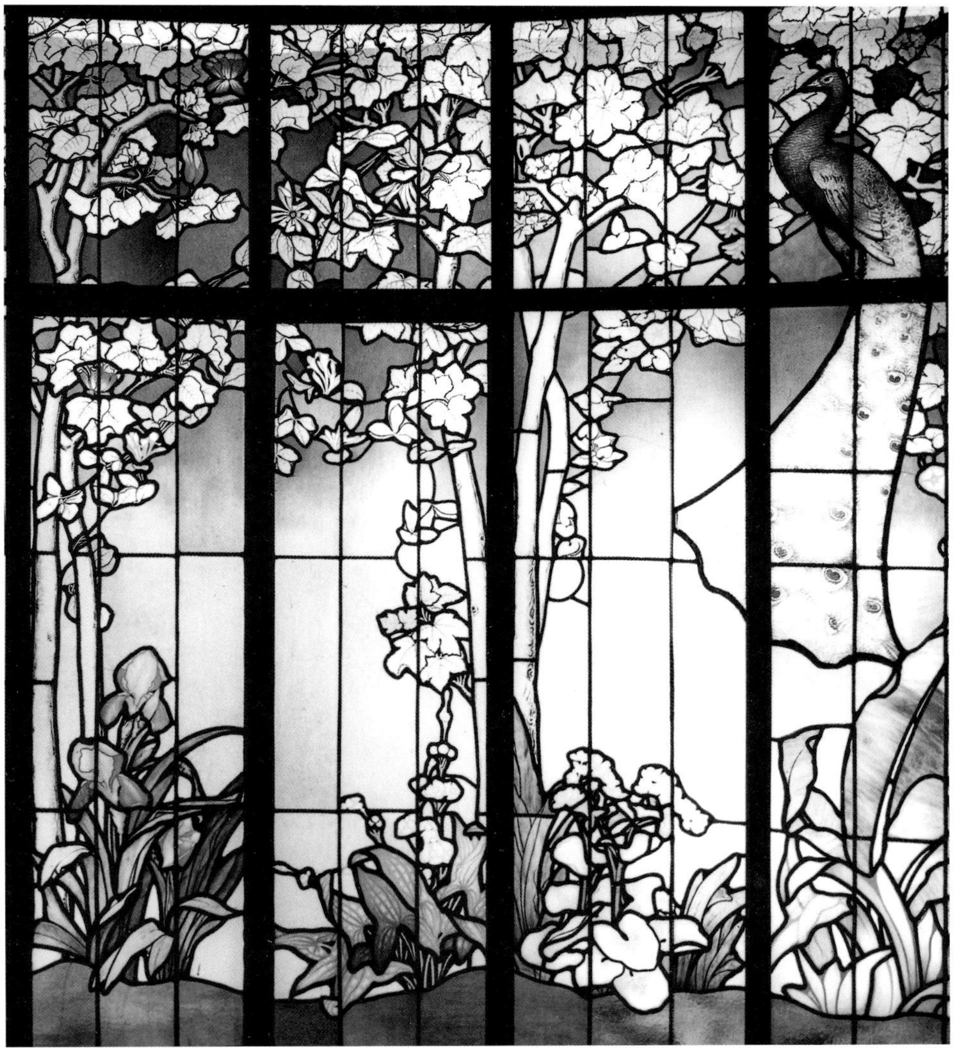

444. Jacques Gruber. Veranda. c. 1909–10. Detail originally from 4 Rue du Général-Drouot, Nancy

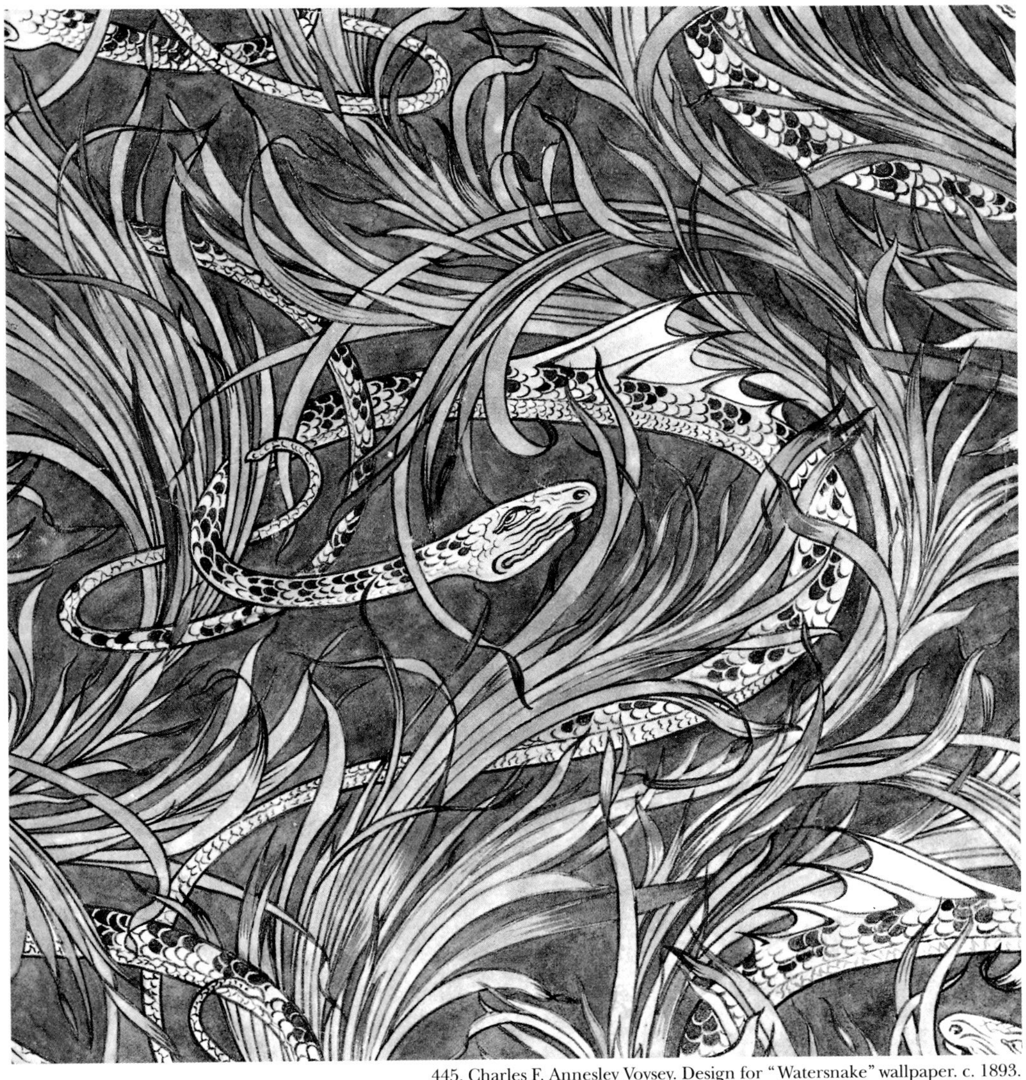

445. Charles F. Annesley Voysey. Design for "Watersnake" wallpaper. c. 1893. Watercolor on paper

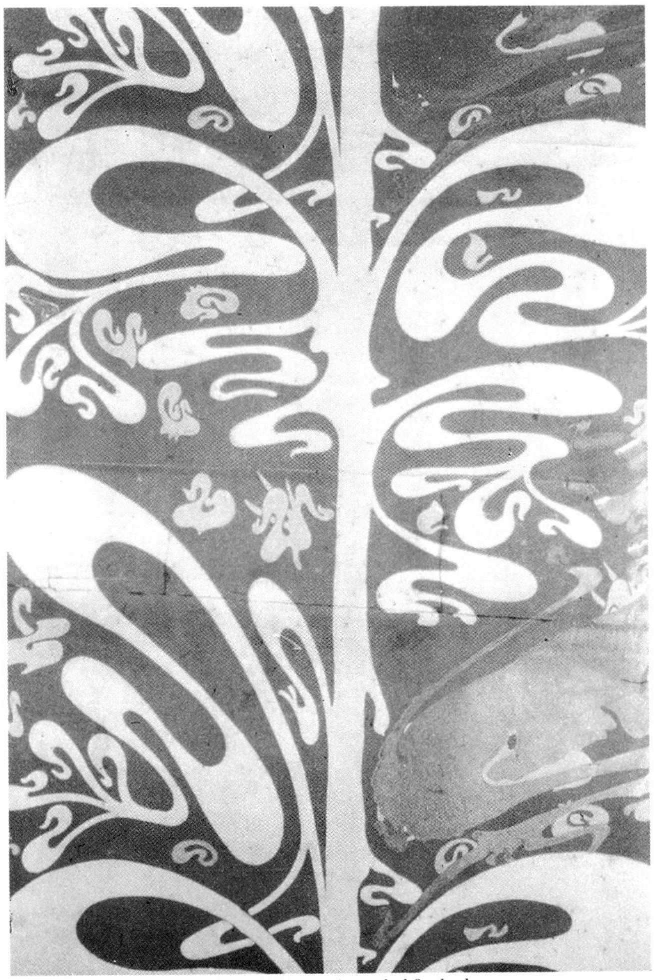

446. Guimard and Le Mardelé. Wallpaper intended for bedrooms in the Castel Béranger. c. 1896–97

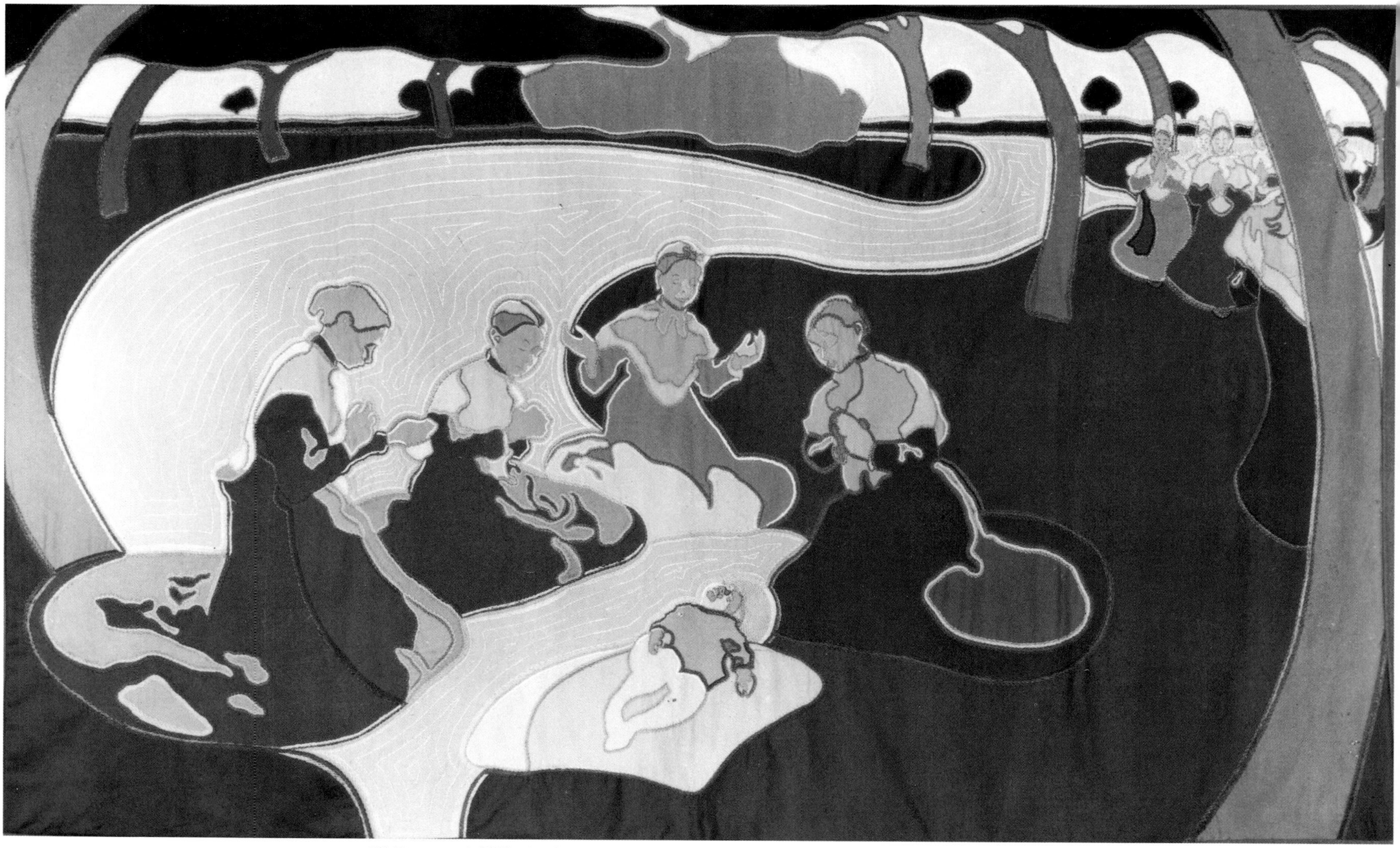

447. Henry van de Velde. *Angels Keep Watch.* 1893. Wall hanging, wool applied work on linen canvas ground

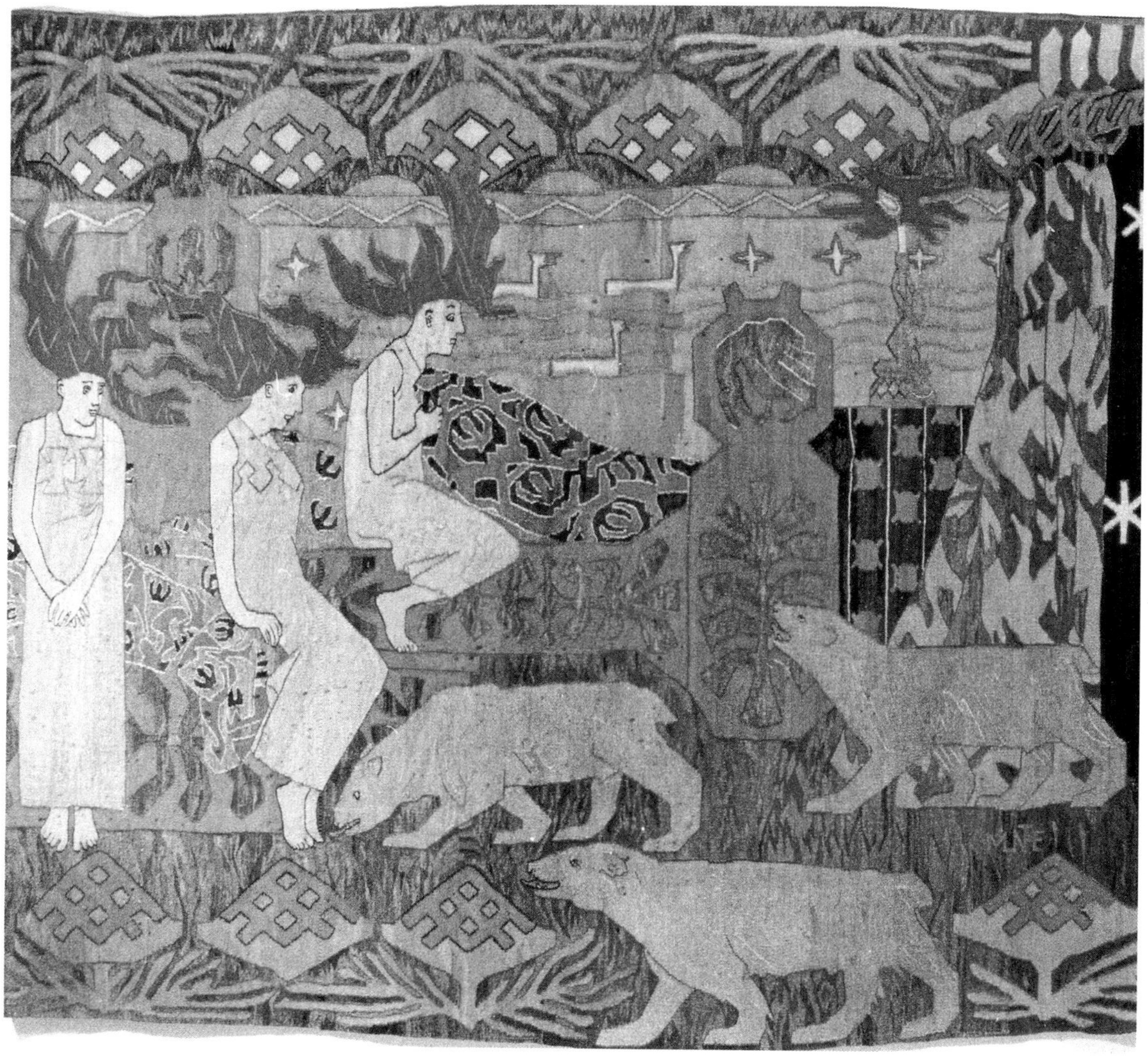

448. Gerhard Munthe and Augusta Christensen. *The Three Suitors.* 1897. Tapestry, wool, and linen

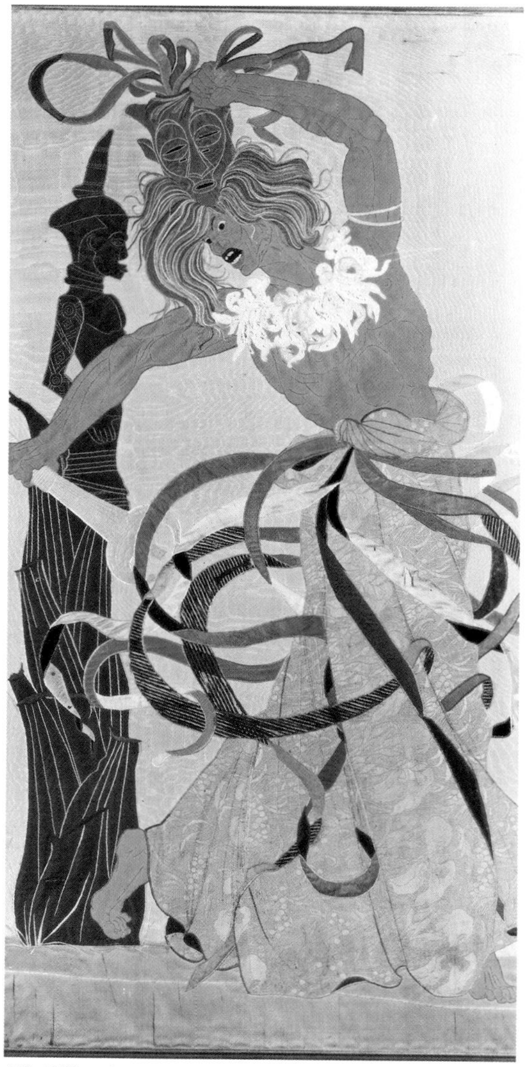

449. Hélène de Rudder. *Fetishism.* 1897. Tapestry, embroidery, and silks

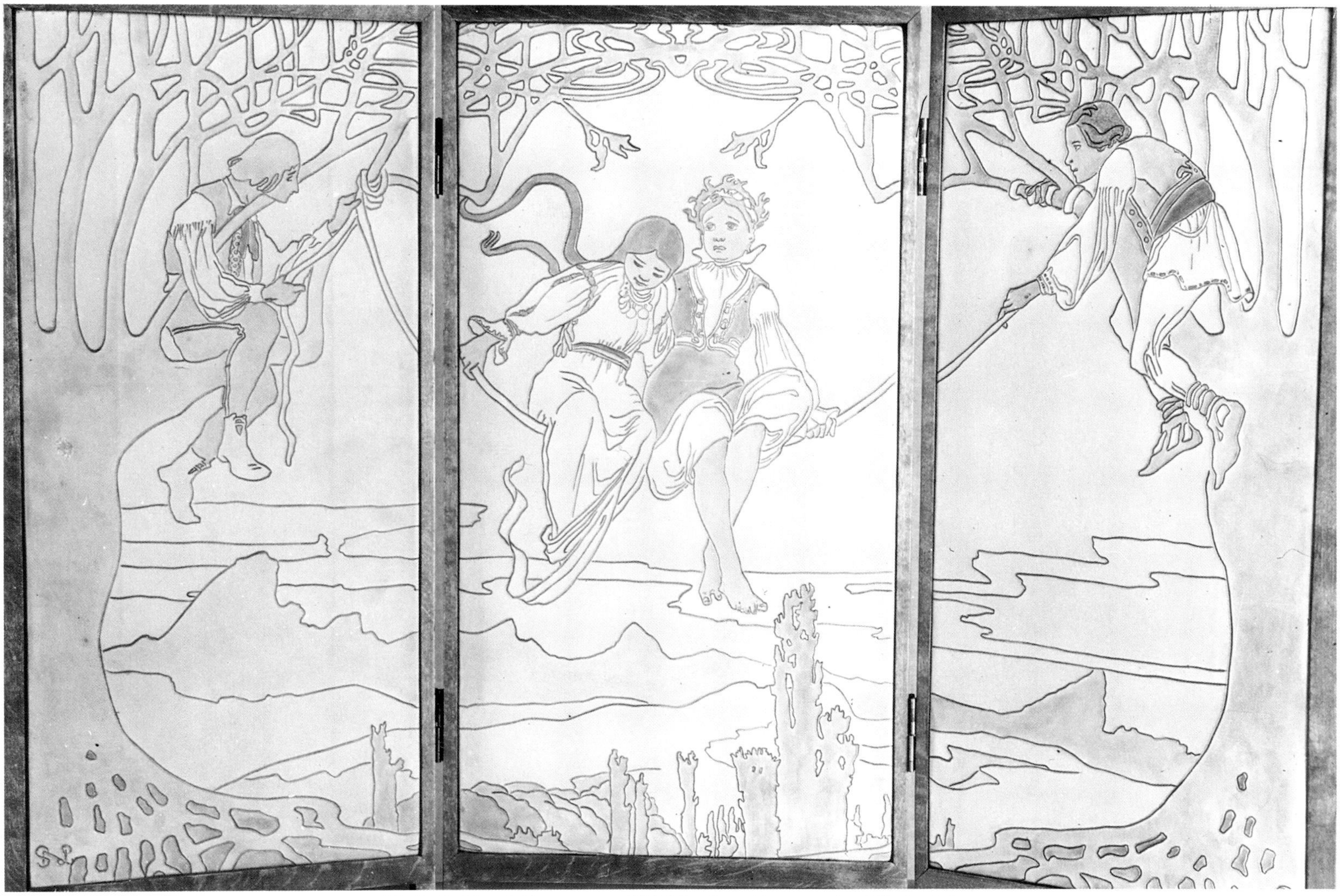

450. Sándor Nagy. Folding screen. c. 1904. Painted goatskin, repoussé and blind-tooled

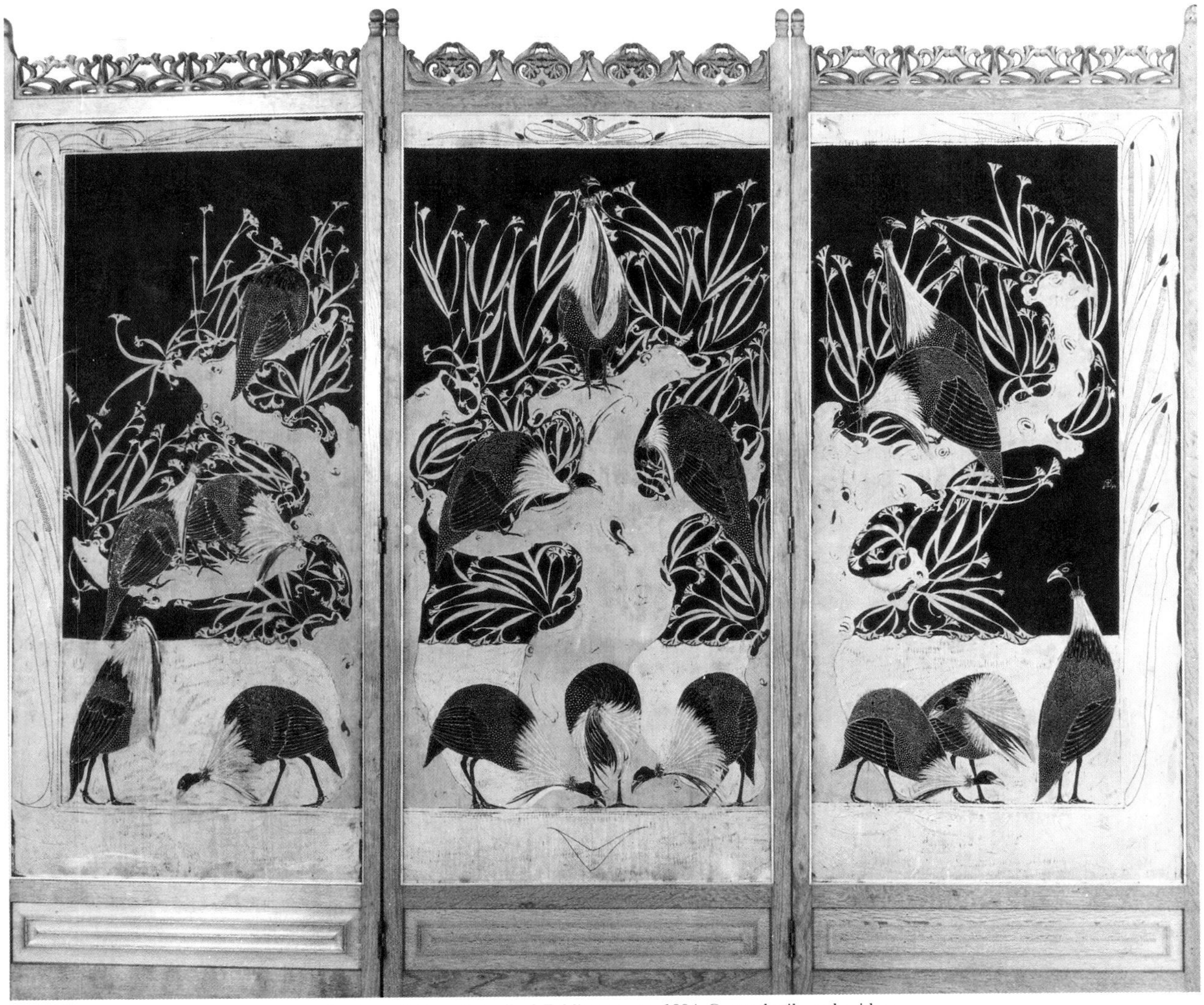

451. Gerrit Willem Dijsselhof. Folding screen. 1894. Cotton batik, embroidery

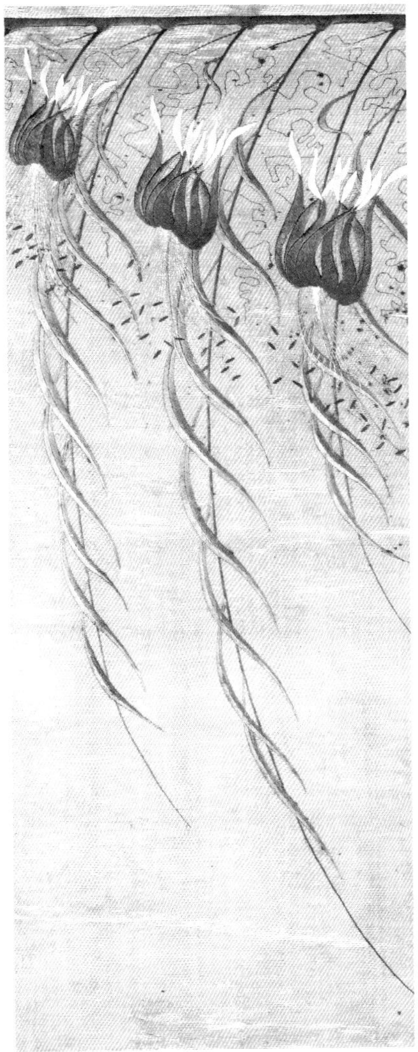

452. Obrist, Ruchet. Orange lilies. 1897. Tapestry

SCULPTURE

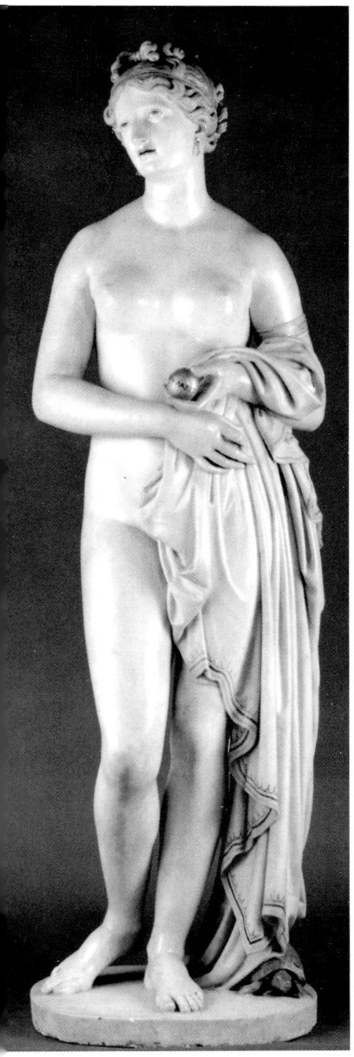

453. John Gibson. *Venus.* 1851–56. Stained marble

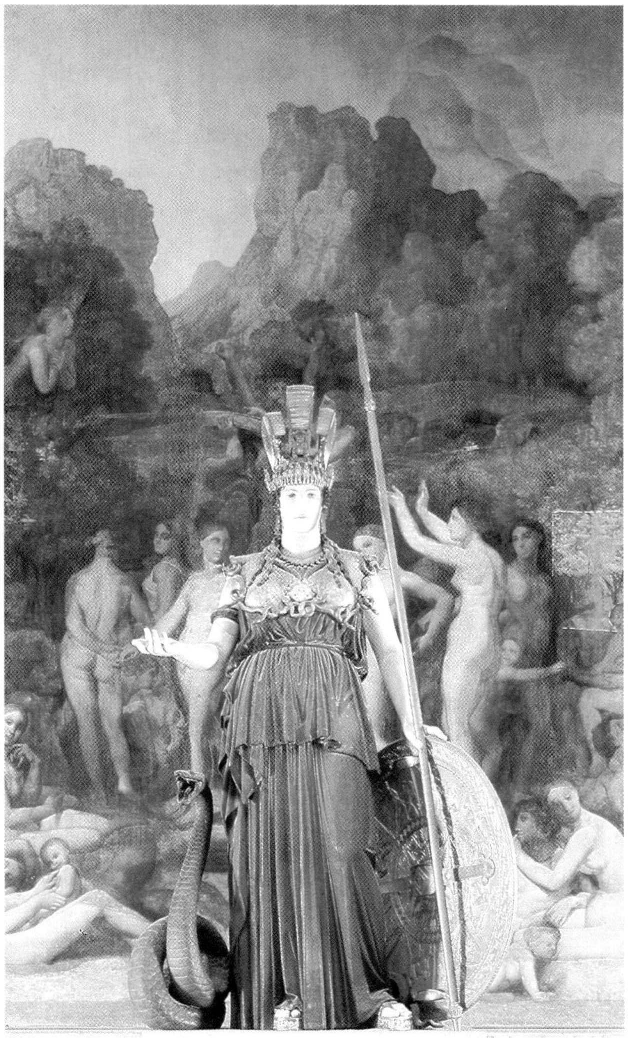

454. Pierre-Charles Simart. *Minerva.* 1855. Chryselephantine

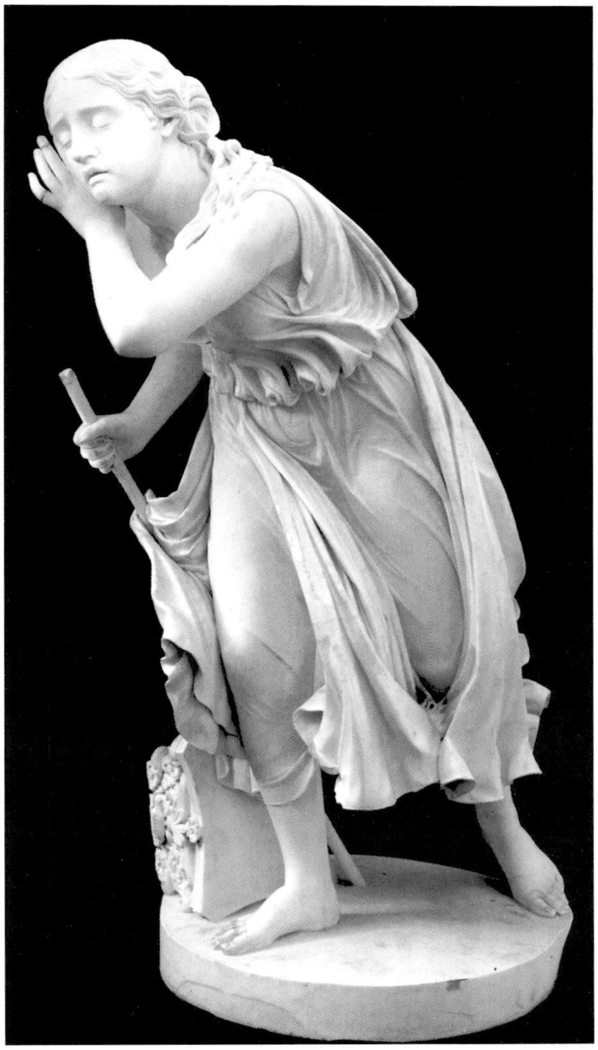

455. Randolph Rogers. *Nydia.* 1856. Marble

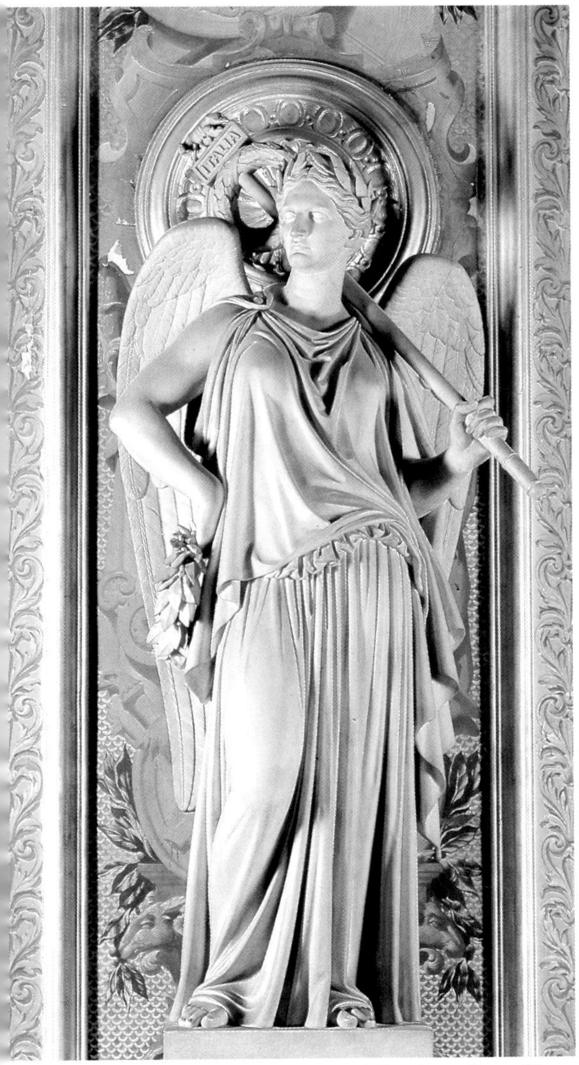

456. Francisque Duret. *Victory.* 1857. Marble

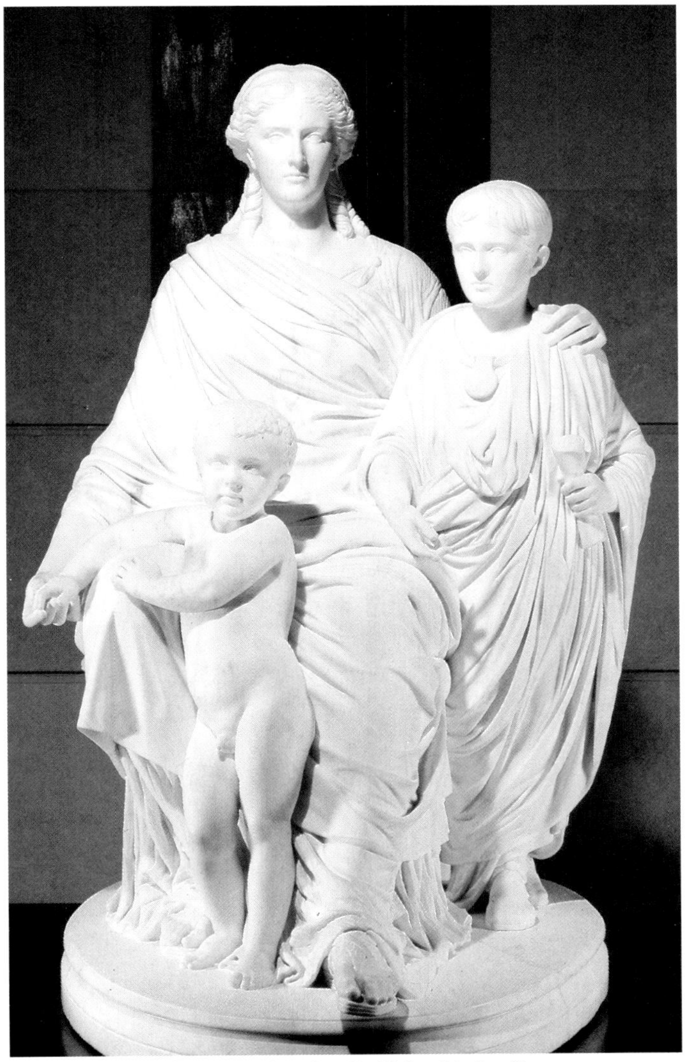

457. Jules Cavelier. *Cornelia, Mother of the Gracchi.* 1861. Marble

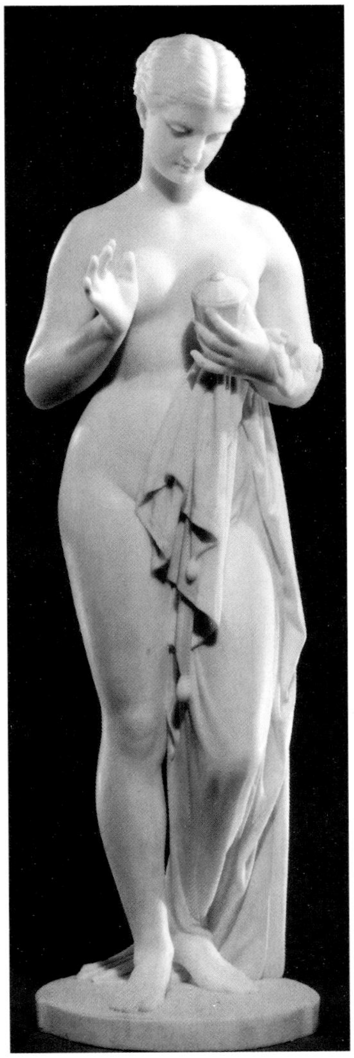

458. Chauncey Ives. *Pandora.* 1863. Marble

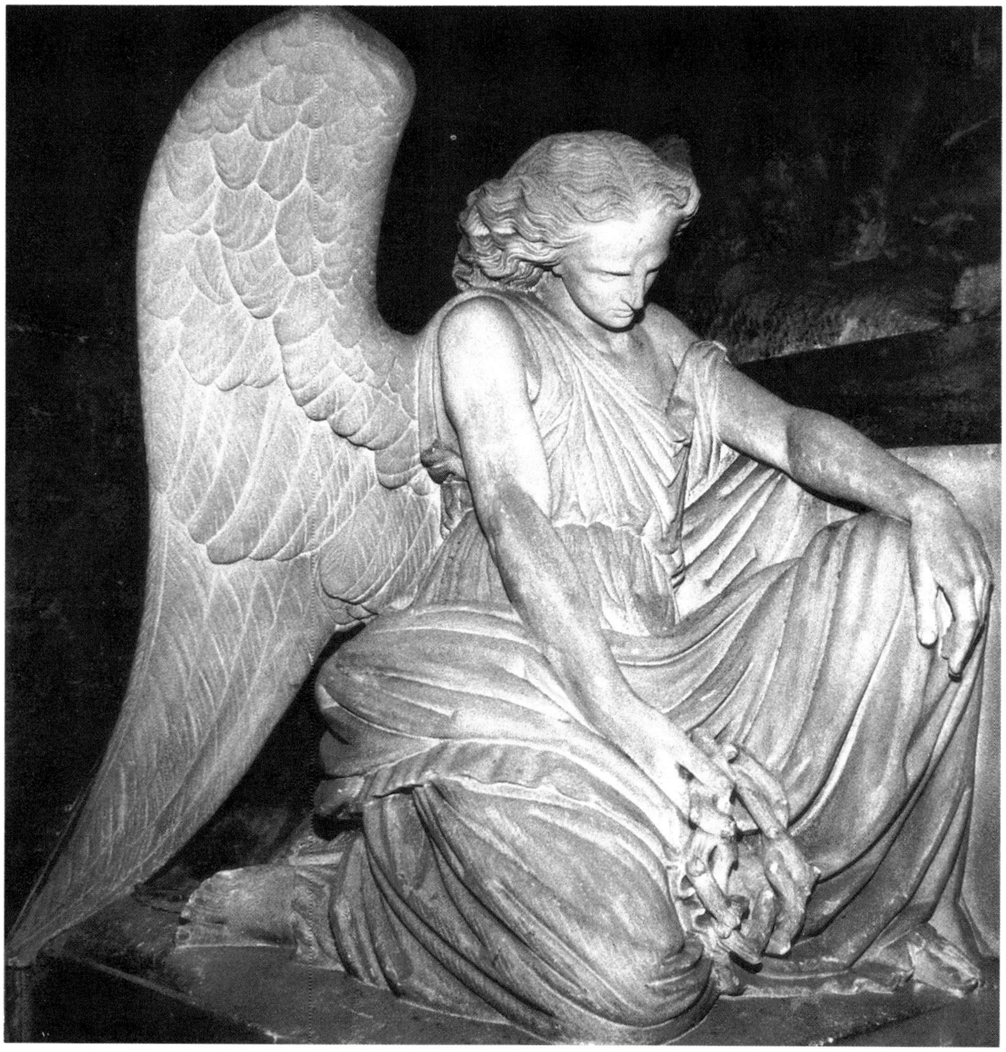

459. Auguste Clésinger. *Angel of Grief.* 1850. Stone

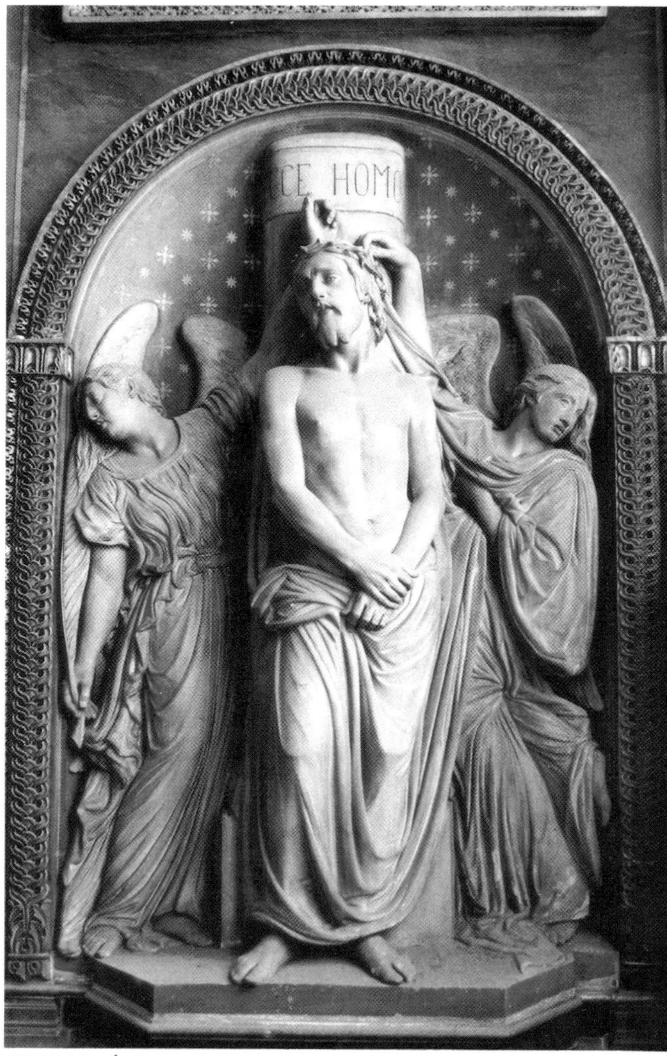

460. Antoine Étex. *Ecce Homo.* 1856. Marble

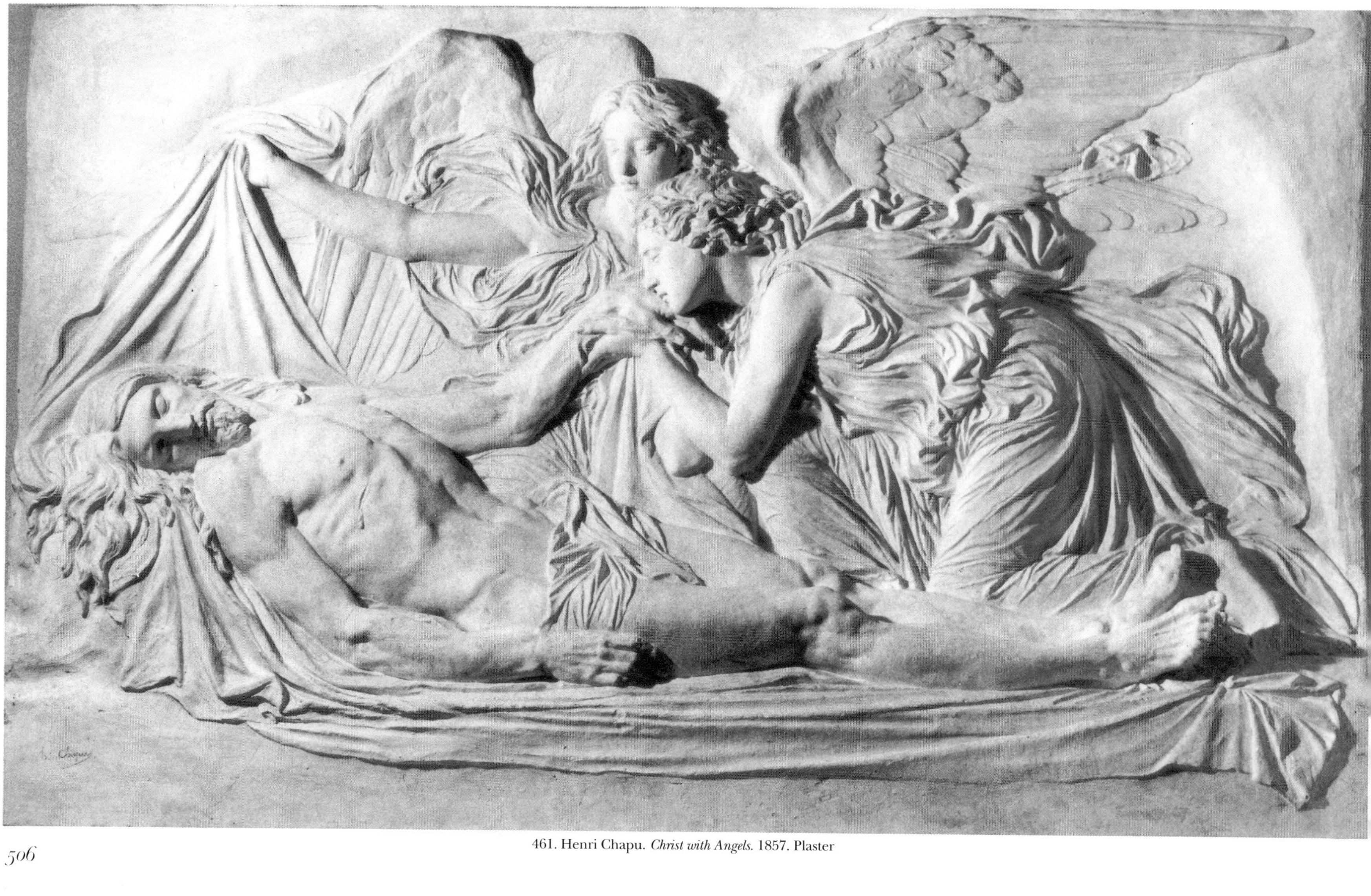

461. Henri Chapu. *Christ with Angels.* 1857. Plaster

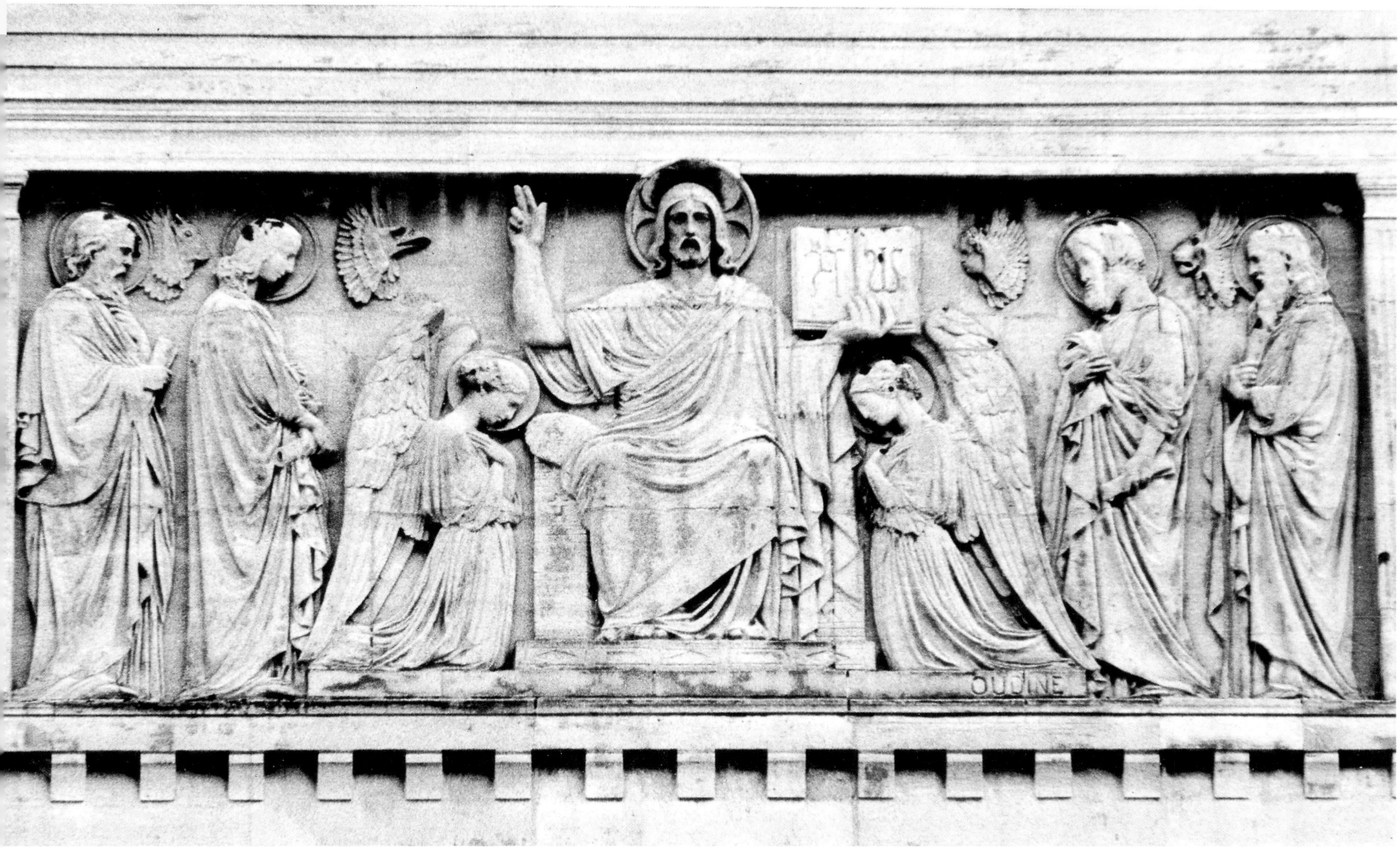

462. Eugène Oudiné. *Christ Between Two Angels and the Four Evangelists.* Model at 1853 Salon. Stone

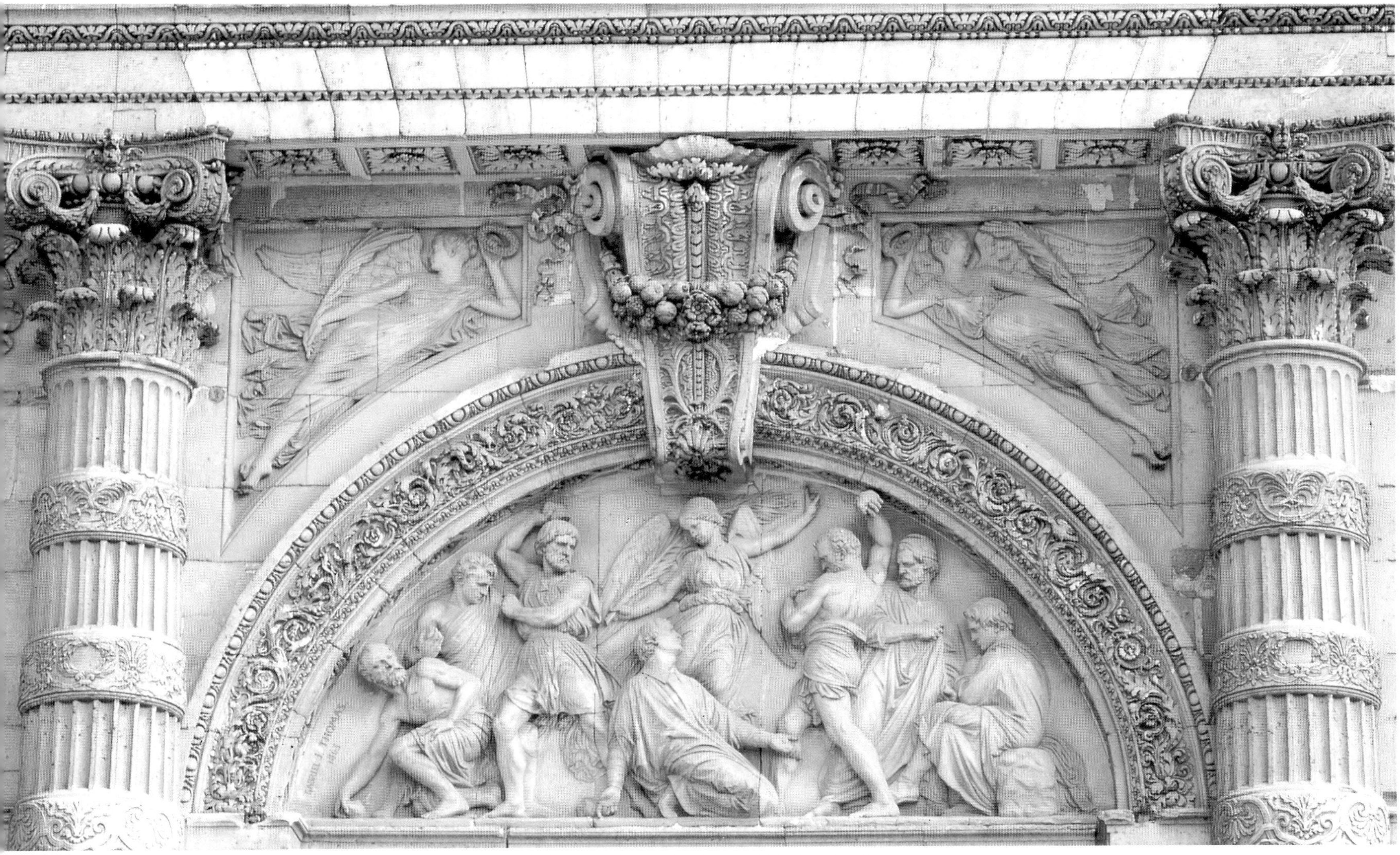

463. Gabriel-Jules Thomas. *The Stoning of St. Stephen.* 1863. Stone

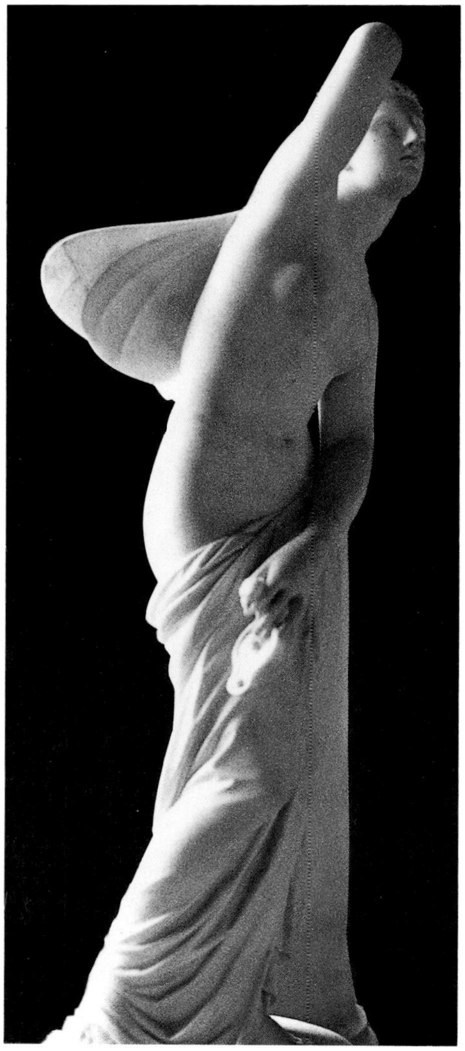

464. Alexander von Bok. *Psyche.* 1864. Marble

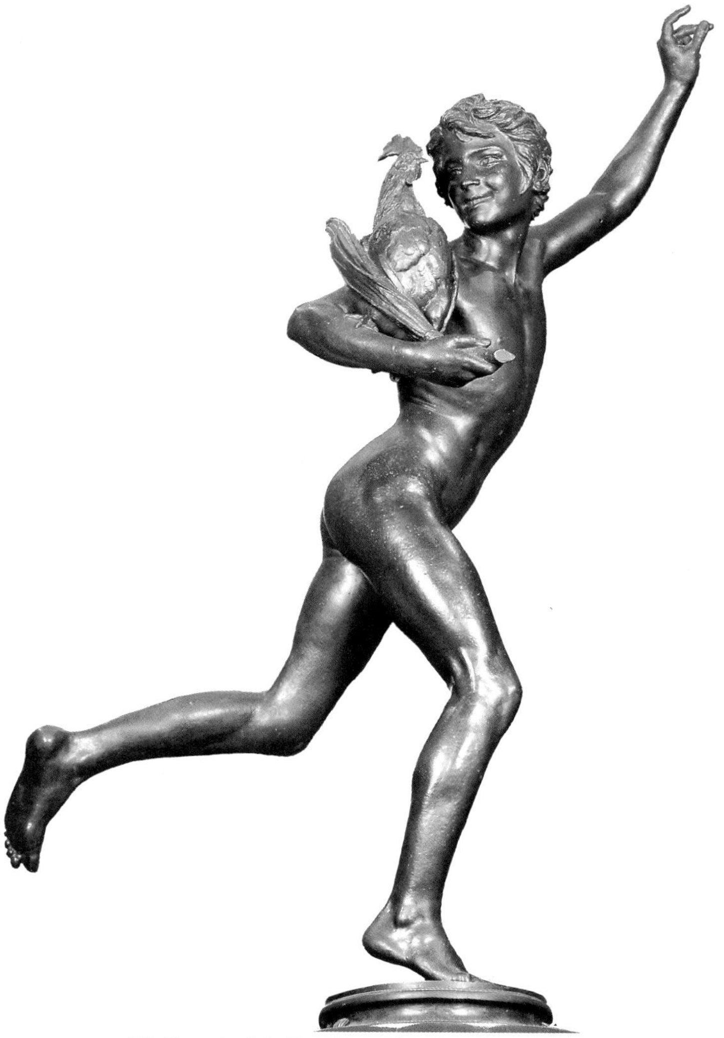

465. Alexandre Falguière. *Winner of the Cockfight.* 1864. Bronze

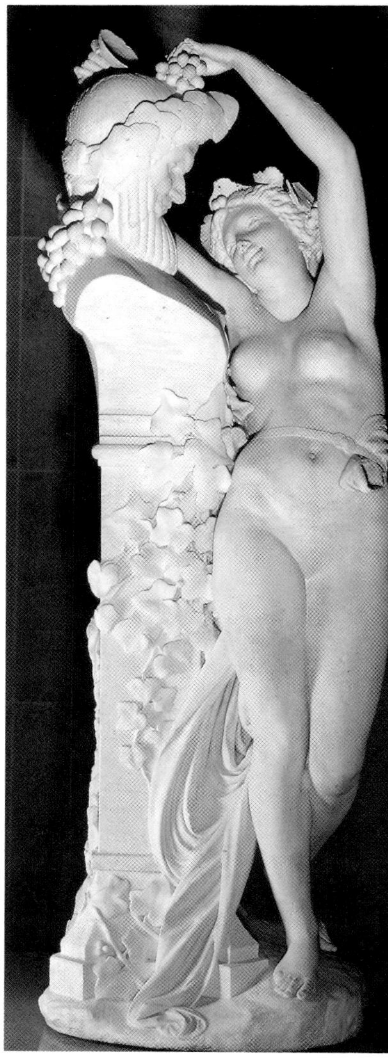

466. Albert-Ernest Carrier-Belleuse. *Bacchante.* 1863. Marble

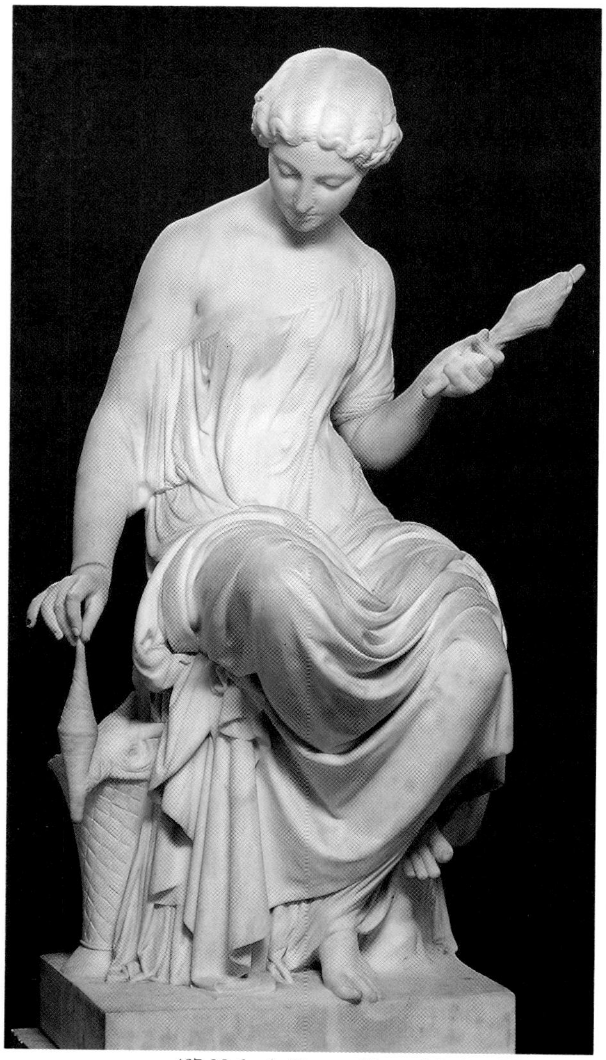

467. Mathurin Moreau. *Woman Spinning.* 1861. Marble

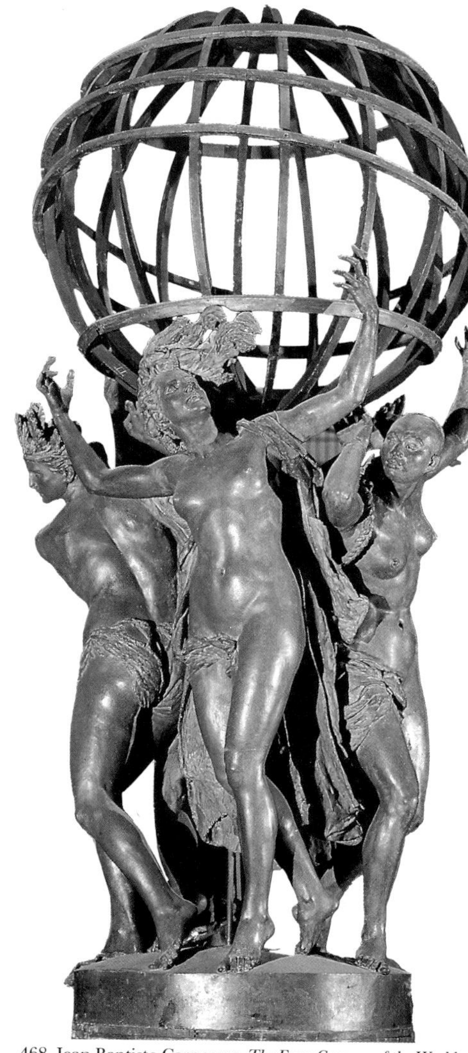

468. Jean-Baptiste Carpeaux. *The Four Corners of the World Supporting the Celestial Sphere.* 1872

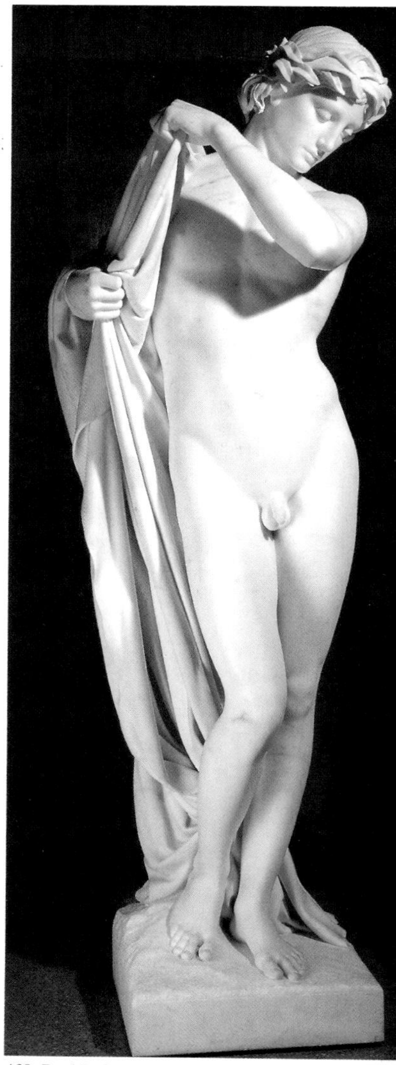

469. Paul Dubois. *Narcissus.* Copy. 1867. Marble

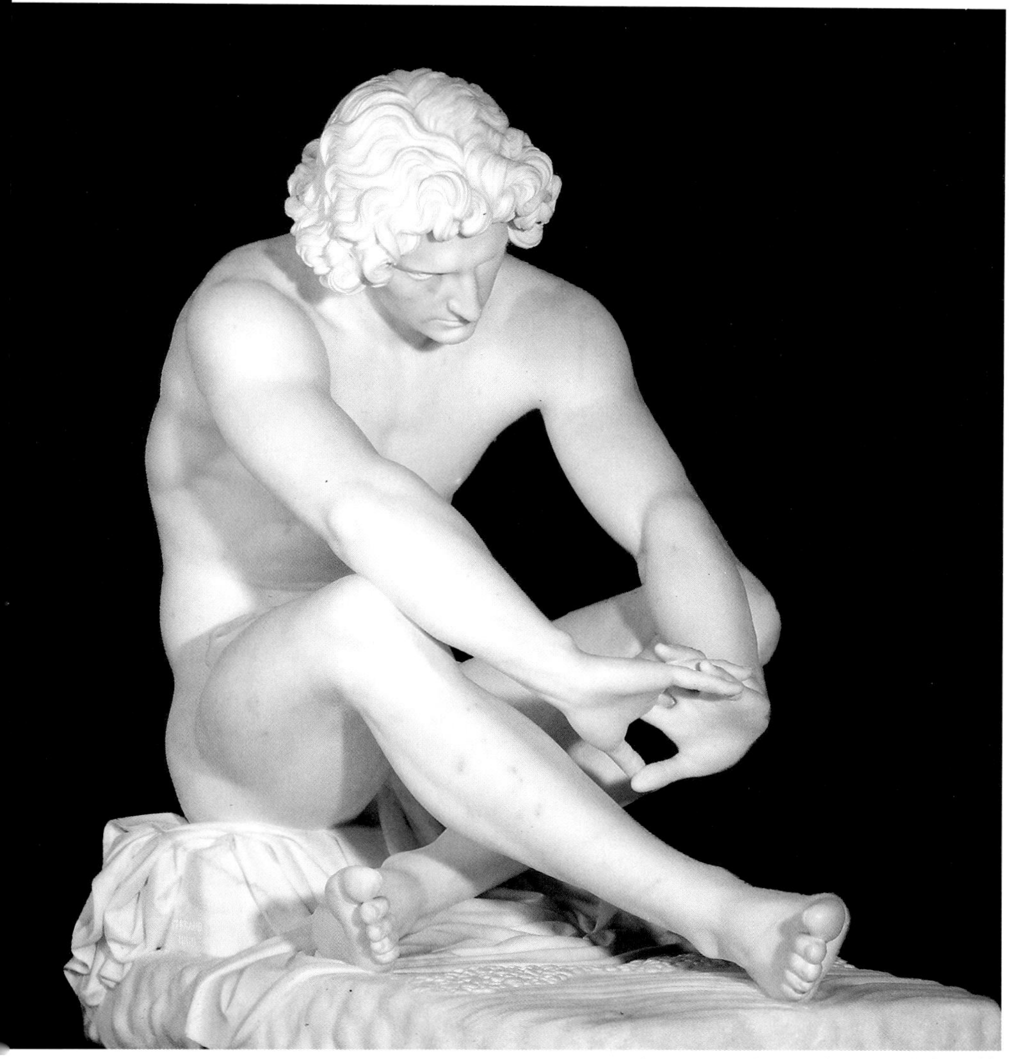

470. Jean-Joseph Perraud. *Despair.* 1869. Marble

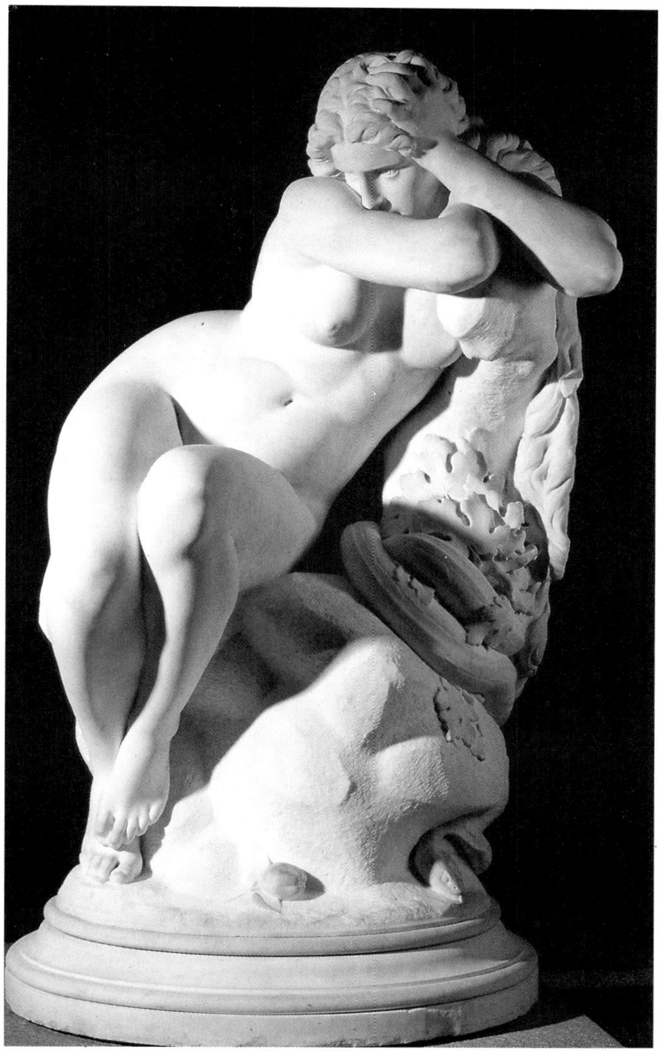

471. Eugène Delaplanche. *Eve After Sinning.* 1869. Marble

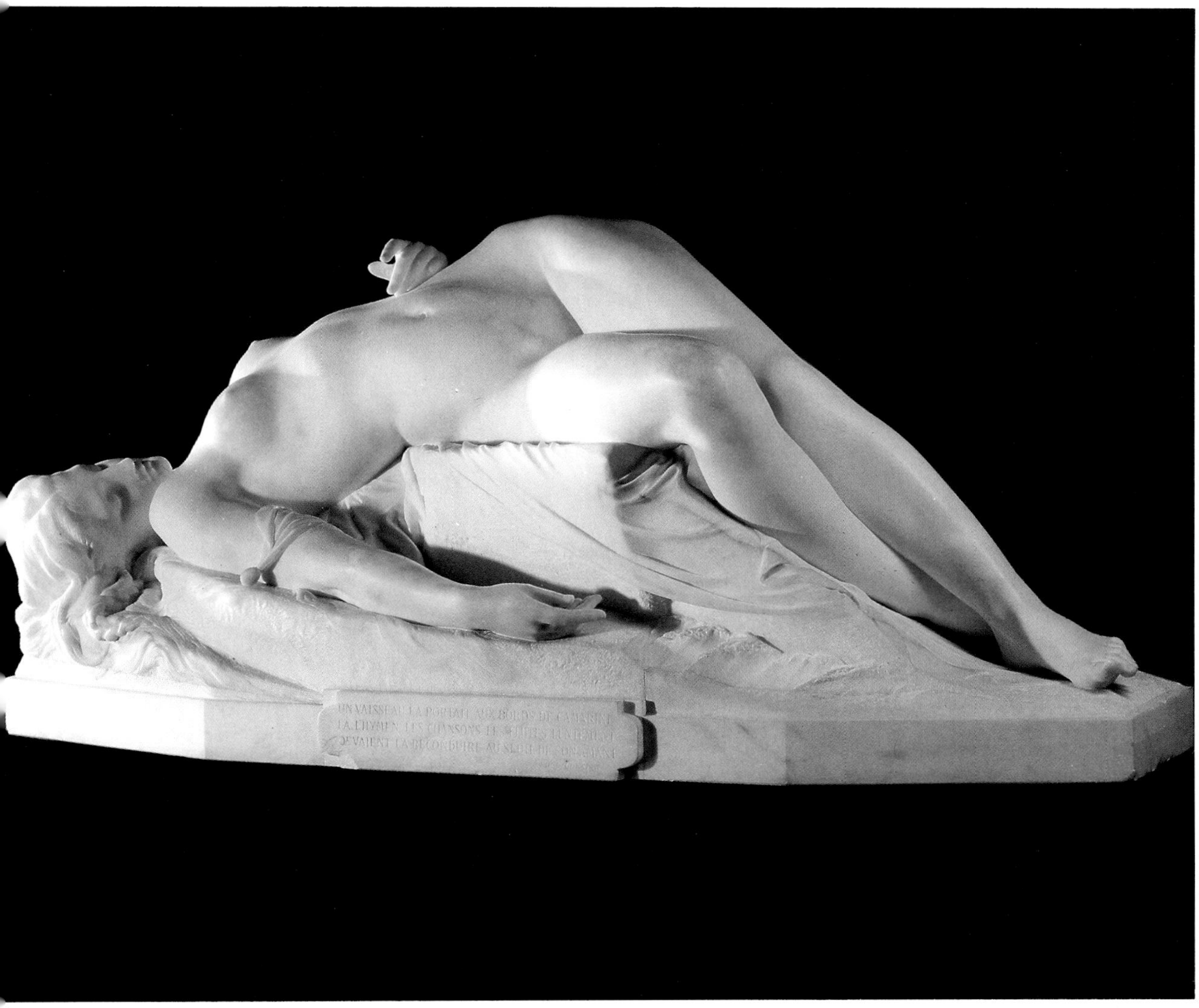

472. Alexandre Schoenewerk. *The Tarantine Girl.* 1871. Marble

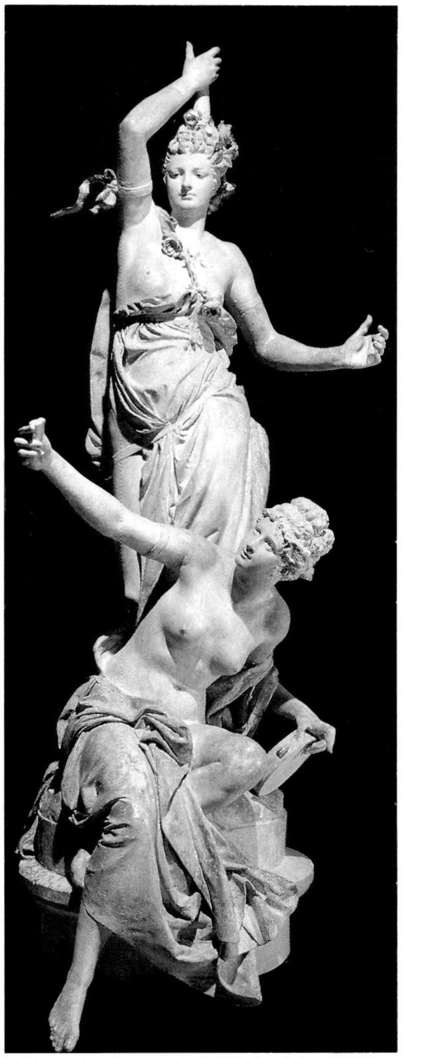

473. Albert-Ernest Carrier-Belleuse. *Torchère* (for the Opéra in Paris). 1873. Plaster

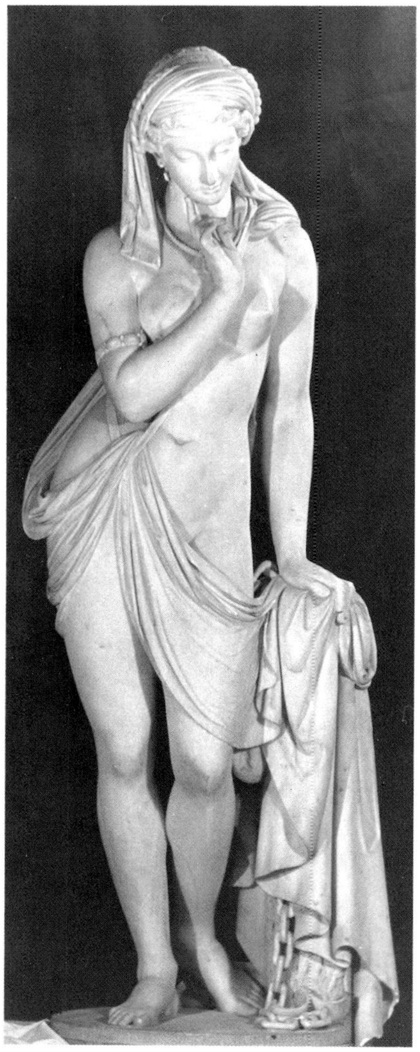

474. Scipione Tadolini. *Greek Slave.* 1862. Marble

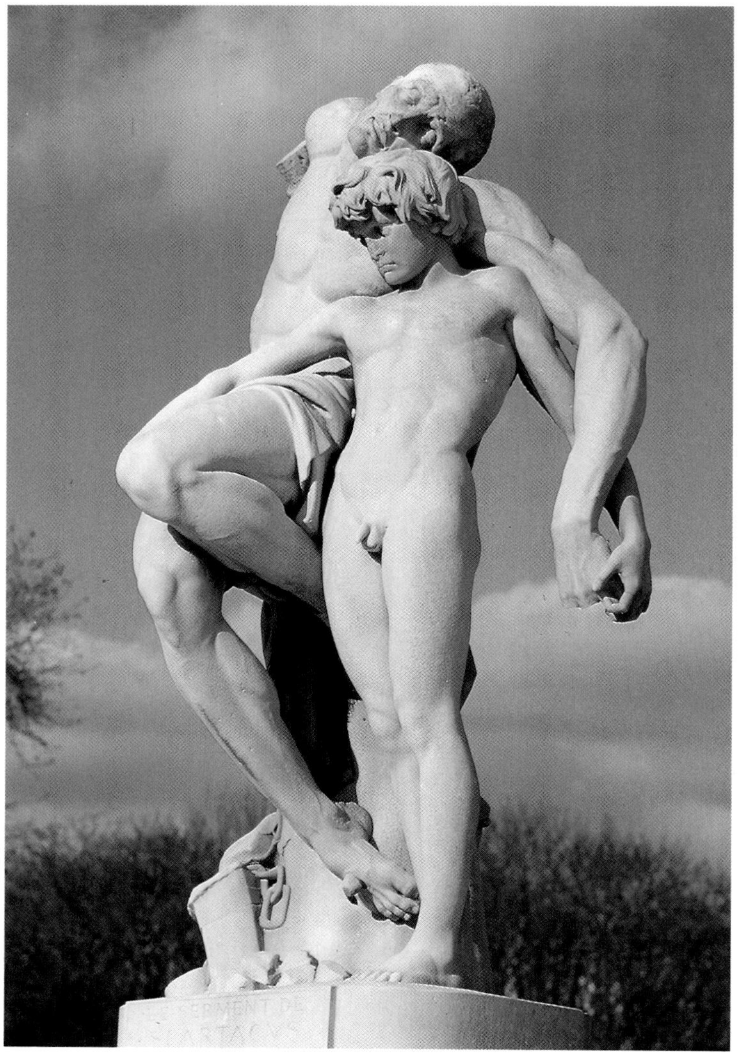

475. Louis-Ernest Barrias. *The Oath of Spartacus.* 1872. Marble

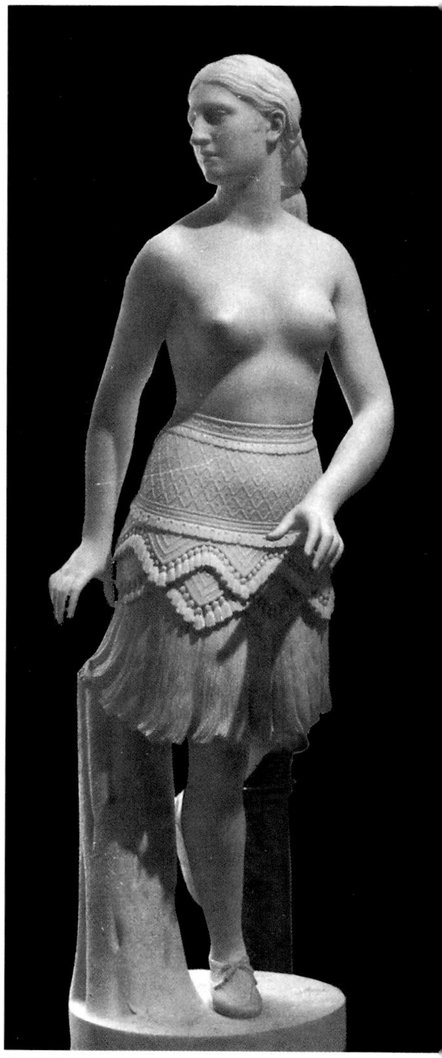

476. Hiram Powers. *Last of the Tribe.* 1870–72. Marble

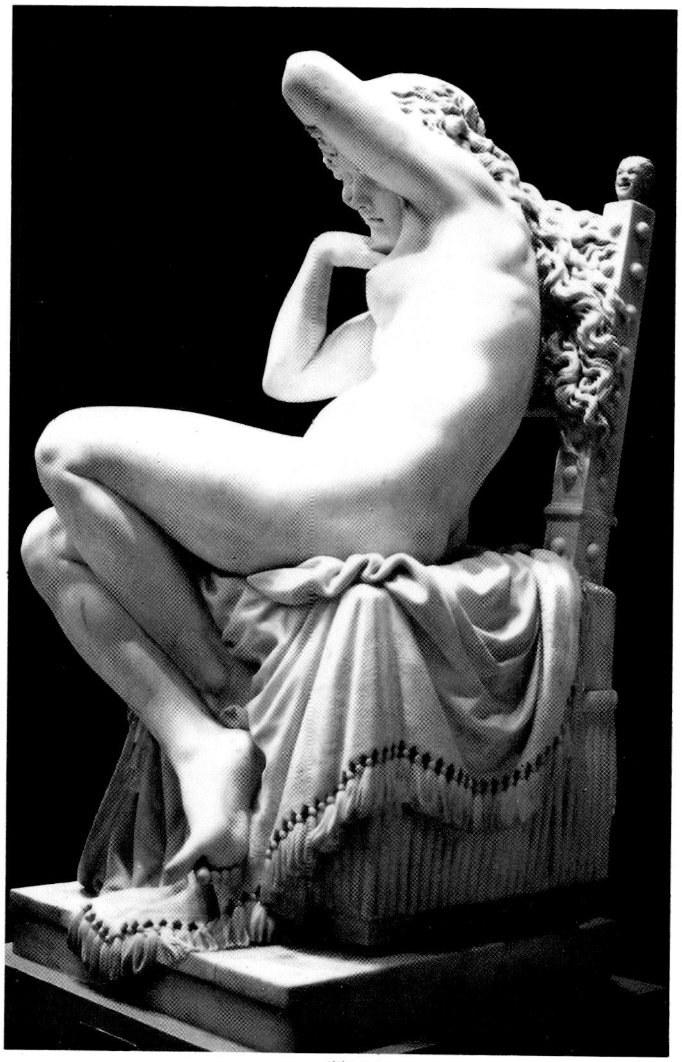

477. Edward Roberts. *First Pose.* 1876. Marble

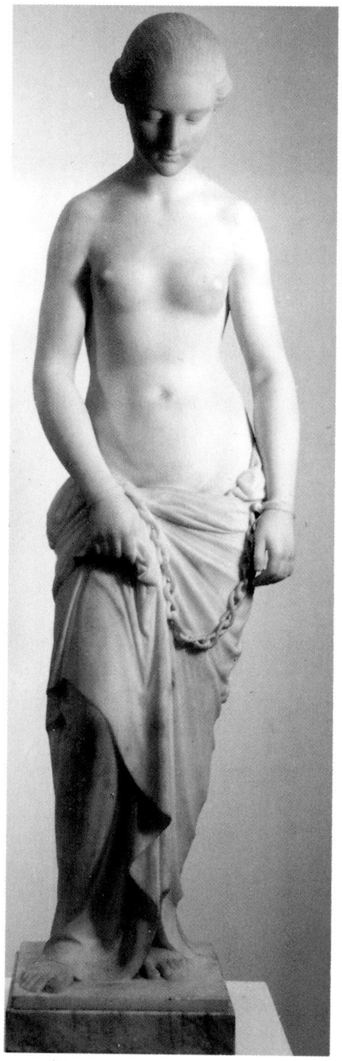

478. Jens Adolph Jerichau. *Slave.* 1871. Marble

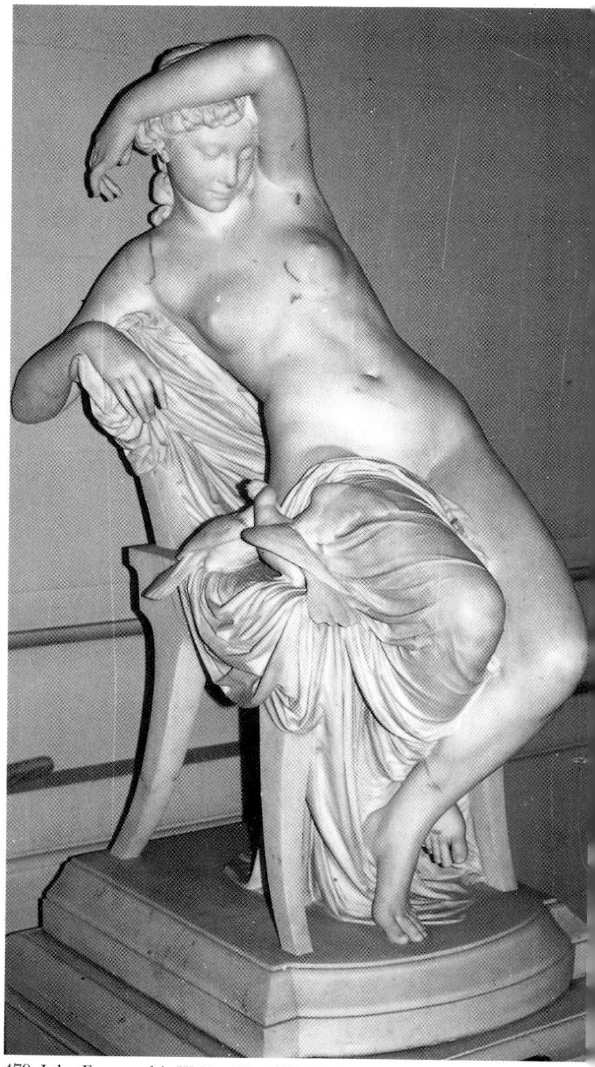

479. Jules Franceschi. *Waking Up.* 1873. Marble

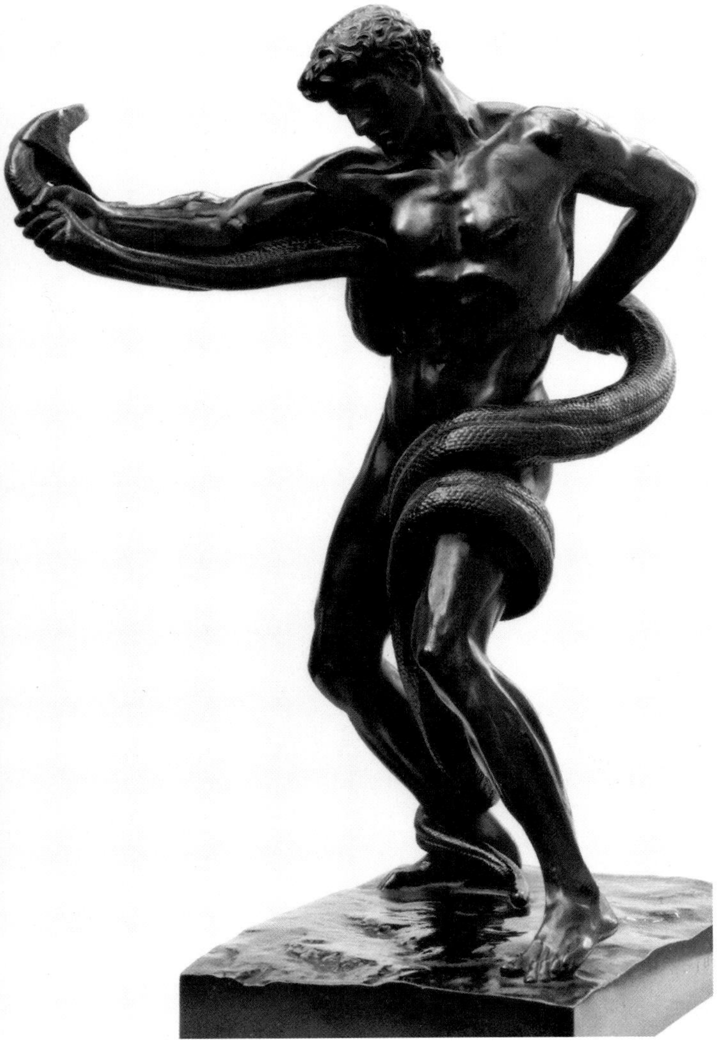

480. Frederic Leighton. *Athlete Struggling with a Python.* 1877. Bronze

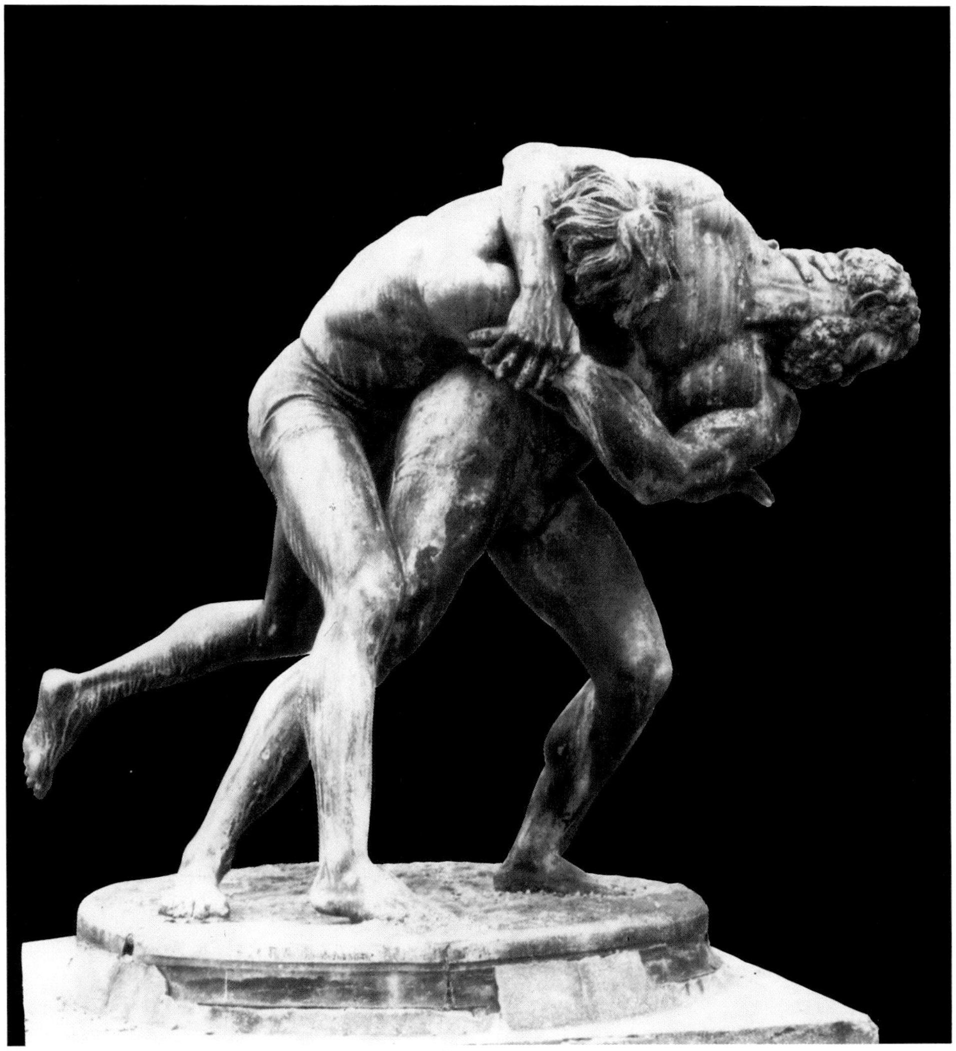

481. Auguste Ottin. *Modern Wrestling: The Hip Throw.* 1867. Bronze

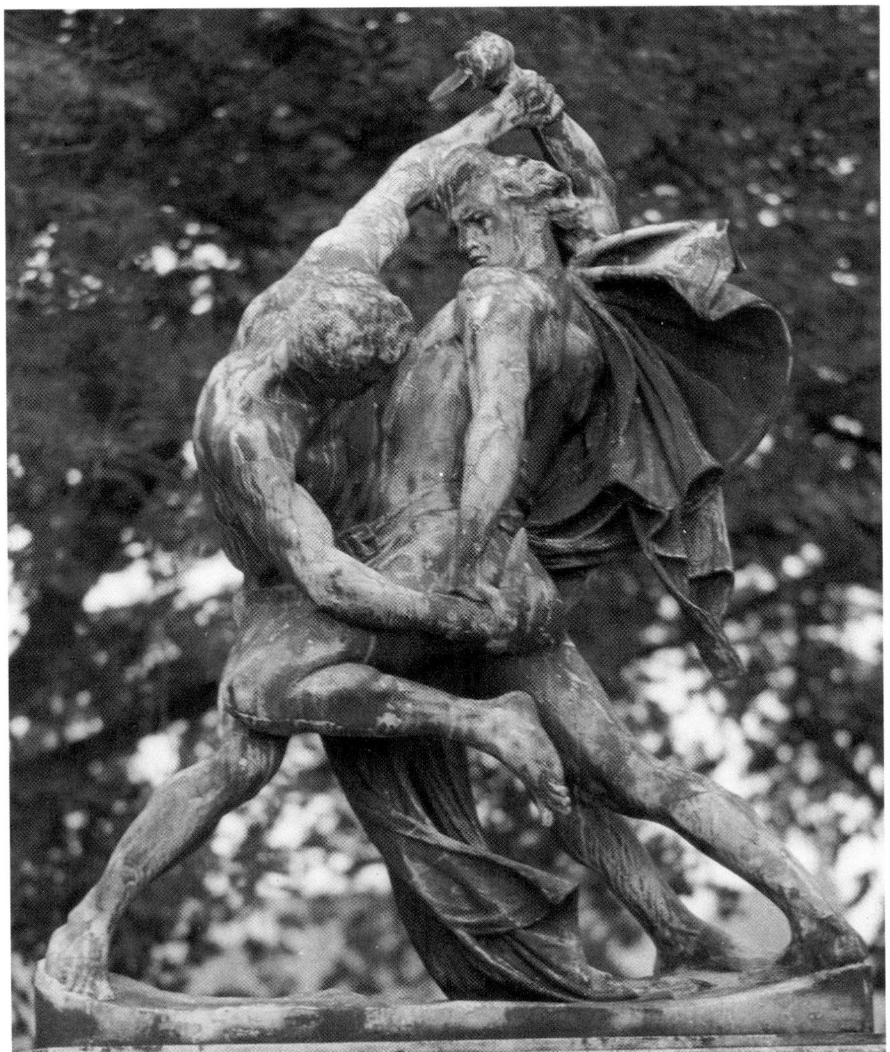

482. Johann Peter Molin. *Knife Fight.* 1858–59. Bronze

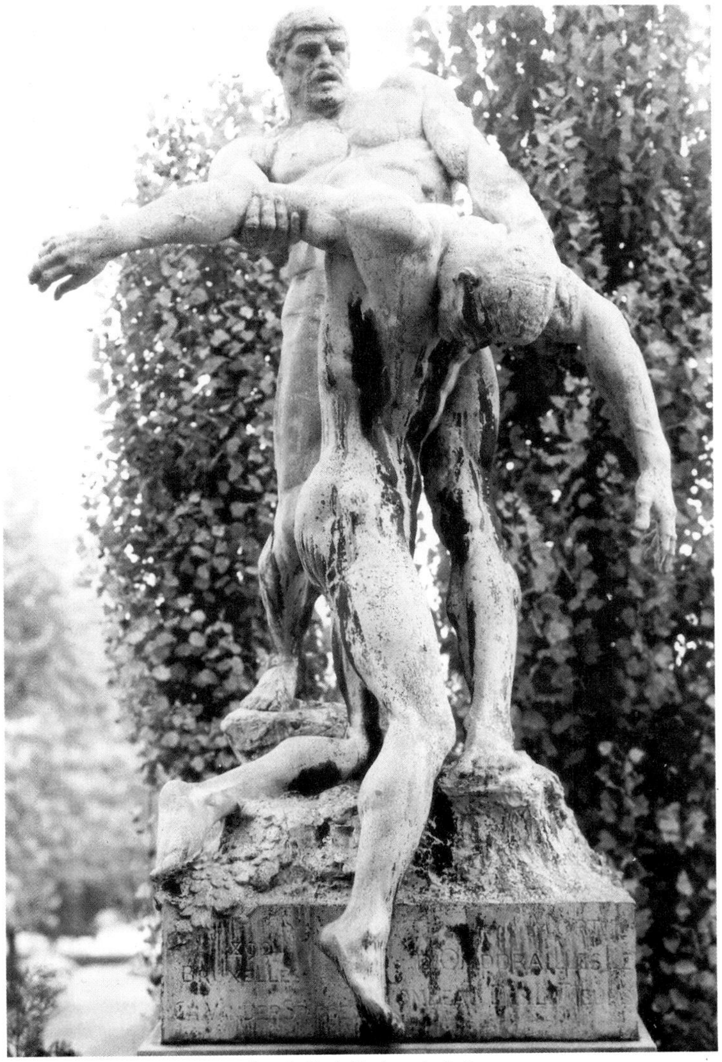

483. Charles van der Stappen. *Ompdrailles-le-Tombeau-des-Lutteurs.* 1892. Bronze

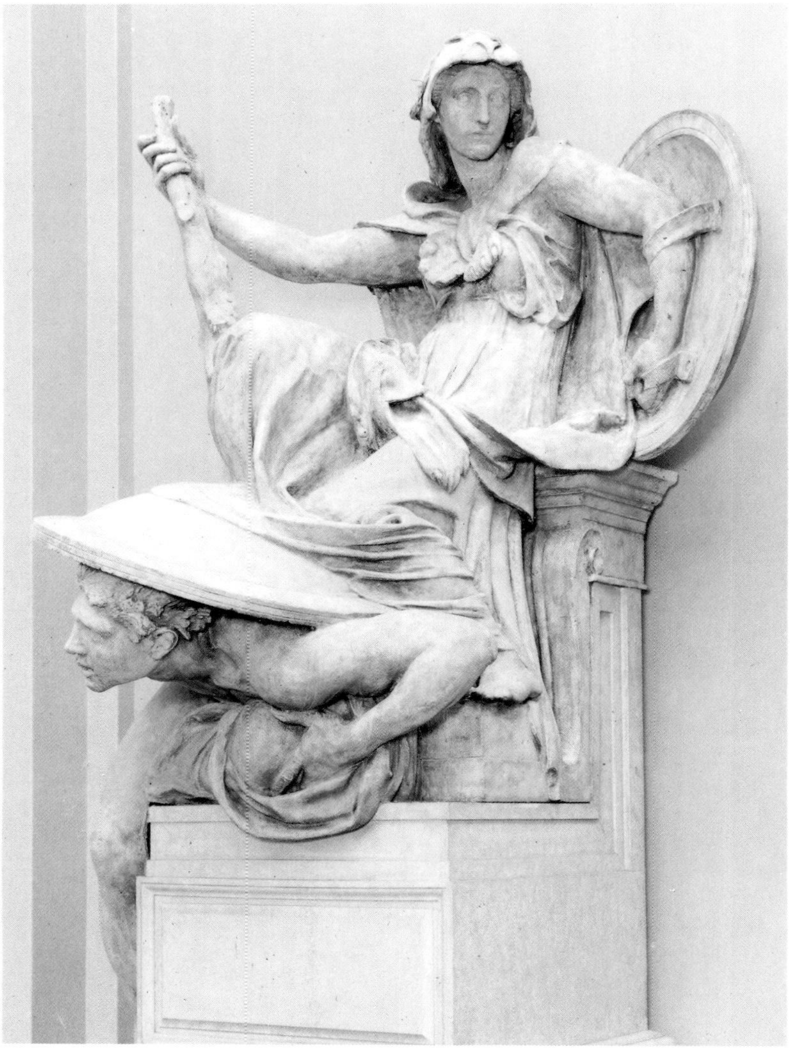

484. Alfred Stevens. *Courage and Cowardice.* 1858–67. Plaster

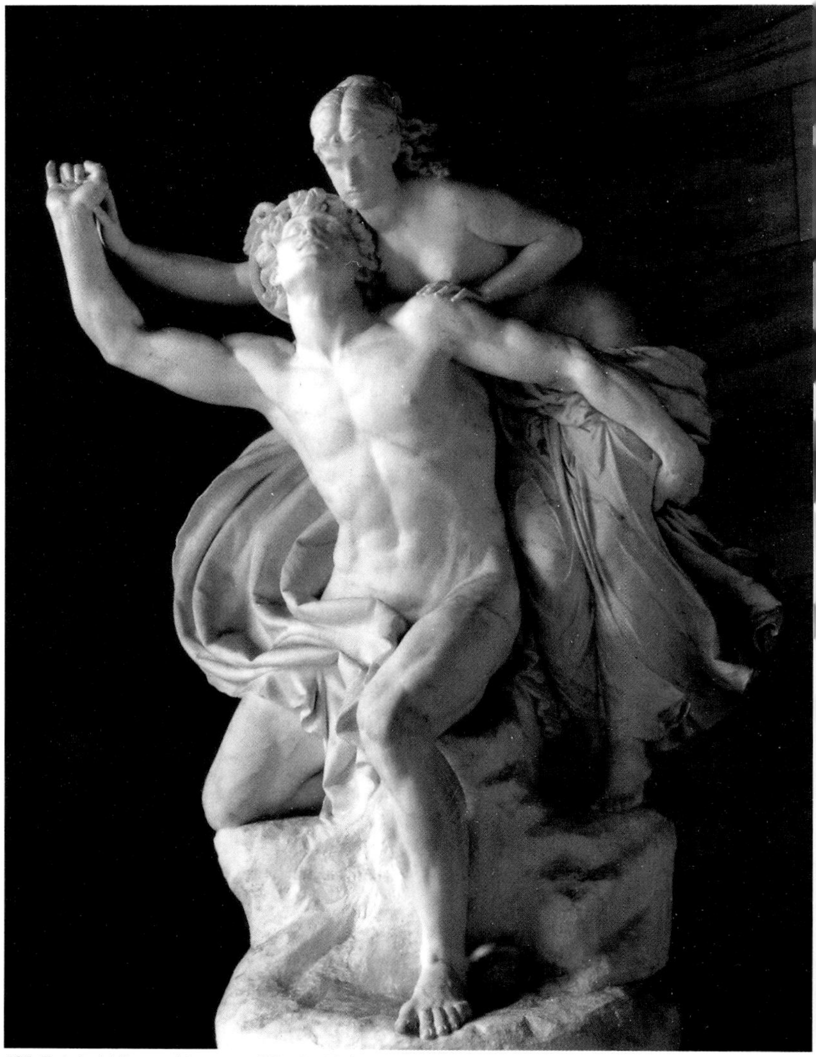

485. Reinhold Begas. *Mercury and Psyche.* 1857. Marble

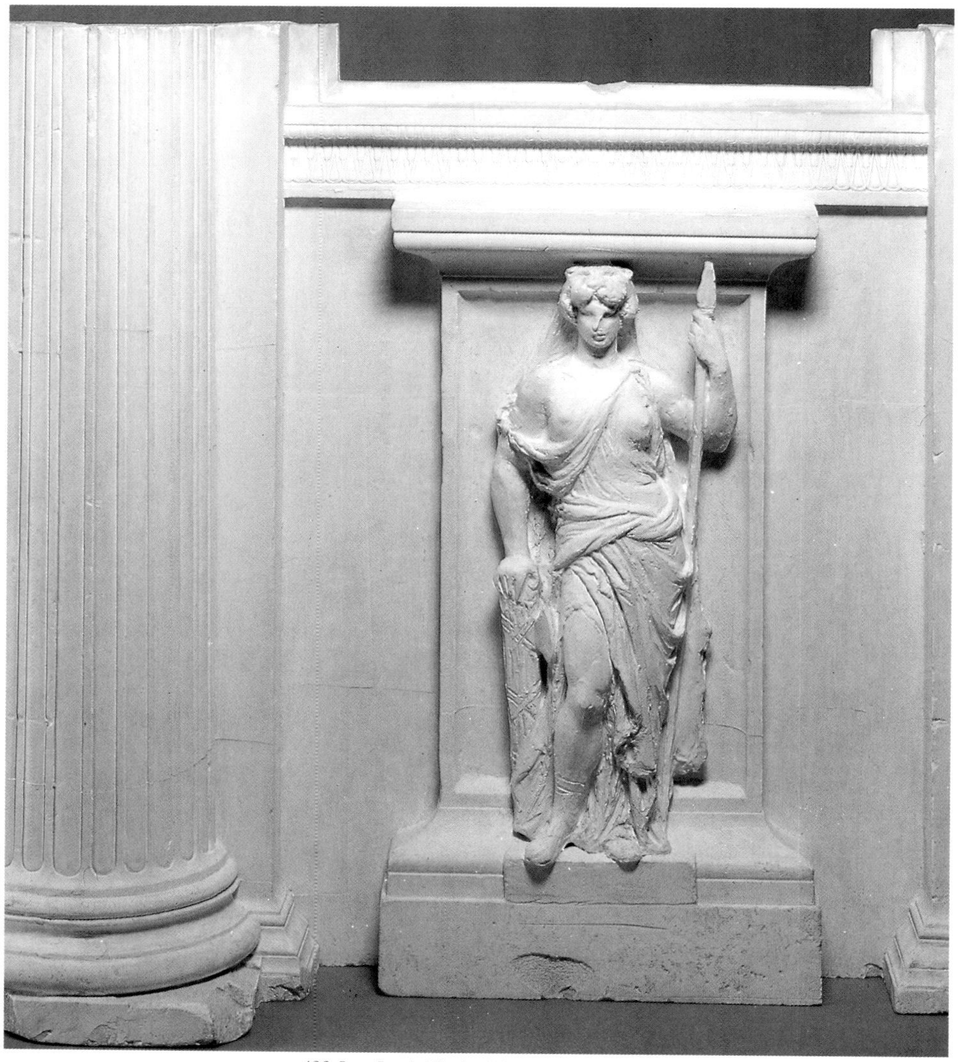

486. Jean-Louis-Nicolas Jaley. *Strength* (for the facade of the Palais de Justice, Paris). 1858–59. Plaster

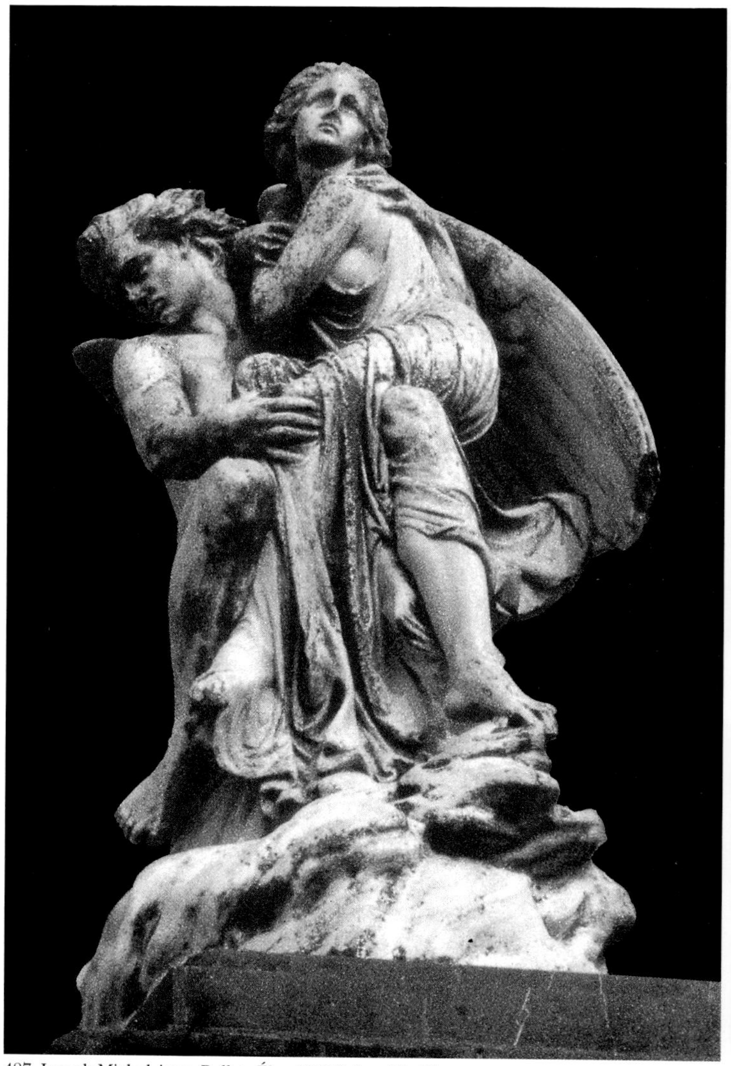

487. Joseph-Michel-Ange Pollet. *Éloa.* 1869 Salon. Marble

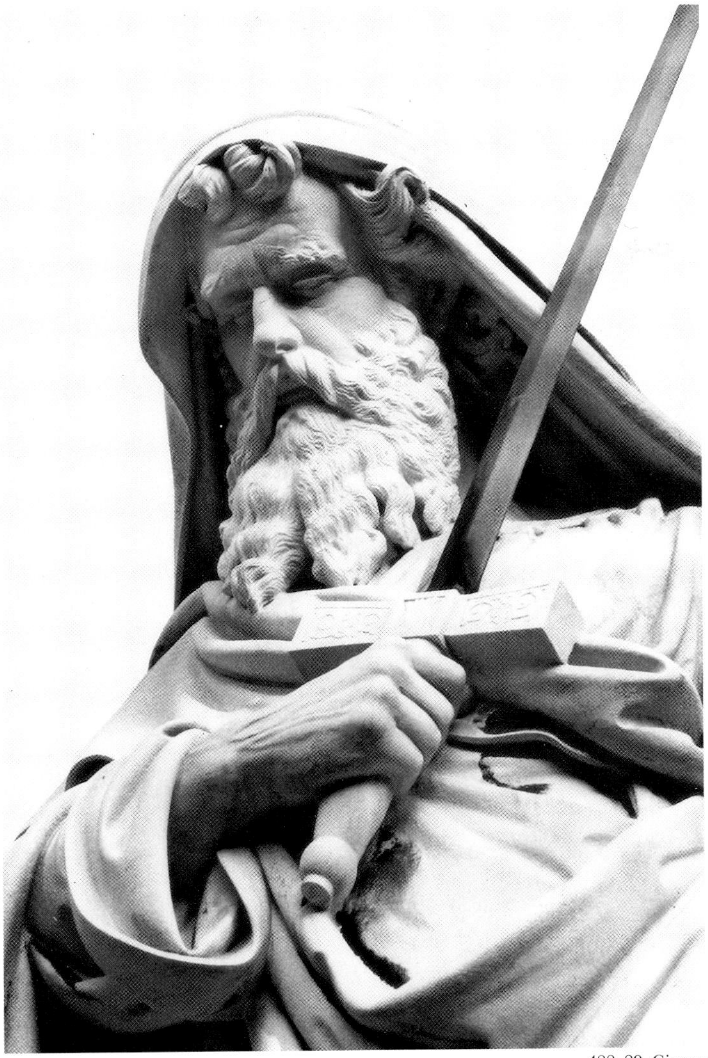

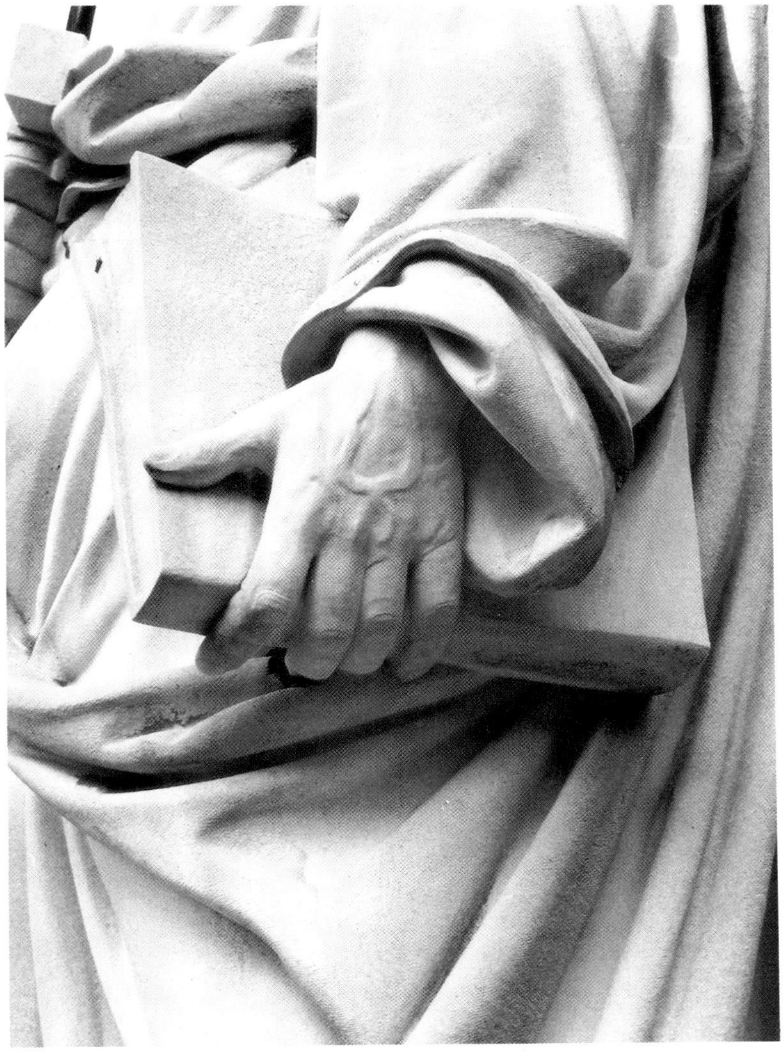

488–89. Giuseppe Obici. *St. Paul* (details). Marble

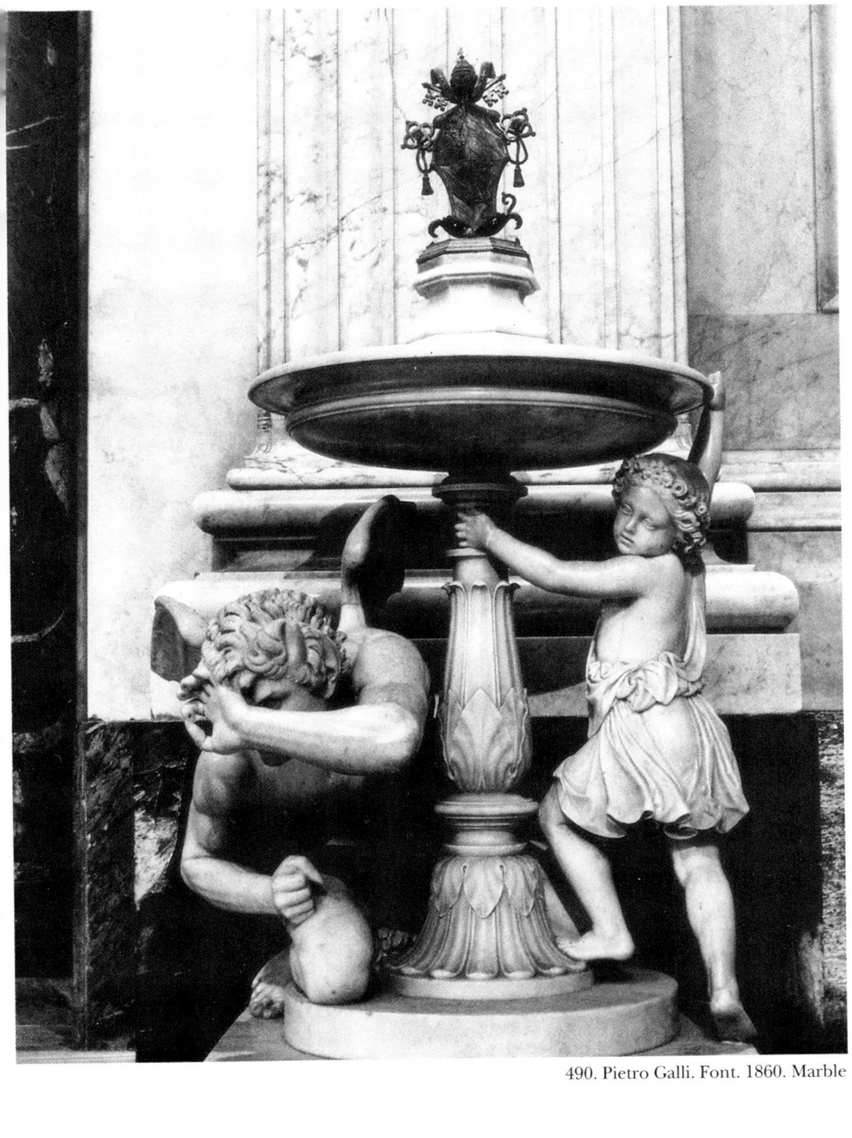

490. Pietro Galli. Font. 1860. Marble

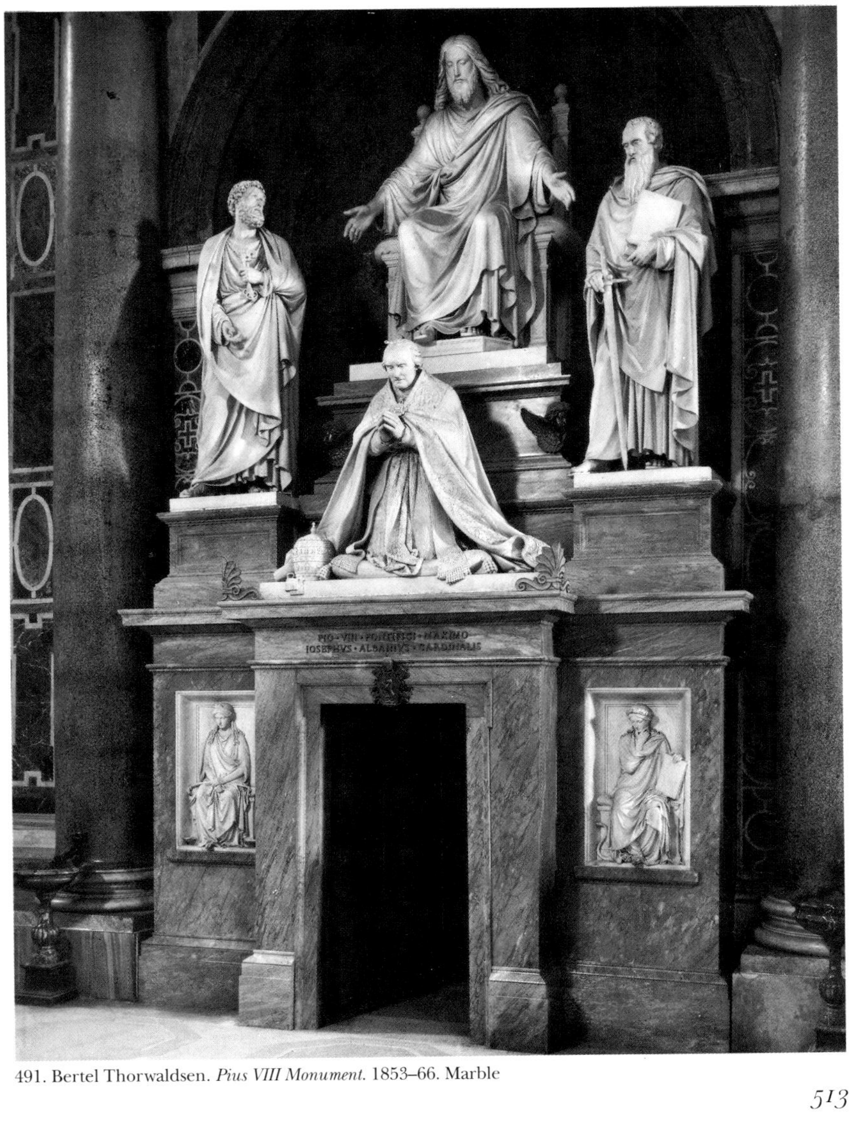

491. Bertel Thorwaldsen. *Pius VIII Monument*. 1853–66. Marble

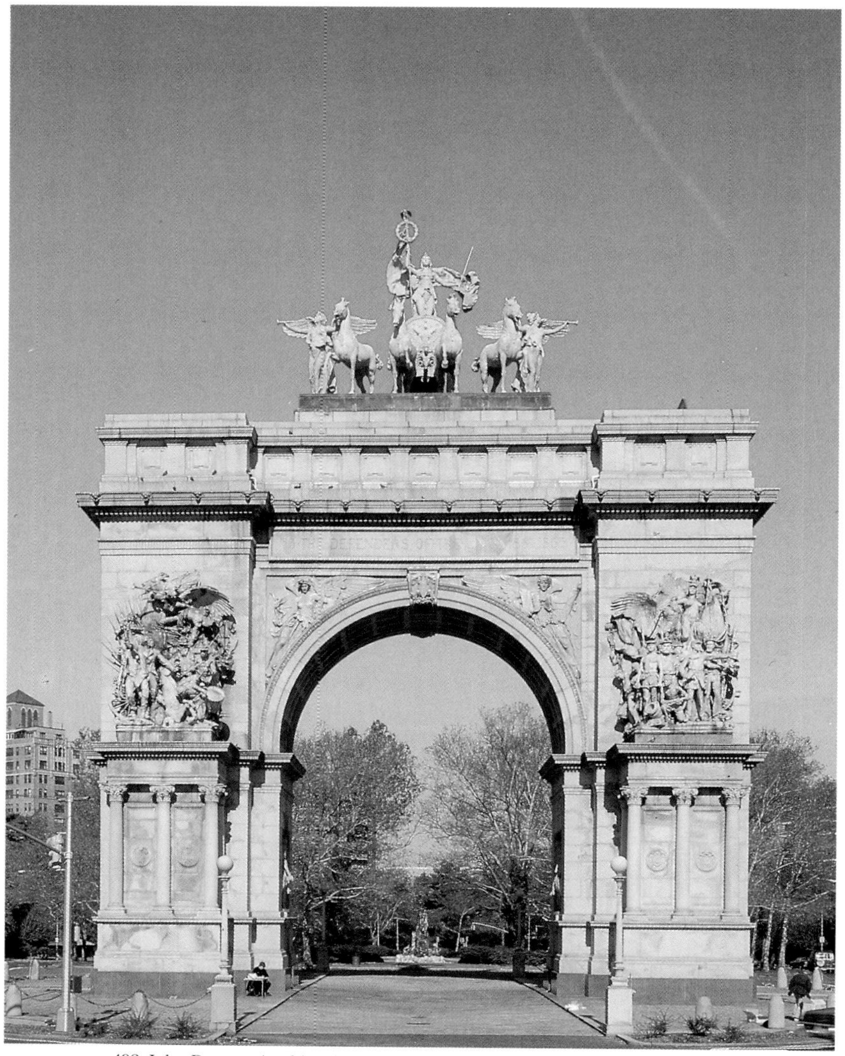

492. John Duncan (architect), Frederick MacMonnies (sculptor). Soldiers' and Sailors' Arch. 1889–92. Grand Army Plaza, Brooklyn

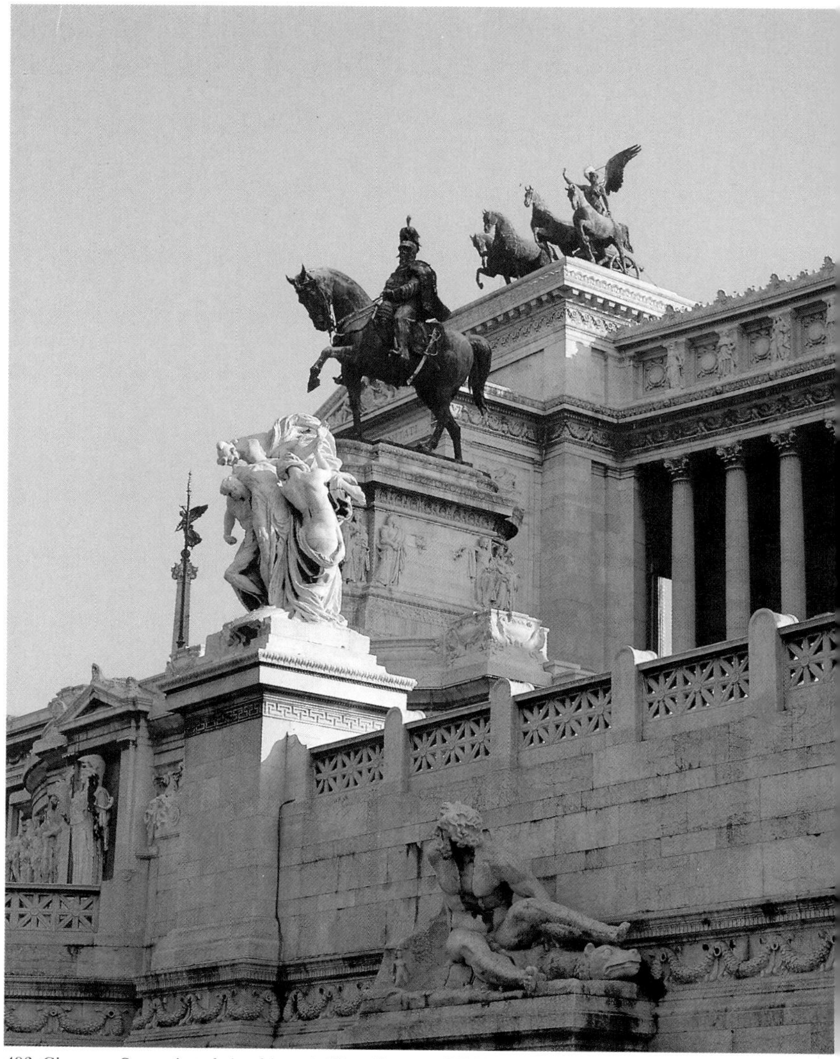

493. Giuseppe Sacconi et al. (architects). *Victor Emmanuel II Monument*, Piazza di Venezia, Rome. 1885–1911. Bartolini: *Quadriga of Liberty*; Chiaradia: *Victor Emmanuel II*; Bistolfi: *Sacrifice*

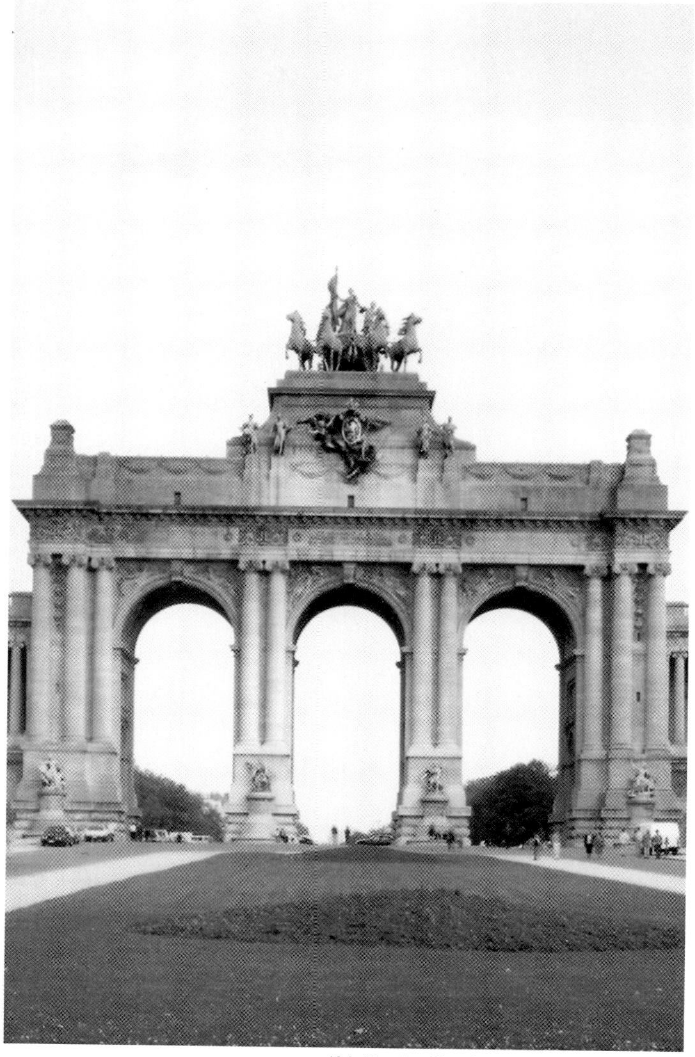

494. Charles Girault. Triumphal Arch. 1904–5. Parc du Cinquantenaire, Brussels

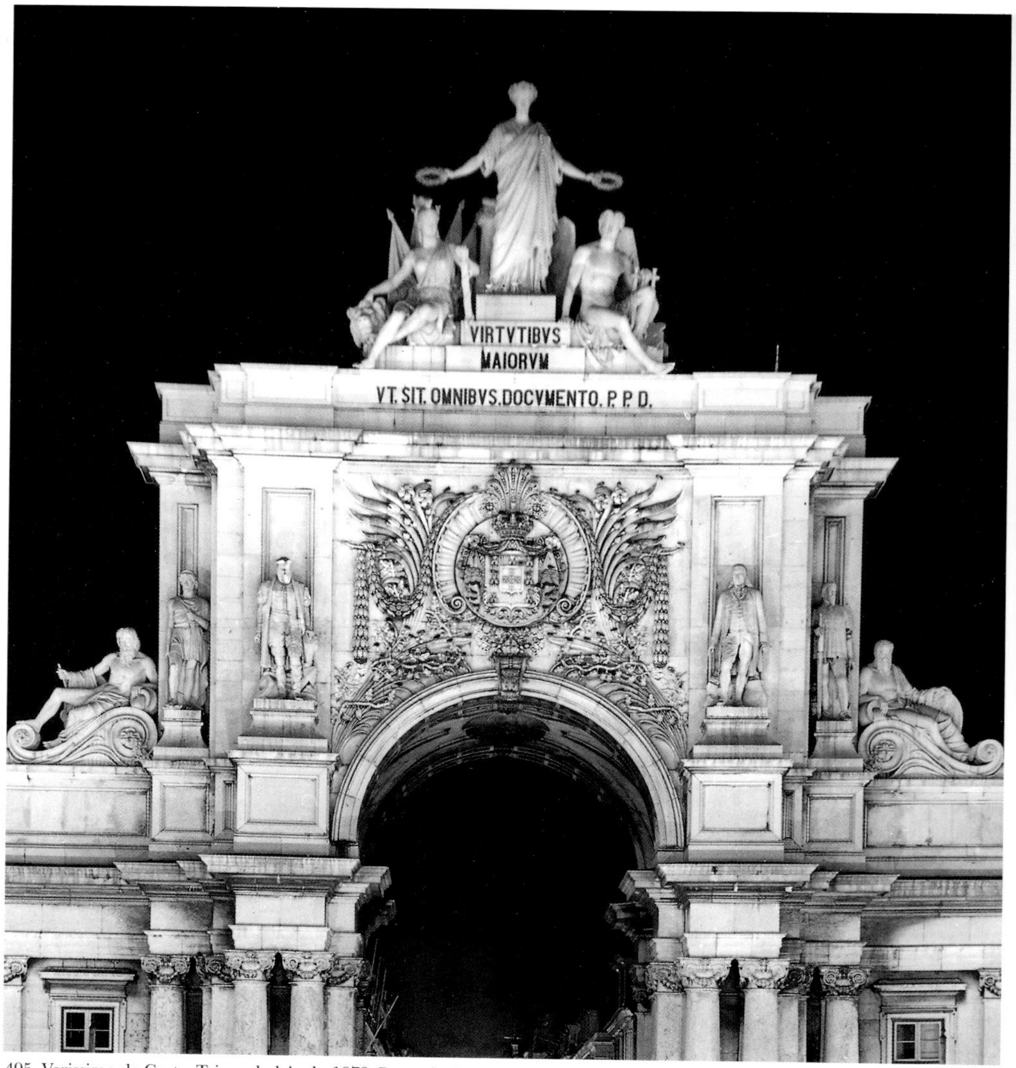

495. Verissimo da Costa. Triumphal Arch. 1872. Praça do Comércio, Lisbon. Célestin Calmels. *Fame Rewarding Valor and Genius*. stone

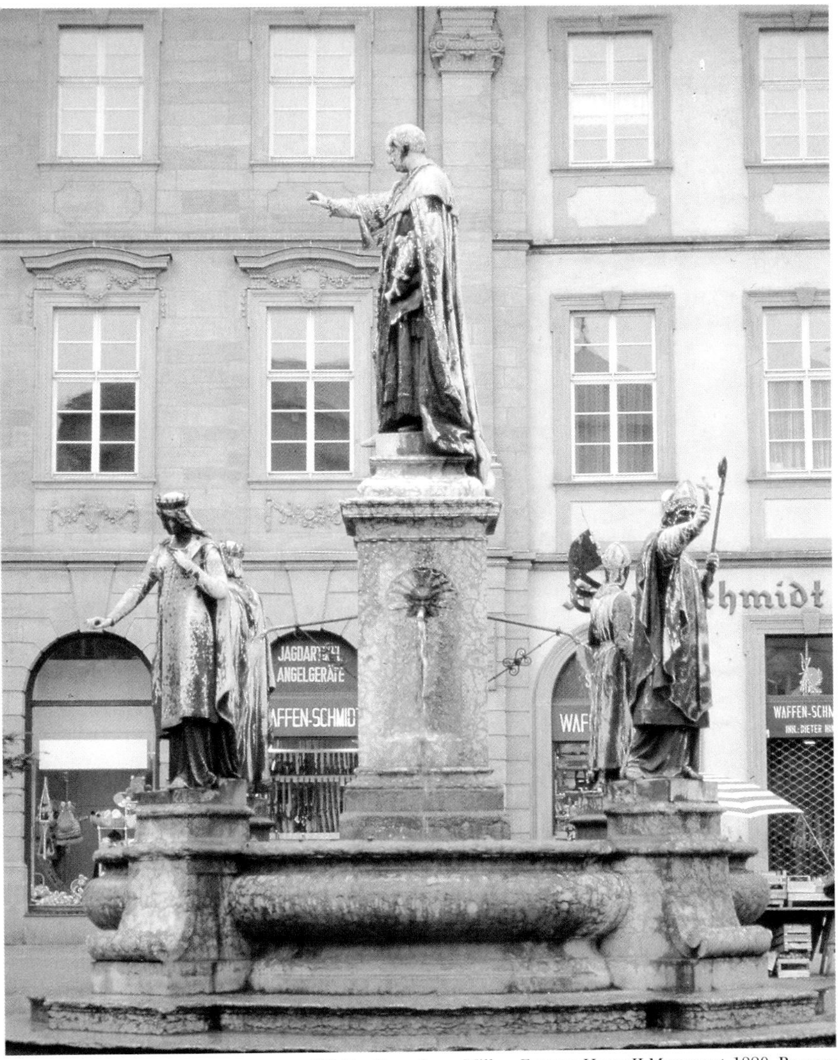

496. Ferdinand von Miller. *Emperor Henry II Monument.* 1880. Bronze.
Maximilianplatz, Bamberg

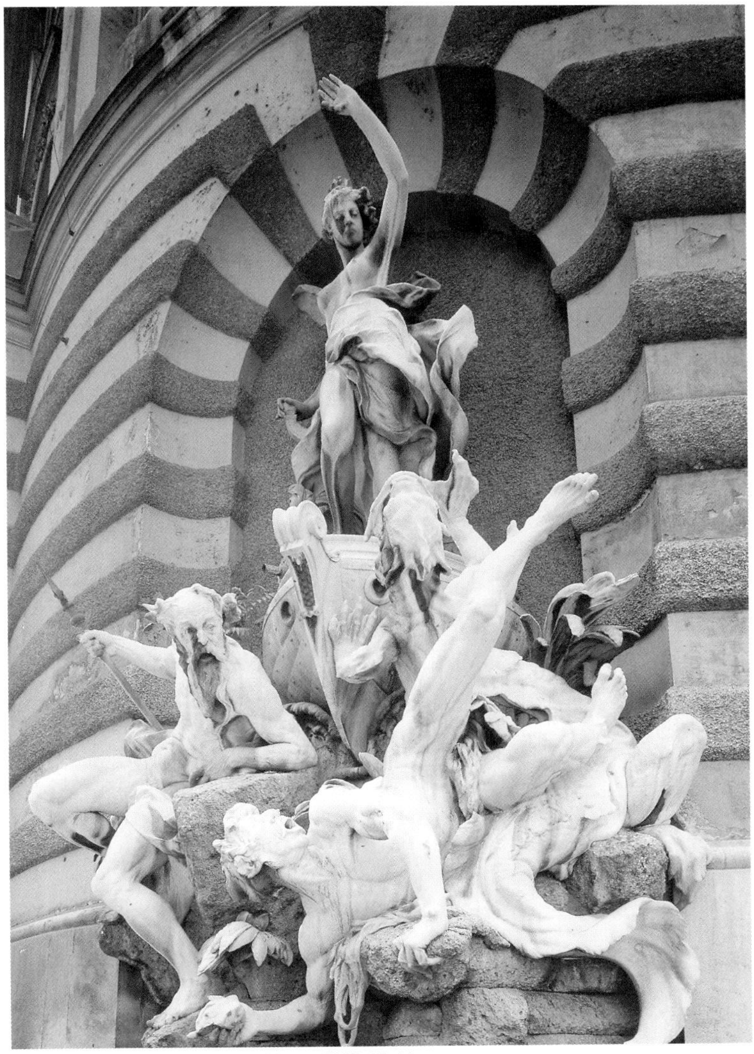

497. Edmund von Hellmer. *Land Power.* 1897. Marble.
Hofburg, Michaelerplatz, Vienna

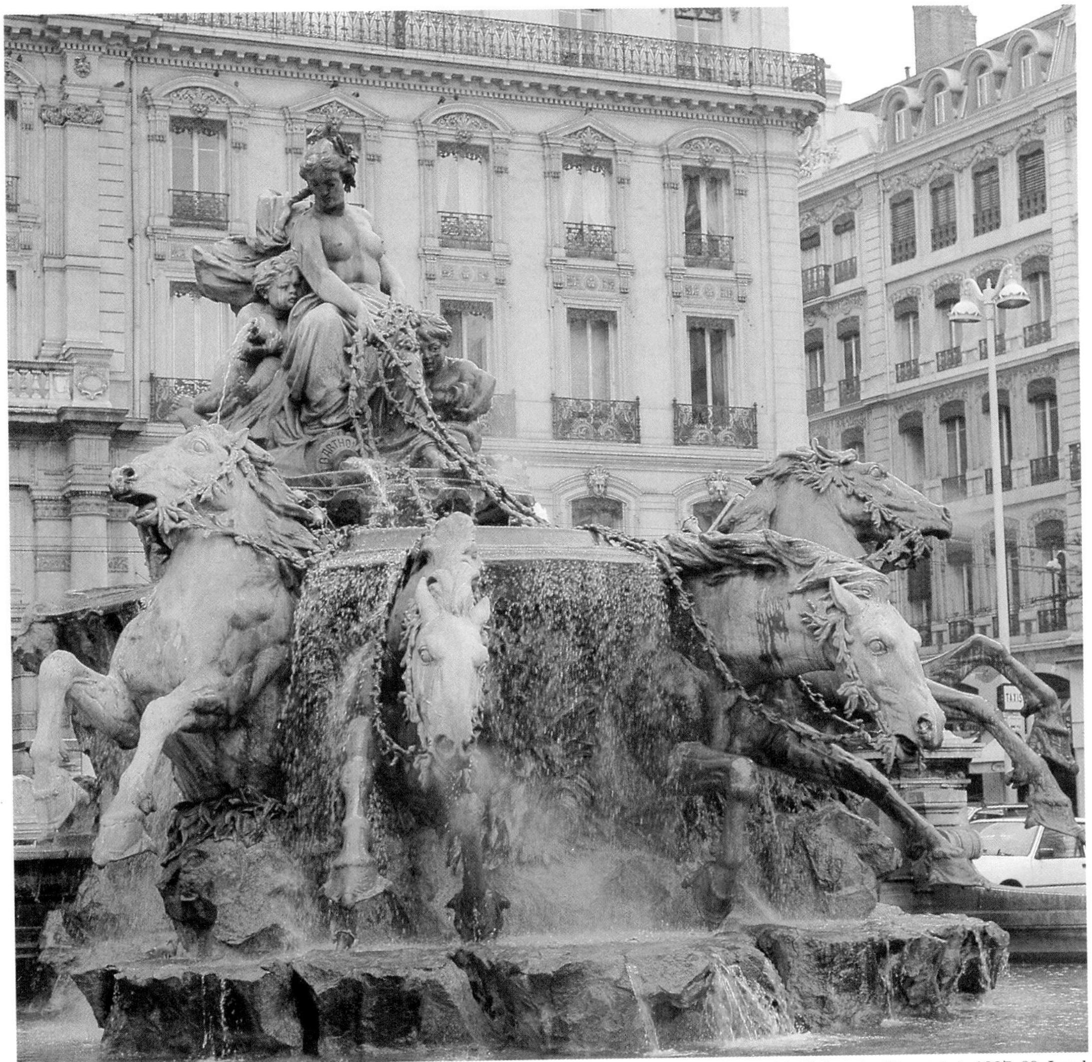

498. Auguste Bartholdi. *The Saône and its Tributaries* (fountain). 1887–89. Lead.
Place des Terraux, Lyon

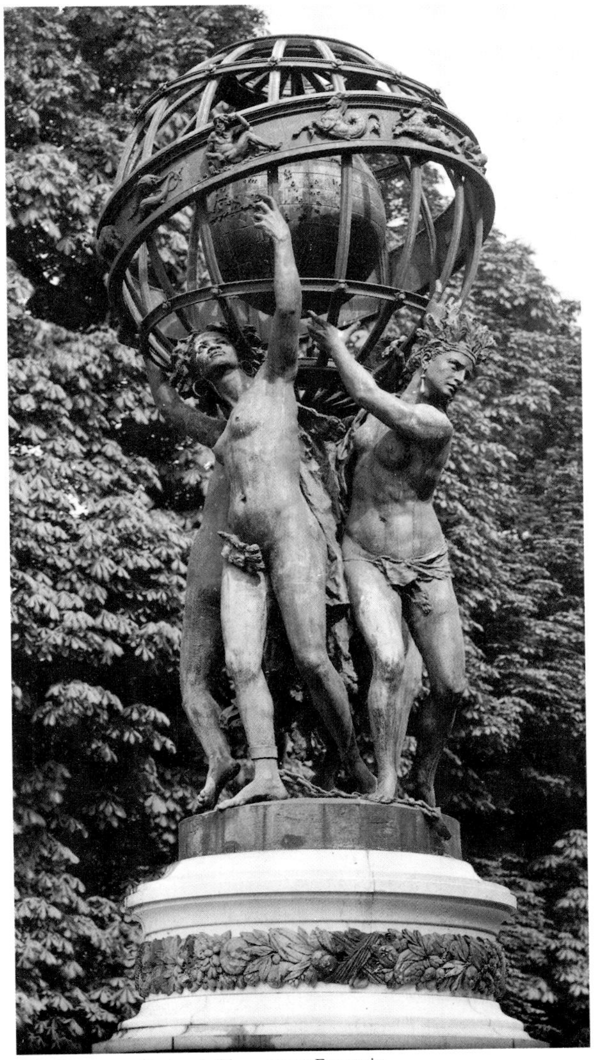

499. Carpeaux, Davioud. Observatory Fountain,
Jardin de l'Observatoire, Paris. 1867–73. Bronze

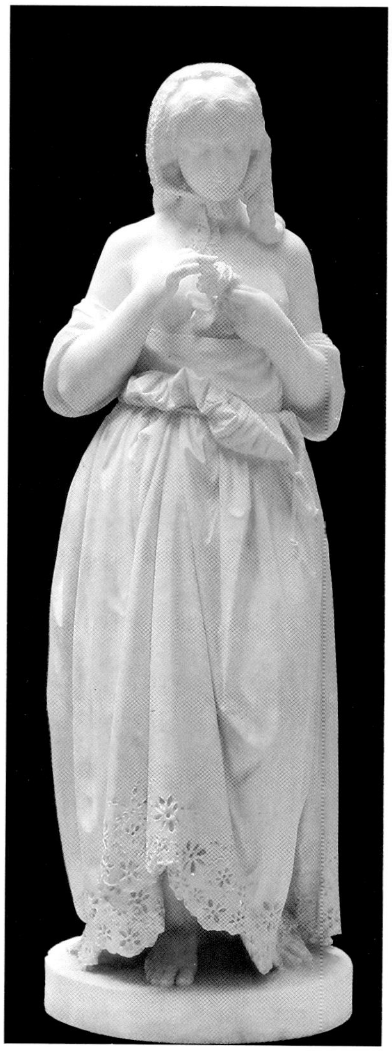

500. Alfonso Balzico. *Margarete.*
1852. Marble

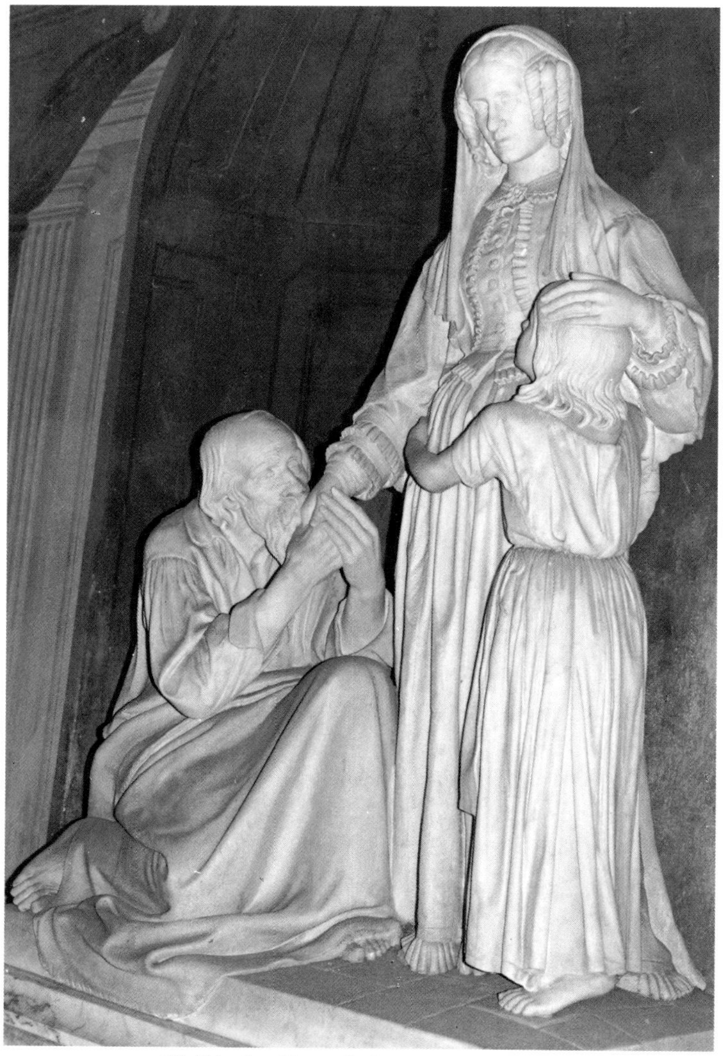

501. Cristoforo Marzaroli. *Contessa Sanvitale.* Marble.
San Giovanni Evangelista Church, Parma

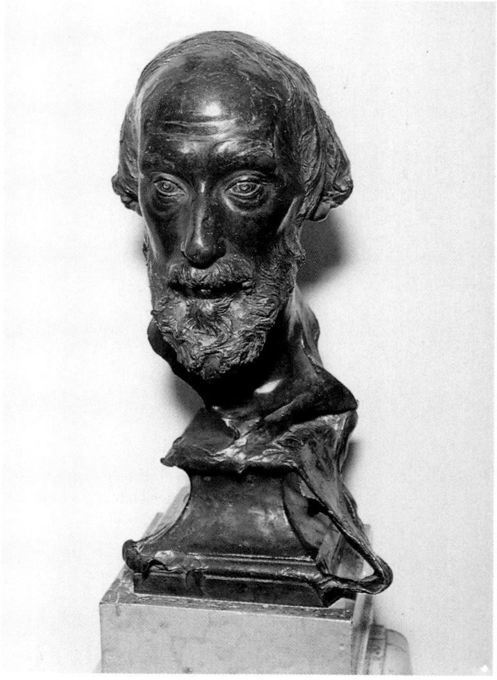

502. Jean Carriès. *Auguste Vacquerie.*
1887. Bronze

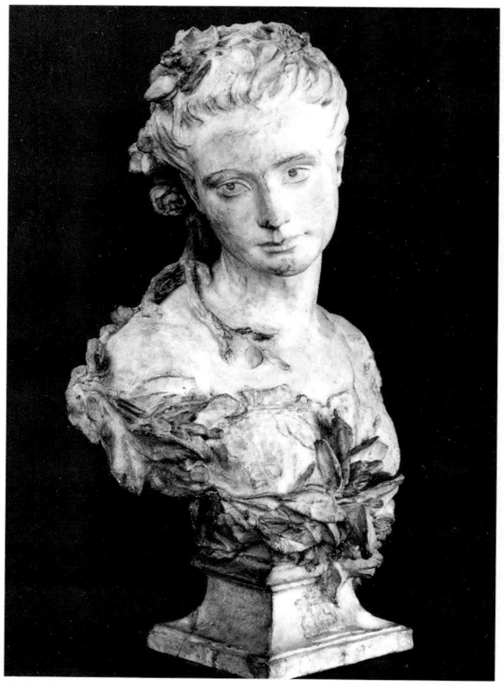

503. Carpeaux. *Amélie de Montfort Dressed as a Bride.*
1869. Plaster

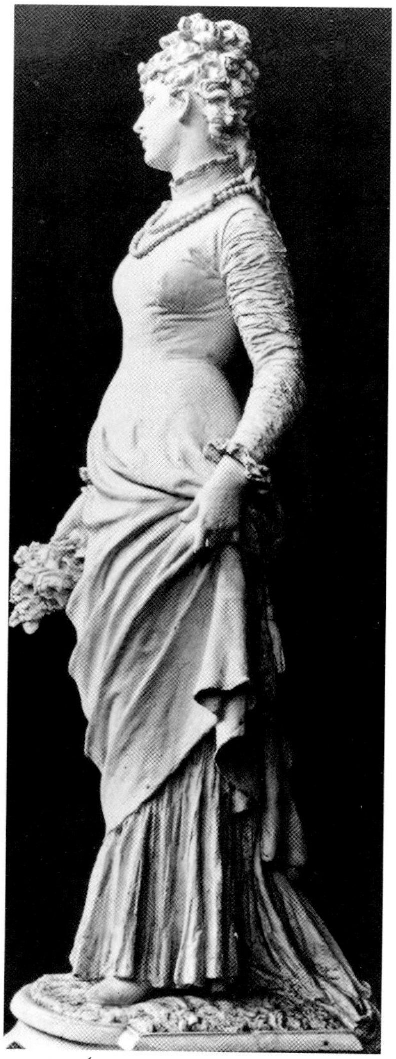

504. Émile Chatrousse. *The Parisian Woman.*
1876 Salon. Plaster

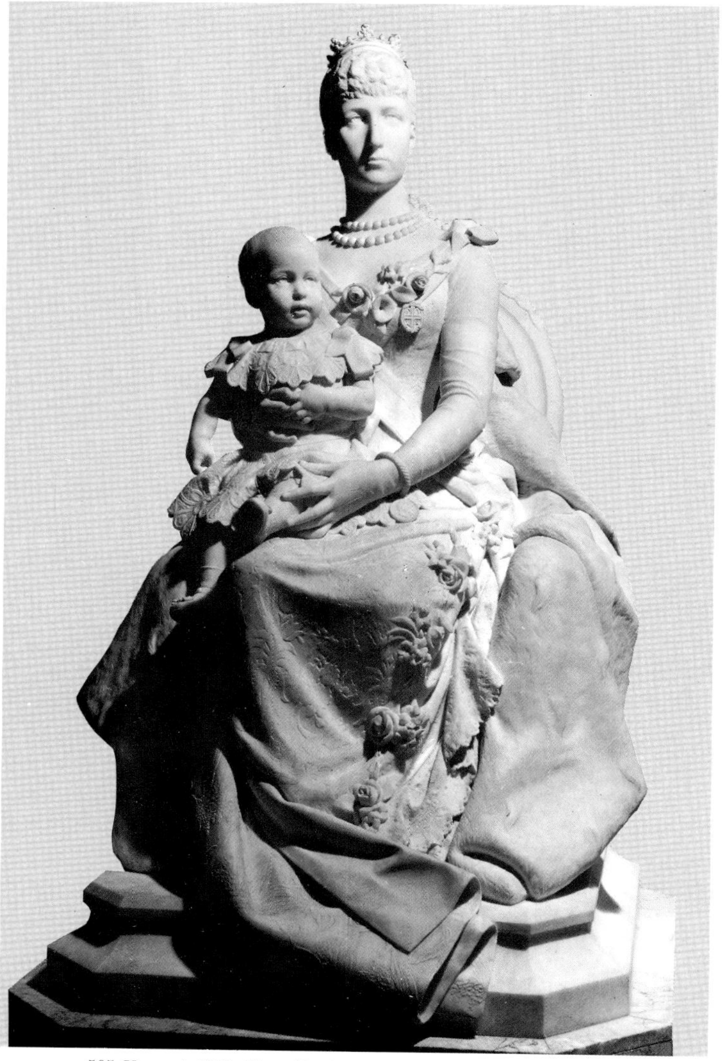

505. Venancio Vallmitjana i Barbany. *Queen María Cristina de Habsburgo with Prince Alfonso.* 1888. Terra cotta

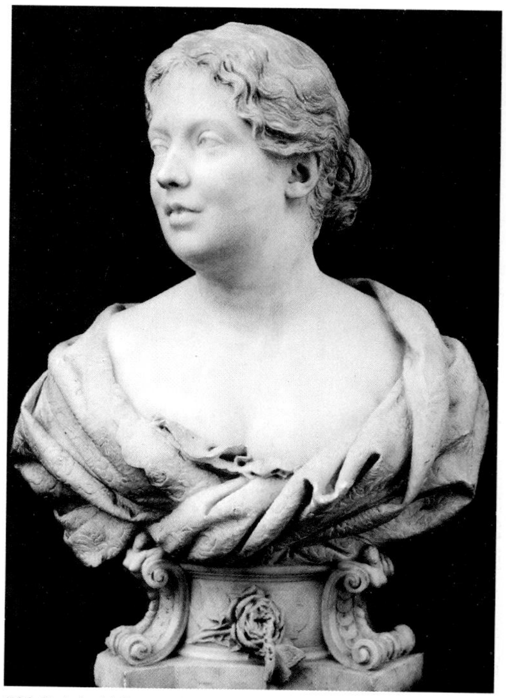

506. Reinhold Begas. *Frau von Hopfen.*
1877. Marble

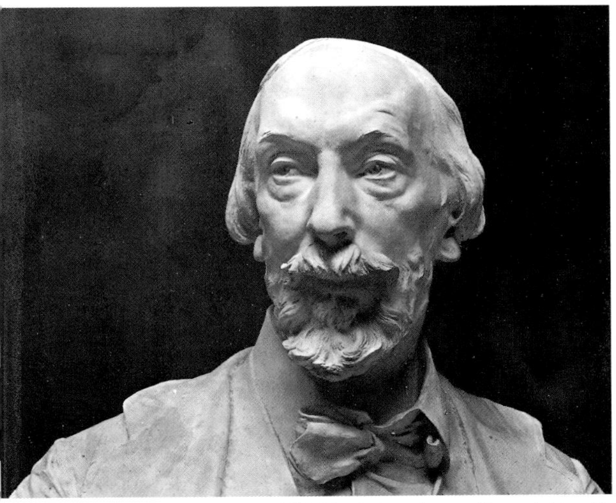
507. Jules Dalou. *Auguste Vacquerie* (detail). 1887. Plaster

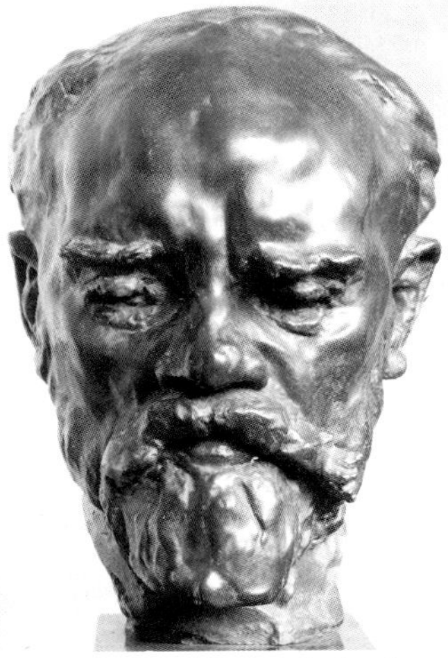
508. Josef Maratka. *Antonin Dvorák.* 1906. Bronze

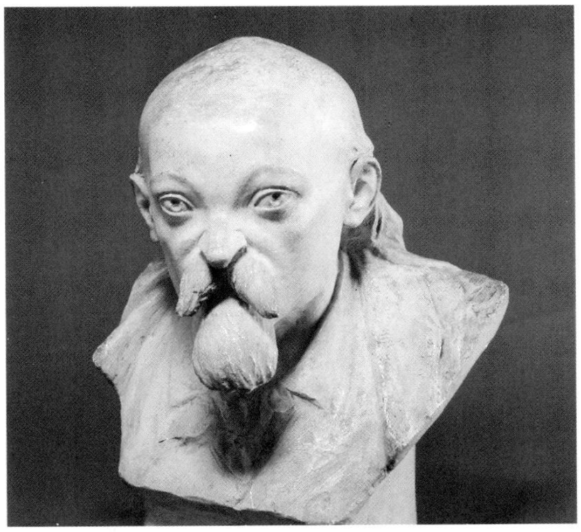
509. Philippe Solari. *Paul Cézanne.* 1904–5. Plaster

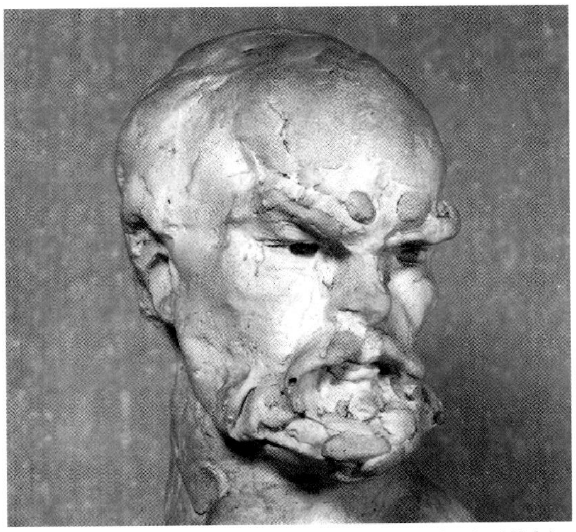
510. Rodo. *Paul Verlaine.* c. 1894. Plaster

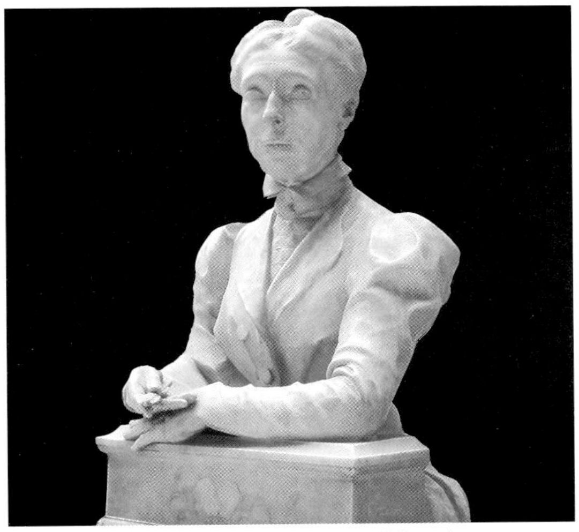
511. Pietro Canonica. *Elisabetta di Sassonia, Duchess of Genoa.* 1898. Marble

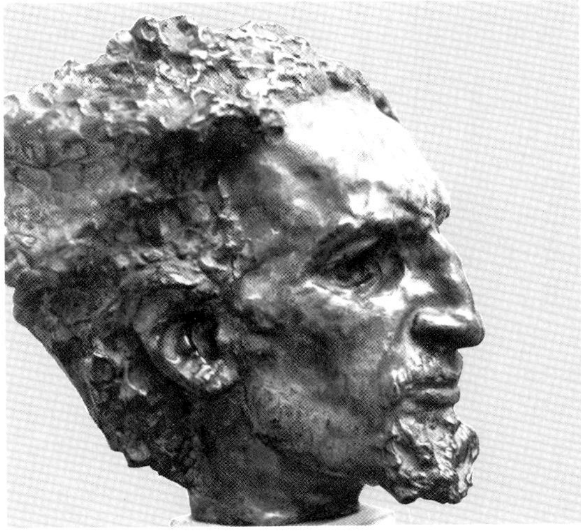
512. Seraphin Sudbinin. *Horrible.* 1906. Bronze

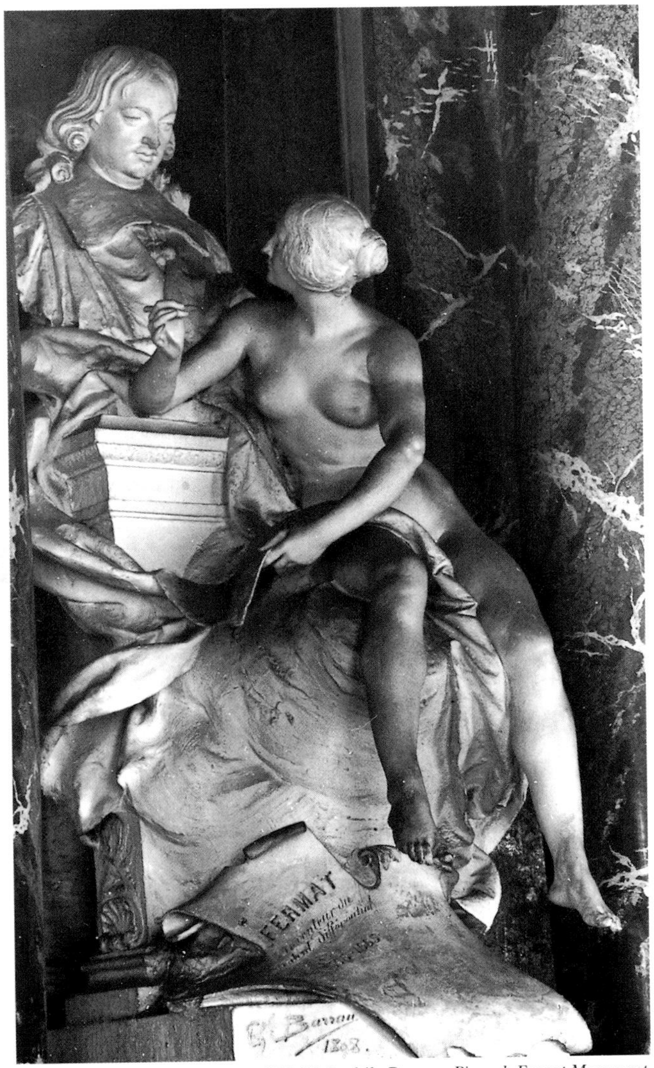

513. Théophile Barrau. *Pierre de Fermat Monument.* 1898. Marble

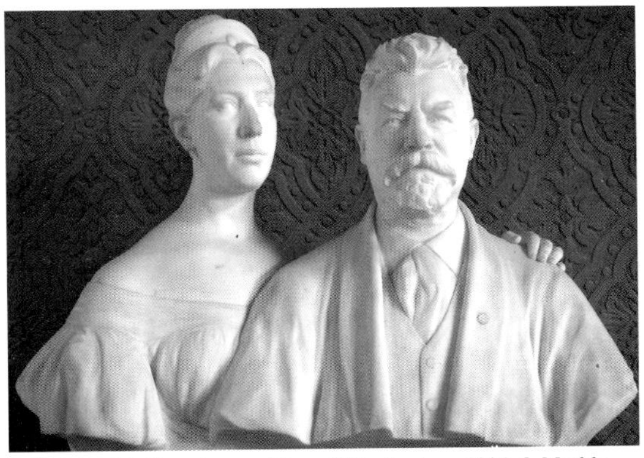
514. Ludvig Brandstrup. *Mr. and Mrs. Jacobsen.* 1904–6. Marble

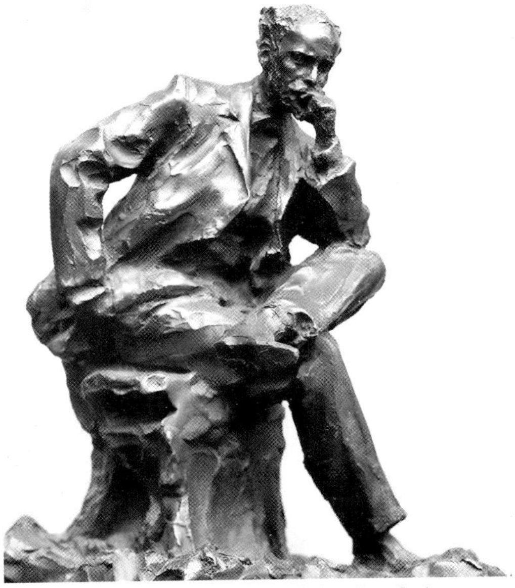
515. Paul Trubetskoy. *The Painter, Isaac Levitan.* 1899. Bronze

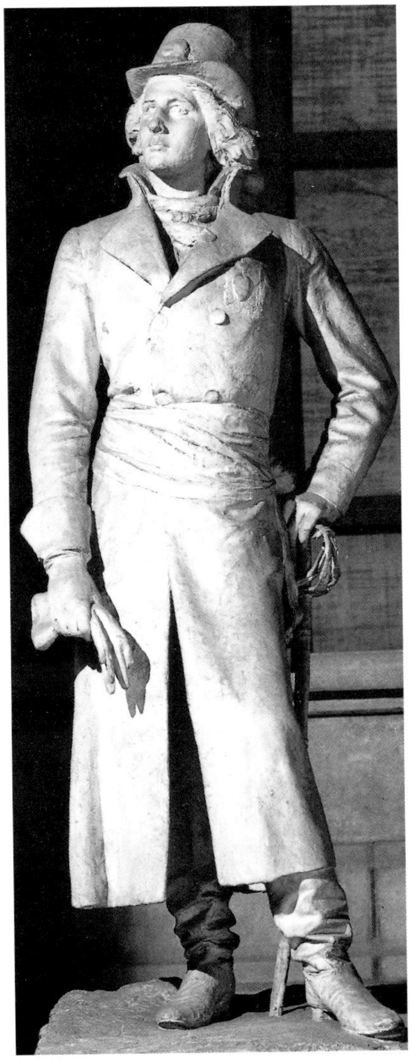
516. Alexandre Falguière. *Henri de la Rochejaquelein.* 1895. Plaster

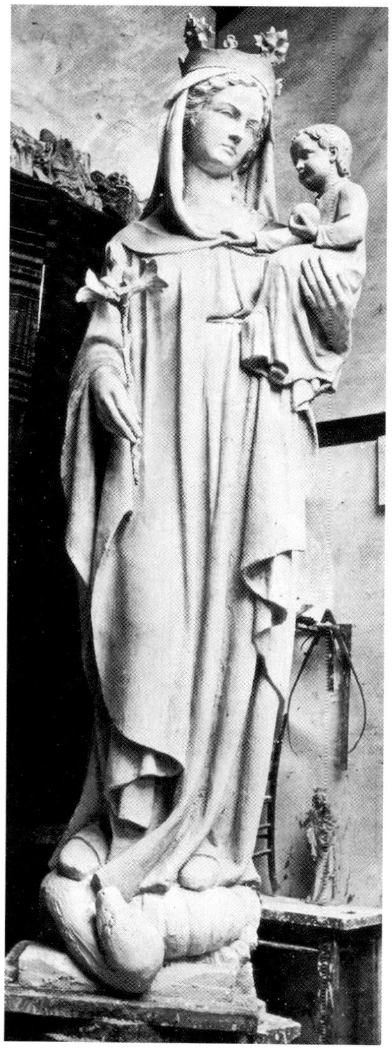

517. François-Antoine Zoegger. *Notre-Dame du Retour* (in the artist's studio)

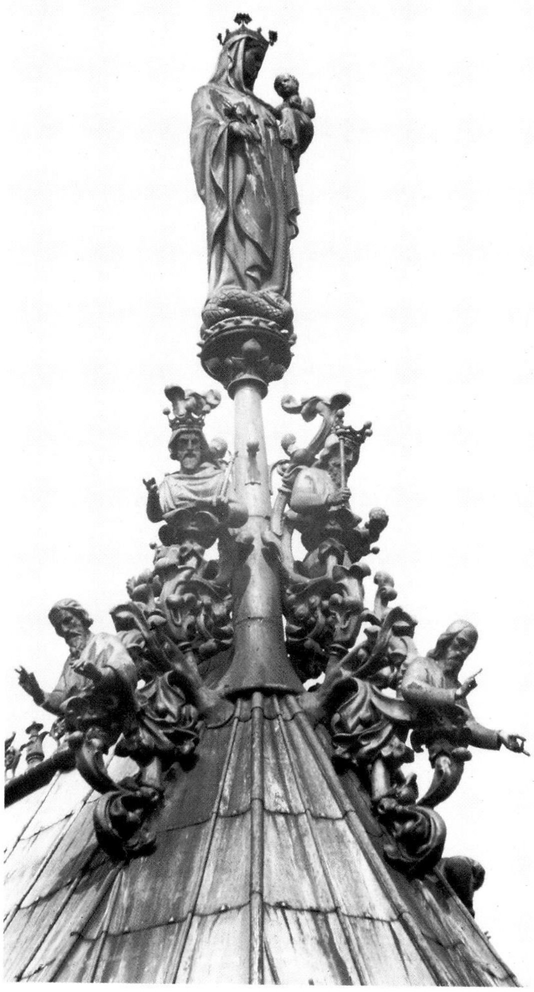

518. François-Antoine Zoegger. *The Virgin and the Prophets.* 1873. Embossed copper

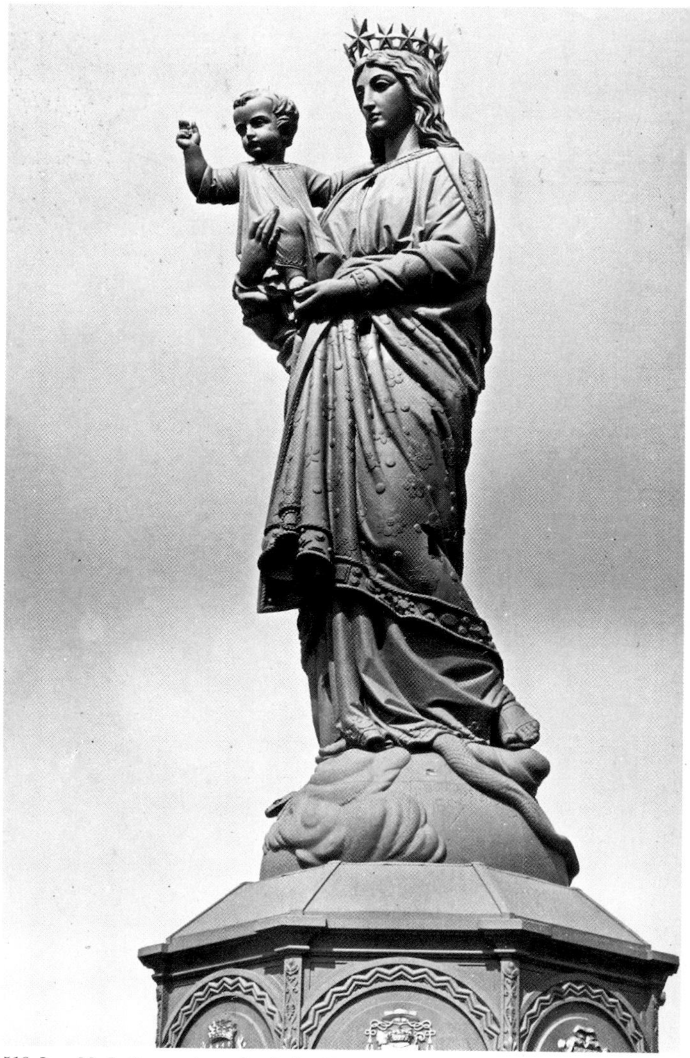

519. Jean-Marie Bonnassieux. *Our Lady of France.* 1860–64. Bronze

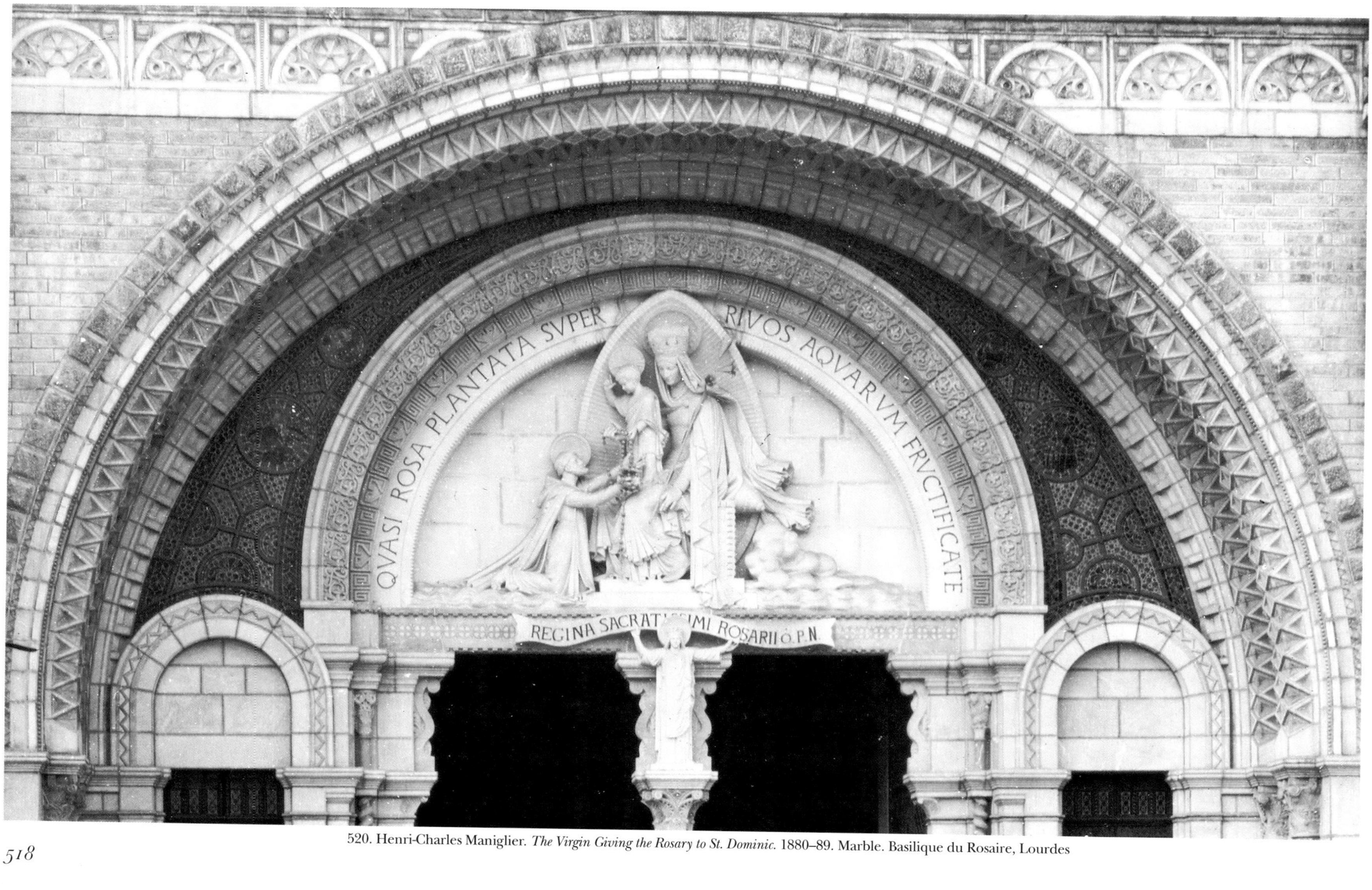

520. Henri-Charles Maniglier. *The Virgin Giving the Rosary to St. Dominic.* 1880–89. Marble. Basilique du Rosaire, Lourdes

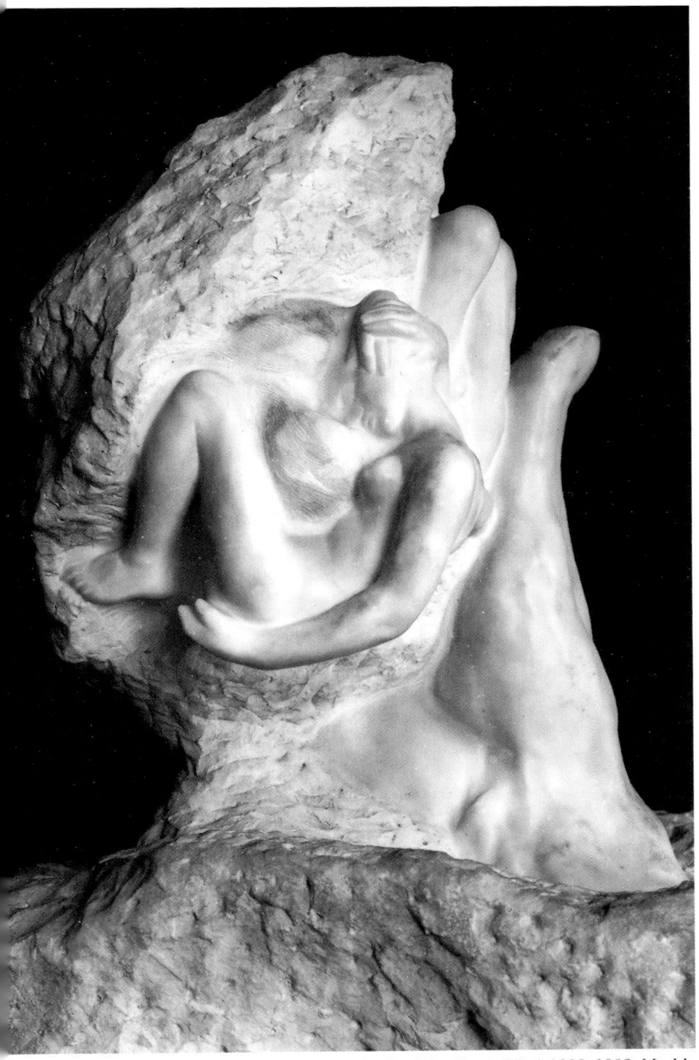

521. Auguste Rodin. *The Hand of God.* 1898–1902. Marble

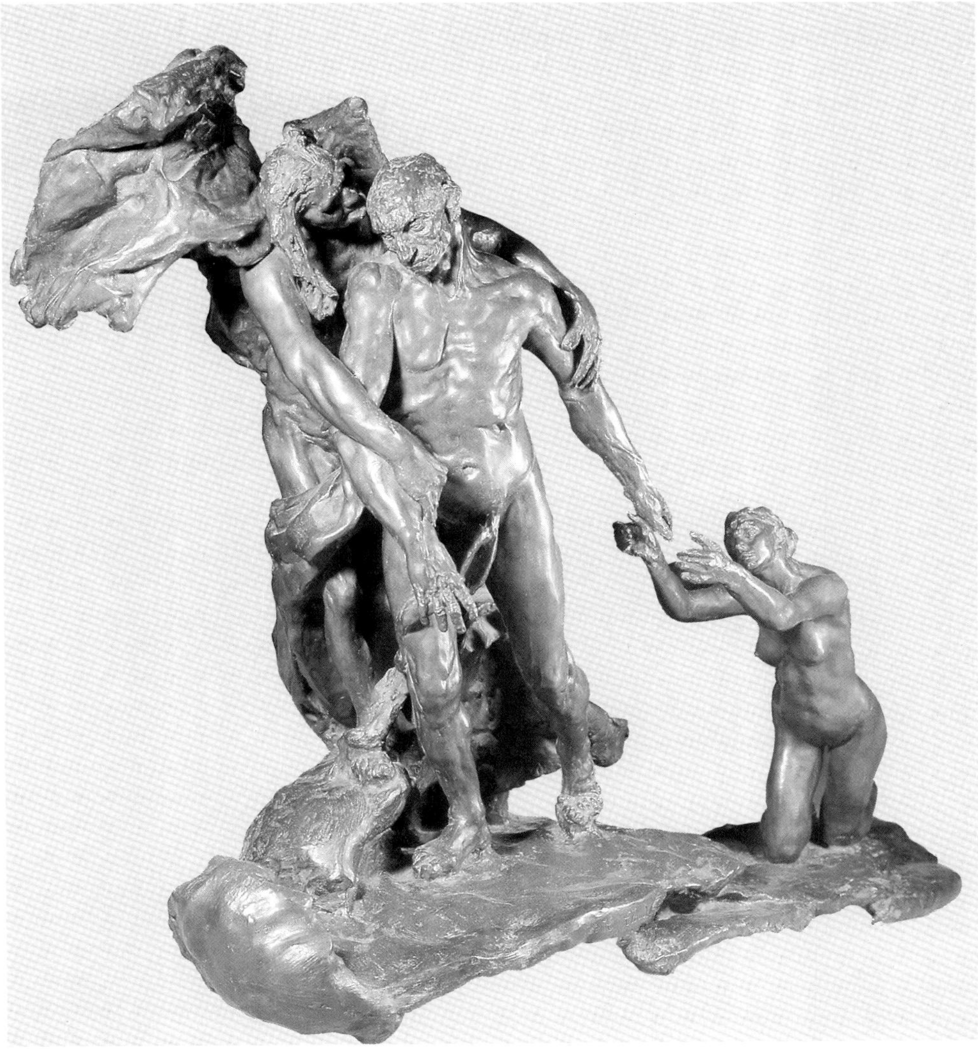

522. Camille Claudel. *Middle Age.* 1899–1903. Bronze

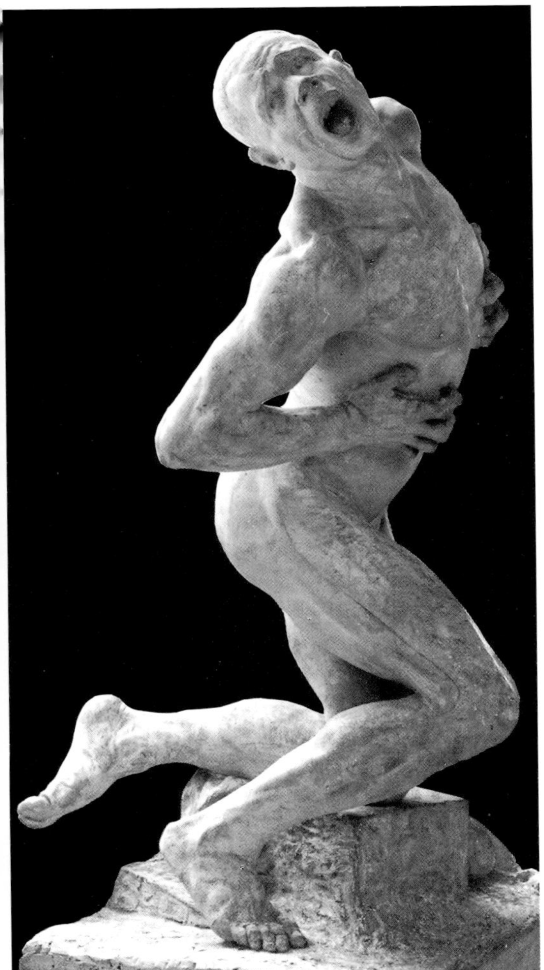

523. Albert Miserey. *The Poison of the Borgias.* 1894. Plaster

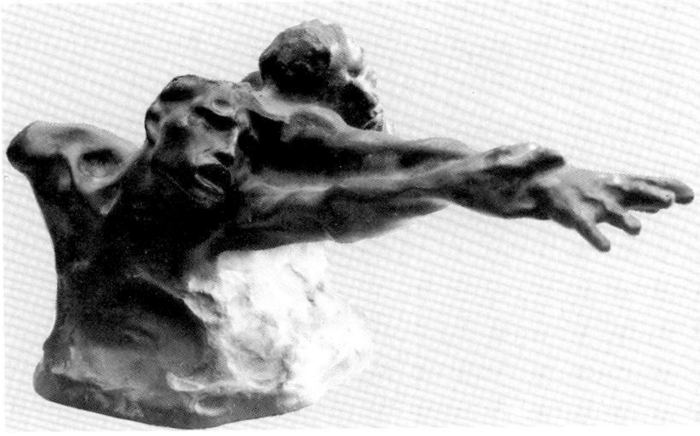

524. Carl Millès. *The Struggle for Existence.* 1903. Bronze

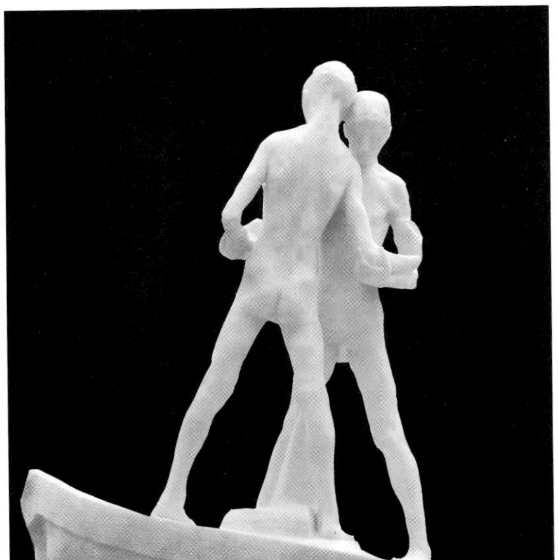

525. Georges Minne. *Solidarity.* 1898. Marble

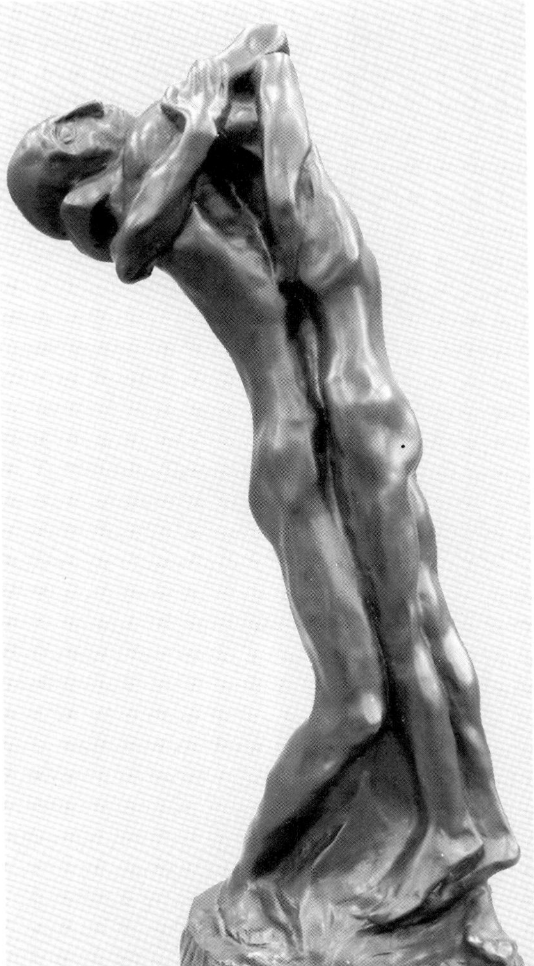

526. Georges Minne. *The Prodigal Son.* 1896. Bronze

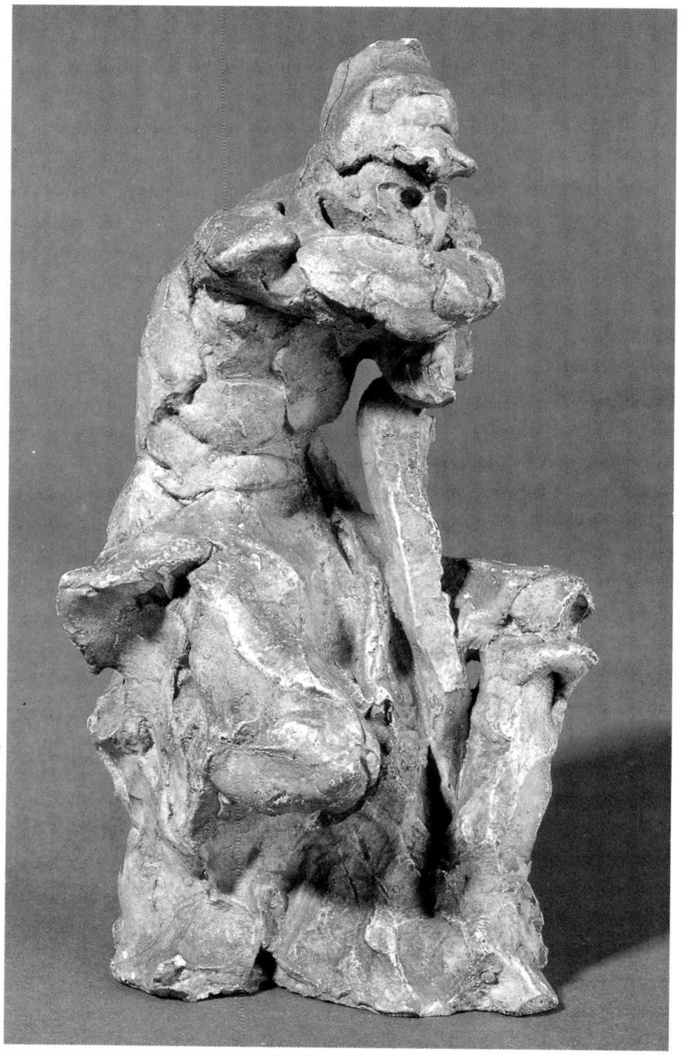

527. Jean-Baptiste Carpeaux. *Pensive Warrior.* Plaster

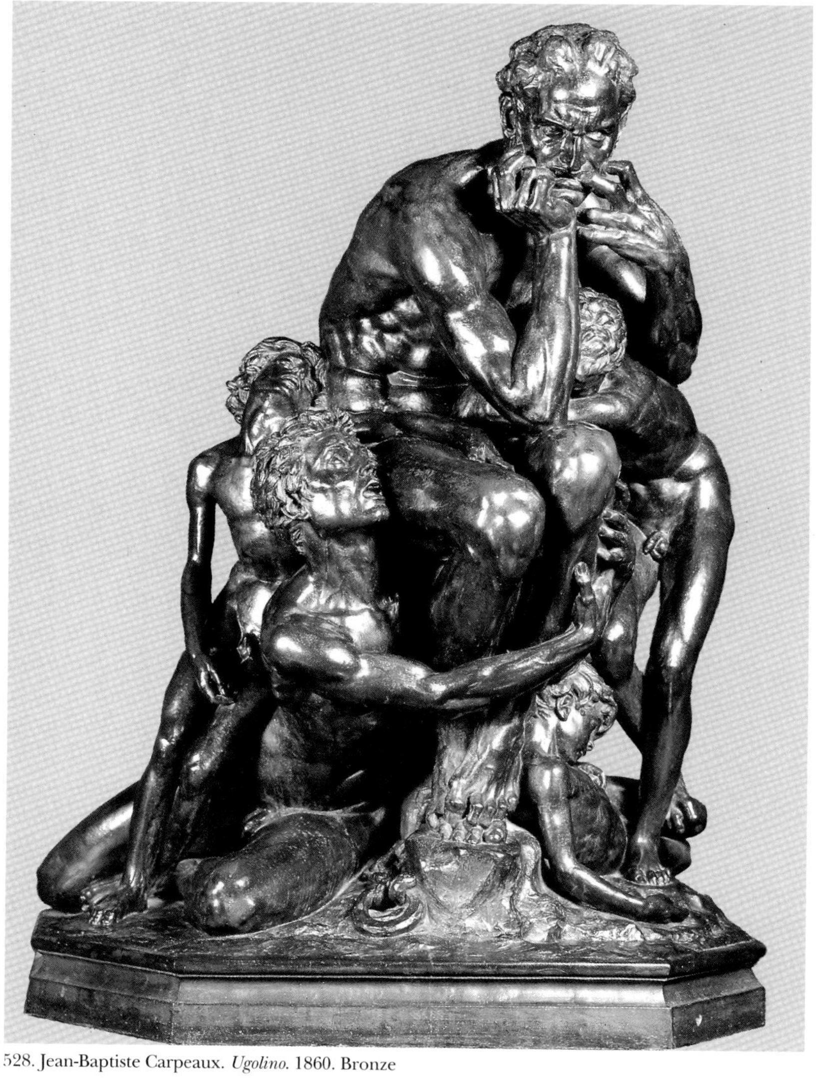

528. Jean-Baptiste Carpeaux. *Ugolino.* 1860. Bronze

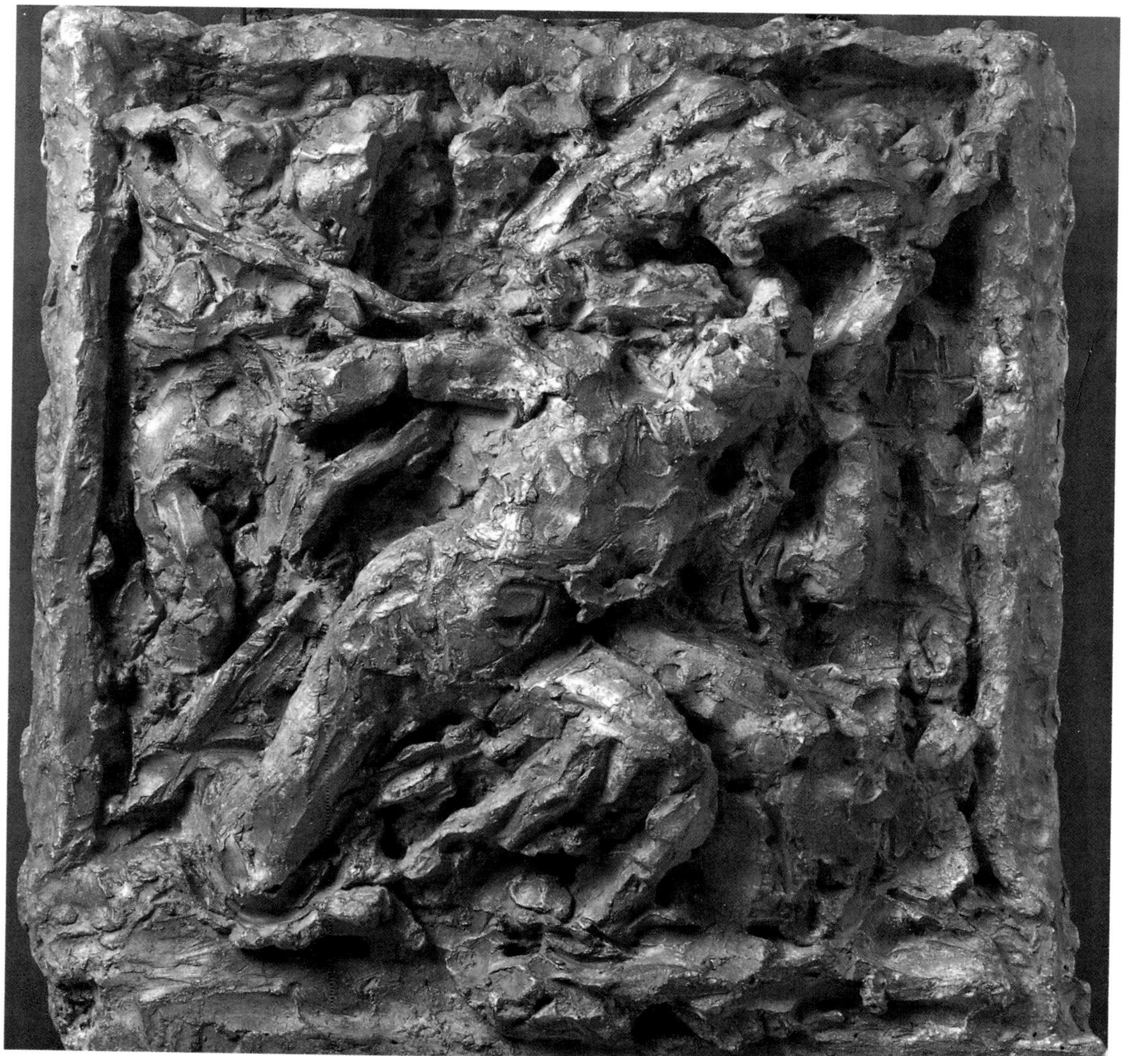

529. Jean-Baptiste Carpeaux. *The Town of Valenciennes Defending its Ramparts.* 1868. Plaster

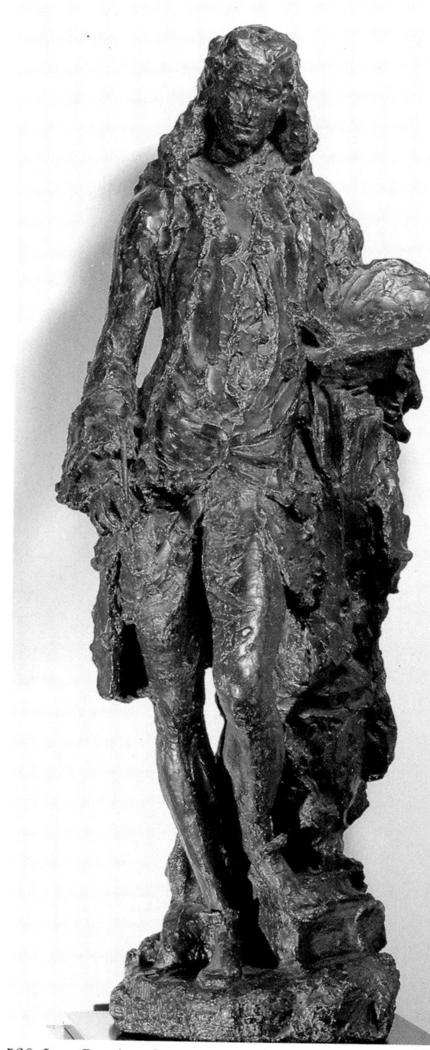

530. Jean-Baptiste Carpeaux. *Antoine Watteau.* c. 1863–64. Bronze

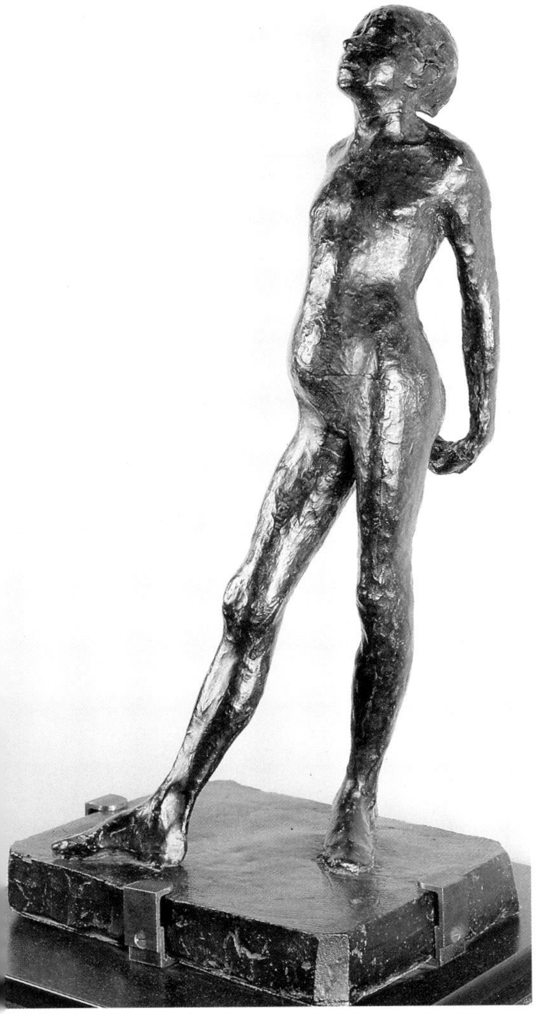

531. Edgar Degas. *Nude Study for the Little Fourteen-Year-Old Dancer.* c. 1880. Bronze

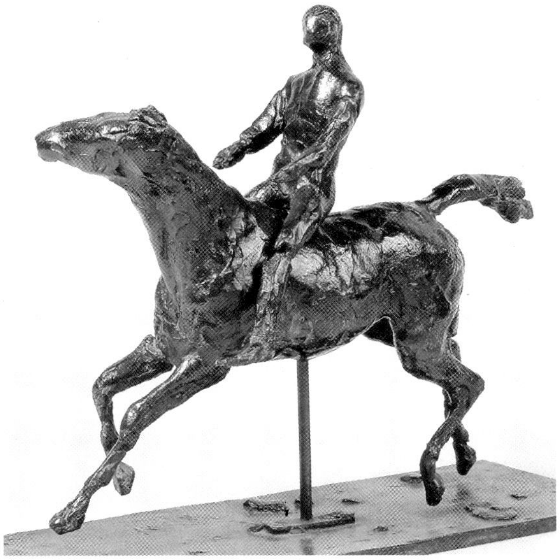

532. Edgar Degas. *Horse and Rider.* Bronze

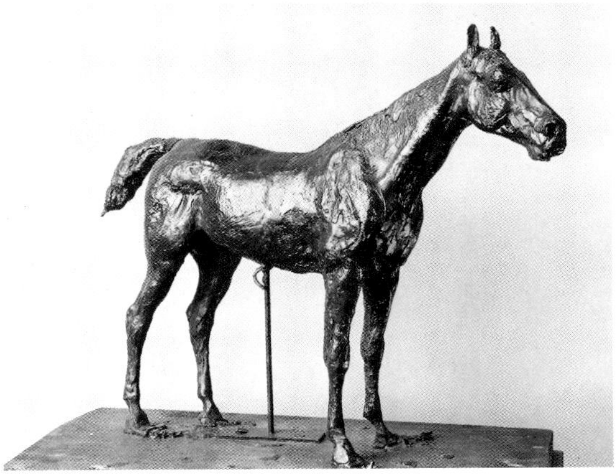

533. Edgar Degas. *Horse Standing.* Wax

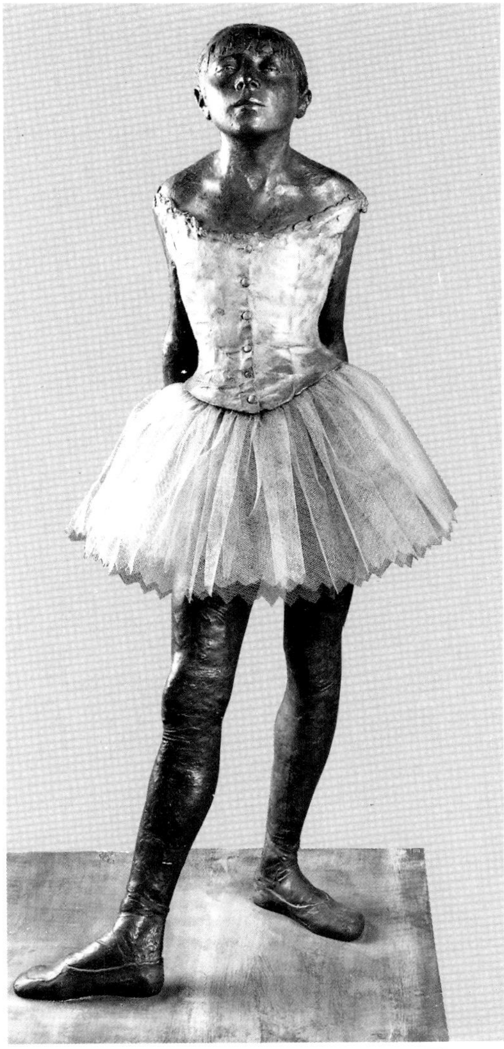

534. Edgar Degas. *The Little Fourteen-Year-Old Dancer, 1880.* 1881. Bronze, tulle, and satin

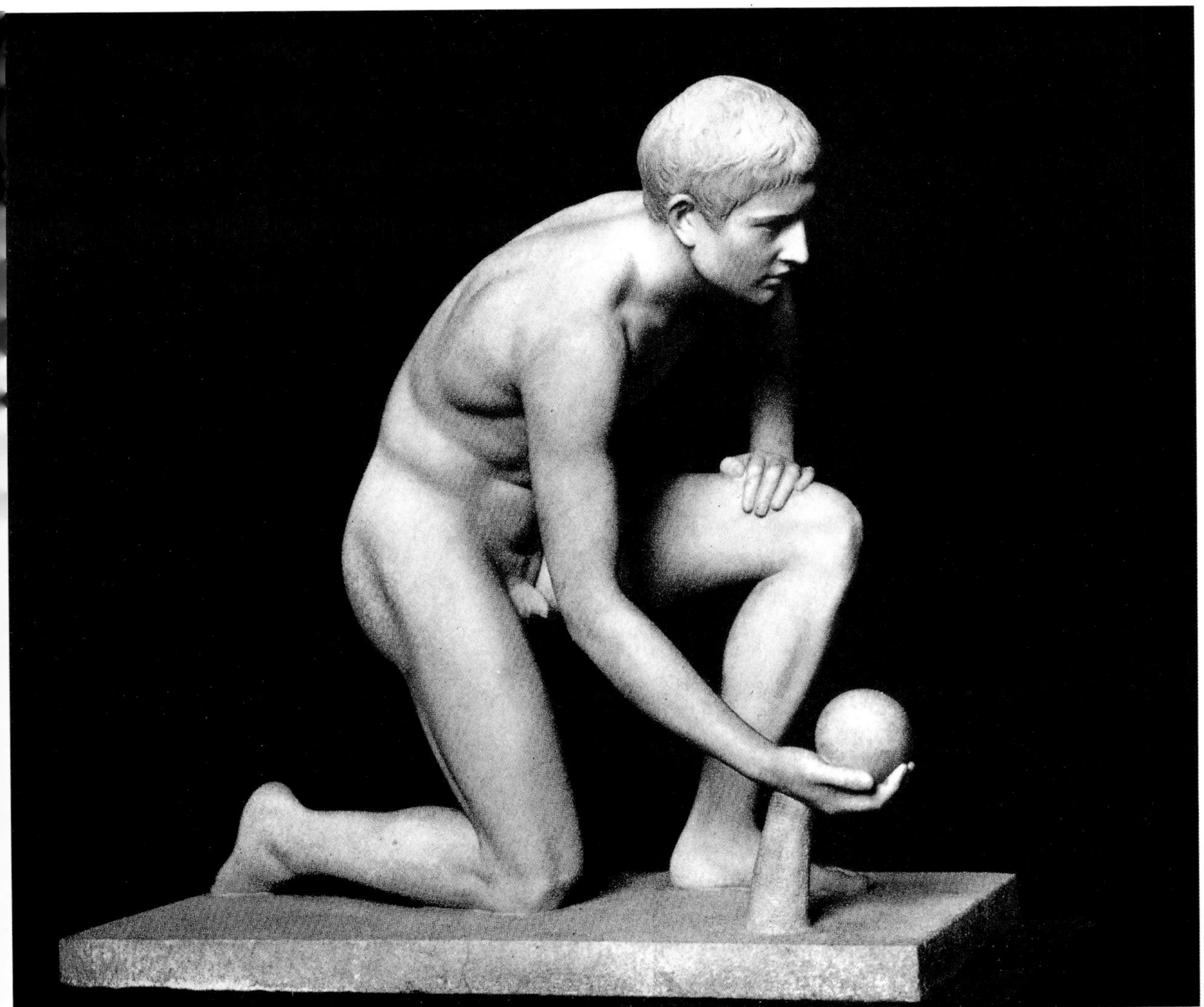

535. Adolf von Hildebrand. *The Bowls Player.* 1887. Marble

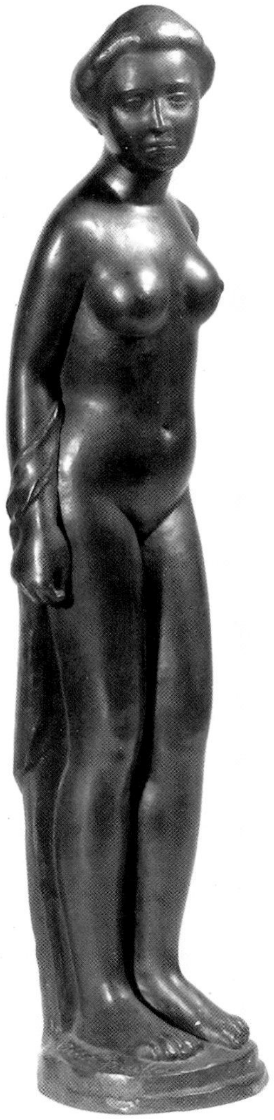

536. Aristide Maillol. *Standing Bather.* 1899. Bronze

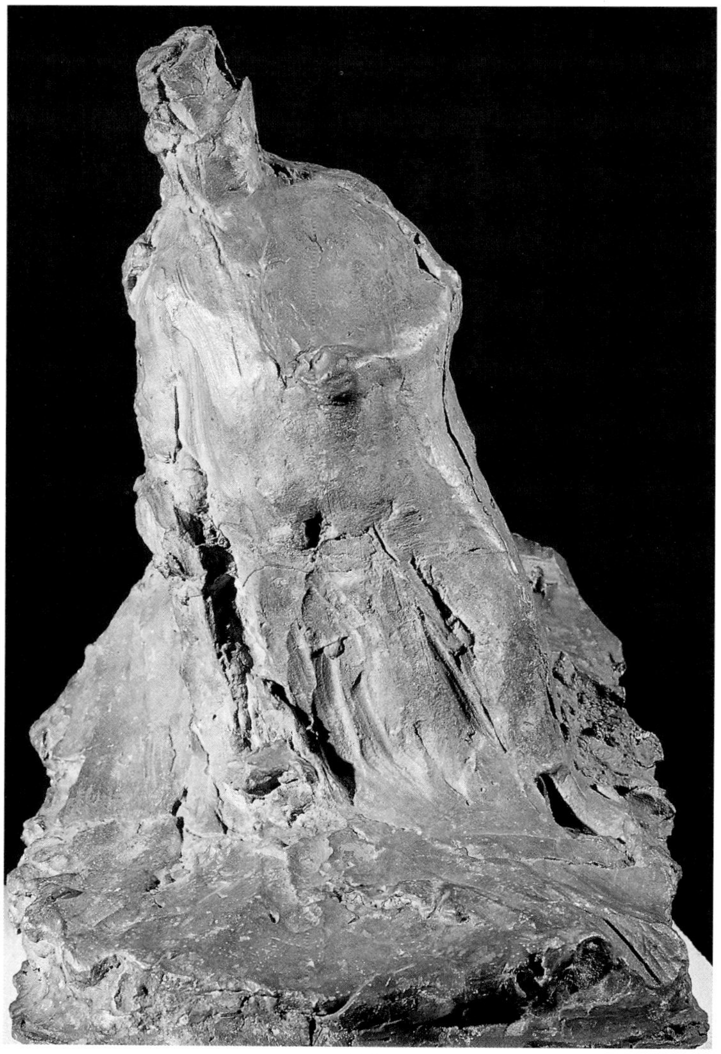

537. Medardo Rosso. *The Bookmaker.* 1894. Wax

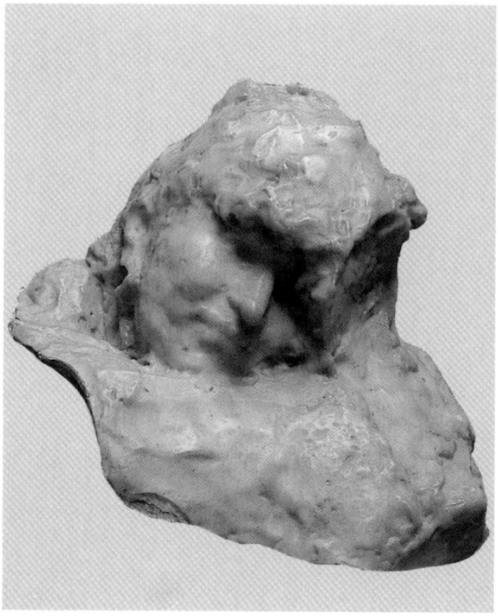

538. Medardo Rosso. *The Flesh of Others.* 1883. Plaster

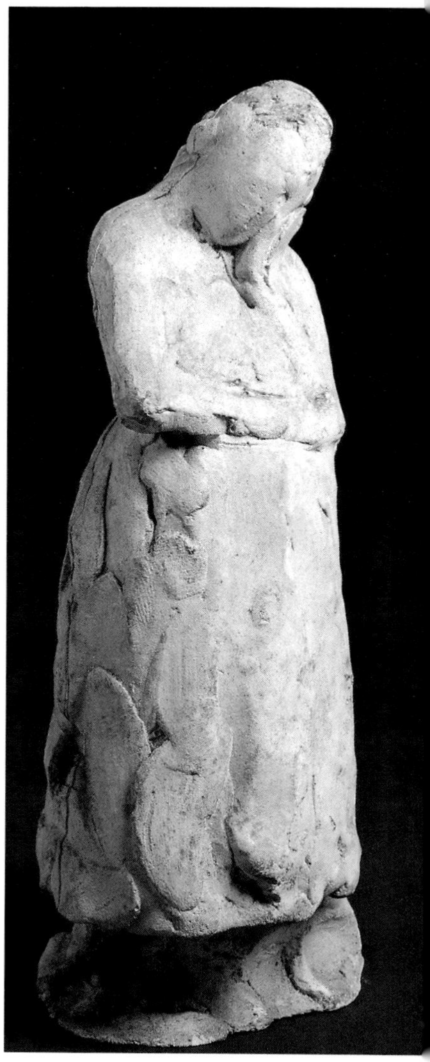

539. François Pompon. *Pensive Countrywoman.* 1905. Plaster

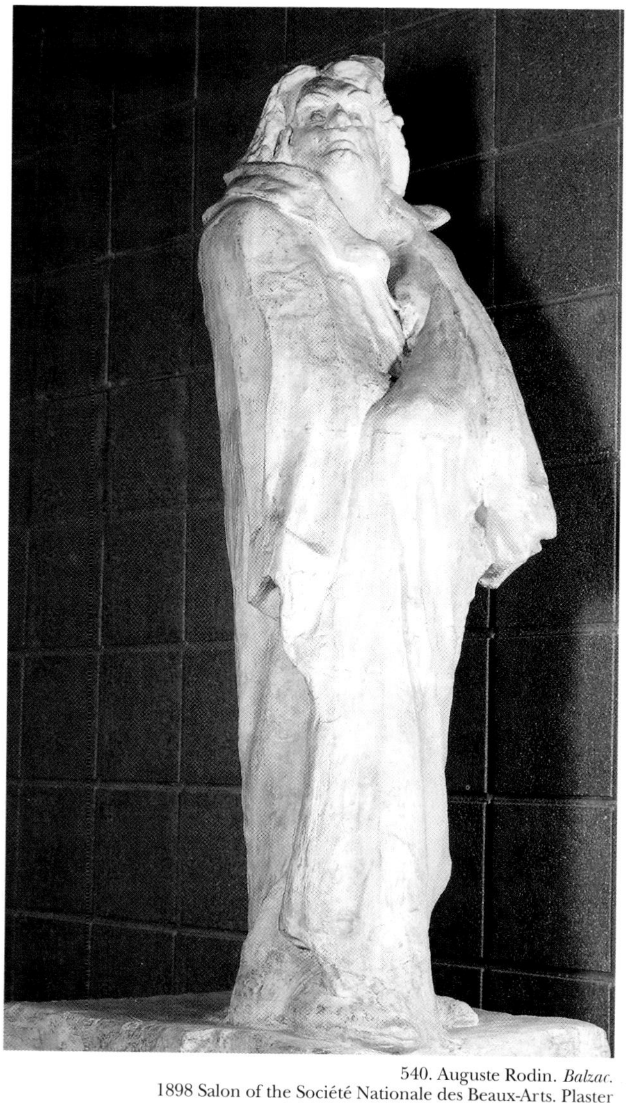

540. Auguste Rodin. *Balzac.* 1898 Salon of the Société Nationale des Beaux-Arts. Plaster

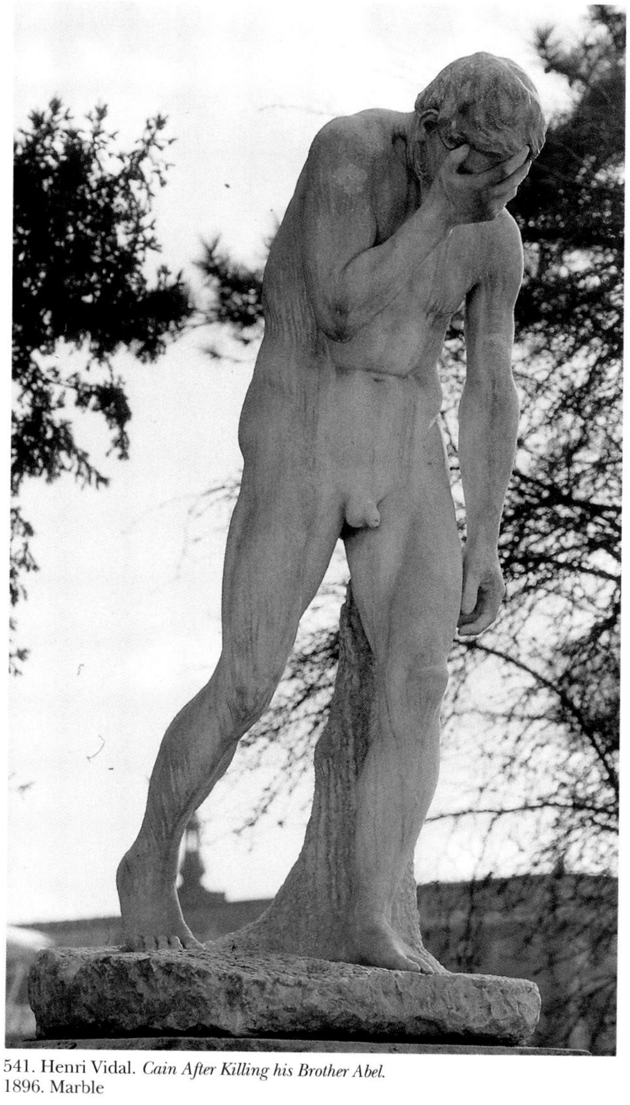

541. Henri Vidal. *Cain After Killing his Brother Abel.* 1896. Marble

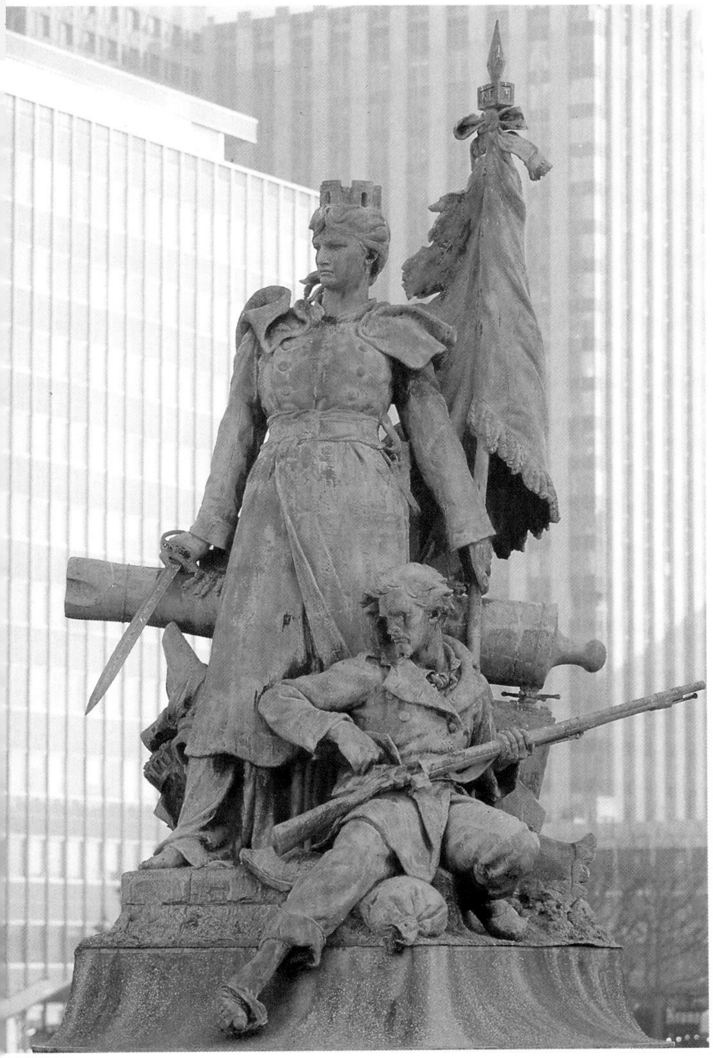

542. Louis-Ernest Barrias. *Monument to the Defense of Paris.* 1879–83. Bronze

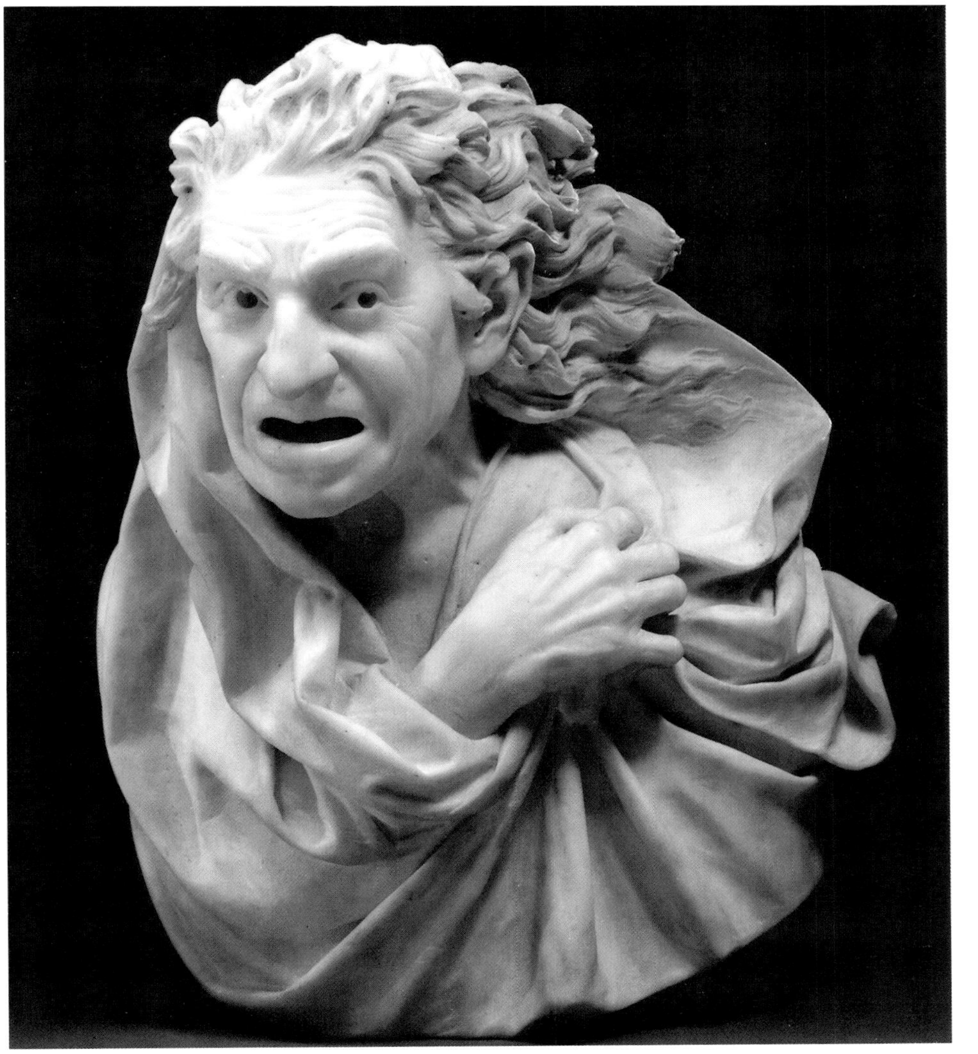

543. Edward Thaxter. *Meg Merrilies Furies.* 1881. Marble

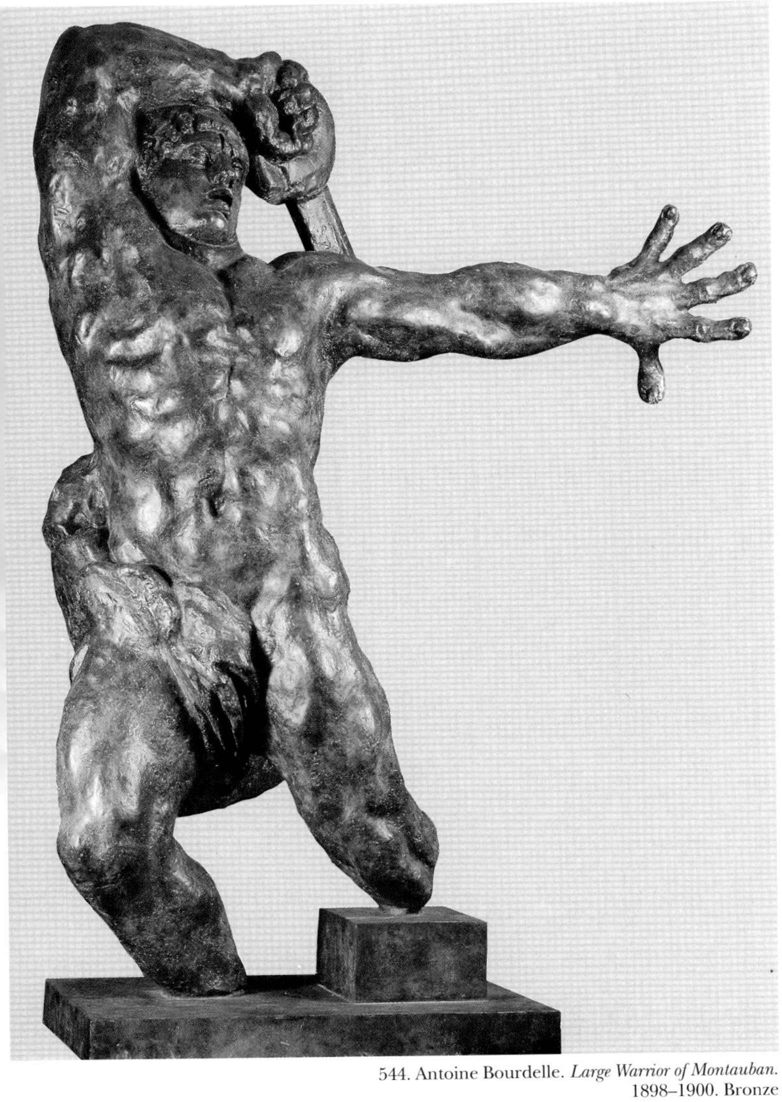

544. Antoine Bourdelle. *Large Warrior of Montauban.* 1898–1900. Bronze

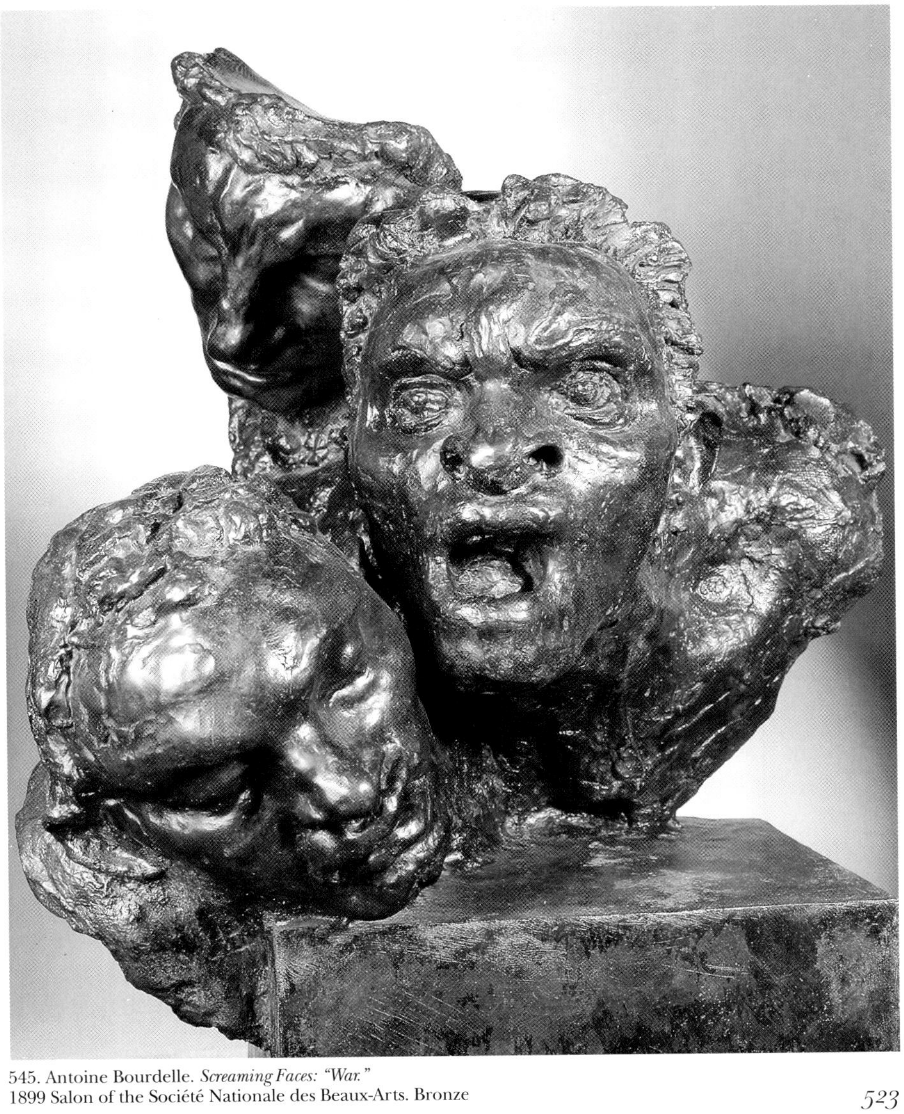

545. Antoine Bourdelle. *Screaming Faces: "War."* 1899 Salon of the Société Nationale des Beaux-Arts. Bronze

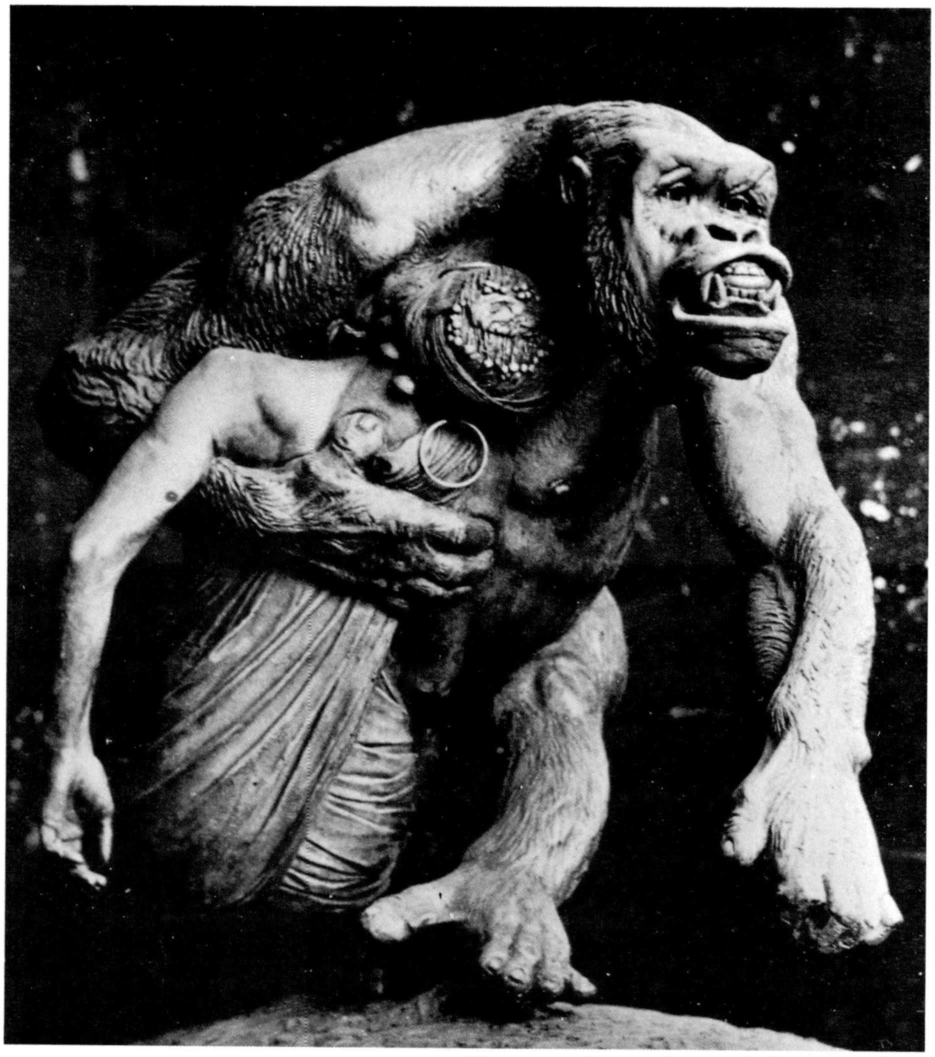

546. Emmanuel Fremiet. *Female Gorilla Carrying off a Negress.*
1859 Salon. Plaster

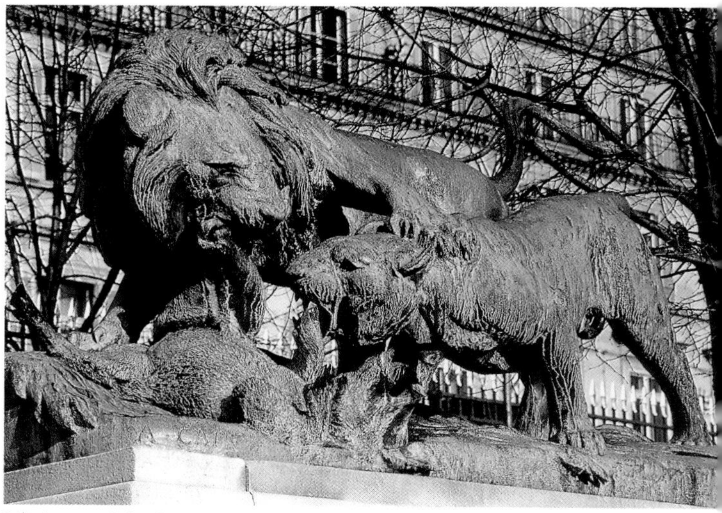

547. Auguste Cain. *Lion and Lioness Fighting Over a Boar.*
1882. Bronze

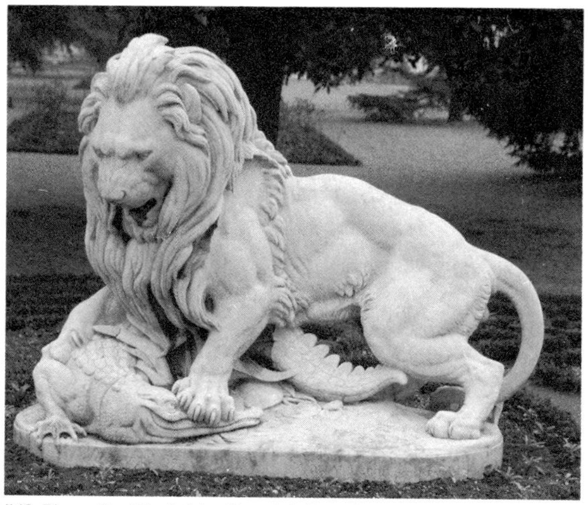

548. Pierre Rouillard. *Lion Overwhelming a Crocodile.* 1864. Marble.
Beylerbeyi Palace Gardens, Istanbul

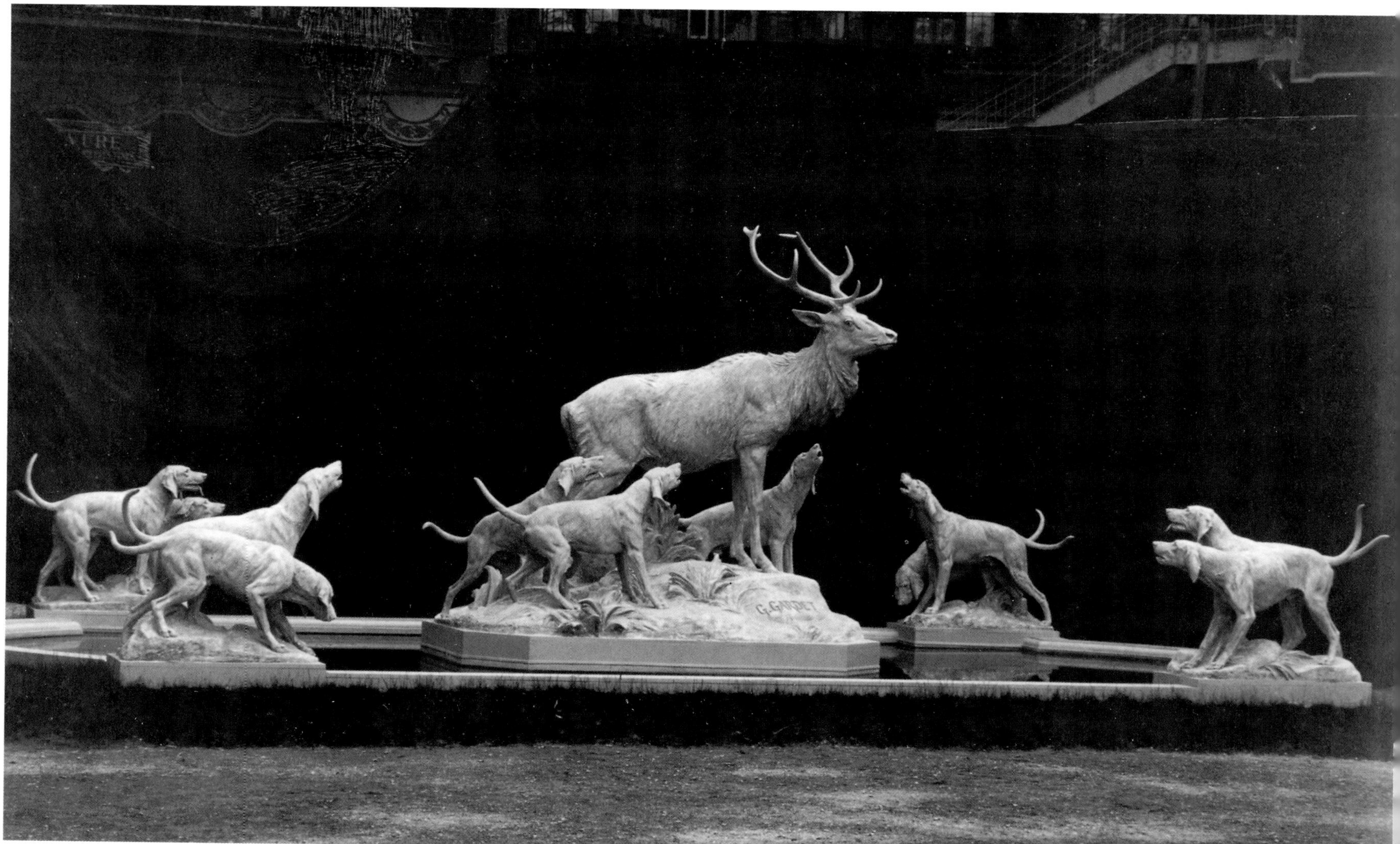

549. Georges Gardet. *The Kill.* 1912. Bronze

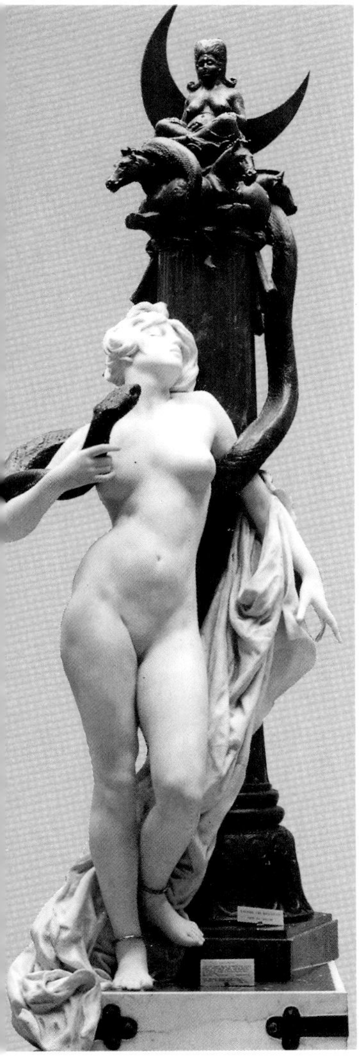

550. Maurice-Désiré Ferrary. *Salammbô.* 1899. Marble and bronze

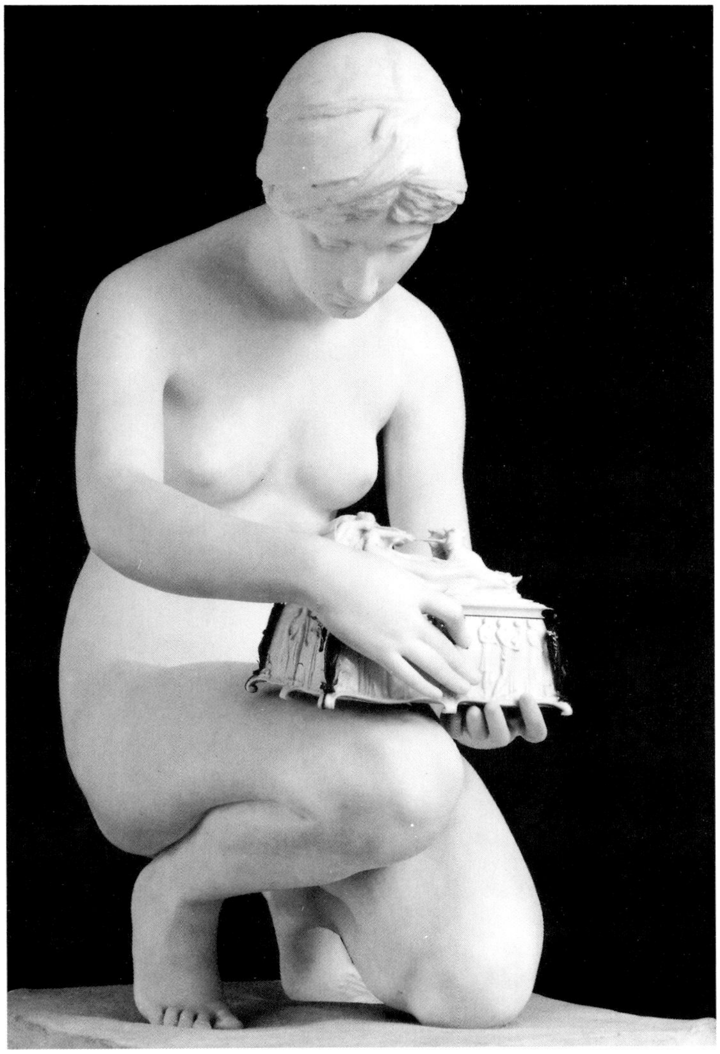

551. Harry Bates. *Pandora.* 1890. Marble, ivory, and bronze

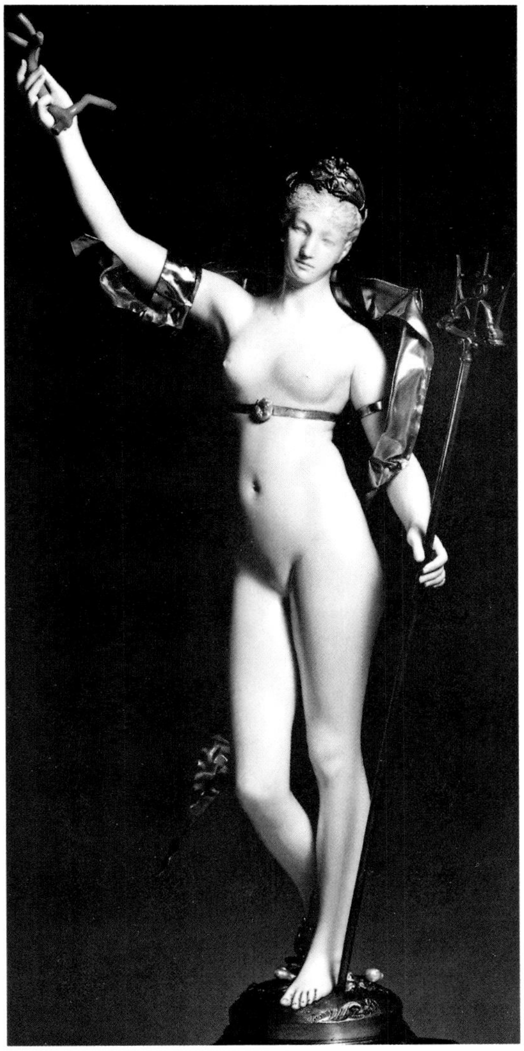

552. Antonin Mercié. *Amphitrite.* 1900. Ivory, silver, and gold

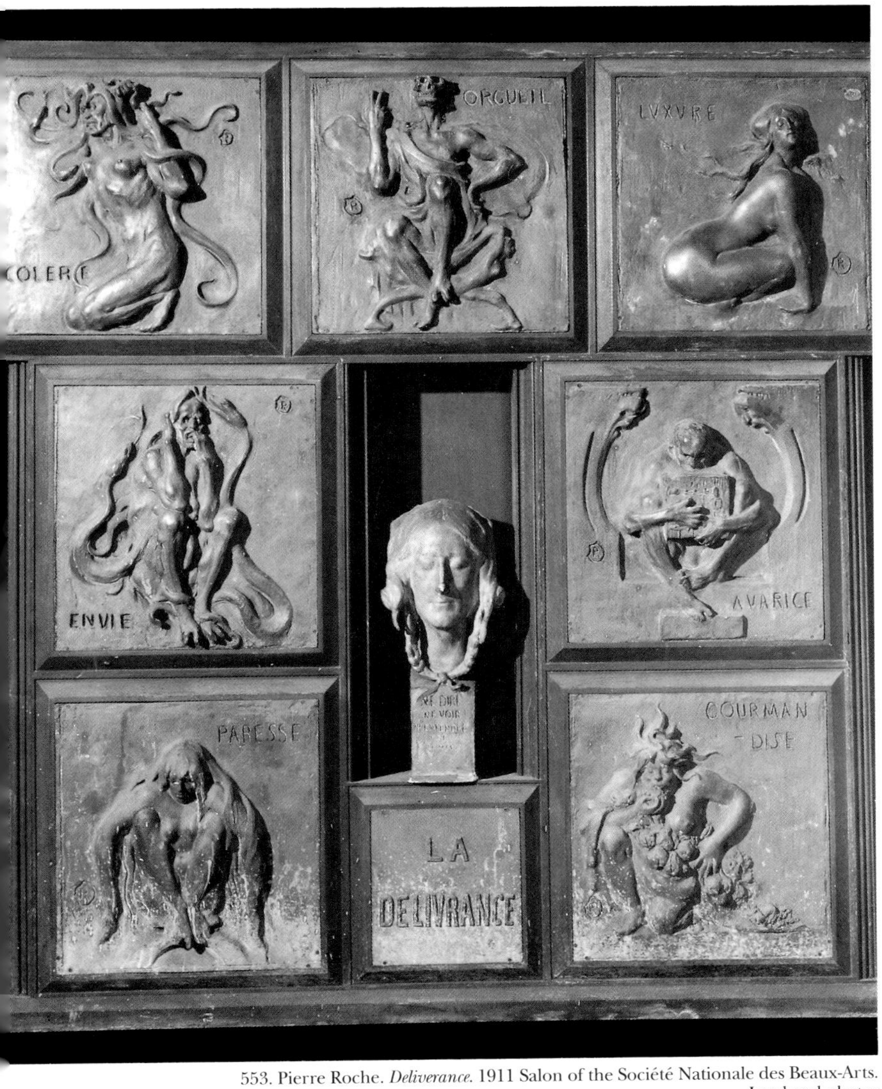

553. Pierre Roche. *Deliverance.* 1911 Salon of the Société Nationale des Beaux-Arts. Lead and plaster

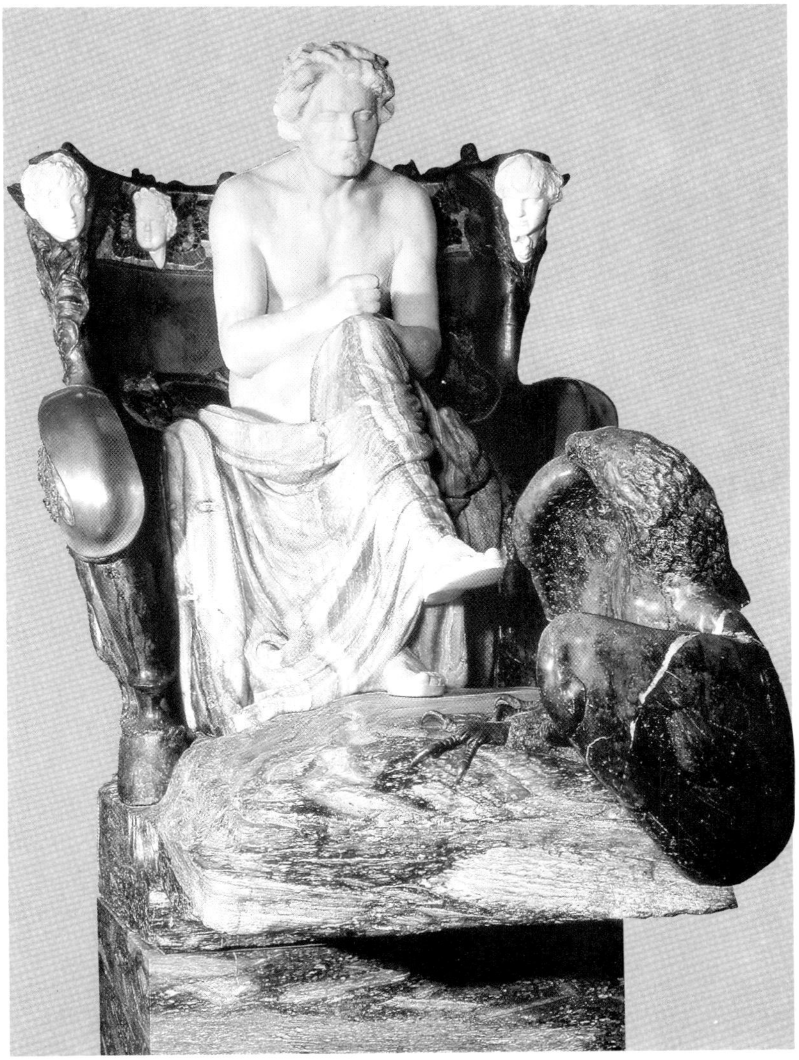

554. Max Klinger. *Beethoven Monument.* 1899–1902. White, black, and purple marble, alabaster, ivory, and bronze

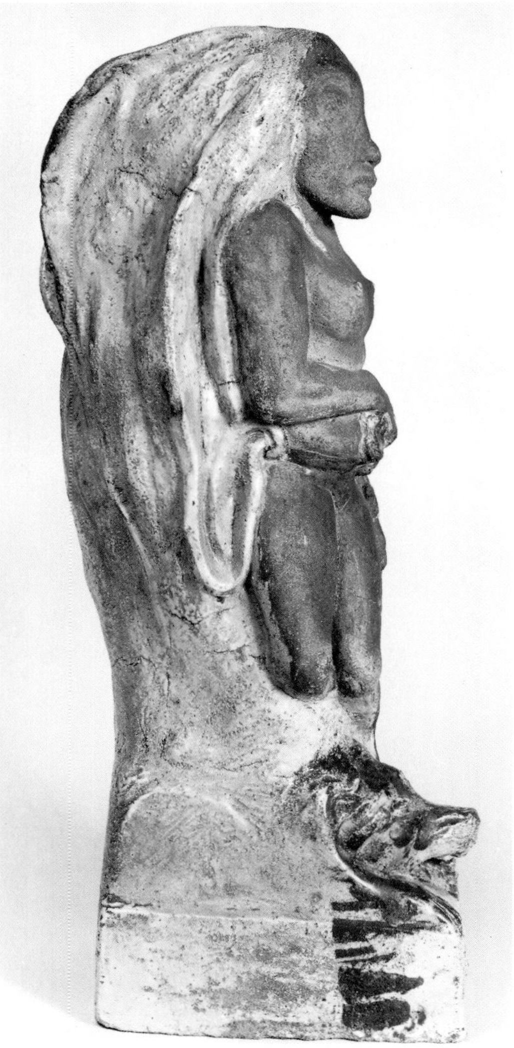

555. Paul Gauguin. *Oviri.* 1894. Stoneware

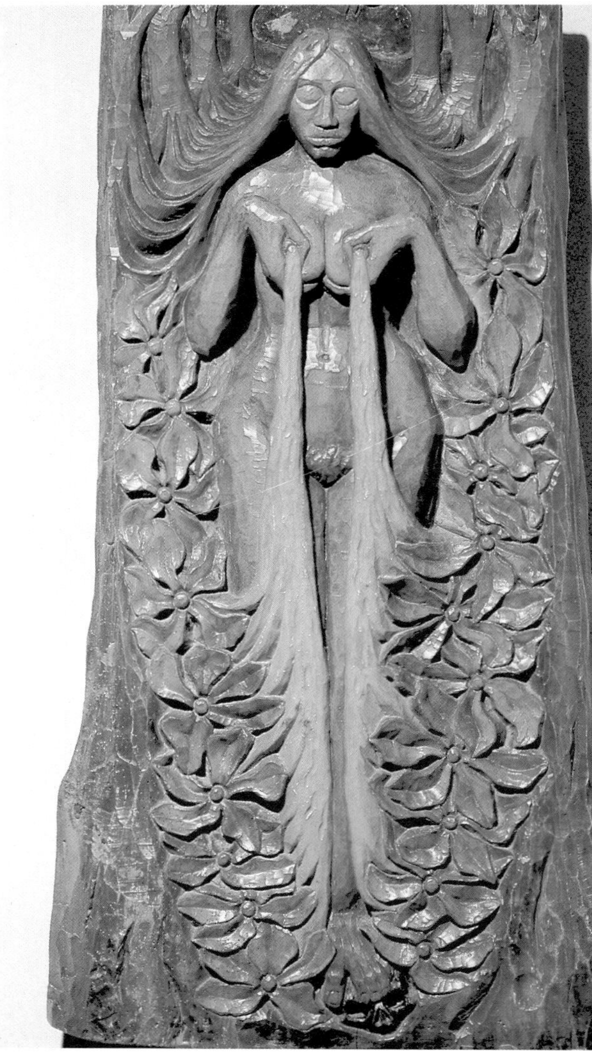

556. Georges Lacombe. *Isis.* 1895 Salon des Indépendants. Polychrome wood

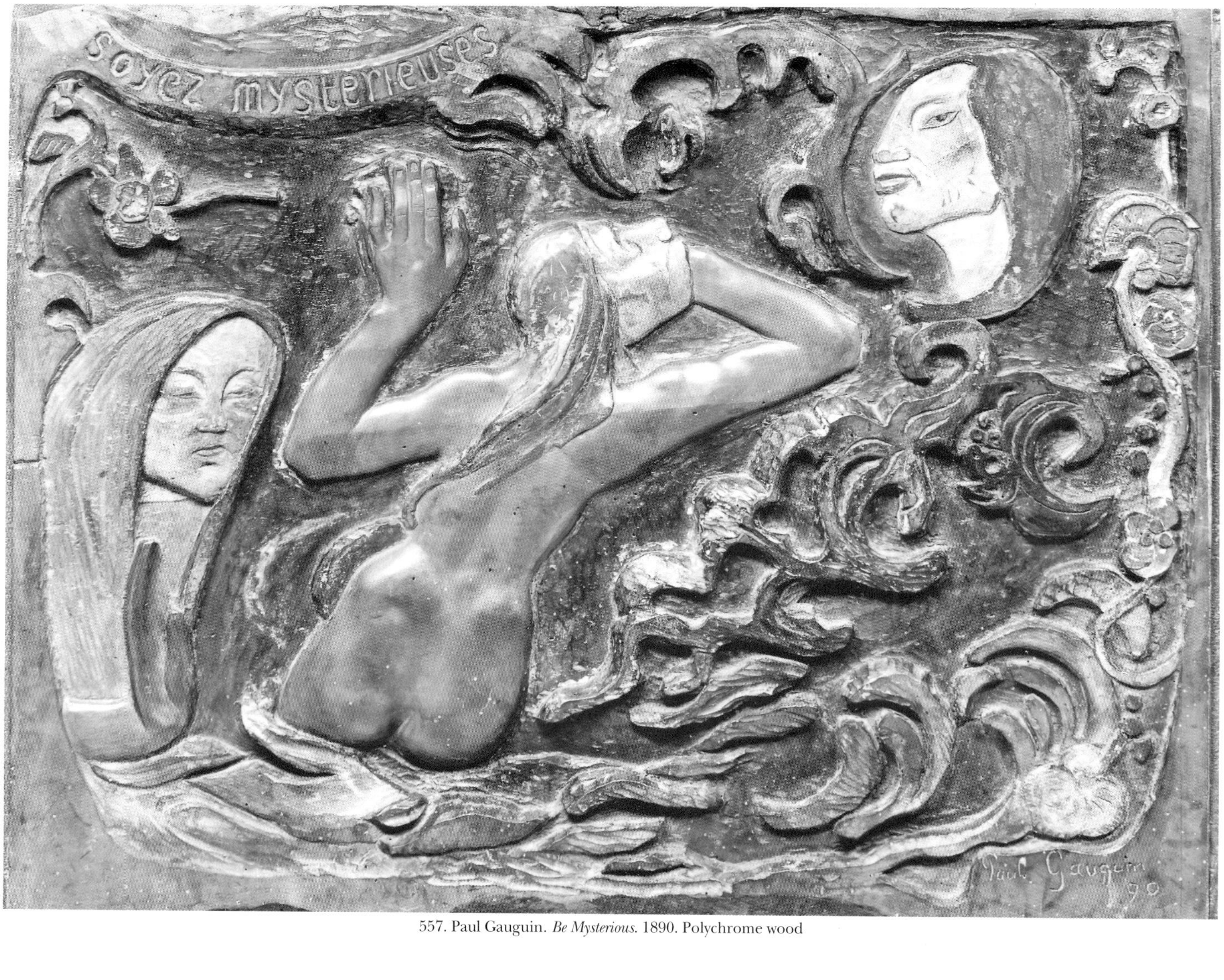

557. Paul Gauguin. *Be Mysterious.* 1890. Polychrome wood

PAINTING

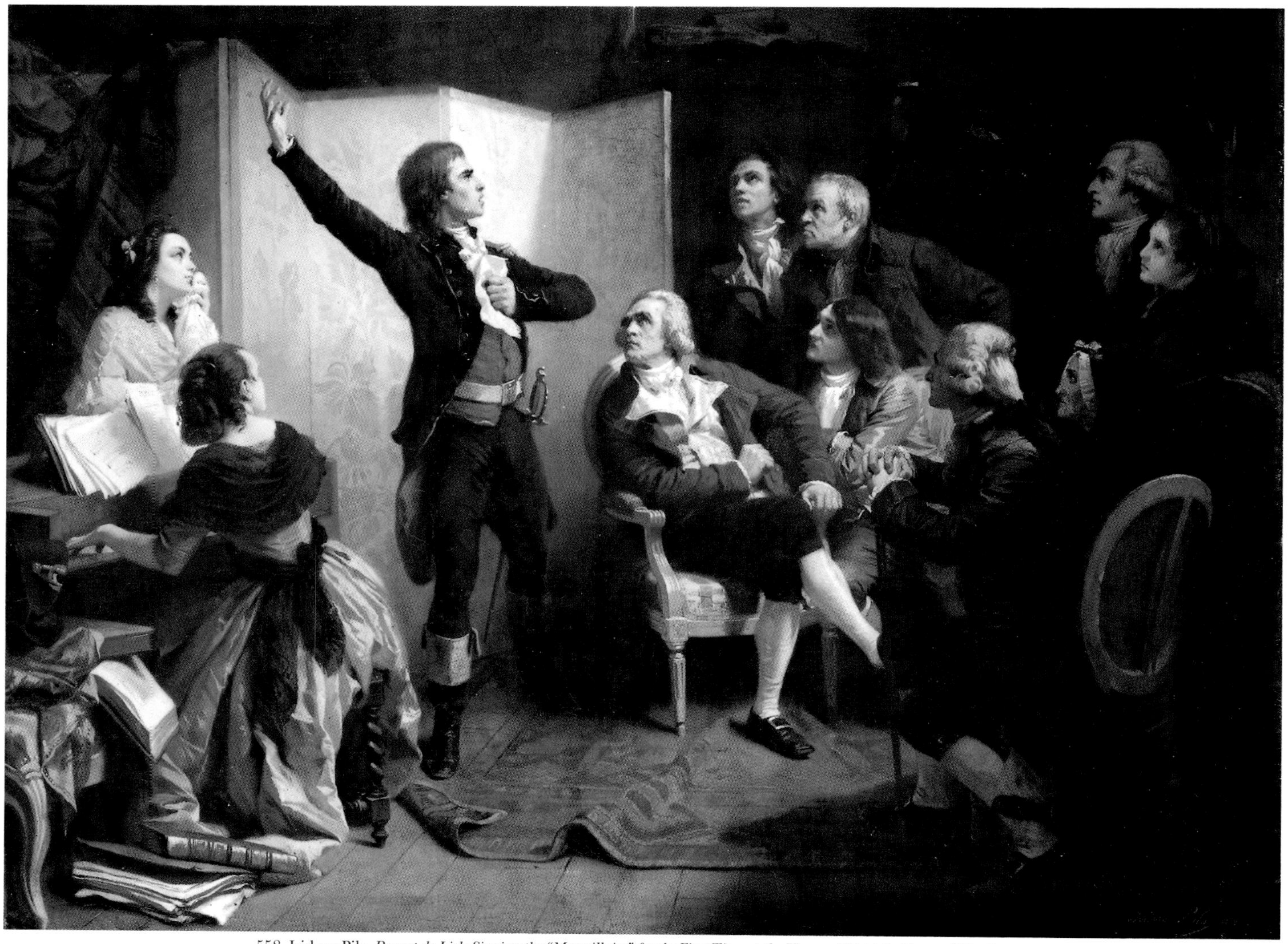

558. Isidore Pils. *Rouget de Lisle Singing the "Marseillaise" for the First Time at the House of Dietrick, Mayor of Strasbourg.* 1849 Salon. Oil on canvas

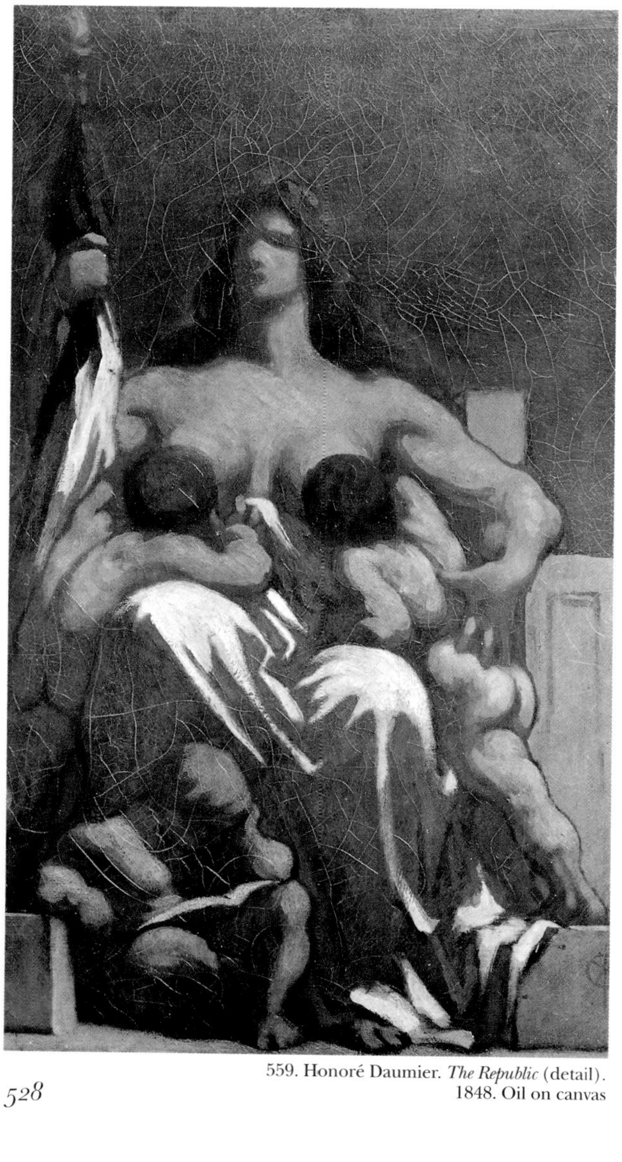

559. Honoré Daumier. *The Republic* (detail). 1848. Oil on canvas

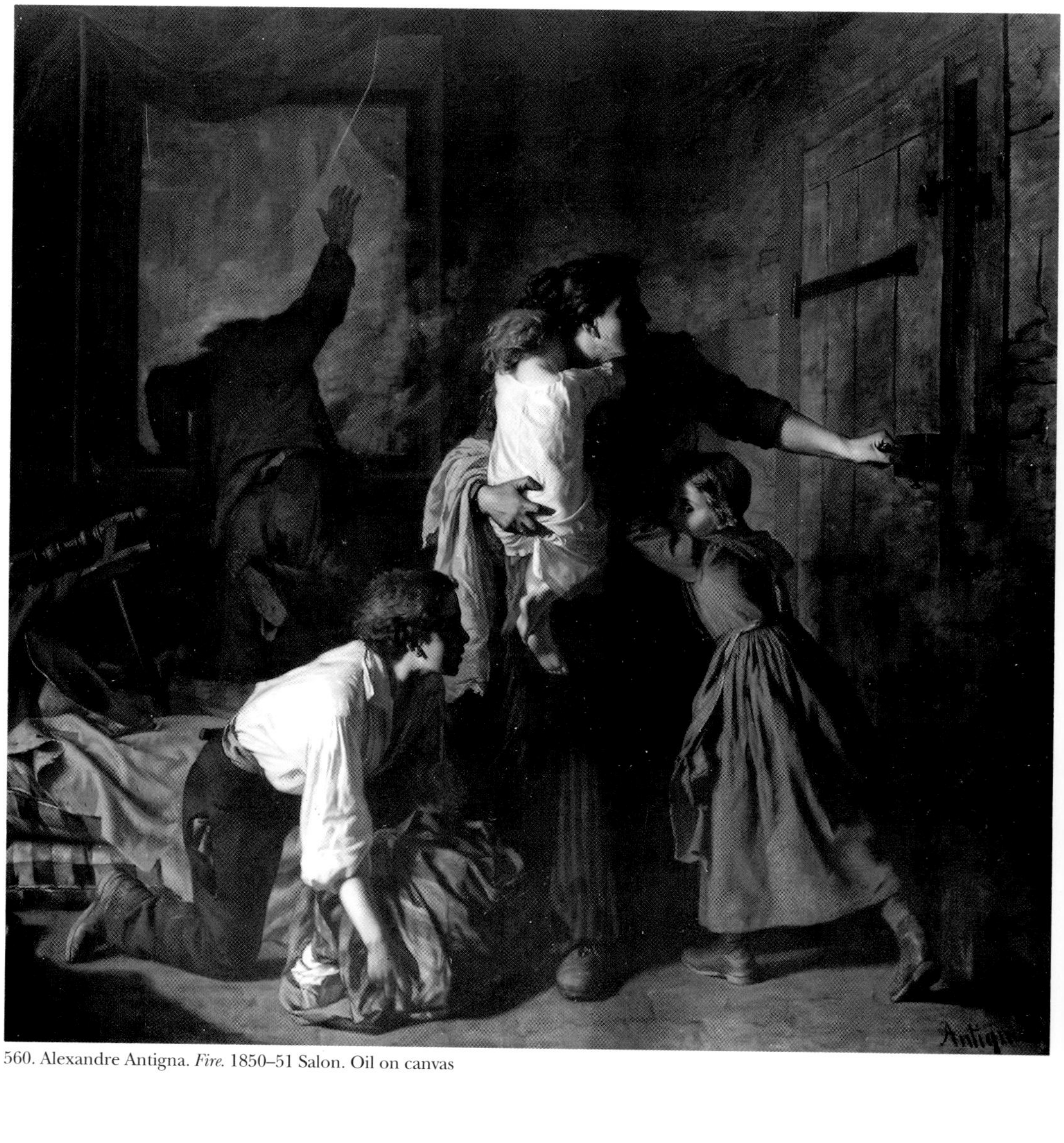

560. Alexandre Antigna. *Fire.* 1850–51 Salon. Oil on canvas

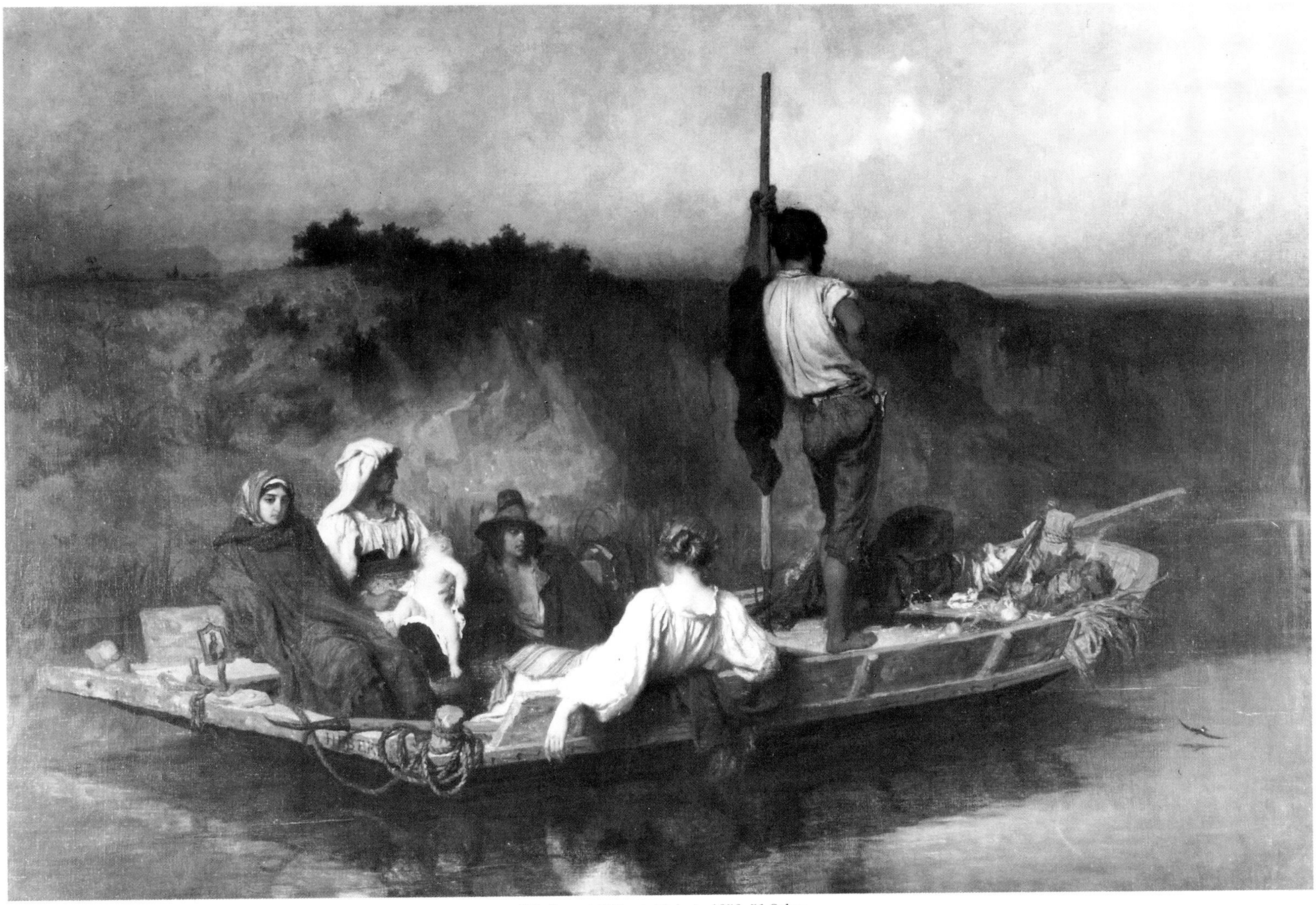
561. Ernest Hébert. *Malaria.* 1850–51 Salon

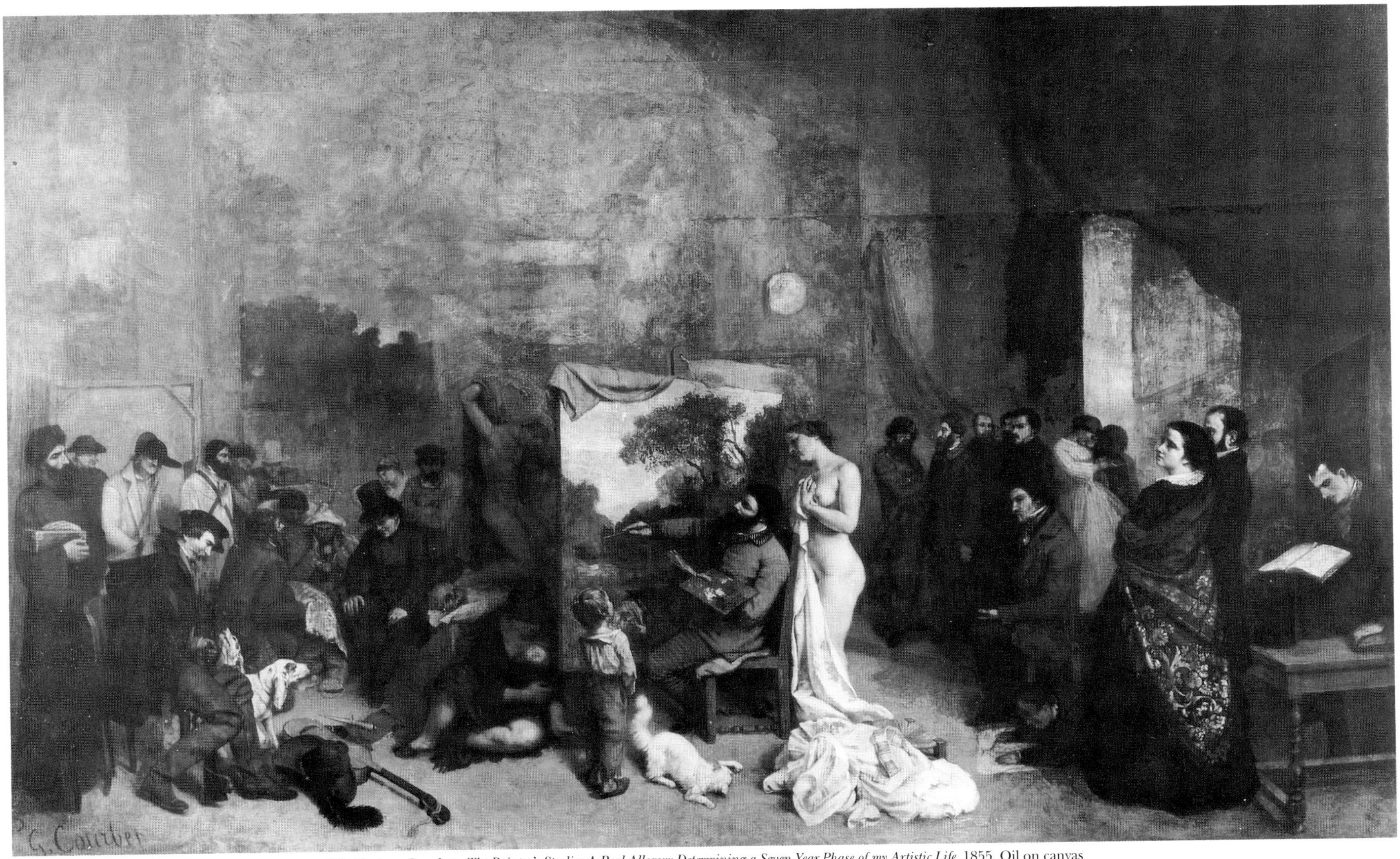
562. Gustave Courbet. *The Painter's Studio: A Real Allegory Determining a Seven-Year Phase of my Artistic Life.* 1855. Oil on canvas

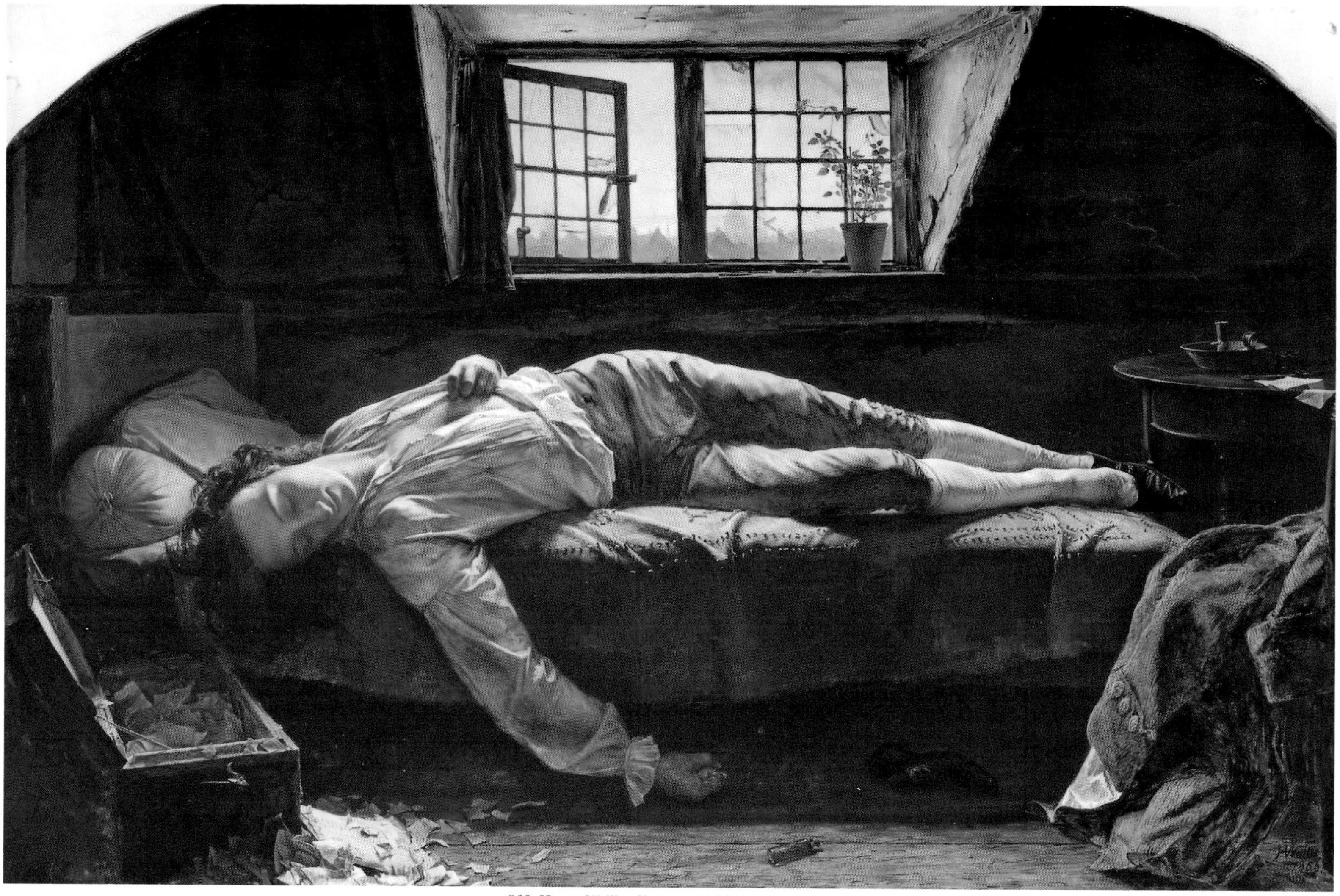

563. Henry Wallis. *Chatterton.* 1856. Oil on canvas

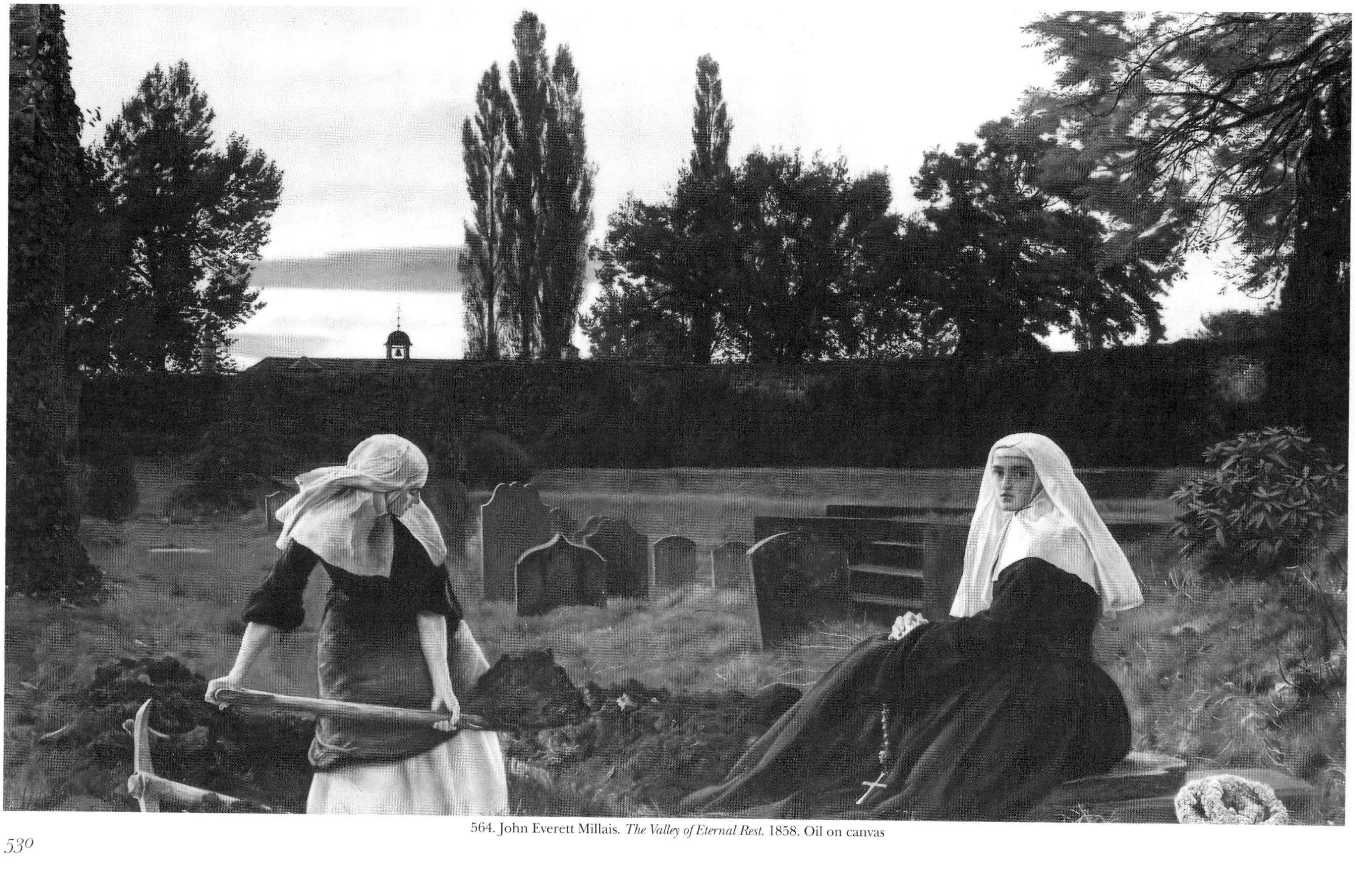

564. John Everett Millais. *The Valley of Eternal Rest.* 1858. Oil on canvas

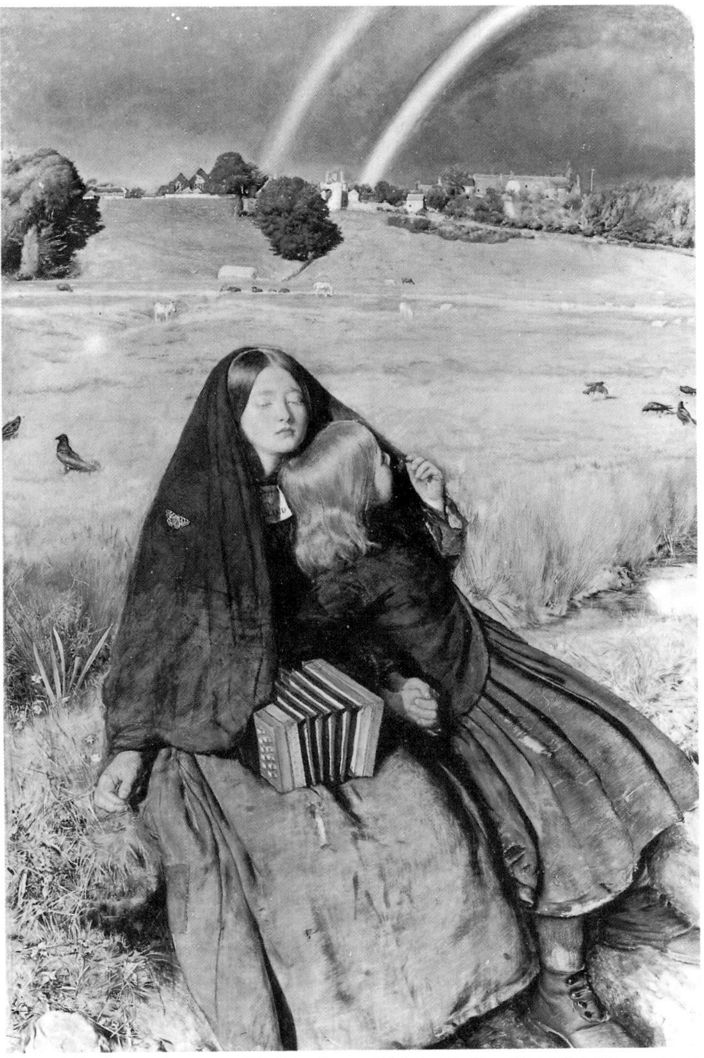

565. John Everett Millais. *The Blind Girl.* 1856. Oil on canvas

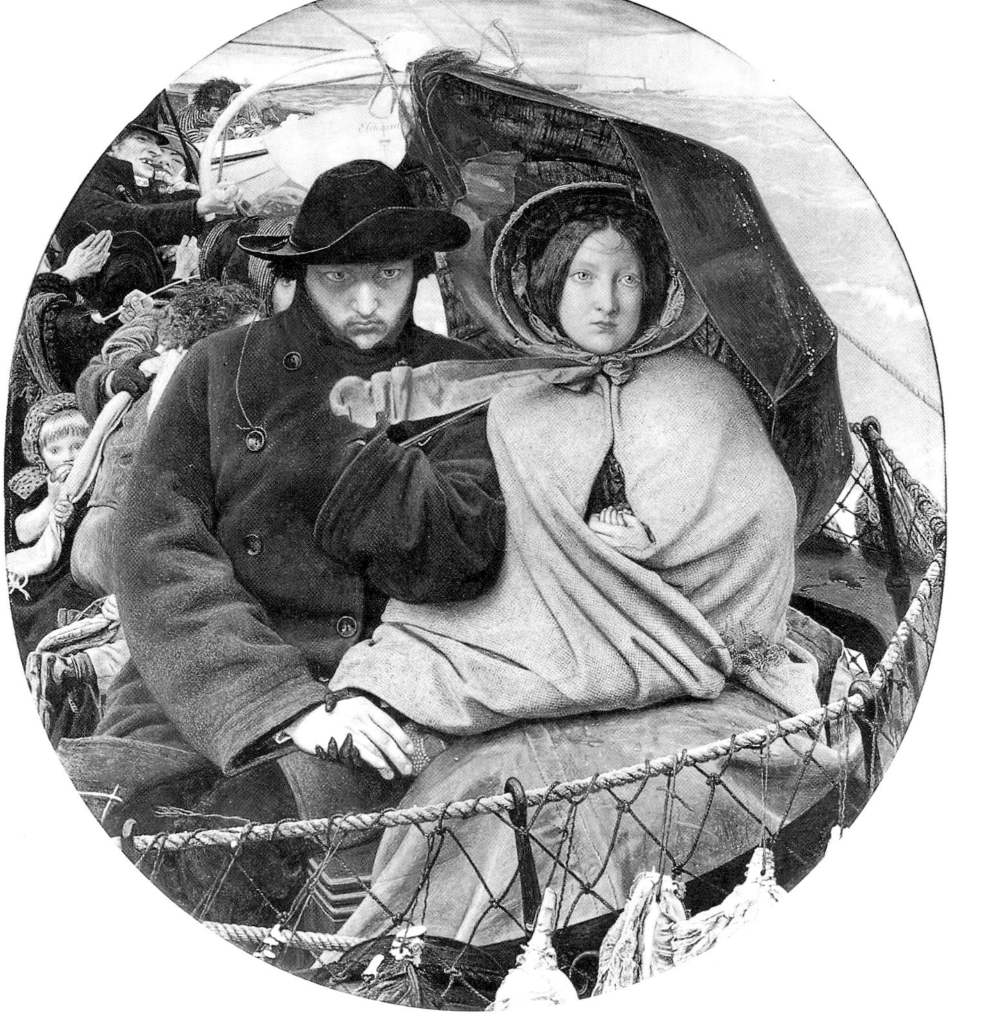

566. Ford Madox Brown. *The Last of England.* 1855. Oil on canvas

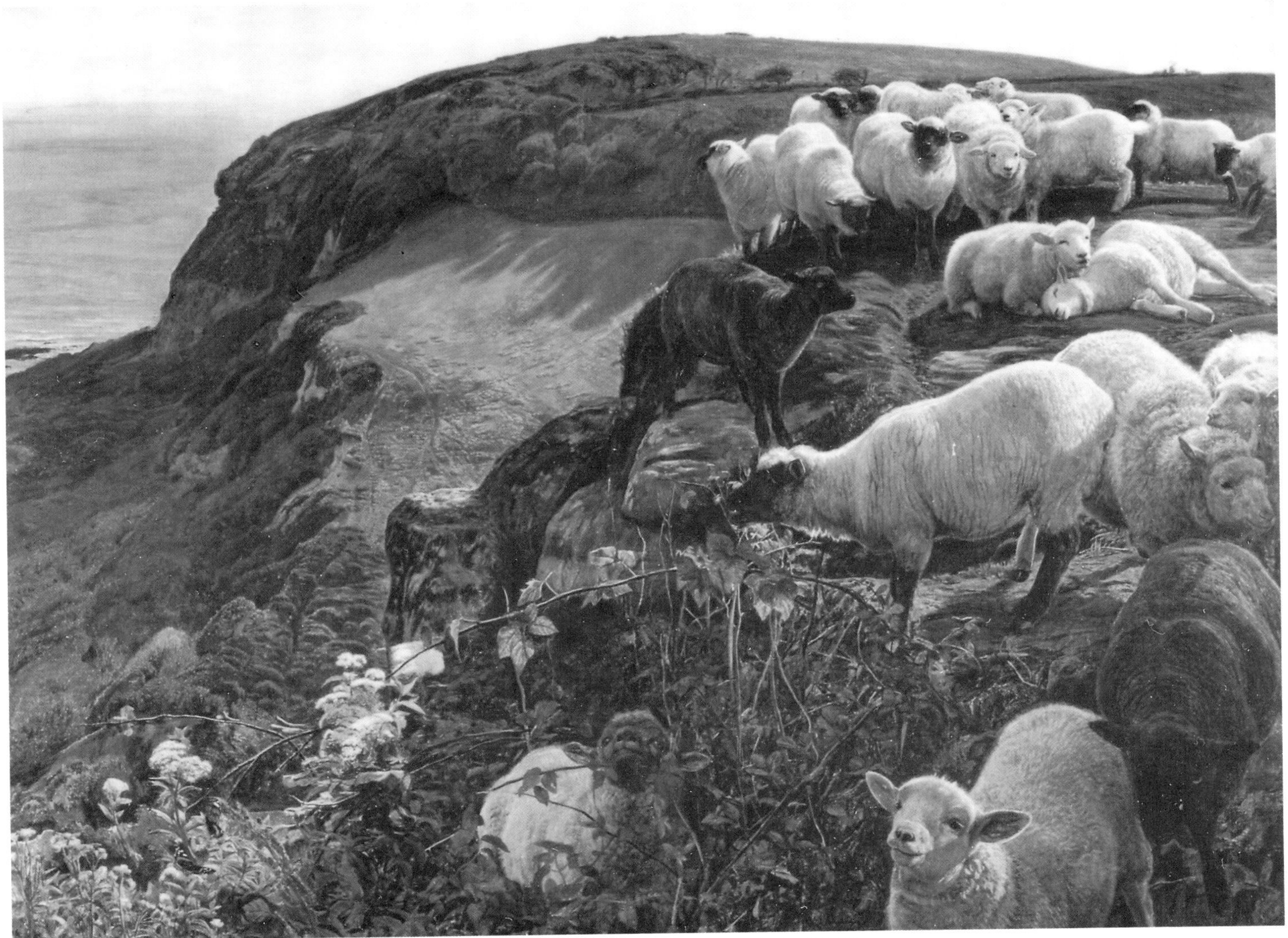

567. William Holman Hunt. *Our English Coasts* or *Lost Sheep.* 1852. Oil on canvas

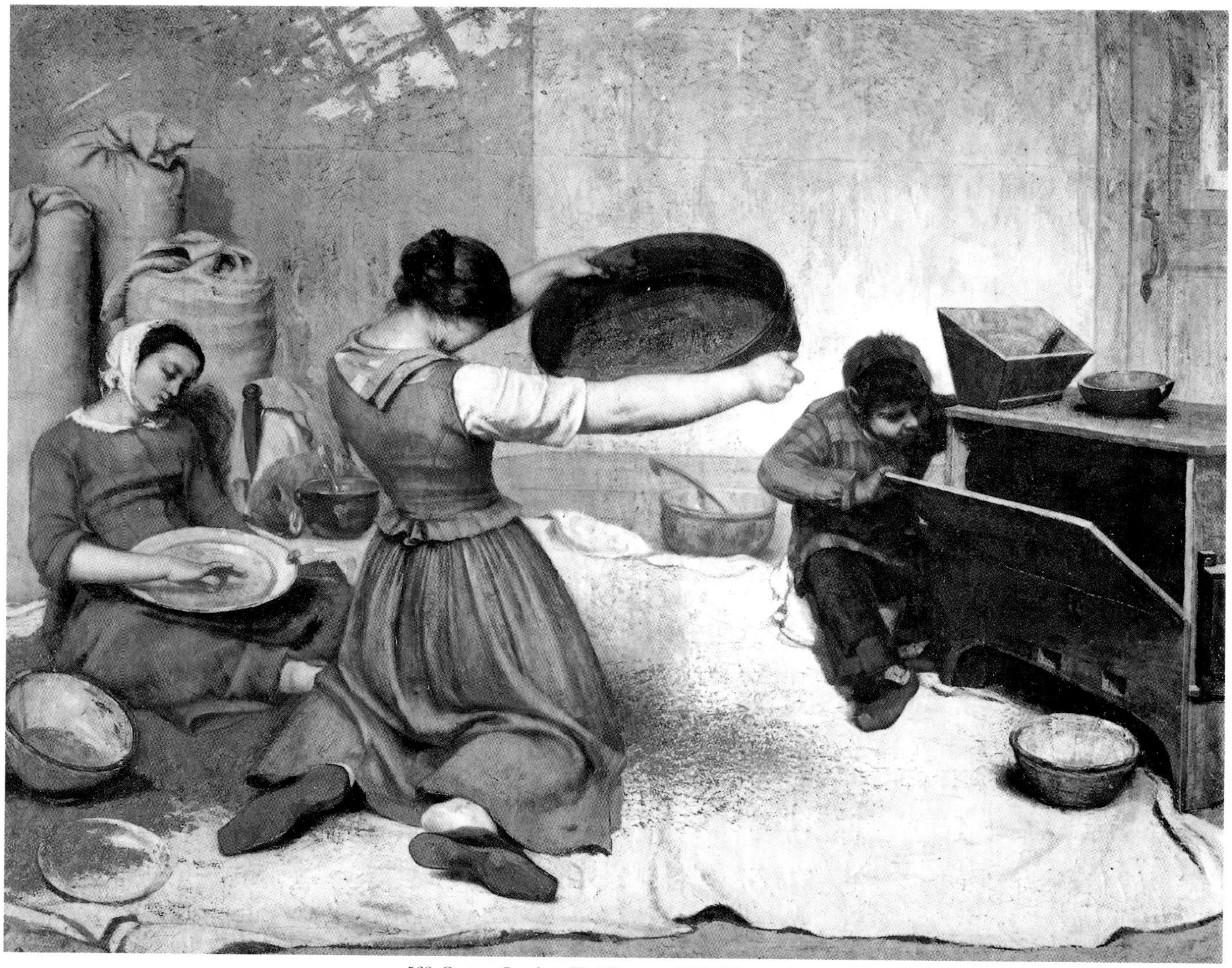

568. Gustave Courbet. *The Winnowers.* 1855. Oil on canvas

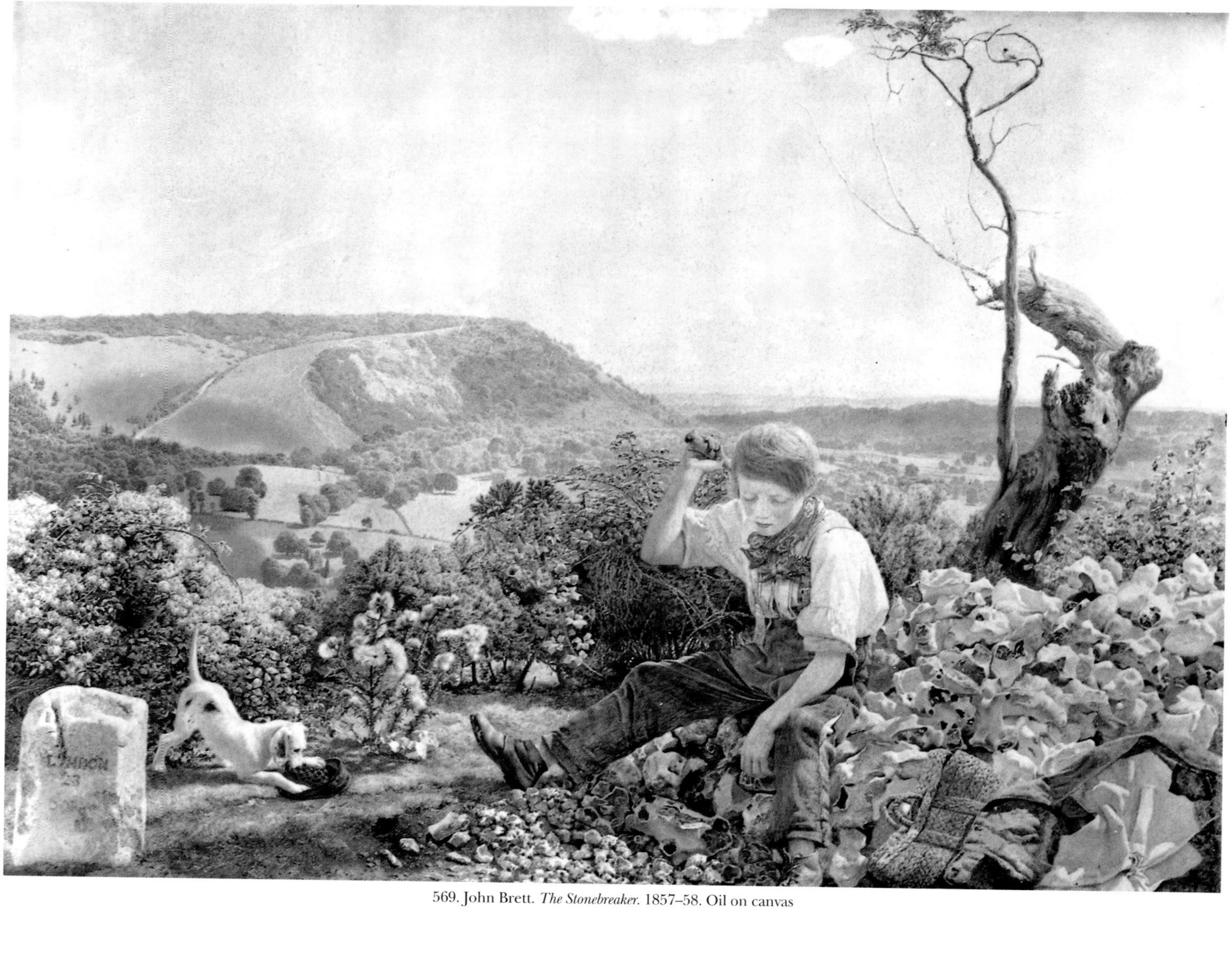

569. John Brett. *The Stonebreaker.* 1857–58. Oil on canvas

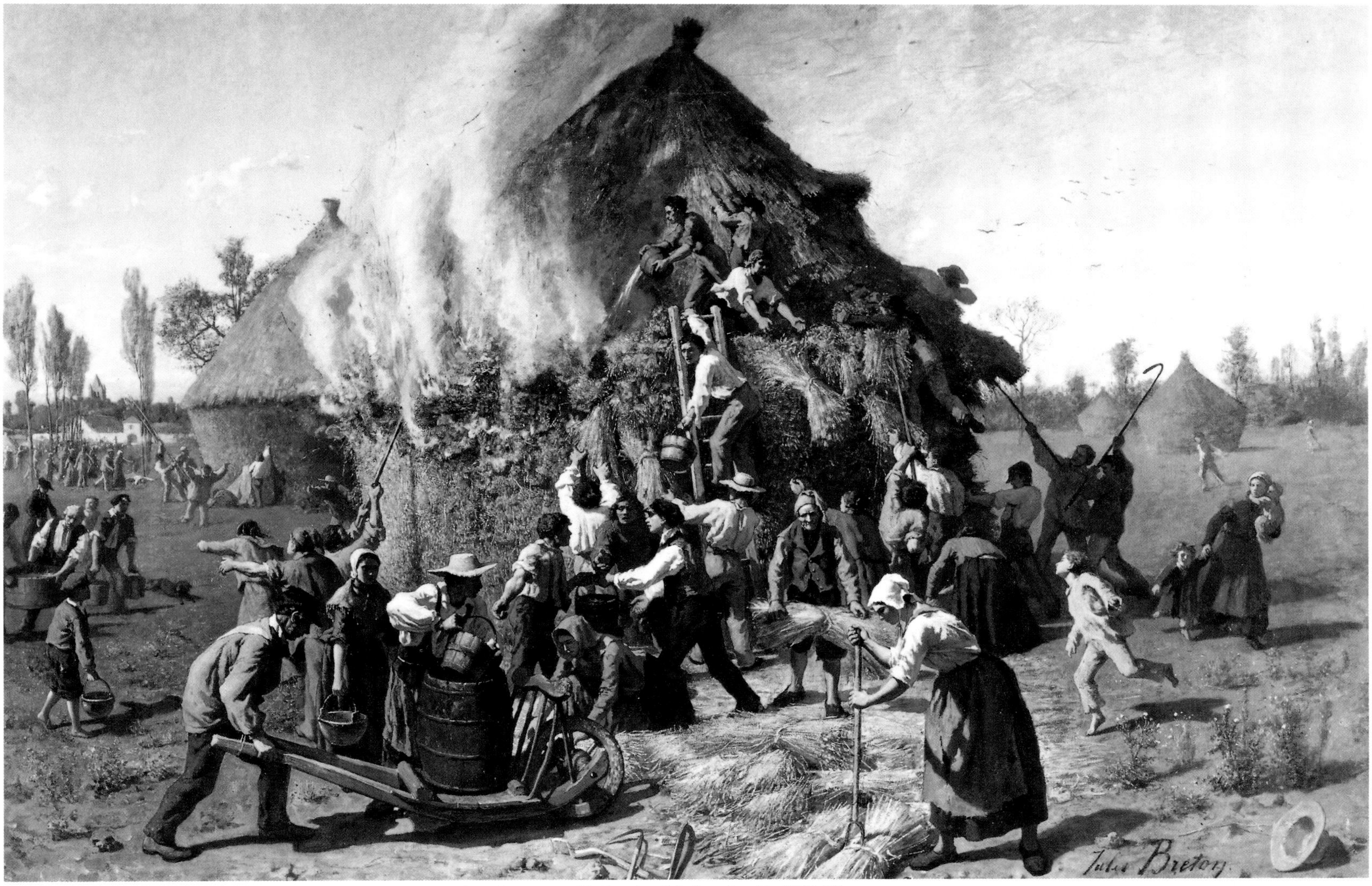

570. Jules Breton. *The Burning Rick.* Completed in 1856. Oil on canvas

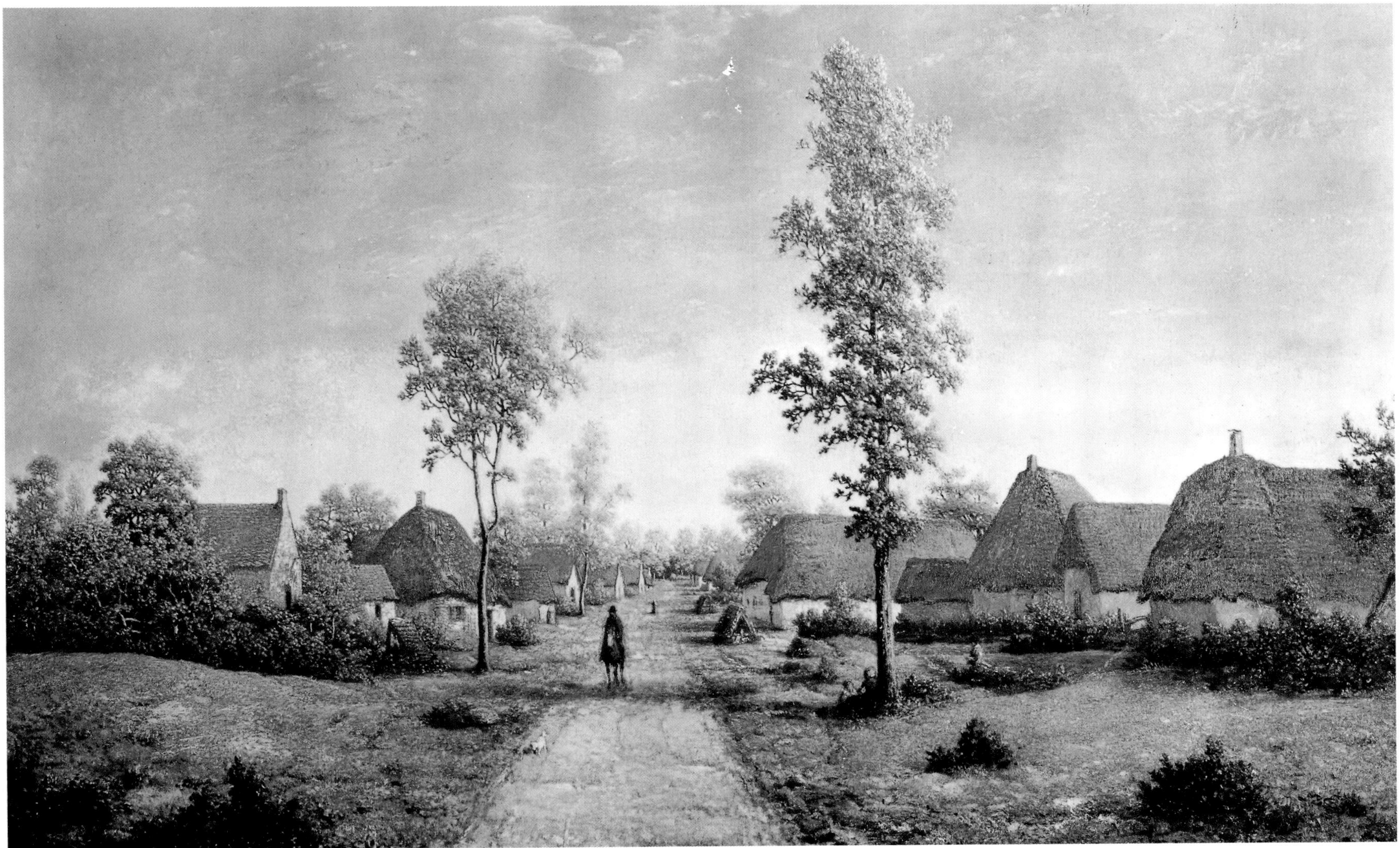

571. Théodore Rousseau. *The Village of Becquigny.* 1864 Salon. Oil on wood

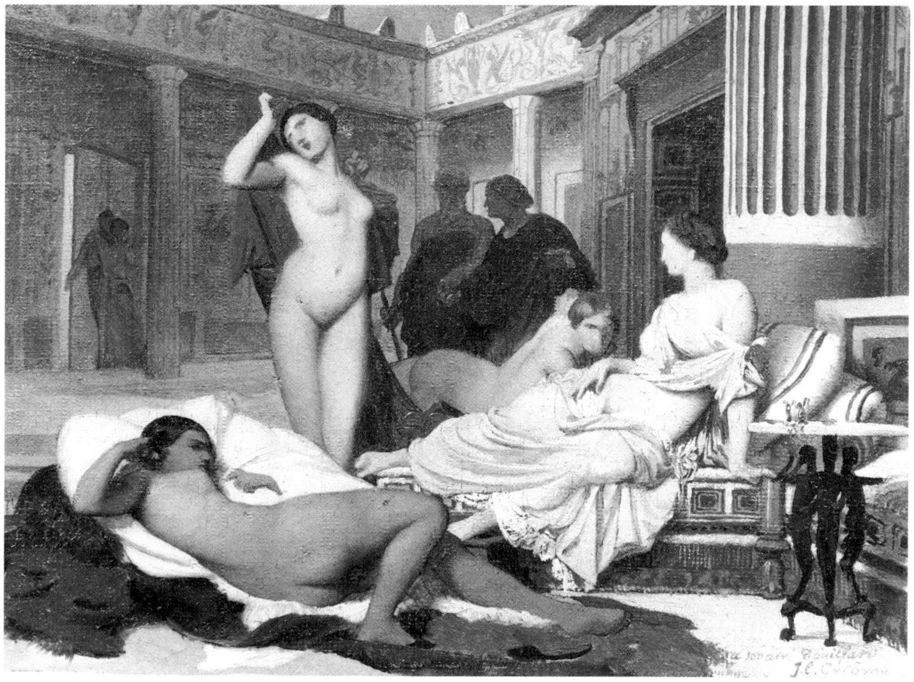

572. Jean-Léon Gérôme. *Greek Interior.* 1848. Oil on canvas

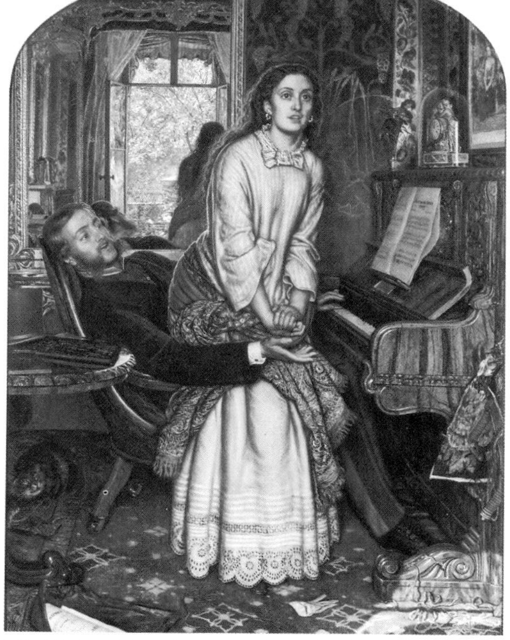

573. William Holman Hunt. *The Awakening Conscience.* 1853–54. Oil on canvas

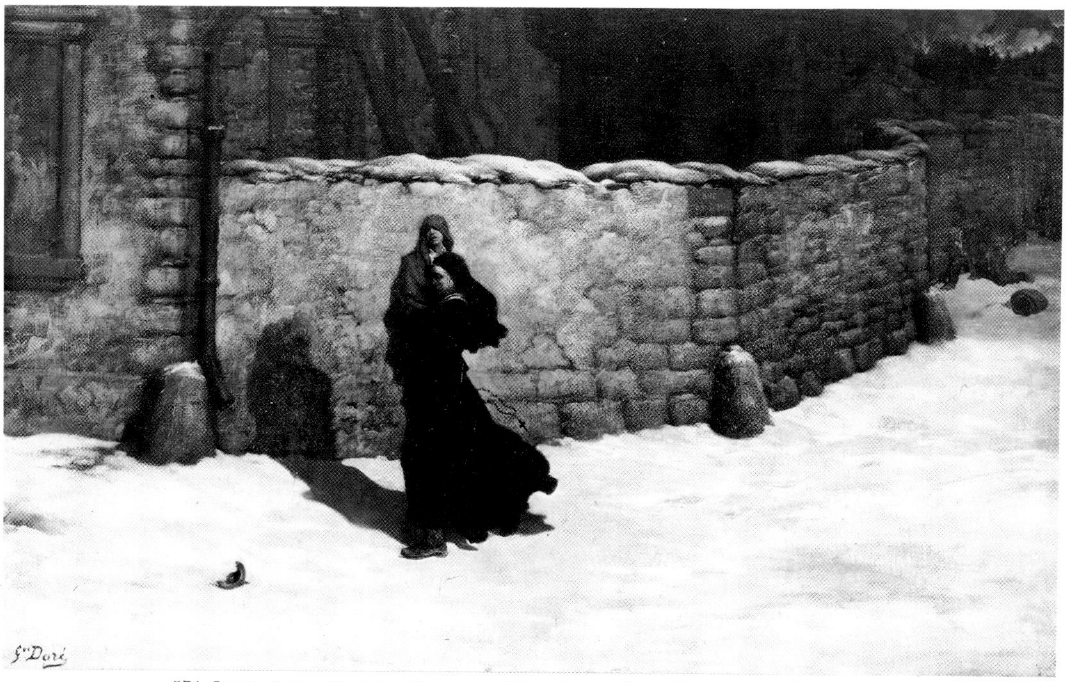

574. Gustave Doré. *The Sister of Charity. An Episode from the Siege of Paris in 1870.* Oil on canvas

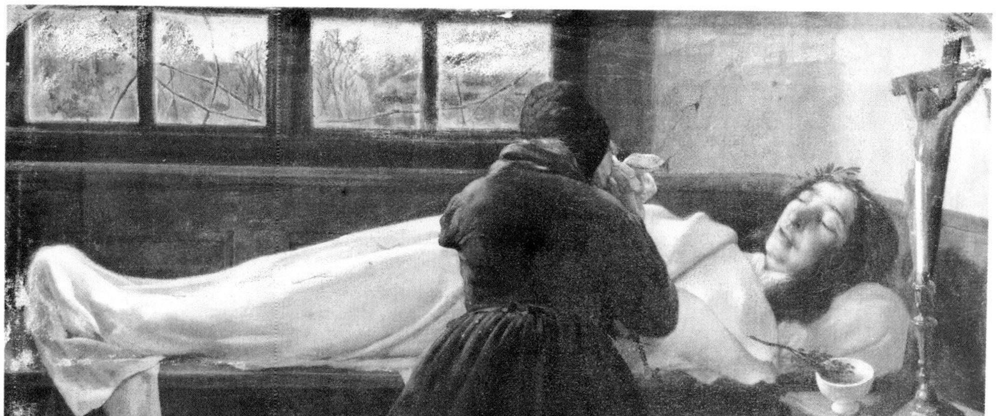

575. Jean-Jacques Henner. *The Artist's Mother Praying Beside the Body of her Daughter Madeleine.* c. 1852. Oil on canvas

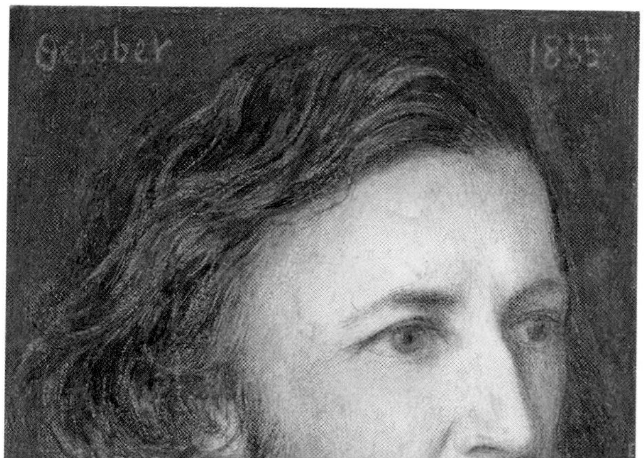

576. Dante Gabriel Rossetti. *Robert Browning.* October 1855. Watercolor, pencil, and colored chalk

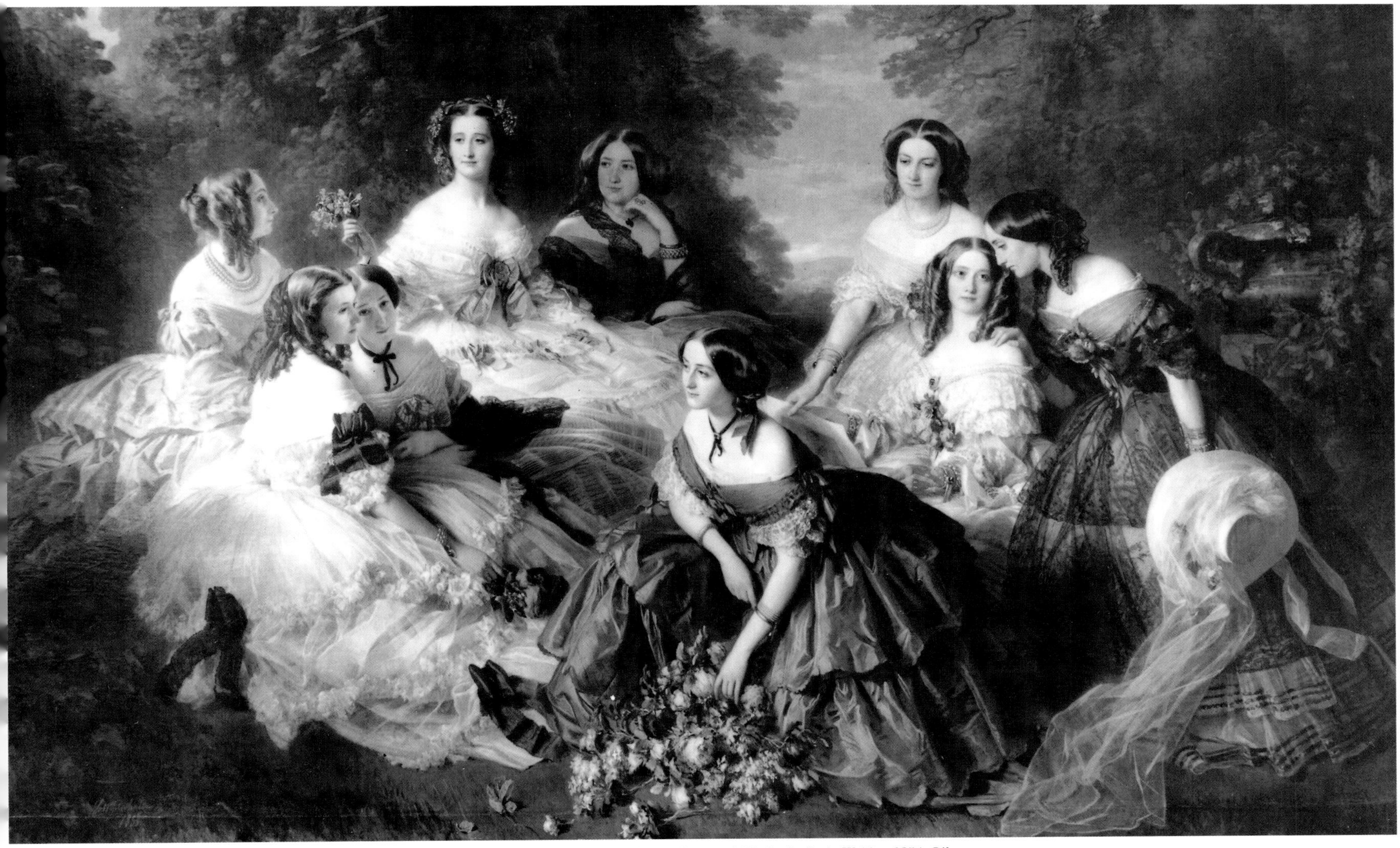

577. Franz Xaver Winterhalter. *Empress Eugénie Surrounded by her Ladies-in-Waiting.* 1854. Oil on canvas

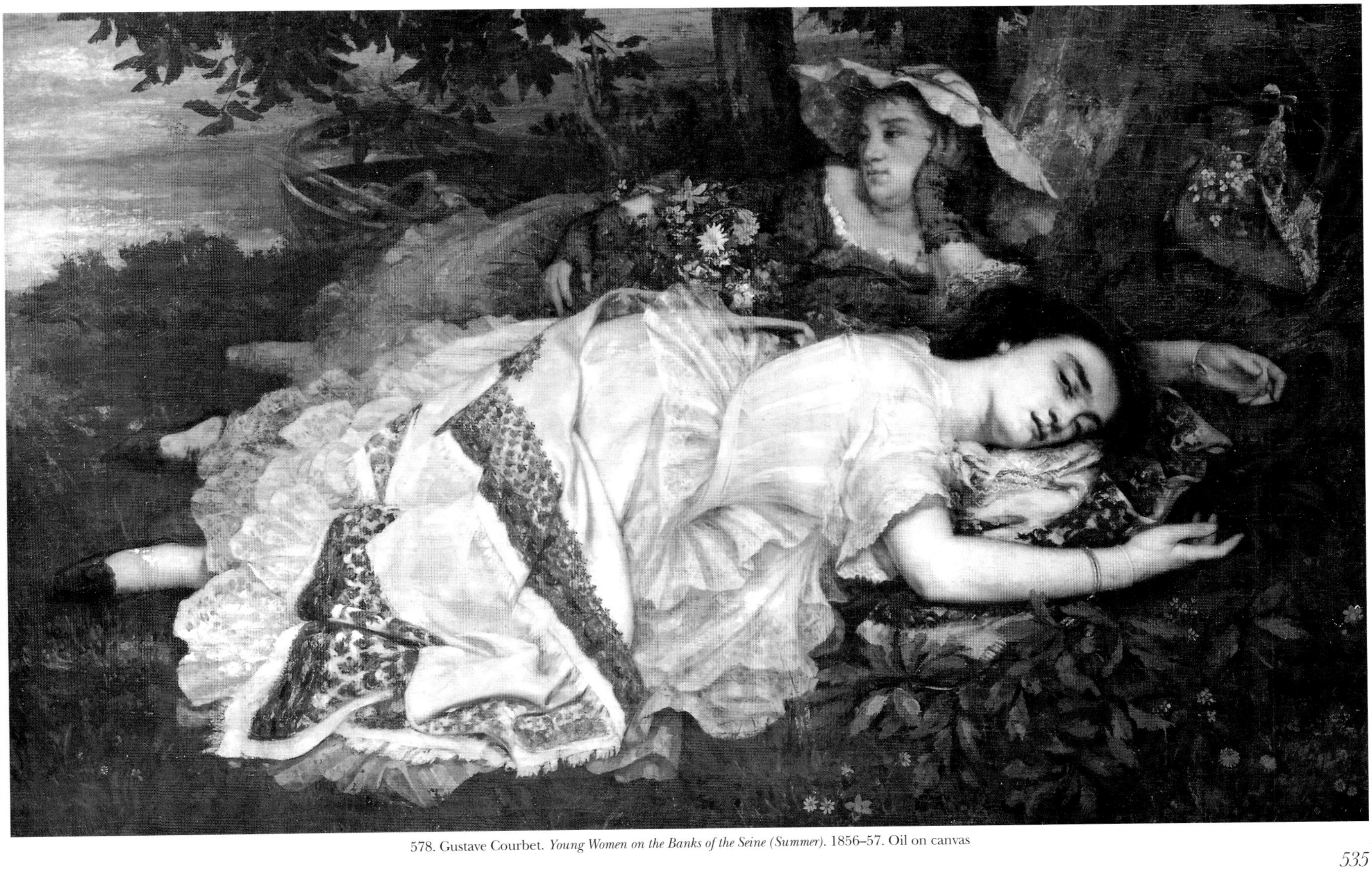

578. Gustave Courbet. *Young Women on the Banks of the Seine (Summer).* 1856–57. Oil on canvas

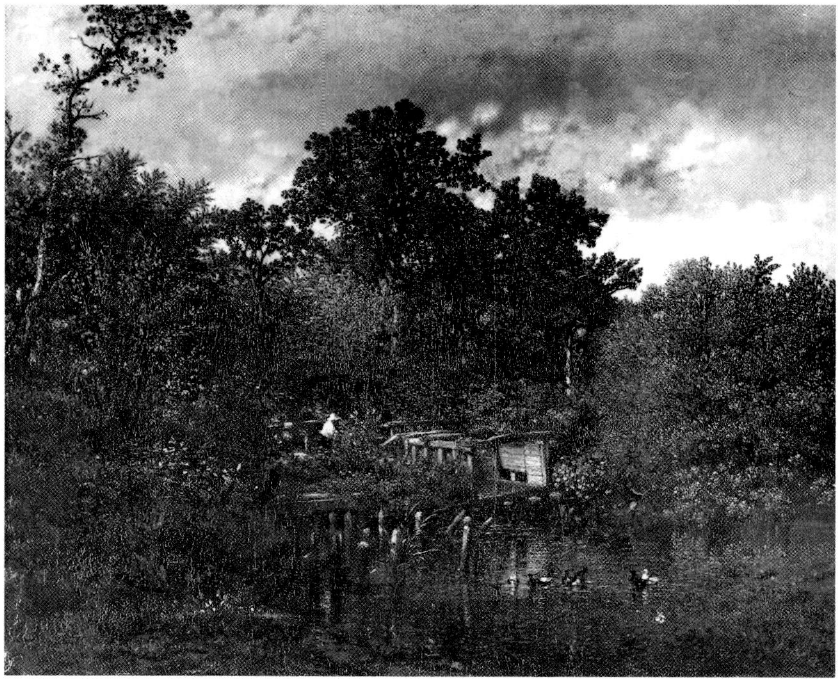

579. Jules Dupré. *The Sluice Gate.* c. 1855–60. Oil on canvas

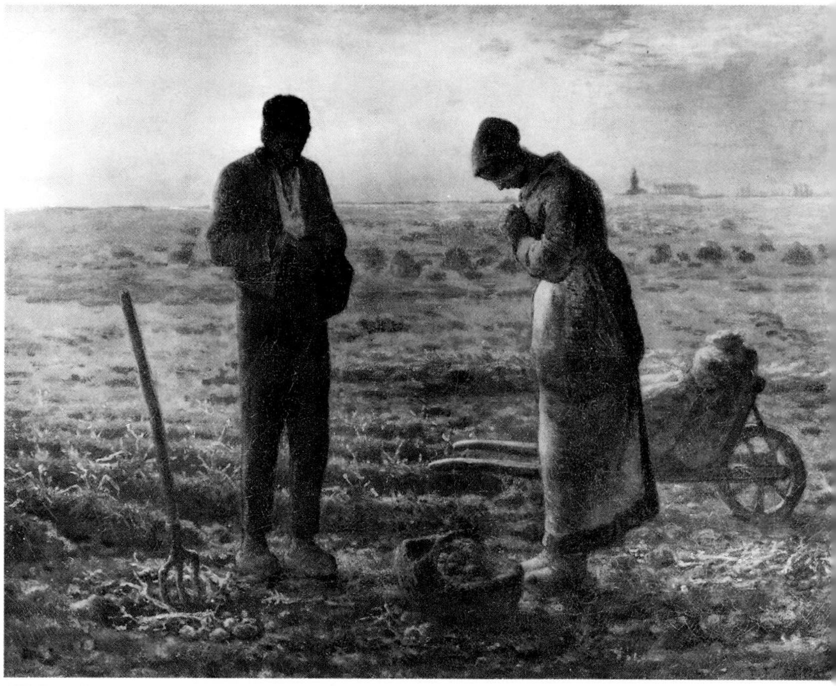

580. Jean-François Millet. *The Angelus.* 1857–59. Oil on canvas

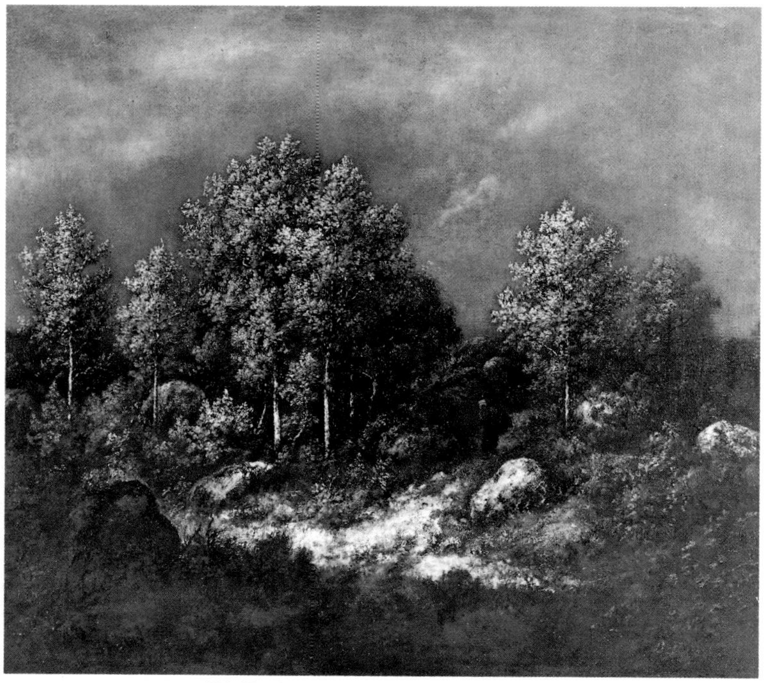

581. Narcisse Diaz de la Peña. *Jean de Paris Heights, Forest of Fontainebleau.* 1867. Oil on canvas

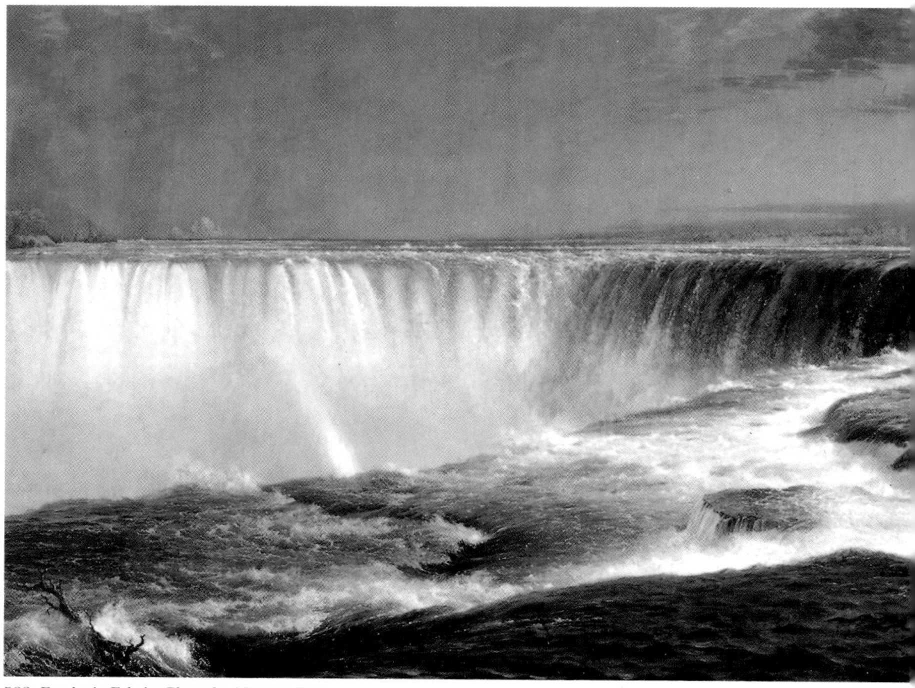

582. Frederic Edwin Church. *Niagara Falls.* 1857. Oil on canvas

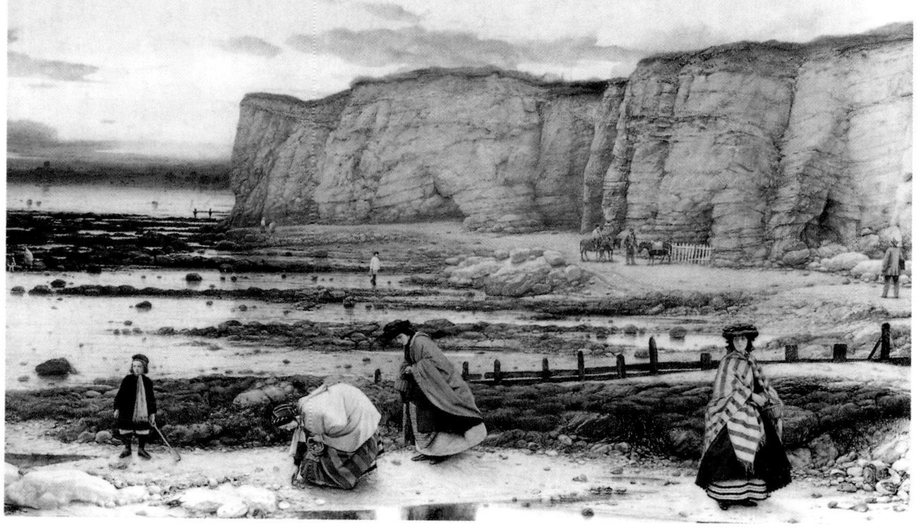

583. William Dyce. *Pegwell Bay, Memory of 5 October 1858.* Royal Academy 1860. Oil on canvas

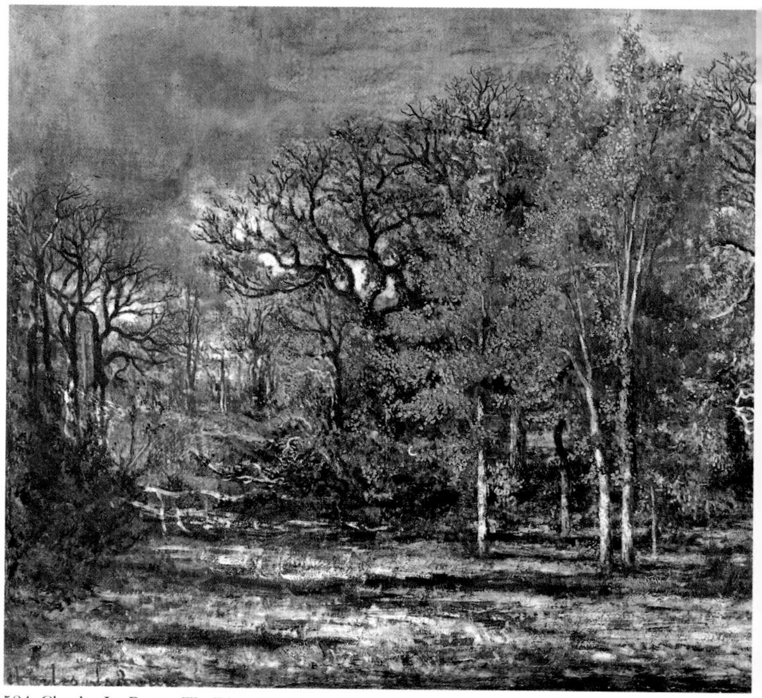

584. Charles Le Roux. *The Edge of the Wood, Cherry Trees in Autumn* (detail). 1855 Exposition Universelle. Oil on canvas

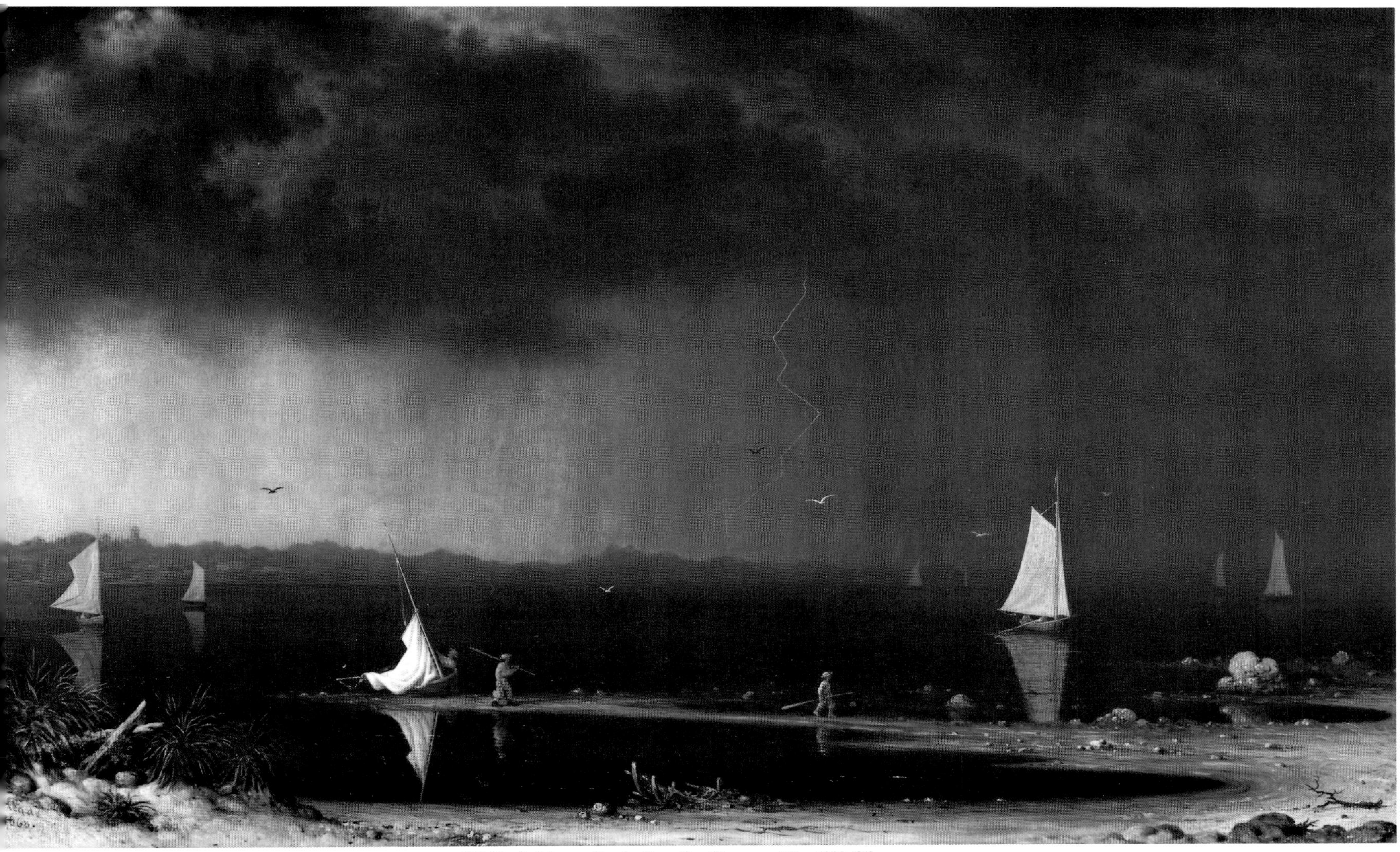

585. Martin Johnson Heade. *Storm Over Narragansett Bay.* 1868. Oil on canvas

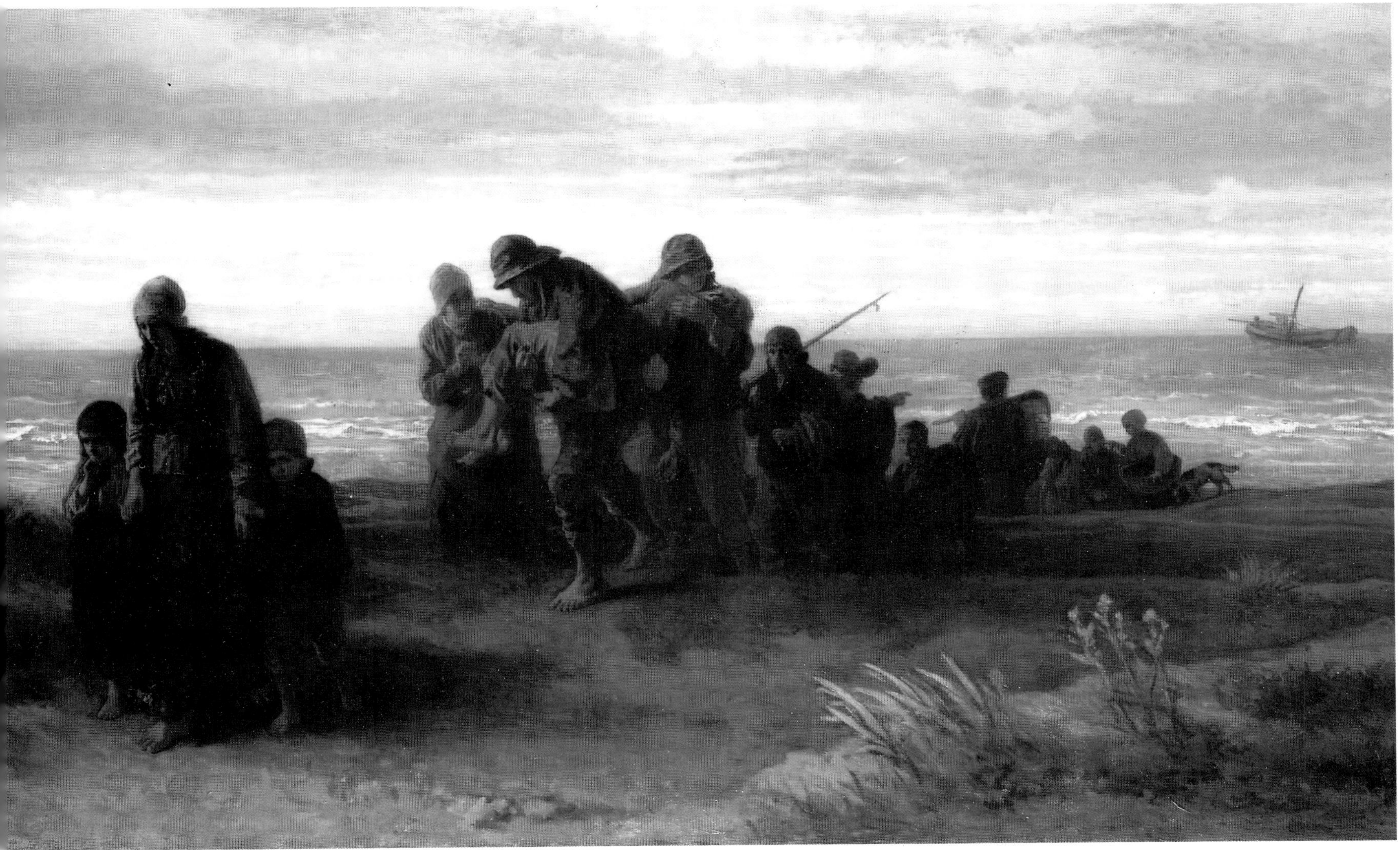

586. Jozef Israëls. *The Shipwreck Victim.* 1861 Salon. Oil on canvas

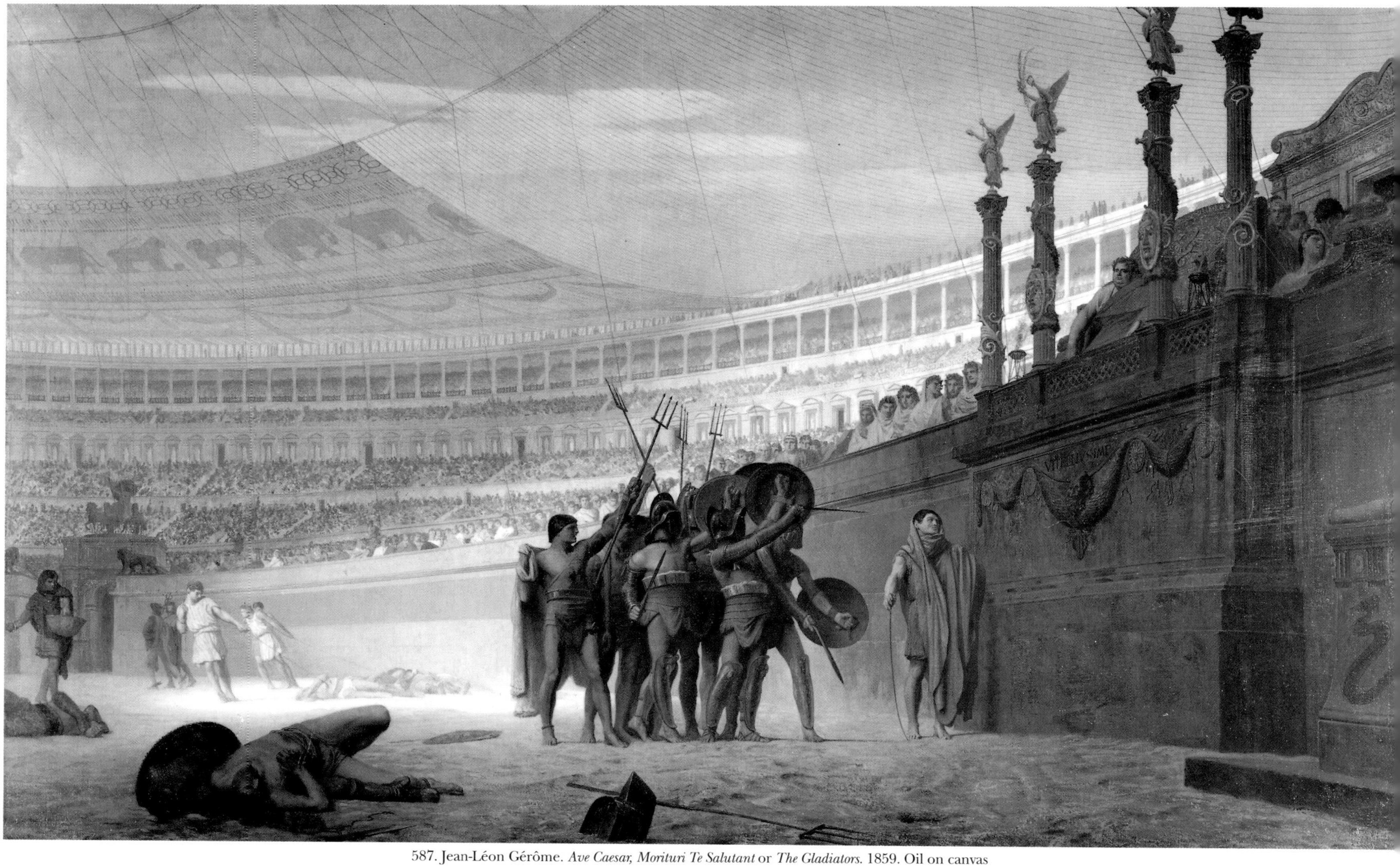

587. Jean-Léon Gérôme. *Ave Caesar, Morituri Te Salutant* or *The Gladiators.* 1859. Oil on canvas

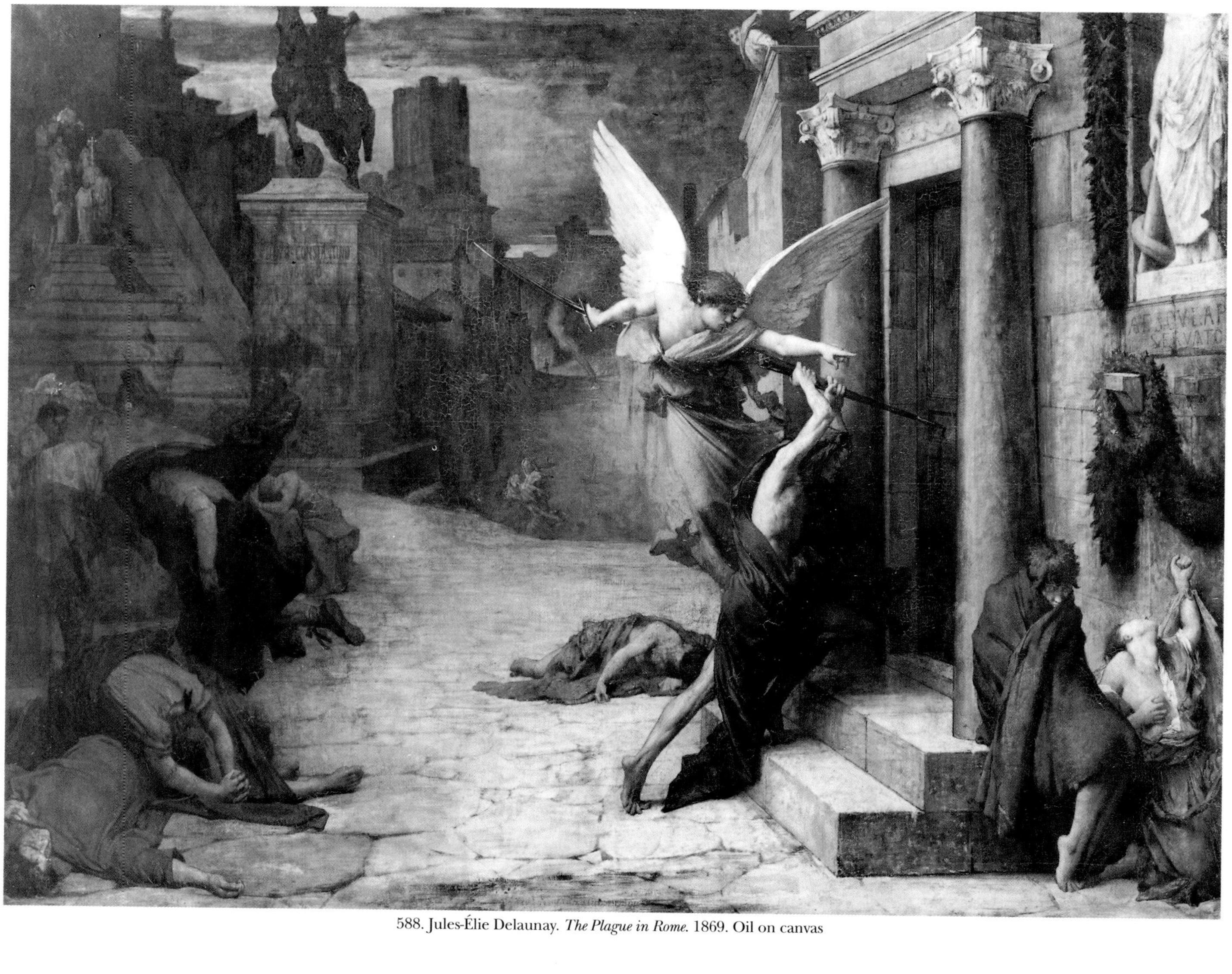

588. Jules-Élie Delaunay. *The Plague in Rome.* 1869. Oil on canvas

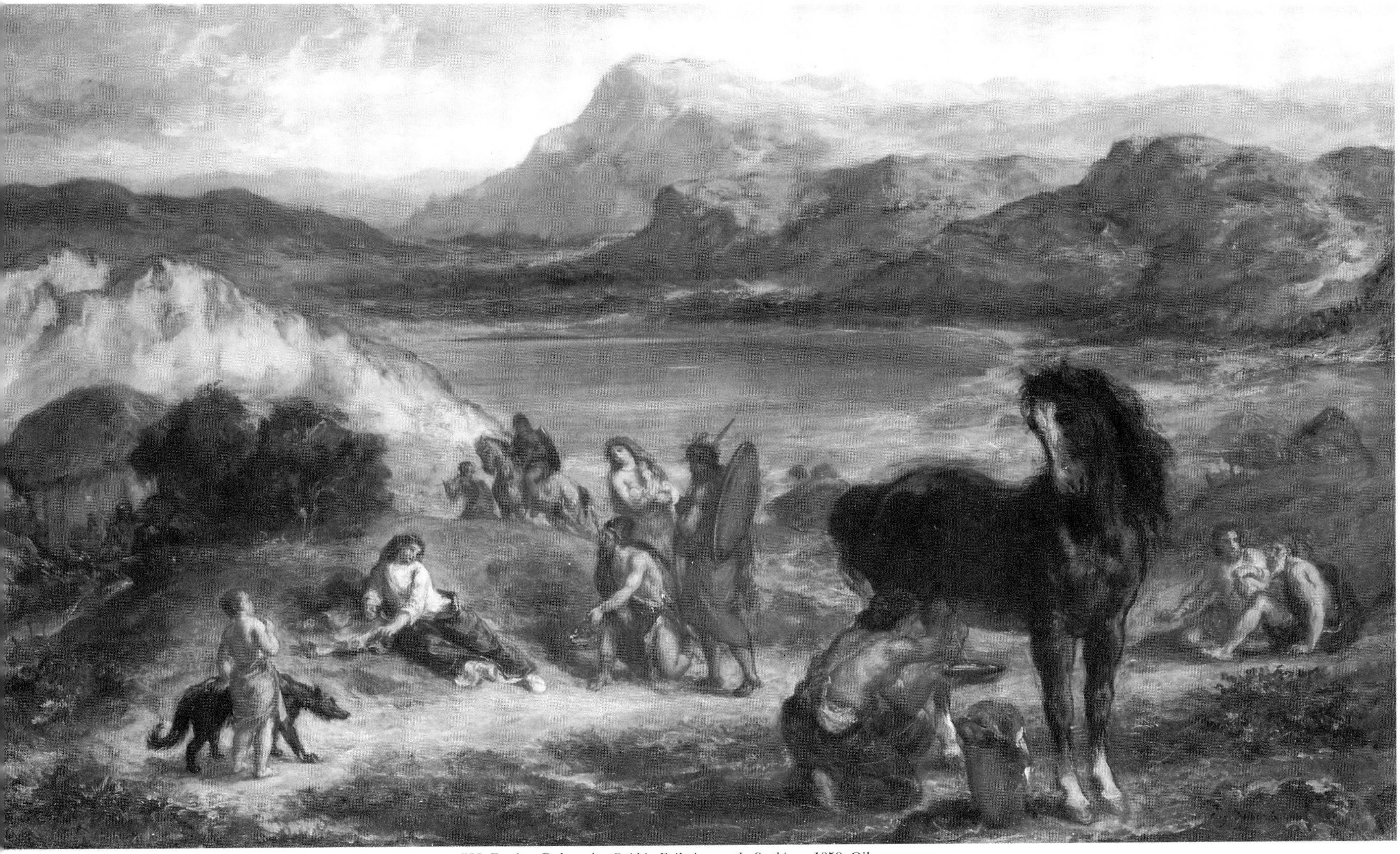

589. Eugène Delacroix. *Ovid in Exile Among the Scythians.* 1859. Oil on canvas

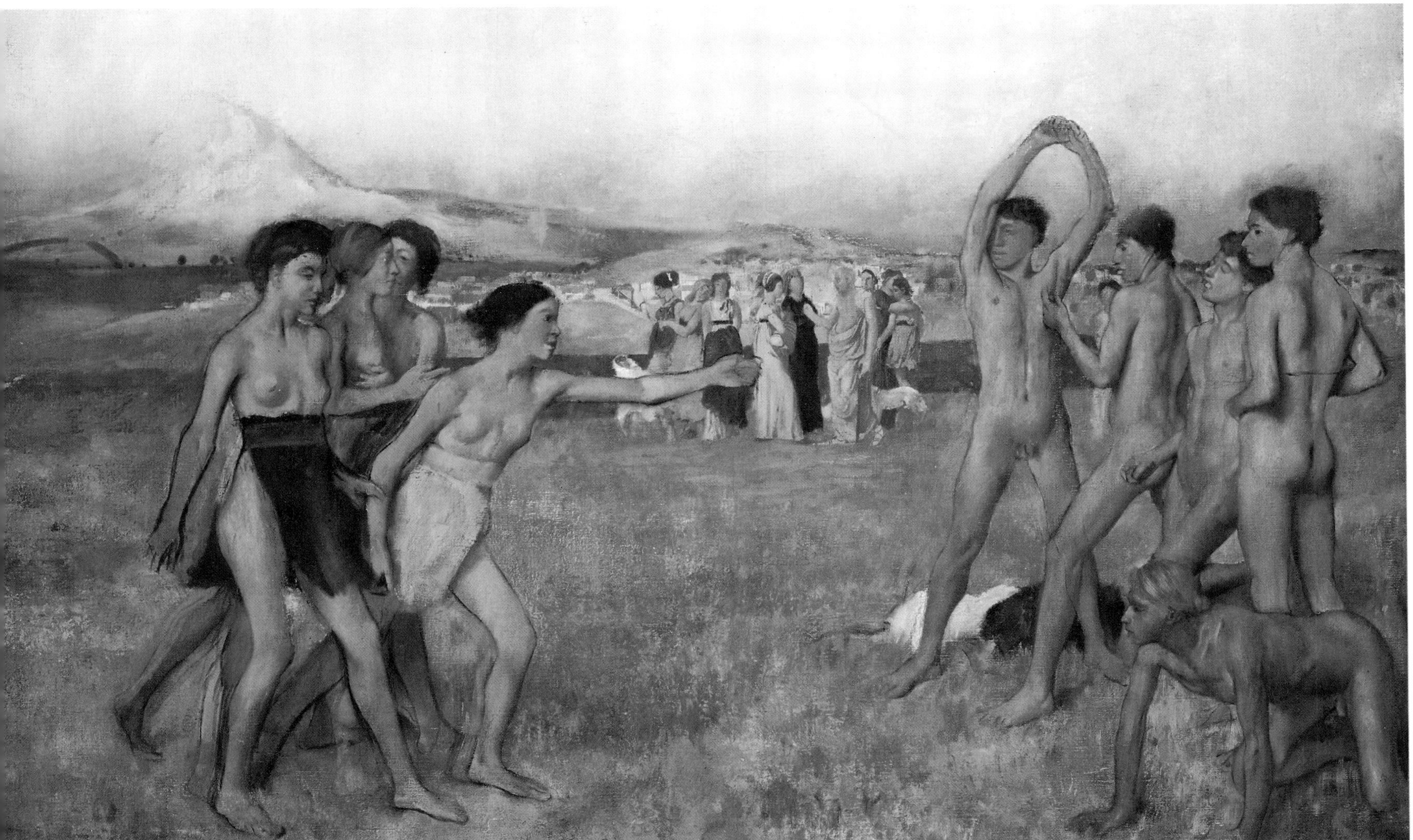

590. Edgar Degas. *Spartan Girls Provoking Boys.* c. 1860–62; reworked before 1880. Oil on canvas

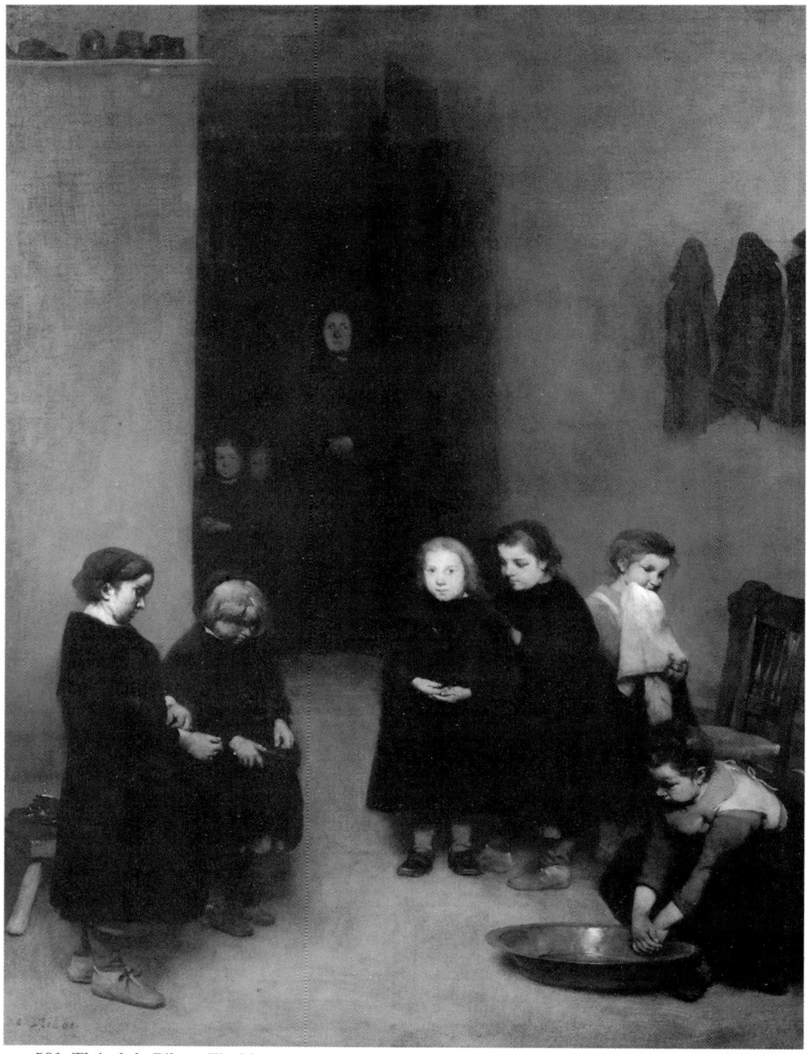

591. Théodule Ribot. *The Morning Wash.* 1863 Salon. Oil on canvas

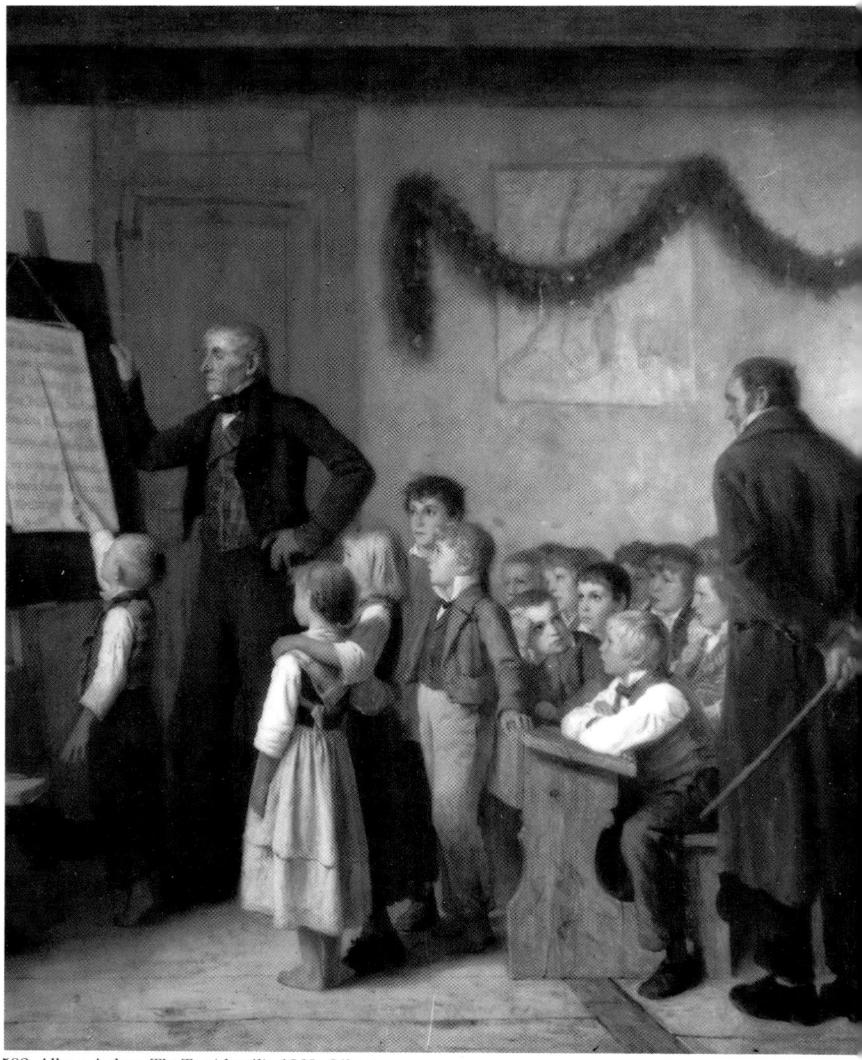

592. Albert Anker. *The Test* (detail). 1862. Oil on canvas

593. Constant Troyon. *Grape Harvest Beside the Seine at Suresnes.* 1862. Oil on canvas

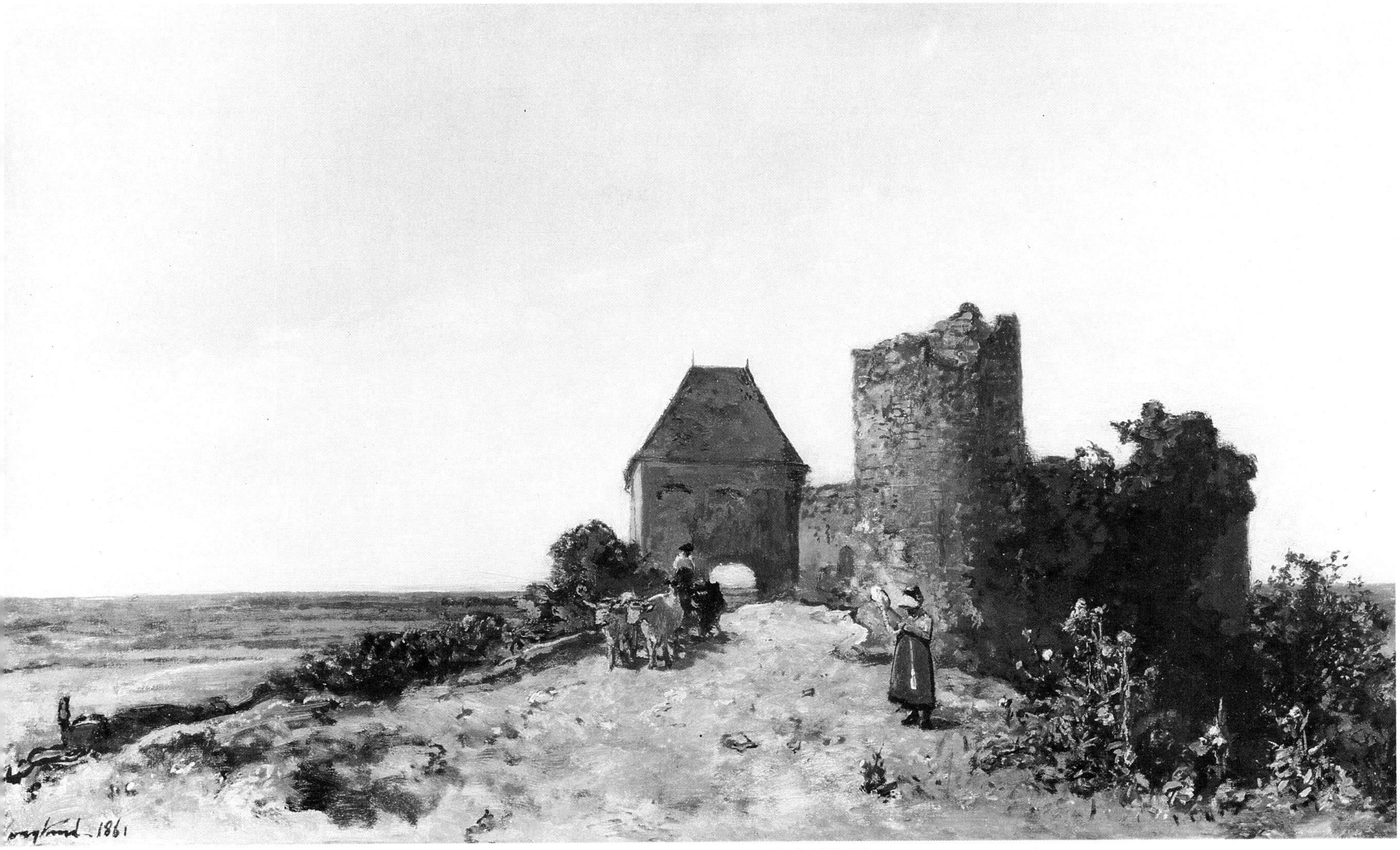

594. Johan Barthold Jongkind. *Ruins of Rosemont Castle.* 1861. Oil on canvas

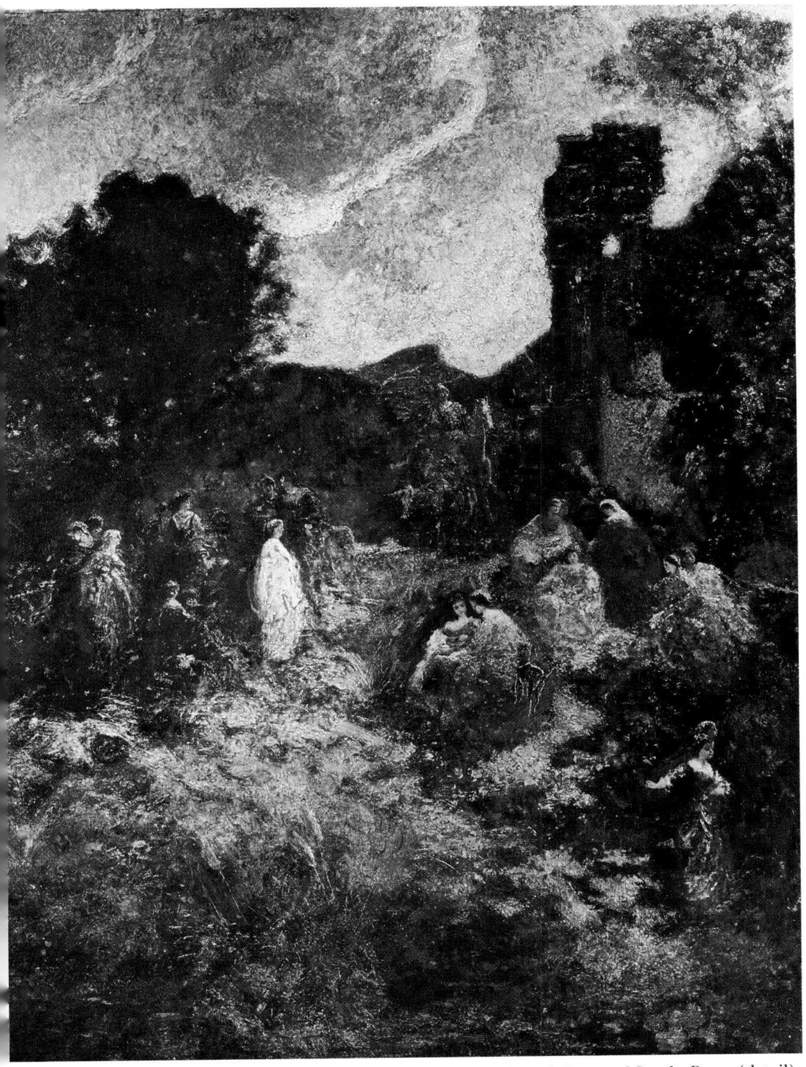

595. Adolphe Monticelli. *Don Quixote and Sancho Panza* (detail). c. 1865. Oil on canvas

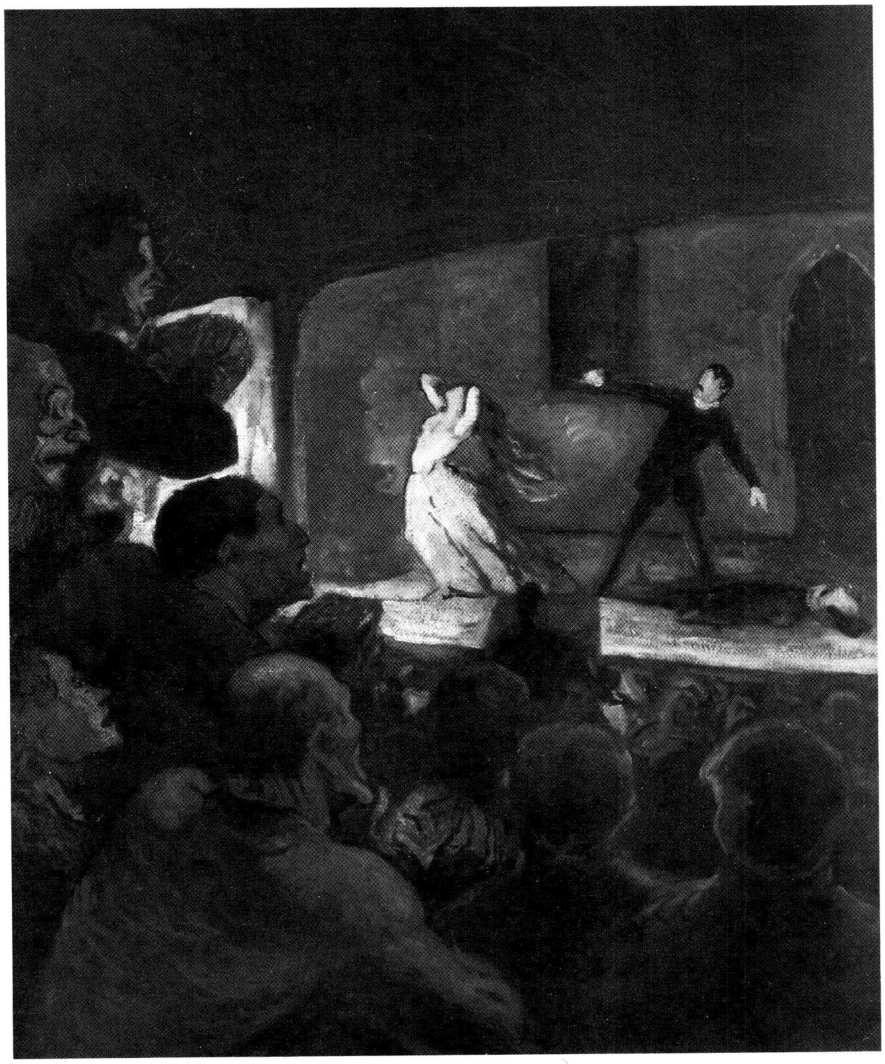

596. Honoré Daumier. *At the Theater.* c. 1864. Oil on canvas

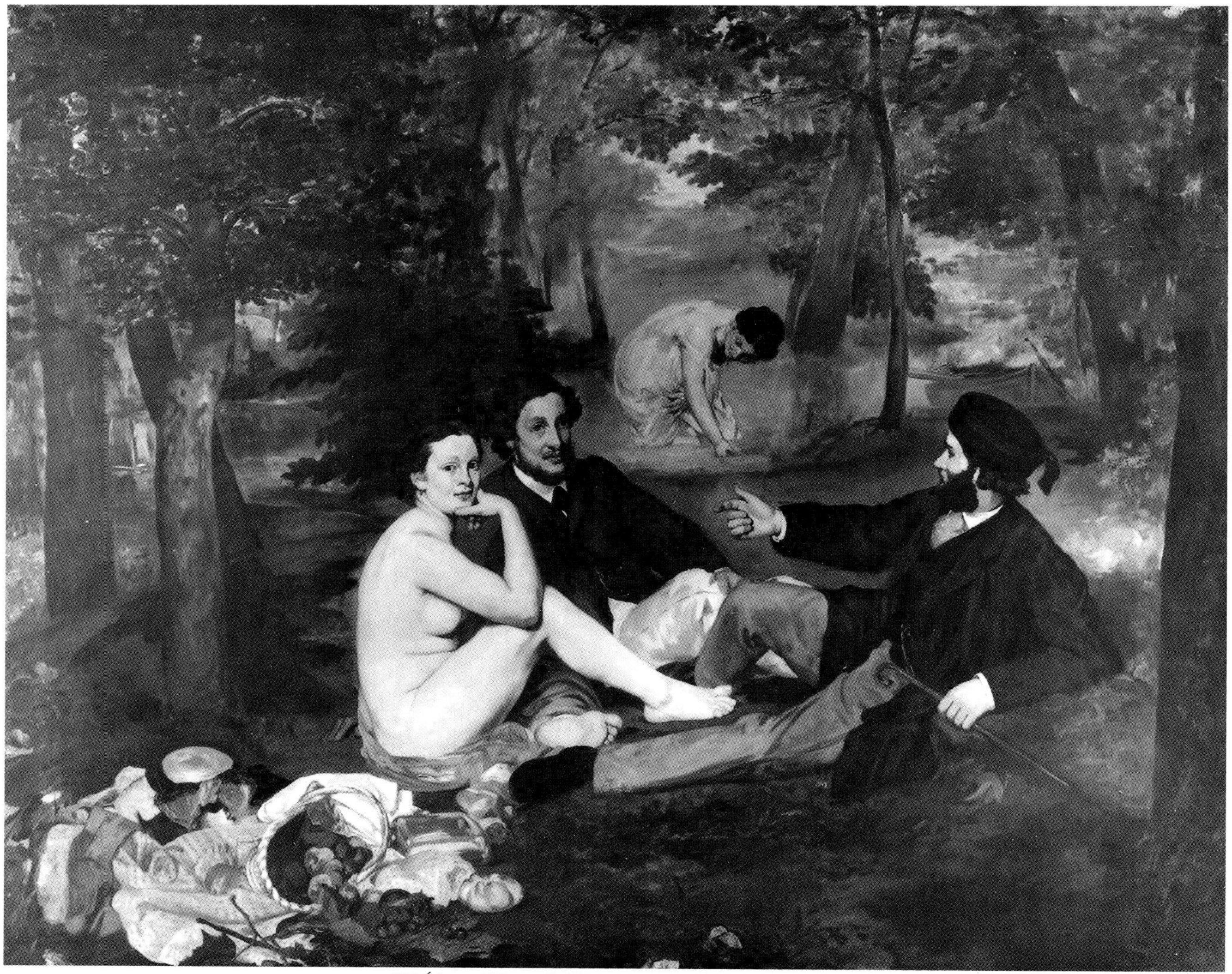

597. Édouard Manet. *Le Déjeuner sur l'herbe.* 1863. Oil on canvas

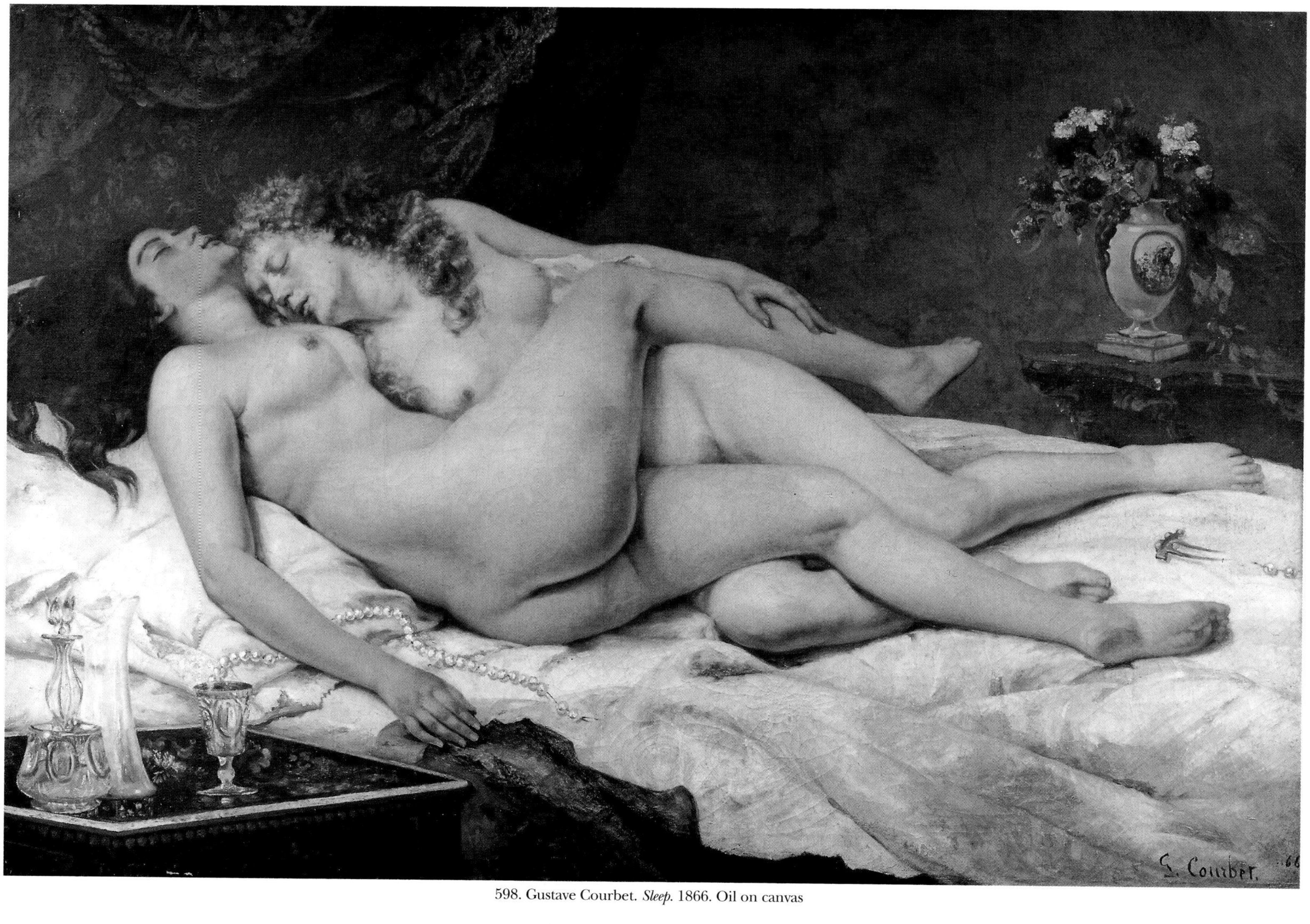

598. Gustave Courbet. *Sleep.* 1866. Oil on canvas

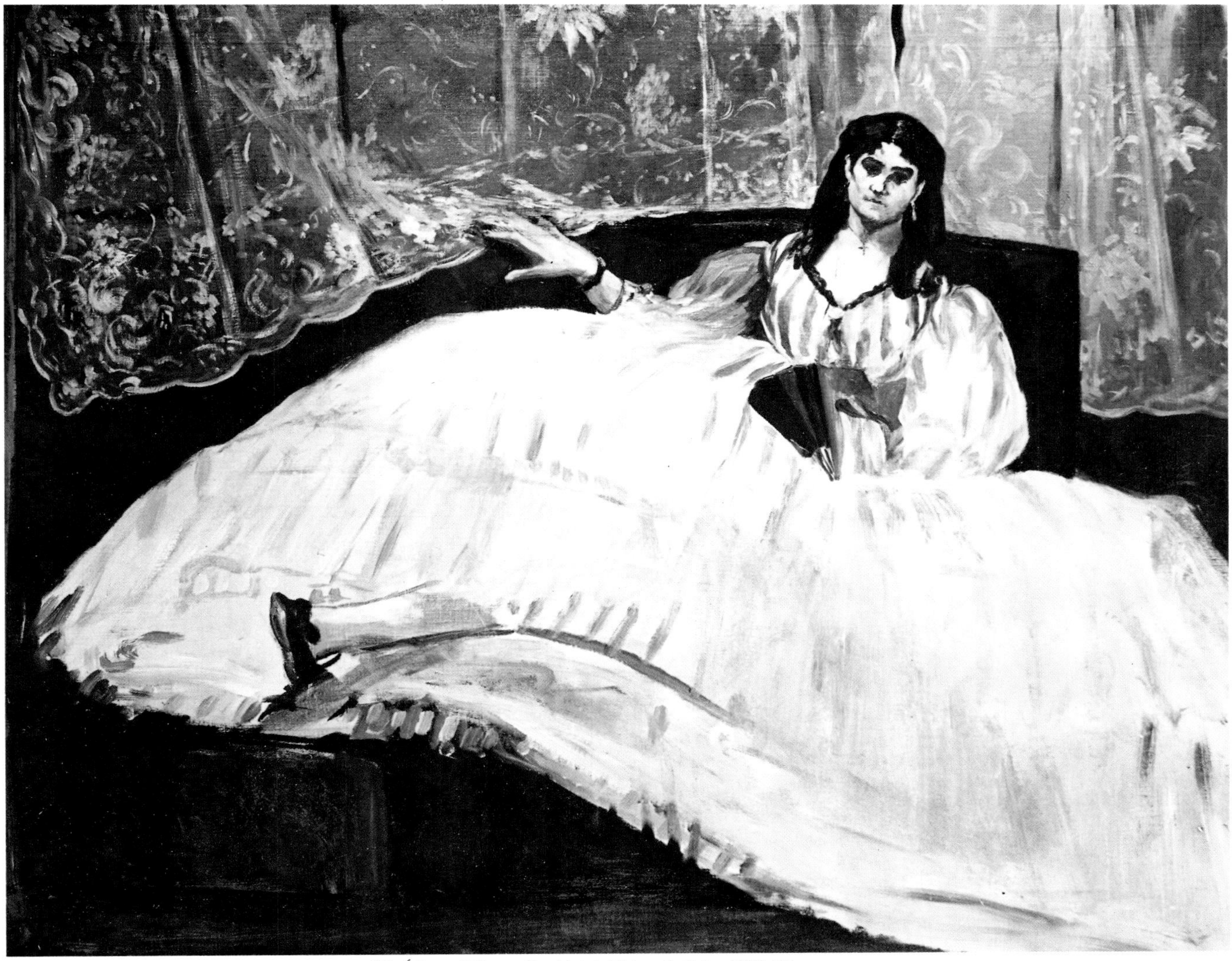

599. Édouard Manet. *Baudelaire's Mistress Reclining.* 1862. Oil on canvas

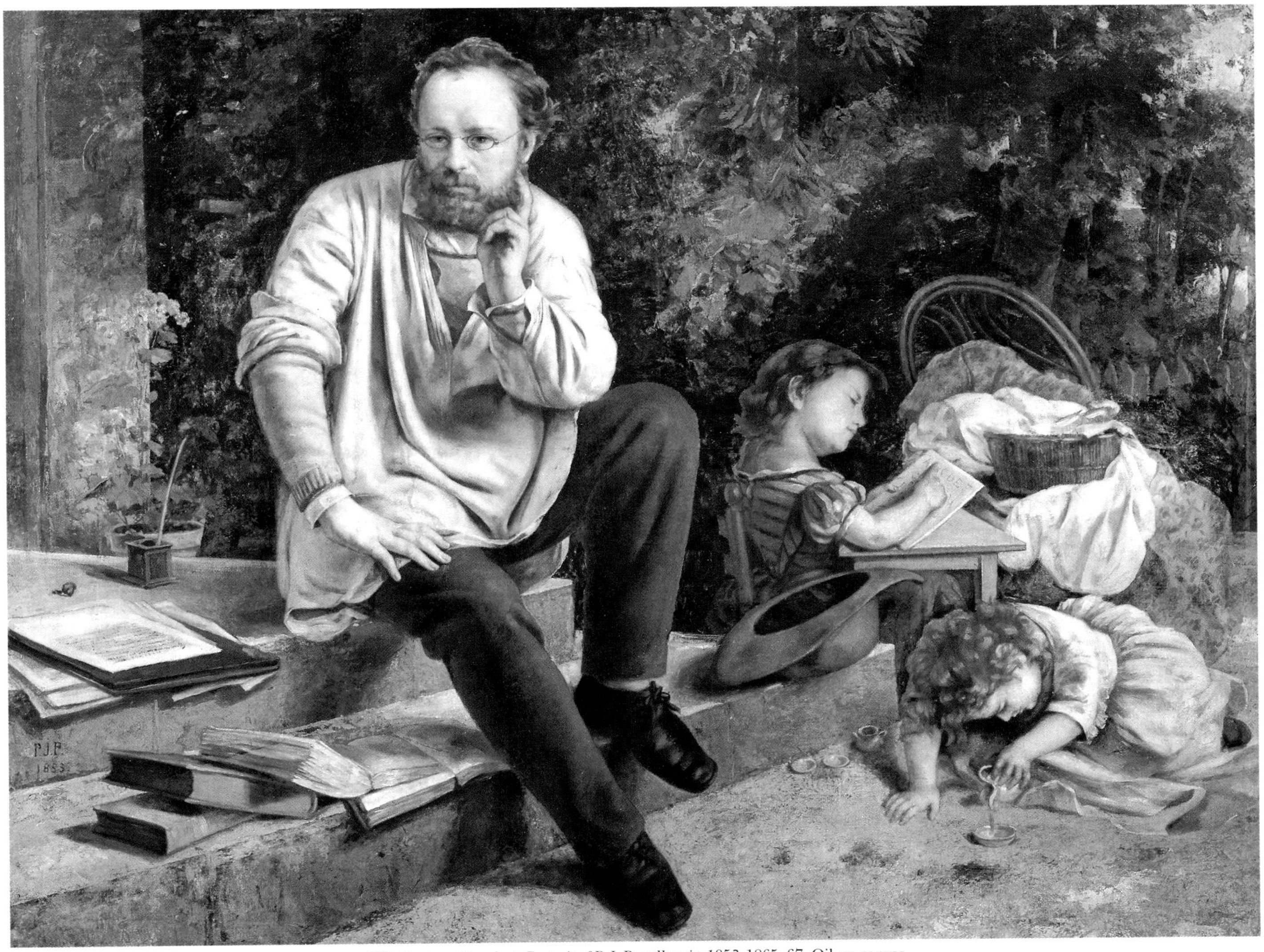

600. Gustave Courbet. *Portrait of P. J. Proudhon in 1853.* 1865–67. Oil on canvas

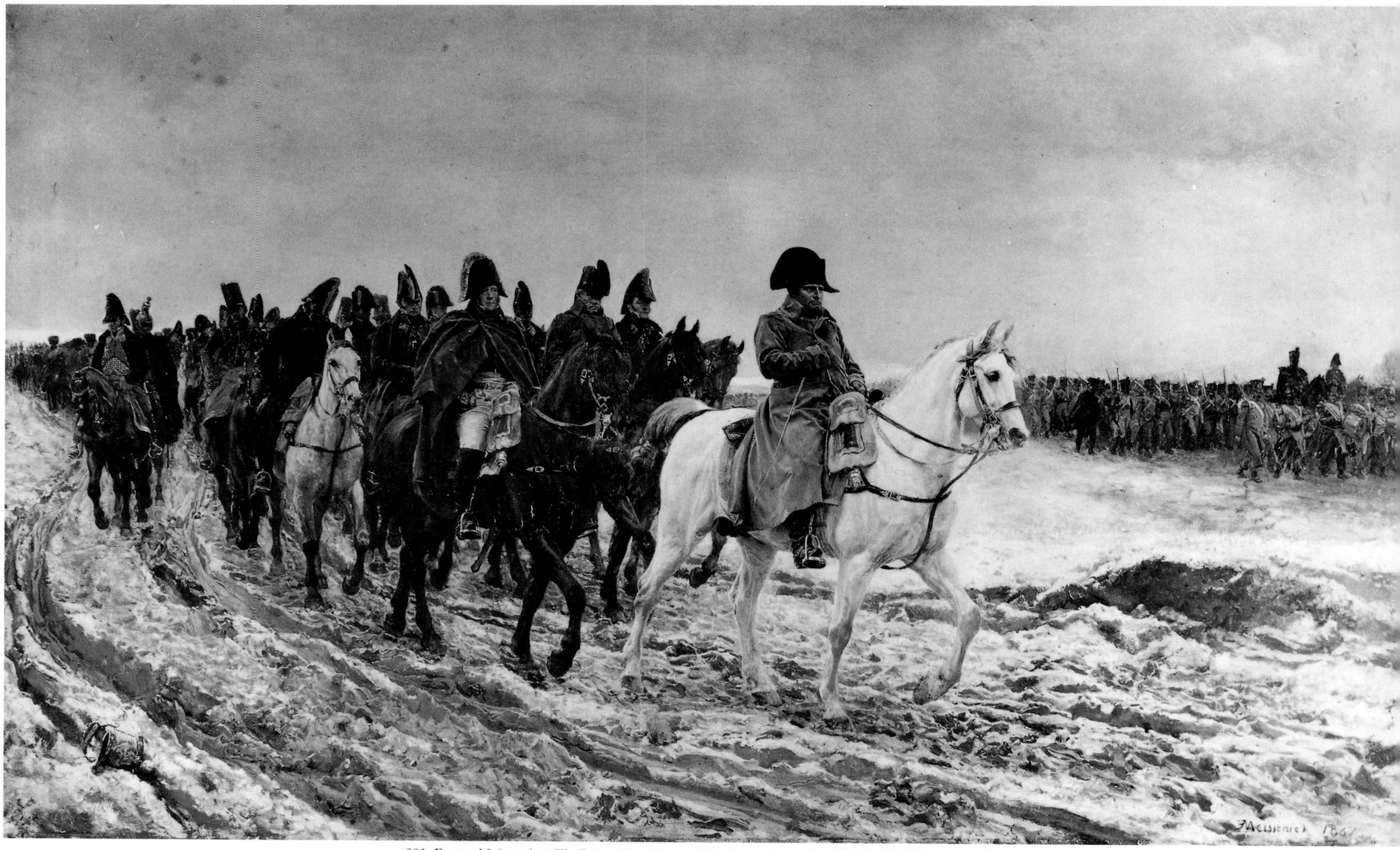

601. Ernest Meissonier. *The Retreat from Moscow (The French Campaign, 1814).* 1864. Oil on wood

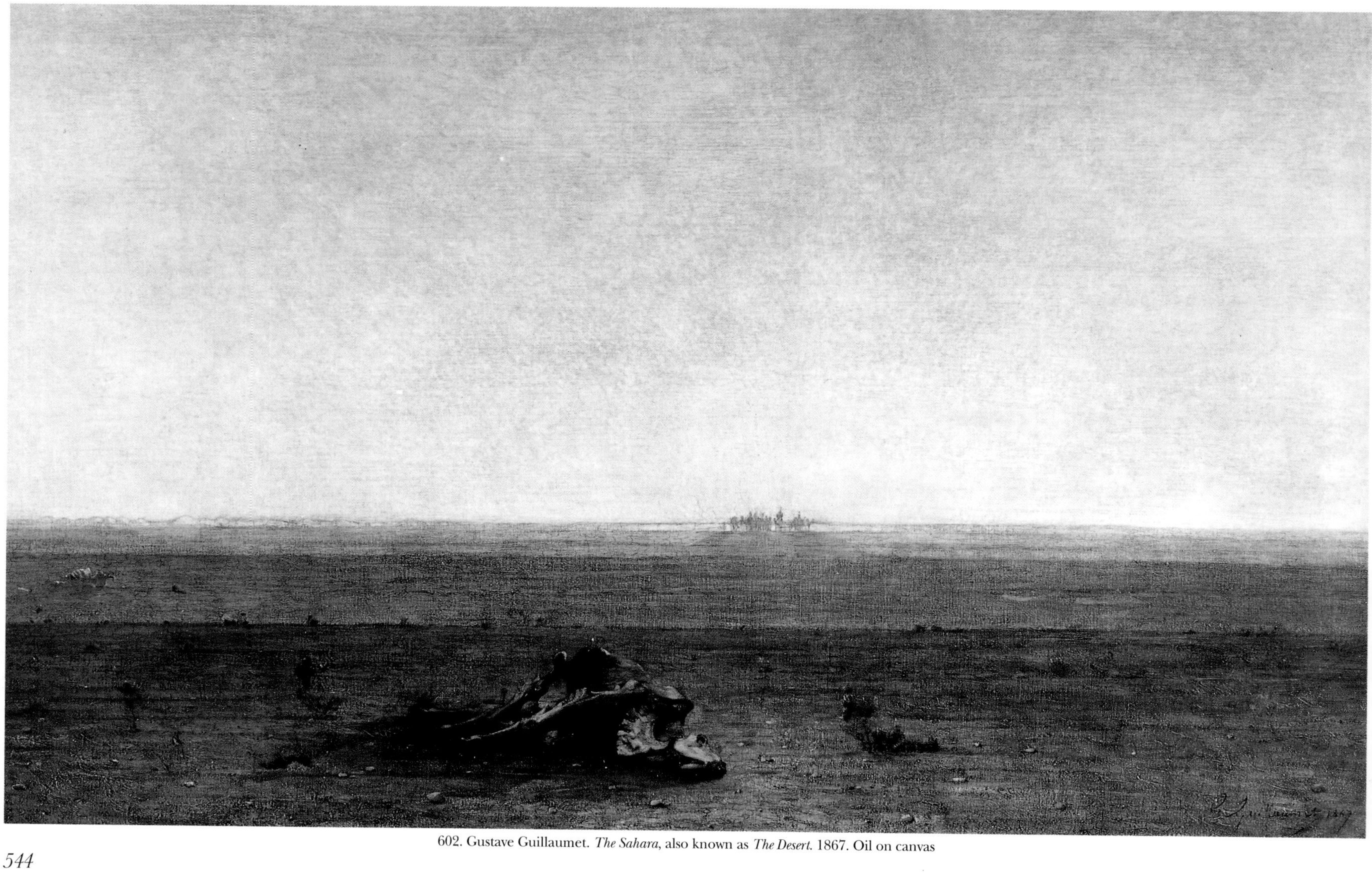

602. Gustave Guillaumet. *The Sahara,* also known as *The Desert.* 1867. Oil on canvas

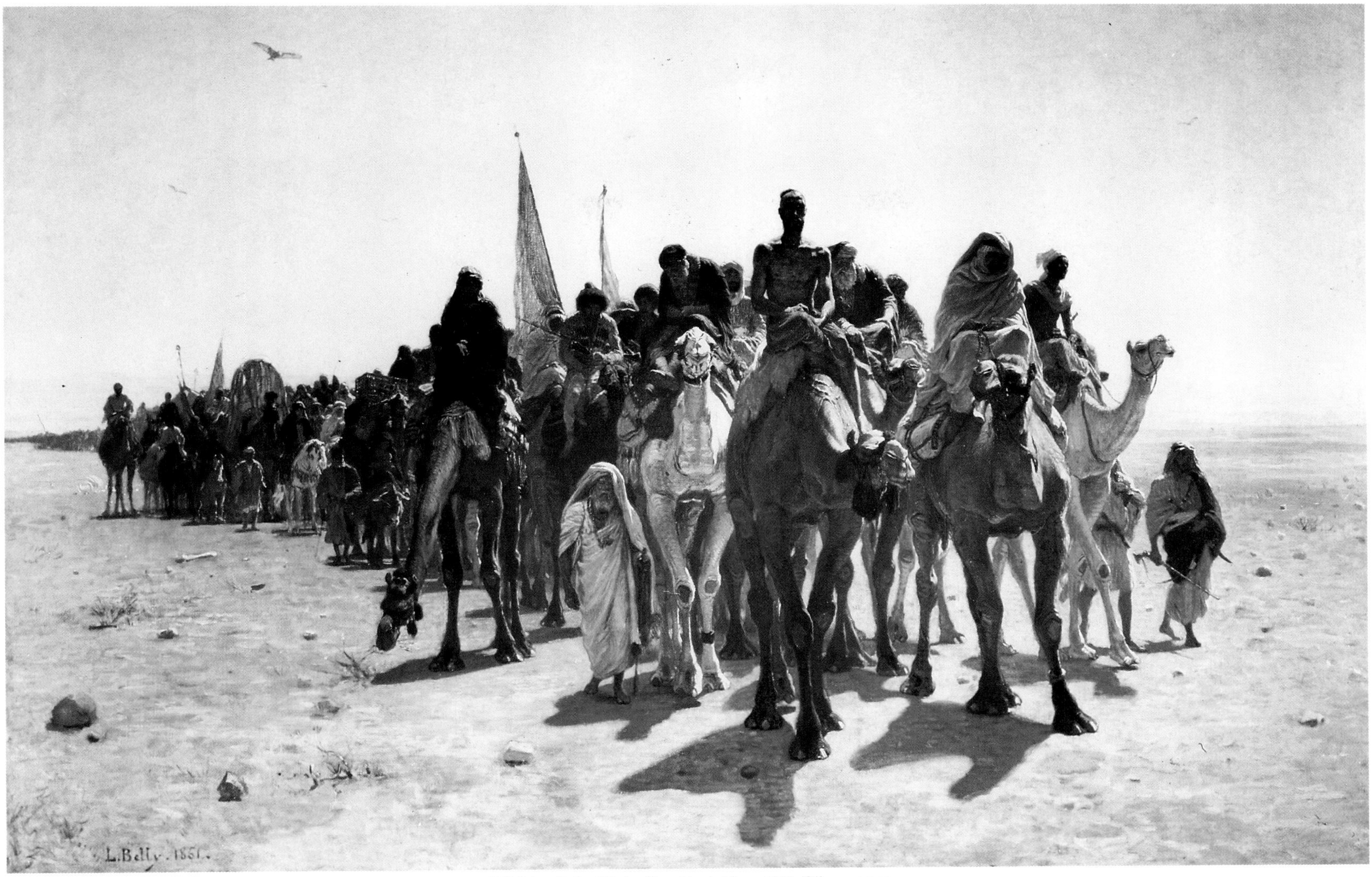

603. Léon Belly. *Pilgrims Traveling to Mecca.* 1861. Oil on canvas

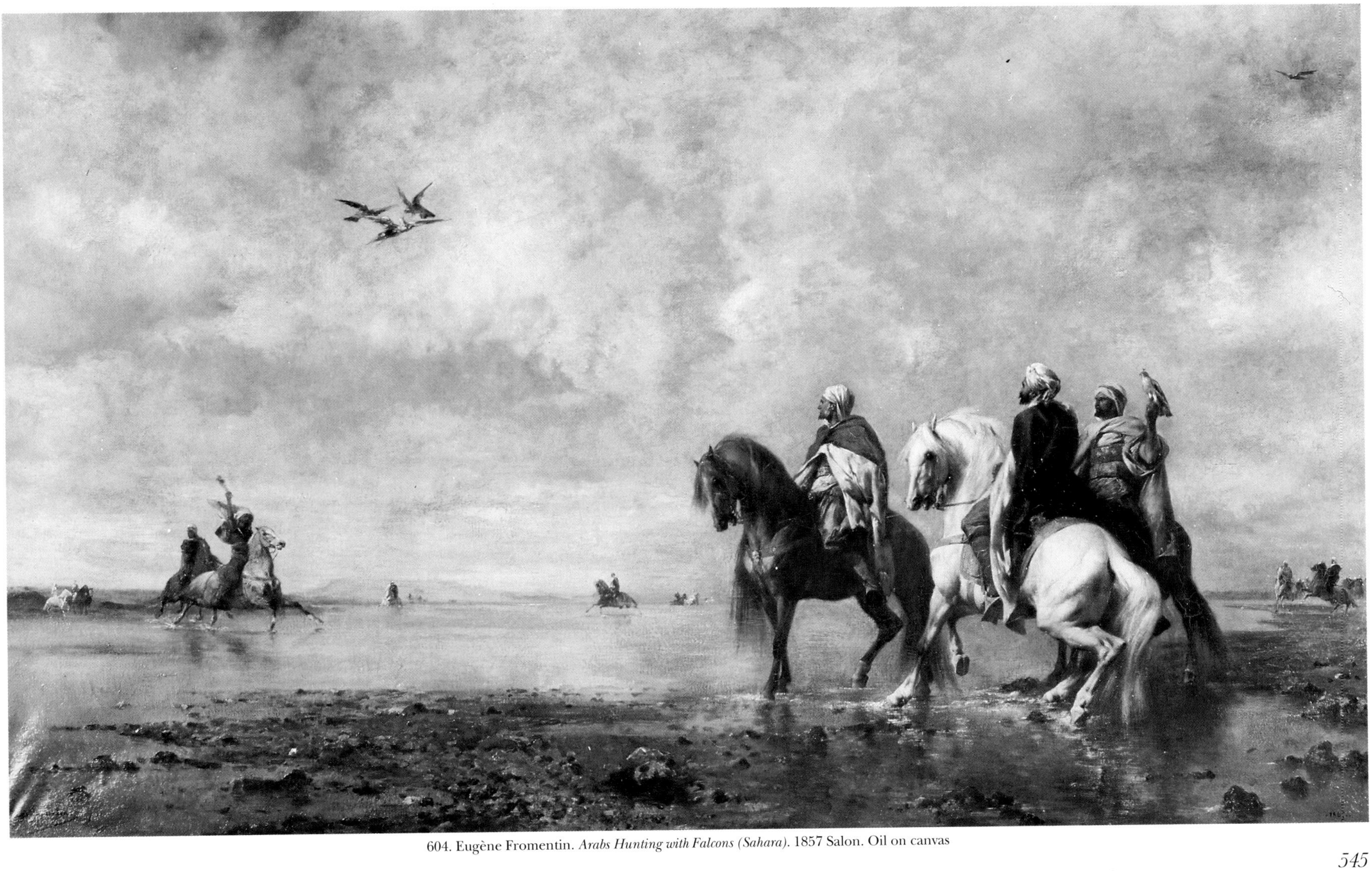

604. Eugène Fromentin. *Arabs Hunting with Falcons (Sahara).* 1857 Salon. Oil on canvas

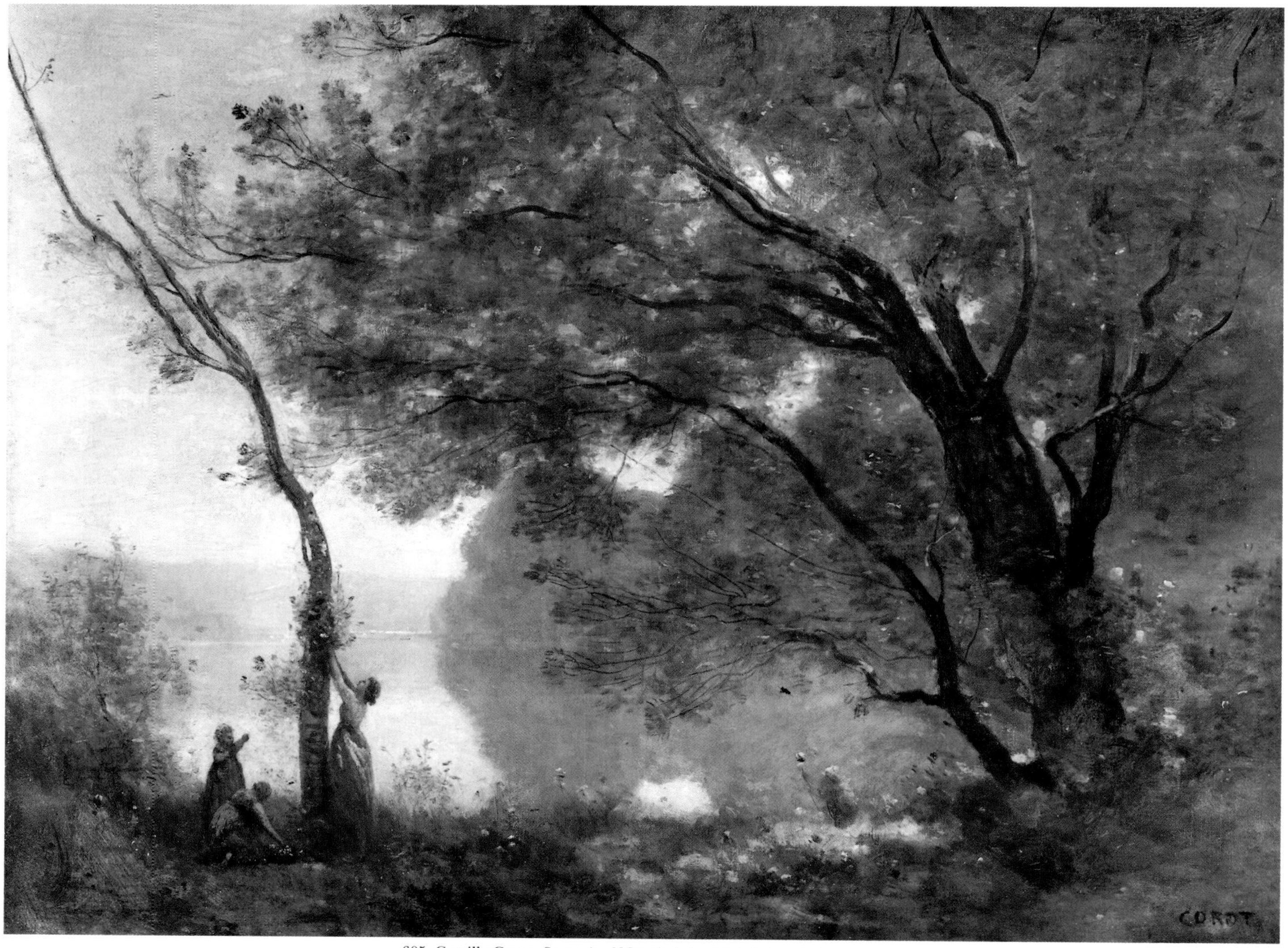

605. Camille Corot. *Souvenir of Mortefontaine.* 1864 Salon. Oil on canvas

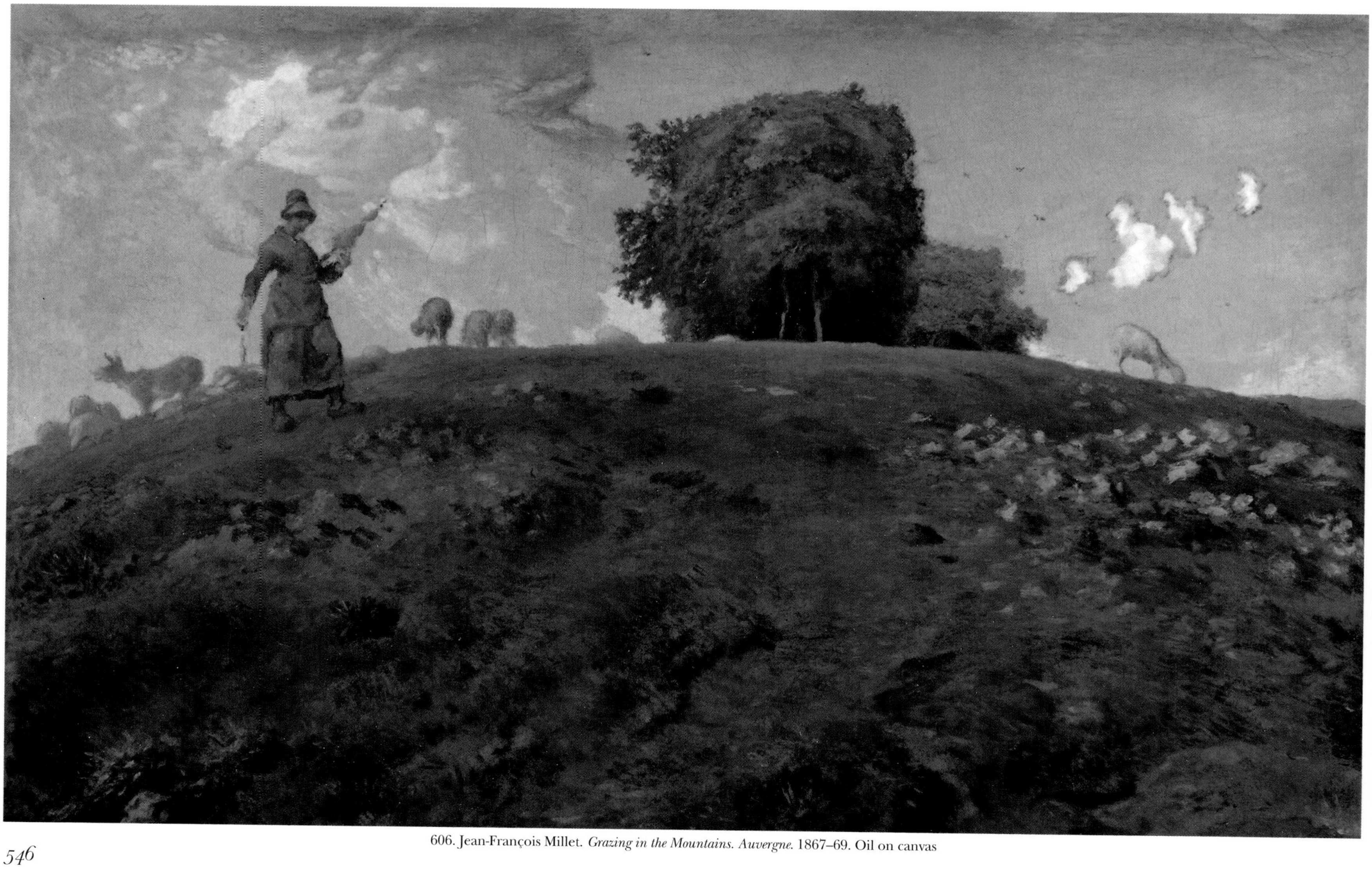

606. Jean-François Millet. *Grazing in the Mountains. Auvergne.* 1867–69. Oil on canvas

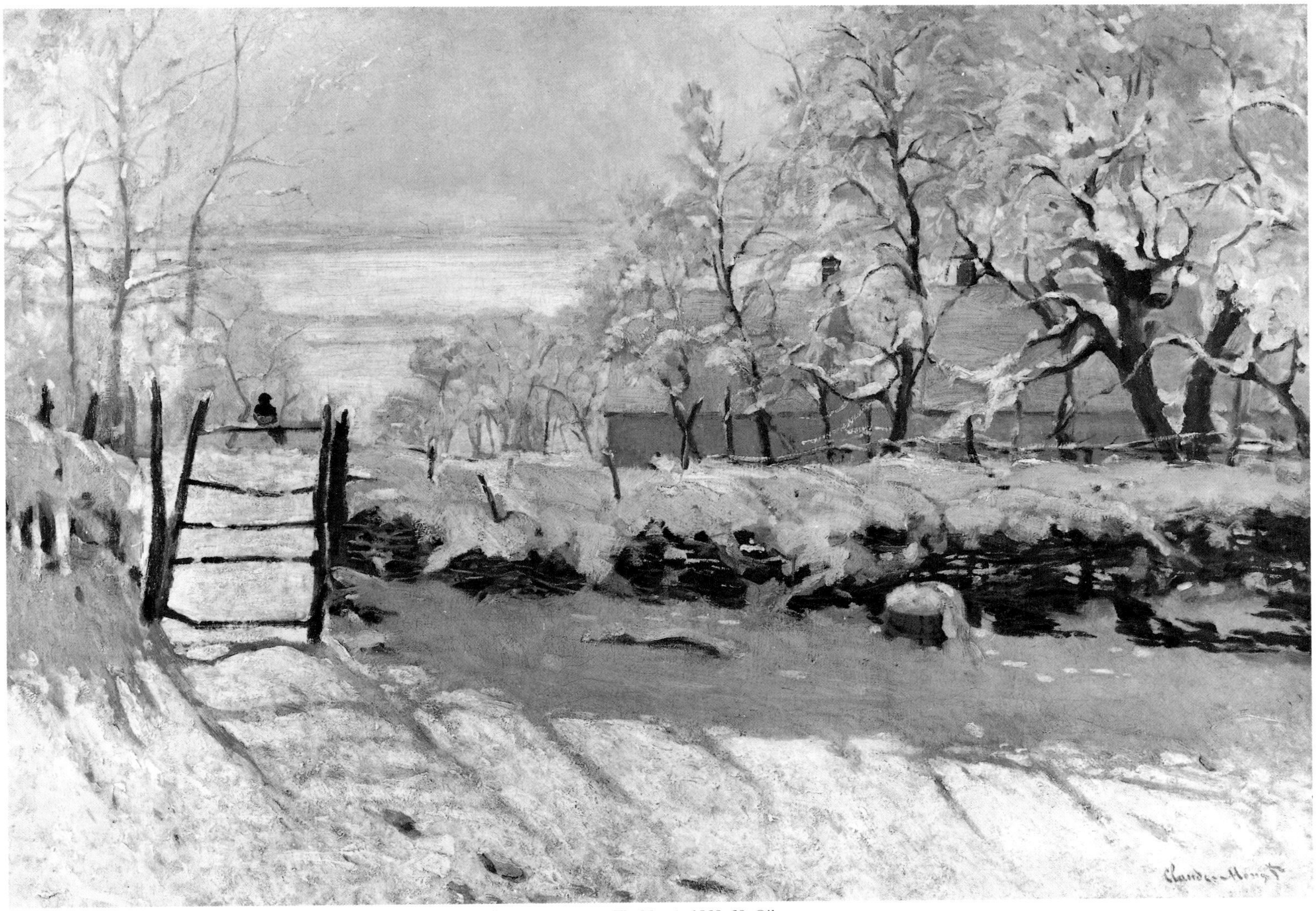

607. Claude Monet. *The Magpie.* 1868–69. Oil on canvas

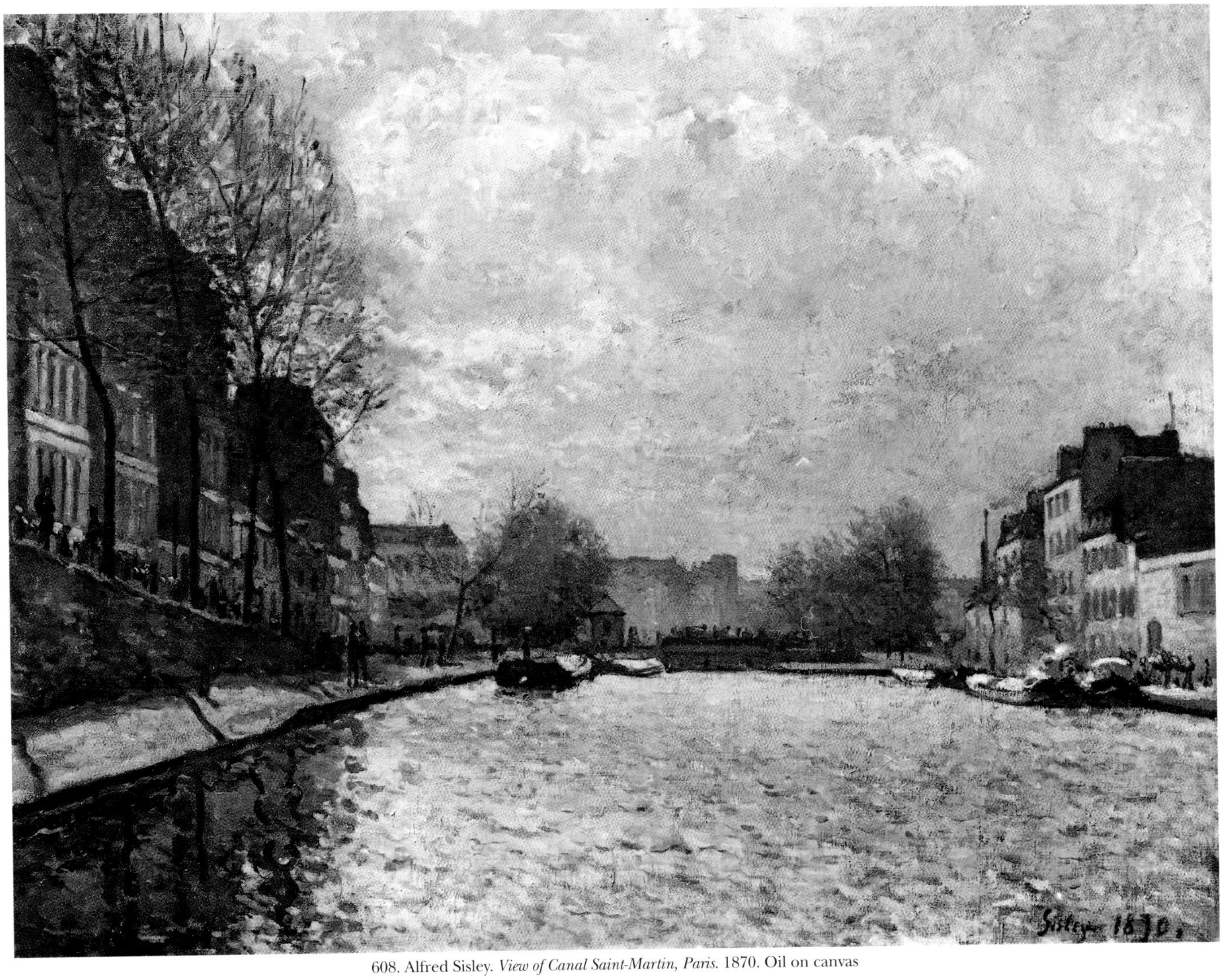

608. Alfred Sisley. *View of Canal Saint-Martin, Paris.* 1870. Oil on canvas

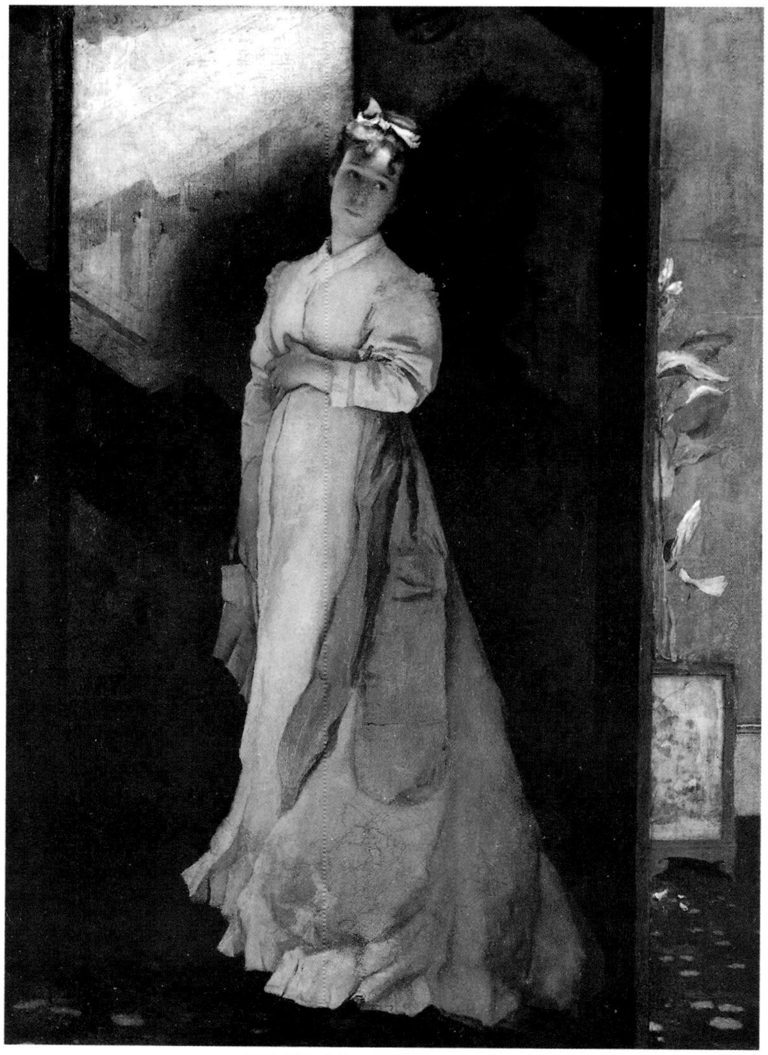

609. Alfred Stevens. *The Letter Breaking It Off.* c. 1867. Oil on canvas

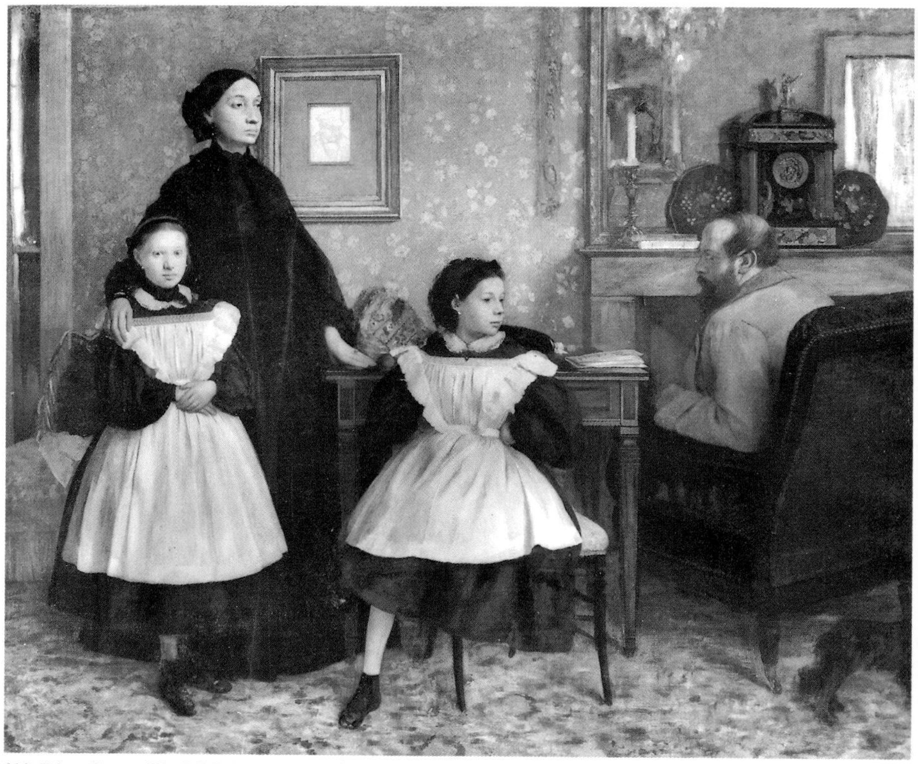

610. Edgar Degas. *The Bellelli Family.* 1858–67. Oil on canvas

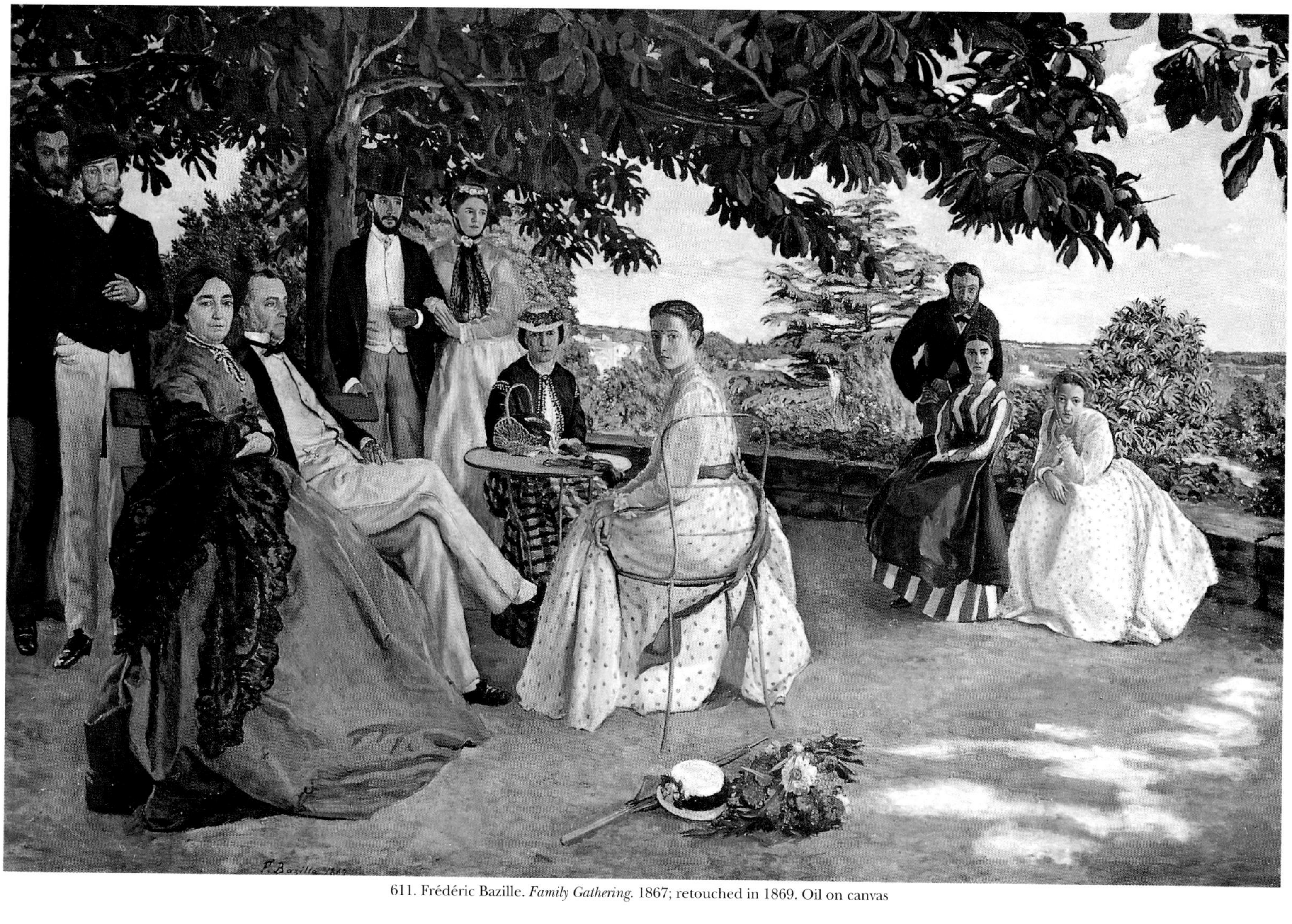

611. Frédéric Bazille. *Family Gathering.* 1867; retouched in 1869. Oil on canvas

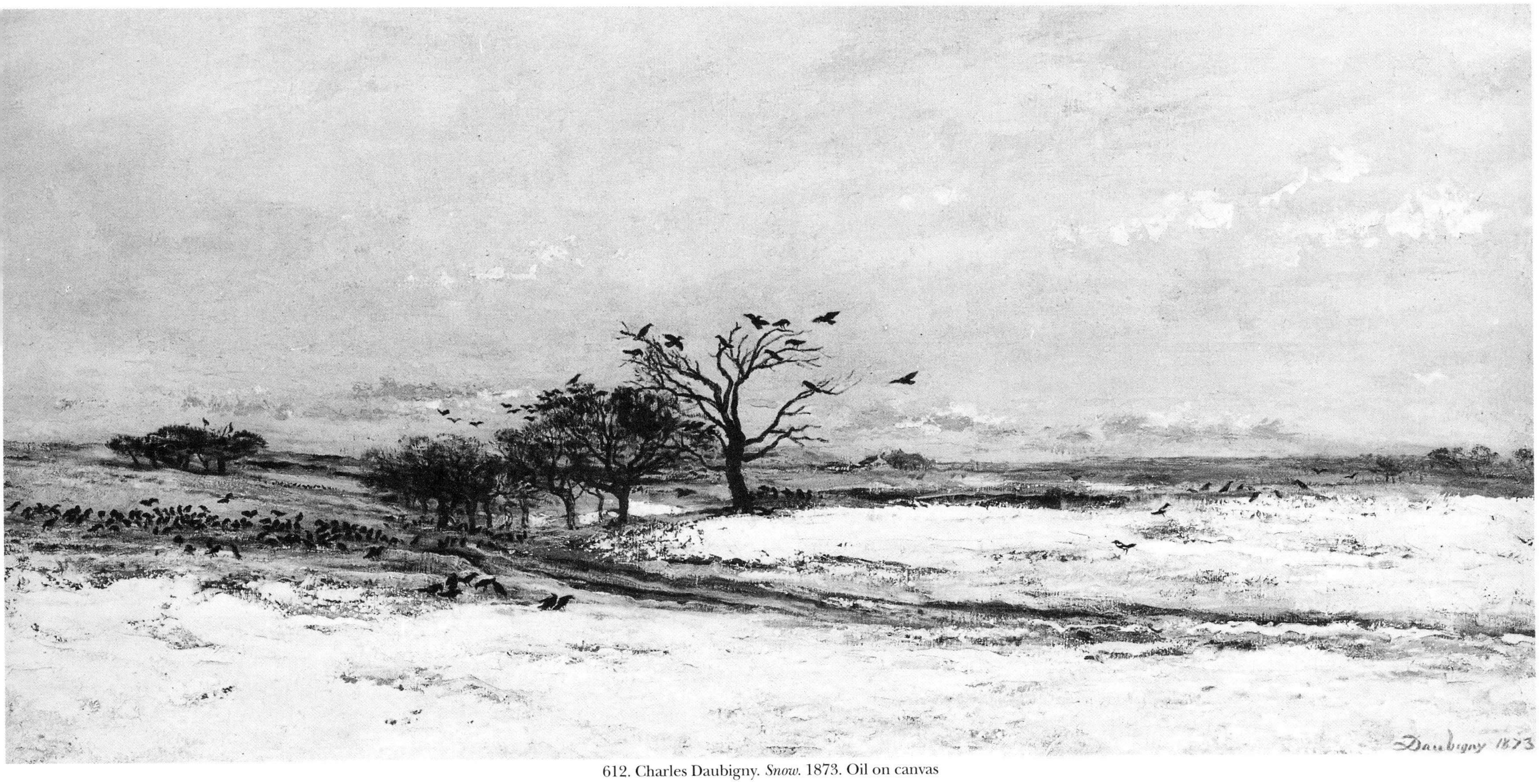

612. Charles Daubigny. *Snow.* 1873. Oil on canvas

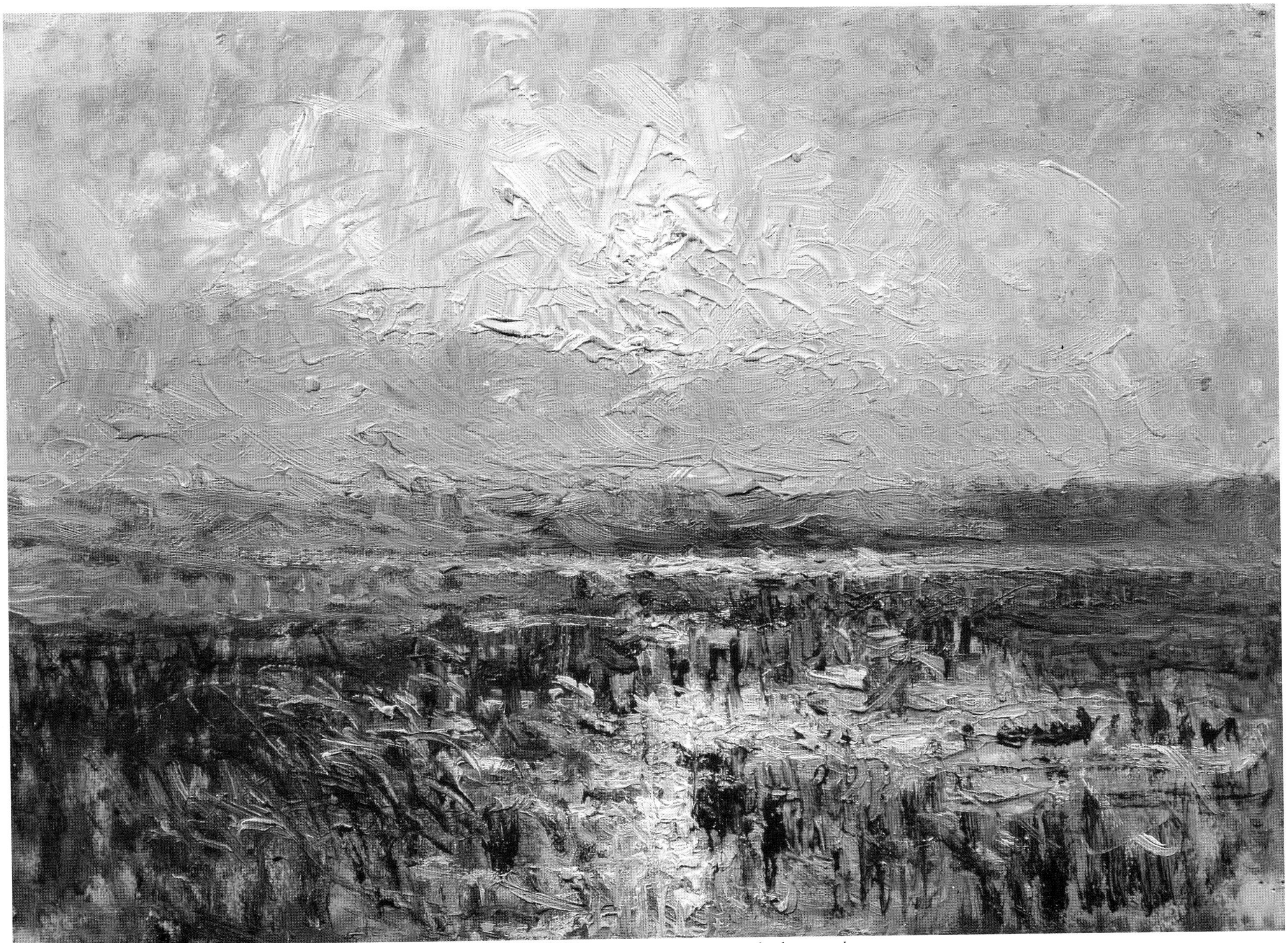

613. Auguste Ravier. *Marsh at Sunset.* Oil on paper, glued onto card

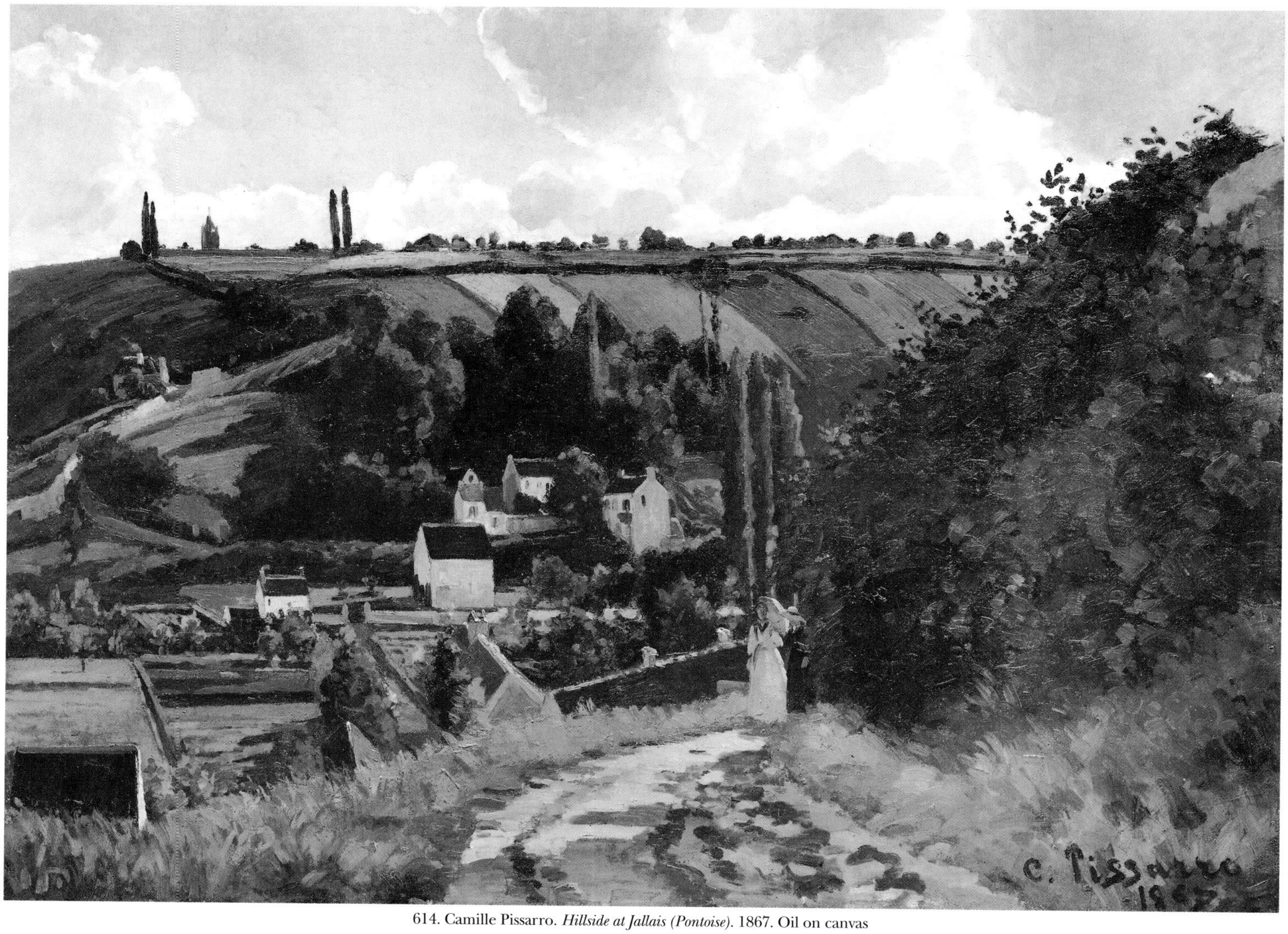

614. Camille Pissarro. *Hillside at Jallais (Pontoise)*. 1867. Oil on canvas

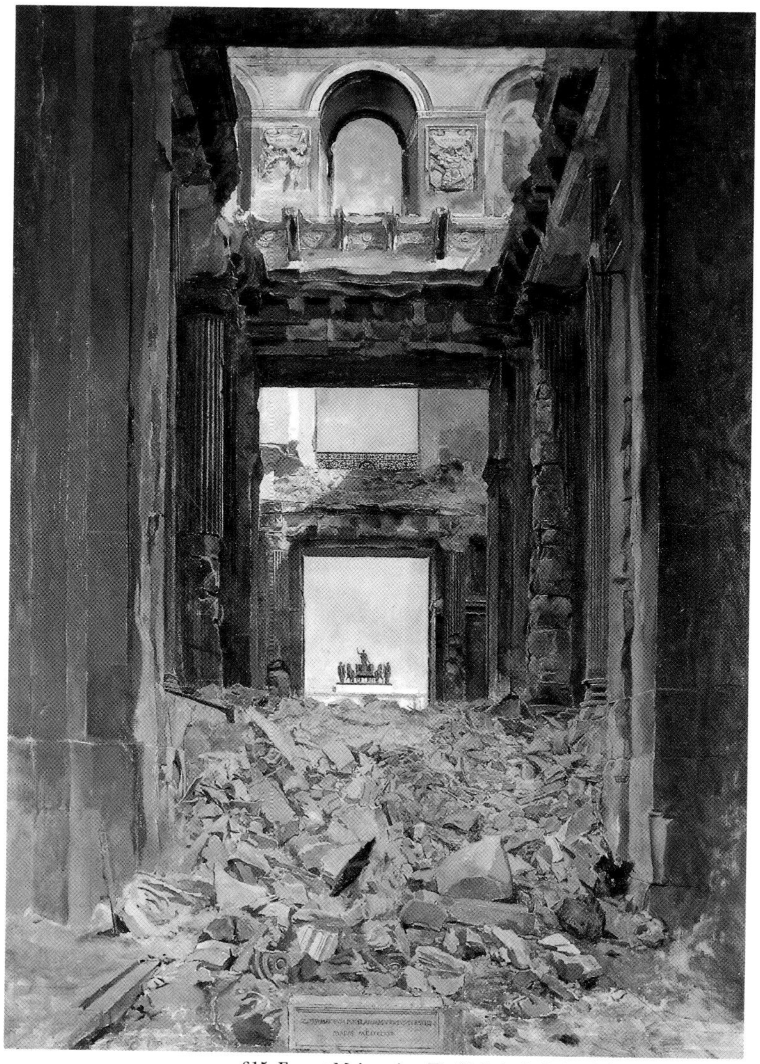

615. Ernest Meissonier. *The Tuileries in Ruins*. 1871. Oil on canvas

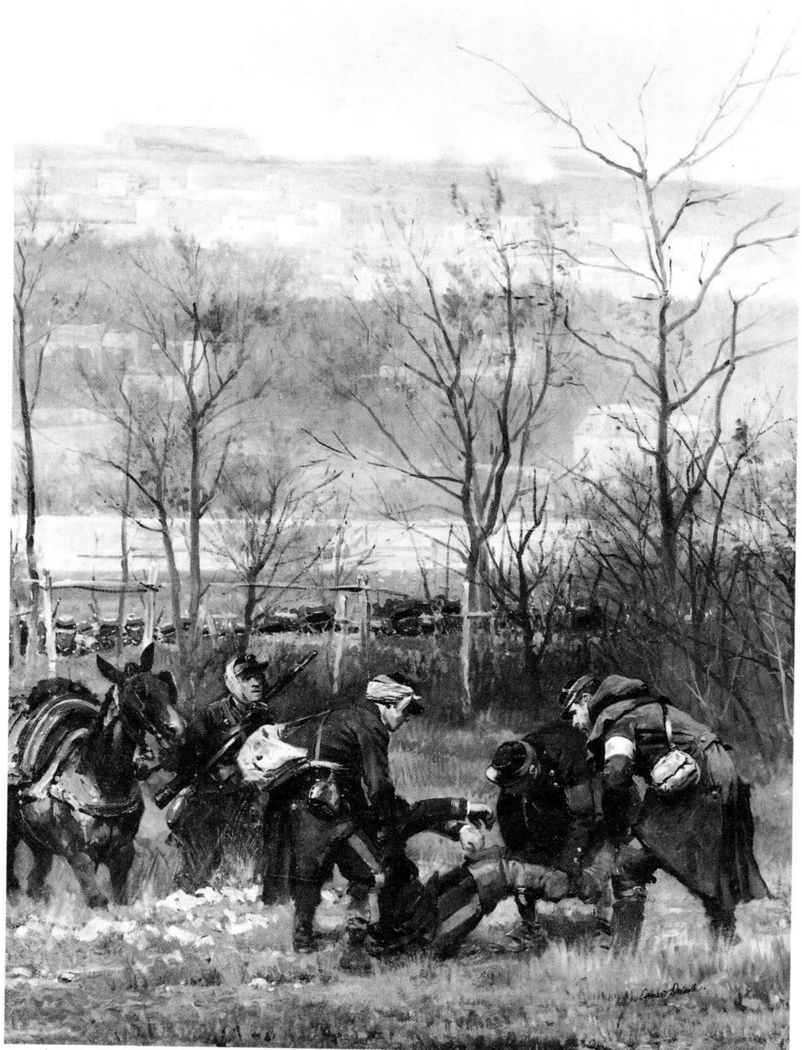

616. Édouard Detaille. *Picking up a Wounded Soldier, Battle of Champigny (November 1870)* (fragment of *Panorama of Champigny*). 1880–82. Oil on canvas

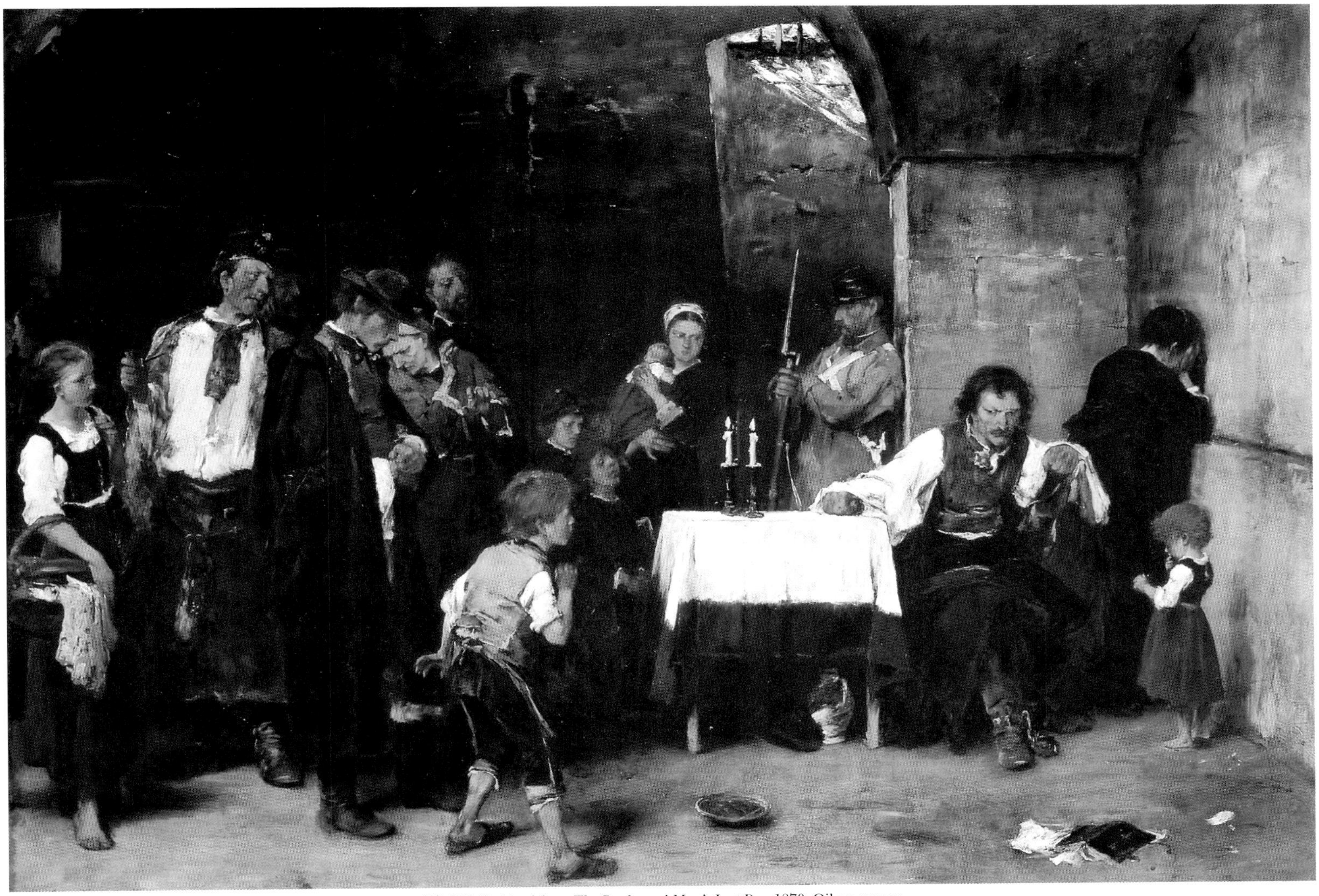

617. Mihály Munkácsy. *The Condemned Man's Last Day*. 1870. Oil on canvas

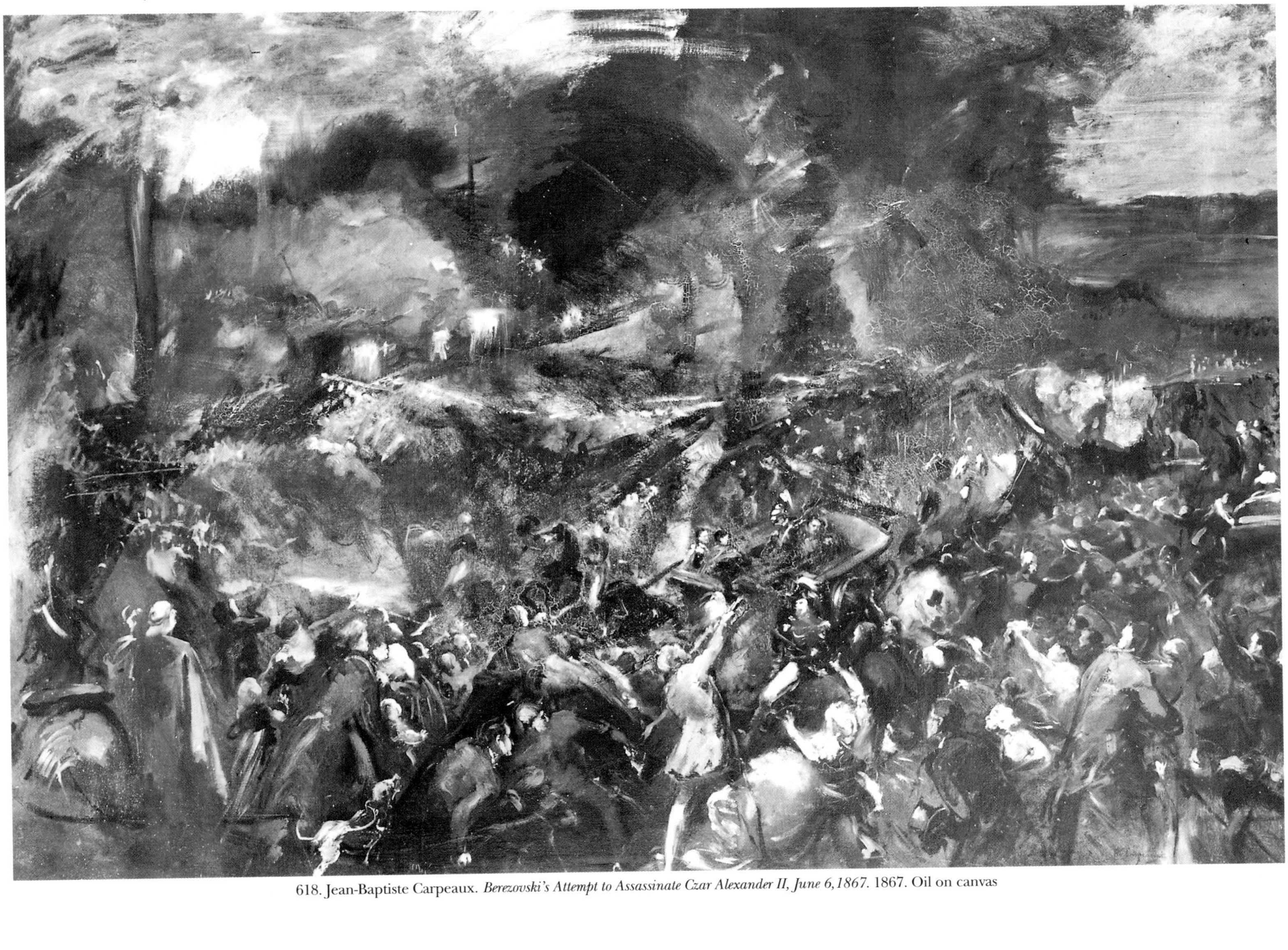

618. Jean-Baptiste Carpeaux. *Berezovski's Attempt to Assassinate Czar Alexander II, June 6,1867*. 1867. Oil on canvas

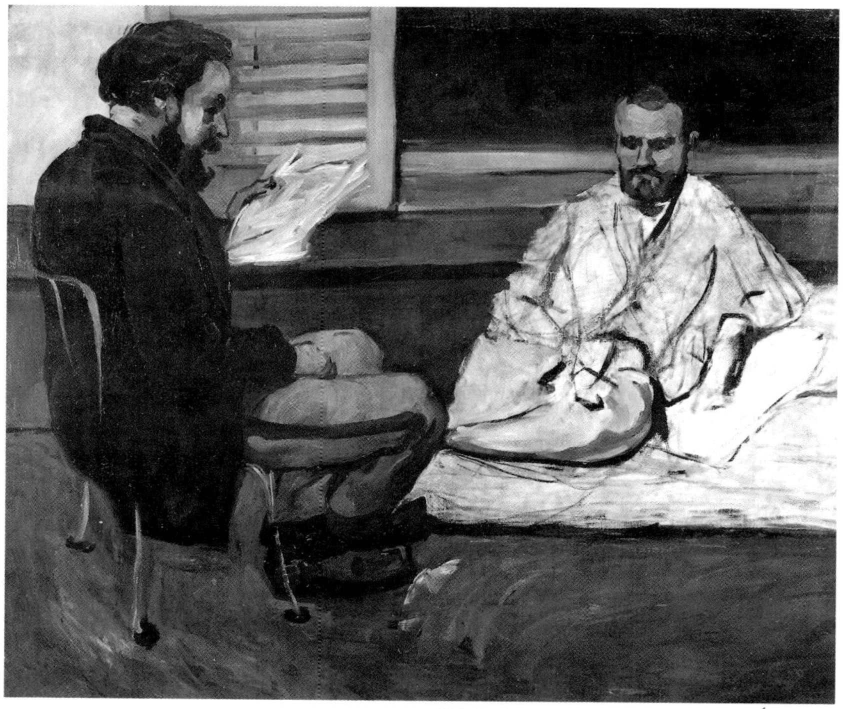

619. Paul Cézanne. *Paul Alexis Reading to Émile Zola.* c. 1869–70. Oil on canvas

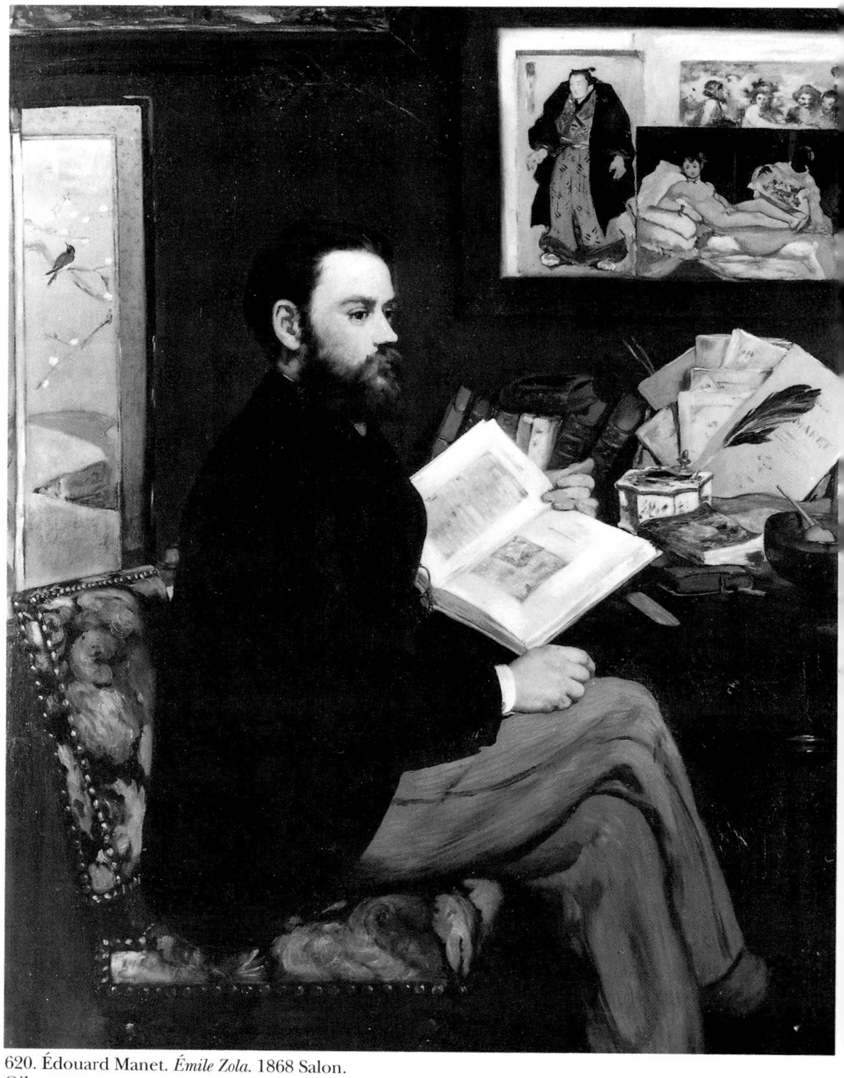

620. Édouard Manet. *Émile Zola.* 1868 Salon. Oil on canvas

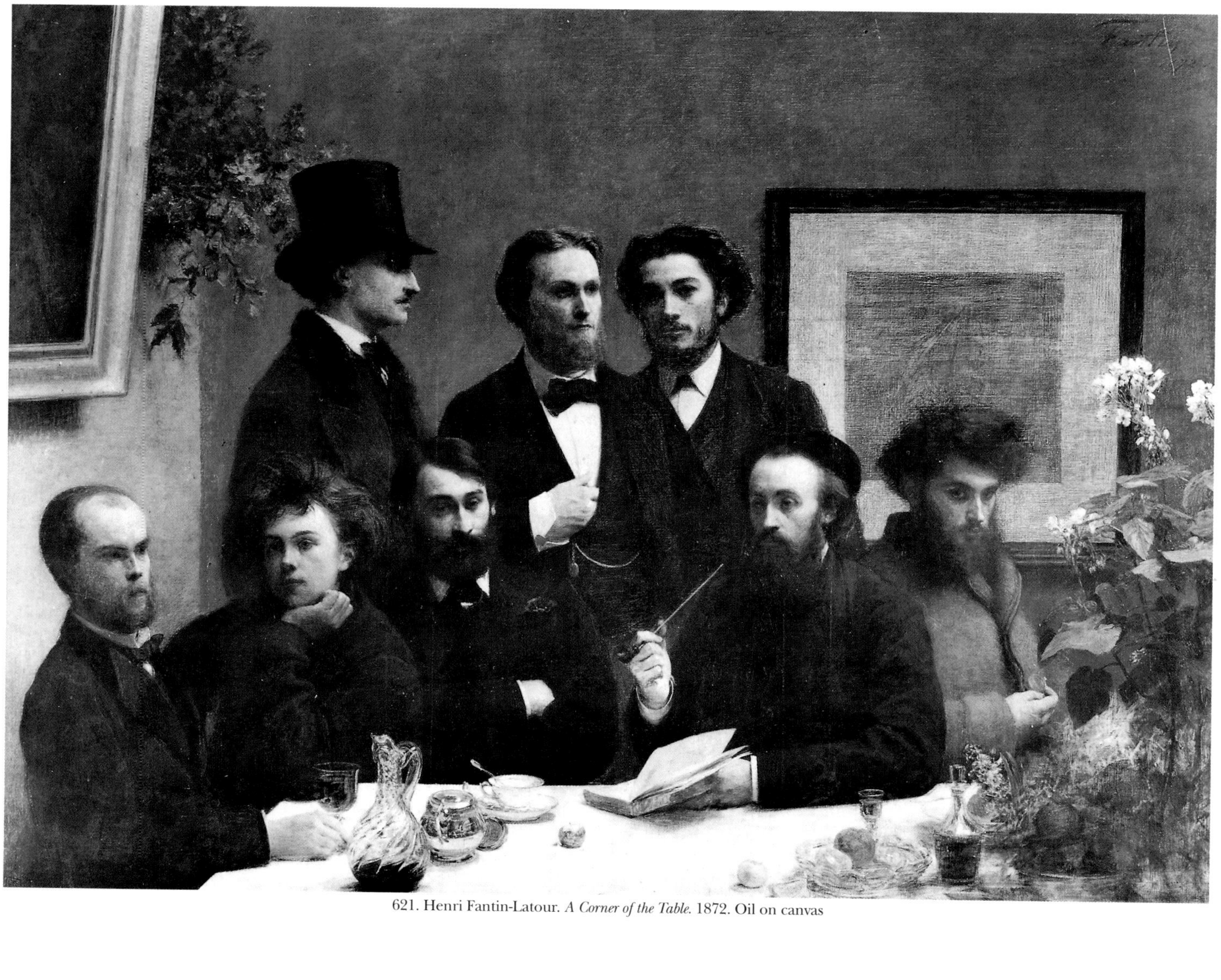

621. Henri Fantin-Latour. *A Corner of the Table.* 1872. Oil on canvas

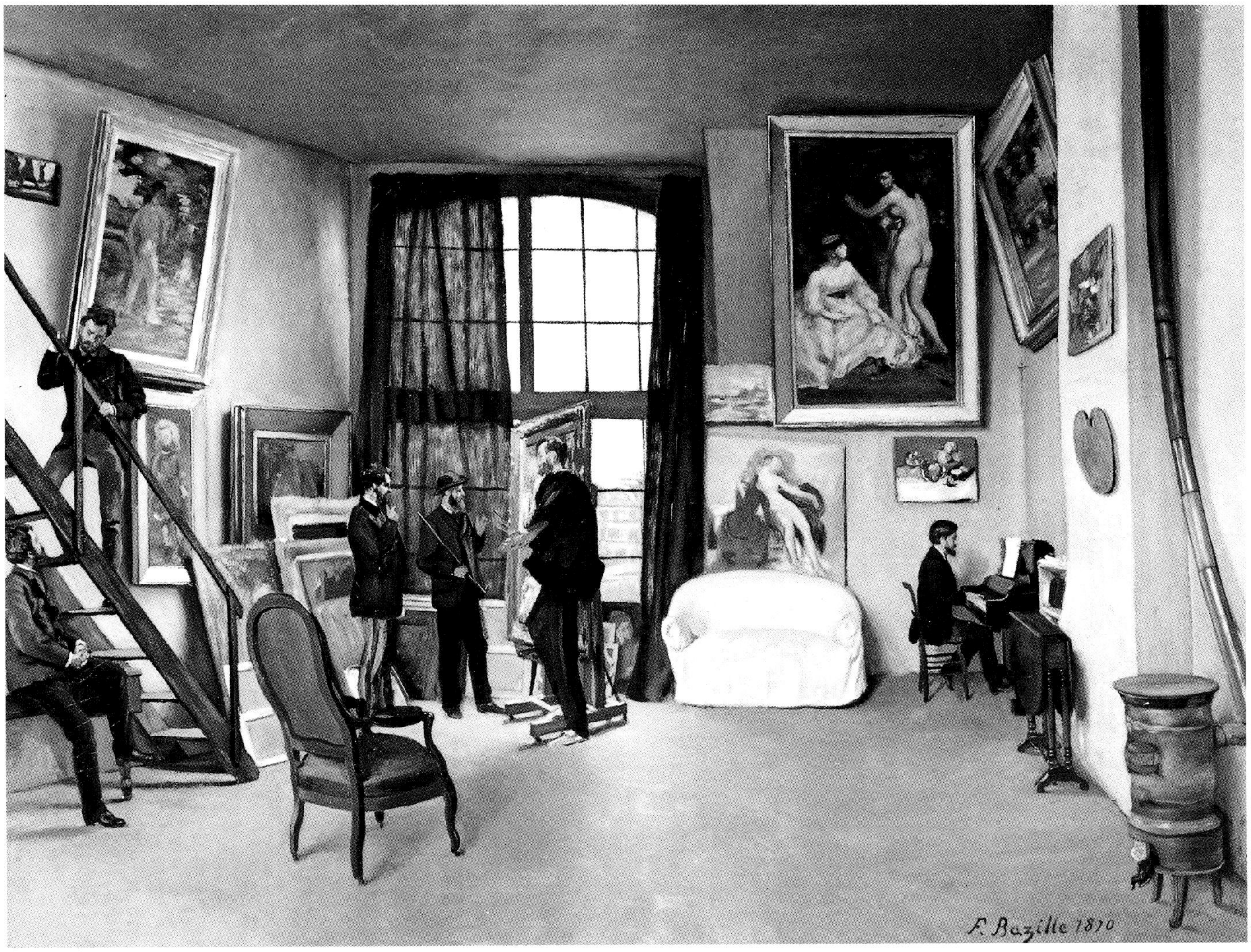

622. Frédéric Bazille. *Studio in Rue de la Condamine* (the figure of Bazille, standing to the right of the easel, may have been painted by Manet). 1870. Oil on canvas

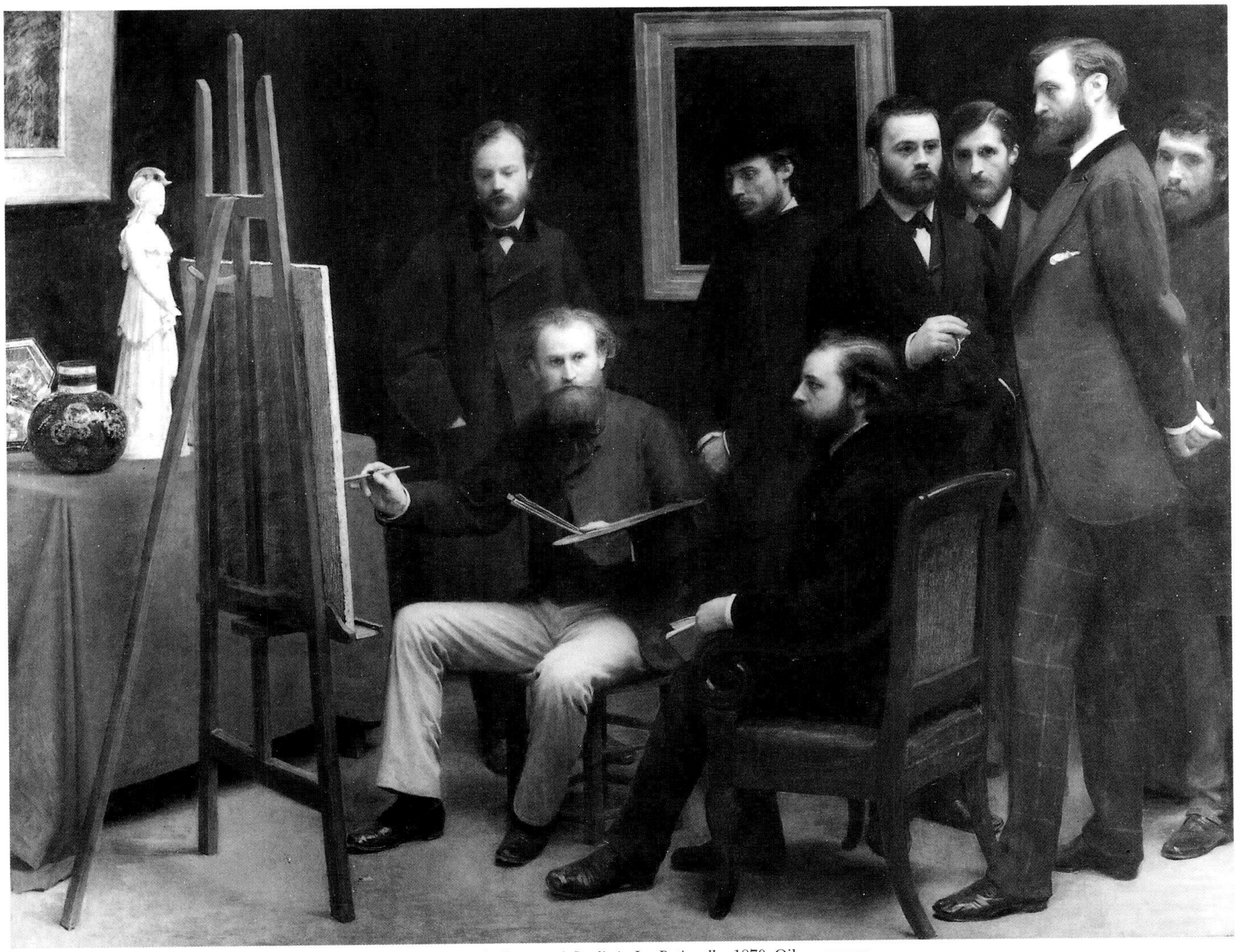

623. Henri Fantin-Latour. *A Studio in Les Batignolles.* 1870. Oil on canvas

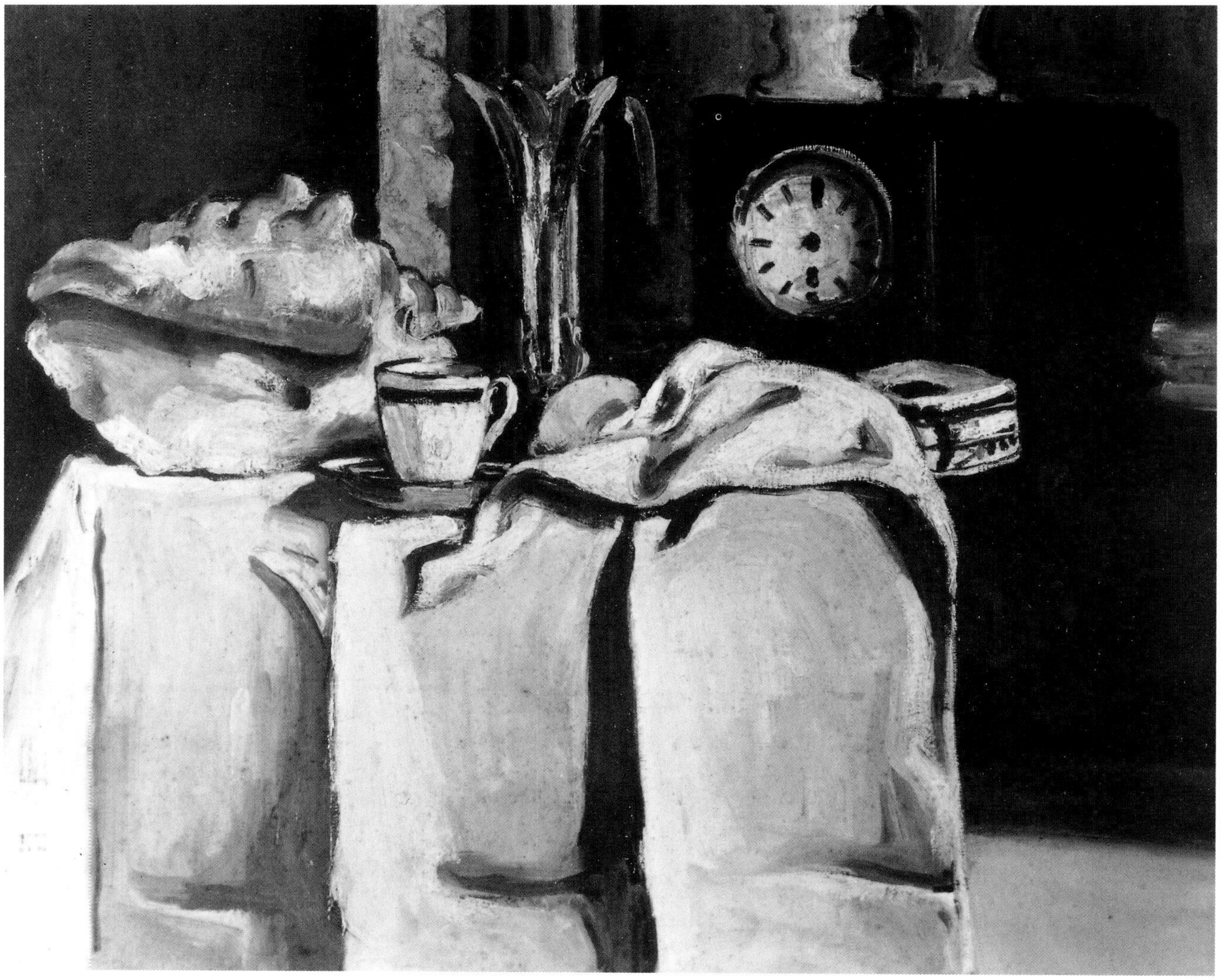

624. Paul Cézanne. *The Black Clock*. c. 1870. Oil on canvas

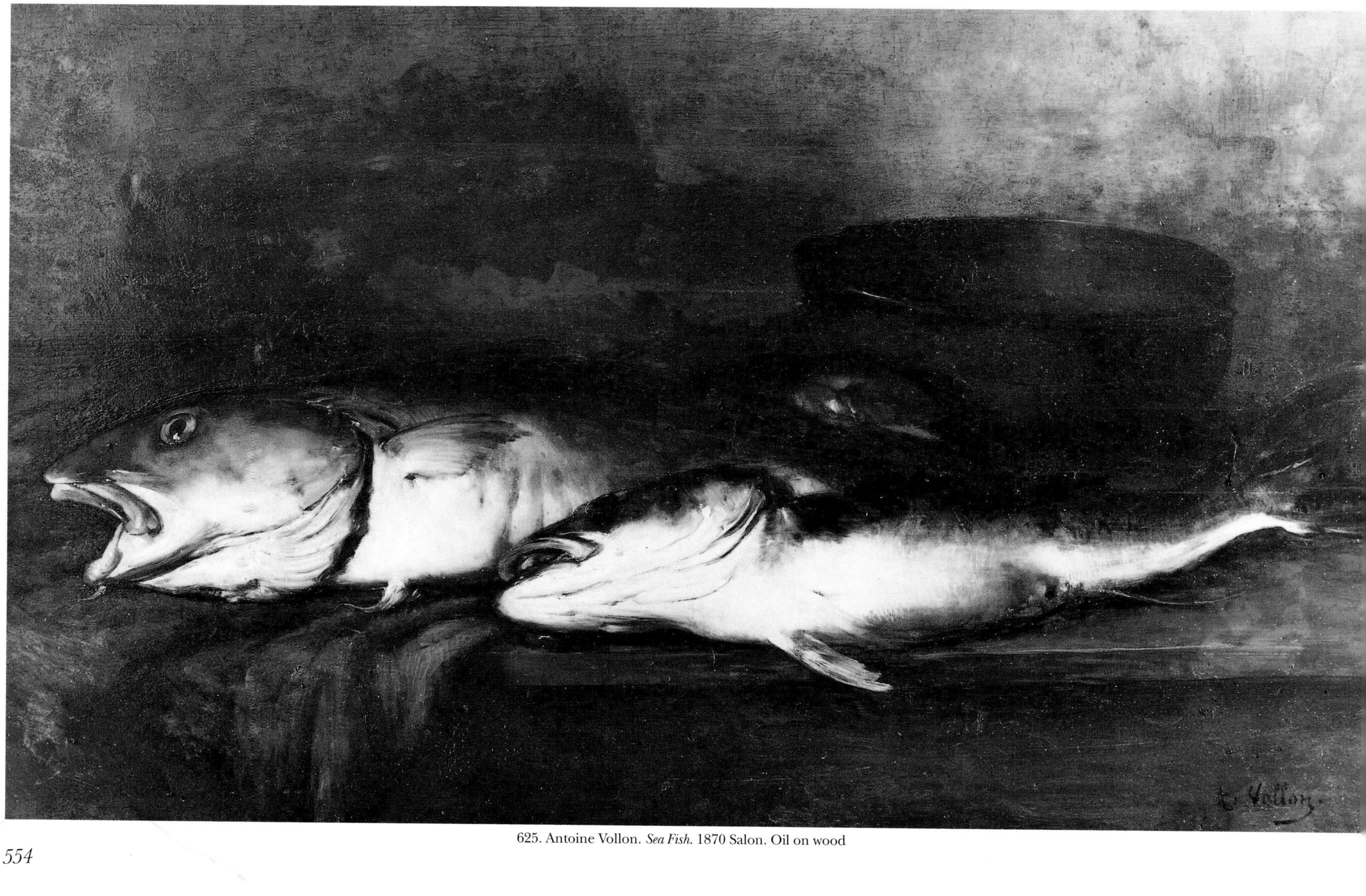

625. Antoine Vollon. *Sea Fish*. 1870 Salon. Oil on wood

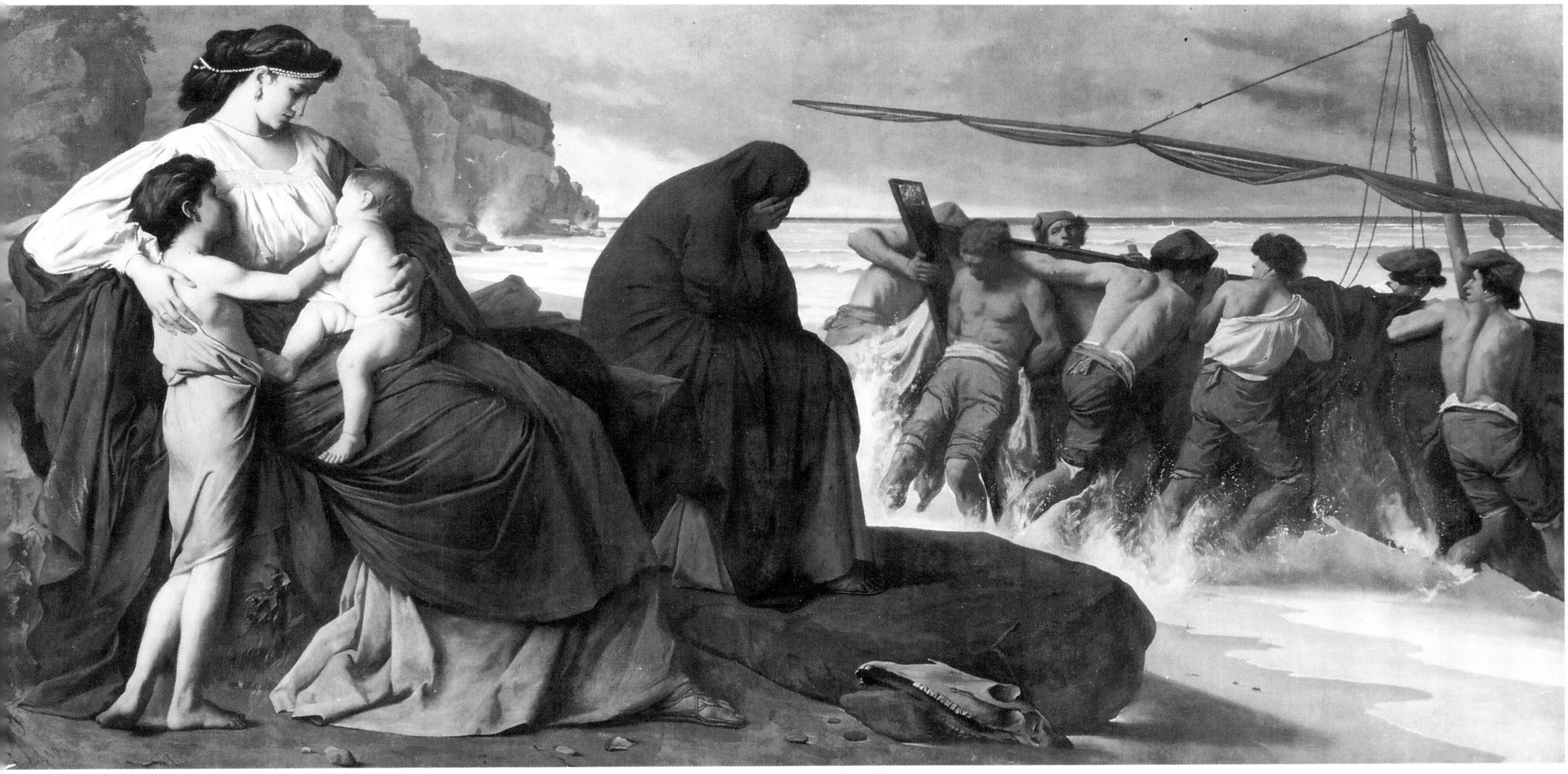

626. Anselm Feuerbach. *Medea.* 1870. Oil on canvas

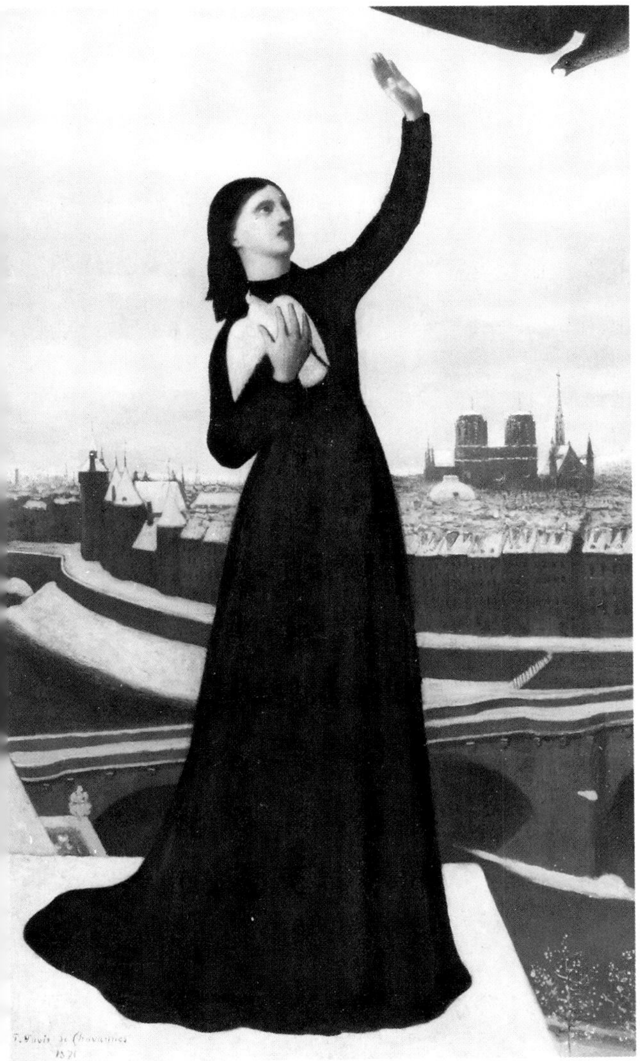

627. Pierre Puvis de Chavannes. *The Pigeon.* 1871. Oil on canvas

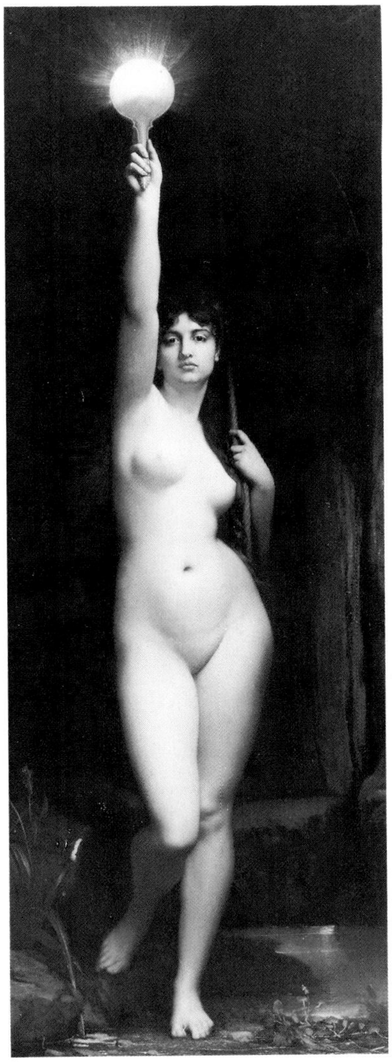

628. Jules Lefebvre. *Truth.* 1870. Oil on canvas

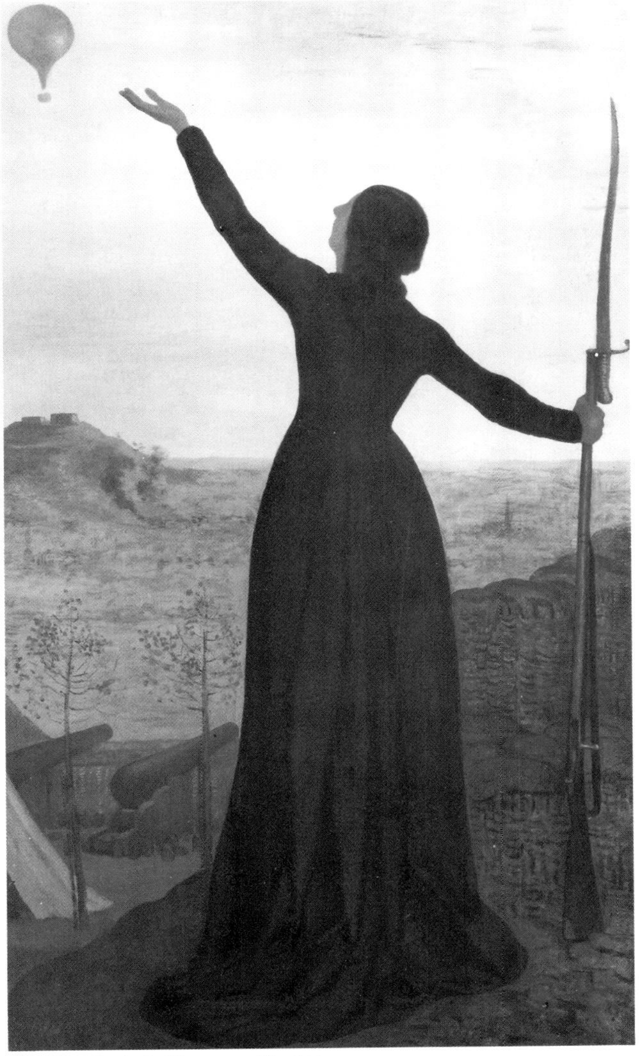

629. Pierre Puvis de Chavannes. *The Balloon.* 1870. Oil on canvas

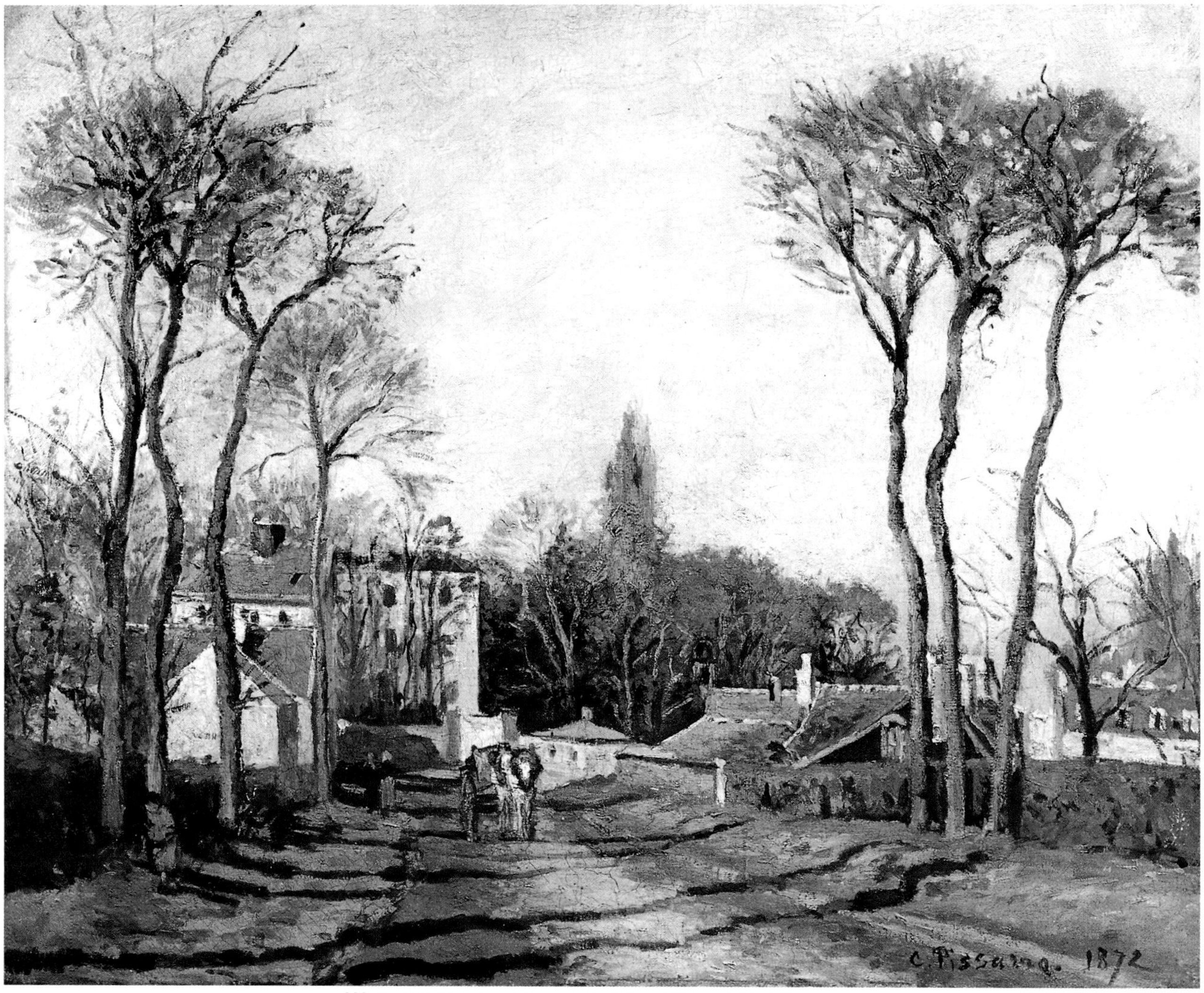

630. Camille Pissarro. *Entrance to the Village of Voisins.* 1872. Oil on canvas

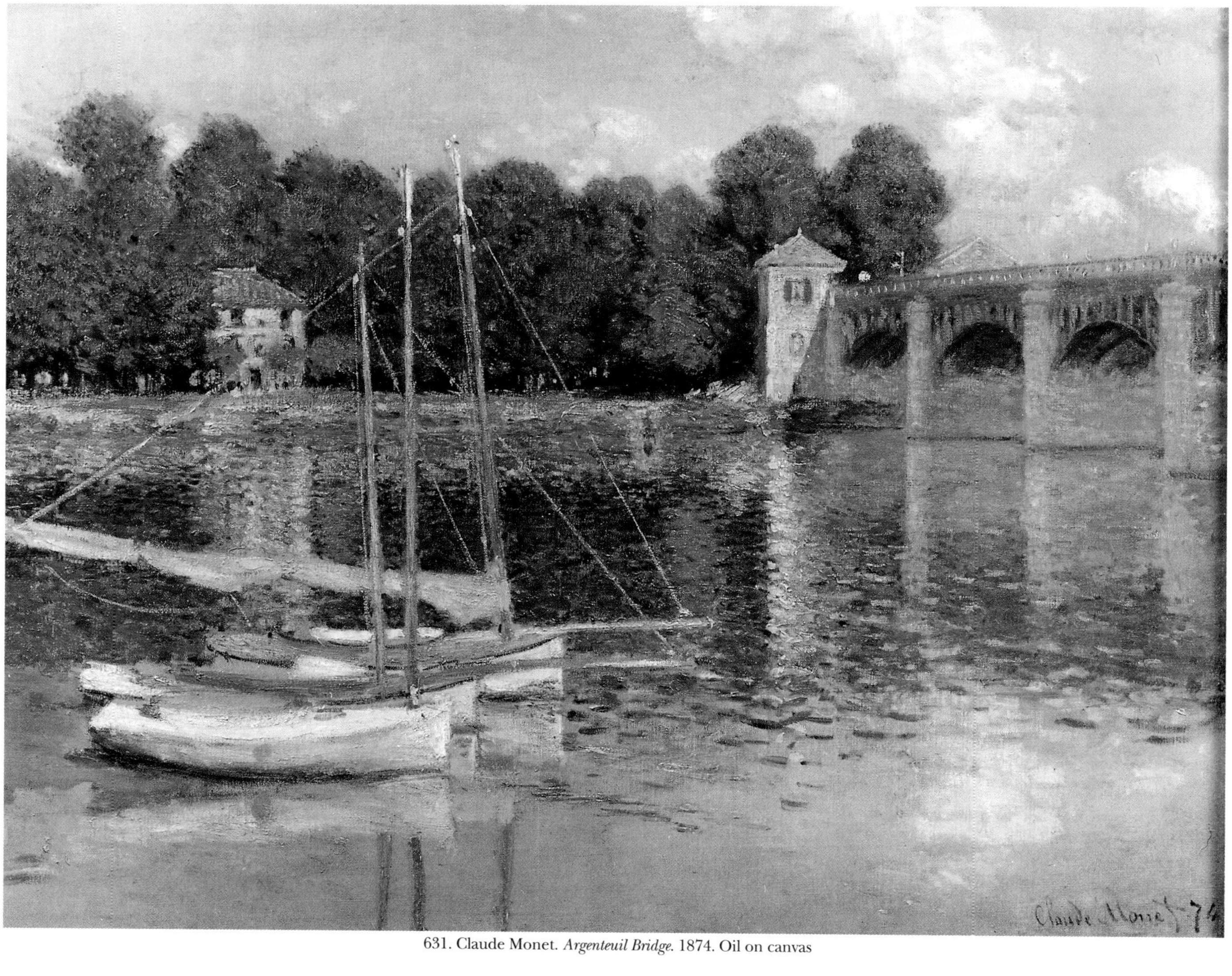

631. Claude Monet. *Argenteuil Bridge.* 1874. Oil on canvas

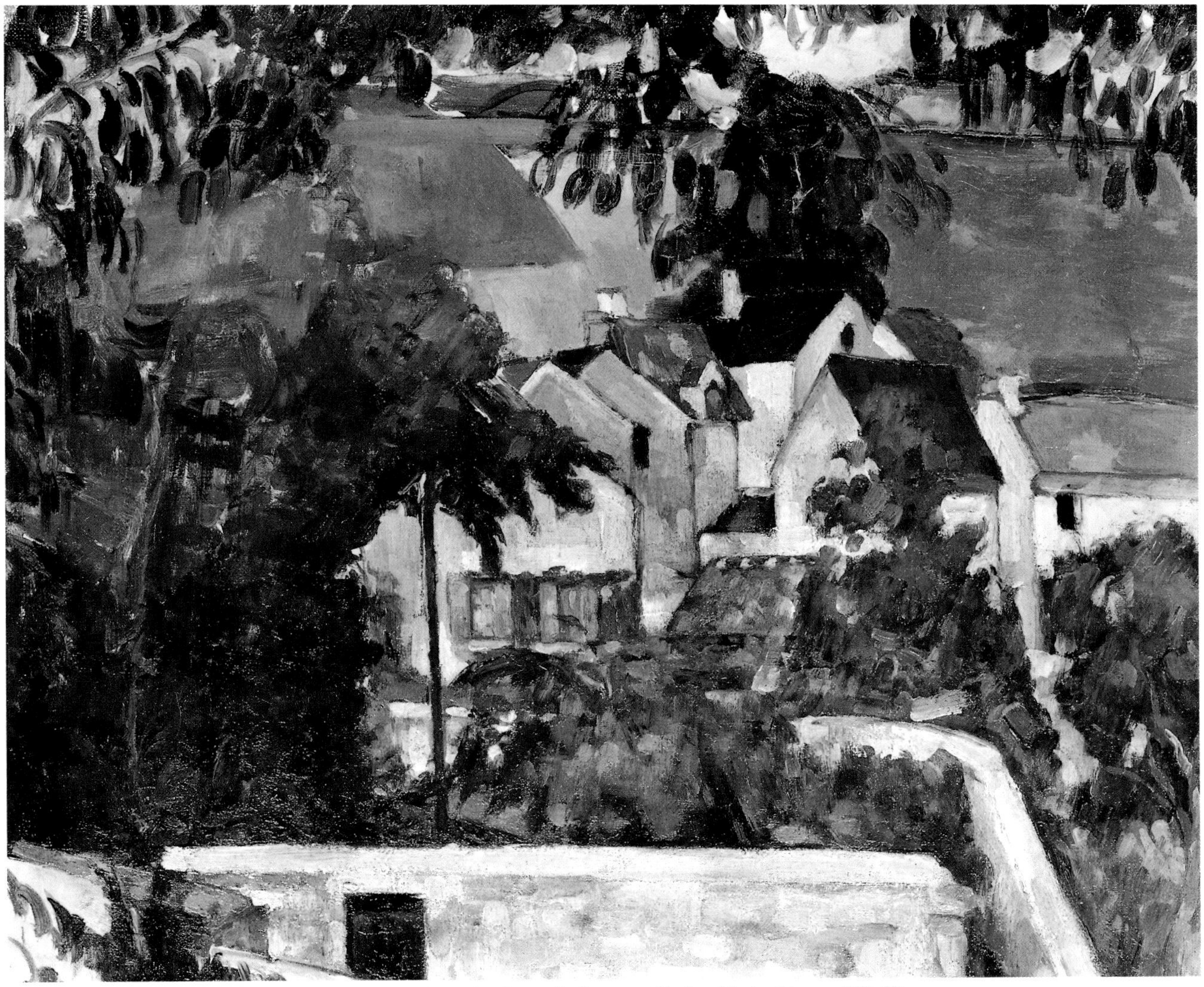

632. Paul Cézanne. *Study: Auvers Landscape*, also known as *The Four District of Auvers*. 1873. Oil on canvas

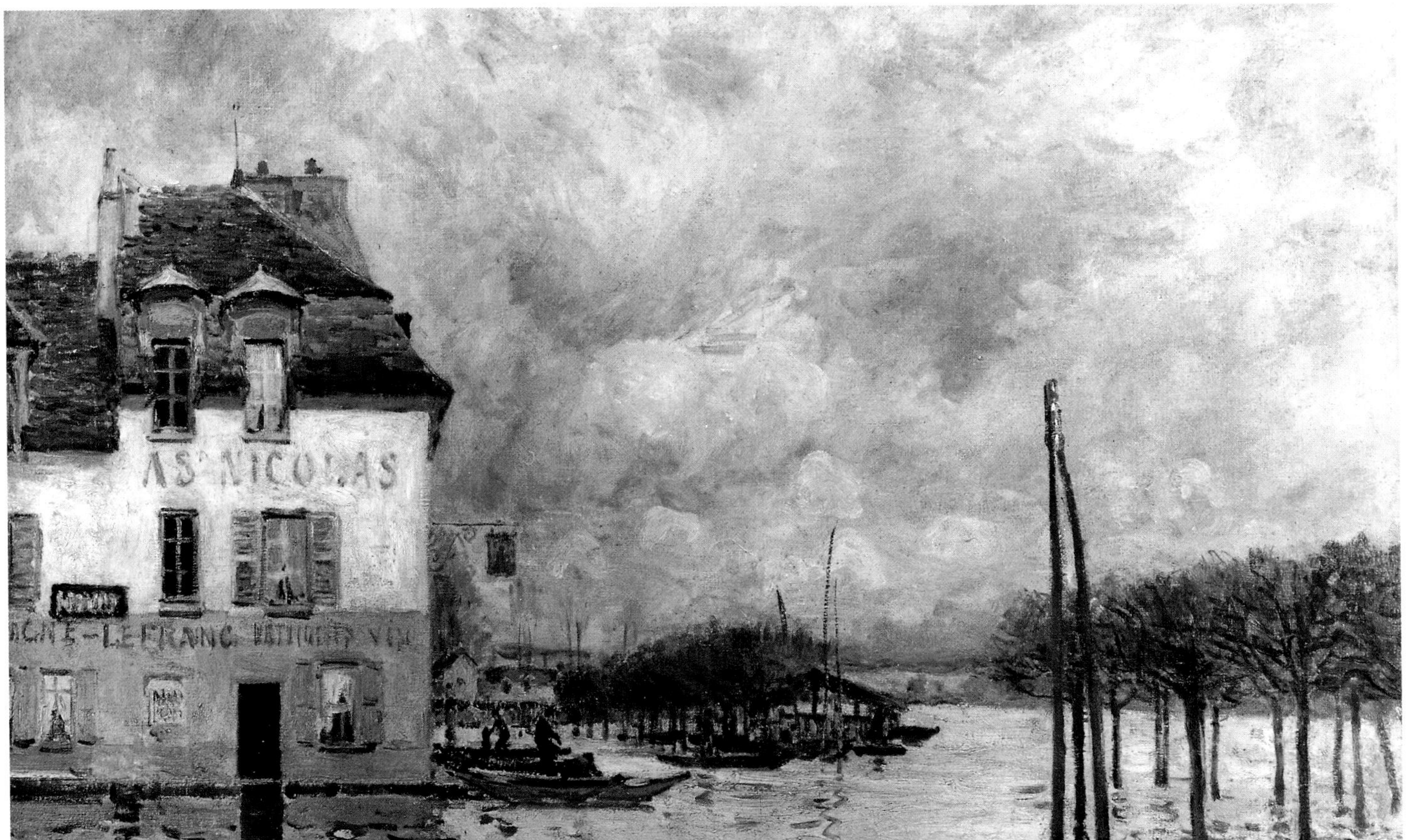

633. Alfred Sisley. *The Flood at Port-Marly*. 1876. Oil on canvas

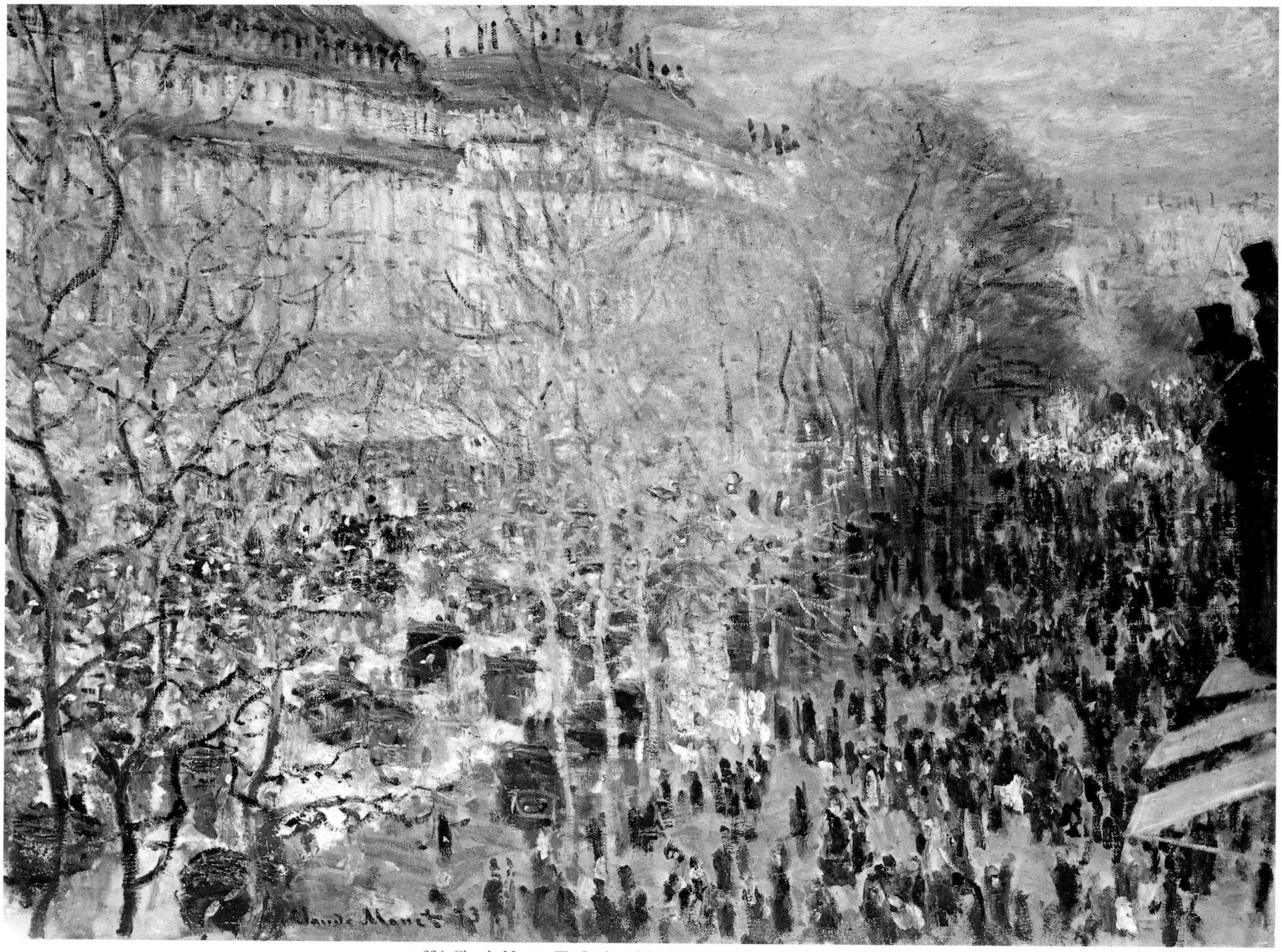

634. Claude Monet. *The Boulevard des Capucines.* 1873. Oil on canvas

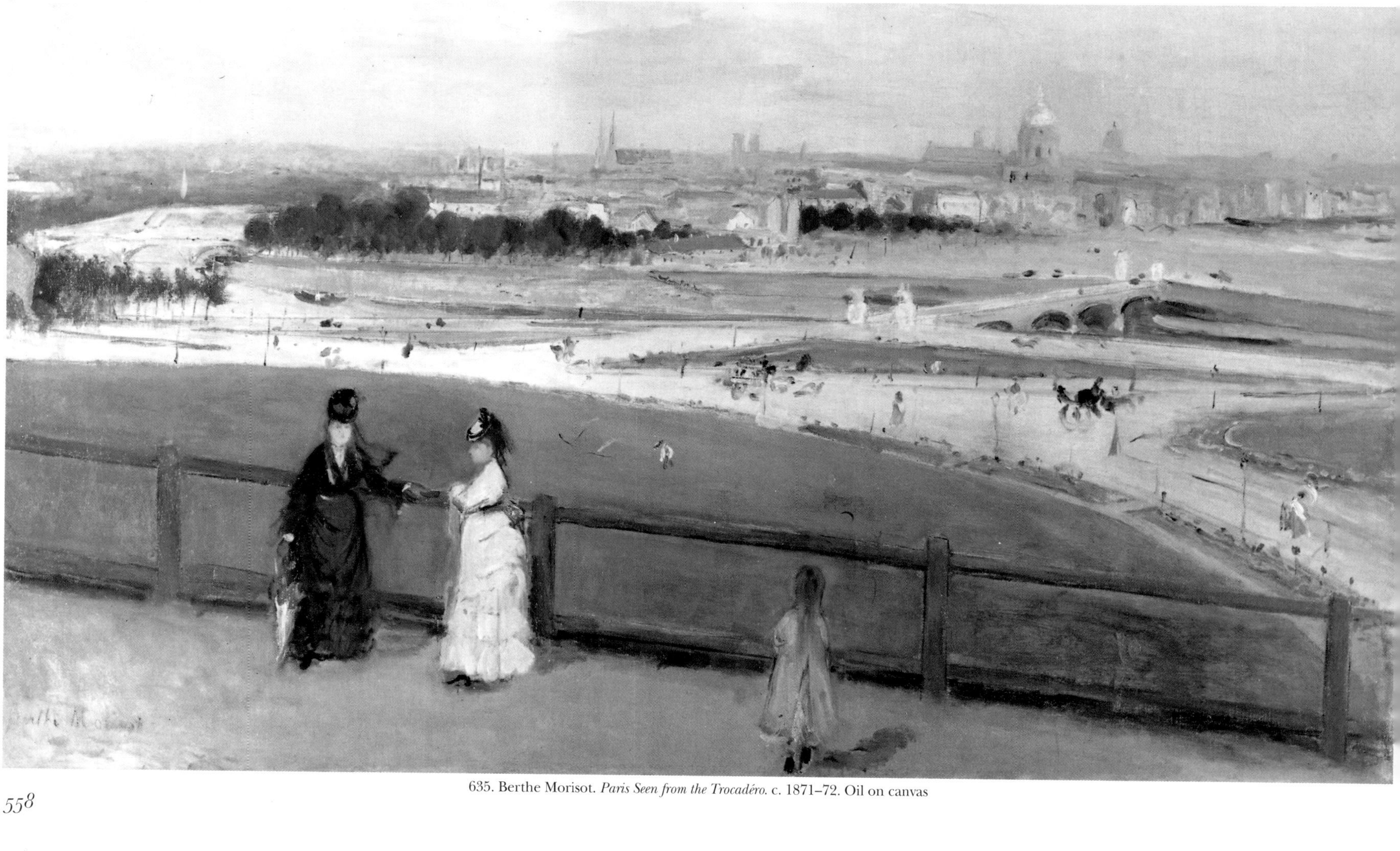

635. Berthe Morisot. *Paris Seen from the Trocadéro.* c. 1871–72. Oil on canvas

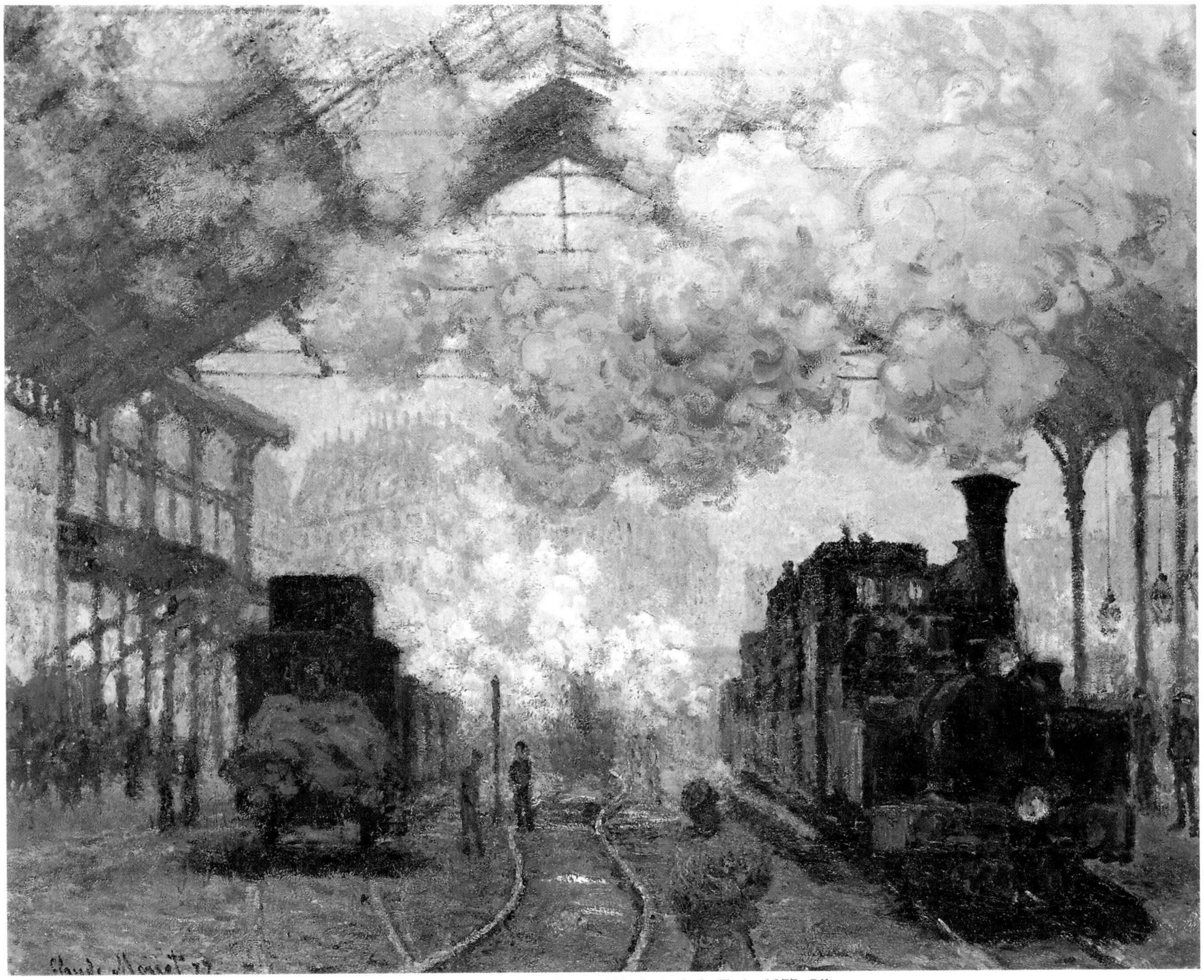

636. Claude Monet. *The Gare Saint-Lazare, The Arrival of a Train*. 1877. Oil on canvas

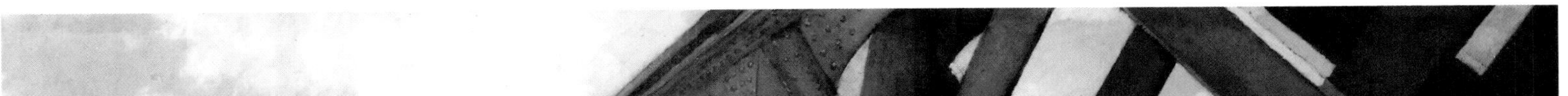

637. Gustave Caillebotte. *The Pont de l'Europe*. 1876. Oil on canvas

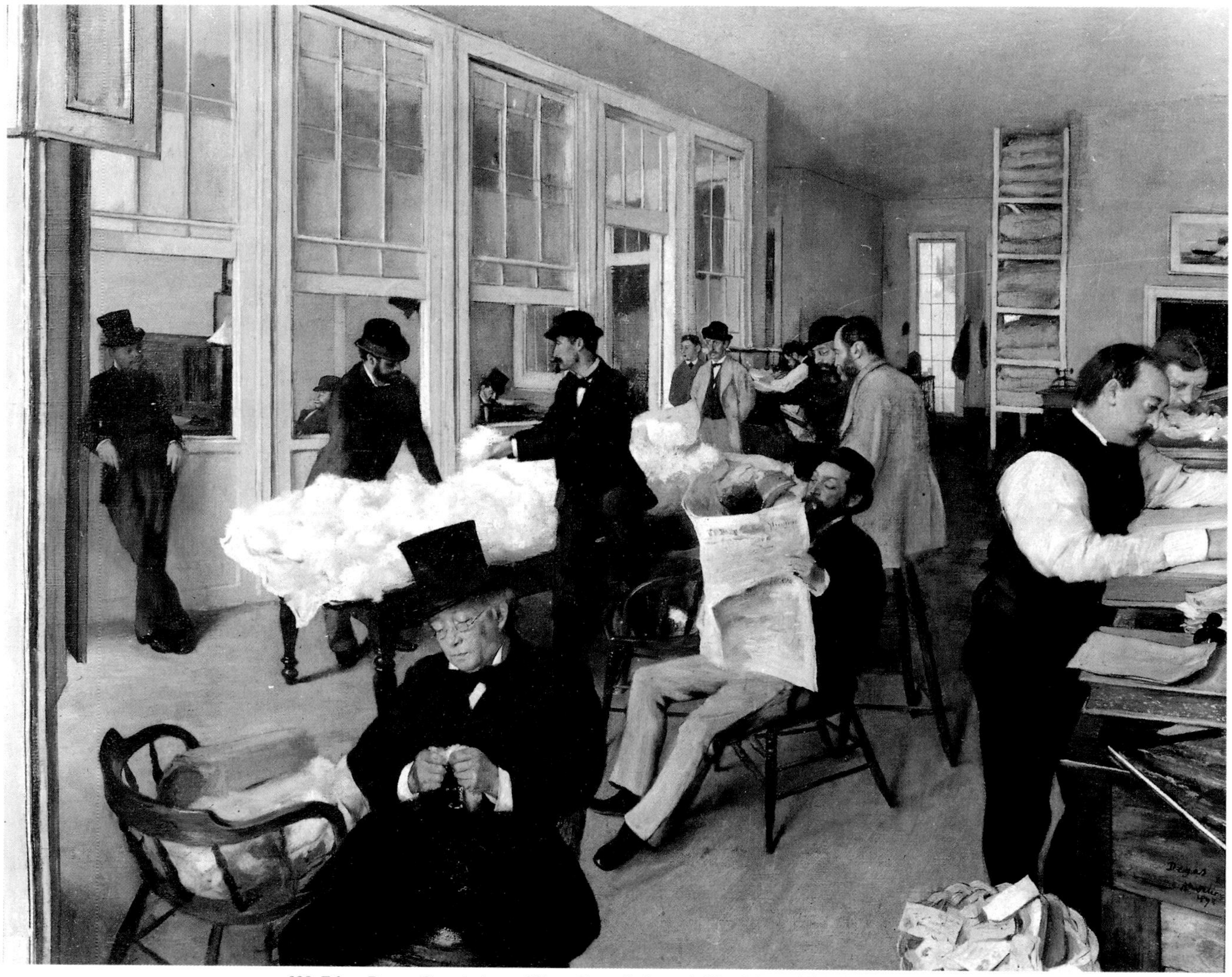

638. Edgar Degas. *Portraits in an Office—Cotton Exchange in New Orleans.* 1873. Oil on canvas

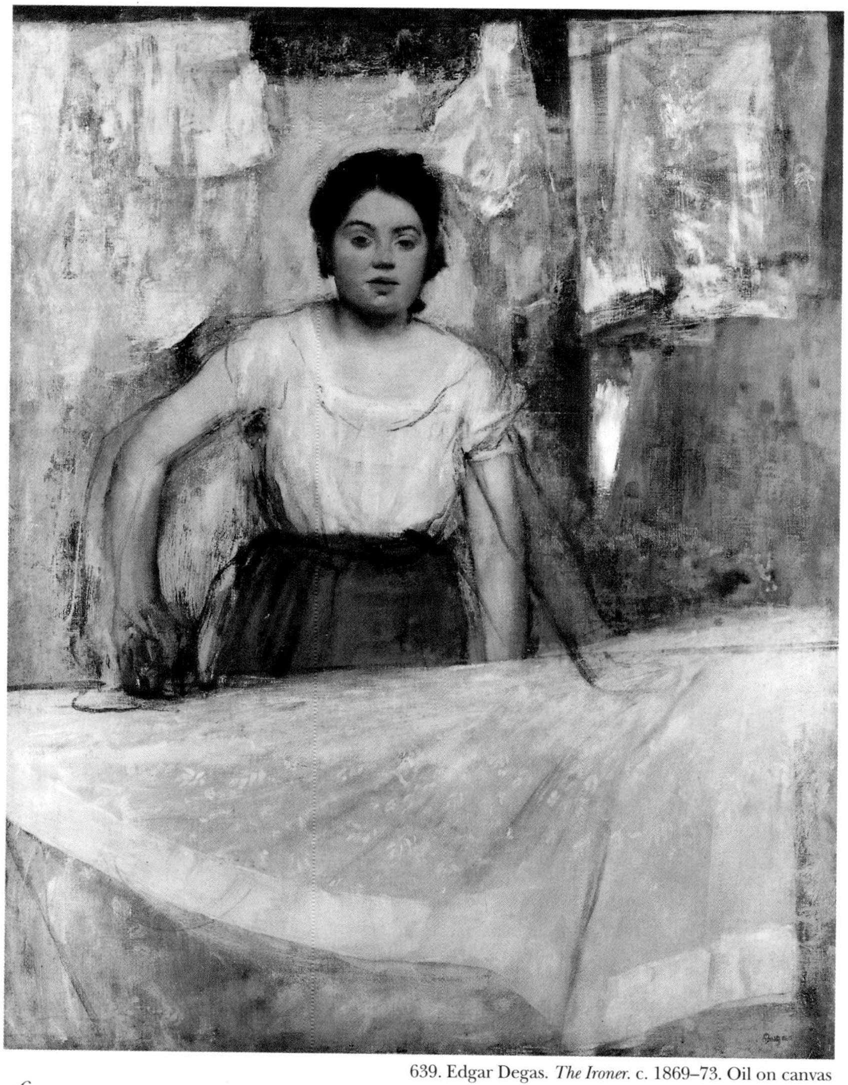

639. Edgar Degas. *The Ironer.* c. 1869–73. Oil on canvas

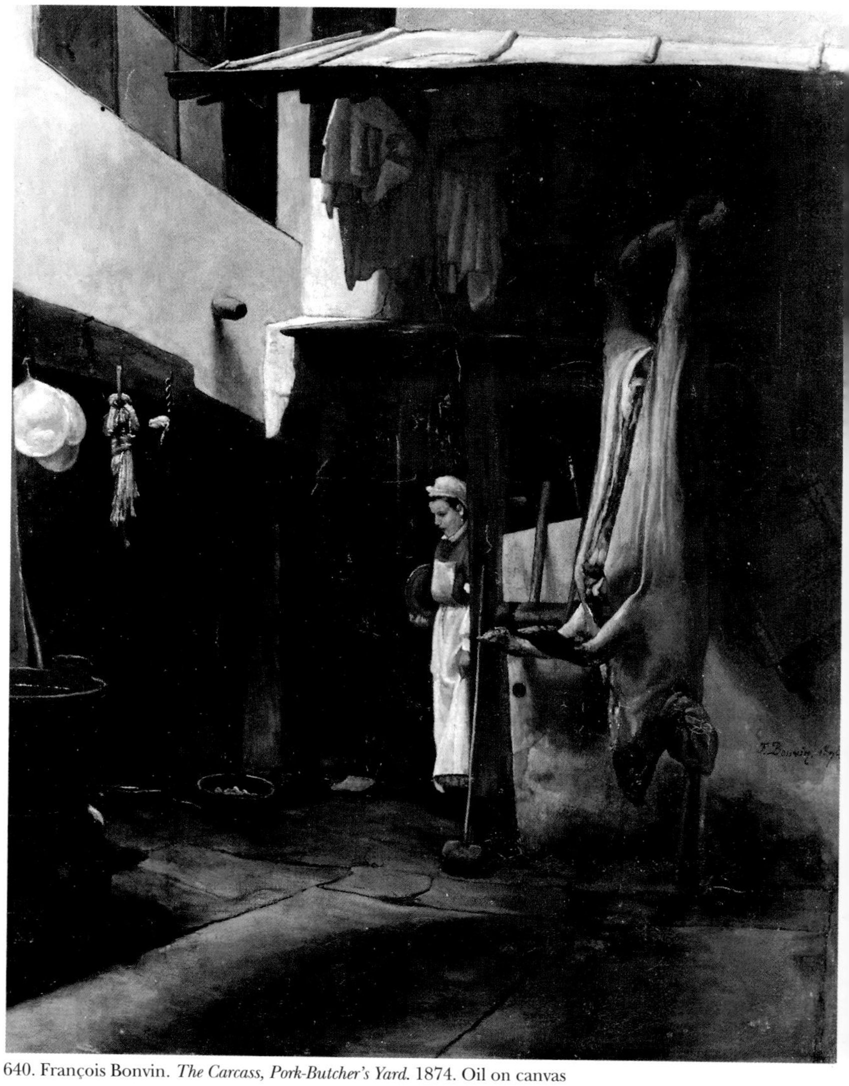

640. François Bonvin. *The Carcass, Pork-Butcher's Yard.* 1874. Oil on canvas

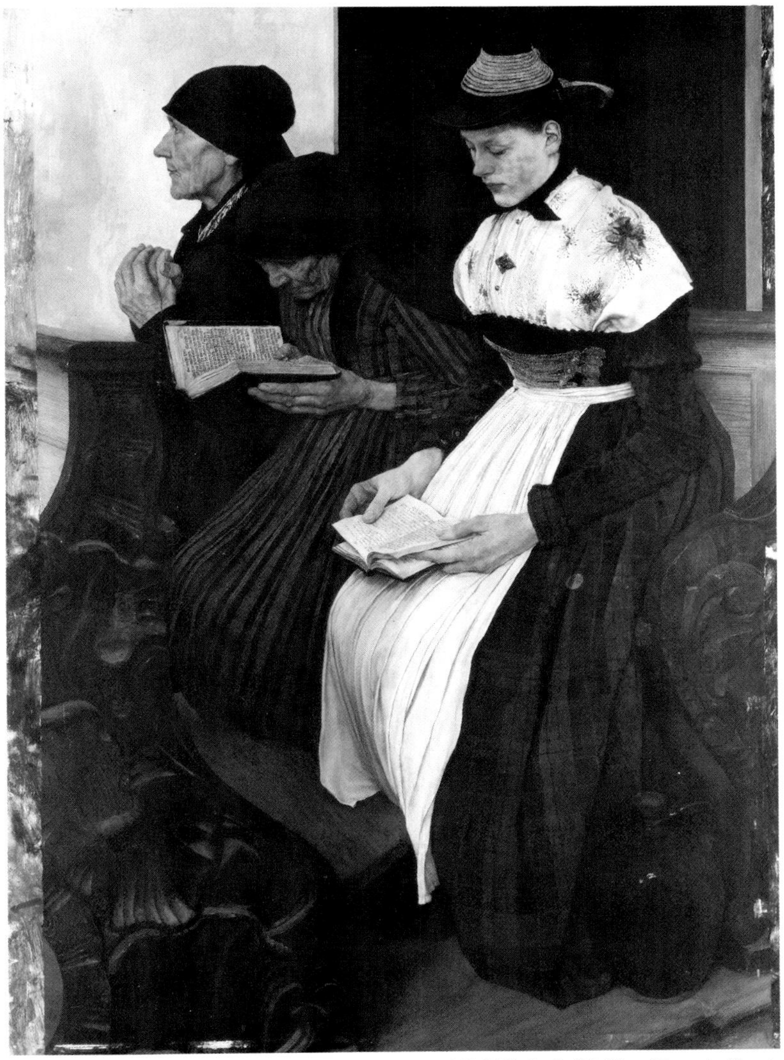

641. Wilhelm Leibl. *Three Women in Church.* 1882. Oil on wood

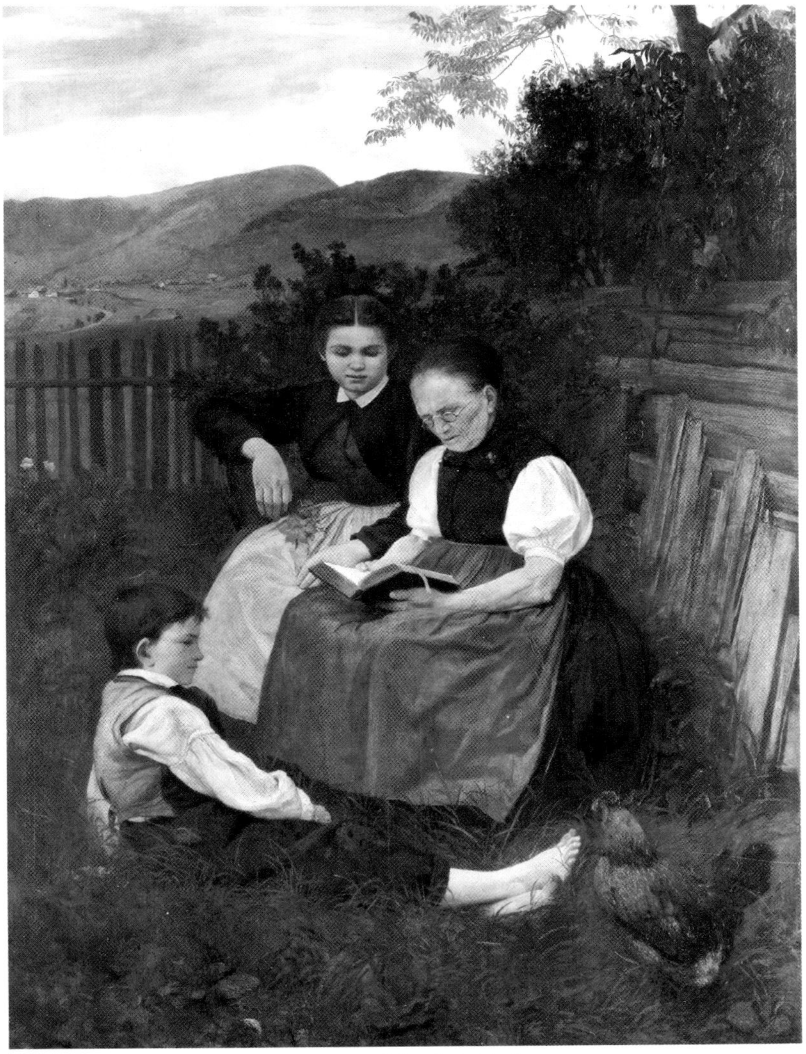

642. Hans Thoma. *Evening, The Artist's Mother and Sister in the Garden.* 1868. Oil on canvas

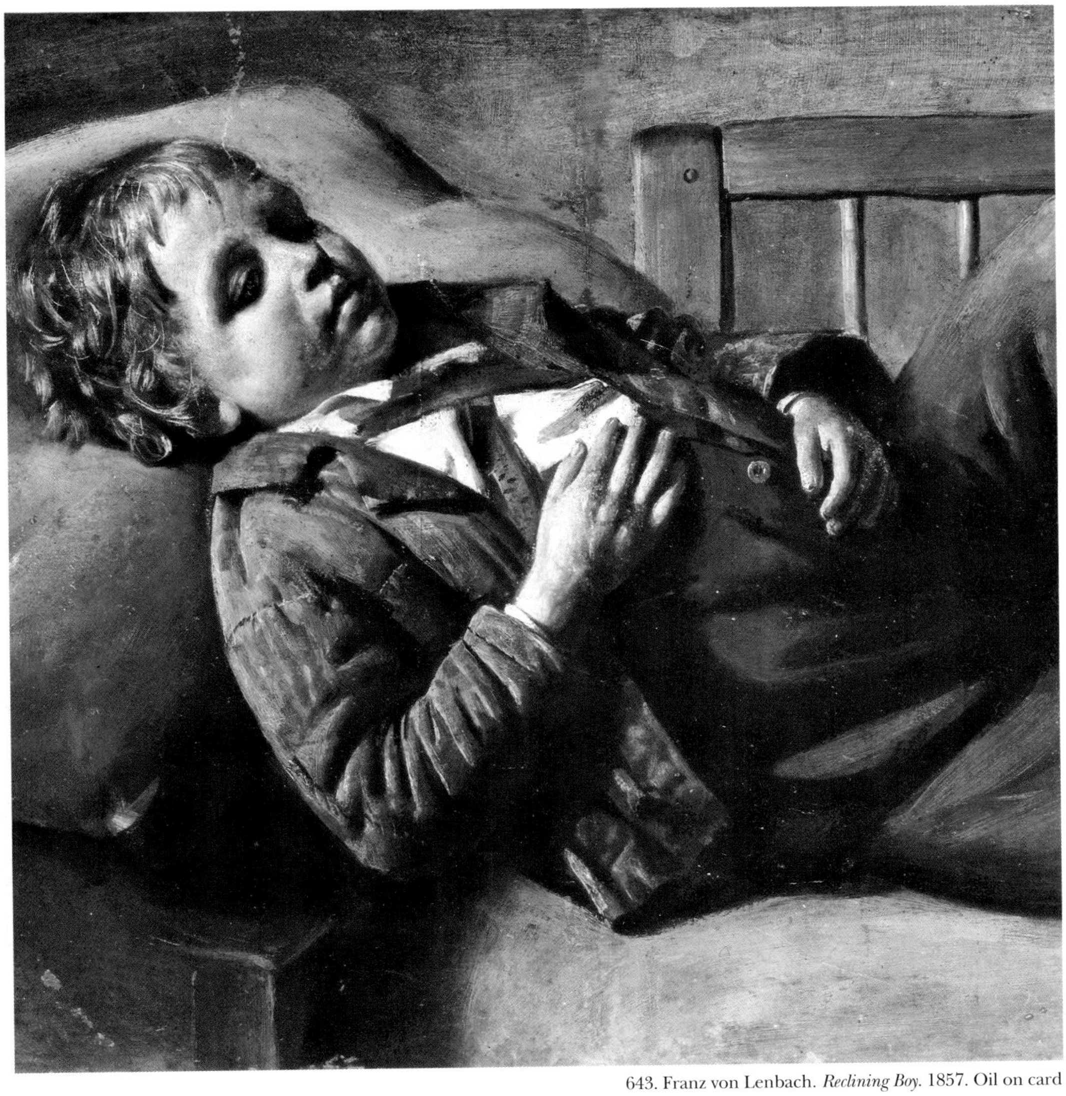

643. Franz von Lenbach. *Reclining Boy.* 1857. Oil on card

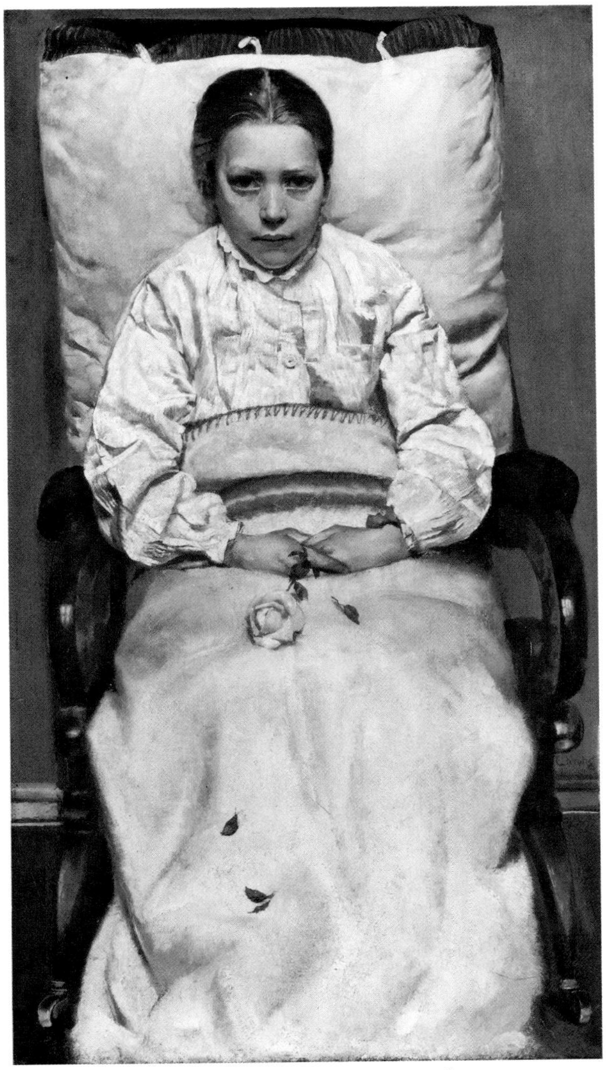

644. Christian Krohg. *The Sick Girl.* 1880–81. Oil on wood

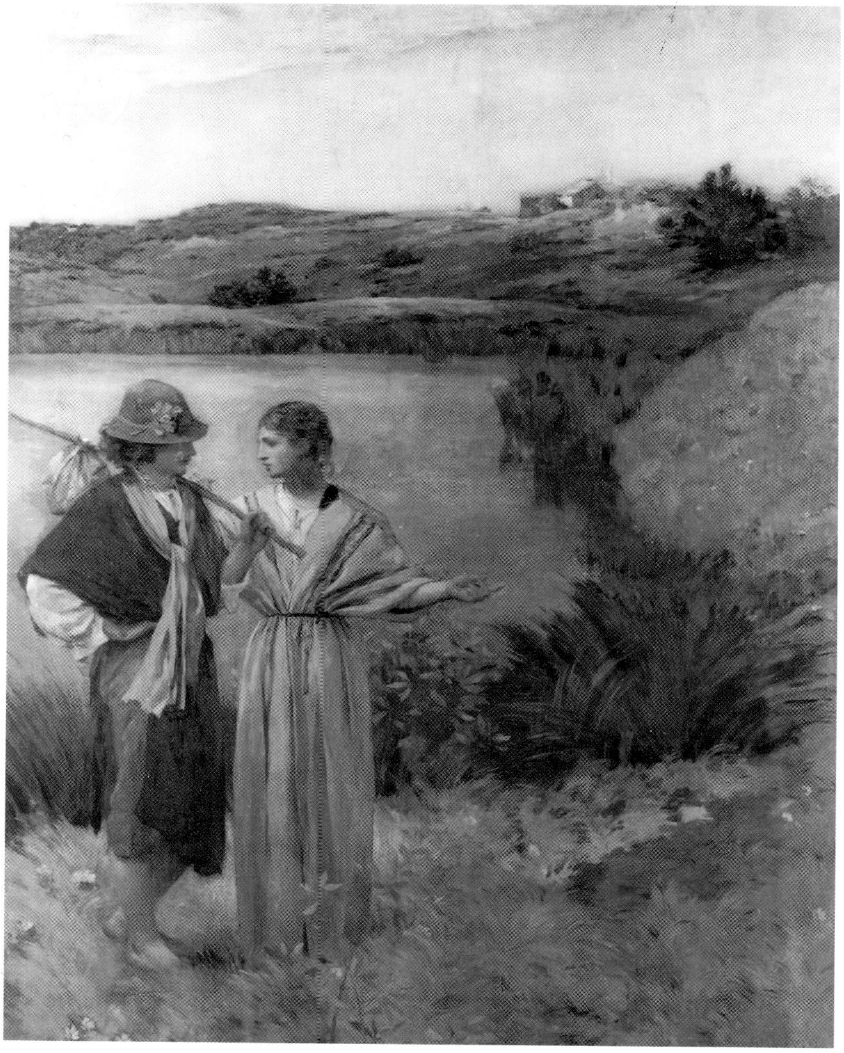

645. Jean-Charles Cazin. *Tobias and the Angel.* 1880. Oil on canvas

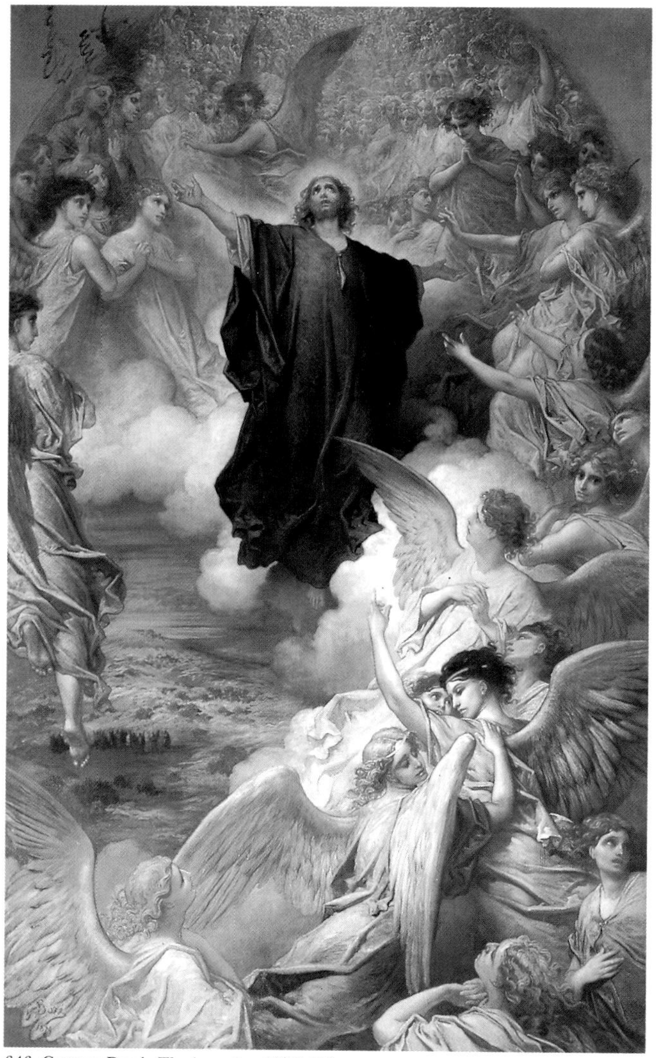

646. Gustave Doré. *The Ascension.* 1879. Oil on canvas

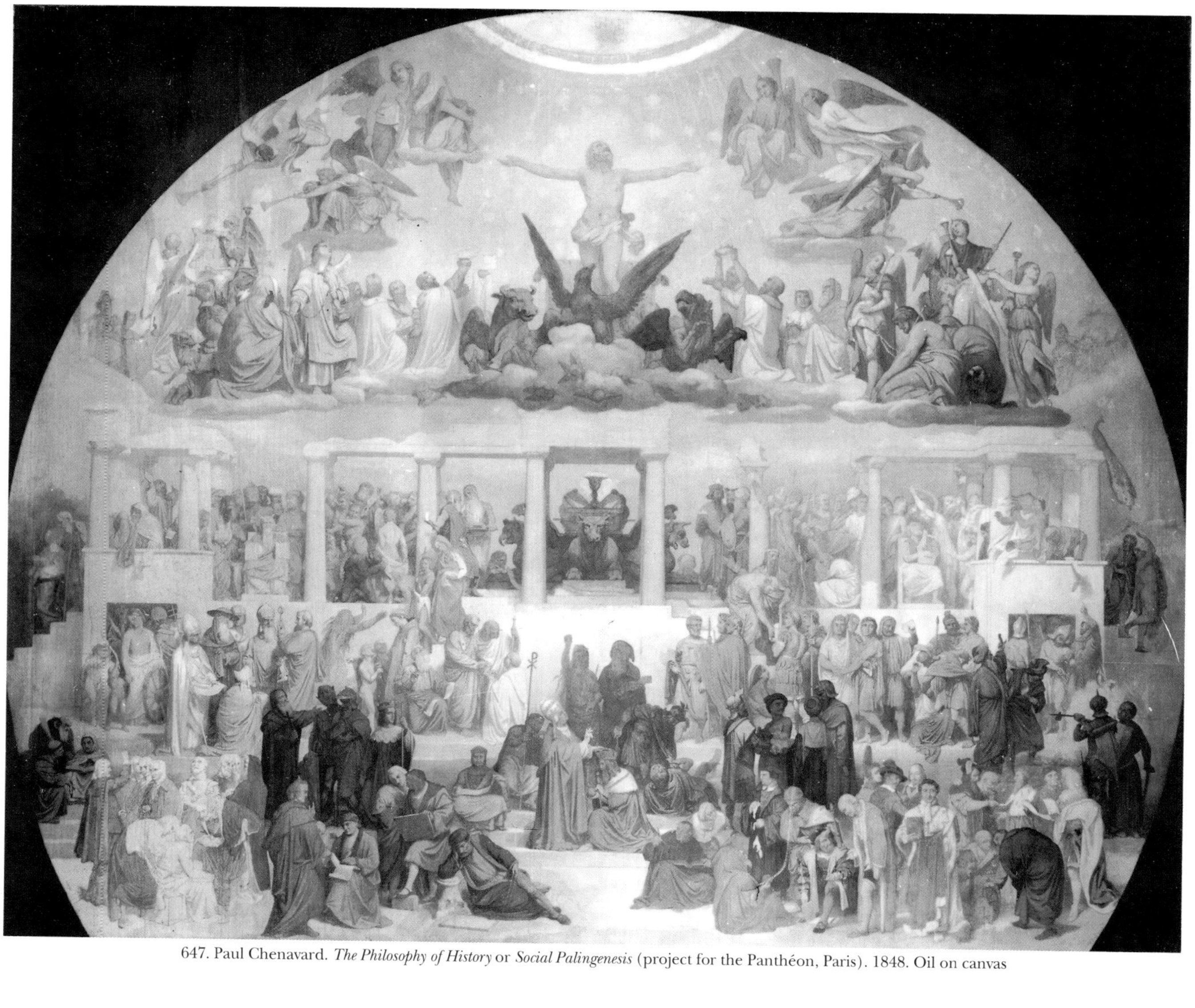

647. Paul Chenavard. *The Philosophy of History* or *Social Palingenesis* (project for the Panthéon, Paris). 1848. Oil on canvas

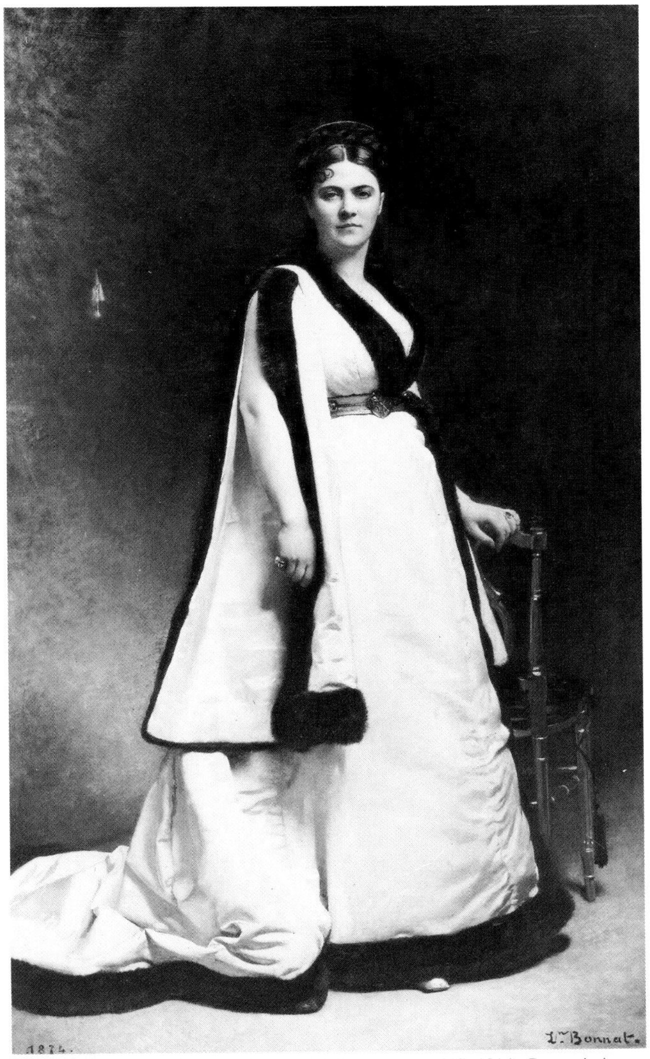

648. Léon Bonnat. *Madame Pasca (1835–1914), Dramatic Actress.* 1874. Oil on canvas

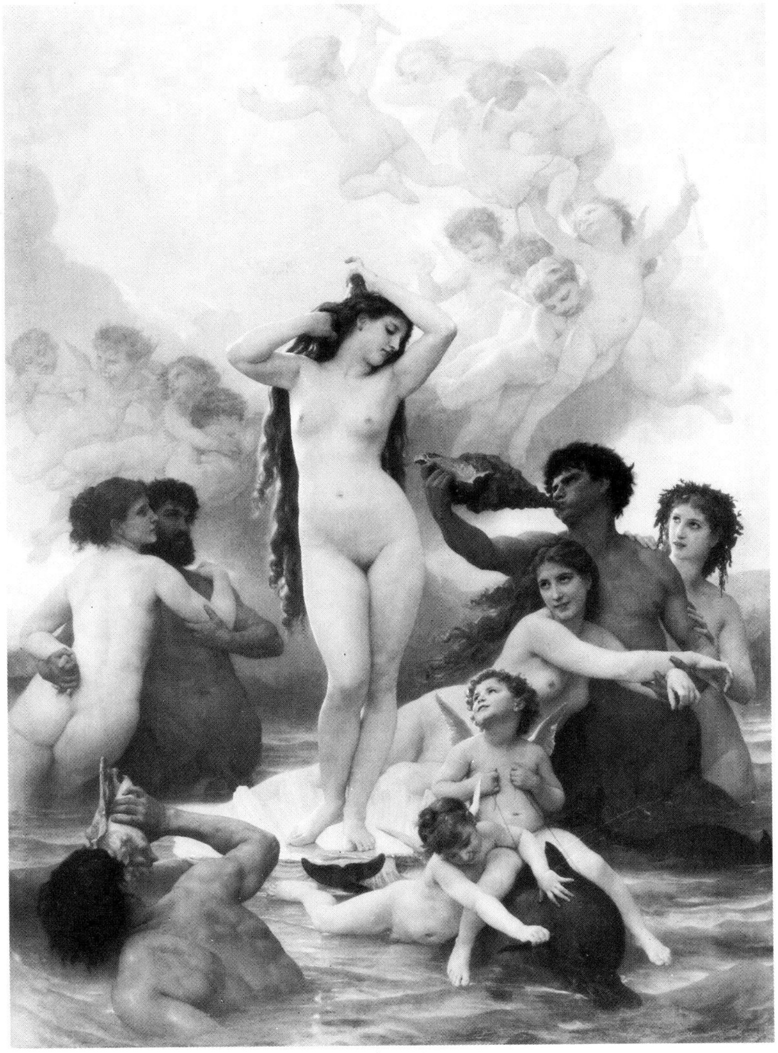

649. William Bouguereau. *The Birth of Venus.* 1879. Oil on canvas

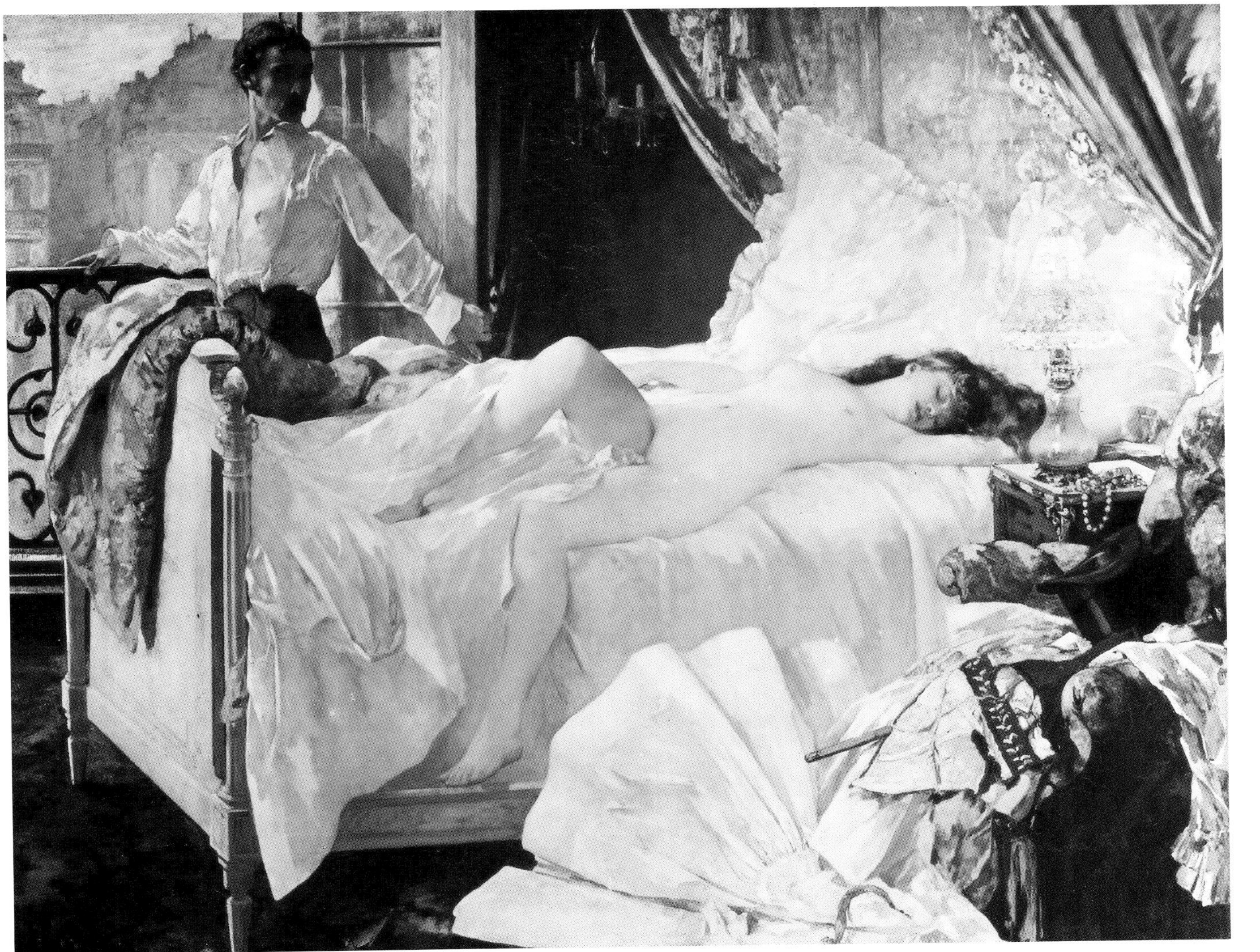

650. Henri Gervex. *Rolla.* 1878. Oil on canvas

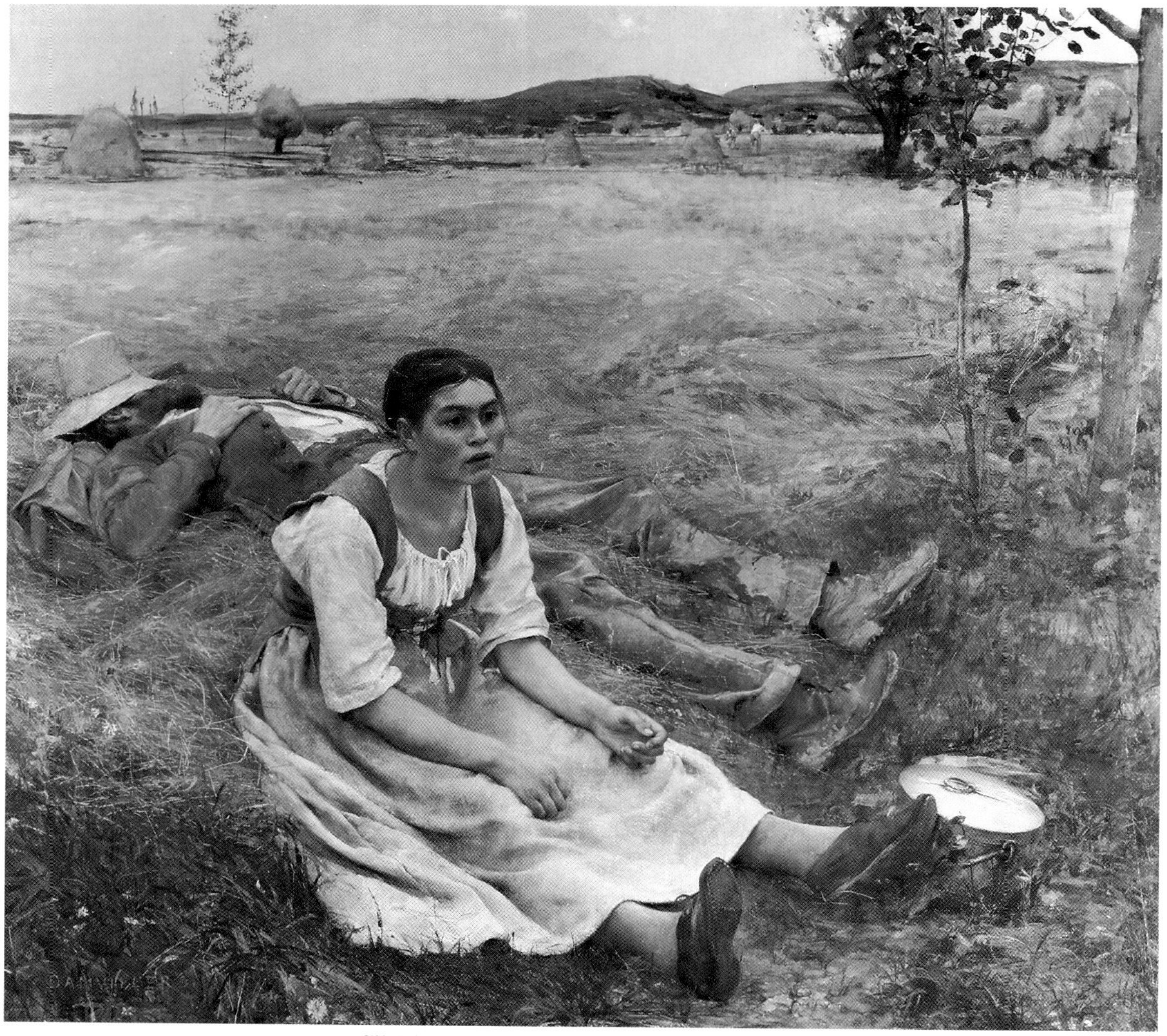

651. Jules Bastien-Lepage. *Haymakers.* 1877. Oil on canvas

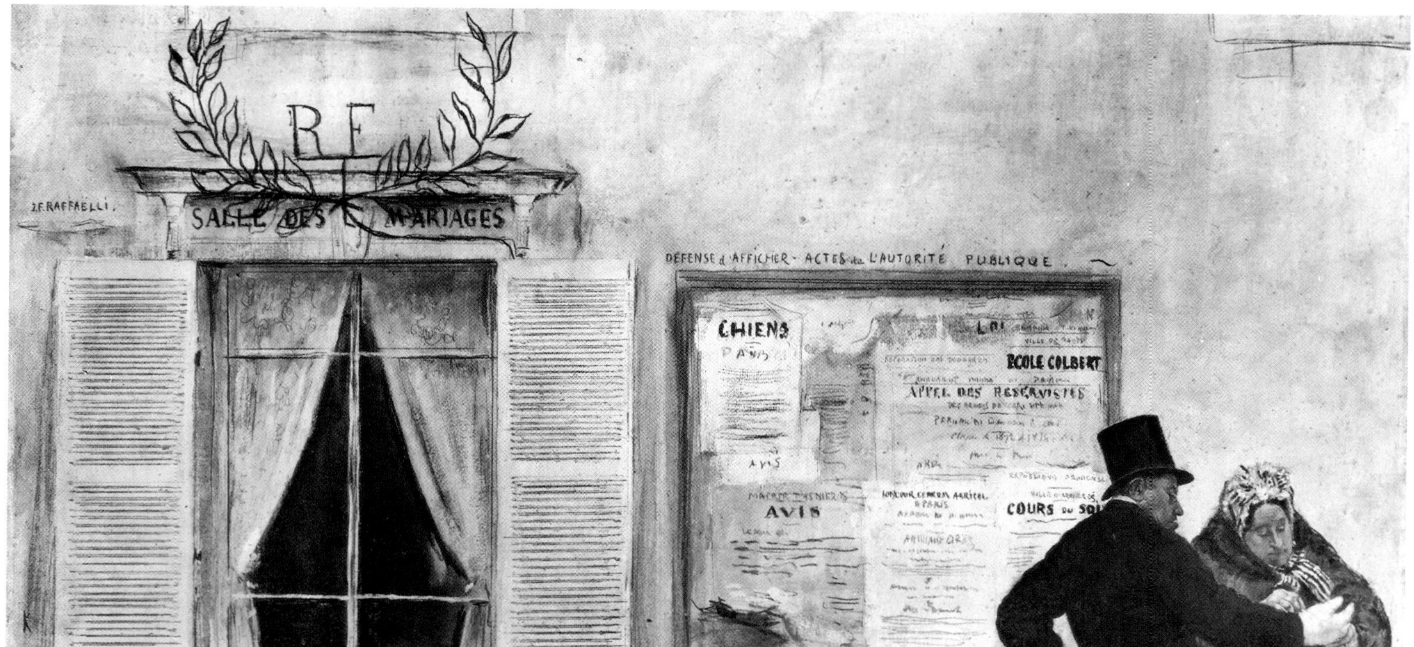

652. Jean-François Raffaëlli. *The Guests Waiting for the Wedding.* Before 1884. Oil on canvas

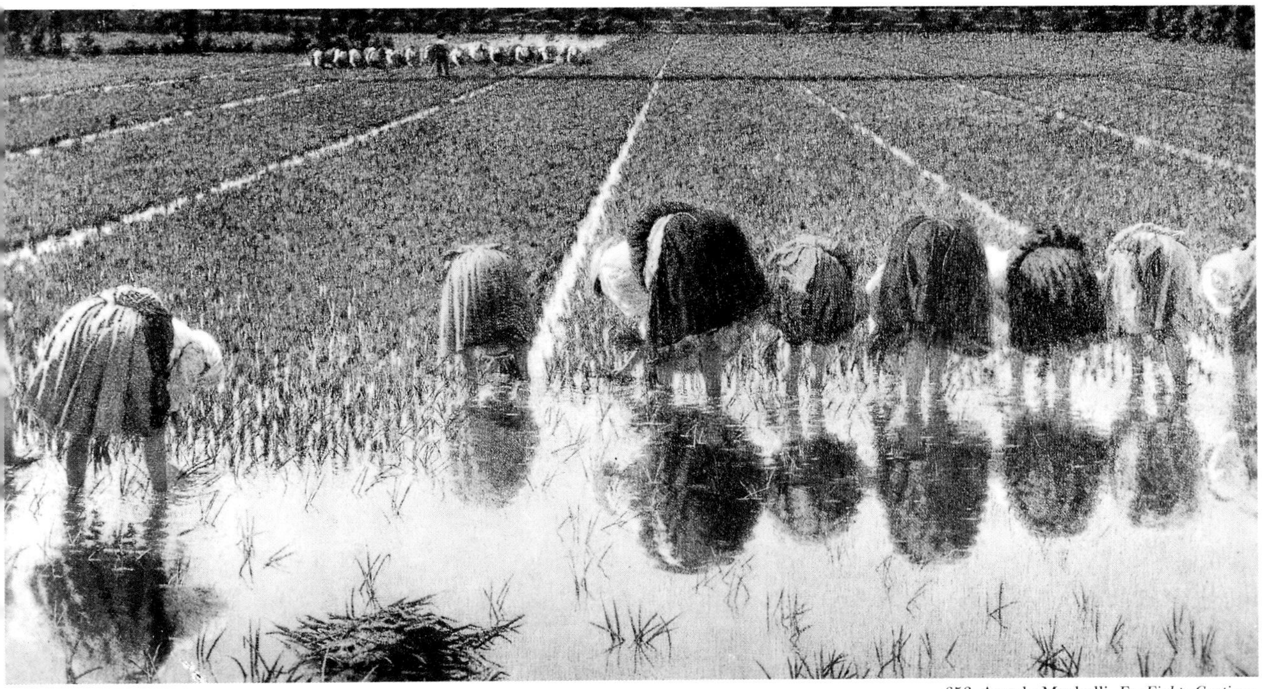

653. Angelo Morbelli. *For Eighty Centimes.* 1894–95. Oil on canvas

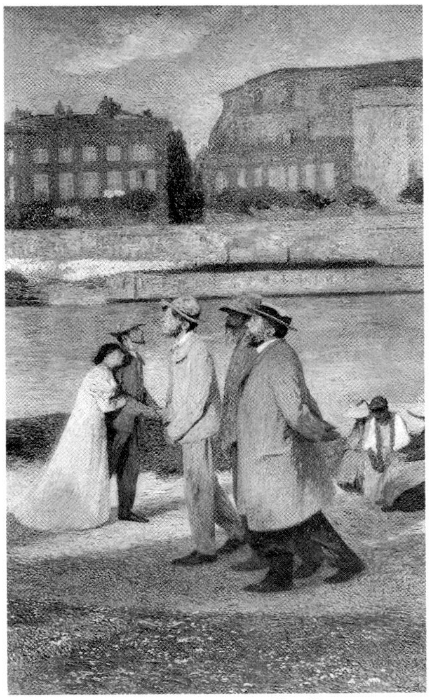

654. Henri Martin. *The Dreamers* (detail). 1903. Oil on canvas

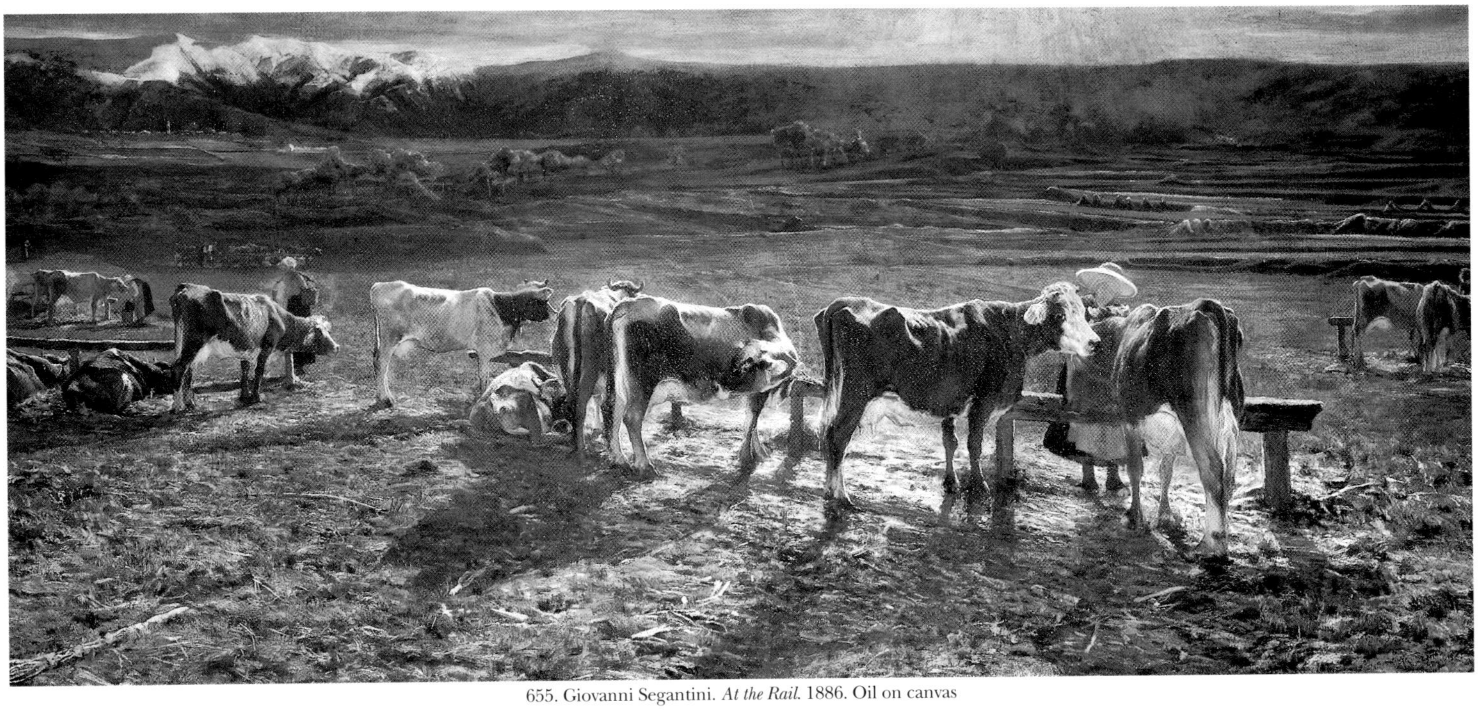

655. Giovanni Segantini. *At the Rail.* 1886. Oil on canvas

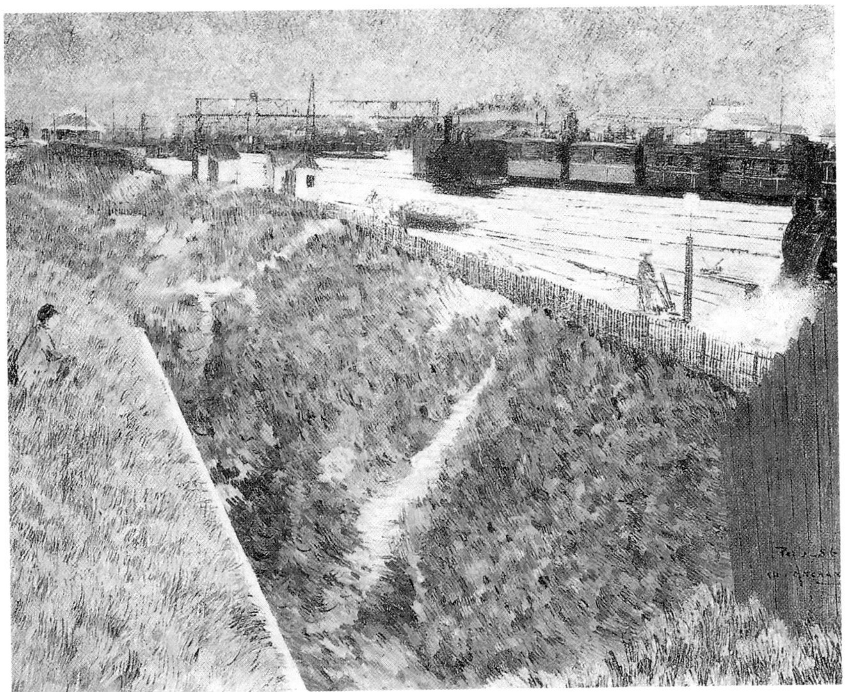

656. Charles Angrand. *The Western Line.* 1886. Oil on canvas

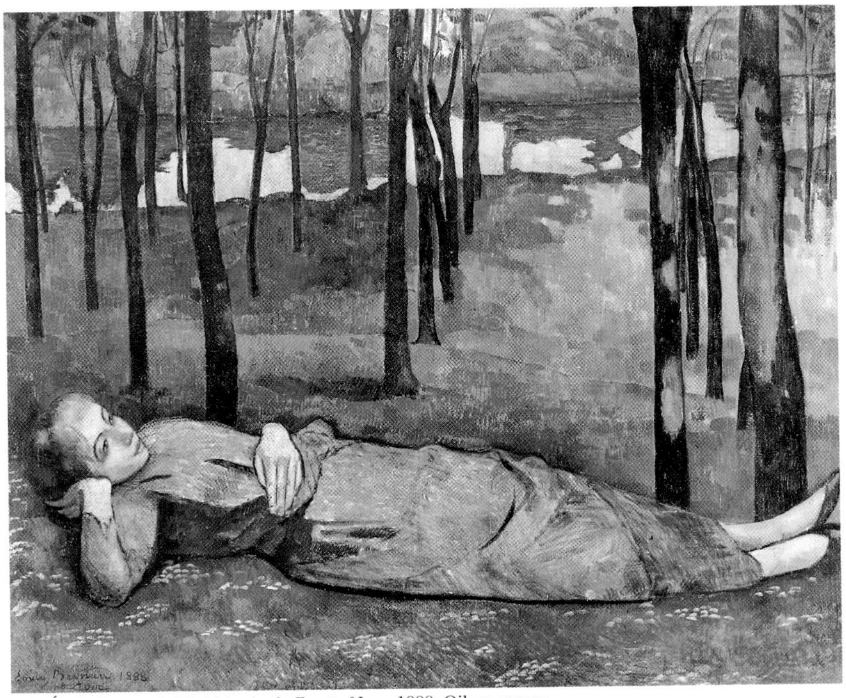

657. Émile Bernard. *Madeleine in the Forest of Love.* 1888. Oil on canvas

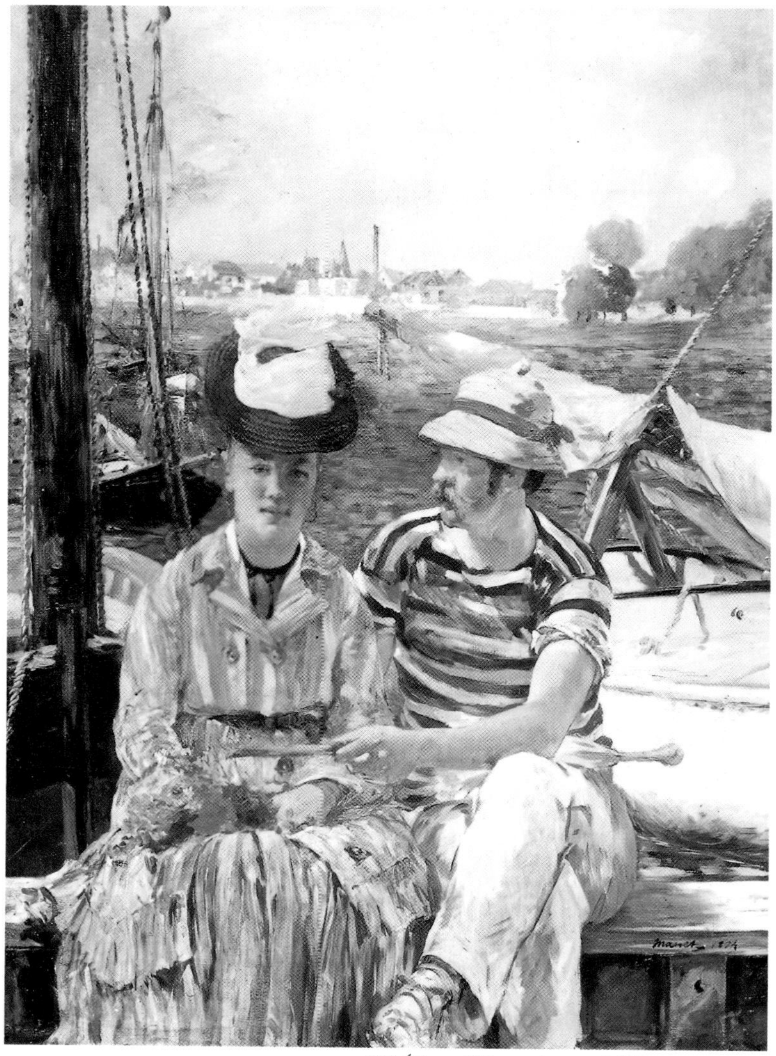
658. Édouard Manet. *Argenteuil.* 1874. Oil on canvas

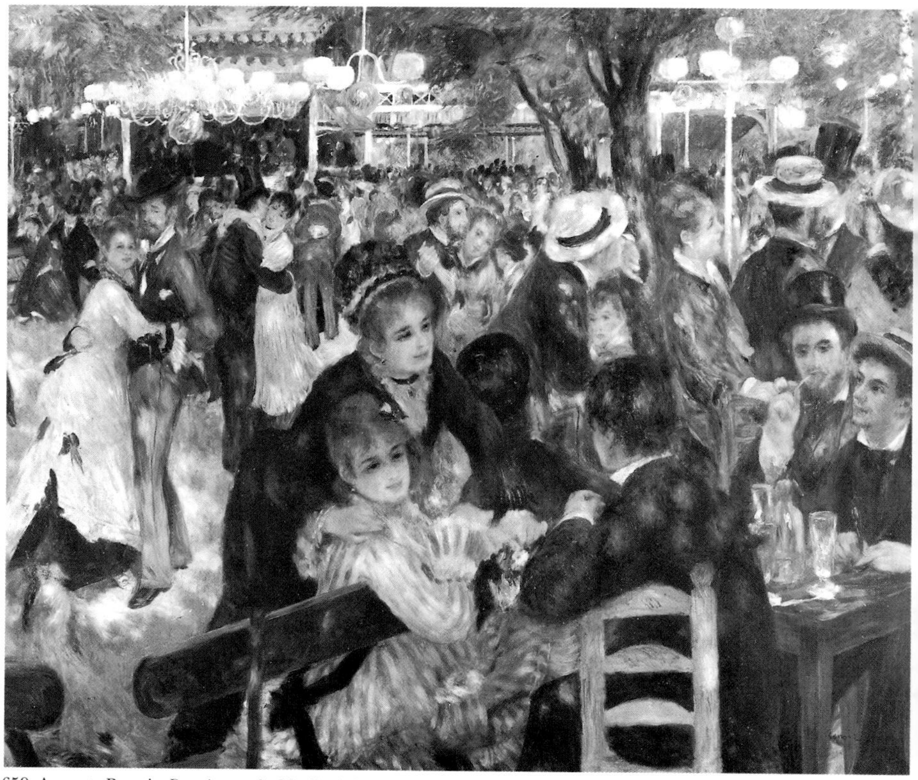
659. Auguste Renoir. *Dancing at the Moulin de la Galette, Montmartre.* 1876. Oil on canvas

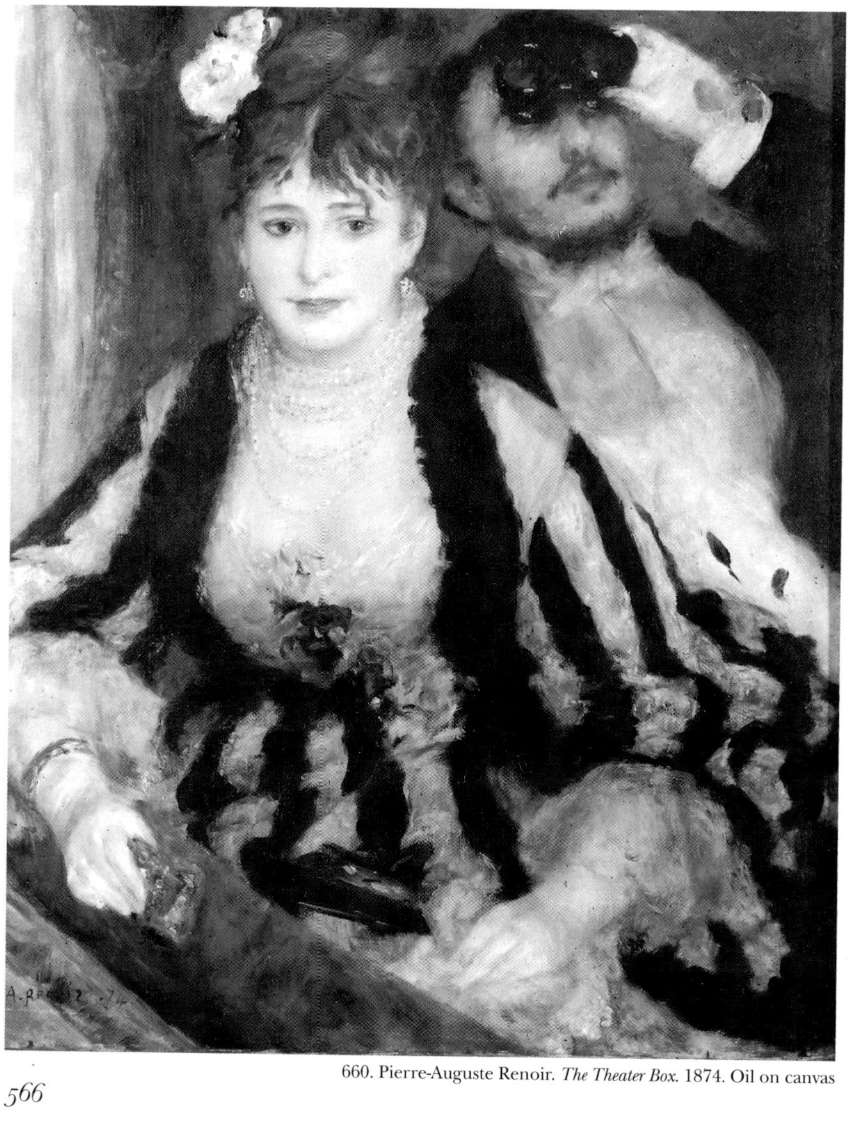
660. Pierre-Auguste Renoir. *The Theater Box.* 1874. Oil on canvas

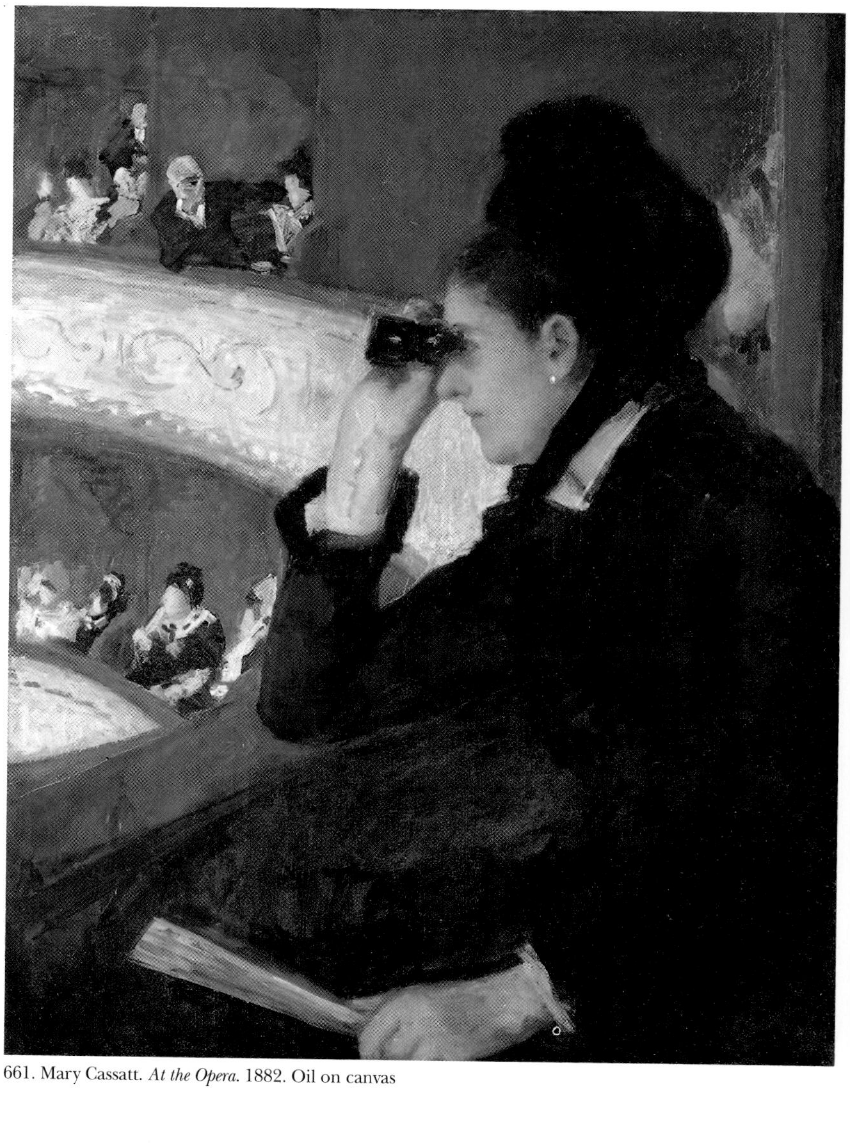
661. Mary Cassatt. *At the Opera.* 1882. Oil on canvas

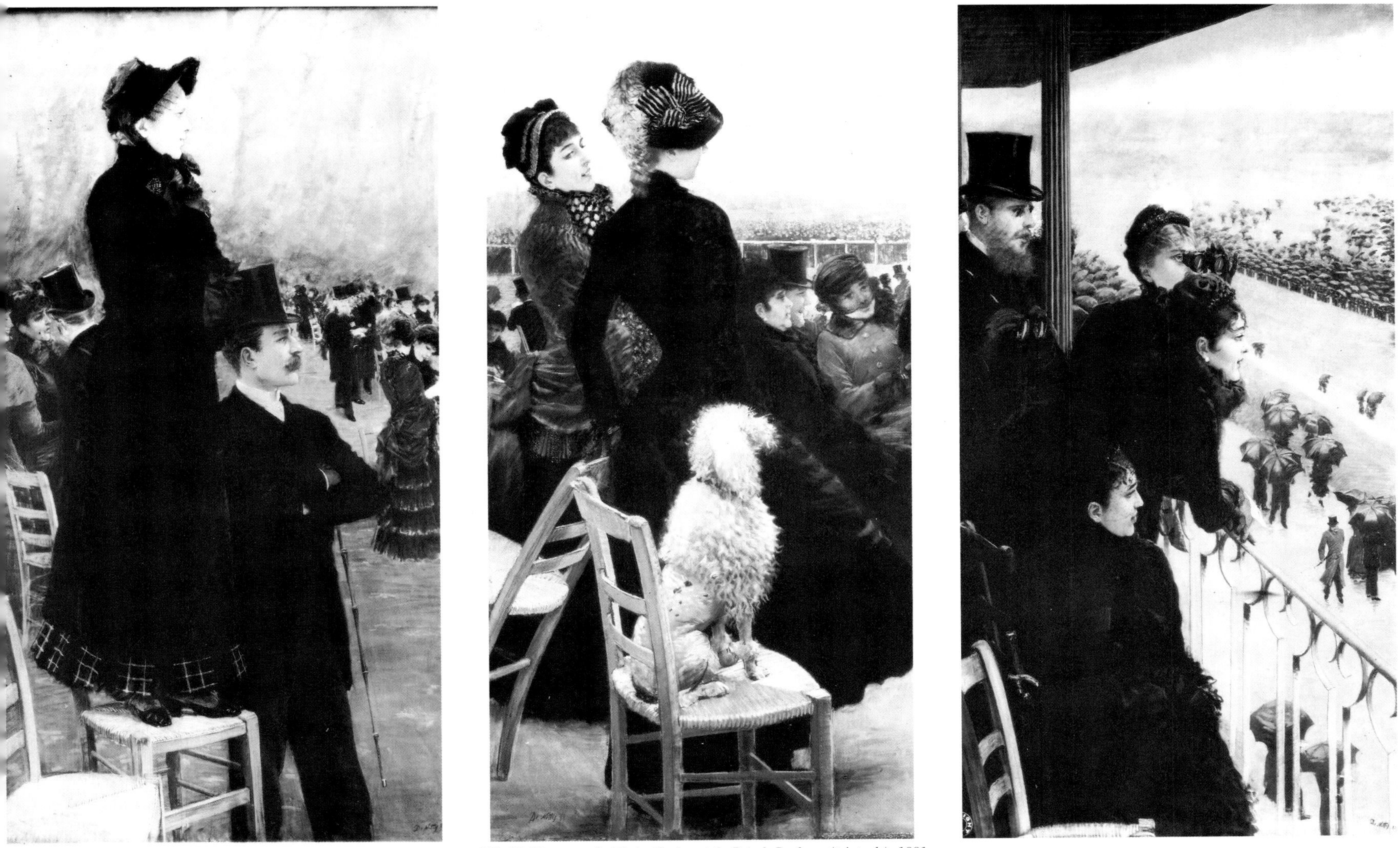

662–64. Giuseppe de Nittis. *Racing at the Bois de Boulogne* (triptych). 1881

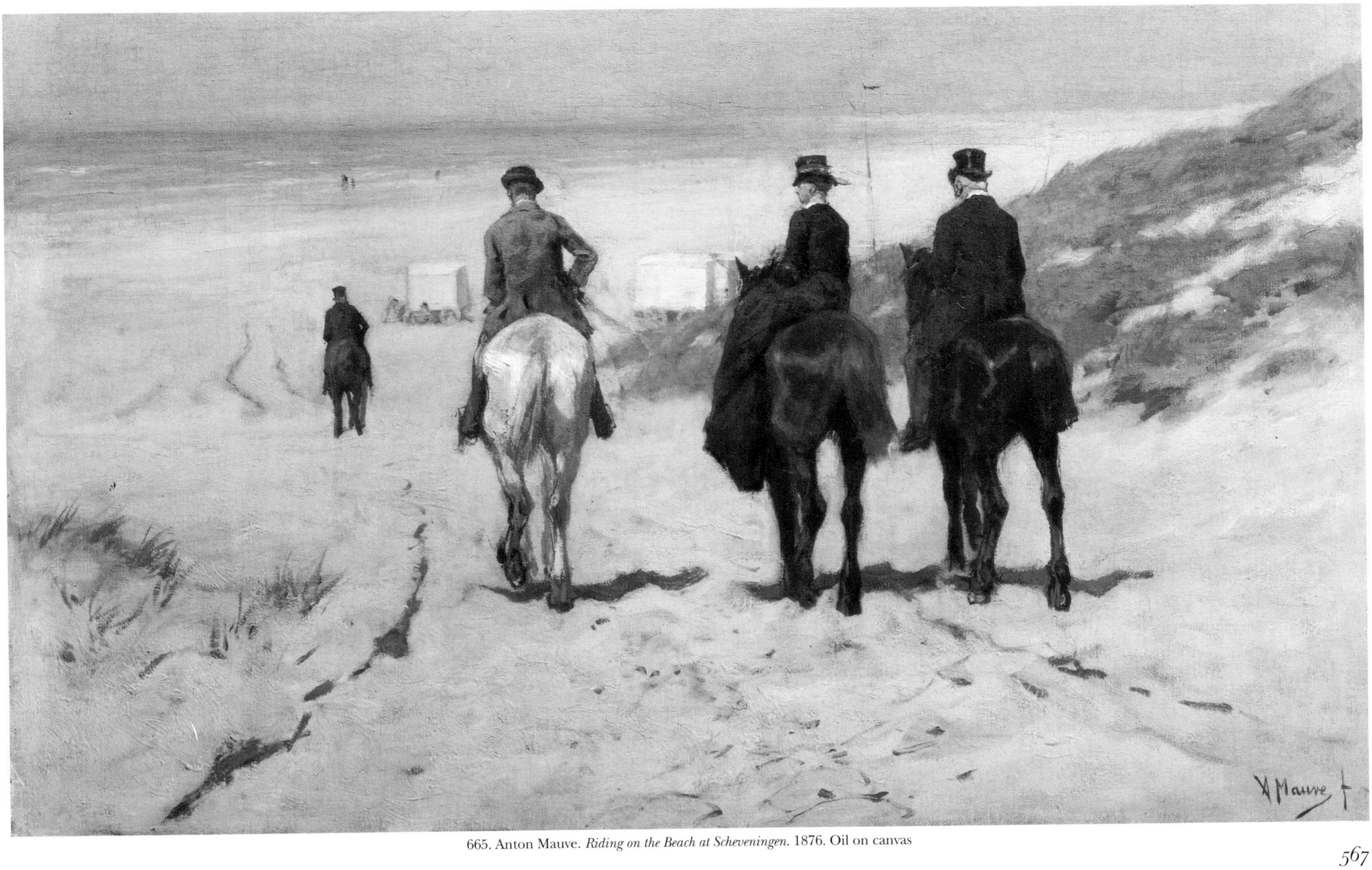

665. Anton Mauve. *Riding on the Beach at Scheveningen.* 1876. Oil on canvas

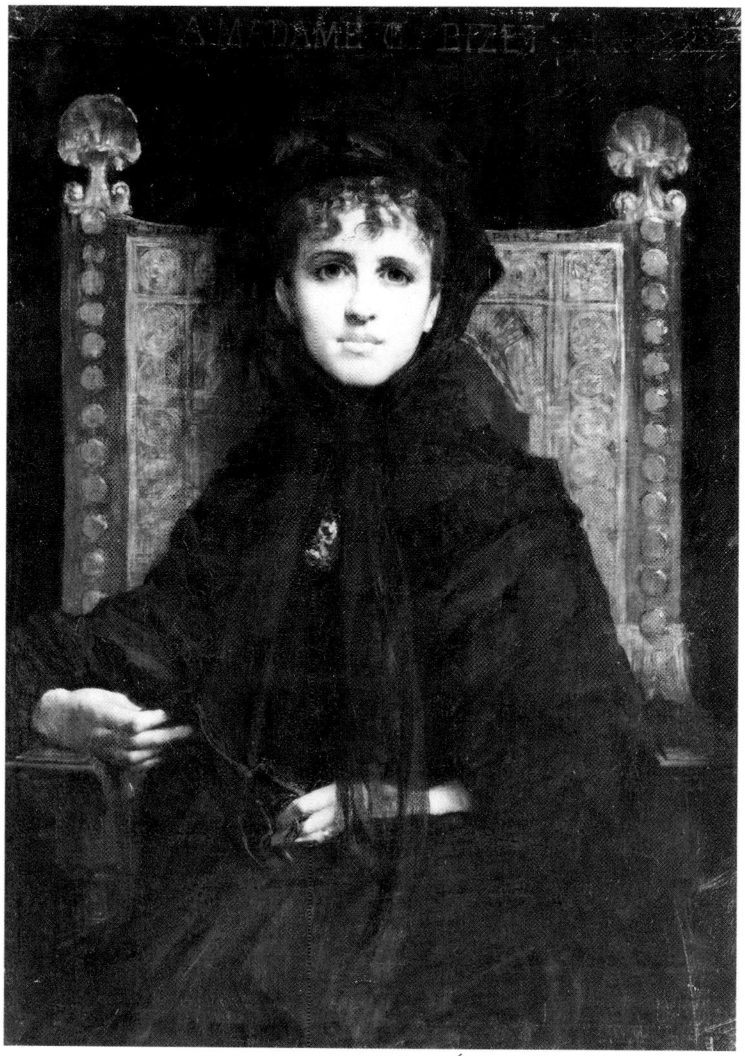

666. Jules-Élie Delaunay. *Madame Georges Bizet.*
1878. Oil on canvas

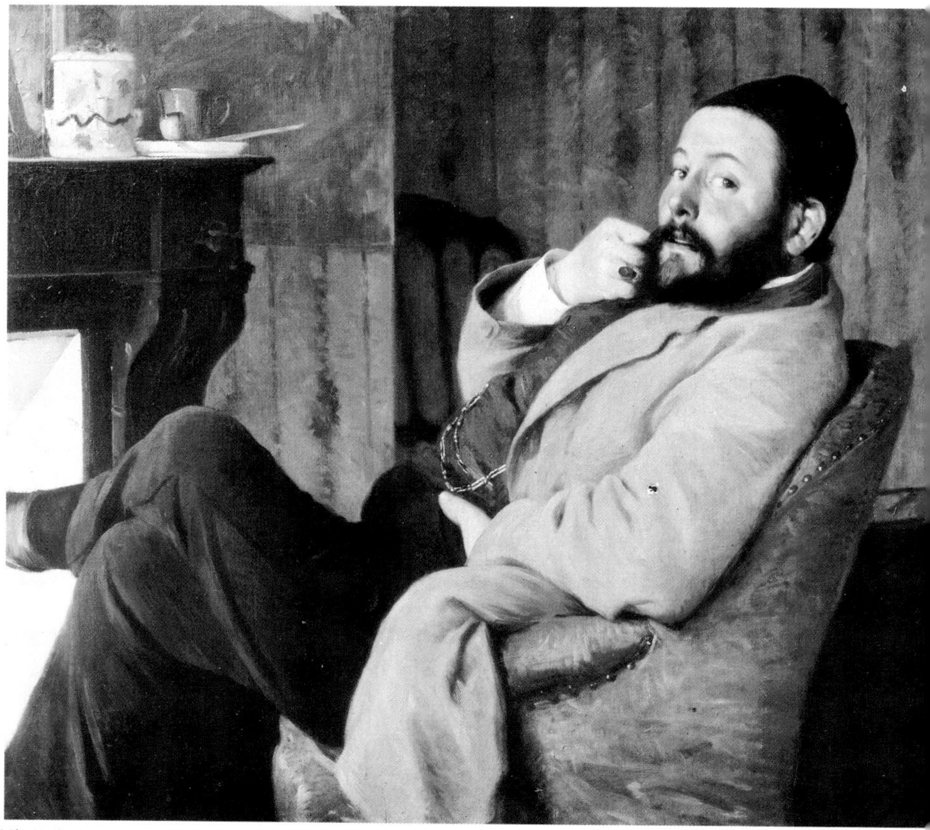

667. Federico Zandomeneghi. *Portrait of Diego Martelli.*
1879. Oil on canvas

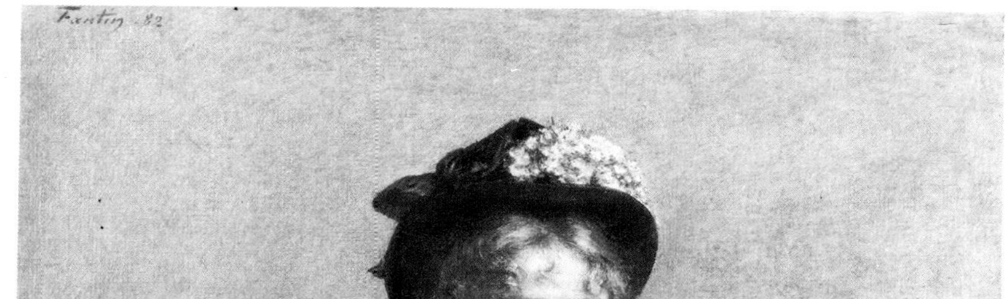

668. Henri Fantin-Latour. *Portrait of Charlotte Dubourg, the Artist's Sister-in-law.*
1882. Oil on canvas

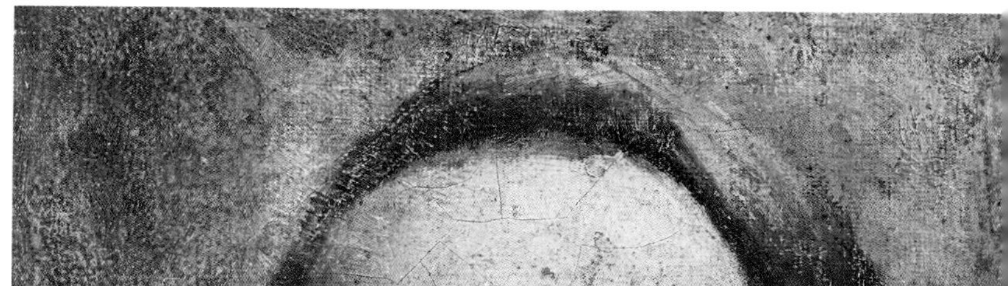

669. Édouard Vuillard. *Portrait of the Artist.*
c. 1889. Oil on canvas

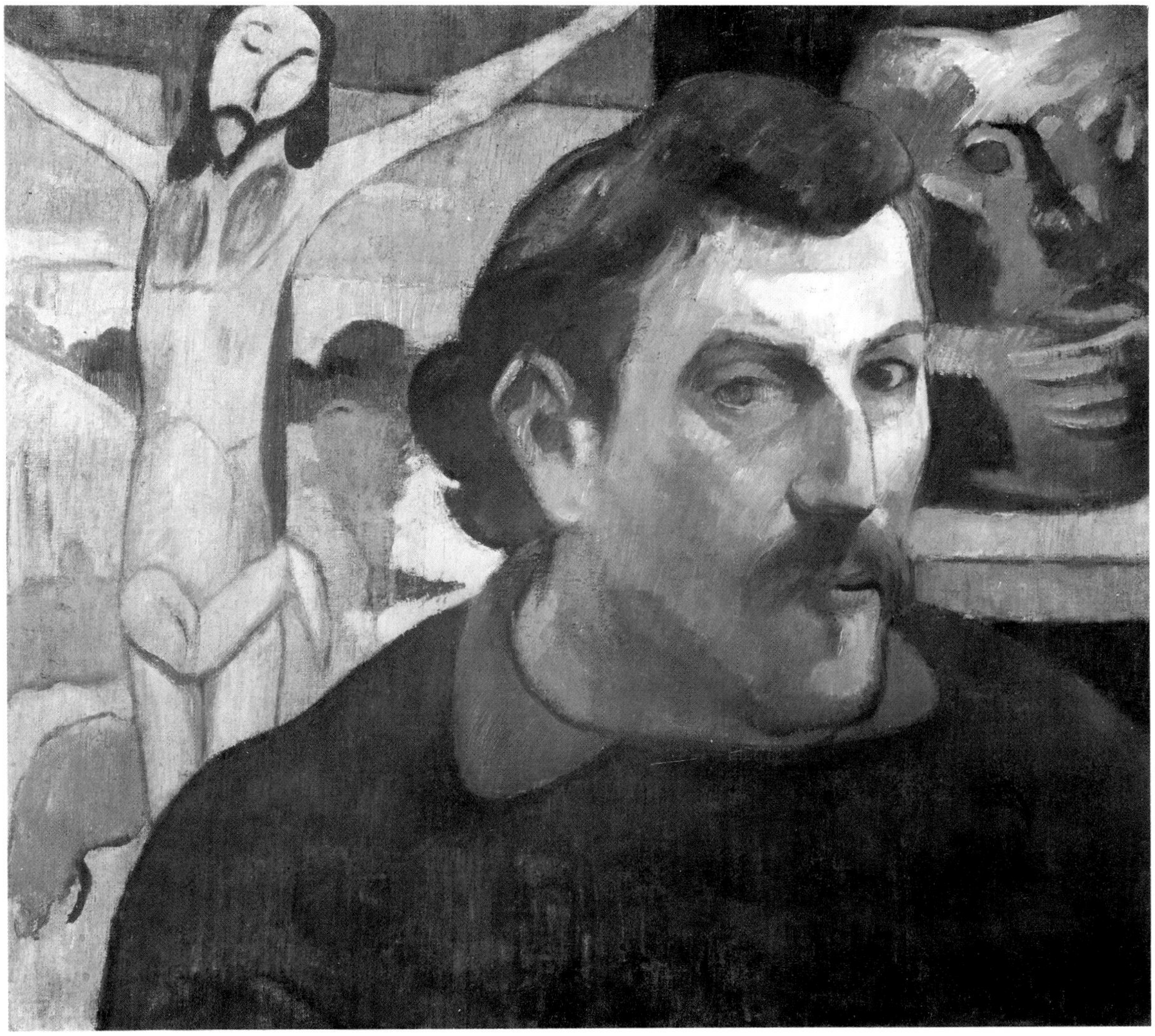

670. Paul Gauguin. *Self-Portrait.* 1889. Oil on canvas

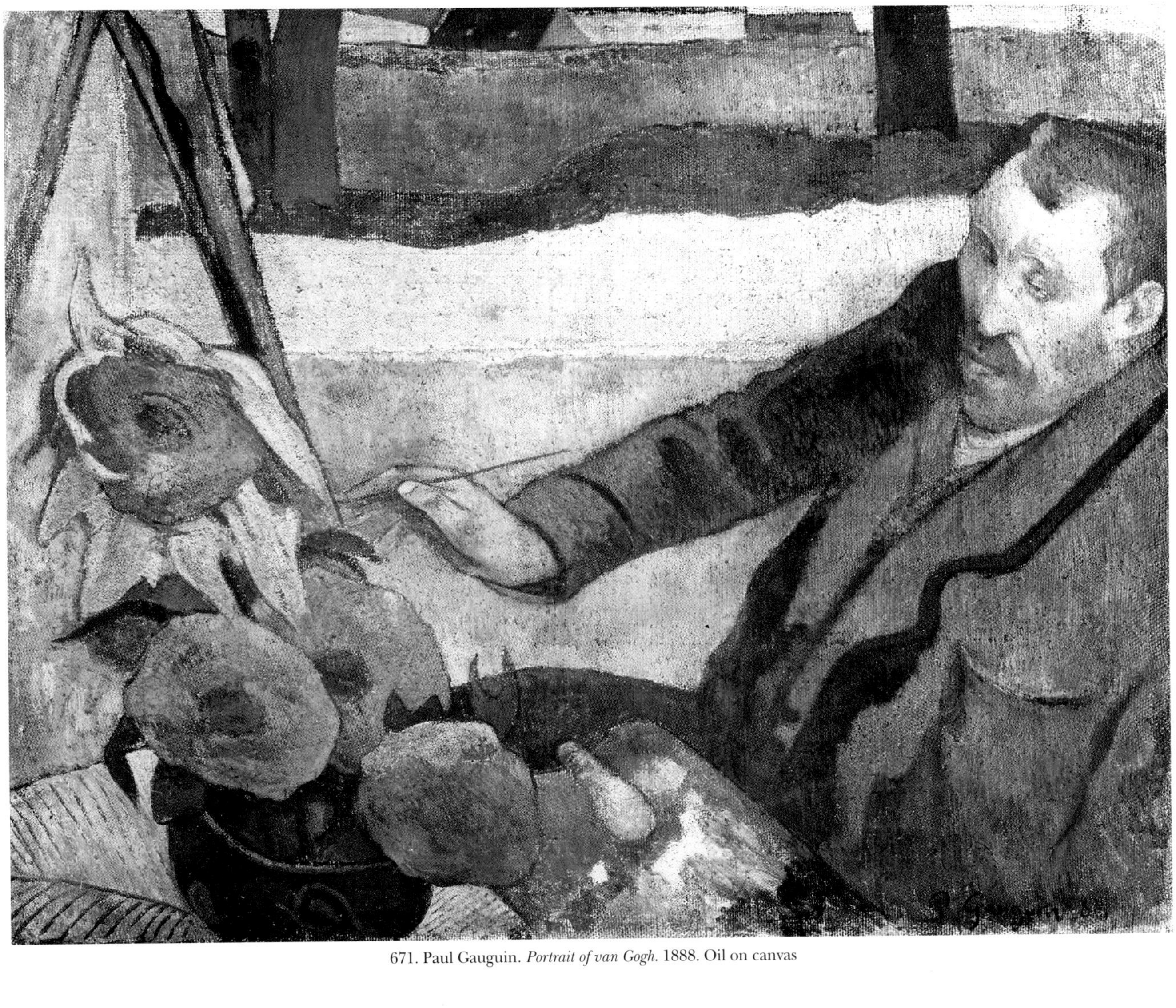

671. Paul Gauguin. *Portrait of van Gogh.* 1888. Oil on canvas

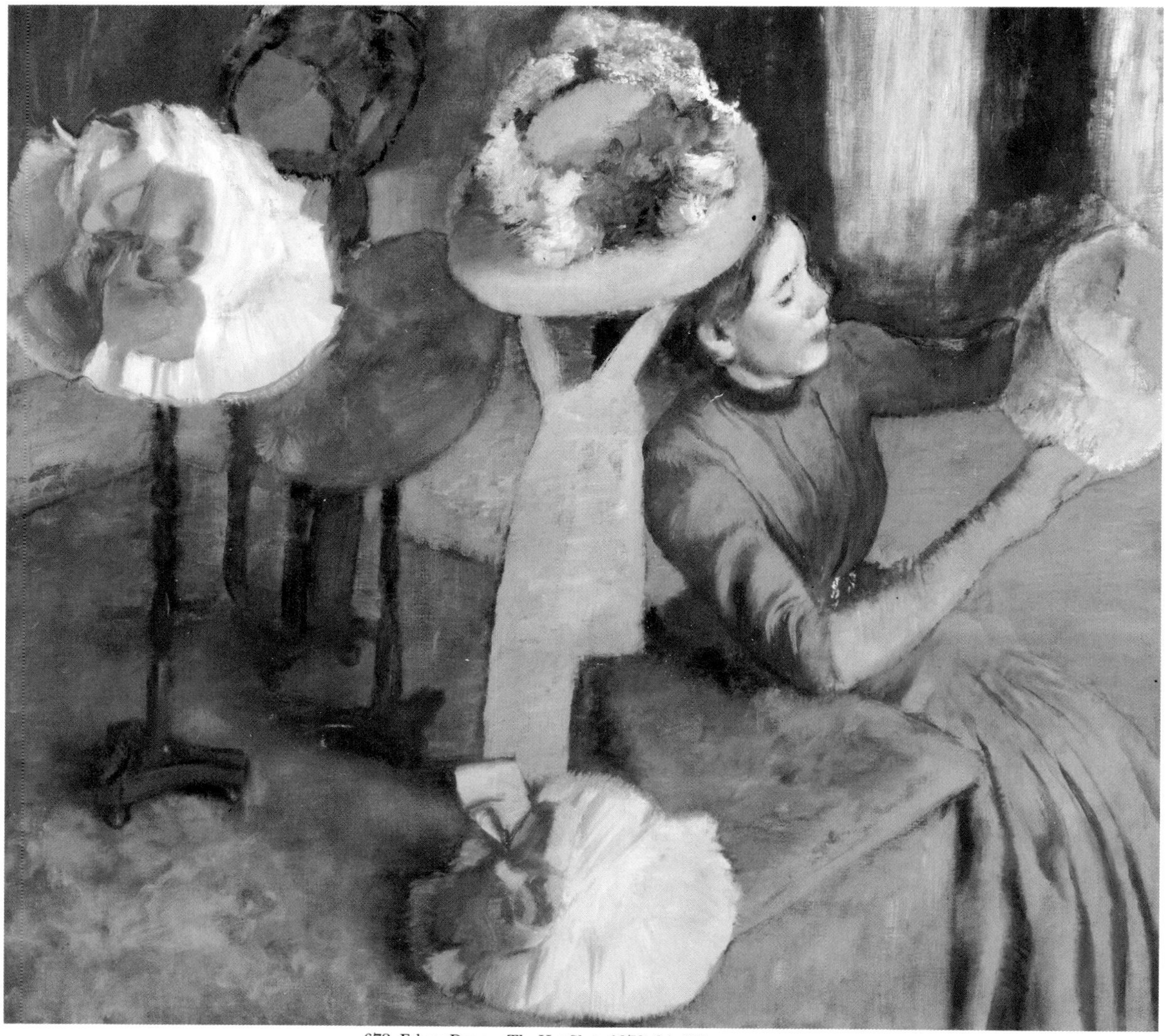

672. Edgar Degas. *The Hat Shop*. 1879–84. Oil on canvas

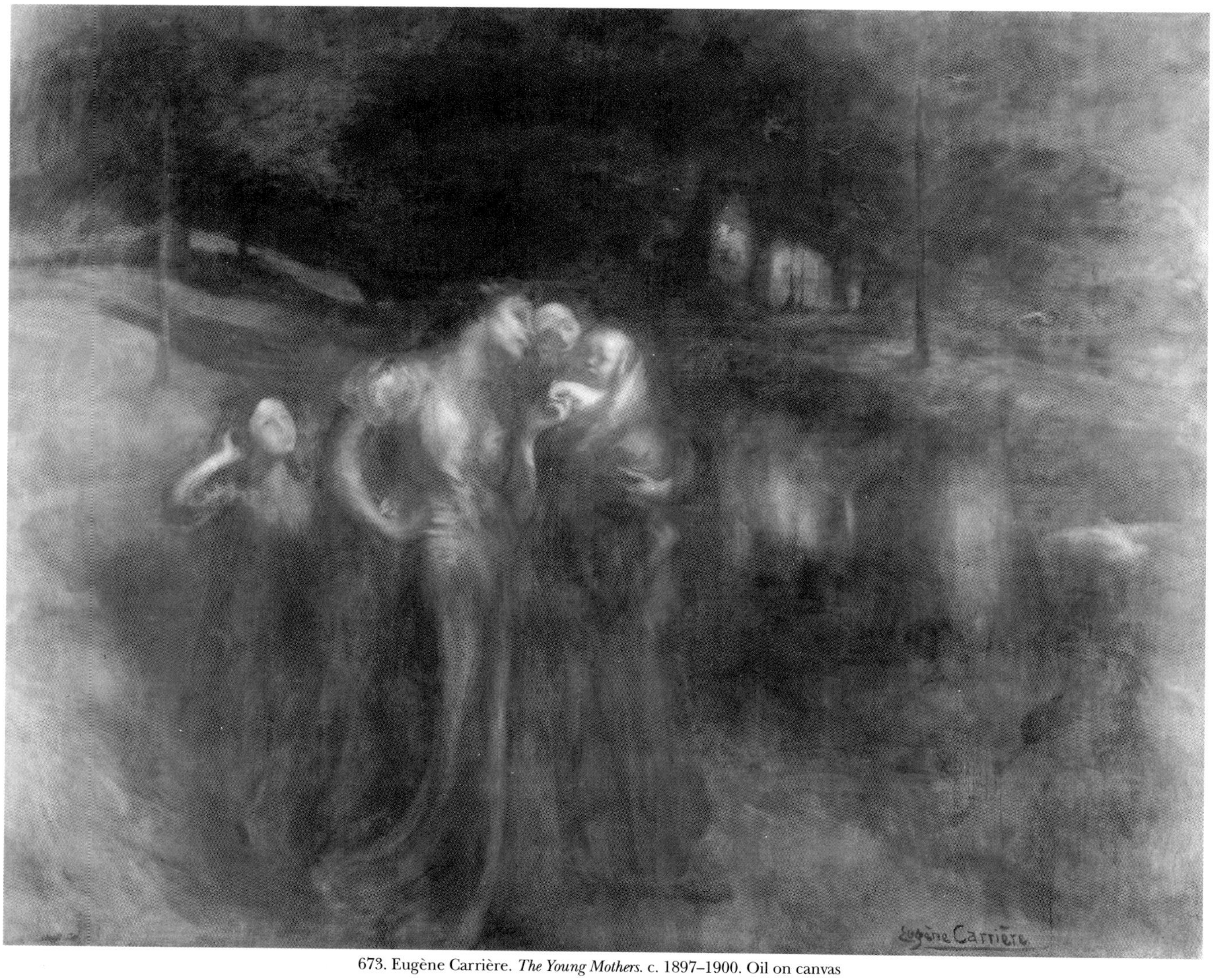

673. Eugène Carrière. *The Young Mothers*. c. 1897–1900. Oil on canvas

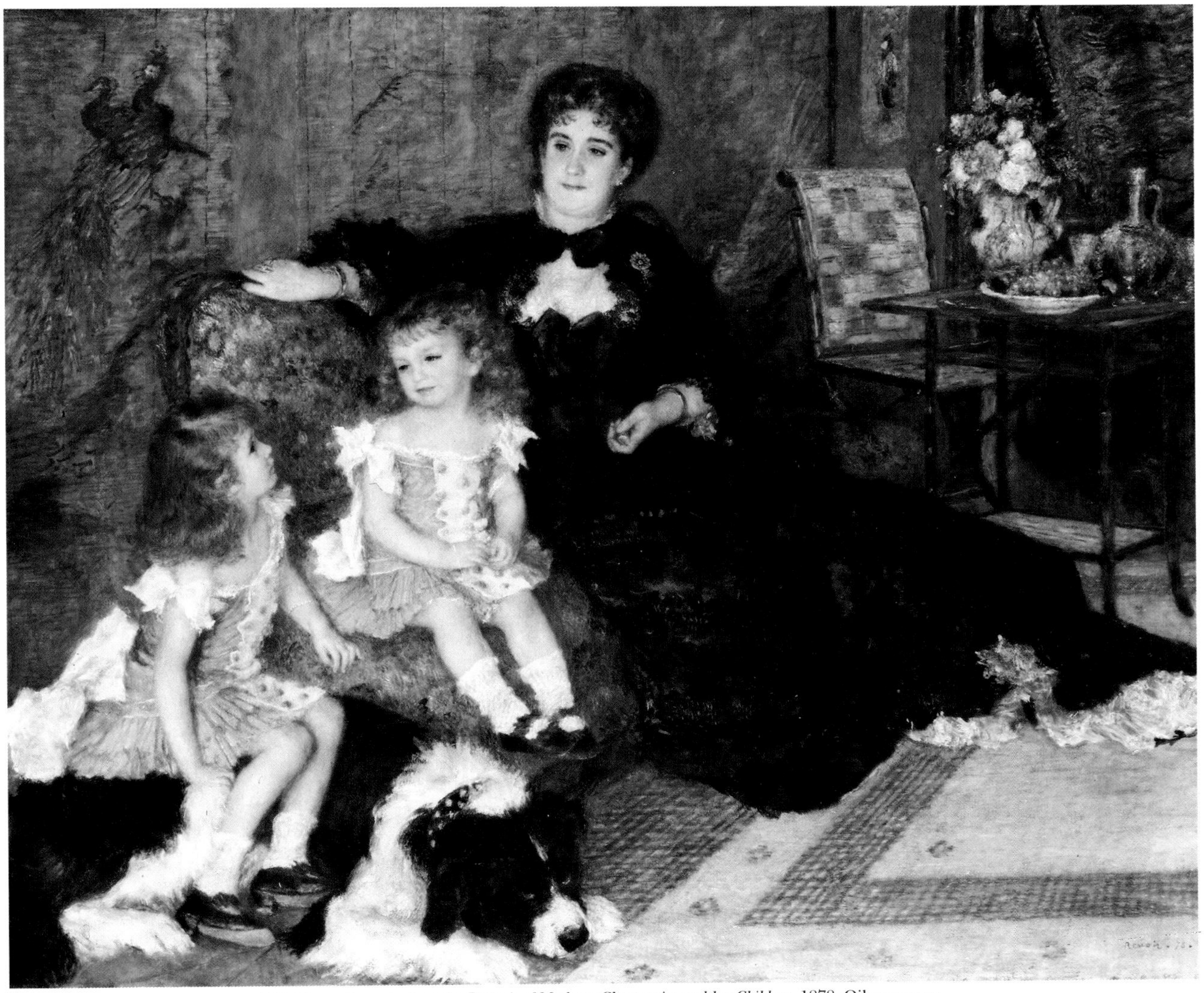

674. Pierre-Auguste Renoir. *Portrait of Madame Charpentier and her Children*. 1878. Oil on canvas

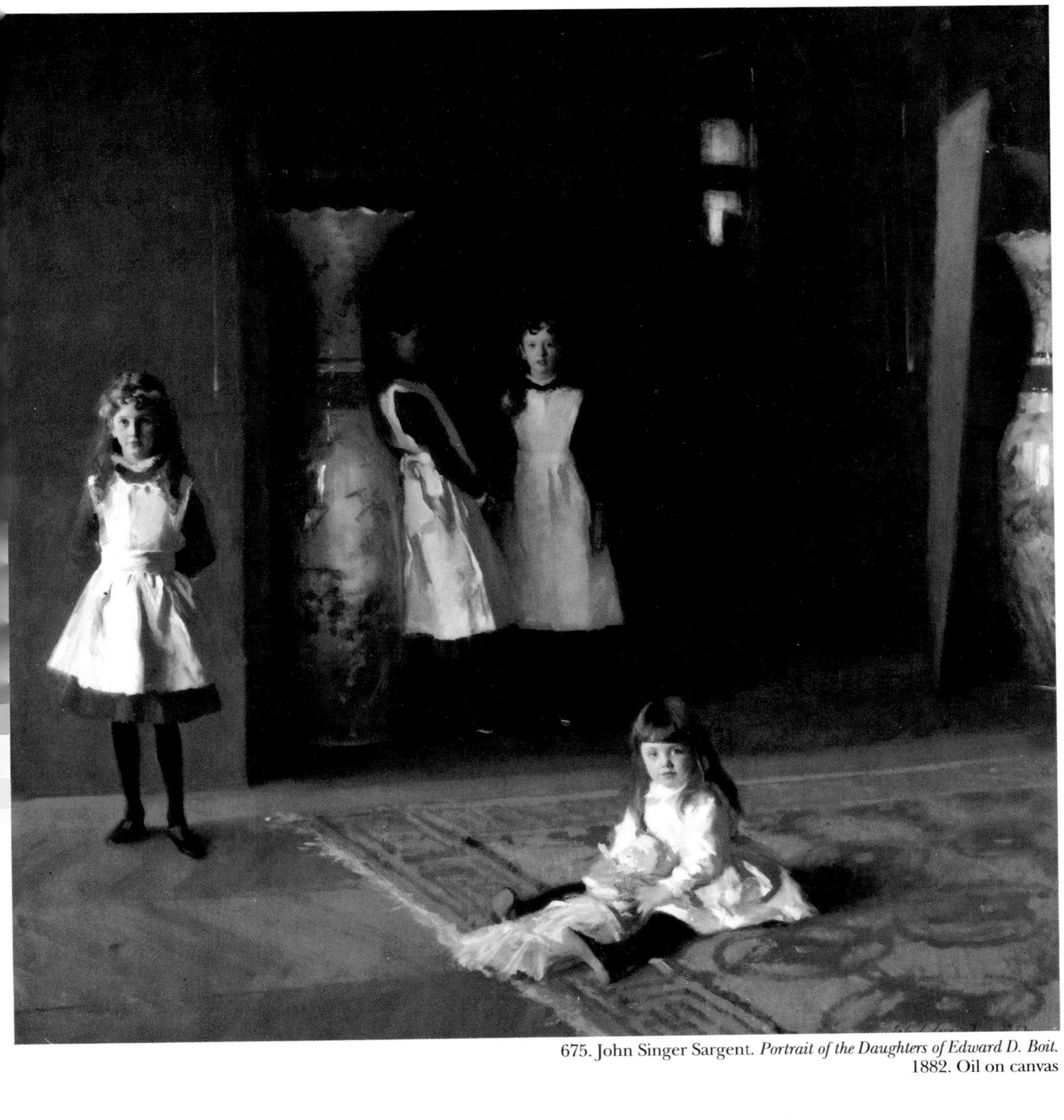

675. John Singer Sargent. *Portrait of the Daughters of Edward D. Boit*. 1882. Oil on canvas

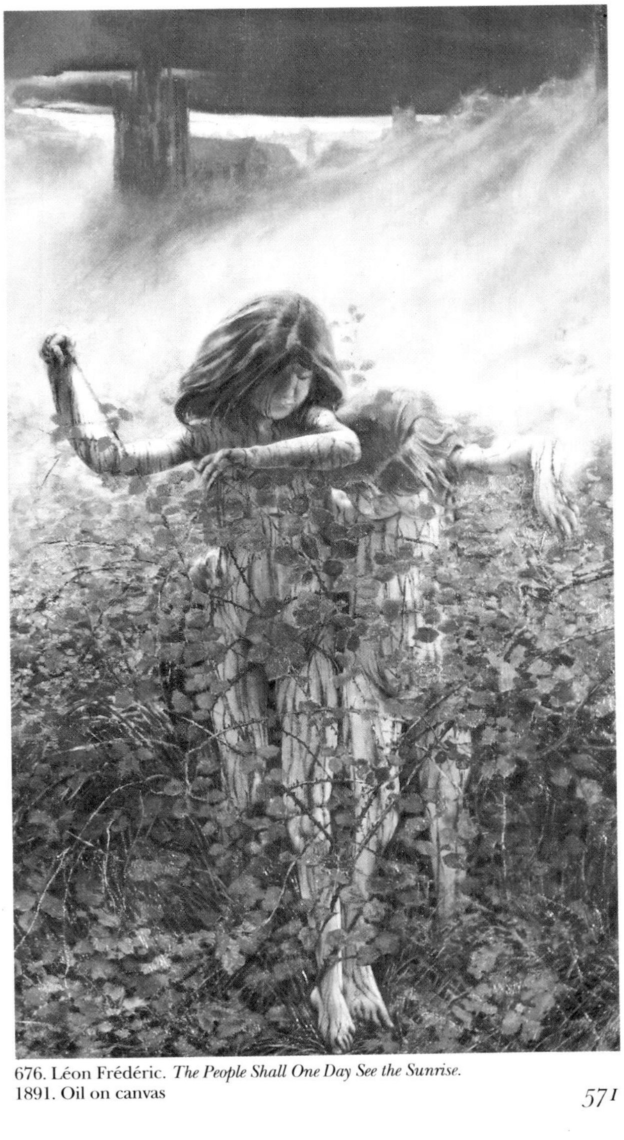

676. Léon Frédéric. *The People Shall One Day See the Sunrise*. 1891. Oil on canvas

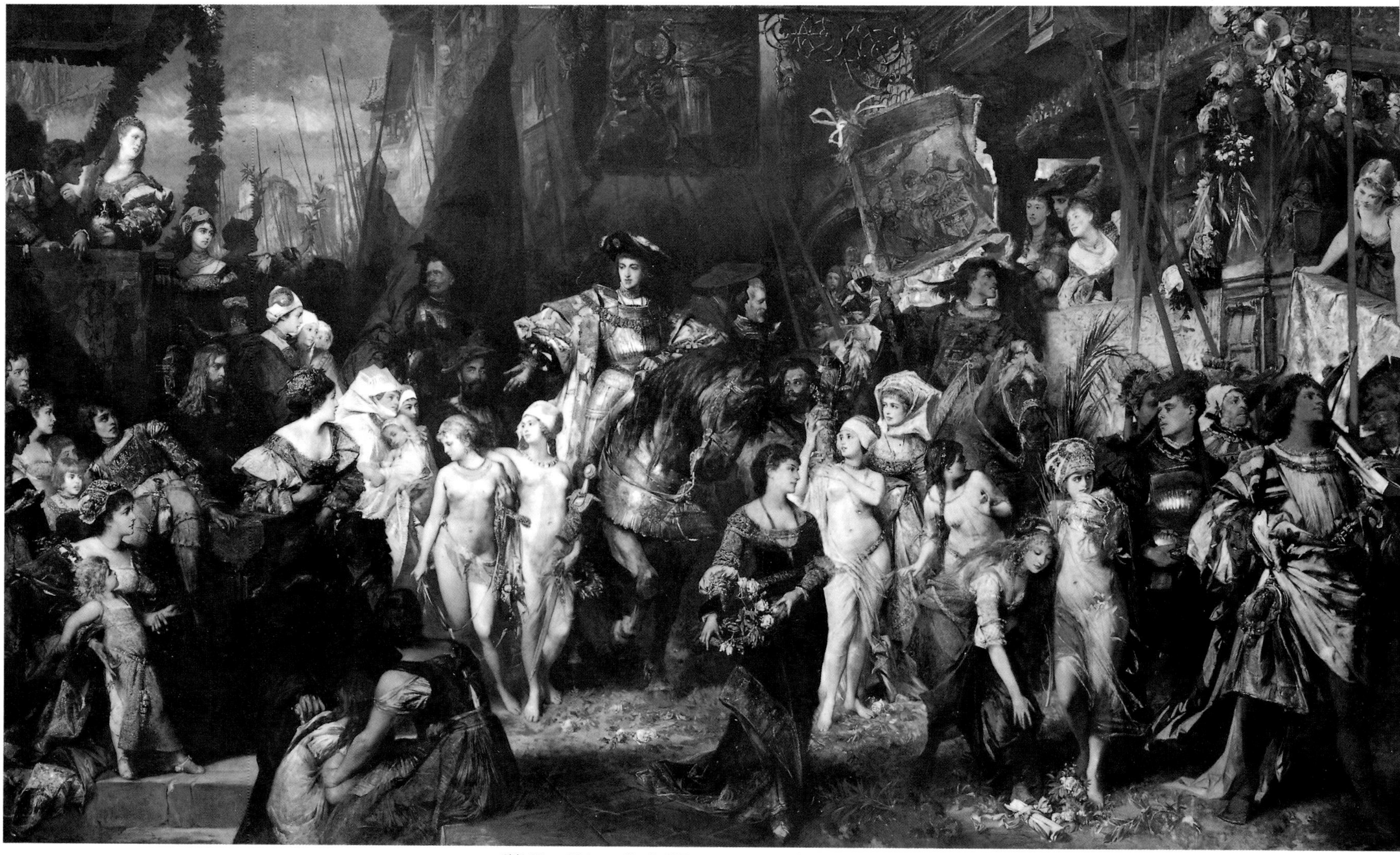

677. Hans Makart. *Charles V Entering Antwerp.* 1878. Oil on canvas

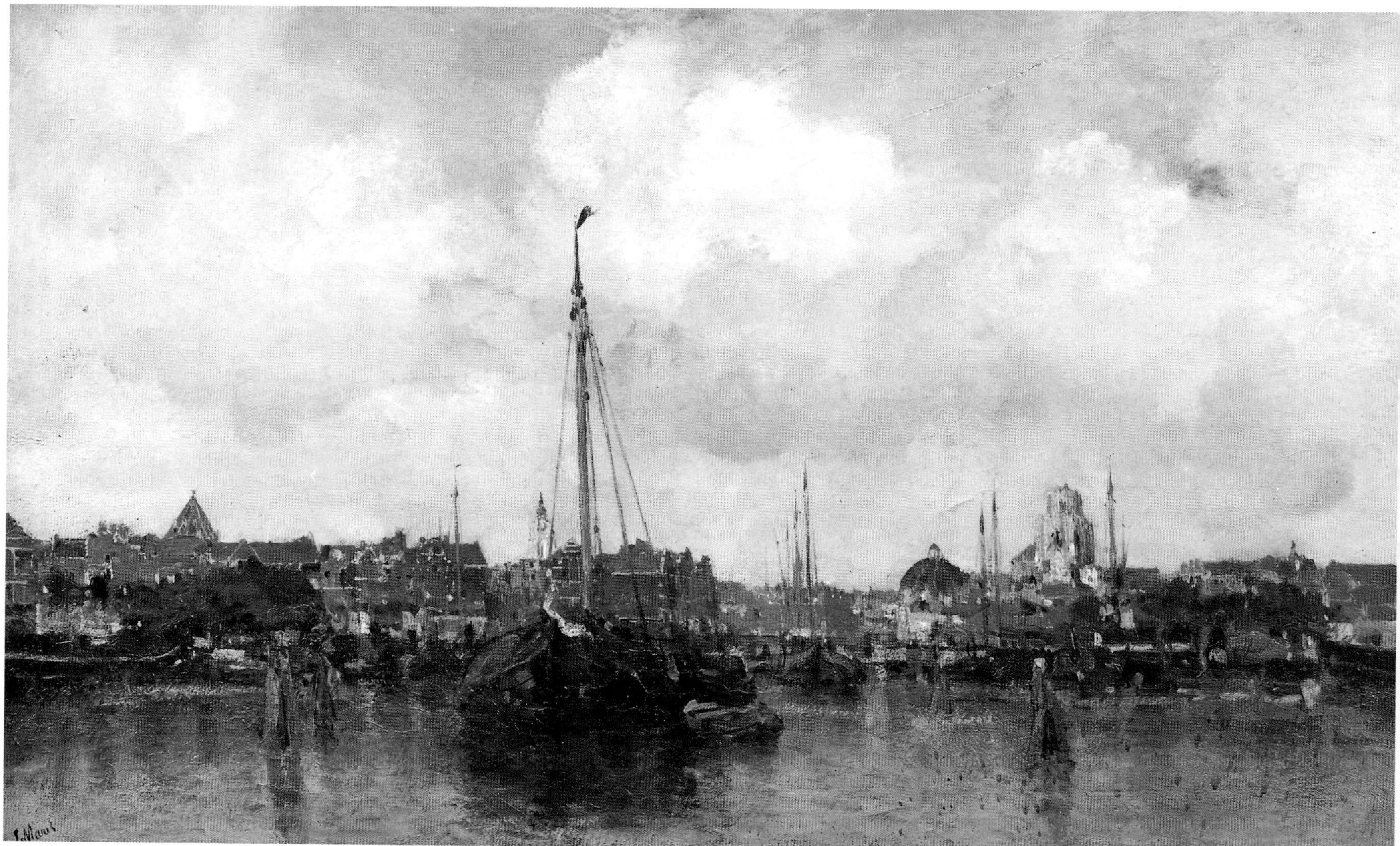

678. Jacob Maris. *Dutch Riverside Town.* 1883. Oil on canvas

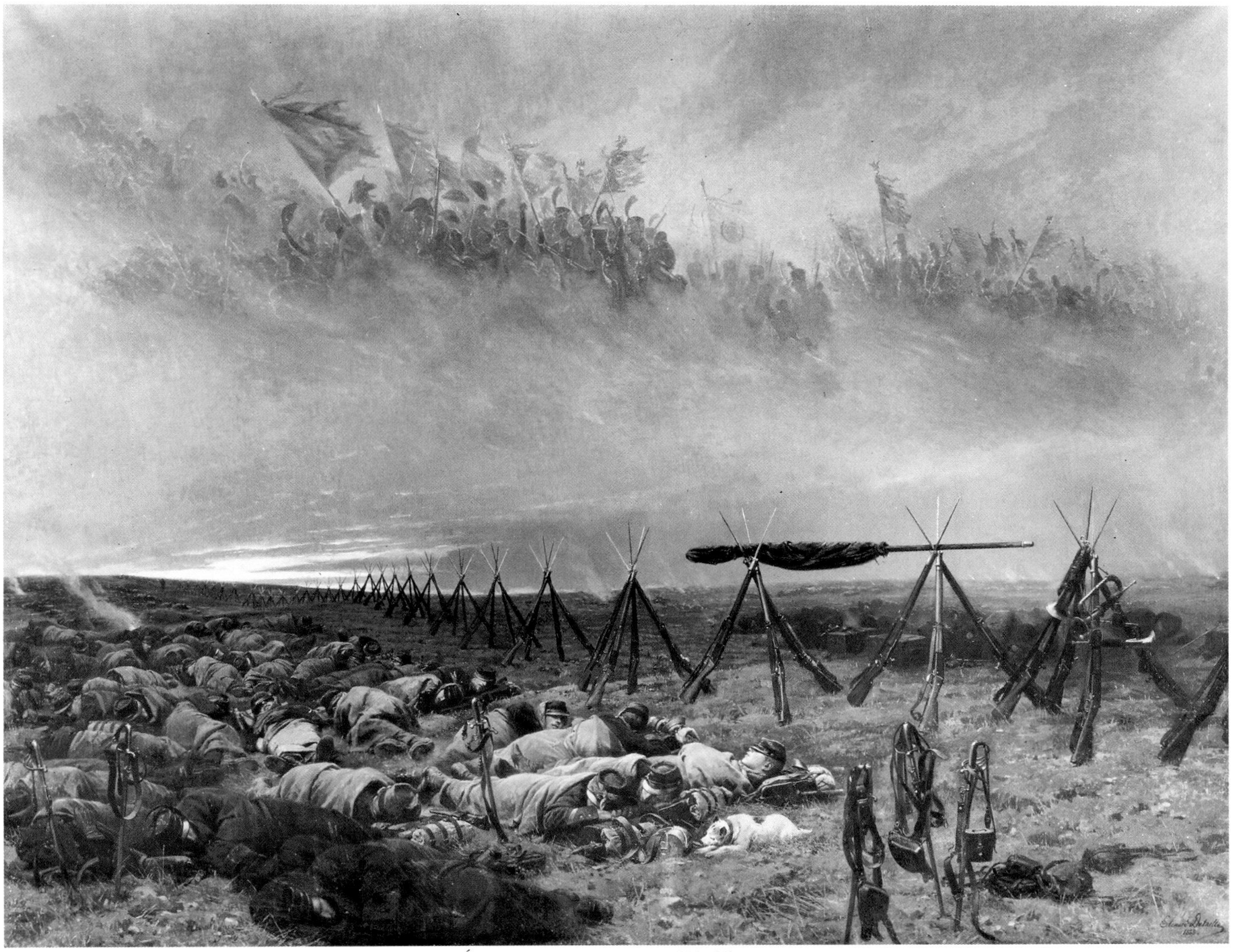

679. Édouard Detaille. *The Dream.* 1888. Oil on canvas

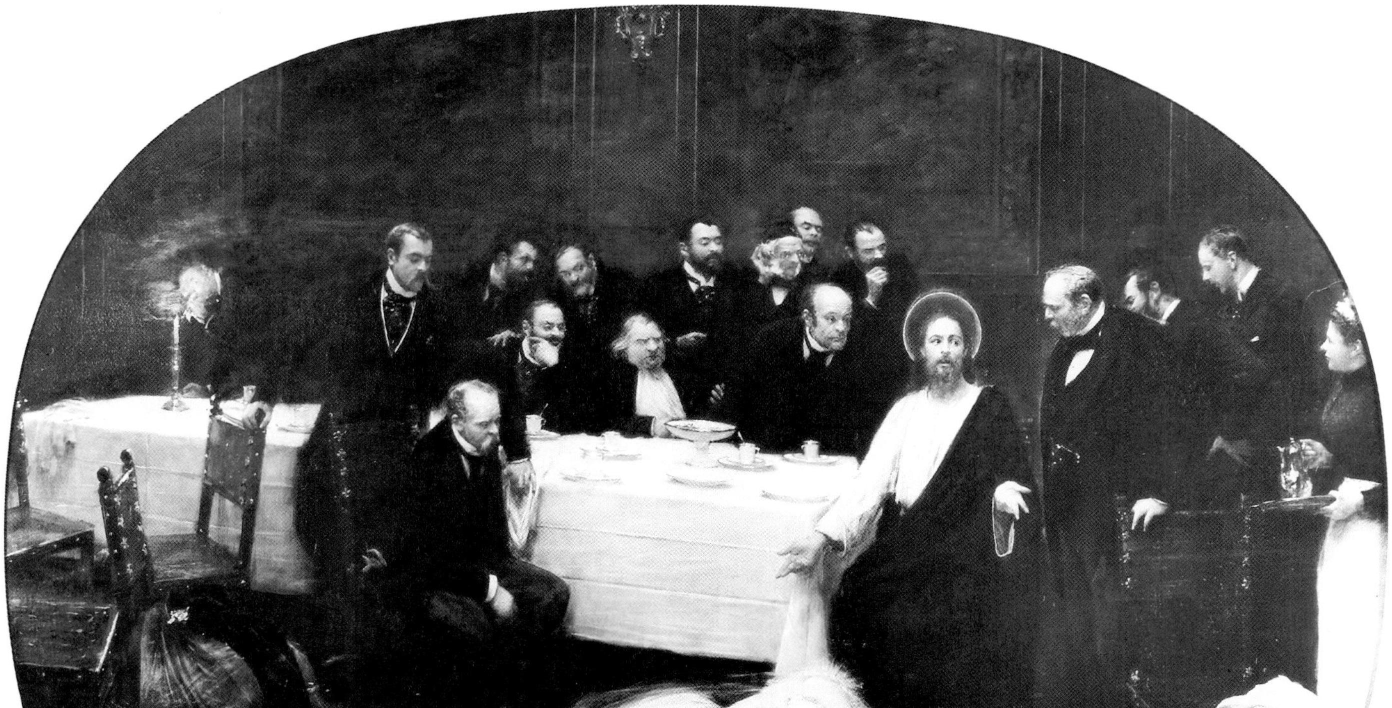

680. Jean Béraud. *Mary Magdalene at the House of the Pharisee.* 1891. Oil on canvas

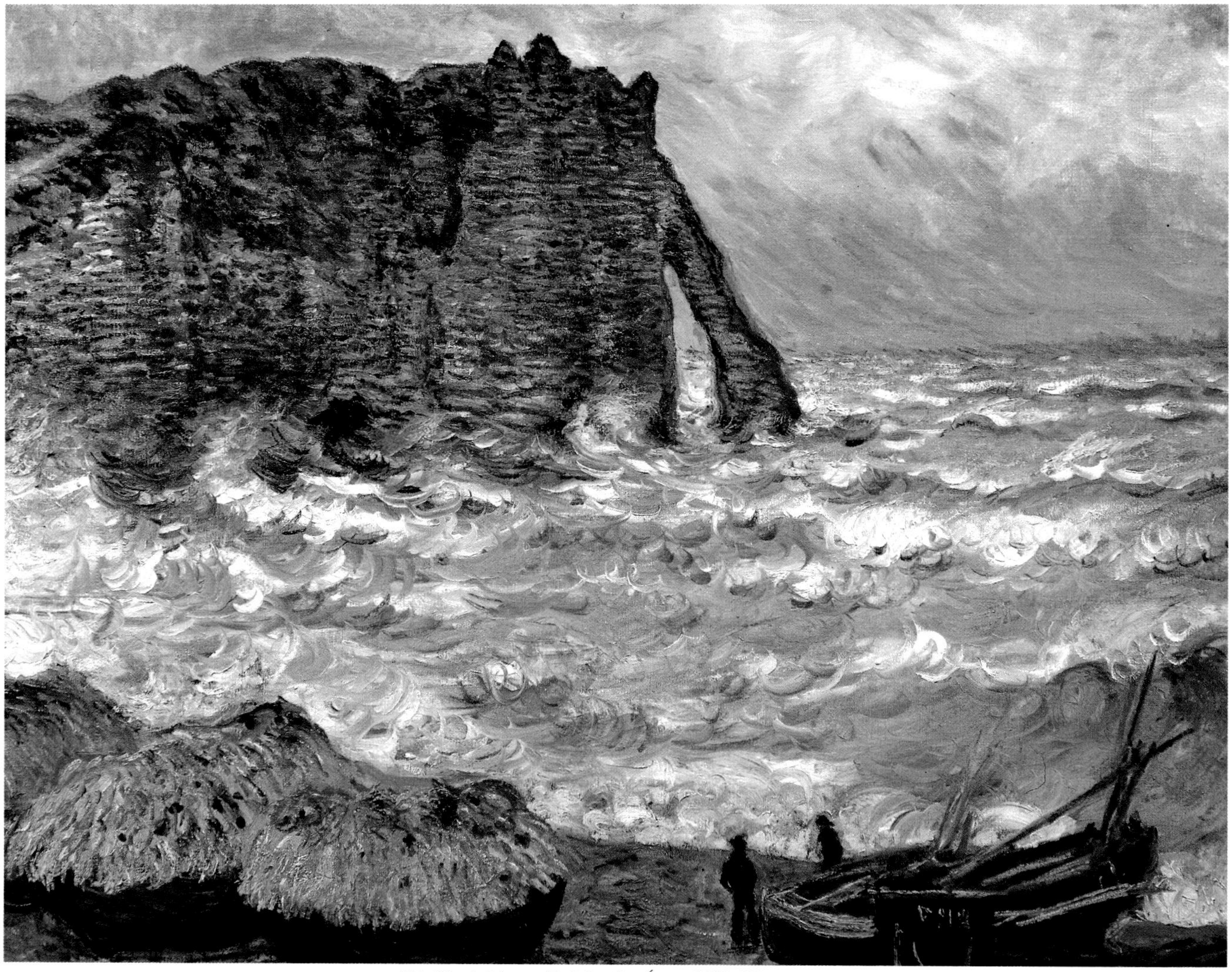

681. Claude Monet. *Turbulent Sea, Étretat.* 1883. Oil on canvas

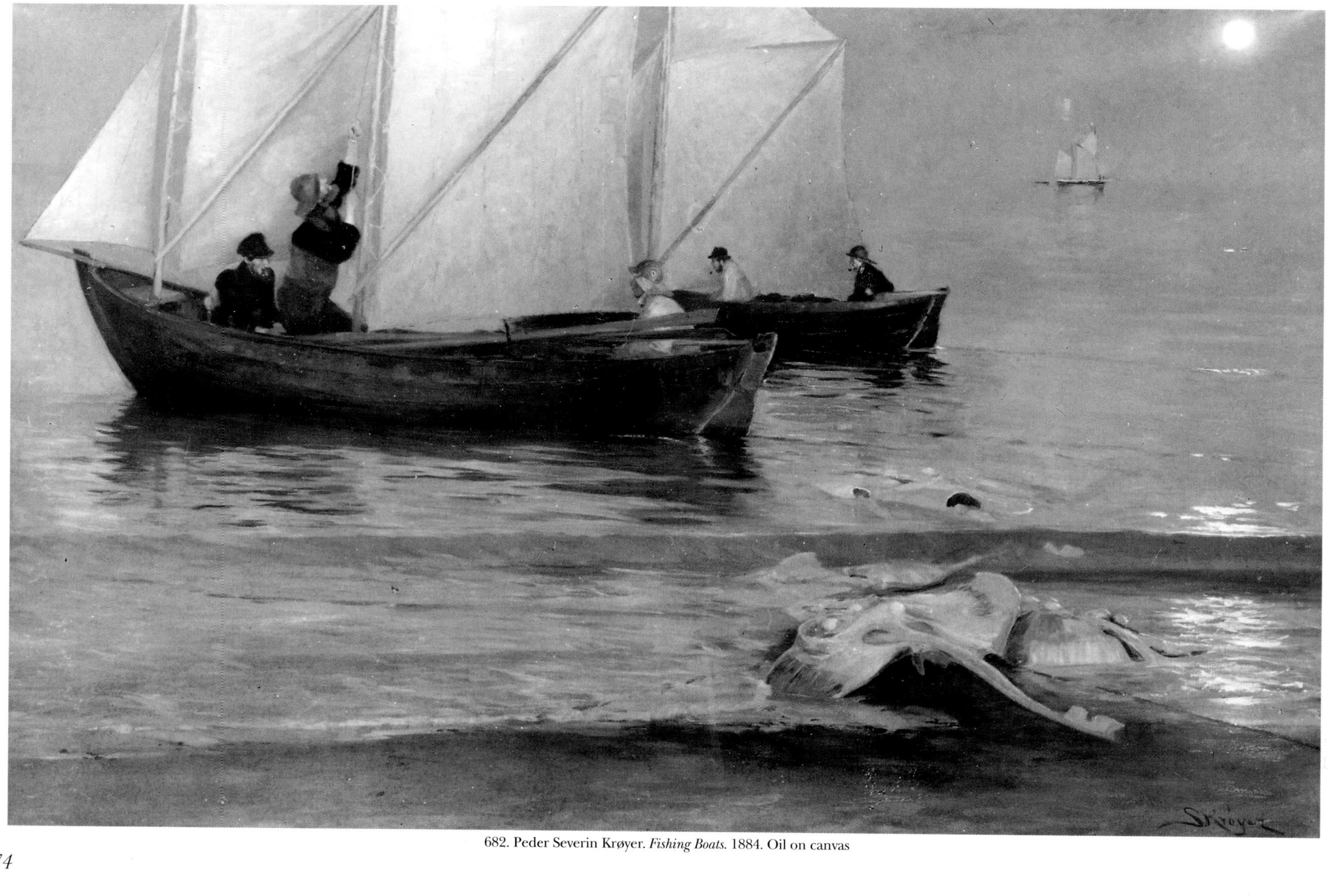

682. Peder Severin Krøyer. *Fishing Boats.* 1884. Oil on canvas

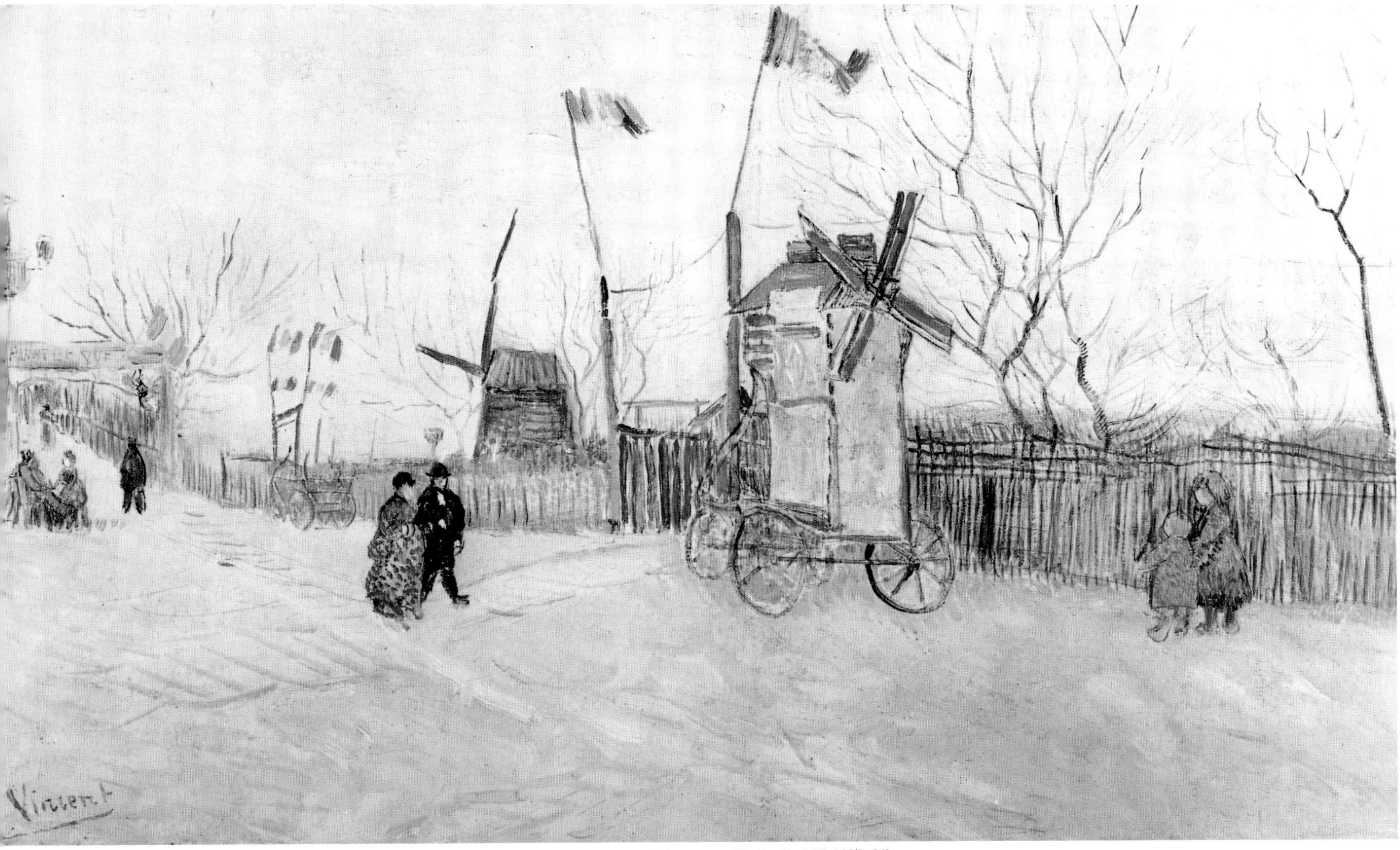

683. Vincent van Gogh. *A Corner of Montmartre, The Powder Mill*. 1887. Oil on canvas

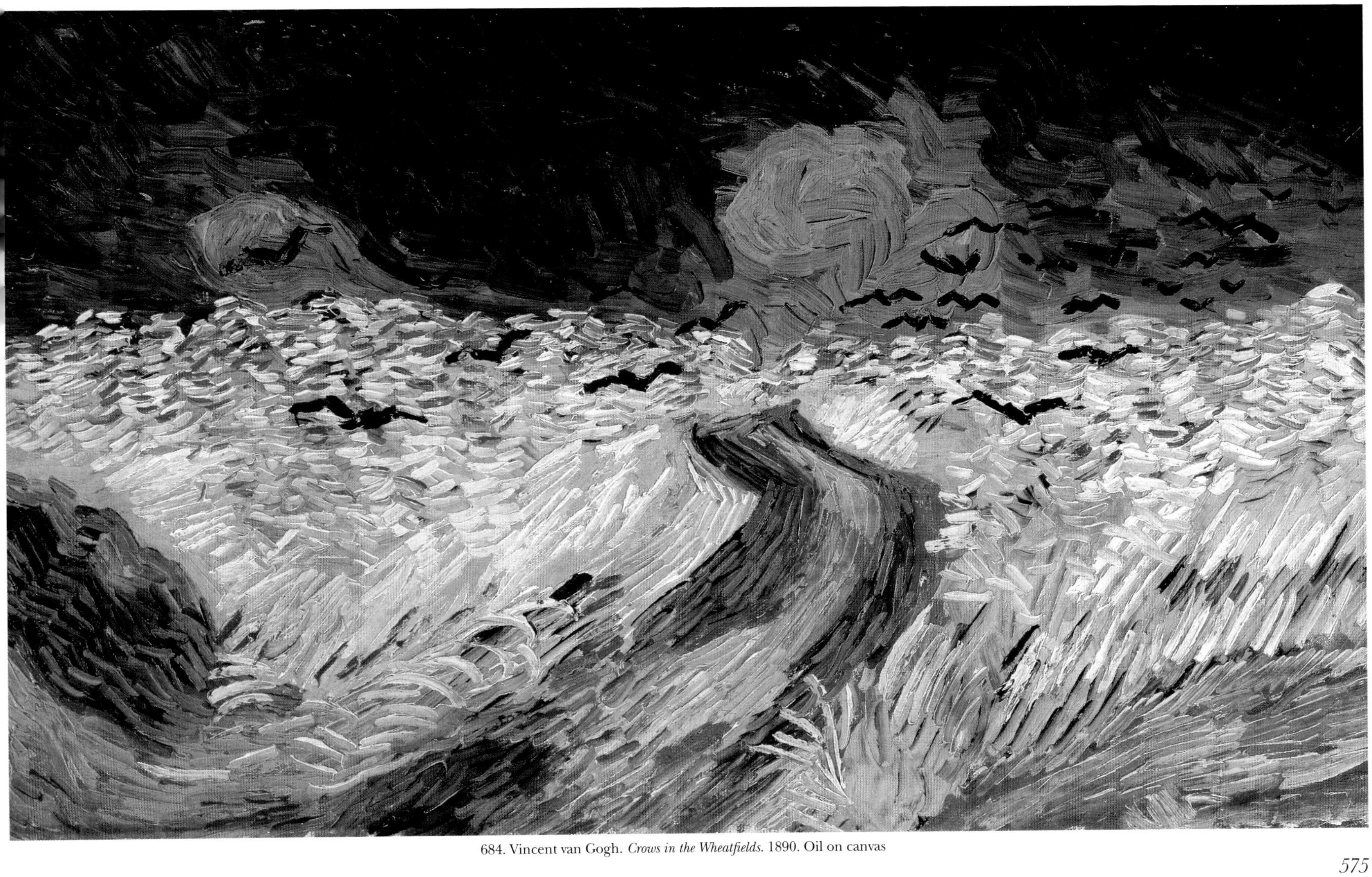

684. Vincent van Gogh. *Crows in the Wheatfields*. 1890. Oil on canvas

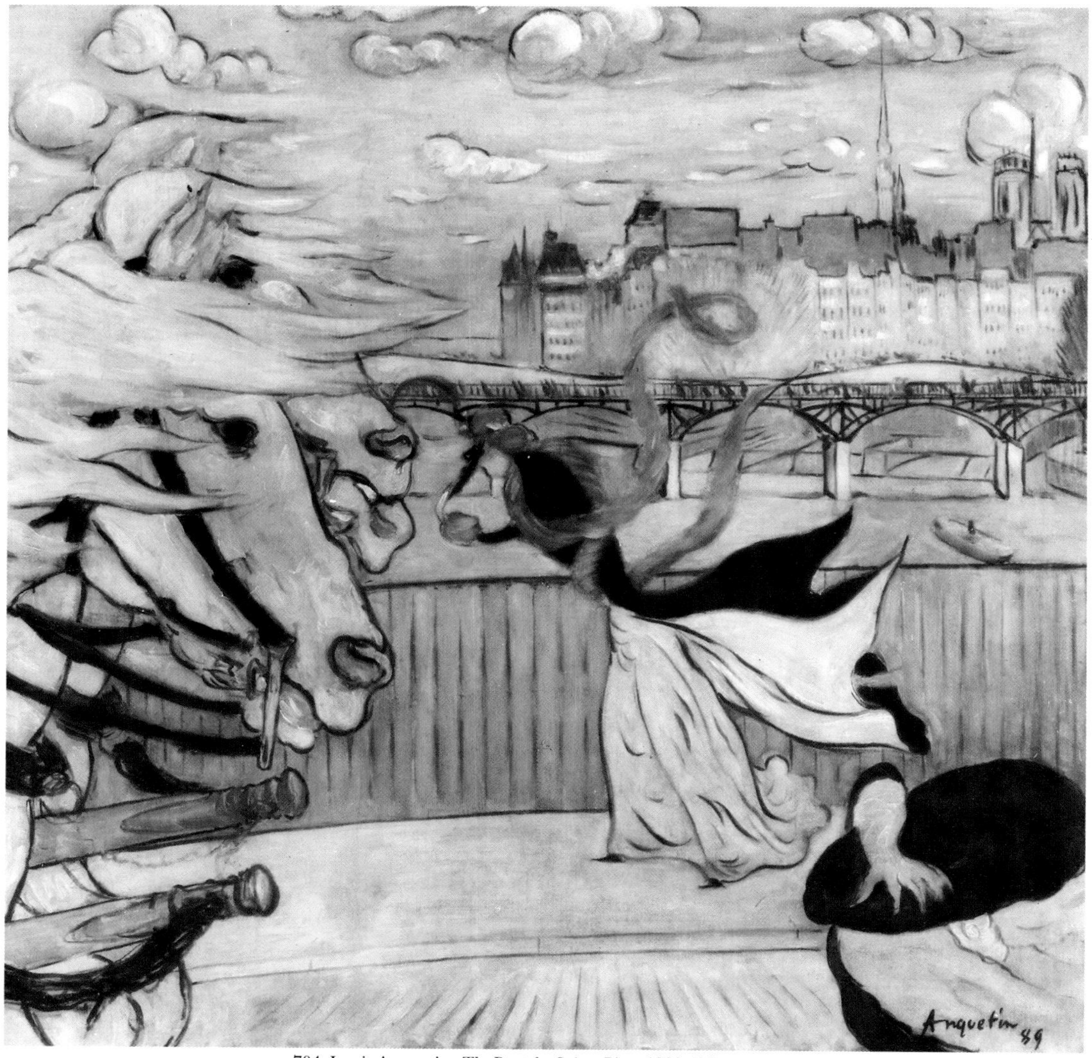

704. Louis Anquetin. *The Pont des Saints-Pères.* 1889. Oil on canvas

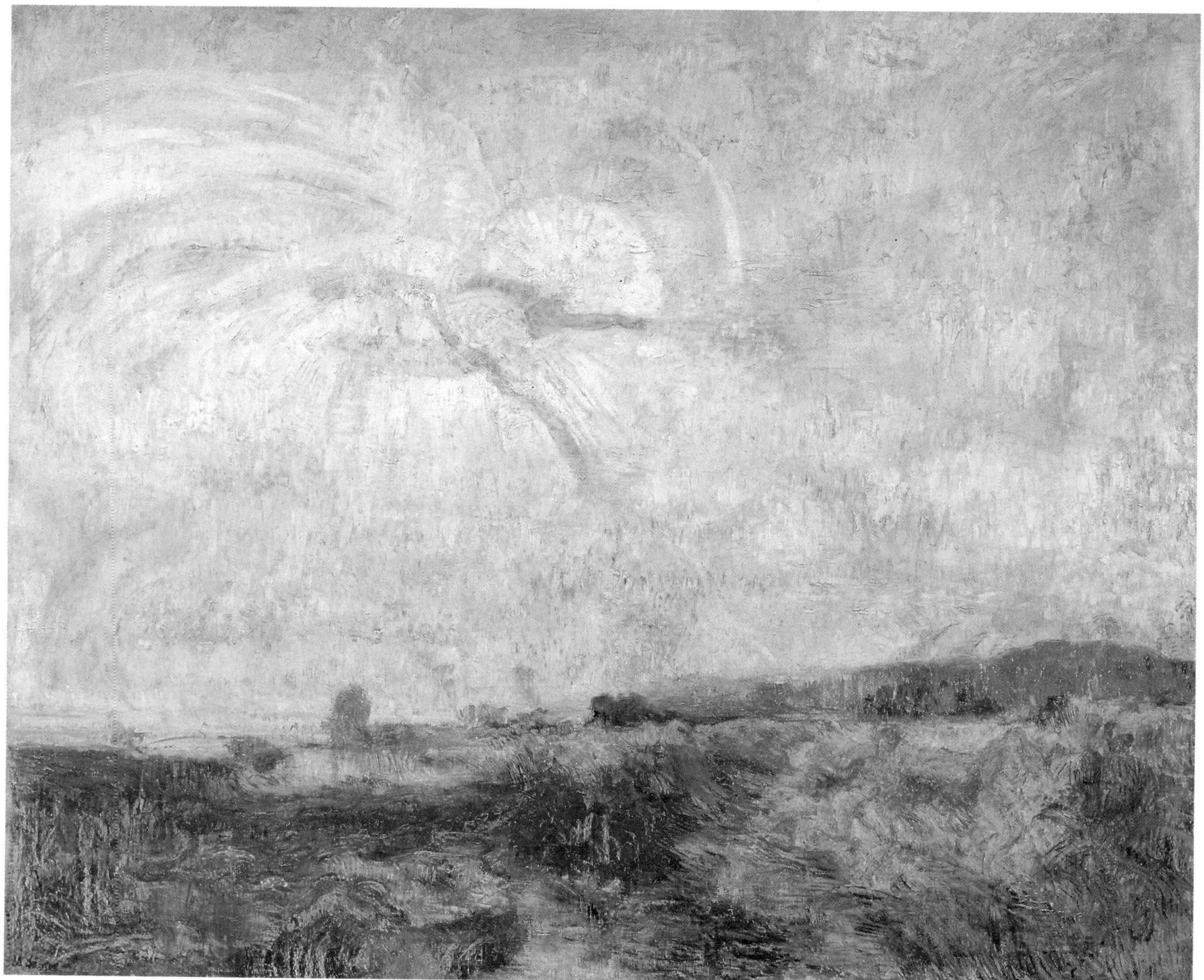

705. James Ensor. *Adam and Eve Being Driven from Paradise.* 1887. Oil on canvas

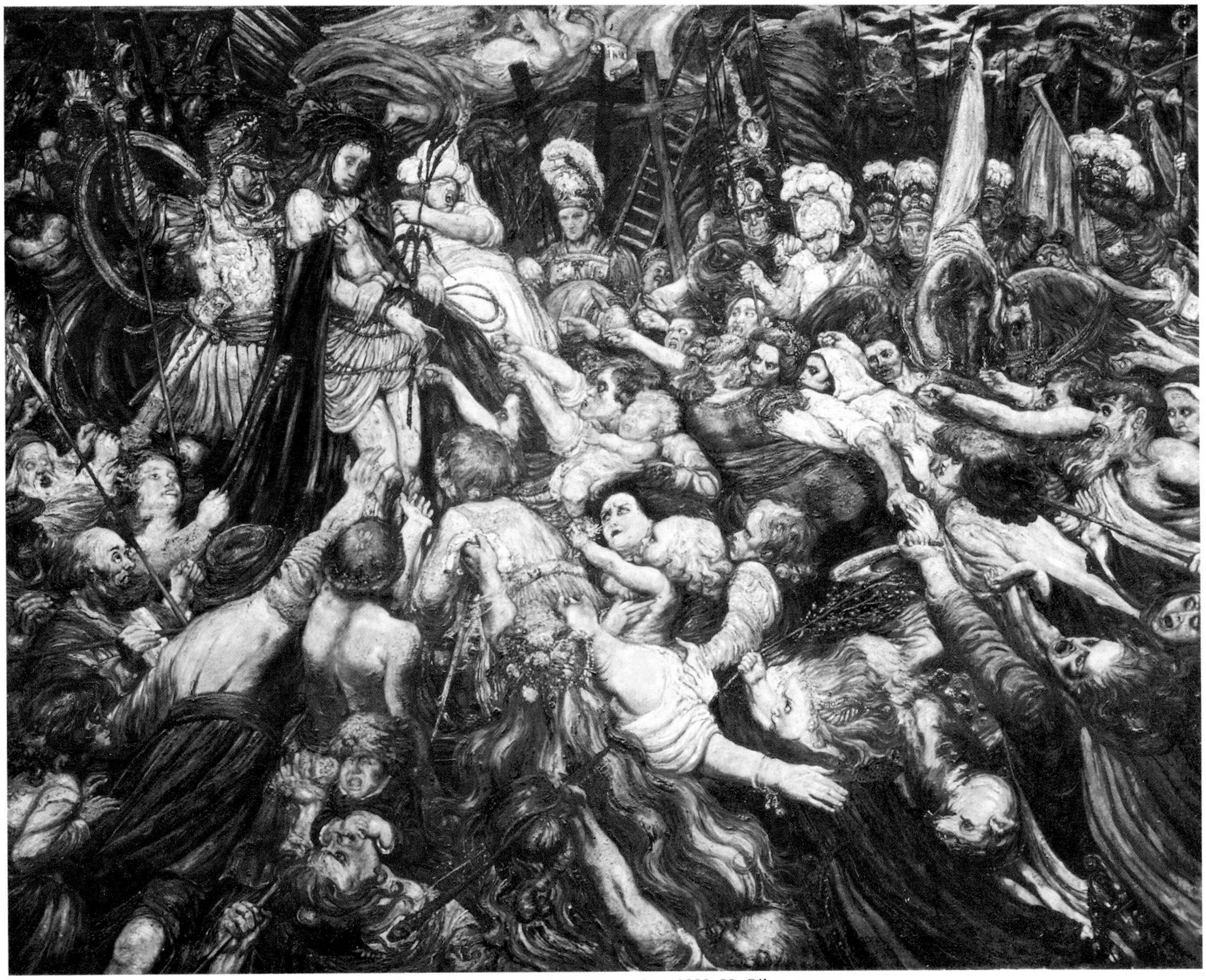

706. Henry de Groux. *Christ Suffering Abuse.* 1888–89. Oil on canvas

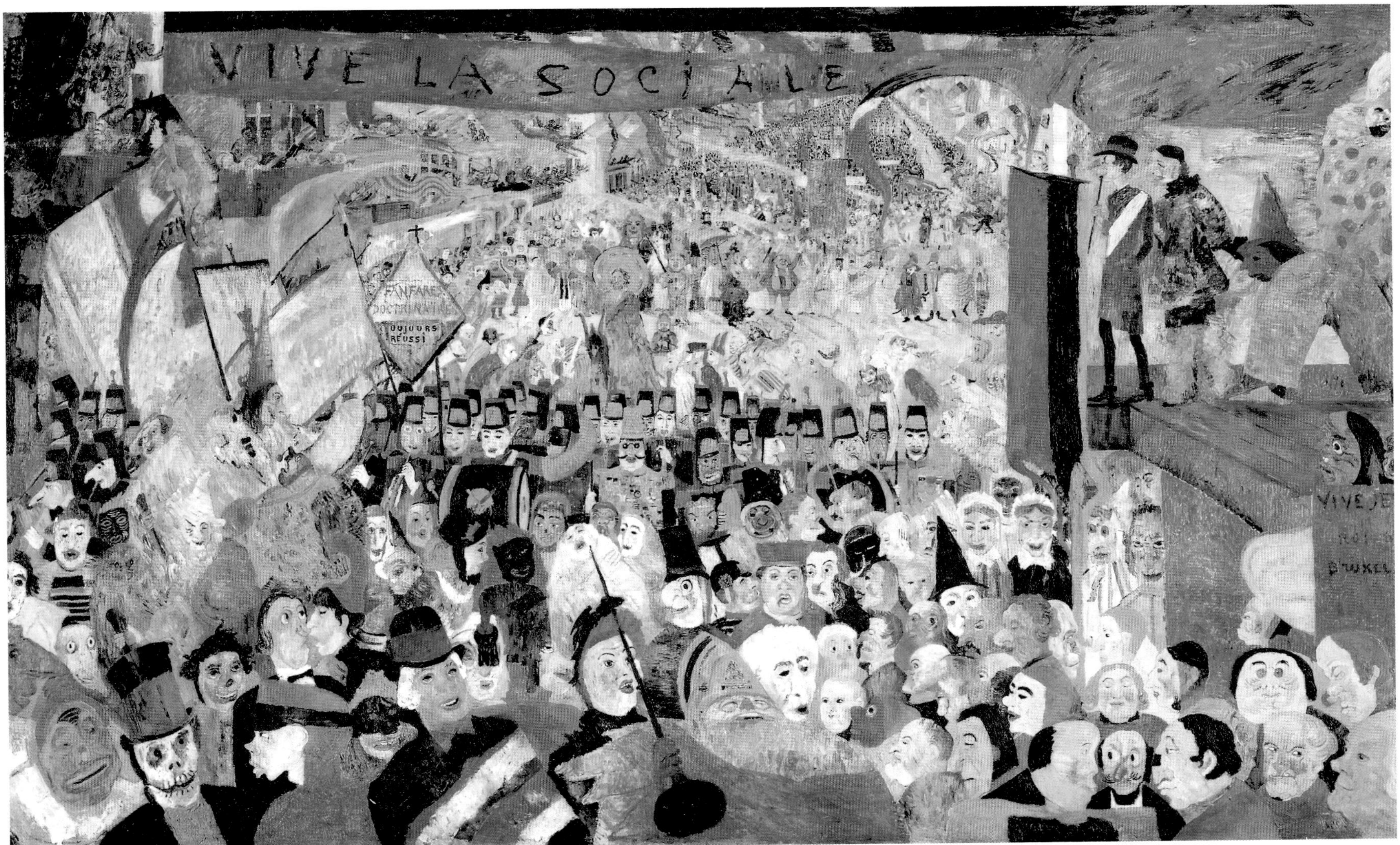

707. James Ensor. *Christ's Entry into Brussels in 1889.* 1888–89. Oil on canvas

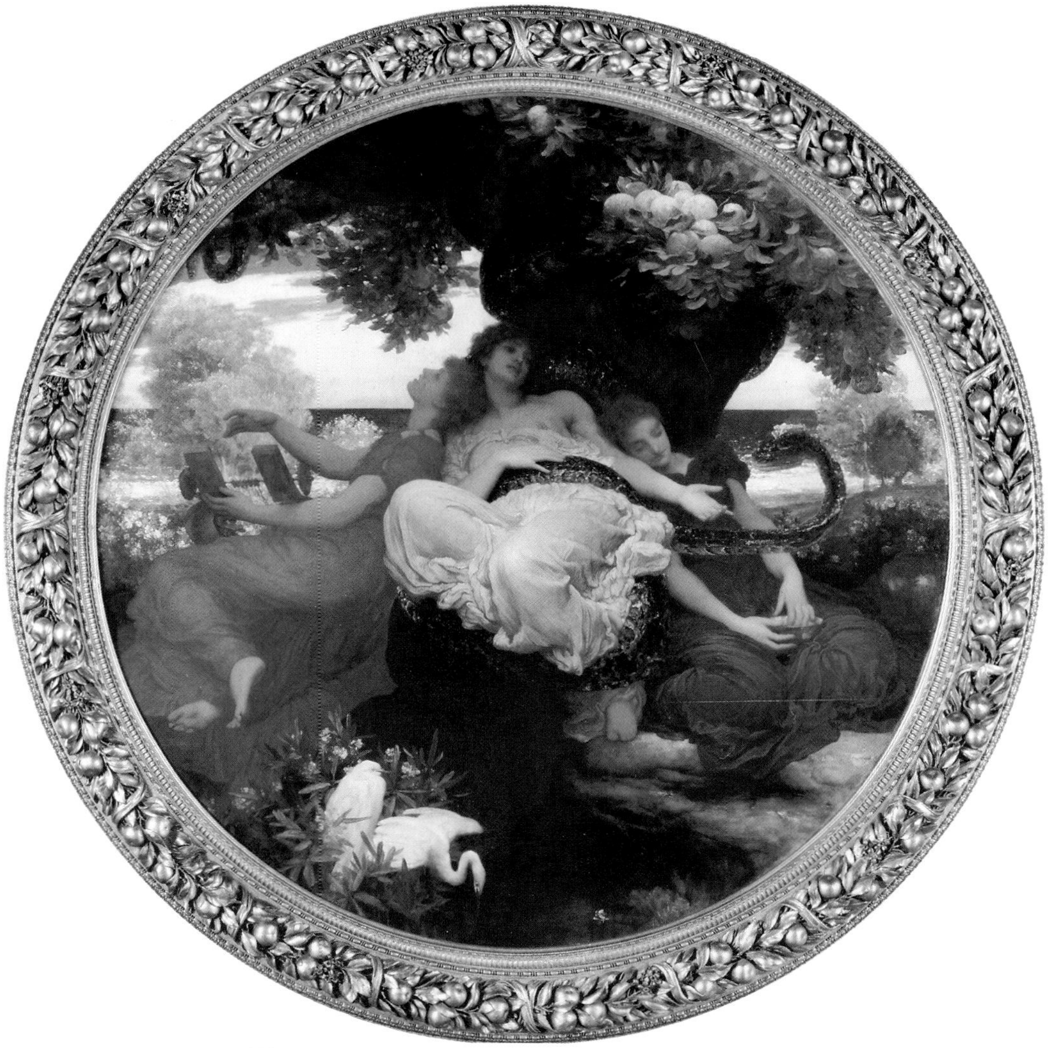

708. Frederic Leighton. *The Garden of the Hesperides.* 1892. Oil on canvas

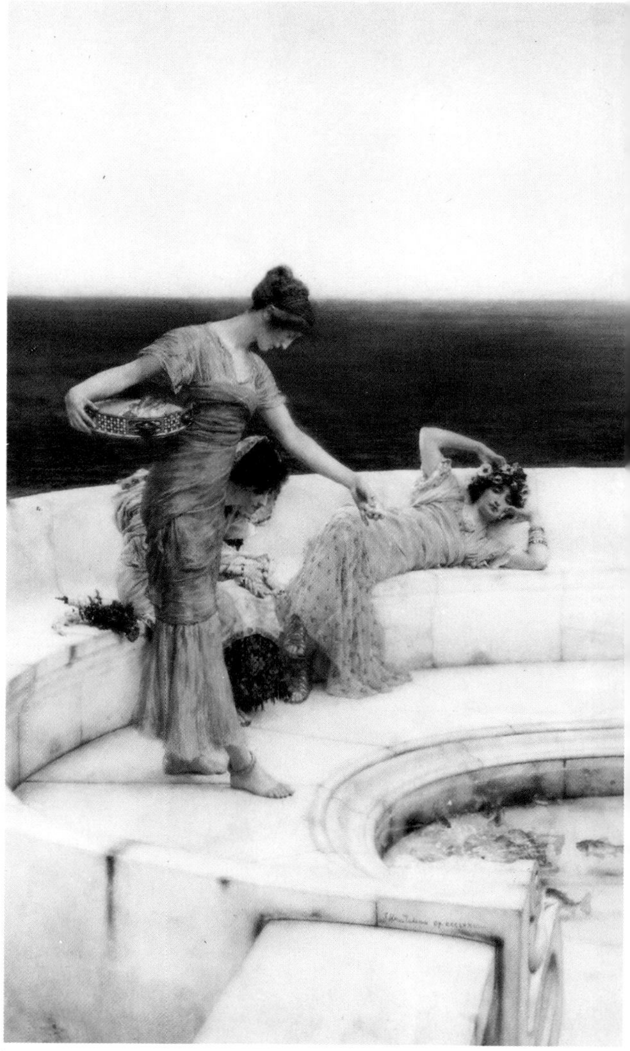

709. Lawrence Alma-Tadema. *Silver Favorites.* 1903. Oil on panel

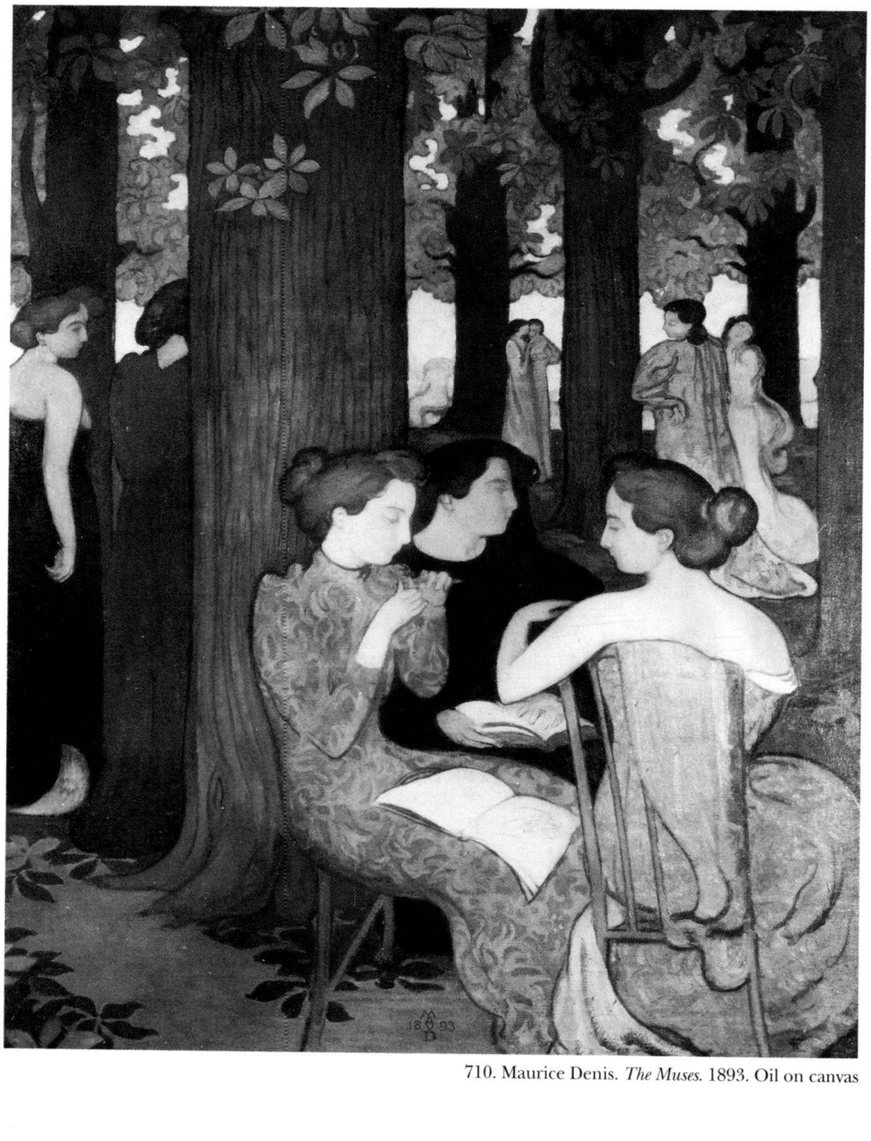

710. Maurice Denis. *The Muses.* 1893. Oil on canvas

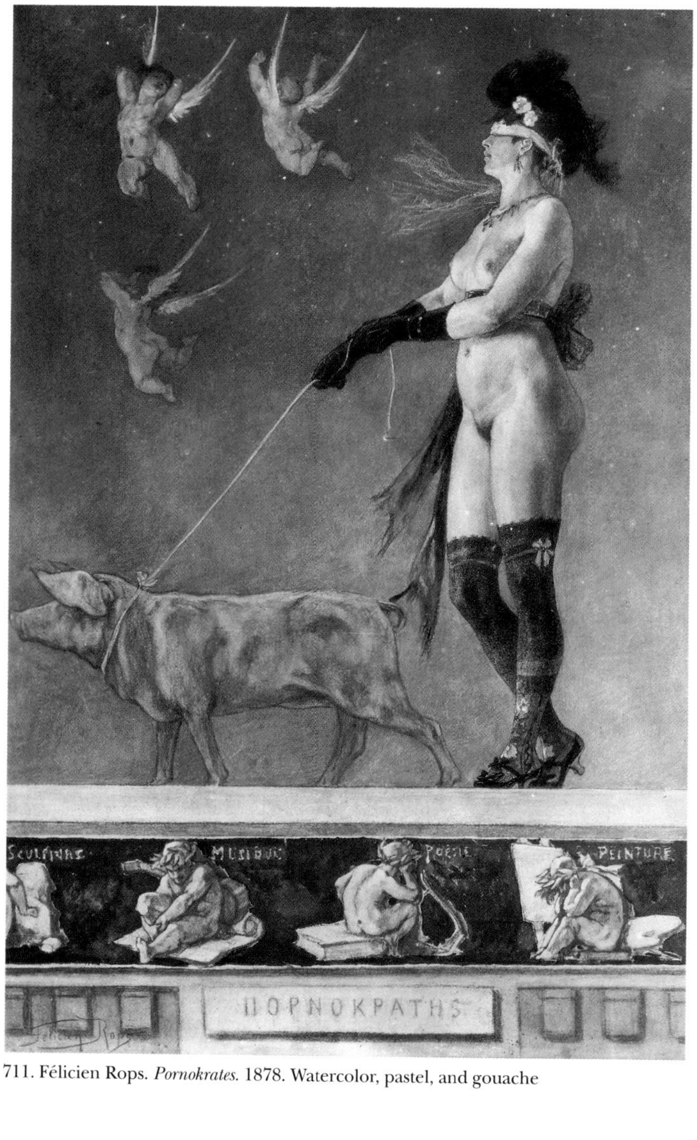

711. Félicien Rops. *Pornokrates.* 1878. Watercolor, pastel, and gouache

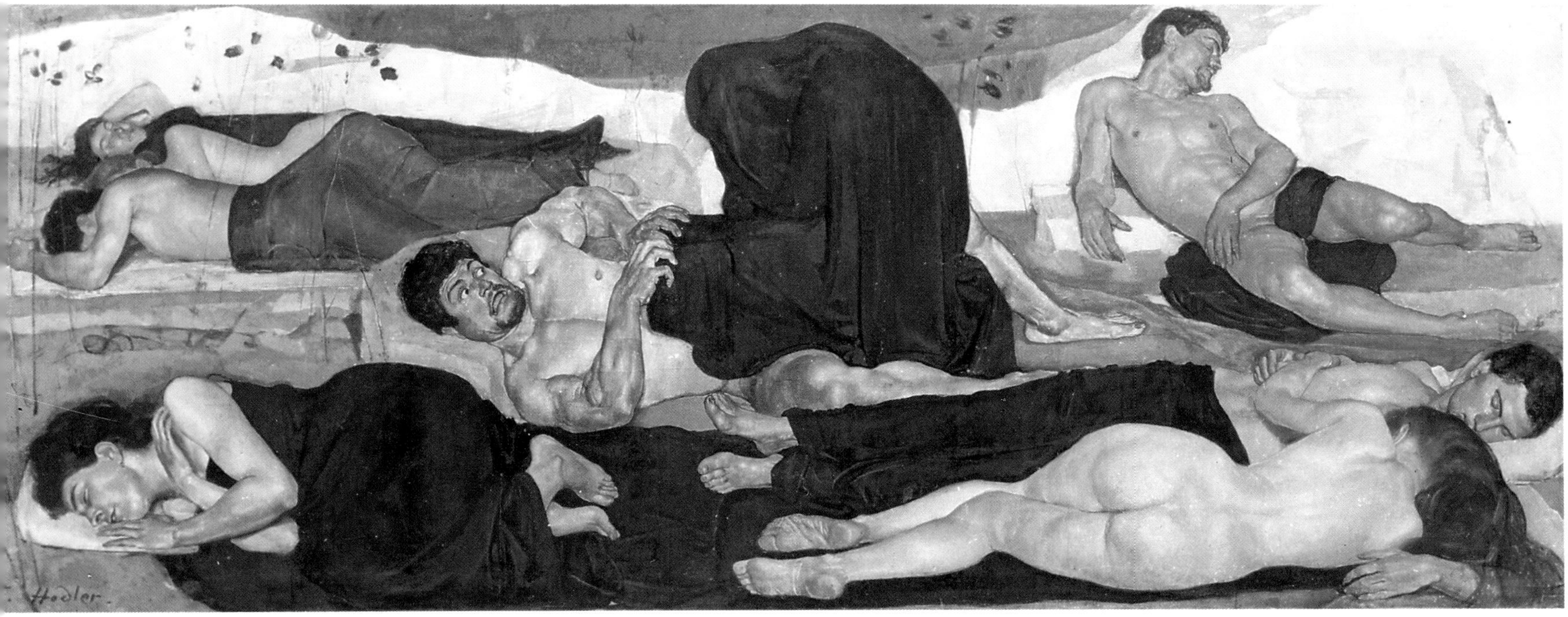

712. Ferdinand Hodler. *Night.* 1890. Oil on canvas

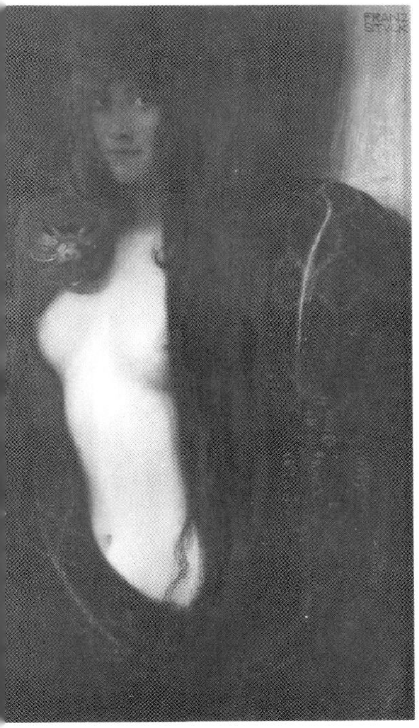

713. Franz von Stück. *Sin.* 1893. Oil on canvas

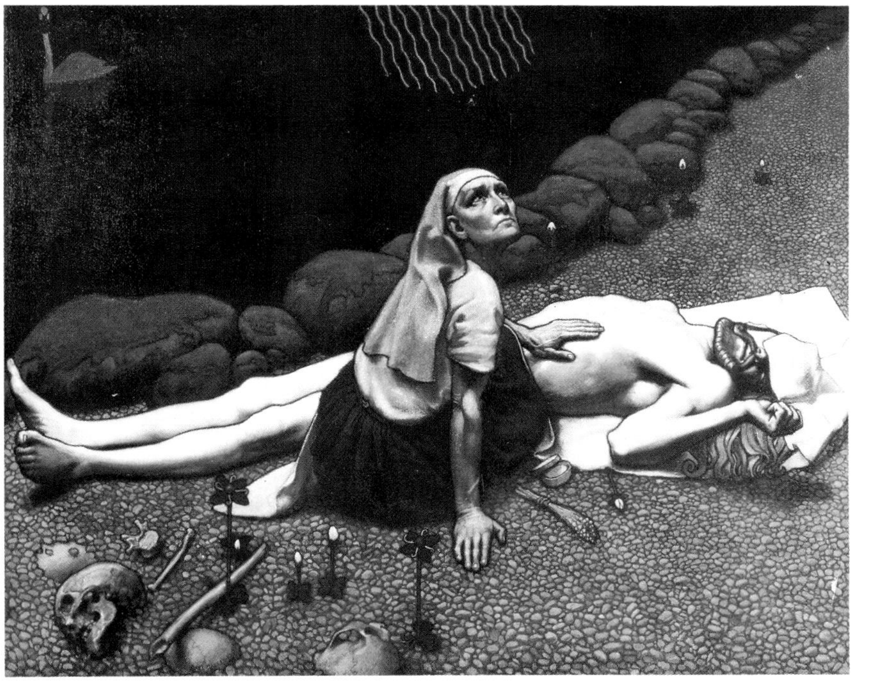

714. Akseli Gallén-Kallela. *Lemminkäinen's Mother.* 1897. Tempera

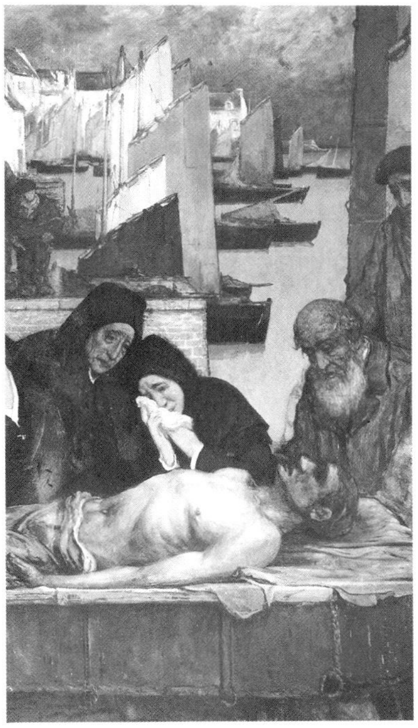

715. Charles Cottet. *Grief Beside the Sea* (detail). 1908. Oil on canvas

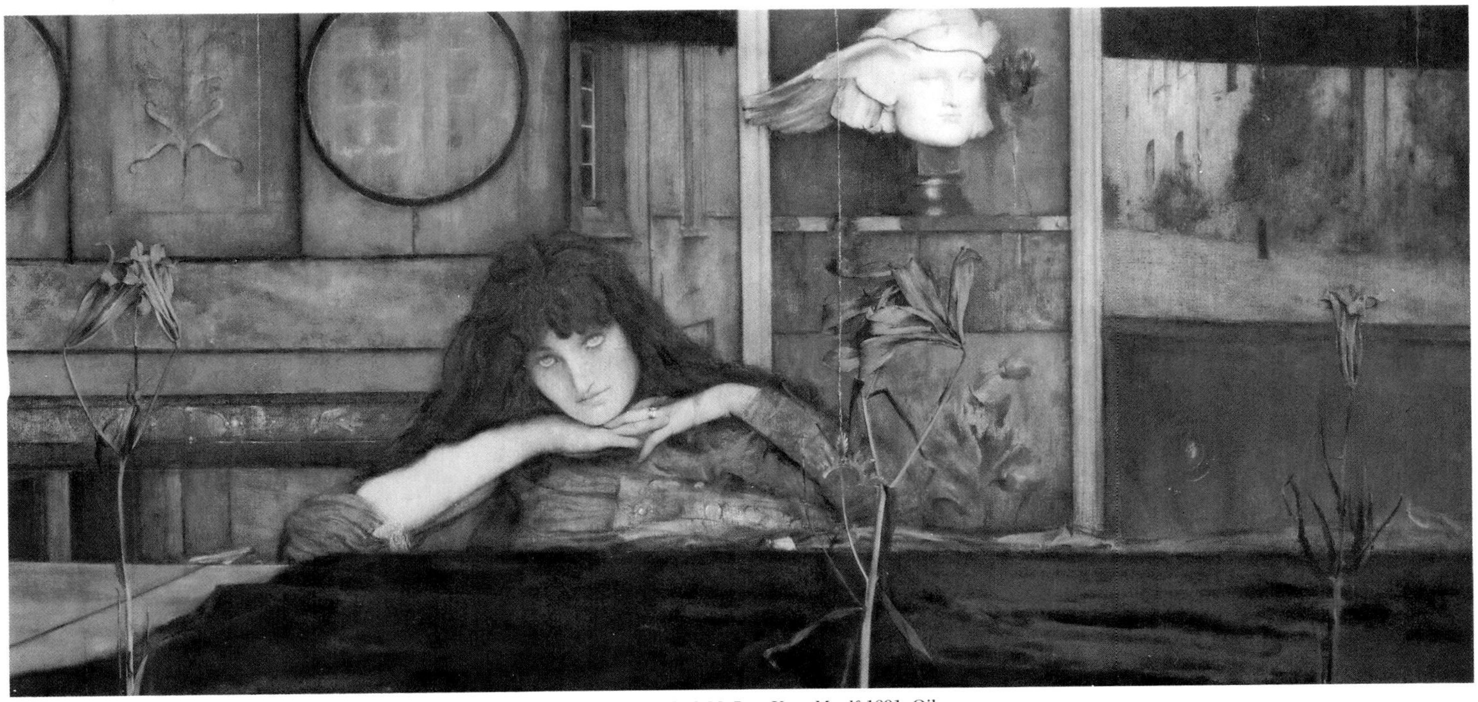

716. Fernand Khnopff. *I Lock My Door Upon Myself.* 1891. Oil on canvas

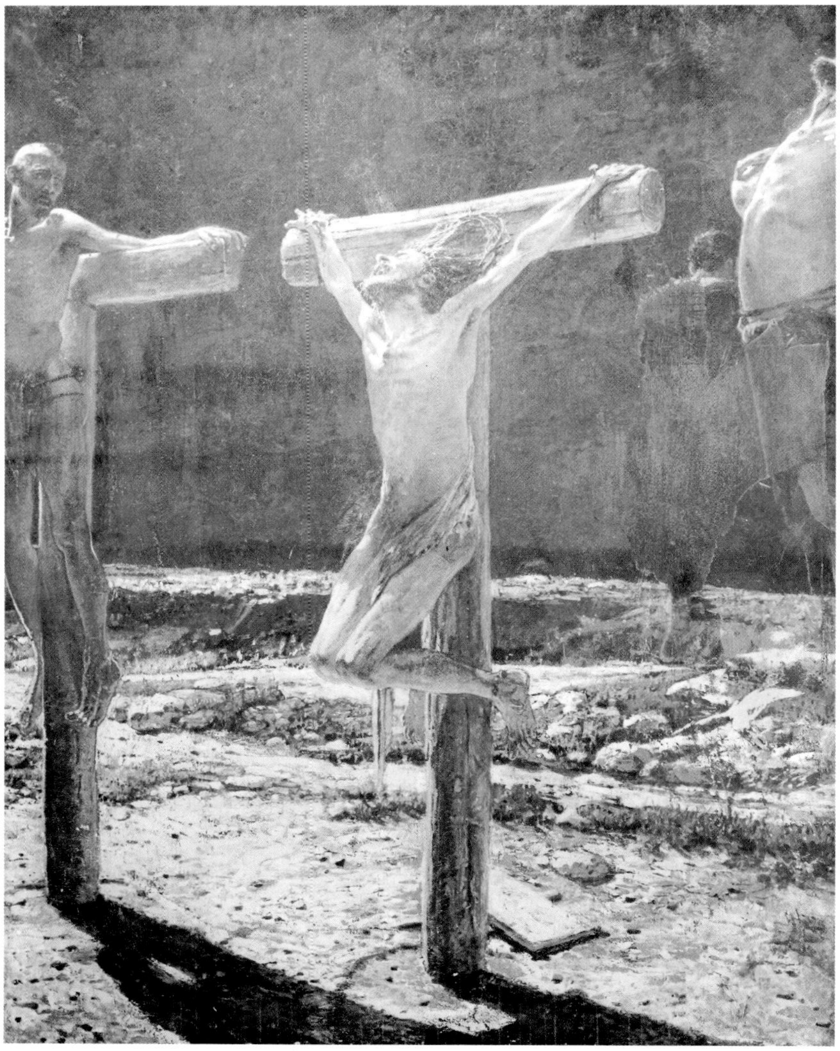

717. Nicolas Gay. *Calvary*, also known as *Golgotha*. 1892. Oil on canvas

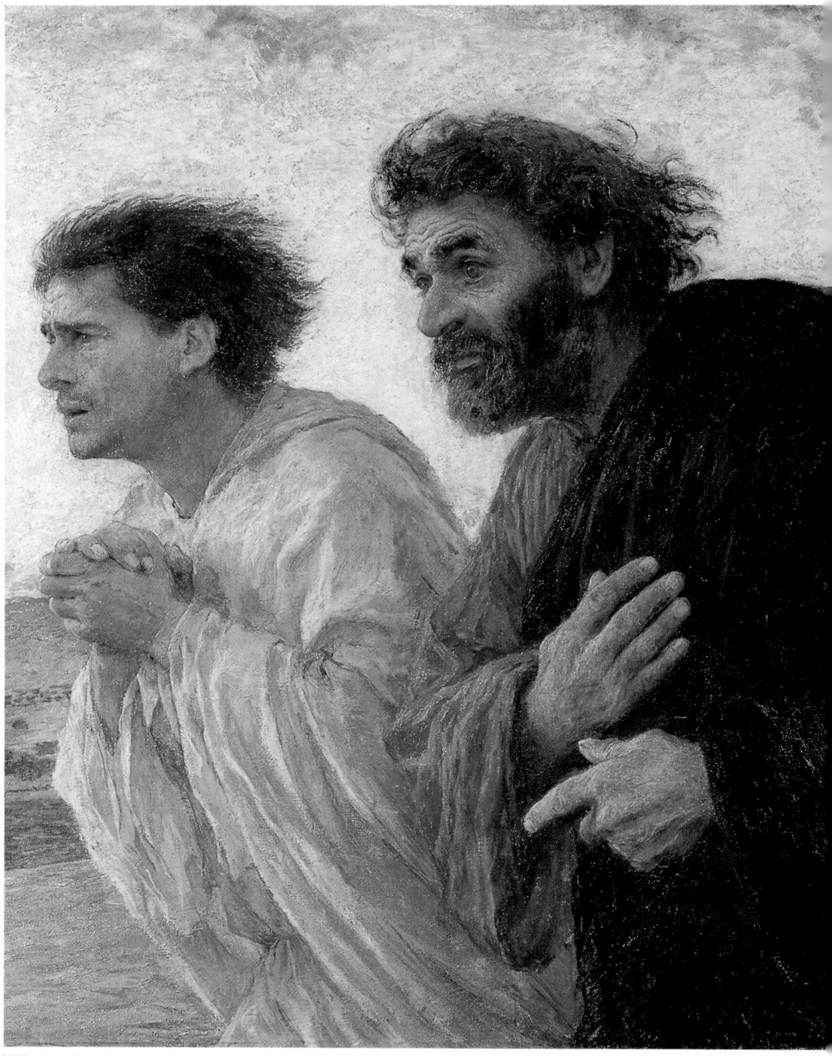

718. Eugène Burnand. *The Disciples Peter and John Running to the Tomb on the Morning of the Resurrection* (detail). 1898. Oil on canvas

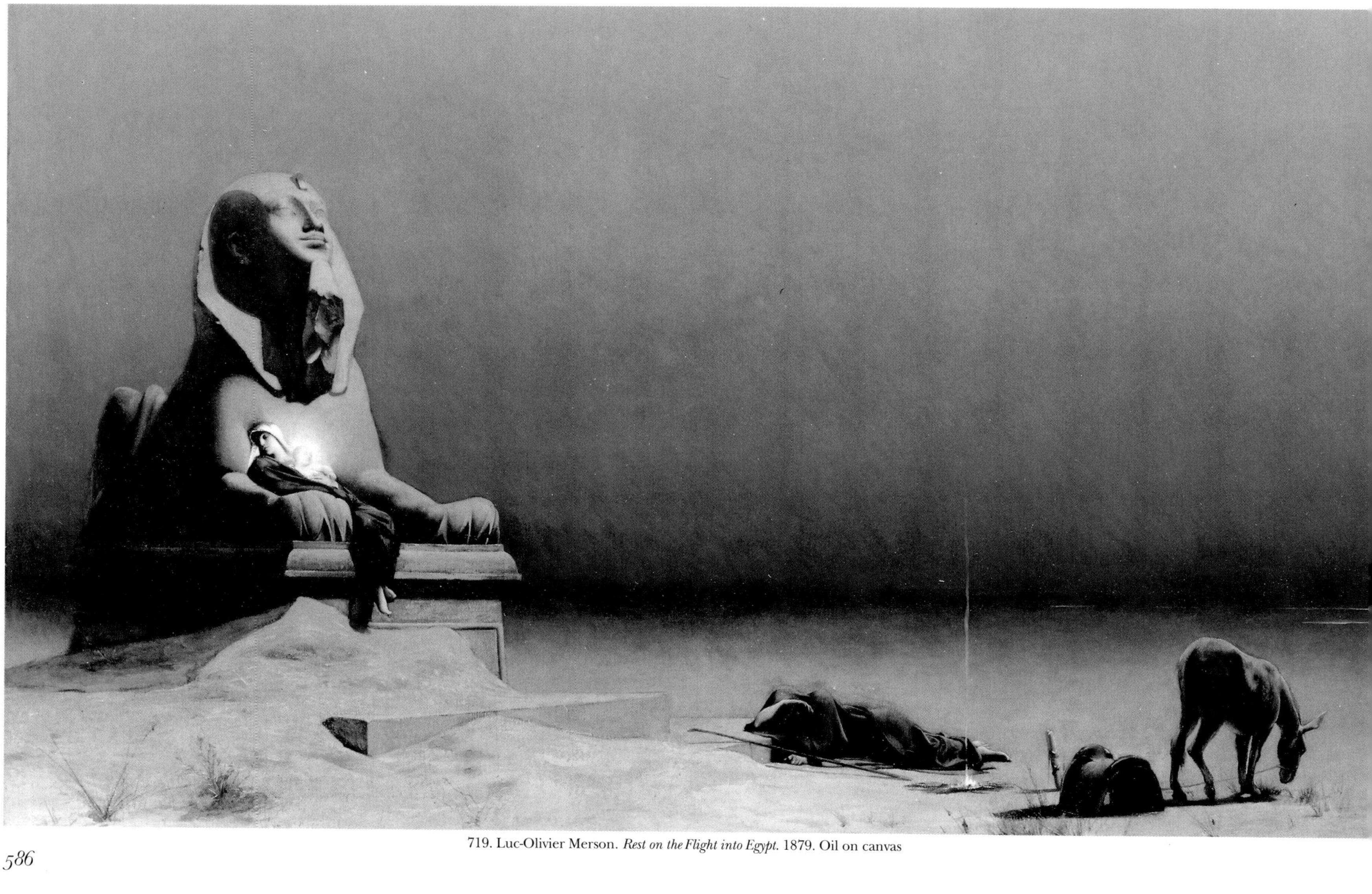

719. Luc-Olivier Merson. *Rest on the Flight into Egypt*. 1879. Oil on canvas

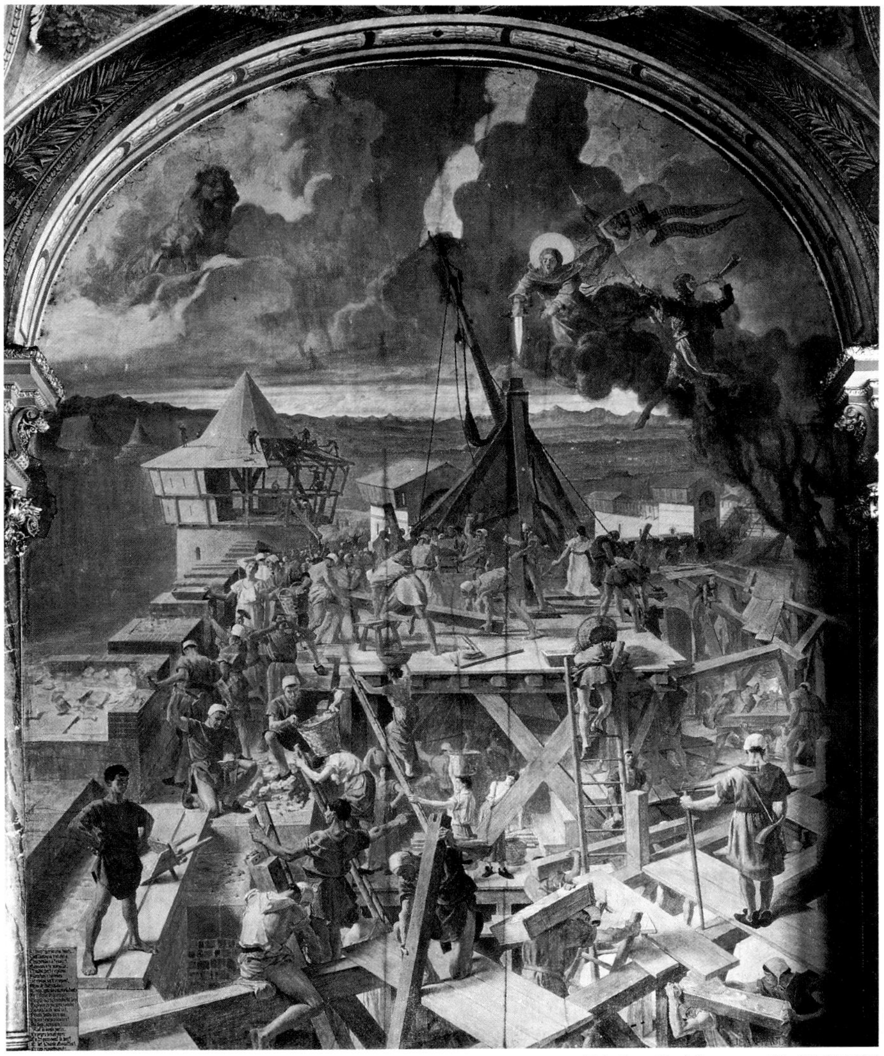

720. Jean-Paul Laurens. *The Wall.* 1895

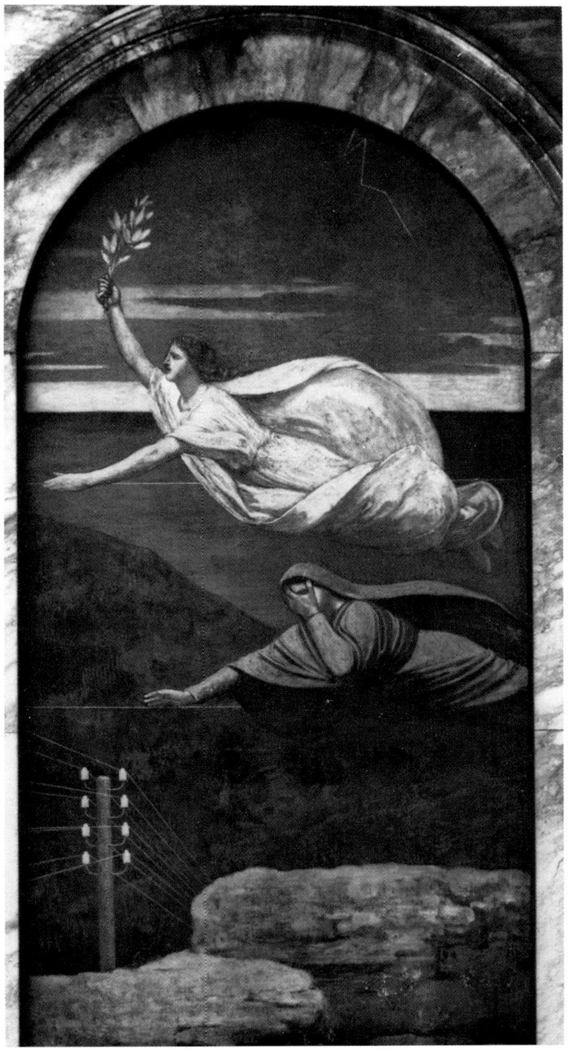

721. Pierre Puvis de Chavannes. *Physics.* 1896

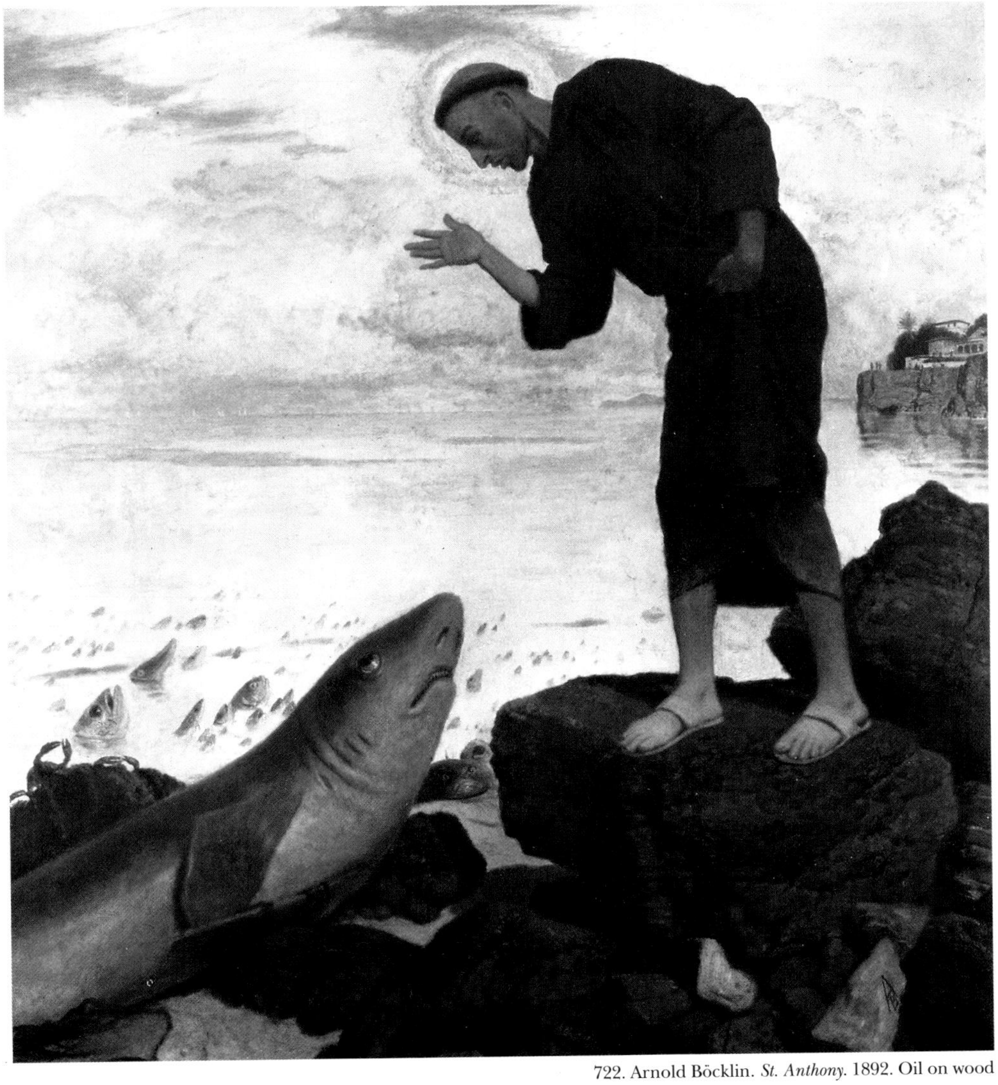

722. Arnold Böcklin. *St. Anthony.* 1892. Oil on wood

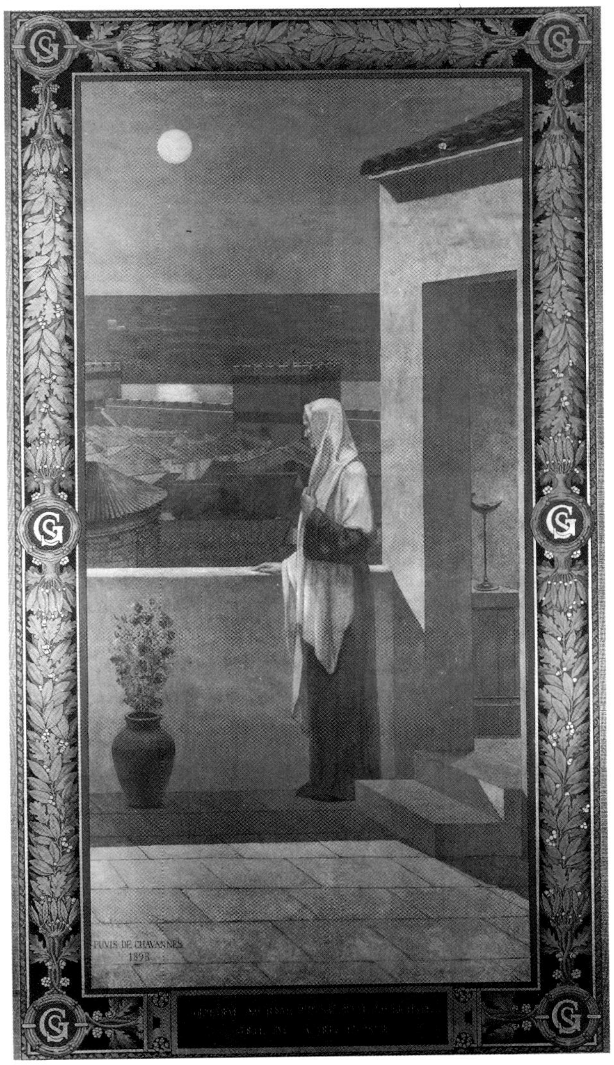

723. Pierre Puvis de Chavannes. *St. Geneviève Watching over the Sleeping Paris.* 1897. Panthéon, Paris

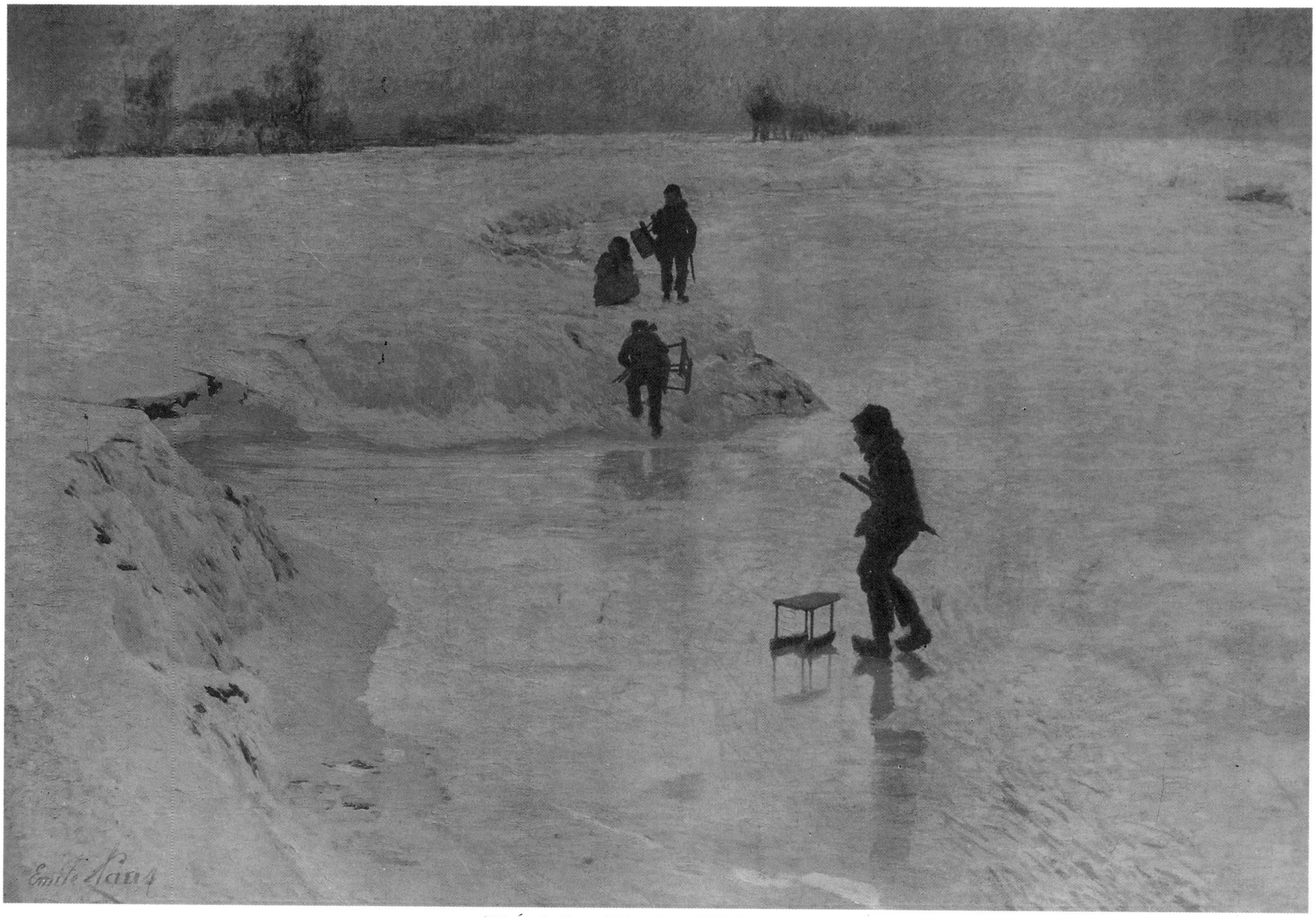

724. Émile Claus. *Halcyon Days.* 1892. Oil on canvas

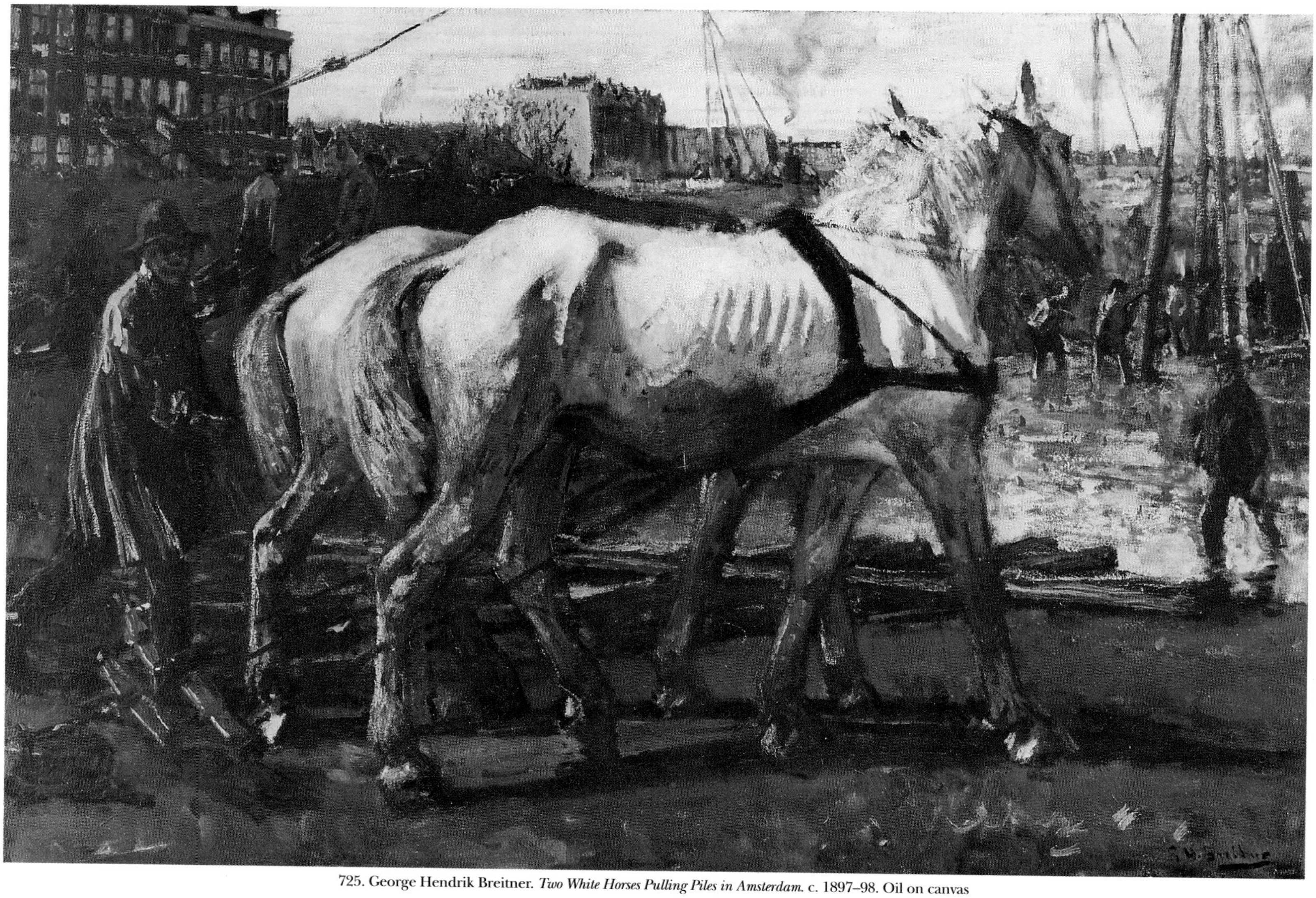

725. George Hendrik Breitner. *Two White Horses Pulling Piles in Amsterdam.* c. 1897–98. Oil on canvas

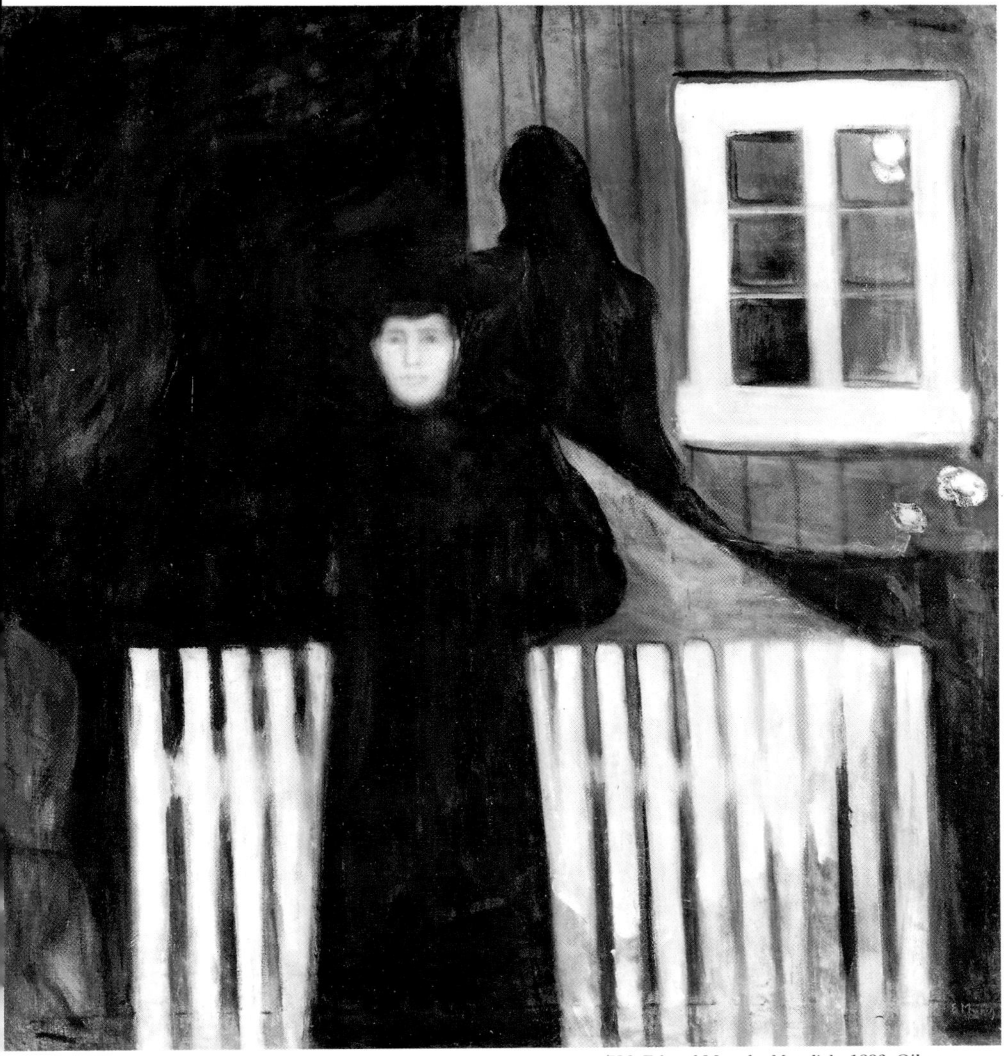

726. Edvard Munch. *Moonlight.* 1893. Oil on canvas

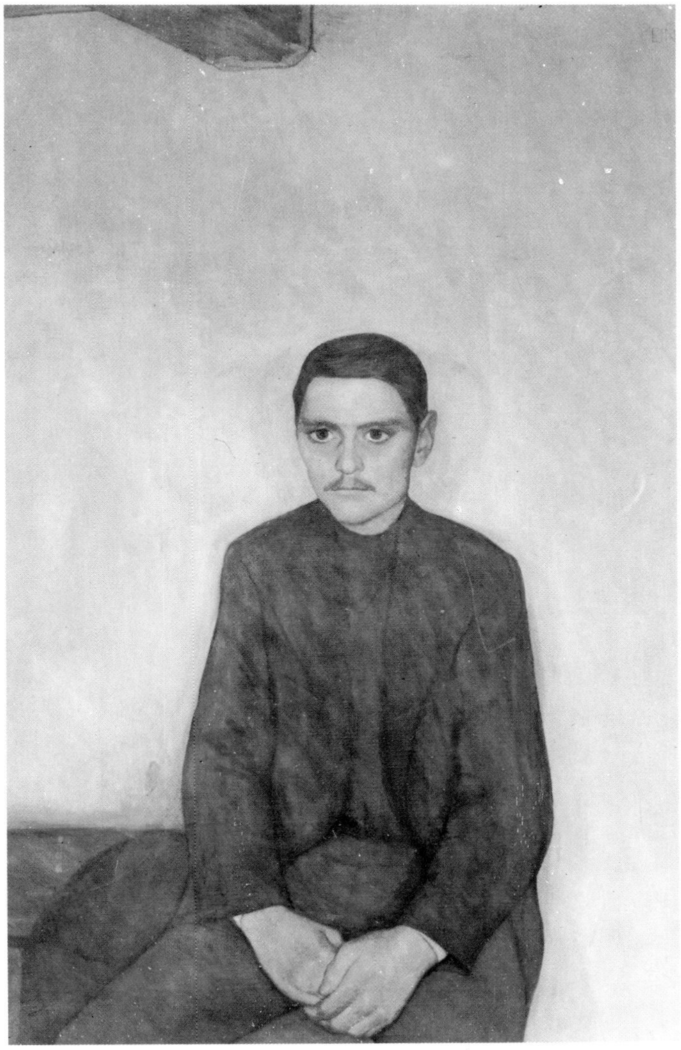

727. Ejnar Nielsen. *And In His Eyes I Saw Death* (detail). 1897. Oil on canvas

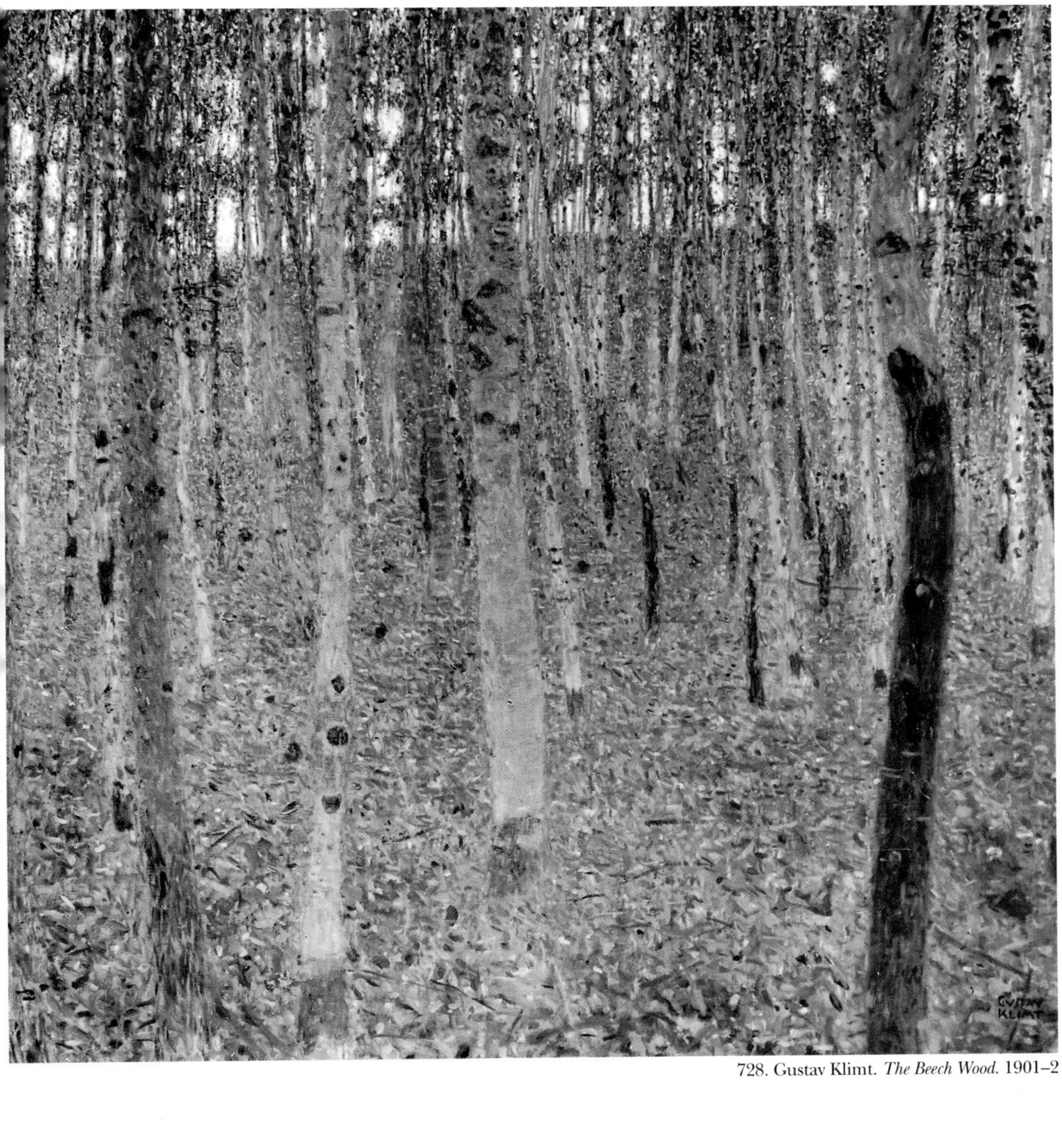

728. Gustav Klimt. *The Beech Wood.* 1901–2

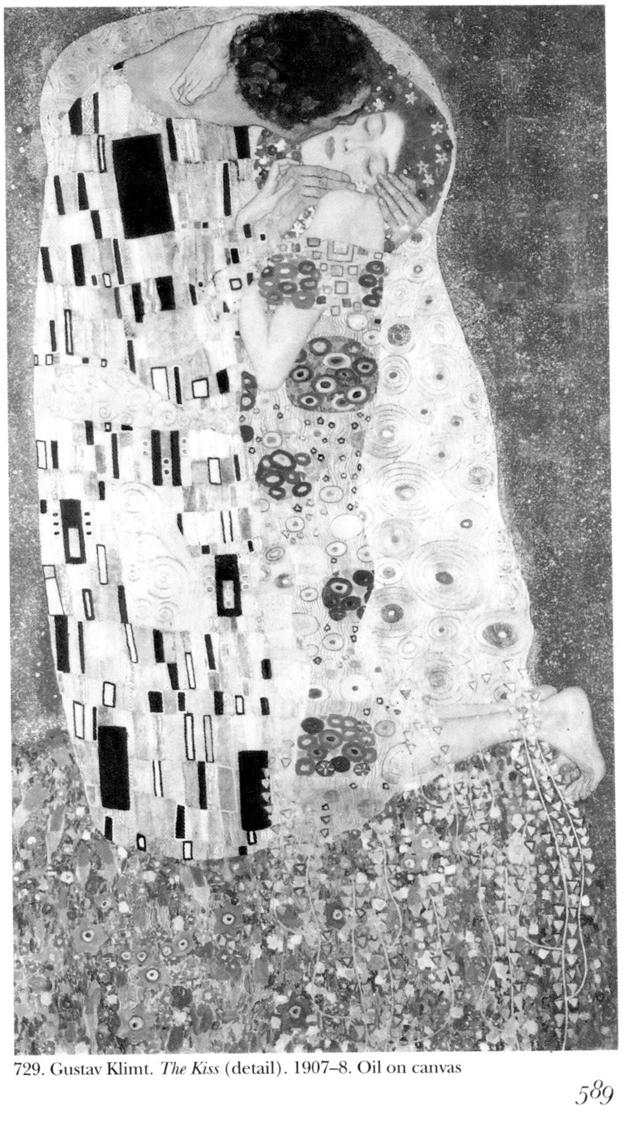

729. Gustav Klimt. *The Kiss* (detail). 1907–8. Oil on canvas

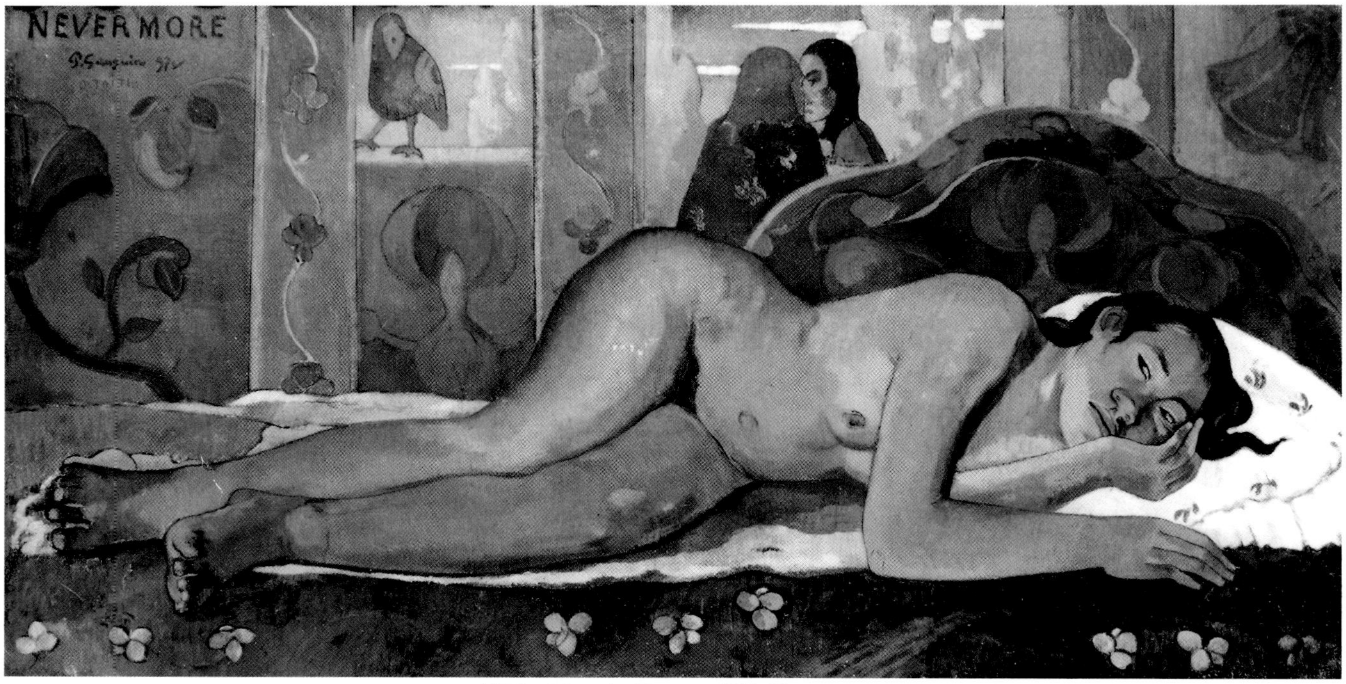

730. Paul Gauguin. *Nevermore.* 1897. Oil on canvas

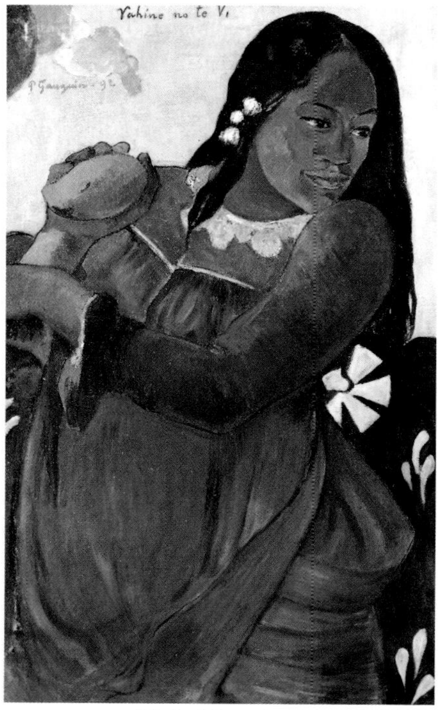

731. Paul Gauguin. *Woman with Mango.* 1892. Oil on canvas

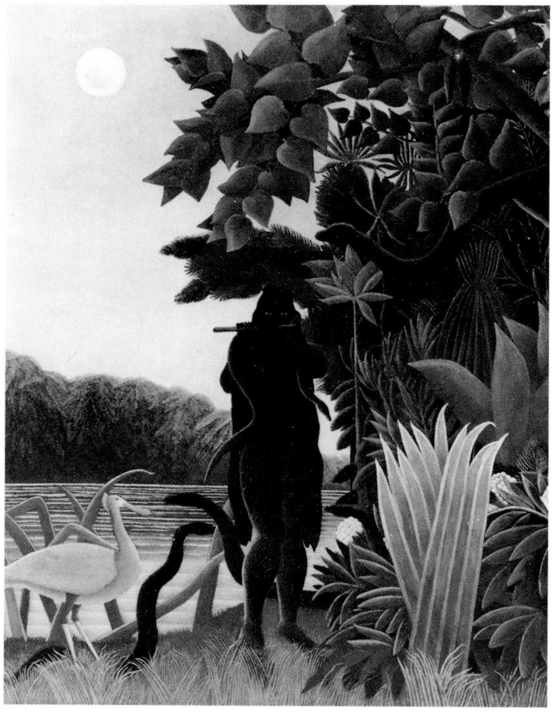

732. Henri Rousseau. *The Snake Charmer.* 1907. Oil on canvas

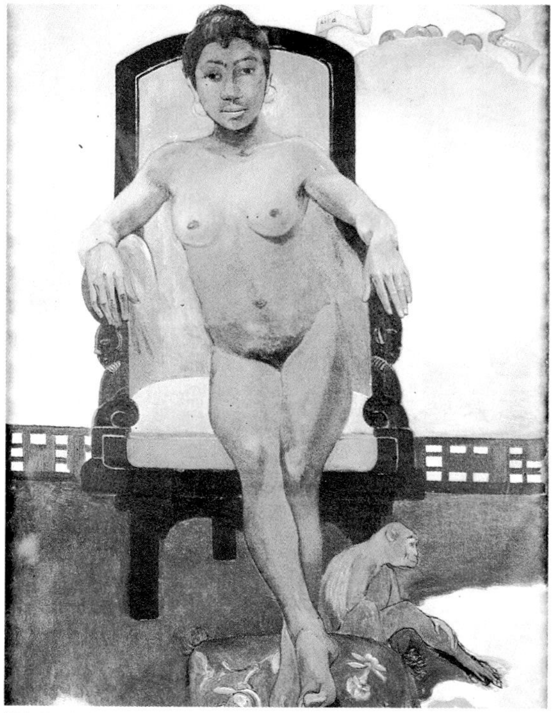

733. Paul Gauguin. *Anna, the Javanese.* 1893. Oil on canvas

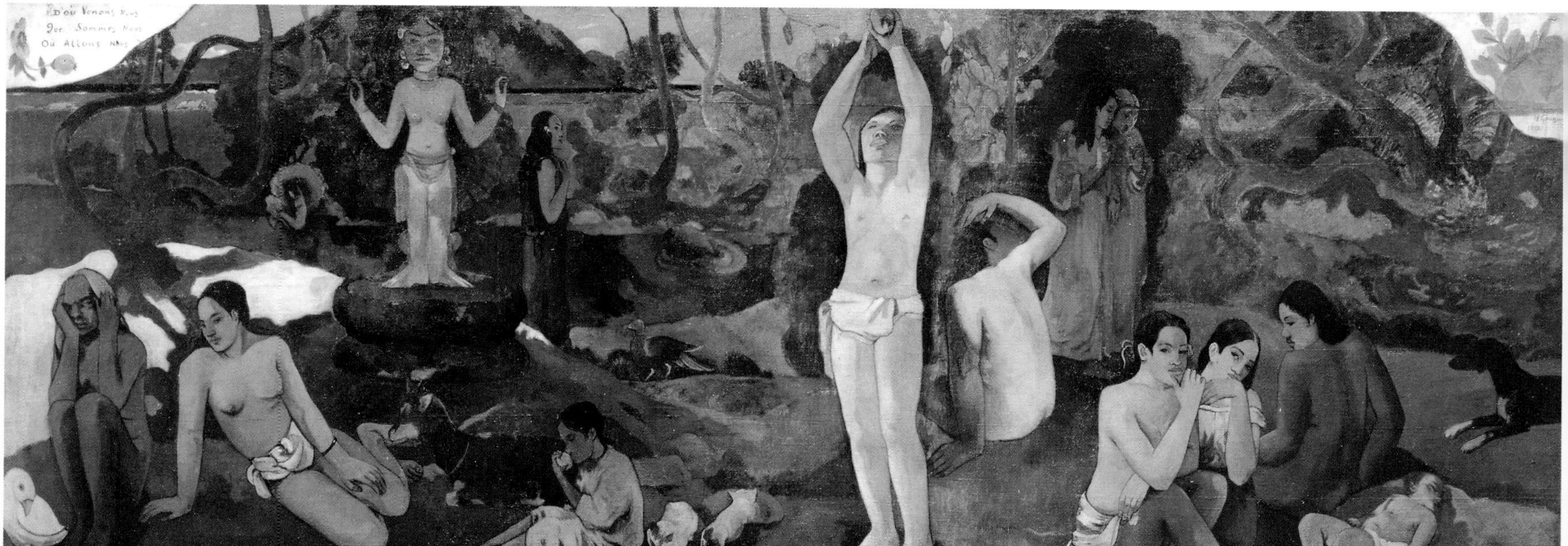

734. Paul Gauguin. *Where Do We Come From? What Are We? Where Are We Going?* 1897. Oil on canvas

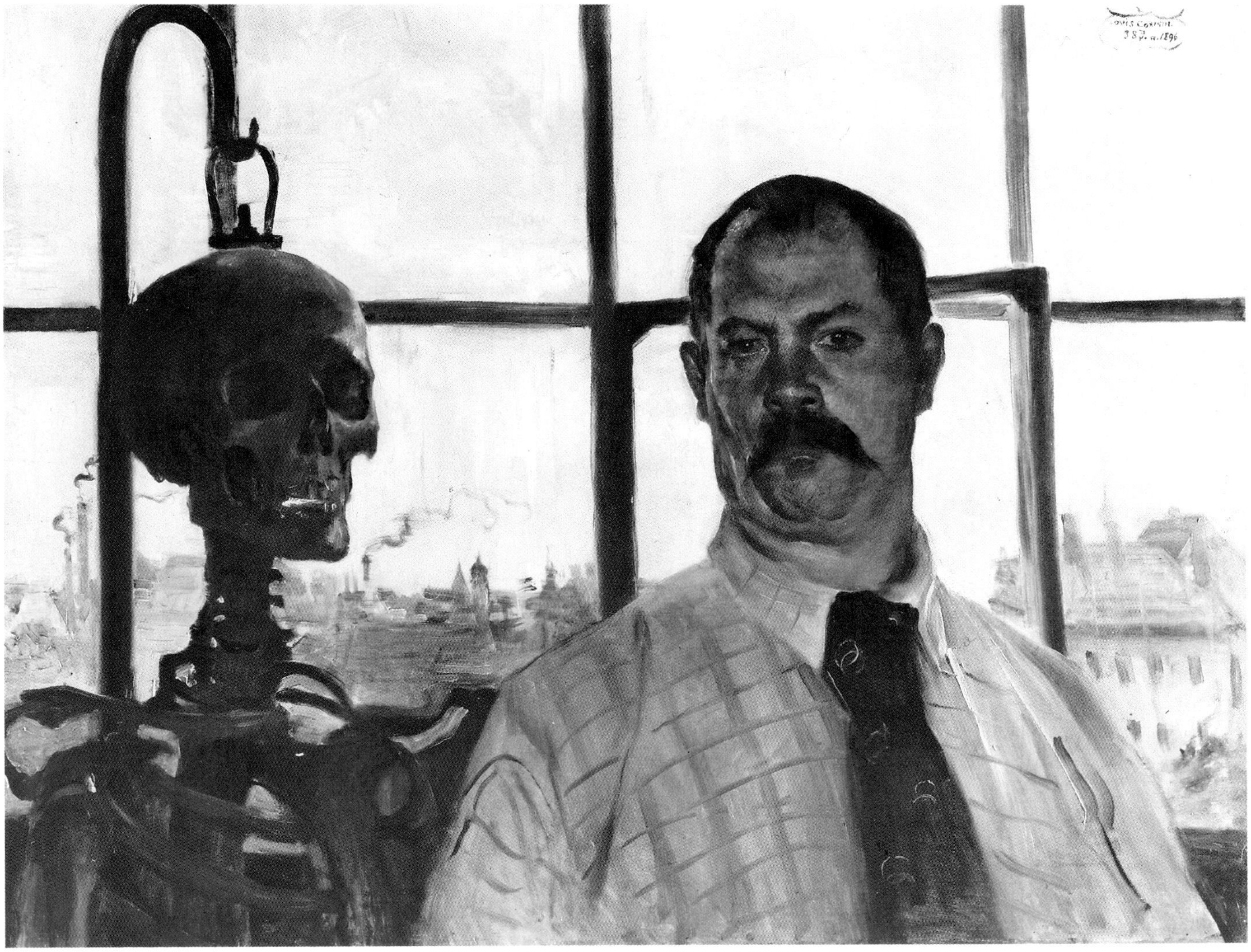

735. Lovis Corinth. *Self-Portrait with Skeleton.* 1896. Oil on canvas

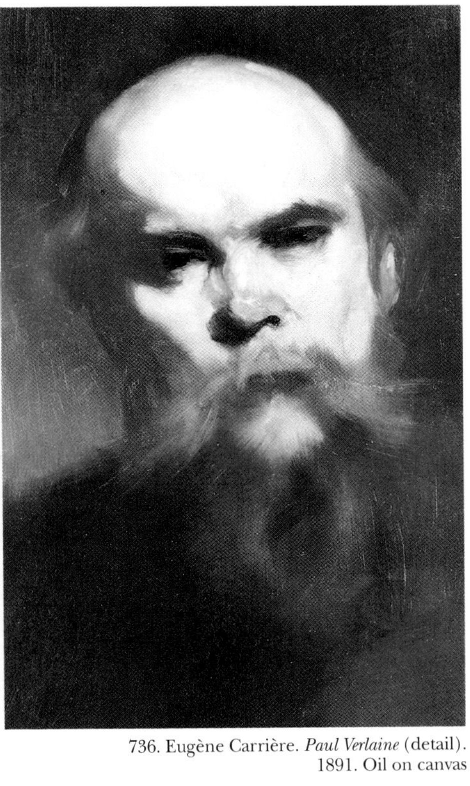

736. Eugène Carrière. *Paul Verlaine* (detail). 1891. Oil on canvas

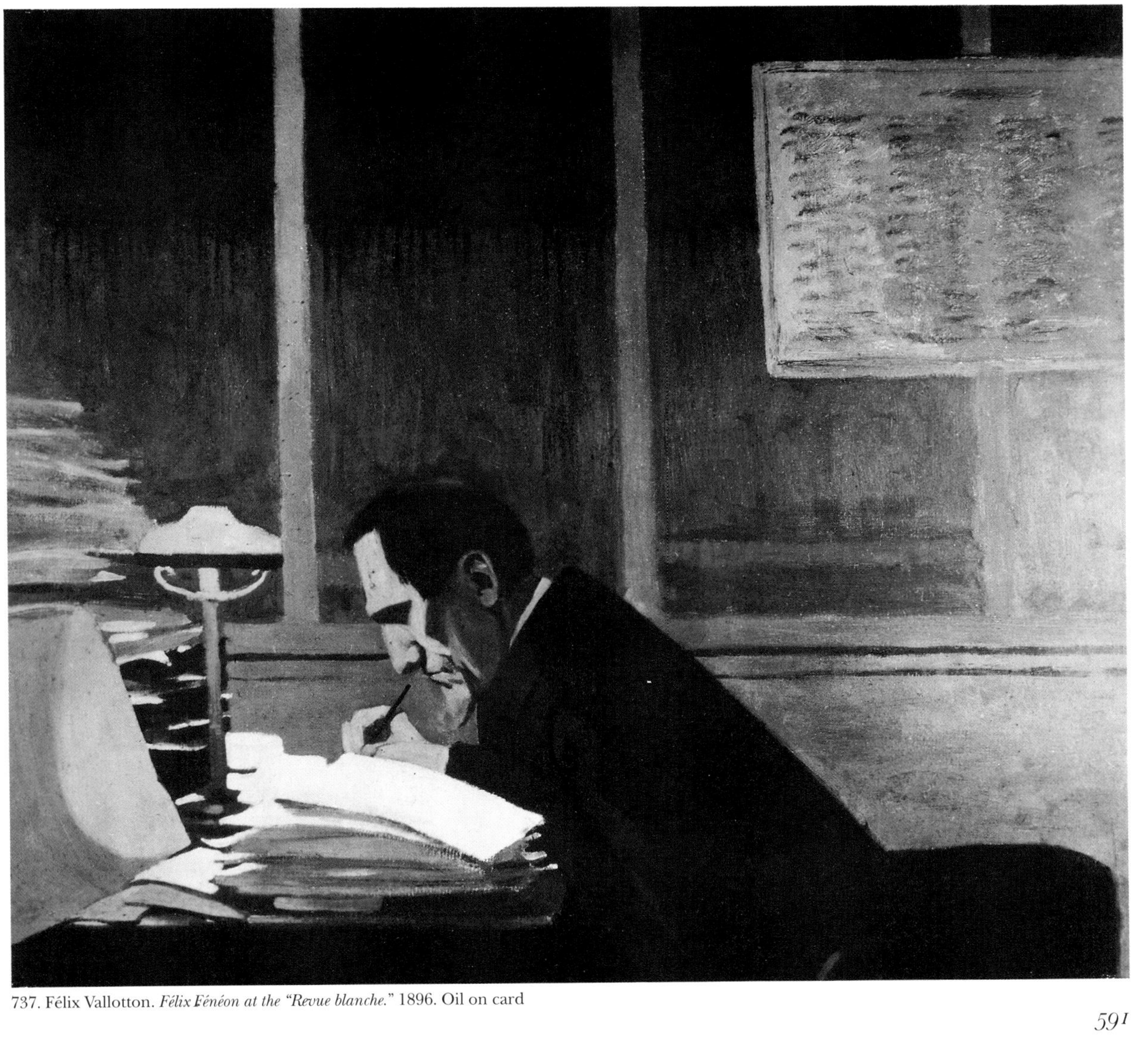

737. Félix Vallotton. *Félix Fénéon at the "Revue blanche."* 1896. Oil on card

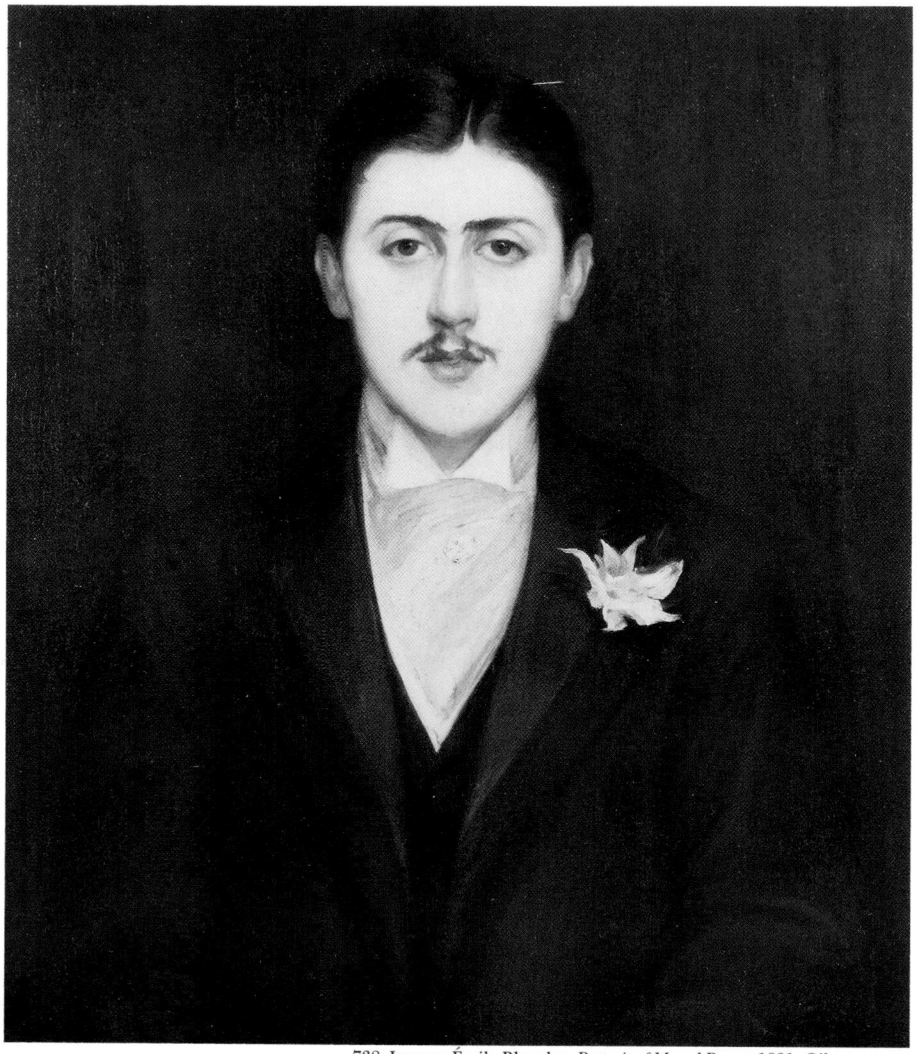

738. Jacques-Émile Blanche. *Portrait of Marcel Proust.* 1891. Oil on canvas

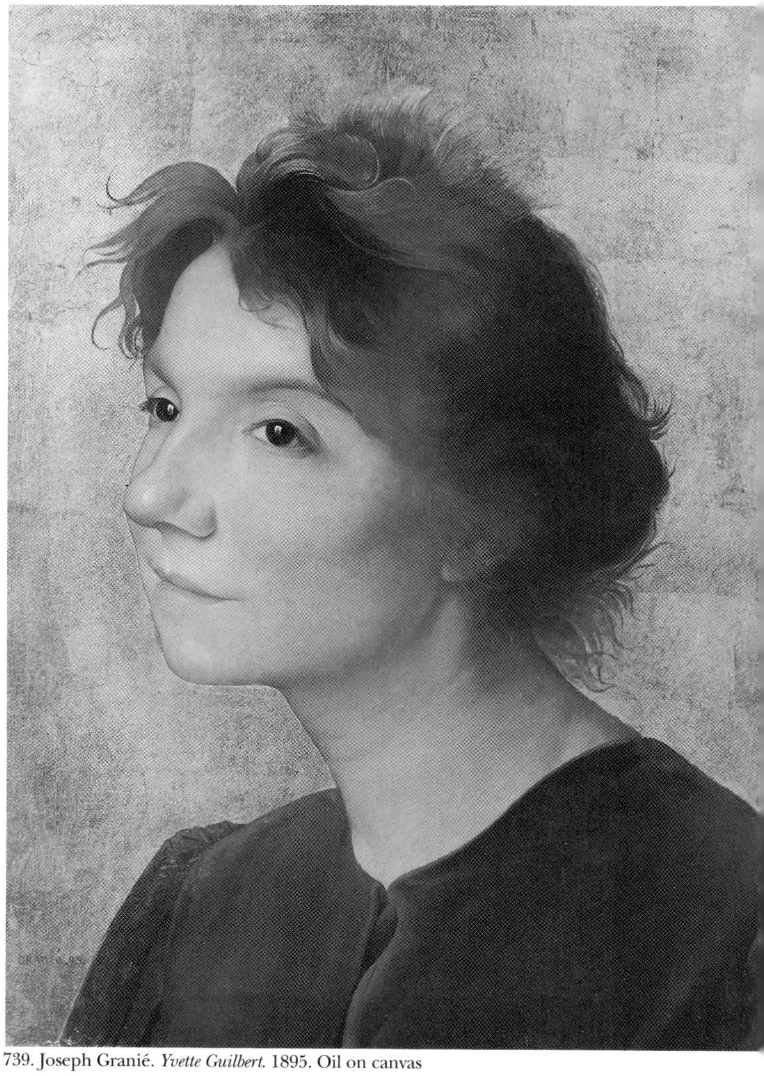

739. Joseph Granié. *Yvette Guilbert.* 1895. Oil on canvas

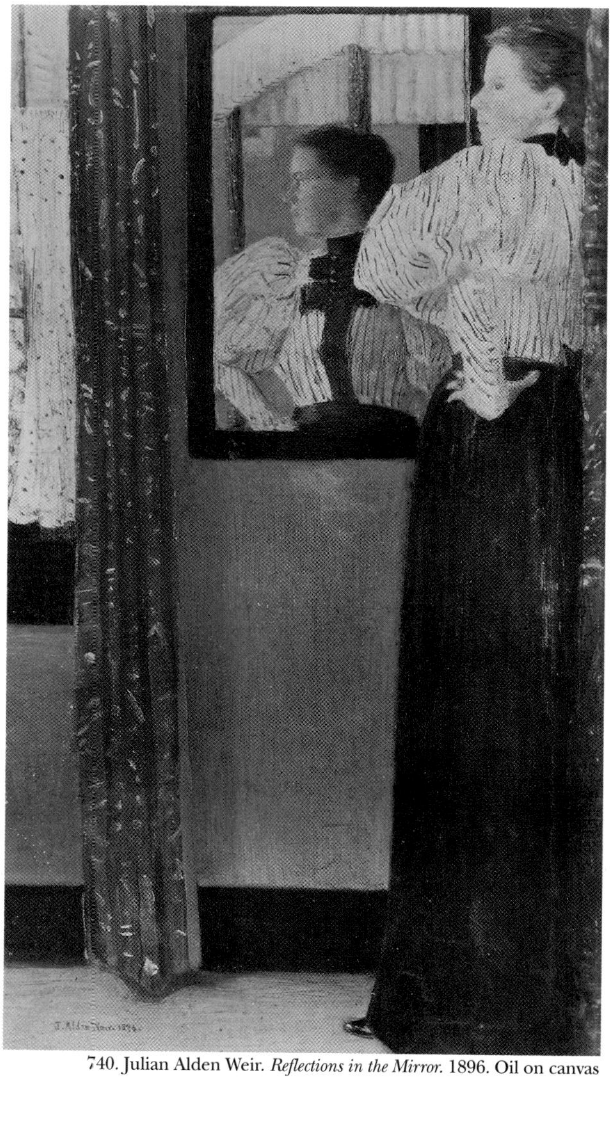

740. Julian Alden Weir. *Reflections in the Mirror.* 1896. Oil on canvas

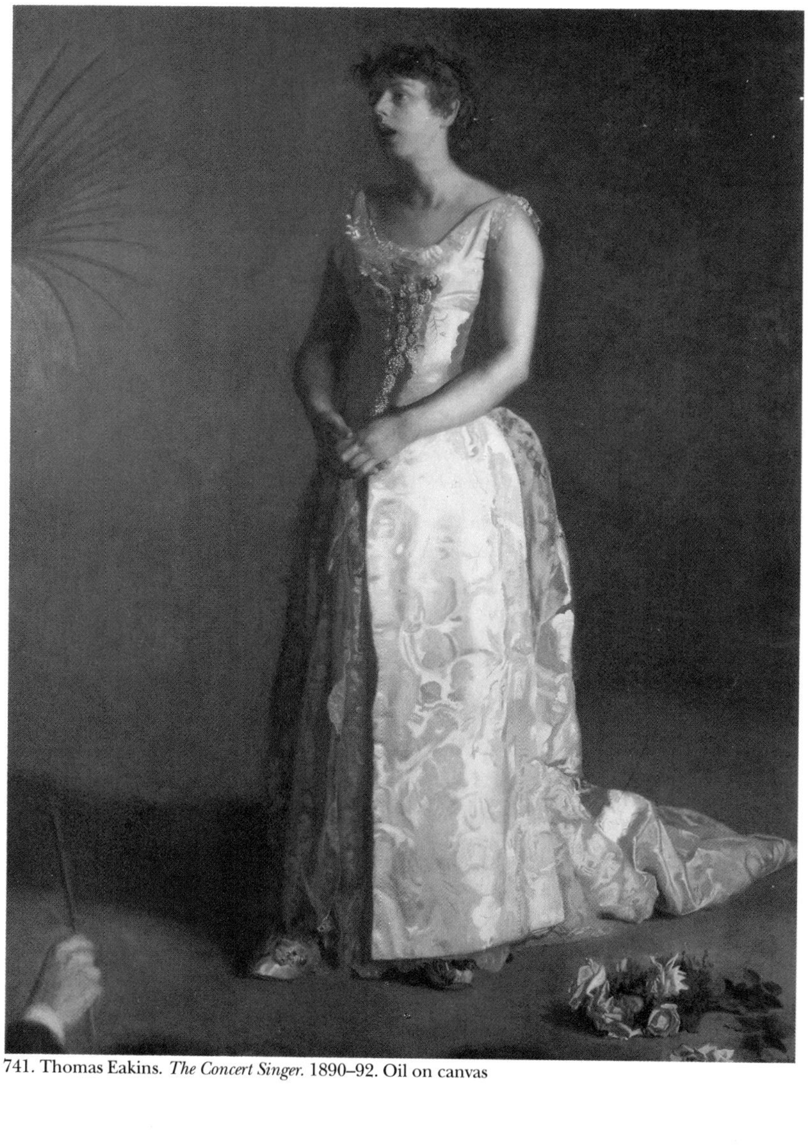

741. Thomas Eakins. *The Concert Singer.* 1890–92. Oil on canvas

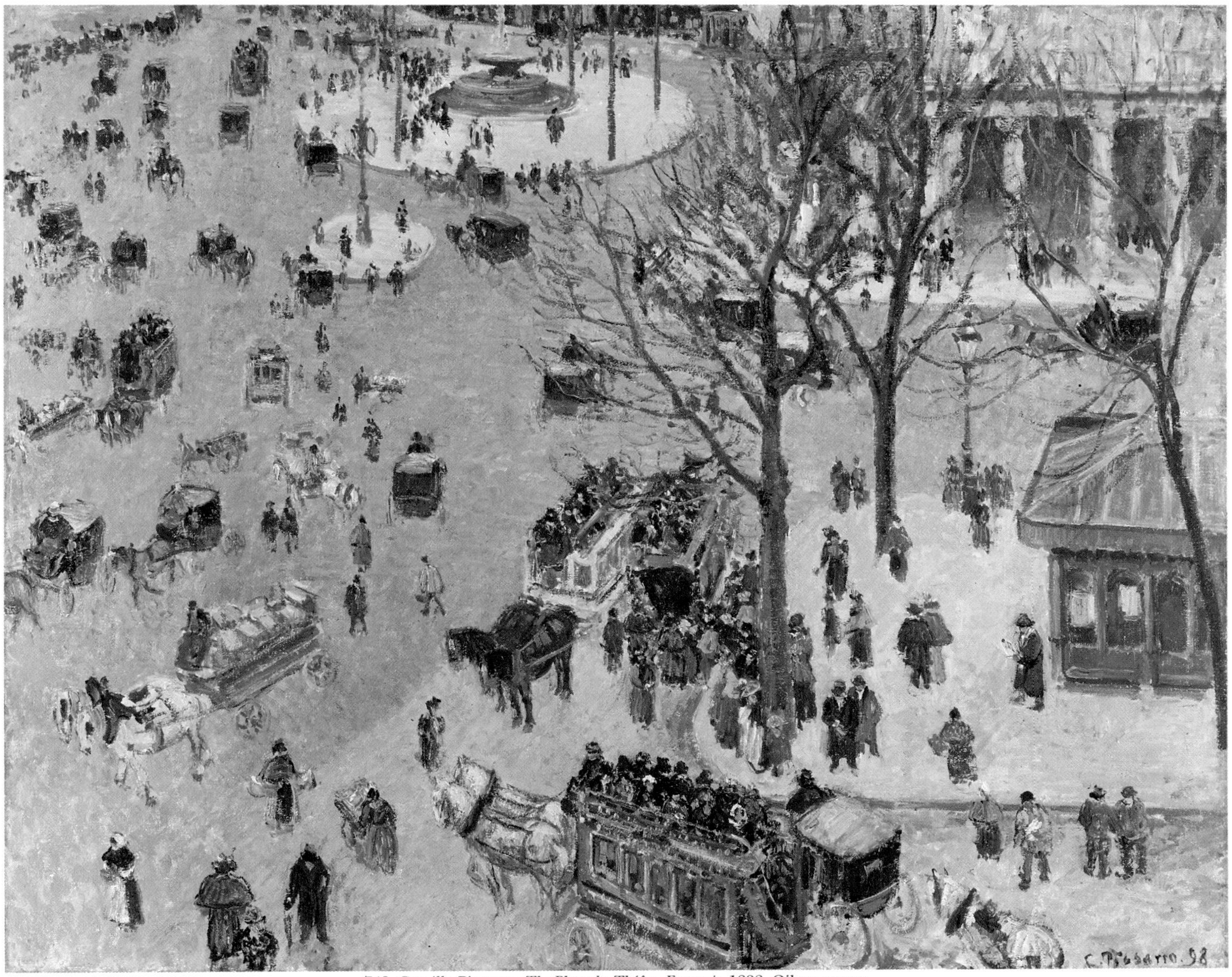

742. Camille Pissarro. *The Place du Théâtre Français.* 1898. Oil on canvas

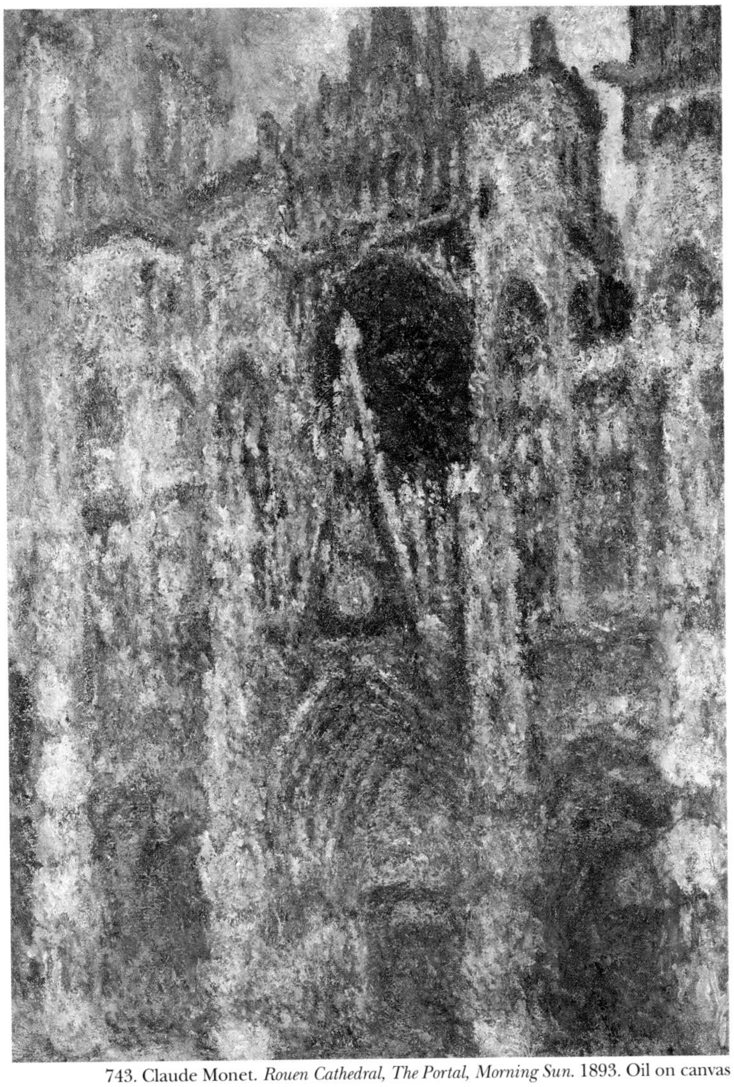

743. Claude Monet. *Rouen Cathedral, The Portal, Morning Sun.* 1893. Oil on canvas

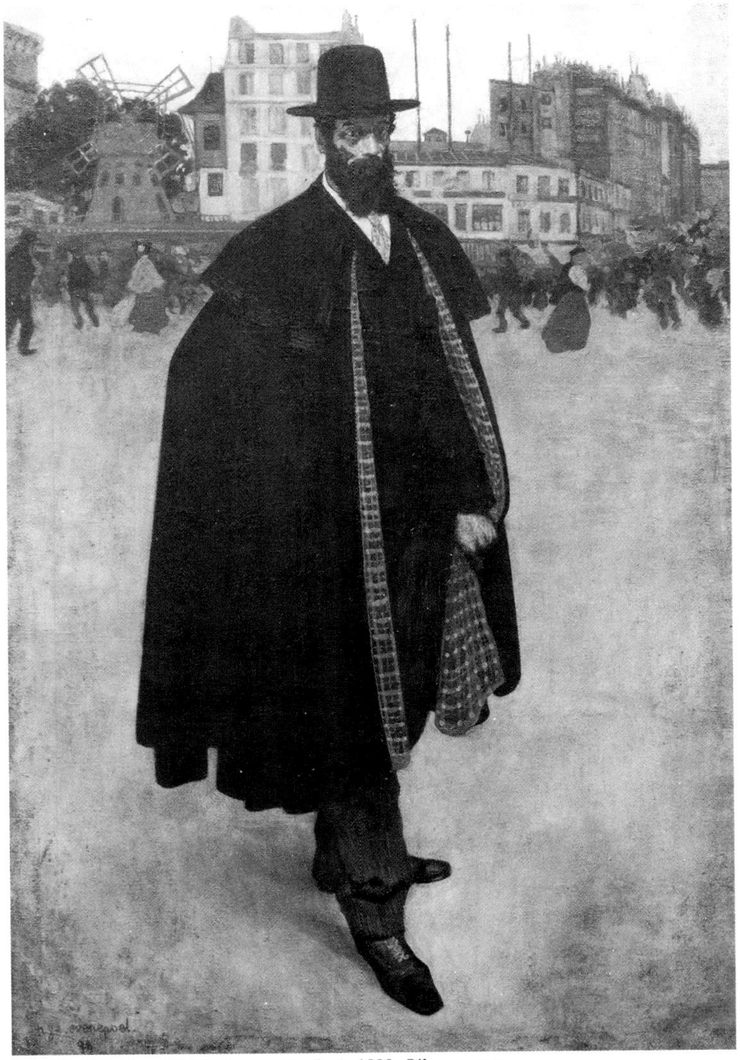

744. Henri Evenepoel. *The Spaniard in Paris.* 1899. Oil on canvas

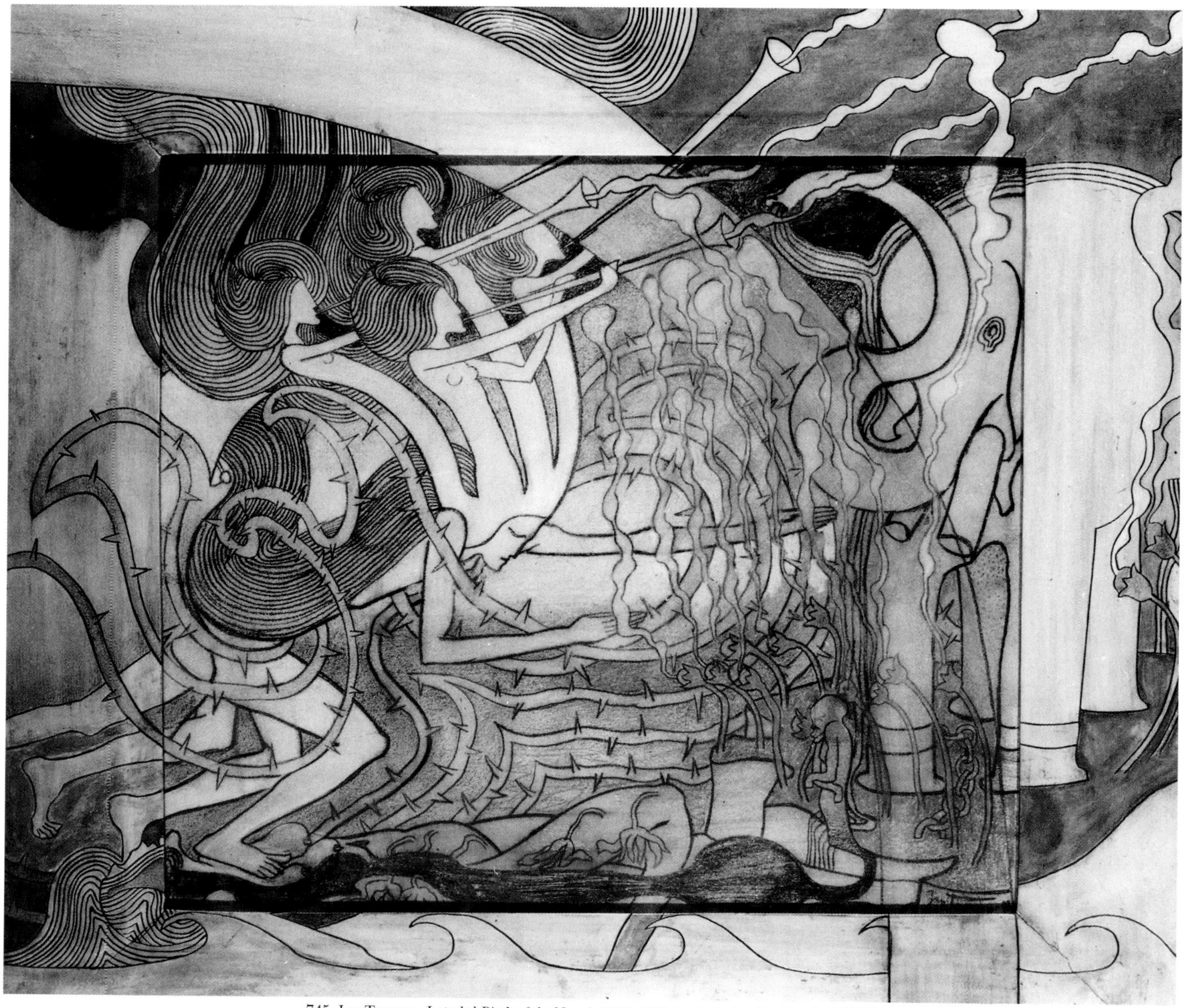

745. Jan Toorop. *Impeded Birth of the New Art (The Old Art Ousted by Modern Art)*. 1893. Black and colored chalks on paper

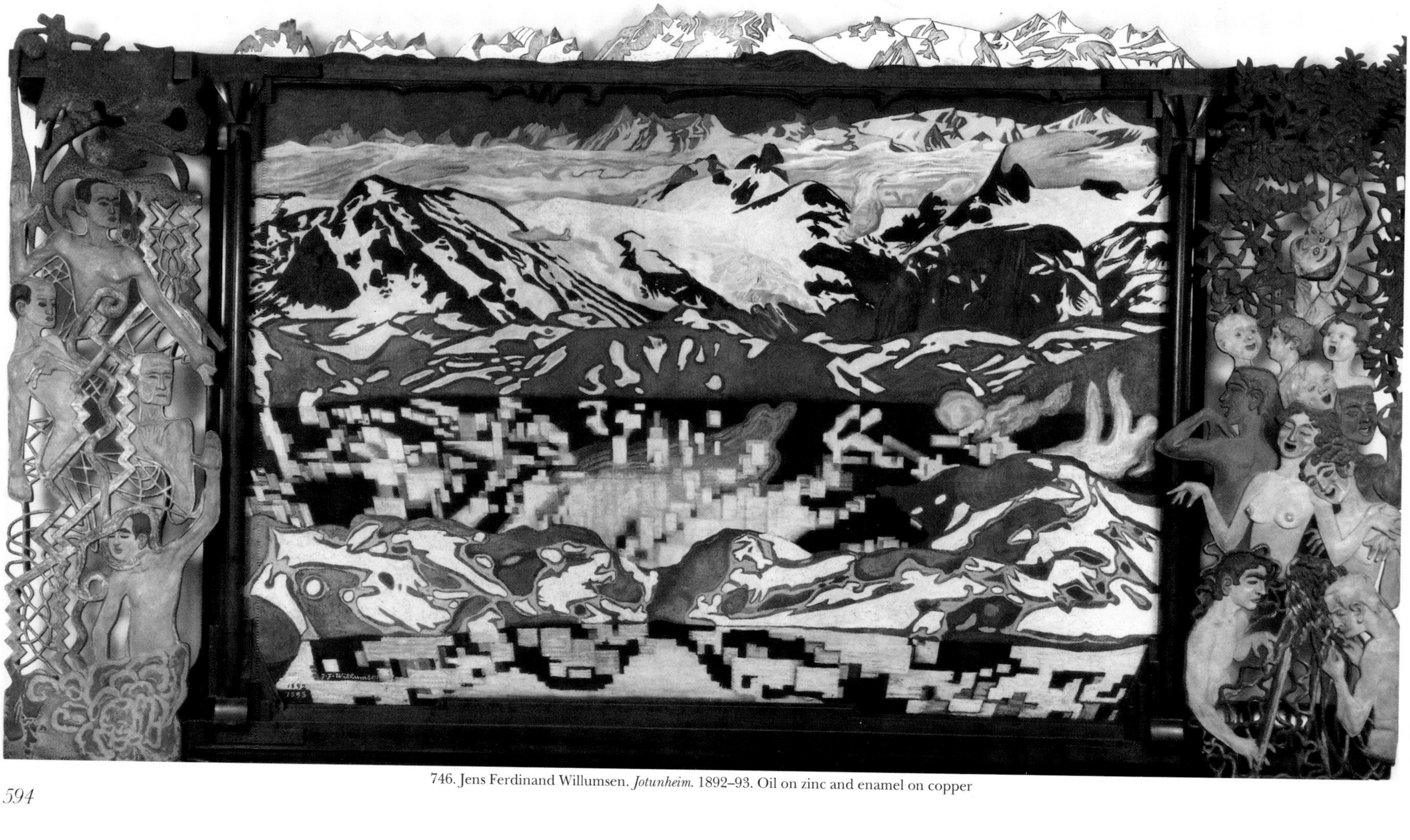

746. Jens Ferdinand Willumsen. *Jotunheim*. 1892–93. Oil on zinc and enamel on copper

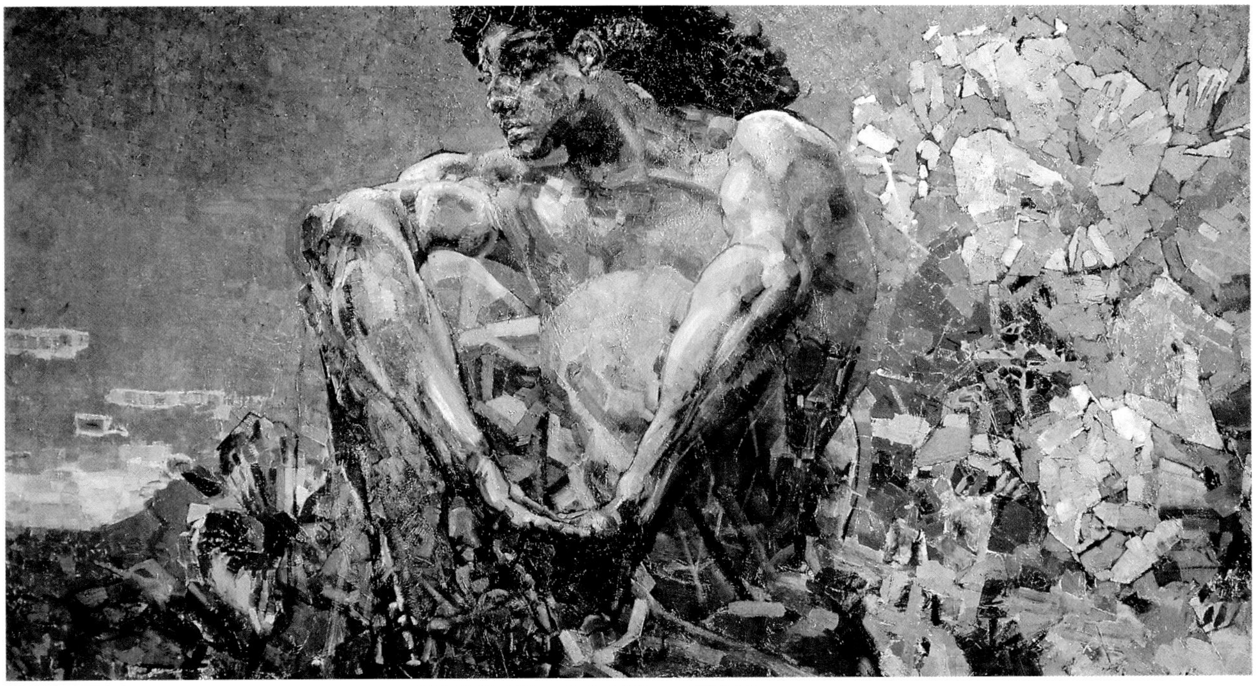

747. Mikhail Vrubel. *Seated Demon.* 1890. Oil on canvas

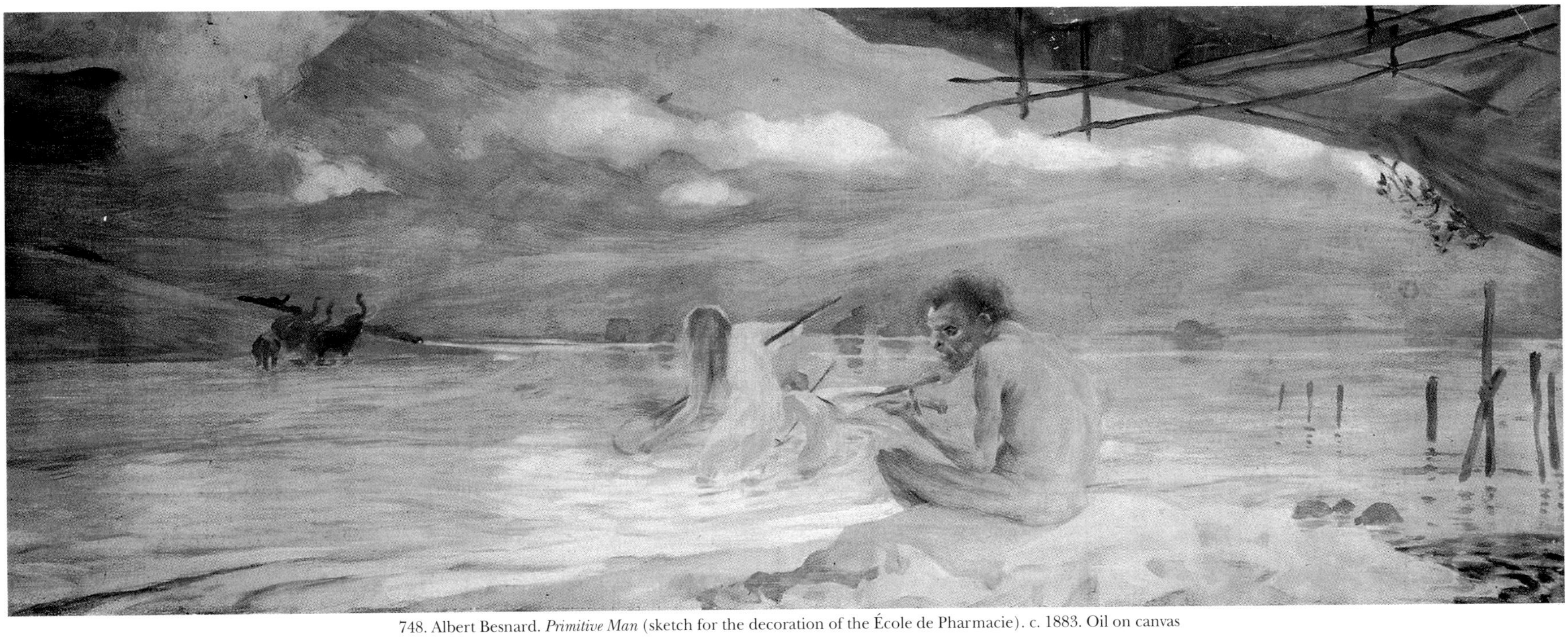

748. Albert Besnard. *Primitive Man* (sketch for the decoration of the École de Pharmacie). c. 1883. Oil on canvas

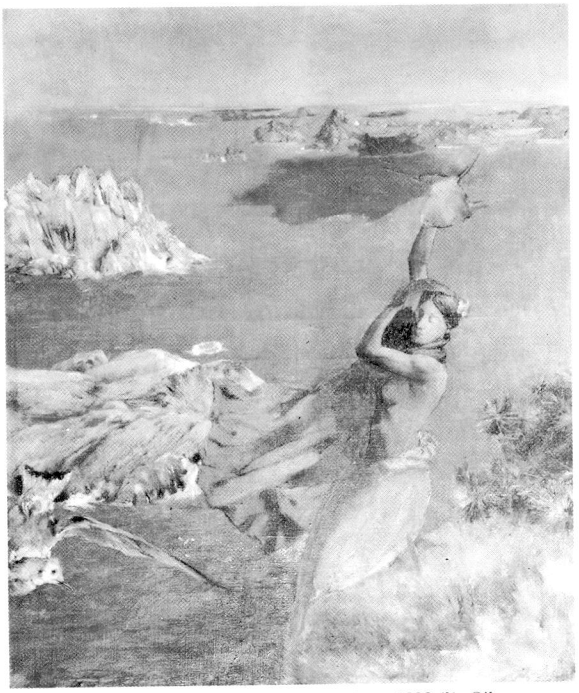

749. Ary Renan. *Sappho.* c. 1893 (?). Oil on canvas

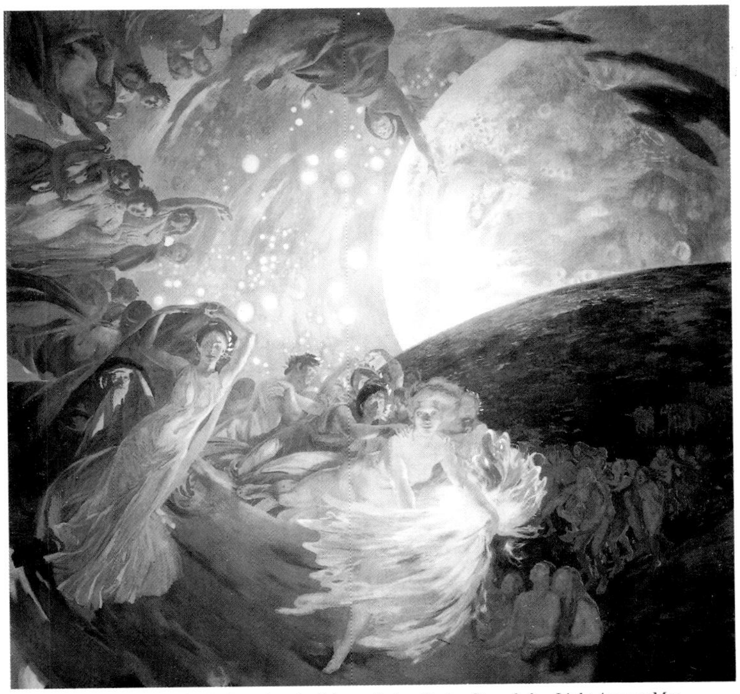

750. Albert Besnard. *Truth, Drawing the Sciences in her Train, Spreads her Light Among Men.* 1890. Hôtel de Ville, Paris

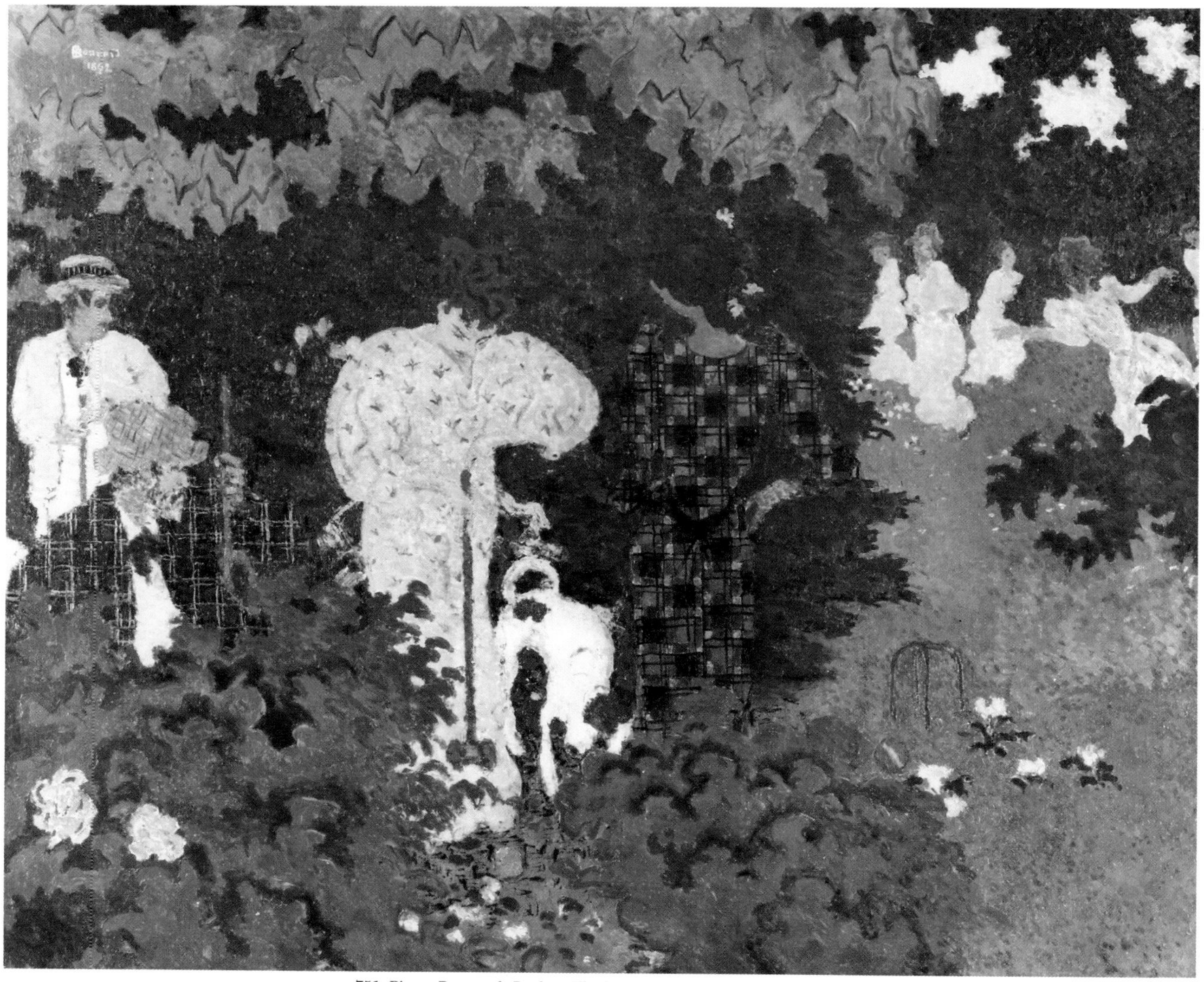

751. Pierre Bonnard. *Dusk* or *The Croquet Game.* 1892. Oil on canvas

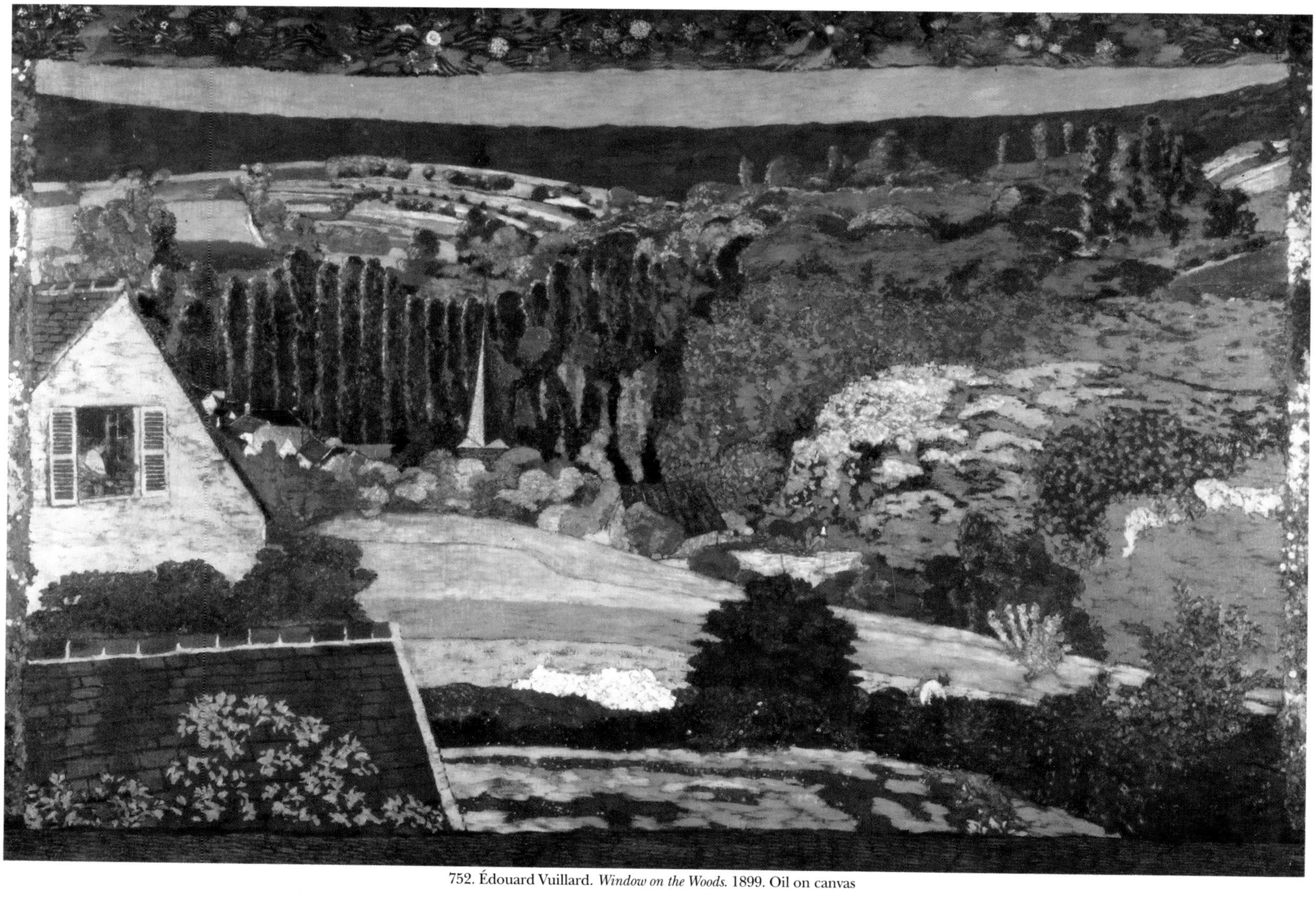

752. Édouard Vuillard. *Window on the Woods.* 1899. Oil on canvas

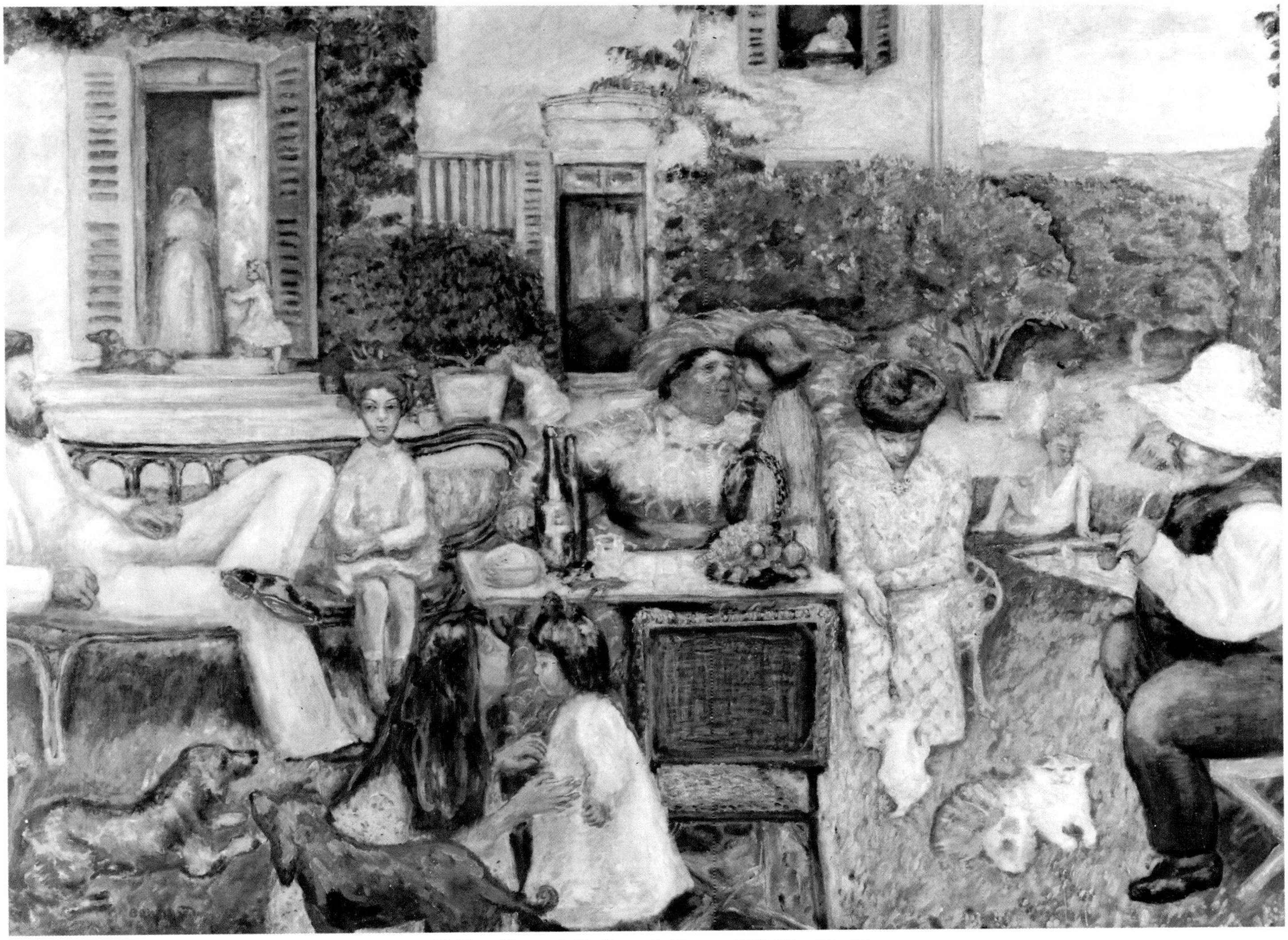

753. Pierre Bonnard. *The Bourgeois Afternoon*. 1900. Oil on canvas

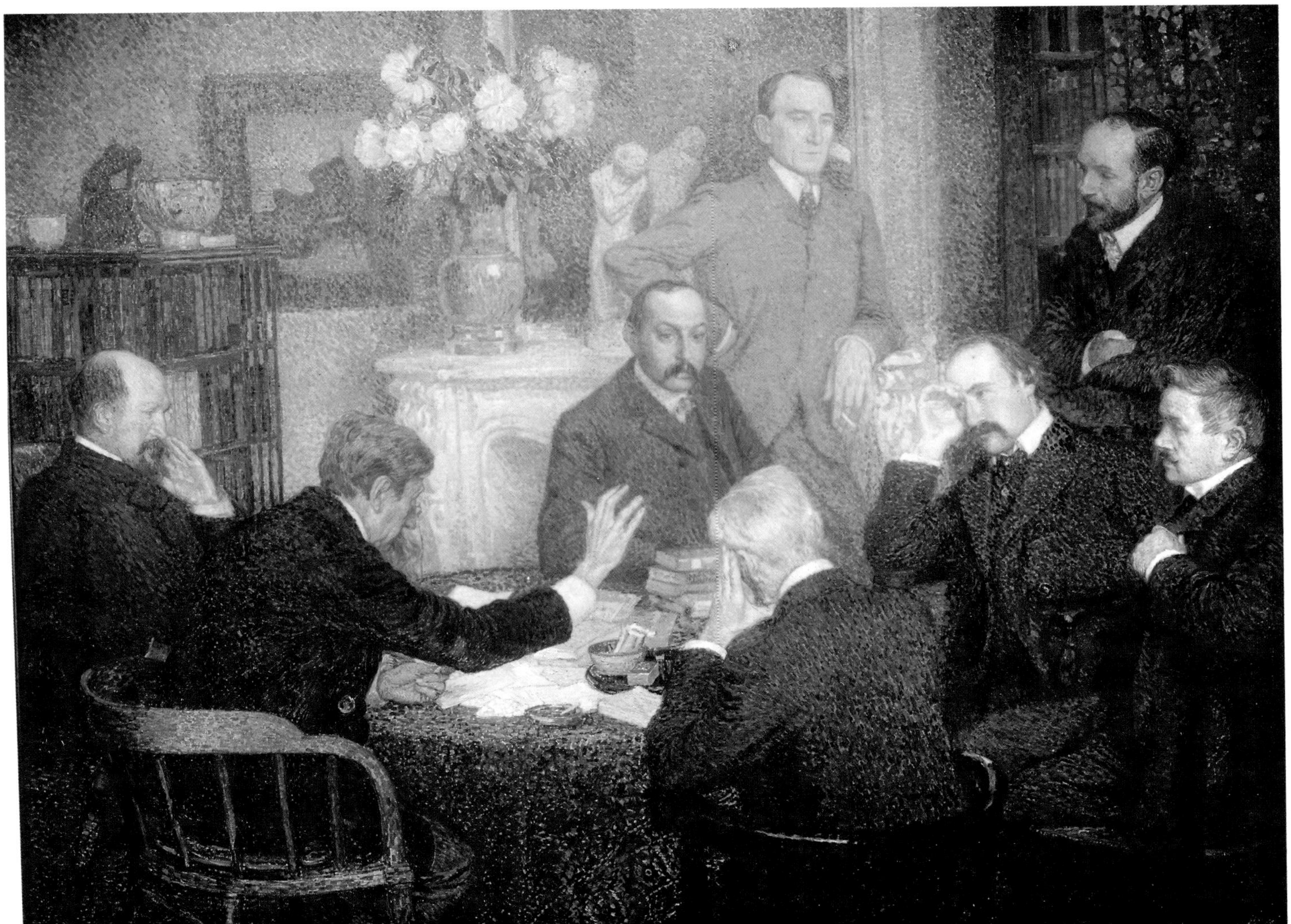

754. Théo van Rysselberghe. *Émile Verhaeren Reading*. 1903. Oil on canvas

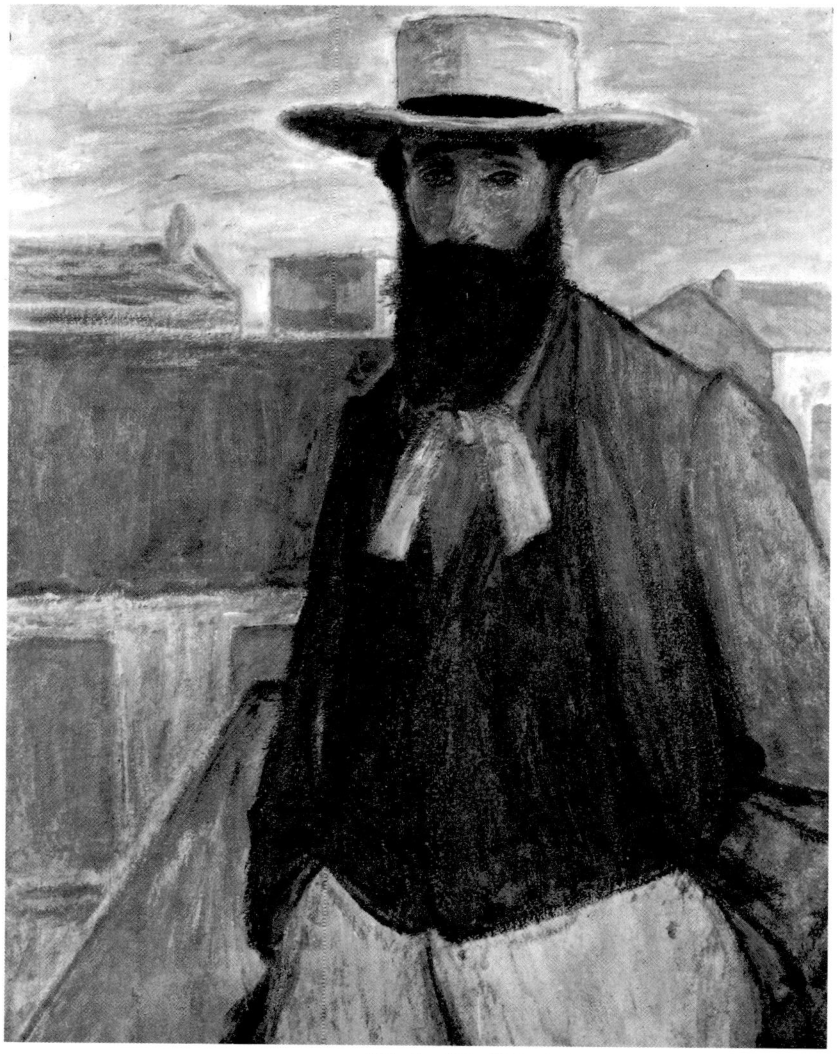

755. József Rippl-Rónai. *Aristide Maillol.* 1899. Oil on canvas

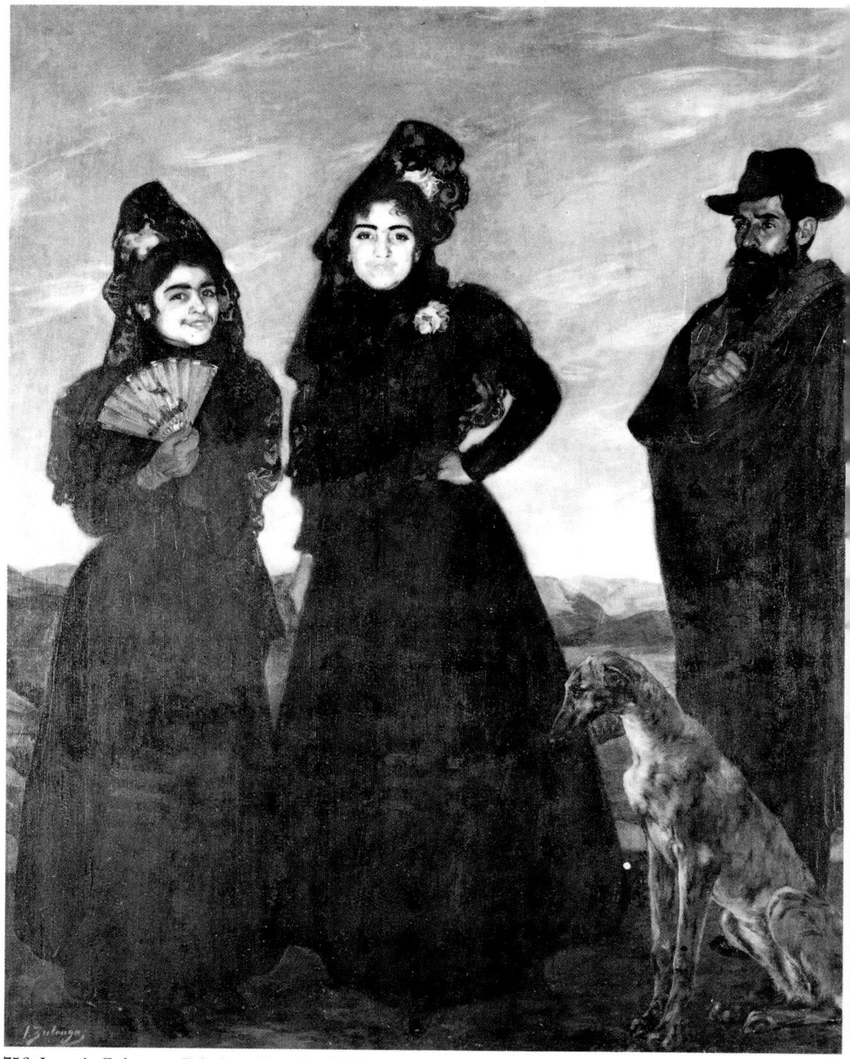

756. Ignacio Zuloaga y Zabaleta. *Portraits: My Uncle and My Two Cousins.* 1899. Oil on canvas

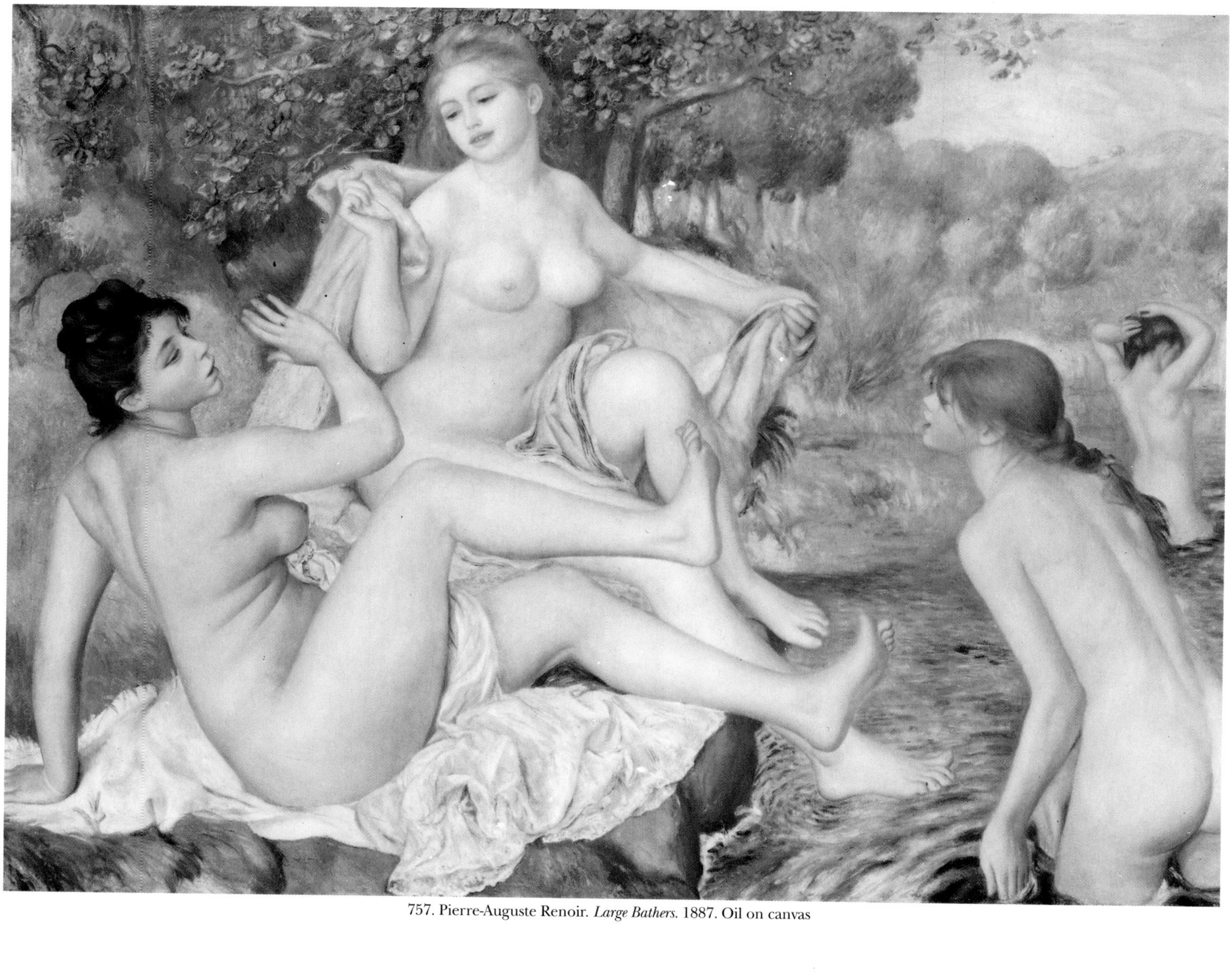

757. Pierre-Auguste Renoir. *Large Bathers.* 1887. Oil on canvas

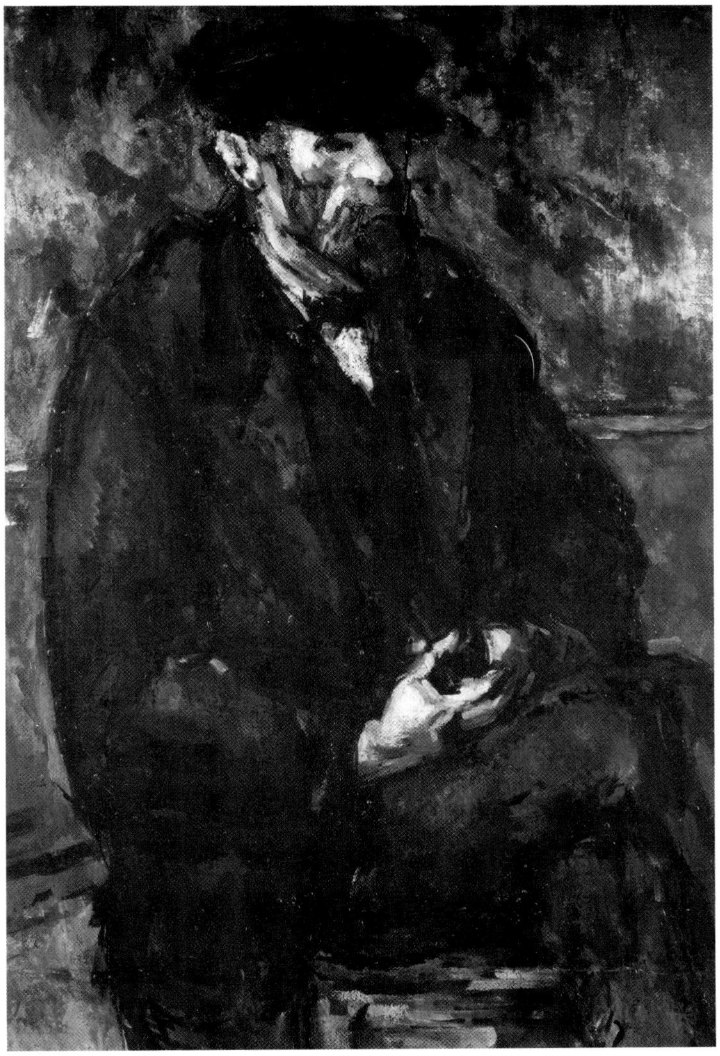

758. Paul Cézanne. *Portrait of Vallier.* 1904–5. Oil on canvas

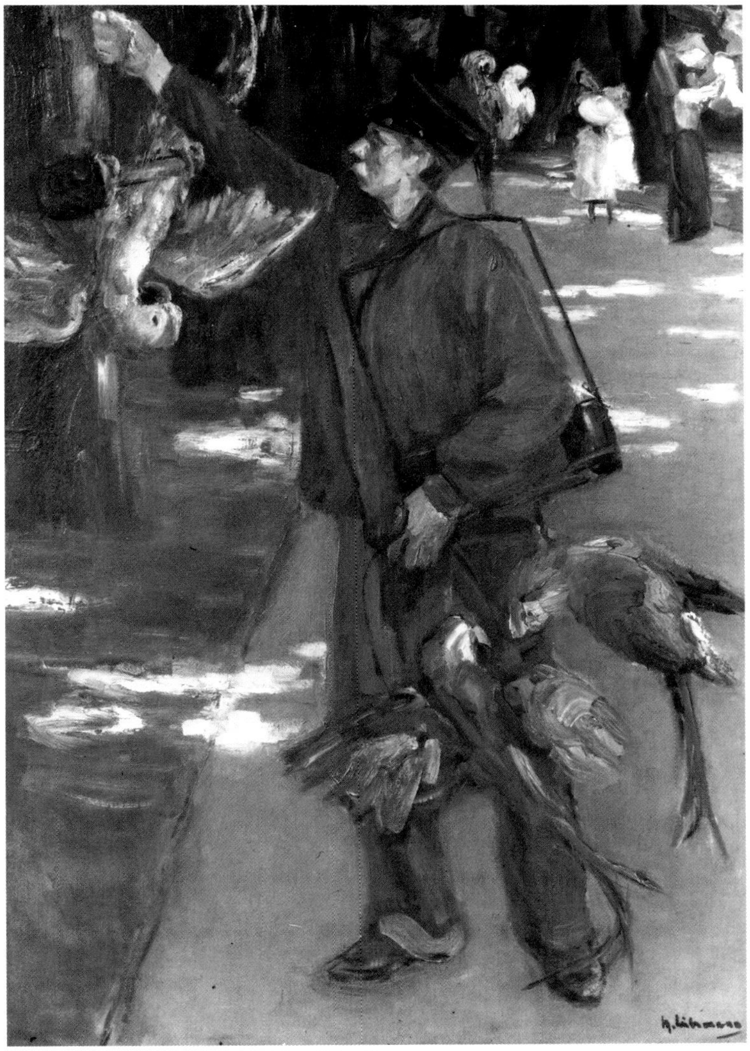

759. Max Liebermann. *The Parrot Man.* 1902. Oil on canvas

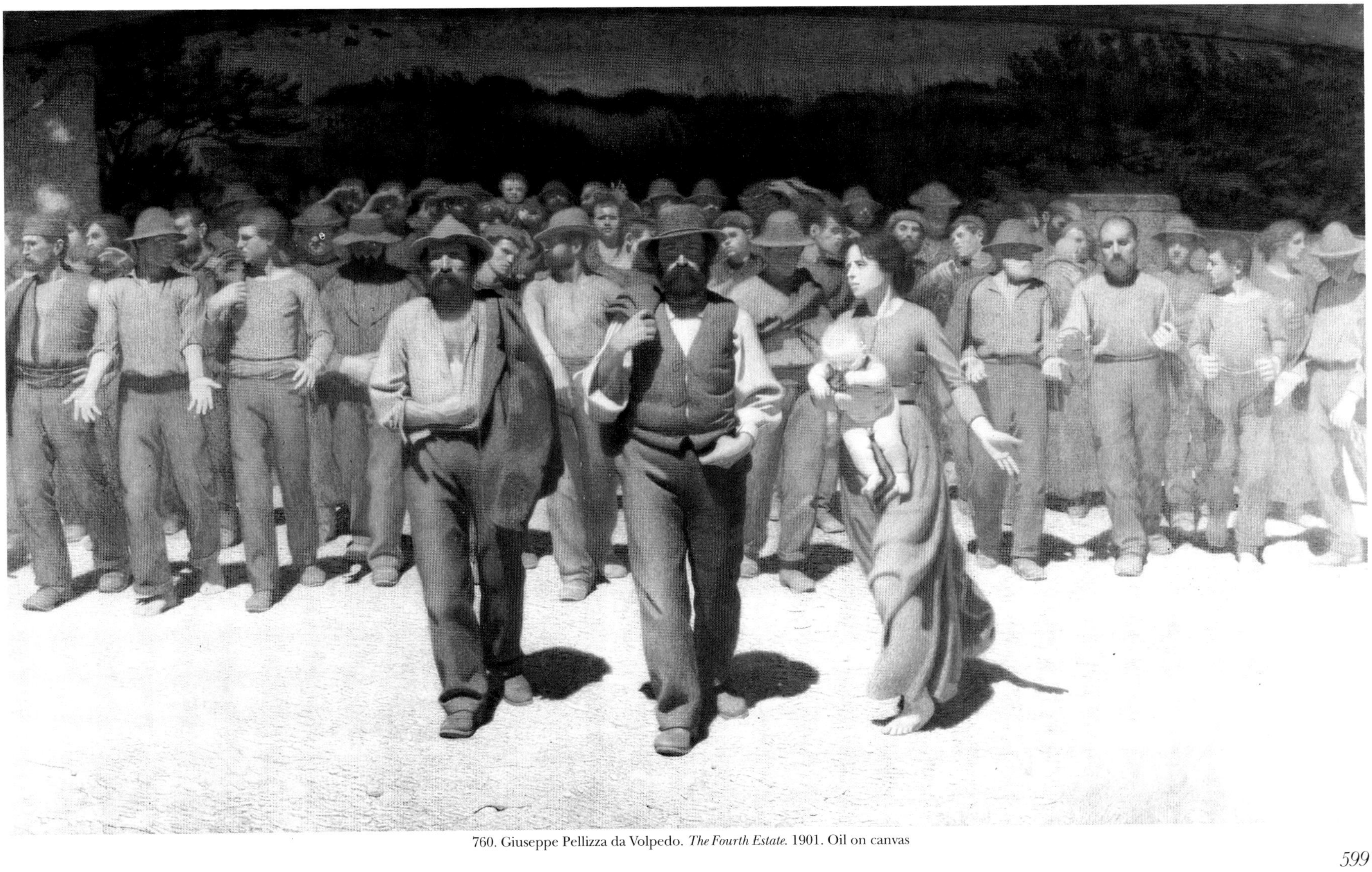

760. Giuseppe Pellizza da Volpedo. *The Fourth Estate.* 1901. Oil on canvas

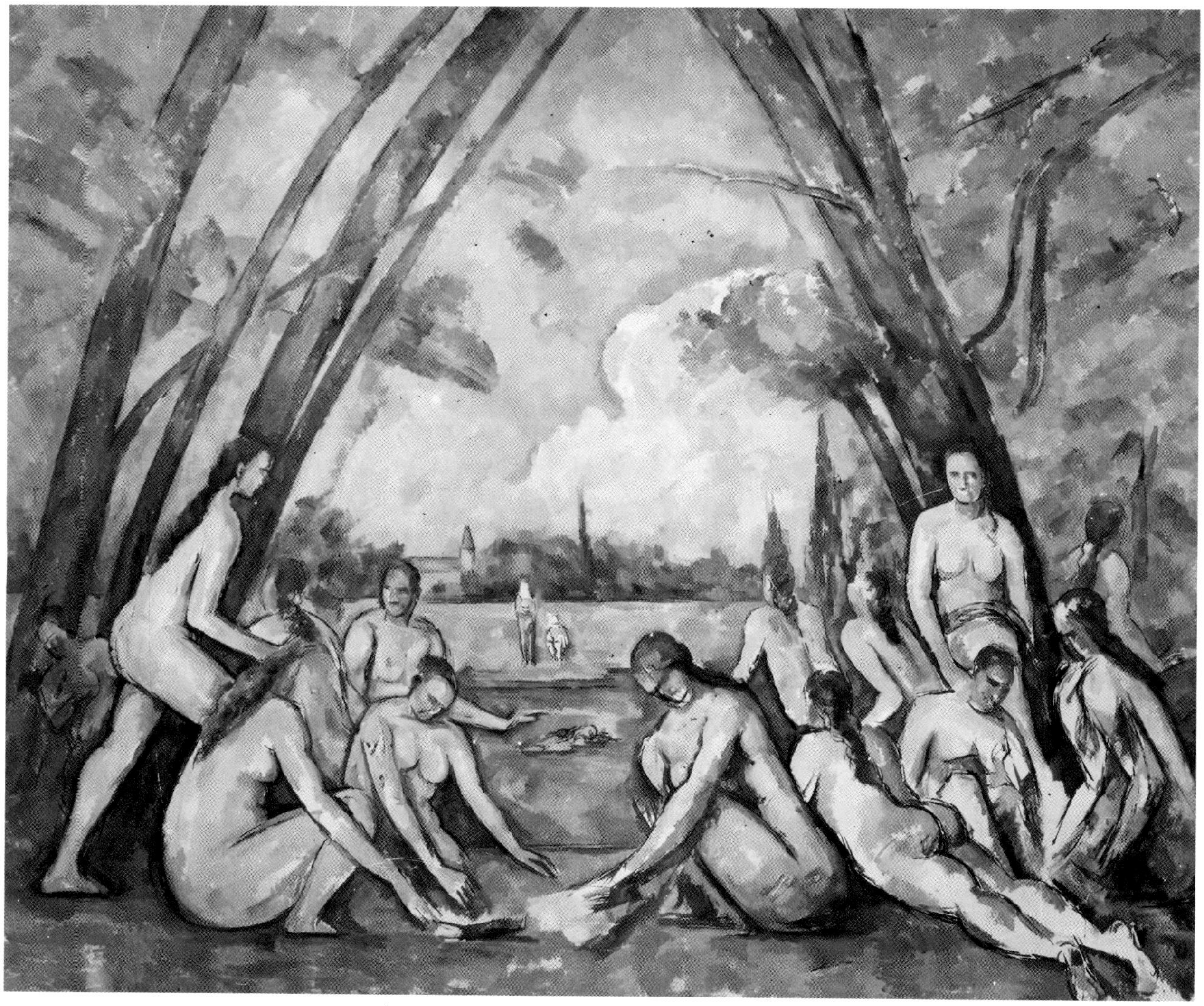

761. Paul Cézanne. *Large Bathers.* 1898–1905. Oil on canvas

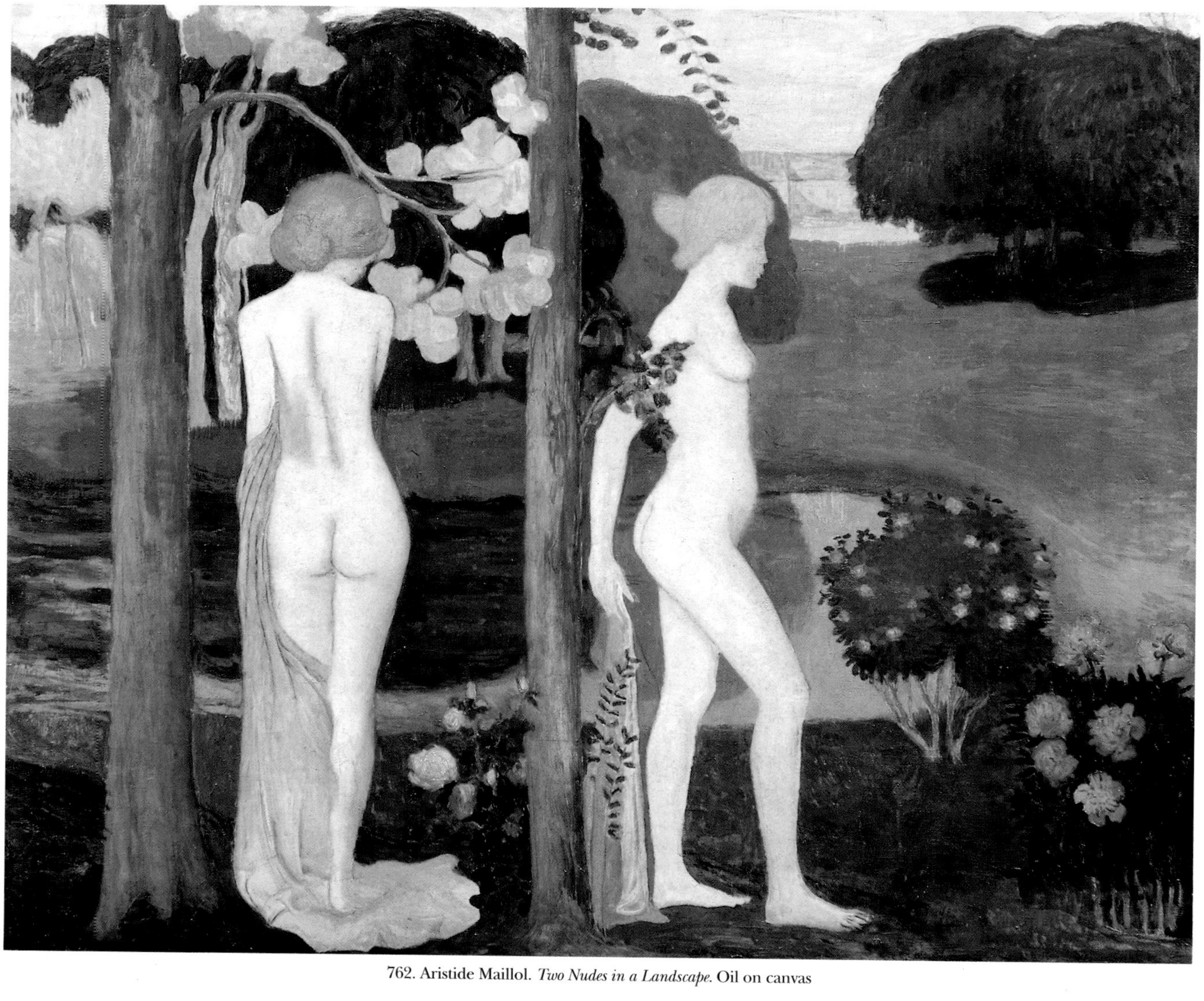

762. Aristide Maillol. *Two Nudes in a Landscape.* Oil on canvas

DOCUMENTATION FOR THE ILLUSTRATIONS

BIBLIOGRAPHY

INDEX

DOCUMENTATION FOR THE ILLUSTRATIONS

280 Alfred-Nicolas Normand
Vestibule in Prince Napoleon's Maison Pompéienne in the Avenue Montaigne, Paris (section across frontage)
c. 1882
Watercolor
Musée des Arts Décoratifs, Paris
(Museum photo)

281 Eugène Lami
Decoration of the Great Hall, Château de Ferrières (plan)
c. 1860
Watercolor
Musée des Arts Décoratifs, Paris
(Museum photo)

282 Paris, plan of the principle roads laid out by Haussmann, 1852–70
1, The Louvre; 2, Palais de l'Industrie; 3, Saint-Augustin Church; 4, La Trinité; 5, Basilique du Sacré-Coeur; 6, Gare du Nord; 7, Gare de l'Est; 8, Saint-Laurent Church; 9, Bibliothèque Nationale; 10, Saint-Eustache Church; 11, Les Halles (main covered market); 12, Palais de Justice (central law courts); 13, Tribunal de Commerce (commercial court); 14, Saint-Michel Fountain; 15, La Santé (prison); 16, Saint-Pierre-de-Montrouge Church
(Drawing by Ferrante Ferranti after Poisson)

283 Charles Garnier
Paris Opéra (plan)
1861–75

284 Hector Horeau
Project to roof the old boulevards
Plan for a covered boulevard in front of the Grand Hôtel in Paris, 1866
Ink and watercolor
62 x 445 cm
Académie d'Architecture, Paris
(Photo Musée d'Orsay, Paris)

285 Pellegrini and Lavalle
Colon Theater at Buenos Aires (plan)
Begun 1857
(Drawing by Ferrante Ferranti after A. Grimbeos)

286 Vienna, plan of the Ringstrasse
1859–88
A, Alte Hofburg (old Imperial Palace); B, Neue Hofburg (new Imperial Palace); C, Staatsoper (opera house); D, Kunsthistorisches Museum (Art History Museum); E, Naturhistorisches Museum (Natural History Museum); F, central law courts; G, Parliament; H, City Hall; I, Burgtheater (City Theater); J, University; K, Votivkirche (Votive Church); L, Börse (Stock Exchange)
(Drawing by Ferrante Ferranti after L. Benevolo)

287 Gottfried Semper and Carl von Hasenauer
Project for joining the Hofburg to the Kunsthistorisches and Naturhistorisches Museums (bird's-eye view)
1869
Pen and wash, 43 x 63 cm
Plan D 4, Planarchiv Burghauptmannschaft, Haus-, Hof-, Staatsarchiv, Vienna
(Photo Museen der Stadt Wien)

288 Edward William Godwin
The White House (plan for the house and studio of the painter James McNeill Whistler)
Pen and black ink, watercolor
Victoria and Albert Museum, London
(Museum photo)

289 Jens Vilhelm Dahlerup
Ny Carlsberg Glyptotek, Copenhagen (main and rear facades) 1890
Watercolor
(Photo Ole Woldbye)

290 T. Royal after Louis-Auguste Boileau
Project for a church using metal (section)
Pen and wash
62.1 x 73.3 cm
École Nationale des Beaux-Arts, Paris
(Photo Musée d'Orsay, Paris)

291 Ernest Lhereux
Library at the École de Droit, Paris (demolished)
From Félix Narjoux, *Paris, Monuments élevés par la ville*, vol. 2, 1850–80
(Photo Musée d'Orsay, Paris)

292 Édouard Durandelle
The Eiffel Tower under construction
May 15, 1888
Musée d'Orsay, Paris (Eiffel Collection)
(Photo Musée d'Orsay, Paris)

293 Arman Bourgade
"La Tour de 300 mètres construite en 300 vers"
["The 300-meter tower constructed in 300 lines of verse"]
1889
Engraving
80 x 57 cm
Musée d'Orsay, Paris (Eiffel Collection)
(Photo Musée d'Orsay, Paris)

294 Eugène-Emmanuel Viollet-le-Duc
Covered market
Engraved by C. Sauvageot, plate 21 in *Entretiens de l'architecture*, Paris, 1865
(Photo Musée d'Orsay, Paris)

295 Louis-Charles Boileau, Gustave Eiffel, and Armand-Moisant
Main staircase of the Au Bon Marché department store in Paris (section)
1873–76
Cabinet des Estampes, Bibliothèque Nationale, Paris
(Photo Bibliothèque Nationale)

296 Joseph Vaudemer
Prison of La Santé, Paris
1875
Cabinet des Estampes, Bibliothèque Nationale, Paris
(Photo Bibliothèque Nationale)

297 Victor Baltard
Les Halles Centrales, Paris (main covered market)
1845–70
From Félix Narjoux. *Paris, Monuments élevés par la ville.* Paris, vol. 2, 1850–80
(Photo Musée d'Orsay, Paris)

298 Hector Guimard
First floor of the Hôtel Guimard, 122 Avenue Mozart, Paris (plan)
1902–10
A, dining room; B, large drawing room; C, reception gallery; D, pantry
(Drawing by Ferrante Ferranti)

299 Xavier Schoellkopf
Town house belonging to Yvette Guilbert, Boulevard Berthier, Paris
1900 (destroyed)
(Photo collection Viollet/Roger Viollet)

300 Hector Guimard
Ground floor, Castel Béranger, Rue La Fontaine, Paris (plan)
1894–98
(Drawing by Ferrante Ferranti after an original drawing)

301 Jules Lavirotte
Ground floor of the building, 29 Avenue Rapp, Paris (plan)
1900–1
(Drawing by Ferrante Ferranti)

302 Victor Horta
Hôtel Tassel, Brussels (plan)
1893
(Drawing by Ferrante Ferranti)

303 Henry van de Velde
Bloemenwerf House, Uccle (plan)
1895
(Drawing by Ferrante Ferranti after an original drawing)

304 Antoni Gaudí i Cornet
Casa Milá, Barcelona (plan)
1905–10
(Drawing by Ferrante Ferranti)

305 Victor Horta
Ground floor, Hôtel Aubecq, Brussels (plan)
A, dining room; B, living room; C, gallery; D, vestibule; E, hall; F, pantry; G, kitchen
(Drawing by Ferrante Ferranti)

306 Ernesto Basile
Villino Florio, Palermo (plan)
1899–1903
(Drawing by Ferrante Ferranti after an original drawing)

307 Antoni Gaudí i Cornet
Palau Güell, Barcelona (cross section)
1886–91
(Drawing by Ferrante Ferranti after an original drawing)

308 Perspective view of project to join the Louvre to the Tuileries Gardens
After the official plans by L. Visconti
Print
Bibliothèque Nationale, Paris
(Photo Bibliothèque Nationale)

309 Hector Lefuel
New Louvre, Paris (west front elevation of the Pavillon de l'Horloge)
c. 1854
Wash on tracing paper
58 x 38 cm
Service d'Architecture, Palais du Louvre, Paris
(Photo Bulloz)

310 Hector Lefuel practice
Project for monumental gates, new Louvre
Service d'Architecture, Palais du Louvre, Paris
(Photo Bulloz)

311 Pierre Manguin
Hôtel de la Païva, Paris (facade)
1856–68
(Photo Dominique Genet)

312 Charles Garnier
Paris Opéra (detail of the facade)
1861–75
(Photo Dominique Genet)

313 Jules Dalou
Diana
Dining room ceiling, Hôtel de la Païva, Paris
1856–68
Wood
(Photo Dominique Genet)

314 Albert-Ernest Carrier-Belleuse
Bedroom fireplace, Hôtel de la Païva, Paris
1865
Silvered bronze, malachite, and glazed tiles
(Photo Dominique Genet)

315 Great drawing room, Hôtel de la Païva, Paris
Ceiling painting *Day Pursuing Night* by Paul Baudry, and on the mantlepiece, *Harmony* and *Music*, marble, by Eugène Delaplanche
1865
(Photo Dominique Genet)

316 William Bouwens van der Boijen (architect), Henri Lombard, Édouard Pépin, Antonin Carles, and Désiré Ferrary *The Hours of the Day*
Crédit Lyonnais, Boulevard des Italiens, Paris
1881
(Photo Dominique Genet)

317 Jacques-Ignace Hittorff
Cirque Impérial, Paris (elevation of the main facade)
1862
Lead pencil, pen and black ink, watercolor
88 x 56 cm
Musée d'Orsay, Paris
(Photo Réunion des Musées Nationaux)

318 Auguste-Joseph Magne
Théâtre du Vaudeville, Paris (elevation of the main facade)
1866–69
Lead pencil, pen and black ink, gray ink wash, watercolor, gouache and gold highlights
81.4 x 50 cm
Musée d'Orsay, Paris
(Photo Réunion des Musées Nationaux)

319 Gabriel Veugny
Cité Napoléon housing project, Rue Rochechouart, Paris (detail)
1849–54
Bibliothèque Nationale, Paris
(Photo Bibliothèque Nationale)

320 Karabet Balyan and Nikogos Balyan
Dolma Batce Palace, Istanbul
1844–56
(Photo Foto Marburg)

321 Imre Steidl
Országház (Hungarian Parliament Building)
1882–1903
Budapest
(Photo Foto Marburg)

322 McKim, Mead and White
Public Library, Boston
1882–92
(Photo Benoît Roland)

323 John MacArthur Jr. (architect), Alexander Milne Calder (sculptor)
City Hall, Philadelphia (facade, upper section)
1868–93
(Photo Benoît Roland)

324 Dankmar Adler and Louis Henry Sullivan
Auditorium Building, Chicago
1886–89
(Photo Benoît Roland)

325 Jean-Camille Formigé
Columbarium
1887
Père-Lachaise Cemetery, Paris
(Photo Dominique Genet)

326 Pierre Bossan and Sainte-Marie Perrin
Basilica Notre-Dame de Fourvière, Lyon (main facade)
1872–1914
(Photo Dominique Genet)

327 Léon Vaudoyer, then Henri Espérandieu, Henri-Antoine Revoil, and Alfred Vaudoyer
Cathedral Sainte-Marie-Majeure, Marseille
1872–93
(Photo Alfred Wolf)

328 Alphonse Balat
Winter garden (detail), Royal Glasshouses at Laeken, Brussels
1875–76
(Photo C. Bastin and J. Evrard)

329 Gustave Eiffel
Maria Pia Bridge over the river Douro, Portugal
Constructed 1875–77
Photograph of a painting by an anonymous artist
Musée d'Orsay, Paris (Eiffel Collection)
(Photo Réunion des Musées Nationaux)

330 Ferdinand Dutert (architect) and Victor Contamin (engineer)
Galerie des Machines, Paris (interior)
Revue technique de l'exposition universelle
École Centrale, Paris
(Photo Musée d'Orsay, Paris)

331 Thomas Deane and Benjamin Woodward
University Museum, Oxford (detail of arched iron braces and wrought-iron capitals)
1855–60
(Photo A. F. Kersting)

332 Otto Wagner
Majolikahaus, 40 Linke Wienzeile, Vienna
1898–99
(Photo C. Bastin and J. Evrard)

333 Jules Saulnier
Menier Chocolate Factory (general view), Noisiel, Seine-et-Marne
1871–72
(Photo Harlingue-Viollet/Roger-Viollet)

334 Edmund Berninger and Gustave Krafft
Store, Place Broglie, Strasbourg
1901
In Raguenet, *Monographie des bâtiments modernes*

335 Otto Wagner
Österreichisches Postsparkasse, Vienna
1904–6
(Photo C. Bastin and J. Evrard)

336 Charles Rennie Mackintosh
Glasgow School of Art
1897–1908
(Photo A. F. Kersting)

337 Hendrick Petrus Berlage
Beurs (Stock Exchange), Amsterdam
1898–1903
(Photo Foto Marburg)

338 Peter Behrens
Behrens's House, Mathildenhöhe, Darmstadt
1901
(Photo Foto Marburg)

339 August Endell
Photoatelier Elvira, Munich
1897–98 (destroyed)
(Photo Foto Marburg)

340 Joseph Maria Olbrich
Hochzeitstürm, Mathildenhöhe, Darmstadt
Built from 1905
(Photo Foto Marburg)

341 Henry van de Velde
Store for Havana Tobacco Co., Berlin
1899–1900 (destroyed)
(Photo Foto Marburg)

342 Louis Marnez and Trézel
Restaurant "Chez Maxim's" Rue Royale, Paris
1899
(Photo Alfred Wolf)

343 Ernesto Basile
Villa Igea, Palermo (interior)
1899
(Photo Ferrante Ferranti)

344 Louis Henry Sullivan
Carson, Pirie, Scott & Co. Store, Chicago (detail of decoration)
1899–1904
The Art Institute of Chicago, Chicago
(Museum photo)

345 Josef Hoffmann
Palais Stoclet, 281 Avenue de Tervueren, Brussels
1905–11
(Photo Benoît Roland)

346 Frank Lloyd Wright
Darwin D. Martin Residence, Buffalo
1904
(Photo Benoît Roland)

347 Paul Saintenoy
Old England Store, Brussels
1899
(Photo C. Bastin and J. Evrard)

348 Gustave Strauven
11 Square Ambiorix, Brussels
1903
(Photo C. Bastin and J. Evrard)

349 Paul Hankar
Ciamberlani House, Brussels
1897
(Photo Viollet/Roger-Viollet)

350 Henry van de Velde
Bloemenwerf House, Uccle
1895
(Photo C. Bastin and J. Evrard)

351 Paul Cauchie
5 Rue des Francs, Brussels
1905
(Photo C. Bastin and J. Evrard)

352 Adolf Loos
Building on the Michaelplatz, Vienna
1909–11
(Photo Angelo Hornak)

353 Victor Horta
Dining room, Hôtel Solvay, Rue Américaine, Brussels
1898
(Photo C. Bastin and J. Evrard)

354 Victor Horta
Hôtel Solvay, Rue Américaine, Brussels
Begun 1894
(Photo C. Bastin and J. Evrard)

355 Victor Horta
Hôtel Max-Hallet, Brussels (rear facade)
1906
(Photo C. Bastin and J. Evrard)

356 Hector Guimard
Castel Henriette, Sèvres
1899–1900 (destroyed)
(Photo Archive Georges Vigne)

357 Henri Sauvage
Villa Majorelle, 1 Rue Louis-Majorelle, Nancy
1898–1901
(Photo Ferrante Ferranti)

358 Anonymous
Pharmacy, Douvres-la-Délivrande, Calvados, France
(Photo Dominique Genet)

359 J. Baunier and Pichereau
Villa "Les Bossettes," Dives-sur-Mer, Calvados
1891
(Photo Dominique Genet)

360 Émile André
Town house, 92–92 bis Quai Claude-le-Lorrain, Nancy
1903
(Photo Ferrante Ferranti)

361 Antoni Gaudí i Cornet
Casa Milá, Barcelona
1906–10
(Photo Ferrante Ferranti)

362 Antoni Gaudí i Cornet
Parc Güell (gallery walkway), Barcelona
1900–14
(Photo Ferrante Ferranti)

363 Lluís Domènech i Montaner
Palau de la Música Catalana (concert hall), Barcelona
1905–8
(Photo Ferrante Ferranti)

364 Georges Chedanne
Hôtel de Voyageurs, Avenue des Champs-Élysées, Paris
(Now the headquarters of the Crédit Commercial de France bank)
(Photo Dominique Genet)

365 Charles Plumet
Building, 50 Avenue Victor-Hugo, Paris
1901
(Photo Dominique Genet)

366 Wagon
Building, Place Félix-Faure, Paris
(Photo Dominique Genet)

367 Henry van de Velde and Auguste Perret
Théâtre des Champs-Élysées, Paris
1913
(Photo Dominique Genet)

368 Hector Guimard
Entrance to the Métropolitain subway station Gare de la Bastille in Paris
1900
(Photo Archives Georges Vigne)

369 Jules Lavirotte
Ceramic Hôtel, 34 Avenue de Wagram, Paris
1904
(Photo Dominique Genet)

370 Charles Massa
Building, Avenue MacMahon, Paris
(Photo Dominique Genet)

371 Henri Sauvage
Building with staggered frontage, 12 Rue Vavin, Paris
1912–19
(Photo Dominique Genet)

372 Charles-Jean Avisseau and Octave-Guillaume de Rochebrune
Footed bowl on dish
1855
Faience fine with molded and inset decoration
Goblet: height 34.5 cm, diameter 26.5 cm; dish: diameter 51.5 cm
Musée d'Orsay, Paris
(Photo Réunion des Musées Nationaux)

373 Firm of Ferdinand Barbedienne
Perfume-burner
1855
Silvered and anodized bronze
51 x 255 cm; tray: diameter 29 cm
Victoria and Albert Museum, London
(Museum photo)

374 Alexandre Henry Dufresne de Saint-Léon
Shield
c. 1856–65
Patinated steel, decoration partially engraved and gilt
Height 14 cm, diameter 52.5 cm
Musée d'Orsay, Paris
(Photo Réunion des Musées Nationaux)

375 Choisey-le-Roi Manufacture (Hippolyte Boulenger)
Dish
c. 1873
Faience fine with printed and enamel-painted decoration, diameter 26 cm
Kunstgewerbemuseum, Berlin
(Photo Staatliche Museen Preussischer Kulturbesitz)

376 J. & L. Lobmeyr Manufacture
Lidded bowl and dish
c. 1873
Colored glass, gilt engraved decoration, white enamel highlights
Bowl: height 19.5 cm; dish: diameter 20.2 cm
Museum für Kunst und Gewerbe, Hamburg
(Museum photo)

377 Théodore Deck
Bowl
1867
Glazed faience
Height 50.5 cm, diameter 7.5 cm
Musée d'Orsay, Paris
(Photo Réunion des Musées Nationaux)

378 Manufacture Nationale de Sèvres in collaboration with Léopold-Jules-Joseph Gély
"Bijou" vase
1871
Hard-paste porcelain and ornamental paste decoration
19.5 x 12.5 cm
Musée d'Orsay, Paris
(Photo Réunion des Musées Nationaux)

379 Wilhelm Hoffmann
Vase
c. 1873
Opaline with engraved and painted decoration
195 x 125 cm
Kunstgewerbemuseum, Berlin
(Photo Funke/Staatliche Museen Preussischer Kulturbesitz)

380 Manufacture Nationale de Sèvres in collaboration with Albert-Ernest Carrier-Belleuse (sculptor)
"Buire de Blois" figural ewer
1883
Hard-paste porcelain, height 43 cm
Musée des Arts Décoratifs, Paris
(Photo Sully-Jaulmes/Musée des Arts Décoratifs)

381 Claudius Popelin
"Gallia"
1867
Enamel-painted copper and ebonized pearwood, 68.5 x 53 cm
Musée d'Orsay, Paris
(Photo Réunion des Musées Nationaux)

382 Eugène Fontenay in collaboration with Eugène Richet (enameler)
Perfume-burner
1878
Gold, enamel, lapis lazuli, and diamonds, 21 x 11 cm
Musée d'Orsay, Paris
(Photo Réunion des Musées Nationaux)

383 Charles Lepec in collaboration with Frères Fannière
Nef
c. 1867
Enameled gold and gilt silver
32.5 x 35.5 cm
Badisches Landesmuseum, Karlsruhe
(Museum photo)

384 Maison Fourdinois
Cabinet
c. 1867
Ebony, boxwood, pearwood, lapis lazuli, jasper, and marble
251 x 153 cm
Victoria and Albert Museum, London

385 Charles-Guillaume Diehl in collaboration with Brandely (draftsman) and Emmanuel Fremiet (sculptor)
Medal cabinet
1867
Cedarwood, walnut inlay, ebony and ivory, silver-plated bronze and copper, 238 x 151 x 60 cm
Musée d'Orsay, Paris
(Photo Dominique Genet)

386 Edward Burne-Jones
The Adoration of the Magi
Cartoon painted c. 1888–90
Wool tapestry made by Morris & Co., Merton Abbey
254 x 381 cm
Museum für Kunst und Gewerbe, Hamburg
(Museum photo)

387 William Burges; made by Harland and Fischer in collaboration with E. J. Poynter (painter)
Secretary
1858
Painted and gilt wood, 213 x 139 x 38 cm
Victoria and Albert Museum, London
(Museum photo)

388 Manufacture Poussielgue-Rusand
Monstrance
1856
Gilt and enameled silver, 83 x 39.2 cm
Musée d'Orsay, Paris
(Photo Réunion des Musées Nationaux)

389 Torolf Prytz and J. Tostrup
Jardiniere
1900
Chased and repoussé silver
35 x 53 cm
Kunstindustrimuseet, Oslo
(Museum photo)

390 Josep Puig i Cadafalch and Gaspar Homar i Mezquida
Dresser from the Casa Amattler
c. 1900
Oak, 298 x 113 x 58 cm
Instituto Amattler de Arte Hispanico, Barcelona
(Photo Mas)

391 Veuve Ferdinand Duvinage (Maison A. Giroux)
Cabinet
c. 1878
Rosewood, inlay of ivory, various woods and metals, patinated, silvered, and gilt bronze, 130 x 68 x 38 cm
Musée d'Orsay, Paris
(Photo Réunion des Musées Nationaux)

392 Manufacture Creil and Montereau for Eugène Rousseau, in collaboration with F. Bracquemond
Soup tureen
1866
Faience fine, printed and painted decoration, 28 x 40 cm
Musée d'Orsay, Paris
(Photo Réunion des Musées Nationaux)

393 Frères Fannière
Beer service
c. 1865
Chased and repoussé silver
Jug: height 23 cm; tumblers: height 13.7 cm; tray: diameter 32 cm
Musée d'Orsay, Paris
(Photo Réunion des Musées Nationaux)

394 Émile Gallé
"Winter Flora" glass-fronted cabinet
1889
Walnut and Amboyna bur, inlay of various woods, gilt copper, and engraved glass, 255 x 128 x 63 cm
Musée d'Orsay, Paris
(Photo Giraudon)

395 John Henry Belter
Sofa
c. 1856
Veneered and carved rosewood
148.6 x 232.4 x 114.5 cm
Victoria and Albert Museum, London
(Museum photo)

396 Émile Gallé
"Clair de Lune" vase
1878
Blown glass, enamel-painted decoration
Height 28 cm, diameter 23 cm
Musée des Arts Décoratifs, Paris
(Photo Sully-Jaulmes)

397 Tiffany & Co. under the direction of Edward Chandler Moore
Large jug
c. 1878
Hammered silver, chased decoration inlaid with colored alloy, 22 x 17.2 cm
Musée d'Orsay, Paris
(Photo Réunion des Musées Nationaux)

398 Théodore Deck
Plate
c. 1878
Enamel-painted faience, diameter 29.9 cm
Victoria and Albert Museum, London
(Museum photo)

399 Minton's Art Pottery Studio
Plate
1872
Enamel-painted faience with gold highlights, diameter 56 cm
Collection P. Rose and A. Gallichan
(Photo McNeill)

400 Elkington & Co. Ltd.
Dish with handles
c. 1870–73
Enameled copper, silvered and anodized bronze
Österreichisches Museum für Angewandte Kunst, Vienna
(Museum photo)

401 Manufacture Christofle under the direction of Émile Reiber
Jardiniere
c. 1878
Patinated, gilt, and silvered copper plate and bronze, 13 x 32 cm
Musée d'Orsay, Paris
(Photo Réunion des Musées Nationaux)

402 Edward William Godwin
Sideboard
c. 1877
Wood, black varnish, silvered metal, and printed paper, 180 x 259 x 56 cm
Victoria and Albert Museum, London
(Museum photo)

403 Lawrence Alma-Tadema; made by Johnstone, Norman & Co.
Armchair
c. 1884
Cedarwood, ebony, ivory, and mother-of-pearl, height 93 cm
Victoria and Albert Museum, London
(Photo Fine Arts Society, London)

404 Herter Brothers
Wardrobe
c. 1880–85
Cherrywood, black varnish, inlay of various woods, and gilt bronze, 199.4 x 125.7 x 66 cm
Metropolitan Museum of Art, New York. Gift of Kenneth O. Smith
(Museum photo)

405 Gebrüder Thonet
Chair
1867
Bent beechwood
Firmenmuseum, Bistritz
(Museum photo)

406 Jan Kastner
Chair
c. 1899–1900
Oak, walnut, maple, copper, and mother-of-pearl inlay, 92 cm
Uměleckoprùmyslové Muzeum, Prague
(Museum photo)

407 Georg Jakob Hunzinger
Chair
c. 1876
Maple and steel, 84.5 x 50.8 x 54 cm
Victoria and Albert Museum, London
(Photo Richard P. Goodbody)

408 Josef Fanta and Jan Navrátil
Armchair
Exposition Universelle, Paris, 1900
Maple, chased and hammered copper, small bronze plaques
Uměleckoprùmyslové Muzeum, Prague
(Museum photo)

409 Otto Wagner
Armchair
1900
Walnut, mother-of-pearl inlay, modern leather upholstery, 84 x 69 x 60 cm
Victoria and Albert Museum, London
(Museum photo)

410 Paul Hankar
Chair
1900
Oak and leather, 115 x 59 x 58 cm
Museum voor Sierkunst, Ghent
(Photo Studio Claerhout)

411 Akseli Gallén-Kallela and Iris workshop
Fauteuil
Exposition Universelle, Paris, 1900
Birchwood, original cloth upholstery with applied work embroidery
Museum für Kunst und Gewerbe, Hamburg
(Museum photo)

412 Gustave Serrurier-Bovy
Chair "Craftsman's Bedroom" model
1895
Oak and straw-bottoming, 94 x 47 x 47 cm
Musée d'Orsay, Paris
(Photo Réunion des Musées Nationaux)

413 François-Rupert Carabin
Bookcase
1890
Walnut and wrought iron, 290 x 215 x 54 cm
Musée d'Orsay, Paris
(Photo Dominique Genet)

414 Eugène Gaillard
Sideboard
Exposition Universelle, Paris, 1900
Walnut and copper, 254 x 210 x 54 cm
Kunstindustrimuseum, Copenhagen
(Photo Ole Woldbye)

415 Gaspar Homar i Mezquida and Josep Pey i Farriol
Cabinet with sofa, from the Casa Lleo Morera
c. 1904
Walnet, inlaid with various woods
259 x 268 x 50 cm
Museu Nacional d'Art Modern de Catalunya, Barcelona
(Museum photo)

416 Frances Macdonald
"Honesty" mirror frame
c. 1896–97
Repoussé metal, 73 x 73.6 cm
Museum and Art Gallery, Glasgow

417 Lluis Masriera
"St. George" pendant
c. 1905
Gold, enamel, and diamonds, 45 x 36 cm
Museu Nacional d'Art Modern de Catalunya, Barcelona
(Museum photo)

418 Alfred Gilbert
Pendant
1891–97
Gilt silver, pearls, and crystal
Royal Institute of Painters in Watercolour, London
(Photo Institute)

419 Archibald Knox and Liberty
Cigar box
1903
Silver and opal on wood, width 21.6 cm
Victoria and Albert Museum, London
(Museum photo)

420 Joseph Maria Olbrich
Jewel casket
1900
Unstained and stained maple, boxwood, and silver, 32 x 36 x 34 cm
Österreichisches Museum für Angewandte Kunst, Vienna
(Musuem photo)

421 Philippe Wolfers
"La Parure" cabinet
1905
Silver, ivory, enamel, pearls, and opals, 42 x 30 x 20 cm
Musées Royaux d'Art et d'Histoire, Brussels
(Photo A.C.L)

422 Peter Behrens and M. J. Rückert
Three-piece cutlery set
1901
Chased silver, knife: 205 cm; fork: 185 cm; spoon: 14 cm
Hessisches Landesmuseum, Darmstadt
(Museum photo)

423 Christopher Dresser and J. W. Hukin & J. J. Heath
Soup tureen
Model patented 1880
Silvered metal and ebony, 21 x 31 x 235 cm
Musée d'Orsay, Paris
(Museum photo)

424 Josef Ladislav Némec
Dress comb
c. 1900
Gilt silver, horn, and mother-of-pearl, 13 cm
Uměleckoprùmyslové Muzeum, Prague
(Museum photo)

425 Joseph Maria Olbrich and Edward Hulek
Candlestick
c. 1902–3
Pewter, 36.4 cm
Badisches Landesmuseum, Karlsruhe
(Museum photo)

426 Gorham Company
Athenic vase
1895–1900
Silver, copper, and enamel, 33 cm
Chrysler Museum, Norfolk
(Museum photo)

427 Georges de Feure
Candlestick
1902
Silvered metal, 26 cm
Musée des Arts Décoratifs, Paris
(Museum photo)

428 Henry van de Velde and Theodor Müller
Samovar
1902
Silver, 38 cm
Kunstgewerbemuseum, Zürich (Sammlung Museum Bellerive)
(Museum photo)

429 Charles Robert Ashbee and the Guild of Handicraft
Bowl with lid
1902
Chased, repoussé, and enameled silver
11.5 x 10.5 cm
Kunstgewerbemuseum, Zürich (Sammlung Museum Bellerive)
(Museum photo)

430 Jan Eisenloeffel
Coffee pot
c. 1902
Copper, 33 cm
Haags Gemeentemuseum, The Hague
(Museum photo)

431 Frans Zwollo
Goblet
1898
Chased, repoussé, and hammered silver, 16.3 cm
Boymans-Van Beuningen Museum, Rotterdam
(Photo Dick Wolters)

432 Zsolnay Manufacture
Vase
1899
Lusterware, 34 cm
Iparmüveszeti Múzeum, Budapest
(Museum photo)

433 Rozenburg Manufacture
Vase
Exposition Universelle, Paris, 1900
Porcelain, underglazed *petit feu* decoration, 27.8 x 13.4 cm
Museum für Kunst und Gewerbe, Hamburg
(Museum photo)

434 Alf Wallander and Schreuder & Olsson
Wine jug
1899
Chased and repoussé pewter, 37 cm
Nationalmuseum, Stockholm
(Museum photo)

435 Rockwood Pottery
Vase
1904
Faience with underglaze decoration, 27 cm
Cooper-Hewitt Museum, New York
(Museum photo)

436 Louis Comfort Tiffany
Vase
Exposition Universelle, Paris, 1900
Favrile glass, 24 cm
Museum für Kunst und Gewerbe, Hamburg
(Museum photo)

437 Rörstrand porcelain factory
Vase
1897
Porcelain with underglazed *grand feu* decoration, 23.5 cm
Kunstgewerbemuseum, Berlin
(Museum photo)

438 Bing and Grøndhal factory
Potpourri vase
c. 1898
Porcelain with underglazed *grand feu* decoration, 28 cm
Musée National de Céramique, Sèvres
(Photo Dominique Genet)

439 Società Ceramica Richard-Ginori
Vase
Exhibition of Applied Arts, Turin, 1902
Hard-paste porcelain, 115 cm
Museo della Porcellane di Doccia, Sesto Fiorentino
(Museum photo)

440 Josef Hoffmann and Wiener Werkstätte
Vase with handle
c. 1905
Perforated iron sheet, painted white, 24.5 cm
Österreichisches Museum für Angewandte Kunst, Vienna
(Musuem photo)

441 Émile Gallé
Model for crystal-glass vase decorated with pine branches
1903
Watercolor and ink on paper, 49.3 x 32.1 cm
Musée d'Orsay, Paris
(Photo Réunion des Musées Nationaux)

442 Josep Pey i Farriol and Antoni Serra
Vase
c. 1907
Porcelain with *grand feu* decoration, 14 cm
Museu Nacional d'Art Modern de Catalunya, Barcelona
(Museum photo)

443 Louis Comfort Tiffany
View of Oyster Bay
c. 1905
Stained glass from the William Skinner Residence, Fifth Avenue, New York, 184 x 168 cm
Metropolitan Museum of Art, New York (from the collection of the Charles Hosmer Morse Museum)
(Museum photo)

444 Jacques Gruber
Veranda
c. 1909–10
Detail originally from 4 Rue du Général-Drouot, Nancy
Opalescent and iridescent glass, wheel-engraved, engraved, and overlaid "American glass," grisaille, 265 x 150 cm
Musée de l'École de Nancy, Nancy
(Photo Gilbert Mangin)

445 Charles F. Annesley Voysey
Design for "Watersnake" wallpaper
c. 1893
Watercolor on paper, 78 x 56 cm
The British Architectural Library, London
(Library photo)

446 Hector Guimard and Le Mardelé
Wallpaper intended for bedrooms in the Castel Béranger
c. 1896–97
83 x 50 cm
Bibliothèque Forney, Paris
(Library photo)

447 Henry van de Velde
Angels Keep Watch
1893
Wall hanging, wool applied work on linen canvas ground, 140 x 233 cm
Kunstgewerbemuseum, Zürich (Sammlung Museum Bellerive)
(Museum photo)

448 Gerhard Munthe and Augusta Christensen
The Three Suitors
1897
Tapestry, wool, and linen, 183 x 221 cm
Vestlandske Kunstindustrimuseum, Bergen
(Museum photo)

449 Hélène de Rudder
Fetishism
1897
Tapestry, embroidery, and silks, 232 x 122 cm
Musées Royaux d'Art et d'Histoire, Brussels
(Photo A.C.L)

450 Sándor Nagy
Folding screen
c. 1904
Painted goatskin, repoussé and blind-tooled, 48 x 74 cm
Iparmüveszeti Múzeum, Budapest
(Museum photo)

451 Gerrit Willem Dijsselhof
Folding screen
1894
Cotton batik, embroidery, 155 x 215 cm
Stedelijk Museum, Amsterdam
(Museum photo)

452 Hermann Obrist and Berthe Ruchet
Orange lilies
1897
Tapestry, embroidery on silk and cotton, gold thread, 98 x 48 cm
Stadtmuseum, Munich
(Museum photo)

453 John Gibson
Venus
1851–56
Stained marble
Walker Art Gallery, Liverpool
(Museum photo)

454 Pierre-Charles Simart
Minerva
Exposition Universelle, 1855
Chryselephantine, height approx. 300 cm
Château de Dampierre
(Photo Dominique Genet)

455 Randolph Rogers
Nydia
1856
Marble, height 145 cm
Museum of Fine Arts, Boston
(Museum photo)

456 Francisque Duret
Victory
1857
Marble, height 200 cm
Musée d'Orsay, Paris
(Photo Dominique Genet)

457 Jules Cavelier
Cornelia, Mother of the Gracchi
1861
Marble, height 171 cm
Musée d'Orsay, Paris
(Photo Dominique Genet)

458 Chauncey Ives
Pandora
Copy made before 1891 from an 1863 model
Marble, height 95 cm
Museum of Fine Arts, Boston
(Museum photo)

459 Auguste Clésinger
Angel of Grief
1850
Stone
Saint-Sulpice Church, Paris
(Photo Ferrante Ferranti)

460 Antoine Étex
Ecce Homo
1856
Marble, height 250 cm
Saint-Eustache Church, Paris
(Photo Ferrante Ferranti)

461 Henri Chapu
Christ with Angels
1857
Plaster, 150 x 240 cm
Musée Chapu, Le Mée

462 Eugène Oudiné
Christ Between Two Angels and the Four Evangelists
Model at 1853 Salon
Stone
Church, Gennevilliers

463 Gabriel-Jules Thomas
The Stoning of St. Stephen
1863
Stone
Saint-Étienne-du-Mont Church, Paris
(Photo Dominique Genet)

464 Alexander von Bok
Psyche
1864
Marble
Russian Museum, St. Petersburg
(Photo Musée d'Orsay)

465 Alexandre Falguière
Winner of the Cockfight
1864
Bronze, height 174 cm
Musée d'Orsay, Paris
(Photo Dominique Genet)

466 Albert-Ernest Carrier-Belleuse
Bacchante
1863
Marble, height 180 cm
Musée d'Orsay, Paris
(Photo Dominique Genet)

467 Mathurin Moreau
Woman Spinning
1861
Marble, height 137 cm
Main staircase, Senate, Paris
(Photo Dominique Genet)

468 Jean-Baptiste Carpeaux
The Four Corners of the World Supporting the Celestial Sphere
1872 Salon
Original plaster model, height 280 cm
(Photo Dominique Genet)

469 Paul Dubois
Narcissus
1867 copy of the marble (1863–66) in the Cour Carrée of the Louvre, Paris
Marble, height 185 cm
Musée d'Orsay, Paris
(Photo Dominique Genet)

470 Jean-Joseph Perraud
Despair
1869
Marble, height 108 cm
Musée d'Orsay, Paris
(Photo Dominique Genet)

471 Eugène Delaplanche
Eve After Sinning
1869
Marble, height 145 cm
Musée d'Orsay, Paris
(Photo Dominique Genet)

472 Alexandre Schoenewerk
The Tarantine Girl
From the poem by André Chenier
1871
Marble, height 74 cm, length 171 cm
Musée d'Orsay, Paris
(Photo Dominique Genet)

473 Albert-Ernest Carrier-Belleuse
Torchère (for the Opéra in Paris)
1873
Plaster, height 260 cm
Musée d'Orsay, Paris
(Photo Dominique Genet)

474 Scipione Tadolini
Greek Slave
1862
Marble
Museo de Bellas Artes, Seville
(Photo Pedro Feria)

475 Louis-Ernest Barrias
The Oath of Spartacus
1872
Marble, height 213 cm
Tuileries Gardens, Paris
(Photo Dominique Genet)

476 Hiram Powers
Last of the Tribe
1870–72
Marble
National Collection of Fine Arts, Washington, D.C.
(Photo Musée d'Orsay)

477 Edward Roberts
First Pose
1876
Marble, height 130 cm
Museum of Art, Philadelphia
(Photo Musée d'Orsay)

478 Jens Adolph Jerichau
Slave
1871
Marble
Kunstmuseum, Randers
(Museum photo)

479 Jules Franceschi
Waking Up
1873
Marble, height 130 cm
Musée des Beaux-Arts, Nîmes
(Photo Musée d'Orsay)

480 Frederic Leighton
Athlete Struggling with a Python
1877
Bronze
Leighton House (indefinite loan from the Tate Gallery)
(Photo Musée d'Orsay)

481 Auguste Ottin
Modern Wrestling: The Hip Throw
1867
Bronze, height 145 cm
Barentin
(Photo Musée d'Orsay)

482 Johann Peter Molin
Knife Fight
1858–59
Bronze, height 223 cm
Nationalmuseum, Stockholm
(Photo Per-Anders Allstein)

483 Charles van der Stappen
Ompdrailles-le-Tombeau-des-Lutteurs
1892
Bronze
Rond-point d'Ixelles, Brussels
(Photo Benoît Roland)

484 Alfred Stevens
Courage and Cowardice
1858–67
Plaster, height 61.5 cm
Victoria and Albert Museum, London
(Museum photo)

485 Reinhold Begas
Mercury and Psyche
1857
Marble
Staatliche Museen, Berlin
(Photo Ferrante Ferranti)

486 Jean-Louis-Nicolas Jaley
Strength (for the facade of the Palais de Justice, Paris)
1858–59
Plaster, height 55.7 cm
Musée d'Orsay, Paris
(Photo Dominique Genet)

487 Joseph-Michel-Ange Pollet
Eloa
1869 Salon
Marble
Oued-Zenati, Algeria
(Photo Anne Pingeot)

488–89 Giuseppe Obici
St. Paul (details)
Marble
Atrium of basilica of S. Paolo Fuori le Mura, Rome
(Photos Ferrante Ferranti)

490 Pietro Galli
Font
1860
Marble
Basilica of S. Paolo Fuori le Mura, Rome
(Photo Ferrante Ferranti)

491 Bertel Thorwaldsen
Pius VIII Monument
1853–66
Marble
Saint Peter's Basilica, Rome
(Photo Alinari-Brogi-Giraudon)

492 John Duncan (architect), Frederick MacMonnies (sculptor)
Soldiers' and Sailors' Arch
1889–92
Grand Army Plaza, Brooklyn
(Photo Benoît Roland)

493 Giuseppe Sacconi et al. (architects)
Victor Emmanuel II Monument
1885–1911
Paolo Bartolini, *Quadriga of Liberty*, bronze
Enrico Chiaradia, *Victor Emmanuel II*, bronze
Leonardo Bistolfi, *Sacrifice*, marble
Piazza di Venezia, Rome
(Photo Cuchi White)

494 Charles Girault (architect), Thomas Vinçotte and Jules Lagae (sculptors)
Triumphal Arch
1904–5
Parc du Cinquantenaire, Brussels
(Photo Benoît Roland)

495 Verissimo da Costa (architect)
Triumphal Arch
1872
Célestin Calmels, *Fame Rewarding Valor and Genius*, stone
Praça do Comércio, Lisbon
(Photo Yan)

496 Ferdinand von Miller
Emperor Henry II Monument
1880
Bronze
Maximilianplatz, Bamberg
(Photo CESA)

497 Edmund von Hellmer
Land Power
1897
Marble
Hofburg, Michaelerplatz, Vienna
(Photo Angelo Hormak)

498 Auguste Bartholdi
The Saône and its Tributaries (fountain)
1887–89
Lead
Place des Terraux, Lyon
(Photo Dominique Genet)

499 Jean-Baptiste Carpeaux and Gabriel Davioud
The Four Corners of the World (Observatory Fountain)
1867–73
Bronze
Jardin de l'Observatoire, Paris
(Photo Bulloz)

500 Alfonso Balzico
Margarete (from Goethe's *Faust*)
1852
Marble
Galleria Nazionale d'Arte Moderna, Rome
(Photo Cuchi White)

501 Cristoforo Marzaroli
Contessa Sanvitale
Marble
San Giovanni Evangelista Church, Parma
(Photo Musée d'Orsay)

502 Jean Carriès
Auguste Vacquerie
1887
Bronze
Théâtre de l'Odéon, Paris
(Photo Dominique Genet)

503 Jean-Baptiste Carpeaux
Amélie de Montfort Dressed as a Bride
1869
Plaster, height 67.5 cm
Musée d'Orsay, Paris
(Photo Réunion des Musées Nationaux)

504 Émile Chatrousse
The Parisian Woman
1876 Salon
Plaster
City of Paris sculpture repository, Ivry (France)
(Photo Musée d'Orsay)

505 Venancio Vallmitjana i Barbany
Queen María Cristina de Habsburgo with Prince Alfonso
1888
Terra cotta
Museu Nacional d'Art Modern de Catalunya, Barcelona
(Photo MAS)

506 Reinhold Begas
Frau von Hopfen
1877
Marble, height 67 cm
Nationalgalerie, Berlin
(Museum photo)

507 Jules Dalou
Auguste Vacquerie (detail)
1887
Plaster, overall height 69 cm
Petit Palais, Paris
(Photo Giraudon)

508 Josef Maratka
Antonín Dvořák
1906
Bronze, height 33 cm
Narodni Galerie
(Gallery photo)

509 Philippe Solari
Paul Cézanne
1904–5
Plaster, height 49.5 cm
Musée d'Orsay, Paris
(Photo Dominique Genet)

510 Rodo (real name, Auguste de Niederhäusern)
Paul Verlaine (study for the marble in the Luxembourg Gardens)
c. 1894
Plaster, height 23 cm
Private collection
(Photo Bulloz)

511 Pietro Canonica
Elisabetta di Sassonia, Duchess of Genoa
1898
Marble
Galleria Nazionale d'Arte Moderna, Rome
(Photo Cuchi White)

512 Seraphin Sudbinin
Horrible
1906
Bronze
Russian Museum, St. Petersburg
(Photo Musée d'Orsay)

513 Théophile Barrau
Pierre de Fermat Monument
1898
Marble
Salle des Illustres, Capitole, Toulouse
(Photo Yan-Jean Dieuzaide)

514 Ludvig Brandstrup
Mr. and Mrs. Jacobsen
1904–6
Marble, height 72 cm
Ny Carlsberg Glyptotek, Copenhagen
(Museum photo)

515 Paul Trubetskoy
The Painter, Isaac Levitan
1899
Bronze, height 36 cm
Tretyakov Gallery, Moscow
(Museum photo)

516 Alexandre Falguière
Henri de la Rochejaquelein
1895
Plaster, height 216 cm
Musée des Augustins, Toulouse
(Photo André Berthelemy/studio Jean Cousin)

517 François-Antoine Zoegger
Notre-Dame du Retour (in the artist's studio)
Model of *Virgin* designed for Clermont-Ferrand
(Contemporary photo, supplied by Musée d'Orsay)

518 François-Antoine Zoegger
The Virgin and the Prophets
Model of *Virgin* at 1873 Salon
Embossed copper
Gable of cathedral, Clermont-Ferrand (France)
(Photo Arch. Phot. Paris/Spadem)

519 Jean-Marie Bonnassieux
Our Lady of France
1860–64
Bronze, height 22.70 m
Rocher Corneille, Le Puy (France)
(Photo Roger-Viollet)

520 Henri-Charles Maniglier
The Virgin Giving the Rosary to St. Dominic
1880–89
Marble
Basilique du Rosaire, Lourdes
(Photo L. L. Roger-Viollet)

521 Auguste Rodin
The Hand of God
1898–1902
Marble, height 94 cm
Musée Rodin, Paris
(Photo Bulloz)

522 Camille Claudel
Middle Age
1899–1903
Bronze, height 114 cm
Musée d'Orsay, Paris
(Photo Dominique Genet)

523 Albert Miserey
The Poison of the Borgias
1894
Plaster, height 205 cm
Musée Municipal, Bernay
(Photo Anne Pingeot)

524 Carl Millès
The Struggle for Existence
1903
Bronze, height 20 cm
Private collection
(Photo Musée d'Orsay)

525 Georges Minne
Solidarity
1898
Marble, height 67.9 cm
Cleveland Museum of Art, Cleveland
(Photo Cuchi White)

526 Georges Minne
The Prodigal Son
1896
Bronze, height 58.5 cm
Private collection
(Photo Musée d'Orsay)

527 Jean-Baptiste Carpeaux
Pensive Warrior
Plaster, height 15.5 cm
Petit Palais, Paris
(Photo Dominique Genet)

528 Jean-Baptiste Carpeaux
Ugolino
1860
Bronze, height 194 cm, width 148 cm
Musée d'Orsay, Paris
(Photo Dominique Genet)

529 Jean-Baptiste Carpeaux
The Town of Valenciennes Defending its Ramparts
1868
Plaster, height 60 cm, width 56 cm
Musée des Beaux-Arts, Valenciennes
(Photo Réunion des Musées Nationaux)

530 Jean-Baptiste Carpeaux
Antoine Watteau
c. 1863–64
Bronze, height 123 cm
Musée d'Orsay, Paris
(Photo Musée d'Orsay)

531 Edgar Degas
Nude Study for the Little Fourteen-Year-Old Dancer
c. 1880
Bronze, height 73.5 cm
Musée d'Orsay, Paris
(Photo Dominique Genet)

532 Edgar Degas
Horse and Rider
Bronze, height 24.8 cm
Musée d'Orsay, Paris
(Photo Dominique Genet)

533 Edgar Degas
Horse Standing
Wax, height 29 cm
Musée d'Orsay, Paris
(Museum photo)

534 Edgar Degas
The Little Fourteen-Year-Old Dancer, 1880
1881 (sixth Impressionist exhibition)
Bronze, tarlatan, and satin, height 103.8 cm
Musée d'Orsay, Paris
(Photo Réunion des Musées Nationaux)

535 Adolf von Hildebrand
The Bowls Player
1887 (destroyed during the war)
Marble
Staatliche Museen, Berlin
(Museum photo)

536 Aristide Maillol
Standing Bather
1899
Bronze, height 63 cm
Musée d'Art Moderne, Troyes
(Photo Dominique Genet)

537 Medardo Rosso
The Bookmaker
1894
Wax, height 43 cm
Museo Medardo Rosso, Barzio
(Photo Fabbri)

538 Medardo Rosso
The Flesh of Others
1883
Plaster
Museo Medardo Rosso, Barzio
(Photo Cuchi White)

539 François Pompon
Pensive Countrywoman
1905
Plaster, height 16.9 cm
Musée d'Orsay, Paris
(Photo Dominique Genet)

540 Auguste Rodin
Balzac
1898 Salon of the Société Nationale des Beaux-Arts
Plaster, height 275 cm
Musée d'Orsay (indefinite loan from the Musée Rodin), Paris
(Photo Dominique Genet)

541 Henri Vidal
Cain After Killing his Brother Abel
1896
Marble, height 195 cm
Tuileries Gardens, Paris
(Photo Dominique Genet)

542 Louis-Ernest Barrias
Monument to the Defense of Paris
1879–83
Bronze, height 4 m
Parvis de la Défense, Courbevoie
(Photo Dominique Genet)

543 Edward Thaxter
Meg Merrilies Furies
1881
Marble, height 64.5 cm
Museum of Fine Arts, Boston
(Museum photo)

544 Antoine Bourdelle
Large Warrior of Montauban
1898–1900
Bronze, height 211 cm
Musée Bourdelle, Paris
(Photo Dominique Genet)

545 Antoine Bourdelle
Screaming Faces: "War"
1899 Salon of the Société Nationale des Beaux-Arts
Bronze, height 93 cm
Musée Bourdelle, Paris
(Photo Dominique Genet)

546 Emmanuel Fremiet
Female Gorilla Carrying off a Negress
1859 Salon
Plaster (destroyed)
(Photo Musée d'Orsay, Paris)

547 Auguste Cain
Lion and Lioness Fighting Over a Boar
1882
Bronze, height 160 cm, length 330 cm
Tuileries Gardens, Paris
(Photo Dominique Genet)

548 Pierre Rouillard
Lion Overwhelming a Crocodile
1864
Marble
Beylerbeyi Palace Gardens, Istanbul
(Photo Laure de Margerie)

549 Georges Gardet
The Kill
1912
Bronze, central group, height 270 cm, width 285, depth 200
Installed in the middle of a pond on a private estate in Cognac, France, in 1919
(Contemporary photo, supplied by Musée d'Orsay)

550 Maurice-Désiré Ferrary
Salammbô
1899
Marble and bronze
Lady Lever Art Gallery, Port Sunlight, Merseyside
(Museum photo)

551 Harry Bates
Pandora
1890
Marble, ivory, and bronze, height 94 cm, width 50.8 cm
Tate Gallery, London
(Museum photo)

552 Antonin Mercié
Amphitrite
1900
Ivory, silver, and gold
Walter Art Gallery, Baltimore
(Museum photo)

553 Pierre Roche
Deliverance
1911 Salon of the Société Nationale des Beaux-Arts
Lead and plaster
Height 195 cm, width 195 cm
Musée d'Art et d'Industrie, Roubaix
(Photo Yves Desbuquois)

554 Max Klinger
Beethoven Monument
1899–1902
White, black, and purple marble, alabaster, ivory, and bronze, height 310 cm
Museum der Bildenden Künste, Leipzig
(Photo Christoph Sandig)

555 Paul Gauguin
Oviri
1894
Stoneware, height 74 cm
Musée d'Orsay, Paris
(Photo Réunion des Musées Nationaux)

556 Georges Lacombe
Isis
1895 Salon des Indépendants
Polychrome wood, height 111.5 cm
Musée d'Orsay, Paris
(Photo Dominique Genet)

557 Paul Gauguin
Be Mysterious
1890
Polychrome wood
Height 40 cm, width 153 cm
Musée d'Orsay, Paris
(Photo Réunion des Musées Nationaux)

558 Isidore Pils
Rouget de Lisle Singing the "Marseillaise" for the First Time at the House of Dietrick, Mayor of Strasbourg
1849 Salon
Oil on canvas, 74 x 91 cm
Musée Historique, Strasbourg
(Photo Lauros-Giraudon)

559 Honoré Daumier
The Republic (detail)
1848
Oil on canvas, overall dimensions 73 x 60 cm
Musée d'Orsay, Paris (Moreau-Nélaton Donation)
(Photo Réunion des Musées Nationaux)

560 Alexandre Antigna
Fire
1850–51 Salon
Oil on canvas, 262 x 282 cm
Musée des Beaux Arts, Orléans
(Photo Lauros-Giraudon)

561 Ernest Hébert
Malaria
1850–51 Salon
Oil on canvas, 135 x 193 cm
Musée d'Orsay, Paris
(Photo Réunion des Musées Nationaux)

562 Gustave Courbet
The Painter's Studio: A Real Allegory Determining a Seven-Year Phase of my Artistic Life
1855
Oil on canvas, 361 x 598 cm
Musée d'Orsay, Paris
(Photo Réunion des Musées Nationaux)

563 Henry Wallis
Chatterton
1856
Oil on canvas, 60.2 x 91.2 cm
Tate Gallery, London
(Museum photo)

564 John Everett Millais
The Valley of Eternal Rest
1858
Oil on canvas, 103 x 172 cm
Tate Gallery, London
(Museum photo)

565 John Everett Millais
The Blind Girl
1856
Oil on canvas, 82.6 x 62.2 cm
Museum and Art Gallery, Birmingham
(Museum photo)

566 Ford Madox Brown
The Last of England
1855
Oil on canvas, 82.5 x 75 cm (oval)
Museum and Art Gallery, Birmingham
(Museum photo)

567 William Holman Hunt
Our English Coasts or *Lost Sheep*
1852
Oil on canvas, 43.2 x 58.4 cm
Tate Gallery, London
(Museum photo)

568 Gustave Courbet
The Winnowers
1855
Oil on canvas, 131 x 167 cm
Musée des Beaux-Arts, Nantes
(Photo Lauros-Giraudon)

569 John Brett
The Stonebreaker
1857–58
Oil on canvas, 48.8 x 66.2 cm
Walker Art Gallery, Liverpool
(Museum photo)

570 Jules Breton
The Burning Rick
Completed in 1856
Oil on canvas, 139.7 x 209.6 cm
Institute of Arts (Robert H. Tannahill Foundation Fund), Detroit
(Museum photo)

571 Théodore Rousseau
The Village of Becquigny
1864 Salon
Oil on wood, 64.5 x 101 cm
Frick Collection, New York
(Museum photo)

572 Jean-Léon Gérôme
Greek Interior
1848
Oil on canvas, 15.5 x 21 cm
Musée d'Orsay, Paris
(Photo Réunion des Musées Nationaux)

573 William Holman Hunt
The Awakening Conscience
1853–54; retouched several times from 1856 to 1886
Oil on canvas, 76.2 x 55.9 cm
Tate Gallery, London
(Museum photo)

574 Gustave Doré
The Sister of Charity. An Episode from the Siege of Paris in 1870
Oil on canvas, 97 x 130 cm
Musée des Beaux-Arts André Malraux, Le Havre
(Photo Panorama)

575 Jean-Jacques Henner
The Artist's Mother Praying Beside the Body of her Daughter Madeleine
c. 1852
Oil on canvas, 46 x 66 cm
Musée National Jean-Jacques Henner, Paris
(Photo Réunion des Musées Nationaux)

576 Dante Gabriel Rossetti
Robert Browning
October 1855
Watercolor, pencil, and colored chalk, 12.1 x 10.8 cm
Fitzwilliam Museum, Cambridge
(Museum photo)

577 Franz Xaver Winterhalter
Empress Eugénie Surrounded by her Ladies-in-Waiting
1854
Oil on canvas, 300 x 420 cm
Musée National du Château, Compiègne
(Photo Dominique Genet)

578 Gustave Courbet
Young Women on the Banks of the Seine (Summer)
1856–57
Oil on canvas, 174 x 200 cm
Petit Palais, Paris
(Photo Dominique Genet)

579 Jules Dupré
The Sluice Gate
c. 1855–60
Oil on canvas, 51 x 69 cm
Musée d'Orsay, Paris
(Photo Réunion des Musées Nationaux)

580 Jean-François Millet
The Angelus
1857–59
Oil on canvas, 55.5 x 66 cm
Musée d'Orsay, Paris
(Photo Réunion des Musées Nationaux)

581 Narcisse Diaz de la Peña
Jean de Paris Heights, Forest of Fontainebleau
1867
Oil on canvas, 84 x 106 cm
Musée d'Orsay, Paris
(Photo Réunion des Musées Nationaux)

582 Frederic Edwin Church
Niagara Falls
1857
Oil on canvas, 108 x 229.9 cm
Corcoran Gallery of Art, Washington, D.C.
(Museum photo)

583 William Dyce
Pegwell Bay, Memory of 5 October 1858
Royal Academy 1860
Oil on canvas, 63.5 x 88.9 cm
Tate Gallery, London
(Museum photo)

584 Charles Le Roux
The Edge of the Wood, Cherry Trees in Autumn (detail)
1855 Exposition Universelle
Oil on canvas, overall dimensions 47.5 x 75 cm
Musée d'Orsay, Paris
(Photo Réunion des Musées Nationaux)

585 Martin Johnson Heade
Storm Over Narragansett Bay
1868
Oil on canvas, 81.6 x 138.4 cm
Amon Carter Museum, Fort Worth (Texas)
(Museum photo)

586 Jozef Israëls
The Shipwreck Victim
1861 Salon
Oil on canvas, 128.9 x 143.8 cm
National Gallery, London
(Museum photo)

587 Jean-Léon Gérôme
Ave Caesar, Morituri Te Salutant or *The Gladiators*
1859
Oil on canvas, 92.9 x 145.4 cm
Yale University Art Gallery, New Haven (Conn.)
(Museum photo)

588 Jules-Élie Delaunay
The Plague in Rome
1869
Oil on canvas, 131 x 176.5 cm
Musée d'Orsay, Paris
(Photo Réunion des Musées Nationaux)

589 Eugène Delacroix
Ovid in Exile Among the Scythians
1859
Oil on canvas, 88 x 130 cm
National Gallery, London
(Museum photo)

590 Edgar Degas
Spartan Girls Provoking Boys
c. 1860–62; reworked before 1880
Oil on canvas, 109 x 155 cm
National Gallery, London
(Museum photo)

591 Théodule Ribot
The Morning Wash
1863 Salon
Oil on canvas, 72.5 x 59 cm
Musée des Beaux-Arts, Montreal
(Photo Marilyn Aitken, MBAM)

592 Albert Anker
The Test (detail)
1862
Oil on canvas, overall dimensions 103 x 175 cm
Kunstmuseum, Bern
(Museum photo)

593 Constant Troyon
Grape Harvest Beside the Seine at Suresnes
1862
Oil on canvas, 97 x 139 cm
Musée d'Orsay, Paris
(Photo Réunion des Musées Nationaux)

594 Johan Barthold Jongkind
Ruins of Rosemont Castle
1861
Oil on canvas, 34 x 56.5 cm
Musée d'Orsay, Paris
(Photo Réunion des Musées Nationaux)

595 Adolphe Monticelli
Don Quixote and Sancho Panza (detail)
c. 1865
Oil on canvas, overall dimensions 96.5 x 130 cm
Musée d'Orsay, Paris
(Photo Réunion des Musées Nationaux)

596 Honoré Daumier
At the Theater
c. 1864
Oil on canvas, 97.5 x 90.4 cm
Neue Pinakothek, Munich
(Museum photo)

597 Édouard Manet
Le Déjeuner sur l'herbe
1863
Oil on canvas, 208 x 264.5 cm
Musée d'Orsay, Paris
(Photo Réunion des Musées Nationaux)

598 Gustave Courbet
Sleep
1866
Oil on canvas, 135 x 200 cm
Petit Palais, Paris
(Photo Dominique Genet)

599 Édouard Manet
Baudelaire's Mistress Reclining
1862
Oil on canvas, 90 x 113 cm
Szépművészeti Muzeum, Budapest
(Photo A. Szenczi Maria)

600 Gustave Courbet
Portrait of P. J. Proudhon in 1853
1865–67
Oil on canvas, 147 x 198 cm
Petit Palais, Paris
(Photo Dominique Genet)

601 Ernest Meissonier
The Retreat from Moscow (The French Campaign, 1814)
1864
Oil on wood, 51.5 x 76.5 cm
Musée d'Orsay, Paris
(Photo Réunion des Musées Nationaux)

602 Gustave Guillaumet
The Sahara, also known as *The Desert*
1867
Oil on canvas, 110 x 200 cm
Musée d'Orsay, Paris
(Photo Réunion des Musées Nationaux)

603 Léon Belly
Pilgrims Traveling to Mecca
1861
Oil on canvas, 161 x 242 cm
Musée d'Orsay, Paris
(Photo Réunion des Musées Nationaux)

604 Eugène Fromentin
Arabs Hunting with Falcons (Sahara)
1857 Salon
Oil on canvas, 99 x 142 cm
Musée Condé, Chantilly
(Photo Lauros-Giraudon)

605 Camille Corot
Souvenir of Mortefontaine
1864 Salon
Oil on canvas, 65 x 89 cm
Louvre, Paris
(Photo Réunion des Musées Nationaux)

606 Jean-François Millet
Grazing in the Mountains: Auvergne
1867–69
Oil on canvas, 79.3 x 98 cm
Art Institute of Chicago (Potter Palmer Collection), Chicago
(Museum photo)

607 Claude Monet
The Magpie
1868–69
Oil on canvas, 89 x 130 cm
Musée d'Orsay, Paris
(Photo Réunion des Musées Nationaux)

608 Alfred Sisley
View of Canal Saint-Martin, Paris
1870
Oil on canvas, 50 x 65 cm
Musée d'Orsay, Paris
(Photo Réunion des Musées Nationaux)

609 Alfred Stevens
The Letter Breaking It Off
c. 1867
Oil on canvas, 74.5 x 54.5 cm
Musée d'Orsay, Paris
(Photo Réunion des Musées Nationaux)

610 Edgar Degas
The Bellelli Family
1858–67
Oil on canvas, 200 x 250 cm
Musée d'Orsay, Paris
(Photo Réunion des Musées Nationaux)

611 Frédéric Bazille
Family Gathering
1867; retouched in 1869
Oil on canvas, 152 x 230 cm
Musée d'Orsay, Paris
(Photo Réunion des Musées Nationaux)

612 Charles Daubigny
Snow
1873
Oil on canvas, 100 x 200 cm
Musée d'Orsay, Paris
(Photo Réunion des Musées Nationaux)

613 Auguste Ravier
Marsh at Sunset
Oil on paper, glued onto card, 21 x 27.9 cm
Musée des Beaux-Arts, Lyon
(Photo Dominique Genet)

614 Camille Pissarro
Hillside at Jallais (Pontoise)
1867
Oil on canvas, 87 x 114 cm
Metropolitan Museum of Art, New York
(Museum photo)

615 Ernest Meissonier
The Tuileries in Ruins
1871
Oil on canvas, 136 x 96 cm
Musée National du Château, Compiègne
(Photo Dominique Genet)

616 Édouard Detaille
Picking up a Wounded Soldier, Battle of Champigny (November 1870) (fragment of *Panorama of Champigny*)
1880–82
Oil on canvas, 202 x 150 cm
Musée d'Orsay, Paris
(Photo Réunion des Musées Nationaux)

617 Mihály Munkácsy
The Condemned Man's Last Day
1870
Oil on canvas, 87 x 115.7 cm
Hungarian National Gallery, Budapest
(Museum photo)

618 Jean-Baptiste Carpeaux
Berezovski's Attempt to Assassinate Czar Alexander II, June 6, 1867
1867
Oil on canvas, 131 x 195 cm
Musée d'Orsay, Paris
(Photo Réunion des Musées Nationaux)

619 Paul Cézanne
Paul Alexis Reading to Émile Zola
c. 1869–70
Oil on canvas, 130 x 160 cm
Museu de Arte, São Paolo
(Photo Giraudon)

620 Édouard Manet
Émile Zola
1868 Salon
Oil on canvas, 146.5 x 114 cm
Musée d'Orsay, Paris
(Photo Réunion des Musées Nationaux)

621 Henri Fantin-Latour
A Corner of the Table
1872
Oil on canvas, 160 x 225 cm
Musée d'Orsay, Paris
(Photo Réunion des Musées Nationaux)

622 Frédéric Bazille
Studio in Rue de la Condamine (the figure of Bazille, standing to the right of the easel, may have been painted by Manet)
1870
Oil on canvas, 98 x 128.5 cm
Musée d'Orsay, Paris
(Photo Réunion des Musées Nationaux)

623 Henri Fantin-Latour
A Studio in Les Batignolles
1870
Oil on canvas, 204 x 273.5 cm
Musée d'Orsay, Paris
(Photo Réunion des Musées Nationaux)

624 Paul Cézanne
The Black Clock
c. 1870
Oil on canvas, 55 x 74 cm
Private collection
(Photo A. C. Cooper)

625 Antoine Vollon
Sea Fish
1870 Salon
Oil on wood, 83 x 119.5 cm
Musée d'Orsay, Paris
(Photo Réunion des Musées Nationaux)

626 Anselm Feuerbach
Medea
1870
Oil on canvas, 197 x 395 cm
Neue Pinakothek, Munich
(Museum photo)

627 Pierre Puvis de Chavannes
The Pigeon
1871
Oil on canvas, 136.7 x 86.5 cm
Musée d'Orsay, Paris
(Photo Réunion des Musées Nationaux)

628 Jules Lefebvre
Truth
1870
Oil on canvas, 264.7 x 111.8 cm
Musée d'Orsay, Paris
(Photo Réunion des Musées Nationaux)

629 Pierre Puvis de Chavannes
The Balloon
1870
Oil on canvas, 136.7 x 86.5 cm
Musée d'Orsay, Paris
(Photo Réunion des Musées Nationaux)

630 Camille Pissarro
Entrance to the Village of Voisins
1872
Oil on canvas, 46 x 55.5 cm
Musée d'Orsay, Paris
(Photo Réunion des Musées Nationaux)

631 Claude Monet
Argenteuil Bridge
1874
Oil on canvas, 60 x 80 cm
Musée d'Orsay, Paris
(Photo Réunion des Musées Nationaux)

632 Paul Cézanne
Study: Auvers Landscape (also known as *The Four District of Auvers*)
1873
Oil on canvas, 46.3 x 55.2 cm
Museum of Art (Samuel S. White III and Vera White Collection), Philadelphia
(Museum photo)

633 Alfred Sisley
The Flood at Port-Marly
1876
Oil on canvas, 60 x 81 cm
Musée d'Orsay, Paris
(Photo Réunion des Musées Nationaux)

634 Claude Monet
The Boulevard des Capucines
1873
Oil on canvas, 61 x 80 cm
Pushkin Museum, Moscow
(Museum photo)

635 Berthe Morisot
Paris Seen from the Trocadéro
c. 1871–72
Oil on canvas, 46 x 81.5 cm
Santa Barbara Museum of Art, Santa Barbara. Gift of Mrs. Hugh N. Kirkland
(Museum photo)

636 Claude Monet
The Gare Saint-Lazare, The Arrival of a Train
1877
Oil on canvas, 83.1 x 101.5 cm
Fogg Art Museum (Collection of Maurice Wertheim), Cambridge (Mass.)
(Museum photo)

637 Gustave Caillebotte
The Pont de l'Europe
1876
Oil on canvas, 131 x 181 cm
Musée du Petit Palais, Geneva
(Museum photo)

638 Edgar Degas
Portraits in an Office—Cotton Exchange in New Orleans
1873
Oil on canvas, 73 x 92 cm
Musée des Beaux-Arts, Pau
(Photo Giraudon)

639 Edgar Degas
The Ironer
c. 1869–73
Oil on canvas, 92.5 x 74 cm
Neue Pinakothek, Munich
(Museum photo)

640 François Bonvin
The Carcass, Pork-Butcher's Yard
1874
Oil on canvas, 61.5 x 50 cm
Musée St. Denis, Reims
(Photo Giraudon)

641 Wilhelm Leibl
Three Women in Church
1882
Oil on wood, 113 x 77 cm
Kunsthalle, Hamburg
(Photo Elke Walford)

642 Hans Thoma
Evening, The Artist's Mother and Sister in the Garden
1868
Oil on canvas, 157 x 115.3 cm
Kunsthalle, Hamburg
(Photo Elke Walford)

643 Franz von Lenbach
Reclining Boy
1857
Oil on card, 39 x 52.5 cm
Nieder Sächsiche Landesgalerie, Städtische Galerie, Hanover
(Museum photo)

644 Christian Krohg
The Sick Girl
1880–81
Oil on wood, 102 x 58 cm
Nasjonalgalleriet, Oslo
(Photo Jacques Lathion)

645 Jean-Charles Cazin
Tobias and the Angel
1880
Oil on canvas, 186 x 142 cm
Musée des Beaux-Arts, Lille
(Photo Lauros-Giraudon)

646 Gustave Doré
The Ascension
1879
Oil on canvas, 690 x 411 cm
Petit Palais, Paris
(Photo Dominique Genet)

647 Paul Chenavard
The Philosophy of History or *Social Palingenesis* (project for the Panthéon, Paris)
1848
Oil on canvas, 303 x 380 cm
Musée des Beaux-Arts, Lyon
(Museum photo)

648 Léon Bonnat
Madame Pasca (1835–1914), Dramatic Actress
1874
Oil on canvas, 222.5 x 132 cm
Musée d'Orsay, Paris
(Photo Réunion des Musées Nationaux)

649 William Bouguereau
The Birth of Venus
1879
Oil on canvas, 300 x 215 cm
Musée d'Orsay, Paris
(Photo Réunion des Musées Nationaux)

650 Henri Gervex
Rolla
1878
Oil on canvas, 175 x 220 cm
Musée des Beaux-Arts, Bordeaux
(Photo Giraudon)

651 Jules Bastien-Lepage
Haymakers
1877
Oil on canvas, 160 x 195 cm
Musée d'Orsay, Paris
(Photo Réunion des Musées Nationaux)

652 Jean-François Raffaëlli
The Guests Waiting for the Wedding
Before 1884
Oil on canvas, 52.5 x 68.5 cm
Musée d'Orsay, Paris
(Photo Réunion des Musées Nationaux)

653 Angelo Morbelli
For Eighty Centimes
1894–95
Oil on canvas, 69 x 124.5 cm
Civico Museo Borgogna, Vercelli
(Museum photo)

654 Henri Martin
The Dreamers (detail)
1903
Oil on canvas
Capitole, Toulouse
(Photo Jan/Jean Dieuzaide)

655 Giovanni Segantini
At the Rail
1886
Oil on canvas, 169 x 389.5 cm
Galleria Nazionale d'Arte Moderna, Rome
(Photo Scala)

656 Charles Angrand
The Western Line
1886
Oil on canvas, 73 x 92 cm
Josefowitz Collection
(Photo Réunion des Musées Nationaux)

657 Émile Bernard
Madeleine in the Forest of Love
1888
Oil on canvas, 138 x 163 cm
Musée d'Orsay, Paris
(Photo Réunion des Musées Nationaux)

658 Édouard Manet
Argenteuil
1874
Oil on canvas, 149 x 115 cm
Musée des Beaux-Arts, Tournai
(Photo Jules Messiaen)

659 Pierre-Auguste Renoir
Dancing at the Moulin de la Galette, Montmartre
1876 (exhibited 1877)
Oil on canvas, 131 x 175 cm
Musée d'Orsay, Paris
(Photo Réunion des Musées Nationaux)

660 Pierre-Auguste Renoir
The Theater Box
1874
Oil on canvas, 80 x 63 cm
Courtauld Institute, London
(Photo Giraudon)

661 Mary Cassatt
At the Opera
1882
Oil on canvas, 80 x 64.8 cm
Museum of Fine Arts, Boston
(Museum photo)

662 Giuseppe de Nittis
–64 *Racing at the Bois de Boulogne* (triptych)
1881
Galleria Nazionale d'Arte Moderna, Rome
(Photos Anderson-Giraudon)

665 Anton Mauve
Riding on the Beach at Scheveningen
1876
Oil on canvas, 45 x 70 cm
Rijksmuseum, Amsterdam
(Museum photo)

666 Jules-Élie Delaunay
Madame Georges Bizet
1878
Oil on canvas, 104 x 75 cm
Musée d'Orsay, Paris
(Photo Réunion des Musées Nationaux)

667 Federico Zandomeneghi
Portrait of Diego Martelli
1879
Oil on canvas, 72 x 92 cm
Galleria d'Arte Moderna di Palazzo Pitti, Florence
(Photo Gabinetto Fotografico)

668 Henri Fantin-Latour
Portrait of Charlotte Dubourg, the Artist's Sister-in-law
1882
Oil on canvas, 118 x 92.5 cm
Musée d'Orsay, Paris
(Photo Réunion des Musées Nationaux)

669 Édouard Vuillard
Portrait of the Artist
c. 1889
Oil on canvas, 24.5 x 19 cm
Musée d'Orsay, Paris
(Photo Réunion des Musées Nationaux)

670 Paul Gauguin
Self-Portrait
1889
Oil on canvas, 38 x 46 cm
Private collection
(Photo Lauros-Giraudon)

671 Paul Gauguin
Portrait of van Gogh
1888
Oil on canvas, 73 x 92 cm
Rijksmuseum Vincent van Gogh, Amsterdam
(Museum photo)

672 Edgar Degas
The Hat Shop
1879-84
Oil on canvas, 100 x 110.7 cm
Art Institute of Chicago (Mr. and Mrs. Lewis Larned Coburn Memorial Collection), Chicago
(Institute photo)

673 Eugène Carrière
The Young Mothers
c. 1897–1900
Oil on canvas, 279 x 357 cm
Petit Palais, Paris
(Photo Pierrain/Musées de la Ville de Paris)

674 Pierre-Auguste Renoir
Portrait of Madame Charpentier and her Children
1878
Oil on canvas, 154 x 190 cm
Metropolitan Museum of Art (Catherine Lorillard Wolfe Collection), New York
(Museum photo)

675 John Singer Sargent
Portrait of the Daughters of Edward D. Boit
1882
Oil on canvas, 221 x 221 cm
Museum of Fine Arts, Boston
(Museum photo)

676 Léon Frédéric
The People Shall One Day See the Sunrise (detail from the left-hand panel of a triptych)
1891
Oil on canvas, overall dimensions 106 x 138.5 cm
Collection of the Administration of Cultural Affairs of the French Community in Belgium, Brussels
(Photo A.C.L.)

677 Hans Makart
Charles V Entering Antwerp
1878
Oil on canvas, 520 x 952 cm
Kunsthalle, Hamburg
(Photo Elke Walford)

678 Jacob Maris
Dutch Riverside Town
1883
Oil on canvas, 73 x 127 cm
Musée d'Orsay, Paris
(Photo Réunion des Musées Nationaux)

679 Édouard Detaille
The Dream
1888
Oil on canvas, 300 x 400 cm
Musée d'Orsay, Paris
(Photo Réunion des Musées Nationaux)

680 Jean Béraud
Mary Magdalene at the House of the Pharisee
1891
Oil on canvas, 104 x 131 cm
Musée d'Orsay, Paris
(Photo Lauros-Giraudon)

681 Claude Monet
Turbulent Sea, Étretat
1883
Oil on canvas, 81 x 100 cm
Musée des Beaux-Arts, Lyon
(Photo Dominique Genet)

682 Peder Severin Krøyer
Fishing Boats
1884
Oil on canvas, 160 x 245 cm
Musée d'Orsay, Paris
(Photo Réunion des Musées Nationaux)

683 Vincent van Gogh
A Corner of Montmartre, The Powder Mill
1887
Oil on canvas, 35 x 64.5 cm
Rijksmuseum Vincent van Gogh, Amsterdam
(Museum photo)

684 Vincent van Gogh
Crows in the Wheatfields
1890
Oil on canvas, 50 x 100 cm
Rijksmuseum Vincent van Gogh, Amsterdam
(Museum photo)

685 George Clausen
The Stone-Gatherers
1887
Oil on canvas, 106.5 x 79 cm
Laing Art Gallery, Newcastle-upon-Tyne
(Museum photo)

686 Alfred Roll
Manda Lamétrie, Farmer's Wife
1887
Oil on canvas, 214.5 x 161 cm
Musée d'Orsay, Paris
(Photo Réunion des Musées Nationaux)

687 Émile Bernard
The Breton Round
1892
Oil on canvas, 54 x 81 cm
Musée des Beaux-Arts, Quimper
(Photo Giraudon)

688 Paul Sérusier
The Shower
1893
Oil on canvas, 73 x 60 cm
Musée d'Orsay, Paris
(Photo Réunion des Musées Nationaux)

689 Paul Cézanne
Pots of Geraniums
c. 1885
Black lead and watercolor, 31 x 27 cm
Mr. and Mrs. Paul Mellon Collection, Upperville (Va.)
(Collection photo)

690 Paul Cézanne
House and Farm of Jas de Bouffan
1885–87
Oil on canvas, 60 x 73 cm
Národní Galerie, Prague
(Gallery photo)

691 Vincent van Gogh
Branch of an Almond Tree in Blossom
1890
Oil on canvas, 73 x 92 cm
Rijksmuseum Vincent van Gogh, Amsterdam
(Museum photo)

692 Georges Seurat
Une baignade, Asnières
1883–84
Oil on canvas, 201 x 301.5 cm
National Gallery, London
(Museum photo)

693 Paul Signac
Saint-Tropez Harbor
1893
Oil on canvas, 56 x 46.5 cm
Von der Heydt Museum, Wuppertal
(Photo Giraudon)

694 Georges Seurat
Le Chahut
1889–90
Oil on canvas, 169 x 141 cm
Rijksmuseum Kröller-Müller, Otterlo
(Museum photo)

695 Henry van de Velde
Blankenberge Beach with Huts
1888
Oil on canvas, 71 x 100 cm
Kunsthaus, Zürich
(Museum photo)

696 Henri-Edmond Cross
Nocturne
1896
Oil on canvas, 65 x 92 cm
Musée du Petit Palais, Geneva
(Museum photo)

697 Henri de Toulouse-Lautrec
At the Moulin-Rouge
1892
123 x 141 cm
Art Institute of Chicago, Chicago
(Photo Giraudon)

698 Henri de Toulouse-Lautrec
"Ambassadeurs, Aristide Bruant"
1892
Six-color poster, 150 x 100 cm
Musée des Beaux-Arts, Orléans
(Photo Lauros-Giraudon)

699 Henri de Toulouse-Lautrec
At the Fernando Circus: The Rider
1888
Oil on canvas, 98 x 161 cm
Art Institute of Chicago, Chicago
(Photo Giraudon)

700 Vincent van Gogh
Portrait of Père Tanguy
1887
Oil on canvas, 92 x 75 cm
Musée Rodin, Paris
(Photo Giraudon)

701 Edgar Degas
Hélène Rouart
1886
Oil on canvas, 162 x 123 cm
National Gallery, London
(Museum photo)

702 Henri de Toulouse-Lautrec
Portrait of Vincent van Gogh
1887
Pastel, 57 x 46.5 cm
Rijksmuseum Vincent van Gogh, Amsterdam
(Museum photo)

703 Georges Seurat
The Black Bow
c. 1882–83
Conté crayon, 31 x 23 cm
Département des Arts Graphiques, Louvre/Musée d'Orsay, Paris
(Photo Réunion des Musées Nationaux)

704 Louis Anquetin
The Pont des Saints-Pères
1889
Oil on canvas, 119.5 x 126 cm
Kunsthalle, Bremen
(Museum photo)

705 James Ensor
Adam and Eve Being Driven from Paradise
1887
Oil on canvas, 205 x 245 cm
Koninklijk Museum, Antwerp
(Museum photo)

706 Henry de Groux
Christ Suffering Abuse
1888–89
Oil on canvas, 293 x 353 cm
Fondation Flandreysy-Espérandieu, Avignon
(Photo Daspet)

707 James Ensor
Christ's Entry into Brussels in 1889
1888–89
Oil on canvas, 257 x 430 cm
The J. Paul Getty Museum, Malibu
(Museum photo)

708 Frederic Leighton
The Garden of the Hesperides
1892
Oil on canvas, diameter 167.6 cm
Lady Lever Art Gallery, Port Sunlight, Merseyside
(Photo National Museums and Galleries on Merseyside, Liverpool)

709 Lawrence Alma-Tadema
Silver Favorites
1903
Oil on panel, 69.1 x 42.2 cm
City Art Galleries, Manchester
(Museum photo)

710 Maurice Denis
The Muses
1893
Oil on canvas, 171.5 x 137.5 cm
Musée d'Orsay, Paris
(Photo Réunion des Musées Nationaux)

711 Félicien Rops
Pornokrates
1878
Watercolor, pastel, and gouache, 75 x 48 cm
Private collection
(Photo A.C.L.)

712 Ferdinand Hodler
Night
1890
Oil on canvas, 116 x 239 cm
Kunstmuseum, Bern
(Museum photo)

713 Franz von Stück
Sin
1893
Oil on canvas, 124.5 x 95.5 cm (including frame)
Neue Pinakothek, Munich
(Museum photo)

714 Akseli Gallén-Kallela
Lemminkäinen's Mother
1897
Tempera, 85 x 118 cm
Ateneumin Taidemuseo, Helsinki
(Museum photo)

715 Charles Cottet
Grief Beside the Sea (detail)
1908
Oil on canvas, overall dimensions 264 x 345 cm
Musée d'Orsay, Paris
(Photo Réunion des Musées Nationaux)

716 Fernand Khnopff
I Lock My Door Upon Myself
1891
Oil on canvas, 72 x 140 cm
Neue Pinakothek, Munich
(Museum photo)

717 Nicolas Gay
Calvary, also known as *Golgotha*
1892
Oil on canvas, 278 x 223 cm
Musée d'Orsay, Paris
(Photo Réunion des Musées Nationaux)

718 Eugène Burnand
The Disciples Peter and John Running to the Tomb on the Morning of the Resurrection (detail)
1898
Oil on canvas, overall dimensions 82 x 134 cm
Musée d'Orsay, Paris
(Photo Réunion des Musées Nationaux)

719 Luc-Olivier Merson
Rest on the Flight into Egypt
1879
Oil on canvas, 71.8 x 128.4 cm
Museum of Fine Arts, Boston
(Museum photo)

720 Jean-Paul Laurens
The Wall
1895
Capitole, Toulouse
(Photo Jan/Jean Dieuzaide)

721 Pierre Puvis de Chavannes
Physics
1896
Public Library, Boston
(Photo Geoffrey Stein)

722 Arnold Bôcklin
St. Anthony
1892
Oil on wood, 152.5 x 105 cm
Kunsthaus, Zürich
(Museum photo)

723 Pierre Puvis de Chavannes
St. Geneviève Watching over the Sleeping Paris
1897
Panthéon, Paris
(Photo Giraudon)

724 Émile Claus
Halcyon Days
1892
Oil on canvas, 148 x 205 cm
Museum voor Schone Kunsten, Ghent
(Museum photo)

725 George Hendrik Breitner
Two White Horses Pulling Piles in Amsterdam
c. 1897–98
Oil on canvas, 100 x 152 cm
Musée d'Orsay, Paris
(Photo Réunion des Musées Nationaux)

726 Edvard Munch
Moonlight
1893
Oil on canvas, 140.5 x 135 cm
Nasjonalgalleriet, Oslo
(Photo Jacques Lathion)

727 Ejnar Nielsen
And In His Eyes I Saw Death (detail)
1897
Oil on canvas, overall dimensions 137 x 188 cm
Statens Museum for Kunst, Copenhagen
(Photo Hans Pedersen)

728 Gustav Klimt
The Beech Wood
1901–2
100 x 100 cm
Gemäldegalerie, Dresden
(Photo Deutsche Fotothek)

729 Gustav Klimt
The Kiss (detail)
1907–8
Oil on canvas, overall dimensions 180 x 180 cm
Österreichische Galerie, Vienna
(Museum photo)

730 Paul Gauguin
Nevermore
1897
Oil on canvas, 60 x 116 cm
Courtauld Institute, London
(Institute photo)

731 Paul Gauguin
Woman with Mango
1892
Oil on canvas, 70 x 45 cm
Museum of Art, Baltimore
(Museum photo)

732 Henri Rousseau
The Snake Charmer
1907
Oil on canvas, 169 x 189.5 cm
Musée d'Orsay, Paris
(Photo Réunion des Musées Nationaux)

733 Paul Gauguin
Anna, the Javanese
1893
Oil on canvas, 116 x 81 cm
Private collection
(Photo A. C. Cooper)

734 Paul Gauguin
Where Do We Come From? What Are We? Where Are We Going?
1897
Oil on canvas, 139 x 374.5 cm
Museum of Fine Arts, Boston
(Museum photo)

735 Lovis Corinth
Self-Portrait with Skeleton
1896
Oil on canvas, 66 x 86 cm
Städtische Galerie im Lehnbachhaus, Munich
(Museum photo)

736 Eugène Carrière
Paul Verlaine (detail)
1891
Oil on canvas, overall dimensions 61 x 51 cm
Musée d'Orsay, Paris
(Photo Réunion des Musées Nationaux)

737 Félix Vallotton
Félix Fénéon at the "Revue blanche"
1896
Oil on card, 52.5 x 65 cm
Josefowitz Collection, Lausanne
(Collection photo)

738 Jacques-Émile Blanche
Portrait of Marcel Proust
1891
Oil on canvas, 73.5 x 60.5 cm
Musée d'Orsay, Paris
(Photo Réunion des Musées Nationaux)

739 Joseph Granié
Yvette Guilbert
1895
Oil on canvas, 41 x 31 cm
Musée d'Orsay, Paris
(Photo Réunion des Musées Nationaux)

740 Julian Alden Weir
Reflections in the Mirror
1896
Oil on canvas, 61.5 x 34.5 cm
Rhode Island School of Design, Providence
(Museum photo)

741 Thomas Eakins
The Concert Singer
1890–92
Oil on canvas, 191 x 138 cm
Museum of Art, Philadelphia
(Museum photo)

742 Camille Pissarro
The Place du Théâtre Français
1898
Oil on canvas, 72.4 x 92.7 cm
County Museum of Art (Mr. and Mrs. George Gard de Sylva Collection), Los Angeles
(Museum photo)

743 Claude Monet
Rouen Cathedral, The Portal, Morning Sun
1893
Oil on canvas, 91 x 63 cm
Musée d'Orsay, Paris
(Photo Réunion des Musées Nationaux)

744 Henri Evenepoel
The Spaniard in Paris
1899
Oil on canvas, 215 x 150 cm
Museum voor Schone Kunsten, Ghent
(Museum photo)

745 Jan Toorop
Impeded Birth of the New Art (The Old Art Ousted by Modern Art)
1893
Black and colored chalks on paper, 62 x 68 cm (including frame)
Haags Gemeentemuseum, The Hague
(Museum photo)

746 Jens Ferdinand Willumsen
Jotunheim
1892–93
Oil on zinc and enamel on copper, 105 x 277 cm
J. F. Willumsens Museum, Frederiksund
(Photo P. Schandorf)

747 Mikhail Vrubel
Seated Demon
1890
Oil on canvas, 115 x 212.5 cm
Tretyakov Gallery, Moscow
(Photo Scala)

748 Albert Besnard
Primitive Man (sketch for the decoration of the École de Pharmacie)
c. 1883
Oil on canvas, 50 x 132 cm
Private collection, Boulogne-Billancourt (Paris)
(Photo Dominique Genet)

749 Ary Renan
Sappho
c. 1893 (?)
Oil on canvas, 120 x 100 cm
Scheffer-Renan Collection, Paris
(Photo Dominique Genet)

750 Albert Besnard
Truth, Drawing the Sciences in her Train, Spreads her Light Among Men
1890
Hôtel de Ville, Paris
(Photo Lauros-Giraudon)

751 Pierre Bonnard
Dusk or *The Croquet Game*
1892
Oil on canvas, 130 x 162.5 cm
Musée d'Orsay, Paris
(Photo Réunion des Musées Nationaux)

752 Édouard Vuillard
Window on the Woods
1899
Oil on canvas, 249.2 x 378.5 cm
Art Institute of Chicago, Chicago
(Museum photo)

753 Pierre Bonnard
The Bourgeois Afternoon
1900
Oil on canvas, 139 x 212 cm
Musée d'Orsay, Paris
(Photo Réunion des Musées Nationaux)

754 Théo van Rysselberghe
Émile Verhaeren Reading
1903
Oil on canvas, 181 x 241 cm
Museum voor Schone Kunsten, Ghent

755 Jószef Rippl-Rónai
Aristide Maillol
1899
Oil on canvas, 100 x 75 cm
Musée d'Orsay, Paris
(Photo Réunion des Musées Nationaux)

756 Ignacio Zuloaga y Zabaleta
Portraits: My Uncle and My Two Cousins
1899
Oil on canvas, 95 x 167.5 cm
Musée d'Orsay, Paris
(Photo Réunion des Musées Nationaux)

757 Pierre-Auguste Renoir
Large Bathers
1887
Oil on canvas, 115 x 170 cm
Museum of Art, Philadelphia
(Museum photo)

758 Paul Cézanne
Portrait of Vallier
1904–5
Oil on canvas, 107.4 x 74.5 cm
National Gallery, Washington, D.C.
(Museum photo)

759 Max Liebermann
The Parrot Man
1902
Oil on canvas, 102.3 x 72.3 cm
Museum Folkwang, Essen
(Museum photo)

760 Giuseppe Pellizza da Volpedo
The Fourth Estate
1901
Oil on canvas, 283 x 550 cm
Galleria Civica d'Arte Moderna, Milan
(Museum photo)

761 Paul Cézanne
Large Bathers
1898–1905
Oil on canvas, 208 x 249 cm
Museum of Art, Philadelphia
(Museum photo)

762 Aristide Maillol
Two Nudes in a Landscape
Oil on canvas, 97 x 122 cm
Petit Palais, Paris
(Photo Dominique Genet)

BIBLIOGRAPHY

PAINTING

Abélès, Luce. *Fantin-Latour. Coin de table* (Les Dossiers du Musée d'Orsay 18). Paris, 1987

Adam, Paul. "Peintres impressionistes." *Revue contemporaine* (May 1886)
———. "Les Artistes indépendants." *La Vogue* (September 6–13, 1886)

Adriani, G. *Toulouse-Lautrec. The Complete Graphic Works. A Catalogue Raisonné.* Exhibition catalogue. Royal Academy of Arts, London, 1988

A Golden Age. Art and Society in Hungary 1896–1914. Exhibition catalogue. Barbican Art Gallery, London, 1989

Aurier, Georges-Albert. "Le Symbolisme en peinture. Paul Gauguin." *Mercure de France* (March 1891)
———. *Œuvres posthumes.* Paris, 1893

Bacou, Roseline. *Odilon Redon.* Geneva, 1956

Bantens, Robert James. *Eugène Carrière, His Work and His Influence.* Ann Arbor, 1983

Bellier de la Chavignerie, Émile, and Louis Auvray. *Dictionnaire général des artistes de l'école française depuis l'origine des arts du dessin jusqu'à nos jours.* Paris, 1882 (vol. 1), 1885 (vol. 2), 1886 (supplement)

Bénédite, Léonce. *Great Painters of the XIXth Century and their Paintings.* London, 1910

Bernard, Émile. *L'Aventure de ma vie.* Geneva, 1954
———. *Souvenirs sur Paul Cézanne et lettres.* Paris, n.d.

Émile Bernard. Exhibition catalogue. Städtische Kunsthalle, Mannheim, 1990

Arnold Böcklin 1827–1901. Exhibition catalogue. Mathildenhöhe, Darmstadt, 1977

Boime, Albert. *The Academy and French Painting in the Nineteenth Century.* London and New York, 1971

Bonnard, Vuillard et les nabis 1888–1903. Exhibition catalogue. Musée National d'Art Moderne, Paris, 1955

Burne-Jones. Exhibition catalogue. Galleria Nazionale d'Arte Moderna, Rome, 1986

Cachin, Françoise. *Gauguin.* Paris, 1988–89

Chaudonneret, Marie-Claude. *La Figure de la République. Le concours de 1848* (Notes et Documents des Musées de France 13). Paris, 1987

Cogeval, Guy. *Les Années post-impressionistes.* Paris, 1986

Compin, Isabelle, Geneviève Lacambre, Anne Roquebert et al. *Musée d'Orsay. Catalogue sommaire illustré des peintures.* 2 vols. Paris, 1990

Gustave Courbet. Exhibition catalogue. Grand Palais, Paris, 1977–78

Courbet Reconsidered. Exhibition catalogue. Brooklyn Museum, New York, 1988

Degas. Exhibition catalogue. Paris, Detroit, and New York, 1988–89

Delevoy, Robert L. *Journal du symbolisme.* Geneva, 1977

Delevoy, Robert L., Catherine de Croës, and Gisèle Ollinger-Zinque. *Fernand Knopff.* Brussels, 1987

Denis, Maurice. "L'époque du symbolisme." *Gazette des Beaux-Arts* (March 1934): 165
———. *Du symbolisme au classicisme.* Paris, 1964

Desnoyers, Fernand. *Salon des Refusés, la peinture en 1863.* Paris, 1863

Distel, Anne. *Les Collectionneurs des impressionistes: amateurs et marchands.* Paris, 1989

Divisionismo italiano and *L'età del divisionismo.* Exhibition catalogue. Palazzo delle Albere, Trento, 1990

Dorra, Henri, and John Rewald. *Seurat.* Paris, 1959

L'École de la Haye. Les maîtres hollandais du XIXe siècle. Exhibition catalogue. Grand Palais, Paris, 1983

Eggum, Arne. *Edvard Munch.* Paris, 1983

Exhibitions of the Rosicrucian Salon (facsimile reprints of the catalogues of the Rosicrucian Salons). New York and London, 1981

Exigences de réalisme dans la peinture française entre 1830 et 1870. Exhibition catalogue. Musée des Beaux-Arts, Chartres, 1983

Fantin-Latour. Exhibition catalogue. Grand Palais, Paris, 1982–83

Fehrer, Catherine. *The Julian Academy, Paris: 1868–1939.* Exhibition catalogue. Shepherd Gallery, New York, 1989

Fénéon, Félix. *Œuvres plus que complètes.* Edited by Joan U. Halperin. Geneva and Paris, 1970

Ferdinand Hodler. Exhibition catalogue. Petit Palais, Paris, 1983

Fèvre, Jeanne. *Mon oncle Degas.* Geneva, 1949

Focillon, Henri. *La Peinture aux XIXe et XXe siècles. Du réalisme à nos jours.* Paris, 1928

Foucart, Bruno. *Le Renouveau de la peinture religieuse en France (1800–1860).* Paris, 1987

From Realism to Symbolism, Whistler and his World. Museum of Art, Philadelphia, 1971

Gamboni, Dario. "Après le régime du sabre, le régime de l'homme de lettres: la critique d'art comme pouvoir et comme enjeu." *La Critique d'art en France 1850–1900.* St.-Étienne, 1989

Gauguin. Exhibition catalogue. Grand Palais, Paris, 1989

Geffroy, Gustave. *La Vie artistique.* 8 vols. Paris, 1892–1903
———. *Claude Monet, sa vie, son œuvre.* Paris, 1980

Herbert, Robert L. *L'Impressionisme, les plaisirs et les jours.* Paris, 1988

Hofstätter, H. H. *Symbolismus und die Kunst der Jahrhundertwende.* Cologne, 1973

Holt, Elizabeth Gilmore. *The Art of All Nations, 1850–1873. The Emerging Role of Exhibitions and Critics.* New York, 1981
———. *The Expanding World of Art, 1874–1902.* Vol. 1: *Universal Expositions and State-Sponsored Fine Arts Exhibitions.* New Haven and London, 1988

James Ensor. Exhibition catalogue. Petit Palais, Paris, 1990

Jean-Aubry, G. *Eugène Boudin.* Paris, 1922

Jullian, René. *Le Mouvement des arts du romantisme au symbolisme: arts visuels, musique, littérature.* Paris, 1979

Kahn, Gustave. "Seurat." *L'Art moderne* (April 5, 1891): 108

Lacambre, Geneviève. "Les institutions du Second Empire et le Salon des Refusés." *Saloni, Gallerie, Musei e loro influenza sullo sviluppo dell'arte dei secole XIXe XXe.* Bologna, 1981

Lamberti, Maria Mimita. *Storia dell'arte italiana. Il novecento.* Turin, 1982

L'Art en France sous le Second Empire. Exhibition catalogue. Grand Palais, Paris, 1979

Legrand, Francine-Claire. *Le Symbolisme en Belgique.* Brussels, 1971

Le Japonisme. Exhibition catalogue. Grand Palais, Paris, 1988

Lorrain, Jean. "Pall Mall semaine." *L'Écho de Paris* (March 23, 1895)

Lumières du nord. La peinture scandinave au XIXe siècle. Exhibition catalogue. Petit Palais, Paris, 1987

Maas, Jeremy. *Victorian Painters.* London, 1978

Max Liebermann in seiner Zeit. Exhibition catalogue. Bayerische Staatsgemäldesammlungen, Munich, 1979–80

McLaren Young, Andrew, Margaret MacDonald, Robin Spencer, and Hamish Miles. *The Paintings of James McNeill Whistler.* 2 vols. New Haven and London, 1980

Manet. Exhibition catalogue. Grand Palais, Paris, 1983

Mathieu, Pierre-Louis. *Gustave Moreau, sa vie, son œuvre.* Fribourg, 1976

Maurice Denis. Exhibition catalogue. Orangerie, Paris, 1970

Maus, Madeleine Octave. *Trente années de lutte pour l'art. 1884–1914.* Brussels, 1926

Meier-Graefe, Julius. *Modern Art.* New York and London, 1908

Millet. Exhibition catalogue. Grand Palais, Paris, 1975

Le Musée du Luxembourg en 1874. Peintures. Exhibition catalogue. Grand Palais, Paris, 1974

Muther, Richard. *Geschichte der Malerei im XIX. Jahrhundert.* 3 vols. Munich, 1893–94
———. *The History of Modern Painting.* 4 vols. New York and London, 1907

Needham, Gerald. *19th Century Realist Art.* New York, 1988

Neo-Impressionism. Exhibition catalogue. Guggenheim Museum, New York, 1969

The New Painting. Impressionism 1874–1886. Exhibition catalogue. Fine Arts Museum, San Francisco, 1986

Nordau, Max. *Degeneration.* Lincoln, Nebr., 1993

The Orientalists—Delacroix to Matisse. European Painters in North Africa and the Near East. Exhibition catalogue. Royal Academy of Arts, London, 1984

Parsons, Christopher, and Martha Ward. *A Bibliography of Salon Criticism in Second Empire Paris.* Cambridge, 1986

Pissarro. Exhibition catalogue. Grand Palais, Paris, 1981

Post-Impressionism. Cross-currents in European Painting. Exhibition catalogue. Royal Academy of Arts, London, 1979–80

The Pre-Raphaelites. Exhibition catalogue. Tate Gallery, London, 1984

Puvis de Chavannes. Exhibition catalogue. Grand Palais, Paris, 1976–77

Redon, Odilon. *À soi-même, journal. Notes sur la vie, l'art et les artistes.* Paris, 1922

Renoir. Exhibition catalogue. Grand Palais, Paris, 1985

Rewald, John. "Extraits du journal inédit de Signac." *Gazette des Beaux Arts* (July-Sept 1949, April 1952, July-Aug 1953)
———. *The History of Impressionism.* 4th. ed. New York, 1973
———. *Post-Impressionism. From van Gogh to Gauguin.* 3rd ed. New York, 1978
———. *Cézanne, a Biography.* New York, 1986

Rey, Robert. *La Renaissance du sentiment classique dans la peinture française à la fin du XIXe siècle.* Paris, 1921

Félicien Rops. Exhibition catalogue. Centre Culturel de la Communauté Française, Brussels, 1985

Rosen, Charles, and Henri Zerner. *Romanticism and Realism. The Mythology of Nineteenth Century Art.* London and Boston, 1984

Rosenblum, Robert, and Horst W. Janson. *Art of the Nineteenth Century. Painting and Sculpture.* London, 1984

Russische Malerei im 19. Jahrhundert. Realismus, Impressionismus, Symbolismus. Exhibition catalogue. Kunsthaus, Zürich, 1989

Segantini. Exhibition catalogue. Palazzo delle Albere, Trento, 1990

Sensier, Alfred. *Souvenirs sur Théodore Rousseau.* Paris, 1872

Spate, Virginia. *The Colour of Time. Claude Monet.* London, 1992

Sutter, Jean. *Les Néo-Impressionistes.* Paris and Neuchâtel, 1970

Symboles et Réalités. La peinture allemande 1848–1905. Exhibition catalogue. Petit Palais, Paris, 1984

Le Symbolisme en Europe. Exhibition catalogue. Grand Palais, Paris, 1976

Symbolism in Polish Painting 1890–1914. Exhibition catalogue. Institute of Art, Detroit, 1984

Tschechische Kunst 1878–1914: auf dem Weg in der Moderne. Exhibition catalogue. Mathildenhöhe, Darmstadt, 1984–85

Terrasse, Antoine. *Pierre Bonnard.* Paris, 1967

Terrasse, Michel. *Bonnard. Du dessin au tableau.* Paris, 1996

Thompson, Belinda. *The Post-Impressionists.* Oxford, 1983
———. *Vuillard.* Oxford, 1988

Thuillier, Jacques. *Peut-on parler d'une peinture "pompier"?* Paris, 1984

Toulouse-Lautrec. Gemälde und Bildstudien. Exhibition catalogue. Kunsthalle, Tübingen, 1986–87

Un nouveau monde. Chefs-d'œuvre de la peinture américaine 1760–1910. Exhibition catalogue. Grand Palais, Paris, 1984

Vincent van Gogh and the Birth of Cloisonism. Exhibition catalogue. Art Gallery of Ontario, Toronto, 1981

Van Gogh. Exhibition catalogue. Rijksmuseum Vincent van Gogh, Amsterdam, 1990

Verkade, Jan. *Le Tourment de Dieu.* Paris, 1926

Watkins, Nicholas. *Bonnard.* London, 1994

Weisberg, Gabriel P. *The Realist Tradition. French Painting and Drawing, 1830–1900.* Exhibition catalogue. Cleveland Museum of Art, Cleveland, 1980
———, ed. *The European Realist Tradition.* Bloomington, 1982

William Bouguereau 1825–1905. Exhibition catalogue. Petit Palais, Paris, 1984

Worpswede. Eine deutsche Künstlerkolonie um 1900. Fischershude, 1986

SCULPTURE

Adams, Henry. *The Education of Henry Adams, an Autobiography.* Boston and New York, 1924

Adhémar, Jean. "Before the Degas Bronzes." *Art News* (November 1955): 35, 36, 70

L'Âge mûr de Camille Claudel. Exhibition catalogue. Musée d'Orsay, Paris, and Musée des Beaux-Arts, Lyon, 1988–89

Alexandre, Arsène. *Jean Carriès, imagier et potier. Étude d'une œuvre et d'une vie.* Paris, 1895

Alfred Gilbert, Sculptor and Goldsmith. Exhibition catalogue. Royal Academy of Arts, London, 1986

L'Art en France sous le Second Empire. Exhibition catalogue. Museum of Art, Philadelphia, Institute of Arts, Detroit, and Grand Palais, Paris, 1978–79

Auguste Rodin. Le Monument des Bourgeois de Calais, 1884–95. Exhibition catalogue. Paris, 1977

Aurier, Georges-Alfred. "Le Symbolisme en peinture." *Mercure de France* (March 1891): 155–56

Beattie, Susan. *Alfred Stevens, 1817–1875.* London, 1975
———. *The New Sculpture.* New Haven and London, 1983

Bénédite, Léonce. "Les Salons de 1904. La Sculpture." *Revue de l'art ancien et moderne* (June 1904): 431–40

Benoist, Luc. *La Sculpture romantique à travers l'art français.* Paris, 1928. New ed., Paris, 1994

Blanc, Charles. "Salon de 1866." *Gazette des Beaux-Arts* 2nd sem. (1866): 58–64

Blühm, Andreas, ed. *The Colour of Sculpture 1840–1910.* Amsterdam and Leeds, 1996–97

Bonnat, Léon. "Barye." *Gazette des Beaux-Arts* 1st sem. (1889): 374–82

Borel, Pierre. *Les Sculptures inédites de Degas. Choix de cires originales.* Geneva, 1949

Bresc, Geneviève, and Anne Pingeot. *Sculptures des jardins du Louvre, du Carrousel et des Tuileries.* 2 vols. Paris, 1986

Bruel, André. *Les Carnets de David d'Angers.* 2 vols. Paris, 1958

Burollet, Thérèse. "Le dépôt des sculptures de la Ville de Paris ou la survie de la statuaire parisienne." *Gazette des Beaux-Arts* no. 95 (1979): 114–24

Byvanck, W. G. C. *Un Hollandais à Paris en 1891. Sensations de littérature et d'art.* Preface by Anatole France. Paris, 1892

Camille Claudel. Exhibition catalogue. Musée Rodin, Paris, 1951

Cantrel, Émile. "Salon de 1863." *L'Artiste* (1863): 185–95

Caso, Jacques de. "D'un désespoir à l'autre: Perraud et Rodin." *"Il se rendit en Italie," Études offertes à André Chastel* (1987): 605–16

Centenaire de la reconstruction de l'Hôtel de Ville, 1882–1982. Exhibition catalogue. Hôtel de Ville, Paris, 1982

Ceschi, Carlo. *Le Chiese di Roma dagli inizi del neoclassicismo al 1961.* N.p., 1963

Chatrousse, Émile. "Les statuaires français à l'Exposition universelle de Londres." *L'Artiste* (1862): 121–26

Chesneau, Ernest. "Auguste Préault." *L'Art* 2 (1879): 3–15

Cladel, Judith. *Maillol, sa vie, son œuvre, ses idées.* Paris, 1937
———. *Rodin, sa vie glorieuse, sa vie inconnue.* Paris, 1950

Claris, Edmond. *De l'impressionisme en sculpture.* Paris, 1902

Claudet, Max. *Perraud statuaire.* 1877

Clément-Carpeaux, Louise. *La Vérité sur l'œuvre et la vie de J. B. Carpeaux.* Paris, 1934

Le Corps en morceaux. Exhibition catalogue. Musée d'Orsay, Paris, and Kunsthalle, Frankfurt, 1990

Crane, Sylvia E. *White Silence: Greenough, Powers and Crawford. American Sculptors in Nineteenth-Century Italy.* Coral Gables, 1972

Craven Wayne. *Sculpture in America.* New York, 1968

La "Danse" de Carpeaux. Exhibition catalogue. Musée d'Orsay, Paris, 1969

La "Danse" de Joseph Bernard. Exhibition catalogue. Musée d'Orsay, Paris, 1989

De Carpeaux à Matisse. La Sculpture française de 1850–1914 dans les musées et les collections publiques du nord de la France. Exhibition catalogue. Musée des Beaux-Arts, Calais, Musée des Beaux-Arts, Lille, Musée des Beaux-Arts, Arras, Musée des Beaux-Arts et d'Archéologie, Boulogne, and Musée Rodin, Paris, 1982–83

Dédicaces à Paul Verlaine. Exhibition catalogue. Metz, 1996

Degas scultore. Exhibition catalogue. Centro Mostre, Florence, and Palazzo Forti, Verona, 1986

Degas. Exhibition catalogue. Grand Palais, Paris, Musée des Beaux-Arts du Canada, Ottawa, and Metropolitan Museum of Art, New York, 1988–89

Delaborde, Henri. "L'art français au Salon de 1859." *Revue des Deux Mondes* (1859): 497–532

Delacroix, Eugène. *Journal 1822–1863.* Paris, 1980

Dreyfous, Maurice. *Dalou, sa vie et son œuvre.* Paris, 1903

Durand-Révillon, Jeanine. "Un promoteur de la sculpture polychrome sous le Second Empire: Charles-Henri-Joseph Cordier (1827–1905)." *Bulletin de la Société d'art français* (1984): 181–98

Emmanuel Fremiet, "La main et le multiple." Exhibition catalogue. Musée des Beaux-Arts, Dijon, 1988–89

Escholier, Raymond. *Matisse ce vivant.* Paris, 1956

Exposition commémorative du centenaire de la statue de la Liberté. Exhibition catalogue. National Library, New York, and Musée des Arts Décoratifs, Paris, 1986–87

Fumet, Stanislas. *Histoire de Dieu dans ma vie.* Paris, 1978

Gaborit, Jean-René, and Jack Ligot. *Sculptures en cire de l'ancienne Égypte à l'art abstrait.* Paris, 1987

Gardner, Albert Ten Eyck. *American Sculpture: a Catalogue of the Collection of the Metropolitan Museum of Art.* New York, 1965

Garnier, Charles. *Le Nouvel Opéra de Paris.* N.p., 1878–81

Gauguin, Paul. *Lettres de Gauguin à sa femme et à ses amis.* Edited by Maurice Malingue. Paris, 1946

Gauguin. Exhibition catalogue. National Gallery of Art, Washington, D.C., Art Institute of Chicago, Chicago, and Grand Palais, Paris, 1988–89

Geffroy, Gustave. "Auguste Rodin." *La Vie artistique* 3rd ser., vol. 2 (1893): 62–115

Geist, Sydney. *Brancusi: A Study of the Sculpture.* New York, 1968

George, Waldemar. *Aristide Maillol et l'âme de la sculpture.* Paris, 1977

Goode, James M. *The Outdoor Sculpture of Washington D.C. A Comprehensive Historical Guide.* Washington, D.C., 1974

Gray, Christopher. *Sculpture and Ceramics of Paul Gauguin.* Baltimore, 1963

Greenthal, Kathryn, Paula M. Kozol, and Jan Seidler Ramirez. *American Figurative Sculpture in the Museum of Fine Arts, Boston.* Boston, 1986

Guérin, Marcel. *L'Œuvre gravée de Gauguin.* Paris, 1927

Haesaerts, Paul. *Renoir sculpteur.* Hermes, n.d.

Hamel, Maurice. "Le Salon de 1887." *Gazette des Beaux-Arts* 2nd sem. (1887): 35–56

Havemeyer, Louisine. *Sixteen to Sixty. Memoirs of a Collector.* New York, 1961

Heilmeyer, Alexander. *Adolf von Hildebrand.* Munich, 1922

Bernhard Hoetger 1874–1949. Plastiken aus den Pariser Jahren 1900–1910. Exhibition catalogue. Kunsthandel Wolfgang Werner KG, Graphisches Kabinett, Bremen, 1977

"La pêche à la sardine." *L'Illustration* (July 1880): 49

L'Impressionisme nelle scultura. Exhibition catalogue. Galleria Peter Coray, Lugano, 1989

Janson, Horst W. *19th Century Sculpture.* New York, 1985

Jianou, Ionel, and Michel Dufet. *Bourdelle.* 3rd ed. Paris, 1984

Jouin, Jules. *David d'Angers, sa vie, son œuvre, ses écrits et ses contemporains.* 2 vols. Paris, 1878

Jullian, Philippe. "Les Roses-Croix." *Connaissance des arts* (August 1969)

Jullian, René, Jean Bernard, Lucien Stoenesco, and Pascale Grémont-Gervaise. *Joseph Bernard.* Fondation de Coubertin, 1989

Kjellberg, Pierre. *Les Bronzes du XIXᵉ siècle. Dictionnaire des sculpteurs.* Paris, 1987

Lagrange, Léon. "Le Salon de 1861." *Gazette des Beaux-Arts* 2nd sem. (1861): 159–71
———. "Le Salon de 1864." *Gazette des Beaux-Arts* 2nd sem. (1864): 5–44

Lami, Stanislas. *Dictionnaire des sculpteurs de l'école française au XIXᵉ siècle.* 4 vols. Paris, 1914–21

Lapaire, Claude. "Le Monument Verlaine par Auguste de Niederhäusern, dit Rodo." *Genava* vol. 37 (1989): 195–208
———. "Auguste de Niederhäusern—Rodo. Sculpteur de Verlaine." *Dédicaces à Paul Verlaine.* Metz, 1996

The Last Romantics. The Romantic Tradition in British Art. Exhibition catalogue. Barbican Art Gallery, London, 1989

Lemoine-Molimard, Marie-France. "Le décor extérieur du Nouveau Louvre sous Napoléon III: la série des *Hommes illustres*" *Revue du Louvre* nos. 5–6 (1978): 374–49

Le Normand-Romain, Antoinette, Anne Pingeot, Reinhold Hohl, Barbara Rose, and Jean-Luc Daval. *La Sculpture. L'aventure de la sculpture moderne—XIXᵉ et XXᵉ siècles.* Geneva, 1986

Mantz, Paul. "Salon de 1859. 4ᵉ article." *Gazette des Beaux-Arts* 2nd sem. (1859): 363–71
———. "Salon de 1863." *Gazette des Beaux-Arts* 2nd sem. (1863): 32–64
———. "Salon de 1865." *Gazette des Beaux-Arts* 2nd sem. (1865): 33–42
———. "Salon de 1869." *Gazette des Beaux-Arts* 2nd sem. (1869): 16–23
———. "Salon de 1872." *Gazette des Beaux-Arts* 2nd sem. (1872): 55–66

Margerie, Laure de. *Carpeaux, la fièvre créatrice.* Paris, 1989

Matisse, Henri. "Notes d'un peintre." *La Grande Revue* (December 25, 1908): 731–45

Ménard, René. "Salon de 1870." *Gazette des Beaux-Arts* vol. 52 (1870): 61–71

Michel, André. *Exposition universelle de 1900. Rapport du jury international. Classe 9, sculpture et gravure en médailles et en pierres fines.* Paris, 1902

Morhardt, Mathias. "Mlle Camille Claudel." *Mercure de France* (March 1898): 709–55

Muybridge, Eadweard. *The Human Figure in Motion.* New York, 1955
———. *Animals in Motion.* New York, 1957

New York City Public Sculpture by 19th Century American Artists. Exhibition catalogue. Metropolitan Museum of Art, New York, 1974

Ormond, Léonée and Richard. *Lord Leighton.* New Haven and London, 1975

Paolo Troubetzkoy 1866–1938. Exhibition catalogue. Museo del Paesaggio, Verbania Pallanza, 1990

Paris, Reine-Marie, and Arnaud de la Chapelle. *L'Œuvre de Camille Claudel.* Paris 1990

Pingeot, Anne. "Le décor de la Cour carrée du Louvre, les statues des niches du rez-de-chaussée." *Proceedings of the 24th International Congress on Art History* vol. 4. Bologna (1979): 119–42
———. "Les Gaulois sculptés." *Actes du colloque international de Clermont-Ferrand, 23–25 juin 1980* new ser., vol. 13 (1980): 255–82
———. *Les Vierges colossales du Second Empire.* Exhibition catalogue. Paris, 1986
———. "Le décor extérieur du Louvre sur la Cour carrée et la rue de Rivoli (1851–1936)." *Revue du Louvre* no. 2 (1989): 112–22
———. *Degas Sculptures.* Photographs by Frank Horvat. Paris, 1991

Pingeot, Anne, Antoinette Le Normand-Romain, and Laure de Margerie. *Catalogue sommaire illustré des sculptures du musée d'Orsay.* Paris, 1986

Pingeot, Anne, Philippe Durey, Antoinette Le Normand-Romain, and Isabelle Leroy-Jay-Lemaistre. *La Sculpture française au XIXᵉ siècle.* Exhibition catalogue. Grand Palais, Paris, 1986

Potvin, Jules. *Julien Dillens statuaire.* Brussels, 1913

Quand Paris dansait avec Marianne, 1879–1889. Exhibition catalogue. Petit Palais, Paris, 1989

Read, Benedict, *Victorian Scupture.* New Haven and London, 1982

Reff, Theodore. *The Note Books of Edgar Degas.* New York, 1985

Rencontres de l'école du Louvre. La sculpture du XIXe siècle. Une mémoire retrouvée. Les fonds de sculpture. Paris, 1986

Rewald, John. *Maillol.* Paris, 1939

Riccoboni, A. *Roma nell'arte.* Rome, 1942

Rivière, Anne, Bruno Gaudichon, and Danielle Ghanassia. *Camille Claudel, catalogue raisonné.* Paris, 1996

Rodin, Auguste. *L'Art. Entretiens réunis par Paul Gsell.* Paris, 1911. New ed., Paris, 1951

———. *Le Monument des Bourgeois de Calais (1884–1895).* Exhibition catalogue. Musée des Beaux-Arts, Calais, and Musée Rodin, Paris, 1977–78

The Romantics to Rodin. Exhibition catalogue. County Museum, Los Angeles, Institute of Arts, Minneapolis, Institute of Arts, Detroit, and Museum of Art, Indianapolis, 1980–81

Roquebert, Anne. *La Sculpture française au XIXe siècle.* Paris, 1986

Rubin, William, ed. *"Primitivism" in 20th Century Art. Affinity of the Tribal and the Modern.* Exhibition catalogue. Museum of Modern Art, New York, 1984

Salmson, Jules. *Entre deux coups de ciseau: Souvenirs d'un sculpteur.* Geneva and Paris, 1892

Scheyer, Ernst. "The Adams Memorial by Augustus Saint-Gaudens." *The Art Quarterly* (summer 1956): 178–98

Schmoll, General Eisenwerth Joseph. "Denkmäler der Arbeit-Entwürfe und Planungen." *Epochengrenzen und Kontinuität.* Munich, 1985: 175–216

"La Scultura nel XIX secolo." *Proceedings of the 24th International Congress of Art History.* 6th section edited by Horst W. Janson. Bologna, 1979

Shedd, Meredith. "A polychrome *effigie* in Paris: Eugène Guillaume's statue of St. Louis at the Palais de Justice." *Gazette des Beaux-Arts* (July—August 1988): 51–60

Sizeranne, Robert de la. "Notes et impressions." *L'Illustration* 2 (1902): 51

Sur les traces de Jean-Baptiste Carpeaux. Exhibition catalogue. Grand Palais, Paris, 1975

Nectoux, Jean-Michel, and Antoinette Le Normand-Romain. *1913. Le Théâtre des Champs-Élysées.* Exhibition catalogue. Musée d'Orsay, Paris, 1987

Thiébault-Sisson. "Au jour le jour, d'une vie d'artiste, Emmanuel Fremiet." *Le Temps* 2 (3 January 1896)

———. "Degas sculpteur raconté par lui-même." *Le Temps* (May 23, 1921)

Thompson, Richard. "The Sculpture of Camille Pissarro." *Sources. Notes in History of Art* (1983): 25–28

Thoré, Théophile. *Les Salons de W. Burger, 1861–1868.* Paris, 1870

Valéry, Paul. "Degas danse dessin."*Œuvres.* Vol. 2. Paris, 1960

Vermersch, E. "Le groupe de M. Carpeaux." *Le Figaro.* August 21, 1869

Villard, Nina de. *Le Courrier du soir.* April 23, 1881

Vollard, Ambroise. *Degas (1834–1917).* Paris, 1924

Wennberg, Bo. *French and Scandinavian Sculpture in the Nineteenth Century. A Study of Trends and Innovations.* Stockholm and Atlantic Highlands, N.J., 1978

Werth, Léon. "Aristide Maillol." *L'Art décoratif* (February 1913): 61–76

Yriarte, Charles. "Exposition des Beaux-Arts. Sculpture." *Le Monde illustré* 2nd sem. (1863): 46–47

Zgorniak, Marek. "Le château de Swierklaniec, œuvre oubliée d'Hector Lefuel. À propos d'un dessin du musée d'Orsay." *Revue du Louvre* no. 1 (1989): 46–52

PHOTOGRAPHY

Alland, Alexandre. *Jacob A. Riis, Photographer & Citizen.* New York, 1974

Ameluxen, Hubertus von. *Die aufgehobene Zeit.* Exhibition catalogue. Berlin, 1988

Buckland, Gail. *Fox Talbot and the Invention of Photography.* Boston, 1980

Cobb, Joséphine. "Alexander Gardner." *Image* no. 62 (June 1958)

Christ, Yvan, and Marcel Bovis. *150 ans de photographie française.* Paris, 1979

Dodier, Virginia. *Lady Hawarden.* Trans. by Françoise Heilbrun. Exhibition catalogue. Musée d'Orsay, Paris, 1990

Fossier, Françoise, Françoise Heilbrun, and Philippe Néagu. *Henri Rivière, graveur et photographe.* Exhibition catalogue. Musée d'Orsay, Paris, 1988

Frizot, Michel. *Avant le cinématographe la chronophotographie.* Beaune, 1984

Frizot, Michel, and Jean-Claude Gautrand. *Hippolyte Bayard, naissance de l'image photographique.* Amiens, 1986

Galassi, Peter. *Before Photography: Painting and the Invention of Photography.* Exhibition catalogue. Museum of Modern Art, New York, 1981

Gernsheim, Helmut. *Lewis Carroll, Photographer.* London and New York, 1949

———. *Julia Margaret Cameron, Her Life and Photographic Work.* New York, 1975

Gernsheim, Helmut and Alison. *L.Y.M. Daguerre: the History of the Diorama and the Daguerreotype.* London and New York, 1956

———. *Coburn, Photographer: an Autobiography.* New York, 1966

Greaves, Roger. *Nadar ou le paradoxe vital.* Paris, 1980

Green, Jonathan. *Camera Work, a Critical Anthology.* New York, 1973

Harker, Margaret F. *Henry Peach Robinson.* London, 1988

Heilbrun, Françoise. *Charles Nègre, photographe, 1820–1880.* Exhibition catalogue. Musée d'Orsay, Paris, 1980

———. "Auguste Salzmann, photographe malgré lui." *F. de Saulcy 1807–1880 et la Terre Sainte.* Paris, 1982

Heilbrun, Françoise, and Philippe Néagu. "Baldus: paysages, architecture." *Photographies* 1 (1983)

———. *Pierre Bonnard, photographe.* Exhibition catalogue. Musée d'Orsay, Paris, 1987

Horan, James D. *Timothy O'Sullivan, America's Forgotten Photographer.* New York, 1966

Huberman, Georges Didi. *Invention de l'hystérie, Charcot et l'iconographie de la Salpêtrière.* Paris, 1982

Jammes, André, and Eugenia Parry Janis. *The Art of French Calotype.* Princeton, 1983

Jammes, Bruno. "John B. Greene, an American calotypist." *History of Photography.* October 1981

Jammes, Isabelle. *Blanquart-Évrard et les origines de l'édition photographique en France.* Paris, 1981

Janis, Eugenia Parry, and Josiane Sartre. *Henry Le Secq, photographe de 1850 à 1860.* Paris, 1986

Janis, Eugenia Parry. *The Photography of Gustave Le Gray.* Exhibition catalogue. Chicago, 1987

Jay, Paul. *Niepce, genèse d'une invention.* Chalon-sur-Saône, 1988

Jones, Edgar Yoxall. *Father of Art Photography, O. G. Rejlander 1813–1875.* Newton Abbott, 1973

MacCauley, Anne. "The Career of Charles Aubry." *The J. Paul Getty Museum Journal* vol. 14 (1986): 157–72

Marbot, Bernard. *Une invention du XIXe siècle, expression et technique: la photographie.* Exhibition catalogue. Bibliothèque Nationale, Paris, 1976

Meredith, Roy. *Mr. Lincoln's Cameraman, Mathew B. Brady.* New ed., New York, 1974

Naef, Weston J. *Fifty Pioneers of Modern Photography, the Collection of Alfred Stieglitz.* New York, 1978

Naef, Weston J., and James N. Wood. *Era of Exploration: the Rise of Landscape Photography in the American West 1860–1885.* Exhibition catalogue. Metropolitan Museum of Art, New York, 1975

Naef, Weston J., and Bernard Marbot. *Regards sur la photographie en France au XIXe siècle.* Exhibition catalogue. Petit Palais, Paris, 1980

Néagu, Philippe, and Jean-Jacques Poulet-Allamgny. *Nadar.* Vol. 2. Paris, 1979

Newhall, Beaumont. *Photography 1839–1937.* Exhibition catalogue. Museum of Modern Art, New York, 1937

———. *Frederick H. Evans.* New York, 1973

Norman, Dorothy. *Alfred Stieglitz: An American Seer.* New York, 1973

Ranke, Winfried. *Heinrich Zille, Photographien Berlin 1890–1910.* Munich, 1975

Scharf, Aaron. *Art and Photography.* London, 1968

Stevenson, Sara. *David Octavius Hill and Robert Adamson. Catalogue of their Calotypes Taken between 1843 and 1847 in the Collection of the Scottish National Portrait Gallery.* Edinburgh, 1981

Szarkowski, John, and Maria Morris. *The Work of Atget.* Vols. 1–4. New York, 1981–83

Turner, Peter, and Richard Wood. *P. H. Emerson, Photographer of Norfolk.* London, 1974

Vitali, Lamberto. *Un fotografo fin de siècle: Il conte Primoli.* Turin, 1968

Zola, Émile-François. *Zola photographe.* Paris, 1979

THE DECORATIVE ARTS

Alcouffe, Daniel. "Les émailleurs français à l'Exposition universelle de 1867." *Antologia di Belle Arti* vol. 4 (1980): 102–21

Alcouffe, Daniel, Marc Bascou, A. Dion-Tenenbaum, and Philippe Thiébaut. *Le arti decorative alli grandi esposizioni universali, 1851–1900.* Milan, 1988

L'Anjou religieux et les orfèvres du XIXe siècle. Exhibition catalogue. Musée des Beaux-Arts, Angers, 1983

Architect-Designers. Pugin to Mackintosh. Exhibition catalogue. Fine Art Society, London, 1981

Art & Design in Europe and America. 1800–1900. Exhibition catalogue. Victoria and Albert Museum, London, 1987

L'Art en France sous le Second Empire. Exhibition catalogue. Grand Palais, Paris, 1979

Art Nouveau Belgium France. Exhibition catalogue. Institute of the Arts, Rice University, Houston, 1976

Art nouveau en Belgique. Exhibition catalogue. Palais des Beaux-Arts, Brussels, 1980–81

Art Nouveau in Munich. Exhibition catalogue. Philadelphia Museum of Art, Philadelphia, 1988

The Arts & Crafts Movement. Exhibition catalogue. Fine Art Society, London, 1973

Aslin, Elizabeth. *The Aesthetic Movement. Prelude to Art Nouveau.* New York, 1969

Barten, Sigrid. *René Lalique. Schmuck und Objets d'art 1890–1910.* Munich, 1977

Bascou, Marc. "Émile Reiber, Le Japon pour tous." *L'Objet d'art* 13 (1989): 52–61

———. "A Newly Rediscovered Credence by A. H. Sauvrezy for the Paris Universal Exhibition of 1867." *Decorative Arts Society Journal* 16 (1992): 44–49

———. *L'émail français au XIXè siècle. 1860–1890.* Exhibition catalogue. Musée Municipal de l'Evêché, Limoges, 1994

Bayer, Patricia. *The Art of René Lalique.* London, 1991

Becker, Vivienne. *Art Nouveau Jewelry.* London, 1985

Billcliffe, Roger. *Charles Rennie Mackintosh. The Complete Furniture, Furniture Drawings & Interior Designs.* London, 1979

Bossaglia, Rossana. *Il Liberty in Italia.* Milan, 1968

Bouilhet, Henri. *L'Orfèvrerie française au XVIIIe et XIXe siècles.* Paris, 1908–12

Bouillon, Jean. *Journal de l'Art nouveau.* Geneva, 1985

Bouvier, Roselyne. *Majorelle. Une aventure moderne.* Paris, 1991

Burty, Philippe. *Chefs-d'œuvre des arts industriels. Céramique, verrerie et vitraux, émaux, métaux, orfèvrerie et bijouterie, tapisserie.* Paris, 1866

———. "Les Industries de luxe à l'exposition de l'Union centrale." *Gazette des Beaux-Arts* (December 1869): 529–46

Cervera, Juan. *Modernismo, the Catalan Renaissance of the Arts.* New York, 1976

Charpentier, Françoise-Thérèse. *Émile Gallé, industriel et poète, 1846–1904.* Nancy, 1978

———, ed. *Art nouveau. L'École de Nancy.* Paris, 1987

Les Chefs-d'œuvre d'art à l'Exposition universelle, 1878. Edited by Bergerat. Paris, 1878

Cirici-Pellicer, Alexandre. *El Arte Modernista Catalan.* Barcelona, 1951

Clouzot, Henri. *Le Style Louis-Philippe-Napoléon III.* Paris, 1939

Constantine, Mildred, ed., and Peter Selz. *Art Nouveau. Art at the Turn of the Century.* New York, 1959

Cooper, Jeremy. *Victorian and Edwardian Furniture and Interiors.* London, 1987

Culme, John. *Nineteenth-Century Silver.* London, 1977

Die Bugattis. Exhibition catalogue. Museum für Kunst und Gewerbe, Hamburg, 1983

Durant, Stuart. *Ornament. A Survey of Decoration since 1830.* London, 1986

Ein Dokument Deutscher Kunst—Darmstadt 1901–1976. Exhibition catalogue. Hessisches Landesmuseum, Darmstadt, 1976

Europa 1900. Exhibition catalogue. Musée des Beaux-Arts, Ostend, 1967

Exposition universelle de 1855. Rapports du jury mixte international. Paris, 1856

Exposition universelle de 1867 à Paris. Rapports du jury international. Paris, 1868

Exposition universelle de 1878. Les Beaux-Arts et les arts décoratifs. Edited by Louis Gonse. Paris, 1879

Exposition universelle de 1889 à Paris. Rapports du jury international. Paris, 1891

Faÿ-Hallé, Antoinette, and Barbara Mundt. *La Porcelaine européenne au XIXe siècle.* Fribourg and Paris, 1983

Fenz, Werner. *Kolo Moser, Internationaler Jugendstil und Wiener Sezession.* Salzburg, 1984

Francastel, Pierre. *Art et technique du XIXe.* Geneva, 1956

Gallé. Exhibition catalogue. Musée du Luxembourg, Paris, 1985–86

Gallé, Émile. *Le Décor symbolique.* Nancy, 1900

Gans, Louis. *Nieuwe kunst. De Nederlandse Bijdrage tot de Art Nouveau.* Utrecht, 1960

Gere, Charlotte, and Michael Whiteway. *Nineteenth Century Design, from Pugin to Mackintosh.* London, 1993

Glass from World's Fairs 1851–1904. Exhibition catalogue. Corning Museum of Glass, 1986

Goldschmiede Arbeiten des Historismus in Köln. Exhibition catalogue. Stadtmuseum, Cologne, 1980

Guimard. Exhibition catalogue. Musée d'Orsay, Paris, 1992

Henderson, Philip. *William Morris, His Life, Work and Friends.* London, 1967

Henry van de Velde, 1863–1957. Exhibition catalogue. Palais des Beaux-Arts, Brussels, 1963

Herter Brothers. Furniture and Interiors for a Gilded Age. Exhibition catalogue. Museum of Fine Arts, Houston, 1994, and Metropolitan Museum of Art, New York, 1995

High Victorian Design. Le style de la grande époque victorienne. Exhibition catalogue. Art Gallery, Winnipeg, 1974–75

Historismus. Kunsthandwerk und Industrie im Zeitalter der Weltausstellungen. Exhibition catalogue. Kunstgewerbemuseum, Berlin, 1973

Hohe Kunst zwischen Biedermeier und Jugendstil: Historismus. Exhibition catalogue. Museum für Kunst und Gewerbe, Hamburg, 1977

Homage to Barcelona—The City and its Art 1888–1936. Exhibition catalogue. Hayward Gallery, London, 1985–86

Howarth, Thomas. *Charles Rennie Mackintosh and the Modern Movement.* London, 1952

100 Jahre Österreichisches Museum für Angewandte Kunst. Kunstgewerbe des Historismus. Österreichisches Museum für Angewandte Kunst, Vienna, 1964–65

Il Liberty italiano e ticinese. Exhibition catalogue. Lugano, 1981

In Pursuit of Beauty. Americans and the Aesthetic Movement. Exhibition catalogue. Metropolitan Museum of Art, New York, 1986

Johnson, Diane Chambers. *American Art Nouveau.* New York, 1979

Jugendstil. Exhibition catalogue. Palais des Beaux-Arts, Brussels, 1977

Kempton, Richard. *Art Nouveau, an Annotated Bibliography.* Los Angeles, 1977

Koch, Robert. *Louis C. Tiffany. Rebel in Glass.* New York, 1964

Laborde, Léon de. *De l'union des arts et de l'industrie.* Paris, 1856

Leben und Arbeiten im Industrie-Zeitalter. Exhibition catalogue. Germanisches Nationalmuseum, Nuremberg, 1985

Ledoux-Lebard, Denise. *Les Ébénistes du XIXe siècle, 1795–1889, leurs œuvres et leurs marques.* Paris, 1984

Lenning, Henry F. *The Art Nouveau.* The Hague, 1951

Les Sources du XXe siècle. Exhibition catalogue. Musée National d'Art Moderne, Paris, 1960–61

Levy, Mervyn. *Liberty Style. The Classic Years: 1898–1910.* London, 1986

London, International Exhibition of 1851. The Art-Journal Illustrated Catalogue. The Industry of all Nations, 1851. London, 1851

London, International Exhibition of 1862. The Art-Journal Illustrated Catalogue of the International Exhibition, 1862. London, 1862

London, International Exhibition of 1871. The Art-Journal Catalogue to the International Exhibition, 1871. London, 1871–72

L'orfèvrerie française au XIXè siècle. XVème Rencontres de l'École du Louvre, La Documentation française (1994)

Loze, Pierre. *Belgian Art Nouveau.* Ghent, 1991

Luchet, Auguste. *L'Art industriel à l'Exposition universelle de 1867.* Paris, 1868

Madsen, Stephan Tschudi. *Sources of Art Nouveau.* Oslo, 1956

Mainardi, Patricia. *Art and Politics of the Second Empire.* New Haven and London, 1987

Mérimée, Prosper. "Considérations sur l'application de l'Art à l'Industrie à l'Exposition universelle." *Exposition universelle de Londres de 1862. Rapports des membres de la section française du jury international.* Vol. 6. Paris, 1862–64: 247–62

Mesnard, Jules. *Les Merveilles de l'Exposition universelle de 1867.* Paris, 1867

Minton, 1798–1910. Exhibition catalogue. Victoria and Albert Museum, London, 1976

Mundt, Barbara. *Historismus. Kunstgewerbe zwischen Biedermeier und Jugendstil.* Munich, 1981

Nancy 1900. Exhibition catalogue. Münchner Stadtmuseum, Munich, 1981

19th Century America: Furniture and Other Decorative Arts. Exhibition catalogue. Metropolitan Museum of Art, New York, 1970

Nocq, Henri. *Tendances nouvelles.* Paris, 1896

Opstad, Jan Lanitz. *Norsk Art Nouveau.* Oslo, 1979

Payne, Christopher. *19th Century European Furniture.* Antique Collectors' Club, 1985

Pecher, Wolfgang D. *Henry Van de Velde. Das Gesamtwerk.* Vol. 1. Munich, 1981

Porcelaines de Sèvres au XIXe siècle. Exhibition catalogue. Musée National de Céramique, Sèvres, 1975

Pugin. A Gothic Passion. Exhibition catalogue. Victoria and Albert Museum, London, 1994

René Lalique. Bijoux, verre. Exhibition catalogue. Musée des Arts Décoratifs, Paris, 1991

Samoyault-Verlet, Colombe. "Furniture in France under the Second Empire." *The Connoisseur* vol. 199 (1978): 264–71

Schmalenbach, Fritz. *Jugendstil. Ein Beitrag zu Theorie und Geschichte der Flächenkunst.* Würzburg, 1935

Schmutzler, Robert. *Art Nouveau—Jugendstil.* Stuttgart, 1962

Schweiger, W. J. *Wiener Werkstätte.* Vienna, 1982

Seling, Helmut, ed. *Jugendstil. Der Weg ins 20. Jahrhundert.* Heidelberg, 1959

Snowman, Kenneth, ed. *The Master Jewelers.* London. 1990

The Strange Genius of William Burges. Exhibition catalogue. National Museum of Wales, Cardiff, and Victoria and Albert Museum, London, 1981

Torino 1902. Le arti décorative internazionale del nuovo secolo. Exhibition catalogue. Galleria Civica d'Arte Moderna e Contemporanea, Turin, 1994

Verlet, Pierre. *Styles, meubles, décors.* Paris, 1972

Victorian and Edwardian Decorative Art. The Handley-Read Collection. Exhibition catalogue. Royal Academy of Arts, London, 1972

Victorian Church Art. Exhibition catalogue. Victoria and Albert Museum, London, 1971–72

Waring, J. B. *Masterpieces of Industrial Art and Sculpture at the International Exhibition, 1862.* London, 1863

Watelet, Jacques-Grégoire. *Gustave Serrurier-Bovy, architecte et décorateur, 1858–1910.* Brussels, 1975

Weisberg, Gabriel P. *Art Nouveau Bing. Paris Style 1900.* New York, 1986

Weltkulturen und Moderne Kunst. Exhibition catalogue. Munich, 1972

Werner, J., and W. Schweiger. *Wiener Werkstätte.* London, 1984

Wichmann, Siegfried. *Jugendstil.* Munich, 1977

———. *Japonisme.* London, 1981

———. *Jugendstil Floral Funktional.* Hernsching, 1984

William Morris. Exhibition catalogue. Victoria and Albert Museum, London 1994

ARCHITECTURE

Aboville, Christine d'. *Sur les traces de l'art nouveau—Architecture 1900 au Havre.* Le Havre, 1987

Amery, Colin, and Gavin Stamp. *Victorian Buildings of London, 1857–1887, an Illustrated Guide.* London, 1980

"Istanbul." *Archives d'Architecture moderne.* Brussels, 1982

Art Nouveau—Art and Design at the Turn of the Century. New York, 1959. New ed., New York, 1975

Art Nouveau—Belgium-France. Exhibition catalogue. Rice Museum, Houston, and Art Institute of Chicago, Chicago, 1976

Baker, Paul. *Richard Morris Hunt.* Boston, 1980

Benevolo, Léonardo. *Histoire de l'architecture moderne.* Vol. 1: *La Révolution industrielle. Espace et Architecture.* Paris, 1978

Blanc, Charles. "La Rue des Nations." *L'Art et l'industrie de tous les peuples à l'Exposition universelle de 1878.* Paris, 1878

Borsi, Franco. *Bruxelles 1900.* Brussels, 1979

Borsi, Franco, and Ezio Godoli. *Vienne architecture 1900.* Paris, 1985

———. *Paris Art nouveau—Architecture et décoration.* Paris, 1989

Borsi, Franco, and Paolo Portoghesi. *Victor Horta.* Brussels, 1977

Bouillon, Jean-Paul. *Journal de l'Art nouveau 1870–1914.* Geneva, 1985

Bracco, Patrick. *L'Architecture néo-romane en France au XIXe siècle.* Master's diss. under Bruno Foucart. Nanterre, 1975

Brunhammer, Yvonne. *Pionniers du XIXe siècle—Guimard—Horta—Van de Velde.* Exhibition catalogue. Musée des Arts Décoratifs, Paris, 1971

Brunhammer, Yvonne, and Gillian Naylor et al. *Hector Guimard.* Architectural Monographs. N.p., 1978

Burnham, Daniel, and Edward H. Bennett. *Plan of Chicago.* Edited by Charles Moore. Chicago, 1909

La Carrière de l'architecte au XIXe siècle. Exhibition catalogue. Musée d'Orsay, Paris, 1986–87

Casati, G. C. "Vienne et ses constructions nouvelles." *Le Moniteur des architectes* col. 1–4, vol. 5, 2nd ser. (July 15, 1869)

Cassou, Jean, Émile Langui, and Nikolaus Pevsner. *Les Sources du vingtième siècle.* Paris, 1961

Champigneulle, Bernard. *L'Art nouveau.* Paris, 1972

Chemetov, Paul, and Bernard Marrey. *Architectures. Paris—1848–1914.* Paris, 1980

Chicago, naissance d'une métropole, 1872–1922. Exhibition catalogue. Musée d'Orsay, Paris, 1987–88

Culpepper, Ralph. *Hector Guimard Bibliographie.* Société des Amis de la Bibliothèque Forney, notes et documents 4 (March 1975)

Dali, Salvador. "De la beauté terrifiante et comestible de l'architecture modern' style," *Minotaure* 3–4 (December 1933): 69–76

Daval, Jean-Luc. *Journal de l'Art moderne—1884–1914—Les années décisives.* Geneva, 1979

Gabriel Davioud, architecte de Paris. Exhibition catalogue. Hôtel de Sully, Paris, 1982

Drexler, Arthur. *The Architecture of the École des Beaux-Arts.* London, 1977

Duchamp-Villon, Raymond. "L'architecture et le fer." Lecture published in *Poème et Drame* (January–March 1914)

Dufournet, Paul. *Horeau précurseur.* Paris, 1980

Foucart, Bruno. "La cathédrale synthétique de Louis-Auguste Boileau." *Revue de l'art* 3 (1969): 49–66

Foucart, Bruno, and Véronique Noël-Bouton. "Saint-Nicolas de Nantes. Bataille et triomphe du néo-gothique." *Congrès archéologique de Haute-Bretagne.* Paris, 1968: 136–81

Frontisi, Claude. *Guimard Hector architectures.* Les amis d'Hector Guimard, 1985?

Gaillard, Jeanne. *Paris, la ville 1852–1870.* Paris, 1977

Garnier, Charles. *Le Nouvel Opéra de Paris.* Paris, 1878

Giedion, Sigfried. *Space, Time and Architecture.* Cambridge, Mass., 1941. 5th ed., Cambridge, Mass., 1967

Gromort, Georges, André Fontanas, and Louis Vauxcelles. *Histoire générale de l'art français de la Révolution à nos jours.* Vol. 2. Paris, n.d.

Guerrand, Roger-Henry. *L'Art nouveau en Europe.* Preface by Aragon. Paris, 1965

Hautecœur, Louis. *Histoire de l'architecture classique en France.* Vol. 6: *La Restauration et la Monarchie de Juillet, 1815–1848*; vol. 7: *La Fin de l'architecture classique en France, 1848–1900.* Paris, 1957

Hitchcock, Henry-Russell. *Architecture, Nineteenth and Twentieth Centuries.* Harmondsworth, 1958. 2nd ed., Harmondsworth, 1977

Hittorff, un architecte du XIXe siècle. Exhibition catalogue. Musée Carnavalet, Paris, 1986–87

Hector Horeau 1801–1872. Exhibition catalogue. Supplement to *Cahiers de la Recherche architecturale* 3. Musée des Arts Décoratifs, Paris

Henri Sauvage 1873–1932. Exhibition catalogue. Société des Architectes Diplômés par le Gouvernement, Paris, and École Nationale Supérieure d'Architecture et des Arts Visuels, Brussels, 1976–77

Kahane, Martine. *L'Ouverture du nouvel Opéra.* Exhibition catalogue. Musée d'Orsay, Paris, 1986–87
———. *Le Foyer de la dance.* Exhibition catalogue. Musée d'Orsay, Paris, 1988

Kunst und Dekoration, 1851–1914. Exhibition catalogue. Darmstadt, 1976–77

Le Japonisme. Exhibition catalogue. Grand Palais, Paris, and National Museum of Western Art, Tokyo, 1988

Le Corbusier. *Urbanisme.* Paris, 1925

Lemoine, Bertrand. *Les Halles de Paris.* Paris, 1980
———. *L'Architecture du fer, France: XIXe siècle.* Paris, 1986

Leniaud, Jean-Michel. *Jean-Baptiste Lassus ou le temps retrouvé des cathédrales.* Paris, 1980

Le Livre des expositions universelles. Exhibition catalogue. Musée des Arts Décoratifs, Paris, 1983

Loyer, François. *Le Siècle de l'industrie, 1789–1914.* Paris, 1983
———. *Paris, XIXe siècle, l'immeuble et la rue.* Paris, 1987

Loyrette, Henri. *Gustave Eiffel.* Paris, 1986

Madsen, Stephan Tschudi. *Sources of Art Nouveau.* Oslo, 1956. New ed., Oslo, 1975

Magne, Henri-Marcel. *L'Architecture.* Paris, 1922

Mannoni, Edith, and Chantal Bizot. *Mobilier 1900–1925.* Paris, n.d.

Marrey, Bernard, *Les Grands Magasins.* Paris, 1979

Marrey, Bernard, and Paul Chemetov. *Architectures, Paris 1848–1914, familièrement inconnues.* Paris, n.d.

Martel, Pierre, and Nicolas Sainte Fare Garnot. *L'Architecture hospitalière au XIXe siècle. L'exemple parisien.* Exhibition catalogue. Musée d'Orsay, Paris, 1987

Meeks, Carroll. *The Railroad Station.* New Haven and London, 1956. New ed., 1978

Mémoires du baron Haussmann. Grands travaux de Paris. 2 vols. Paris, 1979

Middleton, Robin, and David Watkin. *Neoclassical and Nineteenth-Century Architecture.* New York, 1980

Mignot, Claude. *L'Architecture au XIXe siècle.* Fribourg, 1983

1889. La Tour Eiffel et l'Exposition universelle. Exhibition catalogue. Musée d'Orsay, Paris, 1989

Morizet, André. *Du vieux Paris au Paris moderne. Haussmann et ses prédécesseurs.* Paris, 1937

Nancy—architecture 1900. Paris, 1976

Nocq, Henry. *Tendances nouvelles.* Paris, 1896

Novotny, Fritz, and Renate Wagner-Rieger, eds. *Die Wiener Ringstrasse.* 11 vols. Vienna, 1969–81

Paul Abadie, architecte, 1812–1884. Exhibition catalogue. Musée des Monuments Français, Paris, 1988

Pevsner, Nikolaus. *Pioneers of Modern Design from William Morris to Walter Gropius.* Harmondsworth, 1960
———. *A History of Building Types.* London, 1976

Poelart et son temps. Exhibition catalogue. Palais de Justice, Brussels, 1980

Poncetton, François. *Gustave Eiffel, le magicien du fer.* Paris, 1939

Rheims, Maurice. *L'Objet 1900.* Paris, 1964
———. *L'Art 1900 ou le style Jules Verne.* Paris, 1965

Richard Morris Hunt, architecte, 1827–1895. Exhibition catalogue. Hôtel de Sully, Paris, 1989

Russell, Frank, ed., Tim Benton, François Loyer, and Ezio Godoli. *L'Architecture de l'Art nouveau.* Paris, 1979

Saint-Félix, M. de. "Les installations orientales dans le parc." *L'Exposition universelle de 1867 illustrée.* 2 vols. Paris, 1867

Schmutzler, Robert. *Art Nouveau.* London, 1977

Sédille, Paul. "Vienne et ses constructions nouvelles." *Le Moniteur des architectes,* 1884

Le Siècle de l'éclectisme—Lille 1830–1930. Paris and Brussels, 1979

Le XVIe arrondissement, mécène de l'Art nouveau 1895–1914. Exhibition catalogue. Paris, Beauvais, and Brussels, 1984

Steinhauser, Monika. *Der Pariser Oper.* Munich, 1969

Thiébaut, Philippe et al. *Art nouveau—L'école de Nancy.* Paris, 1987

Victor Laloux, l'architecte de la gare d'Orsay. Exhibition catalogue. Musée d'Orsay, Paris, 1987

Viollet-le-Duc, Eugène-Emmanuel. *Entretiens sur l'architecture, 1863–1872.* Brussels and Liège, 1977. Translated as *Discourses on Architecture.* Boston, 1876

Viollet-le-Duc. Exhibition catalogue. Grand Palais, Paris, 1980

Vogüé, Eugène Melchior de. *Remarques sur l'Exposition du Centenaire.* Paris, 1889

Zerbst, Rainer. *Gaudi (1852–1926). Une vie en architecture.* Cologne, 1988

LITERARY SOURCES

Amicis, Edmondo de. *Souvenirs de Paris et de Londres.* Paris, 1880

Baudelaire, Charles. *Les Fleurs du mal* (1857). In *Œuvres complètes.* Vol. 1. Paris, 1975: 1–145
———. "Salon de 1856." *Écrits sur l'art.* 2 vols. Paris, 1971
———. *Œuvres complètes.* Vol. 2. Paris, 1976

Barbey d'Aurevilly, Jules. *Sensations d'art.* Paris, 1886

Castagnary, Jules. *Salons 1857–78.* 2 vols. Paris, 1892
———. *Le Salon de 1864.* Paris, 1864
———. "Salon de 1869." *Le Siècle* (June 25, 1869)

Champfleury. *Œuvres posthumes. Salons 1846–1851.* Paris, 1894

Claudel, Paul. "Rodin ou l'homme de génie." *Œuvres en prose.* Paris, 1965: 285–88

Debussy, Claude. *Lettres à deux amis.* Paris, 1942

Du Camp, Maxime. *Le Salon de 1857.* Paris, 1857
———. *Le Salon de 1859.* Paris, 1859
———. "Le Salon de 1863." *Revue des Deux Mondes* (1863): 907–12
———. *Souvenirs littéraires.* Paris, 1882–83

Flaubert, Gustave. *Salammbô.* Paris, 1863

Gautier, Théophile. *Les Beaux-Arts en Europe.* Paris, 1855
———. "Salon de 1857." *L'Artiste.* Paris, 1857
———. "Variétés. Exposition de 1859." *Le Moniteur universel,* September 21, 1859

Gide, André. "Promenade au Salon d'Automne." *Gazette des Beaux-Arts* 2nd sem. (1905): 475–85
———. *Incidences.* Paris, 1924

Goncourt, Edmond de. *La Faustin.* Paris, 1862

Goncourt, Jules and Edmond de. *Le Salon de 1852.* Paris, 1852
———. *Journal. Mémoires de la vie littéraire.* 4 vols. Paris, 1956

Gourmont, Remy de. *Sixtine.* Paris, 1890

Huysmans, Joris-Karl. *Certains, 1889.* Paris, 1986
———. *L'Art moderne.* Paris, 1883. New ed., 1975
———. *L'Art moderne. Certains.* Paris, 1976
———. *À rebours.* Paris, 1884. Eng. trans., *Against the Grain.* New York, 1930

Mirbeau, Octave. *Des artistes.* Paris, 1986

Renard, Jules. *Journal. 1887–1910.* Paris, 1965. New ed., 1984

Rilke, Rainer Maria. "Auguste Rodin" (1903), in *Œuvres I. Prose.* Paris, 1966: 391–457

Valéry, Paul. *Degas, Danse, Dessin.* Paris, 1936

Vallès, Jules. *L'Art,* May 29, 1868. Reprinted in *L'Œuvre.* Vol. I. Paris, 1975: 1058–60

Zola, Émile. *Œuvres complètes.* Paris, 1927–29
———. *La Curée.* Paris, 1960
———. *Le Ventre de Paris.* Paris, 1960
———. *Pot-Bouille.* Paris, 1989
———. *Au bonheur des dames.* Paris, 1883
———. *Le Bon Combat. De Courbet aux impressionistes.* Paris, 1974
———. "Une nouvelle manière en peinture. Édouard Manet." *Revue du XIXe siècle,* January 1, 1867. Reprinted as *Édouard Manet. Étude biographique et critique.* Paris, 1867

INDEX

Note: Figure numbers, shown in *italic* type, follow page numbers. An asterisk * after the page number indicates an important discussion of the subject. Buildings are shown as subentries under the place or site where they are located.

C

D

E

F

G

H

I

J

K

L

M

Q

R

S

T

U

V

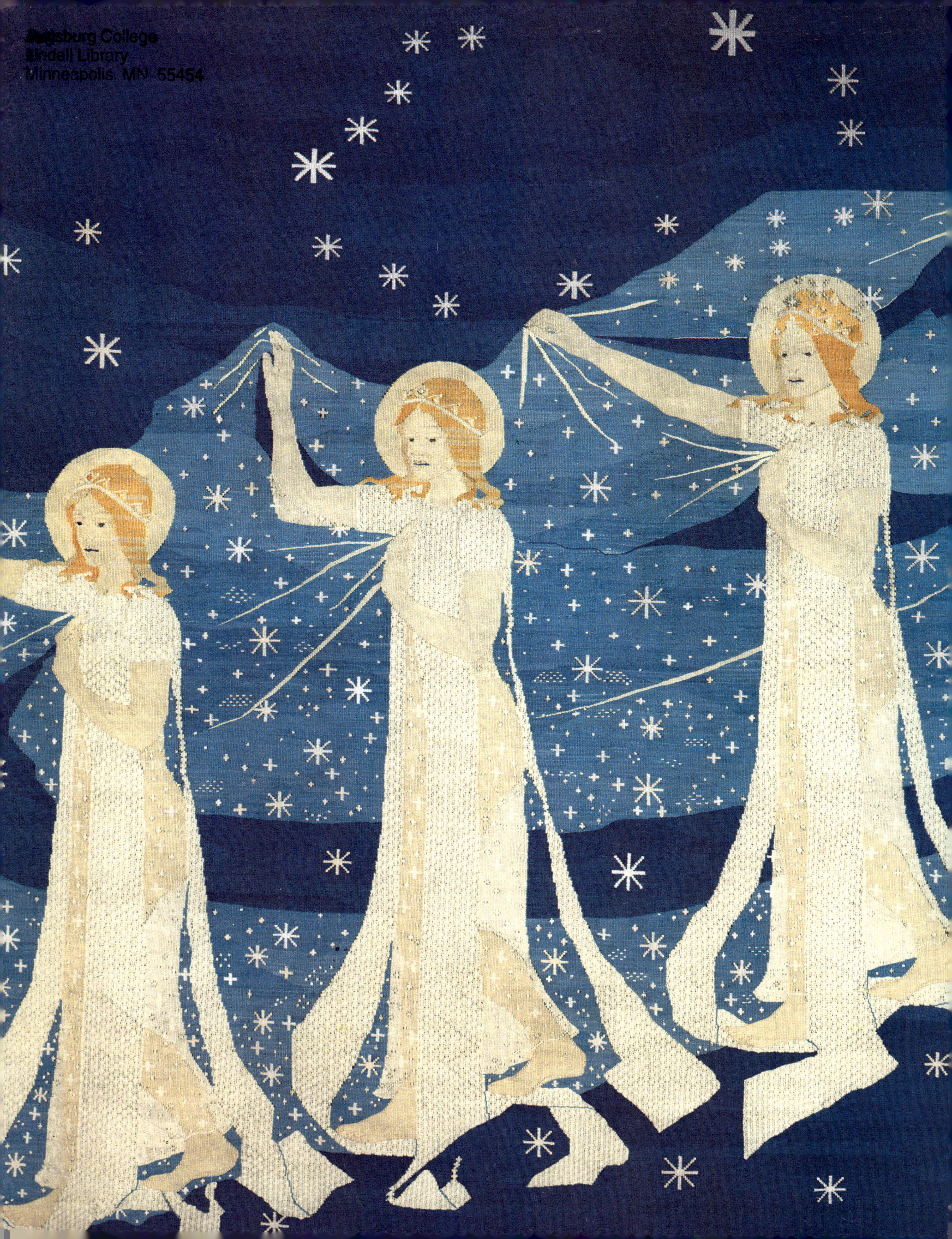